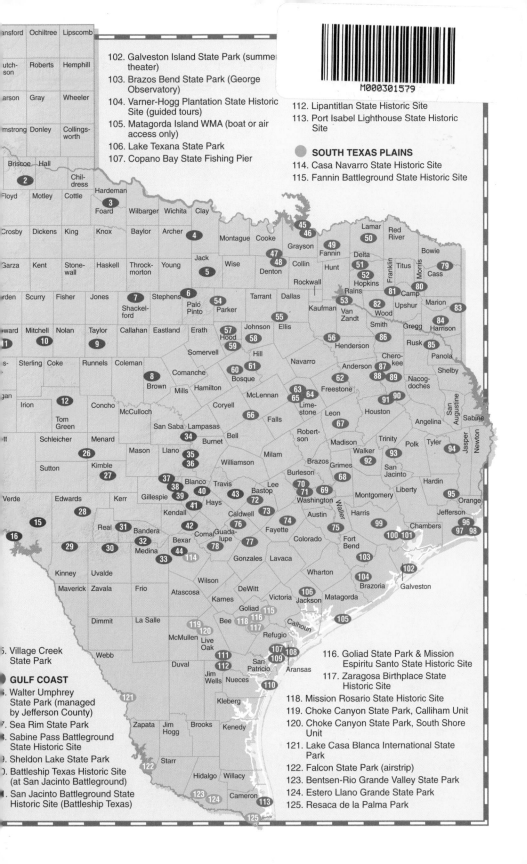

ansford | Ochiltree | Lipscomb

utch-son | Roberts | Hemphill

arson | Gray | Wheeler

mstrong | Donley | Collings-worth

Briscoe | Hall | Chil-dress
2

Floyd | Motley | Cottle | Hardeman
3
Foard | Wilbarger | Wichita | Clay

Crosby | Dickens | King | Knox | Baylor | Archer
4
Montague | Cooke
Grayson

Garza | Kent | Stone-wall | Haskell | Throck-morton | Young
5
Jack | Wise | Denton

rden | Scurry | Fisher | Jones
7
Shackel-ford
Stephens
6
Palo Pinto
54
Parker
Tarrant | Dallas
55
Kaufman

ward | Mitchell | Nolan | Taylor | Callahan | Eastland | Erath
57
Hood
58
Johnson
59
Ellis
56
1 | 10 | 9
Somervell
Hill

s- | Sterling | Coke | Runnels | Coleman
8
Comanche
60
Bosque
61
Navarro

gan | Irion
12
Brown
Mills | Hamilton
McLennan
Freestone
62

Tom Green
Concho | McCulloch
Coryell
66
Falls
63 64
65
Lime-stone

tt | Schleicher | Menard
26
San Saba | Lampasas
34
Burnet
Bell
Robert-son
67
Leon

Sutton | Mason | Llano
35 36
Williamson
Milam
Brazos

Kimble
27
37
38
Blanco
40
Travis
43
Lee
Bastop
72
70 71 69
Washington

Verde | Edwards | Kerr
28
Gillespie
39
41
Hays
Montgomery

15 | Real
31
Bandera
42
Caldwell
73
Austin
Harris
75
99

16
29 | 30
Medina
32
Bexar
44
114
Gonzales
Lavaca
Colorado
Fort Bend
103

Kinney | Uvalde
33
Wilson
Wharton
104
102

Maverick | Zavala | Frio | Atascosa
DeWitt
106
Brazoria | Galveston

Karnes
Victoria | Jackson | Matagorda

Goliad | 115
105

Dimmit | La Salle
119 120
Bee
118 116 117
Refugio
Calhoun

McMullen | Live Oak
111
San Patricio | Aransas
107 109 108

Webb | Duval
112
Jim Wells | Nueces
110

121 | Zapata | Jim Hogg | Brooks | Kenedy
Kleberg

122 | Starr
Hidalgo | Willacy
123 124 | Cameron | 113
125

102. Galveston Island State Park (summer theater)
103. Brazos Bend State Park (George Observatory)
104. Varner-Hogg Plantation State Historic Site (guided tours)
105. Matagorda Island WMA (boat or air access only)
106. Lake Texana State Park
107. Copano Bay State Fishing Pier

112. Lipantitlan State Historic Site
113. Port Isabel Lighthouse State Historic Site

● SOUTH TEXAS PLAINS
114. Casa Navarro State Historic Site
115. Fannin Battleground State Historic Site

116. Goliad State Park & Mission Espiritu Santo State Historic Site
117. Zaragosa Birthplace State Historic Site
118. Mission Rosario State Historic Site
119. Choke Canyon State Park, Calliham Unit
120. Choke Canyon State Park, South Shore Unit
121. Lake Casa Blanca International State Park
122. Falcon State Park (airstrip)
123. Bentsen-Rio Grande Valley State Park
124. Estero Llano Grande State Park
125. Resaca de la Palma Park

. Village Creek State Park

● GULF COAST

. Walter Umphrey State Park (managed by Jefferson County)
. Sea Rim State Park
. Sabine Pass Battleground State Historic Site
. Sheldon Lake State Park
. Battleship Texas Historic Site (at San Jacinto Battleground)
. San Jacinto Battleground State Historic Site (Battleship Texas)

Barnes & Noble Booksellers #2744
9521 Viscount
El Paso, TX 79925
915-590-1932

R:2744 REG:005 TRN:2351 CSHR:Yoli 0

andom House Webster's C
9780375425639
(1 @ 12.95)   12.95
ew York Times Almanac 2
9780143117018
(1 @ 12.95)   12.95
exas Almanac, 2010-2011
9780876112403
(1 @ 29.95)   29.95

Subtotal   55.85
ales Tax (8.250%)   4.61
OTAL   60.46
ASH   100.00
ASH CHANGE   39.54-

MEMBER WOULD HAVE SAVED   8.59

Want to read your books on a dream
vacation? Write a review at bn.com and
be entered for a chance to win one!
No purchase necessary. See official
rules and details at bn.com/reviews.

.101.20   05/03/2010 12:41PM

CUSTOMER COPY

May 3 2010   12:41 PM

29.95

★ THE SOURCE FOR ALL THINGS TEXAN SINCE 1857 ★

TEXAS ALMANAC
2010 ★ 2011

 PUBLISHED BY TEXAS STATE HISTORICAL ASSOCIATION

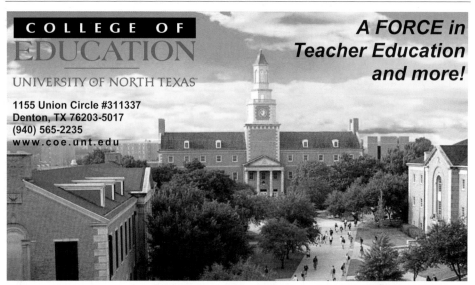

TEXAS ALMANAC
2010 - 2011

Elizabeth Cruce Alvarez
Editor

Robert Plocheck
Associate Editor

Cover and Title Page Design
David Timmons Design
Austin, Texas

Back Cover Credits

✶ Texas Capitol photo courtesy of Ron Billings; Texas Forest Service

✶ Lady Bird and Lyndon Johnson photo courtesy of the Lyndon Baines Johnson Library and Museum, Austin, Texas

✶ Map of Bell County, Texas; see page 220

ISBN (hardcover) 978-0-87611-240-3
ISBN (paperback) 978-0-87611-241-0

Library of Congress Control Number: 2009926425

Copyright © 2010
The Texas State Historical Association
1155 Union Circle #311580
Denton, TX 76203-5017
940-369-5200

www.texasalmanac.com

Distributed by Texas A&M University Press Consortium
4354 TAMU, College Station, Texas 77843-4354

To order by telephone, call 1-800-826-8911

To order online, log onto:
http://www.tamupress.com/product/Texas-Almanac-2010-2011,5223.aspx

THE SOURCE FOR ALL THINGS TEXAN SINCE 1857

Preface

With the publication of the 65th edition of the Texas Almanac, a new chapter begins for this historic book.

In May 2008, the Texas Almanac was acquired by the Texas State Historical Association, itself a 112-year-old organization, and this is the first edition published under the TSHA imprint.

The Almanac was launched in 1857 by the *Galveston News,* and 16 editions were published by the *News* during the 19th century — even during the Civil War. Publication ceased after editor Willard Richardson's death but started up again in 1904 in Dallas as part of *The Dallas Morning News.* There the Almanac remained through 48 editions.

Now the tradition of chronicling "all things Texan" continues as part of TSHA — a long-standing and respected historical organization. Finding a home at TSHA is a perfect fit for the Texas Almanac, and that new home also includes new offices on the beautiful campus of the University of North Texas in Denton.

With each edition of the Almanac, we update facts, figures, articles and all of the hundreds of state and county maps. With their incredible detail, our county maps are the best traveling companion when driving through the Lone Star State.

The *Texas Almanac 2010–2011* also includes hundreds of color photographs taken all around the state. Associate Editor Robert Plocheck took a good many of these photos during his travels, and we also want to thank Ron Billings of the Texas Forest Service for supplying the Almanac with many more beautiful and fresh photos of flora, fauna and landmarks.

The Texas Almanac Web site also has been redesigned and contains a history timeline and feature articles, tables and maps from previous editions. Visit the Almanac's Web site at www.texasalmanac.com.

The Web site includes the Texas Almanac's Searchable Town Database,® which contains more than 17,000 town names, existing and defunct.

In addition to the hospitality shown to us by UNT, the university's Willis Library has begun a project to digitize all previous editions of the Texas Almanac. Check our Web site for information on how to access these historic Almanacs online once the digitization project is complete.

We hope readers enjoy this edition of the Texas Almanac, use it at work and take it along when traveling across our great state.

Lamberto Alvarez photo

Elizabeth Cruce Alvarez
Editor, 2009

The Texas State Historical Association: Past and Future

The Texas State Historical Association began on February 13, 1897, when ten individuals met on the University of Texas campus to discuss founding an organization to promote the discovery, collection, preservation, and publication of historical material pertaining to Texas. The assemblage included academic and nonacademic historians, a blend of membership that has been preserved to the present.

The Association's first director (or secretary, as he was called at the time) was history professor George P. Garrison of the University of Texas, and he brought together the most respected names in Texas to help him with his endeavor. Many of the organization's founding members were veterans of the Texas Revolution, Mexican War, and Civil War. Many held political offices. Some were well known writers and historians. Year after year, the Association's membership grew as it recruited not only the writers, but also the makers of Texas history.

For more than a century, the Texas State Historical Association has played a leadership role in Texas history research and education, helping to identify, collect, preserve, and tell the stories of Texas. It has now entered into a new collaboration with the University of North Texas to carry on and expand its work. In the coming years these two organizations, with their partners and members, will create a collaborative whole that is greater than the sum of its parts. The collaboration will provide passion, talent, and long-term support for the dissemination of scholarly research, educational programs for the K-12 community, and opportunities for public discourse about the complex issues and personalities of our heritage.

The TSHA is proud to add the *Texas Almanac* to its list of core programs that include the *Southwestern Historical Quarterly*, the oldest continuously published scholarly journal in Texas; the *Handbook of Texas Online*, the most comprehensive and authoritative state encyclopedia in the country; a book program that publishes new titles and reprints of Texas history classics; and an Education Program that reaches out to students and teachers at all levels throughout the state. Further information about the programs can be found throughout this edition of the Almanac.

We believe the Almanac is a perfect complement to everything else that we do because it deals not only

University of North Texas in Denton. Robert Plocheck photo.

with the history of the state but also with its present. Assiduously updated every two years in an extraordinary range of categories covering everything from environment to weather to sports and recreation to state and local government to culture, agriculture, education, religion, business, and much more, the Almanac provides an in-depth portrait of the current state of the Lone Star State. Once its archive is available online, we believe it will offer an extraordinary resource for those interested discovering where we have been and how rapidly we are changing.

In the midst of this rapid change, the Texas State Historical Association endeavors to provide a future for our heritage and to ensure that the lessons of our history continue to serve as a resource for the people of Texas. We encourage the readers of the *Texas Almanac* to become members of the Association and to help us in our ongoing efforts.

J. Kent Calder
Executive Director

Southwestern

TSHA Board of Directors, 2009–2010

Officers

Walter L. Buenger	President
College Station	
Dianne Powell	Vice President
San Antonio	
Merline Pitre	Second Vice President
Houston	
Frances B. Vick	Past President
Dallas	(2008)
Frank de la Teja	Past President
Austin	(2007)

Board Members

Watson Arnold, M.D.	(2007–2010)
Fort Worth	
John C. Britt	(2007–2010)
Baytown	
Gregg Cantrell	(2007–2010)
Fort Worth	
Caroline Castillo Crimm	(2007–2010)
Huntsville	
Light T. Cummins	(2009–2012)
Sherman	
Joseph S. (Joe) Fletcher Jr.	(2007–2010)
McAllen	
Joe R. Fulton	(2008–2011)
Corpus Christi	

Sarita A. Hixon	(2008–2011)
Houston	
J. Scott Morris	(2007–2010)
Austin	
Jack Niland	(2008–2011)
El Paso	
B. Byron Price	(2007–2010)
Norman, Oklahoma	
Mary Kelley Scheer	(2007–2010)
Beaumont	
John Schoellkopf	(2008–2011)
Dallas	
Gayle Strange	(2009–2012)
Denton	
Lonn Taylor	(2009–2012)
Fort Davis	
Cecil E. (Eddie) Weller Jr.	(2007–2010)
Houston	
Jenkins Garrett	Honorary Life Board Member
Fort Worth	
John Crain	Honorary Life Board Member
Dallas	
Mary Margaret Amberson	Secretary
San Antonio	
Randolph (Mike) Campbell	Chief Historian
Denton	(ex officio)
J. Kent Calder	Executive Director
Denton	(ex officio)

Table of Contents

Contents

Index of Maps

Index of Tables

TSHA EDUCATIONAL SERVICES

The hallmark of TSHA's education program remains its student programs. These currently include the following:

Junior Historians of Texas

Since 1939, Junior Historians has fostered an interest in state and local history through activities, trips, research and more. Usually organized into clubs or chapters, these elementary and secondary students serve their schools and communities while learning history. Chapters receive a variety of materials and benefits including newsletters, notification of upcoming opportunities, and the group's journal, the *Texas Historian,* through their affiliation with TSHA and its partner organization National History Club. A collegiate version of this program exists as the Walter Prescott Webb Historical Society.

Texas History Day

Texas History Day, a yearlong program for students in Grades 6-12, is affiliated with National History Day. Students in the junior division (Grades 6-8) and the senior division (Grades 9-12) prepare projects based on an annual theme while developing critical thinking skills. Though primarily a teaching methodology, the contest aspect of the program coordinated by the TSHA helps provide motivation for students who have consistently been recognized as some the best in the nation.

Texas Quiz Show

The Texas Quiz Show is an annual academic competition for middle school students about all things Texas, conducted in a game show format. The program is designed to provide a fun and easy way to recognize Texas History Month, as required by public law in HB 294, while encouraging students to do additional research and reading in Texas history. Most questions are drawn from the *Texas Almanac* and *Handbook of Texas Online.*

In addition to student oriented programs, TSHA provides services to educators and others including: workshops, travel seminars, lesson plans, a Speakers Bureau, and other resources. TSHA is proud to provide Teaching Texas, a new resource to assist educators in finding the multitude of resources available to teach social studies in Texas located at www.TeachingTexas.org.

For information about all TSHA education programs, visit
www.TSHAonline.org/education

Texas
The Lone Star State

On this and the following page, is a demographic and geographic profile of the second-largest, second-most-populous state in the United States. Look in the Index to find more-detailed information on each subject.

★ The Government

Capital: Austin

Government: Bicameral Legislature

28th State to enter the Union: Dec. 29, 1845

Present Constitution adopted: 1876

State motto: Friendship (1930)

State symbols:
  Flower: Bluebonnet (1901)
  Bird: Mockingbird (1927)
  Tree: Pecan (1919)
  Song: "Texas, Our Texas" (1929)

Origin of name: Texas, or Tejas, was the Spanish pronunciation of a Caddo Indian word meaning "friends" or "allies."

Nickname: Texas is called the Lone Star State because of the design of the state flag: a broad vertical blue stripe at left centered by a single white star, and at right, horizontal bars of white (top) and red.

★ The People

Population (July 2008 U.S. Census Bureau estimate) **24,326,974**

Population, 2000 U.S. Census **20,851,820**

Population, 1990 U.S. Census **16,986,510**

Population increase, 1990–2000 .... **22.8%**

Population increase, 2000–2008 .... **16.7%**

Ethnicity, 2007 (for explanation of categories, see page 210):

	Number	Percent
Anglo	11,337,714	47.4%
Hispanic	8,791,986	36.8%
Black	2,782,876	11.6%
Other	991,804	4.1%

Population density (2008) .... **90.6 per sq. mi.**

Voting-age population (2008) **17,735,442**

(U.S. Census Bureau, State Data Center, Texas Secretary of State.)

On an Average Day in Texas in 2005:

There were **1,056** resident live **births**.
There were **427** resident **deaths**.
There were **629** more births than deaths.
There were **484** marriages.
There were **208** divorces.

(2005 Texas Vital Statistics, Dept. of State Health Services)

★ Ten Largest Cities

Houston (Harris Co.)	2,149,948
San Antonio (Bexar Co.)	1,336,040
Dallas (Dallas Co.)	1,248,184
Austin (Travis Co.)	736,172
Fort Worth (Tarrant Co.)	688,222
El Paso (El Paso Co.)	609,327
Arlington (Tarrant Co.)	374,948
Corpus Christi (Nueces Co.)	285,600
Plano (Collin Co.)	279,607
Laredo (Webb Co.)	222,482

(January 2008 State Data Center estimate)

Number of counties 254
Largest by pop. ....3,984,349.........Harris Co.
Smallest by pop. ....42.........Loving Co.

Number of incorporated cities 1,210
Number of cities of 100,000 pop. or more 31
Number of cities of 50,000 pop. or more 62
Number of cities of 10,000 pop. or more 237

★ Business

Gross State Product (2008) .... $1.215 trillion
Per Capita Personal Income (2007) $37,038
Civilian Labor Force (Dec. 2008) 11,833,270

(GSP: Texas Comptroller of Public Accounts and U.S. Bureau of Economic Analysis; per capita income: U.S. Bureau of Economic Analysis; civilian labor force: Texas Workforce Commission.)

★ The Natural Environment

Area (total) .... 268,581 sq. miles
(171,891,840 acres)

Land area................................ 261,797 sq. miles
(167,550,080 acres)

Water area .... 6,784 sq. miles
(4,341,760 acres)

Geographic center: About 15 miles northeast of Brady in northern McCulloch County.

Highest point: Guadalupe Peak (8,749 ft.) in Culberson County in far West Texas.

Lowest point: Gulf of Mexico (sea level).

Normal average annual precipitation range: From 60.57 inches at Jasper County in far East Texas, to 9.43 inches at El Paso, in far West Texas.

Record highest temperature:
Seymour, Aug. 12, 1936 .... 120°F
Monahans, June 28, 1994 .... 120°F

Record lowest temperature:
Tulia, Feb. 12, 1899 .... −23°F
Seminole, Feb. 8, 1933........................ −23°F

★ Principal Products

Manufactures: Chemicals and allied products, petroleum and coal products, food and kindred products, transportation equipment.

Farm products: Cattle, cotton, vegetables, fruits, nursery and greenhouse, dairy products.

Minerals: Petroleum, natural gas and natural gas liquids.

Finance (as of 12/31/2008):
Number of banks 594
Total deposits....................$199,988,476,000
Number of savings & loan associations......22
Total assets.........................$87,572,855,000
Number of savings banks 28
Total assets............................$3,988,377,000

(Banks: Federal Reserve Bank of Dallas; savings and loans and savings banks: Texas Savings and Loan Department)

Agriculture:
Total farm marketings, 2008 .... $19.7 billion
Number of farms, 2007 229,000
Land in farms (acres, 2007)....... 129.5 million
Cropland (acres, 2006).................22,617,000
Pastureland (acres, 2000) 15,914,000
Rangeland (acres, 2000) 95,745,000

(The Statistical Abstract of the United States 2009)

The Welcome Center on Interstate 10 at Orange on the Louisiana border. Ron Billings photo; Texas Forest Service.

Texas' Rank Among the United States

Texas' rank among the United States in selected categories are given below. Others categories are covered in other sections, such as, Agriculture, Business, Transportation, Science and Health.

Source (unless otherwise noted): The 2009 Statistical Abstract, U.S. Census Bureau; www.census.gov/compendia/statab

★ Ten Most Populous States, 2008

Rank	State	Population 2008	%Change 2000–2008
1.	California	36,756,666	8.5
2.	**Texas**	**24,326,974**	**16.7**
3.	New York	19,490,297	2.7
4.	Florida	18,328,340	14.7
5.	Illinois	12,901,563	3.9
6.	Pennsylvania	12,448,279	1.4
7.	Ohio	11,485,910	1.2
8.	Michigan	10,003,422	0.7
9.	Georgia	9,685,744	18.3
10.	North Carolina	9,222,414	14.6

(United States, ...304,059,724 .... 8.0)

★ Ten Fastest Growing States, 2008

Rank	State	Population Change 2000–2008
1.	Nevada	30.1%
2.	Arizona	26.7%
3.	Utah	22.5%
4.	Georgia	18.3%
5.	Idaho	17.8%
6.	**Texas**	**16.7%**
7.	Colorado	14.8%
8.	Florida	14.7%
9.	North Carolina	14.6%
10.	South Carolina	11.7%

★ Highest Immigration, 2000–2008

Rank	State	International Migrants
1.	California	1,825,697
2.	New York	876,969
3.	**Texas**	**851,909**
4.	Florida	694,850
5.	Illinois	425,893
6.	New Jersey	384,687
7.	Georgia	243,788
8.	Arizona	216,347
9.	Massachusetts	212,930
10.	North Carolina	192,099

(United States...........................8,114,516)

★ States with Most Live Births, 2006

Rank	State	Births
1.	California	562,431
2.	**Texas**	**399,612**
3.	New York	250,091
4.	Florida	236,882
5.	Illinois	180,583
6.	Ohio	150,590

(United States................. 4,265,996)

★ States with Highest Birth Rates, 2006

Rank	State	Births per 1,000 Pop.
1.	Utah	21.0
2.	**Texas**	**17.0**
3.	Arizona	16.6
4.	Idaho	16.5
5.	Alaska	16.4
6.	Nevada	16.1

(United States................. 14.2)

★ States with Most Farms, 2007

Rank	State	No. of Farms
1.	**Texas**	**229,000**
2.	Missouri	105,000
3.	Iowa	88,000
4.	Kentucky	83,000
4.	Oklahoma	83,000
5.	Minnesota	79,000
5.	Tennessee	79,000

(United States................. 2,076,000)

★ States with Most Land in Farms, 2007

Rank	State	Farm Acreage
1.	**Texas**	**129,500,000**
2.	Montana	60,000,000
3.	Kansas	47,200,000
4.	Nebraska	45,600,000
5.	New Mexico	45,000,000
6.	South Dakota	43,700,000

(United States................. 930,920,000)

State Flags and Symbols

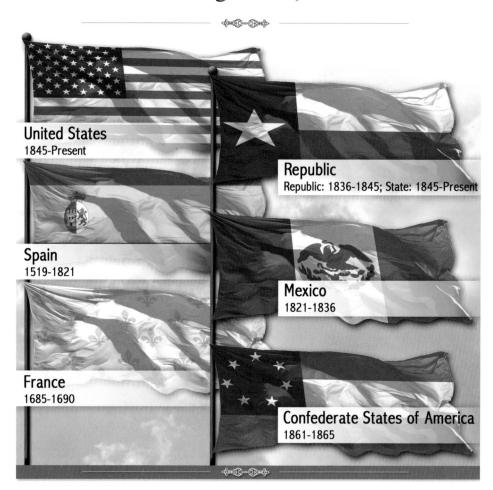

United States
1845-Present

Republic
Republic: 1836-1845; State: 1845-Present

Spain
1519-1821

Mexico
1821-1836

France
1685-1690

Confederate States of America
1861-1865

Texas often is called the **Lone Star State** because of its state flag with a single star. The state flag was also the **flag of the Republic of Texas**. The following information about historic Texas flags, the current flag and other Texas symbols may be supplemented by information available from the **Texas State Library** in Austin. (On the Web: **www.texasalmanac.com/flags. htm and www.tsl.state.tx.us/ref/abouttx/index. html#flags**)

Six Flags of Texas

Six different flags have flown over Texas during eight changes of sovereignty. The accepted sequence of these flags follows:

Spanish — 1519–1821
French — 1685–1690
Mexican — 1821–1836
Republic of Texas — 1836–1845
Confederate States of America — 1861–1865
United States — 1845 to the present.

Evolution of the Lone Star Flag

The Convention at Washington-on-the-Brazos in March 1836 allegedly adopted a flag for the Republic that was designed by Lorenzo de Zavala. The design of de Zavala's flag is unknown, but the convention journals state that a "Rainbow and star of five points above the western horizon; and a star of six points sinking below" was added to de Zavala's flag.

There was a suggestion the letters "T E X A S" be placed around the star in the flag, but there is no evidence that the Convention ever approved a final flag design. Probably because of the hasty dispersion of the Convention and loss of part of the Convention notes, nothing further was done with the Convention's proposals for a national flag. A **so-called "Zavala flag"** is sometimes flown in Texas today that consists of a blue field with a white five-pointed star in the center and letters "T E X A S" between the star points, but there is no historical evidence to support this flag's design.

The **first official flag of the Republic**, known as the **National Standard of Texas** or **David G. Burnet's** flag, was adopted by the Texas Congress and approved by President Sam Houston on Dec. 10, 1836. The design "shall be an azure ground with a large golden star central."

The Lone Star Flag

On Jan. 25, 1839, President Mirabeau B. Lamar approved the adoption by Congress of a new national flag. This flag consisted of "a blue perpendicular stripe of the width of one third of the whole length of the flag, with a white star of five points in the centre thereof, and two horizontal stripes of equal breadth, the upper stripe white, the lower red, of the length of two thirds of the length of the whole flag." This is the **Lone Star Flag,** which later became the state flag.

Although Senator William H. Wharton proposed the adoption of the Lone Star Flag in 1838, no one knows who actually designed the flag. The legislature in 1879 inadvertently repealed the law establishing the state flag, but the legislature adopted a new law in 1933 that legally re-established the flag's design.

The red, white and blue of the state flag stand, respectively, for bravery, purity and loyalty. The proper finial for use with the state flag is either a star or a spearhead. Texas is one of only two states that has a flag that formerly served as the flag of an independent nation. The other is Hawaii.

Rules for Display of the State Flag

The Texas Flag Code was first adopted in 1933 and completely revised in 1993. Laws governing display of the state flag are found in sections 3100.051 through 3100.072 of the Texas Government Code. (On the Web: **www.tsl.state.tx.us/ref/abouttx/flagcode. html**). A summary of those rules follows:

The Texas flag should be displayed on state and national holidays and on special occasions of historical significance, and it should be displayed at every school on regular school days. **When flown out-of-doors**, the Texas flag should not be flown earlier than sunrise nor later than sunset unless properly illuminated. It should not be left out in inclement weather unless a weatherproof flag is used. It should be flown with the white stripe uppermost except in case of distress.

No flag other than the **United States flag** should be placed above or, if on the same level, to the state flag's right (observer's left). The state flag should be underneath the national flag when the two are flown from the same halyard. **When flown from adjacent flagpoles**, the national flag and the state flag should be of approximately the same size and on flagpoles of equal height; the national flag should be on the flag's own right (observer's left).

If the state flag is displayed with the flag of another U.S. state, a nation other than the U.S., or an international organization, the state flag should be, from an observer's perspective, to the left of the other flag on a separate flagpole or flagstaff, and the state flag should not be above the other flag on the same flagpole or flagstaff or on a taller flagpole or flagstaff. If the state flag and the U.S. flag are displayed from crossed flagstaffs, the state flag should be, from an observer's perspective, to the right of the U.S. flag and the state flag's flagstaff should be behind the U.S. flag's flagstaff.

When the flag is displayed horizontally, the white stripe should be above the red stripe and, from an observer's perspective, to the right of the blue stripe. **When the flag is displayed vertically**, the blue stripe should be uppermost and the white stripe should be to the state flag's right (observer's left).

If the state and national flags are both **carried in a procession**, the national flag should be on the marching right and state flag should be on the national flag's left (observer's right).

On Memorial Day, the state flag should be displayed at half-staff until noon and at that time raised to the peak of the flagpole. **On Peace Officers Memorial Day** (May 15), the state flag should be displayed at half-staff all day, unless that day is also Armed Forces Day.

The state flag should not touch anything beneath it or be dipped to any person or things except the U.S. flag. Advertising should not be fastened to a flagpole, flagstaff or halyard on which the state flag is displayed. If a state flag is no longer used or useful as an emblem for display, it should be destroyed, preferably by burning. A **flag retirement ceremony** is set out in the Texas Government Code at the Texas State Library Web site mentioned above.

Pledge to the Texas Flag

A pledge to the Texas flag was adopted in 1933 by the 43rd Legislature. It contained a phrase, "Flag of 1836," which inadvertently referred to the David G. Burnet flag instead of the Lone Star Flag adopted in 1839. In 2007, the 80th Legislature changed the pledge to its current form:

Honor the Texas flag; I pledge allegiance to thee, Texas, one state under God, one and indivisible.

A person reciting the pledge to the state flag should face the flag, place the right hand over the heart and remove any easily removable hat.

The pledge to the Texas flag may be recited at all public and private meetings at which the pledge of allegiance to the national flag is recited and at state historical events and celebrations. The pledge to the Texas flag should be recited after the pledge of allegiance to the United States flag if both are recited.

State Song

The state song of Texas is **"Texas, Our Texas."** The music was written by the late William J. Marsh (who died Feb. 1, 1971, in Fort Worth at age 90), and the words by Marsh and Gladys Yoakum Wright, also of Fort Worth. It was the winner of a state song contest sponsored by the 41st legislature and was adopted in 1929. The wording has been changed once: Shortly after Alaska became a state in Jan. 1959, the word "Largest" in the third line was changed by Mr. Marsh to "Boldest."

The text follows:

Texas, Our Texas

Texas, our Texas! All hail the mighty State!
Texas, our Texas! So wonderful, so great!
Boldest and grandest, Withstanding
    ev'ry test;
O Empire wide and glorious, You stand
    supremely blest.

Chorus
God bless you Texas!
And keep you brave and strong,
That you may grow in power and worth,
Thro'out the ages long.

Refrain
Texas, O Texas! Your freeborn single star,
Sends out its radiance to nations near and far.
Emblem of freedom! It sets our hearts aglow,
With thoughts of San Jacinto and
    glorious Alamo.

Texas, dear Texas! From tyrant grip now free,
Shines forth in splendor your star
    of destiny!
Mother of heroes! We come your
    children true,
Proclaiming our allegiance, our faith, our love
    for you.

State Motto

The state motto is "**Friendship**." The word Texas, or Tejas, was the Spanish pronunciation of a Caddo Indian word meaning "friends" or "allies." (41st Legislature in 1930.)

State Citizenship Designation

The people of Texas usually call themselves Texans. However, **Texian** was generally used in the early period of the state's history.

State Seal

The design of the **obverse (front)** of the State Seal consists of "a star of five points encircled by olive and live oak branches, and the words, 'The State of Texas'." (State Constitution, Art. IV, Sec. 19.) This design is a slight modification of the Great Seal of the Republic of Texas, adopted by the Congress of the Republic, Dec. 10, 1836, and readopted with modifications in 1839.

Front of Seal

Back of Seal

An official design for the **reverse (back)** of the seal was adopted by the 57th Legislature in 1961, but there were discrepancies between the written description and the artistic rendering that was adopted at the same time. To resolve the problems, the 72nd Legislature in 1991 adopted an official design.

The 73rd Legislature in 1993 finally adopted the reverse by law. The current description is in the Texas Government Code, section 3101.001:

"(b) The reverse side of the state seal contains a shield displaying a depiction of:

(1) the Alamo; (2) the cannon of the Battle of Gonzales; and (3) Vince's Bridge. (c)

The shield on the reverse side of the state seal is encircled by:

(1) live oak and olive branches; and (2) the unfurled flags of: (A) the Kingdom of France; (B) the Kingdom of Spain; (C) the United Mexican States: (D) the Republic of Texas; (E) the Confederate States of America; and (F) the United States of America. (d) Above the shield is emblazoned the motto, "REMEMBER THE ALAMO," and beneath the shield are the words, "TEXAS ONE AND INDIVISIBLE." (e) A white five-pointed star hangs over the shield, centered between the flags."

Texas State Symbols

State Bird — The **mockingbird** (*Mimus polyglottos*) is the state bird of Texas, adopted by the 40th Legislature of 1927 at the request of the Texas Federation of Women's Clubs.

State Flower — The state flower of Texas is the **bluebonnet**, also called **buffalo clover**, **wolf flower** and *el conejo* (the rabbit). The bluebonnet was adopted as the state flower, at the request of the Society of Colonial Dames in Texas, by the 27th Legislature in 1901. The original resolution made *Lupinus subcarnosus* the state flower, but a resolution by the 62nd Legislature in 1971 provided legal status as the state flower of Texas for "*Lupinus Texensis* and any other variety of bluebonnet."

State Tree — The **pecan tree** (*Carya illinoinensis*) is the state tree of Texas. The sentiment that led to its official adoption probably grew out of the request of Gov. James Stephen Hogg that a pecan tree be planted at his grave. The 36th Legislature in 1919 adopted the pecan tree.

Other Symbols

(In 2001, the Texas Legislature placed restrictions on the adoption of future symbols by requiring that a joint resolution to designate a symbol must specify the item's historical or cultural significance to the state.)

State Air Force — The **Commemorative Air Force** (formerly known as the Confederate Air Force), based in Midland at Midland International Airport, was proclaimed the state air force of Texas by the 71st Legislature in 1989.

State Bluebonnet City — The city of **Ennis** in Ellis County was named state bluebonnet city by the 75th Legislature in 1997.

State Bluebonnet Festival — The **Chappell Hill Bluebonnet Festival**, held in April, was named state bluebonnet festival by the 75th Legislature in 1997.

State Bluebonnet Trail — The city of Ennis was named state bluebonnet trail by the 75th Legislature in 1997.

State Bread — *Pan de campo*, translated "camp bread" and often called cowboy bread, was named the state bread by the 79th Legislature in 2005. It is a simple baking-powder bread that was a staple of early Texans and often baked in a Dutch oven.

State Cooking Implement — The **cast iron Dutch oven** was named the cooking implement of Texas by the 79th Legislature in 2005.

State Dinosaur — *Paluxysaurus jonesi* was designated the state dinosaur by the 81st Legislature in 2009.

State Dish — **Chili** was proclaimed the Texas state dish by the 65th Legislature in 1977.

State Dog Breed — The **Blue Lacy** was designated the state dog breed by the 79th Legislature in 2005. The Blue Lacy is a herding and hunting breed descended from greyhound, scent-hound, and coyote stock and developed by the Lacy brothers, who left Kentucky and settled near Marble Falls in 1858.

State Epic Poem — "**The Legend of Old Stone Ranch**," written by John Worth Cloud, was named the epic poem of Texas by the 61st Legislature in 1969. The work is a 400-page history of the Albany–Fort Griffin area written in verse form.

STATE BIRD

Mockingbird
Mimus Polyglottos

STATE FLOWER

Bluebonnet
Lupinus Texensis

STATE TREE

Pecan Tree
Carya Illinoinensis

STATE DISH

Chili

STATE DOG BREED

Blue Lacy

STATE FIBER AND FABRIC

Cotton

STATE FRUIT

Texas Red Grapefruit

STATE INSECT

Monarch Butterfly
Danaus Plexippus

STATE SMALL MAMMAL

Armadillo
Dasypus Novemcinctus

STATE NATIVE PEPPER

Chiltepin

State Fiber and Fabric — Cotton was designated the state fiber and fabric by the 75th Legislature in 1997.

State Fish — The **Guadalupe bass**, a member of the genus *Micropterus* within the sunfish family, was named the state fish of Texas by the 71st Legislature in 1989. It is one of a group of fish collectively known as black bass.

State Flower Song — "**Bluebonnets**," written by Julia D. Booth and Lora C. Crockett, was named the state flower song by the 43rd Legislature in 1933.

State Folk Dance — The **square dance** was designated the state folk dance by the 72nd Legislature in 1991.

State Fruit — The **Texas red grapefruit** was designated the state fruit by the 73rd Legislature in 1993.

State Gem — **Texas blue topaz**, the state gem of Texas, is found in the Llano uplift area in Central Texas, especially west to northwest of Mason. It was designated by the 61st Legislature in 1969.

State Gemstone Cut — The **Lone Star Cut** was named the state gemstone cut by the 65th Legislature in 1977.

State Grass — **Sideoats grama** (*Bouteloua curtipendula*), a native grass found on many different soils, was designated the state grass of Texas by the 62nd Legislature in 1971.

State Health Nut — The **pecan** was designated the state nut by the 77th Legislature in 2001.

State Insect — The **Monarch butterfly** (*Danaus plexippus*) was

designated the state insect by the 74th Legislature in 1995.

State Mammals — The **armadillo** (*Dasypus novemcinctus*) was designated the state **small mammal**; the **longhorn** was designated the state **large mammal**; and the **Mexican free-tailed bat** (*Tadarida brasiliensis*) was designated the state flying mammal by the 74th Legislature in 1995.

State Musical Instrument — The **guitar** was named the state musical instrument by the 75th Legislature in 1997.

State Native Pepper — The **chiltepin** was named the native pepper of Texas by the 75th Legislature in 1997.

State Native Shrub — The **Texas purple sage** (*leucophyllum frutescens*) was designated the state native shrub by the 79th Legislature in 2005.

State Pepper — The **jalapeño pepper** was designated the state pepper by the 74th Legislature in 1995.

State Plant — The **prickly pear cactus** was named the state plant by the 74th Legislature in 1995.

State Plays — The four official state plays of Texas are *The Lone Star, Texas, Beyond the Sundown*, and *Fandangle*. They were designated by the 66th Legislature in 1979.

State Precious Metal — Silver was named the

The longhorn is the official state large mammal.

official precious metal by the 80th Legislature in 2007.

State Railroad — The **Texas State Railroad** was designated the state railroad by the 78th Legislature in 2003. The Texas State Railroad is a steam powered tourist excursion train operated by the Texas Parks & Wildlife Department. Its 25 miles of track meander through the East Texas piney woods and across the Neches River between the towns of Rusk and Palestine.

State Reptile — The **Texas horned lizard** (*Phrynosoma cornutum*) was named the state reptile by the 73rd Legislature in 1993.

State Seashell — The **lightning whelk** (*Busycon perversum pulleyi*) was named the state seashell by the 70th Legislature in 1987. One of the few shells that open on the left side, the lightning whelk is named for its colored stripes. It is found only on the Gulf Coast.

State Ship — The battleship **USS Texas** was designated the state ship by the 74th Legislature in 1995. The USS Texas was launched on May 18, 1912, from Newport News, VA, and commissioned on March 12, 1914. In 1919, it became the first U.S. battleship to launch an aircraft, and in 1939 it received the first commercial radar in the U.S. Navy. In 1940, the Texas was designated flagship of the U.S. Atlantic Fleet and was the last of the battleships to participate in both World Wars I and II. It was decommissioned on April 21, 1948, and is a National Historic Landmark and a National Mechanical Engineering Landmark.

State Shoe — The cowboy boot was named the state shoe by the 80th Legislature in 2007.

State Shrub — The **crape myrtle** (*Lagerstroemia*

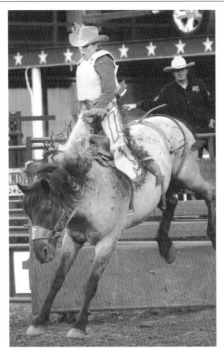

Rodeo was named the State Sport in 1997. Dallas Morning News photo.

indica) was designated the official state shrub by the 75th Legislature in 1997.

State Snack — **Tortilla chips and salsa** was designated the official state snack by the 78th Legislature in 2003 at the request of second-grade students in Mission.

State Sport — **Rodeo** was named the state sport of Texas by the 75th Legislature in 1997.

State Stone — **Petrified palmwood**, found in Texas principally in eastern counties near the Texas Gulf Coast, was designated the state stone by the 61st Legislature in 1969.

State Tall Ship — The **Elissa** was named the state tall ship by the 79th Legislature in 2005. The 1877 ship makes its home at the Texas Seaport Museum at the port of Galveston.

State Tartan — The **Texas Bluebonnet Tartan** was named the official state tartan by the 71st Texas Legislature in 1989.

State Tie — The bolo tie was designated the state tie by the 80th Legislature in 2007.

State Vegetable — The **Texas sweet onion** was designated the state vegetable by the 75th Legislature in 1997.

State Vehicle — The **chuck wagon** was named the state vehicle by the 79th Legislature in 2005. Texas rancher Charles Goodnight is created with inventing the chuck wagon to carry cowboys food and supplies on trail drives.

State 10K — The **Texas Roundup 10K** was named the state 10K by the 79th Legislature in 2005 to encourage Texans to exercise and incorporate physical activity into their daily lives.

STATE PLANT

STATE PEPPER

Jalapeño Pepper

Prickly Pear Cactus

STATE REPTILE

Texas Horned Lizard
Phrynosoma Cornutum

STATE TARTAN

Texas Bluebonnet Tartan

University of North Texas Press

History

Lady Bird Johnson. Photos courtesy of the Lyndon Baines Johnson Library and Museum.

Lady Bird Johnson

A Brief Sketch of Texas History

Prehistory to Annexation

Annexation to 1980

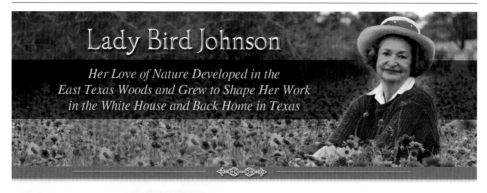

Lady Bird Johnson

*Her Love of Nature Developed in the
East Texas Woods and Grew to Shape Her Work
in the White House and Back Home in Texas*

The Brick House, Lady Bird Johnson's childhood home in Karnack.

By Jan Jarboe Russell

The seeds of all that Lady Bird Johnson accomplished as First Lady and environmentalist were planted in the deep woods of her native East Texas. She was born on Dec. 22, 1912, in the Brick House, a two-story, 17-room antebellum house that sits on an isolated rise facing a double wall of pine trees near the tiny town of Karnack.

Her father, Thomas Jefferson Taylor, owned a 65,000-acre cotton plantation, two country stores and was the richest man in Harrison County. Her mother, Minnie Lee Pattillo Taylor, a dreamy woman from a genteel Alabama family, named her only daughter Claudia Alta. However, Alice Tittle, the nursemaid, took one look at the six-and-one-half-pound, dark-haired baby and pronounced her "as purty as a lady bird." The nickname stuck.

On Sept. 14, 1918, Minnie Taylor suffered a miscarriage after an accidental fall as she descended the staircase at the Brick House and died. Lady Bird was 5 years old and at home. Her two older brothers, Tommy and Tony, were both in boarding school in the Catskills of New York. Lady Bird was left in the care of her father and her Aunt Effie, her mother's unmarried sister, who

Claudia Alta Taylor at about 6 months with Alice Tittle, who nicknamed her "Lady Bird."

came from Alabama to live at the Brick House.

Her Mother's Influence

Lady Bird had few memories of her mother. In one, she remembered her as a "tall graceful" lady who "wore white quite a lot . . . went around the house in a great rush, and loved to read." In another, her mother walked barefoot through the woods, her white skirt damp with dew, carrying a hand-picked nosegay of wildflowers.

As a young girl, Lady Bird took to the same woods, exploring ancient trees, exotic plants and dark bayous. "Growing up rather alone," Lady Bird said, "I took my delights in the gifts nature offered me daily."

One of her favorite places was Caddo Lake, the largest natural lake in Texas. "On Caddo Lake, I loved to paddle in those dark bayous, where time itself seemed ringed around by silence and ancient cypress trees, rich in festoons of Spanish moss," recalled Lady Bird. "Now and then an alligator would surface like a gnarled log. It was a place for dreams."

Lady Bird at age 3.

As a young adolescent, she roamed the woods near the Brick House in the spring looking for the first daffodil and named that daffodil "queen."

Her mother demonstrated concern for the environment in many ways. She built a birdbath in the front yard of the Brick House and fed the birds all year round. In 1910, she sponsored a Save the Quail

Claudia "Lady Bird" Taylor loved to roam the woods and bayous near her childhood home in East Texas.

Society, and to protect the quail from hunters, she posted "no hunting" signs on several thousand acres of her husband's property. Neighbors considered Minnie "strange" for these behaviors, which became part of Lady Bird's emotional inheritance.

An Isolated Childhood

Until she went to high school in nearby Marshall, Lady Bird lived an isolated life. Her primary playmates were two African-American girls, whose parents worked for her father and who also had nicknames: Doodle Bug and Stuff.

While growing up, Lady Bird poured over her mother's books, many of them leather-bound travel books. She inherited her mother's bookish nature and excelled in school. In 1928, the year she graduated from high school, the prediction of her classmates in the yearbook was not that she would marry and have children — normal ambitions for Southern girls of her age and class — but that Lady Bird would be an explorer, a "second Halliburton, poking her nose in unknown places in Asia."

Graduation day in 1934 at the University of Texas at Austin.

By the time she graduated from the University of Texas with two degrees — a bachelor of arts in 1933 and bachelor of journalism in 1934 — Lady Bird's world became much larger. She had many friends and increased confidence. Her ambition was to become a reporter, preferably a drama critic for *The Washington Post.* If that didn't work out, she intended to apply for teaching jobs "in some faraway romantic spot — Hawaii or Alaska."

Lyndon and Politics

Instead, romance soon found Lady Bird. One of her college friends introduced her to Lyndon Johnson, the tall, lanky aide to U.S. Rep. Richard Kleberg, the King Ranch's member of Congress. They had their first date in October and for the next seven weeks, they carried on a long-distance romance in letters and telephone calls. In October, Lady Bird was worried about his future career. "Lyndon, please tell me as soon as you can what the deal is . . . I am afraid it's politics," she wrote in a letter.

After eloping to San Antonio on November 17, 1934, for a small wedding, Lady Bird moved to a one-bedroom apartment in Washington, D.C., and set about conquering her fear of politics. The practical virtues instilled in her by her father — thriftiness

Honeymooning in Xochimilco, Mexico.

Lynda Bird, Lady Bird, Luci Baines and LBJ at home on Election Day in 1948.

and a keen business sense — served both her and Johnson well.

In 1937, when Johnson ran his first race for Congress, she asked how much the campaign would cost. "About $10,000," she was told. She telephoned her father in Karnack and received the entire amount from her mother's inheritance. Five years later, she used more of her mother's inheritance to buy KTBC, a failing low-power, daytime-only Austin radio station, and built it into a communications empire worth millions of dollars that she personally managed well into her eighties.

Campaigning for LBJ's U.S. Senate race in June 1941.

Her support of her husband's political career defined her. In 1941, when Johnson volunteered for the U.S. Navy during World War II, Lady Bird ran his Congressional office. She campaigned for him in every race. When their two daughters, Lynda Bird and Luci Baines, were still young, Lady Bird packed up her dishes and her household belongings at the start of every congressional session and commuted back and forth in a station wagon from Austin to Washington.

During the 1948 race for the U.S. Senate, she joined her husband on a helicopter blitz through Texas towns, taking photographs of rallies on a handheld 16-millimeter camera. During the 1960 presidential campaign when Johnson ran as John F. Kennedy's running mate, Lady Bird went to Dallas four days before the election to campaign for Kennedy and confronted an angry crowd of women who were opposed to Kennedy, who spit at her and carried signs that said, "Let's Ground Lady Bird." The Kennedy-Johnson ticket carried Texas and therefore the election. "Lady Bird carried Texas for us," said Robert Kennedy, brother to the new president.

On Nov. 22, 1963, when Kennedy was assassinated in Dallas, Lady Bird was in the motorcade and at the hospital when Kennedy was

declared dead. On
her drive back to
the airport to board
Air Force One,
Lady Bird saw a
flag flying at half-
mast and realized
her life was never
going to be the
same. She stood by
her husband on the
airplane when he
was sworn in as the
36th president. "I
have moved onstage
to a part I never
rehearsed," Lady Bird told Liz Carpenter, her closest
aide.

President Johnson and
Lady Bird move into the White
House on Dec. 7, 1963.
Cecil Stoughton photo.

On the day she moved into the White House, she
found a bouquet of flowers from Mrs. Kennedy with
a note that said: "I wish you a happy arrival in your
new house, Lady Bird — Remember —you will be
happy here. Love, Jackie."

Finding Consolation in Nature

Amid the turmoil of the 1960s when the nation
was bitterly divided over race and the Vietnam
War, Lady Bird reached back to the source of her
childhood consolation — nature — to find a cause
that brought her moments of happiness in the White
House. She put a sign on her desk in the East Wing
that said "can do" and went to work on her signature
issue — the environment. It started with the planting
of pansies on the mall in Washington, D.C., followed
by azaleas, dogwood, cherry trees and daffodils that
are still in evidence in Washington's parks and green
spaces.

In 1965, Congress passed "Lady Bird's Bill"
that limited junkyards and billboards on the
nation's highways and encouraged the planting
of wildflowers. She used her influence to prevent
construction of dams in the Grand Canyon, to create
Redwoods National Park, to purchase more parkland
and to protect rivers. "The environment is where we
all meet, where we all have a mutual interest," she
said. "It is what we all share."

One of the most significant events as First Lady
came during the 1964 presidential race, three months

Lady Bird and two young people among blooming azaleas during a Beautification of Washington, D.C., tour in
April 1966. Robert Knudsen photo.

after Johnson signed the Civil Rights Act, which
made him a traitor to many white Southerners.
Lady Bird took a 1,628-mile train trip through eight
Southern states. "Don't give me the easy towns," she
told Carpenter. "Anyone can get into Atlanta. Let me
take the tough ones."

The issue of civil rights was one that Lady Bird
took personally. She'd grown up in the segregated
South and witnessed racial prejudice first-hand.
As a child, she'd heard about how a group of white
vigilantes had cornered a black man near Karnack
and accused him of some
crime. The man was
terrified and ran. The
vigilantes shot him in the
back. Even as a child,
she knew such behavior
was wrong and thought to
herself, "Someone should
do something about this."
With the passage of the
Civil Rights Act of 1964,
her husband did.

Rafting the Snake
River in Grand Teton
National Park with
Interior Secretary Stew-
art Udall in August 1964.
Robert Knudsen photo.

During the train trip,
called the Lady Bird
Special, Lady Bird made
47 speeches in four days,
and her message was that
unless the South accepted
the Civil Rights Act and
put an end to segregation,
its economy would be
ruined and its fate consigned to the past. She faced
angry hecklers, many carrying signs that said,
"Black Bird. Go home." There were threats on her
life; at one point, the Secret Service made sure the
railroad tracks were swept for bombs. When hecklers

Portrait in the White
House in May 1968.
Robert Knudsen photo.

drowned her out, she stood
on the back of the train and
said: "You've had your say.
But I've come all this way.
If you're finished, now I'd
like to talk." Ultimately, her
message was heard.

In speeches, Lady
Bird reminded audiences
that First Ladies aren't
elected by anyone but
served by accident of
marriage and answered to a
constituency of one — their
husbands. Throughout their
39-year marriage, Lady
Bird took care of LBJ's
personal needs — bringing
him coffee in bed, laying out his clothes — but
she did more than that. She helped draft speeches,
finance campaigns and served as one of his closest
advisors. Just before his announcement in 1968 that
he would not seek another term in office, Lady Bird
walked over to Johnson's desk in the Oval Office a
few seconds before he started speaking and told him,
"Remember — pacing and drama."

On the last night that Lady Bird spent in the
White House, a line of poetry from *India's Love*

"*The environment is where we all meet, where we all have a mutual interest. It is what we all share.*"

Groundbreaking for the National Wildflower Research Center near Austin, Dec. 22, 1982. Frank Wolfe photo.

Visiting a Project Head Start classroom in March 1968. Robert Knudsen photo.

Lyrics drifted through her mind before she went to sleep:

> *I seek to celebrate my glad release, the Tents of Silence and the Camp of Peace.*

The following day, she and Johnson moved back home to the LBJ Ranch near Stonewall, which was for Lady Bird a camp of peace. Four years and two days later, on Jan. 22, 1973, Johnson died of a heart attack at the ranch. Lady Bird soon seeded pasture after pasture with wildflowers.

During her widowhood, Lady Bird served as the chief steward of her husband's memory, presiding over events at the LBJ Library and Museum in Austin. She became the driving force behind building the 10-mile hike and bike trail around the Town Lake portion of the Colorado River. On her 70th birthday, she founded the National Wildflower Research Center near Austin.

After she died at age 94 on July 11, 2007, 10,000 mourners filed past her casket at the LBJ Library. On July 15, a cortege procession left the Texas State Capitol and thousands of people lined the route through downtown Austin and along the shores of Town Lake, which had been renamed Lady Bird Lake, to pay their respects. Many held wildflowers in their hands.

Jan Jarboe Russell, Texas journalist, is the author of Lady Bird, A Biography of Mrs. Johnson, *published by Scribner's in 1999.*

All photographs are courtesy of the LBJ Library and Museum in Austin; some are family photos by unknown photographers and others are credited in the captions to individual photographers.

Sources:
Dallek, Robert. *Lone Star Rising: Lyndon Johnson and His Times, 1908–1960.* New York: Oxford University Press, 1991.

Johnson, Lady Bird. *A White House Diary.* New York: Holt, Rinehart and Winston, 1970; and Austin: University of Texas Press, 2007.

Middleton, Harry. *Lady Bird Johnson, A Life Well Lived.* Austin: The Lyndon Baines Johnson Foundation, 1992.

Russell, Jan Jarboe. *Lady Bird, A Biography of Mrs. Johnson.* New York: Scribner's, 1999.

Arriving for the annual wreath-laying ceremony at the Lyndon B. Johnson State Historic Site in August 2002. Dallas Morning News photo.

Timeline of the Life of Claudia Alta Taylor "Lady Bird" Johnson
1912–2007

DEC. 22, 1912 — Claudia Alta Taylor is born to Thomas Jefferson Taylor and Minnie Pattillo Taylor in Karnack, Texas.

SEPT. 14, 1918 — Minnie Taylor dies after falling down the stairs at the family home.

1918–1923 — Attends grade school in Karnack and Jefferson, Texas, and, briefly, in Alabama.

1928 — Graduates from Marshall Public High School at age 15, third in her class.

1928 — Attends Saint Mary's Episcopal School for Girls in Dallas, graduating in 1930.

1933 — Graduates from The University of Texas at Austin with a bachelor of arts in history.

1934 — Receives a bachelor of journalism, *cum laude,* from UT Austin, as well as a teacher's certificate.

AUG. 31, 1934 — Meets Lyndon Baines Johnson through a mutual friend.

OCTOBER 1934 — First date with LBJ, an aide to U.S. Rep. Richard Kleberg.

NOV. 17, 1934 — Marries LBJ at St. Mark's Episcopal Church in San Antonio and honeymoons in Mexico.

1937 — Uses part of her maternal inheritance to finance LBJ's first run for Congress from Austin's 10th District. He serves six terms.

1941 — Runs LBJ's Congressional office when he volunteers for the U.S. Navy during World War II.

1943 — Buys a failing Austin radio station, KTBC, with inheritance from her mother, which she builds into the LBJ Holding Company, a successful group of radio and TV stations.

MARCH 19, 1944 — Gives birth to Lynda Bird Johnson in Virginia.

JULY 2, 1947 — Gives birth to Luci Baines Johnson in Virginia.

Lady Bird and Aunt Effie Pattillo.

Early 1930s.

In Washington, circa 1934.

1948 — Campaigns for her husband during his successful run for the U.S. Senate.

1956 — Campaigns for her husband during his successful re-election to the U.S. Senate.

1960 — Substitutes for the pregnant Jacqueline Kennedy, at John F. Kennedy's request, and travels 35,000 miles over 71 days campaigning for the Kennedy-Johnson presidential ticket.

NOV. 22 1963 — Is a witness as LBJ is sworn in as the 36th President of the United States on Air Force One after the assassination of President Kennedy.

At the U.S. Capitol, August 1958.

Swearing-in on Air Force One. Cecil Stoughton photo.

1964 — Creates the First Lady's Committee for a More Beautiful National Capital, which she later expands to a national program.

1964 — Travels through eight Southern states on a whistle-stop train, the Lady Bird Special, campaigning for the Johnson-Humphrey presidential ticket and promoting the Civil Rights Act of 1964.

September 1967 on the banks of the Pedernales River. Yoichi Okamoto photo.

SUMMER 1964 — Accompanies Secretary of the Interior Stewart Udall on several trips to the American West and develops a deep interest in conservation. Dedicates the Flaming Gorge Dam in Utah and tells audiences that natural beauty is their greatest resource and must be protected.

JAN. 20, 1965— Creates a new tradition at the presidential inauguration when she holds the Bible on which her husband placed his hand while repeating the presidential oath of office.

FEB. 4, 1965 — Launches her "Beautification" effort.

OCT. 7, 1965 — LBJ signs the Highway Beautification Act of 1965, nicknamed "Lady Bird's Bill."

1965 — Chairs Project Head Start for preschool children in the President's War on Poverty.

June 1965 ceremony for National Head Start Day.

JULY 26, 1968 — During the signing of a Department of the Interior Appropriations Bill, is thanked by LBJ for her dedication to conservation and is presented with 50 pens used to sign dozens of laws relating to conservation and beautification.

JANUARY 1969 — Returns to Texas with LBJ at the end of his term in office.

1969 — Columbia Island in the Potomac River is renamed Lady Bird Johnson Park.

1969 — Begins many years of service on the advisory boards of numerous National Parks, Historic Sites, Buildings and Monuments and encourages the beautification of Texas highways.

1970 — Publishes her memoir, *A White House Diary*, and co-authors *Wildflowers Across America* with Carlton Lees.

1971 — Chairs the Town Lake Beautification Project in Austin, is appointed to the UT System Board of Regents and helps

New Year's Eve 1972 at the LBJ Ranch. Frank Wolfe photo.

plan the LBJ Library and Museum and the LBJ School of Public Affairs in Austin, which is dedicated on May 22, 1971.

DECEMBER 1972 — She and the President give the LBJ Ranch house and surrounding property to the people of the United States as a National Historic Site.

JAN. 22, 1973 — LBJ dies of a heart attack at his Stonewall ranch.

1977 — Receives Medal of Freedom from President Gerald Ford.

Lynda Bird, Luci Baines and Lady Bird at Wildflower Center groundbreaking. Frank Wolfe photo.

DEC. 22, 1982 — On her 70th birthday, donates $125,000 and 60 acres of land near Austin to establish, along with her friend actress Helen Hayes, the National Wildflower Research Center.

1984 — Inducted into the Texas Women's Hall of Fame.

APRIL 28, 1988 — Receives Congressional Gold Medal from President Ronald Reagan.

1992 — LBJ Foundation creates the Lady Bird Johnson Conservation Award.

1995 — The wildflower center moves to the Hill Country southwest of Austin on land donated by Mrs. Johnson.

DECEMBER 1997 —The National Wildflower Research Center is renamed the Lady Bird Johnson Wildflower Center in honor of her 85th birthday.

2006 — The Lady Bird Johnson Wildflower Center becomes part of The University of Texas at Austin.

JULY 11, 2007 — Lady Bird dies at age 94 at home in Austin.

AUG. 6, 2007 — Town Lake is officially renamed Lady Bird Lake.

Sources: The Handbook of Texas Online, www.tshaonline. org; National First Ladies Library, www.firstladies.org; Lyndon Baines Johnson Library and Museum, www.lbjlib. utexas.edu; Austin City Connection, www.ci.austin.tx.us.

June 1991 on the LBJ Ranch. Frank Wolfe photo.

A Brief Sketch of Texas History

This two-part sketch of Texas' past, from prehistoric times to 1980, is based on "A Concise History of Texas" by former *Texas Almanac* editor Mike Kingston. Mr. Kingston's history was published in the 1986–1987 edition of the *Texas Almanac*, which marked Texas' sesquicentennial. Robert Plocheck, associate editor of the *Texas Almanac*, edited and expanded Mr. Kingston's history.

PREHISTORY TO ANNEXATION

Prehistoric Texas

Early Texans are believed to have been descendants of Asian groups that migrated across the Bering Strait during the Ice Ages of the past 50,000 years.

At intermittent periods, enough water accumulated in massive glaciers worldwide to lower the sea level several hundred feet. During these periods, the Bering Strait became a 1,300-mile-wide land bridge between North America and Asia.

These early adventurers worked their way southward for thousands of years, eventually getting as far as Tierra del Fuego in South America about 10,000 years ago.

Biologically, they were completely modern homo sapiens. No evidence has been found to indicate that any evolutionary change occurred in the New World.

Four basic stages reflecting cultural advancement of early inhabitants are used by archeologists in classifying evidence. These stages are the Paleo-Indian (20,000 to 7,000 years ago), Archaic (7,000 years ago to about the time of Christ), Woodland (time of Christ to 800–1,000 years ago), and Neo-American or Late Prehistoric (800–1,000 years ago until European contact).

Not all early people advanced through all these stages in Texas. Much cultural change occurred in adaptation to changes in climate. The Caddo tribes of East Texas, for example, reached the Neo-American stage before the Spanish and French explorers made contact in the 1500s and 1600s.

Pictographs can be seen on outcroppings near Paint Rock in Concho County. The earliest paintings date to prehistoric times. Matthew Minard photo.

Others, such as the Karankawas of the Gulf Coast, advanced no further than the Archaic stage of civilization at the same time. Still others advanced and then regressed in the face of a changing climate.

The earliest confirmed evidence indicates that humans were in Texas between 10,000 and 13,000 years ago.

Paleo-Indians were successful big-game hunters. Artifacts from this period are found across the state but not in great number, indicating that they were a small, nomadic population.

As Texas' climate changed at the end of the Ice Age about 7,000 years ago, inhabitants adapted. Apparently the state experienced an extended period of warming and drying, and the population during the **Archaic** period increased.

These Texans began to harvest fruits and nuts, and to exploit rivers for food, as indicated by the freshwater mussel shells in ancient garbage heaps.

The **Woodland** stage is distinguished by the development of settled societies, with crops and local wild plants providing much of their diet. The bow and arrow came into use, and the first pottery is associated with this period.

Pre-Caddoan tribes in East Texas had formed villages and were building distinctive mounds for burials and for ritual.

The **Neo-American** period is best exemplified by the highly civilized Caddoes, who had a complex culture with well-defined social stratification. They were fully agricultural and participated in trade over a wide area of North America.

The Spanish Explorations

Spain's exploration of North America was one of the first acts of a vigorous nation that was emerging from centuries of campaigns to oust the Islamic Moors from the Iberian Peninsula.

In early **1492**, the Spanish forces retook the province of Granada, completing the reconquista or reconquest.Later in the year, the Catholic royals of the united country, Ferdinand and Isabella, took a major stride toward shaping world history by commissioning Christopher Columbus for the voyage that was to bring Europeans to America.

As early as **1519, Capt. Alonso Alvarez de Pineda**, in the service of the governor of Jamaica, mapped the coast of Texas.

The **first recorded exploration of today's Texas** was made in the 1530s by **Alvar Núñez Cabeza de Vaca**, along with two other Spaniards and a Moorish slave named Estevanico. They were members of an expedition commanded by Panfilo de Narváez that left Cuba in 1528 to explore what is now the southeastern United States. Ill-fated from the beginning, many members of the expedition lost their lives, and others, including Cabeza de Vaca, were shipwrecked on the Texas coast. Eventually the band wandered into Mexico in 1536.

In **1540**, Francisco Vázquez de Coronado was commissioned to lead an exploration of the American Southwest. The quest took him to the land of the Pueblo Indians in what is now New Mexico. Native Americans, who had learned it was best to keep Europeans away from their homes, would suggest vast

Francisco Vasquez de Coronado explored the Texas High Plains looking for gold and silver. This drawing entitled Coronado's March — Colorado *(circa 1897) by Frederic Remington is courtesy of the Library of Congress.*

riches could be found in other areas. So Coronado pursued a fruitless search for gold and silver across the **High Plains of Texas**, Oklahoma and Kansas.

While Coronado was investigating Texas from the west, Luis de Moscoso Alvarado approached from the east. He assumed leadership of Hernando de Soto's expedition when the commander died on the banks of the Mississippi River. In **1542**, Moscoso's group ventured as far west as **Central Texas** before returning to the Mississippi.

Forty years passed after the Coronado and Moscoso expeditions before Fray Agustín Rodríguez, a Franciscan missionary, and Francisco Sánchez Chamuscado, a soldier, led an expedition into Texas and New Mexico.

Following the Río Conchos in Mexico to its confluence with the Rio Grande near present-day **Presidio** and then turning northwestward up the great river's valley, the explorers passed through the El Paso area in **1581**.

Juan de Oñate was granted the right to develop this area populated by Pueblo Indians in 1598. He blazed a trail across the desert from Santa Barbara, Chihuahua, to intersect the Rio Grande at the Pass of the North. For the next 200 years, this was the supply route from the interior of Mexico that served the northern colonies.

Texas was attractive to the Spanish in the 1600s. Small expeditions found trade possibilities, and missionaries ventured into the territory. Frays Juan de Salas and Diego López responded to a request by the Jumano Indians for religious instruction in **1629**, and for a brief time priests lived with the Indians near present-day **San Angelo**.

The first permanent settlement in Texas was established in **1681–1682** after New Mexico's Indians rebelled and drove Spanish settlers southward. The colonists retreated to the **El Paso** area, where the mis-

This engraving by Jan Van Vianen, created in 1698, shows La Salle, several priests and others on shore as supplies are unloaded from a ship. While exploring near the Trinity River, LaSalle was murdered by some of his men. Image courtesy of the Library of Congress.

sions of Corpus Christi de la Isleta and Nuestra Señora del Socorro — each named for a community in New Mexico — were established. Ysleta pueblo originally was located on the south side of the Rio Grande, but as the river changed its course, the pueblo ended up on the north bank. Now part of El Paso, the community is considered the oldest European settlement in Texas.

French Exploration

In 1682, **René Robert Cavelier, Sieur de La Salle**, explored the Mississippi River to its mouth at the Gulf of Mexico. La Salle claimed the vast territory drained by the river for France.

Two years later, La Salle returned to the New World with four ships and enough colonists to establish his country's claim. Guided by erroneous maps, this second expedition overshot the mouth of the Mississippi by 400 miles and ended up on the Texas coast. Though short of supplies because of the loss of two of the ships, the French colonists established Fort Saint Louis on Garcitas Creek several miles inland from Lavaca Bay.

In 1687, La Salle and a group of soldiers began an overland trip to find French outposts on the Mississippi River. Somewhere west of the Trinity River, the explorer was murdered by some of his men. His grave has never been found. (A more detailed account of La Salle's expedition can be found in the *Texas Almanac 1998–1999* and on the *Texas Almanac* Web site.)

In 1689, Spanish authorities sent **Capt. Alonso de León**, the governor of Coahuila (which at various times included Texas in its jurisdiction), into Texas to

confront the French. He headed eastward from present-day **Eagle Pass** and eventually found the tattered remnants of Fort Saint Louis.

Indians had destroyed the settlement and killed many colonists. León continued tracking survivors of the ill-fated colony into East Texas.

Spanish Rule

Father **Damián Massanet** accompanied León on this journey. The priest was fascinated with tales about the "Tejas" Indians of the region.

Tejas meant *friendly*, but at the time the term was considered a tribal name. Actually these Indians were members of the Caddo Confederacy that controlled parts of four present states: Texas, Louisiana, Arkansas and Oklahoma.

The Caddo religion acknowledged one supreme god, and when a Tejas chief asked Father Massanet to stay and instruct his people in his faith, the Spaniards promised to return and establish a mission.

The pledge was redeemed in **1690** when the mission San Francisco de los Tejas was founded near present-day Weches in Houston County.

Twin disasters struck this missionary effort. Spanish government officials quickly lost interest when the French threat at colonization diminished. And as was the case with many New World Indians who had no resistance to European diseases, the Tejas soon were felled by an epidemic. The Indians blamed the new religion and resisted conversion. The mission languished, and it was difficult to supply it from other Spanish outposts in northern Mexico. In 1693, the Spanish officials closed the mission effort in **East Texas.**

Although Spain had not made a determined effort to settle Texas, great changes were coming to the territory. Spain introduced horses into the Southwest. By the late 1600s, Comanches were using the horses to expand their range southward across the plains, displacing the Apaches. In the **1720s**, the **Apaches** moved onto the lower Texas Plains, usurping the traditional hunting grounds of the Jumanos and others. The nomadic Coahuiltecan bands were particularly hard hit.

In 1709, Fray Antonio de San Buenaventura y Olivares had made an initial request to establish a mission at San Pedro Springs (today's San Antonio) to minister to the Coahuiltecans. Spanish officials denied the request. However, new fears over the French movement into East Texas changed that.

Another Franciscan, **Father Francisco Hidalgo**, who had earlier served at the missions in East Texas, returned to them when he and **Father Antonio Margil de Jesús** accompanied **Capt. Diego Ramón** on an expedition to the area in 1716. In that year, the mission of San Francisco de los Neches was established near the site of the old San Francisco de los Tejas mission. Nuestra Señora de Guadalupe was located at the present-day site of Nacogdoches, and Nuestra Señora de los Dolores was placed near present-day San Augustine.

The East Texas missions did little better on the second try, and supplying the frontier missions remained difficult. It became apparent that a way station between northern Mexico and East Texas was needed.

In 1718, Spanish officials consented to Fray Olivares' request to found a mission at San Pedro Springs. That mission, called **San Antonio de Valero**, was later to be known as the **Alamo**. Because the Indians of the region often did not get along with each other, other missions were established to serve each group.

These missions flourished and each became an early ranching center. But the large herds of cattle and horses attracted trouble. The San Antonio missions began to face the wrath of the Apaches. The mission system, which attempted to convert the Indians to Christianity and to "civilize" them, was partially successful in subduing minor tribes but not larger tribes like the Apaches.

The Spanish realized that more stable colonization efforts must be made. Indians from Mexico, such as the Tlascalans who fought with Cortés against the Aztecs, were brought into Texas to serve as examples of "good" Indians for the wayward natives.

In **1731**, Spanish colonists from the **Canary Islands** were brought to Texas and founded the **Villa of San Fernando de Béxar**, the first civil jurisdiction in the province and today's **San Antonio**.

In the late 1730s, Spanish officials became concerned over the vulnerability of the large area between the Sierra Madre Oriental and the Gulf Coast in northern Mexico. The area was unsettled, a haven for runaway Indian slaves and marauders, and it was a wide-open pathway for the English or French to travel from the Gulf to the rich silver mines in Durango.

For seven years, the search for the right colonizer went on before **José de Escandón** was selected in 1746. A professional military man and successful administrator, Escandón earned a high reputation by subduing Indians in central Mexico. On receiving the assignment, he launched a broad land survey of the area running from the mountains to the Gulf and from the Río Pánuco in Tamaulipas, Mexico, to the Nueces River in Texas.

In 1747, he began placing colonists in settlements throughout the area. **Tomás Sánchez** received a land grant on the Rio Grande in 1755 from which **Laredo** developed. And other small Texas communities along the river sprang up as a result of Escandón's well-executed plan. Many old Hispanic families in Texas hold title to their land based on grants in this period.

In the following decades, a few other Spanish colonists settled around the old missions and frontier forts. **Antonio Gil Ybarbo** led one group that settled **Nacogdoches** in the **1760s and 1770s**.

The Demise of Spain

Spain's final 60 years of control of the province of Texas were marked with a few successes and a multitude of failures, all of which could be attributed to a breakdown in the administrative system.

Charles III, the fourth of the Bourbon line of kings, took the Spanish throne in 1759. He launched a series of reforms in the New World. The king's choice of administrators was excellent. In 1765, José de Gálvez was dispatched to New Spain (an area that then included all of modern Mexico and much of today's American West) with instructions to improve both the economy and the defense of the area.

Gálvez initially toured parts of the vast region, gaining first-hand insight into the practical problems of the colony. There were many that could be traced to Spain's basic concepts of colonial government. Texas, in particular, suffered from the mercantilist economic system that attempted to funnel all colonial trade through ports in Mexico.

But administrative reforms by Gálvez and his nephew, Bernardo Gálvez, namesake of Galveston, were to be followed by ill-advised policies by successors.

Problems with the Comanches, Apaches and "Norteños," as the Spanish called some tribes, continued to plague the province, too.

About the same time, Spain undertook the administration of the Louisiana Territory. One of the terms

The Ybarbo Ranch House on the grounds of Stephen F. Austin State University in Nacogdoches was built around 1774 by Antonio Gil Ybarbo, a Spanish lieutenant governor and commander of the militia in Nacogdoches in the late eighteenth century. Image courtesy of the Library of Congress.

of the cession by France was that the region would enjoy certain trading privileges denied to other Spanish dependencies. So although Texas and Louisiana were neighbors, trade between the two provinces was banned.

The Spanish crown further complicated matters by placing the administration of Louisiana under authorities in Cuba, while Texas remained under the authorities in Mexico City.

The death of Charles III in 1788 and the beginning of the French Revolution a year later weakened Spain's hold on the New World dominions. Charles IV was not as good a sovereign as his predecessor, and his choice of ministers was poor. The quality of frontier administrators declined, and relations with Indians soured further.

Charles IV's major blunder, however, was to side with French royalty during the revolution, earning Spain the enmity of Napoleon Bonaparte. Spain also allied with England in an effort to thwart Napoleon, and in this losing cause, the Spanish were forced to cede Louisiana back to France.

In 1803, Napoleon broke a promise to retain the territory and sold it to the United States. Spain's problems in the New World thereby took on an altogether different dimension. Now, Anglo-Americans cast longing eyes on the vast undeveloped territory of Texas.

With certain exceptions for royalists who left the American colonies during the revolution, Spain had maintained a strict prohibition against Anglo or other non-Spanish settlers in their New World territories. But they were unprepared to police the eastern border of Texas after removing the presidios in the 1760s. What had been a provincial line became virtually overnight an international boundary, and an ill-defined one at that.

American Immigrants

Around **1800, Anglo-Americans** began to probe the Spanish frontier. Some settled in East Texas and others crossed the Red River and were tolerated by authorities.

Others, however, were thought to have nefarious designs. Philip Nolan was the first of the American filibusters to test Spanish resolve. Several times he entered Texas to capture wild horses to sell in the United States.

But in 1801, the Spanish perceived an attempted insurrection by Nolan and his followers. He was killed in a battle near present-day Waco, and his company was taken captive to work in the mines in northern Mexico.

Spanish officials were beginning to realize that the economic potential of Texas must be developed if the Anglo-Americans were to be neutralized. But Spain's centuries-long role in the history of Texas was almost over.

Resistance to Spanish rule had developed in the New World colonies. Liberal ideas from the American and French revolutions had grown popular, despite the crown's attempts to prevent their dissemination.

In Spain, three sovereigns — Charles IV, Napoleon's brother Joseph Bonaparte, and Ferdinand VII — claimed the throne, often issuing different edicts

Col-lee, chief of a band of Cherokees. As early as 1818, Cherokees settled in Texas north of Nacogdoches on land between the Trinity and Sabine rivers. Photo from the Smithsonian Institution.

simultaneously. Since the time of Philip II, Spain had been a tightly centralized monarchy with the crown making most decisions. Now, chaos reigned in the colonies.

As Spain's grip on the New World slipped between 1790 and 1820, Texas was almost forgotten, an internal province of little importance. Colonization was ignored; the Spanish government had larger problems in Europe and in Mexico.

Spain's mercantile economic policy penalized colonists in the area, charging them high prices for trade goods and paying low prices for products sent to markets in the interior of New Spain. As a result, settlers from central Mexico had no incentives to come to Texas. Indeed, men of ambition in the province often prospered by turning to illegal trade with Louisiana or to smuggling. On the positive side, however, Indians of the province had been mollified through annual gifts and by developing a dependence on Spain for trade goods.

Ranching flourished. In **1795**, a census found **69 families** living on 45 ranches in the **San Antonio** area. A census in **1803** indicated that there were **100,000 head of cattle** in Texas. But aside from a few additional families in Nacogdoches and La Bahía (near present-day Goliad), the province was thinly populated.

The largest group of early immigrants from the

United States was not Anglo, but Indian.

As early as **1818, Cherokees** of the southeastern United States came to Texas, settling north of Nacogdoches on lands between the Trinity and Sabine rivers. The Cherokees had been among the first U.S. Indians to accept the federal government's offers of resettlement. As American pioneers entered the newly acquired lands of Georgia, Alabama and other areas of the Southeast, the Indians were systematically removed, through legal means or otherwise.

Some of the displaced groups settled on land provided in Arkansas Territory, but others, such as the Cherokees, came to Texas. These Cherokees were among the "Five Civilized Tribes" that had adopted agriculture and many Anglo customs in an unsuccessful attempt to get along with their new neighbors. Alabama and Coushatta tribes had exercised squatters' rights in present-day Sabine County in the early 1800s, and soon after the Cherokees arrived, groups of Shawnee, Delaware and Kickapoo Indians came from the United States.

A **second wave of Anglo** immigrants began to arrive in Texas, larger than the first and of a different character. These Anglos were not so interested in agricultural opportunities as in other schemes to quickly recoup their fortunes.

Spain recognized the danger represented by the unregulated colonization by Americans. The Spanish Cortes' colonization law of 1813 attempted to build a buffer between the eastern frontier and northern Mexico. Special permission was required for Americans to settle within 52 miles of the international boundary, although this prohibition often was ignored.

As initially envisioned, Americans would be allowed to settle the interior of Texas. Colonists from Europe and Mexico would be placed along the eastern frontier to limit contact between the Americans and the United States. Spanish officials felt that the Americans already in Texas illegally would be stable if given a stake in the province through land ownership.

Moses Austin, a former Spanish subject in the vast Louisiana Territory, applied for the first empresario grant from the Spanish government. With the intercession of Baron de Bastrop, a friend of Austin's from Missouri Territory, the request was approved in January **1821**.

Austin agreed to settle **300 families** on land bounded by the Brazos and Colorado rivers on the east and west, by El Camino Real (the old military road running from San Antonio to Nacogdoches) on the north, and by the Gulf Coast.

But Austin died in June 1821, leaving the work to his son, **Stephen F. Austin**. Problems began as soon as the first authorized colonists arrived in Texas the following December when it was learned that Mexico had gained independence from Spain.

Mexico, 1810–1836

Mexico's war for independence, 1810–1821, was savage and bloody in the interior provinces, and Texas suffered as well.

In early 1812, Mexican revolutionary **José Bernardo Gutiérrez de Lara** traveled to Natchitoches, La., where, with the help of U.S. agents, an expedition was organized. **Augustus W. Magee**, a West Point graduate, commanded the troop, which entered Texas in August 1812. This "Republican Army of the North" easily took Nacogdoches, where it gathered recruits.

After withstanding a siege at La Bahía, the army took San Antonio and proclaimed the First Republic of Texas in April 1813. A few months later, the republican forces were bloodily subdued at the Battle of Medina River.

Royalist Gen. Joaquín de Arredondo executed a staggering number of more than 300 republicans, including some Americans, at San Antonio, and a young lieutenant, **Antonio López de Santa Anna**, was recognized for valor under fire.

When the war finally ended in Mexico in 1821, little more had been achieved than separation from Spain.

Sensing that liberal reforms in Spain would reduce the authority of royalists in the New World, Mexican conservatives had led the revolt against the mother country. They also achieved early victories in the debate over the form of government the newly independent Mexico should adopt.

An independent Mexico was torn between advocates of centralist and federalist forms of government. The former royalists won the opening debates, settling Emperor Agustín de Iturbide on the new Mexican throne. But he was overthrown and the Constitution of 1824, a federalist document, was adopted.

The Mexican election of 1828 was a turning point in the history of the country when the legally elected administration of Manuel Gómez Pedraza was overthrown by supporters of Vicente Guerrero, who in turn was ousted by his own vice president Anastasio Bustamante. Mexico's most chaotic political period followed. Between 1833 and 1855, the Mexican presidency changed hands 36 times.

Texas, 1821–1833

Mexico's **land policy,** like Spain's, differed from the U.S. approach. Whereas the United States sold land directly to settlers or to speculators who dealt with the pioneers, the Mexicans retained tight control of the property transfer until predetermined agreements for development were fulfilled.

But a 4,428-acre *sitio* — a square league — and a 177-acre *labor* could be obtained for only surveying costs and administrative fees as low as $50. The empresario was rewarded with grants of large tracts of land, but only when he fulfilled his quota of families to be brought to the colonies.

Considering the prices the U.S. government charged, Texas' land was indeed a bargain and a major attraction to those Americans looking for a new start.

More than 25 empresarios were commissioned to settle colonists. Empresarios included **Green DeWitt** and **Martín de León**, who in 1824 founded the city of Guadalupe Victoria (present-day Victoria).

By 1830, Texas boasted an estimated population of 15,000, with Anglo-Americans outnumbering Hispanics by a margin of four to one.

Stephen F. Austin was easily the most successful empresario. After his initial success, Austin was authorized in 1825 to bring 900 more families to Texas, and in 1831, he and his partner, **Samuel Williams**, received another concession to bring 800 Mexican and European families. Through Austin's efforts, 1,540 land titles were issued to settlers.

In the early years of colonization, the settlers busied themselves clearing land, planting crops, building homes and fending off Indian attacks. Many were successful in establishing a subsistence economy.

One weakness of the Mexican colonial policy was that it did not provide the factors for a market economy. Although towns were established, credit, banks and good roads were not provided by the government.

Ports were established at Galveston and Matagorda bays after Mexican independence, but the colonists felt they needed more, particularly one at the mouth of the Brazos. And foreign ships were barred from coastwise trade, which posed a particular hardship because Mexico had few merchant ships.

To settle in Texas, pioneers had to become Mexican citizens and to embrace Roman Catholicism. Most of the Americans were Protestants, if they adhered to any religion, and they were fiercely defensive of the right to **religious freedom** enjoyed in the United States.

Although no more than one-fourth of the Americans ever swore allegiance to the Catholic Church, the requirement was a long-standing irritation.

Slavery, too, was a point of contention. Mexico prohibited the introduction of slavery after December 1827. Nevertheless, several efforts were made to evade the government policy. Austin got the state Legislature to recognize labor contracts under which slaves were technically free but bound themselves to their masters for life. Often entire families were covered by a single contract. While many early Anglo colonists were not slaveholders, they were Southerners, and the ownership of slaves was a cultural institution that they supported. The problem was never settled during Texas' colonial period despite the tensions it generated.

Most of the early Anglo-American colonists in Texas intended to fulfill their pledge to become good Mexican citizens. But the political turmoil following the 1828 presidential election raised doubts in the Americans' minds about the ability of Mexico to make representative government function properly.

On a tour of Texas in 1827 and 1828, Gen. Manuel Mier y Terán noted that the Texans "carried their constitutions in their pockets." And he feared the Americans' desire for more rights and liberties than the government was prepared to offer would lead to rebellion. Unrest increased in Texas when Gen. Mier y Terán

A statue of Moses Austin stands in front of City Hall in San Antonio. Robert Plocheck photo.

began reinforcing existing garrisons and establishing new ones.

But a major factor in the discontent of Americans came with the **decree of April 6, 1830**, when the Mexican government in essence banned further American immigration into Texas and tried to control slavery. (For an account of how Texans opposed this decree at Fort Anahuac, see Texas History Features on the *Texas Almanac* Web site.)

Austin protested that the prohibition against American immigration would not stop the flow of Anglos into Texas; it would stop only stable, prosperous Americans from coming.

Austin's predictions were fulfilled. Illegal immigrants continued to come. By 1836, the estimated number of people in Texas had reached 35,000.

Prelude to Revolution

In the midst of all the turmoil, Texas was prospering. By 1834, some 7,000 bales of cotton with a value of $315,000 were shipped to New Orleans. In the middle of the decade, Texas exports, including cotton and beaver, otter and deer skins, amounted to $500,000.

Trade ratios were out of balance, however, because $630,000 in manufactured goods were imported. And, there was little currency in Texas. Ninety percent of the business transactions were conducted with barter or credit.

In 1833 and 1834, the **Coahuila y Texas** legislature was diligently trying to respond to the complaints of the Texas colonists. The English language was recognized for official purposes. Religious toleration was approved. The court system was revised, providing Texas with an appellate court and trial by jury.

In Mexico City, however, a different scenario was developing. **Santa Anna** assumed supreme authority in April 1834 and began dismantling the federalist government. Among the most offensive changes dictated by Santa Anna was the reduction of the state militias to one man per each 500 population. The intent was to eliminate possible armed opposition to the emerging centralist government.

But liberals in the state of Zacatecas in central Mexico rebelled. Santa Anna's response was particularly brutal, as he tried to make an example of the rebels. Troops were allowed to sack the state capital after the victory over the insurgents.

Trouble also was brewing closer to the Texans. In March 1833, the Coahuila y Texas legislature moved the state capital from Saltillo to Monclova. The Monclova legislature in 1834 gave the governor authority to sell 400 *sitios* — or 1.77 million acres of land — to finance the government and to provide for protection. A year later the lawmakers criticized Santa Anna's reputation on federalism. Seeing a chance to regain lost prestige, Saltillo declared for Santa Anna and set up an opposition government. In the spring of 1835, Santa Anna sent his brother-in-law, Martín Perfecto de Cos, to break up the state government at Monclova.

Texans were appalled by the breakdown in state government, coming on the heels of so many assurances that the political situation was to improve.

Texas politics were polarizing. A "war party" advocated breaking away from Mexico altogether, while a "peace party" urged calm and riding out the political storm. Most of the settlers, however, aligned with neither group.

In January 1835, Santa Anna sent a detachment of soldiers to Anahuac to reinforce the customs office, but duties were being charged irregularly at various ports on the coast. William B. Travis, in an act not supported by all colonists, led a contingent of armed colonists against the Mexican soldiers, who withdrew without a fight.

Although some members of the peace party wrote Mexican Gen. **Martín Perfecto de Cos**, stationed at Matamoros, apologizing for the action, he was not compromising. Cos demanded that the group be arrested and turned over to him. The Texans refused.

The committees of correspondence, organized at the Convention of 1832 (which had asked that Texas be separated from Coahuila), began organizing another meeting. Because the term "convention" aroused visions of revolution in the eyes of Mexican officials, the gathering at Washington-on-the-Brazos in October 1835 was called a "consultation." But with the breakdown of the state government and with Santa Anna's repeal of the Constitution of 1824, the American settlers felt well within their rights to provide a new framework with which to govern Texas.

Fresh from brutally putting down the rebellion in Zacatecas, Santa Anna turned his attention to Texas. Gen. Cos was determined to regarrison the state, and the settlers were equally determined to keep soldiers out.

Col. **Domingo de Ugartechea**, headquartered at San Antonio, became concerned about armed rebellion when he heard of the incident at Anahuac. He recalled a six-pound cannon that had been given DeWitt colonists to fight Indians.

Ugartechea ordered Cpl. Casimira de León with five men to Gonzales to retrieve the weapon. No problems were expected, but officials at Gonzales refused to surrender the weapon. When the Mexicans reinforced Cpl. León's men, a call was sent out for volunteers to help the Gonzales officials. Dozens responded.

Oct. 2, 1835, the Texans challenged the Mexicans with a **"come-and-take-it"** flag over the cannon. After a brief skirmish, the Mexicans withdrew, but the first rounds in the Texas Revolution had been fired.

Winning Independence

As 1836 opened, Texans felt in control of their destiny and secure in their land and their liberties. The Mexican army had been driven from their soil.

But tragedy loomed. Easy victories over government forces at Anahuac, Nacogdoches, Goliad, Gonzales and San Antonio in the fall of 1835 had given them a false sense of security. That independent mood was their undoing, for no government worthy of the name coordinated the defense of Texas. Consequently, as the Mexican counterattack developed, no one was in charge. Sam Houston was titular commander-in-chief of the Texas forces, but he had little authority.

Some even thought the Mexicans would not try to re-enter Texas. Few Texans counted on the energy and determination of Santa Anna, the dictator of Mexico.

The status of the strongholds along the San Antonio River was of concern to Houston. In mid-January, Houston sent **James Bowie** to San Antonio to determine if the Alamo was defensible. If not, Bowie had orders to destroy it and withdraw the men and artillery to Gonzales and Copano.

On Feb. 8, David Crockett of Tennessee, bringing 12 men with him, arrived to aid the revolutionaries.

On Feb. 12, 1836, Santa Anna's main force crossed the Rio Grande headed for San Antonio. The Mexican battle plan had been debated. But Mexico's national pride was bruised by the series of defeats the nation's army had suffered in 1835, capped by Gen. Cos's ouster from San Antonio in December.

On Feb. 11, the Consultation's "governor of the government" **Henry Smith**, sent **William B. Travis** to San Antonio. Immediately a split in command at the **Alamo** garrison arose. Most were American volunteers who looked to the Houston-appointed Bowie as their leader. Travis had only a handful of Texas army regulars. Bowie and Travis agreed to share the command of 150 men.

Arriving at the Alamo on Feb. 23, Santa Anna left no doubt regarding his attitude toward the defenders.

Members of the San Antonio Living History Association fire a volley during a pre-dawn memorial service at Alamo Plaza in San Antonio March 6, 2007. The 13-day Battle of the Alamo ended the morning of March 6, 1936. Eric Gay/AP photo.

He hoisted a blood-red flag, the traditional Mexican symbol of no quarter, no surrender, no mercy. Travis and Bowie defiantly answered the display with a cannon shot.

Immediately the Mexicans began surrounding the Alamo and bombarding it. Throughout the first night and nights to come, Santa Anna kept up a continual din to destroy the defenders' morale.

On Feb. 24, Bowie became ill and relinquished his share of command to Travis. Although the Mexican bombardment of the Alamo continued, none of the defenders was killed. In fact, they conducted several successful forays outside the fortress to burn buildings that were providing cover for the Mexican gunners and to gather firewood.

Messengers also successfully moved through the Mexican lines at will, and 32 reinforcements from Gonzales made it into the Alamo without a loss on March 1.

Historians disagree over which flag flew over the defenders of the Alamo.

Mexican sources have said that Santa Anna was outraged when he saw flying over the fortress a Mexican tricolor, identical to the ones carried by his troops except with the numbers "1 8 2 4" emblazoned upon it. Some Texas historians have accepted this version because the defenders of the Alamo could not have known that Texas' independence had been declared on March 2. To the knowledge of the Alamo's defenders, the last official position taken by Texas was in support of the Constitution of 1824, which the flag symbolized. But the only flag found after the battle, according to historian Walter Lord, was one flown by the **New Orleans Greys**.

By March 5, Santa Anna had 4,000 men in camp,

a force he felt sufficient to subdue the Alamo.

Historians disagree on the date, but the story goes that on March 3 or 5, Travis called his command together and explained the bleak outlook. He then asked those willing to die for freedom to stay and fight; those not willing could try to get through enemy lines to safety. Even the sick Jim Bowie vowed to stay. Only Louis (Moses) Rose, a veteran of Napoleon's retreat from Moscow slipped out of the Alamo that night.

At dawn March 6, Santa Anna's forces attacked. When the fighting stopped between 8:30 and 9 a.m., all the defenders were dead. Only a few women, children and black slaves survived the assault. **Davy Crockett**'s fate is still debated. Mexican officer Enrique de la Peña held that Crockett was captured with a few other defenders and was executed by Santa Anna.

Santa Anna's victory came at the cost of almost one-third his forces killed or wounded. Their deaths in such number set back Santa Anna's timetable. The fall of the Alamo also brutally shook Texans out of their lethargy.

Sam Houston, finally given command of the entire Texas army, left the convention at **Washington-on-the-Brazos** on the day of the fall of the Alamo.

On March 11, he arrived at Gonzales to begin organizing the troops. Two days later, **Susanna Dickinson**, the wife of one of the victims of the Alamo, and two slaves arrived at Houston's position at Gonzales with the news of the fall of the San Antonio fortress.

Houston then ordered **James Fannin** to abandon the old presidio **La Bahía** at Goliad and to retreat to Victoria. Fannin had arrived at the fort in late January with more than 400 men. As a former West Pointer, he had a background in military planning, but Fannin had refused Travis' pleas for help, and after receiving

Houston's orders, Fannin waited for scouting parties to return.

Finally, on March 19, he left, but too late. Forward elements of Gen. José de Urrea's troops caught Fannin's command on an open prairie. After a brief skirmish Fannin surrendered.

Santa Anna was furious when Gen. Urrea appealed for clemency for the captives. The Mexican leader issued orders for their execution. On March 27, a Palm Sunday, most of the prisoners were divided into groups and marched out of Goliad, thinking they were being transferred to other facilities. When the executions began, many escaped. But about 350 were killed.

On March 17, Houston reached the Colorado near the present city of La Grange and began receiving reinforcements. Within a week, the small force of several hundred had become almost respectable, with 1,200-1,400 men in camp.

By the time Houston reached the Colorado, the convention at Washington-on-the-Brazos was completing work. **David Burnet**, a New Jersey native, was named interim president of the new Texas government, and **Lorenzo de Zavala**, a Yucatán native, was named vice president.

On March 27, Houston moved his men to San Felipe on the Brazos. The Texas army was impatient for a fight, and there was talk in the ranks that, if action did not develop soon, a new commander should be elected.

As the army marched farther back toward the San Jacinto River, two Mexican couriers were captured and gave Houston the information he had hoped for. Santa Anna in his haste had led the small Mexican force in front of Houston. Now the Texans had an opportunity to win the war.

Throughout the revolt, Houston's intelligence system had operated efficiently. Scouts, commanded by **Erastus "Deaf" Smith**, kept the Texans informed of Mexican troop movements. **Hendrick Arnold**, a free black, was a valuable spy, posing as a runaway slave to enter Mexican camps to gain information.

Early on April 21, Gen. Cos reinforced Santa Anna's troops with more than 500 men. The new arrivals, who had marched all night, disrupted the camp's routine for a time, but soon all the soldiers and officers settled down for a midday rest.

About 3 p.m., Houston ordered his men to parade

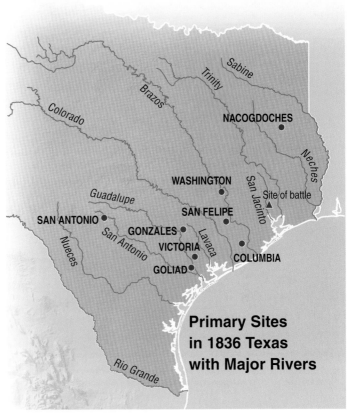

Primary Sites in 1836 Texas with Major Rivers

and the battle was launched at 4:30 p.m.

A company of Mexican-Texans, commanded by Juan Seguín, had served as the rear guard for Houston's army through much of the retreat across Texas and had fought many skirmishes with the Mexican army in the process.

Perhaps fearing the Mexican-Texans would be mistaken for Santa Anna's soldiers, Houston had assigned the company to guard duty as the battle approached. But after the men protested, they fought in the battle of San Jacinto.

Historians disagree widely on the number of troops on each side. Houston probably had about 900 while Santa Anna had between 1,100 and 1,300.

But the Texans had the decided psychological advantage. Two thirds of the fledging Republic's army were "old Texans" who had family and land to defend. They had an investment of years of toil in building their homes. And they were eager to avenge the massacre of men at the Alamo and Goliad.

In less than 20 minutes they set the Mexican army to rout. More than 600 Mexicans were killed and hundreds more wounded or captured. Only nine of the Texans died in the fight.

It was not until the following day that Santa Anna was captured. One Texan noticed that a grubby soldier his patrol found in the high grass had a silk shirt under his filthy jacket. Although denying he was an officer,

Independence Hall, a reconstructed version of the building where the Texas Declaration of Independence was signed on March 2, 1836, at Washington-on-the-Brazos. Robert Plocheck photo.

he was taken back to camp, where he was acknowledged with cries of "El Presidente" by other prisoners.

Santa Anna introduced himself when taken to the wounded Houston.

President Burnet took charge of Santa Anna, and on May 14 the dictator signed **two treaties at Velasco**, a public document and a secret one. The public agreement declared that hostilities would cease, that the Mexican army would withdraw to south of the **Rio Grande**, that prisoners would be released and that Santa Anna would be shipped to Veracruz as soon as possible.

In the secret treaty, Santa Anna agreed to recognize Texas' independence, to give diplomatic recognition, to negotiate a commercial treaty and to set the Rio Grande as the new Republic's boundary.

Republic of Texas, 1836–1845

Sam Houston was easily the most dominant figure throughout the nearly 10-year history of the Republic of Texas. While he was roundly criticized for the retreat across Texas during the revolution, the victory at San Jacinto endeared him to most of the new nation's inhabitants.

Houston handily defeated Henry Smith and Stephen F. Austin in the election called in September 1836 by the interim government, and he was inaugurated as president on Oct. 22.

In the same September election, voters overwhelmingly approved a proposal to request annexation to the United States.

The first cabinet appointed by the new president represented an attempt to heal old political wounds. Austin was named secretary of state and Smith was secretary of the treasury. But Texas suffered a major tragedy in late December 1836 when Austin, the acknowledged **"Father of Texas,"** died of pneumonia.

A host of problems faced the new government. Santa Anna was still in custody, and public opinion favored his execution. Texas' leadership wisely kept Santa Anna alive, first to keep from giving the Mexicans an emotional rallying point for launching another invasion. Second, the Texas leaders hoped that the dictator would keep his promise to work for recognition of Texas.

Santa Anna was released in November 1836 and made his way to Washington, D.C. Houston hoped the dictator could persuade U.S. President **Andrew Jackson** to recognize Texas. Jackson refused to see Santa Anna, who returned to Mexico, where he had fallen from power.

Another major challenge was the Texas army. The new commander, Felix Huston, favored an invasion of Mexico, and the troops, made up now mostly of American volunteers who came to Texas after the battle of San Jacinto, were rebellious and ready to fight.

President Houston tried to replace Felix Huston with **Albert Sidney Johnston**, but Huston seriously wounded Johnston in a duel. In May 1837, Huston was asked to the capital in Columbia to discuss the invasion. While Huston was away from the troops, Houston sent **Thomas J. Rusk**, the secretary of war, to furlough the army without pay — but with generous land grants. Only 600 men were retained in the army.

The Republic's other problems were less tractable. The economy needed attention, Indians still were a threat, Mexico remained warlike, foreign relations had to be developed, and relations with the United States had to be solidified.

The greatest disappointment in Houston's first term was the failure to have the Republic annexed to the United States. Henry Morfit, President Jackson's agent, toured the new Republic in the summer of 1836. Although impressed, Morfit reported that Texas' best chance at continued independence lay in the "stupidity of the rulers of Mexico and the financial embarrassment of the Mexican government." He recommended that annexation be delayed.

Houston's foreign policy achieved initial success when **J. Pinckney Henderson** negotiated a trade treaty with Great Britain. Although the agreement was short of outright diplomatic recognition, it was progress. In the next few years, France, Belgium, The Netherlands and some German states recognized the new Republic.

Under the constitution, Houston's first term lasted only two years, and he could not succeed himself. His successor, **Mirabeau B. Lamar**, had grand visions and was a spendthrift. Houston's first term cost Texas only about $500,000, while President Lamar and the Congress spent $5 million in the next three years.

Early in 1839, Lamar gained recognition as the **"Father of Education"** in Texas when the Congress granted each of the existing 23 counties three leagues of land to be used for education. Fifty leagues of land were set aside for a university.

Despite the lip service paid to education, the government did not have the money for several years to set up a school system. Most education during the Republic was provided by private schools and churches.

Lamar's Indian policies differed greatly from those under Houston. Houston had lived with Cherokees as a youth, was adopted as a member of a tribe and advocated Indian rights long before coming to Texas. Lamar reflected more the frontier attitude toward American Indians. His first experience in public life was as secretary to Gov. George Troup of Georgia, who successfully opposed the federal government's policy of assimilation of Indians at the time. Indians were simply removed from Georgia.

Texans first tried to negotiate the Cherokees' removal from the region, but in July 1839, the Indians were forcibly ejected from Texas at the **Battle of the Neches River** in Van Zandt County. Houston's close friend, the aging Cherokee chief **Philip Bowles**, was killed in the battle while Houston was visiting former President Jackson in Tennessee. The Cherokees moved on to Arkansas and Indian Territory.

Houston was returned to the presidency of the Republic in 1841. His second administration was even more frugal than his first; soon income almost matched expenditures.

Houston re-entered negotiations with the Indians in Central Texas in an attempt to quell the raids on settlements. A number of trading posts were opened along the frontier to pacify the Indians.

War fever reached a high pitch in Texas in 1842, and Houston grew increasingly unpopular because he would not launch an offensive war against Mexico.

In March 1842, Gen. **Rafael Vásquez** staged guerrilla raids on San Antonio, Victoria and Goliad, but quickly left the Republic.

A force of 3,500 Texas volunteers gathered at San Antonio demanding that Mexico be punished. Houston urged calm, but the clamor increased when Mexican **Gen. Adrian Woll** captured San Antonio in September. He raised the Mexican flag and declared the reconquest of Texas.

Ranger Capt. **Jack Hays** was camped nearby. Within days 600 volunteers had joined him, eager to drive the Mexican invaders from Texas soil. Gen. Woll withdrew after the **Battle of Salado**.

Alexander Somervell was ordered by Houston to follow with 700 troops and harass the Mexican army. He reached Laredo in December and found no Mexican troops. Somervell crossed the Rio Grande to find military targets. A few days later, the commander returned home, but 300 soldiers decided to continue the raid under the command of William S. Fisher. On Christmas day, this group attacked the village of **Mier**, only to be defeated by a Mexican force that outnumbered them 10-to-1.

After attempting mass escape, the survivors of the Mier expedition were marched to Mexico City where Santa Anna, again in political power, ordered their execution. When officers refused to carry out the order, it was amended to require execution of one of every 10 Texans. The prisoners drew beans to determine who would be shot; bearers of **black beans** were executed. Texans again were outraged by the treatment of prisoners, but the war fever soon subsided.

As Houston completed his second term, the United States was becoming more interested in annexation. Texas had seriously flirted with Great Britain and France, and the Americans did not want a rival republic with close foreign ties on the North American continent. Houston orchestrated the early stages of the final steps toward annexation. It was left to his successor, **Anson Jones**, to complete the process.

The Republic of Texas' main claim to fame is simply endurance. Its settlers, unlike other Americans who had military help, had cleared a large region of Indians by themselves, had established farms and communities and had persevered through extreme economic hardship.

Adroit political leadership had gained the Republic recognition from many foreign countries. Although dreams of empire may have dimmed, Texans had established an identity on a major portion of the North American continent. The frontier had been pushed to a line running from Corpus Christi through San Antonio and Austin to the Red River.

The U.S. presidential campaign of 1844 was to make Texas a part of the Union. ☆

Annexation

Annexation to the United States was far from automatic for Texas once independence from Mexico was gained in 1836. Sam Houston noted that Texas "was more coy than forward" as negotiations reached a climax in 1845.

William H. Wharton was Texas' first representative in Washington. His instructions were to gain diplomatic recognition of the new Republic's independence.

After some squabbles, the U.S. Congress appropriated funds for a minister to Texas, and President Andrew Jackson recognized the new country in one of his last acts in office in March 1837.

Texas President **Mirabeau B. Lamar** (1838–41) opposed annexation. He held visions of empire in which Texas would rival the United States for supremacy on the North American continent.

During his administration, Great Britain began a close relationship with Texas and made strenuous efforts to get Mexico to recognize the Republic. This relationship between Great Britain and Texas raised fears in the United States that Britain might attempt to make Texas part of its empire.

Southerners feared for the future of slavery in Texas, which had renounced the importation of slaves as a concession to get a trade treaty with Great Britain, and American newspapers noted that trade with Texas had suffered after the Republic received recognition from European countries.

In Houston's second term in the Texas presidency, he instructed **Isaac Van Zandt**, his minister in Washington, to renew the annexation negotiations. Although U.S. President **John Tyler** and his cabinet were eager to annex Texas, they were worried about ratification in the U.S. Senate. The annexation question was put off.

In January 1844, Houston again gave Van Zandt instructions to propose annexation talks. This time the United States agreed to Houston's standing stipulation that, for serious negotiations to take place, the United States must provide military protection to Texas. U.S. naval forces were ordered to the Gulf of Mexico and U.S. troops were positioned on the southwest border close to Texas.

On April 11, 1844, Texas and the United States

During his second term as president of the Republic of Texas, Sam Houston renewed negotiations to annex Texas to the United States. This 67-foot-tall statue of Sam Houston was designed and constructed by artist David Adickes and dedicated to the City of Huntsville in 1994. Lamberto Alvarez photo.

signed a treaty for annexation. Texas would enter the Union as a territory, not a state, under terms of the treaty. The United States would assume Texas' debt up to $10 million and would negotiate Texas' southwestern boundary with Mexico.

On June 8, 1844, the U.S. Senate rejected the treaty with a vote of 35-16, with much of the opposition coming from the slavery abolition wing of the Whig Party.

But **westward expansion** became a major issue in the U.S. presidential election that year. James K.

Polk, the Democratic nominee, was a supporter of expansion, and the party's platform called for adding Oregon and Texas to the Union.

After Polk won the election in November, President Tyler declared that the people had spoken on the issue of annexation, and he resubmitted the matter to Congress.

Several bills were introduced in the U.S. House of Representatives containing various proposals.

In **February 1845**, the U.S. Congress approved a resolution that would bring Texas into the Union as a state. Texas would cede its public property, such as forts and custom houses, to the United States, but it could keep its public lands and must retain its public debt. The region could be divided into four new states in addition to the original Texas. And the United States would negotiate the Rio Grande boundary claim.

British officials asked the Texas government to delay consideration of the U.S. offer for 90 days to attempt to get Mexico to recognize the Republic. The delay did no good: Texans' minds were made up.

President Anson Jones, who succeeded Houston in 1844, called a convention to write a **state constitution** in Austin on July 4, 1845.

Mexico finally recognized Texas' independence, but the recognition was rejected. **Texas voters overwhelmingly accepted** the U.S. proposal and approved the new constitution in a referendum.

On **Dec. 29, 1845**, the U.S. Congress accepted the state constitution, and Texas became the 28th state in the Union. The first meeting of the Texas Legislature took place on Feb. 16, 1846.

1845–1860

The entry of Texas into the Union touched off the **War with Mexico**, a war that some historians now think was planned by President James K. Polk to obtain the vast American Southwest.

Gen. **Zachary Taylor** was sent to Corpus Christi, just above the Nueces River, in July 1845. In February 1846, right after Texas formally entered the Union, the general was ordered to move troops into the disputed area south of the Nueces to the mouth of the Rio Grande. Mexican officials protested the move, claiming the status of the territory was under negotiation.

Seventy years after the Texas Revolution, veterans of the Battle of San Jacinto and other revolution battles, met at Goliad in 1906. By the next year, there were not enough survivors to hold a reunion. Texas Almanac file photo.

After Gen. Taylor refused to leave, Mexican President **Mariano Paredes** declared the opening of a defensive war against the United States on April 24, 1846.

After initial encounters at **Palo Alto and Resaca de la Palma**, both a few miles north of today's **Brownsville**, the war was fought south of the Rio Grande.

President Polk devised a plan to raise 50,000 volunteers from every section of the United States to fight the war. About 5,000 Texans saw action in Mexico.

Steamboats provided an important supply link for U.S. forces along the Rio Grande. Historical figures such as **Richard King**, founder of the legendary King Ranch, and **Mifflin Kenedy**, another rancher and businessman, first came to the **Lower Rio Grande Valley** as steamboat operators during the war.

Much farther up the Rio Grande, the war was hardly noticed. U.S. forces moved south from Santa Fe, which had been secured in December 1846. After a minor skirmish with Mexican forces north of El Paso, the U.S. military established American jurisdiction in this part of Texas.

Gen. **Winfield Scott** brought the war to a close in March 1847 with the capture of Mexico City.

When the **Treaty of Guadalupe Hidalgo** was signed on Feb. 2, 1848, the United States had acquired the American Southwest for development. And in Texas, the Rio Grande became an international boundary.

Europeans, of whom the vast majority were **German**, rather than Anglos, were the first whites to push the Texas frontier into west Central Texas after annexation. **John O. Meusebach** became leader of the German immigration movement in Texas, and he led a wagon train of some 120 settlers to the site of **Fredericksburg** in May 1846.

Germans also migrated to the major cities, such as San Antonio and Galveston, and by 1850 there were more people of German birth or parentage in Texas than there were Mexican-Texans.

The estimated population of 150,000 at annexation grew to 212,592, including 58,161 slaves, in the first U.S. census count in Texas in 1850.

As the state's population grew, the regions developed distinct population characteristics. The southeast and eastern sections attracted immigrants from the Lower South, the principal slaveholding states. Major plantations developed in these areas.

North Texas got more Upper Southerners and Midwesterners. These immigrants were mostly small farmers and few owned slaves.

Mexican-Texans had difficulty with Anglo immigrants. The **"cart war"** broke out in 1857. Mexican teamsters controlled the transportation of goods from the Gulf coast to San Antonio and could charge lower rates than their competition.

A campaign of terror was launched by Anglo haulers, especially around Goliad, in an attempt to drive the Mexican-Texans out of business. Intervention by the U.S. and Mexican governments finally brought the situation under control, but it stands as an example of the attitudes held by Anglo-Texans toward Mexican-Texans.

Cotton was by far the state's largest money crop, but corn, sweet potatoes, wheat and sugar also were produced. **Saw milling** and grain milling became the major industries, employing 40 percent of the manufacturing workers.

Land disputes and the public-debt issue were settled with the **Compromise of 1850**. Texas gave up claims to territory extending to Santa Fe and beyond in exchange for $10 million from the federal government. That sum was used to pay off the debt of the Republic.

Personalities, especially Sam Houston, dominated elections during early statehood, but, for most Texans, politics were unimportant. Voter turnouts were low in the 1850s until the movement toward secession gained strength.

Secession

Texas' population almost tripled in the decade between 1850 and 1860, when 604,215 people were counted, including 182,921 slaves.

Many of these new settlers came from the Lower South, a region familiar with slavery. Although three-quarters of the Texas population and two-thirds of the farmers did not own slaves, slaveowners controlled 60 to 70 percent of the wealth of the state and dominated the politics.

In 1850, 41 percent of the state's officeholders were from the slaveholding class; a decade later, more than 50 percent of the officeholders had slaves.

In addition to the political power of the slaveholders, they also provided role models for new immigrants to the state. After these newcomers got their first land, they saw slave ownership as another step up the economic ladder, whether they owned slaves or not. Slave ownership was an economic goal.

This attitude prevailed even in areas of Texas where slaveholding was not widespread or even practical.

These factors were the wind that fanned the flames of the secessionist movement throughout the late 1850s.

The appearance of the **Know-Nothing Party**, which based its platform on a pro-American, anti-immigrant foundation, began to move Texas toward party politics. Because of the large number of foreign-born settlers, the party attracted many Anglo voters.

In 1854, the Know-Nothings elected candidates to city offices in San Antonio, and a year later, the mayor of Galveston was elected with the party's backing.

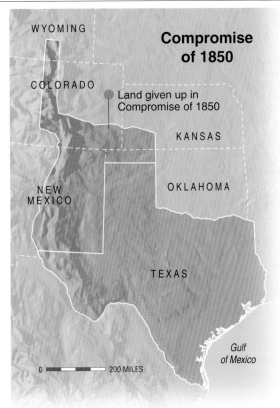

Compromise of 1850

WYOMING

COLORADO

● Land given up in Compromise of 1850

KANSAS

NEW MEXICO

OKLAHOMA

TEXAS

Gulf of Mexico

0 ▆▭▆▭▆ 200 MILES

Also in 1855, the Know-Nothings elected 20 representatives and five senators to the Legislature.

The successes spurred the **Democrats** to serious party organization for the first time. In 1857, **Hardin Runnels** was nominated for governor at the Democratic convention held in Waco.

Sam Houston sought the governorship as an independent, but he also got Know-Nothing backing. Democrats were organized, however, and Houston was dealt the only election defeat in his political career.

Runnels was a strong states'-rights Democrat who irritated many Texans during his administration by advocating reopening the slave trade. His popularity on the frontier also dropped when Indian raids became more severe.

Most Texans still were ambivalent about secession. The Union was seen as a protector of physical and economic stability. No threats to person or property were perceived in remaining attached to the United States.

In 1859, Houston again challenged Runnels, basing his campaign on Unionism. Combined with Houston's personal popularity, his position on the secession issue apparently satisfied most voters, for they gave him a solid victory over the more radical Runnels. In addition, Unionists **A.J. Hamilton** and **John H. Reagan** won the state's two congressional seats. Texans gave the states'-rights Democrats a sound whipping at the polls.

Within a few months, however, events were to change radically the political atmosphere of the state. On the frontier, the army could not control Indian raids, and with the later refusal of a Republican-controlled Congress to provide essential aid in fighting Indians, the federal government fell into disrepute.

Secessionists played on the growing distrust. Then in the summer of 1860, a series of fires in the cities around the state aroused fears that an abolitionist plot was afoot and that a slave uprising might be at hand — a traditional concern in a slaveholding society.

Vigilantes lynched blacks and Northerners across Texas, and a siege mentality developed.

When **Abraham Lincoln** was elected president (he was not on the ballot in Texas), secessionists went to work in earnest.

Pleas were made to Gov. Houston to call the Legislature into session to consider secession. Houston refused, hoping the passions would cool. They did not. Finally, **Oran M. Roberts** and other secessionist leaders issued a call to the counties to hold elections and send delegates to a convention in Austin. Ninety-two of 122 counties responded, and on Jan. 28, 1861, the meeting convened.

Only eight delegates voted against secession, while 166 supported it. An election was called for Feb. 23, 1861, and the ensuing campaign was marked by intolerance and violence. Opponents of secession were often intimidated — except the governor, who courageously stumped the state opposing withdrawal from the Union. Houston also argued that if Texas did secede it should revert to its status as an independent republic and not join the Confederacy.

Only one-fourth of the state's population had been in Texas during the days of independence, and the argument carried no weight. On election day, 76 percent of 61,000 voters favored secession.

President Lincoln, who took office within a couple of weeks, reportedly sent the Texas governor a letter offering 50,000 federal troops to keep Texas in the Union. But after a meeting with other Unionists, Houston declined the offer. "I love Texas too well to bring strife and bloodshed upon her," the governor declared.

On March 16, Houston refused to take an oath of loyalty to the Confederacy and was replaced in office by **Lt. Gov. Edward Clark.**

See the Texas Almanac Web site for results of the Referendum on Ordinance of Secession of 1861.

Civil War

Texas did not suffer the devastation of its Southern colleagues in the Civil War. On but a few occasions did Union troops occupy territory in Texas, except in the El Paso area.

The state's cotton was important to the Confederate war effort because it could be transported from Gulf ports when other Southern shipping lanes were blockaded.

Some goods became difficult to buy, but unlike other states of the Confederacy, Texas still received consumer goods because of the trade that was carried on through Mexico during the war.

Although accurate figures are not available, historians estimate that between 70,000 and 90,000 Texans fought for the South, and between 2,000 and 3,000, including some former slaves, saw service in the Union army.

Texans became disenchanted with the Confederate government early in the war. State taxes were levied for the first time since the Compromise of 1850, and by war's end, the Confederacy had collected more than $37 million from the state.

But most of the complaints about the government centered on Brig. Gen. **Paul O. Hebert**, the Confederate commander of the Department of Texas.

In April 1862, Gen. Hebert declared martial law without notifying state officials. Opposition to the South's new conscription law, which exempted persons owning more than 15 slaves among other categories of exemptions, prompted the action.

The violence against suspected Union sympathizers reached its zenith with the **"Great Hanging at Gainesville,"** when 40 men were tried and hanged at Gainesville in October 1862. Two others were shot as they tried to escape. Although the affair reached its climax in Cooke County, men were killed in neighboring Grayson, Wise and Denton counties. Most were accused of treason or insurrection, but evidently few had actually conspired against the Confederacy, and many were innocent of the abolitionist sentiments for which they were tried.

In November 1862, Gen. Hebert prohibited the export of cotton except under government control, and this proved a disastrous policy.

The final blow came when the commander failed to defend **Galveston** and it fell into Union hands in the fall of 1862.

Maj. Gen. **John B. Magruder**, who replaced Hebert, was much more popular. The new commander's first actions were to combat the Union offensive against Texas ports. Sabine Pass had been closed in September 1862 by the Union blockade, and Galveston was in Northern hands.

On Jan. 1, 1863, Magruder retook Galveston with the help of two steamboats lined with cotton bales. Sharpshooters aboard proved devastating in battles against the Union fleet. Three weeks later, Magruder used two other cotton-clad steamboats to break the Union blockade of Sabine Pass, and two of the state's major ports were reopened.

Late in 1863, the Union launched a major offensive against the Texas coast that was partly successful. On Sept. 8, however, Lt. **Dick Dowling** and 42 men fought off a 1,500-man Union invasion force at **Sabine Pass**. In a brief battle, Dowling's command sank two Union gunboats and put the other invasion ships to flight.

Federal forces were more successful at the mouth of the Rio Grande. On Nov. 1, 1863, 7,000 Union troops landed at **Brazos Santiago**, and five days later, Union forces entered Brownsville.

Members of the 9th Texas Infantry Civil War reenactors march past the Denton County Courthouse during John B. Denton Days in July. Gary Payne photo.

Texas Unionists led by **E.J. Davis** were active in the Valley, moving as far upriver as Rio Grande City. Confederate Col. **John S. "Rip" Ford**, commanding state troops, finally pushed the Union soldiers out of Brownsville in July 1864, reopening the important port for the Confederacy.

Most Texans never saw a Union soldier during the war. The only ones they might have seen were in the **prisoner-of-war camps**. The largest, **Camp Ford**, near Tyler, housed 5,000 prisoners. Others operated in Kerr County and at Hempstead.

As the war dragged on, the mood of Texans changed. Those on the homefront began to feel they were sacrificing loved ones and suffering hardship so cotton speculators could profit.

Public order broke down as refugees flocked to Texas. And slaves from other states were sent to Texas for safekeeping. When the war ended, there were an estimated 400,000 slaves in Texas, more than double the number counted in the 1860 census.

Morale was low in Texas in early 1865. Soldiers at Galveston and Houston began to mutiny. At Austin, Confederate soldiers raided the state treasury in March and found only $5,000 in specie. Units began breaking up, and the army was beginning to dissolve before Gen. **Robert E. Lee** surrendered at **Appomattox** in April 1865. He surrendered the Army of Northern Virginia, and while this assured Union victory, the surrender of other Confederate units was to follow until the last unit gave up in Oklahoma at the end of June.

The last land battle of the Civil War was fought at **Palmito Ranch** near Brownsville on May 13, 1865. After the Confederate's victory, they learned the governors of the Western Rebel states had authorized the disbanding of armies, and, a few days later, they accepted a truce with the Union forces.

Reconstruction

On June 19, 1865, **Gen. Gordon Granger**, under the command of Gen. Philip M. Sheridan, arrived in Galveston with 1,800 federal troops to begin the Union occupation of Texas. Gen. Granger proclaimed the emancipation of the slaves.

A.J. Hamilton, a Unionist and former congressman from Texas, was named provisional governor by President Andrew Johnson.

Texas was in turmoil. Thousands of the state's men had died in the conflict. Indian raids had caused as much damage as the skirmishes with the Union army, causing the frontier to recede up to 100 miles eastward in some areas.

Even worse, confusion reigned. No one knew what to expect from the conquering forces.

Gen. Granger dispatched troops to the population centers of the state to restore civil authority. But only a handful of the 50,000 federal troops that came to Texas was stationed in the interior. Most were sent to the Rio Grande as a show of force against the French forces in Mexico, and clandestine aid was supplied to Mexican President Benito Juarez in his fight against the French and Mexican royalists.

The **frontier forts**, most of which were built during the early 1850s by the federal government to protect western settlements, had been abandoned by the U.S. Army after secession. These were not remanned, and a prohibition against a militia denied settlers a means of self-defense against Indian raids. *(For an overview of the frontier forts, see Texas Almanac 2004–2005.)*

Thousands of freed black slaves migrated to the cities, where they felt the federal soldiers would provide protection. Still others traveled the countryside, seeking family members and loved ones from whom they had been separated during the war.

The **Freedman's Bureau**, authorized by Congress in March 1865, began operation in September 1865 under Gen. E.M. Gregory. It had the responsibility to provide education, relief aid, labor supervision and judicial protection for the newly freed slaves.

The bureau was most successful in opening schools for blacks. Education was a priority because 95 percent of the freed slaves were illiterate.

The agency also was partially successful in getting blacks back to work on plantations under reasonable labor contracts.

Some plantation owners harbored hopes that they would be paid for their property loss when the slaves were freed. In some cases, the slaves were not released from plantations for up to a year.

To add to the confusion, some former slaves had the false notion that the federal government was going to parcel out the plantation lands to them. These blacks simply bided their time, waiting for the division of land.

Under pressure from President Johnson, Gov. Hamilton called for an election of delegates to a constitutional convention in January 1866. Hamilton told the gathering what was expected: Former slaves were to be given civil rights; the secession ordinance had to be repealed; Civil War debt had to be repudiated; and slavery was to be abolished with ratification of the Thirteenth Amendment.

Many delegates to the convention were former secessionists, and there was little support for compromise.

J.W. Throckmorton, a Unionist and one of eight men who had opposed secession in the convention of 1861, was elected chairman of the convention. But a coalition of conservative Unionists and Democrats controlled the meeting. As a consequence, Texas took limited steps toward appeasing the victorious North.

Slavery was abolished, and blacks were given some civil rights. But they still could not vote and were barred from testifying in trials against whites.

No action was taken on the Thirteenth Amendment because, the argument went, the amendment already had been ratified.

Otherwise, the constitution that was written followed closely the constitution of 1845. President Johnson in August 1866 accepted the new constitution and declared insurrection over in Texas, the last of the states of the Confederacy so accepted under **Presidential Reconstruction**.

Throckmorton was elected governor in June, along with other state and local officials. However, Texans had not learned a lesson from the war.

When the Legislature met, a series of laws limiting the rights of blacks were passed. In labor disputes, for example, the employers were to be the final arbitrators. The codes also bound an entire family's labor, not just the head of the household, to an employer.

Funding for black education would be limited to what could be provided by black taxpayers. Since few blacks owned land or had jobs, that provision effectively denied education to black children. However, the thrust of the laws and the attitude of the legislators was clear: Blacks simply were not to be considered full citizens.

Many of the laws later were overturned by the Freedman's Bureau or military authorities when, in March 1867, Congress began a **Reconstruction plan** of its own. The Southern states were declared to have no legal government and the former Confederacy was divided into districts to be administered by the military until satisfactory Reconstruction was effected. Texas and Louisiana made up the Fifth Military District under the command of Gen. Philip H. Sheridan.

Gov. Throckmorton clashed often with Gen. Sheridan. The governor thought the state had gone far enough in establishing rights for the newly freed slaves and other matters. Finally in August 1867, Throckmorton and other state officials were removed from office by Sheridan because they were considered an "impediment to the reconstruction." **E.M. Pease**, the former two-term governor and a Unionist, was named provisional governor by the military authorities.

A **new constitutional convention** was called by Gen. Winfield S. Hancock, who replaced Sheridan in November 1867. For the first time, blacks were allowed to participate in the elections that selected delegates. A total of 59,633 whites and 49,497 blacks registered. The elected delegates met on June 1, 1868. Deliberations got bogged down on partisan political matters, however, and the convention spent $200,000, an astronomical sum for the time.

This constitution of 1869, as it came to be known, granted full rights of citizenship to blacks, created a system of education, delegated broad powers to the

Members of the first exploration of the Big Bend portion of the Rio Grande are photographed on Oct. 28, 1899, near Langtry in Val Verde County. Left to right: James MacMahon, boatman; Robert T. Hill, party leader; Prentice B. Hill, assistant; Shorty Franklin, boatman; Henry J. Ware, boatman; and Serafino Torrez, cook. USGS photo.

governor and generally reflected the views of the state's Unionists.

Gov. Pease, disgusted with the convention and with military authorities, resigned in September 1869. Texas had no chief executive until January 1870, when the newly elected **E.J. Davis** took office.

Meeting in February 1870, the Legislature created a **state militia** under the governor's control; created a **state police force**, also controlled by the governor; postponed the 1870 general election to 1872; enabled the governor to appoint more than 8,500 local office-holders; and granted subsidized **bonds for railroad construction** at a rate of $10,000 a mile.

For the first time, a system of public education was created. The law required compulsory attendance at school for four months a year, set aside one-quarter of the state's annual revenue for education and levied a poll tax to support education. Schools also were to be integrated, which enraged many white Texans.

The Davis administration was the most unpopular in Texas' history. In fairness, historians have noted that Davis did not feel that whites could be trusted to assure the rights of the newly freed blacks.

Violence was rampant in Texas. One study found that between the close of the Civil War and mid-1868, 1,035 people were murdered in Texas, including 486 blacks, mostly victims of white violence.

Gov. Davis argued that he needed broad police powers to restore order. Despite their unpopularity, the state police and militia — blacks made up 40 percent of the police and a majority of the militia — brought the lawlessness under control in many areas.

Democrats, aided by moderate Republicans, regained control of the Legislature in the 1872 elections, and, in 1873, the lawmakers set about stripping the governor of many of his powers.

The political turmoil ended with the gubernatorial election of 1873, when **Richard Coke** easily defeated Davis. Davis tried to get federal authorities to keep him in office, but President Grant refused to intervene.

In January of 1874, Democrats were in control of state government again. The end of Reconstruction concluded the turbulent Civil War era, although the attitudes that developed during the period lasted well into the 20th century.

Capital and Labor

A **constitutional convention** was called in 1875 to rewrite the 1869 constitution, a hated vestige of Radical Republican rule.

Every avenue to cutting spending at any level of government was explored. Salaries of public officials were slashed. The number of offices was reduced. Judgeships, along with most other offices, were made elective rather than appointive.

The state road program was curtailed, and the immigration bureau was eliminated.

Perhaps the worst change was the destruction of the statewide school system. The new charter created a "community system" without a power of taxation, and schools were segregated by race.

Despite the basic reactionary character, the new constitution also was visionary. Following the lead of several other states, the Democrats declared railroads to be common carriers and subject to regulation.

To meet the dual challenge of lawlessness and Indian insurrection, Gov. Coke in 1874 re-established the **Texas Rangers**.

While cowboys and cattle drives are romantic subjects for movies on the Texas of this period, the fact is that the simple cotton farmer was the backbone of the state's economy.

But neither the farmer nor the cattleman prospered throughout the last quarter of the 19th century. At the root of their problems was federal monetary policy and the lingering effects of the Civil War.

Although the issuance of paper money had brought about a business boom in the Union during the war, inflation also increased. Silver was demonetized in 1873. Congress passed the Specie Resumption Act in 1875 that returned the nation to the gold standard in 1879.

Almost immediately a contraction in currency began. Between 1873 and 1891, the amount of national bank notes in circulation declined from $339 million to $168 million.

The reduction in the money supply was devastating in the defeated South. Land values plummeted. In 1870, Texas land was valued at an average of $2.62 an acre, compared with the national average of $18.26 an acre.

With the money supply declining and the national economy growing, farm prices dropped. In 1870, a bushel of wheat brought $1. In the 1890s, wheat was 60 cents a bushel. Except for a brief spurt in the early 1880s, cattle prices followed those of crops.

Between 1880 and 1890, the number of farms in Texas doubled, but the number of tenants tripled. By 1900, almost half the state's farmers were tenants.

The much-criticized crop-lien system was developed following the war to meet credit needs of the small farmers. Merchants would extend credit to farmers through the year in exchange for liens on their crops. But the result of the crop-lien system, particularly when small farmers did not have enough acreage to operate efficiently, was a state of continual debt and despair.

The work ethic held that a man would benefit from his toil. When this apparently failed, farmers looked to the monetary system and the railroads as the causes. Their discontent hence became the source of the agrarian revolt that developed in the 1880s and 1890s.

The entry of the Texas & Pacific and the Missouri-Kansas-Texas **railroads** from the northeast changed trade patterns in the state.

Since the days of the Republic, trade generally had flowed to Gulf ports, primarily Galveston. Jefferson in Northeast Texas served as a gateway to the Mississippi River, but it never carried the volume of trade that was common at Galveston.

The earliest railroad systems in the state also were centered around Houston and Galveston, again directing trade southward. With the T&P and Katy lines, North Texas had direct access to markets in St. Louis and the East.

Problems developed with the railroads, however. In 1882, Jay Gould and Collis P. Huntington, owner of the Southern Pacific, entered into a secret agreement that amounted to creation of a monopoly of rail service in Texas. They agreed to stop competitive track extensions; to divide under a pooling arrangement freight moving from New Orleans and El Paso; to purchase all competing railroads in Texas; and to share the track between Sierra Blanca and El Paso.

The Legislature made weak attempts to regulate railroads, as provided by the state constitution. Gould thwarted an attempt to create a commission to regulate the railroads in 1881 with a visit to the state during the Legislature's debate.

The railroad tycoon subdued the lawmakers' interest with thinly disguised threats that capital would abandon Texas if the state interfered with railroad business.

As the 19th century closed, Texas remained an agricultural state. But the industrial base was growing. Between 1870 and 1900, the per capita value of manufactured goods in the United States rose from $109 to $171. In Texas, these per capita values increased from $14 to $39, but manufacturing values in Texas industry still were only one-half of annual agricultural values.

In 1886, a new breed of Texas politician appeared. **James Stephen Hogg** was not a Confederate veteran, and he was not tied to party policies of the past.

As a reform-minded attorney general, Hogg had actively enforced the state's few railroad regulatory laws. With farmers' support, Hogg was elected governor in 1890, and at the same time, a debate on the constitutionality of a **railroad commission** was settled when voters amended the constitution to provide for one.

The reform mood of the state was evident. Voters returned only 22 of the 106 members of the Texas House in 1890.

Despite his reputation as a reformer, Hogg accepted the growing use of **Jim Crow laws** to limit blacks' access to public services. In 1891, the Legislature responded to public demands and required railroads to provide separate accommodations for blacks and whites.

The stage was being set for one of the major political campaigns in Texas history, however. Farmers did not think that Hogg had gone far enough in his reform program, and they were distressed that Hogg had not appointed a farmer to the railroad commission. Many began to look elsewhere for the solutions to their problems. The **People's Party** in Texas was formed in August 1891.

The 1892 general election was one of the most spirited in the state's history. Gov. Hogg's supporters shut conservative Democrats out of the convention in Houston, so the conservatives bolted and nominated railroad attorney George Clark for governor.

The People's Party, or **Populists**, for the first time had a presidential candidate, James Weaver, and a gubernatorial candidate, T.L. Nugent.

Texas Republicans also broke ranks. The party's strength centered in the black vote. After the death of former Gov. E.J. Davis in 1883, **Norris Wright Cuney**, a black, was party leader. Cuney was considered one of the most astute politicians of the period, and he controlled federal patronage.

White Republicans revolted against the black leadership, and these "Lily-whites" nominated **Andrew Jackson Houston**, son of Sam Houston, for governor.

Black Republicans recognized that alone their strength was limited, and throughout the latter part of the 19th century, they practiced fusion politics, backing candidates of third parties when they deemed it appropriate. Cuney led the Republicans into a coalition with the conservative Democrats in 1892, backing George Clark.

The election also marked the first time major Democratic candidates courted the black vote. Gov. Hogg's supporters organized black voter clubs, and the governor got about half of the black vote.

Black farmers were in a quandary. Their financial

problems were the same as those small farmers who backed the Populists.

White Populists varied in their sympathy with the racial concerns of blacks. On the local level, some whites showed sympathy with black concerns about education, voting and law enforcement. Black farmers also were reluctant to abandon the Republican Party because it was their only political base in Texas.

Hogg was re-elected in 1892 with a 43 percent plurality in a field of five candidates.

Populists continued to run well in state races until 1898. Historians have placed the beginning of the party's demise in the 1896 presidential election in which national Populists fused with the Democrats and supported **William Jennings Bryan**.

Although the Populist philosophy lived on, the party declined in importance after 1898. Farmers remained active in politics, but most returned to the Democratic Party, which usurped many of the Populists' issues.

Oil

Seldom can a people's history be profoundly changed by a single event on a single day. But Texas' entrance into the industrial age can be linked directly to the discovery of oil at **Spindletop**, three miles from **Beaumont**, on Jan. 10, 1901.

From that day, Texas' progress from a rural, agricultural state to a modern industrial giant was steady.

1900–1920

One of the greatest natural disasters ever to strike the state occurred on Sept. 8, 1900, when a **hurricane devastated Galveston**, killing 6,000 people. (For a more detailed account, see "After the Great Storm" in the 1998-1999 *Texas Almanac*). In rebuilding from that disaster, Galveston's civic leaders fashioned the **commission form of municipal government**.

Amarillo later refined the system into the council-manager organization that is widely used today.

The great Galveston storm also reinforced arguments by Houston's leadership that an inland port should be built for protection against such tragedies and disruptions of trade. The **Houston Ship Channel** was soon a reality.

The reform spirit in government was not dead after the departure of Jim Hogg. In 1901, the Legislature prohibited the issuing of railroad passes to public officials. More than 270,000 passes were issued to officials that year, and farmers claimed that the free rides increased their freight rates and influenced public policy as well.

In 1903, state Sen. **A.W. Terrell** got a major **election-reform law** approved, a measure that was further modified two years later. A was established to replace a hodgepodge of practices for nominating candidates that had led to charges of irregularities after each election.

Also in the reform spirit, the Legislature in 1903 prohibited abuse of **child labor** and set minimum ages at which children could work in certain industries. The action preceded federal child-labor laws by 13 years.

However, the state, for the first time, imposed the **poll tax** as a requirement for voting. Historians differ on whether the levy was designed to keep blacks or poor whites — or both — from voting. Certainly the poll tax cut election turnouts. Black voter participation dropped from about 100,000 in the 1890s to an estimated 5,000 in 1906.

The Democratic State Executive Committee also recommended that county committees limit participation in primaries to whites only, and most accepted the suggestion.

The election of **Thomas M. Campbell** as governor in 1906 marked the start of a progressive period in Texas politics. Interest revived in controlling corporate influence.

Under Campbell, the state's **antitrust laws** were strengthened and a **pure food and drug bill** was passed. Life insurance companies were required to invest in Texas 75 percent of their reserves on policies in the state. Less than one percent of the reserves had been invested prior to the law.

Some companies left Texas. But the law was beneficial in the capital-starved economy. In 1904, voters amended the constitution to allow the state to charter **banks** for the first time, and this eased some of the farmers' credit problems. In 1909, the Legislature approved a bank-deposit insurance plan that predated the federal program.

With corporate influence under acceptable control, attention turned to the issue of prohibition of alcohol. Progressives and prohibitionists joined forces against the conservative establishment to exert a major influence in state government for the next two decades.

Prohibitionists had long been active in Texas. They had the **local-option clause** written into the Constitution of 1876, which allowed counties or their subdivisions to be voted dry. But in 1887, a prohibition amendment to the state constitution had been defeated by a two-to-one margin, and public attention had turned to other problems.

In the early 20th century, the prohibition movement gathered strength. Most of Texas already was dry because of local option. When voters rejected a prohibition amendment by a slim margin in 1911, the state had 167 dry counties and 82 wet or partially wet counties. The heavily populated counties, however, were wet. Prohibition continued to be a major issue.

Problems along the U.S.-Mexico border escalated in 1911 as the decade-long **Mexican Revolution** broke out. Soon the revolutionaries controlled some northern Mexican states, including Chihuahua. Juarez and El Paso were major contact points. El Paso residents could stand on rooftops to observe the fighting between revolutionaries and government troops. Some Americans were killed.

After pleas to the federal government got no action, Gov. Oscar Colquitt sent state militia and Texas Rangers into the Valley in 1913 to protect Texans after Matamoros fell to the rebels. Unfortunately, the Rangers killed many innocent Mexican-Texans during the operation. In addition to problems caused by the fighting and raids, thousands of Mexican refugees flooded Texas border towns to escape the violence of the revolution.

In 1914, **James E. Ferguson** entered Texas politics and for the next three decades, "Farmer Jim" was one of the most dominating and colorful figures on the political stage. Ferguson, a banker from Temple, skirted the prohibition issue by pledging to veto any legislation pertaining to alcoholic beverages.

His strength was among farmers, however. Sixty-two percent of Texas' farmers were tenants, and Ferguson pledged to back legislation to limit tenant rents. Ferguson also was a dynamic orator. He easily won the primary and beat out three opponents in the general election.

Ferguson's first administration was successful. The Legislature passed the law limiting tenants' rents, although it was poorly enforced, and aid to rural schools was improved.

In 1915, the border problems heated up. A Mexican national was arrested in the Lower Rio Grande Valley carrying a document outlining plans for Mexican-Americans, Indians, Japanese and blacks in Texas and the Southwest to eliminate all Anglo males over age 16 and create a new republic. The document, whose author was never determined, started a bloodbath in the Valley. Mexican soldiers participated in raids across the Rio Grande, and Gov. Ferguson sent in the Texas Rangers.

Historians differ on the number of people who were killed, but a safe assessment would be hundreds. Gov. Ferguson and Mexican President Venustiano Carranza met at Nuevo Laredo in November 1915 in an attempt to improve relations. The raids continued.

Pancho Villa raided Columbus, N.M., in early 1916; two small Texas villages in the Big Bend, Glenn Springs and Boquillas, also were attacked. In July, President **Woodrow Wilson** determined that the hostilities were critical and activated the National Guard.

Soon 100,000 U.S. troops were stationed along the border. **Fort Bliss** in El Paso housed 60,000 men, and **Fort Duncan** near Eagle Pass was home to 16,000 more.

With the exception of Gen. John J. Pershing's pursuit of Villa into Northern Mexico, few U.S. troops crossed into Mexico. But the service along the border gave soldiers basic training that was put to use when the United States entered World War I in 1917.

Ferguson was easily re-elected in 1916, and he worked well with the Legislature the following year. But after the Legislature adjourned, the governor got into a dispute with the board of regents of the **University of Texas**. The disagreement culminated in the governor's vetoing all appropriations for the school.

As the controversy swirled, the Travis County grand jury indicted Ferguson for misappropriation of funds and for embezzlement. In July 1917, Speaker of the Texas House F.O. Fuller called a special session of the Legislature to consider **impeachment** of the governor.

The Texas House voted 21 articles of impeachment, and the Senate in August 1917 convicted Ferguson on 10 of the charges. The Senate's judgment not only removed Ferguson from office, but also barred him from seeking office again. Ferguson resigned the day before the Senate rendered the decision in an attempt to avoid the prohibition against seeking further office.

Texas participated actively in **World War I**. Almost 200,000 young Texans, including 31,000 blacks, volunteered for military service, and 450 Texas women served in the nurses' corps. Five thousand lost their lives overseas, either fighting or in the **influenza pandemic** that swept the globe.

Texas also was a major training ground during the conflict, with 250,000 soldiers getting basic training in the state.

On the negative side, the war frenzy opened a period of intolerance and nativism in the state. German-Texans were suspect because of their ancestry. A law was passed to prohibit speaking against the war effort. Persons who failed to participate in patriotic activities often were punished. Gov. William P. Hobby even vetoed the appropriation for the German department at the University of Texas.

Ferguson's removal from office was a devastating blow to the anti-prohibitionists. Word that the former governor had received a $156,000 loan from members of the brewers' association while in office provided ammunition for the progressives.

In February 1918, a special session of the Legislature prohibited saloons within a 10-mile radius of military posts and ratified the national prohibition amendment, which had been introduced in Congress by Texas Sen. **Morris Sheppard**.

Women also were given the **right to vote in state primaries** at the same session.

Although national prohibition was to become effective in early 1920, the Legislature presented a prohibition amendment to voters in May 1919, and it was approved, bringing prohibition to Texas earlier than to the rest of the nation. At the same time, a woman suffrage amendment, which would have granted women the right to vote in all elections, was defeated.

Although World War I ended in November 1918, it brought many changes to Texas. Rising prices during the war had increased the militancy of labor unions.

Blacks also became more militant after the war. Discrimination against black soldiers led in 1917 to a riot in Houston in which several people were killed.

With the election of Mexican President Alvaro Obregón in 1920, the fighting along the border subsided.

In 1919, state Rep. J.T. Canales of Brownsville initiated an investigation of the **Texas Rangers**' role in the border problems. As a result of the study, the Rangers' manpower was reduced from 1,000 members to 76, and stringent limitations were placed on the agency's activities. Standards for members of the force also were upgraded.

By 1920, although still a rural state, the face of Texas was changing. Nearly one-third of the population was in the cities.

Pat M. Neff won the gubernatorial election of 1920, beating Sen. Joseph W. Bailey in the primary. As a former prosecuting attorney in McLennan County, Neff made law and order the major thrust of his administration. During his tenure the state took full responsibility for developing a **highway system**, a **gasoline tax** was imposed, and a state **park board** was established.

In 1921, a group of West Texans threathened to form a new state because Neff vetoed the creation of a new college in their area. Two years later, **Texas Technological College** (now Texas Tech University) was authorized in Lubbock and opened its doors in 1925.

Although still predominantly a rural state, Texas cities were growing. In 1900, only 17 percent of the population lived in urban areas; by 1920, that figure had almost doubled to 32 percent. A discontent developed with the growth of the cities. Rural Texans had long seen cities as hotbeds of vice and immorality. Simple rural values were cherished, and it seemed that those values were threatened in a changing world. After World War I, this transition accelerated.

KKK and Minorities

In addition, "foreigners" in the state became suspect; nativism reasserted itself. German-Texans were associated with the enemy in the war, and Mexican-Texans were mostly Roman Catholics and likened to the troublemakers along the border. Texas was a fertile ground for the new **Ku Klux Klan** that entered the state in late 1920. The Klan's philosophy was a mixture of patriotism, law-and-order, nativism, white supremacy and Victorian morals. Its influence spread quickly across the state, and reports of Klan violence and murder were rampant.

Prohibition had brought a widespread disrespect for law. Peace officers and other officials often ignored speakeasies and gambling. The Klan seemed to many Texans to be an appropriate instrument for restoring law and order and for maintaining morality in towns and cities. By 1922, many of the state's large communities were under direct Klan influence, and a Klan-backed candidate, Earle Mayfield, was elected to the U.S. Senate, giving Texas the reputation as the most powerful Klan bastion in the Union. Hiram Wesley Evans of Dallas also was elected imperial wizard of the national Klan in that year.

The Klan became more directly involved in politics and planned to elect the next governor in 1924. Judge Felix Robertson of Dallas got the organization's backing in the Democratic primary. Former governor Jim Ferguson filed to run for the office, but the Texas Supreme Court ruled that he could not because of his impeachment conviction. So Ferguson placed his wife, Miriam A. Ferguson, on the ballot. Several other prominent Democrats also entered the race.

The Fergusons made no secret that Jim would have a big influence on his wife's administration. One campaign slogan was, "Two governors for the price of one." Mrs. Ferguson easily won the runoff against Robertson when many Texans decided that "Fergusonism" was preferable to the Klan in the governor's office.

Minorities began organizing in Texas to seek their civil rights. The National Association for the Advancement of Colored People (**NAACP**) opened a Texas chapter in 1912, and by 1919, there were chapters in 31 Texas communities. Similarly, Mexican-Texans formed Orden Hijos de America in 1921, and in 1929, the **League of United Latin American Citizens** (LU-LAC) was organized in Corpus Christi.

The Klan dominated the Legislature in 1923, passing a law barring blacks from participation in the Democratic primary. Although blacks had in fact been barred from voting in primaries for years, this law gave **Dr. Lawrence A. Nixon**, a black dentist from El Paso, the opportunity to go to court to fight the all-white primary. IIn 1927, the U.S. Supreme Court overturned the statute, but that was only the beginning of several court battles, which were not resolved until 1944.

Disgruntled Democrats and Klansmen tried to beat Mrs. Ferguson in the general election in 1924, but she was too strong. Voters also sent 91 new members to the Texas House, purging it of many of the Klan-backed representatives. After that election, the Klan's power ebbed rapidly in Texas.

Mrs. Ferguson named Emma Grigsby Meharg as Texas' first woman secretary of state in 1925. The governors Ferguson administration was stormy. Jim was accused of cronyism in awarding highway contracts and in other matters. And "Ma" returned to her husband's practice of liberal clemency for prisoners. In two years, Mrs. Ferguson extended clemency to 3,595 inmates.

Although Jim Ferguson was at his bombastic best in the 1926 Democratic primary, young Attorney General **Dan Moody** had little trouble winning the nomination and the general election.

At age 33, Moody was the youngest person ever to become governor of Texas. Like many governors during this period, he was more progressive than the Legislature, and much of his program did not pass. Moody was successful in some government reorganization. He also cleaned up the highway department, which had been criticized under the Fergusons, and abandoned the liberal clemency policy for prisoners. And Moody worked at changing Texas' image as an anti-business state. "The day of the political trust-buster is gone," he told one Eastern journalist.

Progressives and prohibitionists still had a major influence on the Democratic Party, and 1928 was a watershed year for them. Moody easily won renomination and re-election. But the state party was drifting away from the direction of national Democrats. When **Al Smith**, a wet and a Roman Catholic, won the presidential nomination at the national Democratic convention in Houston, Texans were hard-pressed to remain faithful to the "party of the fathers." Moody, who had been considered a potential national figure, ruined his political career trying to straddle the fence, angering both wets and drys, Catholics and Protestants. Former governor O.B. Colquitt led an exodus of so-called "**Hoovercrats**" from the state Democratic convention in 1928, and for the first time in its history, Texas gave its electoral votes to a Republican, Herbert Hoover, in the general election.

Through the 1920s, oil continued to increase in importance in Texas' economy. New discoveries were made at Mexia in 1920, Luling in 1922, Big Lake in Reagan Conty in 1923, in the Wortham Field in 1924 and in Borger in 1926. But oil still did not dominate the state's economic life.

As late as **1929**, meat packing, cottonseed processing and various milling operations exceeded the added value of petroleum refining. And as the 1920s ended, lumbering and food processing shared major economic roles with the petroleum industry. During the decade, Texas grew between 35 and 42 percent of U.S. cotton and 20-30 percent of the world crop. Irrigation and mechanization opened the South Plains to cotton growing. Eight years later, more than 1.1 million bales were grown in the region, mostly around Lubbock.

Dust storms added to the problems of the Great Depression. Here, a dust storm plows into Spearman in Hansford County on April 14, 1935. Photo courtesy of the NOAA Historic National Weather Service Collection/MCT.

But Texas, with the rest of the nation, was on the threshhold of a major economic disaster that would have irreversible consequences. The **Great Depression** was at hand.

Depression Years

Historians have noted that the state's economic collapse was not as severe as that which struck the industrialized states. Texas' economy had sputtered through the decade of the 1920s, primarily because of the fluctuation of the price of cotton and other agricultural products. But agricultural prices were improving toward the end of the decade.

The Fergusons attempted a political comeback in the gubernatorial election of 1930. But Texans elected **Ross S. Sterling**, the founder of Humble Oil Co. Early in the Depression, Texans remained optimistic that the economic problems were temporary, another of the cyclical downturns the nation experienced periodically. Indeed, some Texans even felt that the hardships would be beneficial, ridding the economy of speculators and poor businessmen. Those attitudes gave way to increasing concern as the poor business conditions dragged on.

A piece of good luck turned into a near economic disaster for the state in late 1930. **C.M. "Dad" Joiner** struck oil near Kilgore, and soon the **East Texas oil boom** was in full swing. Millions of barrrels of new oil flooded the market, making producers and small landowners wealthy. Soon the glut of new oil drove market prices down from $1.10 a barrel in 1930 to 10 cents in 1931. Many wells had to be shut in around the state because they could not produce oil profitably at the low prices.

The Texas Railroad Commission attempted in the spring of 1931 to control production through proration, which assigned production quotas to each well (called the allowable). The first proration order limited each well to about 1,000 barrels a day of production. **Proration** had two goals: to protect reserves through conservation and to maintain prices by limiting production. But, on July 28, a federal court ruled that proration was an illegal attempt to fix prices.

In August 1931, Gov. Sterling placed four counties of the East Texas field under martial law and briefly shut down oil production there altogether. A federal court later ruled the governor's actions illegal. Gov. Sterling was roundly criticized for sending troops. Opponents said the action was taken to aid the major oil companies to the disadvantage of independent producers.

In 1932, Gov. Sterling appointed **Ernest O. Thompson** to a vacancy on the railroad commission. Thompson, who had led a coalition in favor of output regulation, is credited with fashioning a compromise between independents and major oil companies. In April 1933, the railroad commission prorated production on the basis, in part, of bottom-hole pressure in each well, and the courts upheld this approach. But enforcement remained a problem.

Finally in 1935, Texas' Sen. **Tom Connally** authored the Hot Oil Act, which involved the federal government in regulation by prohibiting oil produced in violation of state law from being sold in interstate commerce. Thereafter, Texas' producers accepted the concept of proration. Since Texas was the nation's largest oil producer, the railroad commission could set the national price of oil through proration for several decades thereafter.

Despite these problems, the oil boom helped East Texas weather the Depression better than other parts of the state. Farmers were hit particularly hard in 1931. Bumper crops had produced the familiar reduction in prices. Cotton dropped from 18 cents per pound in 1928 to six cents in 1931. That year Louisiana Gov. **Huey Long** proposed a ban on growing cotton in 1932 to eliminate the surplus. The Louisiana legislature enacted the ban, but Texas was the key state to the plan since it led the nation in cotton production. Gov. Sterling was cool to the idea, but responded to public support of it by calling a special session of the Legislature. The lawmakers passed a **cotton acreage limitation** bill in 1931, but the law was declared unconstitutional the following year.

One feature of the Depression had become the number of transients drifting from city to city looking for work. Local governments and private agencies tried to provide relief for the unemployed, but the effort was soon overwhelmed by the number of persons needing help. In Houston, blacks and Mexican-Texans were warned not to apply for relief because there was not enough money to take care of whites, and many Mexicans returned to Mexico voluntarily and otherwise.

To relieve the local governments, Gov. Sterling proposed a bond program to repay counties for highways they had built and to start a public-works program. Texans' long-held faith in self-reliance and rugged individualism was put to a severe test.

By **1932**, many were looking to the federal government to provide relief from the effects of the Depression.

U.S. Speaker of the House **John Nance Garner** of Texas was a presidential candidate when the Democrats held their national convention. To avoid a deadlocked convention, Garner maneuvered the Texans to change strategy. On the fourth ballot, the Texas delegation voted for the eventual nominee, New York Gov. **Franklin D. Roosevelt**. Garner got the second place on the ticket that swept into office in the general election.

In Texas, **Miriam Ferguson** was successful in unseating Gov. Sterling in the Democratic primary, winning by about 4,000 votes. Her second administration was less turbulent than the first. State government costs were reduced, and voters approved $20 million in so-called "bread bonds" to help provide relief. In 1933, **horse racing** came to the state, authorized through a rider on an appropriations bill legalizing pari-mutuel betting. The law was repealed in 1937. Prohibition also was repealed in 1933, although much of Texas remained dry under the **local-option** laws and the prohibition against open saloons.

State government faced a series of financial problems during Mrs. Ferguson's second term. The annual deficit climbed to $14 million, and the state had to default on the interest payments on some bonds. Voters aggravated the situation by approving a $3,000 **homestead exemption**. Many property owners were losing their homes because they could not pay taxes. And while the exemption saved their homesteads, it worsened the state's financial problems.

Many Texas banks failed during the Depression, as did banks nationally. One of Roosevelt's first actions was to declare a national bank holiday in 1933. Gov. Ferguson closed state banks at the same time, although she had to "assume" authority that was not in the law.

The New Deal

In Washington, Texans played an important role in shaping Roosevelt's **New Deal**. As vice president, Garner presided over the Senate and maneuvered legislation through the upper house. **Texans** also chaired major committees in the House: **Sam Rayburn**, Interstate and Foreign Commerce; **Hatton W. Sumners**, Judiciary; **Fritz G. Lanham**, Public Buildings and Grounds; **J.J. Mansfield**, Rivers and Harbors; and **James P. Buchanan**, Appropriations. With this influence, the Texas delegation supported the president's early social programs. In addition, **Jesse Jones** of Houston served as director of the Reconstruction Finance Corporation, the Federal Loan Administration and as Secretary of Commerce. Jones was one of the most influential men in Washington and second only to Roosevelt in wielding financial power to effect recovery.

Poor conservation practices had left many of the state's farmlands open to erosion. During the **Dust Bowl** days of the early and mid-1930s, for example, the weather bureau in Amarillo reported 192 dust storms within a three-year period. Cooperation between state and federal agencies helped improve farmers' conservation efforts and reduced the erosion problem by the end of the decade.

Mrs. Ferguson did not seek re-election in 1934, and Attorney General **James V. Allred** was elected. Under his administration, several social-welfare programs were initiated, including old-age pensions, teachers' retirement and worker's compensation. Allred was re-elected in 1936.

Some of the New Deal's luster dimmed when the nation was struck by another recession in 1937.

Although Texas' economic condition improved toward the end of the decade, a full recovery was not realized until the beginning of World War II — when the state went through another industrial revolution.

Tragedy struck the small East Texas town of **New London** in Rusk County on March 18, 1937. At 3:05 p.m., natural gas, which had seeped undetected into an enclosed area beneath a school building from a faulty pipe connection, exploded when a shop teacher turned on a sander. Approximately 298 of the 540 students and teachers in the school died, and all but 130 of the survivors were injured. The disaster prompted the Legislature to pass a law requiring that a malodorant be added to gas so leaks could be detected by smell.

In 1938, voters elected one of the most colorful figures in the state's political history to the governor's office. **W. Lee "Pappy" O'Daniel**, a flour salesman and leader of a radio hillbilly band, came from nowhere to defeat a field of much better known candidates in the Democratic primary and to easily win the general election. When re-elected two years later, O'Daniel became the first candidate to poll more than one million votes in a Texas election.

But O'Daniel's skills of state did not equal his campaigning ability, and throughout his administration, the governor and the Legislature were in conflict.

In early **1941**, long-time U.S. Senator Morris Sheppard died, and O'Daniel wanted the office. He appointed Andrew Jackson Houston, Sam Houston's aged son, to fill the vacancy. Houston died after only 24 days in office. O'Daniel won the special election for the post in a close race with a young congressman, **Lyndon B. Johnson**.

Lt. Gov. **Coke R. Stevenson** succeeded O'Daniel as governor and brought a broad knowledge of government to the office. Stevenson was elected to two full terms. Thanks to frugal management and greatly increasing revenues during the war years, he left the state treasury with a surplus in 1947. Voters also solved the continuing deficit problem by approving a pay-as-you-go amendment to the constitution in 1942. It requires the state comptroller to certify that tax revenues will be available to support appropriations. Otherwise the money cannot be spent.

World War II

As in every war after Texas entered the Union, young Texans flocked to military service when the United States entered World War II. More than 750,000 served, including 12,000 women in the auxiliary services. In December 1942, U.S. Secretary of the Navy Frank Knox said Texas contributed the largest percentage of its male population to the armed forces of any state. Thirty Texans won Congressional Medals of Honor in the fighting. **Audie Murphy**, a young farm boy from Farmersville, became one of the most decorated soldiers of the war. Dallas-born **Sam Dealey** was the most-decorated Navy man.

Important contributions also were made at home. Texas was the site of 15 training posts, at which more than one and a quarter million men were trained, and of several prisoner-of-war camps.

World War II irrevocably changed the face of Texas. During the decade of the 1940s, the state's population switched from predominantly rural to 60 percent urban. The number of **manufacturing** workers almost doubled. And as had been the dream of Texas leaders for more than a century, the state began to attract new industries.

Conservatives vs. Liberals

The state's politics became increasingly controlled by conservative Democrats after Gov. Allred left office. In 1946, **Beauford H. Jester**, a member of the railroad commission, gained the governorship. Under Jester in 1947, the Legislature passed the state's right-to-work law, prohibiting mandatory union membership, and reorganized public education with passage of the **Gilmer-Aikin Act**.

During the Jester administration several major constitutional amendments were adopted. Also, one of Texas' greatest tragedies occurred on April 16, 1947, when the French ship SS Grandcamp, carrying a load of ammonium nitrate, exploded at **Texas City**. More than 500 died and 4,000 sustained injuries. Property damage exceeded $200 million.

In **1948**, Sen. W. Lee O'Daniel did not seek re-election. Congressman Lyndon Johnson and former Gov. Coke Stevenson vied for the Democratic nomination. In the runoff, Johnson won by a mere **87 votes** in the closest — and most hotly disputed — statewide election in Texas' history. Johnson quickly rose to a leadership position in the U.S. Senate, and, with House Speaker Sam Rayburn, gave Texas substantial influence in national political affairs.

Although re-elected in 1948, Jester died in July 1949, the only Texas governor to die in office, and Lt. Gov. **Allan Shivers** succeeded him. During Shivers' administration, state spending more than doubled, reaching $805.7 million in 1956, as the governor increased appropriations for public-health institutions, school salaries, retirement benefits, highways and old-age pensions.

Shivers broke with tradition, successfully winning three full terms as governor after completing Jester's unexpired term. Shivers also led a revolt by Texas Democrats against the national party in **1952**. The governor, who gained both the Democratic and Republican nominations for the office under the law that allowed cross-filing that year, supported Republican Dwight Eisenhower for the presidency. Many Texas Democrats broke with the national party over the so-called "**Tidelands issue**." Texas claimed land 12 miles out into the Gulf as state lands. The issue was important because revenue from oil and natural gas production from the area supported public education in the state.

Major oil companies also backed Texas' position because state royalties on minerals produced from the land were much lower than federal royalties. President Harry S. Truman vetoed legislation that would have given Texas title to the land. Democratic presidential nominee Adlai Stevenson was no more sympathetic to the issue, and Texas gave its electoral votes to Republican Dwight Eisenhower in an election that attracted a two million-vote turnout for the first time in Texas. President Eisenhower signed a measure into law guaranteeing Texas' tidelands.

Scandal struck state government in 1954 when irregularities were discovered in the handling of funds in the veterans' land program in the General Land Office. Land Commissioner Bascom Giles was convicted of several charges and sent to prison. Several insurance companies also went bankrupt in the mid-1950s, prompting a reorganization of the State Board of Insurance in 1957.

In 1954, the U.S. Supreme Court ruled unconstitutional the segregation of schools, and for the next quarter-century, **school integration** became a major political issue. By the late 1960s, most institutions were integrated, but the state's major cities continued to wage court battles against forced busing of students to attain racial balance. Blacks and Mexican-Texans also made gains in voting rights during the 1950s.

Shivers had easily defeated **Ralph W. Yarborough** in the Democratic primary in 1952, but the divisions between the party's loyalists and those who bolted ranks to join Republicans in presidential races were growing. Shivers barely led the first 1954 primary over Yarborough and won the nomination with 53 percent of the vote in the runoff. Yarborough ran an equally close race against **Price Daniel**, a U.S. Senator who sought the governorship in 1956. Upon election as governor, Daniel left the Senate, and Yarborough won a special election to fill the vacancy in 1957. Yarborough won re-election in 1964 before losing to **Lloyd Bentsen** in 1970 in the Democratic primary. Although a liberal, Yarborough proved to be unusually durable in Texas' conservative political climate.

The state budget topped $1 billion for the first time in 1958. The Legislature met for 205 days in regular and special sessions in 1961–62 and levied, over Gov. Daniel's opposition, the state's first broad-based **sales tax in 1962**.

Technological Growth

Through the 1950s and 1960s, Texas' industrial base had expanded and diversified. Petroleum production and refining remained the cornerstones, but other industries grew. Attracted by cheap electricity, the aluminum industry came to Texas. Starting from the base developed during World War II, defense industries and associated high-tech firms, specializing in electronics and computers, centered on the Dallas–Fort Worth area and Houston. One of the most important scientific breakthroughs of the century came in 1958 in Dallas. **Jack Kilby**, an engineer at **Texas Instruments**, developed and patented the integrated circuit that became the central part of computers.

Sen. Lyndon Johnson unsuccessfully sought the Democratic presidential nomination in 1960, and **John F. Kennedy** subsequently selected the Texan as his running mate. Johnson is credited with keeping several Southern states, including Texas, in the Democratic column in the close election. Kennedy was a Roman Catholic and a liberal, a combination normally rejected by the Southern states. When Johnson left the Senate to assume his new office in 1961, **John Tower** won a special election that attracted more than 70 candidates. Tower became the first Republican since Reconstruction to serve as a Texas senator.

During the early 1960s, Harris County was chosen as the site for the National Aeronautics and Space Administration's manned spacecraft center. The acquisition of **NASA** further diversified Texas' industrial base.

In 1962, **John B. Connally**, a former aide to LBJ and Secretary of the Navy under Kennedy, returned to Texas to seek the governorship. Gov. Daniel sought an unprecedented fourth term and was defeated in the Democratic primary. Connally won a close Democratic runoff over liberal **Don Yarborough** and was elected easily. As governor, Connally concentrated on improving **public education, state services** and **water development**. He was re-elected in 1964 and 1966.

Lee Harvey Oswald, center, is shot by Jack Ruby, right, two days after the assassination of President John F. Kennedy in Dallas. Dallas Morning News photo.

The Assassination

One of the major tragedies in the nation's history occurred in Dallas on **Nov. 22, 1963**, when President Kennedy was assassinated while riding in a motorcade. Gov. Connally also was seriously wounded. Lyndon Johnson was administered the oath of the presidency by Federal Judge Sarah T. Hughes of Dallas aboard Air Force One at Love Field. Lee Harvey Oswald was arrested for the murder of the president on the afternoon of the assassination, but Oswald was killed by Dallas nightclub operator Jack Ruby two days later.

An extensive investigation into the assassination of President Kennedy was conducted by the Warren Commission. The panel concluded that Oswald was the killer and that he acted alone. Ruby, who was convicted of killing Oswald, died of cancer in the Dallas County jail in 1967 while the case was being appealed.

The assassination damaged the Republican Party in Texas, however. Building strength in Texas' conservative political atmosphere in 1962, eight Republicans, the most in decades, had been elected to the Texas House. And two Republicans — Ed Foreman of Odessa and Bruce Alger of Dallas — served in Congress. All were defeated in the 1964 general election.

In the emotional aftermath of the tragedy, Johnson, who won the presidency outright in a **landslide election in 1964**, persuaded the Congress to pass a series of civil-rights and social-welfare programs that changed the face of the nation. Texas was particularly affected by the civil-rights legislation and a series of lawsuits challenging election practices. During the 1960s, the state constitutional limitation of urban representation in the Legislature was overturned. The poll tax was declared unconstitutional, and the practice of electing officials from at-large districts fell to the so-called "one-man, one-vote" ruling. As a result, more Republican, minority and liberal officials were elected, particularly from urban areas. In 1966, **Curtis Graves** and **Barbara Jordan** of Houston and **Joe Lockridge** of Dallas became the first blacks to serve in the Texas Legislature since 1898.

Lyndon Johnson did not seek re-election in 1968. The nation had become involved in an unpopular war in Vietnam, and Johnson bowed out of the race in the interest of national unity.

Sharpstown Scandal

Democrats stayed firmly in control of state government. **Preston Smith** was elected governor, and **Ben Barnes** gained the lieutenant governorship. Both were re-elected in 1970. Although state spending continued to increase, particularly on education, the Legislature otherwise was quiet. A minimum-wage law was approved, and public kindergartens were authorized in 1969.

At a special session, the **Sharpstown scandal**, one of the state's major scandals developed. Gov. Smith allowed the lawmakers to consider special banking legislation supported by Houston banker Frank Sharp. Several public officials were implicated in receiving favors from the banker for seeing that the legislation passed. Texas House Speaker Gus Mutscher and Rep. Tommy Shannon were convicted of conspiracy to accept bribes in a trial held in Abilene.

Voters in **1972** demanded a new leadership in the state capital. Smith and Barnes were defeated in the Democratic primary, and **Dolph Briscoe** was elected governor. In the fall, Texans gave presidential candidate Richard Nixon the state's electoral votes. Nixon carried 246 counties over Democrat George McGovern and received more than 65 percent of the popular vote.

The Legislature in 1973 was dominated by a reform atmosphere in the wake of the Sharpstown scandal. Price Daniel Jr., son of the former governor, was selected speaker of the House, and several laws concerning ethics and disclosure of campaign donations and spending were passed. Open meetings and open records statutes also were approved.

By 1970, Texas had become an even more urban state. The census found almost 11.2 million people in the state, ranking it sixth nationally. Three Texas cities, Houston, Dallas and San Antonio, were among the 10 largest in the nation.

Through the first half of the 1970s, several major changes were made in state policy. **Liquor-by-the-drink** became legal and the age of majority was lowered from 20 to 18, giving young people the right to vote. Also, the state's first Public Utilities Commission was created, hearing its initial case in September 1976.

Prosperity

Texas entered a period of unparalleled prosperity in 1973 when the Organization of Petroleum Exporting Countries (OPEC) boycotted the U.S. market. Severe energy shortages resulted, and the price of oil and natural gas skyrocketed. The federal government had allowed foreign oil to be imported through the 1960s, severely reducing the incentives to find and produce domestic oil. Consequently, domestic producers could not compensate for the loss in foreign oil as a result of the boycott. The Texas Railroad Commission had long complained about the importation of foreign oil, and in 1972, the panel had removed proration controls from wells in the state, allowing 100 percent production. For the rest of the decade, domestic producers mounted a major exploration effort, drilling thousands of wells. Nevertheless, **Texas' oil and gas production peaked in 1970** and has been declining since. Newly discovered oil and gas have not replaced the declining reserves. While Texans suffered from the inflation that followed, the state prospered. Tax revenues at all levels of government increased, and state revenues, basically derived from oil and gas taxes, spiraled, as did the state budget.

With the new revenue from inflation and petroleum taxes, state spending rose from $2.95 billion in 1970 to $8.6 billion in 1979, and education led the advance, moving from 42 percent of the budget to 51.5 percent. But there was no increase in state tax rates.

It was no surprise that **education** was one of the major beneficiaries of increased state spending. After World War II, more emphasis was placed on education across the state. **Community colleges** sprang up in many cities, and a total of 109 colleges were established between the end of the war and 1980. Quantity did not assure quality, however, and Texas' public and higher education seldom were ranked among national leaders.

In 1972, voters approved an amendment authorizing the Legislature to sit as a **constitutional convention** to rewrite the 1876 charter. The lawmakers met for several months and spent $5 million, but they failed to propose anything to be considered by voters. The public was outraged, and in 1975, the Legislature presented the work of the convention to voters in the form of eight constitutional amendments. All were defeated in a special election in November 1975.

Texas voters participated in their **first presidential primary in 1976**. Jimmy Carter of Georgia won the Democratic primary, and eventually the presidency. Ronald Reagan carried the state's Republicans, but lost the party's nomination to President Gerald Ford.

The state proved politically volatile in **1978**. First, Attorney General **John Hill** defeated Gov. Dolph Briscoe in the Democratic primary. A political newcomer, Dallas businessman **William P. Clements**, upset Hill in the general election, giving Texas its first Republican governor since Reconstruction. Also for the first time since Reconstruction, state officials were elected to **four-year terms**. ☆

Environment

Guadalupe River State Park in Comal and Kendall counties. Ron Billings photo; Texas Forest Service.

Physical Regions

Where in Texas Are We?

Geology

Earthquakes

Soils

Aquifers, Rivers, Lakes

Plant Life

Forests & Grasslands

Wildlife

The Physical State of Texas

Area of Texas

Texas occupies about 7 percent of the total water and land area of the United States. Second in size among the states, **Texas has a land and water area of 268,580 square miles** as compared with Alaska's 663,267 square miles, according to the United States Bureau of the Census. California, the third largest state, has 163,696 square miles. Texas is as large as all of New England, New York, Pennsylvania, Ohio and North Carolina combined.

The **state's total area** consists of 261,797 square miles of land and 6,783 square miles of water.

Length and Breadth

The **longest straight-line distance** in a general north-south direction is 801 miles from the northwest corner of the Panhandle to the extreme southern tip of Texas on the Rio Grande below Brownsville. The greatest east-west distance is 773 miles from the extreme eastward bend in the Sabine River in Newton County to the extreme western bulge of the Rio Grande just above El Paso.

The **geographic center** of Texas is southwest of Mercury in northern McCulloch County at approximately 99° 20' West longitude and 31° 08' North latitude.

Texas' Boundary Lines

The boundary of Texas by segments, including only larger river bends and only the great arc of the coastline, is as follows:

BOUNDARY	MILES
Rio Grande	889.0
Coastline	367.0
Sabine River, Lake and Pass	180.0
Sabine River to Red River	106.5
Red River	480.0
East Panhandle line	133.6
North Panhandle line	167.0
West Panhandle line	310.2
Along 32nd parallel	209.0
TOTAL	**2,842.3**

Following the smaller meanderings of the rivers and the tidewater coastline, the following are the boundary measurements:

BOUNDARY	MILES
Rio Grande	1,254.0
Coastline (tidewater)	624.0
Sabine River, Lake and Pass	292.0
Sabine River to Red River	106.5
Red River	726.0
East Panhandle line	133.6
North Panhandle line	167.0
West Panhandle line	310.2
Along 32nd parallel	209.0
TOTAL	**3,822.3**

Latitude and Longitude

The extremes of latitude and longitude are as follows:

— From **25° 50' North latitude** at the extreme southern turn of the Rio Grande on the south line of Cameron County to **36° 30' North latitude** along the north line of the Panhandle, and

— from **93° 31' West longitude** at the extreme eastern point on the Sabine River on the east line of Newton County to **106° 38' West longitude** on the extreme westward point on the Rio Grande above El Paso.

Elevation Highs and Lows

The highest point in the state is **Guadalupe Peak** at **8,749 feet** above sea level. Its twin, **El Capitan**, stands at **8,085** feet and also is located in Culberson County near the New Mexico state line.

Both are in Guadalupe Mountains National Park, which includes the scenic McKittrick Canyon.

The elevations used on this page are from various sources, including the U.S. Geological Survey, the National Park Service, and the Texas Department of Transportation.

Named Peaks in Texas Above 8,000 Feet

The named peaks above 8,000 feet and the counties in which they are located are listed below.

NAME	COUNTY	ELEVATION
Guadalupe Peak	Culberson	8,749
Bush Mountain	Culberson	8,631
Shumard Peak	Culberson	8,615
Bartlett Peak	Culberson	8,508
Mount Livermore (Baldy Peak)	Jeff Davis	8,378
Hunter Peak (Pine Top Mtn.)	Culberson	8,368
El Capitan	Culberson	8,085

TOWN: Fort Davis in Jeff Davis County is the **highest town** of any size in Texas at 5,050 feet above sea level, and the county has the **highest average elevation.**

HIGHWAY: The **highest state highway point** also is in Jeff Davis County at **McDonald Observatory** on **Mount Locke** where the road reaches 6,781 feet above sea level, as determined by the Texas Department of Transportation.

RAILWAY: The **highest railway point** is Paisano Pass, which is 5,074 above sea level, 14 miles east of Marfa in Presidio County.

LOWEST: Sea level is the **lowest elevation** determined in Texas, and it can be found in all the coastal counties. No point in the state has been found by the geological survey to be below sea level. ☆

Bluebonnets and Mexican paintbrush cover a hill near Independence in Washington County, part of the Gulf Coastal Plains. Ron Billings photo; Texas Forest Service.

Physical Regions

This section was reviewed by Dr. David R. Butler, professor of geography at Texas State University–San Marcos.

The principal physical regions of Texas are usually listed as follows (see also **Vegetational Areas** and **Soils**):

I. GULF COASTAL PLAINS

Texas' Gulf Coastal Plains are the western extension of the coastal plain extending from the Atlantic to beyond the Rio Grande. Its characteristic rolling to hilly surface covered with a heavy growth of pine and hardwoods extends into East Texas. In the increasingly arid west, however, its forests become secondary in nature, consisting largely of post oaks and, farther west, prairies and brushlands.

The interior limit of the Gulf Coastal Plains in Texas is the line of the **Balcones Fault and Escarpment**. This geologic fault or shearing of underground strata extends eastward from a point on the Rio Grande near Del Rio. It extends to the northwestern part of Bexar County where it turns northeastward and extends through Comal, Hays and Travis counties, intersecting the Colorado River immediately above Austin. The fault line is a single, definite geologic feature, accompanied by a line of southward- and eastward-facing hills.

The resemblance of the hills to balconies when viewed from the plain below accounts for the Spanish name for this area: *balcones.*

North of Waco, features of the fault zone are sufficiently inconspicuous that the interior boundary of the Coastal Plain follows the traditional geologic contact between upper and lower Cretaceous rocks. This contact is along the western edge of the **Eastern Cross Timbers**.

This fault line is usually accepted as the boundary between lowland and upland Texas. Below the fault line, the surface is characteristically coastal plains. Above the Balcones Fault, the surface is characteristically interior rolling plains.

A. Pine Belt or "Piney Woods"

The Pine Belt, called the **"Piney Woods,"** extends 75 to 125 miles into Texas from the east. From north to south, it extends from the Red River to within about 25 miles of the Gulf Coast. Interspersed among the pines are some hardwood timbers, usually in valleys of rivers and creeks. This area is the source of practically all of Texas' commercial timber production *(see Texas Forest Resources, page 105).* It was settled early in Texas' history and is an older farming area of the state.

This area's soils and climate are adaptable to production of a variety of fruit and vegetable crops. Cattle raising is widespread, accompanied by the development of pastures planted to improved grasses. Lumber production is the principal industry. There is a large iron-and-steel industry near Daingerfield in Morris County based on nearby iron deposits. Iron deposits are also worked in Rusk and one or two other counties.

A great oil field discovered in Gregg, Rusk and Smith counties in 1931 has done more than anything else to contribute to the economic growth of the area. This area has a variety of clays, lignite and other minerals as potentials for development.

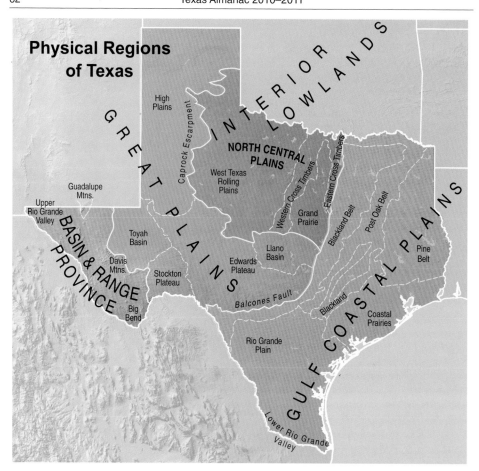

Physical Regions of Texas

High Plains

Caprock Escarpment

INTERIOR LOWLANDS

NORTH CENTRAL PLAINS

GREAT PLAINS

Guadalupe Mtns.

Upper Rio Grande Valley

BASIN & RANGE PROVINCE

Toyah Basin

Davis Mtns.

Stockton Plateau

Big Bend

West Texas Rolling Plains

Western Cross Timbers

Eastern Cross Timbers

Grand Prairie

Llano Basin

Edwards Plateau

Balcones Fault

Blackland Belt

Post Oak Belt

Pine Belt

Blackland

Coastal Prairies

GULF COASTAL PLAINS

Rio Grande Plain

Lower Rio Grande Valley

B. Post Oak Belt

The main Post Oak Belt of Texas is wedged between the Pine Belt on the east, Blacklands on the west, and the Coastal Prairies on the south, covering a considerable area in East Central Texas. The principal industry is diversified farming and livestock raising. Throughout, it is spotty in character, with some insular areas of blackland soil and some that closely resemble those of the Pine Belt. There is a small isolated area of loblolly pines in Bastrop County known as the **"Lost Pines,"** the westernmost southern pines in the United States. The Post Oak Belt has lignite, commercial clays and some other minerals.

C. Blackland Belt

The Blackland Belt stretches from the Rio Grande to the Red River, lying just below the line of the **Balcones Fault**, and varying in width from 15 to 70 miles. It is narrowest below the segment of the Balcones Fault from the Rio Grande to Bexar County and gradually widens as it runs northeast to the Red River. Its rolling prairie, easily turned by the plow, developed rapidly as a farming area until the 1930s and was the principal cotton-producing area of Texas. Now, however, other Texas areas that are irrigated and mechanized lead in farming.

Because of the early growth, the Blackland Belt is still the most thickly populated area in the state and contains within it and along its border more of the state's large and middle-sized cities than any other area. Primarily because of this concentration of population, this

belt has the most diversified manufacturing industry of the state.

D. Coastal Prairies

The Texas Coastal Prairies extend westward along the coast from the Sabine River, reaching inland 30 to 60 miles. Between the Sabine and Galveston Bay, the line of demarcation between the prairies and the Pine Belt forests to the north is very distinct. The Coastal Prairie extends along the Gulf from the Sabine to the Lower Rio Grande Valley.

The eastern half is covered with a heavy growth of grass; the western half, which is more arid, is covered with short grass and, in some places, with small timber and brush. The soil is heavy clay. Grass supports the densest cattle population in Texas, and cattle ranching is the principal agricultural industry. Rice is a major crop, grown under irrigation from wells and rivers. Cotton, grain sorghum and truck crops are also grown.

Coastal Prairie areas have seen the greatest industrial development in Texas history since World War II. Chief concentration has been from Orange and Beaumont to Houston, and much of the development has been in petrochemicals and the aerospace industry.

Corpus Christi, in the Coastal Bend, and Brownsville, in the Lower Rio Grande Valley, have seaports and agricultural and industrial sections. Cotton, grain, vegetables and citrus fruits are the principal crops. Cattle production is significant, with the famed King Ranch and other large ranches located here.

E. Lower Rio Grande Valley

The deep alluvial soils and distinctive economy cause the Lower Rio Grande Valley to be classified as a subregion of the Gulf Coastal Plain. The Lower Valley, as it is called locally, is Texas' greatest citrus-winter vegetable area because of the normal absence of freezing weather and the rich delta soils of the Rio Grande. Despite occasional damaging freezes the Lower Valley ranks high among the nation's fruit-and-truck regions. Much of the acreage is irrigated, although dry-land farming also is practiced.

F. Rio Grande Plain

This may be roughly defined as lying south of San Antonio between the Rio Grande and the Gulf Coast. The Rio Grande Plain shows characteristics of both the Gulf Coastal Plain and the North Mexico Plains because there is similarity of topography, climate and plant life all the way from the Balcones Escarpment in Texas to the Sierra Madre Oriental in Mexico, which runs past Monterrey about 160 miles south of Laredo.

The Rio Grande Plain is partly prairie, but much of it is covered with a dense growth of **prickly pear, mesquite, dwarf oak, catclaw, guajillo, huisache, blackbrush, cenizo** and other cactus and wild shrubs. It is devoted primarily to raising cattle, sheep and goats. The Texas Angora goat and mohair industry centers in this area and on the **Edwards Plateau,** which borders it on the north. San Antonio and Laredo are its chief commercial centers, with San Antonio dominating trade.

There is some farming, and the **Winter Garden,** centering in Dimmit and Zavala counties north of Laredo, is irrigated from wells and streams to produce vegetables in late winter and early spring. Primarily, however, the central and western part of the Rio Grande Plain is devoted to livestock raising.

The rainfall is less than 25 inches annually and the hot summers bring heavy evaporation, so that cultivation without irrigation is limited.

Over a large area in the central and western parts of the Rio Grande Plain, the growth of **small oaks, mesquite, prickly pear (Opuntia) cactus** and a variety of wild shrubs is very dense and it is often called the **Brush Country.** It is also referred to as the **chaparral** and the **monte.** (*Monte* is a Spanish word, one meaning of which is dense brush.)

II. INTERIOR LOWLANDS

North Central Plains

The North Central Plains of Texas are a southwestern extension into Texas of the **interior, or central, lowlands** that extend northward to the Canadian border, paralleling the Great Plains to the West. The North Central Plains of Texas extend from the Blackland Belt on the east to the Caprock Escarpment on the west. From north to south they extend from the Red River to the Colorado.

A. West Texas Rolling Plains

The West Texas Rolling Plains, approximately the western two-thirds of the North Central Plains in Texas, rise from east to west in altitude from about 750 feet to 2,000 feet at the base of the **Caprock Escarpment.** Annual rainfall ranges from about 30 inches on the east to 20 on the west. In general, as one progresses westward in Texas the precipitation not only declines but also becomes more variable from year to year. Temperature varies rather widely between summer's heat and winter's cold.

This area still has a large cattle-raising industry with many of the state's largest ranches. However, there is much level, cultivable land.

Cows graze near Westlake in Tarrant County on the east edge of the Interior Lowlands. Lamberto Alvarez photo.

B. Grand Prairie

Near the eastern edge of the North Central Plains is the **Grand Prairie,** extending south from the Red River in an irregular band through Cooke, Montague, Wise, Denton, Tarrant, Parker, Hood, Johnson, Bosque, Coryell and some adjacent counties. It is a limestone-based area, usually treeless except along the numerous streams, and adapted primarily to livestock raising and staple-crop growing. Sometimes called the **Fort Worth Prairie,** it has an agricultural economy and largely rural population, with no large cities except Fort Worth on its eastern boundary.

C. Eastern and Western Cross Timbers

Hanging over the top of the Grand Prairie and dropping down on each side are the Eastern and Western Cross Timbers. The two southward-extending bands are connected by a narrow strip along the Red River. The **Eastern Cross Timbers** extend southward from the Red River through eastern Denton County and along the boundary between Dallas and Tarrant counties. It then stretches through Johnson County to the Brazos River and into Hill County.

The much larger **Western Cross Timbers** extend from the Red River south through Clay, Montague, Jack, Wise, Parker, Palo Pinto, Hood, Erath, Eastland, Comanche, Brown and Mills counties to the Colorado River, where they meet the Llano Basin. Their soils are adapted to fruit and vegetable crops, which reach considerable commercial production in some areas in Parker, Erath, Eastland and Comanche counties.

III. GREAT PLAINS

A. High Plains

The Great Plains, which lie to the east of the base of the Rocky Mountains, extend into northwestern Texas. This area, commonly known as the **High Plains,** is a vast, flat, high plain covered with thick layers of alluvial material. It is also known as the **Staked Plains** or the Spanish equivalent, *Llano Estacado.*

Historians differ as to the origin of this name. Some say it came from the fact that the explorer Coronado's expedition used stakes to mark its route across the trackless sea of grass so that it would be guided on its return trip. Others think that the *estacado* refers to the **palisaded appearance** of the Caprock in many places, especially the west-facing escarpment in New Mexico.

The **Caprock Escarpment** is the dividing line between the High Plains and the Lower Rolling Plains of West Texas. Like the Balcones Escarpment, the Caprock Escarpment is a striking physical feature, rising abruptly 200, 500 and in some places almost 1,000 feet above the plains. Unlike the **Balcones Escarpment,** the Caprock was caused by surface erosion.

Where rivers issue from the eastern face of the Caprock, there frequently are notable canyons, such as **Palo Duro Canyon** on the **Prairie Dog Town Fork of the Red River, Blanco Canyon on the White River,** as well as the breaks along the Canadian River as it crosses the Panhandle north of Amarillo.

Along the eastern edge of the Panhandle, there is a gradual descent of the land's surface from high to low plains; but at the Red River, the Caprock Escarpment becomes a striking surface feature. It continues as an east-facing wall south through Briscoe, Floyd, Motley, Dickens, Crosby, Garza and Borden counties, gradually decreasing in elevation. South of Borden County, the escarpment is less obvious, and the boundary between the High Plains and the Edwards Plateau occurs where the alluvial cover of the High Plains disappears.

Stretching over the largest level plain of its kind in the United States, the High Plains rise gradually from about 2,700 feet on the east to more than 4,000 in spots along the New Mexico border.

Chiefly because of climate and the resultant agriculture, subdivisions are called the North Plains and South Plains. The **North Plains,** from Hale County north, has primarily wheat and grain sorghum farming, but with significant ranching and petroleum developments. Amarillo is the largest city, with Plainview on the south and Borger on the north as important commercial centers.

The **South Plains,** also a leading grain sorghum region, **leads Texas in cotton production.** Lubbock is the principal city, and Lubbock County is one of the state's largest cotton producers. Irrigation from underground reservoirs, centered around Lubbock and Plainview, waters much of the crop acreage.

B. Edwards Plateau

Geographers usually consider that the Great Plains at the foot of the Rocky Mountains actually continue southward from the High Plains of Texas to the Rio Grande and the Balcones Escarpment. This southern and lower extension of the Great Plains in Texas is known as the **Edwards Plateau.**

It lies between the Rio Grande and the Colorado River. Its southeastern border is the **Balcones Escarpment** from the Rio Grande at Del Rio eastward to San Antonio and thence to Austin on the Colorado River. Its upper boundary is the Pecos River, though the **Stockton Plateau** is geologically and topographically classed with the Edwards Plateau.

The Edwards Plateau varies from about 750 feet high at its southern and eastern borders to about 2,700 feet in places. Almost the entire surface is a thin, limestone-based soil covered with a medium to thick growth of **cedar, small oak** and **mesquite** with a varying growth of **prickly pear.** Grass for cattle, weeds for sheep and tree foliage for the browsing goats support three industries — **cattle, goat and sheep raising** — upon which the area's economy depends. It is the **nation's leading Angora goat and mohair producing region** and one of the nation's leading sheep and wool areas. A few crops are grown.

Hill Country

The Hill Country is a popular name for the **eastern portion of the Edwards Plateau** south of the Llano Basin. Its notable large springs include **Barton Springs** at Austin, **San Marcos Springs** at San Marcos, **Comal Springs** at New Braunfels, several springs at San Antonio, and a number of others.

The Hill Country is characterized by rugged hills with relatively steep slopes and thin soils overlying limestone bedrock. High gradient streams combine with these steep hillslopes and occasionally heavy precipitation to produce an area with a significant flash-flood hazard.

C. Toyah Basin

To the northwest of the Edwards and Stockton plateaus is the Toyah Basin, a broad, flat remnant of an old sea floor that occupied the region as recently as Quaternary time. Located in the **Pecos River Valley,** this region, in relatively recent time, has become important for many agricultural products as a result of irrigation. Additional economic activity is afforded by local oil fields.

D. Llano Basin

The Llano Basin lies at the junction of the Colorado and Llano rivers in Burnet and Llano counties. Earlier, this was known as the **"Central Mineral Region,"** because of the evidence there of a large number of minerals.

On the Colorado River in this area, a succession of dams impounds two large and five small reservoirs. Uppermost is **Lake Buchanan,** one of the large reservoirs, between Burnet and Llano counties. Below it in the west-

Cactus near Alpine in Brewster County in the Basin and Range Province. Ron Billings photo; Texas Forest Service.

ern part of Travis County is **Lake Travis**. Between these two large reservoirs are three smaller ones, **Inks, L.B. Johnson** (formerly Granite Shoals) and **Marble Falls** reservoirs, used primarily to produce electric power from the overflow from Lake Buchanan. **Lake Austin** is along the western part of the city of Austin. Still another small lake, **Lady Bird Lake** (formerly Town Lake), is formed by a low-water dam in Austin.

The recreational area around these lakes has been called the **Highland Lakes Country**. This is an interesting area with Precambrian and Paleozoic rocks found on the surface. Granitic domes, exemplified by **Enchanted Rock** north of Fredericksburg, form the core of this area of ancient rocks.

IV. BASIN and RANGE PROVINCE

The Basin and Range province, with its center in Nevada, surrounds the Colorado Plateau on the west and south and enters far West Texas from southern New Mexico on the east. It consists of broad interior drainage basins interspersed with scattered fault-block mountain ranges.

Although this is the only part of Texas regarded as mountainous, these should not be confused with the Rocky Mountains. Of all the independent ranges in West Texas, only the Davis Mountains resemble the Rockies, and there is much debate about this.

Texas west of the Edwards Plateau, bounded on the north by New Mexico and on the south by the Rio Grande, is distinctive in its physical and economic conditions. Traversed from north to south by fault-block mountains, it contains all of Texas' true mountains and also is very interesting geologically.

A. Guadalupe Mountains

Highest of the Trans-Pecos Mountains is the **Guadalupe Range**, which enters the state from New Mexico. It comes to an abrupt end about 20 miles south of the boundary line, where **Guadalupe Peak**, (8,749 feet, highest in Texas) and **El Capitan** (8,085 feet) are situated. El Capitan, because of perspective, appears to the observer on the plain below to be higher than Guadalupe.

Lying just west of the Guadalupe range and extending to the **Hueco Mountains** a short distance east of El Paso is the **Diablo Plateau** or basin. It has no drainage outlet to the sea. The runoff from the scant rain that falls on its surface drains into a series of salt lakes that lie just west of the Guadalupe Mountains. These lakes are dry during periods of low rainfall, exposing bottoms of solid salt, and for years they were a source of **commercial salt**.

B. Davis Mountains

The Davis Mountains are principally in Jeff Davis County. The highest peak, **Mount Livermore** (8,378 feet), is **one of the highest in Texas**; there are several others more than 7,000 feet high. These mountains intercept the moisture-bearing winds and receive more precipitation than elsewhere in the Trans-Pecos, so they have more vegetation than the other Trans-Pecos mountains. Noteworthy are the **San Solomon Springs** at the northern base of these mountains.

C. Big Bend

South of the Davis Mountains lies the Big Bend country, so called because it is encompassed on three sides by a great southwALT swing of the Rio Grande. It is a mountainous country of scant rainfall and sparse population. Its principal mountains, the **Chisos**, rise to 7,825 feet in **Mount Emory**.

Along the Rio Grande are the **Santa Elena, Mariscal** and **Boquillas canyons** with rim elevations of 3,500 to 3,775 feet. They are among the noteworthy canyons of the North American continent.

Because of its remarkable topography and plant and animal life, the southern part of this region along the Rio Grande is home to **Big Bend National Park**, with headquarters in a deep valley in the Chisos Mountains. It is a favorite recreation area.

D. Upper Rio Grande Valley

The Upper Rio Grande (El Paso) Valley is a narrow strip of irrigated land running down the river from El Paso for a distance of 75 miles or more. In this area are the historic towns and missions of **Ysleta, Socorro** and **San Elizario, oldest in Texas**. Cotton is the chief product of the valley, much of it the long-staple variety. This limited area has a dense urban and rural population, in marked contrast to the territory surrounding it. ☆

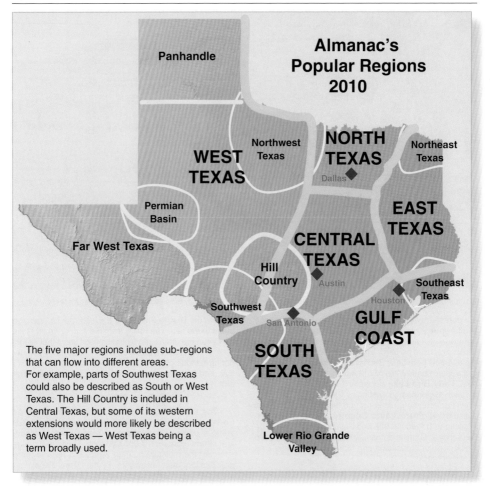

Almanac's Popular Regions 2010

Panhandle

Northwest Texas

NORTH TEXAS

Northeast Texas

WEST TEXAS

Dallas

Permian Basin

EAST TEXAS

Far West Texas

CENTRAL TEXAS

Hill Country

Austin

Southwest Texas

San Antonio

Southeast Texas

Houston

GULF COAST

SOUTH TEXAS

Lower Rio Grande Valley

The five major regions include sub-regions that can flow into different areas. For example, parts of Southwest Texas could also be described as South or West Texas. The Hill Country is included in Central Texas, but some of its western extensions would more likely be described as West Texas — West Texas being a term broadly used.

Where in Texas Are We?

Southwest Texas State University in San Marcos changed its name in 2003 to Texas State University–San Marcos.

The college is in Central Texas, not Southwest Texas, argued the late, longtime president of the institution, Jerome Supple, during the consideration of the name change.

In fact, how the regions within the state are perceived changes. Although many today would agree with Dr. Supple, in the 1880s the popular view was that Southwest Texas included San Marcos, and sometimes El Paso, as well.

In 1902, *The Dallas Morning News* reported on the effects of the boil weevil in "Southwest Texas." Included under that category were counties from Wilson, southeast of San Antonio, to Lee, east of Austin, even Brewster County, as well as Hays County, home of San Marcos.

"Geographers define regions in three different basic ways," says the National Geographics Xpeditions Web site. These are:

"Formal — characterized by common

properties, such as economy or climate." [Examples; citrus-growing areas of southern Texas or the areas of desert climate.]

"Functional — organized around a focal point with surrounding areas linked by communication systems or economic association." [Example; the Dallas-Fort Worth metropolitan area.]

"Perceptual — a construct that reflects human feelings and attitudes about areas and is therefore defined by people's shared subjective images of those areas. It tends to reflect the element of people's mental maps."

These perceptual regions of the state can be defined in many ways, including directional, and here we present some maps showing various interpretions of the regions within Texas.

Terry G. Jordan, in his study published in *Texas, A Geography*, polled 4,000 college students in 1977 for their self-descriptions of their home regions. The results are shown in his preceptual and directional regions maps, following.

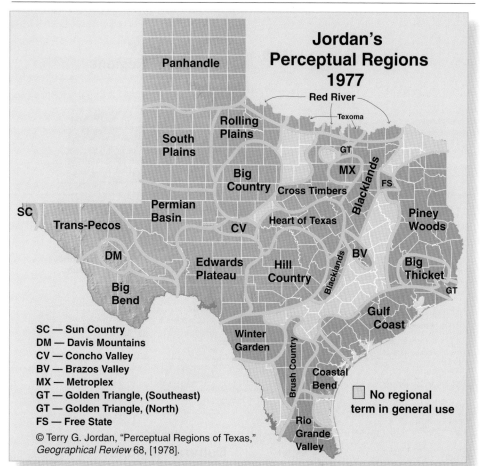

Jordan's Perceptual Regions 1977

Panhandle

Red River

Texoma

Rolling Plains

South Plains

GT

Big Country

Cross Timbers

MX

Blacklands

FS

Permian Basin

CV

Heart of Texas

Piney Woods

SC

Trans-Pecos

DM

Edwards Plateau

Hill Country

Blacklands

BV

Big Thicket

GT

Big Bend

Gulf Coast

Winter Garden

Brush Country

Coastal Bend

No regional term in general use

Rio Grande Valley

SC — Sun Country
DM — Davis Mountains
CV — Concho Valley
BV — Brazos Valley
MX — Metroplex
GT — Golden Triangle, (Southeast)
GT — Golden Triangle, (North)
FS — Free State

© Terry G. Jordan, "Perceptual Regions of Texas,"
Geographical Review 68, [1978].

Dr. Jordan pointed out that regions with environmental terms as a rule are the oldest. "Cross Timbers, for example, was in use at least by 1840." But many environmental terms are now nearly or completely forgotten. Redlands, for example, was a belt centered on San Augustine County in East Texas.

These environmental terms don't necessarily describe the real physical characteristics of the region. The Lower Rio Grande Valley is not a valley but a delta, and the Permian Basin in not a topographic basin, but, rather, the term refers to the geological formation underneath.

Some regions have political terms, such as Texoma (Texhoma), which combines the names of Texas and Oklahoma. Free State is a 19th century term for Van Zandt County that has various explanations for its origin.

Also included in Dr. Jordan's study were promotional names which appeared after World War II, such as Big Country around Abilene and the Metroplex of Dallas-Fort Worth.

Over time the area considered within the Hill Country has expanded, perhaps because of its attraction to travelers. The Almanac in the past defined the Hill Country as "an area of hills and spring-fed streams along the edge of the Balcones Escarpment

in the southeast portion of the Edwards Plateau." Possibly related to the appealing sound of Hill Country, the term Texas Forest Country now has been coined to refer to the Piney Woods of East Texas.

As the National Geographic points out, these definitions are always changing:

"Some regions, especially formal regions, tend to be stable in spatial definition, but may undergo change in character. Others, especially functional regions, my retain certain basic characteristics, but may undergo spatial redefinition over time.

"Yet other regions, particularly **perceptual** regions, are likely to vary over time in both spatial extent and character."

And not everyone will agree on the names. As Dr. Jordan found in 1977:

"Unlikely as it may seem, the majority of home county students at East Texas State University [now Texas A&M–Commerce], in Hunt County, did not place their county in East Texas, nor were those at West Texas State [now West Texas A&M] or Southwest Texas State universities swayed by the names of their institutions. Only North Texas State [now University of North Texas] students voted in a predictable manner and even there the majority was rather small." — RP.

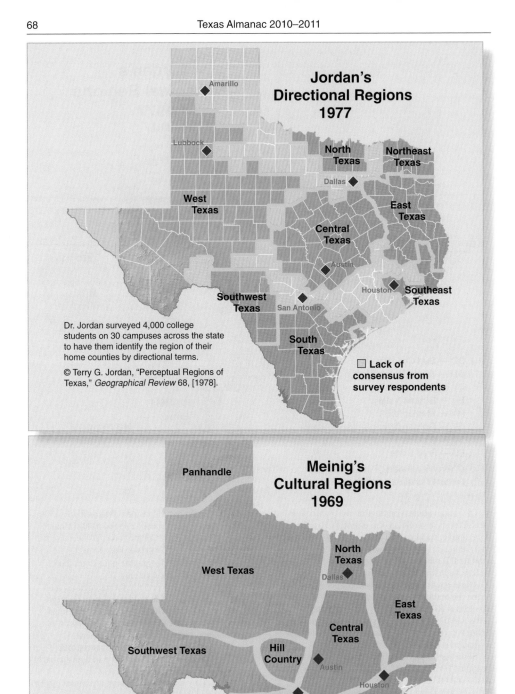

Jordan's Directional Regions 1977

Amarillo

Lubbock

North Texas

Northeast Texas

Dallas

West Texas

East Texas

Central Texas

Austin

Southwest Texas

Houston

Southeast Texas

San Antonio

Dr. Jordan surveyed 4,000 college students on 30 campuses across the state to have them identify the region of their home counties by directional terms.

© Terry G. Jordan, "Perceptual Regions of Texas," *Geographical Review* 68, [1978].

South Texas

☐ Lack of consensus from survey respondents

Meinig's Cultural Regions 1969

Panhandle

West Texas

North Texas

Dallas

East Texas

Central Texas

Southwest Texas

Hill Country

Austin

Houston

San Antonio

Gulf Coast

Geographer D.W. Meinig defined the cultural regions of Texas, referring to the Hill Country as German Hill Country.

From *Imperial Texas: An Interpretive Essay in Cultural Geography* by D.W. Meinig, © 1969, renewed 1997. Used by permission of author and the University of Texas Press.

South Texas

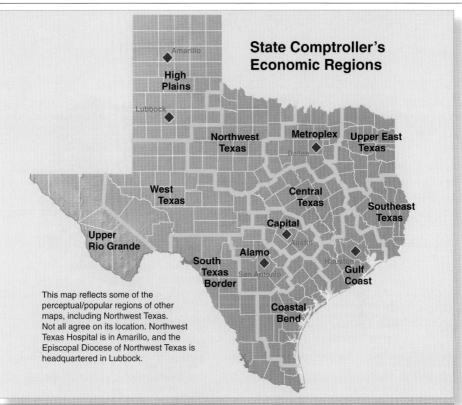

State Comptroller's Economic Regions

High Plains

Amarillo

Lubbock

Northwest Texas

Metroplex

Dallas

Upper East Texas

West Texas

Central Texas

Southeast Texas

Capital

Austin

Upper Rio Grande

Alamo

San Antonio

South Texas Border

Houston

Gulf Coast

Coastal Bend

This map reflects some of the perceptual/popular regions of other maps, including Northwest Texas. Not all agree on its location. Northwest Texas Hospital is in Amarillo, and the Episcopal Diocese of Northwest Texas is headquartered in Lubbock.

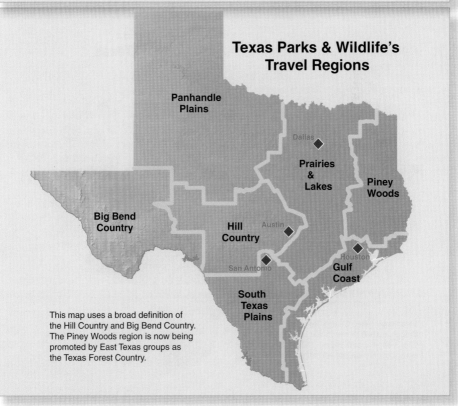

Texas Parks & Wildlife's Travel Regions

Panhandle Plains

Dallas

Prairies & Lakes

Piney Woods

Big Bend Country

Hill Country

Austin

San Antonio

Gulf Coast

Houston

South Texas Plains

This map uses a broad definition of the Hill Country and Big Bend Country. The Piney Woods region is now being promoted by East Texas groups as the Texas Forest Country.

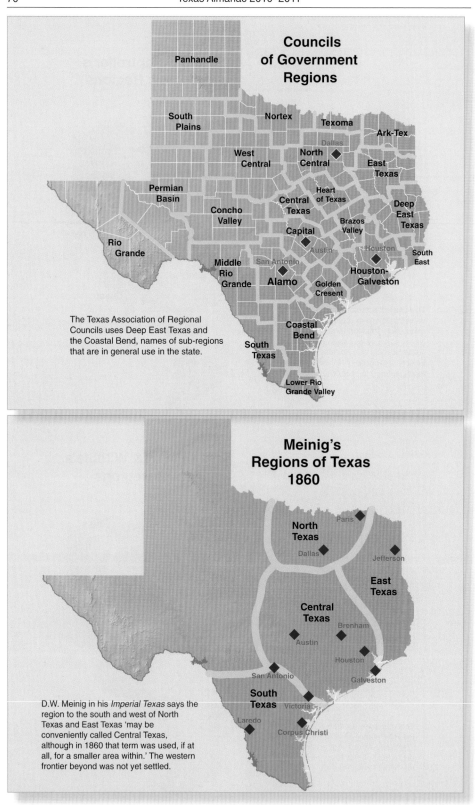

Councils of Government Regions

Panhandle

South Plains

Nortex

Texoma

Ark-Tex

West Central

North Central

Dallas

East Texas

Permian Basin

Heart of Texas

Central Texas

Concho Valley

Deep East Texas

Brazos Valley

Capital

Rio Grande

Austin

Houston

South East

Middle Rio Grande

San Antonio

Alamo

Houston-Galveston

Golden Cresent

Coastal Bend

South Texas

Lower Rio Grande Valley

The Texas Association of Regional Councils uses Deep East Texas and the Coastal Bend, names of sub-regions that are in general use in the state.

Meinig's Regions of Texas 1860

North Texas

Paris

Dallas

Jefferson

East Texas

Central Texas

Brenham

Austin

Houston

San Antonio

Galveston

South Texas

Victoria

Laredo

Corpus Christi

D.W. Meinig in his *Imperial Texas* says the region to the south and west of North Texas and East Texas 'may be conveniently called Central Texas, although in 1860 that term was used, if at all, for a smaller area within.' The western frontier beyond was not yet settled.

Geology of Texas

Source: Bureau of Economic Geology, The University of Texas at Austin; www.beg.utexas.edu/

History in the Rocks

Mountains, seas, coastal plains, rocky plateaus, high plains, forests — all this physiographic variety in Texas is controlled by the varied rocks and structures that underlie and crop out across the state. The fascinating geologic history of Texas is recorded in the rocks — both those exposed at the surface and those penetrated by holes drilled in search of oil and natural gas.

The rocks reveal a dynamic, ever-changing earth — ancient mountains, seas, volcanoes, earthquake belts, rivers, hurricanes and winds. Today, the volcanoes and great earthquake belts are no longer active, but rivers and streams, wind and rain, and the slow, inexorable alterations of rocks at or near the surface continue to change the face of Texas.

The geologic history of Texas, as documented by the rocks, began more than a billion years ago. Its legacy is the mineral wealth and varied land forms of modern Texas.

Geologic Time Travel

The story preserved in rocks requires an understanding of the origin of strata and how they have been deformed. **Stratigraphy** is the study of the composition, sequence and origin of rocks: what rocks are made of, how they were formed and the order in which the layers were formed.

Structural geology reveals the architecture of rocks: the locations of the mountains, volcanoes, sedimentary basins and earthquake belts.

The map on the following page shows where rocks of various geologic ages are visible on the surface of Texas today. History concerns events through time, but geologic time is such a grandiose concept, most find it difficult to comprehend. So geologists have named the various chapters of earth history.

Precambrian Eon

Precambrian rocks, more than 600 million years old, are exposed at the surface in the Llano Uplift of Central Texas and in scattered outcrops in West Texas, around and north of Van Horn and near El Paso.

These rocks, some more than a billion years old, include complexly deformed rocks that were originally formed by cooling from a liquid state as well as rocks that were altered from pre-existing rocks.

Precambrian rocks, often called the "basement complex," are thought to form the foundation of continental masses. They underlie all of Texas. The outcrop in Central Texas is only the exposed part of the **Texas Craton**, which is primarily buried by younger rocks. (A craton is a stable, almost immovable portion of the earth's crust that forms the nuclear mass of a continent.)

Paleozoic Era

During the early part of the Paleozoic Era (approximately 600 million to 350 million years ago), broad, relatively shallow seas repeatedly inundated the Texas Craton and much of North and West Texas. The evidence for these events is found exposed around the Llano Uplift and in far West Texas near Van Horn and El Paso, and also in the subsurface throughout most of West and North Texas. The evidence includes early Paleozoic rocks — sandstones, shales and limestones, similar to sediments that form in seas today — and the

Volcanic and intrusive igneous rocks are well exposed in arid areas of the Trans-Pecos, such as Grapevine Hills in Big Bend National Park. Ron Billings photo; Texas Forest Service.

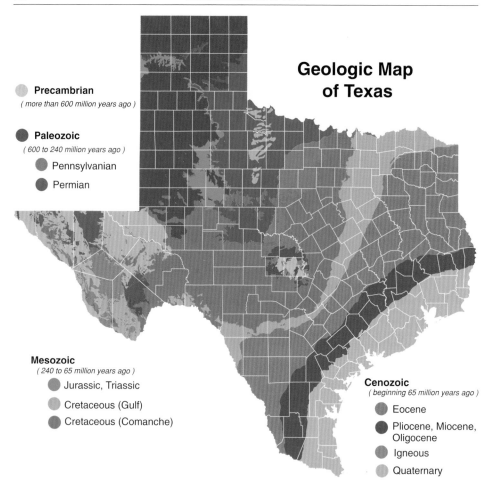

Geologic Map of Texas

Precambrian
(more than 600 million years ago)

Paleozoic
(600 to 240 million years ago)

Pennsylvanian

Permian

Mesozoic
(240 to 65 million years ago)

Jurassic, Triassic

Cretaceous (Gulf)

Cretaceous (Comanche)

Cenozoic
(beginning 65 million years ago)

Eocene

Pliocene, Miocene, Oligocene

Igneous

Quaternary

fossils of animals, similar to modern crustaceans — the brachiopods, clams, snails and related organisms that live in modern marine environments.

By late Paleozoic (approximately 350 million to 240 million years ago), the Texas Craton was bordered on the east and south by a long, deep marine basin called the Ouachita Trough. Sediments slowly accumulated in this trough until late in the Paleozoic Era. Plate-tectonic theory postulates that the collision of the North American Plate (upon which the Texas Craton is located) with the European and African–South American plates uplifted the thick sediments that had accumulated in the trough to form the Ouachita Mountains.

At that time, the once-majestic Ouachita Mountain chain extended across Texas, southeast Oklahoma and southwest Arkansas. Today, much of the Texas portion is buried by younger sediments, although uplift and erosion have exposed remnants in the Marathon Basin, which can be seen in Post Park, south of Marathon.

During the **Pennsylvanian Period**, however, the Ouachita Mountains bordered the eastern margin of shallow inland seas that covered most of West Texas. Rivers flowed westward from the mountains to the seas bringing sediment to form deltas along an ever-changing coastline.

The sediments were then reworked by the waves and currents of the inland sea. Today, these fluvial, delta and shallow marine deposits compose the late

Paleozoic rocks that crop out and underlie the surface of North-Central Texas.

Broad marine shelves divided the West Texas seas into several sub-basins, or deeper areas, that received more sediments than accumulated on the limestone shelves. Limestone reefs rimmed the deeper basins. Today, these reef limestones are important oil reservoirs in West Texas.

These seas gradually withdrew from Texas, and by the late **Permian Period**, all that was left in West Texas were shallow basins and wide tidal flats in which salt, gypsum and red muds accumulated in a hot, arid land. Strata deposited during the Permian Period are exposed today along the edge of the Panhandle, as far east as Wichita Falls and south to Concho County, and in the Trans-Pecos.

Mesozoic Era

Approximately 240 million years ago, the major geologic events in Texas shifted from West Texas to East and Southeast Texas. The European and African–South American plates, which had collided with the North American plate to form the Ouachita Mountains, began to separate from North America.

A series of faulted basins, or rifts, extending from Mexico to Nova Scotia were formed. These rifted basins received sediments from adjacent uplifts. As Europe and the southern continents continued to drift away

Visitors gather at the entrance to Natural Bridge Caverns in Comal County, a National Natural Landmark and one of the largest caverns in Texas. The caverns are composed of layers of limestone that accumulated during the Cretaceous period. Coastal settling that formed the Balcones Fault Zone also created joints, or cracks, in the limestone, and underground water moving along the joints eventually carved the passages at Natural Bridge Caverns. Ron Billings photo; Texas Forest Service.

from North America, the Texas basins were eventually buried beneath thick deposits of marine salt within the newly formed East Texas and Gulf Coast basins.

Jurassic and **Cretaceous** rocks in East and Southeast Texas document a sequence of broad limestone shelves at the edge of the developing Gulf of Mexico. From time to time, the shelves were buried beneath deltaic sandstones and shales, which built the northwestern margin of the widening Gulf of Mexico to the south and southeast.

As the underlying salt was buried more deeply by dense sediments, the salt became unstable and moved toward areas of least pressure. As the salt moved, it arched or pierced overlying sediments forming, in some cases, columns known as "salt domes." In some cases, these salt domes moved to the surface; others remain beneath a sedimentary overburden. This mobile salt formed numerous structures that would later serve to trap oil and natural gas.

By the early **Cretaceous** (approximately 140 million years ago), the shallow Mesozoic seas covered a large part of Texas, eventually extending west to the Trans-Pecos area and north almost to present-day state boundaries. Today, the limestone deposited in those seas are exposed in the walls of the magnificent canyons of the Rio Grande in the Big Bend National Park area and in the canyons and headwaters of streams that drain the Edwards Plateau, as well as in Central Texas from San Antonio to Dallas.

Animals of many types lived in the shallow Mesozoic seas, tidal pools and coastal swamps. Today these lower Cretaceous rocks are some of the most fossiliferous in the state. Tracks of **dinosaurs** occur in several places, and remains of **terrestrial**, **aquatic** and **flying reptiles** have been collected from Cretaceous rocks in many areas.

During most of the late Cretaceous, much of Texas lay beneath marine waters that were deeper than those of the early Cretaceous seas, except where rivers, deltas and shallow marine shelves existed.

River delta and strandline sandstones are the reservoir rocks for the most prolific oil field in Texas. When discovered in 1930, this East Texas oil field contained recoverable reserves estimated at 5.6 billion barrels.

The chalky rock that we now call the "Austin Chalk" was deposited when the Texas seas became deeper. Today, the chalk (and other Upper Cretaceous rocks) crops out in a wide band that extends from near Eagle Pass on the Rio Grande, east to San Antonio, north to Dallas and east to the Texarkana area. The Austin Chalk and other upper Cretaceous rocks dip southeastward beneath the East Texas and Gulf Coast basins.

The late Cretaceous was the time of the last major seaway across Texas, because mountains were forming in the western United States that influenced areas as far away as Texas.

A **chain of volcanoes** formed beneath the late Cretaceous seas in an area roughly parallel to and south and east of the old, buried Ouachita Mountains. The eruptions of these volcanoes were primarily on the sea floor and great clouds of steam and ash likely accompanied them.

Between eruptions, invertebrate marine animals built reefs on the shallow volcanic cones. Pilot Knob, located southeast of Austin, is one of these old volcanoes that is now exposed at the surface.

Cenozoic Era

At the dawn of the Cenozoic Era, approximately 65 million years ago, deltas fed by rivers were in the northern and northwestern margins of the East Texas Basin. These streams flowed eastward, draining areas to the north and west. Although there were minor incursions of the seas, the Cenozoic rocks principally document extensive seaward building by broad deltas, marshy lagoons, sandy barrier islands and embayments.

Thick vegetation covered the levees and areas between the streams. Coastal plains were taking shape under the same processes still at work today.

The Mesozoic marine salt became buried by thick sediments in the coastal plain area. The salt began to form ridges and domes in the Houston and Rio Grande areas. The heavy load of sand, silt and mud deposited by the deltas eventually caused some areas of the coast to subside and form large fault systems, essentially parallel to the coast.

Many of these coastal faults moved slowly and probably generated little earthquake activity. However, movement along the Balcones and Luling-Mexia-Talco zones, a **complex system of faults** along the western and northern edge of the basins, likely generated large earthquakes millions of years ago.

Predecessors of modern animals roamed the Texas Cenozoic coastal plains and woodlands. Bones and teeth of **horses, camels, sloths, giant armadillos, mammoths, mastodons, bats, rats, large cats** and other modern or extinct mammals have been excavated from coastal plain deposits.

Vegetation in the area included varieties of plants and trees both similar and dissimilar to modern ones. **Fossil palmwood**, the Texas "**state stone**," is found in sediments of early Cenozoic age.

The Cenozoic Era in Trans-Pecos Texas was entirely different. There, **extensive volcanic eruptions** formed great calderas and produced copious lava flows. These eruptions ejected great clouds of volcanic ash and rock particles into the air — many times the amount of material ejected by the 1980 eruption of Mount St. Helens.

Ash from the eruptions drifted eastward and is found in many of the sand-and-siltstones of the Gulf Coastal Plains. **Lava** flowed over older Paleozoic and Mesozoic rocks, and igneous intrusions melted their way upward into crustal rocks. These volcanic and intrusive igneous rocks are well exposed in arid areas of the Trans-Pecos today.

In the Texas Panhandle, streams originating in the recently elevated southern Rocky Mountains brought floods of gravel and sand into Texas. As the braided streams crisscrossed the area, they formed great alluvial fans.

These fans, which were deposited on the older **Paleozoic** and **Mesozoic** rocks, occur from northwestern Texas into Nebraska. Between 1 million and 2 million years ago, the streams of the Panhandle were isolated from their Rocky Mountain source, and the eastern edge of this sheet of alluvial material began to retreat westward, forming the **Caprock** of the modern High Plains.

Late in the Cenozoic Era, a great **Ice Age** descended on the northern North American continent. For more than 2 million years, there were successive advances and retreats of the thick sheets of glacial ice. Four periods of extensive glaciation were separated by warmer interglacial periods. Although the glaciers never reached as far south as Texas, the state's climate and sea level underwent major changes with each period of glacial advance and retreat.

Sea level during times of glacial advance was 300 to 450 feet lower than during the warmer interglacial periods because so much sea water was captured in the ice sheets. The climate was both more humid and cooler than today, and the major Texas rivers carried more water and more sand and gravel to the sea. These deposits underlie the outer 50 miles or more of the Gulf Coastal Plain.

Approximately 3,000 years ago, sea level reached its modern position. The rivers, deltas, lagoons, beaches and barrier islands that we know as coastal Texas today have formed since that time. ☆

Oil and natural gas, as well as nonfuel minerals, are important to the Texas economy. For a more detailed discussion, see pages 622, and 625–645.

In the Texas Panhandle, streams originating in the southern Rocky Mountains brought floods of gravel and sand into Texas during the Cenozoic Era, as seen in this Hutchinson County landscape. Robert Plocheck photo.

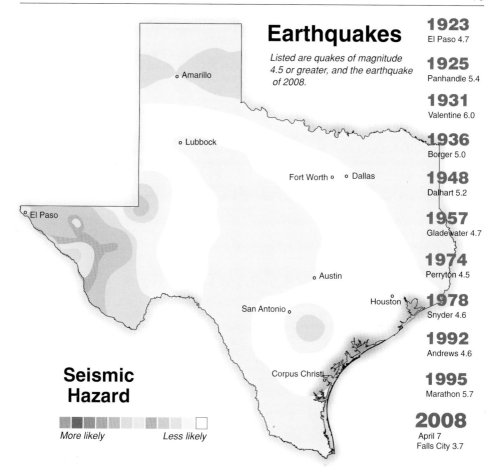

Earthquakes

1923
El Paso 4.7

Listed are quakes of magnitude 4.5 or greater, and the earthquake of 2008.

1925
Panhandle 5.4

1931
Valentine 6.0

1936
Borger 5.0

1948
Dalhart 5.2

1957
Gladewater 4.7

1974
Perryton 4.5

1978
Snyder 4.6

1992
Andrews 4.6

1995
Marathon 5.7

2008
April 7
Falls City 3.7

Seismic Hazard

More likely   Less likely

As the map above shows, except for the Trans-Pecos region of West Texas, most of the state has a relatively small probability of experiencing an earthquake. However, more than 100 tremors of magnitude 3.0 or greater have occurred. The map is based on the U.S. Geological Survey Seismic Hazard map.

Notable Earthquakes Shake Texas on Occasion

This adapted article was prepared for the Texas Almanac 1986-1987 by Dr. Wayne D. Pennington and Scott D. Davis, both of the Institute of Geophysics of the University of Texas at Austin.

Texas has experienced more than 100 earthquakes of magnitude 3 or greater since 1847. However, because the density of both seismographs and people has been very low in Texas, knowledge of the state's seismicity is undoubtedly incomplete.

The largest known earthquake in Texas occurred on Aug. 16, 1931, near the town of Valentine in Jeff Davis County. The total felt area exceeded one million square kilometers (about 400,000 square miles). *(See accompanying list, Significant Earthquakes, for details.)*

Ten earthquakes had epicenters near El Paso. Several of these shocks have produced minor damage. One earthquake on March 7, 1923, caused an adobe house to collapse and led to the suffocation of a man in Juarez, Mex. This is the only known death caused

by a Texas earthquake. Seismic activity in this area of Texas may be related to known faults that have been interpreted as part of the Rio Grande rift zone, a zone of crustal extension.

Notable earthquakes in the Texas Panhandle are probably associated with an ancient zone of crustal weakness that has been reactivated in recent times. Although the largest known earthquakes in the Panhandle have not exceeded magnitude 5.4, the potential for very large earthquakes remains uncertain.

Historic earthquakes in East and Central Texas include the 1847 Seguin, 1873 Manor, 1887 Paige, 1902 Creedmoor, 1932 Mexia-Wortham and the 1934 quake near Paris. These earthquakes were all fairly small and probably occurred as a result of sediment loading and resulting flexure in the Gulf of Mexico.

Earthquakes also have been located in Southeast Texas. The 1887 Wellborn, 1910 Hempstead and 1914 Anderson shocks may have been related to salt dome growth or minor adjustments from sediment loading in the Gulf. The 1891 Rusk and the 1981 Center and Jacksonville earthquakes in Northeast Texas were all located on or near an 80-kilometer segment of the Mount Enterprise fault system.

Fluid withdrawal is usually associated with aseismic subsidence and faulting such as occurs in the Houston area. However, small earthquakes are sometimes reported. In 1925, small shocks were associated with subsidence produced from oil production at the Goose Creek old field near Houston.

Larger earthquakes in East Texas also may have resulted from fluid withdrawal. Tentative relations between withdrawal and seismicity have been proposed for the 1932 Mexia-Wortham and the 1957 Gladewater earthquakes. More convincing evidence exists for the earthquakes in some oil and gas fields in South Texas.

The injection of fluids into the earth's crust for disposal or for secondary recovery of oil also has been known to produce earthquakes in other states. Some earthquakes, none very damaging, may be associated with fluid injection in the Permian Basin of West Texas.

An account of Texas' seismicity would not be complete without considering the effects of earthquakes from neighboring regions. Popular legend holds that the New Madrid, Mo., earthquakes of 1811-1812 were responsible for the formation of Caddo Lake. However, there exist accounts of the lake's existence as a swampy area as early as 1722. Whether the shocks deepened the lake is not known. In any case, it is likely that moderately high intensities of shock waves were experienced in Northeast Texas.

The Sonora, Mex., earthquake of 1887 cracked several buildings in El Paso and caused a general panic in the population of that city. Seismic surface waves from the Alaskan earthquake of 1964 damaged a water well in the Texas Panhandle and produced waves, which damaged several boats in channels along the Gulf Coast. ☆

Significant Earthquakes in Texas

Listed chronologically are the significant earthquakes in Texas, followed by the magnitude — commonly called the Richter scale, and known details about the earthquake.

1811 (8.1) — The first of this series of earthquakes at New Madrid, Mo., occurred on Dec. 16, 1811, magnitude 8.1. The second occurred on Jan. 12, 1812, with a magnitude of 7.8, and the third occurred on Feb. 7, 1812, with a magnitude of 8.0. All three were felt over an area of 5,000,000 square kilometers and were probably felt in Texas, but no verifiable accounts are known.

1847 (3.6) — The Feb. 14, 1847, earthquake was centered near Seguin. Newspapers reported cracked timber in houses at Seguin and New Braunfels.

1873 (3.1) — The May 1, 1873, earthquake was at Manor near Austin.

1882 (5.6) — The Oct. 22, 1882, earthquake felt in Texas, was probably centered in Oklahoma or Arkansas; the total felt area covered about 375,000 square kilometers. At Sherman heavy machinery vibrated, bricks were thrown from chimneys, and movable objects overturned.

1887 (4.1) — The Jan. 5, 1887, earthquake was at Paige in Bastrop County. The felt area was 4,600 square kilometers.

1887 (3.3) — The Jan. 31, 1887, earthquake was at Wellborn near College Station.

1887 (7.4) — A May 3, 1887, earthquake in Sonora, Mex., was felt strongly in West Texas, including El Paso and Fort Davis.

1891 (4.0) — On Jan. 8, 1891, violent shaking of buildings and a few toppled chimneys were reported from Rusk. These effects were evaluated as intensity VI, although other towns in East Texas along a northeast-southwest line through Rusk experienced tornadoes and sudden, violent wind storms producing effects similar to, and in some cases more damaging than, those in Rusk.

1902 (3.9) — The Oct. 9, 1902, earthquake was near Creedmoor, south of Austin. The felt area was 5,600 square kilometers.

1907 (3.6) — In April 1907, an earthquake near Amarillo occurred. Newspapers reported a window broken.

1910 (3.8) — The May 8, 1910, earthquake was at Hempstead. The felt area was 2,900 square kilometers.

1914 (3.3) — The Dec. 30, 1914, earthquake was at Anderson.

1917 (3.9) — A locally damaging earthquake occurred at Panhandle on March 28, 1917. Some cracked plaster was reported and children were evacuated from a school building.

1923 (4.7) — An earthquake on March 7, 1923, caused an adobe house to collapse and led to the suffocation of a man in Juarez, Mex., a few miles from the Texas border. This is the only known death caused by a Texas earthquake.

1925 (5.4) — Another disturbance occurred at Panhandle on July 30, 1925. There were three distinct shocks over a period of 15 seconds. Major problems were the shaking of dishes on shelves and rattling and creaking of furniture. The shocks were felt over an area of approximately 518,000 square kilometers including Roswell, N.M., Tulsa, Okla., and Leavenworth, Kan.

1931 (6.0) — This West Texas earthquake heavily damaged buildings in Valentine. The first shock occurred at 5:40 a.m. on Aug. 16. Although people were panic stricken, there were no fatalities and only a few minor injuries from falling adobe. Even though Valentine bore the brunt of the shock, damage was reported from widely scattered points in Brewster, Culberson, Jeff Davis and Presidio counties. Cracked walls and damaged chimneys were reported from several towns. The total felt area covered about 1,000,000 square kilometers in Texas, New Mexico and Mexico. The earthquake was accompanied by rumbling subterranean sounds heard over practically the entire affected area. The shock was strongly recorded on all seismographs in North America and at stations all over the world. Numerous aftershocks were felt in the epicentral region; the strongest, on Aug. 18, was magnitude 4.2 at Alpine, Lobo, Pecos and Valentine. A minor aftershock was felt at Valentine on Nov. 3.

1932 (4.0) — Slight damage resulted from an earthquake in the Mexia-Wortham area on April 9, 1932. Loose bricks were thrown down and some plaster cracked. The shock was also felt in Coolidge, Currie, Groesbeck, Hillsboro, Teague and Richland.

1934 (4.2) — A moderate earthquake affected an area of about 7,700 square kilometers in northeastern Texas near Paris and an adjoining portion of Oklahoma on April 11, 1934. The tremor was most distinctly felt at Arthur City, Chicota and Powderly. Many persons who felt the shock reported having heard a roaring or rumbling noise. Two shocks were recognized by many observers.

1936 (5.0) — Widely felt earthquake shocks with an epicenter in the Panhandle near Borger occurred June 19, 1936. Effects were noted at Gruver, White Deer and outside Borger.

1948 (5.2) — On March 11, 1948, a shock in the northern Panhandle near Dalhart caused minor damage, consisting mainly of cracked plaster. The effects were reported from Amarillo, Channing, Dalhart, Panhandle and Perryton.

1951 (4.2) — The Panhandle area was the center for another moderate shock on June 20, 1951. Damage to plaster occurred at Amarillo and Hereford. The felt region extended from Lubbock to Borger.

1952 (5.5) — This earthquake in central Oklahoma near El Reno on April 9, 1952, caused furniture to sway in North Texas and was felt as far south as Austin.

1957 (4.7) — Four shocks over six hours affected an area of about 26,000 square kilometers in bordering portions of Arkansas and Louisiana on March 19, 1957. Press reports noted that a few objects were upset and at least one or two windows were broken. Newspaper office and police station switchboards were swamped with called from alarmed residents. Effects were felt in Gladewater, Diana, Elkhart, Marshall, Nacogdoches and Troup.

1964 (4.4) — A series of moderate earthquakes in the Texas-Louisiana border region near Hemphill started on April 23, 1964. Epicenters were determined on April 23, 24, 27 and 28. There were numerous additional shocks reported felt at Pineland, Hemphill and Milam. The only damage reported was from the magnitude 4.4 earthquake on April 28 — wall paper and plaster cracked at Hemphill. The magnitude of the other epicenters changed from 3.2 to 3.7. Shocks were also felt at Pineland on April 30 and May 7. On June 2, three more shocks were reported in the same area. The strongest was measured at magnitude 4.2. Another moderate earthquake on Aug. 16 awakened several people at Hemphill and there were some reports of cracked plaster. The shock was also felt at Bronson, Geneva, Milam and Pineland.

1966 (4.1) — The Texas Panhandle region experienced another tremor on July 20, 1966. The earthquake knocked books from a shelf in one home and was felt by nearly all in Borger. Effects were felt Amarillo.

1966 (3.4) — Several street signs were knocked down and windows were broken at Kermit on Aug. 14, 1966. The shock was also felt at Wink.

1969 (3.9) — Four small earthquakes occurred near El Paso on May 12, 1969. One house in El Paso had hairline cracks in the ceiling and cracks in the cement driveway.

1974 (4.5) — On Feb. 15, 1974, an earthquake in the Texas Panhandle caused plaster cracks at Perryton, Booker, Darrouzett and Texhoma.

1978 (4.6) — An earthquake occurred on June 16, 1978 centered near Synder. Windows broke at Snyder, Fluvanna and Peacock, and cracked plaster was reported at Justiceburg.

1981 (3.2) — On June 9, 1981, an earthquake at Center, near the border with Louisiana.

1981 (3.3) — On Nov. 6, 1981, an earthqake at Jacksonville. The felt area of 800 square kilometers.

1992 (4.6) — An earthquake centered in Andrews County occurred on Jan. 2, 1992. Although felt over a wide area, 440,000 square kilometers, only minored damage was reported.

1995 (5.7) — An earthquake occurred on April 14, 1995 in Brewster County. There were broken water mains, cracked walls and windows and broken dishes. Broken gas mains resulted in several small fires. Landslides were reported, most notably from the peak of Cathedral Mountain.

Sources: Principally, the U.S. Geological Survey and the Institute for Geophysics at the University of Texas at Austin. Also, previous Texas Almanacs.

Soils of Texas

Source: Natural Resources Conservation Service, U.S. Department of Agriculture, Temple, Texas; www.tx.nrcs.usda.gov/

Soil is one of Texas' most important natural resources. Texas soils are complex because of the wide diversity of climate, vegetation, geology and landscape. **More than 1,300 different kinds of soil** are recognized in Texas. Each has a specific set of properties that affect its use.

Soil maps and information about soils and their uses are available for almost all Texas counties. The official soil information for soils in Texas is found at: **http://web-soilsurvey.nrcs.usda.gov/app/** and at **http://soildata-mart.nrcs.usda.gov/County.aspx?State=TX.**

Also contact the Natural Resources Conservation Service for more information: 101 S. Main, Temple 76501-7602; phone: 254-742-9850 or go to **www. tx.nrcs.usda.gov;** click on "Information About: Soils."

Soil Conservation

The vast expanse of Texas soils encouraged wasteful use of soil and water throughout much of the state's history. About 21 percent of all land area in Texas has been classified as prime farmland. Settlers, attracted by these rich soils and the abundant water of the eastern half of the region, used them to build an agriculture and agribusiness of vast proportions, and then found their abuse had created critical problems.

In the 1930s, interest in soil and water conservation began to mount. In 1935, the Soil Conservation Service, now called the **Natural Resources Conservation Service**, was created in the U.S. Department of Agriculture. In 1939, the **Texas Soil Conservation Law** made it possible for landowners to organize local soil and water conservation districts.

As of July 2009, Texas had **216 conservation districts**, which manage conservation functions within the district. A subdivision of state government, each district is governed by a board of five elected landowners. Technical assistance in planning and applying conservation work is provided through the USDA, Natural Resources Conservation Service. State funds are administered through the **Texas State Soil and Water Conservation Board**.

The 1997 National Resources Inventory showed that **land use** in Texas consisted of about 57 percent rangeland, 16 percent cropland, 9 percent pastureland, 6 percent forestland, 5 percent developed land, 2 percent federal land, 2 percent land in the conservation reserve program (CRP), 1 percent miscellaneous land and 2 percent water.

Major Soil Areas

Texas can be divided into 21 **Major Land Resource Areas** that have similar or related soils, vegetation, topography, climate and land uses. Brief descriptions of these areas follow.

Trans-Pecos Soils

The 18.7 million acres of the Trans-Pecos, mostly west of the Pecos River, are diverse plains and valleys intermixed with mountains. Surface drainage is slow to rapid. This arid region is used mainly as rangeland. A small amount of irrigated cropland is on the more fertile soils along the Rio Grande and the Pecos River. Vineyards are a more recent use of these soils, as is the disposal of large volumes of municipal wastes.

Upland soils are mostly well-drained, light reddish-brown to brown clay loams, clays and sands (some have a large amount of gypsum or other salts). Many areas have shallow soils and rock outcrops, and sizable areas have deep sands. Bottomland soils are deep, well-drained, dark grayish-brown to reddish-brown silt loams, loams, clay loams and clays. Lack of soil moisture and wind erosion are the major soil-management problems. Only irrigated crops can be grown on these soils, and most areas lack an adequate source of good water.

Upper Pecos, Canadian Valleys and Plains Soils

The Upper Pecos and Canadian Valleys and Plains area occupies a little over a half-million acres and is in

Some areas of the Trans-Pecos have a large amount of gypsum or other salts, such as the Salt Basin in Hudspeth County at the base of the Guadalupe Mountains. Robert Plocheck photo.

Dickens County in the West Texas Rolling Plains has outcrops of red beds that give the region the name "Red Plains." This area is used mostly for rangeland. Robert Plocheck photo.

the northwest part of Texas near the Texas-New Mexico border. It is characterized by broad rolling plains and tablelands broken by drainageways and tributaries of the Canadian River. It includes the **Canadian Breaks**, which are rough, steep lands below the adjacent High Plains. The average annual precipitation is about 15 inches, but it fluctuates widely from year to year. Surface drainage is slow to rapid.

The soils are well drained and alkaline. The mostly reddish-brown clay loams and sandy loams were formed mostly in material weathered from sandstone and shale. Depths range from shallow to very deep.

The area is used mainly as rangeland and wildlife habitat. Native vegetation is mid- to short-grass prairie species, such as hairy grama, sideoats grama, little bluestem, alkali sacaton, vine-mesquite, and galleta in the plains and tablelands. Juniper and mesquite grow on the relatively higher breaks. Soil management problems include low soil moisture and brush control.

High Plains Soils

The High Plains area comprises a vast high plateau of more than 19.4 million acres in northwestern Texas. It lies in the southern part of the Great Plains province that includes large similar areas in Oklahoma and New Mexico. The flat, nearly level treeless plain has few streams to cause local relief. However, several major rivers originate in the High Plains or cross the area. The largest is the Canadian River, which has cut a deep valley across the Panhandle section.

Playas, small intermittent lakes scattered through the area, lie up to 20 feet below the surrounding plains. A 1965 survey counted more than 19,000 playas in 44 counties occupying some 340,000 acres. Most runoff from rainfall is collected in the playas, but only 10 to 40 percent of this water percolates back to the Ogallala Aquifer. The aquifer is virtually the exclusive water source in this area.

Upland soils are mostly well-drained, deep, neutral to alkaline clay loams and sandy loams in shades of brown or red. Sandy soils are in the southern part. Many soils have large amounts of lime at various depths and some are shallow over caliche. Soils of bottomlands are

minor in extent.

The area is used mostly for cropland, but significant areas of rangeland are in the southwestern and extreme northern parts. Millions of cattle populate the many large feedlots in the area. The soils are moderately productive, and the flat surface encourages irrigation and mechanization. Limited soil moisture, constant danger of wind erosion and irrigation water management are the major soil-management problems, but the region is Texas' leading producer of three important crops: cotton, grain sorghums and wheat.

Rolling Plains Soils

The Rolling Plains include 21.7 million acres east of the High Plains in northwestern Texas. The area lies west of the North Central Prairies and extends from the edge of the Edwards Plateau in Tom Green County northward into Oklahoma. The landscape is nearly level to strongly rolling, and surface drainage is moderate to rapid. Outcrops of red beds, geologic materials and associated reddish soils led some scientists to use of the name "**Red Plains.**" Limestone underlies the soils in the southeastern part. The eastern part contains large areas of badlands.

Upland soils are mostly deep, pale-brown through reddish-brown to dark grayish-brown, neutral to alkaline sandy loams, clay loams and clays; some are deep sands.

Many soils have a large amount of lime in the lower part, and a few others are saline; some are shallow and stony. Bottomland soils are mostly reddish-brown and sandy to clayey; some are saline.

This area is used mostly for rangeland, but cotton, grain sorghums and wheat are important crops. The major soil-management problems are brush control, wind erosion, low fertility and lack of soil moisture. Salt spots are a concern in some areas.

North Central Prairie Soils

The North Central Prairie occupies about 7 million acres in North Central Texas. Adjacent to this area on the north is the rather small area (less than 1 million acres) called **Rolling Red Prairies**, which extends into

Oklahoma and is included here because the soils and land use are similar. This area lies between the Western Cross Timbers and the Rolling Plains. It is predominantly grassland intermixed with small wooded areas. The landscape is undulating with slow to rapid surface drainage.

Upland soils are mostly deep, well-drained, brown or reddish-brown, slightly acid loams over neutral to alkaline, clayey subsoils. Some soils are shallow or moderately deep to shale. Bottomland soils are mostly well-drained, dark-brown or gray loams and clays.

This area is used mostly as rangeland, but wheat, grain sorghums and other crops are grown on the better soils. Brush control, wind and water erosion and limited soil moisture are the major soil-management concerns.

Edwards Plateau Soils

The 22.7 million acres of the Edwards Plateau are in South Central Texas east of the Trans-Pecos and west of the Blackland Prairie. Uplands are nearly level to undulating except near large stream valleys where the landscape is hilly with deep canyons and steep slopes. Surface drainage is rapid.

Upland soils are mostly shallow, stony or gravelly, dark alkaline clays and clay loams underlain by limestone. Lighter-colored soils are on steep sideslopes and deep, less-stony soils are in the valleys. Bottomland soils are mostly deep, dark-gray or brown, alkaline loams and clays.

Raising beef cattle is the main enterprise in this region, but it is also the center of Texas' and the nation's mohair and wool production. The area is a major deer habitat; hunting leases produce income. Cropland is mostly in the valleys on the deeper soils and is used mainly for growing forage crops and hay. The major soil-management concerns are brush control, large stones, low fertility, excess lime and limited soil moisture. There are many **Cedar Brakes**.

Central/Llano Basin Soils

The Central Basin, also known as the Llano Basin, occupies a relatively small area in Central Texas. It includes parts or all of Llano, Mason, Gillespie and adjoining counties. The total area is about 1.6 million acres of undulating to hilly landscape.

Upland soils are mostly shallow, reddish-brown to brown, mostly gravelly and stony, neutral to slightly acid sandy loams over granite, limestone, gneiss and schist bedrock. Large boulders are on the soil surface in some areas. Deeper, less stony sandy-loam soils are in the valleys. Bottomland soils are minor areas of deep, dark-gray or brown loams and clays.

Ranching is the main enterprise, with some farms producing peaches, grain sorghum and wheat. The area provides excellent deer habitat, and hunting leases are a major source of income. Brush control, large stones and limited soil moisture are soil-management concerns.

Northern Rio Grande Plain Soils

The Northern Rio Grande Plain comprises about 6.3 million acres in South Texas extending from Uvalde to Beeville. The landscape is nearly level to rolling, mostly brush-covered plains with slow to rapid surface drainage.

The major upland soils are deep, reddish-brown or dark grayish-brown, neutral to alkaline loams and clays. Bottomland soils are mostly dark-colored loams.

The area is mostly rangeland with significant areas of cropland. Grain sorghums, cotton, corn and small grains are the major crops. Crops are irrigated in the western part, especially in the Winter Garden area, where vegetables such as spinach, carrots and cabbage are grown. Much of the area is good deer and dove habi-

tat; hunting leases are a major source of income. Brush control, soil fertility, and irrigation-water management are the major soil-management concerns.

Western Rio Grande Plain Soils

The Western Rio Grande Plain comprises about 5.3 million acres in an area of southwestern Texas from Del Rio to Rio Grande City. The landscape is nearly level to undulating except near the Rio Grande where it is hilly. Surface drainage is slow to rapid.

The major soils are mostly deep, brown or gray alkaline clays and loams. Some are saline.

Most of the soils are used for rangeland. Irrigated grain sorghums and vegetables are grown along the Rio Grande. Hunting leases are a major source of income. Brush control and limited soil moisture are the major soil-management problems.

Central Rio Grande Plain Soils

The Central Rio Grande Plain comprises about 5.9 million acres in an area of South Texas from Live Oak County to Hidalgo County. It Includes the **South Texas Sand Sheet**, an area of deep, sandy soils and active sand dunes. The landscape is nearly level to gently undulating. Surface drainage is slow to rapid. Upland soils are mostly deep, light-colored, neutral to alkaline sands and loams. Many are saline or sodic. Bottomland soils are of minor extent.

Most of the area is used for raising beef cattle. A few areas, mostly in the northeast part, are used for growing grain sorghums, cotton and small grains. Hunting leases are a major source of income. Brush control is the major soil-management problem on rangeland; wind erosion and limited soil moisture are major concerns on cropland.

Lower Rio Grande Valley Soils

The Lower Rio Grande Valley comprises about 2.1 million acres in extreme southern Texas. The landscape is level to gently sloping with slow surface drainage.

Upland soils are mostly deep, grayish-brown, neutral to alkaline loams; coastal areas are mostly gray, silty clay loam and silty clay; some are saline. Bottomland soils are minor in extent.

Most of the soils are used for growing irrigated vegetables and citrus, along with cotton, grain sorghums and sugar cane. Some areas are used for growing beef cattle. Irrigation water management and wind erosion are the major soil-management problems on cropland; brush control is the major problem on rangeland.

Western Cross Timbers Soils

The Western Cross Timbers area comprises about 2.6 million acres. It includes the wooded section west of the Grand Prairie and extends from the Red River southward to the north edge of Brown County. The landscape is undulating and is dissected by many drainageways including the Brazos and Red rivers. Surface drainage is rapid.

Upland soils are mostly deep, grayish-brown, slightly acid loams with loamy and clayey subsoils. Bottomland soils along the major rivers are deep, reddish-brown, neutral to alkaline silt loams and clays.

The area is used mostly for grazing beef and dairy cattle on native range and improved pastures. Crops are peanuts, grain sorghums, small grains, peaches, pecans and vegetables. The major soil-management problem on grazing lands is brush control. Waste management on dairy farms is a more recent concern. Wind and water erosion are the major problems on cropland.

Eastern Cross Timbers Soils

The Eastern Cross Timbers area comprises about 1 million acres in a long narrow strip of wooded land that

A windmill sculpture in Montague County. This area lies between the Western Cross Timbers and the Rolling Plains and is predominantly grassland. Robert Plocheck photo.

separates the northern parts of the Blackland Prairie and Grand Prairie and extends from the Red River southward to Hill County. The landscape is gently undulating to rolling and is dissected by many streams, including the Red and Trinity rivers. Sandstone-capped hills are prominent in some areas. Surface runoff is moderate to rapid.

The upland soils are mostly deep, light-colored, slightly acid sandy loams and loamy sands with reddish loamy or clayey subsoils. Bottomland soils are reddish-brown to dark gray, slightly acid to alkaline loams or gray clays.

Grassland consisting of native range and improved pastures is the major land use. Peanuts, grain sorghums, small grains, peaches, pecans and vegetables are grown in some areas. Brush control, water erosion and low fertility are the major soil concerns in management.

Grand Prairie Soils

The Grand Prairie comprises about 6.3 million acres in North Central Texas. It extends from the Red River to about the Colorado River. It lies between the Eastern and Western Cross Timbers in the northern part and just west of the Blackland Prairie in the southern part. The landscape is undulating to hilly and is dissected by many streams including the Red, Trinity and Brazos rivers. Surface drainage is rapid.

Upland soils are mostly dark-gray, alkaline clays; some are shallow over limestone and some are stony. Some areas have light-colored loamy soils over chalky limestone. Bottomland soils along the Red and Brazos rivers are reddish silt loams and clays. Other bottomlands have dark-gray loams and clays.

Land use is a mixture of rangeland, pastureland and cropland. The area is mainly used for growing beef cattle. Some small grain, grain sorghums, corn and hay are grown. Brush control and water erosion are the major management concerns.

Blackland Prairie Soils

The Blackland Prairies consist of about 12.6 million acres of east-central Texas extending southwesterly from the Red River to Bexar County. There are smaller areas to the southeast. The landscape is undulating with few scattered wooded areas that are mostly in the bottomlands. Surface drainage is moderate to rapid.

Both upland and bottomland soils are deep, dark-gray to black alkaline clays. Some soils in the western part are shallow to moderately deep over chalk. Some soils on the eastern edge are neutral to slightly acid, grayish clays and loams over mottled clay subsoils (sometimes called graylands). Blackland soils are known as "cracking clays" because of the large, deep cracks that form in dry weather. This high shrink-swell property can cause serious damage to foundations, highways and other structures and is a safety hazard in pits and trenches.

Land use is divided about equally between cropland and grassland. Cotton, grain sorghums, corn, wheat, oats and hay are grown. Grassland is mostly improved pastures, with native range on the shallower and steeper soils. Water erosion, cotton root rot, soil tilth and brush control are the major management problems.

Claypan Area Soils

The Claypan Area consists of about 6.1 million acres in east-central Texas just east of the Blackland Prairie. The landscape is a gently undulating to rolling, moderately dissected woodland also known as the **Post Oak Belt** or **Post Oak Savannah**. Surface drainage is moderate.

Upland soils commonly have a thin, light-colored, acid sandy loam surface layer over dense, mottled red, yellow and gray claypan subsoils. Some deep, sandy soils with less clayey subsoils exist. Bottomlands are deep, highly fertile, reddish-brown to dark-gray loamy to clayey soils.

Land use is mainly rangeland. Some areas are in improved pastures. Most cropland is in bottomlands that are protected from flooding. Major crops are cotton, grain sorghums, corn, hay and forage crops, most of which are irrigated. Brush control on rangeland and irrigation water management on cropland are the major management problems. Water erosion is a serious problem on the highly erosive claypan soils, especially where they are overgrazed.

The southmost place on Texas highways is on FM 1419 in Cameron County. Lower Rio Grande Valley soils are mostly used for growing irrigated crops. Robert Plocheck photo.

East Texas Timberland Soils

The East Texas Timberlands area comprises about 16.1 million acres of the forested eastern part of the state. The land is gently undulating to hilly and well dissected by many streams. Surface drainage is moderate to rapid.

This area has many kinds of upland soils but most are deep, light-colored, acid sands and loams over loamy and clayey subsoils. Deep sands are in scattered areas and red clays are in areas of "redlands." Bottomland soils are mostly brown to dark-gray, acid loams and some clays.

The land is used mostly for growing commercial pine timber and for woodland grazing. Improved pastures are scattered throughout and are used for grazing beef and dairy cattle and for hay production. Some commercial hardwoods are in the bottomlands. Woodland management problems include seedling survival, invasion of hardwoods in pine stands, effects of logging on water quality and control of the southern pine beetle. Lime and fertilizers are necessary for productive cropland and pastures.

Coast Prairie Soils

The Coast Prairie includes about 8.7 million acres near the Gulf Coast. It ranges from 30 miles to 80 miles in width and parallels the coast from the Sabine River in Orange County in Southeast Texas to Baffin Bay in Kleberg County in South Texas. The landscape is level to gently undulating with slow surface drainage.

Upland soils are mostly deep, dark-gray, neutral to slightly acid clay loams and clays. Lighter-colored and more-sandy soils are in a strip on the northwestern edge; some soils in the southern part are alkaline; some are saline and sodic. Bottomland soils are mostly deep, dark-colored clays and loams along small streams but are greatly varied along the rivers.

Land use is mainly grazing lands and cropland. Some hardwood timber is in the bottomlands. Many areas are also managed for wetland wildlife habitat. The nearly level topography and productive soils encourage farming. Rice, grain sorghums, cotton, corn and hay are the main crops. Brush management on grasslands and removal of excess water on cropland are the major management concerns.

Coast Saline Prairies Soils

The Coast Saline Prairies area includes about 3.2 million acres along a narrow strip of wet lowlands adjacent to the coast; it includes the barrier islands that extend from Mexico to Louisiana. The surface is at or only a few feet above sea level with many areas of salt-water marsh. Surface drainage is very slow.

The soils are mostly deep, dark-colored clays and loams; many are saline and sodic. Light-colored sandy soils are on the barrier islands. The water table is at or near the surface of most soils.

Cattle grazing is the chief economic use of the various salt-tolerant cordgrasses and sedges. Many areas are managed for wetland wildlife. Recreation is popular on the barrier islands. Providing fresh water and access to grazing areas are the major management concerns.

Gulf Coast Marsh Soils

This 150,000-acre area lies in the extreme southeastern corner of Texas. The area can be subdivided into four parts: freshwater, intermediate, brackish, and saline (saltwater) marsh. The degree of salinity of this system grades landward from saltwater marshes along the coast to freshwater marshes inland. Surface drainage is very slow.

This area contains many lakes, bayous, tidal channels, and man-made canals. About one-half of the marsh is fresh, and one-half is salty. Most of the area is susceptible to flooding either by fresh water drained from lands adjacent to the marsh or by saltwater from the Gulf of Mexico.Most of the soils are very poorly drained, continuously saturated, soft and can carry little weight. In general, the organic soils have a thick layer of dark gray, relatively undecomposed organic material over a gray, clayey subsoil. The mineral soils have a surface of dark gray, highly decomposed organic material over a gray, clayey subsoil.

Most of the almost treeless and uninhabited area is in marsh vegetation, such as grasses, sedges and rushes. It is used mainly for wildlife habitat. Part of the fertile and productive estuarine complex that supports marine life of the Gulf of Mexico, it provides wintering ground for waterfowl and habitat for many fur-bearing animals and alligators. A significant acreage is firm enough to support livestock and is used for winter grazing of cattle. The major management problems are providing fresh water and access to grazing areas.

Flatwoods Soils

The Flatwoods area includes about 2.5 million acres of woodland in humid Southeast Texas just north of the Coast Prairie and extending into Louisiana. The landscape is level to gently undulating. Surface drainage is slow.

Upland soils are mostly deep, light-colored, acid loams with gray, loamy or clayey subsoils. Bottomland soils are deep, dark-colored, acid clays and loams. The water table is near the surface at least part of the year.

The land is mainly used for forest, although cattle are grazed in some areas. Woodland management problems include seedling survival, invasion of hardwoods in pine stands, effects of logging on water quality and control of the southern pine beetle. ☆

Water Resources

Sources: Texas Water Development Board, www.twdb.state.tx.us; U.S. Geological Survey, http://tx.usgs.gov/

Texas has historically relied on its wealth of fresh to slightly saline water that underlies more than 81 percent of the state. About 59 percent of the approximately 16 million acre-feet of water used yearly in Texas is derived from underground formations that make up 9 major and 21 minor aquifers.

Nearly 79 percent of the groundwater produced in 2003 was used for irrigating crops, especially in the Panhandle region. Groundwater also supplies about 36 percent of the state's municipal needs.

Major Aquifers of Texas

Ogallala

The Ogallala aquifer extends under 47 counties of the Texas Panhandle and is the southernmost extension of the largest aquifer (High Plains aquifer) in North America. The Ogallala Formation of late Miocene to early Pliocene age consists of heterogeneous sequences of coarse-grained sand and gravel in the lower part, grading upward into clay, silt and fine sand. In Texas, the Panhandle is the most extensive region irrigated with groundwater. In 2000, almost 97 percent of the water pumped from the Ogallala was used for irrigation.

Water-level declines are occurring in part of the region because of extensive pumping that far exceeds recharge. Water-conservation measures by agricultural and municipal users are being promoted. Computer models of the northern and southern portions of the Ogallala aquifer were completed by the Texas Water Development Board and its contractor. Several agencies are investigating playa recharge and agricultural re-use projects over the aquifer.

Gulf Coast Aquifer

The Gulf Coast aquifer forms an irregularly shaped belt that parallels the Texas coastline and extends through 54 counties from the Rio Grande northeastward to the Louisiana border. The **aquifer system** is composed of the water-bearing units of the Catahoula, Oakville, Fleming, Goliad, Willis, Lissie, Bentley, Montgomery and Beaumont formations.

This system has been divided into three major water-producing components referred to as the **Chicot, Evangeline** and **Jasper** aquifers. In 2000, municipal uses accounted for 43 percent and irrigation accounted for 39 percent of the total pumpage from the aquifer.

Water quality is generally good northeast of the San Antonio River basin, but deteriorates to the southwest. Years of heavy pumpage have caused significant water-level declines in portions of the aquifer. Some of these declines have resulted in significant **land-surface subsidence**, particularly in the Houston-Galveston area.

Edwards (Balcones Fault Zone)

The Edwards (BFZ) aquifer forms a narrow belt extending through nine counties from a groundwater divide in Kinney County through the San Antonio area northeastward to the Leon River in Bell County. A poorly defined groundwater divide in Hays County hydrologically separates the aquifer into the San Antonio and Austin regions. Water in the aquifer occurs in fractures, honeycomb zones (or intergranular pores) and solution channels in the Edwards and associated limestone formations of Cretaceous age.

In 2000, about 55 percent of pumpage was for municipal use, while irrigation was the principal use in the western segment. San Antonio is one of the largest cities in the world that relies solely on a single groundwater

Water Regulation

In Texas, water law has been historically different for surface water and groundwater. Surface water belongs to the state and, except for limited amounts of water for household and on-farm livestock use, requires permits for use.

In general, groundwater is considered the property of the surface landowner by "right of capture," meaning the landowner may pump as much water from beneath his land as he can for any beneficial use. This right may be limited only through the creation of ground-water conservation districts, which may make rules to protect and conserve groundwater supplies within their boundaries.

The **Texas Commission on Environmental Quality** is responsible for permitting and adjudicating surface-water rights and uses. It is the primary regulator of surface water and polices contamination and pollution of both surface and groundwater.

The **Texas Water Development Board** collects data on occurrence, availability and water quality within the state; plans for future water supply and use; and administers the state's funds for grants and loans to finance future water development and supply.

In January 2007, the Texas Water Development Board released a comprehensive **statewide water plan**, which the 75th Texas Legislature in 1997 required the board to complete every five years. The TWDB divided the state into 16 regional water-planning areas, and each area's Regional Water Planning Group is required to adopt a water plan that addresses conservation of water supplies, and that looks at how to meet future water needs and how to respond to future droughts.

source for its municipal supply. The aquifer also feeds several well-known recreational springs and underlies some of Texas' most environmentally sensitive areas.

In 1993, the Edwards Aquifer Authority was created by the legislature to regulate aquifer pumpage to benefit all users from Uvalde County through a portion of Hays County. Barton Springs-Edwards Aquifer Conservation District provides aquifer management for the rest of Hays and southern Travis counties.

The EAA has an active program to educate the public on water conservation and also operates several active groundwater recharge sites. The San Antonio River Authority also has a number of flood-control structures that effectively recharge the aquifer.

Conservation districts are promoting more-efficient irrigation techniques, and market-based, voluntary transfers of unused agricultural water rights to municipal uses are more common.

Carrizo-Wilcox

Extending from the Rio Grande in South Texas northeastward into Arkansas and Louisiana, the Carrizo-Wilcox aquifer provides water to all or parts of 66 counties. The Wilcox Group and overlying Carrizo Sand form a hydrologically connected system of sand locally interbedded with clay, silt, lignite and gravel.

Throughout most of its extent in Texas, the aquifer

yields fresh to slightly saline water that is used mainly for irrigation in the **Winter Garden District** of South Texas and for public supply and industrial use in Central and Northeast Texas.

Excessive pumping has lowered the water level, particularly in the artesian portion of the Winter Garden District of Atascosa, Frio and Zavala counties and in municipal and industrial areas in Angelina and Smith counties.

Trinity

The Trinity aquifer consists of basal Cretaceous-age Trinity Group formations extending from the Red River in North Texas to the Hill Country of Central Texas. Formations comprising the aquifer include the **Twin Mountains, Glen Rose, Paluxy, Hosston Sand** and **Hensel Sand**. Where the Glen Rose thins or is absent, the Twin Mountains and Paluxy formations coalesce to form the **Antlers Formation**. In the south, the Trinity includes the Glen Rose and underlying **Travis Peak** formations. Water from the Antlers portion is used mainly for irrigation in the outcrop area of North and Central Texas.

Elsewhere, water from the Trinity aquifer is used primarily for municipal and domestic supply. Extensive development of the Trinity aquifer in the Dallas-Fort Worth and Waco areas has resulted in water-level declines of 350 to more than 1,000 feet.

Edwards-Trinity (Plateau)

This aquifer underlies the Edwards Plateau, extending from the Hill Country of Central Texas westward to the Trans-Pecos region. It consists of sandstone and limestone formations of the Trinity formations, and limestones and dolomites of the Edwards and associated limestone formations. Groundwater movement is generally toward the southeast.

Near the plateau's edge, flow is toward the main streams, where the water issues from springs. Irrigation, mainly in the northwestern portion of the region, accounted for about 70 percent of total aquifer use in 2000 and has resulted in significant water-level declines in Glasscock and Reagan counties. Elsewhere, the aquifer supplies fresh but hard water for municipal, domestic and livestock use.

Seymour

This aquifer consists of isolated areas of alluvium found in parts of 25 north-central and Panhandle counties in the upper Red River and Brazos River basins. Eastward-flowing streams during the Quaternary Period deposited discontinuous beds of poorly sorted gravel, sand, silt and clay that were later dissected by erosion, resulting in the isolated remnants of the formation. Individual accumulations vary greatly in thickness, but most of the Seymour is less than 100 feet.

The lower, more permeable part of the aquifer produces the greatest amount of groundwater. Irrigation pumpage accounted for 93 percent of the total use from the aquifer in 1994. Water quality generally ranges from fresh to slightly saline. However, the salinity has increased in many heavily pumped areas to the point

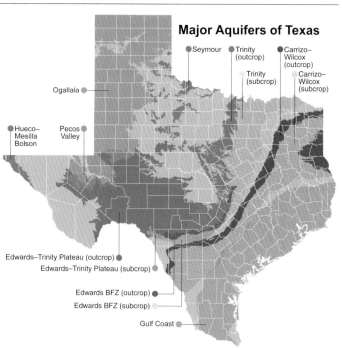

Major Aquifers of Texas

- Seymour
- Trinity (outcrop)
- Trinity (subcrop)
- Carrizo–Wilcox (outcrop)
- Carrizo–Wilcox (subcrop)
- Ogallala
- Hueco–Mesilla Bolson
- Pecos Valley
- Edwards–Trinity Plateau (outcrop)
- Edwards–Trinity Plateau (subcrop)
- Edwards BFZ (outcrop)
- Edwards BFZ (subcrop)
- Gulf Coast

where the water has become unsuitable for domestic and municipal use. Natural salt pollution in the upper reaches of the Red and Brazos river basins precludes the full utilization of these water resources.

Hueco-Mesilla Bolson

These aquifers are located in El Paso and Hudspeth counties in far western Texas and occur in Tertiary and Quaternary basin-fill deposits that extend northward into New Mexico and westward into Mexico. The Hueco Bolson, located on the eastern side of the Franklin Mountains, consists of up to 9,000 feet of clay, silt, sand and gravel and is an important source of drinking water for both El Paso and Juarez, Mexico.

Located west of the Franklin Mountains, the Mesilla Bolson reaches up to 2,000 feet in thickness and contains three separate water-producing zones. Groundwater depletion of the Hueco Bolson has become a serious problem.

Historical large-scale groundwater withdrawals, especially for the municipal uses of El Paso and Juarez, have caused major water-level declines and significantly changed the direction of flow, causing a deterioration of the chemical quality of the groundwater in the aquifer, according to El Paso Water Utilities and the USGS.

Pecos Valley

Located in the upper Pecos River Valley of West Texas, this aquifer, formerly called the Cenozoic Pecos Alluvium, is the principal source of water for irrigation in Reeves and northwestern Pecos counties and for industrial uses, power supply and municipal use elsewhere. Consisting of up to 1,500 feet of alluvial fill, the aquifer occupies two hydrologically separate basins: the Pecos Trough in the west and the Monument Draw Trough in the east.

Water is generally hard and contains dissolved-solids concentrations ranging from less than 300 to more than 5,000 parts per million. Water-level declines in excess of 200 feet have historically occurred in Reeves and Pecos counties, but have moderated since the mid-1970s with the decrease in irrigation pumpage. ☆

Major Rivers of Texas

Some 11,247 named Texas streams are identified in the U.S. Geological Survey Geographic Names Information System. Their combined length is about 80,000 miles, and they drain 263,513 square miles within Texas. Fourteen major rivers are described below, starting with the southernmost and moving northward:

Rio Grande

The Pueblo Indians called this river **P'osoge**, which means the "river of great water." In 1582, **Antonio de Espejo** of Nueva Vizcaya, Mexico, followed the course of the **Río Conchos** to its confluence with a great river, which Espejo named **Río del Norte (River of the North)**. The name **Rio Grande** was first given the stream apparently by the explorer **Juan de Oñate**, who arrived on its banks near present-day El Paso in 1598.

Thereafter the names were often consolidated, as **Río Grande del Norte**. It was shown also on early Spanish maps as **Río San Buenaventura** and **Río Ganapetuan**. In its lower course it early acquired the name **Río Bravo**, which is its name on most Mexican maps. At times it has also been known as **Río Turbio**, probably because of its muddy appearance during its frequent rises. Some people erroneously call this watercourse the Rio Grande River.

This river **forms the boundary of Texas** and international U.S.-Mexican boundary for **889** or **1,254** river miles, depending upon method of measurement. (See **Texas Boundary Lines, page 60.**)

The **U.S. Geological Survey** figure for the total length from its headwaters to its mouth on the Gulf of Mexico is **1,900** miles.

According to the USGS, the Rio Grande is tied with the St. Lawrence River (also 1,900 miles) as the **fourth-longest** North American river, exceeded only by the Missouri-Mississippi, McKenzie-Peace and Yukon. Since all of these except the Missouri-Mississippi are partly in Canada, the Rio Grande is the **second-longest river entirely within or bordering the United States**. It is

Texas' longest river.

The snow-fed flow of the Rio Grande is used for irrigation in Colorado below the San Juan Mountains, where the river rises at the Continental Divide. Turning south, it flows through a canyon in northern New Mexico and again irrigates a broad valley of central New Mexico. Southern New Mexico impounds Rio Grande waters in Elephant Butte Reservoir for irrigation of the valley above and below El Paso.

The valley near El Paso is thought to be the **oldest irrigated area in Texas** since Indians were irrigating crops here when Spanish explorers arrived in the early 1500s.

From source to mouth, the Rio Grande drops 12,000 feet to sea level as a mountain torrent, desert stream and meandering coastal river. Along its banks and in its valley Europeans established some of their first North American settlements. Here are situated **three of the oldest towns in Texas — Ysleta, Socorro and San Elizario**.

Because of the extensive irrigation, the Rio Grande virtually ends at the lower end of the El Paso valley, except in seasons of above-normal flow.

The river starts again as a perennially flowing stream where the Río Conchos of Mexico flows into it at Presidio-Ojinaga. Through the **Big Bend,** the Rio Grande flows through three successive **canyons**, the **Santa Elena**, the **Mariscal** and the **Boquillas**. The Santa Elena has a river bed elevation of 2,145 feet and a canyon-rim elevation of 3,661. Corresponding figures for Mariscal are 1,925 and 3,625, and for Boquillas, 1,850 and 3,490. The river here flows for about 100 miles around the base of the **Chisos Mountains** as the southern boundary of **Big Bend National Park**.

Below the Big Bend, the Rio Grande gradually emerges from mountains onto the Coastal Plains. A 191.2-mile strip on the U.S. side from Big Bend National Park downstream to the Terrell-Val Verde County line has federal designation as the **Rio Grande Wild and Scenic River**.

At the confluence of the Rio Grande and Devils

The Rio Grande separates Mexico, at left, from Zapata County. Robert Plocheck photo.

River, the United States and Mexico have built **Amistad Dam**, to impound 3,151,267 acre-feet of water, of which Texas' share is 56.2 percent. **Falcon Reservoir**, also an international project, impounds 2,653,636 acre-feet of water, of which Texas' share in Zapata and Starr counties is 58.6 percent.

The Rio Grande, where it joins the Gulf of Mexico, has created a fertile delta called the **Lower Rio Grande Valley**, a major vegetable- and fruit-growing area. The river drains 49,387 square miles of Texas and has an average annual flow of 645,500 acre-feet.

Principal tributaries flowing from the Texas side are the **Pecos** and **Devils** rivers. On the Mexican side are **Río Conchos**, **Río Salado** and **Río San Juan**. About three-fourths of the water running into the Rio Grande below El Paso comes from the Mexican side.

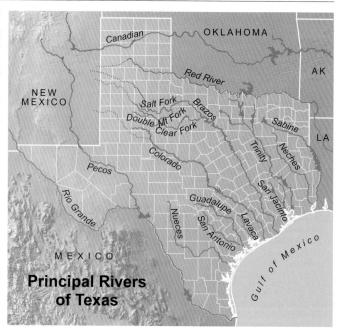

Principal Rivers of Texas

Pecos River

The Pecos, one of the major tributaries of the Rio Grande, rises on the western slope of the Santa Fe Mountains in the **Sangre de Cristo Range** of northern New Mexico. It enters Texas as the boundary between Loving and Reeves counties and flows **350 miles** southeast as the boundary for several other counties, entering Val Verde County at its northwestern corner and angles across that county to its mouth on the **Rio Grande**, northwest of Del Rio.

According to the Handbook of Texas the origins of the river's several names began with Antonio de Espejo, who called the river the **Río de las Vacas** ("river of the cows") because of the number of buffalo in the vicinity. Gaspar Castaño de Sosa, who followed the Pecos northward, called it the **Río Salado** because of its salty taste, which caused it to be shunned by men and animals alike.

It is believed that the name "Pecos" first appears in Juan de Oñate's reports concerning the Indian pueblo of Cicuye, now known as the **Pecos Pueblo** in New Mexico, and is of unknown origin.

Through most of its **926-mile**-long course from its headwaters, the Pecos River parallels the Rio Grande. The total drainage area of the Pecos in New Mexico and Texas is about 44,000 square miles. Most of its tributar-

ies flow from the west; these include the **Delaware River** and **Toyah Creek**.

The topography of the river valley in Texas ranges from semiarid irrigated farmlands, desert with sparse vegetation, and, in the lowermost reaches of the river, deep canyons.

Nueces River

The Nueces River rises in two forks in Edwards and Real counties and flows **315 miles** to Nueces Bay on the Gulf near Corpus Christi. Draining 16,700 square miles, it is a beautiful, **spring-fed stream** flowing through **canyons** until it issues from the **Balcones Escarpment** onto the Coastal Plains in northern Uvalde County.

Alonso de León, in 1689, gave it its name. **Nueces**, plural of *nuez*, means nuts in Spanish. (More than a century earlier, Cabeza de Vaca had referred to a **Río de las Nueces** in this region, but that is now thought to have been the Guadalupe.)

The original Indian name seems to have been **Chotilapacquen**. Crossing Texas in 1691, Terán de los Rios named the river **San Diego**.

The Nueces was the boundary line between the Spanish provinces of Texas and Nuevo Santander. After the Revolution of 1836, both Texas and Mexico claimed

AVERAGE ANNUAL FLOW		
	RIVER	**ACRE-FEET***
1.	Brazos	6,074,000
2.	Sabine	5,864,000
3.	Trinity	5,727,000
4.	Neches	4,323,000
5.	Red	3,464,000
6.	Colorado	1,904,000

*One acre-foot equals 325,851 gallons of water.
Source: Texas Water Development Board, 2007 State Water Plan.

LENGTHS OF MAJOR RIVERS		
	RIVER	**LENGTHS/MILES***
1.	Rio Grande	1,900
2.	Red	1,290
3.	Brazos	1,280
4.	Pecos	926
5.	Canadian	906
6.	Colorado	865

*Length from the original headwaters where the name defines the complete length to its outflow point. *Source: U.S. Geological Survey, 2008.*

the territory between the Nueces and the Rio Grande, a dispute which was settled by the **Treaty of Guadalupe Hidalgo** in 1848, which fixed the international boundary at the Rio Grande.

Average runoff of the Nueces is about 539,700 acre-feet a year. Principal water conservation projects are **Lake Corpus Christi** and **Choke Canyon Reservoir**. Principal tributaries of the Nueces are the **Frio** and the **Atascosa**.

San Antonio River

The San Antonio River has at its source **large springs** within and near the city limits of San Antonio. It flows **180 miles** across the Coastal Plains to a junction with the **Guadalupe** near the Gulf Coast. Its channel through San Antonio has been developed into a parkway known as the River Walk.

Its principal tributaries are the **Medina River** and **Cibolo Creek**, both spring-fed streams, and this, with its own spring origin, gives it a remarkably clear water and makes it one of the steadiest of Texas rivers. Including the Medina River headwaters, it is **238 miles** in length.

The river was first named the **León** by Alonso de León in 1689; the name was not for himself, but he called it "lion" because its channel was filled with a rampaging flood.

Because of its limited and arid drainage area (4,180 square miles) the average runoff of the San Antonio River is relatively small, about 562,700 acre-feet annually.

Guadalupe River

The Guadalupe rises in its North and South forks in the western Kerr County. A **spring-fed stream**, it flows eastward through the Hill Country until it issues from the **Balcones Escarpment** near New Braunfels. It then crosses the Coastal Plains to San Antonio Bay. Its total length is **409 miles**, and its drainage area is 5,953 square miles. Its principal tributaries are the **San Marcos**, another spring-fed stream, which joins it in Gonzales County; the **San Antonio**, which joins it just above its mouth on San Antonio Bay; and the **Comal**, which joins it at New Braunfels.

There has been power development on the Guadalupe near Gonzales and Cuero for many years, and there is also power generation at **Canyon Lake**. Because of its springs, and its considerable drainage area, the Guadalupe has an average annual runoff of more than 1.42 million acre-feet.

The name Guadalupe is derived from **Nuestra Señora de Guadalupe**, the name given the stream by Alonso de León.

Lavaca River

The Lavaca rises in extreme southeastern Fayette County and flows **117 miles** into the Gulf through Lavaca Bay. Without a spring-water source and with only a small watershed, including that of its principal tributary, the **Navidad**, its flow is intermittent. Runoff averages about 277,000 acre-feet yearly.

The Spanish called it the Lavaca (cow) because of the numerous bison found near it. It is the principal stream running to the Gulf between the Guadalupe and the Colorado, and drains 2,309 square miles. The principal lake on the **Navidad** is **Lake Texana**.

Colorado River

Rising in east central Dawson County, the Colorado River, which flows **865 miles** to Matagorda Bay, is the **longest river within Texas**. Its drainage area, which extends into New Mexico, is 42,318 square miles.

Its average annual runoff reaches a volume of 1.9 million acre-feet near the Gulf. Its name is a Spanish word meaning "**reddish**." There is evidence that Spanish explorers originally named the muddy Brazos "Colorado," but Spanish mapmakers later transposed the two

names.

The river flows through a rolling, mostly prairie terrain to the vicinity of San Saba County, where it enters the rugged **Hill Country** and **Llano Basin**. It passes through a picturesque series of **canyons** until it issues from the **Balcones Escarpment** at Austin and flows across the Coastal Plains.

In the Hill Country a remarkable series of reservoirs has been built to provide hydoelectric power. The largest of these are **Lake Buchanan** in Burnet and Llano counties and **Lake Travis** in Travis County. Between the two in Burnet County are three smaller reservoirs: **Inks, Lyndon B. Johnson** (formerly Granite Shoals) and **Marble Falls**. Below Lake Travis is the older **Lake Austin**, largely filled with silt, whose dam is used to produce power from waters flowing down from the lakes above. **Lady Bird Lake** (formerly Town Lake) is in the City of Austin. This area has been known as the **Highland Lakes Country**.

As early as the 1820s, Anglo-Americans settled on the banks of the lower Colorado, and in 1839 the **Capital Commission of the Republic of Texas** chose the picturesque area where the river flows from the **Balcones Escarpment** as the site of a new capital of the Republic — now **Austin**, capital of the state.

The early colonists encouraged navigation along the lower channel with some success. However, a **natural log raft** that formed 10 miles from the Gulf blocked river traffic after 1839, although shallow-draught vessels occasionally ventured as far upstream as Austin.

Conservation and utilization of the waters of the Colorado are under jurisdiction of three agencies created by the Legislature; the **Lower**, **Central** and **Upper Colorado River Authorities**.

The principal tributaries of the Colorado River are the several prongs of the **Concho River** on its upper course, **Pecan Bayou** (farthest west "bayou" in the United States) and the **Llano**, **San Saba** and **Pedernales** rivers. All except Pecan Bayou flow into the Colorado from the **Edwards Plateau** and are spring-fed, perennially flowing. In the numerous mussels found along these streams, **pearls** occasionally have been found. On early Spanish maps, the Middle Concho was called **Río de las Perlas**.

Brazos River

The Brazos River proper is considered as beginning where the **Double Mountain** and **Salt Forks** flow together in **northeastern Stonewall County**, and it then flows **840 miles** across Texas. The **U.S. Geological Survey** puts the **total length** from the New Mexico source of its longest upper prong at **1,280 miles**.

With a drainage area of about 42,805 square miles, it is the second-largest river basin in Texas, after the Rio Grande. It flows directly into the Gulf southwest of Freeport in Brazoria County. **Its average annual flow exceeds 6 million acre-feet, the largest volume of any river in the state.**

The Brazos' third upper fork is the **Clear Fork**, which joins the main stream in Young County, just above **Possum Kingdom Lake**. The Brazos crosses most of the main physiographic regions of Texas — High Plains, West Texas Rolling Plains, Western Cross Timbers, Grand Prairie and Gulf Coastal Plains.

The original name of this river was **Brazos de Dios**, meaning "Arms of God." There are several legends as to why. One is that the Coronado expedition, wandering on the trackless **Llano Estacado**, exhausted its water and was threatened with death from thirst. Arriving at the bank of the river, they gave it the name "Brazos de Dios" in thankfulness. Another is that a ship exhausted its water supply and its crew was saved when they found the mouth of the Brazos. Still another story is that miners on the San Saba were forced by drought to seek water near present-day Waco and in gratitude called it Brazos de Dios.

Much early Anglo-American colonization of Texas took place in the Brazos Valley. Along its channel were **San Felipe de Austin**, capital of Austin's colony; **Washington-on-the-Brazos**, where Texans declared independence; and other historic settlements. There was some navigation of the **lower channel** of the Brazos in this period. Near its mouth it intersects the **Gulf Intracoastal Waterway**, which provides connection with the commerce on the Mississippi.

Most of the Brazos Valley lies within the boundaries of the **Brazos River Authority**, which conducts a multipurpose program for development. A large reservoir on the Brazos is **Lake Whitney** (553,344 acre-feet capacity) on the main channel, where it is the boundary line between Hill and Bosque counties. **Lake Waco** on the Bosque and **Belton Lake** on the Leon are among the principal reservoirs on its tributaries. In addition to its three upper forks, other chief tributaries are the **Paluxy, Little** and **Navasota** rivers.

San Jacinto River

The San Jacinto is a short river with a drainage basin of 3,936 square miles and an average annual runoff of nearly 1.36 million acre-feet. It is formed by the junction of its East and West forks in northeastern Harris County and runs to the Gulf through Galveston Bay. Its total length, including the East Fork, is about **85 miles**.

The Guadalupe River flows through Kendall County. Robert Plocheck photo.

Lake Conroe is on the **West Fork**, and **Lake Houston** is located at the junction of the West Fork and the East Fork. The **Houston Ship Channel** runs through the lower course of the San Jacinto and its tributary, **Buffalo Bayou**, connecting the Port of Houston to the Gulf.

There are two stories of the origin of its name. One is that when early explorers discovered it, its channel was choked with hyacinth ("**jacinto**" is the Spanish word for hyacinth). The other is that it was discovered on Aug. 17, St. Hyacinth's Day. The **Battle of San Jacinto** was fought on the shore of this river on April 21, 1836, when Texas won its independence from Mexico. **San Jacinto Battleground State Historic Site and monument** commemorate the battle.

Trinity River

The Trinity rises in its East Fork, Elm Fork, West Fork and Clear Fork in Grayson, Montague, Archer and Parker counties, respectively. The main stream begins with the junction of the Elm and West forks at Dallas. Its length is **550 miles**, and its drainage area is 17,913 square miles. Because of moderate to heavy rainfall over its drainage area, it has a average annual flow of 5.7 million acre-feet near its mouth on Trinity Bay.

The Trinity derives its name from the Spanish "**Trinidad.**" Alonso de León named it **La Santísima Trinidad** (the Most Holy Trinity).

Navigation was developed along its lower course with several riverport towns, such as **Sebastopol** in Trinity County. For many years there has been a basin-wide movement for navigation, conservation and utilization of its water. The **Trinity River Authority** is a state agency and the **Trinity Improvement Association** is a publicly supported nonprofit organization that has advocated its development.

The Trinity has in its valley **more large cities, greater population and more industrial development** than any other river basin in Texas. On the Coastal Plains there is large use of its waters for **rice irrigation**. Large reservoirs on the Elm Fork are **Lewisville Lake** and **Ray Roberts Lake**. There are four reservoirs above Fort Worth: **Lake Worth, Eagle Mountain Lake** and **Lake Bridgeport** on the West Fork and **Benbrook Lake** on the Clear Fork.

Lake Lavon in southeast Collin County and **Lake Ray Hubbard** in Collin, Dallas, Kaufman and Rockwall counties are on the East Fork. **Lake Livingston** is in Polk, San Jacinto, Trinity and Walker counties. Two other reservoirs in the Trinity basin below the Dallas-Fort Worth area are **Cedar Creek Reservoir** and **Richland-Chambers Reservoir.**

Neches River

The Neches rises in Van Zandt County in East Texas and flows **416 miles** to **Sabine Lake** near Port Arthur. It has a drainage area of 9,937 square miles. Abundant rainfall over its entire basin gives it an average annual flow near the Gulf of about 4.3 million acre-feet a year. The river takes its name from the **Neches Indians** that the early Spanish explorers found living along its banks. Principal tributary of the Neches, and comparable with the Neches in length and flow above their confluence, is the **Angelina River**, so named from **Angelina (Little Angel)**, a Hainai Indian girl who converted to Christianity and played an important role in the early development of this region.

Both the Neches and the Angelina run most of their courses in the **Piney Woods**, and there was much settlement along them as early as the 1820s.

Sam Rayburn Reservoir, near Jasper on the Angelina River, was completed and dedicated in 1965. It has a storage capacity of 2.85 million acre-feet. Reservoirs located on the Neches River include **Lake Palestine** in the upper basin and **B. A. Steinhagen Lake** located at the junction of the Neches and the Angelina rivers.

Sabine River

The Sabine River is formed by three forks rising in Collin and Hunt counties. From its sources to its mouth on **Sabine Lake**, it flows approximately **360 miles** and drains 7,570 square miles.

Sabine comes from the **Spanish word** for cypress, as does the name of the **Sabinal River**, which flows into the Frio in Southwest Texas. The Sabine has an average annual flow volume of 5.86 million acre-feet, the second-largest in the state after the Brazos.

Throughout most of Texas history the lower Sabine has been the **eastern Texas boundary line**, though for a while there was doubt as to whether the Sabine or the Arroyo Hondo, east of the Sabine in Louisiana, was the boundary. For a number of years the outlaw-infested **neutral ground** lay between them. There was also a **boundary dispute** in which it was alleged that the Neches was really the Sabine and, therefore, the boundary.

Travelers over the part of the **Camino Real** known as the **Old San Antonio Road** crossed the Sabine at the **Gaines Ferry** in Sabine County, and there were crossings for the **Atascosito Road** and other travel and trade routes of that day.

Two of Texas' largest reservoirs have been created by dams on the Sabine River. The first of these is **Lake Tawakoni**, in Hunt, Rains and Van Zandt counties, with a storage capacity of 888,126 acre-feet.

Toledo Bend Reservoir impounds 4.47 million acre-feet of water on the Sabine in Newton, Panola, Sabine and Shelby counties. It is the **largest lake** lying wholly or partly in Texas and the **9th-largest reservoir (in capacity by volume) in the United States**. This is a joint project of Texas and Louisiana, through the **Sabine River Authority**.

Red River

The Red River, with a length of **1,290 miles** from its headwaters, is exceeded in length only by the Rio Grande among rivers associated with Texas. Its original source is water in Curry County, New Mexico, near the Texas boundary, forming a definite channel as it crosses Deaf Smith County, Texas, in tributaries that flow into **Prairie Dog Town Fork of the Red River**. These waters carve the spectacular **Palo Duro Canyon** of the High Plains before the Red River leaves the **Caprock Escarpment**, flowing eastward.

Where the Red River crosses the 100th meridian at the bottom of the Panhandle the river becomes the **Texas-Oklahoma boundary** and is soon joined by Buck Creek to form the main channel, according to the U.S. Geological Survey. Its length in Texas is **695 miles**, before it flows into Arkansas, where it swings south to flow through Louisiana.

The Red River, which drains 24,297 square miles in Texas, is a part of the **Mississippi drainage basin**, and at one time it emptied all of its water into the Mississippi. In recent years, however, part of its water, especially at flood stage, has flowed to the Gulf via the **Atchafalaya**.

The Red River takes its name from the red color of the current. This caused every explorer who came to its banks to call it "red" regardless of the language he spoke — Río **Rojo** or Río **Roxo** in Spanish, **Rivière Rouge** in French. At an early date, the river became the axis for French advance from Louisiana northwestward as far as present-day Montague County. There was consistent **early navigation** of the river from its mouth on the Mississippi to Shreveport, above which navigation was blocked by a **natural log raft**.

A number of important gateways into Texas from the North were established along the stream such as **Pecan Point** and **Jonesborough** in Red River County, **Colbert's Ferry** and **Preston** in Grayson County and, later, **Doan's Store Crossing** in Wilbarger County. The river was a menace to the early traveler because of both its variable current and its **quicksands**, which brought disaster to many a trail-herd cow as well as ox team and covered wagon.

The largest water conservation project on the Red River is **Lake Texoma**, with a conservation storage capacity of 2.51 million acre-feet.

Red River water's high content of salt and other minerals limits its usefulness along its upper reaches. Ten **salt springs** and tributaries in Texas and Oklahoma contribute most of these minerals.

The uppermost tributaries of the Red River in Texas are **Tierra Blanca Creek**, which rises in Curry County, N.M., and flows easterly across Deaf Smith and Randall counties to meet **Palo Duro Creek** and form the **Prairie Dog Town Fork** a few miles east of Canyon.

Other principal tributaries in Texas are the **Pease** and the **Wichita** in North Central Texas and the **Sulphur** in Northeast Texas, which flows through **Wright Patman Lake,** then into the Red River after it has crossed the boundary line into Arkansas.

The last major tributary in Northeast Texas is the **Cypress Creek system**, which flows into Louisiana before joining with the Red River. Major reservoirs in this basin are **Lake O' the Pines** and **Caddo Lake**.

From Oklahoma the principal tributary is the **Washita**, which has its headwaters in Roberts County, Texas. The **Ouachita**, a river with the same pronunciation though spelled differently, is the principal tributary to the Red River's lower course in Arkansas.

The Red River **boundary dispute**, a long-standing feud between Oklahoma and Texas, was finally settled in **2000** when the boundary was set at the vegetation line on the south bank, except for Lake Texoma where the boundary was set within the channel of the lake.

Canadian River

The Canadian River heads near **Raton Pass** in northern New Mexico near the Colorado boundary line and flows into Texas on the west line of Oldham County. It crosses the Texas Panhandle into Oklahoma and there flows into the Arkansas River, a total distance of **906 miles**. It drains 12,865 square miles in Texas, and much of its **213-mile course across the Panhandle** is in a deep gorge.

A tributary, the **North Canadian River**, drips briefly into the Texas Panhandle in Sherman County, before it joins the main channel in Oklahoma.

One of several theories as to how the Canadian got its name is that some early explorers thought it flowed into Canada. **Lake Meredith**, formed by **Sanford Dam** on the Canadian, provides water for several Panhandle cities.

Because of the **deep gorge** and the **quicksand** that occurs in many places, the Canadian River has been a particularly difficult stream to bridge. It is known, especially in its lower course in Oklahoma, as outstanding among the streams of the country for the great amount of quicksand in its channel. ☆

Secondary Streams of Texas

In addition to the principal rivers discussed elsewhere, Texas has many other streams of various size. The following list gives a few of these streams as designated by the U.S. Geological Survey, with additional information from the new Handbook of Texas and previous *Texas Almanacs*.

Alamito Creek — Formed by confluence of North, South forks 3 mi. N Marfa in Presidio County. Flows SE 82 mi. to Rio Grande 5 mi. S Presidio.

Angelina River — Rises in central Rusk County; flows SE 120 mi. through Cherokee, Nacogdoches, Angelina, San Augustine counties into Sam Rayburn Reservoir, then into Jasper County to the Neches River 12 mi. west of Jasper. A meandering stream through forested country.

Aransas River — Formed 2 mi. N Skidmore in SC Bee County by union of Poesta and Aransas creeks; flows SE 40 mi. forming boundary between San Patricio and Refugio counties; then briefly into Aransas County where it empties into Copano Bay.

Atascosa River — Formed NW Atascosa County by confluence of North, West prongs, flows SE 92 mi. through Atascosa and Live Oak counties into Frio River 2 mi. NW Three Rivers.

Attoyac Bayou — Rises 2.8 mi. NE Mount Enterprise in SE Rusk County; flows SE 67 mi. through Shelby, San Augustine and Nacogdoches counties into Angelina River at Sam Rayburn Reservoir.

Barton Creek — Rises NE of Henly in NW Hays County; flows E 40 mi. through Travis County to Colorado River at Lady Bird Lake in Austin.

Beals Creek — Formed by confluence of Sulphur Springs and Mustang draws 4 mi. W Big Spring SW Howard County; flows E 55 mi. into Mitchell County to mouth on Colorado River.

Big Cypress Creek — Forms in SE Hopkins County E of Pickton; flows SE 60 mi. to mouth on Big Cypress Bayou 3 mi. E Jefferson in Marion County and just before the bayou flows into Caddo Lake. The creek forms the boundary lines between Camp and Titus, Camp and Morris, and Morris and Upshur counties. It passes through Lake Cypress Springs, Lake Bob Sandlin, and Lake O' the Pines. Part of the Red River drainage basin.

Blackwater Draw — Rises in Curry County, N.M.; flows into Texas in extreme NW Bailey County; flows SE through Lamb, Hale, and Lubbock counties to junction with Yellow House Draw to form North Fork of the Double Mountain Fork Brazos River. Length, 100 mi.

Blanco Creek — Rises near the intersection of Bee, Goliad and Karnes county lines in extreme S Karnes County; flows SE 45 mi. forming boundary of Bee and Goliad counties. Joins Medio Creek in Refugio County to form Mission River.

Blanco Creek — Rises E of Concan in Uvalde County; flows S 44 mi. to Frio River.

Blanco Creek — Rises W Lindendale in NE Kendall County; flows SE 64 mi. through Blanco and Hay counties; joins San Marcos River, a tributary of the Guadalupe; fed by many springs.

Bosque River — Flows from Lake Waco in McLennan County 5 mi. into Brazos River.

Bosque River, North — Formed at Stephenville by the union of North, South forks in Erath County; flows generally SE 96 mi. through Hamilton, Bosque and McLennan counties into Lake Waco.

Bosque River, South — Rises near Coryell-McLennan county line; flows NE 24 mi. into Lake Waco.

Brady Creek — Rises 14 mi. SW Eden in SW Concho County; flows 90 mi. through McCulloch and San Saba counties into San Saba River 10 mi. SW of Richland Springs.

Brazos River, Clear Fork — Rises 8 mi. E Snyder in Scurry County; flows NE 180 mi. through Fisher, Jones, Haskell, Throckmorton, Shackelford and Stephens counties into Brazos River in S Young County; drainage area 5,728 sq. mi.

Brazos River, Double Mountain Fork — Rises 12 mi. SE Tahoka, Lynn County; flows E 175 mi. through Garza, Kent, Fisher and Haskell counties to confluence with Salt Fork of the Brazos, north of Old Glory in Stonewall County.

Brazos River, North Fork Double Mountain Fork— Formed by union of Yellow House and Blackwater draws in Lubbock; flows SE 75 miles through Crosby, Garza and Kent counties to junction with Double Mountain Fork Brazos River.

Brazos River, Salt Fork — Rises in SE Crosby County; flows 150 mi. through Garza and Kent counties to confluence with Double Mountain Fork in NE Stonewall County to form the main stream of Brazos River.

Buck Creek — Also called Spiller Creek. Rises SE Donley County; flows SE 49 mi. through Collingsworth and Childress counties to Texas-Oklahoma boundary; then 3 mi. through Oklahoma to junction with Prairie Dog Town Fork of Red River NW Hardeman County to form main stream of the Red River.

Buffalo Bayou — Rises in extreme N Fort Bend County; flows E 46 mi. through Houston into San Jacinto River in Harris County. Part of Houston Ship Channel.

California Creek — Rises 10 mi. NE Roby in Fisher County; flows NE 70 mi. through Jones County into Paint Creek in E Haskell County.

Caney Creek — Rises near Wharton in Wharton County; flows 75 mi. through Matagorda County into east end of Matagorda Bay. Centuries ago, the current Caney Creek channel was the channel for the Colorado River.

Capote/Wildhorse Draw — Rises N of Van Horn in Culberson County; runs 86 mi. S through Jeff Davis County to SW of Marfa in Presidio County. One of a number of streams in this area with no outlet to the sea.

Cedar Bayou — Rises 11 mi. NW Liberty in Liberty County; flows 46 mi. S as boundary between Harris County and Liberty and Chambers counties, and into Trinity Bay.

Chambers Creek — Formed SW Waxahachie in Ellis County by union North, South forks; flows SE 45 mi. through Navarro County into Richland Creek at Richland-Chambers Reservoir.

Cibolo Creek — Rises 7 mi. W Boerne in Kendall County; flows SE through Bexar, Comal, Guadalupe and Wilson counties into San Antonio River in Karnes County; 96 mi. in length. Spring-fed, perennially flowing stream.

Coleto Creek — Formed SW of Mission Valley in NW Victoria County by union of Twelve Mile and Fifteen Mile creeks forming boundary between Victoria and Goliad counties. From Coleto Creek Reservoir flows to Guadalupe River in Victoria County.

Comal River — Rises in Comal Springs in City of New Braunfels and flows SE about 2.5 miles to Guadalupe River. Shortest river in Texas.

Concho River — Formed at San Angelo by conjunction North, South Concho rivers; flows E 24 mi. through Tom Green County, then 29 mi. through Concho County into Colorado River 12 m. NE Paint Rock. Drainage basin, including North and South Concho, 6,613 sq. mi. A spring-fed stream.

Concho River, Middle — Rises SW Sterling County; flows S, then E 66 mi. through Tom Green panhandle, Irion and Reagan counties into South Concho River at Lake Nasworthy near Tankersley in Tom Green County.

Concho River, North — Rises in S Howard County; flows 137 mi. through Glasscock, Sterling and Coke counties to confluence with South Concho to form Concho River in Tom Green County. Drainage basin, 1,510 sq. mi.

Tubing on the South Llano River near Junction in Kimble County. Ron Billings photo; Texas Forest Service.

Concho River, South — Rises in C Schleicher County; flows N through Lake Nasworthy to confluence with North Concho River in Tom Green County; length, 41 mi.; drainage basin area 3, 866 sq. mi. Perennial flow from springs.

Cowleech Fork Sabine River — Rises 2 mi. NW Celeste NW Hunt County; flows SE 40 mi. to Lake Tawakoni.

Deep Creek — Rises SE Baird, Callahan County; flows N 55 mi. into Hubbard Creek in Shackelford County near McCatherine Mountain.

Deep Creek — Rises 4 mi. N Fluvanna NW Scurry County; flows SSE 70 mi. to mouth on Colorado River in extreme N Mitchell County.

Delaware River — Rises eastern slope Delaware Mountains in N Culberson County; flows in NE course; crosses Texas-New Mexico state line and enters Pecos River; length, 50 mi.

Devils River — Formed SW Sutton County by union Dry Devils River and Granger Draw; flows SE 95 mi. through Val Verde County into Rio Grande at Amistad Reservoir. Spring-fed, perennially flowing stream throughout most of its course.

Elm Creek — Rises 3 mi. SE Nolan in Nolan County; flows NE 60 mi., passes through Lake Abilene, Buffalo Gap and Abilene in Taylor County and through Lake Fort Phantom Hill into Clear Fork Brazos River near Nugent SE Jones County.

Frio River — Formed at Leakey in Real County by union of West and East Frio rivers; flows S 190 mi. through Uvalde, Medina, Frio, La Salle, McMullen counties (Choke Canyon Reservoir); joins Nueces River S of Three Rivers in Live Oak County. Drainage area, 7,310 sq. mi. Fed by springs in northern part, where it flows through picturesque canyon.

Greens Bayou — Rises 9 mi. W Aldine, C Harris County; flows ESE into Houston Ship Channel; 42 mi. long.

Hondo Creek — Rises 7.5 mi. NW Tarpley C Bandera County; flows SSE 67 mi. through Medina and Frio counties to Frio River 5 mi. NW Pearsall.

Howard Draw — Rises at Crockett-Reagan county line; flows SSW 45 mi. through Val Verde County to Pecos River near Pandale.

Hubbard Creek — Rises 3 mi. NW Baird N Callahan County; flows NE 62 mi. through Shackelford County; then into Stephens County (Hubbard Creek Reservoir) and joins Clear Fork of the Brazos River 10 NW Breckenridge.

James River — Rises SE Kimble County; flows NE 37 mi. to join Llano River in Mason County.

Jim Ned Creek — Rises 10 mi. NW Tuscola SC Taylor County; flows SE 71 mi. through Callahan and Coleman counties to Brown County to join Pecan Bayou, a tributary of Colorado River.

Johnson Draw — Rises NE Crockett County; runs SSE 66 miles to mouth on Devils River in Val Verde County.

Lampasas River — Rises NW Mills County; flows SE 100 miles through Hamilton, Lampasas, Burnet and Bell counties (Stillhouse Hollow Lake); unites with Leon River to form Little River.

Leon River — Formed by confluence North, Middle and South Forks in NC Eastland County; flows SE 185 mi. through Comanche, Hamilton and Coryell counties to junction with Lampasas River to form Little River in Bell County.

Leona River — Rises N Uvalde in central Uvalde County; flows SE 83 mi. through Zavala County into Frio River in Frio County.

Limpia Creek — Heads in the Davis Mountains on the NE slope of Mount Livermore in Jeff Davis County and flows 52 mi. E, NE and E through Limpia Canyon to disappear at the head of Barrilla Draw in Pecos County. Part of course through Limpia Canyon noted for its scenic beauty.

Little Brazos River — Rises 5 mi. SW Thornton, SW Limestone County; flows 72 mi. SE through Falls and Robertson counties into Brazos River in Brazos County.

Little River — Formed central Bell County by union Leon, Lampasas rivers; flows 75 mi. SE through Milam County into Brazos River.

Llano River — Formed C Kimble County by union North, South Llano rivers; flows E 100 mi. through Mason, Llano counties to Colorado River. Drainage area, including North, South Llano rivers, 4,460 sq. mi. A spring-fed stream of the Edwards Plateau, known for scenic beauty.

Llano River, North — Rises C Sutton County; flows E 40 mi. to union with South Llano River at Junction in Kimble County.

Llano River, South — Rises in NC Edwards County; flows

55 mi. NE to confluence with North Llano River at Junction in Kimble County.

Los Olmos Creek — Rises central Duval County; flows SE 71 mi. through Jim Wells and Brooks counties; forms boundary between Kenedy and Kleberg counties; into Baffin Bay.

Madera Canyon — Rises N slope Mount Livermore, Jeff Davis County, at altitude of 7,500 ft.; flows 40 mi. NE to join Aguja Creek at Reeves County line to form Toyah Creek, tributary through Pecos River to Rio Grande. Intermittent stream. Noteworthy for its beauty.

Medina River — Rises in North, West prongs in W Bandera County; flows SE 116 mi. through Medina and Bexar counties to San Antonio River. A spring-fed stream. Scenically beautiful along upper course.

Medio Creek — Rises S Karnes County; flows SE 2 mi. through Karnes County, then 7 mi. along boundary Karnes and Bee counties, then SE 37 mi. through Bee County, SE 7 mi. through Refugio County to junction with Blanco Creek to form Mission River.

Mission River — Formed by confluence of Blanco and Medio creeks in C Refugio County; flows SE 24 mi. to mouth on Mission Bay, an inlet of Copano Bay.

Mulberry Creek — Rises NW Armstrong County at Fairview; flows SE 58 mi. through Donley and Briscoe counties into Prairie Dog Town Fork Red River in NW Hall County.

Navasota River — Rises SE Hill County; flows SE 125 mi. through Limestone County and along boundary Leon, Madison, Robertson, Brazos and Grimes counties to Brazos River near Navasota.

Navidad River — Forms at juncture of East and West Navidad rivers in NE Lavaca County; flows 74 mi. through Lavaca and Jackson counties into Lake Texana near Ganado; then joins Lavaca River.

Nolan River — Rises in NW Johnson County; flows S 30 mi. through Lake Pat Cleburne and into Hill County where is empties into Brazos River at Lake Whitney.

Onion Creek — Rises 1 mi. W of Hays-Blanco county line SE Blanco County; flows SE 37 mi. through N Hays County; then 22 mi. through S Travis County into Colorado River near Garfield.

Paint Creek — Rises in extreme NW Jones County near Tuxedo; flows NE, then SE 53 mi. through SE corner of Stonewall County; then across S Haskell County (Lake Stamford) and into W Throckmorton County to mouth on Clear Fork Brazos River.

Palo Blanco Creek — Rises SE Hebbronville in N Jim Hogg County; flows SE 59 mi. through Duval and Brooks, where it passes through Laguna Salada; then into NW Kenedy County.

Palo Duro Creek — Rises in W Deaf Smith County; flows E 45 mi. into C Randall County to junction with Tierra Blanca Creek near Canyon to form the Prairie Dog Town Fork of the Red River. Lends its name to the notable canyon.

Paluxy River — Formed in E Erath County by convergence of North and South branches at Bluff Dale; flows SE 29 mi. through Hood and Somervell counties to mouth on Brazos River. Dinosaur Valley State Park at a large bend of the river in Somervell County is site of 100-million-year-old dinosaur tracks.

Pease River — Formed by union of North and Middle Pease rivers in NE Cottle County; flows E 100 mi. through Hardeman, Foard and Wilbarger counties into Red River 8 mi. NE of Vernon.

Pease River, Middle — Rises 8 mi. NW Matador in WC Motley County; flows E 63 miles into North Pease River to form the Pease River in NE Cottle County.

Pease River, North — Rises 9 mi. SE Cedar Hill in E Floyd County; flows E 60 mi. through Motley, Hall and Cottle counties. Joins Middle Pease to form Pease River near Garfield.

Pease River, South — Also called Tongue River. Rises 11 mi. SW Roaring Springs in SW Motley County; flows ENE 40 mi. to mouth on Middle Pease River in W Cottle County.

Pecan Bayou — Formed by union of South, North prongs in SC Callahan County; flows SE 90 mi. through Coleman, Brown (Lake Brownwood) and Mills counties into Colorado River SW Goldthwaite. Westernmost bayou.

Pedernales River — Rises NE corner of Kerr County; flows E 106 mi. through Kimble, Gillespie, Blanco, Hays and Travis counties into Colorado River at Lake Travis. Spring-fed; a beautiful stream.

Pine Island Bayou — Rises near Rye NE Liberty County; flows 76 mi. SE through Hardin and Jefferson counties into Neches River.

Red River, Prairie Dog Town Fork — Formed by union of Palo Duro and Tierra Blanca creeks in Randall County; flows E 160 mi. through Armstrong, Briscoe, Hall, and Childress counties to junction with Buck Creek to form Red River in NW corner of Hardeman County. Palo Duro Canyon is along course of this stream as it descends from Great Plains.

Red River, North Fork — Rises W Gray County; flows SE 180 mi. through Wheeler County into Oklahoma to junction with the Red River NE Vernon in Wilbarger County.

Red River, Salt Fork — Rises N Armstrong County; flows SE 155 mi. through Donley and Collingsworth counties and into Oklahoma. It joins the Red River opposite the northernmost point of Wilbarger County.

Richland Creek — Rises 3.5 mi. E Itasca N Hill County; flows E 50 mi. through Ellis and Navarro counties, through Navarro Mills Lake and Richland-Chambers Reservoir; then into the Trinity River in Freestone County.

Running Water Draw — Rises 24 mi. WNW Clovis, N.M.; flows ESE into Texas in C Parmer County; then through Castro, Lamb, Hale and Floyd counties to join Callahan Draw 8 mi. W Floydada at head of White River, a tributary of the Brazos River.

Sabana River — Rises at Callahan-Eastland county line; flows SE 50 through Comanche County into Leon River at Proctor Lake.

Sabinal River — Rises 7 mi. N Vanderpool in NW Bandera County; flows S 60 mi. to junction with Frio River in SE Uvalde County. The West Sabinal River, which rises in Real County, joins the main stream at the Bandera-Uvalde county line.

San Bernard River — Rises 1 mi. S New Ulm in W Austin County; flows SE, forming boundary Austin and Colorado counties, 31 mi.; Austin and Wharton counties, 8 mi.; Wharton and Fort Bend counties, 28 mi.; approaches Gulf of Mexico in Brazoria County. Total length, 120 mi. (For more than 100 years locals have reported hearing the wail of a violin from the river. The mystery has never been solved, although some say the musical sounds are caused by escaping gas. The phenomenon has caused the stream to be called the Singing River — *Handbook of Texas*.)

San Gabriel River — Formed at Georgetown in C Williamson County by union of North and South forks; flows NE 50 mi. into Milam County to join Little River. Originally called San Xavier River.

San Jacinto River, East — Rises E Walker County; flows SE and S 69 mi. through San Jacinto, Liberty, Montgomery and Harris counties into Lake Houston and San Jacinto River.

San Jacinto River, West — Rises E Grimes County NE Shiro; flows SE 90 mi. through Walker County; into Lake Conroe in Montgomery County; then through Montgomery County to Lake Houston in Harris County.

San Marcos River — Formed near N limits City of San Marcos, Hays County, by several large springs, although watershed extends about 10 mi. NE of springs; Blanco River joins the San Marcos River 4 mi. downstream; flows SE 59 mi. as boundary between Guadalupe and Caldwell counties; then through Gonzales County to join Guadalupe River 2 mi. W Gonzales.

Sandy Creek — Rises SW Colorado County; flows SSE 42 mi. through Lavaca, Wharton and Jackson counties into Lake Texana.

San Saba River — Formed W Fort McKavett at Schleicher-Menard county line by union of North Valley and Middle Valley prongs; flows NE 140 mi. through Menard, Mason, McCulloch and San Saba counties into Colorado River 8 mi. NE San Saba. One of the picturesque streams of the Edwards Plateau.

Spring Creek — Rises NE Waller County near Fields Store; flows E 64 mi. forming boundary between Waller and Harris counties, and Montgomery and Harris counties to junction with West Fork San Jacinto River and Lake Houston.

Sulphur River — Formed E Delta County by junction North, South branches; flows E 183 miles forming boundary between Franklin and Red River counties; Titus and Red River counties; Morris and Red River and Bowie counties; then between Bowie and Cass counties, where it flows into Wright Patman Lake; continues on into Red River in S Miller County, Ark.

Sulphur River, North — Rises 1 mi. SW Gober S Fannin County; flows SE, E 54 mi. as boundary between Delta and Lamar counties and to union with South Sulphur River to form Sulphur River.

Sulphur River, South — Rises N Leonard S Fannin County; flows ESE 50 mi. through Hunt County; then as boundary between Hopkins and Delta counties (through Cooper Lake) to union with North Sulphur to form Sulphur River.

Sulphur Springs Draw — Rises in E Lea County, N.M.; enters Texas W Yoakum County at Bronco; flows SE 100 mi. through Terry, Gaines, Dawson, Martin, and Howard counties to confluence with Mustang Creek to form Beals Creek, a tributary of Colorado River.

Sweetwater Creek — Rises 2 mi. W Maryneal C Nolan County; flows NE 45 mi. through Fisher and Jones counties into Clear Fork Brazos River.

Terlingua Creek — Rises WC Brewster County; flows S 83 mi. into Rio Grande just E Santa Elena Canyon.

Tierra Blanca Creek — Rises N Curry County, N.M.; flows E across Texas state line in SW Deaf Smith County and 75 mi. through Deaf Smith, Parmer and Randall counties to junction with Palo Duro Creek where it forms Prairie Dog Town Fork Red River.

Toyah Creek — Forms near boundary Jeff Davis-Reeves counties; flows NE 50 mi. into Pecos River NC Reeves County.

Trinity River, Clear Fork — Rises NW Poolville in NW Parker County; flows SE 56 mi. through Tarrant County into West Fork Trinity River at Fort Worth.

Trinity River, East Fork — Rises 1.5 mi. NW Dorchester in SC Grayson County; flows S 85 mi. through Collin County (Lake Lavon and Lake Ray Hubbard); then Rockwall and Dallas counties into Trinity River in SE Kaufman County.

Trinity River, Elm Fork — Rises 1 mi. NW Saint Jo in E Montague County; flows 85 mi. SE through Cooke, Denton counties (Ray Roberts Lake and Lewisville Lake) to junction with West Fork to form Trinity River proper at Irving in WC Dallas County.

Trinity River, West Fork — Rises in SC Archer County; flows SE 145 mi. through Jack, Wise (Lake Bridgeport) and Tarrant (Eagle Mountain Lake and Lake Worth) counties to conjunction with Elm Fork to form Trinity River proper in WC Dallas County.

Tule Creek — Formed in Swisher County by union of North, Middle and South Tule draws; flows E 40 mi. through Mackenzie Reservoir and Briscoe County into Prairie Dog Town Fork Red River. Remarkably beautiful Tule Canyon along lower course.

Turkey Creek — Rises near Turkey Mountain EC Kinney County; flows SE 54 mi. through Uvalde, Zavala, Dimmit counties to Nueces River.

Washita River — Rises SE Roberts County; flows E 35 mi. through Hemphill County to Oklahoma state line, then SE to Red River at Lake Texhoma. Total length, 295 mi.

White River — Formed 8 mi. W Floydada in WC Floyd County by union of Running Water and Callahan draws; flows SE 62 mi. through Blanco Canyon and White River Lake in Crosby County; then through Garza and Kent counties into Salt Fork Brazos River; principal tributary to Salt Fork.

Wichita River — Formed NE Knox County by union North, South Wichita rivers; flows NE 90 mi. through Baylor (Lake Kemp and Lake Diversion), Archer, Wichita and Clay counties to Red River N Byers.

Wichita River, Little — Formed in C Archer County by union of its North, Middle and South forks; flows NE 62 mi. through Clay County (Lake Arrowhead) into Red River.

Wichita River, North — Rises 6 mi. E East Afton in NE Dickens County; flows E through King, Cottle, Foard counties; then as boundary for Foard and Knox counties; then briefly into Baylor County to junction with South Wichita River to form Wichita River proper NE Vera in Knox County. Length, 100 mi.

Wichita River, South — Rises 10 mi. E Dickens in EC Dickens County; flows E 85 mi. through King and Knox counties to junction with North Wichita to form Wichita River.

Yellow House Draw — Rises in SE Bailey County; flows SE 80 mi. through Cochran, Hockley and Lubbock counties to confluence with Blackwater Draw at Lubbock to form the North Fork of Double Mountain Fork Brazos River. ☆

Terlingua Creek in Brewster County just before its junction with the Rio Grande. Robert Plocheck photo.

Artificial Lakes and Reservoirs

Sources: U.S. Geological Survey, Texas Water Development Board, New Handbook of Texas, Texas Parks & Wildlife, U.S. Army Corps of Engineers, previous Texas Almanacs, various river basin authorities, Websites of owner of reservoirs.

The large increase in the number of reservoirs in Texas during the past half-century has greatly improved water conservation and supplies.

As late as 1913, Texas had only four major reservoirs with a total storage capacity of 277,600 acre-feet. Most of this capacity was in Medina Lake in southwest Texas, with 254,000 acre-feet* capacity, created by a dam completed in May 1913.

By January 2007, Texas had 196 major reservoirs (those with a normal capacity of 5,000 acre-feet or larger) existing, with a total conservation surface area of 1,666,856 acres and a conservation storage capacity of 37,179,139 acre-feet.

According to the U.S. Statistical Abstract of 2001, Texas has **4,959 square miles of inland water**, ranking it first in the 48 contiguous states, followed by Minnesota, with 4,780 sq. mi.; Florida, 4,683; and Louisiana, 4,153.

There are about **6,736 reservoirs** in Texas with a normal storage capacity of 10 acre-feet or larger.

Natural Lakes

There are many natural lakes in Texas, though none is of great size. The largest designated natural lake touching the border of Texas is Sabine Lake, into which the Sabine and Neches rivers discharge. It is more properly a bay of the Gulf of Mexico. Also near the coast, in Calhoun County, is Green Lake, which at about 10,000 acre-feet is one of the state's largest natural freshwater lakes.

Caddo Lake, on the Texas-Louisiana border, was a natural lake originally, but its present capacity and surface area are largely due to dams built to raise the surface of the original body of water. Natural Dam Lake, in Howard County, has a similar history.

In East Texas are many small natural lakes formed by "horse-shoe" bends that have been eliminated from the main channel of a river. There are also a number of these "horse-shoe" lakes along the Rio Grande in the lower valley, where they are called resacas.

On the South Plains and west of San Angelo are lakes, such as Big Lake in Reagan County, that are usually dry.

The following table lists reservoirs in Texas having more than 5,000 acre-feet capacity. With few exceptions, the listed reservoirs are those that were completed by Jan. 1, 2009. *Reservoirs that are normally dry are in italics.* Some industrial cooling reservoirs are not included.

Conservation storage capacity as of 2009 is used; the surface area used is that area at conservation elevation only. Because sediment deposition constantly reduces reservoir volumes over time, these are figures from the most recent surveys available.

Various methods of computing capacity area are used, and detailed information may be obtained from the Texas Water Development Board, Austin, from the U.S.

Army Corps of Engineers, or from local sources. It should be noted that boundary reservoir capacities include water designated for Texas and non-Texas water, as well.

Information is in the following order: (1) Name of lake or reservoir; (2) year of first impounding of water; (3) county or counties in which located; (4) river or creek on which located; (5) location with respect to some city or town; (6) purpose of reservoir; (7) owner of reservoir.

Some of these items, when not listed, are not available. For the larger lakes and reservoirs, the dam impounding water to form the lake bears the same name, unless otherwise indicated.

Lakes and Reservoirs, Date of Origin	Surface Area (Acres)	Storage Capacity (Acre-Ft.*)
Abilene, L. — (1919) Taylor Co.; Elm Cr.; 6 mi. NW Tuscola; (M-In.-R); City of Abilene	595	6,099
Addicks Reservoir — (1948) Harris Co.; South Mayde Cr.; 1 mi. E of Addicks; (FC only) USAE	16,423	200,800
Alan Henry, L. — (1993) Garza Co.; Double Mountain Fork Brazos River; 10 mi. E Justiceburg; (M-In.-Ir.); City of Lubbock	2,741	94,808
Alcoa L. — (1952) Milam Co.; Sandy Cr.; 7 mi. SW Rockdale; (In.-R); Alcoa Aluminum (also called Sandow L.)	914	15,650
Amistad Reservoir, International — (1969) Val Verde Co.; Rio Grande; an international project of the U.S. and Mexico; 12 mi. NW Del Rio; (C-R-Ir.-P-FC); International Boundary and Water Com. (Texas'share of conservation capacity is 56.2 percent.) (Formerly Diablo Reservoir)	65,597	3,275,532
Amon G. Carter, L. — (1961) Montague Co.; Big Sandy Cr.; 6 mi. S Bowie; (M-In.); City of Bowie	1,540	19,902
Anahuac, L. — (1936, 1954) Chambers Co.; Turtle Bayou; near Anahuac; (Ir.-In.-Mi.); Chambers-Liberty Counties Navigation District. (also called Turtle Bayou Reservoir)	5,035	33,348
Anzalduas Channel Dam — Hidalgo Co.; Rio Grande; 11 mi. upstream from Hidalgo; (Ir.-FC); United States and Mexico	1,472	13,910
Aquilla L. — (1983) Hill Co.; Aquilla Cr.; 10.2 mi. W of Hillsboro; (FC-M-Ir.-In.-R); USAE-Brazos R. Auth	3,066	44,460
Arlington, L. — (1957) Tarrant Co.; Village Cr.; 7 mi. W Arlington; (M-In.); City of Arlington	1,926	40,156
Arrowhead, L. — (1966) Clay-Archer counties.; Little Wichita R.; 13 mi. SE Wichita Falls; (M); City of Wichita Falls	14,969	235,997
Athens, L. — (1962) Henderson Co.; 8 mi. E Athens; (M-FC-R); Athens Mun. Water Authority (formerly Flat Creek Reservoir)	1,799	29,435

*An acre-foot is the amount of water necessary to cover an acre of surface area with water one foot deep. The **years** in the table refer to first impounding of water. **Double years** refer to later, larger dams. **Abbreviations are:** L., lake; R., river; Co., county; Cr., creek; (C) conservation; (FC) flood control; (R) recreation; (P) power; (M) municipal; (D) domestic; (Ir.) irrigation; (In.) industry; (Mi.) mining, including oil production; (FH) fish hatchery; USAE, United States Army Corps of Engineers; WC&ID, Water Control and Improvement District; WID, Water Improvement District; USBR, United States Bureau of Reclamation; Auth., Authority; LCRA, Lower Colorado River Authority; TP&WD, Texas Parks & Wildlife Dept.; USDA, United States Department of Agriculture; Imp., impounded.

A bright fall day at Caddo Lake State Park. Ron Billings photo; Texas Forest Service.

Lakes and Reservoirs, Date of Origin	Surface Area (Acres)	Storage Capacity (Acre-Ft.*)
Austin, L. — (1893, 1915, 1939) Travis Co.; Colorado R.; W Austin city limits; (M-In.-P); City of Austin, leased to LCRA (Imp. by Tom Miller Dam)......................	1,599	21,804
(In 1893, the first dam was completed. It broke in 1900. In 1915, a second dam was partially built but not completed. In 1939, the present Tom Miller Dam was completed.)		
Ballinger/Moonen, L. — (1947) Runnels Co.; Valley Creek; 5 mi. W Ballinger; (M); City of Ballinger...............	500	6,850
Balmorhea, L. — (1917) Reeves Co.; Sandia Cr.; 3 mi. SE Balmorhea; (Ir.); Reeves Co. WID No. 1	573	6,350
Bardwell L. — (1965) Ellis Co.; Waxahachie Cr.; 3 mi. SE Bardwell; (FC-C-R); USAE	3,138	46,122
Barker Reservoir — (1945) Harris Co.; above Buffalo Bayou ; (FC only) USAE...........	16,739	209,000
Bastrop, L. — (1964) Bastrop Co.; Spicer Cr.; 3 mi. NE Bastrop; (In.); LCRA..	906	16,590
Baylor Creek L. — (1950) Childress Co.; 10 mi. NW Childress; (M-R); City of Childress	610	9,220
Belton L. — (1954) Bell-Coryell counties; Leon R.; 3 mi. N. Belton; (M-FC-In.-Ir.); USAE-Brazos R. Auth.	12,135	435,225
Benbrook L. — (1952) Tarrant Co.; Clear Fk. Trinity R.; 10 mi. SW Fort Worth; (FC-R); USAE........................	3,635	85,648
Big Creek Reservoir — (1987) Delta Co; Big Creek; 1 mi. N Cooper; (M); City of Cooper..............................	512	4,890
Bivins, L. — (1927) Randall Co.; Palo Duro Cr.; 8 mi. NW Canyon; (M); Amarillo; City of Amarillo (also called Amarillo City Lake)..	379	5,120
Bob Sandlin, L. — (1977) Titus-Wood-Camp-Franklin counties; Big Cypress Cr.; 5 mi. SW Mount Pleasant; (In.-M-R); Titus Co. FWSD No. 1 (Imp. by Fort Sherman Dam)	9,004	200,579
Bonham, L. — (1969) Fannin Co.; Timber Cr.; 5 mi. NE Bonham; (M); Bonham Mun. Water Auth.	1,012	11,026
Brady Creek Reservoir — (1963) McCulloch Co.; Brady Cr.; 3 mi. W Brady; (M-In.); City of Brady................	2,020	29,110
Brandy Branch Reservoir — (1983) Harrison Co.; Brandy Br.; 10 mi. SW Marshall; (In.); AEP- Southwestern Electric Power Co..	1,242	29,513
Braunig L., Victor — (1962) Bexar Co.; Arroyo Seco; 15 mi. SE San Antonio; (In.); Pub. Svc. Bd./San Antonio	1,350	26,500
Brazoria Reservoir — (1954) Brazoria Co.; off-channel reservoir; 1 mi. NE Brazoria; (In.); Dow Chemical Co.	1,865	21,970
Bridgeport, L. — (1932) Wise-Jack counties; W. Fk. of Trinity R.; 4 mi. W Bridgeport; (M-In.-FC-R); Tarrant Regional Water Dist.	11,954	366,236
Brownwood, L. — (1933) Brown Co.; Pecan Bayou; 8 mi. N Brownwood; (M-In.-Ir.); Brown Co. WC&ID No. 1	6,587	131,429
Bryan L. — (1977) Brazos Co.; unnamed stream; 6 mi. NW Bryan; (R-In.); City of Bryan	829	15,227

*An acre-foot is the amount of water necessary to cover an acre of surface area with water one foot deep. The **years** in the table refer to first impounding of water. **Double years** refer to later, larger dams. **Abbreviations are:** L., lake; R., river; Co., county; Cr., creek; (C) conservation; (FC) flood control; (R) recreation; (P) power; (M) municipal; (D) domestic; (Ir.) irrigation; (In.) industry; (Mi.) mining, including oil production; (FH) fish hatchery; USAE, United States Army Corps of Engineers; WC&ID, Water Control and Improvement District; WID, Water Improvement District; USBR, United States Bureau of Reclamation; Auth., Authority; LCRA, Lower Colorado River Authority; TP&WD, Texas Parks & Wildlife Dept.; USDA, United States Department of Agriculture; Imp., impounded.

Lakes and Reservoirs, Date of Origin	Surface Area (Acres)	Storage Capacity (Acre-Ft.*)
Buchanan, L. — (1937) Burnet-Llano-San Saba counties; Colorado R.; 13 mi. W Burnet; (M-Ir.-Mi-P); LCRA	22,137	871,440
Buffalo Lake — *(1938) Randall Co.; Tierra Blanca Cr.; 2 mi. S. Umbarger; (R); U.S. Fish and Wildlife Service; (Imp. by Umbarger Dam)*	*1,900*	*18,150*
Caddo L. — (1873, 1914, 1971) Harrison-Marion counties, Texas, and Caddo Parish, La. An original natural lake, whose surface and capacity were increased by construction of dams	26,800	59,800
(In November 1873, the U.S. Army used nitroglycerin charges to remove the last portion of the Red River raft, a natural logjam. This resulted in the gradual depletion of Caddo water. In 1914, a dam was completed near Mooringsport, La. In 1971, a larger replacement dam was completed.)		
Calaveras L. — (1969) Bexar Co.; Calaveras Cr.; 15 mi. SE San Antonio; (In.); Pub. Svc. Bd. of San Antonio	3,624	63,200
Camp Creek L. — (1949) Robertson Co.; 13 mi. E Franklin; (R); Camp Creek Water Co.	750	6,712
Canyon L. — (1964) Comal Co.; Guadalupe R.; 12 mi. NW New Braunfels; (M-In.-P-FC); Guadalupe- Blanco R. Authority & USAE	8,308	378,781
Casa Blanca L. — (1951) Webb Co.; Chacon Cr.; 3 mi. NE Laredo; (R); Webb Co.; (Imp. by Country Club Dam)	1,680	20,000
Cedar Creek Reservoir — (1965) Henderson-Kaufman counties; Cedar Cr.; 3 mi. NE Trinidad; (M-R); Tarrant Regional Water Dist.; (also called Joe B. Hogsett, L.)	32,873	637,822
Champion Creek Reservoir — (1959) Mitchell Co.; 7 mi. S. Colorado City; (M-In.); City of Colorado City	1,560	41,618
Cherokee, L. — (1948) Gregg-Rusk counties; Cherokee Bayou; 12 mi. SE Longview; (M-In.-R); Cherokee Water Co.	3,467	39,023
Choke Canyon Reservoir — (1982) Live Oak-McMullen counties; Frio R.; 4 mi. W Three Rivers; (M-In.-R-FC); City of Corpus Christi-USBR	25,989	695,262
Cisco, L. — (1923) Eastland Co.; Sandy Cr.; 4 mi. N. Cisco; (M); City of Cisco (Imp. by Williamson Dam)	10,450	26,000
Cleburne, L. Pat — (1964) Johnson Co.; Nolan R.; 4 mi. S. Cleburne; (M); City of Cleburne	1,558	26,008
Clyde, L. — (1970) Callahan Co.; N. Prong Pecan Bayou; 6 mi. S. Clyde; (M); City of Clyde and USDA Soil Conservation Service	449	5,748
Coffee Mill L. — (1939) Fannin Co.; Coffee Mill Cr.; 12 mi. NW Honey Grove; (R); U.S. Forest Service	650	8,000
Coleman, L. — (1966) Coleman Co.; Jim Ned Cr.; 14 mi. N. Coleman; (M-In.); City of Coleman	1,811	38,076
Coleto Creek Reservoir — (1980) Goliad–Victoria counties; Coleto Cr.; 12 mi. SW Victoria; (In); Guadalupe–Blanco River Auth.	3,100	31,040
Colorado City, L. — (1949) Mitchell Co.; Morgan Cr.; 4 mi. SW Colorado City; (M-In.-P); TXU	1,612	31,485
Conroe, L. — (1973) Montgomery-Walker counties; W. Fk. San Jacinto R.; 7 mi. NW Conroe; (M-In.-Mi.); San Jacinto River Authority, City of Houston and Texas Water Dev. Bd.	20,118	416,188
Cooper, L./Olney— (1953) Archer Co.; Mesquite Crk; 8 mi. E Megargel; (W-R); City of Olney; (see L. Olney)	446	6,650
Cooper Lake— (1991) Delta-Hopkins counties; Sulphur R.; 3 mi.SE Cooper; (FC-M-R); USAE; (also called Jim Chapman Lake)	17,958	260,332
Corpus Christi, L. — (1930) Live Oak-San Patricio-Jim Wells counties; Nueces R.; 4 mi. SW Mathis; (P-M-In.-Ir.-Mi.-R.); Lower Nueces River WSD (Imp. by Wesley E. Seale Dam)	18,256	256,961
Cox Creek Reservoir — Calhoun Co.; Cox Creek; 2 mi. E Point Comfort; (In) Alcoa Alumninum; (Also called Raw Water Lake and Recycle Lake)	541	5,034
Crook, L. — (1923) Lamar Co.; Pine Cr.; 5 mi. N. Paris; (M); City of Paris	1,060	9,195
Cypress Springs, L. — (1970) Franklin Co.; Big Cypress Cr.; 8 mi. SE Mount Vernon; (In-M); Franklin Co. WD and Texas Water Development Board (formerly Franklin Co. L.); (Imp. by Franklin Co. Dam)	3,252	66,756
Daniel, L. — (1948) Stephens Co.; Gunsolus Cr.; 7 mi. S Breckenridge; (M-In.); City of Breckenridge; (Imp. by Gunsolus Creek Dam)	924	9,435
Davis, L. — Knox Co.; Double Dutchman Cr.; 5 mi. SE Benjamin; (Ir); League Ranch	585	5,454
Delta Lake Res. Units 1 and 2 — (1939) Hidalgo Co.; Rio Grande (off channel); 4 mi. N. Monte Alto; (Ir.); Hidalgo-Willacy counties WC&ID No. 1 (formerly Monte Alto Reservoir)	2,371	14,000
Diversion, L. — (1924) Archer-Baylor counties; Wichita R.; 14 mi. W Holliday; (M-In.); City of Wichita Falls and Wichita Co. WID No. 2	3,133	33,420
Dunlap, L. — (1928) Guadalupe Co.; Guadalupe R.; 9 mi. NW Seguin; (P); Guadalupe-Blanco R. Auth.; (Imp. by TP-1 Dam)	410	5,900
Eagle L. — (1900) Colorado Co.; Colorado R. (off channel; in Eagle Lake; (Ir.); Lakeside Irrigation Co.	1,200	9,600
Eagle Mountain Lake — (1934) Tarrant-Wise counties; W. Fk. Trinity R.; 14 mi. NW Fort Worth; (M-In.-Ir.); Tarrant Regional Water Dist.	8,694	179,880
Eagle Nest Lake — (1951) Brazoria Co.; off-channel Brazos R.; 12 mi. WNW Angleton; (Ir.); T.M. Smith, et al. (also called Manor Lake)	—	18,000
Eastman Lakes — 8 lakes; Harrison Co.; Sabine R. basin; NW of Longview; Texas Eastman Co.	—	8,135
Electra, L. — (1950) Wilbarger Co.; Camp Cr. and Beaver Cr.; 7 mi. SW Electra; (In.-M); City of Electra	731	5,626
Ellison Creek Reservoir — (1943) Morris Co.; Ellison Cr.; 8 mi. S. Daingerfield; (P-In.); Lone Star Steel	1,516	24,700
Fairfield L. — (1970) Freestone Co.; Big Brown Cr.; 11 mi. NE Fairfield; (In.); TXU; (formerly Big Brown Creek Reservoir)	2,159	44,169
Falcon Reservoir, International — (1954) Starr-Zapata counties; Rio Grande; (International— U.S.-Mexico); 3 mi. W Falcon Heights; (M-In.-Ir.-FC-P-R); International Boundary and Water Com.; (Texas' share of total conservation capacity is 58.6 per cent)	85,194	2,645,646

*An acre-foot is the amount of water necessary to cover an acre of surface area with water one foot deep. The **years** in the table refer to first impounding of water. **Double years** refer to later, larger dams. **Abbreviations are:** L., lake; R., river; Co., county; Cr., creek; (C) conservation; (FC) flood control; (R) recreation; (P) power; (M) municipal; (D) domestic; (Ir.) irrigation; (In.) industry; (Mi.) mining, including oil production; (FH) fish hatchery; USAE, United States Army Corps of Engineers; WC&ID, Water Control and Improvement District; WID, Water Improvement District; USBR, United States Bureau of Reclamation; Auth., Authority; LCRA, Lower Colorado River Authority; TP&WD, Texas Parks & Wildlife Dept.; USDA, United States Department of Agriculture; Imp., impounded.

An aerial view of Canyon Lake in Comal County. Ron Billings photo; Texas Forest Service.

Lakes and Reservoirs, Date of Origin	Surface Area (Acres)	Storage Capacity (Acre-Ft.*)
Fayette Co. Reservoir — (1958) Fayette Co.; Cedar Cr.; 8.5 mi. E. La Grange; (In.); LCRA (also called Cedar Creek Reservoir)	2,400	71,400
Forest Grove Reservoir — (1982) Henderson Co.; Caney Cr.; 7 mi. NW Athens; (In.); TXU, Agent	1,502	20,038
Fort Phantom Hill, Lake — (1938) Jones Co.; Elm Cr.; 5 mi. S. Nugent; (M-R); City of Abilene	4,213	70,030
Georgetown, L. — (1980) Williamson Co.; N. Fk. San Gabriel R.; 3.5 mi. W Georgetown; (FC-M-In.); USAE	1,287	36,823
Gibbons Creek Reservoir — (1981) Grimes Co.; Gibbons Cr.; 9.5 mi NW Anderson; (In.); Texas Mun. Power Agency	2,770	32,084
Gilmer Reservoir — (2001) Upshur Co.; Kelsey Creek; 15 mi. N of Longview; 4 mi. W of Gilmer; (M); City of Gilmer	1,010	12,720
Gladewater, L. — (1952) Upshur Co.; Glade Cr.; in Gladewater; (M-R); City of Gladewater	481	4,637
Gonzales, Lake — (1931) Gonzales Co.; Guadalupe R.; 4.5 mi. SE Belmont; (P); Guadalupe-Blanco R. Auth. (also called H-4 Reservoir)	696	6,500
Graham, L. — (1929) Young Co.; Flint and Salt Creeks; 2 mi. NW Graham; (M-In.); City of Graham	2,444	45,260
Granbury, L. — (1969) Hood Co.; Brazos R.; 8 mi. SE Granbury; (M-In.-Ir.-P); Brazos River Authority (Imp. by DeCordova Bend Dam)	7,945	128,046
Granger L. — (1980) Williamson Co.; San Gabriel R.; 10 mi. NE Taylor; (FC-M-In.); USAE (formerly Laneport L.)	4,064	52,525
Grapevine L. — (1952) Tarrant-Denton counties; Denton Cr.; 2 mi. NE Grapevine; (M-FC-In.-R.); USAE	6,893	164,702
Greenbelt L. — (1967) Donley Co.; Salt Fk. Red R.; 5 mi. N Clarendon; (M-In.); Greenbelt M&I Water Auth.	2,025	59,500
Greenville City Lakes — 6 lakes; Hunt Co.; Conleech Fork, Sabine R.; 2 mi. Greenville; (M-Other); City of Greenville	—	6,864
Halbert, L. — (1921) Navarro Co.; Elm Cr.; 4 mi. SE Corsicana; (M-In-R); City of Corsicana	603	6,033
Harris Reservoir, William — (1947) Brazoria Co.; off-channel between Brazos R. and Oyster Cr.; 8 mi. NW Angleton; (In.); Dow Chemical Co.	1,663	9,200
Hawkins, L. — (1962) Wood Co.; Little Sandy Cr.; 3 mi. NW Hawkins; (FC-R); Wood County; (Imp. by Wood Co. Dam No. 3)	800	11,690
Holbrook, L. — (1962) Wood Co.; Keys Cr.; 4 mi. NW Mineola; (FC-R); Wood County; (Imp. by Wood Co. Dam No. 2)	653	7,790
Hords Creek L. — (1948) Coleman Co.; Hords Cr.; 5 mi. NW Valera; (M-FC); City of Coleman and USAE	504	5,684
Houston, L. — (1954) Harris Co.; San Jacinto R.; 4 mi. N Sheldon; (M-In.-Ir.-Mi.-R); City of Houston	11,854	128,863
Houston County L. — (1966) Houston Co.; Little Elkhart Cr.; 10 mi. NW Crockett; (M-In.); Houston Co. WC&ID No. 1	1,330	17,113

*An acre-foot is the amount of water necessary to cover an acre of surface area with water one foot deep. The **years** in the table refer to first impounding of water. **Double years** refer to later, larger dams. **Abbreviations are:** L., lake; R., river; Co., county; Cr., creek; (C) conservation; (FC) flood control; (R) recreation; (P) power; (M) municipal; (D) domestic; (Ir.) irrigation; (In.) industry; (Mi.) mining, including oil production; (FH) fish hatchery; USAE, United States Army Corps of Engineers; WC&ID, Water Control and Improvement District; WID, Water Improvement District; USBR, United States Bureau of Reclamation; Auth., Authority; LCRA, Lower Colorado River Authority; TP&WD, Texas Parks & Wildlife Dept.; USDA, United States Department of Agriculture; Imp., impounded.

Lakes and Reservoirs, Date of Origin	Surface Area (Acres)	Storage Capacity (Acre-Ft.*)
Hubbard Creek Reservoir — (1962) Stephens Co.; 6 mi. NW Breckenridge; (M-In.-Mi.); West Central Texas Mun. Water Authority	14,922	318,067
Imperial Reservoir — (1912) Reeves-Pecos counties; Pecos R.; 35 mi. N Fort Stockton; (Ir.); Pecos County WC&ID No. 2	1,530	6,000
Inks L. — (1938) Burnet-Llano counties; Colorado R.; 12 mi. W Burnet; (M-Ir.-Mi.-P); LCRA	788	14,074
Jacksonville, L. — (1959) Cherokee Co.; Gum Cr.; 5 mi. SW Jacksonville; (M-R); City of Jacksonville; (Imp. by Buckner Dam)	1,165	25,670
J. B. Thomas, L. — (1952) Scurry-Borden counties; Colorado R.; 16 mi. SW Snyder; (M- In.-R); Colorado River Mun. Water Dist.; (Imp. by Colorado R. Dam)	7,282	199,931
J. D. Murphree Wildlife Management Area Impoundments — Jefferson Co.; off-channel reservoirs between Big Hill and Taylor bayous; at Port Acres; (FH-R); TP&WD (formerly Big Hill Reservoir)	6,881	32,000
Joe Pool Lake — (1986) Dallas-Tarrant-Ellis counties; Mountain Cr.; 14 mi. SW Dallas; (FC-M-R); USAE-Trinity River Auth. (formerly Lakeview Lake)	7,470	142,875
Johnson Creek Reservoir — (1961) Marion Co.; 13 mi. NW Jefferson; (In.); AEP-Southwestern Electric Power Co.	650	10,100
Kemp, L. — (1923) Baylor Co.; Wichita R.; 6 mi. N Mabelle; (M-P-Ir.); City of Wichita Falls; Wichita Co. WID 2	15,357	245,308
Kickapoo, L. — (1945) Archer Co.; N. Fk. Little Wichita R.; 10 mi. NW Archer City; (M); City of Wichita Falls	6,028	85,825
Kiowa, L. — (1967) Cooke Co.; Indian Cr.; 8 mi. SE Gainesville; (R); Lake Kiowa, Inc.	560	7,000
Kirby, L. — (1928) Taylor Co.; Cedar Cr.; 5 mi. S. Abilene; (M); City of Abilene	740	7,620
Kurth, L. — (1950) Angelina Co.; off-channel reservoir; 8 mi. N Lufkin; (In.); Abitibi Consolidated Industries.	726	14,769
Lady Bird Lake (Town Lake) — (1960) Travis Co.; Colorado R.; within Austin city limits; (R); City of Austin	468	6,409
Lake Creek L. — (1952) McLennan Co.; Manos Cr.; 4 mi. SW Riesel; (In.); TXU	550	8,400
Lake Fork Reservoir — (1980) Wood-Rains counties; Lake Fork Cr.; 5 mi. W Quitman; (M-In.); Sabine River Authority	27,264	604,927
Lake O' the Pines — (1959) Marion-Upshur-Morris counties; Cypress Cr.; 9 mi. W Jefferson; (FC-C-R-In.-M); USAE (Imp. by Ferrell's Bridge Dam)	16,919	238,933
Lavon, L. — (1953) Collin Co.; East Fk. Trinity R.; 2 mi. W Lavon; (M-FC-In.); USAE	21,357	443,844
Leon, Lake — (1954) Eastland Co.; Leon R.; 7 mi. S Ranger; (M-In.); Eastland Co. Water Supply Dist.	1,590	26,421
Lewis Creek Reservoir — Montgomery Co.; Lewis Cr.; 10 mi. NW Conroe; (In.); Entergy.	1,010	16,400
Lewisville L. — (1929, 1954) Denton Co.; Elm Fk. Trinity R.; 2 mi. NE Lewisville; (M-FC-In.-R); USAE; (also called Lake Dallas and Garza-Little Elm)	27,175	563,228
Limestone, L. — (1978) Leon-Limestone-Robertson cos.; Navasota R.; 7 mi. NW Marquez; (M-In.-Ir.); Brazos River Authority	12,553	208,015
Livingston, L. — (1969) Polk-San Jacinto-Trinity-Walker counties; Trinity R.; 6 mi. SW Livingston; (M-In.-Ir.); City of Houston and Trinity River Authority	83,277	1,741,867
Loma Alta Lake — Cameron Co.; off-channel Rio Grande; 8 mi. NE Brownsville; (M-In.); Brownsville Navigation Dist.	2,490	26,500
Lost Creek Reservoir — (1990) Jack Co.; Lost Cr.; 4 mi. NE Jacksboro; (M); City of Jacksboro	413	11,950
Lyndon B. Johnson, L. — (1951) Burnet-Llano counties; Colorado R.; 5 mi. SW Marble Falls; (P); LCRA; (Imp. by Alvin Wirtz Dam); (formerly Granite Shoals L.)	6,273	113,323
Mackenzie Reservoir — (1974) Briscoe Co.; Tule Cr.; 9 mi. NW Silverton; (M); Mackenzie Mun. Water Auth.	896	46,429
Marble Falls, L. — (1951) Burnet Co.; Colorado R.; 1.25 mi. SE Marble Falls; (P); LCRA; (Imp. by Max Starcke Dam)	608	7,486
Martin Creek L. — (1974) Rusk-Panola counties; Martin Cr.; 17 mi. NE Henderson; (P); TXU	4,981	75,116
Medina L. — (1913) Medina-Bandera counties; Medina R.; 8 mi. W Rio Medina; (Ir.); Bexar- Medina-Atascosa Co. WID No. 1	6,066	254,823
Meredith, L. — (1965) Moore-Potter-Hutchinson counties; Canadian R.; 10 mi. NW Borger; (M-In.- FC-R); cooperative project for municipal water supply by Amarillo, Lubbock and other High Plains cities. Canadian R. Municipal Water Authority-USBR; (Imp. by Sanford Dam)	16,411	779,556
Millers Creek Reservoir — (1990) Baylor-Throckmorton counties.; Millers Cr.; 9 mi. SE Goree; (M); North Central Texas Mun. Water Auth. and Texas Water Development Board	2,268	27,888
Mineral Wells, L. — (1920) Parker Co.; Rock Cr.; 4 mi. E Mineral Wells; (M); Palo Pinto Co. Mun. WD No. 1	440	7,065
Mitchell County Reservoir — (1993) Mitchell Co.; branch of Beals Creek; (Mi.-In.); Colorado River MWD	1,463	27,266
Monticello Reservoir — (1972) Titus Co.; Blundell Cr.; 2.5 mi. E. Monticello; (In.); TXU	2,001	34,740
Moss L., Hubert H. — (1960) Cooke Co.; Fish Cr.; 10 mi. NW Gainesville; (M-In.); City of Gainesville	1,140	24,058
Mountain Creek L. — (1937) Dallas Co.; Mountain Cr.; 4 mi. SE Grand Prairie; (In.); TXU.	2,710	22,840
Murvaul L. — (1958) Panola Co.; Murvaul Bayou; 10 mi. W Carthage; (M-In.-R); Panola Co. Fresh Water Supply Dist. No. 1	3,529	38,284
Mustang Lake East/West — Brazoria Co.; Mustang Bayou; 6 mi. S Alvin; (Ir.-In.-R); Chocolate Bayou Land & Water Co.	—	6,451
Nacogdoches, L. — (1976) Nacogdoches Co.; Bayo Loco Cr.; 10 mi. W Nacogdoches; (M); City of Nacogdoches.	2,212	39,521
Nasworthy, L. — (1930) Tom Green Co.; S Concho R.; 6 mi. SW San Angelo; (M-In.-Ir); City of San Angelo	1,380	9,615

*An acre-foot is the amount of water necessary to cover an acre of surface area with water one foot deep. The **years** in the table refer to first impounding of water. **Double years** refer to later, larger dams. **Abbreviations are:** L., lake; R., river; Co., county; Cr., creek; (C) conservation; (FC) flood control; (R) recreation; (P) power; (M) municipal; (D) domestic; (Ir.) irrigation; (In.) industry; (Mi.) mining, including oil production; (FH) fish hatchery; USAE, United States Army Corps of Engineers; WC&ID, Water Control and Improvement District; WID, Water Improvement District; USBR, United States Bureau of Reclamation; Auth., Authority; LCRA, Lower Colorado River Authority; TP&WD, Texas Parks & Wildlife Dept.; USDA, United States Department of Agriculture; Imp., impounded.

A wake boarder on Lake Ray Roberts jumps the wake on a warm April day in 2008. The lake, which reaches into Denton, Cooke and Grayson counties, has a storage capacity of nearly 800,000 acre feet. Denton Record-Chronicle photo.

Lakes and Reservoirs, Date of Origin	Surface Area (Acres)	Storage Capacity (Acre-Ft.*)
Natural Dam L. — (1957, 1989) Howard Co.; Sulphur Springs Draw; 8 mi. W Big Spring; An original natural lake, whose surface and capacity were increased by construction of dams; (FC); Wilkinson Ranch & Colorado River MWD	3,605	54,560
Navarro Mills L. — (1963) Navarro-Hill counties; Richland Cr.; 16 mi. SW Corsicana; (M-FC); USAE	4,736	49,826
Nocona, L.— (1960) Montague Co.; 8 mi. NE Nocona; (M-In.-Mi.); No. Montague County Water Supply District (also known as Farmers Creek Reservoir)	1,362	21,445
North Fk. Buffalo Creek Reservoir — (1964) Wichita Co.; 5 mi. NW Iowa Park; (M); Wichita Co. WC&ID No.3.........................	1,392	15,400
North L. — (1957) Dallas Co.; S. Fork Grapevine Cr.; 2 mi. SE Coppell; (In.); TXU	800	9,400
Oak Creek Reservoir — (1952) Coke Co.; 5 mi. SE Blackwell; (M-In.); City of Sweetwater.........................	2,375	39,260
O. C. Fisher L. — (1952) Tom Green Co.; N. Concho R.; 3 mi. NW San Angelo; (M-FC-C- Ir.-R-In.-Mi.); USAE —Upper Colo. River Auth. (formerly San Angelo L.)	5,440	79,483
O. H. Ivie Reservoir — (1990) Coleman-Concho-Runnels counties; 24 mi. SE Ballinger; (M-In.), Colorado R. Mun. Water Dist. (formerly Stacy Reservoir).........................	19,149	554,340
Olmos Reservoir — (1926) Bexar Co.; Olmos Cr.; in San Antonio; (FC only), City of San Antonio	1,050	15,500
Olney, L./Cooper— (1935) Archer Co.; Mesquite Crk; 8 mi. E Megargel; (W-R); City of Olney; (see L. Cooper).........................	446	6,650
Palestine, L. — (1962) Anderson-Cherokee-Henderson-Smith counties; Neches R.; 4 mi. E Frankston; (M-In.-R); Upper Neches R. MWA (Imp. by Blackburn Crossing Dam)	22,656	370,907
Palo Duro Reservoir — (1991) Hansford Co.; Palo Duro Cr.; 12 mi. N Spearman; (M-R); Palo Duro River Auth.........................	2,413	60,897
Palo Pinto, L. — (1964) Palo Pinto Co.; 15 mi. SW Mineral Wells; (M-In.); Palo Pinto Co. Muni. Water Dist. 1	2,176	26,848
Pat Mayse L. — (1967) Lamar Co.; Sanders Cr.; 2 mi. SW Arthur City; (M-In.-FC); USAE	5,638	113,684
Pinkston Reservoir — (1976) Shelby Co.; Sandy Cr.; 12.5 mi. SW Center; (M); City of Center; (formerly Sandy Creek Reservoir)	523	7,380
Possum Kingdom L. — (1941) Palo Pinto-Young-Stephens-Jack counties; Brazos R.; 11 mi. SW Graford; (M-In.-Ir.-Mi.-P-R); Brazos R. Authority; (Imp. by Morris Sheppard Dam).........................	16,716	540,340
Proctor L. — (1963) Comanche Co.; Leon R.; 9 mi. NE Comanche; (M-In.-Ir.-FC); USAE- Brazos River Auth.........................	4,537	55,457
Quitman, L. — (1962) Wood Co.; Dry Cr.; 4 mi. N Quitman; (FC-R); Wood County (Imp. by Wood Co. Dam No.1)	814	7,440
Randell L. — (1909) Grayson Co.; Shawnee Cr.; 4 mi. NW Denison; (M); City of Denison.........................	280	5,860
Ray Hubbard, L. — (1968) Collin-Dallas-Kaufman-Rockwall counties; (formerly Forney Reservoir); E. Fk. Trinity R.; 15 mi. E Dallas; (M); City of Dallas	20,963	452,040
Ray Roberts, L. — (1987) Denton-Cooke-Grayson counties; Elm Fk. Trinity R.; 11 mi. NE Denton; (FC-M-D); City of Denton, Dallas, USAE; (also known as Aubrey Reservoir)	29,350	798,758
Red Bluff Reservoir — (1937) Loving-Reeves counties, Texas; and Eddy Co.; N.M.; Pecos R.; 5 mi. N Orla; (Ir.-P); Red Bluff Water Power Control District.........................	11,193	289,670
Red Draw Reservoir — (1985) Howard Co.; Red Draw; 5 mi. E Bi Spring; (Mi.-In.); Colorado River MWD	374	8,538
Richland-Chambers Reservoir — (1987) Freestone-Navarro counties; Richland Cr.; 20 mi. SE Corsicana; (M); Tarrant Regional Water Dist.........................	43,384	1,087,839
Rita Blanca, L. — (1940) Hartley Co.; Rita Blanca Cr.; 2 mi. S Dalhart; (R) City of Dalhart	524	12,050
River Crest L. — (1953) Red River Co.; off-channel reservoir; 7 mi. SE Bogata; (In.); TXU	555	7,000
Sam Rayburn Reservoir — (1965) Jasper-Angelina-Sabine-Nacogdoches-San Augustine counties; Angelina R.; (FC-P-M-In.-Ir.-R); USAE; (formerly McGee Bend Reservoir)	112,590	2,857,077
San Bernard Reservoirs #1, #2, #3 — Brazoria Co.; Off-Channel San Bernard R.; 3 mi. N Sweeney; (In.); ConocoPhillips	—	8,610
Santa Rosa L. — (1929) Wilbarger Co.; Beaver Cr.; 15 mi. S Vernon; (Mi.); W. T. Waggoner Estate	1,500	11,570

*An acre-foot is the amount of water necessary to cover an acre of surface area with water one foot deep. The **years** in the table refer to first impounding of water. **Double years** refer to later, larger dams. **Abbreviations are:** L., lake; R., river; Co., county; Cr., creek; (C) conservation; (FC) flood control; (R) recreation; (P) power; (M) municipal; (D) domestic; (Ir.) irrigation; (In.) industry; (Mi.) mining, including oil production; (FH) fish hatchery; USAE, United States Army Corps of Engineers; WC&ID, Water Control and Improvement District; WID, Water Improvement District; USBR, United States Bureau of Reclamation; Auth., Authority; LCRA, Lower Colorado River Authority; TP&WD, Texas Parks & Wildlife Dept.; USDA, United States Department of Agriculture; Imp., impounded.

Lakes and Reservoirs, Date of Origin	Surface Area (Acres)	Storage Capacity (Acre-Ft.*)
Sheldon Reservoir — (1943) Harris Co.; Carpenters Bayou; 2 mi. SW Sheldon; (R-FH); TP&WD	1,244	4,224
Smithers L. — (1957) Fort Bend Co.; Dry Creek; 10 mi. SE Richmond; (In.); Texas Genco	2,480	18,700
Somerville L. — (1967) Burleson-Washington-Lee counties; Yegua Cr.; 2 mi. S Somerville; (M-In.-Ir.- FC); USAE-Brazos River Authority	11,555	147,104
South Texas Project Reservoir — (1983) Matagorda Co.; off-channel Colorado R.; 16 mi. S Bay City; (In.); STP Nuclear Operating Co.	7,000	202,600
Spence Reservoir, E. V. — (1969) Coke Co.; Colorado R.; 2 mi. W. Robert Lee; (M-In.-Mi); Colorado R. Mun. Water Dist.; (Imp. by Robert Lee Dam)	14,640	517,272
Squaw Creek Reservoir — (1983) Somervell-Hood counties; Squaw Cr.; 4.5 mi. N Glen Rose; (In.); TXU	3,297	151,367
Stamford, L. — (1953) Haskell Co.; Paint Cr.; 10 mi. SE Haskell; (M-In.); City of Stamford	5,124	51,570
Steinhagen L., B. A. — (1951) Tyler-Jasper counties; Neches R.; 1/2 mi. N Town Bluff; (FC-R-C); USAE (also called Town Bluff Reservoir and Dam B. Reservoir);(Imp. by Town Bluff Dam)	10,687	66,966
Stillhouse Hollow L. — (1968) Bell Co.; Lampasas R.; 5 mi. SW Belton; (M-In.-Ir.-FC); USAE- Brazos River Authority; (also called Lampasas Reservoir)	6,484	227,771
Striker Creek Reservoir — (1957) Rusk-Cherokee counties; Striker Cr.; 18 mi. SW Henderson; (M -In.); Angelina-Nacogdoches WC&ID No. 1	1,920	16,934
Sulphur Springs, L. — (1950) Hopkins Co.; White Oak Cr.; 2 mi. N Sulphur Springs; (M); Sulphur Springs WD; (formerly called White Oak Creek Reservoir)	1,340	17,838
Sulphur Springs Draw Reservoir — (1992) Martin Co.; Sulphur Springs Draw; 12 mi. NE Stanton; (FC); Colorado River MWD	970	7,997
Sweetwater, L. — (1930) Nolan Co.; Bitter Creek; 6 mi. SE Sweetwater (M-R); City of Sweetwater	630	10,006
Tawakoni, L. — (1960) Rains-Van Zandt-Hunt counties; Sabine R.; 9 mi. NE Wills Point; (M-In.-Ir-R); Sabine River Authority; (Imp. by Iron Bridge Dam)	37,879	888,126
Terrell City L. — (1955) Kaufman Co.; Muddy Cedar Cr.; 6 mi. E Terrell; (M-R); City of Terrell	849	8,583
Texana, L. — (1980) Jackson Co.; Navidad R. and Sandy Cr.; 6.8 mi. SE Edna; (M-Ir); USBR, Lavaca-Navidad R. Auth., Texas Water Dev. Bd.; (formerly Palmetto Bend Reservoir)	9,727	153,246
Texoma, L. — (1943) Grayson-Cooke cos., Texas; Bryan-Marshall-Love cos., Okla.; (Imp. by Denison Dam) on Red R. below confluence of Red and Washita rivers; (P-FC-C-R); USAE	74,686	2,516,225
Toledo Bend Reservoir — (1967) Newton-Panola-Sabine-Shelby counties; Sabine R.; 14 mi. NE Burkeville; (M-In.-Ir.-PR); Sabine River Authority (Texas' share of capacity is half amount shown)	181,600	4,472,900
Tradinghouse Creek Reservoir — (1968) McLennan Co.; Tradinghouse Cr.; 9 mi. E Waco; (In.); TXU	2,010	35,110
Travis, L. — (1942) Travis-Burnet counties; Colorado R.; 13 mi. NW Austin; (M-In.-Ir.- Mi.-P-FC-R); LCRA; (Imp. by Mansfield Dam)	19,199	1,113,255
Trinidad L. — (1923) Henderson Co.; off-channel reservoir Trinity R.; 2 mi. S. Trinidad; (P); TXU.	740	6,200
Truscott Brine L. — (1987) Knox Co.; Bluff Cr.; 26 mi. NNW Knox City; (Chlorine Control); Red River Auth.	3,146	111,147
Twin Buttes Reservoir — (1963) Tom Green Co.; Concho R.; 8 mi. SW San Angelo; (M-In. -FC-Ir.-R.); City of San Angelo-USBR-Tom Green Co. WC&ID No. 1	9,080	177,850
Twin Oaks Reservoir — (1982) Robertson Co.; Duck Cr.; 12 mi. N. Franklin; (In) TXU	2,330	30,319
Tyler, L. /Lake Tyler East — (1949/1967) Smith Co.; Prairie and Mud Creeks.; 12 mi. SE Tyler; (M-In) City of Tyler; (Imp. by Whitehouse and Mud Creek dams)	4,737	73,256
Upper Nueces L. — (1926, 1948) Zavala Co.; Nueces R.; 6 mi. N Crystal City; (Ir.); Zavala-Dimmit Co. WID No. 1	316	5,200
Valley Acres Reservoir — (1956) Hidalgo Co.; off-channel Rio Grande; 7 mi. N Mercedes; (Ir-M-FC); Valley Acres Water Dist.	325	1,950
Valley L. — (1961) Fannin-Grayson counties; 2.5 mi. N Savoy; (P); TXU; (formerly Brushy Creek Reservoir)	1,080	16,400
Waco, L. — (1929) McLennan Co.; Bosque R.; 2 mi. W Waco; (M-FC-C-R); City of Waco-USAE Brazos River Authority	8,437	198,943
Walter E. Long, L. — (1967) Travis Co.; Decker Cr.; 9 mi. E Austin; (M-In.-R); City of Austin; (formerly Decker Lake)	1,269	33,940
Waxahachie, L. — (1956) Ellis Co.; S Prong Waxahachie Cr.; 4 mi. SE Waxahachie; (M-In); Ellis County WC&ID No. 1; (Imp. by S. Prong Dam)	656	10,779
Weatherford, L. — (1956) Parker Co.; Clear Fork Trinity River; 7 mi. E Weatherford; (M-In.); City of Weatherford	1,112	17,789
Welsh Reservoir — (1976) Titus Co.; Swauano Cr.; 11 mi. SE Mount Pleasant; (R-In.); AEP-Southwestern Electric Power Co.; (formerly Swauano Creek Reservoir)	1,269	18,431
White River L. — (1963) Crosby Co.; 16 mi. SE Crosbyton; (M-In.-Mi.); White River Municipal Water Dist.	1,642	29,880
White Rock L. — (1911) Dallas Co.; White Rock Cr.; within NE Dallas city limits; (R); City of Dallas	1,088	9,004
Whitney, L. — (1951) Hill-Bosque-Johnson counties; Brazos R.; 5.5 mi. SW Whitney; (FC-P); USAE	23,220	553,349
Wichita, L. — (1901) Wichita Co.; Holliday Cr.; 6 mi. SW Wichita Falls; (M-P-R); City of Wichita Falls	2,200	14,000
Winnsboro, L. — (1962) Wood Co.; Big Sandy Cr.; 6 mi. SW Winnsboro; (FC-R); Wood County; (Imp. by Wood Co. Dam No. 4)	806	8,100
Winters, L. — (1983) Runnels Co.; Elm Cr.; 4.5 mi. E Winters; (M); City of Winters (also known as Elm Creek Lake and New Lake Winters)	643	8,374
Worth, L. — (1914) Tarrant Co.; W. Fk. Trinity R.; in NW Fort Worth; (M); City of Fort Worth	3,458	24,500
Wright Patman L. — (1957) Bowie-Cass-Morris-Titus-Red River counties; Sulphur R.; 8 mi. SW Texarkana; (FC-M); USAE; (formerly Texarkana Lake)	24,438	167,253

*An acre-foot is the amount of water necessary to cover an acre of surface area with water one foot deep. The **years** in the table refer to first impounding of water. **Double years** refer to later, larger dams. **Abbreviations are:** L., lake; R., river; Co., county; Cr., creek; (C) conservation; (FC) flood control; (R) recreation; (P) power; (M) municipal; (D) domestic; (Ir.) irrigation; (In.) industry; (Mi.) mining, including oil production; (FH) fish hatchery; USAE, United States Army Corps of Engineers; WC&ID, Water Control and Improvement District; WID, Water Improvement District; USBR, United States Bureau of Reclamation; Auth., Authority; LCRA, Lower Colorado River Authority; TP&WD, Texas Parks & Wildlife Dept.; USDA, United States Department of Agriculture; Imp., impounded.

Texas Plant Life

This article was updated for the Texas Almanac by Stephan L. Hatch, Director, S.M. Tracy Herbarium and Professor, Dept. of Range-land Ecology and Management, Texas A&M University.

Vegetational Diversity

Variations in amount and frequency of rainfall, in soils and in frost-free days, gives Texas a great variety of vegetation. From the forests of East Texas to the deserts of West Texas, from the grassy plains of North Texas to the semi-arid brushlands of South Texas, plant species change continuously.

More than 100 million acres of Texas are devoted to providing **grazing** for domestic and wild animals. This is the **largest single use for land** in the state. More than 80 percent of the acreage is devoted to range in the Edwards Plateau, Cross Timbers and Prairies, South Texas Plains and Trans-Pecos Mountains and Basins.

Sideoats grama, which occurs on more different soils in Texas than any other native grass, was officially designated as the **state grass of Texas** by the Texas Legislature in 1971.

The **10 principal plant life areas** of Texas, starting in the east, are:

1. Piney Woods

Most of this area of some 16 million acres ranges from about 50 to 700 feet above sea level and receives 40 to 56 inches of rain yearly. Many rivers, creeks and bayous drain the region. Nearly all of Texas' commercial timber comes from this area. There are three native species of **pine**, the principal timber: longleaf, shortleaf and loblolly. An introduced species, the slash pine, also is widely grown. Hardwoods include **oaks, elm, hickory, magnolia, sweet and black gum, tupelo** and others.

The area is interspersed with **native and improved grasslands**. Cattle are the primary grazing animals. **Deer** and **quail** are abundant in properly managed localities. Primary forage plants, under proper graz-ing management, include species of the **bluestems, rossettegrass, panicums, paspalums, blackseed needlegrass, Canada and Virginia wildryes, purple-top, broadleaf and spike woodoats, switchcane, lovegrasses, indiangrass** and numerous **legume** species.

Highly disturbed areas have understory and over-story of undesirable woody plants that suppress growth of pine and desirable grasses. The primary forage grasses have been reduced and the grasslands have been invaded by **threeawns, annual grasses, weeds, broomsedge bluestem, red lovegrass** and shrubby woody species.

2. Gulf Prairies and Marshes

The Gulf Prairies and Marshes cover approximately 10 million acres. There are two subunits: (a) The marsh and salt grasses immediately at tidewater, and (b) a little farther inland, a strip of bluestems and tall grasses, with some gramas in the western part. Many of these grasses make excellent grazing.

Oaks, elm and other hardwoods grow to some extent, especially along streams, and the area has some **post oak** and brushy extensions along its borders. Much of the Gulf Prairies is fertile farmland. The area is well suited for cattle.

Principal grasses of the Gulf Prairies are **tall bunch-grasses**, including **big bluestem, little bluestem, sea-coast bluestem, indiangrass, eastern gamagrass, Texas wintergrass, switchgrass** and **gulf cordgrass**. **Saltgrass** occurs on moist saline sites.

Heavy grazing has changed the native vegetation in many cases so the predominant grasses are the less desirable **broomsedge bluestem, smutgrass, three-awns, tumblegrass** and many other inferior grasses.

Fog rises among loblolly pines in W. Goodrich Jones State Forest in the Piney Woods of East Texas. The Piney Woods comprise about 16 million acres. Ron Billings photo; Texas Forest Service.

Vegetational Areas of Texas

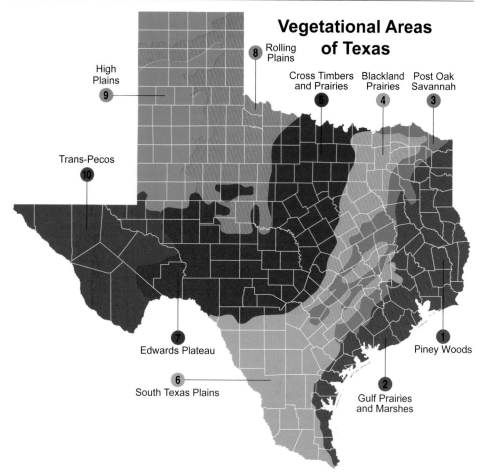

8 Rolling Plains

High Plains 9

Cross Timbers and Prairies 5

Blackland Prairies 4

Post Oak Savannah 3

Trans-Pecos 10

Edwards Plateau 7

South Texas Plains 6

Piney Woods 1

Gulf Prairies and Marshes 2

Other plants that have invaded the productive grasslands include **oak underbrush, Macartney rose, huisache, mesquite, prickly pear, ragweed, bitter sneezeweed, broomweed** and others.

Vegetation of the Gulf Marshes consists primarily of **sedges, bullrush, flat-sedges, beakrush** and other rushes, **smooth cordgrass, marshhay cordgrass, marsh millet** and **maidencane**. The marshes are grazed best during winter.

3. Post Oak Savannah

This secondary forest area, also called the **Post Oak Belt**, covers some 7 million acres. It is immediately west of the primary forest region, with less annual rainfall and a little higher elevation. Principal trees are **post oak, blackjack oak** and **elm. Pecans, walnuts** and other kinds of water-demanding trees grow along streams. The southwestern extension of this belt is often poorly defined, with large areas of prairie.

The upland soils are **sandy and sandy loam**, while the bottomlands are **sandy loams and clays**.

The original vegetation consisted mainly of **little bluestem, big bluestem, indiangrass, switchgrass, purpletop, silver bluestem, Texas wintergrass, spike woodoats, longleaf woodoats, post oak** and **blackjack oak**. The area is still largely native or improved grasslands, with small farms located throughout. Intensive grazing has contributed to dense stands of a woody understory of **yaupon, greenbriar** and **oak** brush.

Mesquite has become a serious problem. Good forage plants have been replaced by such plants as **splitbeard bluestem, red lovegrass, broomsedge bluestem, broomweed, bullnettle** and **western ragweed**.

4. Blackland Prairies

This area of about 12 million acres, while called a "prairie," has much timber along the streams, including a variety of **oaks, pecan, elm, bois d'arc** and **mesquite**. In its native state it was largely a grassy plain — the first native grassland in the westward extension of the Southern Forest Region.

Most of this fertile area has been cultivated, and only small acreages of grassland remain in original vegetation. In heavily grazed pastures, the tall bunchgrass has been replaced by **buffalograss, Texas grama** and other less productive grasses. **Mesquite, lotebush** and other woody plants have invaded the grasslands.

The original grass vegetation includes **big** and **little bluestem, indiangrass, switchgrass, sideoats grama, hairy grama, tall dropseed, Texas wintergrass** and **buffalograss**. Non-grass vegetation is largely legumes and composites.

5. Cross Timbers and Prairies

Approximately 15 million acres of alternating woodlands and prairies, often called the **Western Cross Timbers**, constitute this region. Sharp changes in the vegetational cover are associated with different soils and topography, but the grass composition is rather uniform.

The prairie grasses are **big bluestem, little bluestem, indiangrass, switchgrass, Canada wildrye, sideoats grama, hairy grama, tall grama, tall dropseed, Texas wintergrass, blue grama** and **buffalograss**.

On the Cross Timbers soils, the vegetation is composed of **big bluestem, little bluestem, hooded windmillgrass, sand lovegrass, indiangrass, switchgrass** with many species of legumes. The woody vegetation includes **shinnery, blackjack, post** and **live oaks**.

The entire area has been invaded heavily by woody brush plants of oaks, mesquite, juniper and other unpalatable plants that furnish little forage for livestock.

6. South Texas Plains

South of San Antonio, between the coast and the Rio Grande, are some 21 million acres of subtropical dryland vegetation, consisting of small trees, shrubs, cactus, weeds and grasses. The area is noteworthy for extensive brushlands, known as the **Brush Country**, or the Spanish equivalents of **chaparral** or **monte**. Principal plants are **mesquite, small live oak, post oak, prickly pear (Opuntia) cactus, catclaw, blackbrush, whitebrush, guajillo, huisache, cenizo** and others which often grow very densely.

The original vegetation was mainly perennial warm-season **bunchgrasses** in **post oak, live oak** and **mesquite savannahs**. Other brush species form dense thickets on the ridges and along streams. Long-continued grazing has contributed to the dense cover of brush. Most of the desirable grasses have only persisted under the protection of brush and cacti.

There are distinct differences in the original plant communities on various soils. Dominant grasses on the sandy loam soils are **seacoast bluestem, bristlegrass, paspalum, windmillgrass, silver bluestem, big sandbur** and **tanglehead**. Dominant grasses on the clay and clay loams are **silver bluestem, Arizona cottontop, buffalograss, common curlymesquite, bristlegrass, pappusgrass, gramas, plains lovegrass, Texas cupgrass, vinemesquite**, other **panicums** and **Texas wintergrass**.

Low saline areas are characterized by **gulf cordgrass, saltgrass, alkali sacaton and switchgrass**. In the post oak and live oak savannahs, the grasses are mainly **seacoast bluestem, indiangrass, switchgrass, crinkleawn, paspalums** and **panicums**. Today much of the area has been reseeded to **buffelgrass**.

7. Edwards Plateau

These 25 million acres are rolling to mountainous, with woodlands in the eastern part and grassy prairies in the west. There is a good deal of brushy growth in the central and eastern parts. The combination of grasses, weeds and small trees is ideal for **cattle, sheep, goats, deer and wild turkey**.

This limestone-based area is characterized by the large number of **springfed, perennially flowing streams** which originate in its interior and flow across the **Balcones Escarpment**, which bounds it on the south and east. The soils are shallow, ranging from sands to clays and are calcareous in reaction. This area is predominantly rangeland, with cultivation confined to the deeper soils.

In the east-central portion is the well-marked **Central or Llano Basin** centering in Mason, Llano and Burnet counties, with a mixture of granitic and sandy soils. The western portion of the area comprises the semi-arid **Stockton Plateau**.

Noteworthy is the growth of **cypress** along the perennially flowing streams. Separated by many miles from cypress growth of the moist Southern Forest Belt, they constitute one of Texas' several "islands" of vegetation. These trees, which grow to stately proportions, were commercialized in the past.

The principal grasses of the clay soils are **cane bluestem, silver bluestem, little bluestem, sideoats grama, hairy grama, indiangrass, common curlymesquite, buffalograss, fall witchgrass, plains lovegrass, wildryes** and **Texas wintergrass**.

The rocky areas support tall or mid-grasses with an overstory of **live oak, shinnery oak, juniper and mesquite**. The heavy clay soils have a mixture of **tobosagrass, buffalograss, sideoats grama and mesquite**.

Throughout the Edwards Plateau, **live oak, shinnery oak, mesquite** and **juniper** dominate the woody vegetation. Woody plants have invaded to the degree that they should be controlled before range forage plants can re-establish.

The fallen fruit of the bois d'arc tree, a common sight throughout the Blackland Prairies. This area of about 12 million acres, while called a "prairie," has much timber along the streams, including a variety of oaks, pecan, elm, bois d'arc and mesquite. Robert Plocheck photo.

Yucca and a variety of pines and junipers grow in the Davis Mountains and other mountainous areas of the Trans-Pecos. Ron Billings photo; Texas Forest Service.

8. Rolling Plains

This is a region of approximately 24 million acres of alternating woodlands and prairies. The area is half **mesquite woodland** and half **prairie**. Mesquite trees have steadily invaded and increased in the grasslands for many years, despite constant control efforts.

Soils range from coarse sands along outwash terraces adjacent to streams to tight or compact clays on redbed clays and shales. Rough broken lands on steep slopes are found in the western portion. About two-thirds of the area is rangeland, but cultivation is important in certain localities.

The original vegetation includes **big, little, sand and silver bluestems, Texas wintergrass, indiangrass, switchgrass, sideoats and blue gramas, wildryes, tobosagrass** and **buffalograss** on the clay soils. The sandy soils support **tall bunchgrasses, mainly sand bluestem. Sand shinnery oak, sand sagebrush** and **mesquite** are the dominant woody plants.

Continued heavy grazing contributes to the increase in woody plants, low-value grasses such as **red grama, red lovegrass, tumblegrass, gummy lovegrass, Texas grama, sand dropseed** and **sandbur,** with western **ragweed, croton** and many other weedy forbs. **Yucca** is a problem plant on certain rangelands.

9. High Plains

The High Plains, some 19 million treeless acres, are an extension of the Great Plains to the north. The level nature and porous soils prevent drainage over wide areas.

The relatively light rainfall flows into the numerous shallow **"playa"** lakes or sinks into the ground to feed the great **underground aquifer** that is the source of water for the countless wells that irrigate the surface of the plains. A large part of this area is under irrigated farming, but native grassland remains in about one-half of the High Plains.

Blue grama and **buffalograss** comprise the principal vegetation on the clay and clay loam "hardland" soils. Important grasses on the sandy loam "sandy land" soils are **little bluestem, western wheatgrass, indian-**grass, switchgrass and **sand reedgrass. Sand shinnery oak, sand sagebrush, mesquite** and **yucca** are conspicuous invading brushy plants.

10. Trans-Pecos, Mountains and Basins

With as little as eight inches of annual rainfall, long hot summers and usually cloudless skies to encourage evaporation, this 18-million-acre area produces only drought-resistant vegetation without irrigation. Grass is usually short and sparse.

The principal vegetation consists of **lechuguilla, ocotillo, yucca, cenizo, prickly pear** and other arid land plants. In the more arid areas, **gyp** and **chino** grama, and **tobosagrass** prevail. There is some **mesquite.** The vegetation includes **creosote-tarbush, desert shrub, grama grassland, yucca and juniper savannahs, pine oak forest and saline flats.**

The mountains are 3,000 to 8,749 feet in elevation and support **piñon pine, juniper** and some **ponderosa pine** and other forest vegetation on a few of the higher slopes. The grass vegetation, especially on the higher mountain slopes, includes many **southwestern and Rocky Mountain species** not present elsewhere in Texas. On the desert flats, black grama, burrograss and fluffgrass are frequent.

More productive sites have numerous species of **grama, muhly, Arizona cottontop, dropseed and perennial threeawn grasses**. At the higher elevations, plains **bristlegrass, little bluestem, Texas bluestem, sideoats grama, chino grama, blue grama, piñon ricegrass, wolftail** and several species of needlegrass are frequent.

The common invaders on all depleted ranges are **woody plants, burrograss, fluffgrass, hairy erioneuron, ear muhly, sand muhly, red grama, broom snakeweed, croton, cacti** and several poisonous plants. ☆

For Further Reading

Hatch, S.L., K.N. Gandhi and L.E. Brown, *Checklist of the Vascular Plants of Texas;* MP1655, Texas Agricultural Experiment Station, College Station, 1990.

Texas Forest Resources

Source: Texas Forest Service, Texas A&M University System. On the Web: txforestservice.tamu.edu

Forests resources in Texas are abundant and diverse. Forest land covers roughly 36 percent of the state's land area. According to 2009 figures from the Forest Inventory and Analysis, there are 60.3 million acres of forests and woodlands in Texas, a number much larger than previous Forest Service estimates.

East Texas Piney Woods

The principal forest region in Texas is the East Texas pine-hardwood region, often called the Piney Woods. The 43-county region forms the western edge of the southern pine region, extending from Bowie and Red River counties in northeast Texas to Jefferson, Harris and Waller counties in southeast Texas. The counties contain 12.1 million acres of timberland and produce nearly all of the state's commercial timber.

Following is a summary of the findings of the Forest Inventory of East Texas, completed in 2008 by the Texas Forest Service in cooperation with the USDA Forest Service Southern Research Station.

Timberland Acreage and Ownership

Nearly all (12 million of 12.1 million acres) of the East Texas forest is classified as "timberland," which is suitable for production of timber products and not reserved as parks or wilderness areas. In contrast to the trends in several other Southern states, Texas timberland acreage increased by 1.6 percent between 1992 and 2008. The majority of the new timberland acres came from agricultural lands, such as idle farmland and pasture, which was either intentionally planted with trees or naturally reverted to forest.

Seventy-three percent of East Texas timberland is owned by approximately 210,000 private individuals, families, partnerships and non-wood-using corporations. Nineteen percent is owned by forest-products companies and timber investment groups, and 8 percent is owned by the government. The following table shows acreage of timberland by ownership:

Ownership Class	Thous. Acres
Non-industrial Private	8,731.4
Forest Industry/Corporate	2,243.2
Public:	
National Forest	663.4
Misc. Federal	159.6
State	118.0
County & Municipal	49.3
Total	**11,964.9**

There are distinct regional differences in ownership patterns: 25 percent of the timberland found south of Nacogdoches County is owned by forest industry and other corporations; north of Nacogdoches, the non-industrial private landowner predominates, owning 84 percent of the timberland, with industry owning 11 percent.

Forest Types

Six major forest types are found in the East Texas Piney Woods. Two pine-forest types are most common. The loblolly-shortleaf and longleaf-slash forest types are dominated by the four species of southern yellow pine. In these forests, pine trees make up at least 50 percent of the trees.

Oak-hickory is the second most common forest

Loblolly pines in the Davy Crockett National Forest in Houston County. In Texas, forest land covers about 36 percent of the state's land area. Ron Billings photo; Texas Forest Service.

type. These are upland hardwood forests in which oaks or hickories make up at least 50 percent of the trees, and pine species are less than 25 percent. Oak-pine is a mixed-forest type in which more than 50 percent of the trees are hardwoods, but pines make up 25–49 percent of the trees.

Two forest types, oak-gum-cypress and elm-ash-cottonwood, are bottomland types that are commonly found along creeks, river bottoms, swamps and other wet areas. The oak-gum-cypress forests are typically made up of many species including blackgum, sweet-gum, oaks and southern cypress. The elm-ash-cotton-wood bottomland forests are dominated by those trees but also contain many other species, such as willow, sycamore and maple. The following table shows the breakdown in acreage by forest type:

Forest Type Group	Thous. Acres
Southern Pine:	
Loblolly-shortleaf	4,923.0
Longleaf-slash	191.4
Oak-pine	1,511.2
Oak-hickory	2,906.0
Bottomland Hardwood:	
Oak-gum-cypress	1,411.4
Elm-ash-cottonwood	639.3
Other	382.6
Total	**11,964.9**

Southern pine plantations, established by tree planting and usually managed intensively to maximize timber production, are an increasingly important source of wood fiber. Texas forests include 2.5 million acres of pine plantations, 62 percent of which are on forest-industry-owned land, 34 percent on non-industrial private, and 4 percent on public land. Genetically superior tree seedlings, produced at industry and Texas Forest Service nurseries, are usually planted to improve survival and growth.

Timber Volume and Number of Trees

Texas timberland contains 16 billion cubic feet of timber "growing-stock" volume. One billion cubic feet of growing stock produces roughly enough lumber to build a 2,000-square-foot home for one out of every three Texans. The inventory of softwood increased from 9.2 billion cubic feet in 2003 to 9.3 billion cubic feet in 2008. The hardwood inventory increased from 6.4 billion cubic feet to 6.6 billion cubic feet between 2003 and 2008.

There are an estimated 7.7 billion live trees in East Texas, according to the 2008 survey. This includes 2.2 billion softwoods and 5.6 billion hardwoods. The predominant species are loblolly and shortleaf pine; 2 billion pine trees are found in East Texas.

Timber Growth and Removals

Between 2003 and 2008, an annual average of 721.3 million cubic feet of growing stock timber was removed from the inventory either through harvest or land-use changes. Meanwhile, 929.3 million cubic feet of growing stock were added to the inventory through growth each year.

For pine, an average of 560.2 million cubic feet was removed during those years, while 657.3 million cubic feet were added by growth. For hardwoods, 161.1 million cubic feet were removed, while 272 million cubic feet were added by growth.

The 2007 Timber Harvest

Total Removals

There was a 3.6 percent decrease in total removal of growing stock in East Texas in 2006, including both pine and hardwood. The total volume removed from the 43-county region was 619.3 million cubic feet in 2007, compared to 641.3 million in 2006. Included in the total removal was timber harvested for industrial

Beyond the Piney Woods: Texas' Other Tree Regions

Compared to commercially important East Texas, relatively little data are available for the other tree regions of Texas. However, these areas are environmentally important with benefits of wildlife habitat, improved water quality, recreation and aesthetics.

Following is a brief description of these areas.

• **Post Oak Belt**: The Post Oak Belt forms a band of wooded savannah mixed with pasture and cropland immediately west of the Piney Woods region. It extends from Lamar and Red River counties southwest as far as Bee and Atascosa counties. Predominant species include post oak, blackjack oak and elm. An interesting area called the "**Lost Pines**" forms an isolated island of southern-pine forest in Bastrop, Caldwell, Fayette,and Lee counties just a few miles southeast of Austin.

• **Eastern and Western Cross Timbers**: The Eastern and Western Cross Timbers cover an area of about 3 million acres in North Central Texas. The term "cross timbers" originated with the early settlers who, in their travels from east

to west, crossed alternating patches of oak forest and prairies and so affixed the name "cross timbers" to these forests.

• **Cedar Brakes**: Farther south in the Edwards Plateau region are the cedar brakes, which extend over 3.7 million acres. Cedar, live oak and mesquite dominate these steep slopes and rolling hills. Mesquite is often harvested for cooking wood, knick-knacks and woodworking. Live oak in this region is declining because of the oak wilt disease.

• **Mountain Forests**: The mountain forests of the Trans-Pecos region of Texas, including Jeff Davis County and the Big Bend, are rugged and picturesque. Several western tree species, including piñon pine, ponderosa pine, southwestern white pine and even Douglas fir are found there, along with aspen and several species of oak.

• **Coastal Forests**: The coastal forests of the southern Gulf Coast are characterized by a mix of brush and short, scrubby trees. Common species include mesquite, live oak and acacia. Some of these scrub forests are particularly important as migratory bird habitat.

A log truck arrives at a wood yard in Tyler County. Ron Billings photo; Texas Forest Service.

use and an estimate of logging residue and other timber removals.

Industrial roundwood harvest in Texas, the portion of the total removal that was subsequently utilized in the manufacture of wood products, totaled 501.2 million cubic feet for pine and 127.6 million cubic feet for hardwood. The pine industrial roundwood harvest was down 0.2 percent and the hardwood roundwood harvest was down 13.9 percent from 2006. The combined harvest dropped 3 percent to 628.8 million cubic feet. Top producing counties included Polk, Tyler, Cass, Nacogdoches and Newton.

Total Harvest Value

Stumpage value of the East Texas timber harvest in 2007 was $496.9 million, a 16.2-percent increase

from 2006. The delivered value of timber was up 2.7 percent to $834.5 million. Pine timber accounted for 88.1 percent of the total stumpage value and 82.6 percent of the total delivered value.

The harvest of sawlogs for production of lumber was down 4.4 percent in 2007 to 1.42 billion board feet. The pine sawlog cut totaled 1.23 billion board feet, down 0.8 percent, and the hardwood sawlog harvest decreased 13.9 percent to 127.6 million board feet. Cass, Jasper and Angelina counties were the top producers of sawlogs.

Timber cut for the production of structural panels, including both plywood and OSB (oriented strand board) and hardwood veneer, totaled 164.2 million cubic feet, a 9.5 percent decrease from 2006. Polk, Tyler,

Texas Forest Products Production 1997–2007

| Year | Lumber* (thousand board feet) | | Paper (short tons) | | | Structural Panel |
	Pine	Hardwood	Paper	Paperboard*	Total Paper Products	Pine (thousand square feet*)
1997	1,316,762	160,553	1,116,018	2,052,153	3,168,171	3,200,317
1998	1,293,432	191,165	1,126,648	1,933,906	2,925,856	3,169,713
1999	1,279,487	225,570	1,079,397	1,979,592	3,058,989	3,260,055
2000	1,410,999	184,172	955,117	2,037,148	2,992,265	3,265,644
2001	1,293,823	213,795	599,902	2,083,326	2,683,228	2,732,940
2002	1,425,613	223,932	551,367	2,179,423	2,730,790	2,818,356
2003	1,490,311	287,062	255,462	2,170,185	2,425,647	2,723,225
2004	1,591,109	324,663	0**	2,560,480	2,560,480	2,859,012
2005	1,733,314	230,090	0**	2,512,262	2,512,262	3,249,558
2006	1,676,461	240,214	0**	2,781,865	2,781,865	2,935,637
2007	1,550,716	180,713	0**	2,788,308	2,788,308	2,503,941
	*Includes tie volumes.		*Includes fiberboard and miscellaneous products. **There was no paper or market pulp production due to the closure of a major paper mill.			*3/8-inch basis

Trinity and Angelina counties were the top producers of veneer and panel roundwood.

Harvest of timber for manufacture of pulp and paper products showed little change from 2006 and remained at 2.86 million cords in 2007. Cass, Newton and Tyler counties were the top producers of pulpwood.

Other roundwood harvest, including posts, poles and pilings, totaled 2.8 million cubic feet in 2007, a 17.9-percent decrease from 2006.

Import-Export Trends

Texas was a net importer of timber products in 2007. The total import from other states was 80.8 million cubic feet, while the total export was 71.7 million cubic feet. The net export was 1.4 percent of the total roundwood production in Texas.

Production of Forest Products

Lumber

Texas sawmills produced 1.7 billion board feet of lumber in 2007, a decrease of 9.7 percent over 2006. Production of pine lumber decreased 7.5 percent to 1.6 billion board feet in 2007, while hardwood lumber production dropped 24.7 percent, to 180.7 million board feet in 2007.

Structural Panel Products

Production of structural panels, including plywood and OSB, decreased to 2.5 billion square feet in 2007.

Total Timber Production and Value by County in Texas, 2007

County	Pine	Hardwood	Total	Stumpage Value	Delivered Value
	Cubic feet			Thousand dollars	
Anderson	7,929,044	1,593,416	9,522,460	$ 8,558	$ 13,606
Angelina	26,531,565	5,934,283	32,465,848	27,033	44,220
Bowie	5,282,776	7,099,491	12,382,267	8,097	15,339
Camp	777,474	652,559	1,430,033	1,016	1,832
Cass	24,661,572	13,064,294	37,725,866	29,386	49,838
Chambers	79,431	26,497	105,928	121	175
Cherokee	24,483,065	6,594,173	31,077,238	25,392	42,339
Franklin	190,789	542,744	733,533	457	921
Gregg	980,373	1,671,255	2,651,628	2,046	3,749
Grimes	1,481,718	9,799	1,491,517	1,894	2,541
Hardin	17,422,635	4,874,421	22,297,056	15,290	27,620
Harris	1,105,075	149,230	1,254,305	1,513	2,101
Harrison	17,942,577	5,363,848	23,306,425	18,692	31,088
Henderson	936,929	1,000,460	1,937,389	1,460	2,677
Houston	14,573,473	2,631,769	17,205,242	14,755	23,688
Jasper	24,575,641	1,536,220	26,111,861	21,863	35,378
Jefferson	125,824	79,826	205,650	219	333
Leon	1,686,055	344,061	2,030,116	2,151	3,181
Liberty	10,045,962	4,780,863	14,826,825	11,992	20,175
Madison	466,534	3,440	469,974	451	679
Marion	9,697,813	6,223,681	15,921,494	11,448	20,367
Montgomery	5,004,144	1,993,281	6,997,425	6,766	10,390
Morris	1,157,078	1,049,095	2,206,173	1,529	2,795
Nacogdoches	30,763,710	3,379,036	34,142,746	27,618	45,545
Newton	31,612,454	3,752,127	35,364,581	25,607	44,672
Orange	2,034,601	1,733,003	3,767,604	2,516	4,687
Panola	22,570,819	6,289,457	28,860,276	21,548	37,112
Polk	38,941,122	3,582,079	42,523,201	37,812	59,305
Red River	5,270,050	7,316,617	12,586,667	7,922	15,415
Rusk	12,343,731	4,345,477	16,689,208	13,488	22,689
Sabine	21,891,490	1,812,006	23,703,496	18,586	31,050
San Augustine	19,951,352	1,981,798	21,933,150	15,604	27,422
San Jacinto	13,153,328	2,147,684	15,301,012	12,941	20,833
Shelby	19,642,374	1,684,140	21,326,514	14,185	25,797
Smith	6,861,962	3,743,005	10,604,967	7,208	13,423
Titus	366,337	1,030,635	1,396,972	971	1,868
Trinity	16,070,467	1,695,691	17,766,158	13,179	22,675
Tyler	32,625,139	7,447,607	40,072,746	29,681	51,272
Upshur	8,699,124	3,386,338	12,085,462	9,973	16,513
Van Zandt	28,897	122,918	151,815	100	209
Walker	16,353,186	1,474,247	17,827,433	19,549	27,909
Waller	79,637	1,342	80,979	105	140
Wood	3,154,643	1,396,064	4,550,707	4,033	6,401
Other Counties	1,649,477	2,079,864	3,729,341	2,193	4,553
Totals	**501,201,447**	**127,619,841**	**628,821,288**	**$496,949**	**$834,526**

Paper Products

Production of paperboard totaled 2.8 million tons in 2007, almost the same level as in 2006. There was no paper or market pulp production in Texas in 2007.

Treated Wood

There was a 5.8 percent decrease in the volume of wood processed by Texas wood treaters in 2007 from 2006. The total volume treated in 2007 was 45.6 million cubic feet. Among major treated products, lumber accounted for 71.7 percent of the total volume; crossties accounted for 15.1 percent; utility poles and fence posts each accounted for 7.3 percent and 3.9 percent, respectively.

Surrounded by charred brush and smoke, a white-tail deer jumps a fence as wildfires burn in March 2006 near Alanreed, Gray County, in the Panhandle. Daron Dean photo.

Primary Mill Residue

Total mill residue, including chips, sawdust, shavings and bark in primary mills, such as sawmills, panel mills and chip mills, was 5.9 million short tons in 2007, a decrease of 8.5 percent from 2006. Eighty-four percent of the residue was from pine species and 16 percent was from hardwood species. Chips accounted for 50.6 percent of mill residue, followed by bark (35.3 percent), sawdust (8 percent), and shavings (6.1 percent).

Reforestation

A total of 105,936 acres was planted during the winter 2006 and spring 2007 planting season, a 15-percent increase over the 2004–2005 season. Industrial landowners planted 67,910 acres, up 5.4 percent from the previous season.

The Family Forest owners planted 37,229 acres in 2006–2007, up 39.4 percent percent over 2004–2005. Public landowners only planted 797 acres. The divestiture of industry lands into the non-industrial private sector will eventually lead to a sharp reduction in industry reforestation acreage. Non-industrial ownerships typically reforest less than industry.

Fire Protection

During the 2008 fire season, Texas Forest Service and local fire departments responded to 12,082 fires that threatened 86 communities and burned 1.4 million acres.

Texas has a tiered approach to emergencies such as wildland fires, with response coming from local, district, state and federal levels. When a fire surpasses the capabilities of local fire departments, the Texas Forest Service steps in to help. Texas Forest Service personnel respond to 15 percent of the wildland fires that burn across the state; however, those fires burn 70 percent of total acres lost to wildland fires each year.

Forest Pests

The **southern pine beetle** is the most destructive insect pest in the 12 million acres of commercial forests in East Texas. Typically, this bark beetle kills more timber annually than forest fires.

Currently, this destructive insect is at very low levels in East Texas and has been for the past several years. The Texas Forest Service coordinates all southern pine beetle control activity on state and private forestlands in Texas. These activities include detecting infestations from the air, checking infestations on the ground to evaluate the need for control, and notifying landowners and providing technical assistance when control is warranted.

Recent efforts have focused on prevention of southern pine beetle infestations. Since 2003, the Texas Forest Service has offered federal cost shares to private forest landowners in East Texas as an incentive to thin the young pine stands that are most susceptible to bark beetles. Thinning dense forests to promote vigorous tree growth is the preferred long-run method to reduce tree losses caused by bark beetles.

Extensive mortality of live oaks in Central Texas is causing considerable public concern. A vascular wilt disease, called **oak wilt**, is the major cause of the live oak mortality. A suppression project, administered by Texas Forest Service Forest Pest Management personnel, provides technical assistance and education for affected landowners.

Urban Forests

Because an estimated 86 percent of Texans now live in urban areas, urban trees and forests play an even more important role in the lives of Texans.

Trees reduce the urban heat island effect by shading and evaporative cooling. They also purify the air by absorbing pollutants, slowing the chemical reactions that produce harmful ozone, and filtering dust. Urban forests reduce storm water runoff and soil erosion and buffer against noise, glare and strong winds, while providing habitat for urban wildlife.

Environmental benefits from a single tree may be worth more than $275 each year. The value to real estate and the emotional and psychological benefits of urban trees raise the value of our urban trees even higher. ☆

Public Forests and Grasslands in Texas

Sources: U.S. Forest Service, Lufkin and Albuquerque, NM; www.fs.fed.us/r8/texas/ and the Texas Forest Service, Texas A&M University System; txforestservice.tamu.edu

There are **four national forests** and all or part of **five national grasslands** in Texas. These federally owned lands are administered by the U.S. Department of Agriculture Forest Service and by district rangers.

The national forests cover 637,472 acres in parts of 12 Texas counties. The national grasslands cover 117,394 acres in six Texas counties. Two of these grasslands extend into Oklahoma, as well.

Supervision of the East Texas forests and the two North Texas grasslands is by the Forest Supervisor of the division known as the National Forests and Grasslands in Texas (415 S. 1st St., Ste. 110, Lufkin 75901-3801; 936-639-8501).

The three West Texas grasslands (Black Kettle, McClellan Creek and Rita Blanca) are administered by the Forest Supervisor in Albuquerque, N.M., as units of the Cibola National Forest.

The following list gives the name of the forest or grassland, the administrative district(s) for each, the acreage in each county and the total acreage:

National Forests

Angelina National Forest — Angelina Ranger District (Zavalla); Angelina County, 58,520 acres; Jasper, 21,013; Nacogdoches, 9,238; San Augustine, 64,389. Total, 153,160 acres.

Davy Crockett National Forest — Davy Crockett District (Ratcliff); Houston County, 93,320 acres; Trinity, 67,313. Total, 160,633 acres.

Sabine National Forest — Sabine District (Hemphill); Jasper County, 64 acres; Newton, 1,781; Sabine, 95,454; San Augustine, 4,287; Shelby, 59,212. Total, 160,798 acres.

Sam Houston National Forest — Sam Houston District (New Waverly); Montgomery County, 47,801 acres; San Jacinto, 60,632; Walker, 54,597. Total, 163,030 acres.

National Grasslands

Lyndon B. Johnson National Grassland and Caddo National Grassland — District Ranger at Decatur; Fannin County, 17,873 acres; Montague, 61; Wise, 20,252. Total, 38,186 acres.

Black Kettle National Grassland — Lake Marvin District Ranger in Cheyenne, Okla.; Hemphill County, 576 acres; Roger Mills County, 30,724 acres. Total, 31,300 acres.

McClellan Creek National Grassland — District Ranger in Cheyenne, Okla.; Gray County, 1,449 acres. Total, 1,449 acres.

Rita Blanca National Grassland — District Ranger at Clayton, N.M.; Dallam County, 77,183 acres; Cimarron County, Okla., 15,639 acres. Total, 92,822 acres.

Forests and Grasslands in Texas

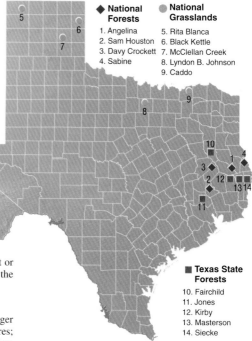

◆ National Forests   **● National Grasslands**

1. Angelina
2. Sam Houston
3. Davy Crockett
4. Sabine

5. Rita Blanca
6. Black Kettle
7. McClellan Creek
8. Lyndon B. Johnson
9. Caddo

■ Texas State Forests
10. Fairchild
11. Jones
12. Kirby
13. Masterson
14. Siecke

Establishment of National Forests and Grasslands

National forests in Texas were established by invitation of the Texas Legislature by an Act of 1933, authorizing the purchase of lands in Texas for the establishment of national forests. President Franklin D. Roosevelt proclaimed these purchases on Oct. 15, 1936.

The national grasslands were originally submarginal Dust Bowl project lands, purchased by the federal government primarily under the Bankhead-Jones Farm Tenant Act (1937). Today they are well covered with grasses and native shrubs.

Forests and Grasslands Uses

The national forests are managed to achieve sustainable conditions and provide wildlife habitat, outdoor recreation, water, wood, minerals and forage for public use while retaining the esthetic, historic and spiritual qualities of the land.

In 1960, the Multiple Use-Sustained Yield Act put into law what had been practiced in Texas for almost 30 years; that resources on public lands will be managed so that they are used in ways that best meet the needs of the people, that the benefits obtained will exist indefinitely, and that each natural resource will be managed in balance with other resources.

However, even the most carefully planned system of management cannot foresee factors that can cause drastic changes in a forest. Fire, storms, insects and disease, for example, can prompt managers to deviate from land management plans and can alter the way a forest is managed.

1. Timber Production

About 486,000 acres of the national forests in Texas are suitable for timber production. Sales of sawtimber, pulpwood and other forest products are initiated to implement forest plans and objectives. The estimated net growth is more than 200 million board feet per year and is valued at $40 million. A portion of this growth is normally removed by cutting.

2. Cattle Grazing

Permits to graze cattle on national grasslands are granted to the public for an annual fee. About 600 head of cattle are grazed on the Caddo–Lyndon B. Johnson National Grasslands annually. On the Rita Blanca National Grasslands, 5,425 head of cattle are grazed each year, most of them in Texas.

3. Hunting and Fishing

State hunting and fishing laws and regulations apply to all national forest land. Game law enforcement is carried out by Texas Parks and Wildlife. A wide variety of fishing opportunities are available on the Angelina, Sabine, Neches and San Jacinto rivers; the Sam Rayburn and Toledo Bend reservoirs; Lake Conroe; and many small streams. Hunting is not permitted on the McClellan Creek National Grassland nor at the Lake Marvin Unit of the Black Kettle National Grassland.

4. Recreational Facilities

An estimated 3 million people visit the recreational areas in the national forests and grasslands in Texas each year, primarily for picnicking, swimming, fishing, camping, boating and nature enjoyment.

The Sabine and Angelina National Forests are on the shores of Toledo Bend and Sam Rayburn reservoirs, two large East Texas lakes featuring fishing and other water sports. Lake Conroe and Lake Livingston offer water-related outdoor recreation opportunities on and near the Sam Houston National Forest. *Recreational activities offered in the National Forests are listed in the Recreation section on page 178.*

State Forests

Texas has **five state forests**, all of which are used primarily for demonstration and research. They are all game sanctuaries with no firearms or hunting allowed. Recreational opportunities, such as horseback riding, hiking, bird watching and picnicking, are available in all but the Masterson Forest. *See page 175 for recreation information.*

I.D. Fairchild State Forest — Texas' largest forest is located west of Rusk in Cherokee County. This forest was transferred from the state prison system in 1925. Additional land was obtained in 1963 from the Texas State Hospitals and Special Schools for a total acreage of 2,740.

W. Goodrich Jones State Forest — Located south of Conroe in Montgomery County, it comprises 1,733 acres. It was purchased in 1926 and named for the founder of the Texas Forestry Association.

John Henry Kirby Memorial State Forest — This 600-acre forest in Tyler County was donated by lumberman John Henry Kirby in 1929, as well as later donors. Revenue from this forest is given to the Association of Former Students of Texas A&M University for student-loan purposes.

Paul N. Masterson Memorial Forest — Mrs. Leonora O'Neal Masterson of Beaumont donated this 519 acres in Jasper County in 1984 in honor of her husband, who was a tree farmer and an active member of the Texas Forestry Association.

E.O. Siecke State Forest — The first state forest, it was purchased by the state in 1924. It contains 1,722 acres of pine land in Newton County. An additional 100 acres was obtained by a 99-year lease in 1946. ☆

Jerry and Ruth Hooper of Tyler walk the 4C National Recreation Trail in the Davy Crockett National Forest. The 20-mile trail connects the Ratcliff Recreation Area to the Neches Bluff overlook. Ron Billings photo; Texas Forest Service.

Texas Big Tree Registry

This partial list of the largest trees in Texas is from the Texas Forest Service. The list, last updated in January 2007, contains species native or naturalized to the state. *Source: Texas Forest Service, texasforestservice.tamu.edu.*

Status	Common Name	Latin Name	County	Circum-ference (inches)	Height (feet)	Crown Spread (feet)
*	Ash, Berlandier (Mexican-)	*Fraxinus berlandierana*	Cameron	252	48	72
	Ash, Green (Red Ash)	*Fraxinus pennsylvanica*	Navarro	324	55	95
*	Ash, Texas (Mountain Ash)	*Fraxinus texensis*	Bandera	76	72	67
	Ash, White	*Fraxinus americana*	Polk	150	116	66
	Aspen, Quaking	*Populus tremuloides*	Culberson	33	67	14
	Baldcypress	*Taxodium distichum var. distichum*	Real	438	96	112
*	Bladcypress, Montezuma	*Taxodium mucronatum*	Cameron	287	68	89
	Beech, American	*Fagus grandifolia*	Sabine	150	132	66
	Birch, River	*Betula nigra*	Red River	101	86	56
	Birch, River	*Betula nigra*	Lamar	118	65	69
	Boxelder (Ashleaf Maple)	*Acer negundo*	Tarrant	106	52	59
#	Buckeye, Texas	*Aesculus glabra var. arguta*	Gillespie	59	39	35
**	Cherry, Escarpment	*Prunus serotina var. eximia*	Real	102	51	53
**	Cherry, Escarpment	*Prunus serotina var. eximia*	Kerr	102	51	53
	Cherry, Southwestern Black	*Prunus serotina var. rufula*	Jeff Davis	111	40	46
Δ	Chinaberry	*Melia azedarach*	San Augustine	117	53	46
	Cottonwood, Eastern	*Populus deltoides var. deltoides*	Bandera	372	80	100
*	Cottonwood, Meseta	*Populus fremontii var. mesetae*	Brewster	211	49	84
	Cottonwood, Plains	*Populus deltoides var. occidentalis*	Lipscomb	264	62	96
*	Cottonwood, Rio Grande	*Populus fremontii var. wislizeni*	Jeff Davis	367	92	118
	Crabapple, Prairie (Blanco-)	*Malus ioensis*	Blanco	13	12	14
	Cypress, Arizona	*Cupressus arizonica var. arizonica*	Brewster	134	91	33
	Dogwood, Flowering	*Cornus florida*	Rusk	72	34	41
	Dogwood, Roughleaf	*Cornus drummondii*	Dallas	18	19	20
	Douglas-Fir, Rocky Mountain	*Pseudotsuga menziesii var. glauca*	Culberson	120	98	29
	Elm, American	*Ulmus americana*	Cherokee	256	80	110
	Elm, Cedar	*Ulmus crassifolia*	Kendall	131	73	72
	Elm, Slippery	*Ulmus rubra*	Ellis	85	90	67
	Elm, Winged	*Ulmus alata*	Leon	135	64	88
	Hackberry (Common-)	*Celtis occidentalis*	Titus	137	79	59
	Hackberry, Netleaf	*Celtis reticulata*	Culberson	76	30	52
	Hackberry, Spiny	*Celtis pallida*	Hidalgo	11	27	16
*	Hawthorn, Blueberry (Blue Haw)	*Crataegus brachyacantha*	Nacogdoches	98	36	46
*	Hawthorn, Texas	*Crataegus texana*	Harris	28	25	28
*	Hawthorn, Tracy (Mountain-)	*Crataegus tracyi*	Jeff Davis	42	27	26
	Hickory, Bitternut	*Carya cordiformis*	Tyler	140	133	110
*	Hickory, Black	*Carya texana*	Sabine	118	127	70
	Hickory, Nutmeg	*Carya myristiciformis*	Franklin	111	115	66
	Hickory, Water (Bitter Pecan)	*Carya aquatica*	Harrison	133	113	76
	Holly, American	*Ilex opaca var. opaca*	Houston	126	53	57
*	Huisache (Sweet Acacia)	*Acacia fornesiana*	Atascosa	160	29	43
*	Juniper, Ashe (Mountain Cedar)	*Juniperus ashei*	Comal	139	41	49
	Madrone, Texas	*Arbutus texana*	Uvalde	118	41	48
	Magnolia, Southern	*Magnolia grandiflora*	Smith	223	67	90
	Magnolia, Sweetbay (Swamp-)	*Magnolia virginiana*	Hardin	118	94	52
	Maple, Canyon (Bigtooth-)	*Acer grandidentatum*	Bandera	85	40	45
	Maple, Florida (Southern Sugar Maple)	*Acer barbatum*	Tyler	125	43	55
	Maple, Red	*Acer rubrum*	Morris	105	79	60
	Maple, Sugar	*Acer saccharum*	Jasper	84	73	64

* National Champion   ** National Co-Champion   # Nominated for national champion   Δ Naturalized species

Status	Common Name	Latin Name	County	Circum-ference (inches)	Height (feet)	Crown Spread (feet)
*	Mesquite, Honey	Prosopis glandulosa var. glandulosa	Real	172	55	89
	Mulberry, Red (Moral)	Morus rubra	Dallas	182	53	54
*	Mulberry, Texas	Morus microphylla	Presidio	100	30	48
Δ	Mulberry, White	Morus alba	Wilbarger	240	36	36
*	Oak, Bigelow (Shin Oak)	Quercus durandii var. breviloba	Travis	113	41	52
	Oak, Black	Quercus velutina	Harrison	125	65	66
	Oak, Black	Quercus velutina	Van Zandt	129	60	62
	Oak, Blackjack	Quercus marilandica	Franklin	113	57	65
**	Oak, Bluejack (Sandjack-)	Quercus incana	Cherokee	83	68	45
**	Oak, Bluejack (Sandjack-)	Quercus incana	Wood	87	61	45
	Oak, Bur (Mossycup-)	Quercus macrocarpa	Tarrant	218	81	105
	Oak, Cherrybark	Quercus falcata var. pagodifolia	Panola	242	118	124
	Oak, Compton	Quercus x comptoniae	Newton	238	88	120
	Oak, Durand	Quercus durandii var. durandii	Liberty	142	75	56
*	Oak, Graves (Chisos Red-)	Quercus gravesii	Val Verde	145	51	41
*	Oak, Havard (Havard Shin-)	Quercus havardii	Yoakum	58	33	30
*	Oak, Lacey (Blue-)	Quercus glaucoides	Comal	114	53	74
	Oak, Laurel	Quercus laurifolia	San Jacinto	154	96	85
	Oak, Live (Encino)	Quercus virginiana var. virginiana	Brazoria	386	67	100
*	Oak, Mohr	Quercus mohriana	Culberson	37	18	20
	Oak, Post	Quercus stellata var. stellata	Bowie	208	92	104
	Oak, Southern Red	Quercus falcata var. falcata	Shelby	268	87	68
*	Oak, Texas (Spanish Oak)	Quercus shumardii var. texana	Tarrant	198	70	82
*	Oak, Texas Live	Quercus virginiana var fusiformis	Young	357	48	80
	Oak, Water	Quercus nigra	Freestone	238	75	108
	Oak, White	Quercus alba	Newton	204	110	69
	Oak, Willow	Quercus phellos	Bowe	235	95	76
	Osage-Orange (Bois-d'Arc)	Maclura poomifera	Bowie	256	61	83
**	Palmetto, Dwarf	Sabal minor (S. louisiana)	Brazoria	43	28	13
**	Palmetto, Dwarf	Sabal minor (S. louisiana)	Brazoria	42	24	12
**	Palmetto, Mexican	Sabal mexicana	Hidalgo	61	50	15
**	Palmetto, Mexican	Sabal mexicana	Cameron	61	45	20
	Pawpaw	Asimina triloba	San Augustine	20	41	22
	Pecan	Carya illinoensis	Parker	258	91	117
	Persimmon, Common	Diospyros virginiana	Cass	79	80	50
*	Persimmon, Texas (Chapote)	Diospyros texana	Uvalde	71	25	36
#	Pine, Arizona	Pinus arizonica var. stormiae	Brewster	110	94	47
	Pine, Loblolly	Pinus taeda	Rusk	159	137	40
	Pine, Longleaf	Pinus palustris	Sabine	117	115	33
	Pine, Longleaf	Pinus palustris	Sabine	123	102	44
**	Pine, Mexican Pinyon	Pinus cembroides	Brewster	67	57	40
**	Pine, Mexican Pinyon	Pinus cembroides	Brewster	74	49	37
	Pine, Pinyon (Nut Pine)	Pinus edulis	Hudspeth	71	40	39
	Pine, Rocky Mountain Ponderosa	Pinus ponderosa var. scopulorum	Jeff Davis	134	110	46
	Pine, Shortleaf	Pinus echinata	Smith	151	91	68
	Plum, Chickasaw (Sand-)	Prunus angustifolia	Lubbock	23	18	28
**	Mexican Plum	Prunus mexicana	Harris	65	21	31
**	Mexican Plum	Prunus mexicana	Hood	68	17	17
*	Plum, Wildgoose (Munson -)	Prunus munsoniana	Dallas	25	36	35
	Redbud, Eastern (Judas-Tree)	Cercis canadensis var. canadensis	Upshur	78	42	40
#	Redbud, Texas	Cercis canadensis var. texensis	Parker	81	20	39
	Redcedar, Eastern	Juniperus virginiana	San Augustine	187	78	47
	Redcedar, Southern	Juniperus silicicola	Mongomery	123	68	46
Δ	Russian-Olive	Elaeagnus angustifolia	Lubbock	82	39	39

* National Champion   ** National Co-Champion   # Nominated for national champion   Δ Naturalized species

Status	Common Name	Latin Name	County	Circum-ference (inches)	Height (feet)	Crown Spread (feet)
*	Saffron-Plum (Coma)	*Bumelia celastrina*	Hidalgo	55	30	32
	Sassafras	*Sassafras albidum*	San Augustine	208	64	68
Δ	Silktree (Mimosa)	*Albizia julibrissin*	Red River	117	36	71
*	Soapberry, Western	*Sapindus drummondii*	Aransas	108	61	65
	Sparkleberry (Farkleberry)	*Vaccinium arboreum*	Houston	62	18	31
	Sparkleberry (Farkleberry)	*Vaccinium arboreum*	Smith	33	32	27
	Sugarberry (Sugar Hackberry)	*Celtis laevigata*	Nacogdoches	162	92	79
#	Sumac, Evergreen	*Rhus virens*	Uvalde	37	15	16
*	Sumac, Evergreen	*Rhus virens*	Comal	31	14	27
*	Sumac, Prairie (Flameleaf-)	*Rhus lanceolata*	Gillespie	71	26	45
	Sumac, Smooth	*Rhus glabra*	Dallas	14	24	16
	Sweetgum	*Liquidambar styraciflua*	Van Zandt	244	91	96
	Sycamore (Am. Planetree)	*Platanus occidentalis*	Houston	333	82	84
	Sycamore (Am. Planetree)	*Platanus occidentalis*	Van Zandt	302	93	65
Δ	Tallowtree (Chinese-)	*Sapium sebiferum*	Orange	40	54	41
*	Tupelo (Blackgum)	*Nyssa sylvatica var. sylvatica*	Wood	232	110	81
	Tupelo, Water (Swamp-)	*Nyssa aquatica*	Jasper	151	110	61
	Walnut, Arizona	*Juglans major*	Blanco	169	78	76
	Walnut, Black	*Juglans nigra*	Bowie	169	66	105
	Walnut, Little (Nogalito)	*Juglans microcarpa*	Jeff Davis	137	48	56
	Willow, Black	*Salix nigra*	Dallas	229	45	58
	Willow, Yewleaf	*Salix taxifolia*	Presidio	74	27	33
	Witch-Hazel	*Hamamelis virginiana*	Tyler	6	26	10
	Yaupon	*Ilex vomitoria*	Hardin	32	21	24
#	Yucca, Beaked	*Yucca rostrata*	Dallas	57	19	11
*	Yucca, Carneros (Spanish Dagger)	*Yucca carnerosana*	Hudspeth	51	25	10
*	Yucca, Faxon	*Yucca faxoniana*	Hudspeth	91	18	9
*	Yucca, Trecul	*Yucca treculeana*	Cameron	24	30	9

* National Champion   ** National Co-Champion   # Nominated for national champion   Δ Naturalized species

Authorities measure Texas' largest live oak in the San Bernard National Wildlife Refuge. AP/Todd Yates photo.

Texas' Threatened and Endangered Species

Endangered species are those the Texas Parks and Wildlife Department (TPWD) has named as being at risk of statewide extinction. Threatened species are likely to become endangered in the future. The following species are either endangered or threatened as of July 15, 2009. This list varies slightly from the federal list. Contact Endangered Resources Branch, Texas Parks and Wildlife, 4200 Smith School Road, Austin 78744; 800-792-1112; www.tpwd.state.tx.us/nature/endang/endang.htm.

Endangered Species

Mammals

Bats: greater long-nosed and Mexican long-nosed bats. **Marine Mammels**: West Indian manatee; black right, blue, finback and sperm whales. **Carnivores**: black-footed ferret; jaguar; jaguarundi; ocelot; gray and red wolves.

Birds

Raptors: peregrine, American peregrine and northern aplomado falcons. **Shorebirds**: Eskimo curlew; interior least tern. **Upland Birds**: Attwater's greater prairie chicken. **Waterbirds**: Whooping crane; eastern brown pelican. **Woodpeckers**: ivory-billed and red-cockaded woodpeckers. **Songbirds**: southwestern willow flycatcher; black-capped vireo; Bachman's and golden-cheeked warblers.

Reptiles

Turtles: Atlantic hawksbill, leatherback and Kemp's ridley sea turtles.

Amphibians

Salamanders: Barton Springs and Texas blind salamanders. **Frogs & Toads**: Houston toad.

Fishes

Killifishes: Comanche Springs and Leon Springs pupfishes. **Livebearers**: Big Bend, Clear Creek, Pecos and San Marcos gambusias. **Minnows**: Rio Grande silvery minnow. **Perches**: Fountain darter.

TPWD employees transport green sea turtles, a threatened species, back to sea after a cold snap in February 2007 stunned the turtles and they washed up on Texas beaches. Texas Parks & Wildlife photo.

Invertebrates

Crustaceans: Peck's cave amphipod. **Mollusks**: Ouachita rock pocketbook mussel.

Vascular Plants

Cacti: Black lace, Nellie Cory, Sneed pincushion, star and Tobusch fishhook cacti; Davis' green pitaya. **Grasses**: little aguja pondweed; Texas wild-rice. **Orchids**: Navasota ladies'-tresses. **Trees, Shrubs & Sub-shrubs**: Texas ayenia; Johnston's frankenia; Walker's manioc; Texas snowbells. **Wildflowers**: South Texas ambrosia; Zapata and white bladderpod; Terlingua Creek cat's-eye; ashy dogweed; Texas trailing phlox; Texas poppy-mallow; Texas prairie dawn; slender rush-pea; large-fruited sand verbena.

Threatened Species

Mammals

Bats: Rafinesque's big-eared, southern yellow, and spotted bats. **Carnivores**: black and Louisiana black bears; white-nosed coati; margay. **Marine Mammals**: Atlantic spotted and rough-toothed dolphins; dwarf sperm, false killer, Gervais' beaked, goose-beaked, killer, pygmy killer, pygmy sperm and short-finned pilot whales. **Rodents**: Palo Duro mouse; Coues' rice and Texas kangaroo rats.

Birds

Raptors: bald eagle; Arctic peregrine falcon; common black, gray, white-tailed and zone-tailed hawks; swallow-tailed kite; Mexican spotted owl; cactus ferruginous pygmy-owl. **Shorebirds**: piping plover; sooty tern. **Songbirds**: rose-throated becard; tropical parula; Bachman's, Texas Botteri's and Arizona Botteri's sparrows; northern beardless tyrannulet. **Waterbirds**: reddish egret; white-faced ibis; wood stork.

Reptiles

Lizards: reticulated gecko; mountain short-horned, reticulate collared and Texas horned lizards. **Snakes**: speckled racer; black-striped, Brazos water, Chihuahua desert lyre, indigo, Louisiana pine, northern cat-eyed, smooth green, scarlet and Trans-Pecos black-headed snakes; timber (canebrake) rattlesnake. **Turtles**: loggerhead and green sea turtles; Texas tortoise; alligator snapping, Cagle's map and Chihuahuan mud turtles.

Amphibians

Salamanders: black-spotted newt; Blanco blind, Cascade Caverns, Comal blind and San Marcos salamanders; South Texas siren (large form). **Frogs & Toads**: sheep and white-lipped frogs; Mexican treefrog; Mexican burrowing toad.

Fishes

Catfishes: toothless blindcat and widemouth blindcat. **Coastal Fishes**: opossum pipefish; river and blackfin goby. **Large River Fish**: paddlefish and shovelnose sturgeon. **Livebearers**: blotched gambusia. Killifishes: Conchos and Pecos pupfishes. **Minnows**: Rio Grande chub; Devils River minnow; Arkansas River, bluehead, bluntnose, Chihuahua and proserpine shiners; Mexican stoneroller. **Perches**: blackside and Rio Grande darters. **Suckers**: blue sucker and creek chubsucker.

Vascular Plants

Cacti: Bunched cory, Chisos Mountains hedgehog and Lloyd's mariposa cacti. **Trees, Shrubs & Sub-shrubs**: Hinckley's oak. **Wildflowers**: Pecos Puzzle sunflower, tinytim. ☆

Texas Wildlife

Source: Texas Parks and Wildlife, Austin.

Texas has many native animals and birds, as well as introduced species. More than **540 species of birds** — about three fourths of all different species found in the United States — have been identified in Texas.

Some **142 species of animals**, including some that today are extremely rare, are found in Texas. A list of plant and animal species designated as threatened or endangered by state wildlife officials is found elsewhere in this chapter.

A few of the leading land mammals of Texas are described here. Those marked by an asterisk (*) are non-native species. Information was provided by the **Nongame and Urban Program**, Texas Parks and Wildlife, and updated using the online version of *The Mammals of Texas* by William B. Davis and David J. Schmidly: **www.nsrl.ttu.edu/tmot1/contents.htm**; the print version was published by Texas Parks and Wildlife Press, Austin, 1994. For additional wildlife information on the Web: **www.tpwd.state.tx.us/nature/wild/wild.htm**.

Mammals

Armadillo — The **nine-banded armadillo** *(Dasypus novemcinctus)* is one of Texas' most interesting mammals. It is found in most of the state except the western Trans-Pecos. It is now common as far north and east as Oklahoma and Mississippi.

Badger — The **badger** *(Taxidea taxus)* is found throughout the state, except the extreme eastern parts. It is a fierce fighter, and it is valuable in helping control the rodent population.

Bat — Thirty-two species of these winged mammals have been found in Texas, more than in any other state in the United States. Of these, 27 species are known residents, though they are seldom seen by the casual observer. The **Mexican**, or **Brazilian**, **free-tailed bat** *(Tadarida brasiliensis)* and the **cave myotis** *(Myotis velifer)* constitute most of the cave-dwelling bats of Central and West Texas.

They have some economic value for their deposits of nitrogen-rich **guano**. Some commercial guano has been produced from **James River Bat Cave**, Mason County; **Beaver Creek Cavern**, Burnet County; and from large deposits in other caves including **Devil's Sinkhole** in Edwards County, **Blowout Cave** in Blanco County and **Bandera Bat Cave**, Bandera County. The largest concentration of bats in the world is found at **Bracken Cave** in Comal County, thought to hold between 20 and 40 million bats. The **big brown bat** *(Eptesicus fuscus)*, the **red bat** *(Lasiurus borealis)* and the **evening bat** *(Nycticeius humeralis)* are found in East and Southeast Texas. The evening and big brown bats are forest and woodland dwelling mammals.

Most of the rarer species of Texas bats have been found along the Rio Grande and in the Trans-Pecos. Bats can be observed at dusk near a water source, and many species may also be found foraging on insects attracted to street lights. Everywhere bats occur, they are the main predators of night-flying insects, including mosquitoes and many crop pests. On the Web: **www.batcon.org/**

Bear — The **black bear** *(Ursus americanus)*, formerly common throughout most of the state, is now surviving in remnant populations in portions of the Trans-Pecos.

Beaver — The **American beaver** *(Castor canadensis)* is found over most of the state except for the Llano Estacado and parts of the Trans-Pecos.

Bighorn — (See **Sheep**.)

Bison — The largest of native terrestrial wild mammals of North America, the **American bison** *(Bos bison)*, commonly called **buffalo**, was formerly found in the western two-thirds of the state. Today it is extirpated or confined on ranches. Deliberate slaughter of this majestic animal for hides and to eliminate the Plains Indians' main food source reached a peak about 1877-78, and the bison was almost eradicated by 1885. Estimates of the number of buffalo killed vary, but as many as 200,000 hides were sold in Fort Worth at a single two-day sale. Except for the interest of the late **Col. Charles Goodnight** and a few other foresighted men, the bison might be extinct.

Cat — The **jaguar** *(Felis onca)* is probably now extinct in Texas and, along with the **ocelot, jaguarundi** and **margay**, is listed as rare and endangered by both federal and state wildlife agencies. The **mountain lion** *(Felis concolor)*, also known as **cougar** and **puma**, was once found statewide. It is now found in the mountainous areas of the Trans-Pecos and the dense Rio Grande Plain brushland. The **ocelot** *(Felis pardalis)*, also known as the **leopard cat**, is found usually along the border. The **red-and-gray cat**, or **jaguarundi** *(Felis yagouaroundi Geoffroy)* is found, rarely, in extreme South Texas. The **margay** *(Felis wiedii)* was reported in the 1850s near Eagle Pass. The **bobcat** *(Lynx rufus)* is found over the state in large numbers.

Chipmunk — The **gray-footed chipmunk** *(Tamias canipes)* is found at high altitudes in the Guadalupe and Sierra Diablo ranges of the Trans-Pecos (see also

A beaver on its lodge at Caddo Lake. The American beaver is found across most of the state except the Llano Estacado and the Trans-Pecos. John Winn photo.

A herd of bighorn sheep ranges in the Elephant Mountain Wildlife Management Area in West Texas. Years of restoration efforts have brought the species back in the region. Texas Parks & Wildlife photo.

Ground Squirrel, with which it is often confused in public reference).

Coati — The **white-nosed coati** *(Nasua narica)*, a relative of the raccoon, is occasionally found in southern Texas from Brownsville to the Big Bend. It inhabits woodland areas and feeds both on the ground and in trees. The coati, which is on the list of threatened species, is also found occasionally in Big Bend National Park.

Coyote — The **coyote** *(Canis latrans)*, great in number, is the most destructive Texas predator of livestock. On the other hand, it is probably the most valuable predator in the balance of nature. It is a protection to crops and range lands by its control of rodents and rabbits. It is found throughout the state, but is most numerous in the brush country of Southwest Texas. It is the second-most important fur-bearing animal in the state.

Deer — The **white-tailed deer** *(Odocoileus virginianus)*, found throughout the state in brushy or wooded areas, is the most important Texas game animal. Its numbers in Texas are estimated at more than 3 million. The **mule deer** *(Odocoileus heminous)* is found principally in the Trans-Pecos and Panhandle areas. It has increased in number in recent years. The little **Del Carmen deer** *(white-tailed subspecies)* is found in limited numbers in the high valleys of the Chisos Mountains in the Big Bend. The only native **elk** in Texas *(Cervus merriami)*, found in the southern Guadalupe Mountains, became extinct about the turn of the 20th century. The **wapiti** or **elk** *(Cervus elaphus)*, was introduced into the same area about 1928. There are currently several herds totalling several hundred individuals.

A number of exotic deer species have been introduced, mostly for hunting purposes. The **axis deer*** *(Cervus axix)* is the most numerous of the exotics. Native to India, it is found mostly in Central and South Texas, both free-ranging and confined on ranches. **Blackbuck*** *(Antilope cervicapra)*, also native to India, is the second-most numerous exotic deer in the state and is found on ranches in 86 counties. **Fallow deer*** *(Cervus dama)*, native to the Mediterranean, has been introduced to 93 counties, while the **nilgai*** *(Boselaphus tragocamelus)*, native of India and Pakistan, is found mostly on ranches in Kenedy and Willacy counties. The **sika deer*** *(Cervus nippon)*, native of southern Siberia, Japan and China, has been introduced in 77 counties in Central and South Texas.

Ferret — The **black-footed ferret** *(Mustela nigripes)* was formerly found widely ranging through the West Texas country of the prairie dog on which it preyed. It is now considered extinct in Texas. It is of the same genus as the weasel and the mink.

Fox — The **common gray fox** *(Urocyon cinereoargenteus)* is found throughout most of the state, primarily in the woods of East Texas, in broken parts of the Edwards Plateau, and in the rough country at the foot of the High Plains. The **kit** or **Swift fox** *(Vulpes velox)* is found in the western one-third of the state. A second species of **kit fox** *(Vulpes macrotis)* is found in the Trans-Pecos and is fairly numerous in some localities. The **red fox*** *(Vulpes vulpes)*, which ranges across Central Texas, was introduced for sport.

Gopher — Nine species of pocket gopher occur in Texas. The **Botta's pocket gopher** *(Thomomys bottae)* is found from the Trans-Pecos eastward across the Edwards Plateau. The **plains pocket gopher** *(Geomys bursarius)* is found from Midland and Tom Green counties east and north to McLennan, Dallas and Grayson counties. The **desert pocket gopher** *(Geomys arenarius)* is found only in the Trans-Pecos, while the **yellow-faced pocket gopher** *(Cratogeomys castanops)* is found in the western one-third of the state, with occasional sightings along the Rio Grande in Maverick and Cameron counties. The **Texas pocket gopher** *(Geomys personatus)* is found in South Texas from San Patricio County to Val Verde County. **Attwater's pocket gopher** *(Geomys attwateri)* and **Baird's pocket gopher** *(Geomys breviceps)* are both found generally in South Central and Coastal Texas from the Brazos River to the San Antonio River and south to Matagorda and San Patricio counties. **Jones' pocket gopher** *(Geomys knoxjonesi)* is found only in far West Texas, while the **Llano pocket gopher** *(Geomys texensis)* is found only in two isolated areas of the Hill Country.

Ground Squirrel — Five or more species of ground squirrel live in Texas, mostly in the western part of the state. The **rock squirrel** *(Spermophilus variegatus)* is found throughout the Edwards Plateau and Trans-Pecos. The **Mexican ground squirrel** *(Spermophilus mexicanus)* is found in southern and western Texas. The **spotted ground squirrel** *(Spermophilus spilosoma)* is found generally in the western half of the state. The **thirteen-lined ground squirrel** *(Spermophilus tridecemlineatus)* is found in a narrow strip from Dallas and Tarrant counties to the Gulf. The **Texas antelope squirrel** *(Ammospermophilus interpres)* is found along the Rio Grande from El Paso to Val Verde County.

Hog, Feral — (see Pig, Feral)

There are millions of feral pigs in Texas, which cause problems for landowners, ranchers and farmers. Ray Sasser photo.

Javelina — The **javelina** or **collared peccary** *(Tayassu tajacu)* is found in brushy semidesert where prickly pear, a favorite food, is found. The javelina was hunted commercially for its hide until 1939. They are harmless to livestock and to people, though they can defend themselves ferociously when attacked by hunting dogs.

Mink — The **mink** *(Mustela vison)* is found in the eastern half of the state, always near streams, lakes or other water sources. Although it is an economically important fur-bearing animal in the eastern United States, it ranked only 13th in numbers and 9th in economic value to trappers in Texas in 1988-89, according to a Texas Parks and Wildlife Department survey.

Mole — The **eastern mole** *(Scalopus aquaticus)* is found in the eastern two-thirds of the state.

Muskrat — The **common muskrat** *(Ondatra zibethica)*, occurs in aquatic habitats in the northern, southeastern and southwestern parts of the state. Although the muskrat was once economically valuable for its fur, its numbers have declined, mostly because of the loss of habitat.

Nutria* — This introduced species *(Myocastor coypus)*, native to South America, is found in the eastern two-thirds of the state. The fur is not highly valued and, since nutria are in competition with muskrats, their spread is discouraged. They have been used widely in Texas as a cure-all for ponds choked with vegetation, with spotty results.

Opossum — A marsupial, the **Virginia opossum** *(Didelphis virginiana)* is found in nearly all parts of the state. The opossum has economic value for its pelt, and its meat is considered a delicacy by some. It is one of the chief contributors to the Texas fur crop.

Otter — A few **river otter** *(Lutra canadensis)* are found in the eastern quarter of the state. It has probably been extirpated from the Panhandle, north-central and southern Texas.

Pig, Feral — Feral pigs are found in most Texas counties but especially in areas of the Rio Grande and Coastal Plains as well as the woods of East Texas. They are descendants of escaped domestic hogs or of European wild hogs that were imported for sport.

Porcupine — The **yellow-haired porcupine** *(Erethizon dorsatum)* is found from the western half of the state east to Bosque County.

Prairie Dog — Until recent years probably no sight was so universal in West Texas as the **black-tailed prairie dog** *(Cynomys ludovicianus)*. Naturalists estimated its population in the hundreds of millions, and prairie-dog towns often covered many acres with thickly spaced burrows. Its destruction of range grasses and cultivated crops has caused farmers and ranchers to destroy many of them, and it is extirpated from much of its former range. It is being propagated in several public zoos, notably the **prairie dog town in Mackenzie Park** at Lubbock. It has been honored in Texas by the naming of the **Prairie Dog Town Fork** of the Red River, along one segment of which is located the beautiful **Palo Duro Canyon.**

Pronghorn — The **Pronghorn** *(Antilocapra americana)* formerly was found in the western two-thirds of the state. It is currently found only in limited areas from the Panhandle to the Trans-Pecos. Despite management efforts, its numbers have been decreasing in recent years.

Rabbit — The **black-tailed jack rabbit** *(Lepus californicus)* is found throughout Texas except in the Big Thicket area of East Texas. It breeds rapidly, and its long hind legs make it one of the world's faster-running animals. The **Eastern cottontail** *(Sylvilagus floridanus)* is found mostly in the eastern three-quarters of the state. The **desert cottontail** *(Sylvilagus auduboni)* is found in the western half of the state, usually on the open range. The **swamp rabbit** *(Sylvilagus aquaticus)* is found in East Texas and the coastal area.

Raccoon — The **raccoon** *(Procyon lotor)* is found throughout Texas, especially along streams and in urban settings. It is the most important fur-bearing animal in the state.

Rats and Mice — There are 40 to 50 species of rats and mice in Texas of varying characteristics, habitats and economic destructiveness. The **Norway rat*** *(Rattus norvegicus)* and the **roof rat*** *(Rattus rattus)*, both non-native species, are probably the most common and the most destructive. They also are instrumental in the transmission of several dread diseases, including bubonic plague and typhus. The **common house mouse*** *(Mus musculis)* is estimated in the hundreds of millions annually. The **Mexican vole** *(Microtus mexicanus guadalupensis)*, also called the **Guadalupe Mountain vole**, is found only in the higher elevations of the Guadalupe Mountains National Park and just over the border into New Mexico.

Ringtail — The **ringtail** *(Bassariscus astutus)* is found statewide but is rare in the Lower Valley and the Coastal Plains.

Sheep — The **mountain sheep** *(Ovis canadensis)*, also called **desert bighorn**, formerly was found in isolated areas of the mountainous Trans-Pecos, but the last native sheep were seen in 1959. They have been recently introduced into the same areas. The **barbary sheep*** *(Ammotragus lervia)*, or **aoudad**, first introduced to the Palo Duro Canyon area in 1957–1958, has become firmly established. Private introductions have brought it into the Edwards Plateau, Trans-Pecos, South Texas, Rolling Plains and Post Oak Savannah regions.

Shrew — Four species are found in Texas: the **southern short-tailed shrew** *(Blarina Carolinensis)*, found in the eastern one-fourth of the state; the **least shrew** *(Cryptotis parva)*, in the eastern and central parts of the state; the **Elliot's short-tailed shrew** *(Blarina hylophaga)*, known only in Aransas, Montague and Bastrop counties); and the **desert shrew** *(Notiosorex crawfordi)*, found in the western two-thirds of the state.

Skunk — There are six species of skunk in Texas. The **Eastern spotted skunk** *(Spilogale putorius)* is found in the eastern half of the state and across north-central Texas to the Panhandle. A small skunk, it is often erroneously called civet cat. This skunk also is found in East Texas and the Gulf area. The **Western spotted skunk** *(Spilogale gracilis)* is found in the southwestern part of the state north to Garza and Howard counties and east to Bexar and Duval counties. The **striped skunk** *(Mephitis mephitis)* is found statewide, mostly in brush or wooded areas. The **hooded skunk** *(Mephitis macroura)* is found in limited numbers in the Big Bend

and adjacent parts of the Trans-Pecos. The **eastern hog-nosed skunk** *(Conepatus leuconotus)*, found in the Gulf Coastal Plains, ranges southward into Mexico. The **common hog-nosed skunk** *(Conepatus mesoleucus)* is found in southwestern, central and southern Texas, north to Collin and Lubbock counties.

Squirrel — The **eastern fox squirrel** *(Sciurus niger)* is found in the eastern two-thirds of the state. The **eastern gray squirrel** *(Sciurus carolinensis)* is found generally in the eastern third of the state. The **flying squirrel** *(Glaucomys volans)* is found in wooded areas of East Texas.

Weasel — The **long-tailed weasel** *(Mustela frenata)*, akin to the mink, is found statewide, but is scarce in West Texas.

Wolf — The **red wolf** *(Canis rufus)* was once found throughout the eastern half of the state. It has now been extirpated from the wild, with the only known remnants of the population now in captive propagation. The **gray wolf** *(Canis lupus)* once had a wide range over the western two-thirds of the state. It is now considered extinct in Texas. The **red wolf** and **gray wolf** are on the federal and state rare and endangered species lists.

Reptiles and Arachnids

Most of the more than **100 species and subspecies of snakes** found in Texas are beneficial, as also are other reptiles. There are **16 poisonous species and subspecies**.

Poisonous reptiles include **three species of copperheads** *(southern, broad-banded and Trans-Pecos)*; one kind of **cottonmouth** *(western)*; **11 kinds of rattlesnakes** (canebrake, western massasauga, desert massasauga, western pigmy, western diamondback, timber, banded rock, mottled rock, northern blacktailed, Mojave and prairie); and the **Texas coral snake**.

Also noteworthy are the **horned lizard**, also called **horned toad**, which is on the list of threatened species; the **vinegarone**, a type of whip scorpion; **tarantula**, a hairy spider; and **alligator**. ☆

An alligator basks in the sun in an Orange County swamp. Ron Billings photo; Texas Forest Service.

National Wildlife Refuges

Source: U.S. Fish and Wildlife Service, U.S. Department of the Interior.

Texas has more than 470,000 acres in 17 national wildlife refuges. Their descriptions, with date of acquisition in parentheses, follow.

Included in this acreage are two conservation easement refuges, which may be visited at different times of the year for bird watching and wildlife viewing, as well as hunting and fishing. Write or call before visiting to check on facilities and days and hours of operation. On the Web: http://southwest.fws.gov/refuges/index.html.

Anahuac (1963): The more than 34,000 acres of this refuge are located along the upper Gulf Coast in Chambers County. Fresh and saltwater marshes and miles of beautiful, sweeping coastal prairie provide wintering habitat for large flocks of waterfowl, including geese, 27 species of ducks and six species of rails. Roseate spoonbills and white ibis are among the other birds frequenting the refuge. Other species include alligator, muskrat and bobcat. Fishing, bird watching, auto tours and hunting are available. Office: Box 278, Anahuac 77514; 409-267-3337.

Aransas (1937): This refuge comprises 70,504 acres on Blackjack Peninsula and three satellite units in Aransas and Refugio counties. The three mainland units consist of oak woodlands, fresh and saltwater marshes and coastal grasslands.

Besides providing wintering grounds for the endangered whooping crane, the refuge is home to many species of waterfowl and other migratory birds — more than 390 different bird species in all.

Refuge is open daily, sunrise to sunset. Interpretive center is open daily, 8:30 a.m. to 4:30 p.m. Other facilities include a 40-foot observation tower, paved auto-tour loop and walking trails. Office: Box 100, Austwell 77950; 361-286-3559.

Attwater Prairie Chicken (1972): Established in 1972 in Colorado County to preserve habitat for the endangered Attwater's prairie chicken, the refuge comprises more than 10,000 acres of native tallgrass prairie, potholes, sandy knolls and some wooded areas. An auto-tour route is available year-round, and 350 acres of marsh are accessible for watching the more than 250 species of birds that visit the refuge. Refuge open sunrise to sunset. Office: Box 519, Eagle Lake 77434; 979-234-3021.

Balcones Canyonlands (1992): This 25,000-acre refuge was dedicated in 1992. Located in Burnet, Travis and Williamson counties northwest of Austin, it was established to protect the nesting habitat of two endangered birds: black-capped vireo and golden-cheeked warbler. Eventually, the refuge will encompass 30,500 acres of oak-juniper woodlands and other habitats. An observation deck can be used for birdwatching. Hunting available. Office: 24518 FM-1431, Box 1, Marble Falls, 78654; 512-339-9432.

Big Boggy (1983): This refuge occupies 5,000 acres of coastal prairie and salt marsh along East Matagorda Bay for the benefit of wintering waterfowl. The refuge is generally closed, and visitors are encouraged to visit nearby San Bernard or Brazoria refuges. Waterfowl hunting is permitted in season. Office: 1212 N. Velasco, #200, Angleton 77515; 979-849-6062.

Brazoria (1966): The 43,388 acres of this refuge, located along the Gulf Coast in Brazoria County, serve as haven for wintering waterfowl and a wide variety of other migratory birds. The refuge also supports many marsh and water birds, from roseate spoonbills and great blue herons to white ibis and sandhill cranes.

Brazoria Refuge is within the Freeport Christmas Bird Count circle, which frequently achieves the highest number of species seen in a 24-hour period. Open daily sunrise to sunset. Hunting and fishing also available. Call for details. Office: 1212 N. Velasco, #200, Angleton 77515; 979-849-6062.

Buffalo Lake (1958): Comprising 7,664 acres in the Central Flyway in Randall County in the Panhandle, this refuge contains some of the best remaining shortgrass prairie in the United States. Buffalo Lake is now dry; a marsh area is artificially maintained for the numerous birds, reptiles and mammals. Available activities include picnicking, auto tour, birding, photography and hiking. Office: Box 179, Umbarger 79091; 806-499-3382.

Hagerman (1946): Hagerman National Wildlife Refuge lies on the Big Mineral arm of Lake Texoma in Grayson County. The 3,000 acres of marsh and water and 8,000 acres of upland and farmland provide a feeding and resting place for migrating waterfowl. Bird watching, fishing and hunting are available. Office: 6465 Refuge Road, Sherman 75092-5817; 903-786-2826.

Laguna Atascosa: Established in 1946 as southernmost waterfowl refuge in the Central Flyway, this

Lake Texoma at Hagerman National Wildlife Refuge in Grayson County. Robert Plocheck photo.

The great blue heron can be found in marshy areas, such as Brazoria Wildlife Refuge. Dallas Morning News photo.

refuge contains more than 45,000 acres fronting on the Laguna Madre in the Lower Rio Grande Valley in Cameron and Willacy counties.

Open lagoons, coastal prairies, salt flats and brushlands support a wide diversity of wildlife. The United States' largest concentration of redhead ducks winters here, along with many other species of waterfowl and shorebirds. White-tailed deer, javelina and armadillo can be found, along with endangered ocelot.

Bird watching and nature study are popular; auto-tour roads and nature trails are available. Camping and fishing are permitted within Adolph Thomae Jr. County Park. Hunting also available. Office: Box 450, Rio Hondo 78583; 956-748-3607.

Lower Rio Grande Valley (1979): The U.S. Fish and Wildlife Service has acquired about half the planned acreage in the Lower Rio Grande Valley for this refuge, which will eventually include 132,500 acres within Cameron, Hidalgo, Starr and Willacy counties.

The refuge will include 11 different habitat types, including sabal palm forest, tidal flats, coastal brushland, mid-delta thorn forest, woodland potholes and basins, upland thorn scrub, flood forest, barretal, riparian woodland and Chihuahuan thorn forest.

Nearly 500 species of birds and over 300 butterfly species have been found there, as well as four of the five cats that occur within the United States: jaguarundi, ocelot, bobcat and mountain lion. Office: Santa Ana/Lower Rio Grande Valley National Wildlife Refuges, Rt. 2, Box 202A, Alamo 78516; 956-784-2500.

Matagorda Island: Matagorda Island is jointly owned and managed by the U.S. Fish and Wildlife Service and the State of Texas under an agreement reached in 1983. For facilities, please check table of Texas Wildlife Management Areas on page 123.

McFaddin (1980): Purchased in 1980, this refuge's 55,000 acres, in Jefferson and Chambers counties, are of great importance to wintering populations of migratory waterfowl. One of the densest populations of alligators in Texas is found here. Activities on the refuge include wildlife observation, hunting, fishing and crabbing. Access best by boat; limited roadways. Office: Box 609, Sabine Pass 77655; 409-971-2909.

Muleshoe (1935): Oldest of national refuges in Texas, Muleshoe provides winter habitat for waterfowl and the continent's largest wintering population of sandhill cranes. Comprising 5,809 acres in the High Plains of Bailey County, the refuge contains playa lakes, marsh areas, caliche outcroppings and native grasslands. A

nature trail, campground and picnic area are available. Office: Box 549, Muleshoe 79347; 806-946-3341.

San Bernard (1968): Located in Brazoria and Matagorda counties on the Gulf Coast near Freeport, this refuge's 27,414 acres attract migrating waterfowl, including thousands of white-fronted and Canada geese and several duck species, which spend the winter on the refuge.

Habitats, consisting of coastal prairies, salt/mud flats and saltwater and freshwater ponds and potholes, also attract yellow rails, roseate spoonbills, reddish egrets and American bitterns. Visitors enjoy auto and hiking trails, photography, bird watching, fishing, and waterfowl hunting in season. Office: 1212 N. Velasco, #200, Angleton, 77515; 979-849-6062.

Santa Ana (1943): Santa Ana is located on the north bank of the Rio Grande in Hidalgo County. Santa Ana's 2,088 acres of subtropical forest and native brushland are at an ecological crossroads of subtropical, Gulf Coast, Great Plains and Chihuahuan desert habitats.

Santa Ana attracts birders from across the United States who can view many species of Mexican birds as they reach the northern edge of their ranges in South Texas. Also found at Santa Ana are ocelot and jaguarundi, endangered members of the cat family. Visitors enjoy a tram or auto drive, bicycling and hiking trails. Office: Rt. 2, Box 202A, Alamo 78516; 956-784-7500.

Texas Point (1980): Texas Point's 8,900 acres are located in Jefferson County on the upper Gulf Coast, 12 miles east of McFaddin NWR, where they serve a large wintering population of waterfowl as well as migratory birds. The endangered southern bald eagle and peregrine falcon may occasionally be seen during peak fall and spring migrations.

Alligators are commonly observed during the spring, summer and fall months. Activities include wildlife observation, hunting, fishing and crabbing. Access to the refuge is by boat and on foot only. Office: Box 609, Sabine Pass 77655; 409-971-2909.

Trinity River (1994): Established to protect remnant bottomland hardwood forests and associated wetlands, this refuge, located in northern Liberty County off State Highway 787 approximately 15 miles east of Cleveland, provides habitat for wintering, migrating and breeding waterfowl and a variety of other wetland-dependent wildlife. Approximately 18,300 acres of the proposed 20,000-acre refuge have been purchased. A tract south of Liberty includes Champion Lake. Office: Box 10015, Liberty 77575; 936-336-9786. ☆

Texas Wildlife Management Areas

Source: Texas Parks and Wildlife Department; www.tpwd.state.tx.us/wma/index.htm.

Texas Parks and Wildlife Department is currently responsible for managing 51 wildlife management areas (WMAs) totaling approximately three quarters of a million acres. Of these, 32 WMAs are owned in fee title, while 19 are managed under license agreements with other agencies.

Wildlife management areas are used principally for hunting, but many are also used for research, fishing, wildlife viewing, hiking, camping, bicycling and horseback riding, when those activities are compatible with the primary goals for which the WMA was established.

Access to WMAs at times designated for public use is provided by various permits, depending on the activity performed.

Hunting permits include Special ($50 or $100), Regular daily ($10), or Annual ($40).

A Limited Public Use Permit ($10) allows access for such activities as birdwatching, hiking, camping or picnicking and on some WMAs under the Texas Conservation Passport (Gold $50, Silver $25). The Gold Passport also allows entry to state parks.

On most WMAs, restrooms and drinking water are not provided; check with the TPWD at the contacts above before you go.

For further information, contact the Texas Parks and Wildlife Department, 4200 Smith School Rd., Austin 78744; 1-800-792-1112, menu #5, selection #1. ☆

Texas Wildlife Management Areas

1. Candy Cain Abshier
2. Alabama Creek
3. Alazan Bayou
4. Angelina-Neches/Dam B
5. Aquilla
6. Atkinson Island
7. Bannister
8. Big Lake Bottom
9. Black Gap
10. Walter Buck
11. Caddo Lake State Park
12. Caddo National Grasslands
13. Cedar Creek Islands
14. Chaparral
15. Cooper
16. James E. Daughtrey
17. Elephant Mountain
18. Gus Engeling
19. Granger
20. Guadalupe Delta
21. Tony Houseman
22. Sam Houston National Forest

Gene Howe
   23. Gene Howe Unit
   24. W.A. Pat Murphy Unit
25. Keechi Creek
26. Kerr

Las Palomas
   27. Lower Rio Grande Valley Units
   28. Anacua Unit
   29. Ocotillo Unit

30. Lower Neches
31. Mad Island
32. Mason Mountain
33. Matador
34. Matagorda Island
35. Pat Mayse
36. Moore Plantation
37. J.D. Murphree
38. The Nature Center
39. M.O. Neasloney
40. North Toledo Bend
41. Old Sabine Bottom
42. Old Tunnel
43. Peach Point

Playa Lakes
   44. Taylor Lakes Unit
   45. Dimmitt and Armstong Units
46. Redhead Pond
47. Richland Creek
48. Ray Roberts
49. Sierra Diablo
50. Somerville
51. Nannie M. Stringfellow
52. Tawakoni
53. Welder Flats
54. White Oak Creek
55. D.R. Wintermann

Texas Wildlife Management Areas

(Acreage)	County	Day Use Only	Hunting	Fishing	Camping	Wildlife Viewing	Hiking	Interpretive Trail	Auto Tour	Bicycling	Horseback Riding	Comments
Candy Cain Abshier (207)	Chambers	★				★						Excellent birding spring and fall
Alabama Creek (14,561)	Trinity		★	★	★	★	★		★	★	★	In Davy Crockett Nat. Forest
Alazan Bayou (2,063)	Nacogdoches		★	★	★	★					★	
Angelina-Neches/Dam B (12,636)	Jasper/Tyler		★	★	★	★	★		★			
Aquilla (9,826)	Hill	★	★	★		★	★		★			
Atkinson Island (150)	Harris	★		★		★						Boat access only
Bannister (25,695)	San Augustine		★	★	★	★			★	★		In Angelina National Forest
Big Lake Bottom (4,071)	Anderson	★	★	★		★						2,870 acres available to public
Black Gap (119,000)	Brewster		★	★	★	★	★		★	★	★	NW of Big Bend National Park
Walter Buck (2,155)	Kimble	★	★			★	★		★			Camping at adjacent state park
Caddo Lake WMA (8,129)	Marion/Harrison		★	★	★	★	★			★	★	
Caddo Natl Grasslands (16,150)	Fannin		★	★	★	★	★				★	
Cedar Creek Islands (160)	Henderson	★		★		★						Access by boat only
Chaparral (15,200)	La Salle/Dimmit	★		★	★	★	★		★	★		
Cooper (14,160)	Delta/Hopkins	★	★	★		★	★					Camping at nearby state park
James E. Daughtrey (4,400)	Live Oak/McMullen	★	★		★	★						Primitive camping for hunters
Elephant Mountain (23,147)	Brewster		★		★	★	★		★			Primitive camping only
Gus Engling (10,958)	Anderson		★	★	★	★	★		★	★	★	
Granger (11,116)	Williamson		★	★	★	★	★			★		Primitive camping only
Guadalupe Delta (6,594)	Calhoun/Refugio	★	★	★		★	★			★		Freshwater Marsh
Tony Houseman (3,313)	Orange		★	★	★	★	★					
Sam Houston Natl Forest (161,508)	San Jacinto/Walker		★	★	★	★	★		★	★	★	Also Montgomery County
Gene Howe (5,882)	Hemphill		★	★	★	★	★		★	★	★	Riding March–August only
Keechi Creek (1,500)	Leon		★									
Kerr (6,493)	Kerr		★	★		★		★	★	★		On Guadalupe River
Las Palomas:												
Anacua Unit (222)	Cameron		★			★						
Lower Rio Grande Valley Units (3,314)	Cameron/Hidalgo	★	★			★	★					Also Starr & Willacy Counties
Ocotillo Unit (2,082)	Presidio	★	★	★	★	★	★					
Lower Neches (7,998)	Orange	★	★			★						Coastal marsh
Mad Island (7,200)	Matagorda	★	★			★						Coastal wetlands
Mason Mountain (5,301)	Mason	★	★									Restricted access
Matador (28,183)	Cottle		★	★	★	★	★	★	★	★	★	Primitive camping
Matagorda Island (43,900)	Calhoun		★	★	★	★	★			★		Access by boat only
Pat Mayse (8,925)	Lamar		★	★	★	★	★			★	★	
Moore Plantation (26,519)	Sabine/Jasper		★	★	★	★	★		★	★	★	In Sabine National Forest
J.D. Murphree (24,250)	Jefferson	★	★	★		★						Access by boat only
The Nature Center (82)	Smith	★				★		★				Primarily for school groups
M.O. Neasloney (100)	Gonzales	★				★	★	★				Primarily for school groups
North Toldeo Bend (3,650)	Shelby		★	★	★	★	★				★	Limited use of horses
Old Sabine Bottom (5,158)	Smith		★	★	★	★	★			★	★	Canoeing
Old Tunnel (16)	Kendall	★				★	★	★				Bat-viewing April–October
Peach Point (10,311)	Brazoria		★	★		★	★	★		★		On Texas Coastal Birding Trail
Playa Lakes (1,492 in 3 units)	Castro/Donley	★	★			★	★					Hunting only on Donley Co. unit
Redhead Pond (37)	Nueces	★				★						Freshwater wetland
Richland Creek (13,796)	Freestone/Navarro		★	★	★	★	★		★	★	★	Primitive camping only
Ray Roberts (40,920)	Cooke/Denton	★	★	★		★	★					Also Grayson Co.
Sierra Diablo (11,625)	Hudspeth/Culberson		★									Restricted acess
Somerville (3,180)	Burleson/Lee	★	★	★		★	★			★		Camping at nearby state park
Nannie M. Stringfellow (3,644)	Brazoria		★									Open for special hunts only.
Tawakoni (2,335)	Hunt/Van Zandt		★	★	★	★	★				★	
Welder Flats (1,480)	Calhoun	★		★		★						Boat access only
White Oak Creek (25,777)	Bowie/Cass/Morris	★	★	★		★	★				★	Also Titus Co.
D.R. Wintermann (246)	Wharton					★						Restricted access; bird refuge

Weather

A post oak silhouetted by the sunset near College Station. Ron Billings photo; Texas Forest Service.

Highlights 2007 & 2008

Monthly Summaries 2007 & 2008

Extremes 2007 & 2008

Temperatures & Precipitation 2007 & 2008

Tornado & Drought Records

Destructive Weather 1766–2008

Records by County

Weather

Source: Unless otherwise noted, this information is provided by Texas State Climatologist John W. Nielsen-Gammon, Assistant State Climatologist Brent McRoberts and undergraduate assistant Zach Adian, Texas A&M University, College Station.

Weather Highlights 2007

March 28: In the Panhandle, 24 tornadoes, including four F-3s, were reported, causing more than $3 million in damage.

April 24: Severe thunderstorms moved across South Texas, producing a nighttime F-3 tornado that killed 10 people along the Texas-Mexico border. The tornado destroyed one elementary school, 59 manufactured homes and 57 houses, resulting in $80 million in damage.

June 17–18: Heavy rain across North Texas produced flooding that led to five deaths and destroyed hundreds of homes. The towns of Sherman and Gainesville sustained the most damage.

June 26–27: Severe storms in Central Texas produced persistent heavy rain, including up to 18 inches around Marble Falls. The Dallas area experienced its second wettest June, after 1928.

Aug. 15–16: Tropical Storm **Erin** developed as a depression in the Gulf of Mexico on the 14th, reaching tropical-storm intensity on the 15th. Erin made landfall near Lamar with maximum sustained winds of 40 mph. About 10 inches of rain fell across Houston and San Antonio. Erin was blamed for 13 deaths and for damaging many homes by flooding.

Sept. 13: Hurricane **Humberto** made landfall just east of Galveston as a Category-1 hurricane, with maximum sustained winds of 85 mph, becoming the first hurricane to make landfall in the United States since 2005. Humberto brought heavy rain to the Texas-Louisiana coastline, was responsible for one death and left about 100,000 residents without power.

Monthly Summaries 2007

In **January,** El Niño conditions were entrenched after forming in mid-September 2006, and every part of Texas experienced above-average precipitation and abnormally cool temperatures. The Edwards Plateau was especially affected and recorded average temperatures more than 4 degrees below normal. The month was initially warm, but on the 11th, a strong Arctic front moved into Texas. It combined with another rain-producing upper-atmospheric system, and icy conditions plagued areas

Climatic Data Regions of Texas

from the DFW Metroplex to Houston. Temperatures remained below freezing in most of the state Jan. 15–17, allowing ice to accumulate. Another front pushed across the state Jan. 21–22. Drought-stricken areas from North-Central to East Texas received beneficial rainfall, relieving some of the drought stress.

February was very dry across the entire state as El Niño continued to weaken. Unlike January, all of Texas reported below-average precipitation, with the Southern, South-Central and the Upper Coast regions receiving less than 10 percent of normal February precipitation. Consequently, February 2007 was the driest February ever recorded in Galveston (0.03 inches); the 2nd driest in College Station and the 4th driest in San Antonio. Mean temperatures remained within 1 degree of February monthly averages in most areas. A strong, dry cold front moved across the state on the 15th, dropping

	Average Temperatures 2007											Precipitation 2007 (Inches)									
	High Plains	Low Plains	North Central	East Texas	Trans-Pecos	Edwards Plateau	South Central	Upper Coast	South Texas	Lower Valley	High Plains	Low Plains	North Central	East Texas	Trans-Pecos	Edwards Plateau	South Central	Upper Coast	South Texas	Lower Valley
Jan.	33.2	38.1	41.6	44.5	42.0	42.2	48.9	51.1	51.0	56.2	1.06	1.55	4.17	8.28	2.03	2.88	6.32	7.52	4.01	2.23
Feb.	40.4	44.3	47.4	48.4	50.8	50.0	55.1	55.3	58.3	62.8	0.23	0.32	0.64	1.66	0.17	0.35	0.20	1.24	0.10	0.46
Mar.	54.6	59.8	62.8	63.7	60.0	62.4	66.5	66.5	68.9	72.5	4.15	4.60	6.84	3.81	1.38	5.75	6.26	5.63	3.23	1.17
April	53.5	58.4	60.6	61.9	62.8	62.4	65.9	66.6	68.8	72.6	1.46	2.04	2.37	2.76	1.13	2.24	2.86	4.86	1.48	0.90
May	64.5	68.5	71.9	73.1	70.5	70.9	75.4	75.8	77.1	79.6	3.88	4.99	8.84	6.67	2.36	6.82	4.90	5.98	6.10	3.54
June	72.6	75.8	77.7	79.5	78.4	77.4	80.8	81.3	82.0	85.0	3.22	5.93	10.10	6.64	2.00	6.17	4.88	4.50	5.75	2.88
July	76.4	78.4	79.6	79.6	78.8	78.2	80.8	80.9	81.6	84.3	1.65	2.08	4.85	8.53	2.61	4.47	12.24	13.72	10.00	8.51
Aug.	78.8	81.2	83.6	83.9	80.1	80.4	83.3	84.1	83.8	85.0	2.33	4.54	1.81	2.46	1.99	4.20	4.17	5.79	2.25	2.36
Sep.	72.1	75.8	77.7	78.3	76.5	76.7	79.8	80.2	80.7	82.7	2.61	1.92	3.84	2.38	2.04	2.57	2.52	4.92	3.16	3.95
Oct.	62.7	66.9	68.2	68.7	67.9	68.6	72.2	72.5	73.9	76.7	0.33	0.38	2.12	2.40	0.27	0.86	1.60	2.60	0.71	1.25
Nov.	48.8	53.8	58.2	59.1	55.5	58.2	63.3	63.7	65.5	69.3	0.26	0.55	1.59	2.85	0.67	1.01	2.12	3.58	0.66	0.40
Dec.	38.9	43.5	46.9	51.1	47.9	49.4	56.8	58.9	59.6	65.8	1.22	1.35	1.73	3.65	0.33	0.49	0.80	1.55	0.19	0.20
Ann.	58.0	62.0	64.7	66.0	64.3	64.7	69.1	69.7	70.9	74.4	22.40	30.25	48.90	52.09	16.98	37.81	48.87	61.89	37.64	27.25

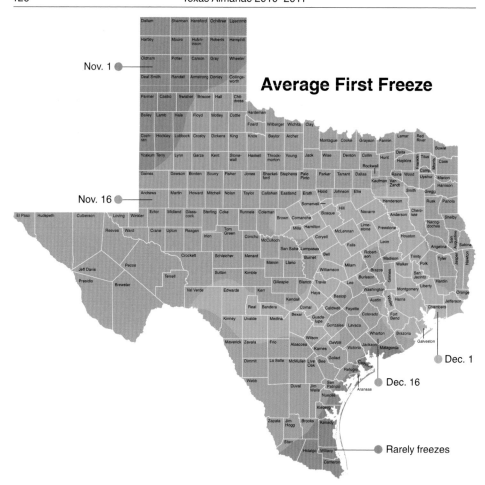

Average First Freeze

Nov. 1 ●

Nov. 16 ●

Dec. 1 ●

Dec. 16 ●

Rarely freezes ●

minimum temperatures to below record levels in many areas, though temperatures warmed considerably later in the month. Severe weather was minimal, but there were three tornado reports, six hail reports, and five severe wind reports.

March brought abundant rainfall to Texas, breaking or approaching records in some areas. Amarillo reported its third-wettest March with 4 inches of rain, and Lubbock had its wettest March ever with 5.94 inches, shattering the old record of 3.56 inches. San Antonio also reported its wettest March ever with a monthly total of 7.06 inches, breaking a record of 6.12 inches set in March 1992. Significant rainfall in March offset the lack of rain in February. Temperatures were above average in all major cities. North-Central Texas had the largest departures from normal March temperatures, including Wichita Falls, which had a mean monthly temperature of 61.4 degrees, 7.2 degrees above normal.

April began slightly warmer than average across the state, but temperatures plunged when a strong cold front moved through on the 7th. Along with numerous record lows, select weather stations reported record snowfall totals, including College Station, which reported its latest spring snowfall ever. Mean temperatures were generally a few degrees below average across the state, though precipitation was more variable. The Trans-Pecos, Low

2007 Weather Extremes	
Lowest Temp.: Bushland, Potter Co., Feb. 15	–4° F
Vega, Oldham Co., Feb. 15	–4° F
Highest Temp.: Terlingua, Brewster Co., June 7	110°F
Wink, Winkler Co., June 18	110°F
Presidio, Presidio Co., June 27	110°F
24-hour Precip.: Sisterdale, Kendall Co., July 17	11.70"
Monthly Precip.: Matagorda, Matagorda Co., July	26.42"
Least Annual Precip.: La Tuna, El Paso Co.	7.12"
Greatest Annual Precip.: Houston Heights, Harris Co.	90.21"

Rolling Plains, Edwards Plateau, Upper Coast and South-Central regions reported above-normal precipitation, while the High Plains, Southern and East Texas regions reported below-normal precipitation. Severe weather reports were numerous, including 49 tornado reports, 189 hail reports and 115 severe wind reports. The 21st was particularly active with 16 tornadoes forming throughout the state.

May was wet across much of the state, though the amount varied. Several weather stations recorded at least 10 days of measurable precipitation. In late May, Waco, Brownsville and Houston each set daily maximum rainfall totals during the same three-day period. Galveston, however, received only half of its normal monthly rainfall. Mean temperatures remained near average, though the North-Central region had temperatures 3–4 degrees cooler than normal and East

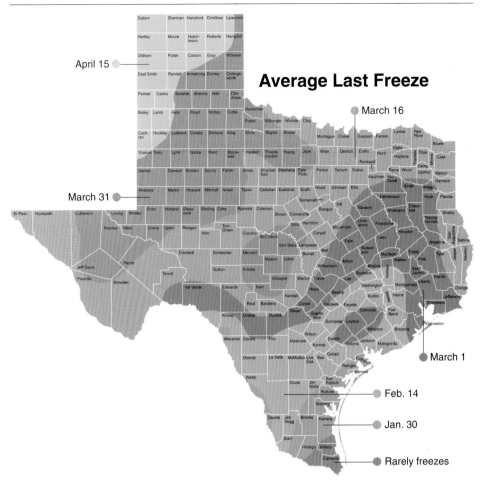

Average Last Freeze

April 15

March 31

March 16

March 1

Feb. 14

Jan. 30

Rarely freezes

Texas was slightly warmer than average. Midland, in particular, was far below average, recording an average maximum temperature of 78.4 degrees, about 8 degrees below normal. Several severe weather events were reported during the month, especially on the 2nd and 30th, when dozens of wind, hail and tornado reports were documented in Central and West Texas.

June began with a series of upper-level disturbances that brought abundant tropical moisture from the Gulf of Mexico. Prolonged periods of excessive rainfall, especially across portions of North Texas and the Hill Country, caused flooding and extensive property damage. Only far North Texas, West Texas and the Upper Coast recorded below-average rainfall. The DFW Metroplex recorded more than 11 inches of rain, while Waco recorded 8.76 inches for the month, including 3.37 inches on the 17th. Although Houston recorded 16 days with measureable precipitation, only 3.07 inches of rain fell, about half of Houston's normal June rainfall. The heavy rainfall and extensive cloud cover kept temperatures near average.

In **July,** an upper-level trough stalled over Texas, resulting in excessive rainfall across much of the state, particularly the Upper Coast and South-Central regions. Victoria and Corpus Christi received precipitation totals of 20.34 inches and 18.13 inches, respectively. Corpus Christi received more than half of its July total on the 2nd, setting a new daily rainfall record. The extreme July rain also soaked portions of the Hill Country, including

11.76 inches reported for the month in San Antonio, its 2nd wettest July on record. The abundant rainfall kept temperatures below average across the state, except in extreme South Texas. Most areas remained well below average, though high pressure late in the month resulted in more typical summer conditions.

During most of **August,** high pressure across the southern plains resulted in more typical summer temperatures than what occurred in July. Temperatures in the Northeast were particularly hot, running about 3.5 degrees above normal, and temperatures in the rest of Texas were close to average. Precipitation patterns varied across the state, the main causes being Tropical Storm Erin, which made landfall on the 16th, and the persistent high pressure in place across Northeast Texas. Erin's path took it toward the Edwards Plateau region, with San Angelo and Abilene recording 6.55 inches and 7.07 inches, respectively, for the month. Houston recorded 2.59 inches of rain on the 16th with Erin's landfall and 8.05 inches overall for August. High pressure left DFW very dry, reporting only 0.35 inches of rain.

September was warm across the entire state due to a persistent ridge of high pressure anchored over the southeastern United States. DFW and Galveston recorded their 10th warmest Septembers on record, while Houston experienced its 8th warmest September. Monthly precipitation totals were highly variable, with most areas receiving anywhere from 50 percent to

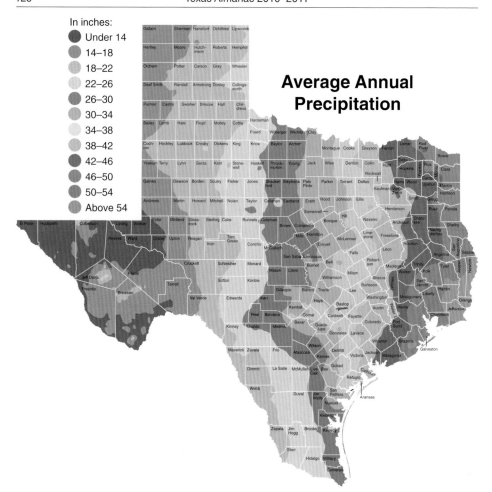

In inches:
- Under 14
- 14–18
- 18–22
- 22–26
- 26–30
- 30–34
- 34–38
- 38–42
- 42–46
- 46–50
- 50–54
- Above 54

Average Annual Precipitation

200 percent of normal monthly precipitation. Hurricane Humberto made landfall as a Category-1 hurricane near High Island, along the Upper Texas Coast, on the morning of the 13th and had maximum sustained winds of 85 mph. Port Arthur received 5.56 inches of rain, sustained winds of 56 mph and gusts up to 84 mph.

October was another warm and dry month. A zonal wind pattern across the U.S. acted as a barrier to any significant cold fronts. Consequently, average daily high temperatures were 5–6 degrees above average, and mean monthly temperatures ranged from 1–5 degrees above average. The warmest areas were the High Plains and North-Central regions. Precipitation totals were low across the state, especially in parts of West Texas, the Panhandle and the Hill County. El Paso received only 0.08 inches of rain, and Midland only 0.16 inches for the month. Half of the major Texas weather stations recorded less than an inch of rain. The first significant cold front of the season arrived in late October, plummeting temperatures to as low as the 30s in some areas.

November weather was similar to October, with above-average mean monthly temperatures keeping the state unseasonably mild. A moderately strong La Niña in the equatorial Pacific is attributed to the numerous record high temperatures recorded in Texas. Similarly, rainfall was limited over much of the state. The Coastal Bend, South-Central and High Plains regions recorded less than half their normal precipitation, though the West

and Southeast regions reported near-normal rainfall. A strong Canadian cold front plowed through Texas over the Thanksgiving weekend, and from the Nov. 22–25, Midland, El Paso, Lubbock and Amarillo set daily snowfall records. El Paso's total snowfall of 4 inches on the 24th broke a record of 2 inches set in 1878. Snow flurries fell as far east as DFW. The end of November brought the return of warmer-than-average temperatures as a series of weak cold fronts moved through the state.

As La Niña conditions continued, **December** remained dry across much of the state, except in the Panhandle and Brazos Valley. The Coastal and Edwards Plateau regions received less than one-fifth their normal December precipitation. Temperatures were above-average for the entire state, especially along the Gulf Coast, where the mean monthly temperatures were 4–5 degrees above average.

Weather Highlights 2008

April 9: Severe weather produced 14 tornadoes across north-central and west-central Texas. Nearly 180,000 homes and business were without power in the Dallas-Fort Worth area. An F-1 tornado near San Angelo caused $6 million in damage, and $2 million of damage occurred elsewhere.

July 23–24: Hurricane **Dolly** strengthened over the warm waters of the Gulf of Mexico to a Category-2 hurricane, with maximum sustained winds near 100

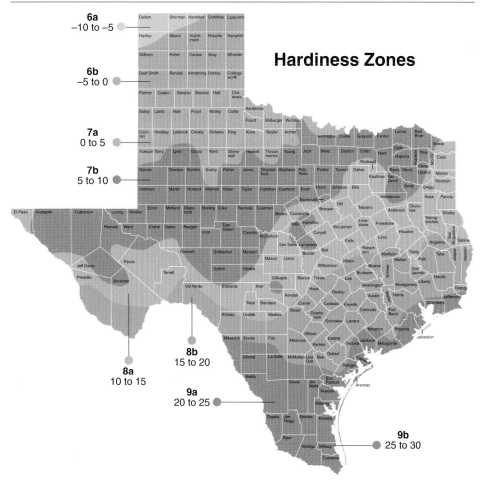

Hardiness Zones

6a
−10 to −5

6b
−5 to 0

7a
0 to 5

7b
5 to 10

8a
10 to 15

8b
15 to 20

9a
20 to 25

9b
25 to 30

mph, before making landfall at South Padre Island. Fifteen inches of rain was reported near Harlingen. Gov. Rick Perry declared 14 counties in South Texas a disaster area, and damage estimates totaled $1.05 billion, including a complete loss of the Rio Grande cotton crop. More than 212,000 customers lost power.

Aug. 5: Tropical Storm **Edouard** developed as a tropical depression in the northern Gulf of Mexico on Aug. 3. It strengthened to a tropical storm later that day, reaching a peak of 65 mph before making landfall east of Galveston. Damage was fairly minor, totaling only about $250,000.

Sept. 13–15: Hurricane **Ike** made landfall over Galveston at 2:10 a.m. on the 13th, causing catastrophic damage in southeast Texas. The Category-2 storm had sustained winds of 110 mph, a storm surge of more than 20 feet and widespread coastal flooding. Thirty-seven people are known to have lost their lives in Texas as a result of Ike and dozens were declared missing. About 100,000 homes were flooded in Texas, with thousands of homes and businesses either heavily damaged or destroyed. Galveston was declared uninhabitable, and an estimated 2.8 million to 4.5 million people were without power for several weeks. Damage from Ike in U.S. coastal and inland areas was estimated at $24 billion, making it the third-costliest U.S. hurricane, behind Andrew, 1992, and Katrina, 2005.

2008 Weather Extremes

Lowest Temp.: Stratford, Sherman Co., Feb. 17–18 .... 0° F
Highest Temp.: Wink, Winkler Co., Aug. 16 ....115°F
Castolon, Brewster Co., Aug. 18 ....115°F
24-hour Precip: New Caney, Montgomery Co., Sept. 14 ..... 11.48"
Monthly Precip.: Santa Rosa, Hidalgo Co., July.................18.67"
Least Annual Precip.: Balmorhea, Reeves Co....................8.24"
Greatest Annual Precip.: Liberty, Liberty Co.....................66.25"

Monthly Summaries 2008

In **January,** La Niña was especially pronounced, with sea surface temperatures as much as 2 degrees below normal. Many major weather stations recorded below-average temperatures, especially in Central and Southeast Texas, an effect typically not seen with La Niña in the South. Though several cold fronts affected the state, the prevailing pattern prevented any significant intrusions of Arctic air. Precipitation followed more typical La Niña patterns in all areas except the Coast. Most of Texas received less than half of normal January precipitation, with west and west-central Texas receiving less than one-tenth of an inch. Upper-level disturbances provided above-average rainfall in coastal areas.

February continued the powerful temperature effects of La Niña. Mean monthly temperatures ranged from 1 degree above normal in Amarillo to 7 degrees above normal in San Antonio. The largest temperature departures occurred in the typically warmest areas: San Antonio's average high was 76.3 degrees, about 9 degrees above normal. Temperatures in San Angelo, Del Rio and areas in the Edwards Plateau were also above normal. No significant cold fronts entered the state, and the dry conditions continued throughout. Parts of West and South Texas were especially dry, with Del Rio and Brownsville receiving only 0.02 inches and 0.04 inches of rain, respectively. East and North Texas received some rain.

March was more active than February, and it continued the trend of above-normal temperatures. Extreme northeast Texas experienced the most above-normal temperatures. The DFW area recorded 3.6 degrees above normal, the highest departure, followed by Wichita Falls, with 3 degrees above normal. Rainfall varied widely across the state with regions in the extreme north, west and south receiving little to no rainfall. A large area of North-Central Texas, however, recorded more than twice its normal March rainfall. San Angelo recorded 4.64 inches, more than 4.5 times normal. Texas experienced several days of severe weather, including hail and high winds across North Texas on the 31st.

La Niña weakened further in **April,** though conditions were still present, and precipitation varied throughout the state. North-Central and Southern regions recorded above-average rainfall, while other regions saw little to no precipitation. Waco recorded more than 5 inches of rain, while El Paso and Del Rio recorded a trace and 0.06 inches, respectively. Temperatures were generally slightly above average. Severe weather events increased in late April. Several hail, high wind and tornado events occurred across north and central Texas, with at least four reports of 4.25-inch or larger hail. The most powerful tornadoes were an F-2 in Bowie County on the 10th and another F-2 in Tarrant County on the 23rd.

May was very dry for most of south and southwestern Texas. Notably dry cities included Galveston, Victoria and El Paso, which received 1 percent, 6 percent, and 8 percent of normal precipitation, respectively. East Texas and the Panhandle saw more rainfall, though most areas did not reach their normal average precipitation for the month. Temperatures across the state ran moderately above average, generally from 1–4 degrees above normal May temperatures. Central Texas was most

Brownsville police officers remove a storefront from Elizabeth Street in downtown Brownsville as Hurricane Dolly blows in on July 23, 2008. Erich Schlegel photo.

affected by the warm weather, while temperatures along the coast, though slightly warmer than normal, were tempered by the sea. Notable severe weather events included 13 tornadoes and nearly 100 hail reports on the May 13–15, and more than 60 hail reports on the 26th, along with some tornadic activity.

June remained dry in all regions except the High Plains and Low Rolling Plains. San Antonio, El Paso and Victoria received 0 percent, 1 percent and 2 percent of normal precipitation for June, respectively. San Antonio and most of South-Central Texas experienced one of its driest Junes on record. An unusually strong cold front made its way through the state in late June, which led to some much-needed rainfall across the state. Temperatures were very warm, with departures from the monthly mean temperature of 3–6 degrees above normal. Only coastal areas did not exceed 100 degrees at least once during the month, though most reached at least 97 degrees.

July's big weather story was Hurricane Dolly, the first hurricane to hit the mainland United States in 2008. Dolly came ashore on July 23 near South Padre Island as a Category-1 hurricane after weakening slightly as it advanced in the Gulf. Rainfall was Dolly's biggest contribution, with Brownsville recording more than 6.5 inches in 24 hours and 13 inches for the month. Corpus Christi received nearly 9 inches of precipitation for the

	Average Temperatures 2008											**Precipitation 2008** (Inches)										
	High Plains	Low Plains	North Central	East Texas	Trans-Pecos	Edwards Plateau	South Central	Upper Coast	South Texas	Lower Valley	High Plains	Low Plains	North Central	East Texas	Trans-Pecos	Edwards Plateau	South Central	Upper Coast	South Texas	Lower Valley
Jan.	38.2	42.6	44.3	45.7	46.0	46.2	51.9	53.1	54.6	59.5	0.06	0.06	0.58	2.45	0.26	0.28	1.82	5.43	0.86	1.68
Feb.	43.7	48.0	51.0	52.8	53.0	53.8	60.5	60.4	64.8	69.0	0.42	0.60	1.47	4.44	0.01	0.20	0.92	2.91	0.11	0.11
Mar.	50.2	54.8	57.5	59.5	57.7	59.1	63.9	63.9	67.7	70.8	0.20	1.74	5.62	6.53	0.11	2.46	2.08	2.65	0.98	0.10
April	57.4	62.6	64.0	65.2	65.1	66.4	69.9	69.8	73.8	76.3	0.62	2.01	4.20	3.45	0.04	1.38	2.33	2.11	1.41	1.68
May	67.4	72.2	73.1	72.6	74.1	75.9	78.2	77.3	81.5	82.5	2.45	2.81	3.33	5.27	0.61	1.65	1.21	1.75	1.84	1.02
June	78.8	82.8	83.0	81.5	83.9	84.0	84.9	83.3	86.5	85.6	2.49	2.94	1.86	3.95	1.19	1.88	0.63	2.83	0.27	0.39
July	77.6	82.3	84.8	83.4	79.1	81.8	83.2	83.0	83.0	82.9	2.57	1.18	0.91	0.95	3.07	1.28	3.61	3.78	6.14	12.73
Aug.	76.1	80.2	82.6	82.0	77.8	81.0	83.8	83.1	84.1	84.8	4.13	4.30	4.31	7.14	2.75	4.79	4.16	7.34	5.84	4.41
Sep.	67.4	71.2	74.0	73.7	69.8	73.1	78.3	78.0	78.9	80.0	2.54	3.68	1.80	4.97	3.35	1.17	0.87	5.73	2.02	7.54
Oct.	58.9	63.0	65.5	64.5	64.2	65.4	70.0	69.5	71.9	75.0	3.81	3.25	2.03	2.68	1.06	1.53	1.40	2.64	0.88	1.32
Nov.	49.7	54.1	57.1	56.5	54.0	56.9	63.4	63.4	64.9	68.9	0.11	0.10	1.64	4.26	0.05	0.22	0.83	3.77	0.23	1.18
Dec.	40.4	44.3	46.3	47.9	47.8	48.6	54.2	55.8	57.0	61.8	0.10	0.04	0.51	2.08	0.11	0.18	0.57	1.53	0.32	0.24
Ann.	58.8	63.2	65.3	65.4	64.4	66.0	70.2	70.1	72.4	74.8	19.50	22.71	28.26	48.17	12.61	17.02	20.43	42.47	20.90	32.40

month. Elsewhere, dry conditions continued, particularly in central Texas areas, where most weather stations received less than 50 percent of normal rainfall. Mean temperatures in the western half of Texas remained slightly below average, while the eastern half was slightly warmer than normal. In West Texas, temperatures were relatively cool in early July, but warmed to near normal by month's end.

August brought above-average precipitation to most of Texas, the only such month in 2008. Tropical Storm Edouard, a weak tropical system, contributed to drought relief as it moved into Southeast Texas. A strong low-pressure system then swept through Texas, bringing rainfall to many areas. Del Rio and Waco received more than 500 percent of their normal rainfall, with record-breaking totals of 11.32 inches and 10.33 inches, respectively. West and North Texas were slightly cooler than average and East Texas slightly warmer than average. Early August was much warmer than usual, while later in the month temperatures were much cooler than normal. Highs around Texas remained in the low- to mid-80s for several days during mid-month, providing relief from the intense heat of the first two weeks.

September began fairly warm, with temperatures a degree or two above average for many areas. In the early morning of the 13th, the eye of Hurricane Ike made landfall in Galveston and brought catastrophic destruction to that city and surrounding coastal cities, including Surfside Beach, which was submerged by Ike's massive surge. This giant Category-2 hurricane (which had been a Category 4) caused more than $30 billion in damage, the third-costliest United States hurricane on record. Statewide temperatures dropped as a cold front arrived during mid-month, after Ike had moved on. Near normal temperatures continued as Texas experienced cloud-free skies until a late front cooled temperatures below average. Temperatures statewide were about 1–3 degrees below average for September as a whole.

October, as is often the case, was a transitional month, with large variability in temperatures and precipitation. Several cold fronts moved through Texas, bringing rain to North Texas in particular and leaving most other areas cooler and drier. Most of South, East and Central Texas recorded below-average temperatures, while some High Plains and West Texas areas were slightly warmer than normal. Most temperatures were near average due to cooler-than-normal minimum temperatures and warmer-than-normal maximum temperatures. Victoria's average minimum temperature ran 6 degrees below normal, the most substantial temperature departure of any major weather station. Because of a dry summer (with the exception of August), several areas experienced large rainfall deficits since the beginning of 2008.

November was very similar to the first half of 2008, with temperatures around 1.5–3 degrees above normal across the state. Most of the warm temperatures were due to relatively large departures of average maximum temperatures. Several weather stations recorded mean maximum temperatures at least 3.5–4.5 degrees above average. While several cold fronts cooled nighttime temperatures substantially, daytime temperatures typically recovered quickly to above-average levels. Precipitation deficits increased as very dry conditions plagued the state. Except for the Upper Coast and areas

Meteorological Data

Source: Updated as of July 2009 by the National Climatic Data Center. Additional data for these locations are listed by county in the table of Texas temperature, freeze, growing season and precipitation records, beginning on page 143.

City	Temperature						Precipitation					Relative Humidity		Wind			Sun
	Record High	Month & Year	Record Low	Month & Year	No. Days Max. 90° and Above	No. Days Min. 32° and Below	Maximum in 24 Hours	Month & Year	Snowfall (Mean Annual)	Max. Snowfall in 24 Hours	Month & Year	6:00 a.m., CST	Noon, CST	Speed, MPH (Mean Annual)	Highest MPH	Month & Year	Percent Possible Sunshine
Abilene	111	8/1943	-9	1/1947	96	51	6.70	9/1961	5.7	9.3	4/1996	73	55	11.9	55	4/1998	70
Amarillo	108	6/1998+	-16	2/1899	62	113	6.75	5/1951	17.9	20.6	3/1934	73	51	13.5	60	6/1994	73
Austin	112	9/2000	-2	1/1949	109	17	15.00	9/1931	0.6	9.7	11/1937	82	62	8.7	52	5/1997	60
Brownsville	106	3/1984	16	12/1989	124	2	12.19	9/1967	**	**	3/1993	89	67	11.3	51	9/1996	60
Corpus Christi	109	9/2000	13	12/1989	110	6	8.92	8/1980	**	2.3	12/2004	89	68	12.0	56	5/1999	60
Dallas-Fort Worth	113	6/1980	-2	1/1949	97	36	5.91	10/1959	2.6	12.1	1/1964	80	61	10.7	73	8/1959	61
Del Rio	112	6/1988	10	12/1989	131	15	17.03	8/1998	1.0	8.6	1/1985	75	62	9.5	60	8/1970	84
El Paso	114	6/1994	-8	1/1962	109	60	6.50	7/1881	6.1	16.8	12/1987	57	27	8.8	84	3/1977	88
Galveston	104	9/2000	8	2/1899	29	5	13.91	10/1901	0.2	15.4	2/1895	83	72	11.0	*100	9/1900	62
†Houston	109	9/2000+	7	12/1989	100	18	11.02	6/2001	0.5	2.0	1/1963	89	67	7.6	51	8/1983	59
Lubbock	114	6/1994	-17	2/1933	80	86	7.46	9/2008	10.4	16.3	1/1983	73	51	12.4	70	3/1952	72
Midland-Odessa	116	6/1994	-11	2/1985+	101	62	5.99	7/1961	5.0	9.8	12/1998	71	48	11.1	67	2/1960	74
Port Arthur-Beaumont	108	8/2000	3	12/1899	82	13	17.16	9/1980	0.3	4.4	2/1960	90	69	9.6	105	8/2005	58
San Angelo	111	7/1960+	-4	12/1989	105	51	6.25	9/1980	3.1	7.4	1/1978	77	55	10.3	75	4/1969	70
San Antonio	111	9/2000	0	1/1949	111	22	13.35	10/1998	0.8	13.2	1/1985	83	60	9.1	48	7/1979	70
Victoria	111	9/2000	9	12/1989	107	11	9.87	4/1991	0.3	2.1	1/1985	90	66	9.9	99	7/1963	49
Waco	112	8/1969	-5	1/1949	111	34	7.98	12/1991	1.1	7.0	1/1949	83	62	11.0	69	6/1961	59
Wichita Falls	117	6/1980	-12	1/1947	103	64	6.22	9/1980	5.5	9.7	3/1989	80	57	11.6	69	6/2002	60
§Shreveport, LA	109	9/2000+	3	1/1962	89	37	10.44	4/1991	1.8	5.6	1/1982	86	63	8.3	63	5/2000	64

*100 mph recorded at 6:15 p.m., Sept. 8, 1900, just before the anemometer blew away. Maximum velocity was estimated to be 120 mph from the northeast between 7:30 p.m. and 8:30 p.m.
†The official Houston station was moved from near downtown to Intercontinental Airport, 12 miles north of the old station.
+ Also recorded on earlier dates, months or years.
§Shreveport is included because it is near the boundary line and its data can be considered representative of Texas' east border.
**Trace, an amount too small to measure.

near Dallas, the state received about one-quarter or less of its normal precipitation. San Antonio reported 0.01 inches, while Midland and Del Rio recorded only a trace of rain. Central Texas was exceptionally dry and received an exceptional drought designation by the U.S. Drought Monitor.

In **December,** drought conditions worsened in the state, with weather stations from the High Plains to the Edwards Plateau recording less than 20 percent of normal monthly precipitation. No major station received even three-quarters of normal precipitation. Fire hazards were most prevalent in the Hill Country, which was under exceptional drought conditions. Except for parts of the Upper Coast, temperatures were warmer than average, especially in the High Plains, Lower Valley and Trans-Pecos. Several cold fronts, including a few bitterly cold Arctic masses, dropped temperatures to single digits on some nights. Amarillo's high temperature on the 15th was 15 degrees, and its low was 9 degrees. ☆

Some homes remain standing while others were destroyed in Crystal Beach along the Bolivar Peninsula following Hurricane Ike, which hit the Texas coast on Sept. 13, 2008. Brad Loper photo.

Extreme Weather Records in Texas

Temperature

Lowest	-23°F	Tulia	Feb. 12, 1899
	-23°F	Seminole	Feb. 8, 1933
Highest	120°F	Seymour	Aug. 12, 1936
	120°F	Monahans	June 28, 1994
Coldest Winter			1898–1899

Wind Velocity

Highest sustained wind

145 mph SE	Matagorda	Sept. 11, 1961
145 mph NE	Port Lavaca	Sept. 11, 1961

Highest peak gust

180 mph SW	Aransas Pass	Aug. 3, 1970
180 mph WSW	Robstown	Aug. 3, 1970

These winds occurred during Hurricane Carla in 1961 and Hurricane Celia in 1970.

Tornadoes

Since 1950, there have been six tornadoes of the F5 category, that is, with winds between 261–318 mph.

Waco	McLennan County	May 11, 1953
Wichita Falls	Wichita County	April 3, 1964
Lubbock	Lubbock County	May 11, 1970
Valley Mills	McLennan County	May 6, 1973
Brownwood	Brown County	April 19, 1976
Jarrell	Williamson County	May 27, 1997

Rainfall

Wettest year statewide		1941	42.62 in.
Driest year statewide		1917	14.30 in.
Most annual	Clarksville	1873	109.38 in.
Least annual	Presidio	1956	1.64 in.
Most in 24 hours†	Alvin	July 25-26, 1979	43.00 in.
Most in 18 hours	Thrall	Sept. 9, 1921	36.40 in.

†Unofficial estimate of rainfall during Tropical Storm Claudette. Greatest 24-hour rainfall at an official site occurred at Albany, Shackelford County, Aug. 4, 1978: 29.05 inches.

Hail

(Hailstones six inches or greater, since 1950)

8.00 in.	Winkler County	May 31, 1960
7.50 in.	Young County	April 14, 1965
6.00 in.	Ward County	May 10, 1991
7.05 in.	Burleson County	Dec. 17, 1995

Snowfall

65.0 in.	Season	Romero*	1923-24
61.0 in.	Month	Vega	Feb. 1956
61.0 in.	Single storm	Vega	Feb. 1-8, 1956
24.0 in.	24 hours	Plainview	Feb. 3-4, 1956
24.2 in.	Annual average	Vega	

*Romero was in southwestern Hartley County.

Source: National Weather Service, Dallas/Fort Worth.

Texas Is Tornado Capital

An average of 132 tornadoes touch Texas soil each year. The annual total varies considerably, and certain areas are struck more often than others.

Tornadoes occur with greatest frequency in the Red River Valley of North Texas.

Tornadoes may occur in any month and at any hour of the day, but they occur with greatest frequency during the late spring and early summer months, and between the hours of 4 p.m. and 8 p.m.

In the period 1959–2008, nearly 62.4 percent of all Texas tornadoes occurred within the three-month period of April, May and June, with almost **one-third of the total tornadoes occurring in May**.

More tornadoes have been recorded in Texas than in any other state, which is partly due to the state's size.

Between 1959 and 2008, 7,657 funnel clouds reached the ground, thus becoming tornadoes.

Texas ranks 11th among the 50 states in the density of tornadoes, with an average of 5.7 tornadoes per 10,000 square miles per year during this period.

The greatest outbreak of tornadoes on record in Texas was associated with **Hurricane Beulah in September 1967**. Within a five-day period, Sept. 19–23, 115 known tornadoes, all in Texas, were spawned by this great hurricane.

Sixty-seven occurred on Sept. 20, a Texas **record for a single day**.

In addition to Hurricane Beulah's 115 tornadoes, there were another 9 tornadoes in September for a total of 124, which is a Texas record for a single month.

The greatest number of tornadoes in Texas in a single year is 232, also in 1967. The second-highest number in a single year is 1995, when 223 tornadoes occurred in Texas.

In 1982, there were 123 tornadoes formed in May, making it the worst outbreak of spring tornadoes in Texas. On average, May has the highest number of tornadoes per month with 39.84. January has the lowest average with 2.24.

A rare winter tornado outbreak occurred on Dec. 29, 2006. There were 27 tornadoes on this day, which is the largest monthly total for December. On average, December has 3.02 tornadoes. ☆

Occurrences by Month, Year

This table, compiled by the National Climatic Data Center, Environmental Data Service and the National Oceanic and Atmospheric Administration, lists tornado occurrences in Texas, by months, for the period 1959–2008.

Source: Office of State Climatologist

Year	January	February	March	April	May	June	July	August	September	October	November	December	ANNUAL
1959	0	0	8	4	32	14	10	3	4	5	6	0	86
1960	4	1	0	8	29	14	3	4	2	11	1	0	77
1961	0	1	21	15	24	30	9	2	12	0	10	0	124
1962	0	4	12	9	25	56	12	15	7	2	0	1	143
1963	0	0	3	9	19	24	8	4	6	4	5	0	82
1964	0	1	6	22	15	11	9	7	3	1	3	0	78
1965	2	5	3	7	43	24	2	9	4	6	0	3	108
1966	0	4	1	21	22	15	3	8	3	0	0	0	77
1967	0	2	11	17	34	22	10	5	124	2	0	5	232
1968	2	1	3	13	47	21	4	8	5	8	11	16	139
1969	0	1	1	16	65	16	6	7	6	8	1	0	127
1970	1	3	5	23	23	9	5	20	9	20	0	3	121
1971	0	20	10	24	27	33	7	20	7	16	4	23	191
1972	1	0	19	13	43	12	19	13	8	9	7	0	144
1973	14	1	29	25	21	24	4	8	5	3	9	4	147
1974	2	1	8	19	18	26	3	9	6	22	2	0	116
1975	5	2	9	12	50	18	10	3	3	3	1	1	117
1976	1	1	8	53	63	11	16	6	13	4	0	0	176
1977	0	0	3	34	50	4	5	5	12	0	6	4	123
1978	0	0	0	34	65	10	13	6	6	1	2	0	137
1979	1	2	24	33	39	14	12	10	4	15	3	0	157
1980	0	2	7	26	44	21	2	34	10	5	0	2	153
1981	0	7	7	9	71	26	5	20	5	23	3	0	176
1982	0	0	6	27	123	36	4	0	3	0	3	1	203
1983	5	7	24	1	62	35	4	22	5	0	7	14	186
1984	0	13	9	18	19	19	0	4	1	5	2	5	95
1985	0	0	5	41	28	5	3	1	1	3	1	2	90
1986	0	12	4	21	50	24	3	5	4	7	1	0	131
1987	1	1	7	0	54	19	11	3	8	0	16	4	124
1988	0	0	0	11	7	7	6	2	42	4	10	0	89
1989	3	0	5	3	70	63	0	6	3	6	1	0	160
1990	3	3	4	56	62	20	5	2	3	0	0	0	158
1991	20	5	2	39	72	36	1	2	3	8	4	0	192
1992	0	5	13	22	43	66	4	4	4	7	21	0	189
1993	1	4	5	17	39	4	4	0	12	23	8	0	117
1994	0	1	1	48	88	2	1	4	3	9	8	0	165
1995	6	0	13	36	66	75	11	3	2	1	0	10	223
1996	7	1	2	21	33	9	3	8	33	8	4	1	130
1997	0	6	7	31	59	50	2	2	1	16	3	0	177
1998	24	15	4	9	11	6	3	5	3	28	1	0	109
1999	22	0	22	23	70	26	3	8	0	0	0	4	178
2000	0	7	49	33	23	8	3	0	0	10	20	1	154
2001	0	0	4	12	36	12	0	7	15	24	27	5	142
2002	0	0	44	25	61	5	1	4	13	8	0	22	183
2003	0	0	4	31	50	29	6	1	4	12	29	0	166
2004	1	1	27	25	29	34	1	5	0	4	55	2	184
2005	0	0	6	7	27	46	15	4	2	0	0	2	109
2006	0	1	4	20	43	7	3	3	0	9	0	27	117
2007	2	1	56	61	43	21	8	4	14	2	1	3	216
2008	0	3	15	48	33	9	5	1	2	3	1	3	123
TOTAL	128	145	540	1,132	2,170	1,128	287	336	445	365	297	168	7,141

Texas Droughts, 1892–2008

The following table shows the extent of drought by major region, 1892–2008, by listing the **percent of normal precipitation**. *Drought here is arbitrarily defined as when there is less than 75 percent of normal precipitation.

Year	High Plains	Low Rolling Plains	North Central	East Texas	Trans-Pecos	Edwards Plateau	South Central	Upper Coast	South Texas	Lower Valley
1892	...	...	...	...	68	...	...	...	73	...
1893	...	...	67	70	...	49	56	64	53	59
1894	...	...	...	68	...	...	...	...	...	...
1897	...	...	...	...	...	...	73	...	72	...
1898	...	...	...	...	...	...	...	...	69	51
1901	...	71	70	...	...	60	62	70	44	...
1902	...	...	...	...	...	...	...	...	65	73
1907	...	...	...	...	...	...	...	...	...	65
1909	...	...	72	68	67	74	70	...	...	...
1910	59	59	64	69	43	65	69	74	59	...
1911	...	...	...	...	...	...	...	...	...	70
1916	...	73	...	74	70	...	73	69	...	...
1917	58	50	63	59	44	46	42	50	32	48
1920	...	...	...	...	...	...	...	...	...	71
1921	...	...	...	72	...	...	...	...	...	73
1922	...	...	...	...	68	...	...	...	...	...
1924	...	...	73	73	...	71	...	72	...	...
1925	...	...	72	...	...	...	72	...	...	...
1927	...	...	...	...	...	...	74	...	...	74
1933	72	...	...	...	62	68	...	...	...	...
1934	66	...	...	...	46	69	...	...	...	...
1937	...	...	...	...	...	...	...	72	...	...
1939	...	...	...	...	...	69	...	...	...	72
1943	...	...	72	...	...	...	...	...	...	...
1948	...	...	73	74	62	...	71	67	...	...
1950	...	...	...	...	...	...	68	...	74	64
1951	...	...	...	...	61	53	...	...	...	...
1952	68	66	...	...	73	...	...	...	56	70
1953	69	...	...	...	49	73	...	...	...	...
1954	70	71	68	73	...	50	50	57	71	...
1956	51	57	61	68	44	43	55	62	53	53
1962	...	...	...	...	...	68	...	...	67	65
1963	...	...	63	68	...	65	61	73	...	...
1964	74	...	...	69	...	...	...	...	...	63
1970	65	63	...	...	...	72	...	...	...	...
1988	...	...	...	...	67	62	67	68	...	...
1989	...	...	...	...	72	...	...	66	64	...
1990	...	...	...	...	...	...	...	...	...	73
1994	...	...	...	...	68	...	...	...	...	...
1996	...	...	...	...	...	71	...	60	70	...
1998	...	69	...	...	71	...	...	...	...	...
1999	...	...	73	...	...	67	69	69	...	...
2000	...	...	...	...	74	...	...	...	67	...
2001	...	...	...	...	56	...	...	...	...	...
2003	65	71	...	...	...	...	...	...	...	...
2005	...	...	68	66	...	...	...	...	72	...
2006	...	...	...	...	...	66	...	...	...	...
2008	...	...	...	...	...	66	61	...	...	...

Drought Frequency

This table shows the number of years of drought and the **number of separate droughts** by region. For example, the High Plains has had 10 drought years, consisting of five 1-year droughts, one 2-year drought and one 3-year drought, a total of 7 droughts.

Years of Drought	High Plains	Low Rolling Plains	North Central	East Texas	Trans-Pecos	Edwards Plateau	South Central	Upper Coast	South Texas	Lower Valley
1	5	8	10	7	7	10	14	10	10	15
2	1	1	2	2	5	5	2	2	3	2
3	1	...	...	...	1	...	...	...	...	...
Total Droughts	7	9	12	9	13	15	16	12	13	17
Drought Years	10	10	14	11	20	20	18	14	16	19

*Drought has proven to be difficult to define and there is no universally accepted definition. The most commonly used drought definitions are based on meteorological, agricultural, hydrological and socioeconomic effects.

Meteorological drought is often defined by a period of substantially **diminished precipitation** duration and/or intensity. The commonly used definition of meteorological drought is an interval of time, generally on the order of months or years, during which the actual moisture supply at a given place consistently falls below the climatically appropriate moisture supply.

Agricultural drought occurs when there is **inadequate soil moisture** to meet the needs of a particular crop at a particular time. Agricultural drought usually occurs after or during meteorological drought but before hydrological drought and can also affect livestock and other dry-land agricultural operations.

Hydrological drought refers to **deficiencies in surface and subsurface water** supplies. It is measured as streamflow and as lake, reservoir and groundwater levels. There is usually a delay between lack of rain and less measurable water in streams, lakes and reservoirs. Therefore, hydrological measurements tend to lag other drought indicators.

Socioeconomic drought occurs when physical water shortages start to affect the health, well-being, and **quality of life** of the people, or when the drought starts to affect the **supply and demand** of an economic product.

Source: New Mexico Drought Planning Team Web site.

Normal Annual Rainfall by Texas Climatic Region

Listed below is the normal annual rainfall in inches for five 30-year periods in each geographical region (See map, p. 125). Normals are given **in the same order** as the regions appear in the tables above.

Region	HP	LRP	NC	ET	TP	EP	SC	UC	ST	LV
1931–1960	18.51	22.99	32.93	45.96	12.03	25.91	33.24	46.19	22.33	24.27
1941–1970	18.59	23.18	32.94	45.37	11.57	23.94	33.03	46.43	21.95	23.44
1951–1980	17.73	22.80	32.14	44.65	11.65	23.52	34.03	45.93	22.91	24.73
1961–1990	18.88	23.77	33.99	45.67	13.01	24.00	34.49	47.63	23.47	25.31
1971–2000	19.64	24.51	35.23	48.08	13.19	24.73	36.21	50.31	24.08	25.43

The Great Galveston Storm of Sept. 8–9, 1900, was the worst natural disaster in U.S. history in terms of human life. Loss of life at Galveston has been estimated at 6,000 to 8,000, but the exact number has never been exactly determined. Sacred Heart Church, above, stands amid the ruins. Texas Almanac file photo.

Significant and Destructive Weather

Source: This list of significant weather events in Texas since 1766 was compiled from ESSA-Weather Bureau information, previous Texas Almanacs, the Handbook of Texas, The Dallas Morning News and other sources.

Sept. 4, 1766: Hurricane. Galveston Bay. Spanish Mission Nuestra Señora de la Luz destroyed.

Sept. 12, 1818: Hurricane. Galveston Island. Salt water flowed four feet deep. Only six buildings remained habitable. Of the six vessels and two barges in the harbor, even the two not seriously damaged were reduced to dismasted hulks. **Pirate Jean Lafitte** moved to one hulk so his **Red House** might serve as a hospital.

Aug. 6, 1844: Hurricane. Mouth of Rio Grande. All houses destroyed at the mouth of the river and at **Brazos Santiago**, eight miles north; 70 lives lost.

Sept. 19, 1854: Hurricane. It struck near **Matagorda**, and moved inland, northwestward over **Columbus**. Main impact fell in **Matagorda and Lavaca bays**. Almost all buildings in Matagorda were destroyed. Four lives were lost in town; more lives were lost on the peninsula.

Oct. 3, 1867: Hurricane. This hurricane moved inland **south of Galveston**, but raked the entire Texas coast **from the Rio Grande to the Sabine. Bagdad and Clarksville**, towns at the mouth of the Rio Grande, were destroyed. Much of Galveston was flooded and property damage there was estimated at $1 million.

Sept. 16, 1875: Hurricane. Struck **Indianola**, Calhoun County. Three-fourths of town swept away; 176 lives lost.

Flooding from the bay caused nearly all destruction.

Aug. 13, 1880: Hurricane. Center struck **Matamoros, Mexico; lower Texas coast** affected.

Oct. 12–13, 1880: Hurricane. Brownsville. City nearly destroyed, many lives lost.

Dec. 29, 1880: Snow. Brownsville. A rare snowstorm in the Lower Rio Grande Valley.

Aug. 23–24, 1882: Torrential rains caused **flooding** on the **North and South Concho and Bosque rivers** (South Concho reported 45 feet above normal level), destroying **Benficklen**, then county seat of Tom Green County, leaving only the courthouse and jail. More than 50 persons drowned in **Tom Green and Erath counties**, with property damage at $200,000 and 10,000 to 15,000 head of livestock lost.

Aug. 19–21, 1886: Hurricane. Indianola. Every house destroyed or damaged. Indianola was never rebuilt.

Oct. 12, 1886: Hurricane. Sabine, Jefferson County. Hurricane passed over Sabine. The inundation extended 20 miles inland and nearly every house in the vicinity was moved from its foundation; 150 persons were drowned.

April 28, 1893: Tornado. Cisco, Eastland County; 23 killed, 93 injured; damage $400,000.

Feb. 1895: Freeze/Snow. Coastal Texas. What is probably the greatest heavy-snow anomaly in the climatic history of the U.S. resulted from a snowstorm along the Texas coast on the 14th–15th. **Houston; Orange; Stafford,** Fort Bend County; and **Columbus,** Colorado County, each reported a snowfall of 20 inches. **Galveston** had a snowfall of 15.4 inches. Snow fell as far south as the Lower Rio Grande Valley, where **Brownsville** received 5 inches. The Lower Valley had lows of **22°F** the 14th through the 17th, destroying the vegetable crops.

May 15, 1896: Tornadoes, Sherman, Grayson County; **Justin** and **Gribble Springs,** Denton County; 76 killed; damage $225,000.

Sept. 12, 1897: Hurricane. Many houses in Port Arthur were demolished; 13 killed, damage $150,000.

May 1, 1898: Tornado. Mobeetie, Wheeler County. Four killed, several injured; damage $35,000.

Feb. 11–13, 1899: Freeze. A disastrous cold wave throughout the state. Newspapers described it as the worst freeze ever known in the state. **Brownsville's** temperature reach 16°F on the 12th and remained below freezing through the 13th. Much destruction of vegetable crops.

June 27–July 1, 1899: Rainstorm. A storm, centered over **the Brazos River watershed,** precipitated an average of 17 inches over 7,000 square miles. At **Hearne,** the gage overflowed at 24 inches; estimated total rainfall was 30 inches. At **Turnersville,** Coryell County, 33 inches were recorded in three days. This rain caused the **worst Brazos River flood on record.** Between 30 and 35 lives were lost. Property damage was estimated at $9 million.

April 5–8, 1900: Rainstorm. This storm began in two centers, over **Val Verde County** on the Rio Grande, and over **Swisher County** on the High Plains, and converged in the vicinity of **Travis County,** causing disastrous floods in the **Colorado, Brazos and Guadalupe rivers.** McDonald Dam on the Colorado River at Austin crumbled suddenly. A wall of water swept through the city taking at least 23 lives. Damage was estimated at $1.25 million.

Sept. 8–9, 1900: Hurricane. Galveston. The Great Galveston Storm was the **worst natural disaster in U.S. history** in terms of human life. Loss of life at Galveston has been estimated at 6,000 to 8,000, but the exact number has never been exactly determined. The island was completely inundated; not a single structure escaped damage. Most of the loss of life was due to drowning by storm tides that reached 15 feet or more. The anemometer blew away when the wind reached 100 mph at 6:15 p.m. on the 8th. Wind reached an estimated maximum velocity of 120 mph between 7:30 and 8:30 p.m. Property damage has been estimated at $30 million to $40 million.

May 18, 1902: Tornado. Goliad. This tornado cut a 250-yard-wide path through town, turning 150 buildings into rubble. Several churches were destroyed, one of which was holding services; all 40 worshippers were either killed or injured. This tornado killed 114, injured 230, and caused an estimated $200,000 in damages.

April 26, 1906: Tornado. Bellevue, Clay County, demolished; considerable damage done at **Stoneburg,** seven miles east in Montague County; 17 killed, 20 injured; damage $300,000.

May 6, 1907: Tornado. North of **Sulphur Springs,** Hopkins County; five killed, 19 injured.

May 13, 1908: Tornado. Linden, Cass County. Four killed, seven injured; damage $75,000.

May 22–25, 1908: Rainstorm; unique because it originated on the Pacific Coast. It moved first into **North Texas** and southern Oklahoma and thence to **Central Texas,** precipitating as much as 10 inches. Heaviest floods were in the upper Trinity basin, but flooding was general as far south as the Nueces. Property damage exceeded $5 million and 11 lives were lost in the Dallas vicinity.

March 23, 1909: Tornado. **Slidell,** Wise County; 11 killed, 10 injured; damage $30,000.

May 30, 1909: Tornado. Zephyr, Brown County; 28 killed, many injured; damage $90,000.

July 21, 1909: Hurricane. Velasco, Brazoria County. One-half of town destroyed, 41 lives lost; damage $2,000,000.

Dec. 1–5, 1913: Rainstorm. This caused the **second major Brazos River flood,** and caused more deaths than

the storm of 1899. It formed over **Central Texas** and spread both southwest and northeast with precipitation of 15 inches at **San Marcos** and 11 inches at **Kaufman.** Floods caused loss of 177 lives and $8.54 million damage.

April 20–26, 1915: Rainstorm. Originated over Central Texas and spread into North and East Texas with precipitation up to 17 inches, causing floods in **Trinity, Brazos, Colorado** and **Guadalupe rivers.** More than 40 lives lost and $2.33 million damage.

Aug. 16–19, 1915: Hurricane. Galveston. Peak wind gusts of 120 miles recorded at Galveston; tide ranged 9.5 to 14.3 feet above mean sea level in the city, and up to 16.1 feet near the causeway. Business section flooded with 5 to 6 feet of water. At least 275 lives lost, damage $56 million. A new seawall prevented a repetition of the 1900 disaster.

Aug. 18, 1916: Hurricane. Corpus Christi. Maximum wind speed 100 mph. 20 Lives lost; damage $1.6 million.

Jan. 10–12, 1918: Blizzard. This was the most severe since that of February, 1899; it was accompanied by zero degree temperature in North Texas and temperatures from 7° to 12° below freezing along the lower coast.

April 9, 1919: Tornado. Leonard, Ector and Ravenna in Fannin County; 20 killed, 45 injured; damage $125,000.

April 9, 1919: Tornado. Henderson, Van Zandt, Wood, Camp, and Red River counties, 42 killed, 150 injured; damage $450,000.

May 7, 1919: Windstorms. Starr, Hidalgo, Willacy and **Cameron counties.** Violent thunderstorms with high winds, hail and rain occurred between **Rio Grande City** and the coast, killing 10 persons. Damage to property and crops was $500,000. Seven were killed at **Mission.**

Sept. 14, 1919: Hurricane. Near **Corpus Christi.** Center moved inland south of Corpus Christi; tides 16 feet above normal in that area and 8.8 feet above normal at **Galveston.** Extreme wind at Corpus Christi measured at 110 mph; 284 lives lost; damage $20.3 million.

April 13, 1921: Tornado. Melissa, Collin County, and **Petty,** Lamar County. Melissa was practically destroyed; 12 killed, 80 injured; damage $500,000.

April 15, 1921: Tornado. Wood, Cass and Bowie counties; 10 killed, 50 injured; damage $85,000.

Sept. 8–10, 1921: Rainstorm. Probably the **greatest rainstorm in Texas history,** it entered Mexico as a hurricane from the Gulf. Torrential rains fell as the storm moved northeasterly across Texas. **Record floods** occurred in **Bexar, Travis, Williamson, Bell and Milam counties,** killing 215 persons, with property losses over $19 million. Five to nine feet of water stood in downtown **San Antonio.** A total of 23.98 inches was measured at the U.S. Weather Bureau station at **Taylor** during a period of 35 hours, with a 24-hour maximum of 23.11 on September 9-10. The **greatest rainfall recorded in United States history during 18 consecutive hours** (measured at an unofficial weather-monitoring site) fell at **Thrall,** Williamson County, 36.40 inches fell on Sept. 9.

April 8, 1922: Tornado. Rowena, Runnels County. Seven killed, 52 injured; damage $55,000.

April 8, 1922: Tornado. Oplin, Callahan County. Five killed, 30 injured; damage $15,000.

April 23–28, 1922: Rainstorm. An exceptional storm entered Texas from the west and moved from the **Panhandle** to **North Central and East Texas.** Rains up to 12.6 inches over Parker, Tarrant and Dallas counties caused severe floods in the Upper Trinity at **Fort Worth;** 11 lives were lost; damage was estimated at $1 million.

May 4, 1922: Tornado. Austin, Travis County; 12 killed, 50 injured; damage $500,000.

May 14, 1923: Tornado. Howard and Mitchell counties; 23 killed, 100 injured; damage $50,000.

April 12, 1927: Tornado. Edwards, Real and Uvalde counties; 74 killed, 205 injured; damage $1.23 million. Most of damage was in **Rocksprings** where 72 deaths occurred and town was practically destroyed.

May 9, 1927: Tornado. Garland; eleven killed; damage $100,000.

May 9, 1927: Tornado. Nevada, Collin County; **Wolfe City,** Hunt County; and **Tigertown,** Lamar County; 28 killed, over 200 injured; damage $900,000.

Jan. 4, 1929: Tornado. Near **Bay City**, Matagorda County. Five killed, 14 injured.

April 24, 1929: Tornado. Slocum, Anderson County; seven killed, 20 injured; damage $200,000.

May 24–31, 1929: Rainstorm. Beginning over **Caldwell County**, a storm spread over much of **Central and Coastal Texas** with maximum rainfall of 12.9 inches, **causing floods in Colorado, Guadalupe, Brazos, Trinity, Neches and Sabine rivers**. Much damage at **Houston** from overflow of bayous. Damage estimated at $6 million.

May 6, 1930: Tornado. Bynum, Irene and Mertens in Hill County; **Ennis**, Ellis County; and **Frost**, Navarro County; 41 killed; damage $2.1 million.

May 6, 1930: Tornado. Kenedy and Runge in Karnes County; **Nordheim**, DeWitt County; 36 killed, 34 injured; damage $127,000.

June 30–July 2, 1932: Rainstorm. Torrential rains fell over the upper watersheds of the **Nueces and Guadalupe rivers**, causing destructive floods. Seven persons drowned; property losses exceeded $500,000.

Aug. 13, 1932: Hurricane. Near **Freeport**, Brazoria County. Wind speed at **East Columbia** estimated at 100 mph; 40 lives lost, 200 injured; damage $7.5 million.

March 30, 1933: Tornado. Angelina, Nacogdoches and San Augustine counties; 10 killed, 56 injured; damage $200,000.

April 26, 1933: Tornado. Bowie County near Texarkana. Five killed, 38 injured; damage $14,000.

April 29, 1933: Dust storm. Panhandle, South Plains. The dust storm extended from **Sweetwater** north to Central Kansas and from Albuquerque, N.M., to Oklahoma. Newspaper accounts described it as the worst sandstorm in years; "as dark as any night" in **Perryton**. Thousands of acres of small grain crops were blown from the soil.

July 22–25, 1933: Tropical Storm. One of the greatest U.S. storms in area and general rainfall. The storm reached the vicinity of **Freeport** late on July 22 and moved very slowly overland across eastern Texas, July 22-25. The storm center moved into northern Louisiana on the 25th. Rainfall averaged 12.50 inches over an area of about 25,000 square miles. Twenty inches or more fell in a small area of eastern Texas and western Louisiana surrounding Logansport, La. The 4-day total at Logansport was 22.30 inches. Property damage was estimated at $1.12 million.

July 30, 1933: Tornado. Oak Cliff section of Dallas, Dallas County. Five killed, 30 injured; damage $500,000.

Sept. 4–5, 1933: Hurricane. Near **Brownsville**. Center passed inland a short distance north of Brownsville, where an extreme wind of 106 mph was measured before the anemometer blew away. Peak wind gusts were estimated at 120 to 125 mph. 40 known dead, 500 injured; damage $16,903,100. About 90 percent of the citrus crop in the **Lower Rio Grande Valley** was destroyed.

July 25, 1934: Hurricane. Near **Seadrift**, Calhoun County, 19 lives lost, many minor injuries; damage $4.5 million. About 85 percent of damage was in crops.

Jan.–March 1935: Dust storms. Amarillo. Seven times, the visibility in Amarillo declined to zero from dust storms. One of these complete blackouts lasted eleven hours. One of the storms raged for 3 1/2 days.

Sept. 15–18, 1936: Rainstorm. Excessive rains over the **North Concho and Middle Concho rivers** caused a sharp rise in the Concho River, which overflowed **San Angelo**. Much of the business district and 500 homes were flooded. Four persons drowned and property losses estimated at $5 million. Four-day storm rainfall at San Angelo measured 25.19 inches; 11.75 inches fell on the 15th.

June 10, 1938: Tornado. Clyde, Callahan County; 14 killed, 9 injured; damage $85,000.

Sept. 23, 1941: Hurricane. Center moved inland near Matagorda, and passed over **Houston** about midnight. Extremely high tides along coast in the **Matagorda to Galveston** area. Heaviest property and crop losses were in counties from Matagorda County to the Sabine River. Four lives lost. Damage was $6.5 million.

April 28, 1942: Tornado. Crowell, Foard County; 11 killed, 250 injured; damage $1.5 million.

Aug. 30, 1942: Hurricane. Matagorda Bay. Highest wind estimated 115 mph at **Seadrift**. Tide at **Matagorda**,14.7 feet. Storm moved west-north-westward and finally diminished over the **Edwards Plateau**; eight lives lost, property damage estimated at $11.5 million, and crop damage estimated at $15 million.

May 10, 1943: Tornado. Laird Hill, Rusk County, and **Kilgore**, Gregg County. Four killed, 25 injured; damage $1 million.

July 27, 1943: Hurricane. Near **Galveston**. Center moved inland across **Bolivar Peninsula and Trinity Bay**. A wind gust of 104 mph was recorded at **Texas City**; 19 lives lost; damage estimated at $16.6 million.

Aug. 26–27, 1945: Hurricane. Aransas-San Antonio Bay area. At **Port O'Connor**, the wind reached 105 mph when the cups were torn from the anemometer. Peak gusts of 135 mph were estimated at **Seadrift, Port O'Connor and Port Lavaca**; three killed, 25 injured; damage $20.1 million.

Jan. 4, 1946: Tornado. Near **Lufkin**, Angelina County and **Nacogdoches**, Nacogdoches County; 13 killed, 250 injured; damage $2.1 million.

Jan. 4, 1946: Tornado. Near **Palestine**, Anderson County; 15 killed, 60 injured; damage $500,000.

May 18, 1946: Tornado. Clay, Montague and Denton counties. Four killed, damage $112,000.

April 9, 1947: Tornado. White Deer, Carson County; **Glazier**, Hemphill County; and **Higgins**, Lipscomb County; 68 killed, 201 injured; damage $1.55 million. Glazier completely destroyed. **One of the largest tornadoes on record**. Width of path, 1 mile at Higgins; length of path, 221 miles across portions of Texas, Oklahoma and Kansas. This tornado also struck Woodward, Okla.

May 3, 1948: Tornado. McKinney, Collin County; three killed, 43 injured; $2 million damage.

May 15, 1949: Tornado. Amarillo and vicinity; six killed, 83 injured. Total damage from tornado, wind and hail, $5.3 million. Total destruction over one-block by three-block area in southern part of city; airport and 45 airplanes damaged; 28 railroad boxcars blown off track.

Jan.–Feb. 1951: Freeze. On Jan. 31.–Feb. 3 and again on Feb. 13–17, cold waves swept over the entire state, bringing **snow and sleet**. Heavy damage was done in the **Lower Rio Grande Valley** to truck and citrus crops, notably in the earlier of these northers. During the norther of Jan. 31–Feb. 3, the temperature went to –19°F **in Dalhart**.

Sept. 8–10, 1952: Rainstorm. Heavy rains over the **Colorado and Guadalupe River watersheds** in southwestern Texas caused major flooding. From 23 to 26 inches fell between **Kerrville, Blanco and Boerne**. Highest stages ever known occurred in the **Pedernales River**; five lives lost, three injured; 17 homes destroyed, 454 damaged. Property loss several million dollars.

March 13, 1953: Tornado. Jud and O'Brien, Haskell County; and **Knox City**, Knox County; 17 killed, 25 injured; damage $600,000.

May 11, 1953: Tornado. Near **San Angelo**, Tom Green County; eleven killed, 159 injured; damage $3.24 million.

May 11, 1953: Tornado. Waco, McLennan County; 114 killed, 597 injured; damage $41.15 million. **One of two most disastrous tornadoes**; 150 homes destroyed, 900 homes damaged; 185 other buildings destroyed; 500 other buildings damaged.

Feb. 1–5, 1956: Blizzard. Northwestern Texas. A major blizzard moved into the Panhandle and South Plains on Feb. 1. Snow and high winds continued through Feb. 5. **Snowfall was the heaviest on record in Texas**. Twenty deaths were attributed to the blizzard.

April 2, 1957: Tornado. Dallas, Dallas County; 10 killed, 200 injured; damage $4 million. Moving through Oak Cliff and West Dallas, it damaged 574 buildings, largely homes.

April–May, 1957: Torrential Rains. Excessive flooding occurred throughout the area **east of the Pecos River to the Sabine River** during the last 10 days of April; 17 lives were lost, and several hundred homes were destroyed. During May, more than 4,000 persons were evacuated from unprotected lowlands on the **West Fork of the Trinity above Fort Worth** and along creeks in Fort Worth. Twenty-nine houses at **Christoval** were damaged or destroyed and 83 houses at **San Angelo** were damaged. Five persons were drowned in floods in **South Central Texas**.

May 15, 1957: Tornado. Silverton, Briscoe County; 21 killed, 80 injured; damage $500,000.

June 27, 1957: Hurricane Audrey. Center crossed the Gulf coast near the Texas-Louisiana line. **Orange** was in the western portion of the eye between 9 and 10 a.m. In Texas, nine lives were lost, 450 persons injured; property damage was $8 million. Damage was extensive in **Jefferson and Orange counties**, with less in **Chambers and Galveston counties**. Maximum wind reported in Texas, 85 m.p.h. at **Sabine Pass**, with gusts to 100 m.p.h.

Oct. 28, 1960: Rainstorm. Rains of 7-10 inches fell in **South Central Texas**; 11 died from drowning in flash floods. In **Austin** about 300 families were driven from their homes. Damage in Austin was estimated at $2.5 million.

Sept. 8–14, 1961: Hurricane Carla. Port O'Connor; maximum wind gust at **Port Lavaca** estimated at 175 mph. Highest tide was 18.5 feet at Port Lavaca. Most damage was to **coastal counties between Corpus Christi and Port Arthur** and inland **Jackson, Harris and Wharton counties**. In Texas, 34 persons died; seven in a tornado that swept across **Galveston Island**; 465 persons were injured. Property and crop damage conservatively estimated at $300 million. The evacuation of an estimated 250,000 persons kept loss of life low. **Hurricane Carla was the largest hurricane of record**.

Jan. 9–12, 1962: Freeze. A disastrous cold wave comparable to the cold waves of 1899 and 1951. Low temperatures ranged from **-15°F in the Panhandle to 10°F at Rio Grande City**. Agricultural losses were estimated at $50 million.

Sept. 7, 1962: Rainstorm. Fort Worth. Rains fell over the Big Fossil and Denton Creek watersheds ranging up to 11 inches of fall in three hours. Extensive damage from flash flooding occurred in **Richland Hills and Haltom City**.

Sept. 16–20, 1963: Hurricane Cindy. Rains of 15 to 23.5 inches fell in portions of **Jefferson, Newton and Orange counties** when Hurricane Cindy became stationary west of **Port Arthur**. Flooding from the excessive rainfall resulted in total property damage of $11.6 million and agricultural losses of $500,000.

April 3, 1964: Tornado. Wichita Falls. Seven killed, 111 injured; damage $15 million; 225 homes destroyed, 50 with major damage, and 200 with minor damage. Sixteen other buildings received major damage.

Sept. 21–23, 1964: Rainstorm. Collin, Dallas and Tarrant counties. Rains of more than 12 inches fell during the first eight hours of the 21st. Flash flooding of tributaries of the Trinity River and smaller creeks and streams resulted in two drownings and an estimated $3 million property damage. Flooding of homes occurred in all sections of **McKinney**. In **Fort Worth**, there was considerable damage to residences along Big Fossil and White Rock creeks.

Jan. 25, 1965: Dust Storm. West Texas. The worst dust storm since February 1956 developed on the **southern High Plains**. Winds, gusting up to 75 mph at **Lubbock**, sent dust billowing to 31,000 feet in the area **from the Texas-New Mexico border eastward to a line from Tulia to Abilene**. Ground visibility was reduced to about 100 yards in many sections. The worst hit was the **Muleshoe, Seminole, Plains, Morton** area on the South Plains. The rain gage at Reese Air Force Base, Lubbock, contained 3 inches of fine sand.

June 2, 1965: Tornado. Hale Center, Hale County. Four killed, 76 injured; damage $8 million.

June 11, 1965: Rainstorm. Sanderson, Terrell County. Torrential rains of up to eight inches in two hours near Sanderson caused a major flash flood that swept through the town. As a result, 26 persons drowned and property losses were estimated at $2.72 million.

April 22–29, 1966: Flooding. Northeast Texas. Twenty to 26 inches of rain fell in portions of Wood, Smith, Morris, Upshur, Gregg, Marion and Harrison counties. Nineteen persons drowned in the rampaging rivers and creeks that swept away bridges, roads and dams, and caused an estimated $12 million damage.

April 28, 1966: Flash flooding. Dallas County. Flash flooding from torrential rains in Dallas County resulted in 14

persons drowned and property losses at $15 million.

Sept. 18–23, 1967: Hurricane Beulah. Near **Brownsville**. The **third largest hurricane of record**, Hurricane Beulah moved inland near the mouth of the Rio Grande on the 20th. Wind gusts of 136 mph were reported during Beulah's passage. Rains 10 to 20 inches over much of the area **south of San Antonio** resulted in record-breaking floods. An unofficial gaging station at **Falfurrias** registered the highest accumulated rainfall, 36 inches. The resultant stream overflow and surface runoff inundated 1.4 million acres. Beulah spawned 115 tornadoes, all in Texas, the **greatest number of tornadoes on record for any hurricane**. Hurricane Beulah caused 13 deaths and 37 injuries, of which five deaths and 34 injuries were attributed to tornadoes. Property losses were estimated at $100 million and crop losses at $50 million.

April 18, 1970: Tornado. Near **Clarendon**, Donley County. Seventeen killed, 42 injured; damage $2.1 million. Fourteen persons were killed at a resort community at Green Belt Reservoir, 7 miles north of Clarendon.

May 11, 1970: Tornado. Lubbock, Lubbock County. Twenty-six killed, 500 injured; damage $135 million. Fifteen square miles, almost one-quarter of the city of Lubbock, suffered damage.

Aug. 3–5, 1970: Hurricane Celia. Corpus Christi. Hurricane Celia was a unique but severe storm. Measured in dollars, it was **the costliest in the state's history to that time**. Sustained wind speeds reached 130 mph, but it was great bursts of kinetic energy of short duration that appeared to cause the severe damage. Wind gusts of 161 mph were measured at the **Corpus Christi** National Weather Service Office. At **Aransas Pass**, peak wind gusts were estimated as high as 180 mph, after the wind equipment had been blown away. Celia caused 11 deaths in Texas, at least 466 injuries, and total property and crop damage in Texas estimated at $453.77 million. Hurricane Celia crossed the Texas coastline midway between Corpus Christi and Aransas Pass about 3:30 p.m. CST on Aug. 3. Hardest hit was the metropolitan area of **Corpus Christi**, including **Robstown, Aransas Pass, Port Aransas** and small towns on the north side of Corpus Christi Bay.

Feb. 20–22, 1971: Blizzard. Panhandle. Paralyzing blizzard, worst since March 22–25, 1957, storm transformed Panhandle into one vast snowfield as 6 to 26 inches of snow were whipped by 40 to 60 mph winds into drifts up to 12 feet high. At **Follett**, 3-day snowfall was 26 inches. Three persons killed; property and livestock losses were $3.1 million.

Sept. 9–13, 1971: Hurricane Fern. Coastal Bend. Ten to 26 inches of rain resulted in some of worst flooding since Hurricane Beulah in 1967. Two persons killed; losses were $30.2 million.

May 11–12, 1972: Rainstorm. South Central Texas. Seventeen drowned at **New Braunfels**, one at **McQueeney**. New Braunfels and **Seguin** hardest hit. Property damage $17.5 million.

June 12–13, 1973: Rainstorm. Southeastern Texas. Ten drowned. Over $50 million in property and crop damage. From 10-15 inches of rain recorded.

Nov. 23–24, 1974: Flash Flooding. Central Texas. Over $1 million in property damage. Thirteen people killed, 10 in **Travis County**.

Jan. 31–Feb. 1, 1975: Flooding. Nacogdoches County. Widespread heavy rain caused flash flooding here, resulting in three deaths; damage over $5.5 million.

May 23, 1975: Rainstorm. Austin area. Heavy rains, high winds and hail resulted in over $5 million property damage; 40 people injured. Four deaths caused by drowning.

April 19, 1976: Tornado. Brownwood. An **F-5** tornado destroyed a few homes and airplanes. Nine persons were injured.

June 15, 1976: Rainstorm. Harris County. Rains in excess of 13 inches caused damage estimated at near $25 million. Eight deaths were storm-related, including three drownings.

Aug. 1–4, 1978: Heavy Rains, Flooding. Edwards Plateau, Low Rolling Plains. Remnants of **Tropical Storm Amelia** caused some of the worst flooding of this century. As much as 30 inches of rain fell near **Albany** in Shackelford

County, where six drownings were reported. In **Bandera, Kerr, Kendall and Gillespie counties**, 27 people drowned and the damage total was at least $50 million.

Dec. 30–31, 1978: Ice Storm. North Central Texas. Possibly the **worst ice storm in 30 years** hit Dallas County particularly hard. Damage estimates reached $14 million, and six deaths were storm-related.

April 10, 1979: The worst single tornado in Texas' history hit **Wichita Falls**. Earlier on the same day, **several tornadoes** hit farther west. The destruction in Wichita Falls resulted in 42 dead, 1,740 injured, over 3,000 homes destroyed and damage of approximately $400 million. An estimated 20,000 persons were left homeless by this storm. In all, the tornadoes on April 10 killed 53 people, injured 1,812 and caused over $500 million damages.

May 3, 1979: Thunderstorms. Dallas County was hit by a wave of the most destructive thunderstorms in many years; 37 injuries and $5 million in damages resulted.

July 25–26, 1979: Tropical storm Claudette caused over $750 million in property and crop damages, but fortunately only few injuries. Near **Alvin**, an estimated 43 inches of rain fell, a new state record for 24 hours.

Aug. 24, 1979: One of the worst **hailstorms** in **West Texas** in the past 100 years; $200 million in crops, mostly cotton, destroyed.

Sept. 18–20, 1979: Coastal flooding from heavy rain, 18 inches in 24 hours at **Aransas Pass**, and 13 inches at **Rockport**.

Aug. 9–11, 1980: Hurricane Allen hit **South Texas** and left three dead, causing $650 million to $750 million in property and crop damages. Over 250,000 coastal residents had to be evacuated. The worst damage occurred along **Padre Island** and in **Corpus Christi**. Over 20 inches of rain fell in **extreme South Texas**, and 29 tornadoes occurred; one of the worst hurricane-related outbreaks.

Summer 1980: One of the hottest summers in the history of the Lone Star State.

Sept. 5–8, 1980: Hurricane Danielle brought rain and flooding to Southeast and Central Texas. Seventeen inches of rain fell at **Port Arthur,** and 25 inches near **Junction.**

May 24–25, 1981: Severe flooding in **Austin** claimed 13 lives, injured about 100 and caused $40 million in damage. Up to 5.5 inches of rain fell in one hour west of the city.

Oct. 11–14, 1981: Record rains in North Central Texas caused by the remains of **Pacific Hurricane Norma**. Over 20 inches fell in some locations.

April 2, 1982: A tornado outbreak in Northeast Texas. The most severe tornado struck **Paris**; 10 people were killed, 170 injured and 1,000 left homeless. Over $50 million in damages resulted. A total of seven tornadoes that day left 11 dead and 174 injured.

May, 1982: Texas recorded **123 tornadoes**, the most ever in May, and one less than the most recorded in any single month in the state. One death and 23 injuries occurred.

Dec. 1982: Heavy snow. El Paso recorded 18.2 inches of snow, the most in any month there.

Aug. 15–21, 1983: Hurricane Alicia was the first hurricane to make landfall in the continental U.S. in three years (Aug. 18), and **one of the costliest in Texas history** ($3 billion). Alicia caused widespread damage to a large section of **Southeast Texas**, including coastal areas near **Galveston** and the entire **Houston** area. Alicia spawned 22 tornadoes, and highest winds were estimated near 130 mph. In all, 18 people were killed and 1,800 injured as a result of the tropical storm.

Jan. 12–13, 1985: A record-breaking snowstorm struck **West and South Central Texas** with up to 15 inches of snow that fell at many locations **between San Antonio and the Rio Grande**. San Antonio recorded 13.2 inches of snow for Jan. 12 (the greatest in a day) and 13.5 inches for the two-day total. **Eagle Pass** reported 14.5 inches of snow.

June 26, 1986: Hurricane Bonnie made landfall between **High Island and Sabine Pass** around 3:45 a.m. The highest wind measured in the area was a gust to 97 m.p.h., which was recorded at the **Sea Rim State Park**. As much as 13 inches of rain fell in **Ace** in southern Polk County. There were several reports of funnel clouds, but no confirmed tornadoes. While the storm caused no major structural damage,

there was widespread minor damage. Numerous injuries were reported.

May 22, 1987: A strong, **multiple-vortex tornado** struck the town of **Saragosa**, Reeves County. Of the town's 183 inhabitants, 30 were killed and 121 were injured. Eight-five percent of the town's structures were destroyed, while total damage topped $1.3 million.

Oct. 15–19, 1994: Extreme amounts of rainfall, up to 28.90 inches over a 4-day period, fell throughout southeastern part of the state. Seventeen lives were lost, most of them victims of flash flooding. Many rivers reached record flood levels. **Houston** was cut off from many other parts of the state, as numerous roads, including Interstate 10, were under water. Damage was estimated to be near $700 million; 26 counties were declared disaster areas.

May 5, 1995: A **thunderstorm** moved across the **Dallas/Fort Worth** area with 70 mph wind gusts and rainfall rates of almost three inches in 30 minutes (five inches in one hour). Twenty people lost their lives as a result of this storm, 109 people were injured by large hail and, with more than $2 billion in damage, NOAA dubbed it the **"costliest thunderstorm event in history."**

May 28, 1995: A **supercell thunderstorm** produced extreme winds and giant hail in **San Angelo**, injuring at least 80 people and causing about $120 million in damage. Sixty-one homes were destroyed, and more than 9,000 were slightly damaged. In some areas, hail was six inches deep, with drifts to two feet.

Feb. 21, 1996: Anomalously **high temperatures** were reported over the **entire state**, breaking records in nearly every region of the state. Temperatures near 100°F shattered previous records by as many as 10°F as Texans experienced heat more characteristic of mid-summer than winter.

May 10, 1996: Hail up to five inches in diameter fell in **Howard County**, causing injuries to 48 people and $30 million worth of property damage.

May 27, 1997: Tornado. Jarrell. A half-mile-wide F-5 tornado struck Jarrell, Williamson County, leveling the Double Creek subdivision, claiming 27 lives, injuring 12 others, and causing more than $40 million in damage.

March–May, 1998: According to the Climate Prediction Center, this three-month period ranks as the **seventh driest** for a region including Texas, Oklahoma, Arkansas, Louisiana and Mississippi. May 1998 has been ranked as both the **warmest and the driest May** in this region.

Aug. 22–25, 1998: Tropical Storm Charley brought torrential rains and flash floods to the **Hill Country**. Thirteen people lost their lives and more than 200 were injured.

Oct. 17–19, 1998: Rainstorm. Hill Country. A massive, devastating flood set all-time records for rainfall and river levels, resulted in the deaths of 25 people, injured more than 2,000 others, and caused more than $500 million damage from the Hill Country to the counties **south and east of San Antonio**.

Jan. 22, 1999: Hail. Brazos County. Golf ball- and softball-sized **hail** fell in the **Bryan-College Station** area, resulting in $10 million in damage to cars, homes and offices.

May 1999: Storms, Tornadoes. East, Central, West Texas. Numerous severe weather outbreaks caused **damaging winds, large hail, dangerous lightning, and numerous tornadoes**. An F-3 tornado moved through downtown area and high school of **De Kalb**, Bowie County, on the 4th, injuring 22 people and causing $125 million in damage to the community. On the same day, **two F-2 tornadoes** roared through **Kilgore** simultaneously. On the 11th, an **F-4** tornado moved through parts of **Loyal Valley**, Mason County, and **Castell**, Llano County, taking the life of one and injuring six. The 25th saw storms produce **2.5-inch hail** in **Levelland** and **Amarillo**. The total cost of damages caused by May storms was more than $157 million.

August 1999: Excessive heat throughout the month resulted in 16 fatalities in the **Dallas/Fort Worth** area. The airport reported 26 consecutive days of 100°F or greater temperatures.

January–October 2000: Drought. A severe drought plagued **most of Texas**. Some regions experienced little to no rain for several months during the summer. **Abilene** saw no rain for **72 consecutive days**, while **Dallas** had **no rain**

for 84 consecutive days during the summer. During July, aquifers hit all-time lows, and lakes and streams fell to critical levels. Most regions had to cut back or stop agricultural activities because of the drought, which resulted in $515 million in agricultural loss, according to USDA figures.

March 28, 2000: Tornado. Fort Worth. A supercell over Fort Worth produced an F-3 tornado, which injured 80 people and caused significant damage. Flooding claimed the lives of two people.

May 20, 2000: Rainstorm. Southeast Texas. A **flash flood** in the **Liberty** and **Dayton** area was caused by 18.3 inches of rain's falling in five hours. Up to 80 people had to be rescued from the flood waters; property damage totalled an estimated $10 million.

July 2000: Excessive heat resulted from a high-pressure ridge, particularly from the 12th to the 21st. **Dallas/Fort Worth** airport reported a **10-day average of 103.3°F. College Station** had **12 consecutive days of 100°F or greater** temperatures. The heat caused 34 deaths in North and Southeast Texas, primarily among the elderly.

Aug. 2, 2000: Storm. Houston. Lightning struck a tree at Astroworld in Houston injuring 17 teens.

Sept. 5, 2000: Excessive heat resulted in at least eight **all-time high temperature** records around the state, one of which was **Possum Kingdom Lake**, which reached 114°F. This day is being regarded as the **hottest day ever in Texas,** considering the state as a whole.

Dec. 13 and 24-25, 2000: Ice/Snow. Two major winter storms blanketed **Northeast Texas** with up to six inches of ice from each storm. Eight inches of snow fell in the **Panhandle,** while areas in North Texas received 12 inches. Thousands of motorists were stranded on Interstate 20 and had to be rescued by the National Guard; 235,000 people lost electric service from the first storm alone. Roads were treacherous, driving was halted in several counties, and the total cost of damages from both storms reached more than $156 million.

Jan. 1–31, 2001: Drought. South Texas. The U.S. Department of Agriculture Farm Service Agency received a **Presidential Disaster Declaration** in December 2000 because of **persistent drought** conditions in **South Texas;** $125 million in damage was reported in the region.

May 2001: Storms. San Antonio, High Plains. Numerous storms causing excessive damage. **Four-inch hail** caused nearly $150 million in damages in **San Antonio** on the 6th. On the 30th, supercell **thunderstorms** in the **High Plains** region produced winds over 100 mph and golf-ball-sized hail caused more than $186 million in damage. All told, storms caused 36 injuries and more than $358 million in damage to property and agriculture.

June–December 2001: Drought. Significant drought-like conditions occurred in Texas from early summer through December. After the yearly drought report was filed, it was determined that the total crop damage across the South Plains region was about $420 million. Consequential losses occurred to crops such as cotton, wheat, grain sorghum and corn.

June 5–10, 2001: Tropical Storm Allison hit the **Houston** area, which dumped large amounts of rain on the city. The storm made landfall on the western end of **Galveston Island** and over the next five days produced record rainfall. These amazing amounts of precipitation led to devastating flooding across southeastern Texas. Some weather stations in the Houston area reported more than 40 inches of rain total and more than 18 inches in a 24-hour period. Twenty-two deaths and $5.2 billion in damage resulted.

July–August 2001: Excessive heat plagued Texas during July and August, which resulted in 17 deaths in the Houston area.

Oct. 12, 2001: Tornado. Hondo. An F2 tornado caused $20 million in damage. The tornado injured 25 people and damaged the National Guard Armory and a large hangar at the Hondo Airport, as well as nearly two dozen aircraft. Some 150 homes in Hondo and 50 on its outskirts were damaged, and nearly 100 mobile homes were damaged.

Nov. 15, 2001: Rainstorms. Central Texas. Storms caused **flash flooding** and some weak **tornadoes** in the Edwards Plateau, South Central and southern portions of

North Central regions. Flash flooding caused 8 deaths and 198 injuries.

March 2002: Storms. Central Texas. Several **violent storms** occurred, which produced hail, tornadoes and strong winds. Hail 1-3/4 inches in diameter caused $16 million in damage to **San Angelo** on the 19th, while 30 people where injured on the same day by an **F2 tornado** in **Somerset,** Bexar County, that also caused $2 million in damage. For the month, there were three fatalities, 64 injuries and more than $37.5 million in damage.

June 30–July 7, 2002: Rainstorm. Central Texas. Excessive rainfall occurred in the **South Central** and **Edwards Plateau** regions, with some areas reporting more than 30 inches of rain. In the South Central region alone nearly $250 million dollars worth of damage was reported from this significant weather event. In Central Texas, 29 counties were devastated by the flooding and declared federal disaster areas by President George W. Bush. The total event damage was estimated at more than $2 billion.

Sept. 5–7, 2002: Tropical Storm Fay. Coastal Plains. The storm made landfall along the coast on the 6th. This system produced extremely heavy rainfall, strong damaging wind gusts and tornadoes. Ten to 20 inches of rain fell in eastern **Wharton County. Brazoria County** was hit the hardest from this system with about 1,500 homes flooded. Tropical Storm Fay produced five tornadoes, flooded many areas and caused significant wind damage. Damage of $4.5 million was reported.

Oct. 24, 2002: Raintorms. South Texas. Severe **thunderstorms** in South Texas produced heavy rain, causing flooding and two tornadoes in **Corpus Christi**. The most extensive damage occurred across **Del Mar College.** The storm caused one death, 26 injuries and total damages exceeded more then $85 million in damage.

Feb. 24–26, 2003: Snow/Ice. North Central Texas. A severe cold front brought **freezing rain, sleet** and **snow** to the **North Central Texas**. Snow accumulations were as high as **5 inches** resulting in $15 million in damages. Most schools and businesses were closed for this period.

April 8, 2003: Rainstorm. Brownsville. A severe thunderstorm caused one of the **most destructive hail events in the history of Brownsville.** Hail exceeded 2.75 inches in diameter and caused $50 million in damages to the city. At least 5 injuries were reported.

July 14–16, 2003: Hurricane Claudette. Port O'Connor. The hurricane made landfall near Port O'Connor in the late morning hours of the 14th. At landfall, wind speeds were more than 90 mph. The system, which moved westward toward Big Bend and northern Mexico, caused 1 death and 2 injuries, and total damages were estimated at more than $100 million.

Sept. 2003: Floods. Upper Coast, South Texas. Persistent flooding during the month caused more than $2 million in damages. The remnants of **Tropical Storm Grace** caused flash flooding along the Upper Coast region near **Galveston** early in September, with rainfall estimates in Matagorda County ranging from 6 to 12 inches. During the second half of the month, **South Texas** was hit with a **deluge of rain caused by a tropical wave** combined with approaching cold fronts, and monthly rainfall totals ranged from 7 to 15 inches throughout the deep south.

June 1–9, 2004: Floods. North Central Texas. Flash flooding due to an upper air disturbance and associated cold front caused damage to more than 1,000 homes through **North Central Texas**. This was the first of many days in which heavy rains fell throughout the state. Estimated damages were more than $7.5 million.

June 21, 2004: Tornadoes. Panhandle. Severe weather kicked up just ahead of a frontal boundary causing damage to **Amarillo** and the surrounding area. Eight tornadoes were reported around the Panhandle, and there were many reports of hail, topping out at 4.25 inches in diameter in Potter County. Thousands of homes were damaged, and the total damage was estimated at more than **$150 million**.

July 28–29, 2004: Rainstorm. North Central Texas. A stationary front lead to torrential rainfall in **Dallas and Waco**. Hundreds of homes were damaged by flash flooding, as 24-hour rainfall totals for the two cities approached 5 inches.

Outlying areas of the cities reported as much as 7 inches of rain in a 12-hour period on the 29th. Damage estimates topped $20 million.

Sept. 14, 2004: Storm. Grapeland. A lightning strike during football practice at Grapeland High School, Houston County, caused one death and injuries to 40 players and coaches.

Dec. 24–26, 2004: Snow. Coastal Texas. Large portions of Southeast and South Texas saw their **first white Christmas in recorded history**. A cold front past over the state a few days prior to Christmas Eve dropping temperatures below freezing. Another cold front brought snow, and it accumulated Christmas Eve night and into Christmas day. Galveston and Houston recorded 4 inches of snow, while areas even further south, such as **Victoria, had 12 inches**. **Brownsville recorded 1.5 inches of snow.**

March 25, 2005: Hail. Austin. In the evening of March 25, the **most destructive hailstorm in 10 years** struck the greater Austin area. The storm knocked out power to 5,000 homes in northwest Austin. Hail of 2 inches in diameter was reported near the Travis County Exposition Center. Total damage was estimated at $100 million.

May 2005–December 2006: Drought. In May, portions of North Central Texas were upgraded from moderate to **severe drought.** By the end of the May, the drought had made significant agricultural and hydrological impacts on the region. In November, many Central Texas counties were added to the drought. The Texas Cooperative Extension estimated statewide drought losses at $4.1 billion, $1.9 billion in North Texas alone.

June 9, 2005: Tornado. Petersburg. An F-3 tornado affected the Petersburg area in southeast Hale County across to portions of southwest and south-central Floyd County. Total damage was estimated at $70 million.

Sept. 23, 2005: Hurrican Rita. Southeast Texas. The eye of **Hurricane Rita** moved ashore in extreme southwest Louisiana between Sabine Pass and Johnson's Bayou in Cameron Parish with maximum sustained winds of 120 mph, category-3 strength. On Sept. 22, Rita had strengthened to a peak intensity of 175 mph winds. In Southeast Texas, Rita resulted in 3 fatalities, 3 injuries, and $159.5 million in property and crop damage. Property damage was estimated at $2.1 billion.

Dec. 27, 2005: Wildfire. Cross Plains. A wildfire in Callahan County caused $11 million in property damages. The fire started just west of Cross Plains and quickly moved east, fanned by winds gusting near 40 mph. The fire moved into Cross Plains quickly and two elderly people were unable to escape the flames; 16 firefighters were also injured while fighting this fire.

Jan. 1, 2006: Wildfires. North Texas. Several wildfires exploded across North Texas due to low humidity, strong winds and the ongoing drought. Fires were reported in Montague, Eastland and Palo Pinto counties. Five injuries were reported as well as $10.8 million in property damage.

March 12–18, 2006: Wildfires. Borger. A wildfire now known as the **Borger wildfire** start four miles southwest of Borger, Hutchinson County. The wildfire burned a total of 479,500 acres. In all, seven people were killed and 28 structures were lost with total property damage at $49.9 million and crop damage at $45.4 million. A second wildfire known as the **Interstate-40 wildfire** burned 427,696 acres. The Texas Forest Service named the two wildfires the East Amarillo Complex. In all, 12 people were killed, total property damage was $49.9 million and crop damage was $45.4 million.

March 19, 2006: Tornado. Uvalde. An **F-2 tornado** moved through the Uvalde area causing $1.5 million in property damage. It was the strongest tornado in South Central Texas since Oct. 12, 2001.

April 11–13, 2006: Wildfire. Canadian. A wildfire 10 miles north of Canadian, Hemphill County, burned 18,000 acres and destroyed crops. Two injuries were reported. Total crop damage was estimated at $90 million.

April 18, 2006: Hail. Gillespie County. Hailstones as large as 2.5 inches in diameter destroyed windows in homes and car windshields between Harper and Doss in Gillespie County. The hail also damaged 70 percent of the area peach

crop, an estimated loss of $5 million.

April 20, 2006: Hail. San Marcos. Hailstones as large at 4.25 inches in diameter (grapefruit-size) was reported south of San Marcos. Damage from this storm was estimated at $100 million with up to 10,000 vehicles damaged and another 7,000 vehicles at homes.

May 4, 2006: Hail. Snyder. Lime-to-baseball-size **hail** fell across Snyder in Scurry County for a least 15 minutes. The hail was blown sideways at times by 60-to-70-mph winds. Total damage was estimated at $15 million.

May 5, 2006: Tornado. Waco. A **tornado** with peak intensity estimated at **low F-2**. Total damage was $3 million.

May 9, 2006: Tornado. Childress. An **F-2 tornado** resulted in significant damage along a one-and-one-half mile path through the north side of Childress during the evening hours. An instrument at Childress High School measured a wind gust of 109 mph. Property damage was estimated at $5.7 million.

Aug. 1, 2006: Thunderstorms. El Paso. Storms in a saturated atmosphere repeatedly developed and moved over mainly the northwest third of El Paso County, concentrating in an area near the Franklin Mountains. Rainfall reports varied from 4–6 inches within 15 hours, with an isolated report of about 8 inches on the western slope of the mountain range. Antecedent conditions from 4 days of heavy rains, combined with terrain effects of the mountains, led to excessive runoff and flooding not seen on such a large scale in the El Paso area in more than 100 years. Property damage was estimated at $180 million.

March 29, 2007: Floods. Corsicana. Flash flooding along Interstate 45 submerged two cars in Navarro County, north of Corsicana, and two feet of water was reported on I-45 and Texas 31, east of town. Damage to businesses, roads and bridges was estimated at $19 million.

April 13, 2007: Hail. Colleyville. Teacup-size hail was reported in Colleyville as strong storms developed in Tarrant County. Hail damage to 5,500 cars and 3,500 homes and businesses was estimated at $10 million.

April 24, 2007: Tornado. Eagle Pass. A large tornado crossed the Rio Grande from Mexico near 6 p.m., striking Rosita Valley, near Eagle Pass. Ten deaths were reported, including a family of five in a mobile home. Golf-ball size hail and the tornado struck Rosita Valley Elementary School, leaving only the interior walls standing. Damage indicated wind speeds near 140 mph and an F-3 level, with a path one-quarter mile wide and four miles long. The tornado also destroyed one 59 manufactured homes and 57 houses. Total damage was estimated at $80 million.

June 17–18, 2007: Floods. North Texas. Torrential rain fell as an upper-level low lingered for several days. In Tarrant County, one person drowned after her rescue boat capsized. Hundreds of people were rescued from high water. In Grayson County, a woman died in floodwaters as she drove under an overpass, and another death occurred in a flooded truck. Three people in Cooke County died when a mobile home was carried away by floodwaters. Damage was estimated at $30 million in Tarrant County, $20 million in Grayson County and $28 million in Cooke County.

June 27, 2007: Floods. Marble Falls. Two lines of thunderstorms produced 10–19 inches of rain in southern Burnet County. Hardest hit was Marble Falls, where two young men died in the early morning when their jeep was swept into high water east of town. Damage to more than 315 homes and businesses was $130 million.

September 13, 2007: Hurricane. Jefferson County. Hurricane Humberto made landfall around 1 a.m. in rural southwestern Jefferson County near McFaddin National Wildlife Refuge. Minimum pressure was around 985 millibars, with maximum winds at 90 mph. Some flash flooding occurred in urban areas between Beaumont and Orange, as 11 inches of rain fell in Jefferson County. Coastal storm tides were 3–5 feet, with the highest storm surge occurring at Texas Point. Humberto caused one death, 12 injuries and $25 million in damage.

March 31, 2008: Hail. Northeast Texas. Severe thunderstorms developed across the Red River valley of northeast Texas, many producing large hail that damaged car windows, skylights and roofs in Texarkana and elsewhere in

The storm surge from Hurricane Ike inundated Galveston with salt water and damaged many of the large live oak trees that characterized the town, above. Texas Forest Service employee Erin Harris (below, on left) and several volunteer Master Gardeners survey affected trees in April 2009 to determine which trees will survive and which will need to be cut down and replaced with saplings. Ron Billings photos; Texas Forest Service.

Bowie County. Damage was estimated at $120 million.

April 10, 2008: Tornadoes. Johnson County. A lone supercell thunderstorm evolved in the afternoon on April 9, producing tornadoes and large hail. A tornado touched down near Happy Hill and traveled northeast 3 miles to Pleasant Point, where it dissipated. The F-1 tornado, with maximum wind speeds of 90–95 mph, destroyed three homes and damaged more than 30 homes and other buildings. Damage was $25 million.

May 14, 2008: Hail. Austin. A severe thunderstorm southwest of Austin moved northeast across downtown Austin causing extensive damage from winds and large hail. Large trees and branches were knocked down, and baseball-size hail and 70–80 mph winds blew out windows in apartments and office buildings, including the State Capitol. Total damage was estimated at $50 million.

August 18, 2008: Floods. Wichita Falls. An unseasonably strong upper-level storm system moved over North Texas, and several waves of heavy thunderstorms caused high precipitation and widespread flooding in the Iowa Park, Burkburnett and Wichita Falls areas. In Wichita Falls, many homes were flooded and residents were evacuated by boat. At least 118 homes were flooded, 19 of which were destroyed. Burkburnett and Iowa Park were isolated for a few hours because of street flooding. Damage was estimated at $25 million, and Gov. Rick Perry declared Wichita County a disaster area.

September 12, 2008: Hurricane. Galveston.

The eye of Hurricane Ike moved ashore near the city of Galveston. The central pressure was 951.6 millibars, with maximum sustained winds around 110 mph, which made Hurricane Ike a strong Category-2 storm. There were 12 deaths directly related to Ike, with 11 occurring in Galveston County from drowning due to the storm surge. In addition, there were at least 25 fatalities indirectly related to Ike, either due to carbon monoxide poisoning from generators, accidents while clearing debris, or house fires from candles. The majority of property damage at the coast was a result of storm tide. Damage from Ike was more typical of a Category-3 or -4 storm, and collectively, damage amounts were near $14 billion over the counties of Harris, Chambers, Galveston, Liberty, Polk, Matagorda, Brazoria, Fort Bend, San Jacinto and Montgomery, with an estimated $8 billion of that due to storm surge in coastal Galveston, Harris and Chambers counties. ☆

Texas Temperature, Freeze, Growing Season and Precipitation Records by County

Data in the table below are from the office of the Texas State Climatologist, Texas A&M University, College Station. Because of the small change in averages, data are revised only at intervals of 10 years. Data below are the latest compilations, as of Feb. 1, 2004, and reflect data compiled during 1971–2000. The table shows temperature, freeze, growing season and precipitation for each county in Texas. Data for counties where a National Weather Service Station has not been maintained long enough to establish a reliable mean are interpolated from isoline charts prepared from mean values from stations with long-established records. Mean maximum temperature for July is computed from the sum of the daily maxima. Mean minimum January is computed from the sum of the daily minima. Weather stations shown in italics do not measure all categories and some data are from the period 1961–1990. An asterisk (*) preceding a record high or low or rainfall extreme denotes a figure that also occurred on an earlier date.

County and Station	Mean Max. July (F.)	Mean Min. January (F.)	Record Highest (F.)	Year	Record Lowest (F.)	Year	Last in Spring	First in Fall	Growing Season (Days)	Jan (In.)	Feb (In.)	Mar (In.)	Apr (In.)	May (In.)	June (In.)	July (In.)	Aug (In.)	Sept (In.)	Oct (In.)	Nov (In.)	Dec (In.)	Annual (In.)	Highest Daily Rainfall (In.)	Mo.-Year
Anderson, Palestine	93.9	37.4	114	1954	-4	1930	Mar. 15	Nov. 18	247	3.60	3.34	3.87	3.80	4.51	4.53	2.55	3.23	3.45	4.90	4.44	4.16	46.38	9.10	08-1991
Andrews, Andrews	94.5	30.4	113	1994	-1	1985	Mar. 29	Nov. 10	226	0.48	0.51	0.52	0.85	1.78	2.12	2.25	1.77	2.21	1.43	0.64	0.59	15.15	7.60	07-1914
Angelina, Lufkin	93.5	37.9	*110	2000	*-2	1951	Mar. 13	Nov. 15	247	4.45	3.17	3.53	3.13	5.29	4.18	2.60	3.08	4.08	4.13	4.54	4.44	46.62	7.47	10-1994
Aransas, Rockport	90.1	44.9	105	2000	12	1983	Feb. 2	Dec. 20	318	2.40	2.18	2.36	2.07	3.66	3.50	2.43	3.13	5.53	4.23	2.56	1.91	35.96	8.15	09-1979
Archer, Archer City	97.0	26.7	114	1980	*-10	1989	Mar. 28	Nov. 9	225	1.13	1.75	2.05	2.46	4.33	4.19	1.79	2.66	3.11	2.66	1.90	1.75	29.78	7.95	10-1981
Armstrong, Claude	90.5	21.2	*108	1980	-16	1905	Apr. 19	Oct. 20	184	0.51	0.58	1.23	1.60	3.34	3.33	3.08	3.00	2.37	1.91	0.82	0.62	22.39	10.27	05-1982
Atascosa, Poteet	95.9	39.0	*110	2000	-1	1949	Feb. 25	Dec. 2	279	1.27	1.83	1.54	2.50	4.09	4.06	1.64	2.69	2.90	3.04	1.79	1.65	29.00	8.75	07-1949
Austin, Sealy	94.9	40.7	111	2000	0	1989	Feb. 18	Dec. 8	291	3.14	2.81	2.61	3.22	4.71	3.85	1.93	3.06	4.33	4.44	3.68	2.90	40.68	11.00	08-1945
Bailey, Muleshoe	91.9	20.2	*110	1944	-21	1933	Apr. 17	Oct. 21	186	0.43	0.50	0.64	1.01	2.04	2.49	2.09	3.07	2.34	1.50	0.67	0.59	17.37	5.25	05-1951
Bandera, Medina	93.9	33.3	109	1980	5	1989	Mar. 22	Nov. 10	233	1.72	1.91	2.27	2.69	4.35	4.29	2.55	3.08	3.66	4.14	2.84	2.28	35.78	9.86	08-1971
Bastrop, Smithville	95.4	36.7	*111	2000	-1	1930	Mar. 4	Nov. 20	260	2.73	2.32	2.56	3.00	5.12	3.66	2.01	2.25	3.56	4.70	3.29	2.84	38.04	16.05	06-1940
Baylor, Seymour	96.5	27.7	120	1936	-14	1947	Mar. 30	Nov. 6	220	1.05	1.56	1.88	1.84	4.13	3.63	1.86	2.58	3.51	2.86	1.48	1.41	27.79	6.20	05-1989
Bee, Beeville	94.6	43.1	111	1939	8	1983	Feb. 14	Dec. 6	294	1.94	1.84	1.90	2.68	3.49	4.19	2.69	3.02	4.30	3.60	2.00	1.83	33.48	10.61	09-1967
Bell, Temple	95.0	34.9	112	1947	*-4	1989	Mar. 3	Nov. 22	264	1.91	2.70	2.65	2.81	4.56	3.71	1.82	2.20	4.00	3.73	3.04	2.68	35.81	9.62	10-1998
Bexar, San Antonio	94.6	38.6	111	2000	0	1949	Feb. 28	Nov. 25	270	1.66	1.75	1.89	2.60	4.72	4.30	2.03	2.57	3.00	3.86	2.58	1.96	32.92	11.26	10-1998
Blanco, Blanco	93.7	34.0	*110	2000	-6	1949	Mar. 20	Nov. 11	235	1.79	2.08	2.63	2.69	4.51	4.18	2.02	2.38	3.26	4.18	2.66	2.37	34.75	17.47	09-1952
Borden, Gail	94.6	28.9	116	1994	-1	1989	Mar. 27	Nov. 8	226	0.58	0.73	0.66	1.20	2.80	2.81	2.03	2.52	2.83	1.77	0.74	0.69	19.68	9.13	10-1960
Bosque, Lake Whitney	96.2	32.7	113	2000	*-3	1989	Mar. 15	Nov. 17	247	1.93	2.39	2.87	3.18	4.29	3.96	2.03	2.37	2.76	3.95	2.67	2.67	35.07	6.22	10-1971
Bowie, Texarkana	93.1	30.7	108	2000	*-6	1989	Mar. 20	Nov. 14	238	3.91	3.80	4.46	4.23	4.97	4.82	3.62	2.41	3.77	4.61	5.69	4.95	51.24	5.45	03-1989
Brazoria, Angleton	91.8	43.7	107	2000	*7	1989	Feb. 15	Dec. 5	290	4.76	3.50	3.76	3.74	5.20	6.44	4.24	4.83	7.49	4.25	4.86	4.17	57.24	14.36	07-1979
Brazos, College Station	95.6	39.8	112	2000	2	1989	Mar. 2	Nov. 29	271	3.32	3.50	2.84	3.20	5.05	2.18	1.92	2.63	3.91	4.22	3.67	3.23	39.67	13.18	09-1983
Brewster, Alpine	88.7	31.3	107	1972	-3	1983	Apr. 8	Nov. 1	207	0.45	0.50	0.34	0.58	1.25	2.18	3.04	2.92	3.23	1.58	0.45	0.67	17.19	3.13	06-1968
Brewster, Chisos Basin	84.2	36.1	103	1972	-3	1949	Mar. 16	Nov. 17	246	0.55	0.69	0.36	0.61	1.60	2.42	3.55	3.72	2.71	1.72	0.66	0.58	19.17	4.29	10-1966
Briscoe, Silverton	90.9	21.6	*109	1994	-9	1963	Apr. 14	Oct. 22	190	0.57	0.78	1.17	1.59	3.22	3.96	2.30	2.76	2.67	1.68	0.90	0.74	22.34	5.25	06-1979
Brooks, Falfurrias	97.0	43.9	115	1998	9	1962	Feb. 6	Dec. 13	311	1.12	1.56	0.86	1.48	2.95	3.25	1.84	2.91	3.84	3.22	1.31	1.08	25.42	10.00	09-1967
Brown, Brownwood	95.0	29.6	111	1964	-6	1989	Mar. 25	Nov. 11	231	1.28	2.09	2.07	2.45	3.62	3.75	1.80	2.28	2.67	3.01	1.62	1.68	28.32	*6.60	06-2000

County and Station	Mean Max. July (F.)	Mean Min. January (F.)	Record Highest (F.)	Year	Record Lowest (F.)	Year	Last in Spring (Mo. Day)	First in Fall (Mo. Day)	Growing Season (Days)	January (In.)	February (In.)	March (In.)	April (In.)	May (In.)	June (In.)	July (In.)	August (In.)	September (In.)	October (In.)	November (In.)	December (In.)	Annual (In.)	Highest Daily Rainfall (In.)	Mo.-Year
Burleson, Somerville	96.7	36.4	114	2000	3	1989	Mar. 3	Nov. 23	264	2.93	2.53	2.62	2.92	4.39	4.21	1.78	2.43	3.59	4.33	3.63	3.14	38.50	15.25	10-1994
Burnet, Burnet	93.6	33.3	*114	1917	*-4	1989	Mar. 20	Nov. 12	237	1.61	2.16	2.33	2.48	4.58	4.09	2.04	2.06	3.15	4.36	2.32	2.15	32.43	9.80	09-1936
Caldwell, Luling	95.8	36.9	*110	2000	-3	1949	Mar. 7	Nov. 20	258	2.27	2.20	2.22	3.06	5.44	4.29	1.70	2.32	3.70	4.36	3.00	2.30	36.86	10.53	10-1998
Calhoun, Port O'Connor	88.2	47.9	105	2000	10	1989	Jan. 29	Dec. 31	338	3.07	2.20	1.73	1.55	3.70	2.77	3.05	2.94	4.97	4.45	2.53	1.82	34.78	12.50	07-1976
Callahan, Putnam	94.9	31.1	110	1964	-8	1989	Mar. 24	Nov. 13	234	1.17	1.55	1.76	1.80	3.13	3.25	1.97	2.02	2.79	3.03	1.64	1.41	25.52	5.00	08-1978
Cameron, Brownsville	92.4	50.5	106	1984	*15	1901	Dec. 25	Jan. 24	>365	1.36	1.18	0.93	1.96	2.48	2.93	1.77	2.99	5.31	3.78	1.75	1.11	27.55	12.09	09-1967
Camp, Pittsburg	94.0	32.0	109		-3		Mar. 21	Nov. 14	238	3.30	3.40	3.40	3.70	4.60	3.30	3.30	2.10	3.30	3.78	3.90	3.90	45.10		
Carson, Panhandle	90.8	19.3	109	1964	*-10	1963	Apr. 18	Oct. 22	186	0.62	0.73	0.64	0.89	3.10	3.54	2.67	2.78	2.21	1.71	0.98	0.64	22.21	8.05	05-1951
Cass, Wright Patman Dam	94.0	31.0	103		8		Mar. 19	Nov. 11	237	3.70	3.60	4.40	4.00	4.50	4.50	3.00	2.60	3.50	4.30	5.30	4.80	48.20		
Castro, Dimmitt	90.1	20.4	111	1983	-9	1986	Apr. 25	Oct. 16	172	0.50	0.51	0.81	0.99	2.76	3.12	2.40	3.06	2.57	1.58	0.71	0.70	19.71	4.38	10-1998
Chambers, Anahuac	91.9	41.7	110	1943	8	1989	Feb. 12	Dec. 9	299	4.84	2.83	3.33	3.56	5.22	4.74	4.59	4.74	6.42	4.31	4.31	4.30	54.08	15.87	08-1945
Cherokee, Rusk	92.8	36.8	110	2000	0	1982	Mar. 10	Nov. 21	255	4.41	3.64	4.12	3.86	4.69	4.34	2.95	2.38	4.01	4.94	4.63	4.53	48.50	10.00	06-2001
Childress, Childress	95.3	26.8	117	1994	*-5	1989	Apr. 1	Nov. 6	218	0.57	0.95	1.41	2.01	3.46	3.51	2.05	2.19	2.51	2.07	1.06	0.86	22.65	5.32	10-1983
Clay, Henrietta	95.0	26.8	*116	1951	*-8	1989	Mar. 30	Nov. 5	220	1.53	2.08	2.45	2.71	4.39	3.72	1.74	2.40	3.35	3.35	1.77	2.17	31.66	6.07	06-1959
Cochran, Morton	91.4	23.1	111	1994	-12	1963	Apr. 14	Oct. 24	193	0.50	0.58	0.64	0.89	1.92	2.90	2.61	2.97	2.66	1.64	0.79	0.62	18.34	6.40	07-1960
Coke, Robert Lee	96.4	29.0	114	2000	*-2	1989	Mar. 26	Nov. 11	230	0.81	1.22	1.05	1.72	3.24	4.05	1.44	2.28	3.46	2.73	1.15	1.00	23.00	8.40	10-1957
Coleman, Coleman	93.7	30.0	114	1943	-5	1930	Mar. 23	Nov. 13	234	1.03	1.75	1.84	2.19	4.11	4.11	1.77	2.58	3.25	3.08	1.57	1.48	28.70	8.55	07-1932
Collin, McKinney	93.1	31.1	110	1936	-7	1930	Mar. 21	Nov. 11	235	2.43	2.91	3.37	3.65	5.68	3.98	2.36	2.16	3.15	4.24	3.71	3.24	41.01	12.10	09-1964
Collingsworth, Wellington	97.9	27.0	113	1994	-6	1989	Apr. 1	Nov. 4	216	0.62	0.73	1.47	2.07	3.88	3.77	2.25	1.85	2.58	3.71	0.89	0.62	22.80	9.50	10-1986
Colorado, Columbus	96.3	36.8	116	2000	*4	1989	Mar. 11	Nov. 16	250	3.61	2.84	2.93	3.57	5.75	5.03	2.64	3.07	3.92	4.16	3.99	3.21	44.72	10.00	06-1973
Comal, New Braunfels	94.7	35.5	112	2000	*2	1989	Mar. 4	Nov. 21	261	1.88	1.98	2.04	2.72	5.01	4.81	1.99	2.32	3.46	4.38	2.71	2.44	35.74	18.35	10-1998
Comanche, Proctor Reservoir	95.5	30.6	113	2000	-8	1989	Mar. 20	Nov. 15	238	1.34	2.02	2.13	2.81	4.75	3.98	1.70	2.22	3.01	3.32	2.07	1.77	31.12	8.37	06-1988
Concho, Paint Rock	97.4	31.9	111	1978	-8	1985	Mar. 31	Nov. 6	219	1.04	1.52	1.35	1.56	3.31	2.90	1.84	2.05	3.55	4.05	1.41	1.29	25.50	8.25	09-1980
Cooke, Gainesville	95.0	28.0	112		-7		Mar. 27	Nov. 8	226	1.80	2.20	3.40	3.20	4.60	3.66	2.00	2.40	4.50	4.60	2.60	1.90	36.90	8.35	06-1964
Coryell, Gatesville	96.4	33.5	*112	2000	-6	1949	Mar. 24	Nov. 13	234	1.65	2.35	2.57	2.90	4.38	3.67	2.36	2.53	2.87	3.30	2.51	2.35	33.43	6.65	06-1991
Cottle, Paducah	96.8	26.2	118	1994	*-7	1989	Mar. 29	Nov. 5	221	0.82	1.11	1.31	1.92	3.31	4.21	1.72	2.63	2.96	2.06	1.08	0.98	24.11	5.55	08-1986
Crane, Crane	95.3	30.6	115	1994	-6	1985	Mar. 23	Nov. 11	232	0.57	0.59	0.34	0.84	1.86	1.71	1.48	2.02	2.95	1.64	0.68	0.70	15.38	5.80	10-1959
Crockett, Ozona	93.0	27.7	*109	1969	-8	1951	Apr. 1	Nov. 2	215	0.68	0.78	1.06	1.36	2.44	1.57	1.57	2.27	2.92	1.91	0.99	0.84	18.95	18.95	06-1913
Crosby, Crosbyton	92.5	25.3	113	1994	*-10	1930	Apr. 2	Nov. 1	212	0.39	0.96	1.03	1.87	3.05	3.10	2.05	3.05	3.46	1.27	0.95	0.53	22.95	5.78	06-1913
Culberson, Van Horn	91.7	27.8	112	1969	-7	1962	Apr. 4	Nov. 5	215	0.35	0.33	0.16	0.24	0.71	1.25	2.11	2.30	2.23	1.32	0.46	0.54	11.98	7.00	08-1966
Dallam, Dalhart	90.0	19.0	*107	1990	-21	1959	Apr. 23	Oct. 16	175	0.40	0.40	1.08	1.35	2.72	2.27	3.11	2.99	1.56	0.71	0.71	0.40	18.57	4.52	08-1985
Dallas, Dallas	96.1	36.4	115	1909	1	1989	Mar. 3	Nov. 25	267	1.89	2.31	3.13	3.46	5.30	3.92	2.43	2.17	2.65	4.65	2.61	2.53	37.05	6.02	03-1977
Dawson, Lamesa	92.9	26.0	114	1994	-12	1933	Apr. 4	Nov. 5	214	0.57	0.77	0.73	0.88	2.35	2.81	2.19	2.00	3.42	1.76	0.82	0.77	19.07	6.24	10-1985
Deaf Smith, Hereford	91.6	21.1	111	1910	-17	1951	Apr. 19	Oct. 19	182	0.50	0.50	0.98	1.02	2.12	2.90	2.06	3.22	2.25	1.59	0.77	0.74	18.65	*5.30	08-1976

COUNTY AND STATION	TEMPERATURE July Mean Max. (F.)	TEMPERATURE January Mean Min. (F.)	Record Highest (F.)	Record Highest Year	Record Lowest (F.)	Record Lowest Year	AVERAGE FREEZE DATES Last in Spring (Mo. Day)	AVERAGE FREEZE DATES First in Fall (Mo. Day)	Growing Season (Days)	Jan. (In.)	Feb. (In.)	Mar. (In.)	Apr. (In.)	May (In.)	June (In.)	July (In.)	Aug. (In.)	Sept. (In.)	Oct. (In.)	Nov. (In.)	Dec. (In.)	Annual (In.)	Highest Daily Rainfall (In.)	Mo.-Year
Delta, Cooper	94.0	30.0	110		-1	1949	Mar. 25	Nov. 13	233	2.70	3.20	4.10	3.60	5.40	4.00	2.90	2.10	3.90	4.80	4.30	4.00	45.00	7.30	05-1982
Denton, Denton	94.1	32.0	*113	1954	*-3	1949	Mar. 18	Nov. 16	243	1.94	2.55	2.82	3.30	5.41	3.29	2.53	2.26	3.35	4.81	2.87	2.66	37.79	12.40	06-1940
DeWitt, Cuero	95.1	41.3	113	2000	7	1989	Feb. 28	Nov. 25	270	2.30	1.95	2.32	2.96	4.74	4.51	2.18	2.25	4.31	3.67	2.66	2.23	36.08	4.70	08-1996
Dickens, Spur	95.4	25.5	117	1933	-17	1933	Apr. 2	Nov. 4	215	0.55	0.70	0.84	1.53	3.18	2.68	1.74	2.12	2.17	1.66	0.82	0.69	18.68	8.78	07-1990
Dimmit, Carrizo Springs	98.3	39.6	114	1942	10	1989	Feb. 14	Dec. 4	292	1.00	0.94	0.89	1.47	2.96	2.78	1.26	2.33	1.95	2.66	1.10	0.87	20.21	9.25	05-2001
Donley, Clarendon	94.7	22.4	117	1936	*-11	1989	Apr. 11	Oct. 25	196	0.64	0.83	1.43	2.25	3.60	3.70	2.37	2.81	2.69	1.78	0.94	0.85	23.89	7.85	09-1971
Duval, Freer	97.3	42.5	116	1998	12	1963	Feb. 13	Dec. 8	297	1.15	1.54	1.58	1.69	3.63	3.70	1.54	2.25	3.06	2.92	1.54	1.05	25.40	7.00	10-1957
Eastland, Eastland	94.9	26.7	*115	1943	*-6	1973	Apr. 1	Nov. 8	221	1.20	1.73	1.93	2.27	3.72	3.40	1.73	2.29	2.67	3.25	1.72	1.62	27.53	4.53	04-1969
Ector, Penwell	96.0	28.7	116	1994	-12	1985	Mar. 30	Nov. 7	222	0.42	0.58	0.42	0.61	2.11	1.56	1.30	1.46	2.35	1.24	0.63	0.61	13.29	9.50	06-1935
Edwards, Rocksprings	91.6	34.3	*108	1980	*3	1951	Mar. 18	Nov. 17	243	0.77	1.31	1.36	1.75	3.23	3.07	2.05	2.84	2.44	3.41	1.50	1.03	24.76	10.80	09-1958
Ellis, Waxahachie	96.0	35.0	115	1909	-4	1989	Mar. 14	Nov. 18	248	2.11	2.63	3.21	3.89	4.85	2.28	2.28	2.26	3.16	4.43	3.04	3.22	38.81		
El Paso, El Paso	94.5	32.9	114	1994	-8	1962	Mar. 22	Nov. 8	230	0.45	0.39	0.26	0.23	0.38	0.87	1.49	1.75	1.61	0.81	0.42	0.77	9.43	2.26	09-1974
Erath, Stephenville	93.6	30.0	111	1925	-8	1989	Mar. 22	Nov. 13	235	1.31	1.86	2.35	2.53	4.35	3.41	1.47	2.41	2.80	3.28	1.97	1.97	29.71	9.71	05-1956
Falls, Marlin	95.0	37.0	*112	1969	-7	1949	Mar. 10	Nov. 17	251	2.49	2.60	3.30	3.19	5.35	3.55	2.09	1.97	3.08	3.90	3.17	3.30	37.99	11.90	07-1903
Fannin, Bonham	92.6	30.2	115	1936	*-5	1930	Mar. 27	Nov. 8	225	2.39	3.01	3.76	3.41	5.57	3.45	2.25	2.13	3.45	5.40	3.94	3.55	44.56	13.30	07-1903
Fayette, La Grange	95.9	41.4	110	2000	3	1989	Feb. 26	Nov. 23	269	3.05	2.88	2.55	2.99	4.82	4.41	2.25	2.81	3.68	4.47	3.36	3.04	40.31	9.41	06-1940
Fisher, Rotan	94.2	27.2	116	1994	*-5	1989	Mar. 29	Nov. 9	225	0.80	1.35	1.30	1.72	3.68	2.74	1.92	2.76	3.45	2.30	1.13	1.07	24.22	6.85	08-1972
Floyd, Floydada	92.3	23.2	111	1994	-9	1963	Apr. 8	Oct. 30	205	0.45	0.72	0.98	1.58	3.01	3.74	2.00	2.50	2.88	1.62	0.84	0.63	20.95	6.51	09-1942
Foard, Crowell			114	1994	-7	1989	Apr. 2	Nov. 7	219	1.00	1.40	1.60	2.10	4.30	3.70	2.00	2.40	3.30	2.40	1.50	1.00	26.40		
Fort Bend, Sugar Land	93.7	41.6	108	1989	*6	1989	Feb. 15	Dec. 10	294	4.06	2.98	3.24	3.48	4.69	5.51	3.30	4.29	5.82	4.03	4.58	3.36	49.34	10.60	06-2001
Franklin, Mount Vernon	92.8	32.2	*108	2000	-1	1989	Mar. 22	Nov. 12	235	2.83	3.41	4.23	3.56	4.71	4.79	3.82	2.19	3.75	4.77	5.10	4.49	47.65	6.10	07-1990
Freestone, Fairfield	95.0	36.4	*110	2000	-2	1989	Mar. 19	Nov. 17	242	2.84	3.29	3.29	3.38	5.04	3.79	2.14	2.56	3.48	4.64	4.16	3.70	42.31	7.90	01-1999
Frio, Pearsall	97.5	37.9	113	2000	*7	1989	Feb. 22	Nov. 25	275	1.30	1.45	1.30	2.15	3.33	3.68	1.58	2.61	2.29	3.20	1.60	1.24	25.73	7.84	06-1946
Gaines, Seminole	94.1	26.7	110	2000	-9	1962	Apr. 2	Nov. 3	215	0.64	0.72	0.61	0.91	2.39	2.45	1.48	2.31	2.73	1.39	0.90	0.71	18.20	5.40	05-1999
Galveston, Galveston	88.7	49.7	102	1994	*14	1989	Jan. 19	Jan. 9	358	4.08	2.61	2.76	2.56	3.70	4.04	3.45	4.22	5.76	3.49	3.64	3.53	43.84	13.63	07-1900
Garza, Post	94.0	27.8	115	1994	*-1	1994	Mar. 30	Nov. 9	223	0.58	0.98	0.76	1.43	3.01	2.83	2.03	2.88	3.07	2.05	0.89	0.78	21.29	6.75	10-1926
Gillespie, Fredericksburg	93.1	36.1	*109	2000	-5	1949	Mar. 18	Nov. 12	238	1.36	1.91	1.86	2.40	4.29	3.97	2.85	2.74	3.07	3.72	1.20	2.14	31.65	8.03	09-1952
Glasscock, Garden City	94.0	36.7	114	1994	-3	1989	Apr. 3	Nov. 3	213	0.73	0.71	0.70	1.14	2.18	1.91	1.86	2.02	2.97	1.66	0.75	0.69	17.32	8.75	07-1945
Goliad, Goliad	95.5	43.3	*112	1998	7	1962	Feb. 25	Nov. 26	273	2.34	2.11	2.00	3.19	4.49	4.96	2.85	3.49	4.56	4.26	2.19	2.14	38.58	9.16	09-1967
Gonzales, Gonzales	93.9	38.7	111	2000	*4	1989	Feb. 26	Dec. 1	277	2.36	2.08	2.22	3.04	5.43	4.24	1.60	2.68	3.20	3.87	2.84	2.46	36.02	16.31	08-1981
Gray, Pampa	92.0	21.9	111	1980	-8	1980	Apr. 13	Oct. 25	195	0.57	0.83	1.50	1.95	3.37	3.52	2.85	2.38	2.29	1.58	1.20	0.70	21.29	3.54	07-1982
Grayson, Sherman	92.7	32.2	113	1936	*-2	1989	Mar. 14	Nov. 14	236	2.11	2.63	3.44	3.49	5.41	4.37	2.34	2.25	4.01	5.15	2.34	3.03	42.04		
Gregg, Longview	94.5	33.7	113	1936	-4	1930	Mar. 19	Nov. 15	240	3.79	3.93	4.11	4.19	4.79	5.03	2.83	2.71	3.81	4.34	4.75	4.78	49.06	8.40	08-1920
Grimes, Richards	96.0	40.0	108		4		Mar. 1	Dec. 4	278	4.10	3.00	3.30	3.40	5.20	3.90	2.20	2.60	4.20	4.40	4.10	4.30	44.70	8.70	03-1989

County and Station	Temperature: Mean Max. July °F	Mean Min. January °F	Record Highest °F	Year	Record Lowest °F	Year	Avg Freeze: Last in Spring Mo. Day	First in Fall Mo. Day	Growing Season Days	Jan. In.	Feb. In.	Mar. In.	Apr. In.	May In.	June In.	July In.	Aug. In.	Sept. In.	Oct. In.	Nov. In.	Dec. In.	Annual In.	Highest Daily Rainfall In.	Mo.-Year
Guadalupe, New Braunfels	95.0	36.0	110		0		Mar. 6	Nov. 28	267	1.90	2.20	1.80	2.60	5.00	4.10	2.00	2.50	4.10	3.50	2.80	2.00	34.50	7.00	07-1960
Hale, Plainview	91.0	24.4	111	1994	-8	1933	Apr. 4	Oct. 31	209	0.59	0.63	0.80	1.52	2.91	3.05	2.45	2.38	2.28	1.72	0.84	0.73	19.90	8.80	06-1960
Hall, Memphis	95.7	25.5	*117	1944	-11	1930	Apr. 1	Nov. 4	217	0.57	0.88	1.52	2.04	3.93	3.51	1.88	2.25	2.45	1.77	0.96	0.75	22.51	8.20	10-1959
Hamilton, Hamilton	94.3	33.4	109	1964	-3	1989	Mar. 16	Nov. 15	243	1.64	1.76	2.61	2.72	3.70	3.71	1.53	1.57	2.85	2.90	2.00	1.60	28.59	5.80	05-1965
Hansford, Spearman	95.5	22.4	111	1936	-22	1959	Apr. 16	Oct. 23	189	0.53	0.62	1.52	1.58	2.83	2.97	2.77	2.38	2.08	1.35	1.01	0.66	20.30	8.03	08-1995
Hardeman, Quanah	96.5	24.6	*119	1994	-15	1989	Apr. 4	Nov. 2	211	0.96	1.17	1.65	2.08	3.86	3.73	2.42	2.57	3.43	2.37	1.40	1.12	26.76	9.95	10-1949
Hardin, Evadale	93.0	37.0	102		12		Mar. 31	Nov. 14	246	5.40	3.70	4.20	4.00	5.50	5.50	4.10	4.20	4.50	5.30	5.00	5.10	56.50	8.58	03-1989
Harris, Houston	93.6	45.2	108	2000	9	1989	Feb. 8	Dec. 20	308	4.25	3.01	3.19	3.46	5.11	6.84	4.36	4.54	5.62	5.26	4.54	3.78	53.96	3.80	12-1997
Harrison, Marshall	92.4	33.4	112	1909	-5	1930	Mar. 20	Nov. 14	236	4.38	4.07	4.33	4.35	5.07	5.23	3.02	2.68	3.89	4.66	4.59	4.95	51.22	14.29	08-1978
Hartley, Channing	90.9	20.0	*108	1981	-9	1979	Apr. 19	Oct. 19	182	0.35	0.45	0.76	1.10	1.88	2.30	2.59	3.50	1.66	1.33	0.61	0.67	17.20	15.78	10-1998
Haskell, Haskell	96.1	28.8	*115	1994	*-6	1989	Mar. 27	Nov. 12	229	0.96	1.47	1.46	1.99	3.32	3.26	1.61	2.74	2.96	2.53	1.26	1.37	24.93	5.15	10-1985
Hays, San Marcos	95.1	38.6	*111	2000	-2	1949	Feb. 28	Nov. 24	268	2.05	2.21	2.09	2.85	5.31	4.84	2.12	2.65	3.46	4.03	3.17	2.41	37.19	7.19	04-1986
Hemphill, Canadian	93.9	18.8	*112	1994	*-14	1942	Apr. 10	Oct. 16	188	0.46	0.71	1.70	1.72	3.75	3.33	2.19	2.36	2.36	1.47	0.94	0.69	21.68	7.81	08-1980
Henderson, Athens	93.4	35.2	*109	2000	-6	1985	Mar. 19	Nov. 14	239	3.37	3.70	3.70	3.47	4.82	3.95	1.74	2.43	3.07	3.88	3.94	4.02	42.03	11.30	09-1936
Hidalgo, McAllen	95.5	48.2	109	1999	17	1962	Jan. 30	Jan. 30	>365	1.20	1.37	0.95	1.36	2.51	2.49	1.70	2.31	4.00	2.76	0.95	1.01	22.61	4.23	06-1999
Hill, Hillsboro	95.7	35.2	113	1917	-6	1989	Mar. 19	Nov. 14	240	2.19	2.67	3.21	3.24	4.65	4.07	2.08	2.19	2.92	4.15	2.70	3.08	37.15		
Hockley, Levelland	92.7	23.7	115	1994	-16	1963	Apr. 08	Oct. 27	201	0.59	0.63	0.58	1.03	2.35	2.78	2.22	2.87	3.24	1.62	0.85	0.82	19.58	8.11	07-1994
Hood, Cresson	97.0	33.0	110		-6		Mar. 26	Nov. 13	232	1.60	2.20	2.60	2.90	5.00	3.90	1.70	2.40	2.60	3.90	2.30	2.30	33.10	9.11	06-2001
Hopkins, Sulphur Springs	94.8	31.1	115	1969	-4	1989	Mar. 25	Nov. 12	232	2.88	3.20	4.27	4.34	5.00	4.64	3.22	2.35	3.35	5.21	4.77	4.46	47.69	4.84	05-1994
Houston, Crockett	93.3	35.9	114	1909	*0	1989	Mar. 10	Nov. 18	252	4.00	3.10	3.45	3.87	4.66	4.46	2.84	2.81	4.12	4.22	3.93	4.02	45.48	3.32	09-1978
Howard, Big Spring	96.6	29.6	*114	1994	*-5	1985	Mar. 23	Nov. 13	235	0.72	0.81	0.73	1.34	3.05	2.58	1.78	2.38	3.51	1.78	0.77	0.67	20.12	6.95	09-1936
Hudspeth, Sierra Blanca	92.0	25.1	*109	1994	-10	1962	Apr. 18	Oct. 29	193	0.49	0.41	0.26	0.29	1.12	1.11	2.11	2.29	2.19	0.44	0.56	0.66	11.93	3.79	05-1959
Hunt, Greenville	93.3	31.2	116	1936	-4	1930	Mar. 23	Nov. 13	235	2.51	3.16	3.67	3.79	5.47	4.03	2.96	2.18	3.56	4.91	3.98	3.48	43.70	9.60	04-1957
Hutchinson, Borger	92.6	23.4	*108	1998	-12	1951	Apr. 14	Oct. 25	193	0.65	0.69	1.56	1.77	3.08	3.20	2.69	3.16	2.00	1.60	0.88	0.70	21.98		
Irion, Funk Ranch	95.0	32.0	108		4		Mar. 27	Nov. 11	229	0.70	1.10	1.00	1.60	2.50	2.50	1.40	1.90	3.10	2.10	1.00	1.00	19.90	9.04	03-1999
Jack, Jacksboro	94.4	29.7	*113	1980	-7	1989	Mar. 21	Nov. 14	237	1.28	1.79	2.38	2.60	4.96	3.18	2.26	2.15	3.18	3.78	2.05	1.83	31.44	5.30	08-1932
Jackson, Edna	94.0	42.0	105		17		Feb. 19	Dec. 6	290	3.10	2.40	2.00	3.10	5.30	4.60	2.90	2.60	4.90	5.00	3.40	2.80	42.10	4.13	05-1984
Jasper, Sam Rayburn Dam	94.5	35.2	109	2000	7	1989	Mar. 17	Nov. 14	241	5.94	4.55	5.29	4.51	5.53	5.81	4.24	3.92	3.97	4.84	5.88	6.09	60.57	12.09	09-1963
Jeff Davis, Fort Davis	89.5	28.4	*107	1998	*0	1985	Apr. 9	Nov. 2	206	0.43	0.35	0.34	0.50	1.46	1.79	2.95	2.97	2.76	1.29	0.49	0.53	15.86	9.40	09-1971
Jeff Davis, Mount Locke	84.5	32.1	104	1994	-10	1962	Apr. 17	Oct. 26	191	0.53	0.49	0.33	0.60	1.73	2.56	3.82	4.02	4.52	0.73	0.56	0.73	20.37	12.14	09-1971
Jefferson, Beaumont	91.6	42.9	108	2000	12	1989	Feb. 14	Dec. 6	295	5.69	3.35	3.75	3.84	5.83	6.58	5.23	4.85	6.10	4.67	4.75	5.25	59.89	9.02	05-1989
Jim Hogg, Hebbronville	97.5	43.8	111	1998	*12	1989	Feb. 8	Dec. 11	307	1.12	1.40	1.14	1.69	3.33	3.13	1.44	2.28	3.68	2.22	1.22	1.10	23.75		
Jim Wells, Alice	96.1	44.1	*111	1998	*12	1989	Jan. 29	Dec. 15	320	1.21	1.51	1.34	1.65	3.16	3.41	1.76	2.70	4.52	3.55	1.50	1.21	27.52		
Johnson, Cleburne	97.0	34.0	114	1939	-5	1989	Mar. 18	Nov. 13	240	1.90	2.29	3.07	3.53	5.11	3.90	2.18	2.36	2.88	3.92	2.54	2.57	36.25		

County and Station	Mean Max. July °F	Mean Min. January °F	Record Highest °F	Year	Record Lowest °F	Year	Last in Spring Mo. Day	First in Fall Mo. Day	Growing Season Days	Jan.	Feb.	Mar.	Apr.	May	June	July	Aug.	Sept.	Oct.	Nov.	Dec.	Annual	Highest Daily Rainfall In.	Mo.-Year
Jones, Anson	96.3	30.7	114	1994	-12	1989	Mar. 28	Nov. 12	228	1.03	1.51	1.21	1.94	3.20	3.13	2.04	2.94	3.93	2.55	1.22	1.30	26.00	5.60	09-1988
Karnes, Karnes City	95.0	41.0	112		7		Feb. 24	Dec. 2	281	1.50	1.70	1.50	2.50	3.40	3.70	1.90	2.40	3.40	3.00	1.90	1.50	28.40		
Kaufman, Kaufman	94.6	32.3	112	1936	*-3	1989	Mar. 19	Nov. 14	240	2.74	3.04	3.37	3.06	4.45	3.31	2.12	1.98	2.77	4.81	3.80	3.45	38.90	13.66	08-1908
Kendall, Boerne	91.9	34.3	112	1925	-4	1949	Mar. 20	Nov. 13	238	1.79	2.24	2.57	2.87	4.66	4.77	2.23	3.05	3.61	4.09	3.11	2.37	37.36	9.04	10-1913
Kenedy, Sarita	95.0	45.0	110		14		Feb. 2	Dec. 18	319	1.10	1.80	1.30	1.60	2.70	3.30	1.50	3.40	4.70	3.40	1.90	1.20	27.90		
Kent, Jayton	95.7	24.9	116	1994	-6	1985	Apr. 2	Nov. 7	218	0.91	1.14	1.12	1.73	3.35	3.21	1.59	2.81	3.04	3.40	0.97	0.90	22.94	6.50	06-1991
Kerr, Kerrville	92.0	32.0	110		-7		Apr. 6	Nov. 6	216	1.30	1.80	2.10	2.30	4.20	4.00	2.20	2.30	3.90	3.80	2.60	2.10	32.60		
Kimble, Junction	94.8	29.3	*110	1984	-11	1929	Apr. 2	Nov. 1	212	0.77	1.43	1.42	1.95	3.23	3.10	1.55	2.20	2.28	2.68	1.37	1.26	23.24	6.10	09-1980
King, Guthrie	96.7	23.9	119	1994	-10	1989	Apr. 6	Nov. 4	211	1.03	1.28	1.26	1.79	3.90	3.17	1.94	2.87	3.25	2.38	1.12	1.01	25.00	8.85	07-1986
Kinney, Brackettville	95.5	37.3	111	1988	4	1962	Mar. 5	Nov. 15	255	0.77	1.16	1.10	1.99	2.87	2.49	1.79	2.29	2.77	2.49	1.41	0.97	22.79	6.05	05-1900
Kleberg, Kingsville	95.5	43.4	*111	2000	10	1989	Feb. 10	Dec. 11	303	1.44	1.71	1.24	1.80	3.53	4.02	1.97	3.05	3.98	3.72	1.50	1.07	29.03	6.67	12-1991
Knox, Munday	96.5	28.1	*111	1994	*-9	1989	Mar. 28	Nov. 12	228	1.00	1.54	1.69	1.91	3.85	3.46	1.70	2.68	3.22	2.73	1.38	1.20	26.36	8.00	06-1930
Lamar, Paris	94.3	29.9	115	1936	*-5	1930	Mar. 18	Nov. 14	240	2.63	3.00	4.11	3.56	4.25	4.25	3.89	2.39	4.42	5.04	4.70	4.20	47.82	7.61	06-1928
Lamb, Littlefield	92.0	22.7	112	1994	-6	1979	Apr. 11	Oct. 25	196	0.55	0.52	0.75	1.11	2.24	2.44	3.89	2.80	2.26	1.52	0.77	0.69	18.69	5.10	06-1999
Lampasas, Lampasas	94.1	30.4	*112	1917	-12	1949	Apr. 1	Nov. 07	219	1.50	2.34	2.31	2.48	4.37	3.49	1.68	2.42	2.61	3.33	2.32	2.23	31.08	6.95	05-1957
La Salle, Fowlerton	98.9	39.1	113	1998	9	1962	Feb. 27	Nov. 26	271	0.93	1.08	1.46	1.84	2.73	2.61	1.53	2.19	2.71	3.15	1.22	1.11	22.56	9.50	10-1986
Lavaca, Hallettsville	94.4	41.8	*111	1980	5	1989	Feb. 25	Nov. 29	277	2.91	2.50	2.46	3.44	5.75	5.02	2.28	2.95	4.49	4.07	3.53	2.83	42.23	11.30	07-1936
Lee, Lexington	93.6	37.3	111	2000	2	1989	Mar. 1	Nov. 22	265	2.40	2.13	2.54	2.48	4.82	3.78	1.63	2.06	3.26	4.69	3.25	2.78	36.02	10.13	10-1994
Leon, Centerville	94.7	34.3	*111	1954	-3	1949	Mar. 17	Nov. 14	242	3.60	3.18	3.51	3.29	4.77	4.12	2.48	2.62	3.50	4.79	3.82	3.60	43.08	8.50	10-1957
Liberty, Liberty	92.2	40.3	108	1913	7	1989	Feb. 18	Dec. 1	285	4.91	3.74	3.84	4.01	5.80	6.88	4.46	4.34	5.92	5.77	5.84	5.01	60.52	18.50	10-1994
Limestone, Mexia	95.8	33.7	112	1909	-5	1989	Mar. 6	Nov. 20	258	2.44	3.08	3.45	3.14	4.91	3.89	1.99	2.56	4.16	4.29	3.64	3.85	41.40	11.80	10-1932
Lipscomb, Lipscomb	94.2	16.2	114	1978	*-18	1974	Apr. 23	Oct. 11	170	0.54	0.81	1.91	2.00	3.85	3.28	2.30	2.52	1.97	1.46	0.81	0.81	22.57	6.62	05-1951
Live Oak, Choke Canyon Dam	97.0	42.0	109		12		Feb. 20	Dec. 6	289	1.20	1.80	1.80	2.40	2.80	3.40	1.60	1.40	2.10	1.70	1.70	1.20	22.00		
Llano, Llano	96.0	32.3	115	1933	-7	1929	Mar. 18	Nov. 12	238	1.08	1.80	1.90	2.19	3.94	3.40	1.84	2.03	2.14	2.88	2.23	1.90	27.33	12.53	09-1952
Loving, Mentone	96.0	28.0	114		-14		Apr. 3	Nov. 8	222	0.30	0.30	0.30	0.20	1.10	0.90	1.80	1.40	1.20	1.00	0.30	0.30	9.10		
Lubbock, Lubbock	91.9	24.4	114	1994	-17	1933	Apr. 3	Nov. 1	211	0.50	0.71	0.76	1.29	2.31	2.98	2.13	2.36	2.57	1.70	0.71	0.67	18.69	5.70	06-1967
Lynn, Tahoka	92.2	25.1	111	1994	-15	1933	Apr. 4	Nov. 1	213	0.66	0.71	0.71	1.48	2.74	2.62	2.22	2.23	2.65	1.73	0.86	0.79	20.48	8.32	10-1913
Madison, Madisonville	96.0	35.8	112	2000	-2	1949	Mar. 7	Nov. 18	255	3.81	2.83	3.24	3.26	5.06	3.89	2.72	2.95	4.20	4.41	4.01	3.62	44.00	8.00	08-1945
Marion, Jefferson	93.1	31.4	108	2000	-5	1989	Mar. 25	Nov. 6	225	4.13	3.96	4.41	4.07	4.60	4.84	2.89	2.93	3.40	4.64	4.68	4.71	49.26	9.10	04-1921
Martin, Lenorah	94.0	30.0	109		-8		Apr. 5	Nov. 6	215	0.70	0.70	0.70	1.20	2.40	2.50	2.00	1.60	3.10	1.80	0.80	0.70	18.20		
Mason, Mason	94.9	30.8	109	1962	*3	1985	Mar. 26	Nov. 9	227	0.91	0.97	1.74	2.05	3.31	2.20	2.00	2.52	3.00	3.01	2.07	1.37	27.95	7.45	09-1952
Matagorda, Bay City	92.4	45.7	*109	2000	*7	1989	Feb. 11	Dec. 13	306	3.89	2.97	3.00	3.18	4.90	4.68	3.89	3.48	5.61	5.13	3.97	3.33	48.03	8.95	09-1961
Maverick, Eagle Pass	98.1	40.1	*115	1944	*10	1962	Feb. 12	Dec. 5	295	0.80	0.94	0.72	1.75	2.95	3.49	2.03	2.01	2.57	2.33	1.08	0.81	21.48	15.60	06-1936
McCulloch, Brady	94.5	32.3	*110	1980	-2	1989	Mar. 21	Nov. 11	235	1.01	1.68	1.63	1.92	3.60	3.26	2.68	2.57	3.26	2.68	1.73	1.61	27.63	6.51	07-1971

COUNTY AND STATION	TEMPERATURE Mean Max. July (F.)	Mean Min. January (F.)	Record Highest (F.)	Year	Record Lowest (F.)	Year	AVERAGE FREEZE DATES Last in Spring	First in Fall	Growing Season Days	MEAN PRECIPITATION January	February	March	April	May	June	July	August	September	October	November	December	Annual	EXTREMES Highest Daily Rainfall (In.)	Mo.-Year
McLennan, Waco	96.7	35.1	112	1969	-5	1949	Mar. 13	Nov. 19	250	1.90	2.43	2.48	2.99	4.46	3.08	2.23	1.85	2.88	3.67	2.61	2.76	33.34	7.98	12-1997
McMullen, Tilden	98.7	40.1	119	1910	5	1989	Feb. 21	Dec. 3	284	1.15	1.27	1.33	1.95	3.10	3.37	1.52	2.56	2.91	2.14	1.38	1.19	23.87	6.93	09-1967
Medina, Hondo	95.0	38.0	112		4		Mar. 6	Nov. 24	263	1.30	1.50	1.60	2.70	3.80	3.60	1.40	1.50	2.80	2.90	1.80	1.40	26.30		
Menard, Menard	94.8	30.7	112	1927	-6	1929	Apr. 7	Oct. 29	204	0.97	1.48	1.60	1.72	3.22	3.38	2.14	2.34	2.69	2.57	1.51	1.28	24.90	6.03	09-1936
Midland, Midland	94.3	29.6	116	1994	-11	1985	Mar. 30	Nov. 12	226	0.53	0.58	0.42	0.73	1.79	1.71	1.89	1.77	2.31	1.77	0.65	0.65	14.80	4.75	05-1968
Milam, Cameron	95.7	39.2	114	1917	-7	1930	Mar. 7	Nov. 22	260	2.29	2.53	2.45	2.88	3.85	3.81	1.94	1.95	3.54	3.71	3.12	2.86	35.52	12.45	09-1921
Mills, Goldthwaite	92.0	35.2	110	1964	-7	1989	Mar. 20	Nov. 15	239	1.26	2.10	2.04	2.28	4.49	2.84	1.76	2.29	2.79	3.13	2.05	1.78	28.78	7.20	10-1969
Mitchell, Colorado City	95.9	27.0	115	1907	-7	1947	Mar. 25	Nov. 7	226	0.44	0.89	1.07	1.33	2.49	2.84	1.81	2.29	3.09	2.22	0.90	0.64	19.43	8.65	04-1900
Montague, Bowie	94.7	25.0	115	1980	-11	1989	Mar. 21	Nov. 12	236	1.47	2.13	2.62	2.89	5.50	3.42	1.23	2.27	3.67	4.20	2.18	2.02	33.72	10.25	05-1989
Montgomery, Conroe	94.3	40.0	109	2000	3		Feb. 27	Nov. 25	270	4.21	2.97	2.94	3.85	4.58	4.58	3.22	3.73	4.46	4.70	4.79	4.37	49.32	14.35	10-1994
Moore, Dumas	91.7	20.8	*109	1980	*-18	1959	Apr. 18	Oct. 22	186	0.47	0.58	1.13	1.31	2.74	2.41	1.81	2.47	1.95	1.11	0.66	0.50	17.75	4.10	05-1988
Morris, Daingerfield	95.0	33.7	112	1998	4	1962	Mar. 3	Nov. 22	263	3.54	3.35	4.64	4.32	4.43	4.24	2.42	2.39	3.29	4.35	4.84	4.39	46.76	7.48	04-1966
Motley, Matador	94.8	27.3	116	1994	-5	1989	Apr. 1	Nov. 8	221	0.67	0.90	1.21	1.81	3.16	3.60	2.98	2.41	3.11	2.09	0.99	0.85	22.90	5.30	10-1983
Nacogdoches, Nacogdoches	94.0	36.0	113	1954	0	1949	Mar. 16	Nov. 12	243	4.40	3.90	4.20	4.10	4.95	5.00	2.10	3.10	3.70	4.00	4.60	4.60	48.40		
Navarro, Corsicana	94.5	34.0	113	1994	-5		Mar. 9	Nov. 23	259	2.49	3.08	3.34	3.39	4.90	3.40	2.90	2.37	3.04	2.53	3.33	3.60	39.48	9.96	05-1968
Newton, Toledo Bend Dam	94.0	35.0	107		7		Mar. 24	Nov. 9	228	5.70	4.40	4.80	4.00	4.90	5.00	3.60	3.40	3.90	3.94	5.00	6.10	54.90		
Nolan, Roscoe	93.8	28.9	113	1994	-11	1947	Mar. 31	Nov. 10	223	1.03	1.18	1.11	1.52	3.04	3.09	1.89	2.59	3.58	1.38	0.99	0.99	23.54	8.28	09-1980
Nueces, Corpus Christi	93.2	46.2	109	2000	13	1989	Feb. 3	Dec. 23	319	1.62	1.84	1.71	2.05	3.33	3.53	2.00	3.54	3.94	3.82	1.74	1.75	32.26	7.92	10-1995
Ochiltree, Perryton	91.4	18.4	111	1981	-17	1988	Apr. 25	Oct. 17	174	0.47	0.62	1.71	1.80	2.47	2.18	2.74	2.22	1.89	1.38	1.09	0.66	20.88	7.11	05-1989
Oldham, Boys Ranch	92.3	20.5	110	1982	-11	1983	Apr. 13	Oct. 16	186	0.49	0.28	0.89	1.13	2.47	2.97	2.96	3.20	1.94	1.48	0.66	0.50	18.18	4.50	09-1990
Orange, Orange	91.0	41.0	104		10		Mar. 16	Nov. 11	240	6.00	3.60	3.90	3.60	5.70	6.20	5.30	4.70	5.60	4.60	4.60	5.20	59.00		
Palo Pinto, Mineral Wells	97.3	33.4	*114	1980	-8	1989	Mar. 23	Nov. 13	233	1.42	1.99	2.69	2.75	4.59	3.25	2.25	2.34	3.04	3.81	2.16	1.74	31.79	6.65	10-1981
Panola, Carthage	93.7	33.9	*109	2000	*1	1989	Mar. 17	Nov. 14	242	4.76	3.88	4.00	4.36	5.05	4.95	3.25	2.92	3.75	4.65	4.93	5.01	51.51	9.25	04-1991
Parker, Weatherford	95.2	29.0	119	1980	*-10	1989	Mar. 29	Nov. 8	223	1.50	2.36	2.79	2.84	4.76	3.93	2.11	2.60	2.85	4.19	2.61	2.16	34.70	7.05	07-1962
Parmer, Friona	89.8	21.7	*108	1990	-15	1963	Apr. 19	Oct. 20	183	0.56	0.53	0.91	1.09	2.19	2.50	2.24	2.89	2.28	1.60	0.80	0.79	18.38	3.90	10-1998
Pecos, Fort Stockton	95.8	31.4	117	1994	-6	1985	Mar. 26	Nov. 12	230	0.50	0.47	0.38	0.72	1.59	1.70	1.34	1.95	2.75	1.45	0.61	0.60	14.06	5.22	10-1986
Polk, Livingston	94.1	35.8	*111	2000	*3	1989	Mar. 17	Nov. 13	241	4.64	3.47	3.89	3.92	5.54	5.20	3.55	3.41	4.73	3.82	4.76	4.92	51.85	10.47	10-1994
Potter, Amarillo	91.0	22.6	*108	1998	-14	1951	Apr. 18	Oct. 20	185	0.63	0.55	1.13	1.33	2.50	3.28	2.68	2.94	1.88	1.50	0.68	0.61	19.71	4.92	06-1984
Presidio, Marfa	88.9	23.9	*106	1994	-2	1972	Apr. 11	Oct. 30	201	0.41	0.47	0.24	0.67	2.89	1.80	2.83	2.70	2.88	1.48	0.39	0.59	15.79	2.93	05-1984
Presidio, Presidio	100.8	34.5	*117	1960	4	1962	Mar. 5	Nov. 20	260	0.31	0.36	0.15	0.31	2.39	1.51	2.01	1.82	1.69	0.99	0.37	0.51	10.76	3.30	04-1979
Rains, Emory	92.4	31.6	110	1964	-5	1989	Mar. 22	Nov. 12	234	3.04	3.34	3.88	5.31	4.19	4.19	2.33	2.23	2.98	4.66	3.89	3.93	50.76	5.65	06-1992
Randall, Canyon	92.6	23.7	*109	1981	-14	1951	Apr. 13	Oct. 22	191	0.46	0.52	0.99	1.08	2.96	2.96	2.39	2.84	1.97	1.78	0.69	0.62	19.19	7.87	08-1968
Reagan, Big Lake	93.4	29.1	110	1998	*1	1989	Apr. 1	Nov. 5	218	0.68	0.92	0.81	1.42	2.39	1.99	1.79	2.18	2.97	1.92	0.88	0.84	19.19	4.85	07-1990
Real, Camp Wood	94.2	33.1	*109	2000	*5	1989	Mar. 22	Nov. 11	233	1.11	1.44	1.55	2.41	3.16	3.68	2.09	3.07	2.87	3.46	1.77	1.38	27.99	8.37	11-2001

COUNTY AND STATION	July Mean Max. (F.)	January Mean Min. (F.)	Record Highest (F.)	Year	Record Lowest (F.)	Year	Last in Spring	First in Fall	Growing Season (Days)	Jan (In.)	Feb (In.)	Mar (In.)	Apr (In.)	May (In.)	June (In.)	July (In.)	Aug (In.)	Sept (In.)	Oct (In.)	Nov (In.)	Dec (In.)	Annual (In.)	Highest Daily Rainfall (In.)	Mo.-Year
Red River, Clarksville	92.2	29.7	115	1936	-7	1930	Mar. 28	Nov. 9	226	2.65	3.17	4.50	4.02	5.43	4.00	3.23	2.07	3.83	4.99	5.43	4.51	47.83	8.30	05-1933
Reeves, Balmorhea	94.7	30.1	112	1939	-9	1933	Mar. 30	Nov. 9	223	0.58	0.56	0.24	0.63	1.45	1.24	1.78	2.29	3.08	1.19	0.54	0.61	14.19	4.13	07-1973
Reeves, Pecos	98.5	28.1	118	1968	-9	1962	Mar. 26	Nov. 7	225	0.47	0.45	0.34	0.47	1.25	1.24	1.35	1.62	2.24	1.10	0.47	0.61	11.61	4.38	05-1992
Refugio, Refugio	94.0	45.0	106		8		Feb. 14	Dec. 15	304	2.50	2.20	1.50	1.90	4.30	4.80	3.30	3.50	7.00	5.20	2.30	1.60	40.10	5.58	10-1985
Roberts, Miami	92.4	20.6	114	1917	*-15	1942	Apr. 15	Oct. 19	186	0.68	0.83	1.74	2.19	3.77	3.26	2.39	2.40	2.38	1.64	1.12	0.90	23.30	7.48	07-1979
Robertson, Franklin	95.1	38.2	112	2000	-1	1989	Mar. 9	Nov. 19	254	2.10	2.86	2.90	3.03	4.81	2.95	2.04	2.60	3.65	4.38	3.26	3.52	39.03		
Rockwall, Rockwall	96.0	33.0	118		-7		Mar. 23	Nov. 14	236	2.70	2.70	3.50	3.60	4.81	3.15	2.30	2.00	3.00	2.52	3.40	3.20	39.60	7.05	05-1946
Runnels, Ballinger	94.3	28.5	116	1907	-6	1949	Mar. 28	Nov. 9	225	0.94	1.32	1.27	1.80	3.38	4.87	1.39	2.40	3.08	4.68	1.31	1.20	23.76	11.05	03-1989
Rusk, Henderson	93.1	33.1	*111	2000	-1	1989	Mar. 20	Nov. 15	239	4.08	3.78	4.00	3.91	4.73	5.00	2.81	2.75	3.71	3.90	4.67	4.23	48.22		
Sabine, Hemphill	93.0	36.0	104		8		Mar. 21	Nov. 12	238	5.50	4.00	5.00	4.20	4.60	4.50	3.80	3.20	3.80	4.40	5.00	6.00	54.40		
San Augustine, Broaddus	93.0	35.0	106		9		Mar. 19	Nov. 12	238	5.30	4.10	4.00	3.40	4.50	5.93	3.00	3.90	4.60	4.40	4.40	5.70	51.10		
San Jacinto, Coldspring	93.8	37.5	110	1998	*3	1989	Mar. 11	Nov. 22	255	4.63	3.44	3.61	3.73	5.40	3.97	2.95	3.52	4.45	4.61	4.89	4.82	51.77	13.50	06-1973
San Patricio, Sinton	91.7	44.2	109	2000	10	1989	Feb. 7	Dec. 13	308	1.91	2.02	1.91	1.99	4.07	3.62	2.98	3.16	5.61	2.82	2.04	1.27	35.54	12.35	04-1930
San Saba, San Saba	95.8	33.4	112	1978	-1	1989	Mar. 20	Nov. 11	236	1.09	1.94	1.96	2.13	3.92	1.90	1.87	2.29	2.38	2.10	2.04	1.66	27.72	11.20	10-1969
Schleicher, Eldorado	93.0	28.0	107		3		Mar. 28	Nov. 12	229	0.69	0.90	0.70	1.70	2.50	3.06	1.60	2.10	3.10	2.34	1.00	0.60	19.00		
Scurry, Snyder	94.6	26.7	115	1936	-11	1985	Apr. 1	Nov. 7	219	1.01	1.03	1.09	1.69	3.01	3.45	2.04	2.55	3.30	3.00	0.91	0.80	22.51	5.26	07-1948
Shackelford, Albany	95.4	28.4	115	1972	-8	1947	Mar. 28	Nov. 6	222	1.60	1.65	1.95	2.34	3.76	4.81	1.91	3.04	3.17	4.64	1.55	1.62	28.45	5.80	07-1953
Shelby, Center	93.9	34.9	112	2000	0	1951	Mar. 20	Nov. 10	234	5.04	4.13	4.21	4.41	5.04	2.26	3.04	3.76	4.20	1.15	4.68	5.05	53.01	9.66	11-1940
Sherman, Stratford	91.1	18.5	*108	1953	*-20	1933	Apr. 26	Oct. 15	171	0.44	0.44	0.44	0.44	2.85	3.70	2.31	2.67	1.71	5.10	0.79	0.56	17.89	5.60	08-1992
Smith, Tyler	94.0	38.0	108		0		Mar. 7	Nov. 21	259	3.30	3.70	4.00	3.70	4.50	4.02	2.20	2.60	3.30	3.83	4.50	4.80	45.40		
Somervell, Glen Rose	97.3	28.9	115	1984	-15	1989	Apr. 11	Oct. 29	200	1.64	2.28	2.80	2.91	5.20	2.94	2.19	2.18	3.15	2.48	2.24	2.38	34.82	8.48	07-1995
Starr, Rio Grande City	99.1	44.5	111	1998	10	1962	Feb. 9	Dec. 14	309	0.97	1.10	0.74	1.22	2.42	3.12	1.27	1.97	4.68	3.44	0.90	0.92	21.61	12.51	09-1967
Stephens, Breckenridge	96.8	30.9	114	1936	-7	1989	Mar. 30	Nov. 10	226	1.30	1.39	2.05	2.17	3.53	1.86	1.86	2.06	2.93	1.84	1.56	1.63	27.04	15.70	10-1981
Sterling, Sterling City	94.7	27.4	112	1994	-13	1985	Apr. 4	Nov. 3	212	0.85	0.91	0.91	1.43	2.79	2.33	1.40	1.87	3.29	2.35	0.85	0.93	19.40	6.53	07-1948
Stonewall, Aspermont	97.4	27.2	117	1994	-10	1989	Mar. 30	Nov. 8	223	0.90	1.31	1.32	1.65	3.44	2.94	1.32	2.77	3.04	2.53	1.17	1.03	23.24	6.92	04-1930
Sutton, Sonora	94.7	27.2	109	1980	-8	1951	Apr. 4	Nov. 3	213	0.84	1.16	1.18	1.57	2.57	2.54	1.93	2.93	3.07	4.14	1.26	0.82	22.40	7.92	09-1976
Swisher, Tulia	91.1	22.2	*110	1994	*-10	1951	Apr. 14	Oct. 24	193	1.10	0.72	1.05	1.31	3.42	3.42	2.32	2.65	2.40	2.90	0.87	0.76	20.71	5.18	06-1985
Tarrant, Benbrook	96.6	31.4	111	1954	-6	1989	Mar. 15	Nov. 17	247	1.70	2.19	2.67	3.17	4.58	3.56	2.29	2.03	2.86	1.75	2.35	2.47	34.01	6.36	10-1991
Taylor, Abilene	94.8	31.8	110	1978	*-7	1989	Mar. 24	Nov. 12	232	0.97	1.13	1.41	1.67	2.83	3.06	1.70	2.63	2.91	2.90	1.30	1.27	23.78	6.30	08-1978
Terrell, Sanderson	91.9	30.5	110	1969	3	1989	Mar. 22	Nov. 10	233	0.39	0.59	0.40	0.86	1.74	2.09	1.52	1.87	2.41	1.50	0.81	0.51	14.94	5.35	06-1965
Terry, Brownfield	92.5	26.1	*111	1994	*-8	1963	Apr. 3	Nov. 3	213	1.00	1.50	1.60	2.10	3.30	3.00	2.31	2.15	2.78	2.90	0.79	0.65	18.89	5.05	10-1983
Throckmorton, Throckmorton	97.0	28.0	114		-11		Mar. 31	Nov. 6	220	1.00	1.50	1.60	2.10	3.30	3.50	1.80	2.60	3.30	2.90	1.50	1.50	26.60		
Titus, Mount Pleasant	94.2	29.3	118	1936	-12	1951	Mar. 29	Nov. 5	220	3.27	3.54	4.42	3.77	5.02	4.89	3.75	2.05	3.56	4.74	5.07	4.49	48.57	8.06	11-1994
Tom Green, San Angelo	94.4	31.8	111	1960	-4	1989	Mar. 28	Nov. 13	230	0.82	1.18	0.99	1.60	3.09	2.52	1.10	2.05	2.95	2.57	1.10	0.94	20.91	6.24	09-1980

County and Station	TEMPERATURE Mean Max. July (°F)	Mean Min. January (°F)	Record Highest (°F)	Year	Record Lowest (°F)	Year	FREEZE DATES Last in Spring	First in Fall	Growing Season (Days)	Jan.	Feb.	March	April	May	June	July	Aug.	Sept.	Oct.	Nov.	Dec.	Annual	Highest Daily Rainfall (In.)	Mo.-Year
Travis, Austin	95.0	40.0	112	2000	-2	1949	Feb. 17	Dec. 6	291	1.89	1.99	2.14	2.51	5.03	3.81	1.97	2.31	2.91	3.97	2.68	2.44	33.65	8.00	06-1941
Trinity, Groveton	94.8	37.1	111	2000	1	1989	Mar. 14	Nov. 14	244	4.17	3.21	3.67	3.13	5.11	5.01	3.48	3.25	4.10	4.07	4.49	4.41	48.10	12.10	10-1994
Tyler, Town Bluff Dam	92.1	38.3	109	2000	6	1989	Mar. 9	Nov. 19	255	5.08	4.02	4.56	4.41	5.61	5.74	3.46	3.42	4.17	3.68	5.08	5.56	54.79	7.50	09-1996
Upshur, Gilmer	93.4	31.4	114	1936	*-4	1989	Mar. 29	Nov. 5	220	3.51	3.58	4.38	4.12	4.41	4.13	3.04	2.50	3.84	4.47	4.75	4.35	47.08	7.88	04-1966
Upton, McCamey	95.6	33.1	*113	1994	-2	1962	Mar. 20	Nov. 12	236	0.47	0.56	0.41	0.93	1.61	1.55	0.94	1.95	2.68	2.06	0.59	0.70	14.45	9.13	10-1986
Uvalde, Uvalde	96.0	37.0	111		6		Mar. 10	Nov. 21	255	1.00	1.10	1.00	2.00	3.30	3.50	1.20	2.60	2.30	2.40	1.60	1.30	23.30		
Val Verde, Del Rio	96.2	39.7	112	1988	10	1989	Feb. 19	Dec. 1	284	0.57	0.96	0.96	1.71	2.31	2.34	2.02	2.16	2.06	2.00	0.96	0.75	18.80	17.03	08-1998
Van Zandt, Wills Point	93.3	31.4	115	1909	*-2	1989	Mar. 14	Nov. 18	248	3.10	3.22	3.74	3.68	4.74	4.45	2.16	2.26	3.39	4.78	4.23	3.93	43.68	7.08	06-1945
Victoria, Victoria	93.4	43.6	111	2000	9	1989	Feb. 9	Dec. 11	305	2.44	2.04	2.25	2.97	5.12	4.96	2.90	3.05	5.00	4.26	2.64	2.47	40.10	9.87	04-1991
Walker, Huntsville	93.8	39.0	108	2000	2	1989	Feb. 23	Nov. 30	279	4.28	3.14	3.47	3.90	5.08	4.66	2.67	3.69	4.73	4.32	4.87	4.10	48.51	10.21	10-1994
Waller, Hempstead	95.0	38.0	107		13		Feb. 28	Dec. 4	283	2.80	2.90	2.10	3.50	4.70	3.60	2.00	2.40	4.60	4.00	3.20	3.00	38.20		
Ward, Monahans	98.6	26.5	*118	1994	-9	1962	Apr. 1	Nov. 7	219	0.51	0.57	0.27	0.55	1.80	1.43	1.31	1.65	2.55	1.39	0.53	0.67	13.23	4.40	09-1980
Washington, Brenham	96.7	39.3	113	2000	*-2	1930	Feb. 20	Dec. 5	288	3.41	2.78	2.93	3.39	5.14	4.66	1.93	3.14	4.83	4.48	4.17	3.29	44.15	10.38	07-1994
Webb, Laredo	101.6	43.7	*114	1998	11	1983	Feb. 9	Dec. 5	299	0.76	0.94	0.92	1.55	2.73	2.99	1.79	2.42	2.73	2.72	1.13	0.85	21.53	6.65	07-1981
Wharton, Pierce	94.3	41.8	112	2000	4	1989	Feb. 19	Dec. 6	290	3.42	2.84	2.74	3.18	5.61	4.69	3.10	3.57	2.83	4.61	3.55	3.23	45.92	8.85	11-1943
Wheeler, Shamrock	93.3	22.9	113	1980	-13	1984	Apr. 6	Oct. 27	203	0.56	0.84	1.88	2.19	3.92	3.74	2.17	2.27	3.19	1.92	1.17	0.83	24.32	8.24	06-1995
Wichita, Wichita Falls	97.2	28.9	117	1980	-12	1947	Mar. 28	Nov. 9	225	1.12	1.58	2.27	2.62	3.92	3.69	1.58	2.39	3.19	3.11	1.68	1.68	28.83	6.19	09-1980
Wilbarger, Vernon	95.7	25.7	119	1943	-9	1989	Mar. 30	Nov. 9	224	1.09	1.34	1.98	2.36	4.11	3.82	1.94	3.07	3.54	2.70	1.48	1.12	28.55	14.82	08-1995
Willacy, Raymondville	95.3	47.5	109	1916	*14	1962	Jan. 19	Jan. 1	347	1.36	1.59	1.44	1.53	2.31	3.22	1.91	3.06	3.54	3.17	1.38	1.11	27.97	9.90	09-1975
Williamson, Taylor	95.3	35.8	*112	2000	-5	1949	Mar. 5	Nov. 20	259	2.09	2.38	2.63	2.68	5.19	3.78	1.62	2.09	3.30	3.83	2.95	2.57	35.11	*6.00	06-1958
Wilson, Floresville	95.7	38.4	111	2000	5	1985	Mar. 8	Nov. 21	257	1.58	1.60	1.65	2.53	3.69	3.24	1.60	2.54	2.61	2.75	2.24	1.57	27.60	9.25	09-1967
Winkler, Wink	96.1	27.8	117	1994	-14	1962	Apr. 2	Nov. 4	215	0.41	0.48	0.32	0.53	1.34	1.83	1.95	1.29	2.14	1.51	0.55	0.57	12.92	5.64	10-1940
Wise, Bridgeport	98.0	30.5	*115	1980	-8	1989	Mar. 30	Nov. 7	222	1.53	2.06	2.63	2.83	5.53	3.54	2.26	2.01	2.73	4.37	2.28	2.01	34.02	9.07	10-1919
Wood, Mineola	93.1	31.2	*110	2000	1	1983	Apr. 1	Nov. 7	219	3.33	3.43	4.05	3.98	4.71	3.99	2.92	2.23	3.67	4.99	4.50	4.08	45.88	6.42	12-1982
Yoakum, Plains	91.7	25.1	111	1994	*-12	1951	Apr. 5	Oct. 29	206	0.49	0.72	0.60	1.15	2.38	2.55	2.34	2.75	2.67	1.24	0.75	0.77	18.41	6.11	07-1960
Young, Graham	96.6	27.1	117	1936	*-8	1989	Apr. 2	Nov. 6	217	1.16	1.79	2.22	2.45	4.52	3.60	2.17	2.32	3.64	3.79	1.88	1.81	31.35	8.22	10-1981
Zapata, Zapata	98.0	45.4	116	1998	13	1911	Jan. 24	Dec. 25	337	0.70	1.04	0.79	1.39	2.27	2.67	1.55	1.80	3.65	1.85	0.94	0.88	19.53	6.10	04-1966
Zavala, Crystal City	97.1	42.6	115	2000	*11	1959	Feb. 16	Dec. 6	292	0.93	1.08	1.08	1.75	2.41	3.25	1.67	2.03	2.10	2.44	1.12	0.84	20.70	6.83	10-1959

Calendar

The Rafes Urban Astronomy Center in Denton is open to the public the first Saturday of each month; www.astronomy.unt.edu. Photo courtesy of the UNT Planetarium and Astronomy Laboratory.

Seasons

Morning & Evening Stars

Eclipses

Major Meteor Showers

Chronological Eras & Cycles

Calendars for 2010 & 2011

Astronomical Calendar for 2010 and 2011

An Explanation of Texas Time

The subsequent calendars were calculated principally from data on the **U.S. Naval Observatory's Web site (http://aa.usno.navy.mil/data/),** and from its publication, ***Astronomical Phenomena for 2010*** and ***Astronomical Phenomena for 2011.***

Times listed here are **Central Standard Time,** except for the period from 2:00 a.m. on the second Sunday in March until 2:00 a.m. on the first Sunday in November, when **Daylight Saving Time,** which is one hour later than Central Standard Time, is in effect.

All of Texas is in the Central Time Zone, except El Paso and Hudspeth counties and the northwest corner of Culberson County, which observe Mountain Time (see map on page 153). Mountain Time is one hour earlier than Central Time.

All times are calculated for the intersection of 99° 20' west longitude and 31° 08' north latitude, which is about 15 miles northeast of Brady, McCulloch County. This point is the **approximate geographical center of the state.**

To get the time of sunrise or sunset, moonrise or moonset for any point in Texas, apply the following rule: Add four minutes to the time given in this calendar for each degree of longitude that the place lies west of the 99th meridian; subtract four minutes for each degree of longitude the place lies east of the 99th meridian.

At times there will be considerable variation for distances north and south of the line of 31° 08' north latitude, but the rule for calculating it is complicated. The formula given above will get sufficiently close results.

The **accompanying map** shows the intersection for which all times given here are calculated, with some major Texas cities and their longitudes. These make it convenient to calculate time at any given point.

The Naval Observatory's Web site allows the calculation of more exact rise and set times of the Sun and Moon at any location for one day or for an entire year.

Planetary Configurations and Phenomena

The phenomena and planetary configurations of heavens for 2010 and 2011 are given in the center column of the calendar on pages 154–159. Below is an explanation of the symbols used in those tables:

☉ The Sun	● The Earth	⛢ Uranus
☾ The Moon	♂ Mars	♆ Neptune
☿ Mercury	♃ Jupiter	♇ Pluto
♀ Venus	♄ Saturn	

Aspects

☌ This symbol appearing between the symbols for heavenly bodies means they are **"in conjunction,"** that is, having the same longitude as applies to the sky and appearing near each other. For example, ♀ ☌ ☾ means that Venus is either **north** or **south** of the moon by a few degrees. Conjunctions listed in this calendar are separated by 8 degrees or less.

☍ This symbol means that the heavenly body listed is in **"opposition"** to the Sun, or that they differ by 180 degrees of longitude.

Common Astronomical Terms

★ **Aphelion** — Point at which a planet's orbit is farthest from the sun.

★ **Perihelion** — Point at which a planet's orbit is nearest the sun.

★ **Apogee** — That point of the moon's orbit farthest from the earth.

★ **Perigee** — That point of the moon's orbit nearest the earth.

The Seasons, 2010 and 2011

2010

The seasons of 2010 begin as follows: **Spring**, March 20, 12:32 p.m. (CDT); **Summer**, June 21, 6:28 a.m. (CDT); **Fall**, Sept. 22, 10:09 p.m. (CDT); **Winter**, Dec. 21, 5:38 p.m. (CST).

2011

The seasons of 2011 begin as follows: **Spring**, March 20, 6:21 p.m. (CDT); **Summer**, June 21, 12:16 p.m. (CDT); **Fall**, Sept. 23, 4:04 a.m. (CDT); **Winter**, Dec. 21, 11:30 p.m. (CST).

Morning & Evening Stars

Morning Stars 2010

Venus — Nov. 4 – Dec. 31
Mars — Jan. 1 – Jan. 29
Jupiter — March 14 – Sept. 21
Saturn — Jan. 1 – March 22; Oct. 19 – Dec. 31

Evening Stars 2010

Venus — Feb. 23 – Oct. 24
Mars — Jan. 29 – Dec. 5
Jupiter — Jan. 1 – Feb. 15; Sept. 21 – Dec. 31
Saturn — March 22 – Sept. 13

Morning Stars 2011

Venus — Jan. 1 – July 11
Mars — April 17 – Dec. 31
Jupiter — April 21 – Oct. 29
Saturn — Jan. 1 – April 4; Oct. 31 – Dec. 31

Evening Stars 2011

Venus — Sept. 23 – Dec. 31
Jupiter — Jan. 1 – March 24; Oct. 29 – Dec. 31
Saturn — April 4 – Sept. 26

Major Meteor Showers

These are approximate dates. Listen to local news/weather broadcasts several days beforehand to determine peak observation days and hours. Generally, viewing is best between midnight and dawn of the date listed.

Meteor shower dates are provided by Ron Dilulio, Planetarium and Astronomy Laboratory director, the University of North Texas, Denton, Texas.

Meteor Shower	Peak 2010	Peak 2011
Quadrantid	Jan. 4	Jan. 4
Lyrid	April 22	April 22
Perseid	Aug. 12	Aug. 13
Orionid	Oct. 22	Oct. 22
Leonid	Nov. 18	Nov. 18
Geminid	Dec. 13	Dec. 13

Eclipses

Eclipses 2010

Jan. 15 — Sun, annular, visible in central Africa, the Indian Ocean, parts of India, Sri Lanka, Bangladesh, Myanmar and China.

June 26 — Moon, partial, visible in parts of Americas, Pacific Ocean, Antarctica, eastern Asia, Australia.

July 11 — Sun, total, visible in the Cook Islands, French Polynesia, southeastern Pacific Ocean, far south Chile and Argentina.

Dec. 21 — Moon, total, visible in Europe, west Africa, the Americas, the Pacific Ocean, eastern Australia, the Phillippines, north-east Asia.

Eclipses 2011

Jan. 4—Sun, partial, visible in Europe, north Africa, Middle East, western Asia, northwest India.

June 1 — Sun, partial, visible in eastern Asia, north Alaska and Canada, north Scandinavia, Greenland.

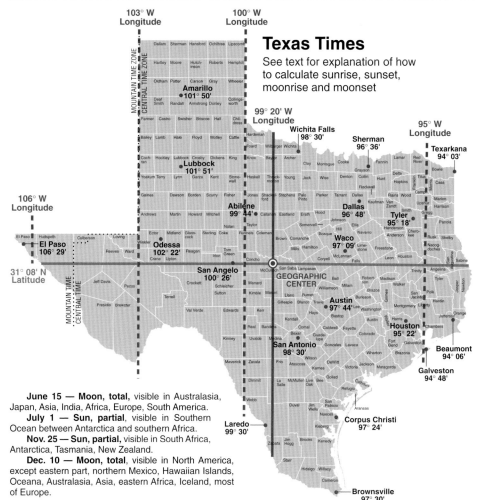

Texas Times

See text for explanation of how to calculate sunrise, sunset, moonrise and moonset

June 15 — **Moon, total,** visible in Australasia, Japan, Asia, India, Africa, Europe, South America.

July 1 — **Sun, partial,** visible in Southern Ocean between Antarctica and southern Africa.

Nov. 25 — **Sun, partial,** visible in South Africa, Antarctica, Tasmania, New Zealand.

Dec. 10 — **Moon, total,** visible in North America, except eastern part, northern Mexico, Hawaiian Islands, Oceana, Australasia, Asia, eastern Africa, Iceland, most of Europe.

Chronological Eras & Cycles

Chronological Eras 2010

The year 2010 of the **Christian** era comprises the latter part of the 234th and the beginning of the 235th year of the independence of the United States of America, and corresponds to the year 6723 of the Julian period. All dates in the list below are given in terms of the Gregorian calendar, in which Jan. 14, 2010, corresponds to Jan. 1, 2010, Julian calendar:

Era	Year	Begins
Byzantine	7519	Sept. 14
Jewish (A.M.)*	5771	Sept. 8
Chinese (Geng-yin)	4647	Feb. 14
Roman (A.U.C.)	2763	Jan. 14
Nabonassar	2759	April 21
Japanese	2670	Jan. 1
Grecian (Seleucidae)	2322	Sept. 14 or Oct. 14
Indian (Saka)	1932	March 22
Diocletian	1727	Sept. 11
Islamic (Hegira)*	1432	Dec. 7

*Year begins at sunset.

Chronological Cycles 2010

Dominical Letter	C	Julian Period	6723
Epact	14	Roman Indiction	3
Golden Number or Lunar Cycle	XVI	Solar Cycle	3

Chronological Eras 2011

The year 2011 of the **Christian** era comprises the latter part of the 235th and the beginning of the 236th year of the independence of the United States of America, and corresponds to the year 6724 of the Julian period. All dates in the list below are given in terms of the Gregorian calendar, in which Jan. 14, 2011, corresponds to Jan. 1, 2011, of the Julian calendar:

Era	Year	Begins
Byzantine	7520	Sept. 14
Jewish (A.M.)*	5772	Sept. 28
Chinese (xin mao)	4648	Feb. 3
Roman (A.U.C.)	2764	Jan. 14
Nabonassar	2760	April 21
Japanese	2671	Jan. 1
Grecian (Seleucidae)	2323	Sept. 14 or Oct. 14
Indian (Saka)	1933	March 22
Diocletian	1728	Sept. 12
Islamic (Hegira)*	1433	Nov. 26

*Year begins at sunset.

Chronological Cycles 2011

Dominical Letter	B	Julian Period	6724
Epact	25	Roman Indiction	4
Golden Number or Lunar Cycle	XVII	Solar Cycle	4

Calendar for 2010

Times are **Central Standard Time,** except from March 14 to Nov. 7, during which **Daylight Saving Time** is observed. **Boldface times for moonrise and moonset indicate p.m.** Times are figured for the point **99° 20' West and 31° 08' North,** the approximate geographical center of the state. **See page 152 for explanation of how to get the approximate time at any other Texas point. (On the Web: http://aa.usno.navy.mil/data/)** Please note: Not all eclipses are visible in United States. For visibility, see listing beginning on page 152.

1st Month — January 2010 — 31 Days

Moon's Phases — *Last Qtr.,* Jan. 7, 4:39 a.m.; *New,* Jan. 15, 1:11 a.m.; *First Qtr.,* Jan. 23, 4:53 a.m.; *Full,* Jan. 30, 12:18 a.m.

Day of: Year	Month	Week	Planetary Configurations and Phenomena	*Hour of: Sunrise	Sunset	Moon-rise	Moon-set
1	1	Fr.	☾ at perigee	7:36	5:46	**7:06**	8:23
2	2	Sa.	● at perihelion	7:36	5:47	**8:19**	9:09
3	3	Su.	♂ ☌ ☾	7:36	5:48	**9:29**	9:49
4	4	Mo.	☿ in inferior ☌	7:36	5:48	**10:36**	10:25
5	5	Tu.		7:37	5:49	**11:40**	10:59
6	6	We.	♄ ☌ ☾	7:37	5:50		11:32
7	7	Th.	Last qtr. ☾	7:37	5:51	12:43	**12:06**
8	8	Fr.		7:37	5:52	1:46	**12:41**
9	9	Sa.		7:37	5:52	2:48	**1:21**
10	10	Su.		7:37	5:53	3:48	**2:04**
11	11	Mo.	♀ in superior ☌	7:37	5:54	4:46	**2:52**
12	12	Tu.		7:37	5:55	5:40	**3:44**
13	13	We.	☿ ☌ ☾	7:37	5:56	6:28	**4:39**
14	14	Th.	♄ stationary	7:36	5:57	7:12	**5:36**
15	15	Fr.	New ☾; eclipse of ☉	7:36	5:58	7:50	**6:32**
16	16	Sa.	☾ at apogee	7:36	5:58	8:23	**7:27**
17	17	Su.	♆ ☌ ☾	7:36	5:59	8:54	**8:21**
18	18	Mo.	♃ ☌ ☾	7:36	6:00	9:22	**9:15**
19	19	Tu.		7:35	6:01	9:49	**10:08**
20	20	We.	⛢ ☌ ☾	7:35	6:02	10:16	**11:03**
21	21	Th.		7:35	6:03	10:45	**11:59**
22	22	Fr.		7:34	6:04	11:16	
23	23	Sa.	First qtr. ☾	7:34	6:05	11:51	12:57
24	24	Su.		7:34	6:06	**12:32**	1:59
25	25	Mo.		7:33	6:07	**1:21**	3:03
26	26	Tu.		7:33	6:07	**2:19**	4:07
27	27	We.	♂ closest approach	7:32	6:08	**3:25**	5:09
28	28	Th.		7:32	6:09	**4:37**	6:06
29	29	Fr.	♂ ☍ ☉	7:31	6:10	**5:51**	6:56
30	30	Sa.	Full ☾ at perigee; ♂ ☌ ☾	7:31	6:11	**7:04**	7:40
31	31	Su.		7:30	6:12	**8:15**	8:19

2nd Month — February 2010 — 28 Days

Moon's Phases — *Last Qtr.,* Feb. 5, 5:48 p.m.; *New,* Feb. 13, 8:51 p.m.; *First Qtr.,* Feb. 21, 6:42 p.m.; *Full,* Feb. 28, 10:38 a.m.

Day of: Year	Month	Week	Planetary Configurations and Phenomena	*Hour of: Sunrise	Sunset	Moon-rise	Moon-set
32	1	Mo.		7:29	6:13	**9:23**	8:55
33	2	Tu.	♄ ☌ ☾	7:29	6:14	**10:30**	9:30
34	3	We.		7:28	6:15	**11:35**	10:04
35	4	Th.		7:27	6:15		10:41
36	5	Fr.	Last qtr. ☾	7:27	6:16	12:39	11:20
37	6	Sa.		7:26	6:17	1:41	**12:02**
38	7	Su.		7:25	6:18	2:40	**12:49**
39	8	Mo.		7:24	6:19	3:36	**1:40**
40	9	Tu.		7:24	6:20	4:26	**2:34**
41	10	We.		7:23	6:21	5:11	**3:30**
42	11	Th.		7:22	6:21	5:50	**4:26**
43	12	Fr.	☿ ☌ ☾; ☾ at apogee	7:21	6:22	6:25	**5:22**
44	13	Sa.	New ☾	7:20	6:23	6:56	**6:16**
45	14	Su.	♆ ☌ ☉	7:19	6:24	7:25	**7:10**
46	15	Mo.		7:18	6:25	7:53	**8:04**
47	16	Tu.	⛢ ☌ ☾	7:18	6:26	8:20	**8:58**
48	17	We.		7:17	6:26	8:48	**9:53**
49	18	Th.		7:16	6:27	9:18	**10:50**
50	19	Fr.		7:15	6:28	9:51	**11:49**
51	20	Sa.		7:14	6:29	10:29	
52	21	Su.	First qtr. ☾	7:13	6:30	11:14	12:51
53	22	Mo.		7:12	6:30	**12:06**	1:53
54	23	Tu.		7:11	6:31	**1:06**	2:54
55	24	We.		7:09	6:32	**2:13**	3:51
56	25	Th.	♂ ☌ ☾	7:08	6:33	**3:23**	4:43
57	26	Fr.		7:07	6:33	**4:36**	5:29
58	27	Sa.	☾ at perigee	7:06	6:34	**5:47**	6:10
59	28	Su.	Full ☾; ♃ ☌ ☉	7:05	6:35	**6:58**	6:48

See text before January calendar for explanation.

3rd Month — March 2010 — 31 Days

Moon's Phases — *Last Qtr.,* March 7, 9:42 a.m.; *New,* March 15, 4:01 p.m; *First Qtr.,* March 23, 6:00 a.m.; *Full,* March 29, 9:25 p.m.

Day of: Year	Month	Week	Planetary Configurations and Phenomena	*Hour of: Sunrise	Sunset	Moon-rise	Moon-set
60	1	Mo.		7:04	6:36	**8:07**	7:23
61	2	Tu.	♄ ☌ ☾	7:03	6:36	**9:15**	7:59
62	3	We.		7:02	6:37	**10:21**	8:36
63	4	Th.		7:01	6:38	**11:27**	9:15
64	5	Fr.		6:59	6:39		9:57
65	6	Sa.		6:58	6:39	12:29	10:44
66	7	Su.	Last qtr. ☾	6:57	6:40	1:28	11:35
67	8	Mo.		6:56	6:41	2:21	**12:28**
68	9	Tu.		6:55	6:41	3:08	**1:24**
69	10	We.		6:53	6:42	3:49	**2:20**
70	11	Th.	♂ stationary	6:52	6:43	4:26	**3:16**
71	12	Fr.	☾ at apogee	6:51	6:43	4:58	**4:10**
72	13	Sa.	♆ ☌ ☾	6:50	6:44	5:28	**5:04**
73	†14	Su.	DST begins; ☿ superior ☌	7:49	7:45	6:56	**6:58**
74	15	Mo.	New ☾	7:47	7:46	7:24	**7:52**
75	16	Tu.		7:46	7:46	7:52	**8:48**
76	17	We.	⛢ ☌ ☉; ♀ ☌ ☾	7:45	7:47	8:22	**9:45**
77	18	Th.		7:44	7:48	8:54	**10:44**
78	19	Fr.		7:42	7:48	9:31	**11:44**
79	20	Sa.	**Equinox**	7:41	7:49	10:13	
80	21	Su.	♄ ☍ ☉	7:40	7:50	11:02	12:46
81	22	Mo.		7:39	7:50	11:58	1:46
82	23	Tu.	First qtr. ☾	7:37	7:51	**1:00**	2:43
83	24	We.		7:36	7:51	**2:07**	3:35
84	25	Th.	♂ ☌ ☾	7:35	7:52	**3:16**	4:21
85	26	Fr.		7:34	7:53	**4:25**	5:03
86	27	Sa.		7:32	7:53	**5:34**	5:41
87	28	Su.	☾ at perigee	7:31	7:54	**6:43**	6:17
88	29	Mo.	Full ☾; ♄ ☌ ☾	7:30	7:55	**7:51**	6:52
89	30	Tu.		7:29	7:55	**8:59**	7:28
90	31	We.		7:27	7:56	**10:06**	8:07

4th Month — April 2010 — 30 Days

Moon's Phases — *Last Qtr.,* April 6, 4:37 a.m.; *New,* April 14, 7:29 a.m.; *First Qtr.,* April 21, 1:20 p.m.; *Full,* April 28, 7:18 a.m.

Day of: Year	Month	Week	Planetary Configurations and Phenomena	*Hour of: Sunrise	Sunset	Moon-rise	Moon-set
91	1	Th.		7:26	7:57	**11:12**	8:49
92	2	Fr.		7:25	7:57		9:35
93	3	Sa.		7:24	7:58	12:14	10:25
94	4	Su.		7:22	7:59	1:11	11:19
95	5	Mo.		7:21	7:59	2:01	**12:15**
96	6	Tu.	Last qtr. ☾; ♇ stationary	7:20	8:00	2:46	**1:12**
97	7	We.		7:19	8:00	3:24	**2:08**
98	8	Th.	☾ at apogee	7:18	8:01	3:58	**3:03**
99	9	Fr.	♆ ☌ ☾	7:16	8:02	4:29	**3:57**
100	10	Sa.		7:15	8:02	4:58	**4:51**
101	11	Su.	♃ ☌ ☾	7:14	8:03	5:26	**5:45**
102	12	Mo.	⛢ ☌ ☾	7:13	8:04	5:54	**6:40**
103	13	Tu.		7:12	8:04	6:23	**7:37**
104	14	We.	New ☾	7:11	8:05	6:55	**8:36**
105	15	Th.	☿ ☌ ☾	7:09	8:06	7:31	**9:37**
106	16	Fr.	♀ ☌ ☾	7:08	8:06	8:12	**10:39**
107	17	Sa.		7:07	8:07	8:59	**11:40**
108	18	Su.	☿ stationary	7:06	8:08	9:54	
109	19	Mo.		7:05	8:08	10:54	12:38
110	20	Tu.		7:04	8:09	11:59	1:31
111	21	We.	First qtr. ☾	7:03	8:10	**1:06**	2:18
112	22	Th.	♂ ☌ ☾	7:02	8:10	**2:13**	3:01
113	23	Fr.		7:01	8:11	**3:20**	3:39
114	24	Sa.	☾ at perigee	7:00	8:12	**4:26**	4:14
115	25	Su.	♄ ☌ ☾	6:59	8:12	**5:32**	4:48
116	26	Mo.		6:58	8:13	**6:39**	5:23
117	27	Tu.		6:57	8:14	**7:45**	6:00
118	28	We.	Full ☾; ☿ in inferior ☌	6:56	8:14	**8:52**	6:40
119	29	Th.		6:55	8:15	**9:56**	7:24
120	30	Fr.		6:54	8:16	**10:57**	8:13

† Daylight Saving Time begins at 2:00 a.m.

Calendar for 2010 (Cont'd.)

5th Month — May 2010 — 31 Days

Moon's Phases — Last Qtr., May 5, 11:15 p.m.; New, May 13, 8:04 p.m.; First Qtr., May 20, 6:43 p.m.; Full, May 27, 6:07 p.m.

Year	Month	Week	Planetary Configurations and Phenomena	Sunrise	Sunset	Moonrise	Moonset
121	1	Sa.		6:53	8:16	11:51	9:07
122	2	Su.		6:52	8:17		10:03
123	3	Mo.		6:51	8:18	12:39	11:01
124	4	Tu.		6:50	8:19	1:20	11:58
125	5	We.	Last qtr. ☾	6:49	8:19	1:56	12:54
126	6	Th.	☾ at apogee	6:48	8:20	2:28	1:48
127	7	Fr.	♆ ☌ ☾	6:48	8:21	2:58	2:42
128	8	Sa.		6:47	8:21	3:26	3:35
129	9	Su.	♃ ☌ ☾; ⛢ ☌ ☾	6:46	8:22	3:54	4:30
130	10	Mo.	☿ stationary	6:45	8:23	4:23	5:26
131	11	Tu.		6:44	8:23	4:54	6:24
132	12	We.	☿ ☌ ☾	6:44	8:24	5:28	7:24
133	13	Th.	New ☾	6:43	8:25	6:08	8:27
134	14	Fr.		6:42	8:25	6:54	9:30
135	15	Sa.		6:42	8:26	7:47	10:31
136	16	Su.	♀ ☌ ☾	6:41	8:27	8:47	11:27
137	17	Mo.		6:40	8:27	9:52	
138	18	Tu.		6:40	8:28	10:59	12:16
139	19	We.		6:39	8:29	12:06	1:00
140	20	Th.	First qtr. ☾ at perigee	6:39	8:29	1:13	1:39
141	21	Fr.		6:38	8:30	2:18	2:15
142	22	Sa.		6:38	8:31	3:22	2:49
143	23	Su.	♄ ☌ ☾	6:37	8:31	4:27	3:23
144	24	Mo.		6:37	8:32	5:31	3:58
145	25	Tu.	☿ greatest elongation W	6:36	8:32	6:37	4:35
146	26	We.		6:36	8:33	7:41	5:17
147	27	Th.	Full ☾	6:36	8:34	8:43	6:04
148	28	Fr.		6:35	8:34	9:40	6:55
149	29	Sa.		6:35	8:35	10:30	7:51
150	30	Su.		6:35	8:35	11:15	8:48
151	31	Mo.	♄ ♆ stationary	6:34	8:36	11:53	9:46

6th Month — June 2010 — 30 Days

Moon's Phases — Last Qtr., June 4, 5:13 p.m.; New, June 12, 6:15 a.m.; First Qtr., June 18, 11:29 p.m.; Full, June 26, 6:30 a.m.

Year	Month	Week	Planetary Configurations and Phenomena	Sunrise	Sunset	Moonrise	Moonset
152	1	Tu.		6:34	8:36		10:43
153	2	We.		6:34	8:37	12:27	11:38
154	3	Th.	☾ at apogee; ♆ ☌ ☾	6:34	8:38	12:58	12:32
155	4	Fr.	Last qtr. ☾	6:33	8:38	1:26	1:26
156	5	Sa.		6:33	8:39	1:54	2:19
157	6	Su.	♃ ⛢ ☌ ☾	6:33	8:39	2:22	3:14
158	7	Mo.		6:33	8:40	2:51	4:10
159	8	Tu.		6:33	8:40	3:24	5:09
160	9	We.		6:33	8:40	4:01	6:11
161	10	Th.	☿ ☌ ☾	6:33	8:41	4:44	7:14
162	11	Fr.		6:33	8:41	5:34	8:17
163	12	Sa.	New ☾	6:33	8:42	6:33	9:16
164	13	Su.		6:33	8:42	7:38	10:10
165	14	Mo.		6:33	8:42	8:46	10:57
166	15	Tu.	☾ at perigee; ♀ ☌ ☾	6:33	8:43	9:56	11:39
167	16	We.		6:33	8:43	11:04	
168	17	Th.	♂ ☌ ☾	6:33	8:43	12:11	12:16
169	18	Fr.	First qtr. ☾	6:33	8:44	1:16	12:51
170	19	Sa.	♄ ☌ ☾	6:34	8:44	2:20	1:25
171	20	Su.		6:34	8:44	3:24	1:59
172	21	Mo.	Solstice	6:34	8:44	4:28	2:35
173	22	Tu.		6:34	8:45	5:31	3:15
174	23	We.		6:34	8:45	6:33	3:59
175	24	Th.		6:35	8:45	7:31	4:48
176	25	Fr.	♇ ☍ ☉	6:35	8:45	8:24	5:41
177	26	Sa.	Full ☾; eclipse of ☾	6:35	8:45	9:10	6:38
178	27	Su.		6:36	8:45	9:51	7:35
179	28	Mo.	☿ in superior ☌	6:36	8:45	10:26	8:33
180	29	Tu.		6:36	8:45	10:58	9:29
181	30	We.	♆ ☌ ☾	6:37	8:45	11:27	10:24

7th Month — July 2010 — 31 Days

Moon's Phases — Last Qtr., July 4, 9:35 a.m.; New, July 11, 2:40 p.m.; First Qtr., July 18, 5:11 a.m.; Full, July 25, 8:37 p.m.

Year	Month	Week	Planetary Configurations and Phenomena	Sunrise	Sunset	Moonrise	Moonset
182	1	Th.	☾ at apogee	6:37	8:45	11:55	11:17
183	2	Fr.		6:38	8:45		12:10
184	3	Sa.	⛢ ♃ ☌ ☾	6:38	8:45	12:23	1:04
185	4	Su.	Last qtr. ☾	6:38	8:45	12:51	1:58
186	5	Mo.	⛢ stationary	6:39	8:45	1:21	2:55
187	6	Tu.	● at aphelion	6:39	8:45	1:56	3:55
188	7	We.		6:40	8:45	2:35	4:56
189	8	Th.		6:40	8:44	3:21	5:59
190	9	Fr.		6:41	8:44	4:15	7:00
191	10	Sa.		6:41	8:44	5:17	7:57
192	11	Su.	New ☾; total eclipse of ☉	6:42	8:44	6:26	8:48
193	12	Mo.	☿ ☌ ☾	6:42	8:43	7:37	9:34
194	13	Tu.	☾ at perigee	6:43	8:43	8:48	10:14
195	14	We.	♀ ☌ ☾	6:43	8:43	9:57	10:51
196	15	Th.		6:44	8:42	11:05	11:26
197	16	Fr.	♂ ♄ ☌ ☾	6:45	8:42	12:11	
198	17	Sa.		6:45	8:42	1:17	12:00
199	18	Su.	First qtr. ☾	6:46	8:41	2:21	12:36
200	19	Mo.		6:46	8:41	3:25	1:15
201	20	Tu.		6:47	8:40	4:27	1:57
202	21	We.		6:48	8:40	5:25	2:44
203	22	Th.		6:48	8:39	6:19	3:36
204	23	Fr.	♃ stationary	6:49	8:39	7:07	4:31
205	24	Sa.		6:49	8:38	7:50	5:28
206	25	Su.	Full ☾	6:50	8:37	8:27	6:25
207	26	Mo.		6:51	8:37	9:00	7:21
208	27	Tu.		6:51	8:36	9:30	8:17
209	28	We.	☾ at apogee; ♆ ☌ ☾	6:52	8:35	9:58	9:10
210	29	Th.		6:52	8:35	10:25	10:03
211	30	Fr.	⛢ ☌ ☾	6:53	8:34	10:53	10:56
212	31	Sa.	♃ ☌ ☾	6:54	8:33	11:22	11:50

8th Month — August 2010 — 31 Days

Moon's Phases — Last Qtr., Aug. 2, 11:59 p.m.; New, Aug. 9, 10:08 p.m.; First Qtr., Aug. 16, 1:14 p.m.; Full, Aug. 24, 12:05 p.m.

Year	Month	Week	Planetary Configurations and Phenomena	Sunrise	Sunset	Moonrise	Moonset
213	1	Su.	♂ ☌ ♄	6:54	8:33	11:54	12:45
214	2	Mo.	Last qtr. ☾	6:55	8:32		1:42
215	3	Tu.		6:56	8:31	12:30	2:42
216	4	We.		6:56	8:30	1:12	3:42
217	5	Th.		6:57	8:29	2:01	4:43
218	6	Fr.	☿ greatest elongation E	6:58	8:28	2:58	5:41
219	7	Sa.		6:58	8:27	4:02	6:35
220	8	Su.		6:59	8:27	5:12	7:23
221	9	Mo.	New ☾; ♀ ☌ ♄	6:59	8:26	6:24	8:06
222	10	Tu.	☾ at perigee	7:00	8:25	7:35	8:45
223	11	We.	☿ ☌ ☾	7:01	8:24	8:46	9:22
224	12	Th.		7:01	8:23	9:55	9:58
225	13	Fr.	♄ ♀ ♂ ☌ ☾	7:02	8:22	11:03	10:35
226	14	Sa.		7:03	8:21	12:10	11:14
227	15	Su.		7:03	8:20	1:16	11:56
228	16	Mo.	First qtr. ☾	7:04	8:19	2:20	
229	17	Tu.		7:04	8:18	3:20	12:42
230	18	We.		7:05	8:17	4:16	1:33
231	19	Th.	☿ stat.; ♀ gr. elong. E	7:06	8:16	5:05	2:26
232	20	Fr.	♆ ☍ ☉	7:06	8:15	5:49	3:23
233	21	Sa.		7:07	8:14	6:28	4:19
234	22	Su.		7:08	8:12	7:02	5:16
235	23	Mo.	♀ ☌ ♂	7:08	8:11	7:33	6:11
236	24	Tu.	Full ☾; ♆ ☌ ☾	7:09	8:10	8:01	7:05
237	25	We.	☾ at apogee	7:09	8:09	8:29	7:58
238	26	Th.		7:10	8:08	8:57	8:51
239	27	Fr.	⛢ ♃ ☌ ☾	7:10	8:07	9:25	9:45
240	28	Sa.		7:11	8:05	9:56	10:39
241	29	Su.		7:12	8:04	10:30	11:35
242	30	Mo.		7:12	8:03	11:09	12:33
243	31	Tu.		7:13	8:02	11:54	1:31

*See text before January calendar for explanation.

☉ The Sun ● The Earth ☾ The Moon ☿ Mercury ♀ Venus ♂ Mars ♃ Jupiter ♄ Saturn ♆ Neptune ⛢ Uranus ♇ Pluto

Calendar for 2010 (Cont'd.)

9th Month — September 2010 — 30 Days

Moon's Phases — *Last Qtr.*, Sept. 1, 12:22 p.m.; *New*, Sept. 8, 5:30 a.m. *First Qtr.*, Sept. 15, 12:50 a.m.; *Full*, Sept. 23, 4:17 a.m.; *Last Qtr.*, Sept. 30, 10:52 p.m.

Day of Year	Day of Month	Day of Week	Planetary Configurations and Phenomena	*Hour of Sunrise	Sunset	Moon-rise	Moon-set
244	1	We.	Last qtr. ☾	7:13	8:01		**2:30**
245	2	Th.		7:14	7:59	12:46	**3:28**
246	3	Fr.	☿ in inferior ☌	7:15	7:58	1:45	**4:22**
247	4	Sa.		7:15	7:57	2:50	**5:11**
248	5	Su.		7:16	7:56	3:59	**5:56**
249	6	Mo.		7:16	7:54	5:10	**6:37**
250	7	Tu.	☾ at perigee	7:17	7:53	6:21	**7:15**
251	8	We.	New ☾	7:17	7:52	7:31	**7:52**
252	9	Th.	♄ ☌ ☾	7:18	7:51	8:41	**8:29**
253	10	Fr.		7:19	7:49	9:51	**9:09**
254	11	Sa.	♂ ♀ ☌ ☾; ☿ stationary	7:19	7:48	10:59	**9:51**
255	12	Su.		7:20	7:47	**12:06**	**10:37**
256	13	Mo.	♇ stationary	7:20	7:46	**1:10**	**11:27**
257	14	Tu.		7:21	7:44	**2:09**	
258	15	We.	First qtr. ☾	7:22	7:43	**3:01**	12:21
259	16	Th.		7:22	7:42	**3:47**	1:17
260	17	Fr.		7:23	7:40	**4:28**	2:14
261	18	Sa.		7:23	7:39	**5:03**	3:11
262	19	Su.	☿ greatest elongation W	7:24	7:38	**5:35**	4:06
263	20	Mo.	♆ ☌ ☾	7:24	7:36	**6:04**	5:00
264	21	Tu.	☾ at apogee; ♃ ⛢ ☍ ☉	7:25	7:35	**6:33**	5:54
265	22	We.	**Equinox;** ♃ ☌ ⛢	7:26	7:34	**7:00**	6:47
266	23	Th.	Full ☾; ♃ ⛢ ☌ ☾	7:26	7:33	**7:29**	7:40
267	24	Fr.		7:27	7:31	**7:59**	8:34
268	25	Sa.		7:27	7:30	**8:33**	9:30
269	26	Su.		7:28	7:29	**9:10**	10:27
270	27	Mo.		7:29	7:27	**9:53**	11:25
271	28	Tu.		7:29	7:26	**10:42**	**12:23**
272	29	We.	♀ ☌ ♂	7:30	7:25	**11:37**	**1:20**
273	30	Th.	Last qtr. ☾; ♄ ☌ ☉	7:30	7:24		**2:14**

10th Month — October 2010 — 31 Days

Moon's Phases — *New*, Oct. 7, 1:44 p.m.; *First Qtr.*, Oct. 14, 4:27 p.m.; *Full*, Oct. 22, 8:36 p.m.; *Last Qtr.*, Oct. 30, 7:46 a.m.

Day of Year	Day of Month	Day of Week	Planetary Configurations and Phenomena	*Hour of Sunrise	Sunset	Moon-rise	Moon-set
274	1	Fr.		7:31	7:22	12:38	**3:03**
275	2	Sa.		7:32	7:21	1:43	**3:48**
276	3	Su.		7:32	7:20	2:50	**4:29**
277	4	Mo.		7:33	7:19	3:58	**5:08**
278	5	Tu.		7:34	7:17	5:07	**5:44**
279	6	We.	☾ at perigee	7:34	7:16	6:16	**6:21**
280	7	Th.	New ☾; ♀ stationary	7:35	7:15	7:26	**7:00**
281	8	Fr.		7:35	7:14	8:36	**7:41**
282	9	Sa.	♀ ♂ ☌ ☾	7:36	7:13	9:45	**8:27**
283	10	Su.		7:37	7:11	10:52	**9:17**
284	11	Mo.		7:37	7:10	11:55	**10:11**
285	12	Tu.		7:38	7:09	**12:52**	**11:08**
286	13	We.		7:39	7:08	**1:42**	
287	14	Th.	First qtr. ☾	7:39	7:07	**2:25**	12:06
288	15	Fr.		7:40	7:06	**3:02**	1:03
289	16	Sa.	☿ in superior ☌	7:41	7:04	**3:36**	1:59
290	17	Su.	♆ ☌ ☾	7:42	7:03	**4:06**	2:54
291	18	Mo.	☾ at apogee	7:42	7:02	**4:35**	3:48
292	19	Tu.		7:43	7:01	**5:03**	4:41
293	20	We.	♃ ⛢ ☌ ☾	7:44	7:00	**5:31**	5:34
294	21	Th.		7:44	6:59	**6:01**	6:28
295	22	Fr.	Full ☾	7:45	6:58	**6:34**	7:23
296	23	Sa.		7:46	6:57	**7:10**	8:20
297	24	Su.		7:47	6:56	**7:52**	9:19
298	25	Mo.		7:47	6:55	**8:40**	10:18
299	26	Tu.		7:48	6:54	**9:33**	11:15
300	27	We.		7:49	6:53	**10:32**	**12:10**
301	28	Th.	♀ in inferior ☌	7:50	6:52	**11:35**	**1:00**
302	29	Fr.		7:50	6:51		**1:46**
303	30	Sa.	Last qtr. ☾	7:51	6:50	12:40	**2:27**
304	31	Su.		7:52	6:50	1:45	**3:04**

See text before January calendar for explanation.

11th Month — November 2010 — 30 Days

Moon's Phases — *New*, Nov. 5, 11:52 p.m.; *First Qtr.*, Nov. 13, 10:39 a.m.; *Full*, Nov. 21, 11:27 a.m.; *Last Qtr.*, Nov. 28, 2:36 p.m.

Day of Year	Day of Month	Day of Week	Planetary Configurations and Phenomena	*Hour of Sunrise	Sunset	Moon-rise	Moon-set
305	1	Mo.		7:53	6:49	2:51	**3:40**
306	2	Tu.		7:54	6:48	3:58	**4:16**
307	3	We.	☾ at perigee	7:54	6:47	5:05	**4:53**
308	4	Th.	♄ ☌ ☾	7:55	6:46	6:13	**5:32**
309	5	Fr.	New ☾	7:56	6:45	7:22	**6:15**
310	6	Sa.		7:57	6:45	8:30	**7:03**
311	†7	Su.	**DST ends;** ♂ ☌ ☾	6:58	5:44	8:36	**6:56**
312	8	Mo.		6:59	5:43	9:37	**7:53**
313	9	Tu.		6:59	5:43	10:31	**8:52**
314	10	We.		7:00	5:42	11:18	**9:51**
315	11	Th.		7:01	5:41	11:59	**10:49**
316	12	Fr.		7:02	5:41	**12:34**	**11:45**
317	13	Sa.	First qtr. ☾	7:03	5:40	**1:06**	
318	14	Su.	♆ ☌ ☾	7:04	5:40	**1:35**	12:39
319	15	Mo.	☾ at apogee	7:04	5:39	**2:03**	1:33
320	16	Tu.	♃ ⛢ ☌ ☾; ♀ stationary	7:05	5:39	**2:32**	2:25
321	17	We.		7:06	5:38	**3:01**	3:19
322	18	Th.		7:07	5:38	**3:33**	4:14
323	19	Fr.	♃ stationary	7:08	5:37	**4:08**	5:10
324	20	Sa.	☿ ☌ ♂	7:09	5:37	**4:48**	6:09
325	21	Su.	Full ☾	7:10	5:37	**5:34**	7:08
326	22	Mo.		7:10	5:36	**6:27**	8:08
327	23	Tu.		7:11	5:36	**7:25**	9:05
328	24	We.		7:12	5:36	**8:28**	9:57
329	25	Th.		7:13	5:35	**9:33**	10:44
330	26	Fr.		7:14	5:35	**10:39**	11:27
331	27	Sa.		7:15	5:35	**11:44**	**12:05**
332	28	Su.	Last qtr. ☾	7:16	5:35		**12:41**
333	29	Mo.		7:16	5:35	12:48	**1:16**
334	30	Tu.	☾ at perigee	7:17	5:35	1:53	**1:51**

12th Month — December 2010 — 31 Days

Moon's Phases — *New*, Dec. 5, 11:36 a.m.; *First Qtr.*, Dec. 13, 7:59 a.m.; *Full*, Dec. 21, 2:13 a.m.; *Last Qtr.*, Dec. 27, 10:18 p.m.

Day of Year	Day of Month	Day of Week	Planetary Configurations and Phenomena	*Hour of Sunrise	Sunset	Moon-rise	Moon-set
335	1	We.	♄ ☌ ☾; ☿ gr. elong. E	7:18	5:35	2:58	**2:27**
336	2	Th.	♀ ☌ ☾	7:19	5:35	4:05	**3:07**
337	3	Fr.		7:20	5:35	5:12	**3:52**
338	4	Sa.	♀ gr. illuminated extent	7:20	5:35	6:18	**4:42**
339	5	Su.	New ☾	7:21	5:35	7:20	**5:37**
340	6	Mo.	⛢ stationary	7:22	5:35	8:18	**6:36**
341	7	Tu.	☿ ☌ ☾	7:23	5:35	9:09	**7:36**
342	8	We.		7:23	5:35	9:53	**8:35**
343	9	Th.		7:24	5:35	10:31	**9:33**
344	10	Fr.	☿ stationary	7:25	5:35	11:04	**10:29**
345	11	Sa.	♆ ☌ ☾	7:26	5:36	11:35	**11:23**
346	12	Su.		7:26	5:36	**12:03**	
347	13	Mo.	First qtr. ☾ at apogee	7:27	5:36	**12:32**	12:16
348	14	Tu.	⛢ ☌ ☾	7:28	5:36	**1:00**	1:09
349	15	We.		7:28	5:37	**1:30**	2:02
350	16	Th.		7:29	5:37	**2:04**	2:58
351	17	Fr.		7:30	5:38	**2:41**	3:55
352	18	Sa.		7:30	5:38	**3:25**	4:54
353	19	Su.	☿ in inferior ☌	7:31	5:38	**4:15**	5:54
354	20	Mo.		7:31	5:39	**5:12**	6:53
355	21	Tu.	**Solstice;** total eclipse ☾	7:32	5:39	**6:15**	7:48
356	22	We.		7:32	5:40	**7:21**	8:39
357	23	Th.		7:33	5:40	**8:29**	9:24
358	24	Fr.		7:33	5:41	**9:36**	10:05
359	25	Sa.	☾ at perigee	7:34	5:41	**10:41**	10:42
360	26	Su.	♇ ☌ ☉	7:34	5:42	**11:46**	11:18
361	27	Mo.	Last qtr. ☾	7:34	5:43		11:52
362	28	Tu.	♄ ☌ ☾	7:35	5:43	12:51	**12:28**
363	29	We.		7:35	5:44	1:56	**1:06**
364	30	Th.	☿ stationary	7:35	5:45	3:01	**1:48**
365	31	Fr.	♀ ☌ ☾	7:36	5:45	4:06	**2:35**

† Daylight Saving Time ends at 2:00 a.m.

☉ The Sun ● The Earth ☾ The Moon ☿ Mercury ♀ Venus ♂ Mars ♃ Jupiter ♄ Saturn ♆ Neptune ⛢ Uranus ♇ Pluto

Calendar for 2011

Times are **Central Standard Time,** except from March 13 to Nov. 6, during which **Daylight Saving Time** is observed. **Boldface times for moonrise and moonset indicate p.m.** Times are figured for the point **99° 20' West and 31° 08' North,** the approximate geographical center of the state. **See page 152 for explanation of how to get the approximate time at any other Texas point. (On the Web: http://aa.usno.navy.mil/data/)** Please note: Not all eclipses are visible in United States. For visibility, see listing on page 152

1st Month — January 2011 — 31 Days

Moon's Phases — *New,* Jan. 4, 3:03 a.m.; *First Qtr.,* Jan. 12, 5:31 a.m.; *Full,* Jan. 19, 3:21 p.m.; *Last Qtr.,* Jan. 26, 6:57 a.m.

Day of Year	Day of Month	Day of Week	Planetary Configurations and Phenomena	Sunrise	Sunset	Moonrise	Moonset
1	1	Sa.		7:36	5:46	5:09	**3:27**
2	2	Su.	♃☌♅; ☿☌☾	7:36	5:47	6:07	**4:23**
3	3	Mo.	● at perihelion	7:36	5:48	7:00	**5:22**
4	4	Tu.	New ☾	7:36	5:48	7:46	**6:22**
5	5	We.		7:37	5:49	8:27	**7:21**
6	6	Th.		7:37	5:50	9:03	**8:17**
7	7	Fr.	♆☌☾	7:37	5:51	9:34	**9:12**
8	8	Sa.	♀ gr. elong. W	7:37	5:51	10:04	**10:06**
9	9	Su.	☿ gr. elong. W	7:37	5:52	10:32	**10:59**
10	10	Mo.	☾ at apogee; ♅♃☌☾	7:37	5:53	11:00	**11:52**
11	11	Tu.		7:37	5:54	11:30	
12	12	We.	First qtr. ☾	7:37	5:55	**12:01**	12:46
13	13	Th.		7:37	5:56	**12:36**	1:41
14	14	Fr.		7:36	5:57	**1:16**	2:38
15	15	Sa.		7:36	5:57	**2:02**	3:37
16	16	Su.		7:36	5:58	**2:55**	4:36
17	17	Mo.		7:36	5:59	**3:55**	5:33
18	18	Tu.		7:36	6:00	**5:01**	6:27
19	19	We.	Full ☾	7:35	6:01	**6:09**	7:15
20	20	Th.		7:35	6:02	**7:19**	7:59
21	21	Fr.	☾ at perigee	7:35	6:03	**8:27**	8:40
22	22	Sa.		7:34	6:04	**9:35**	9:17
23	23	Su.		7:34	6:04	**10:42**	9:53
24	24	Mo.		7:34	6:05	**11:48**	10:29
25	25	Tu.	♄☌☾	7:33	6:06		11:07
26	26	We.	Last qtr. ☾	7:33	6:07	12:54	11:48
27	27	Th.	♄ stationary	7:32	6:08	1:59	**12:33**
28	28	Fr.		7:32	6:09	3:02	**1:23**
29	29	Sa.	♀☌☾	7:31	6:10	4:01	**2:17**
30	30	Su.		7:31	6:11	4:55	**3:14**
31	31	Mo.		7:30	6:12	5:43	**4:13**

2nd Month — February 2011 — 28 Days

Moon's Phases — *New,* Feb. 2, 8:31 p.m.; *First Qtr.,* Feb. 11, 1:18 a.m.; *Full,* Feb. 18, 2:36 a.m.; *Last Qtr.,* Feb. 24, 5:26 p.m.

Day of Year	Day of Month	Day of Week	Planetary Configurations and Phenomena	Sunrise	Sunset	Moonrise	Moonset
32	1	Tu.	☿☌☾	7:30	6:13	6:25	**5:11**
33	2	We.	New ☾	7:29	6:13	7:02	**6:08**
34	3	Th.		7:28	6:14	7:35	**7:04**
35	4	Fr.	♂☌☉	7:28	6:15	8:05	**7:58**
36	5	Sa.		7:27	6:16	8:34	**8:51**
37	6	Su.	☾ at apogee; ♅☌☾	7:26	6:17	9:02	**9:44**
38	7	Mo.	♃☌☾	7:25	6:18	9:31	**10:37**
39	8	Tu.		7:25	6:19	10:01	**11:31**
40	9	We.		7:24	6:20	10:34	
41	10	Th.		7:23	6:20	11:11	12:27
42	11	Fr.	First qtr. ☾	7:22	6:21	11:53	1:23
43	12	Sa.		7:21	6:22	**12:42**	2:21
44	13	Su.		7:20	6:23	**1:37**	3:17
45	14	Mo.		7:20	6:24	**2:38**	4:11
46	15	Tu.		7:19	6:25	**3:45**	5:02
47	16	We.		7:18	6:25	**4:54**	5:48
48	17	Th.	♆☌☉	7:17	6:26	**6:04**	6:31
49	18	Fr.	Full ☾	7:16	6:27	**7:14**	7:10
50	19	Sa.	☾ at perigee	7:15	6:28	**8:23**	7:48
51	20	Su.		7:14	6:29	**9:33**	8:26
52	21	Mo.	♄☌☾	7:13	6:29	**10:41**	9:05
53	22	Tu.		7:12	6:30	**11:49**	9:46
54	23	We.		7:11	6:31		10:31
55	24	Th.	Last qtr. ☾	7:10	6:32	12:54	11:20
56	25	Fr.	☿ in superior ☌	7:09	6:33	1:56	**12:14**
57	26	Sa.		7:08	6:33	2:52	**1:10**
58	27	Su.		7:06	6:34	3:41	**2:08**
59	28	Mo.	♀☌☾	7:05	6:35	4:25	**3:05**

**See text before January calendar for explanation.*

3rd Month — March 2011 — 31 Days

Moon's Phases — *New,* March 4, 2:46 p.m.; *First Qtr.,* March 12, 5:45 p.m.; *Full,* March 19, 1:10 p.m.; *Last Qtr.,* March 26, 7:07 a.m.

Day of Year	Day of Month	Day of Week	Planetary Configurations and Phenomena	Sunrise	Sunset	Moonrise	Moonset
60	1	Tu.		7:04	6:36	5:03	**4:02**
61	2	We.		7:03	6:36	5:37	**4:58**
62	3	Th.		7:02	6:37	6:08	**5:52**
63	4	Fr.	New ☾	7:01	6:38	6:37	**6:45**
64	5	Sa.		7:00	6:38	7:05	**7:38**
65	6	Su.	☾ at apogee; ♃☌☾	6:59	6:39	7:34	**8:31**
66	7	Mo.		6:57	6:40	8:04	**9:25**
67	8	Tu.		6:56	6:41	8:36	**10:20**
68	9	We.		6:55	6:41	9:11	**11:15**
69	10	Th.		6:54	6:42	9:51	
70	11	Fr.		6:53	6:43	10:36	12:11
71	12	Sa.	First qtr. ☾	6:51	6:43	11:27	1:07
72	†13	Su.	**DST begins;**	7:50	7:44	**1:23**	3:00
73	14	Mo.		7:49	7:45	**2:25**	3:50
74	15	Tu.		7:48	7:45	**3:31**	4:37
75	16	We.	☿☌♃	7:46	7:46	**4:38**	5:20
76	17	Th.		7:45	7:47	**5:47**	6:01
77	18	Fr.		7:44	7:47	**6:57**	6:39
78	19	Sa.	Full ☾ at perigee	7:43	7:48	**8:07**	7:17
79	20	Su.	**Equinox;** ♄☌☾	7:41	7:49	**9:18**	7:56
80	21	Mo.	♅☌☉	7:40	7:49	**10:29**	8:38
81	22	Tu.	☿ gr. elong. E	7:39	7:50	**11:38**	9:23
82	23	We.		7:38	7:51		10:12
83	24	Th.		7:36	7:51	12:44	11:06
84	25	Fr.		7:35	7:52	1:44	**12:03**
85	26	Sa.	Last qtr. ☾; ♀☌♆	7:34	7:53	2:37	**1:02**
86	27	Su.		7:33	7:53	3:23	**2:00**
87	28	Mo.		7:31	7:54	4:03	**2:58**
88	29	Tu.		7:30	7:55	4:38	**3:53**
89	30	We.	☿ stationary; ♆☌☾	7:29	7:55	5:10	**4:48**
90	31	Th.	♀☌☾	7:28	7:56	5:40	**5:41**

4th Month — April 2011 — 30 Days

Moon's Phases — *New,* April 3, 9:32 a.m.; *First Qtr.,* April 11, 7:05 a.m.; *Full,* April 17, 9:44 p.m.; *Last Qtr.,* April 24, 9:47 p.m.

Day of Year	Day of Month	Day of Week	Planetary Configurations and Phenomena	Sunrise	Sunset	Moonrise	Moonset
91	1	Fr.		7:26	7:56	6:09	**6:33**
92	2	Sa.	☾ at apogee	7:25	7:57	6:37	**7:26**
93	3	Su.	New ☾ ; ♄☍☉	7:24	7:58	7:07	**8:20**
94	4	Mo.		7:23	7:58	7:38	**9:14**
95	5	Tu.		7:22	7:59	8:13	**10:10**
96	6	We.	♃☌☉	7:20	8:00	8:51	**11:06**
97	7	Th.		7:19	8:00	9:34	
98	8	Fr.		7:18	8:01	10:23	12:01
99	9	Sa.	♇ stationary	7:17	8:02	11:17	12:54
100	10	Su.		7:15	8:02	**12:15**	1:45
101	11	Mo.	First qtr. ☾	7:14	8:03	**1:17**	2:31
102	12	Tu.		7:13	8:04	**2:21**	3:14
103	13	We.		7:12	8:04	**3:27**	3:54
104	14	Th.		7:11	8:05	**4:34**	4:32
105	15	Fr.		7:10	8:06	**5:42**	5:09
106	16	Sa.		7:09	8:06	**6:52**	5:47
107	17	Su.	Full ☾ at perigee; ♄☌☾	7:07	8:07	**8:03**	6:27
108	18	Mo.		7:06	8:08	**9:14**	7:10
109	19	Tu.	☿☌♂	7:05	8:08	**10:23**	7:59
110	20	We.		7:04	8:09	**11:28**	8:52
111	21	Th.		7:03	8:10		9:50
112	22	Fr.	☿ stationary; ♀☌♅	7:02	8:10	12:26	10:50
113	23	Sa.		7:01	8:11	1:17	11:50
114	24	Su.	Last qtr. ☾	7:00	8:12	2:00	**12:50**
115	25	Mo.		6:59	8:12	2:38	**1:47**
116	26	Tu.		6:58	8:13	3:11	**2:42**
117	27	We.	♆☌☾	6:57	8:14	3:42	**3:36**
118	28	Th.		6:56	8:14	4:11	**4:28**
119	29	Fr.	☾ at apogee; ♅☌☾	6:55	8:15	4:40	**5:21**
120	30	Sa.	♀☌☾	6:54	8:16	5:09	**6:14**

† Daylight Saving Time begins at 2:00 a.m.

Calendar for 2011 (Cont'd.)

5th Month — May 2011 — 31 Days

Moon's Phases — *New,* May 3, 1:51 a.m.; *First Qtr.,* May 10, 3:33 p.m.; *Full,* May 17, 6:09 a.m.; *Last Qtr.,* May 24, 1:52 p.m.

Day of Year	Day of Month	Day of Week	Planetary Configurations and Phenomena	*Hour of Sunrise	Sunset	Moon-rise	Moon-set
121	1	Su.	☿☌☾; ♂☌♃; ♃♂☌☾	6:53	8:16	5:40	**7:09**
122	2	Mo.		6:52	8:17	6:13	**8:04**
123	3	Tu.	New ☾	6:51	8:18	6:51	**9:00**
124	4	We.		6:50	8:18	7:33	**9:56**
125	5	Th.		6:49	8:19	8:20	**10:50**
126	6	Fr.		6:49	8:20	9:13	**11:42**
127	7	Sa.	☿ gr. elong. W	6:48	8:20	10:10	
128	8	Su.		6:47	8:21	11:10	12:29
129	9	Mo.		6:46	8:22	**12:13**	1:13
130	10	Tu.	First qtr. ☾; ☿☌♃	6:45	8:22	**1:16**	1:52
131	11	We.	♀☌♃	6:45	8:23	**2:20**	2:30
132	12	Th.		6:44	8:24	**3:26**	3:06
133	13	Fr.		6:43	8:24	**4:32**	3:42
134	14	Sa.	♄☌☾	6:43	8:25	**5:40**	4:19
135	15	Su.	☾ at perigee	6:42	8:26	**6:50**	5:00
136	16	Mo.		6:41	8:27	**8:00**	5:45
137	17	Tu.	Full ☾	6:41	8:27	**9:07**	6:36
138	18	We.		6:40	8:28	**10:10**	7:32
139	19	Th.	☿☌♂	6:39	8:28	**11:05**	8:32
140	20	Fr.		6:39	8:29	**11:53**	9:34
141	21	Sa.		6:38	8:30		10:36
142	22	Su.	♀☌♂	6:38	8:30	12:34	11:36
143	23	Mo.		6:37	8:31	1:10	**12:33**
144	24	Tu.	Last qtr. ☾; ♆☌☾	6:37	8:32	1:42	**1:28**
145	25	We.		6:37	8:32	2:12	**2:21**
146	26	Th.		6:36	8:33	2:41	**3:14**
147	27	Fr.	☾ at apogee; ⛢☌☾	6:36	8:34	3:10	**4:07**
148	28	Sa.		6:35	8:34	3:40	**5:01**
149	29	Su.	♃☌☾	6:35	8:35	4:13	**5:56**
150	30	Mo.	♂☌☾	6:35	8:35	4:49	**6:52**
151	31	Tu.	♀☌☾	6:34	8:36	5:29	**7:49**

6th Month — June 2011 — 30 Days

Moon's Phases — *New,* June 1, 4:03 p.m., *First Qtr.,* June 8, 9:11 p.m.; *Full,* June 15, 3:14 p.m.; *Last Qtr.,* June 23, 6:48 a.m.

Day of Year	Day of Month	Day of Week	Planetary Configurations and Phenomena	*Hour of Sunrise	Sunset	Moon-rise	Moon-set
152	1	We.	New ☾	6:34	8:36	6:15	**8:44**
153	2	Th.		6:34	8:37	7:07	**9:38**
154	3	Fr.	♆ stationary	6:34	8:37	8:04	**10:27**
155	4	Sa.		6:34	8:38	9:04	**11:12**
156	5	Su.		6:33	8:38	10:07	**11:53**
157	6	Mo.		6:33	8:39	11:10	
158	7	Tu.		6:33	8:39	**12:13**	12:31
159	8	We.	First qtr. ☾	6:33	8:40	**1:17**	1:07
160	9	Th.		6:33	8:40	**2:21**	1:42
161	10	Fr.	♄☌☾	6:33	8:41	**3:27**	2:18
162	11	Sa.	☾ at perigee	6:33	8:41	**4:34**	2:56
163	12	Su.	☿ in superior ☌	6:33	8:42	**5:42**	3:38
164	13	Mo.		6:33	8:42	**6:49**	4:25
165	14	Tu.	♄ stationary	6:33	8:42	**7:53**	5:17
166	15	We.	Full ☾	6:33	8:43	**8:51**	6:15
167	16	Th.		6:33	8:43	**9:43**	7:17
168	17	Fr.		6:33	8:43	**10:27**	8:19
169	18	Sa.		6:33	8:44	**11:06**	9:21
170	19	Su.		6:34	8:44	**11:41**	10:20
171	20	Mo.	♆☌☾	6:34	8:44		11:17
172	21	Tu.	**Solstice;**	6:34	8:44	12:12	**12:11**
173	22	We.		6:34	8:44	12:41	**1:05**
174	23	Th.	Last qtr. ☾ at apogee	6:34	8:45	1:10	**1:58**
175	24	Fr.		6:35	8:45	1:40	**2:52**
176	25	Sa.		6:35	8:45	2:12	**3:46**
177	26	Su.	♃☌☾	6:35	8:45	2:46	**4:41**
178	27	Mo.		6:36	8:45	3:24	**5:38**
179	28	Tu.	♇☍☉; ♂☌☾	6:36	8:45	4:08	**6:34**
180	29	We.		6:36	8:45	4:58	**7:29**
181	30	Th.		6:37	8:45	5:53	**8:21**

*See text before January calendar for explanation.

7th Month — July 2011 — 31 Days

Moon's Phases — *New,* July 1, 3:54 a.m.; *First Qtr.,* July 8, 1:29 a.m.; *Full,* July 15, 1:40 a.m.; *Last Qtr.,* July 23, 12:02 a.m.; *New,* July 30, 1:40 p.m.

Day of Year	Day of Month	Day of Week	Planetary Configurations and Phenomena	*Hour of Sunrise	Sunset	Moon-rise	Moon-set
182	1	Fr.	New ☾	6:37	8:45	6:53	**9:08**
183	2	Sa.	☿☌☾	6:37	8:45	7:56	**9:52**
184	3	Su.		6:38	8:45	9:01	**10:31**
185	4	Mo.	● at aphelion	6:38	8:45	10:06	**11:09**
186	5	Tu.		6:39	8:45	11:10	**11:44**
187	6	We.		6:39	8:45	**12:15**	
188	7	Th.	☾ at perigee; ♄☌☾	6:40	8:45	**1:20**	12:20
189	8	Fr.	First qtr. ☾	6:40	8:44	**2:25**	12:57
190	9	Sa.		6:41	8:44	**3:31**	1:36
191	10	Su.	⛢ stationary	6:41	8:44	**4:37**	2:21
192	11	Mo.		6:42	8:44	**5:41**	3:10
193	12	Tu.		6:42	8:44	**6:40**	4:04
194	13	We.		6:43	8:43	**7:34**	5:03
195	14	Th.		6:43	8:43	**8:21**	6:04
196	15	Fr.	Full ☾	6:44	8:43	**9:02**	7:06
197	16	Sa.		6:44	8:42	**9:38**	8:06
198	17	Su.		6:45	8:42	**10:11**	9:04
199	18	Mo.	♆☌☾	6:46	8:41	**10:42**	10:01
200	19	Tu.		6:46	8:41	**11:11**	10:55
201	20	We.	☿ gr. elong. E	6:47	8:40	**11:41**	11:49
202	21	Th.	☾ at apogee; ⛢☌☾	6:47	8:40		**12:42**
203	22	Fr.		6:48	8:39	12:11	**1:36**
204	23	Sa.	Last qtr. ☾; ♃☌☾	6:49	8:39	12:44	**2:30**
205	24	Su.		6:49	8:38	1:20	**3:26**
206	25	Mo.		6:50	8:38	2:01	**4:22**
207	26	Tu.		6:50	8:37	2:47	**5:17**
208	27	We.	♂☌☾	6:51	8:36	3:40	**6:10**
209	28	Th.		6:52	8:36	4:38	**7:00**
210	29	Fr.		6:52	8:35	5:40	**7:46**
211	30	Sa.	New ☾	6:53	8:34	6:45	**8:28**
212	31	Su.		6:54	8:34	7:52	**9:07**

8th Month — August 2011 — 31 Days

Moon's Phases — *First Qtr.,* Aug. 6, 6:08 a.m.; *Full,* Aug. 13, 1:57 p.m.; *Last Qtr.,* Aug. 21, 4:54 p.m.; *New,* Aug. 28, 10:04 p.m.

Day of Year	Day of Month	Day of Week	Planetary Configurations and Phenomena	*Hour of Sunrise	Sunset	Moon-rise	Moon-set
213	1	Mo.	☿☌☾	6:54	8:33	8:58	**9:44**
214	2	Tu.	☾ at perigee; ☿ stationary	6:55	8:32	10:04	**10:21**
215	3	We.		6:55	8:31	11:11	**10:58**
216	4	Th.	♄☌☾	6:56	8:30	**12:17**	**11:37**
217	5	Fr.		6:57	8:30	**1:24**	
218	6	Sa.	First qtr. ☾	6:57	8:29	**2:30**	12:20
219	7	Su.		6:58	8:28	**3:34**	1:07
220	8	Mo.		6:59	8:27	**4:34**	2:00
221	9	Tu.		6:59	8:26	**5:29**	2:56
222	10	We.		7:00	8:25	**6:17**	3:56
223	11	Th.		7:01	8:24	**7:00**	4:56
224	12	Fr.		7:01	8:23	**7:37**	5:56
225	13	Sa.	Full ☾	7:02	8:22	**8:11**	6:54
226	14	Su.	♆☌☾	7:02	8:21	**8:42**	7:51
227	15	Mo.		7:03	8:20	**9:12**	8:46
228	16	Tu.	♀ in superior ☌	7:04	8:19	**9:42**	9:40
229	17	We.	⛢☌☾	7:04	8:18	**10:12**	10:33
230	18	Th.	☾ at apogee	7:05	8:17	**10:44**	11:27
231	19	Fr.		7:05	8:16	**11:18**	**12:21**
232	20	Sa.	♃☌☾	7:06	8:15	**11:57**	**1:15**
233	21	Su.	Last qtr. ☾	7:07	8:14		**2:10**
234	22	Mo.	♆☍☉	7:07	8:13	12:40	**3:05**
235	23	Tu.		7:08	8:12	1:29	**3:58**
236	24	We.		7:09	8:10	2:23	**4:48**
237	25	Th.	♂☌☾; ☿ stationary	7:09	8:09	3:22	**5:35**
238	26	Fr.		7:10	8:08	4:26	**6:19**
239	27	Sa.	☿☌☾	7:10	8:07	5:31	**7:00**
240	28	Su.	New ☾	7:11	8:06	6:38	**7:39**
241	29	Mo.		7:12	8:05	7:46	**8:17**
242	30	Tu.	☾ at perigee ♃ stationary	7:12	8:03	8:55	**8:55**
243	31	We.	♄☌☾	7:13	8:02	10:03	**9:35**

☉ The Sun ● The Earth ☾ The Moon ☿ Mercury ♀ Venus ♂ Mars ♃ Jupiter ♄ Saturn ♆ Neptune ⛢ Uranus ♇ Pluto

Calendar for 2011 (Cont'd.)

9th Month — September 2011 — 30 Days

Moon's Phases — *First Qtr.,* Sept. 4, 12:39 p.m.; *Full,* Sept. 12, 4:27 a.m.; *Last Qtr.,* Sept. 20, 8:39 a.m.; *New,* Sept. 27, 6:09 a.m.

Day of Year	Day of Month	Day of Week	Planetary Configurations and Phenomena	*Hour of Sunrise	Sunset	Moon-rise	Moon-set
244	1	Th.		7:13	8:01	11:12	**10:18**
245	2	Fr.		7:14	8:00	**12:20**	**11:05**
246	3	Sa.	☿ gr. elong. W	7:14	7:58	**1:26**	**11:57**
247	4	Su.	First qtr. ☾	7:15	7:57	**2:28**	
248	5	Mo.		7:16	7:56	**3:25**	12:52
249	6	Tu.		7:16	7:55	**4:15**	1:51
250	7	We.		7:17	7:53	**4:59**	2:50
251	8	Th.		7:17	7:52	**5:37**	3:50
252	9	Fr.		7:18	7:51	**6:12**	4:48
253	10	Sa.	♆☌☾	7:19	7:50	**6:44**	5:44
254	11	Su.		7:19	7:48	**7:14**	6:39
255	12	Mo.	Full ☾	7:20	7:47	**7:44**	7:33
256	13	Tu.	⛢☌☾	7:20	7:46	**8:14**	8:26
257	14	We.		7:21	7:45	**8:45**	9:20
258	15	Th.	☾ at perigee	7:21	7:43	**9:19**	10:14
259	16	Fr.	♇ stationary; ♃☌☾	7:22	7:42	**9:56**	11:08
260	17	Sa.		7:23	7:41	**10:37**	**12:02**
261	18	Su.		7:23	7:39	**11:22**	**12:56**
262	19	Mo.		7:24	7:38		**1:48**
263	20	Tu.	Last qtr. ☾	7:24	7:37	12:13	**2:39**
264	21	We.		7:25	7:35	1:09	**3:26**
265	22	Th.		7:25	7:34	2:08	**4:10**
266	23	Fr.	**Equinox;** ♂☌☾	7:26	7:33	3:11	**4:51**
267	24	Sa.		7:27	7:32	4:16	**5:31**
268	25	Su.	⛢☍☉	7:27	7:30	5:23	**6:09**
269	26	Mo.		7:28	7:29	6:31	**6:47**
270	27	Tu.	New ☾ at perigee	7:28	7:28	7:40	**7:27**
271	28	We.	☿ in superior ☌	7:29	7:26	8:51	**8:10**
272	29	Th.		7:30	7:25	10:02	**8:57**
273	30	Fr.		7:30	7:24	11:12	**9:49**

10th Month — October 2011 — 31 Days

Moon's Phases — *First Qtr.,* Oct. 3, 10:15 p.m.; *Full,* Oct. 11, 9:06 p.m.; *Last Qtr.,* Oct. 19, 10:30 p.m.; *New,* Oct. 26, 2:56 p.m.

Day of Year	Day of Month	Day of Week	Planetary Configurations and Phenomena	*Hour of Sunrise	Sunset	Moon-rise	Moon-set
274	1	Sa.		7:31	7:23	**12:18**	**10:45**
275	2	Su.		7:31	7:21	**1:18**	**11:44**
276	3	Mo.	First qtr. ☾	7:32	7:20	**2:11**	
277	4	Tu.		7:33	7:19	**2:57**	12:45
278	5	We.		7:33	7:18	**3:38**	1:44
279	6	Th.		7:34	7:16	**4:14**	2:43
280	7	Fr.	♆☌☾	7:35	7:15	**4:46**	3:40
281	8	Sa.		7:35	7:14	**5:17**	4:34
282	9	Su.		7:36	7:13	**5:47**	5:28
283	10	Mo.	⛢☌☾	7:37	7:12	**6:16**	6:21
284	11	Tu.	Full ☾	7:37	7:10	**6:47**	7:15
285	12	We.	☾ at apogee	7:38	7:09	**7:20**	8:08
286	13	Th.	♃☌☾; ♄☌☉	7:39	7:08	**7:56**	9:02
287	14	Fr.		7:39	7:07	**8:36**	9:56
288	15	Sa.		7:40	7:06	**9:20**	10:50
289	16	Su.		7:41	7:05	**10:08**	11:43
290	17	Mo.		7:41	7:04	**11:01**	**12:33**
291	18	Tu.		7:42	7:03	**11:58**	**1:20**
292	19	We.	Last qtr. ☾	7:43	7:01		**2:04**
293	20	Th.		7:43	7:00	12:58	**2:45**
294	21	Fr.	♂☌☾	7:44	6:59	2:00	**3:24**
295	22	Sa.		7:45	6:58	3:03	**4:01**
296	23	Su.		7:46	6:57	4:08	**4:39**
297	24	Mo.		7:46	6:56	5:15	**5:17**
298	25	Tu.		7:47	6:55	6:25	**5:58**
299	26	We.	New ☾ at perigee	7:48	6:54	7:36	**6:44**
300	27	Th.	☿☌☾	7:49	6:53	8:47	**7:34**
301	28	Fr.	♀☌☾; ♃☍☉	7:49	6:52	9:57	**8:30**
302	29	Sa.		7:50	6:52	11:03	**9:30**
303	30	Su.		7:51	6:51	**12:01**	**10:33**
304	31	Mo.		7:52	6:50	**12:52**	**11:35**

*See text before January calendar for explanation.

11th Month — November 2011 — 30 Days

Moon's Phases — *First Qtr.,* Nov. 2, 11:38 a.m.; *Full,* Nov. 10, 2:16 p.m.; *Last Qtr.,* Nov. 18, 9:09 a.m.; *New,* Nov. 25, 12:10 a.m.

Day of Year	Day of Month	Day of Week	Planetary Configurations and Phenomena	*Hour of Sunrise	Sunset	Moon-rise	Moon-set
305	1	Tu.		7:53	6:49	**1:36**	
306	2	We.	First qtr. ☾	7:53	6:48	**2:14**	12:35
307	3	Th.		7:54	6:47	**2:48**	1:33
308	4	Fr.	♆☌☾	7:55	6:46	**3:19**	2:29
309	5	Sa.		7:56	6:46	**3:49**	3:23
310	†6	Su.	**DST ends;** ⛢☌☾	6:57	5:45	**3:19**	3:17
311	7	Mo.		6:57	5:44	**3:49**	4:10
312	8	Tu.	☾ at apogee	6:58	5:43	**4:22**	5:03
313	9	We.	♃☌☾; ♆ stationary	6:59	5:43	**4:57**	5:57
314	10	Th.	Full ☾	7:00	5:42	**5:35**	6:51
315	11	Fr.		7:01	5:42	**6:18**	7:45
316	12	Sa.		7:02	5:41	**7:06**	8:39
317	13	Su.		7:03	5:40	**7:57**	9:30
318	14	Mo.	☿ gr. elong. E	7:03	5:40	**8:53**	10:18
319	15	Tu.		7:04	5:39	**9:51**	11:03
320	16	We.		7:05	5:39	**10:51**	11:44
321	17	Th.		7:06	5:38	**11:52**	**12:22**
322	18	Fr.	Last qtr. ☾	7:07	5:38		**12:59**
323	19	Sa.	♂☌☾	7:08	5:37	12:54	**1:34**
324	20	Su.		7:09	5:37	1:57	**2:11**
325	21	Mo.		7:09	5:37	3:03	**2:49**
326	22	Tu.	♄☌☾	7:10	5:36	4:11	**3:31**
327	23	We.	☾ at perigee	7:11	5:36	5:21	**4:18**
328	24	Th.	☿ stationary	7:12	5:36	6:31	**5:11**
329	25	Fr.	New ☾	7:13	5:36	7:40	**6:09**
330	26	Sa.	☿☌☾; ♀☌☾	7:14	5:35	8:43	**7:12**
331	27	Su.		7:15	5:35	9:39	**8:17**
332	28	Mo.		7:15	5:35	10:28	**9:21**
333	29	Tu.		7:16	5:35	11:10	**10:22**
334	30	We.		7:17	5:35	11:46	**11:20**

12th Month — December 2011 — 31 Days

Moon's Phases — *First Qtr.,* Dec. 2, 3:52 a.m.; *Full,* Dec. 10, 8:36 a.m.; *Last Qtr.,* Dec. 17, 6:48 p.m.; *New,* Dec. 24, 12:06 p.m.

Day of Year	Day of Month	Day of Week	Planetary Configurations and Phenomena	*Hour of Sunrise	Sunset	Moon-rise	Moon-set
335	1	Th.	♆☌☾	7:18	5:35	**12:19**	
336	2	Fr.	First qtr. ☾	7:19	5:35	**12:50**	12:16
337	3	Sa.		7:19	5:35	**1:20**	1:10
338	4	Su.	⛢☌☾; ☿ in inferior ☌	7:20	5:35	**1:50**	2:03
339	5	Mo.	☾ at apogee	7:21	5:35	**2:22**	2:56
340	6	Tu.	♃☌☾	7:22	5:35	**2:56**	3:50
341	7	We.		7:23	5:35	**3:33**	4:44
342	8	Th.		7:23	5:35	**4:15**	5:39
343	9	Fr.		7:24	5:35	**5:01**	6:33
344	10	Sa.	Full ☾; ⛢ stationary	7:25	5:35	**5:52**	7:25
345	11	Su.		7:25	5:36	**6:47**	8:15
346	12	Mo.		7:26	5:36	**7:45**	9:02
347	13	Tu.	☿ stationary	7:27	5:36	**8:45**	9:44
348	14	We.		7:27	5:36	**9:46**	10:24
349	15	Th.		7:28	5:37	**10:47**	11:00
350	16	Fr.		7:29	5:37	**11:49**	11:36
351	17	Sa.	Last qtr. ☾; ♂☌☾	7:29	5:37		**12:11**
352	18	Su.		7:30	5:38	12:52	**12:47**
353	19	Mo.		7:31	5:38	1:56	**1:25**
354	20	Tu.	♄☌☾	7:31	5:39	3:03	**2:08**
355	21	We.	**Solstice;** ☾ at perigee	7:32	5:39	4:11	**2:57**
356	22	Th.	☿☌☾; ☿ gr. elong. W	7:32	5:40	5:18	**3:51**
357	23	Fr.		7:33	5:40	6:23	**4:51**
358	24	Sa.	New ☾	7:33	5:41	7:23	**5:55**
359	25	Su.		7:33	5:41	8:15	**7:00**
360	26	Mo.	♃ stationary	7:34	5:42	9:01	**8:04**
361	27	Tu.	♀☌☾	7:34	5:43	9:41	**9:05**
362	28	We.		7:35	5:43	10:17	**10:03**
363	29	Th.	♆☌☾	7:35	5:44	10:49	**10:59**
364	30	Fr.	♇☌☉	7:35	5:44	11:20	**11:54**
365	31	Sa.	⛢☌☾	7:36	5:45	11:51	

† Daylight Saving Time ends at 2:00 a.m.

☉ The Sun ● The Earth ☾ The Moon ☿ Mercury ♀ Venus ♂ Mars ♃ Jupiter ♄ Saturn ♆ Neptune ⛢ Uranus ♇ Pluto

206-Year Calendar, A.D. 1894–2099, Inclusive

Using this calendar, you can find the day of the week for any day of the month and year for the period 1894–2099, inclusive. **To find any day of the week,** first look in the table of Common Years or Leap Years for the year required. Under each month are numbers that refer to the corresponding numbers at the head of each column in the Table of Days, below. For example, to find what day of the week March 2 fell in the year 1918, find 1918 in the table of Common Years. In a parallel line under March is the number 5. Look at column 5 in the Table of Days; there it shows that March 2 fell on Saturday.

Common Years, 1894 to 2099

											Jan.	Feb.	Mar.	Apr.	May	June	July	Aug.	Sept.	Oct.	Nov.	Dec.
1894	1900	...	...	...	...	...	...	...	...	...												
1906	1917	1923	1934	1945	1951	1962	1973	1979	1990	...	1	4	4	7	2	5	7	3	6	1	4	6
2001	2007	2018	2029	2035	2046	2057	2063	2074	2085	2091												
1895	...	...	...	...	...	...	...	...	...	...												
1901	1907	1918	1929	1935	1946	1957	1963	1974	1985	1991	2	5	5	1	3	6	1	4	7	2	5	7
2002	2013	2019	2030	2041	2047	2058	2069	2075	2086	2097												
1897	...	...	...	...	...	...	...	...	...	...												
1909	1915	1926	1937	1943	1954	1965	1971	1982	1993	1999	5	1	1	4	6	2	4	7	3	5	1	3
2010	2021	2027	2038	2049	2055	2066	2077	2083	2094	2100												
1898	1910	1921	1927	1938	1949	1955	1966	1977	1983	1994	6	2	2	5	7	3	5	1	4	6	2	4
2005	2011	2022	2033	2039	2050	2061	2067	2078	2089	2095												
1899	1905	1911	1922	1933	1939	1950	1961	1967	1978	1989	7	3	3	6	1	4	6	2	5	7	3	5
1995	2006	2017	2023	2034	2045	2051	2062	2073	2079	2090												
1902	1913	1919	1930	1941	1947	1958	1969	1975	1986	1997	3	6	6	2	4	7	2	5	1	3	6	1
2003	2014	2025	2031	2042	2053	2059	2070	2081	2087	2098												
1903	1914	1925	1931	1942	1953	1959	1970	1981	1987	1998	4	7	7	3	5	1	3	6	2	4	7	2
2009	2015	2026	2037	2043	2054	2065	2071	2082	2093	2099												

Leap Years, 1896 to 2096

									Jan.	Feb. (29)	Mar.	Apr.	May	June	July	Aug.	Sept.	Oct.	Nov.	Dec.
...	...	1920	1948	1976	2004	2032	2060	2088	4	7	1	4	6	2	4	7	3	5	1	3
...	...	1924	1952	1980	2008	2036	2064	2092	2	5	6	2	4	7	2	5	1	3	6	1
...	...	1928	1956	1984	2012	2040	2068	2096	7	3	4	7	2	5	7	3	6	1	4	6
...	1904	1932	1960	1988	2016	2044	2072	...	5	1	2	5	7	3	5	1	4	6	2	4
1896	1908	1936	1964	1992	2020	2048	2076	...	3	6	7	3	5	1	3	6	2	4	7	2
...	1912	1940	1968	1996	2024	2052	2080	...	1	4	5	1	3	6	1	4	7	2	5	7
...	1916	1944	1972	2000	2028	2056	2084	...	6	2	3	6	1	4	6	2	5	7	3	5

Table of Days

1		2		3		4		5		6		7	
Mon.	1	Tues.	1	Wed.	1	Thurs.	1	Fri.	1	Sat.	1	SUN.	1
Tues.	2	Wed.	2	Thurs.	2	Fri.	2	Sat.	2	SUN.	2	Mon.	2
Wed.	3	Thurs.	3	Fri.	3	Sat.	3	SUN.	3	Mon.	3	Tues.	3
Thurs.	4	Fri.	4	Sat.	4	SUN.	4	Mon.	4	Tues.	4	Wed.	4
Fri.	5	Sat.	5	SUN.	5	Mon.	5	Tues.	5	Wed.	5	Thurs.	5
Sat.	6	SUN.	6	Mon.	6	Tues.	6	Wed.	6	Thurs.	6	Fri.	6
SUN.	7	Mon.	7	Tues.	7	Wed.	7	Thurs.	7	Fri.	7	Sat.	7
Mon.	8	Tues.	8	Wed.	8	Thurs.	8	Fri.	8	Sat.	8	SUN.	8
Tues.	9	Wed.	9	Thurs.	9	Fri.	9	Sat.	9	SUN.	9	Mon.	9
Wed.	10	Thurs.	10	Fri.	10	Sat.	10	SUN.	10	Mon.	10	Tues.	10
Thurs.	11	Fri.	11	Sat.	11	SUN.	11	Mon.	11	Tues.	11	Wed.	11
Fri.	12	Sat.	12	SUN.	12	Mon.	12	Tues.	12	Wed.	12	Thurs.	12
Sat.	13	SUN.	13	Mon.	13	Tues.	13	Wed.	13	Thurs.	13	Fri.	13
SUN.	14	Mon.	14	Tues.	14	Wed.	14	Thurs.	14	Fri.	14	Sat.	14
Mon.	15	Tues.	15	Wed.	15	Thurs.	15	Fri.	15	Sat.	15	SUN.	15
Tues.	16	Wed.	16	Thurs.	16	Fri.	16	Sat.	16	SUN.	16	Mon.	16
Wed.	17	Thurs.	17	Fri.	17	Sat.	17	SUN.	17	Mon.	17	Tues.	17
Thurs.	18	Fri.	18	Sat.	18	SUN.	18	Mon.	18	Tues.	18	Wed.	18
Fri.	19	Sat.	19	SUN.	19	Mon.	19	Tues.	19	Wed.	19	Thurs.	19
Sat.	20	SUN.	20	Mon.	20	Tues.	20	Wed.	20	Thurs.	20	Fri.	20
SUN.	21	Mon.	21	Tues.	21	Wed.	21	Thurs.	21	Fri.	21	Sat.	21
Mon.	22	Tues.	22	Wed.	22	Thurs.	22	Fri.	22	Sat.	22	SUN.	22
Tues.	23	Wed.	23	Thurs.	23	Fri.	23	Sat.	23	SUN.	23	Mon.	23
Wed.	24	Thurs.	24	Fri.	24	Sat.	24	SUN.	24	Mon.	24	Tues.	24
Thurs.	25	Fri.	25	Sat.	25	SUN.	25	Mon.	25	Tues.	25	Wed.	25
Fri.	26	Sat.	26	SUN.	26	Mon.	26	Tues.	26	Wed.	26	Thurs.	26
Sat.	27	SUN.	27	Mon.	27	Tues.	27	Wed.	27	Thurs.	27	Fri.	27
SUN.	28	Mon.	28	Tues.	28	Wed.	28	Thurs.	28	Fri.	28	Sat.	28
Mon.	29	Tues.	29	Wed.	29	Thurs.	29	Fri.	29	Sat.	29	SUN.	29
Tues.	30	Wed.	30	Thurs.	30	Fri.	30	Sat.	30	SUN.	30	Mon.	30
Wed.	31	Thurs.	31	Fri.	31	Sat.	31	SUN.	31	Mon.	31	Tues.	31

Beginning of the Year

The Athenians began the year in June; the Macedonians, in September; the Romans, first in March and later in January; the Persians, on Aug. 11; and the ancient Mexicans, on Feb. 23. The Chinese year, which begins in late January or early February, is similar to the Mohammedan year. Both have 12 months of 29 and 30 days alternating, while in every 19 years, there are seven years that have 13 months. This does not quite fit the planetary movements, hence the Chinese have formed a cycle of 60 years, in which period 22 intercalary (added to the calendar) months occur.

Recreation & Sports

Horseback riders in Jones State Forest in Montgomery County. Texas Forest Service photo.

Texas State Parks & Forests

National Parks, Historical Sites, Recreation Areas

Birding, Fishing & Hunting

Fairs & Festivals

Sports

Texas State Parks

Texas' diverse system of state parks and historic sites offers contrasting attractions — mountains and canyons, arid deserts and lush forests, spring-fed streams, sandy dunes, saltwater surf and fascinating historic sites.

The state park information below was provided by **Texas Parks and Wildlife** (TPW) and the **Texas Historical Commission**. Additional information and brochures on individual parks are available from the TPW's Austin headquarters, 4200 Smith School Rd., Austin 78744; 1-800-792-1112; **www.tpwd.state.tx.us/park/**, and the historical commission, **www.thc.state.tx.us/hsites/hsdefault.shtml**.

The TPW's **Central Reservation Center** can take reservations for almost all state parks that accept reservations. Exceptions are Indian Lodge, the Texas State Railroad and facilities not operated by the TPW. Call the center during usual business hours at 512-389-8900. The TDD line is 512-389-8915.

The **Texas State Parks Pass**, currently costing $60 per year, waives entrance fees for all members and all passengers in member's vehicle to all state parks when entrance fees are required, as well as other benefits. For further information, contact TPW 512-389-8900.

Texas State Parklands Passport is a windshield decal granting discounted entrance to state parks for Texas residents who are senior citizens or are collecting Social Security disability payments and free entrance for disabled U.S. veterans. Available at state parks with proper identification. Details can be obtained at numbers or addresses above.

The following information is a brief glimpse of what each park has to offer. Refer to the **chart on pages 166–167** for a more complete list of available activities and facilities. Entrance fees to state parks range from $1 to $5 per person. There are also fees for tours and some activities. For up-to-date information, call the information number listed above before you go. Road abbreviations used in this list are: IH - interstate highway, US - U.S. Highway, TX - state highway, FM - farm-to-market road, PR - park road.

List of State Parks & Historic Sites

Abilene State Park, 16 miles southwest of Abilene on FM 89 and PR 32 in Taylor County, consists of 529.4 acres that were deeded by the City of Abilene in 1933. A part of the **official Texas longhorn herd** and bison are located in the park. Large groves of pecan trees that once shaded bands of Comanches now shade visitors at picnic tables. Activities include camping, hiking, picnicking, nature study, biking, lake swimming and fishing. In addition to **Lake Abilene, Buffalo Gap**, the original Taylor County seat (1878) and one of the early frontier settlements, is nearby. Buffalo Gap was on the **Western**, or **Goodnight-Loving, Trail**, over which pioneer Texas cattlemen drove herds to railheads in Kansas.

Acton State Historic Site is a .01-acre cemetery plot in Hood County where **Davy Crockett's** second wife, Elizabeth, was buried in 1860. It is 4.5 miles east of Granbury on US 377 to FM 167 south, then 2.4 miles south to Acton. Nearby attractions include **Cleburne, Dinosaur Valley** and **Lake Whitney state parks**.

Admiral Nimitz State Historic Site (see **National Museum of the Pacific War**).

Atlanta State Park is 1,475 acres located 11 miles northwest of Atlanta on FM 1154 in Cass County; adjacent

The Barton Warnock Environmental Education Center in Brewster County. Texas Parks & Wildlife photo.

to **Wright Patman Dam** and **Reservoir**. Land acquired from the U.S. Army in 1954 by license to 2004 with option to renew to 2054. Camping, biking and hiking in pine forests, as well as water activities, such as boating, fishing, lake swimming. Nearby are historic town of **Jefferson** and the **Caddo Lake** and **Daingerfield state parks**.

Balmorhea State Park is 45.9 acres four miles southwest of Balmorhea on TX 17 between Balmorhea and Toyahvale in Reeves County. Deeded in 1934-35 by private owners and Reeves Co. Water Imp. Dist. No. 1 and built by the Civilian Conservation Corps (CCC). Swimming pool (1-3/4 acres) fed by artesian **San Solomon Springs**; also provides water to **aquatic refuge** in park. Activities include swimming, picnicking, camping, scuba and skin diving. Motel rooms available at **San Solomon Springs Courts**. Nearby are city of Pecos, **Fort Davis National Historic Site, Davis Mountains State Park** and **McDonald Observatory.**

Barton Warnock Environmental Education Center consists of 99.9 acres in Brewster County. Originally built by the Lajitas Foundation in 1982 as the Lajitas Museum Desert Gardens, the TPW purchased it in 1990 and renamed it for Texas botanist Dr. Barton Warnock. The center is also the eastern entrance station to **Big Bend Ranch State Park**. Self-guiding botanical and museum tours. On FM 170 one mile east of Lajitas.

Bastrop State Park is 3,503.7 acres one mile east of Bastrop on TX 21 or from TX 71. The park was acquired by deeds from the City of Bastrop and private owners in 1933-35; additional acreage acquired in 1979. Site of famous "**Lost Pines**," isolated region of loblolly pine and hardwoods. **Swimming pool, cabins** and **lodge** are among facilities. Fishing at Lake Bastrop, backpacking, picnicking, canoeing, bicycling, hiking. Golf course adjacent to park. **State capitol** at Austin 32 miles away; 13-mile drive through forest leads to **Buescher State Park.**

Battleship Texas State Historic Site (see **San Jacinto Battleground State Historic Site** and **Battleship Texas)**

Bentsen-Rio Grande Valley State Park, a scenic park, is along the Rio Grande five miles southwest of Mission off FM 2062 in Hidalgo County. The 760 acres of **subtropical resaca woodlands and brushlands** were acquired from private owners in 1944. Park is excellent base from which to tour **Lower Rio Grande Valley** of Texas and adjacent **Mexico**; most attractions within an hour's drive. Hiking trails provide chance to study unique plants and animals of park. Many birds unique to southern United States found here, including **pauraque, groove-billed ani, green kingfisher, rose-throated becard** and **tropical**

parula. Birdwatching tours guided by park naturalists offered daily December–March. Park is one of last natural refuges in Texas for **ocelot** and **jaguarundi**. Trees include **cedar elm, anaqua, ebony** and **Mexican ash**. Camping, hiking, picnicking, boating, fishing also available. Nearby are **Santa Ana National Wildlife Refuge, Falcon State Park** and **Sabal Palm Sanctuary.**

Big Bend Ranch State Park, more than 299,008 acres of **Chihuahuan Desert wilderness** in Brewster and Presidio counties along the Rio Grande, was purchased from private owners in 1988. The purchase more than doubled the size of the state park system, which comprised at that time 220,000 acres. Eastern entrance at Barton Warnock Environmental Education Center one mile east of Lajitas on FM 170; western entrance is at **Fort Leaton State Historic Park** four miles east of Presidio on FM 170. The area includes **extinct volcanoes**, several **waterfalls**, two **mountain ranges**, at least **11 rare species of plants and animals**, and **90 major archaeological sites**. There is little development. Vehicular access limited; wilderness backpacking, hiking, scenic drive, picnicking, fishing and swimming. There are longhorns in the park, although they are not part of the official **state longhorn herd**.

Big Spring State Park is 382 acres located on FM 700 within the city limits of Big Spring in Howard County. Both city and park were named for a natural spring that was replaced by an artificial one. The park was deeded by the City of Big Spring in 1934 and 1935. Drive to top of **Scenic Mountain** provides panoramic view of surrounding country and look at **prairie dog colony**. The "big spring," nearby in a city park, provided watering place for herds of bison, antelope and wild horses. Used extensively also as campsite for early Indians, explorers and settlers.

Blanco State Park is 104.6 acres along the Blanco River four blocks south of Blanco's town square in Blanco County. The land was deeded by private owners in 1933. Park area was used as campsite by early explorers and settlers. Fishing, camping, swimming, picnicking, boating. **LBJ Ranch** and **LBJ State Historic Site, Pedernales Falls** and **Guadalupe River state parks** are nearby.

The pool at Balmorhea State Park in Reeves County is fed by San Solomon Springs and is popular with snorkelers. Randy Eli Grothe photo.

Bonham State Park is a 261-acre park located two miles southeast of Bonham on TX 78, then two miles southeast on FM 271 in Fannin County. It includes a 65-acre lake, **rolling prairies** and **woodlands**. The land was acquired in 1933 from the City of Bonham. Swimming, camping, mountain-bike trail, lighted fishing pier, boating. **Sam Rayburn Memorial Library** in Bonham. **Sam Rayburn Home** and **Valley Lake** nearby.

Brazos Bend State Park in Fort Bend County, eight miles east of Damon off FM 1462 on FM 762, approximately 28 miles south of Houston. The 4,897-acre park was purchased from private owners in 1976–77. **George Observatory** in park. **Observation platform** for spotting and photographing the **270 species of birds, 23 species of mammals, and 21 species of reptiles and amphibians, including American alligator**, that frequent the park. Interpretive and educational programs every weekend. Backpacking, camping, hiking, biking, fishing. Creekfield

A camp site at the 261-acre Bonham State Park in Fannin County. Robert Plocheck photo.

Sunset casts an iridescent glow on the waters of Cooper Lake near the Granny's Neck Screened Shelter Area at the Doctors Creek Unit of Cooper Lake State Park in Delta and Hopkins counties. Gary S. Hickinbotham photo.

Lake Nature Trail.

Buescher State Park, a scenic area, is 1,016.7 acres 2 miles northwest of Smithville off TX 71 to FM 153 in Bastrop County. Acquired between 1933 and 1936, about one-third deeded by private owner; heirs donated a third; balance from City of Smithville. **El Camino Real** once ran near park, connecting **San Antonio de Béxar** with **Spanish missions in East Texas.** Park land was part of **Stephen F. Austin's colonial grant.** Some **250 species of birds** can be seen. Camping, fishing, hiking, boating. Scenic park road connects with **Bastrop State Park** through **Lost Pines** area.

Caddo Lake State Park, north of Karnack one mile off TX 43 to FM 2198 in Harrison County, consists of 483.85 acres along **Cypress Bayou,** which runs into Caddo Lake. A scenic area, it was acquired from private owners in 1933. Nearby Karnack is childhood home of Lady Bird Johnson. Close by is old city of **Jefferson,** famous as commercial center of Northeast Texas during last half of 19th century. Caddo Indian legend attributes formation of Caddo Lake to **a huge flood. Cypress trees, American lotus** and **lily pads,** as well as **71 species of fish,** predominate in lake. **Nutria, beaver, mink, squirrel, armadillo, alligator** and **turtle** abound. Activities include camping, hiking, swimming, fishing, canoeing. Screened shelters, cabins.

Caddoan Mounds State Historic Site in Cherokee County six miles southwest of Alto on TX 21. Total of 93.8 acres acquired in 1975. Open for day visits only, park offers exhibits and interpretive trails through reconstructed **Caddo dwellings and ceremonial areas,** including two temple mounds, a burial mound and a village area typical of people who lived in region for 500 years beginning about A.D. 800. Open Tuesday–Sunday. Nearby are **Jim Hogg** and **Mission Tejas State historic sites** and **Texas State Railroad.**

Caprock Canyons State Park, 100 miles southeast of Amarillo and 3.5 miles north of Quitaque off FM 1065 and TX 86 in Briscoe, Floyd and Hall counties, has 15,313 acres. Purchased in 1975. Scenic escarpment's canyons provided camping areas for **Indians of Folsom culture** more than 10,000 years ago. **Mesquite** and **cacti** in the **badlands** give way to **tall grasses, cottonwood** and **plum thickets** in the bottomlands. Wildlife includes **aou-**

dad sheep, coyote, bobcat, porcupine and **fox.** Activities include scenic drive, camping, hiking, mountain-bike riding, horse riding and horse camping. A **64.25-mile trailway** (hike, bike and equestrian trail) extends from South Plains to Estelline.

Casa Navarro State Historic Site, on .7 acre at corner of S. Laredo and W. Nueva streets in downtown San Antonio, was acquired by donation from San Antonio Conservation Society Foundation in 1975. The furnished **Navarro House** three-building complex, built about 1848, was home of statesman, rancher and Texas patriot **José Antonio Navarro.** Guided tours; exhibits. Open Wednesday through Sunday.

Cedar Hill State Park, an urban park on 1,826 acres 10 miles southwest of Dallas via US 67 and FM 1382 on **Joe Pool Lake,** was acquired by long-term lease from the Army Corp of Engineers in 1982. Camping mostly in wooded areas. Fishing from two lighted jetties and a perch pond for children. Swimming, boating, bicycling, birdwatching and picnicking. Vegetation includes several sections of **tall-grass prairie.** Penn Farm Agricultural History Center includes reconstructed buildings of the **19th-century Penn Farm** and exhibits; self-guided tours.

Choke Canyon State Park consists of two units, South Shore and Calliham, located on 26,000-acre **Choke Canyon Reservoir.** Park acquired in 1981 in a 50-year agreement among Bureau of Reclamation, City of Corpus Christi and Nueces River Authority. Thickets of **mesquite** and **blackbrush acacia** predominate, supporting populations of **javelina, coyote, skunk** and **alligator,** as well as the **crested caracara.** The 385-acre South Shore Unit is located 3.5 miles west of Three Rivers on TX 72 in Live Oak County; the 1,100-acre Calliham Unit is located 12 miles west of Three Rivers, on TX 72, in McMullen County. Both units offer camping, picnicking, boating, fishing, lake swimming, and baseball and volleyball areas. The Calliham Unit also has a hiking trail, wildlife educational center, screened shelters, rentable **gym and kitchen. Sports complex** includes swimming pool and tennis, volleyball, shuffleboard and basketball courts. Across dam from South Shore is North Shore Equestrian and Camping Area; 18 miles of horseback riding trails.

Cleburne State Park is a 528-acre park located 10 miles southwest of Cleburne via US 67 and PR 21 in Johnson

County with 116-acre spring-fed lake; acquired from the City of Cleburne and private owners in 1935 and 1936. **Oak, elm, mesquite, cedar** and **redbud** cover white rocky hills. Bluebonnets in spring. Activities include camping, picnicking, hiking, bicycling, canoeing, swimming, boating, fishing. Nearby are **Fossil Rim Wildlife Center** and **dinosaur tracks** in Paluxy River at **Dinosaur Valley State Park**.

Colorado Bend State Park, a 5,328.3-acre facility, is 28 miles west of Lampasas in Lampasas and San Saba counties. Access is from Lampasas to Bend on FM 580 west, then follow signs (access road subject to flooding). Park site was purchased partly in 1984, with balance acquired in 1987. Primitive camping, fishing, swimming, hiking, biking and picnicking; guided tours to Gorman Falls. Rare and endangered species here include **golden-cheeked warbler, black-capped vireo** and **bald eagle**.

Confederate Reunion Grounds State Historic Site, located in Limestone County on the Navasota River, is 77.1 acres in size. Acquired 1983 by deed from Joseph E. Johnston Camp No. 94 CSA. Entrance is 6 miles south of Mexia on TX 14, then 2.5 miles west on FM 2705. **Historic buildings**, two **scenic footbridges** span creek; hiking trail. Nearby are **Fort Parker State Park** and **Old Fort Parker State Historic Site**.

Cooper Lake State Park, comprises 3,026 acres three miles southeast of Cooper in Delta and Hopkins counties acquired in 1991 by 25-year lease from Army Corps of Engineers. Two units, Doctors Creek and South Sulphur, adjoin 19,300-surface-acre Cooper Lake. Fishing, boating, camping, picnicking, swimming. Screened shelters and cabins. South Sulphur offers equestrian camping and horseback riding trails. Access to Doctors Creek Unit is via TX 24 east from Commerce to Cooper, then east on TX 154 to FM 1529 to park. To South Sulphur Unit, take IH 30 to Exit 122 west of Sulphur Springs to TX 19, then TX 71, then FM 3505.

Copper Breaks State Park, 12 miles south of Quanah on TX 6 in Hardeman County, was acquired by purchase from private owner in 1970. Park features rugged scenic beauty on 1,898.8 acres, two lakes, **grass-covered mesas** and juniper breaks. Nearby **medicine mounds** were important ceremonial sites of Comanche Indians. Nearby **Pease River** was site of 1860 battle in which **Cynthia Ann Parker** was recovered from Comanches. Part of **state longhorn herd** lives at park. Abundant wildlife. Nature, hiking and equestrian trails; natural and historical exhibits; summer programs; horseback riding; camping, equestrian camping.

Daingerfield State Park, off TX 49 and PR 17 southeast of Daingerfield in Morris County, is a 550.9-acre recreational area that includes an 80-surface-acre lake; deeded in 1935 by private owners. This area is center of iron industry in Texas; nearby is Lone Star Steel Co. In spring, **dogwood, redbuds** and **wisteria** bloom; in fall, brilliant foliage of **sweetgum, oaks** and **maples** contrast with dark green pines. Campsites, lodge and cabins.

Davis Mountains State Park is 2,709 acres in Jeff Davis County, 4 miles northwest of Fort Davis via TX 118 and PR 3. The scenic area was deeded in 1933-1937 by private owners. First European, **Antonio de Espejo**, came to area in 1583. Extremes of altitude produce both **plains grasslands** and **piñon-juniper-oak woodlands**. **Montezuma quail**, rare in Texas, visit park. Scenic drives, camping and hiking. **Indian Lodge**, built by the Civilian Conservation Corps during the early 1930s, has 39 rooms, restaurant and swimming pool (reservations: 432-426-3254). Four-mile hiking trail leads to **Fort Davis National Historic Site**. Other nearby points of interest include **McDonald Observatory** and 74-mile scenic loop through **Davis Mountains**. Nearby are scenic **Limpia, Madera, Musquiz** and **Keesey canyons; Camino del Rio**; ghost town of **Shafter**; **Big Bend National Park; Big Bend Ranch State Park; Fort Davis National Historic Site**; and **Fort Leaton State Historic Site**.

Devil's River State Natural Area comprises 19,988.6 acres in Val Verde County, 22 miles off US 277, about

Theropod tracks lead into the Paluxy River at Dinosaur Valley State Park in Somervell County. In 2009, the park celebrated the 100th anniversary of the tracks' discovery with publication of Dinosaur Highway: A History of Dinosaur Valley State Park *by Laurie E. Jasinski, who also wrote the ballad "The Dinosaur Waltz." Gary S. Hickinbotham photo.*

65 miles north of Del Rio on graded road. It is an **ecological and archaeological crossroads**. Ecologically, it is in a **transitional area** between the **Edwards Plateau**, the **Trans-Pecos desert** and the **South Texas brush country**. Archaeological studies suggest occupation and use by cultures from both east and west. Camping, hiking and mountain biking. Canyon and pictograph-site tours by prearrangement only. **Dolan Falls** is nearby and is accessible only through The Nature Conservancy of Texas.

Devil's Sinkhole State Natural Area, comprising 1,859.7 acres about 6 miles northeast of Rocksprings on US 377 in Edwards County, is a **vertical cavern**. The sinkhole, discovered by Anglo settlers in 1867, is a registered **National Natural Landmark**; it was purchased in 1985 from private owners. The cavern opening is about 40 by 60 feet, with a vertical drop of about 140 feet. Access by prearranged tour with Devil's Sinkhole Society (830-683-BATS). Bats can be viewed in summer leaving cave at dusk; no access to cave itself. Contact **Kickapoo Cavern State Park** to arrange a tour.

Dinosaur Valley State Park, located off US 67 four miles west of Glen Rose in Somervell County, is a 1,524.72-acre scenic park. Land was acquired from private own-

Parks text continues on page 168.

☆ Texas State Parks ☆

Park / †Type of Park / Special Features	NEAREST TOWN	Day Use Only	Historic Site/Museum	Exhibit/Interpretive Center	Restrooms	Showers	Trailer Dump Stn.	††Camping	Screened Shelters	Cabins	Group Facilities	Nature Trail	Hiking Trail	Picnicking	Boat Ramp	Fishing	Swimming	Water Skiing	Miscellaneous
Abilene SP	BUFFALO GAP				★	★	★	15	★		BG	★		★			☆	★	L
Acton SHS (Grave of Davy Crockett's wife)	GRANBURY	★	★																
Atlanta SP	ATLANTA				★	★	★	14			DG	★	★	★	★	☆	☆	☆	
Balmorhea SP (San Solomon Springs Courts)	BALMORHEA			★	★	★	★	14			DG			★			★		I
Barton Warnock Environmental Ed. Center	LAJITAS	★		★	★			★				★							
Bastrop SP	BASTROP				★	★	★	10	★		BG	★	★		★		☆	★	G
Battleship Texas HS (At San Jacinto Battleground)	DEER PARK	★	★	★															
Bentsen-Rio Grande Valley SP	MISSION				★	★		10			BG	★	★	★	★	☆			
Big Bend Ranch SP Complex	PRESIDIO			★	★	★		1			NG	★	★			☆	☆		B1, L, E
Big Spring SP	BIG SPRING			★	★			13			BG	★	★	★					
Blanco SP	BLANCO				★	★	★	16	★		DG		★	★			☆	☆	
Boca Chica Beach (Open Beach)	BROWNSVILLE							1					☆			☆	☆		
Bonham SP	BONHAM				★	★	★	14			BG	★	★	★	★	★	☆		B1
Brazos Bend SP (George Observatory)	RICHMOND			★	★	★	★	4	★		BG	★	★	★		★			B1, B2
Buescher SP	SMITHVILLE				★	★	★	14	★		BG	★	★	★		★	☆		B2
Caddo Lake SP	KARNACK			★	★	★	★	15	★	★	BG	★	★	★	★	★	☆	☆	
Caddoan Mounds SHS	ALTO	★	★	★	★							★							
Caprock Canyons SP and Trailway	QUITAQUE			★	★	★	★	8			BG	★	★	★	★	★	☆		B1, E
Casa Navarro SHS	SAN ANTONIO	★	★	★	★														
Cedar Hill SP	CEDAR HILL				★	★	★	12			DG	★	★	★	★	☆	☆		B1
Choke Canyon SP, Calliham Unit	CALLIHAM			★	★	★	★	10	★		BG	★		★	★	★	☆	☆	
Choke Canyon SP, South Shore Unit	THREE RIVERS			★	★	★	★	8			DG		★	★	★	★	☆	☆	B1, E
Cleburne SP	CLEBURNE				★	★	★	16	★		BG	★	★	★	★	★	☆		
Colorado Bend SP (Cave Tours)	BEND			★				1				★	★	★	★	★			B1
Confederate Reunion Grounds SHS	MEXIA	★	★	★				1			BG	★	★			☆			
Cooper Lake SP (Doctors Creek Unit)	COOPER			★	★	★	★	4	★		DG	★	★	★	★	★	★	☆	
Cooper Lake SP (South Sulphur Unit)	SULPHUR SPRINGS			★	★	★	★	14	★	★	DG	★	★	★	★	★		☆	B1, E
Copano Bay SFP ▲	FULTON			★										★	★				
Copper Breaks SP	QUANAH			★	★	★	★	10			BG	★	★		★	★	☆		B1, E, L
Daingerfield SP	DAINGERFIELD				★	★	★	15	★	★	BG	★	★	★	★	★	☆		
Davis Mountains SP (Indian Lodge)	FORT DAVIS			★	★	★	★	11			DG	★	★	★					I, E
Devils River SNA (Use by reservation only)	DEL RIO				★			1			BG					★			B1, E
Devil's Sinkhole SNA (Use by reservation only)	ROCKSPRINGS	_(No access to cavern. Tours of SNA by special request only.)_																	
Dinosaur Valley SP (Dinosaur Footprints)	GLEN ROSE			★	★	★	★	12			DG	★	★	★			☆	☆	B1, E, L
Eisenhower SP (Marina)	DENISON			★	★	★	★	15	★		BG	★	★	★	★	★	☆	☆	B1
Eisenhower Birthplace SHS	DENISON	★	★	★	★						DG								
Enchanted Rock SNA	FREDERICKSBURG				★	★	★	9			DG	★	★	★					R
Fairfield Lake SP	FAIRFIELD				★	★	★	11			DG	★	★	★	★	★	☆	☆	B1
Falcon SP (Airstrip)	ZAPATA				★	★	★	15	★		BG	★		★	★	☆	☆	☆	B1
Fannin Battleground SHS	GOLIAD	★	★	★	★						DG			★					
Fanthorp Inn SHS	ANDERSON	★	★	★	★									★					
Fort Boggy SP	CENTERVILLE	★			★						DG	★	★	★	★	☆	☆		
Fort Griffin SP & HS	ALBANY		★	★	★	★	★	10			BG	★	★	★		☆			L, E
Fort Lancaster SHS	OZONA	★	★	★	★									☆					
Fort Leaton SHS	PRESIDIO	★	★	★	★							★		★					
Fort McKavett SHS	FORT McKAVETT	★	★	★	★							★		★					
Fort Parker SP	MEXIA				★	★	★	14	★		BG	★	★	★	★	★	☆		B1
Fort Richardson SHS & Lost Creek Res. TW	JACKSBORO		★	★	★	★	★	10	★		DG	★	★	★	★	★	★		E
Franklin Mountains SP	EL PASO	★			★			6			DG	★	★						B1, E, R
Fulton Mansion SHS	FULTON	★	★	★										★					
Galveston Island SP (Summer Theater)	GALVESTON			★	★	★	★	4				★		★			☆	☆	B1
Garner SP	CONCAN				★	★	★	14	★	★	BG	★	★	★			☆	☆	B2
Goliad SHS	GOLIAD		★	★	★	★	★	11	★		DG	★	★	★			☆	★	
Goose Island SP	ROCKPORT			★	★	★	★	14			BG	★		★	★	★			
Governor Hogg Shrine SHS	QUITMAN	★	★	★	★						DG	★		★					
Guadalupe River SP/Honey Creek SNA	BOERNE				★	★	★	13				★	★			☆	☆		E
Hill Country SNA	BANDERA							6			NG	★		★		☆	☆		B1, E
Hueco Tanks SHS (Indian Pictographs)	EL PASO	★	★	★	★	★	★	14			DG	★	★	★					R
Huntsville SP	HUNTSVILLE			★	★	★	★	14	★		DG	★	★	★	★	★	☆		B1, B2
Inks Lake SP	BURNET			★	★	★	★	10	★		BG	★	★	★	★	★	☆	☆	G
Jim Hogg SHS	RUSK	★	★	★	★							★		★					
Kickapoo Cavern SP (Use by reservation only)	BRACKETTVILLE	*			★	★		6			NG	★	★						B1

† — TYPES OF PARKS

SP	State Park	SFP	State Fishing Pier
SHS	State Historic Site	TW	Trailway
SNA	State Natural Area		

†† — TYPES OF CAMPING

1-Primitive; 2-Walk-in tent; 3-Tent; 4-Water and Electric; 5-Water, Electric, Sewer; 6-1 & 2; 7-1, 2 & 4; 8-1, 2, 3 & 4; 9-1 & 3; 10-1, 3 & 4; 11-1, 3, 4 & 5; 12-1 & 4; 13-2, 3 & 4; 14-3 & 4; 15-3, 4 & 5; 16-4 & 5; 17-1, 3 & 5.

☆ Texas State Parks ☆

Park / †Type of Park / Special Features	NEAREST TOWN	Day Use Only	Historic Site/Museum	Exhibit/Interpretive Center	Restrooms	Showers	Trailer Dump Stn.	††Camping	Screened Shelters	Cabins	Group Facilities	Nature Trail	Hiking Trail	Picnicking	Boat Ramp	Fishing	Swimming	Water Skiing	Miscellaneous
Lake Arrowhead SP	WICHITA FALLS				★	★	★	10			DG	★	★	★	★	★	☆	☆	E
Lake Bob Sandlin SP	MOUNT PLEASANT				★	★	★	10	★		DG		★	★	★	★	☆	☆	B1
Lake Brownwood SP	BROWNWOOD				★	★	★	15	★	★	BG	★	★	★	★	★	☆	☆	
Lake Casa Blanca International SP	LAREDO				★	★	★	14			DG		★	★	☆	☆	☆	☆	B1
Lake Colorado City SP	COLORADO CITY				★	★	★	14		★	BG	★	★	★	★	★	☆	☆	
Lake Corpus Christi SP	MATHIS				★	★	★	15	★		DG		★	★	★	★	☆	☆	
Lake Houston SP	NEW CANEY				★	★		9			BG	★	★	★		★			B1, E
Lake Livingston SP	LIVINGSTON				★	★	★	15	★		DG	★	★	★	★	★	☆	☆	B1, B2, E
Lake Mineral Wells SP and TW	MINERAL WELLS				★	★	★	10	★		DG	★	★	★	★	★	☆		B1, E, R
Lake Somerville SP & TW, Birch Creek Unit	SOMERVILLE			★	★	★	★	10			BG	★	★	★	★	★	☆	☆	B1, E
Lake Somerville SP & TW, Nails Creek Unit	LEDBETTER			★	★	★	★	10			DG	★	★	★	★	★	☆	☆	B1, E
Lake Tawakoni SP	WILLS POINT				★	★	★	4				★	★	★	★	☆	☆	☆	
Lake Texana SP	EDNA				★	★		14			DG	★	★	★	★	★	☆	☆	B1
Lake Whitney SP (Airstrip)	WHITNEY				★	★	★	15	★		BG		★	★	★	☆	☆	☆	B1
Landmark Inn SHS (Hotel Rooms)	CASTROVILLE	★	★	★	★						DG	★		★		☆			I
Lipantitlan SHS	SAN PATRICIO	★											★						
Lockhart SP	LOCKHART				★	★		16			BG			★			★		G
Longhorn Cavern SP (Cavern Tours) ▲	BURNET	★	★	★	★							★	★	★					
Lost Maples SNA	VANDERPOOL			★	★	★	★	12				★	★	★			☆	☆	
Lyndon B. Johnson SHS	STONEWALL	★	★	★	★						DG	★		★		☆	★		L
Magoffin Home SHS	EL PASO	★	★	★	★									★					
Martin Creek Lake SP	TATUM				★	★	★	12	★	★	DG	★	★	★	★	★	☆	☆	B1
Martin Dies Jr. SP	JASPER				★	★	★	14	★		BG	★	★	★	★	★	☆	☆	B1
Matagorda Island SP (Boat or Air Access Only)	PORT O'CONNOR	★	★	★	★			1			NG	★	★			☆	☆	☆	B1
McKinney Falls SP	AUSTIN		★	★	★	★	★	13	★		BG	★	★	★		☆	☆		B1, B2
Meridian SP	MERIDIAN				★	★	★	13	★		BG	★	★	★	★	☆	☆		
Mission Tejas SHS	WECHES		★		★	★	★	15			BG	★	★	★			☆		
Monahans Sandhills SP	MONAHANS			★	★	★	★	14			DG	★		★					E
Monument Hill/Kreische Brewery SHS	LA GRANGE	★	★	★	★							★		★					
Mother Neff SP	MOODY				★	★	★	10			BG	★	★	★			☆		
Mustang Island SP	PORT ARANSAS				★	★	★	12						★			☆	☆	B1
National Museum of the Pacific War	FREDERICKSBURG	★	★	★	★							★							
Old Fort Parker SP (Managed by Groesbeck city)	GROESBECK	★	★	★				1						★					E
Palmetto SP	LULING				★	★	★	15			BC	★	★	★		★	☆		
Palo Duro Canyon SP (Summer Drama: "Texas")	CANYON			★	★	★	★	8	★			★	★	★		★			B1, E, L
Pedernales Falls SP	JOHNSON CITY				★	★	★	9			NG	★	★	★		☆	☆		B1, E
Port Isabel Lighthouse SHS	PORT ISABEL	★	★																
Possum Kingdom SP	CADDO				★	★	★	10	★			★	★	★	★	★	☆	☆	
Purtis Creek SP	EUSTACE				★	★	★	10				★	★	★	★	★	☆		P
Ray Roberts Lake SP, Isle du Bois Unit	DENTON				★	★	★	13			DG	★	★	★	★	★	☆	☆	B1, B2, E
Ray Roberts Lake SP, Johnson Unit	DENTON				★	★	★	7			DG	★	★	★	★	★	☆	☆	B1, B2
Rusk/Palestine SP (Texas State RR Terminals)	RUSK/PALESTINE				★	★	★	15			DG	★		★		★			
Sabine Pass Battleground SHS	SABINE PASS	★	★	★				★	12						★	★	☆		
Sam Bell Maxey House SHS	PARIS	★	★	★	★									★					
San Angelo SP	SAN ANGELO				★	★	★	8		★	BG	★	★	★	★	★	☆	☆	B1, E, L
San Jacinto Battleground SHS (Battleship Texas)	HOUSTON	★	★	★	★						DG	★		★		☆			
Sea Rim SP	PORT ARTHUR			★	★	★	★	10				★		★	★	☆	★		B1
Sebastopol SHS	SEGUIN	★	★	★										★					
Seminole Canyon SHS (Indian Pictographs)	LANGTRY		★	★	★	★	★	14				★	★	★					B1
Sheldon Lake SP	HOUSTON	★										★	☆	★	★				
South Llano River SP	JUNCTION		★		★	★	★	10				★	★	★		☆	☆		B1
Starr Family SHS	MARSHALL	★	★	★	★									★					
Stephen F. Austin SHS	SAN FELIPE		★		★	★	★	15	★		BG	★	★	★		☆			G
Texas State Railroad SHS	PALESTINE/RUSK	★	★	★	★									★					
Tyler SP	TYLER				★	★	★	15	★		BG	★	★	★	★	★	☆		B1
Varner-Hogg Plantation SHS (Guided Tours)	WEST COLUMBIA	★	★	★	★							★		★		☆			
Village Creek SP	LUMBERTON				★	★	★	13			BG	★	★	★		☆	☆		B1
Walter Umphrey SP	PORT ARTHUR	(Managed by Jefferson County)																	
Washington-on-the-Brazos SHS (Anson Jones Home)	WASHINGTON	★	★	★	★						DG		★	★					
Wyler Aerial Tramway Franklin Mts. SP	EL PASO	★		★	★														

Facilities

▲ Facilities not operated by Parks & Wildlife.
★ Facilities or services available for activity.
☆ Permitted but facilities not provided.

Note: Contact individual parks for information on handicap facilities.

Miscellaneous Codes

B1 Mountain Biking
B2 Surfaced Bike Trail
BG Both Day & Night Group Facilities
DG Day-Use Group Facilities
E Equestrian Trails
G Golf
I Hotel-Type Facilities
L Texas Longhorn Herd
NG Overnight Group Facilities
R Rock Climbing

ers in 1968. **Dinosaur tracks** in bed of Paluxy River and two full-scale dinosaur models, originally created for New York World's Fair in 1964–65, on display. Part of state **longhorn herd** is in park. Camping, picnicking, hiking, mountain biking, swimming, fishing.

Eisenhower Birthplace State Historic Site is 6 acres off US 75 at 609 S. Lamar, Denison, Grayson County. The property was acquired in 1958 from the Eisenhower Birthplace Foundation. Restoration of home of President Dwight Eisenhower includes furnishings of period and some personal effects of Gen. Eisenhower. Guided tour; call for schedule. Park open daily, except Christmas Day and New Year's Day; call for hours. Town of Denison established on **Butterfield Overland Mail** Route in 1858.

Eisenhower State Park, 423.1 acres five miles northwest of Denison via US 75 to TX 91N to FM 1310 on the shores of **Lake Texoma** in Grayson County, was acquired by an Army lease in 1954. Named for the 34th U.S. president, **Dwight D. Eisenhower**. First Anglo settlers came to area in 1835; **Fort Johnson** was established in area in 1840; **Colbert's Ferry** established on Red River in 1853 and operated until 1931. Areas of **tall-grass prairie** exist. Hiking, camping, picnicking, fishing, swimming.

Enchanted Rock State Natural Area is 1,643.5 acres on Big Sandy Creek 18 miles north of Fredericksburg on FM 965 on the line between Gillespie and Llano counties. Acquired in 1978 by The Nature Conservancy of Texas; state acquired from TNCT in 1984. Enchanted Rock is huge **pink granite boulder** rising 425 feet above ground and covering 640 acres. It is **second-largest batholith** (underground rock formation uncovered by erosion) in the United States. Indians believed **ghost fires** flickered at top and were awed by weird creaking and groaning, which geologists say resulted from rock's heating and expanding by day, cooling and contracting at night. Enchanted Rock is a **National Natural Landmark** and is on the **National Register of Historic Places**. Activities include hiking, geological study, camping, **rock climbing** and star gazing.

Estero Llano Grande State Park, part of the World Birding Center network, is a 176-acre wetlands refuge 3.2 miles southeast of Weslaco off FM 1015. Birds seen here include **waders, shorebirds** and **migrating waterfowl,** as well as coastal species such as **Roseate spoonbill** and **Ibis**. Rare spottings include r**ed-crowned parrots** and **green parakeets**. Opened daily. Guided tours offered.

Fairfield Lake State Park is 1,460 acres adjacent to Lake Fairfield, 6 miles northeast of the city of Fairfield off FM 2570 and FM 3285 in Freestone County. It was leased from Texas Utilities in 1971-72. Surrounding woods offer sanctuary for many species of birds and wildlife. Camping, hiking, backpacking, nature study, water-related activities available. Extensive schedule of tours, seminars and other activities.

Falcon State Park is 572.6 acres located 15 miles north of Roma off US 83 and FM 2098 at southern end of Falcon Reservoir in Starr and Zapata counties. Park leased from International Boundary and Water Commission in 1949. Gently rolling hills covered by **mesquite, huisache, wild olive, ebony, cactus**. Excellent **birding** and **fishing**. Camping and water activities also. Nearby are **Mexico, Fort Ringgold** in Rio Grande City and historic city of **Roma. Bentsen-Rio Grande Valley State Park** is 65 miles away.

Fannin Battleground State Historic Site, 9 miles east of Goliad in Goliad County off US 59 to PR 27. The 13.6-acre park site was acquired by the state in 1914; transferred to TPW by legislative enactment in 1965. At this site on March 20, 1836, **Col. James Fannin** surrendered to Mexican **Gen. José Urrea** after **Battle of Coleto**; 342 massacred and 28 escaped near what is now **Goliad State Park**. Near Fannin site is **Gen. Ignacio Zaragoza's Birthplace** and partially restored **Mission Nuestra Señora del Espíritu Santo de Zúñiga** (see also **Goliad State Park** in this list).

Fanthorp Inn State Historic Site includes a historic double-pen cedar-log dogtrot house and 1.4 acres in Anderson, county seat of Grimes County, south of TX 90. Acquired by purchase in 1977 from a Fanthorp descendant and opened to the public in 1987. Inn records report visits from many prominent civic and military leaders, including **Sam Houston, Anson Jones,** and **generals Ulysses S. Grant, Robert E. Lee** and **Stonewall Jackson**. Originally built in 1834, it has been restored to its 1850 use as a family home and travelers' hotel. Tours available Friday, Saturday, Sunday. Call TPW for stagecoach-ride schedule. No dining or overnight facilities.

Fort Boggy State Park is 1,847 acres of wooded, rolling hills in Leon County near Boggy Creek, about 4 miles south of Centerville on TX 75. Land donated to TPWD in 1985 by Eileen Crain Sullivan. Area once home to Keechi and Kickapoo tribes. Log fort was built by set-

Hikers trek up the pink granite batholith at Enchanted Rock State Natural Area. Texas Parks & Wildlife photo.

More Travel Information

Call the **Texas Department of Transporta-tion**'s toll-free number: **1-800-888-8TEX** for:

- The **Texas State Travel Guide**, a free, full-color publication with information about attractions, activities, history and historic sites.
- The official **Texas state highway map**.

On the Internet: **www.traveltex.com**

tlers in 1840s; first settlement north of the Old San Antonio Road and between the Navasota and Trinity rivers. Swimming beach, fishing, picnicking, nature trails for hiking and mountain biking. Fifteen-acre lake open to small craft. Open-air group pavilion overlooking lake can be reserved ($50 per day). Nearby attractions include **Rusk/Palestine**, **Fort Parker**, and **Texas State Railroad** state parks, and **Old Fort Parker Historic Site**. Open Wed.–Sun. for day use only; entrance fee. For reservations, call 512-389-8900.

Fort Griffin State Historic Site is 506.2 acres 15 miles north of Albany off US 283 in Shackelford County. The state was deeded the land by the county in 1935. Portion of **state longhorn herd** resides in park. On bluff overlooking townsite of **Fort Griffin** and **Clear Fork of Brazos River** valley are partially restored ruins of **Old Fort Griffin**, restored bakery, replicas of enlisted men's huts. Fort constructed in 1867, deactivated 1881. Camping, equestrian camping, hiking. Nearby are **Albany** with restored courthouse square, **Abilene** and **Possum Kingdom state parks**. Albany annually holds **"Fandangle"** musical show in commemoration of frontier times.

Fort Lancaster State Historic Site, 81.6-acres located about 8 miles east of Sheffield on TX 290 in Crockett County. Acquired in 1968 by deed from Crockett County; Henry Meadows donated 41 acres in 1975. **Fort Lancaster** established Aug. 20, 1855, to guard San Antonio-El Paso Road and protect movement of supplies and immigrants from Indian hostilities. Site of part of Camel Corps experiment. Fort abandoned March 19, 1861, after Texas seceded from Union. Exhibits on history, natural history and archaeology; nature trail, picnicking. Open daily; day use only.

Fort Leaton State Historic Site, 4 miles southeast of Presidio in Presidio County on FM 170, was acquired in 1967 from private owners. Consists of 23.4 acres, 5 of which are on site of **trading post**. In 1848, **Ben Leaton** built fortified adobe trading post known as Fort Leaton near present Presidio. Ben Leaton died in 1851. Guided tours; exhibits trace history, natural history and archaeological history of area. Serves as western entrance to **Big Bend Ranch State Park**. Day use only.

Fort McKavett State Historic Site, 79.5 acres acquired from 1967 through the mid-1970s from Fort McKavett Restoration, Inc., Menard County and private individuals, is located 23 miles west of Menard off US 190 and FM 864. Originally called **Camp San Saba**, the fort was built by War Department in 1852 to protect frontier settlers and travelers on Upper El Paso Road from Indians. Camp later renamed for **Capt. Henry McKavett**, killed at Battle of Monterrey, Sept. 21, 1846. Fort abandoned March 1859; reoccupied April 1868. A **Buffalo Soldier post**. Abandoned again June 30, 1883. Once called by Gen. Wm. T. Sherman, "the prettiest post in Texas." More than 25 restored buildings, ruins of many others. Interpretive exhibits. Day use only.

Fort Parker State Park includes 1,458.8 acres, including 758.78 land acres and 700-acre lake between Mexia and Groesbeck off TX 14 in Limestone County. Named for the former imprisoned fort built near present park in 1836, the site was acquired from private owners and the City of Mexia 1935-1937. Camping, fishing, swimming, canoeing, picnicking. Nearby is **Old Fort Parker Historic Site**, which

is operated by the City of Groesbeck.

Fort Richardson State Historic Site, located one-half mile south of Jacksboro off US 281 in Jack County, contains 454 acres. Acquired in 1968 from City of Jacksboro. Fort founded in 1867, northernmost of line of federal forts established after Civil War for protection from Indians; originally named **Fort Jacksboro**. In April 1867, fort was moved to its present location from 20 miles farther south; on Nov. 19, 1867, made permanent post at Jacksboro and named for **Israel Richardson**, who was fatally wounded at Battle of Antietam. Expeditions sent from Fort Richardson arrested Indians responsible for **Warren Wagon Train Massacre** in 1871 and fought Comanches in **Palo Duro Canyon**. Fort abandoned in May 1878. Park contains seven restored buildings and two replicas. Interpretive center, picnicking, camping, fishing; **ten-mile trailway**.

Franklin Mountains State Park, created by an act of the legislature in 1979 to protect the mountain range as a wilderness preserve and acquired by TPW in 1981, comprises 24,247.56 acres, all within El Paso city limits. **Largest urban park in the nation**. It includes virtually an entire **Chihuahuan Desert mountain range**, with an elevation of 7,192 feet at the summit. The park is habitat for many Chihuahuan Desert plants including **sotol, lechuguilla, ocotillo, cholla** and **barrel cactus**, and such animals as **mule deer, fox** and an occasional **cougar**. Camping, mountain biking, nature study, hiking, picnicking, rock-climbing. **Wyler Aerial Tramway,** an aerial cable-car tramway on 195 acres of rugged mountain on east side of Franklin Mountains. Purchase tickets at tramway station on McKinley Ave. Check with park for fees and hours; 915-566-6622. Other area attractions include **Hueco Tanks State Historic Site and Magoffin Home State Historic Site**.

Fulton Mansion State Historic Site in Fulton is 3.5 miles north of Rockport off TX Business 35 on South Fulton Beach Rd. in Aransas County. The 2.3 acre-property was acquired by purchase from private owner in 1976. Three-story wooden structure, built in 1874-1877, was home of **George W. Fulton**, prominent in South Texas for economic and commercial influence; mansion derives significance from its innovative construction and Victorian design. Call ahead for days and hours of guided tours; open Wednesday–Sunday; 800-792-1112.

Galveston Island State Park, on the west end of Galveston Island on FM 3005, is a 2,013.1-acre site acquired in 1969 from private owners. Camping, birding, nature study, swimming, bicycling and fishing amid **sand dunes and grassland**. Musical productions in **amphitheater** during summer.

Garner State Park is 1,419.8 acres of recreational facilities on US 83 on the Frio River in Uvalde County 9 miles south of Leakey. Named for **John Nance Garner**, U.S. Vice President, 1933-1941, the park was deeded in 1934-36 by private owners. Camping, hiking, picnicking, river recreation, miniature golf, biking, boat rentals. Cabins available. Nearby is **John Nance "Cactus Jack" Garner Museum** in Uvalde. Nearby also are ruins of historic **Mission Nuestra Señora de la Candelaria del Cañon**, founded in 1749; **Camp Sabinal** (a U.S. Cavalry post and later Texas Ranger camp) established 1856; **Fort Inge**, established 1849.

Goliad State Park and **Mission Espíritu Santo Historic Site** are 188.3 acres one-fourth mile south of Goliad on US 183 and 77A, along the San Antonio River in Goliad County. The land was deeded to the state in 1931 by the City and County of Goliad; transferred to TPW 1949. Nearby are the sites of several battles in the Texas fight for independence from Mexico. The park includes a replica of **Mission Nuestra Señora del Espíritu Santo de Zúñiga**, originally established 1722 and settled at its present site in 1749. **Gen. Ignacio Zaragoza Birthplace State Historic Site**, which is located near **Presidio la Bahía**, across the river. Gen. Zaragoza was the Mexican national hero who led troops against the French at historic **Battle of Puebla** on May 5, 1862. The restored presidio and chapel, **Nuestra Señora de Loreto de la Bahía**, dates to 1749. Adjacent is a memorial shaft marking the common burial site of **Fannin** and victims of Goliad massacre (1836). Located four miles west of Goliad on US 59 is the **Mission Rosario State Historic Site** which contains ruins of **Nuestra Señora del Rosario** mission, established 1754. At Goliad State Park are camping, picnicking, historical exhibits, nature trail. (See also **Fannin Battleground State Historic Site**.)

Goose Island State Park, 321.4 acres 10 miles northeast of Rockport on TX 35 and PR 13 on St. Charles and Aransas bays in Aransas County, was deeded by private owners in 1931-1935 plus an additional seven acres donated in the early 1990s by Sun Oil Co. Located here is "Big Tree" estimated to be a 1,000-year-old **live oak**. Fishing, picnicking and camping, plus excellent birding; no swimming. Rare and endangered **whooping cranes** can be viewed during winter just across St. Charles Bay in **Aransas National Wildlife Refuge**.

Government Canyon State Natural Area is an 8,622-acre area in Bexar County, northwest of San Antonio, 3.5 miles northwest of Loop 1604 and FM 471, then 1.6 miles north on Galm Road. Day use only. No camping. Open Friday–Monday. Trees such as **mounatin laurel, Ashe juniper, Mexican buckeye** and **Escarpment black cherry.**

Gov. Hogg Shrine State Historic Site is a 26.7-acre tract on TX 37 about six blocks south of the Wood County Courthouse in Quitman. Named for **James Stephen Hogg,** first native-born governor of Texas, the park includes museums housing items that belonged to the Hogg and Stinson families. Seventeen acres deeded by the Wood County Old Settlers Reunion Association in 1946; 4.74 acres gift of Miss Ima Hogg in 1970; 3 acres purchased **Gov. James Stephen Hogg Memorial Shrine** created in 1941. Three museums: Gov. Hogg's wedding held in **Stinson Home; Honeymoon Cottage; Miss Ima Hogg Museum** houses both park headquarters and display of representative history of entire Northeast Texas area. Operated by City of Quitman.

Guadalupe River State Park comprises 1,938.7 acres on cypress-shaded Guadalupe River in Kendall and Comal counties, 13 miles east of Boerne on TX 46. Acquired by deed from private owners in 1974. Park has four miles of river frontage with several **white-water rapids** and is located in a stretch of **Guadalupe River** noted for canoeing, tubing. Picnicking, camping, hiking, nature study. Trees include **sycamore, elm, basswood, pecan, walnut, persimmon, willow** and **hackberry** (see also **Honey Creek State Natural Area**).

Hill Country State Natural Area in Bandera and Medina counties, 9 miles west of Bandera on FM 1077. The 5,369.8-acre site acquired by gift from Merrick Bar-O-Ranch and purchased in 1976. Park is located in typical Texas Hill Country on West Verde Creek and contains several **spring-fed streams**. Primitive and equestrian camping, hiking, horseback riding, mountain biking, fishing. Group lodge.

Honey Creek State Natural Area consists of 2,293.7 acres adjacent to **Guadalupe River State Park** (above); entrance is in the park. Acquired from The Nature Conservancy of Texas in 1985 with an addition from private individual in 1988. Diverse plant life includes **agarita, Texas persimmon** and **Ashe juniper** in hills, and **cedar elm, Spanish oak, pecan, walnut** and **Mexican buckeye** in bottomlands. Abundant wildlife includes **ringtail, leopard frog, green kingfisher, golden-cheeked warbler** and **canyon wren**. Schedule varies; call 830-796-4413 for details.

Hueco Tanks State Historic Site, located 32 miles northeast of El Paso in El Paso County on FM 2775 just north of US 62-180, was obtained from the county in 1969, with additional 121 acres purchased in 1970. Featured in this 860.3-acre park are large **natural rock basins** that provided water for archaic hunters, Plains Indians, Butterfield Overland Mail coach horses and passengers, and other travelers in this arid region. In park are **Indian pictographs, old ranch house** and relocated **ruins of**

stage station. **Rock climbing**, picnicking, camping, hiking. Wildlife includes **gray fox, bobcat, prairie falcons, golden eagles.** Visitation is limited. Pictograph tours are by advanced request. Call 1-800-792-112, (Option 3).

Huntsville State Park is 2,083.2-acre recreational area off IH 45 and PR 40 six miles south of Huntsville in Walker County, acquired by deeds from private owners in 1937. Heavily wooded park adjoins **Sam Houston National Forest** and encloses **Lake Raven**. Hiking, camping, fishing, biking, paddle boats, canoeing. At nearby Huntsville are **Sam Houston's old homestead (Steamboat House)**, containing some of his personal effects, and **his grave**. Approximately 50 miles away is **Alabama-Coushatta Indian Reservation** in Polk County.

Inks Lake State Park is 1,201 acres of recreational facilities along Inks Lake, 9 miles west of Burnet on the Colorado River off TX 29 on PR 4 in Burnet County. Acquired by deeds from the Lower Colorado River Authority and private owners in 1940. Camping, hiking, fishing, swimming, boating, golf. **Deer, turkey** and other wildlife abundant. Nearby are **Longhorn Cavern State Park, LBJ Ranch, LBJ State Historic Site, Pedernales Falls State Park** and **Enchanted Rock State Natural Area**. **Granite Mountain** quarry at nearby Marble Falls furnished red granite for **Texas state capitol. Buchanan Dam**, considered the largest multi-arch dam in the nation, located 4 miles from park.

Jim Hogg Historic Site is 178.4 acres of East Texas Pineywoods in Cherokee County, 2 miles east of Rusk off U.S. 84 E. and Fire Tower Road. Memorial to Texas' first native-born governor, James Stephen Hogg, 1891–1895. Remnants of 1880s iron ore mining. Scale replica of Hogg birthplace. Picnicking, historical study, nature study, hiking and bird watching. Self-guided and guided museum tours and nature trail tours. Operated by the City of Rusk; 903-683-4850. Area attractions: **Caddoan Mounds** and **Mission Tejas State historic sites**, Rusk/Palestine, **Texas State Railroad** and **Tyler state parks** and historic Nacogdoches. Day use only; entrance fee.

Kickapoo Cavern State Park is located about 22 miles north of Brackettville on RM 674 on the Kinney/Edwards county line in the southern Edwards Plateau. The park (6,368.4 acres) contains **15 known caves**, two of which are large enough to be significant: **Kickapoo Cavern**, about 1/4 mile in length, has impressive formations, and **Green Cave**, slightly shorter, supports a nursery colony of **Brazilian freetail bats** in summer. Birds include rare species such as **black-capped vireo, varied bunting** and **Montezuma quail**. Reptiles and amphibians include **barking frog, mottled rock rattlesnake** and **Texas alligator lizard**. Tours of Kickapoo and observation of bats available only by special arrangement. Group lodge; primitive camping; hiking and mountain-biking trails. Open only by reservation.

Kreische Brewery State Historic Site (see Monument Hill and Kreische Brewery State Historic Sites).

Lake Arrowhead State Park consists of 524 acres in Clay County, about 14 miles south of Wichita Falls on US 281 to FM 1954, then 8 miles to park. Acquired in 1970 from the City of Wichita Falls. **Lake Arrowhead** is a reservoir on the Little Wichita River with 106 miles of shoreline. The land surrounding the lake is generally semiarid, gently rolling prairie, much of which has been invaded by mesquite in recent decades. Fishing, camping, lake swimming, picnicking, horseback-riding area.

Lake Bob Sandlin State Park, on the wooded shoreline of 9,400-acre Lake Bob Sandlin, is located 12 miles southwest of Mount Pleasant off FM 21 in Titus County. Activities in the 639.8-acre park include picnicking, camping, mountain biking, hiking, swimming, fishing and boating. **Oak, hickory, dogwood, redbud, maple** and **pine** produce spectacular fall color. Eagles can sometimes be spotted in winter months.

Lake Brownwood State Park in Brown County is 537.5 acres acquired from Brown County Water Improvement

Tubing at Lake Somerville State Park in Lee and Burleson counties. Ron Billings Photo; Texas Forest Service.

District No. 1 in 1934. Park reached from TX 279 to PR 15, 16 miles northwest of Brownwood on Lake Brownwood near **geographical center of Texas**. Water sports, hiking, camping. Cabins available.

Lake Casa Blanca International State Park, located one mile east of Laredo off US 59 on Loop 20, was formerly operated by the City of Laredo and Webb County and was acquired by TPW in 1990. Park includes 371 acres on Lake Casa Blanca. **Recreation hall** can be reserved. Camping, picnicking, fishing, ball fields, playgrounds, amphitheater, and tennis courts. County-operated golf course nearby.

Lake Colorado City State Park, 500 acres leased for 99 years from a utility company. It is located in Mitchell County 11 miles southwest of Colorado City off IH 20 on FM 2836. Water sports, picnicking, camping, hiking. Part of **state longhorn herd** can be seen in park.

Lake Corpus Christi State Park, a 14,112-acre park in San Patricio, Jim Wells and Live Oak counties. Located 35 miles northwest of Corpus Christi and four miles southwest of Mathis off TX 359 and Park Road 25. Was leased from City of Corpus Christi in 1934. Camping, picnicking, birding, water sports. Nearby are **Padre Island National Seashore; Mustang Island, Choke Canyon, Goliad and Goose Island state parks; Aransas National Wildlife Refuge, and Fulton Mansion State Historic Site**.

Lake Livingston State Park, in Polk County, about one mile southwest of Livingston on FM 3126 and PR 65, contains 635.5 acres along Lake Livingston. Acquired by deed from private landowners in 1971. Near ghost town of **Swartwout**, steamboat landing on Trinity River in 1830s and 1850s. Camping, picnicking, swimming pool, fishing, mountain biking and stables.

Lake Mineral Wells State Park, located 4 miles east of Mineral Wells on US 180 in Parker County, consists of 3,282.5 acres encompassing Lake Mineral Wells. In 1975, the City of Mineral Wells donated 1,095 land acres and the lake to TPW; the federal government transferred additional land from Fort Wolters army post. Popular for **rock-climbing/rappelling**. Swimming, fishing, boating, camping; the 20-mile **Lake Mineral Wells State Trailway** avaiable for hiking, bicycling, equestrian use.

Lake Somerville State Park, northwest of Brenham in Lee and Burleson counties, was leased from the federal government in 1969. **Birch Creek Unit** (2,365 acres

reached from TX 60 and PR 57) and **Nails Creek Unit** (3,155 acres reached from US 290 and FM 180), are connected by a **13-mile trailway system**, with **equestrian and primitive camp sites**, rest benches, shelters and drinking water. Also camping, birding, picnicking, volleyball and water sports. **Somerville Wildlife Management Area**, 3,180 acres is nearby.

Lake Tawakoni State Park is a 376.3-acre park in Hunt County along the shore of its namesake reservoir. It was acquired in 1984 through a 50-year lease agreement with the Sabine River Authority and opened in 2001. Includes a swimming beach, half-mile trail, picnic sites, boat ramp and campsites. A **40-acre tallgrass prairie** managed in the post-oak woodlands. The park is reached from IH 20 on TX 47 north to FM 2475 about 20 miles past Wills Point.

Lake Texana State Park is 575 acres, 6.5 miles east of Edna on TX 111, halfway between Houston and Corpus Christi in Jackson County, with camping, boating, fishing and picnicking facilities. It was acquired by a 50-year lease agreement with the Bureau of Reclamation in 1977. Good birding in the **oak/pecan woodlands**. **Alligators** are often found in park coves.

Lake Whitney State Park is 1,280.7 acres along the east shore of Lake Whitney west of Hillsboro via TX 22 and FM 1244 in Hill County. Acquired in 1954 by a Department of the Army lease. Located near ruins of **Towash**, early Texas settlement inundated by the lake. Towash Village named for chief of Hainai Indians. Park noted for **bluebonnets** in spring. Camping, hiking, birding, picnicking, water activities.

Landmark Inn State Historic Site, 4.7 acres in Castroville, Medina County, about 15 miles west of San Antonio, was acquired through donation by Miss Ruth Lawler in 1974. Castroville, settled in the 1840s by Alsatian farmers, is called **Little Alsace of Texas**. Landmark Inn built about 1844 as residence and store for **Cesar Monod**, mayor of Castroville 1851-1864. Special workshops, tours and events held at inn; grounds may be rented for receptions, family reunions and weddings. Overnight lodging; all rooms air-conditioned and nonsmoking.

Lipantitlan State Historic Site is 5 acres 9 miles east of Orange Grove in Nueces County off Texas 359, FM 624 and FM 70. The property was deeded by private owners in 1937. Fort constructed here in 1833 by Mexican government fell to Texas forces in 1835. Only facilities are picnic tables. **Lake Corpus Christi State Park** is nearby.

Lockhart State Park is 263.7 acres 4 miles south of Lockhart via US 183, FM 20 and PR 10 in Caldwell County. The land was deeded by private owners between 1934 and 1937. Camping, picnicking, hiking, fishing, 9-hole golf course. After Comanche raid in Linnville, **Battle of Plum Creek** (1840) was fought in area.

Longhorn Cavern State Park, off US 281 and PR 4 about 6 miles west and 6 miles south of Burnet in Burnet County, is 645.62 acres dedicated as a natural landmark in 1971. It was acquired in 1932-1937 from private owners. The cave has been used as a shelter since prehistoric times. Among legends about the cave is that the outlaw **Sam Bass** hid stolen money there. Confederates made gunpowder in the cave during the Civil War. Nature trail; guided tours of cave; picnicking, hiking. Cavern operated by concession agreement. **Inks Lake State Park** and **Lyndon B. Johnson Ranch** located nearby.

Lost Maples State Natural Area consists of 2,174.2 scenic acres on the Sabinal River in Bandera and Real counties, 5 miles north of Vanderpool on FM 187. Acquired by purchase from private owners in 1973-1974. Outstanding example of Edwards Plateau flora and fauna, features isolated stand of uncommon **Uvalde bigtooth maple. Rare golden-cheeked warbler, black-capped vireo** and **green kingfisher** nest and feed in park. Fall foliage can be spectacular (late Oct. through early Nov.). Hiking trails, camping, fishing, picnicking, birding.

Lyndon B. Johnson State Historic Site, off US 290 in Gillespie County 14 miles west of Johnson City near Stonewall, contains 717.9 acres. Acquired in 1965 with private donations. **Home of Lyndon B. Johnson** located north bank of **Pedernales River** across Ranch Road 1 from park; portion of **official Texas longhorn herd** maintained at park. Wildlife exhibit includes **turkey, deer and bison. Living-history demonstrations** at restored **Sauer-Beckmann house.** Reconstruction of **Johnson birthplace** is open to public. Historic structures, swimming pool, tennis courts, baseball field, picnicking. Day use only. Nearby is family cemetery where former president and relatives are buried. In Johnson City is **boyhood home of President Johnson.** (See **National Parks.**)

Magoffin Home State Historic Site, in El Paso, is a 19-room territorial-style adobe on a 1.5-acre site. Purchased by the state and City of El Paso in 1976, it is operated by TPW. Home was built in 1875 by El Pasoan **Joseph Magoffin.** Furnished with original family artifacts. Guided tours; call for schedule. Day use only.

Martin Creek Lake State Park, 286.9 acres, is located 4 miles south of Tatum off TX 43 and CR 2183 in Rusk County. It was deeded to the TPW by Texas Utilities in 1976. Water activities; also cabins, camping, picnicking. Roadbed of **Trammel's Trace**, old Indian trail that became major route for settlers moving to Texas from Arkansas, can be seen. **Hardwood and pine** forest shelters abundant wildlife including **swamp rabbits, gophers, nutria** and numerous species of land birds and waterfowl.

Martin Dies Jr. State Park is 705 acres in Jasper and Tyler counties on B. A. Steinhagen Reservoir between Woodville and Jasper via US 190. Land leased for 50 years from Corps of En-

gineers in 1964. Located at edge of **Big Thicket**. Plant and animal life varied and abundant. Winter **bald eagle census** conducted at nearby Sam Rayburn Reservoir. Camping, hiking, mountain biking, water activities. Wildscape/herb garden. Park is approximately 30 miles from **Alabama and Coushatta Indian Reservation.**

McKinney Falls State Park is 744.4 acres 13 miles southeast of the state Capitol in Austin off US 183. Acquired in 1970 by gift from private owners. Named for Thomas F. McKinney, **one of Stephen F. Austin's first 300 colonists,** who built his home here in the mid-1800s on Onion Creek. Ruins of his homestead can be viewed. Swimming, hiking, biking, camping, picnicking, fishing, guided tours.

Meridian State Park in Bosque County is a 505.4-acre park. The heavily wooded land, on TX 22 three miles southwest of Meridian, was acquired from private owners in 1933-1935. **Texas-Santa Fe expedition** of 1841 passed through Bosque County near present site of park on Bee Creek. **Endangered golden-cheeked warbler** nests here. Camping, picnicking, hiking, fishing, lake swimming, birding, bicycling.

Mission Tejas State Historic Site is a 363.5-acre park in Houston County. Situated 12 miles west of Alto via TX 21 and PR 44, the park was acquired from the Texas Forest Service in 1957. In the park is a representation of **Mission San Francisco de los Tejas,** the first mission in East Texas (1690). It was abandoned, then re-established 1716; abandoned again 1719; re-established again 1721; abandoned for last time in 1730 when the mission was moved to San Antonio. Also in park is restored **Rice Family Log Home,** built about 1828. Camping, hiking, fishing, picnicking.

Monahans Sandhills State Park consists of 3,840 acres of sand dunes, some up to 70 feet high, in Ward and Winkler counties 5 miles northeast of Monahans on IH 20 to PR 41. Land leased by state from private foundation until 2056. Dunes used as meeting place by raiding Indians. Camping, hiking, picnicking, sand-surfing. Scheduled tours. **Odessa meteor crater** is nearby, as is **Balmorhea State Park.**

Monument Hill State Historic Site and **Kreische Brewery State Historic Site** are operated as one park unit. Monument Hill consists of 40.4 acres one mile south of La Grange on US 77 to Spur Road 92 in Fayette County. Monument and tomb area acquired by state in 1907; additional acreage acquired from the Archdiocese of San Antonio in 1956. Brewery and home purchased from private owners in 1977. Monument is dedicated to **Capt. Nicholas Dawson** and his men, who fought at **Salado Creek** in 1842, in Mexican **Gen. Adrián Woll's** invasion

Representation of Mission San Francisco de los Tejas, the first Spanish mission in East Texas, at Mission Tejas State Historic Site. The 363-acre park in Houston County offers camping, hiking, fishing and picnicking. Texas Parks & Wildlife photo.

Pedernales Falls State Park in Blanco County is more than 5,000 acres. Ron Billings photo; Texas Forest Service.

of Texas, and to the men of the **"black bean lottery"** (1843) of the **Mier Expedition**. Remains were brought to **Monument Hill** for reburial in 1848. Kreische Complex, on 36 acres, is linked to Monument Hill through interpretive trail. **Kreische Brewery State Historic Site** includes the brewery and stone-and-wood house built between 1850-1855 on Colorado River. One of **first commercial breweries** in state, it closed in 1884. Smokehouse and barn also in complex. Guided tours of brewery and house; call for schedule. Also picknicking, nature study.

Mother Neff State Park was the **first official state park** in Texas. It originated with 6 acres donated by Mrs. I. E. Neff, mother of **Pat M. Neff**, governor of Texas from 1921 to 1925. Gov. Neff and Frank Smith donated remainder in 1934. The park, located 8 miles west of Moody on FM 107 and TX 236, now contains 259 acres along the Leon River in Coryell County. Heavily wooded. Camping, picnicking, fishing, hiking.

Mustang Island State Park, 3,954 acres on Gulf of Mexico in Nueces County, 14 miles south of Port Aransas on TX 361, was acquired from private owners in 1972. Mustang Island is a barrier island with a complicated ecosystem, dependent upon the sand dune. The foundation plants of the dunes are **sea oats, beach panic grass and soilbind morning glory**. Beach camping, picknicking; sun, sand and water activities. Excellent birding. **Padre Island National Seashore** 14 miles south.

National Museum of the Pacific War and **Admiral Nimitz State Historical Site** is on 7 acres in downtown Fredericksburg. First established as a state agency in 1969 by Texas Legislature; transferred to TPW in 1981. George Bush Gallery opened in 1999. Named for **Adm. Chester W. Nimitz** of World War II fame, it includes the **Pacific War Museum** in the **Nimitz Steamboat Hotel**; the **Japanese Garden of Peace**, donated by the people of Japan; the **History Walk of the Pacific War**, featuring planes, boats and other equipment from World War II; and other special exhibits. Nearby is **Kerrville State Park**.

Old Fort Parker is a 37.5-acre park 4 miles north of Groesbeck on TX 14 in Limestone County. Deeded by private owners in 1936 and originally constructed by the Civilian Conservation Corps (CCC); rebuilt in 1967. Reconstructed fort is pioneer memorial and site of Cynthia Ann Parker abduction on May 19, 1836, by Comanche Indians. Nearby Fort Parker Cemetery has graves of those killed at the fort in the 1836 raid. Historical study and picnicking. Living History events throughout year. Primitive skills classes/campouts by appointment. Groups welcome. Operated by the City of Groesbeck, 254-729-5253.

Palmetto State Park, a scenic park, is 270.3 acres 8 miles southeast of Luling on US 183 and PR 11 along the San Marcos River in Gonzales County. Land deeded in 1934-1936 by private owners and City of Gonzales. Named for **tropical dwarf palmetto** found there. Diverse plant and animal life; excellent birding. Also picnicking, fishing, hiking, pedal boats, swimming. Nearby **Gonzales** and **Ottine** important in early Texas history. Gonzales settled 1825 as center of **Green DeWitt's colonies**.

Palo Duro Canyon State Park consists of 16,402 acres 12 miles east of Canyon on TX 217 in Armstrong and Randall counties. The land was deeded by private owners in 1933 and is the scene of the annual summer production of the musical drama, "Texas." Spectacular one-million-year-old **scenic canyon** exposes rocks spanning about 200 million years of geological time. **Coronado** may have visited canyon in 1541. Canyon officially discovered by **Capt. R. B. Marcy** in 1852. Scene of decisive battle in 1874 between Comanche and Kiowa Indians and U.S. Army troops under **Gen. Ranald Mackenzie**. Also scene of ranching enterprise started by **Charles Goodnight** in 1876. Part of **state longhorn herd** is kept here. Camping, mountain biking, scenic drives, horseback and hiking trails, horse rentals.

Pedernales Falls State Park, 5,211.7 acres in Blanco County about 9 miles east of Johnson City on FM 2766 along Pedernales River, was acquired from private owners in 1970. Typical **Edwards Plateau** terrain, with **live oaks, deer, turkey** and **stone hills**. Camping, picnicking, hiking, swimming, tubing. Falls main scenic attraction.

Port Isabel Lighthouse State Historic Site consists of 0.9 acre in Port Isabel, Cameron County. Acquired by purchase from private owners in 1950, site includes **lighthouse** constructed in 1852; visitors can climb to top. Park is near sites of Civil War battle of **Palmito Ranch** (1865), and Mexican War battles of **Palo Alto** and **Resaca de la Palma** (1846). Operated by City of Port Isabel.

Possum Kingdom State Park, west of Mineral Wells via US 180 and PR 33 in Palo Pinto County, is 1,528.7 acres adjacent to **Possum Kingdom Lake**, in **Palo Pinto Mountains** and **Brazos River Valley**. Rugged canyons home to **deer**, other wildlife. Acquired from the Brazos River Authority in 1940. Camping, picnicking, swimming, fishing, boating. Cabins available.

Purtis Creek State Park is 1,582.4 acres in Henderson and Van Zandt counties 3.5 miles north of Eustace on FM 316. Acquired in 1977 from private owners. Fishing, camping, hiking, picnicking, paddle boats and canoes.

Ray Roberts Lake State Park (Isle du Bois Unit), consists of 2,263 acres on the south side of Ray Roberts Lake on FM 455 in Denton County. **Johnson Branch Unit** contains 1,514 acres on north side of lake in Denton and Cooke counties 7 miles east of IH 30 on FM 3002. There are also six satellite parks. Land acquired in 1984 by lease from Department of the Army. Abundant and varied plant and animal life. Fishing, camping, picnicking, swimming, hiking, biking; tours of 19-century farm buildings at Johnson Branch. Includes Lantana Ridge Lodge on the east side of the lake. It is a full-service lodging facility with restaurant.

Resaca de la Palma State Park, part of the World Birding Center network, is 1,700 semi-tropical acres off US 281, four miles west of Brownsville in Cameron County. Opened Monday-Friday, by appointment and reservations. Birding and natural history tours offered. Colorful neo-tropical and neartic migrant birds have been noted here.

Rusk/Palestine State Park, a total of 136 acres, includes Rusk unit, adjacent to **Texas State Railroad Rusk Depot** off US 84 in Cherokee County, and Palestine unit, off US 84 adjacent to Texas State Railroad Palestine Depot. Fishing, picnicking, camping, tennis courts, playground. Train rides in restored passenger cars (see also **Texas State Railroad State Historic Site**).

Sabine Pass Battleground State Historic Site in Jefferson County 1.5 miles south of Sabine Pass on Dick Dowling Road, contains 57.6 acres acquired from Kountze County Trust in 1972. **Lt. Richard W. Dowling**, with small Confederate force, repelled an attempted 1863 invasion of Texas by Union gunboats. **Monument, World War II ammunition bunkers**. Fishing, picnicking, camping.

Sam Bell Maxey House State Historic Site, at the corner of South Church and Washington streets in Paris, Lamar County, was donated by City of Paris in 1976. Consists of .4 acre with 1868 Victorian Italianate-style frame house, plus outbuildings. Most of furnishings accumulated by Maxey family. Maxey served in Mexican and Civil wars and was two-term U.S. Senator. House is on the **National Register of Historic Places**. Open for tours Friday through Sunday.

San Angelo State Park, on **O.C. Fisher Reservoir** adjacent to the city of San Angelo in Tom Green County, contains 7,677 acres of land, most of which will remain undeveloped. Leased from U.S. Corps of Engineers in 1995. Access is from US 87 or 67, then FM 2288. Highly diversified plant and animal life. Activities include boating, water activities, hiking, mountain biking, horseback riding, camping, picnicking. Part of **state longhorn herd** in park. Nearby is **Fort Concho**.

San Jacinto Battleground State Historic Site and **Battleship Texas State Historic Site** are located 20 miles east of downtown Houston off TX 225 east to TX 134 to PR 1836 in east Harris County. The park is 1,200 acres with 570-foot-tall monument erected in 1936-1939 in honor of Texans who defeated Mexican **Gen. Antonio López de Santa Anna** on April 21, 1836, to win Texas' independence from Mexico. The park is original site of Texans' camp acquired in 1883. Subsequent acquisitions made in 1897, 1899 and 1985. Park transferred to TPW in 1965. Park registered as **National Historic Landmark**. Elevator ride to observation tower near top of monument; museum. Monument known as **tallest free-standing concrete structure in the world** at the time it was erected. Interpretive trail around battleground. Adjacent to park is the **U.S.S. Texas**, commissioned in 1914. The battleship, the only survivor of the dreadnought class and the only surviving veteran of two world wars, was donated to people of Texas by U.S. Navy. Ship was moored in the Houston Ship Channel at the **San Jacinto Battleground** on San Jacinto Day, 1948. Extensive repairs were done 1988-1990. Some renovation is on-going, but ship is open for tours. Ship closed Christmas Eve and Christmas Day.

Sea Rim State Park in Jefferson County, 20 miles south of Port Arthur, off TX 87, contains 4,141 acres of marshland and 5.2 miles of **Gulf beach** shoreline, acquired from private owners in 1972. It is prime wintering area for **waterfowl**. Wetlands also shelter such wildlife as river otter, nutria, alligator, mink, muskrat. Camping, fishing, swimming; wildlife observation; nature trail; boating. **Airboat tours of marsh**. Near **McFaddin National Wildlife Refuge**.

Sebastopol State Historic Site at 704 Zorn Street in Seguin, Guadalupe County, was acquired by purchase in 1976 from Seguin Conservation Society; approximately 2.2 acres. Built about 1856 by **Col. Joshua W. Young** of **limecrete**, concrete made from local gravel and lime, the Greek Revival-style house, which was restored to its 1880 appearance by the TPW, is on National Register of Historic Places. Tours available Friday and Sunday. Also of interest in the area is historic **Seguin**, founded 1838.

Seminole Canyon State Historic Site in Val Verde County, 9 miles west of Comstock off US 90, contains 2,172.5 acres; acquired by purchase from private owners 1973-1977. **Fate Bell Shelter** in canyon contains several important **prehistoric Indian pictographs**. Historic interpretive center. Tours of rock-art sites Wednesday-Sunday; also hiking, mountain biking, camping.

Sheldon Lake State Park & Wildlife Management Area, 2,800 acres in Harris County on Garrett Road 20 miles east of Beltway 8. Acquired by purchase in 1952 from the City of Houston. Freshwater marsh habitat. Activities include nature study, birding, fishing. Wildscape gardens of native plants.

South Llano River State Park, 5 miles south of Junction in Kimble County off US 377, is a 524-acre site. Land donated to the TPW by private owner in 1977. Wooded bottomland along the winding South Llano River is **largest and oldest winter roosting site for the Rio Grande turkey** in Central Texas. Roosting area closed to visitors October-March. Other animals include **wood ducks, javelina, fox, beaver, bobcat** and **armadillo**. Camping, picnicking, tubing, swimming and fishing, hiking, mountain biking.

Starr Family State Historic Site, 3.1 acres at 407 W. Travis in Marshall, Harrison County. Greek Revival-style mansion, **Maplecroft**, built 1870-1871, was home to four generations of Starr family, powerful and economically influential Texans. Two other family homes also in park. Acquired by gift in 1976; additional land donated in 1982. Maplecroft is on National Register of Historic Places. Tours Friday–Sunday or by appointment. Special events during year.

Stephen F. Austin State Historic Site is 663.3 acres along the Brazos River in San Felipe, Austin County, named for the **"Father of Texas."** The area was deeded by the San Felipe de Austin Corporation in 1940. Site of township of San Felipe was seat of government where conventions of 1832 and 1833 and Consultation of 1835 held. These led to **Texas Declaration of Independence**. San Felipe was home of **Stephen F. Austin** and other famous early Texans; home of **Texas' first Anglo newspaper (the Texas Gazette)** founded in 1829; postal system of Texas originated here. Area called **"Cradle of Texas Liberty."** Museum. Camping, picnicking, golf, fishing, hiking.

Texas State Railroad State Historic Site, in Anderson and Cherokee counties between the cities of Palestine and Rusk, adjacent to US 84, contains 499 acres. Acquired by Legislative Act in 1971. Trains run seasonal schedules on 25.5 miles of track. Call for information and reservations: In Texas 1-800-442-8951; outside 903-683-2561. Railroad built by the State of Texas to support the **state-owned iron works** at Rusk. Begun in 1893, and built largely by inmates from the state prison system, the railroad was gradually extended until it reached Palestine in 1909 and established regular rail service between the towns. (See also **Rusk/Palestine State Park**.)

Tyler State Park is 985.5 acres two miles north of IH 20 on FM 14 north of Tyler in Smith County. Includes 64-acre lake. The land was deeded by private owners in 1934–1935. Heavily wooded. Camping, hiking, fishing, boating, lake swimming. Nearby Tyler called **Rose Capital of Nation, with Tyler Rose Garden and annual Tyler Rose Festival**. Also in Tyler are **Caldwell Children's Zoo** and **Goodman Museum**.

Varner-Hogg Plantation State Historic Site is 66 acres in Brazoria County two miles north of West Columbia on FM 2852. Land originally owned by Martin Varner, a member of Stephen F. Austin's **"Old Three Hundred"** colony; later was home of Texas governor **James Stephen Hogg**. Property was deeded to the state in 1957 by Miss Ima Hogg, Gov. Hogg's daughter. **First rum distillery** in Texas established in 1829 by Varner. Mansion tours Tuesday through Saturday. Also picnicking, fishing.

Village Creek State Park, comprising 1,004 heavily forested acres, is located in Lumberton, Hardin County, 10 miles north of Beaumont off US 69 and FM 3513. Purchased in 1979 from private owner, the park contains abundant flora and fauna typical of the Big Thicket area. The **200 species of birds** found here include wood ducks, egrets and herons. Activities include fishing, camping, canoeing, swimming, hiking and picnicking. Nearby is the **Big Thicket National Preserve**.

Walter Umphrey State Park is operated by Jefferson County on the south end of Please Island off TX 82. For RV site reservations, contact SGS Causeway Bait & Tackle, 409-985-4811.

Washington-on-the-Brazos State Historic Site consists of 293.1 acres 7 miles southwest of Navasota in Washington County on TX 105 and FM 1155. Land acquired by deed from private owners in 1916, 1976 and 1996. Park includes the site of the signing on March 2, 1836, of the **Texas Declaration of Independence** from Mexico, as well as the site of the later **signing of the Constitution of the Republic of Texas**. In 1842 and 1845, the land included the **capitol of the Republic. Star of the Republic Museum**. Activities include picnicking and birding. **Barrington Living History Farm** is the home of **Anson Jones, the last president of the Republic of Texas**. Activities are guided by entries that Jones made in his daybook while living there. For further information, contact 916-878-2214 or link to barrington.farm@tpwd. state.tx.us.

Recreation in the State Forests

All Texas State Forests are game sanctuaries with no firearms or hunting allowed. For general information about the Texas State Forests, see page 111 in the Environment section.

I.D. Fairchild State Forest

Located in Cherokee County, recreation includes hiking, horseback riding, picnicking, wildlife viewing and biking.

Special attractions are a **historical fire tower** site with plaque, Red Cockaded Woodpecker Management

Frosty sweetgum leaves in the forests of East Texas. Ron Billings photo; Texas Forest Service.

Area and a pond with picnic area. Forest management demonstration sites throughout the forest. There are no restroom facilities in this forest.

Open year-round during daylight hours. Obtain information and maps at the Palestine District Office, 2203 West Spring St. (US-287 West) or call (903) 729-7738 weekdays.

W. Goodrich Jones State Forest

Recreational opportunities in this forest, located in Montgomery County, include bird watching, hiking, horseback riding, picnicking, wildlife viewing and biking.

Special attractions include **Sweetleaf Nature Trail** with State Champion Sweetleaf Tree, Red Cockaded Woodpecker Management Area, two small lakes with limited fishing and picnicking. Forest management demonstration sites throughout the forest.

Open year-round during daylight hours. Information, maps, permits and restrooms available at the Conroe District Office on FM 1488, 1.5 miles west of I-45. Call (936) 273-2261 for information.

John Henry Kirby Memorial State Forest

Located in Tyler County, forest resource educational opportunities at this forest include demonstrations and nature study. Group education tours available by appointment.

Recreational opportunities include hiking, picnicking, bird and wildlife watching. Special attractions are forest management demonstration sites, small picnic area and **John Henry Kirby Monument**.

Open year-round to foot traffic during daylight hours. Contact the district office prior to entry. Special arrangements are needed for vehicle access. Information and maps can be obtained at the Woodville District Office on Hwy. 69 south or by calling (409) 283-3785 weekdays. No restroom facilities are available in this forest.

Masterson State Forest

All use of this forest in Jasper County is by reservation only. Group resource education tours are available by appointment. No public facilities are available. Information and maps can be obtained at the Kirbyville District Office, FM 82, 4.5 miles southeast of Kirbyville; call weekdays at (409) 423-2890.

E.O. Siecke State Forest

Recreational opportunities in this Newton County forest include hiking, bird watching, nature study, horseback riding, picnicking and wildlife viewing.

Special attractions are a **historic fire tower,** the **oldest slash pine stand in Texas** and a **trout creek.** Forest management demonstration sites throughout.

Open year-round during daylight hours. Limited access by vehicle. Information, maps and restrooms are available at the Kirbyville District Office, located at the state forest on FM 82, 4.5 miles southeast of Kirbyville. Call (409) 423-2890 weekdays for information. ☆

National Parks, Historical Sites, Recreation Areas

Below are listed the facilities in and the activities that can be enjoyed at the two national parks, a national seashore, a biological preserve, several historic sites, memorials and recreation areas in Texas. They are under supervision of the **U.S. Department of Interior**. On the Web: **www.nps.gov/parks/search.htm**; under "Select State," choose "Texas." In addition, the recreational opportunities in the national forests and national grasslands in Texas, under the jurisdiction of the **U.S. Department of Agriculture**, are listed at the end of the article.

Alibates Flint Quarries National Monument consists of 1,371 acres in Potter County. For more than 10,000 years, **pre-Columbian Indians** dug agatized limestone from the quarries to make projectile points, knives, scrapers and other tools. The area is presently undeveloped. You may visit the flint quarries on guided walking tours with a park ranger. Tours are at 10:00 a.m. and 2:00 p.m. from Memorial Day to Labor Day. Off-season tours can be arranged by writing to Lake Meredith National Recreation Area, Box 1460, Fritch 79036, or by calling 806-857-3151.

Amistad National Recreation Area is located on the U.S. side of Amistad Reservoir, an international reservoir on the Texas-Mexico border. The 57,292-acre park's attractions include boating, water skiing, swimming, fishing, camping and archaeological sites. If lake level is normal, visitors can see 4000-year-old prehistoric pictographs in Panther and Parida caves, which are accessible only by boat. Check with park before visiting. The area is one of the densest concentrations of **Archaic rock art** in North America — more than 300 sites. Commercial campgrounds, motels and restaurants nearby. Marinas located at Diablo East and Rough Canyon. Open year round. NPS Administration, 4121 Hwy. 90 W, Del Rio 78840; 830-775-7491.

Big Bend National Park, established in 1944, has spectacular mountain and **desert scenery** and a variety of unusual geological structures. It is the nation's largest protected area of Chihuahuan Desert. Located in the great bend of the Rio Grande, the 801,000-acre park, which is part of the international boundary between the United States and Mexico, was designated a U.S. Biosphere Reserve in 1976. Hiking, birding and float trips are popular. Numerous campsites are located in park, and the Chisos Mountain Lodge has accommodations for approximately 345 guests. Write for reservations to National Park Concessions, Inc., Big Bend National Park, Texas 79834; 915-477-2291; www.chisosmountainslodge.com. Park open year round; facilities most crowded during spring break. PO Box 129, Big Bend National Park 79834; 915-477-2251.

Big Thicket National Preserve, established in 1974, consists of 13 separate units totalling 97,000 acres of diverse flora and fauna, often nicknamed the "biological crossroads of North America." The preserve, which includes parts of seven East Texas counties, has been designated an "International Biosphere Reserve" by the United Nations Educational, Scientific and Cultural Organization (UNESCO). The preserve includes **four different ecological systems:** Southeastern swamps, Eastern forests, Central Plains and Southwestern deserts. The visitor information station is located on FM 420, seven miles north of Kountze; phone 409-951-6725. Open daily from 9 a.m. to 5 p.m. Naturalist activities are available by reservation only; reservations are made through the station. Nine trails, ranging in length from one-half mile to 18 miles, visit a variety of forest communities. The two shortest trails are handicapped accessible. Trails are open year round, but flooding may occur after heavy rains. Horses permitted on the Big Sandy Horse Trail only. Boating and canoeing are popular on preserve corridor units. Park headquarters are at 3785 Milam, Beaumont 77701; 409-246-2337.

Chamizal National Memorial, established in 1963 and opened to the public in 1973, stands as a monument to Mexican-American friendship and goodwill. The memorial, on 52 acres in El Paso, commemorates the peaceful settlement on Aug. 29, 1963, of a 99-year-old boundary dispute between the United States and Mexico. Chamizal uses the **visual and performing arts** as a medium of interchange, helping people better understand not only other cultures but their own, as well. It hosts a variety of programs throughout the year, including: the fall Chamizal Festival musical event; the Siglo de Oro drama festival (early March); the Oñate Historical Festival celebrating the First Thanksgiving (April); and Music Under the Stars (Sundays, June-August). The park has a 1.8-mile walking trail and picnic areas. Phone: 915-532-7273.

Fort Davis National Historic Site in Jeff Davis County was a key post in the West Texas defense system, guarding immigrants and tradesmen on the San

Fort Davis National Historic Site is open year round exept Christmas Day. Robert Plocheck photo.

McKittrick Canyon cuts a slash through the Guadalupe Mountain range, exposing the backbone of the Capitan Reef — one of the most extensive fossil reef formations on earth. Robert Plocheck photo.

Antonio-El Paso road from 1854 to 1891. At one time, Fort Davis was manned by black troops, called **"Buffalo Soldiers"** (because of their curly hair) who fought with great distinction in the Indian Wars. Henry O. Flipper, the first black graduate of West Point, served at Fort Davis in the early 1880s. The 474-acre historic site is located on the north edge of the town of Fort Davis in the Davis Mountains, the second-highest mountain range in the state. The site includes a museum, an auditorium with daily audio-visual programs, restored and refurnished buildings, picnic area and hiking trails. Open year round except Christmas Day. PO Box 1379, Fort Davis 79734; 915-426-3224.

Guadalupe Mountains National Park, established in 1972, includes 86,416 acres in Hudspeth and Culberson counties. The Park contains one of the most extensive fossil reefs on record. Deep canyons cut through this reef and provide a rare opportunity for geological study. Special points of interest are **McKittrick Canyon,** a fragile riparian environment, and **Guadalupe Peak,** the highest in Texas. Camping, hiking on 80 miles of trails, Frijole Ranch Museum, summer amphitheater programs. Orientation, free information and natural history exhibits available at Visitor Center. Open year round. Lodging at Van Horn, Texas, and White's City or Carlsbad, NM. HC 60, Box 400, Salt Flat 79847; 915-828-3251.

Lake Meredith National Recreation Area, 30 miles northeast of Amarillo, centers on a reservoir on the Canadian River, in Moore, Hutchinson and Potter counties. The 50,000-acre recreational area is popular for **water-based activities.** Boat ramps, picnic areas, unimproved campsites. Commercial lodging and trailer hookups available in nearby towns. Open year round. PO Box 1460, Fritch 79036; 806-857-3151.

Lyndon B. Johnson National Historic Site includes two separate districts 14 miles apart. The Johnson City District comprises the boyhood home of the 36th President of United States and the Johnson Settlement, where his grandparents resided during the late 1800s. The LBJ Ranch District can be visited only by taking the National Park Service bus tour starting at the LBJ State Historic Site. The tour includes the reconstructed **LBJ Birthplace,** old school, family cemetery, show barn and a view of the **Texas White House.** Site in Blanco and Gillespie counties was established in 1969, and contains 1,570 acres, 674 of which are federal. Open year round except Thanksgiving, Christmas Day and New Year's Day. No camping on site; commercial campgrounds, motels in area. PO Box 329, Johnson City 78636; 830-868-7128.

Padre Island National Seashore consists of a 67.5-mile stretch of a barrier island along the Gulf Coast; noted for **white-sand beaches,** excellent fishing and abundant bird and marine life. Contains 133,000 acres in Kleberg, Willacy and Kenedy counties. Open year round. One paved campground (fee charged) located north of Malaquite Beach; unpaved (primitive) campground area south on beach. Five miles of beach are accessible by regular vehicles; 55 miles are accessible only by 4x4 vehicles. Off-road vehicles prohibited. Camping permitted in two designated areas. Commercial lodging available on the island outside the National Seashore boundaries. PO Box 181300, Corpus Christi 78480; 361-949-8068.

Palo Alto Battlefield National Historic Site, Brownsville, preserves the site of the first major battle in the Mexican-American War. Fought on May 8, 1846, it is recognized for the innovative use of light or "flying" artillery. Participating in the battle were **three future presidents:** General Zachary Taylor and Ulysses S. Grant on the U.S. side, and Gen. Mariano Arista on the

Mexican. Historical markers are located at the junction of Farm-to-Market roads 1847 and 511. Access to the 3,400-acre site is currently limited. Exhibits at the visitors center interpret the battle as well as the causes and consequences of the war. Phone 956-541-2785.

Rio Grande Wild and Scenic River is a 196-mile strip on the U.S. shore of the Rio Grande in the Chihuahuan Desert, beginning in Big Bend National Park and continuing downstream to the Terrell-Val Verde County line. There are federal facilities in Big Bend National Park only. Contact Big Bend National Park for more information.

San Antonio Missions National Historic Site preserves four Spanish Colonial Missions — **Concepción, San José, San Juan** and **Espada** — as well as the Espada dam and aqueduct, which are two of the best-preserved remains in the United States of the Spanish Colonial irrigation system, and **Rancho de las Cabras,** the colonial ranch of Mission Espada. All were crucial elements to Spanish settlement on the Texas frontier. When Franciscan attempts to establish a chain of missions in East Texas in the late 1600s failed, the Spanish Crown ordered three missions transferred to the San Antonio River valley in 1731.

The missions are located within the city limits of San Antonio, while Rancho de las Cabras is located 25 miles south in Wilson County near Floresville. The four missions, which are **still in use as active parishes,** are open to the public from 9 a.m. to 5 p.m. daily except Thanksgiving, Christmas and New Year's. Public roadways connect the sites; a hike-bike trail is being developed. The visitor center for the mission complex is at San José. For more information, write to 2202 Roosevelt Ave., San Antonio 78210; 210-534-8833 or 210-932-1001.

Recreation in the National Forests

For general information about the National Forests and National Grasslands, see page 110 in the Environment section.

An estimated 3 million people visit the National Forests in Texas for recreation annually. These visitors use established recreation areas primarily for hiking, picnicking, swimming, fishing, camping, boating and nature enjoyment. In the following list of some of these areas, Forest Service Road is abbreviated FSR:

Angelina National Forest

Bouton Lake, 14 miles southeast of Zavalla off Texas 63 and FSR 303, has a 9-acre natural lake with primitive facilities for camping, picnicking and fishing. Boykin Springs, 14 miles southeast of Zavalla, has a 6-acre lake and facilities for hiking, swimming, picnicking, fishing and camping.

Caney Creek on Sam Rayburn Reservoir, 10 miles southeast of Zavalla off FM 2743, offers fishing, boating and camping. Sandy Creek, 15.5 miles east of Zavalla on Sam Rayburn, offers fishing, boating and camping.

The Sawmill Hiking Trail is 2.5 miles long and winds from Aldridge Sawmill trail head to Boykin Springs Recreation Area.

Davy Crockett National Forest

Ratcliff Lake, 25 miles west of Lufkin on Texas 7, includes a 45-acre lake and facilities for picnicking, hiking, swimming, boating, fishing and camping. There is also an amphitheater.

The 20-mile-long 4C National Recreation Trail connects Ratcliff Recreation Area to the Neches Bluff overlook. The Piney Creek Horse Trail, 10 miles long, can be entered approximately 5.5 miles south of Kennard off County Road 4625. There are two horse camps along this trail system.

Sabine National Forest

Indian Mounds Recreation Area, accessible via FM 83 about 12 miles southeast of Hemphill, has camping facilities and a boat-launch ramp. Lakeview, on Toledo Bend Reservoir 21 miles from Pineland, offers camping, hiking and fishing and can be reached via Texas 87, FM 2928 and FSR 120.

Ragtown, 26 miles southeast of Center and accessible by Texas 87 and Texas 139, County Road 3184 and FSR 132, is also on Toledo Bend and has facilities for hiking, camping and boating. Red Hill Lake, 3 miles north of Milam on Texas 87, has facilities for fishing, swimming, camping and picnicking. Willow Oak Recreation Area, on Toledo Bend 13 miles south of Hemphill off Texas 87, offers fishing, picnicking, camping and boating.

Trail Between the Lakes is 28 miles long from Lakeview Recreation Area on Toledo Bend to U.S. 96 near Sam Rayburn Reservoir.

Sam Houston National Forest

Cagle Recreation Area is located on the shores of Lake Conroe, 50 miles north of Houston and 5 miles west of I-45 at FM 1375. Cagle offers camping, fishing, hiking, birding and other recreational opportunities in a forested lakeside setting.

Double Lake, 3 miles south of Coldspring on FM 2025, has facilities for picnicking, hiking, camping, swimming and fishing.

Stubblefield Lake, 15 miles west-northwest of New Waverly off Texas 1375 on the shores of Lake Conroe, has facilities for camping, hiking, picnicking and fishing.

A canoeist paddles by campers on Lake Ratcliff in Davy Crockett National Forest near Lufkin. Ron Billings photo; Texas Forest Service.

The picnic area at Lake Marvin, Black Kettle National Grassland. Robert Plocheck photo.

The Lone Star Hiking Trail, approximately 128 miles long, is located in Sam Houston National Forest in Montgomery, Walker and San Jacinto counties.

Recreation on the National Grasslands

North Texas

Lake Davy Crockett Recreation Area **(Caddo National Grassland)**, 12 miles north of Honey Grove (Fannin County) on FM 409, just off FM 100, has a boat-launch ramp and camping sites on a 450-acre lake.

Coffee Mill Lake Recreation Area has camping and picnicking facilities on a 650-acre lake. This area is 4 miles west of Lake Davy Crockett Recreation Area.

The Caddo Multi-Use Trail system, also 4 miles west of Lake Crockett, offers camping, hiking and horseback riding on 35 miles of trails.

Black Creek Lake Recreation Area **(Lyndon B. Johnson National Grassland)** is 8 miles north of Decatur (Wise County) and has camping, picnic facilities and a boat-launch ramp on a 35-acre lake.

Cottonwood Lake, 13 miles north of Decatur, is around 40 acres and offers hiking, boating and fishing.

The Cottonwood-Black Creek Hiking Trail is 4 miles long and connects the two lakes. It is rated moderately difficult. There are nearly 75 miles of multipurpose trails which run in the Cottonwood Lake vicinity.

TADRA Horse Trail, 10 miles north of Decatur, has camping and 75 miles of horse trails. Restrooms and and parking facilities are available.

West Texas

Lake McClellan **(McClellan Creek National Grassland)** in Gray County, and Lake Marvin, which is part of the **Black Kettle National Grassland** in Hemphill County, receive more than 28,000 recreation visitors annually.

These areas provide camping, picnicking, fishing, birdwatching and boating facilities. Concessionaires operate facilities at Lake McClellan, and a nominal fee is charged for use of the areas. Thompson Grove Picnic Area is 14 miles northeast of Texline.

At the **Rita Blanca National Grassland** (Dallam County), about 4,500 visitors a year enjoy picnicking and hunting. Thompson Grove Picnic Area is 14 miles northeast of Texline. ☆

Recreational Facilities, Corps of Engineers Lakes, 2008
Source: Fort Worth District, Corps of Engineers

Reservoir	Swim Areas	Boat Ramps	Picnic Sites	Camp Sites	Rental Units	Visitor Hours, 2008
Aquilla	0	2	0	0	0	251,400
Bardwell	3	6	47	155	0	691,400
Belton	4	21	368	278	0	11,336,100
Benbrook	3	16	109	186	0	4,259,000
Buffalo Bayou*	0	0	848	0	0	12,360,800
Canyon	5	18	189	497	24	2,337,200
Cooper	2	5	110	329	14	3,777,300
Georgetown	1	3	109	224	0	3,848,500
Granger	2	5	129	143	0	1,448,900
Grapevine	1	14	139	161	6	7,093,300
Hords Creek	3	9	8	136	0	3,328,000
Joe Pool	3	7	315	556	0	7,318,500
Lake O' the Pines	7	33	150	471	0	14,028,800
Lavon	3	22	209	280	0	7,610,300
Lewsville	7	21	432	519	5	21,249,900
Navarro Mills	3	6	26	255	0	5,460,100
O.C. Fisher	0	13	75	61	0	441,800
Pat Mayse**	3	10	0	211	3	1,470,500
Proctor	5	6	39	216	0	2,642,500
Ray Roberts	2	11	294	371	30	25,352,100
Sam Rayburn	5	37	21	737	65	16,618,100
Somerville	2	12	150	949	21	14,139,600
Stillhouse Hollow	3	5	75	67	0	940,400
Texoma**†	6	27	116	825	269	88,214,100
Town Bluff	2	13	81	370	1	3,630,100
Waco	2	12	143	247	0	2,404,300
Wallisville*	0	2	10	0	0	496,800
Whitney	3	23	48	763	0	4,670,800
Wright Patman	4	22	203	578	0	12,408,500
Totals	84	381	4,443	9,585	438	279,829,100

All above lakes managed by the Fort Worth District, U.S. Army Corps of Engineers, with the following exceptions:
* Includes both Addicks and Barker Dams; managed by Galveston District, USACE.
**Managed by Tulsa District, USACE.
†Figures for facilities on Texas side of lake. Visitation is for entire lake.

National Natural Landmarks in Texas

Nineteen Texas natural areas have been listed on the **National Registry of Natural Landmarks**.

The registry was established by the Secretary of the Interior in 1962 to identify and encourage the preservation of geological and ecological features that represent nationally significant examples of the nation's natural heritage.

The registry currently lists a total of 587 national natural landmarks. Texas areas on the list, as of August 2001, and their characteristics, are these (year of listing in parentheses):

Attwater Prairie Chicken Preserve, Colorado County, 55 miles west of Houston in the national wildlife refuge, is rejuvenated Gulf Coastal Prairie, which is habitat for Attwater's prairie chickens. (1968)

Bayside Resaca Area, Cameron County, Laguna Atascosa National Wildlife Refuge, 28 miles north of Brownsville. Excellent example of a resaca, supporting coastal salt-marsh vegetation and rare birds. (1980)

Catfish Creek, Anderson County, 20 miles northwest of Palestine, is undisturbed riparian habitat. (1983)

Caverns of Sonora, Sutton County, 16 miles southwest of Sonora, has unusual geological formations. (1965)

Devil's Sink Hole, Edwards County, 9 miles northeast of Rocksprings, is a deep, bell-shaped, collapsed limestone sink with cave passages extending below the regional water table. (1972)

Dinosaur Valley, Somervell County, in Dinosaur Valley State Park, four miles west of Glen Rose, contains fossil footprints exposed in bed of Paluxy River. (1968)

Enchanted Rock, Gillespie and Llano counties, 12 miles southwest of Oxford, is a classic batholith, composed of coarse-grained pink granite. (1971)

Ezell's Cave, Hays County, within the city limits of San Marcos, houses at least 36 species of cave creatures. (1971)

Fort Worth Nature Center and Refuge, Tarrant County, within the Fort Worth city limits. Contains remnants of the Grand Prairie and a portion of the Cross Timbers, with limestone ledges and marshes. Refuge for migratory birds and other wildlife, and home to 11 buffalo raised by the center's staff. Educational programs offered for youth and adults. Self-guided hiking. (1980)

Greenwood Canyon, Montague County, along a tributary of Braden Branch, is a rich source of Cretaceous fossils. (1975)

High Plains Natural Area, Randall County, Buffalo Lake National Wildlife Refuge, 26 miles southwest of Amarillo, is a grama-buffalo shortgrass area. (1980)

Little Blanco River Bluff, Blanco County, comprises an Edwards Plateau limestone-bluff plant community. (1982)

Longhorn Cavern, Burnet County, 11 miles southwest of Burnet. Formed at least 450 million years ago, cave contains several unusual geologic features. (1971)

Lost Maples State Natural Area, Bandera and Real counties, 61 miles northwest of San Antonio, contains Edwards Plateau fauna and flora, including unusual bigtooth maple. Largest known nesting population of golden-cheeked warbler. (1980)

Muleshoe National Wildlife Refuge, Bailey County, 59 miles northwest of Lubbock, contains playa lakes and typical High Plains shortgrass grama grasslands. (1980)

Natural Bridge Caverns, Comal County, 16 miles west of New Braunfels, is a multilevel cavern system, with beautiful and unusual geological formations. (1971)

Odessa Meteor Crater, Ector County, 10 miles southwest of Odessa, is one of only two known meteor sites in the country. (1965)

Palo Duro Canyon State Park, Armstrong and Randall counties, 22 miles south-southwest of Amarillo. Cut by waters of the Red River, it contains cross-sectional views of sedimentary rocks representing four geological periods. (1976)

Santa Ana National Wildlife Refuge, Hidalgo County, 7 miles south of Alamo, is a lowland forested area with jungle-like vegetation. It is habitat for more than 300 species of birds and some rare mammals. (1966) ☆

The Odessa Meteor Crater visitors center seen from inside the crater. Robert Plocheck photo.

Sea Center Texas

Sea Center Texas is a marine aquarium, fish hatchery and nature center operated by the Texas Parks and Wildlife Department to educate and entertain visitors. The visitor center opened in 1996 and has interpretive displays, a "touch tank" and native Texas habitat exhibits depicting a salt marsh, bay, jetty, reef and open Gulf waters. The Gulf aquarium features "Cooper," a 50-pound grouper; "Slick," the state record green moray eel; a nurse shark; and other offshore species.

Touted as the world's largest redfish hatchery, the facility is one of three marine hatcheries on the Texas coast that produces juvenile red drum and spotted seatrout for enhancing natural populations in Texas bays. The hatchery has the capability to produce 15 million juvenile fish yearly. It also serves as a testing ground for production of other marine species, such as flounder.

A half-acre youth fishing pond introduces youngsters to saltwater fishing through scheduled activities. The pond is handicap accessible and stocked with a variety of marine fish. It also offers guided hatchery tours and educational programs by reservation.

The center's wetland area is part of the Great Texas Coastal Birding Trail, where more than 150 species of birds have been identified. The wetland consists of a one-acre salt marsh and a three-acre freshwater marsh. Damselflies, dragonflies, butterflies, turtles and frogs are frequently sited off the boardwalk. A small outdoor pavilion provides a quiet resting place adjacent to the butterfly and hummingbird gardens.

Sea Center Texas is operated in partnership with The Dow Chemical Company and the Coastal Conservation Association. It is located in Lake Jackson, 50 miles south of Houston off of Texas 288. Admission and parking are free. Open 9 a.m. to 4 p.m. Tuesday through Saturday, and 1 p.m. to 4 p.m. Sunday. Closed Monday and some holidays. Reservations are required for some group tours, nature tours and hatchery tours. For more information call 979-292-0100. www.tpwd. state.tx.us/seacenter. ☆

Youngsters at the Texas State Aquarium reach to pet a stingray. Robert Plocheck photo.

Texas State Aquarium

The Texas State Aquarium, located on 7.3 acres on the southernmost tip of Corpus Christi Beach in Corpus Christi, is operated by the Texas State Aquarium Association, a nonprofit, self-supporting organization established in 1978. Efforts to fund a public aquarium in South Texas first began in 1952. Several nonprofit organizations founded over the years eventually grew into the Texas State Aquarium Association.

Since 1978 the association has raised more than $28 million in private and public funding for the construction and operation of the aquarium. The city of Corpus Christi provided $14.5 million, of which $4 million came from a bond issue.

In 1985 the Sixty-ninth Texas Legislature declared the project the "Official Aquarium of the State of Texas." Construction of the first phase of the project, the Jesse H. and Mary Gibbs Jones Gulf of Mexico Exhibit Building, began in September 1988 and was completed in July 1990.

In 2003 Dolphin Bay opened to house its Atlantic bottlenose dolphins. The same year, the Environmental Discovery Center opened, featuring an expanded library, a Family Learning Center and the Flint Hills Resources Distance Learning Studio.

The aquarium's exhibits and research focus on the plants and animals of the Gulf of Mexico and the Caribbean. The Texas State Aquarium is the first facility in the United States to do so.

There is an admission and parking fee. Open daily 9 a.m. to 5 p.m., Labor Day through March 1, and until 6 p.m. March 1 through Labor Day. For more information call 1-800-477-GULF. www.texasstateaquarium.org.— *New Handbook of Texas and Texas State Aquarium.*

Anglers fish the channel between Bahia Grande and the Brownsville Ship Channel. Robert Plocheck photo.

Recreational Fishing in Texas

Source: Texas Parks and Wildlife Department.

Freshwater

In Texas, 247 species of freshwater fish are found. This includes 78 species that inhabit areas with low salinity and can be found in rivers entering the Gulf of Mexico.

Also included in that total are 18 species that are not native, but were introduced into the state.

The estimated number of freshwater recreational anglers is 1.84 million, with annual expenditures of $1.49 billion annually. Catch-and-release fishing has emerged on the Texas scene as the conservation theme of anglers who desire continued quality fishing.

The most popular fish for recreational fishing are largemouth bass; catfish; crappie; and striped, white and hybrid striped bass.

The Texas Parks and Wildlife Department operates field stations, fish hatcheries and research facilities to support the conservation and management of fishery resources.

TPWD has continued its programs of stocking fish in public waters to increase angling opportunities. The hatcheries operated by TPWD raise largemouth and smallmouth bass, as well as catfish, striped and hybrid striped bass and sunfish.

Saltwater

There are about 1.1 million saltwater anglers in Texas (16 years old and older) who spend an estimated $797 million annually on fishing-related expenditures. In 2008, anglers harvested 2.48 million fish from both Texas bays and the Gulf of Mexico off Texas combined.

The most popular saltwater sport fish in Texas bays are spotted seatrout, sand seatrout, Atlantic croaker, red drum, southern flounder, black drum, sheepshead and gafftopsail catfish.

Offshore, some of the fish anglers target are red snapper, king mackerel, Spanish mackerel, dolphin (fish), spotted seatrout, tarpon and yellowfin tuna.

For Commercial Fishing data, see page 618.

Required Licenses

All **fishing licenses** and stamp endorsements are valid only during the period Sept. 1 through Aug. 31, except lifetime licenses and licenses issued for a specific number of days. If you own any valid freshwater fishing package, you will be able to purchase a saltwater stamp, and, if you own any valid saltwater fishing package, you will be able to purchase a freshwater stamp. An all-water fishing package is also available.

Detailed information concerning licenses, stamps, seasons, regulations and related information can be obtained from Texas Parks and Wildlife, 4200 Smith School Road, Austin 78744; (800) 792-1112 or 512-389-4800.

On the Web, information from TPW: www.tpwd. state.tx.us/fish/fish.htm.

Texas Freshwater Fisheries Center

The Texas Freshwater Fisheries Center in Athens, about 75 miles southeast of Dallas, is an $18 million hatchery and educational center, where visitors can learn about the underwater life.

The interactive Visitors Center includes aquarium displays of fish in their natural environment. Visitors get an "eye-to-eye" view of three authentically designed Texas freshwater habitats: a Hill Country stream, an East Texas pond and a reservoir. A marsh exhibit features live American alligators.

A casting pond stocked with rainbow trout in the winter and catfish in the summer provides a place for visitors to learn how to bait a hook, cast a line and land a fish. The center has conference facilities, hosts groups by appointment. The Texas Freshwater Fisheries Center is open Tuesday through Saturday, 9 a.m. to 4 p.m., and Sunday, 1 to 4 p.m. It is closed on Monday. Admission is charged.

The Center is located 4.5 miles east of Athens on FM 2495 at Lake Athens. Address: 5550 Flat Creek Road, Athens 75751, or call 903-676-2277. ☆

Hunting in Texas

Texas Parks and Wildlife Department reported that for the **year ending Aug. 31, 2007,** there were 510,979 paid hunting-license holders, 1,063,935 sport or recreation fishing-license holders and 590,997 combination-license holders. These licenses, plus stamps, tags or permits, resulted in total revenue to the state of $82,480,064.

For the **year ending Aug. 31, 2008,** there were 506,729 paid hunting-license holders, 1,233,679 sport or recreation fishing-license holders and 614,938 combination-license holders. These licenses, plus stamps, tags or permits, resulted in revenue to the state of $85,781,580.

During the **2006–2007 license year,** TPWD estimated that hunters harvested:

— 449,030 white-tailed deer;
— 5,754 mule deer;
— 19,737 wild turkey in the fall and 23,056 in the spring;
— 5,686,385 mourning dove;
— 623,041 bobwhite quail;
— 13,992 javelina.

During the **2007–2008 license year,** TPWD estimated that hunters harvested:

— 512,852 white-tailed deer;
— 9,141 mule deer;
— 26,005 wild turkey in the fall and 25,079 in the spring;
— 5,918,468 mourning dove;
— 1,541,212 bobwhite quail;
— 25,408 javelina.

As of the 2005–2006 hunting year, rabbits and squirrels are no longer surveyed. ☆

Required Licenses

A **hunting license** is required of Texas residents and nonresidents of Texas who hunt any bird or animal. Hunting licenses and stamp endorsements are valid during the period Sept. 1 through the following Aug. 31 of each year, except lifetime licenses and licenses issued for a specific number of days.

A hunting license (except the nonresident special hunting license and non-resident 5-day special hunting license) is valid for taking all legal species of wildlife in Texas including deer, turkey, javelina, antelope, aoudad (sheep) and all small game and migratory game birds.

Special licenses and tags are required for taking alligators, and a trapper's license is required to hunt fur-bearing animals.

In addition to a valid hunting license,

— an Upland Game Bird Stamp Endorsement is required to hunt turkey, pheasant, quail, lesser prairie chicken or chachalaca. Non-residents who purchase the non-resident spring turkey license are exempt from this stamp endorsement requirement.

— To hunt any migratory game birds (including waterfowl, coot, rail, gallinule, snipe, dove, sandhill crane and woodcock), a Migratory Game Bird Stamp Endorsement is required, in addition to a valid hunting license.

— A valid Federal Duck Stamp and HIP Certification are also required of waterfowl hunters age 16 or older.

On the Web, information from TPW on hunting: www.tpwd.state.tx.us/hunt/hunt.htm.

Hunting for a Lease

A banner across the road in Goldthwaite proclaims, "Welcome Hunters." Hunting leases are important to the economies of many Texas towns. The Texas Parks and Wildlife Department has launched Hunt Texas, a free online connnection between landowners and hunters, at http://www.tpwd.state.tx.us/exptexas/programs/hunt-texas/. Through the Web site, landowners can register their leases and hunters can search by county, game type, length of lease terms, costs and weapons allowed. Robert Plocheck photo.

Birding in Texas

World Birding Center

The World Birding Center comprises nine birding education centers and observation sites in the Lower Rio Grande Valley designed to protect wildlife habitat and offer visitors a view of more than 500 species of birds. The center has partnered with the Texas Parks and Wildlife Department, the U.S. Fish and Wildlife Service and nine communities to turn 10,000 acres back into natural areas for birds, butterflies and other wildlife.

This area in Cameron, Hidalgo and Starr counties is a natural migratory path for millions of birds that move between the Americas. The nine WBC sites are situated along the border with Mexico:

Bird Sighting Regions

Source:
Texas Ornithological Society

Bentsen–Rio Grande Valley State Park

This is the World Birding Center Headquarters and comprises the 760-acre Bentsen-RGV State Park and 1,700 acres of adjoining federal refuge land near **Mission**. The site offers: daily tram service; 4 nature trails ranging in length from 1/4 mile to 2 miles; 2-story high Hawk Observation Tower with a 210-foot-long handicapped access ramp; 2 observation decks; 2 accessible bird blinds; primitive camping sites (by reservation); rest areas; picnic sites with tables; exhibit hall; park store; coffee bar; meeting room (available for rental); catering kitchen; bike rentals (1 and 2 seat bikes). Access within the park is by foot, bike and tram only; (956) 585-1107. **Hours:** 6 a.m. to 10 p.m., seven days a week.

Edinburg Scenic Wetlands

This 40-acre wetlands in **Edinburg** is an oasis for water-loving birds, butterflies and other wildlife. The site is currently offering:walking trails, nature tours and classes; (956) 381-9922. **Hours:** 8 a.m. – 5 p.m., Monday through Wednesday; 8 a.m.–6 p.m., Thursday through Saturday. Closed Sunday.

Estero Llano Grande State Park

This 176-acre refuge in **Weslaco** attracts a wide array of South Texas wildlife with its varied landscape of shallow lake, woodlands and thorn forest; 956-565-3919.

Hours: 8 a.m.–5 p.m., Monday through Friday; 8 a.m.–7:30 p.m., Saturday and Sunday through August.

Harlingen Arroyo Colorado

This site in **Harlingen** is connected by an arroyo waterway, as well as hike-and-bike trails meandering through the city, Hugh Ramsey Nature Park to the east and the Harlingen Thicket to the west; (956) 427-8873. **Hours:** Office, 8 a.m.–5:00 p.m., Monday through Friday. Nature trails are open seven days a week, sunrise to sunset.

Old Hidalgo Pumphouse

Visitors to this museum in **Hidalgo** on the Rio Grande can learn about the steam-driven irrigation pumps that transformed Hidalgo County into a year-round farming area. The museum's grounds feature hummingbird gardens, walking trails and historic tours; (956) 843-8686.

The Old Hidalgo Pumphouse site includes hummingbird gardens. Robert Plocheck photo

Birders along the Rio Grande at Salineño in Starr County. Robert Plocheck photo.

Hours: 10 a.m.–5 p.m., Monday through Friday; 1 p.m.–5 p.m., Sunday. Closed Saturday.

Quinta Mazatlan

This 1930s country estate in **McAllen** is a historic Spanish Revival adobe hacienda surrounded by lush tropical landscaping and native woodland. It is also an urban oasis, where quiet trails wind through more than 15 acres of birding habitat; (956) 688-3370. **Hours:** 8 a.m.–5 p.m., Tuesday through Saturday. Open until sunset on Thursdays. Closed Mondays and holidays.

Resaca de la Palma State Park

More than 1,700 acres of newly opened wilderness near **Brownsville**, this site comprises the largest tract of native habitat in the World Birding Center network. The park offers birding tours and natural history tours. Admission is by appointment and reservation only; (956) 565-3919.

Roma Bluffs

History and nature meet on scenic bluffs above the Rio Grande, where the World Birding Center in **Roma** is located on the old plaza of a once-thriving steamboat port. Part of a national historic district, the WBC Roma Bluffs includes a riverside nature area of three acres in Starr County. The site offers: walking trails, canoe trips, birding tours, natural history tours and classes; (956) 849-4930. **Hours:** 8 a.m.–4:00 p.m. Tuesday through Saturday, although trails are open seven days a week and are free to the public.

South Padre Island Birding and Nature Center

At the southern tip of the world's longest barrier island, **South Padre Island** Birding and Nature Center is a slender thread of land between the shallow Laguna Madre and the Gulf of Mexico. This site offers: a nature trail boardwalk and birding tours; 1-800-SOPADRE.

The Eastern Meadowlark, photographed here at Anahuac National Wildlife Refuge. Natalie Caudill photo.

Hours: 9 a.m.–5 p.m., seven days a week.

Great Texas Coastal Birding Trail

The Great Texas Coastal Birding Trail winds its way through 43 Texas counties along the entire Texas coastal region. The trail, completed in April 2000, is divided into upper, central and lower coastal regions. It includes 308 wildlife-viewing sites and such amenities as boardwalks, parking pullouts, kiosks, observation platforms and landscaping to attract native wildlife.

Color-coded maps are available, and signs mark each site. Trail maps contain information about the birds and habitats likely to be found at each site, the best season to visit, and food and lodging.

For information, contact: Nature Tourism Coordinator, Texas Parks and Wildlife, 4200 Smith School Road, Austin, TX 78744; 512-389-4396. On the Web at www.tpwd.state.tx.us/huntwild/wild/wildlife_trails/. ☆

Fairs, Festivals and Special Events

Fairs, festivals and other special events provide year-round recreation in Texas. Some are of national interest, while many attract visitors from across the state. Each county profile in the Counties section also lists events in the Recreation paragraph and following town names. Information here was furnished by event coordinators.

Abilene — West Texas Fair & Rodeo; September; 1700 Hwy. 36, 79602; www.taylorcountyexpocenter.com. *Since 1897.*

Albany — Fort Griffin Fandangle; June; PO Box 155, 76430; www.fortgriffinfandangle.org. *Since 1938.*

Alvarado — Johnson County Pioneers & Old Settlers Reunion; August; PO Box 217, 76009. *Since 1893.*

Amarillo — Tri-State Fair; September; PO Box 31087, 79120.

Anderson — Grimes County Fair; June; PO Box 435, 77830.

Angleton — Brazoria County Fair; October; PO Box 818, 77516; www.bcfa.org. *Since 1939.*

Aransas Pass — Shrimporee; June, 130 W. Goodnight, 78336; www.aransaspass.org. *Since 1949.*

Arlington — Texas Scottish Festival; June; PO Box 511, 76634; www.texasscottishfestival.com. *Since 1986.*

Athens — Texas Fiddlers' Asso. Reunion; May (last Fri.); PO Box 1441, 75751. *Since 1932.*

Austin — Star of Texas Fair & Rodeo; March; 9100 Decker Lake Rd. 78724; www.rodeoaustin.com. *Since 1937.*

Austin — Austin Fine Arts Festival; April; PO Box 5705, 78763; www.austinfineartsfestival.org.

Bay City — Matagorda County Fair & Livestock Show; February; PO Box 1803, 77404; www.matagorda-countyfair.com. *Since 1945.*

Bay City — Bay City Rice Festival; October; PO Box 867; 77404; www.baycitylions.org.

Beaumont — South Texas State Fair; October; 7250 Wespark Cr., 77705; www.ymbl.org. *Since 1943.*

Bellville — Austin County Fair; October; PO Box 141, 77418; www.austincountyfair.com.

Belton — 4th of July Celebration & PRCA Rodeo; July; PO Box 659, 76513; www.beltonchamber.com.

Belton — Central Texas State Fair; Aug.-Sept.; PO Box 206, 76513; www.centraltexasstatefair.com.

Big Spring — Howard County Fair; September; PO Box 2356, 79721. *Since 1973*

Boerne — Boerne Berges Fest; June; PO Box 748, 78006; www.bergesfest.com.

Boerne — Kendall County Fair; September (Labor Day Wknd.); PO Box 954, 78006; www.kcfa.org. *Since 1906.*

Brackettville — Gunfighter Competition; July; PO Box 528, 78832; www.alamovillage.com.

Brackettville — Western Horse Races & BBQ; September (Labor Day); PO Box 528, 78832; www.alamo-village.com.

Brenham — Washington County Fair; September; 1305 E. Blue Bell Rd., 77833; www.washingtoncofair.com. *Since 1870.*

Brownsville — Charro Days Fiesta; February; PO Box 3247, 78523-3247; www.charrodaysfiesta.com. *Since 1938.*

Burnet — Burnet Bluebonnet Festival; April; 229 S. Pierce; 78611. 222.burnetchamber.org. *Since 1986.*

Burton — Cotton Gin Festival; April (3rd wknd.); PO Box 98; 77835; www.cottonginmuseum.org. *Since 1990.*

Caldwell — Burleson County Fair; September; PO Box 634, 77836.

The Chappell Hill Bluebonnet Festival was named the State Bluebonnet Festival in 1997 by the 75th Texas Legislature. It is held every April in the Washington County town. Ron Billings photo; Texas Forest Service.

Willie Nelson, far right, and his band, including his son Lukas, center, play to a full house at Willie's Place at Carl's Corner for Willie's 76th Birthday Concert in May 2009. Lamberto Alvarez photo.

Canyon — TEXAS! Musical Drama; June–August; 1514 5th Ave., 79015; www.texas-show.com. *Since 1966.*

Carl's Corner — Concerts year-round, including Willie Nelson's 4th of July Picnic and other Nelson events; year-round; www.biowillieusa.com.

Chappell Hill — Bluebonnet Festival; April; 152 Cnty. Rd. 4145, 76634; http://clifton.centraltx.com/heritage.htm.

Clifton — Norse Smorgasbord; November; 152 Cnty. Rd. 4145, 76634; http://clifton.centraltx.com/heritage.htm.

Clute — Great Texas Mosquito Festival; July; PO Box 997, 77531; www.mosquitofestival.com. *Since 1981.*

Columbus — Colorado County Fair; September; PO Box 506, 78933; www.coloradocountyfair.org.

Conroe — Montgomery County Fair; March–April; PO Box 869, 77305-0869; www.mcfa.org. *Since 1957.*

Corpus Christi — Bayfest; September–October; PO Box 1858, 78403-1858; www.bayfesttexas.com.

Corpus Christi — Buc Days; April–May; PO Box 30404, 78463; www.bucdays.com.

Corsicana — Derrick Days; April; 120 N. 12th St., 75110; www.corsicana.org. *Since 1976.*

Crowell — Cynthia Ann Parker Festival; May; PO Box 452, 79227; www.crowelltex.com/CAP/cappage1.html.

Dalhart — XIT Rodeo & Reunion; August (1st full wknd.); PO Box 967, 79022. *Since 1936.*

Dallas — State Fair of Texas; September–October; PO Box 150009, 75315; www.bigtex.com. *Since 1886.*

Decatur — Wise County Old Settlers Reunion; July (last full week); PO Box 203, 76234.

De Leon — De Leon Peach & Melon Festival; August; PO Box 44, 76444-0044; www.cctc.net/~pmdeleon/index.htm. *Since 1917.*

Denton — North Texas State Fair & Rodeo; August; PO Box 1695, 76202; www.ntfair.com. *Since 1929.*

Edna — Jackson County Youth Fair; October; PO Box 457, 77957; www.jcyf.org. *Since 1949.*

Ennis — National Polka Festival; May; PO Box 1177, 75120-1237; www.visitennis.org/festivals.html.

Fairfield — Freestone County Fair; June; PO Box 196; 75840.

Flatonia — Czhilispiel; October (4th full wknd.); PO Box 610, 78941; www.flatoniachamber.com. *Since 1973.*

Fort Worth — Pioneer Days; September; 131 E. Exchange Ave., Ste 100B, 76106; www.fortworthstockyards.org.

Fort Worth — Southwestern Exposition & Livestock Show; January-February; PO Box 150, 76101; www.fwssr.com. *Since 1897.*

Fredericksburg — Night in Old Fredericksburg; July; 302 E. Austin, 78624; www.fredericksburg-texas.com. *Since 1963.*

Fredericksburg — Oktoberfest; October (1st wknd.); PO Box 222, 78624; www.Oktoberfestinfbg.com.

Freer — Freer Rattlesnake Roundup; May; PO Box 717, 78357; www.freerrattlesnake.com. *Since 1966.*

Galveston — Dickens on The Strand; December; 502 20th St., 77550; www.dickensonthestrand.org. *Since 1973.*

Galveston — Galveston Historic Homes Tour; May; 502 20th St., 77550-2014; www.galvestonhistory.org. *Since 1974.*

Gilmer — East Texas Yamboree; October; PO Box 854, 75644; www.yamboree.com. *Since 1937.*

Glen Flora — Wharton County Youth Fair; April; PO Box 167, 77443; www.whartoncountyyouthfair.org. *Since 1976.*

Graham — Art Splash on the Square; May; PO Box 1684, 76450; www.art-splash.com.

Graham — Red, White & You Parade & Festivities; July; PO Box 299; 76450; www.visitgraham.com.

Granbury — Annual July 4th Celebration; July; 116 W. Bridge St., 76048; www.granburychamber.com.

Granbury — Harvest Moon Festival; October; 116 W. Bridge St., 76048; www.hgma.com. *Since 1977.*

Grand Prairie — National Championship Pow-Wow; September; 2602 Mayfield Rd, 75052; www.tradersvillage.com. *Since 1963.*

Greenville — Hunt County Fair; June; PO Box 1071, 75403; www.huntcountyfair.com. *Since 1970.*

Groesbeck — Limestone County Fair; March–April; PO Box 965, 76642.

Hallettsville — Hallettsville Kolache Fest; September; PO Box 313, 77964; www.hallettsville.com. *Since 1995.*

Helotes — Helotes Cornyval; May (1st wknd.); PO Box 376, 78023; www.cornyval.com. *Since 1967.*

Hempstead — Waller County Fair; September–October; PO Box 911, 77445. www.wallercountyfair.com. *Since 1946.*

Hico — Hico Old Settler Reunion; July; PO Box 93, 76457; www.hico-tx.com. *Since 1887.*

Hidalgo — BorderFest; March; PO Box 722; 78557; www.borderfest.com.

Hondo — Medina County Fair; September (3rd wknd.); PO Box 4, 78861. *Since 1980.*

Houston — Harris County Fair; October; 1 Abercrombie Dr, 77084-4233; www.harriscountyfair.net. *Since 1977.*

Houston — Houston International Festival; April–May; 1111 Bagby St., Ste. 2550, 77002; www.ifest.org.

Houston — Houston Livestock Show and Rodeo; March; PO Box 20070; 77225-0070; www.hlsr.com.

Hughes Springs — Wildflower Trails of Texas; April; PO Box 805, 75656. *Since 1970.*

Huntsville — Walker County Fair & Rodeo; March–April; PO Box 1817, 77342; www.walkercountyfair.com. *Since 1979.*

Jefferson — Historical Pilgrimage and Spring Festival; May (1st wknd.); PO Box 301, 75657-0301; www.theexcelsiorhouse.com. *Since 1947.*

Johnson City — Blanco County Fair; August; PO Box 261, 78636-0261; www.lbjcountry.com/

Kenedy — Bluebonnet Days; April; 205 South 2nd St., 78119-2729.

Kerrville — Kerr County Fair; October; PO Box 290842, 78029; www.kerrcountyfair.com. *Since 1980.*

Kerrville — Kerrville Folk Festival; May–June; PO Box 291466, 78029; www.kerrvillefolkfestival.com. *Since 1972.*

Kerrville — The Official Texas State Arts & Crafts Fair; May (Memorial wknd.); 4000 Riverside Dr., 78028, www.tacef.org. *Since 1972.*

Kerrville — Kerrville Wine and Music Festival; September (Labor Day wknd.); PO Box 291466; 78029; www.kerrvillefolkfestival.com. *Since 1991.*

Killeen — Take 190 West: Killeen Salutes the Arts; February; www.take190west.com.

LaGrange — Fayette County Fair; September (Labor Day wknd.); PO Box 544, 78945; www.fayettecountyfair.net. *Since 1926.*

Laredo — Border Olympics; January–March; PO Box 450037, 78044-0037; http://borderolympics.net. *Since 1947.*

Laredo — Laredo International Fair & Expo; March; PO Box 1770, 78043; www.laredofair.com. *Since 1963.*

Laredo — Washington's Birthday Celebration; January–February; 1819 E. Hillside Rd., 78041-3383; www.wbcalaredo.com. *Since 1898.*

Longview — Gregg County Fair & Exposition; September; 1511 Judson Rd., Ste. F, 75601; www.greggcountyfair.com. *Since 1951.*

Lubbock — 4th on Broadway Festival; July; PO Box 1643, 79408; www.broadwayfestivals.com. *Since 1991.*

Lubbock — Lights on Broadway Celebration; December; PO Box 1643, 79408; www.broadwayfestivals.com.

Lubbock — Panhandle-South Plains Fair; September; PO Box 208, 79408; www.southplainsfair.com. *Since 1914.*

Lufkin — Texas Forest Festival; September; 1615 S. Chestnut St., 75901; www.texasforestfestival.com.

Luling — Luling Watermelon Thump; June (last full wknd); PO Box 710, 78648-0710; www.watermelonthump.com. *Since 1953.*

Marshall — Fire Ant Festival; October; PO Box 520, 75671; www.marshall-chamber.com. *Since 1984.*

Marshall — Stagecoach Days Festival; May; PO Box 520, 75671; www.marshall-chamber.com. Since 1973.

Marshall — Wonderland of Lights; November–December; PO Box 520, 75671; www.marshalltxchamber.com.

Mercedes — Rio Grande Valley Livestock Show; March; 1000 N. Texas; www.rgvlivestockshow.com. *Since 1940.*

Mesquite — Mesquite Championship Rodeo; April–September (each Fri. & Sat.); 1818 Rodeo Dr, 75149-3800; www.mesquiterodeo.com. *Since 1958.*

Monahans — Butterfield-Overland Stage Coach and Wagon Festival; July; 401 S. Dwight Ave., 79756 www.butterfield.ws/. *Since 1994.*

Mount Pleasant — Titus County Fair; September; PO Box 1232, 75456-1232; www.tituscountyfair.com.

Nacogdoches — Piney Woods Fair; October; 3805 NW Stallings Dr., 75964; www.nacexpo.net. *Since 1978.*

Nederland — Nederland Heritage Festival; March; PO Box 1176, 77627; www.nederlandhf.org. *Since 1973.*

New Braunfels — Comal County Fair; September; PO Box 310223, 78131-0223; www.comalcountyfair.org. *Since 1894.*

New Braunfels — Wurstfest; October–November; PO Box 310309, 78131-0309; www.wurstfest.com.

Odessa — Permian Basin Fair & Expo; September; 218 W. 46th St., 79764; www.permianbasinfair.com.

Palestine — Dogwood Trails Festival; March–April; PO Box 2828, 75802-2828; www.visitpalestine.com.

Paris — Red River Valley Fair; August–September; 570 E. Center St., 75460; www.rrvfair.org. *Since 1911.*

Pasadena — Pasadena Livestock Show & Rodeo; September–October; 7601 Red Bluff Rd., 77507-1035; www.pasadenarodeo.com.

Plantersville — Texas Renaissance Festival; October–November (8 weekends); 21778 FM 1774, 77363; www.texrenfest.com. *Since 1975.*

Port Arthur — CalOILcade; October; PO Box 2336, 77643; www.portarthur.com/cavoilcade. *Since 1953.*

Port Lavaca — Calhoun County Fair; October (3rd wknd.); PO Box 42, 77979-0042. *Since 1963.*

Poteet — Poteet Strawberry Festival; April; PO Box 227, 78065; www.strawberryfestival.com. *Since 1948.*

Refugio — Refugio County Fair & Rodeo & Livestock Show; March; PO Box 88, 78377. *Since 1961.*

Rio Grande City — Starr County Fair; March (1st full wknd.); PO Box 841, 78582. *Since 1961.*

Rosenberg — Fort Bend County Fair; September–October; PO Box 428, 77471; www.fbcfa.org. *Since 1937.*

Salado — Salado Scottish Games and Competitions; November (2nd wknd); PO Box 36, 76571-0036; www.ctam-salado.org.

San Angelo — San Angelo Stock Show & Rodeo; February; 200 W 43rd St., 76903; www.sanangelorodeo.com. *Since 1932.*

San Antonio — Fiesta San Antonio; April; 2611 Broadway St.; 78215; www.fiesta-sa.org. *Since 1891.*

San Antonio — Texas Folklife Festival; June; 801 S. Bowie, 78205; www.texasfolklifefestival.org. *Since 1972.*

Sanderson — Cinco de Mayo Celebration; May (1st Sat.); PO Box 598, 79848.

Sanderson — 4th of July Celebration; July; PO Box 4810, 79848-4810; www.sandersontx.info. *Since 1908.*

Sanderson — Prickly Pear Pachanga; October; PO Box 410, 79848; www.sandersontx.info. *Since 2001.*

Santa Fe — Galveston County Fair & Rodeo; April; PO Box 889, 77510; www.galvestoncountyfair.com.

Schulenburg — Schulenburg Festival; August (1st full wknd.); PO Box 115; 78956; www.schulenburgfestival.com. *Since 1976.*

Seguin — Guadalupe Agricultural & Livestock Fair; October (2nd wknd); PO Box 334, 78155; www.guadalupecountyfairandrodeo.com. *Since 1885.*

Shamrock — St. Patrick's Day Celebration; March; PO Box 588, 79079. www.shamrocktx.net/site/index-2.html. *Since 1947.*

Stamford — Texas Cowboy Reunion; July; PO Box 948, 79553; www.tcrrodeo.com. *Since 1933.*

Sulphur Springs — Hopkins County Fall Festival; September (3rd Sat.); PO Box 177, 75483. **Sweetwater** — Rattlesnake Roundup; March; PO Box 416, 79556-0416; www.rattlesnakeroundup.net. *Since 1958.*

Terlingua — Terlingua International Chili Championship; November; PO Box 39, 79852; www.chili.org. *Since 1947.*

Texarkana — Four States Fair; September; 3700 E. 50th St., Texarkana AR, 75504; www.fourstatesfair.com.

Tyler — East Texas State Fair; September; 2112 W. Front St., 75702; www.etstatefair.com. *Since 1914.*

Tyler — Texas Rose Festival; Ocober (3rd wknd.); PO Box 8224, 75711; www.texasrosefestival.com. *Since 1933.*

Waco — Heart O' Texas Fair & Rodeo; October; 4601 Bosque Blvd.; 76710; www.hotfair.com. *Since 1954.*

Waxahachie — Gingerbread Trail Tour of Homes; June (1st full wknd); PO Box 706, 75168; www.-rootsweb.com/~txecm/ginger.htm. *Since 1969.*

Waxahachie — Scarborough Renaissance Festival; April–May; PO Box 538, 75168-0538; www.scarboroughrenfest.com. *Since 1980.*

Weatherford — Parker County Peach Festival; July (2nd Sat.); PO Box 310, 76086; www.weatherfordchamber.com. *Since 1985.*

Weatherford — Christmas on the Square; December; PO Box 310, 76086; www.weatherford-chamber.com. *Since 1988.*

West — Westfest; September (Labor Day wknd.); PO Box 123, 76691; www.westfest.com. *Since 1976.*

Winnsboro — Autumn Trails Festival; October (every wkend.); PO Box 464; 75494.

Woodville — Tyler County Dogwood Festival; March–April; PO Box 2151, 75979-2151; www.tylercountydogwoodfestival.org. Since 1944.

Yorktown — Yorktown's Fiesta En La Calle Festival; April (1st Sat.); PO Box 488, 78164-0488; www.yorktowntx.com.

Yorktown — Yorktown's Annual Western Days Celebration; October (3rd full wknd.); PO Box 488, 78164-0488; www.yorktowntx.com. *Since 1959.* ☆

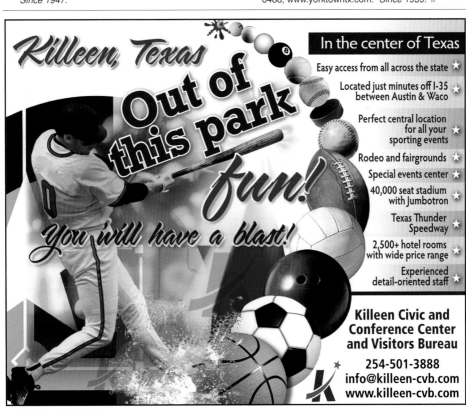

Professional Basketball in Texas

Big-time professional basketball arrived in Texas in 1967 with the formation of the American Basketball Association, which placed franchises in Dallas and Houston.

By 1973, the Dallas Chaparrals had moved to San Antonio to become the Spurs, who were absorbed into the National Basketball Association in 1976.

The ABA Houston Mavericks played two years before moving to North Carolina to become the Cougars.

The San Antonio Spurs have gone on to the NBA finals four times, winning the national championship all four times.

RIGHT, San Antonio Spurs' Tim Duncan (21), teammates David Robinson (50), Mario Elie, lower right, Antonio Daniels, right rear, Sean Elliott (32), Avery Johnson and Mario Elie celebrate after defeating the New York Knicks 78-77 in Game 5 to clinch the 1999 NBA finals at New York's Madison Square Garden. File photo.

Dallas Chaparrals (ABA)

Year	Win	Loss	%	Playoffs
1967-68	46	32	.590	lost ABA semifinals to New Orleans Buccaneers 4-1
1968-69	41	37	.526	lost first round to New Orleans Buccaneers 4-3
1969-70	45	39	.536	lost first round to Los Angeles Stars 4-2
changed name to **Texas Chaparrals**, playing some games in Fort Worth and Lubbock				
1970-71	30	54	.357	lost first round to Utah Stars 4-0
changed name back to **Dallas Chaparrals**				
1971-72	42	42	.500	lost first round to Utah Stars 4-0
1972-73	28	56	.333	
franchise relocated to **San Antonio**, beginning play in 1973 as the Spurs				

San Antonio Spurs (ABA-NBA)

Year	Win	Loss	%	Playoffs
1973-74	45	39	.536	lost first round to Indiana Pacers 4-3
1974-75	51	33	.607	lost first round to Indiana Pacers 4-2
1975-76	50	34	.595	lost first round to New York Nets 4-3
merged into NBA				
1976-77	44	38	.537	lost first round to Boston Celtics 2-0
1977-78	52	30	.634	lost semifinals to Washington Bullets 4-2
1978-79	48	34	.585	lost conference finals to Washington 4-3
1979-80	41	41	.500	lost first round to Houston Rockets 4-2
1980-81	52	30	.634	lost conference semifinals to Houston 4-2
1981-82	48	34	.585	lost conference finals to Los Angeles Lakers 4-0
1982-83	53	29	.646	lost conference finals to Los Angeles Lakers 4-2
1983-84	37	45	.451	

Year	Win	Loss	%	Playoffs
1984-85	41	41	.500	lost first round to Denver Nuggets 3-2
1985-86	35	47	.427	lost first round to Los Angeles Lakers 3-0
1986-87	28	54	.341	
1987-88	31	51	.378	lost first round to Los Angeles Lakers 3-0
1988-89	21	61	.256	
1989-90	56	26	.683	lost conference semifinals to Portland Trailblazers 4-3
1990-91	55	27	.671	lost first round to Golden State Warriors 3-1
1991-92	47	35	.573	lost conference semifinals to Phoenix Suns 3-0
1992-93	49	33	.598	lost conference semifinals to Phoenix Suns 4-2
1993-94	55	27	.671	lost first round to Utah Jazz 3-1
1994-95	62	20	.756	lost conference finals to Houston Rockets 4-2
1995-96	59	23	.720	lost conference semifinals to Utah Jazz 4-2
1996-97	20	62	.244	
1997-98	56	26	.683	lost conference semifinals to Utah Jazz 4-1
1998-99	37	13	.740	won **NBA finals** over New York Knicks 4-1
1999-00	53	29	.646	lost first round to Phoenix Suns 3-1
2000-01	58	24	.707	lost conference finals to Los Angeles Lakers 4-0
2001-02	58	24	.707	lost conference semifinals to Los Angeles Lakers 4-1
2002-03	60	22	.732	won **NBA finals** over New Jersey Nets 4-2
2003-04	57	25	.695	lost conference semifinals to Los Angeles Lakers 4-2
2004-05	59	23	.720	won **NBA finals** over Detroit Pistons 4-3
2005-06	63	19	.768	lost conference semifinals to Dallas Mavericks 4-3
2006-07	58	24	.707	won **NBA finals** over Cleveland Cavaliers 4-0
2007-08	56	26	.683	lost conference finals to Los Angeles Lakers 4-1
2008-09	54	28	.659	lost first round to Dallas Mavericks 4-1

Houston Mavericks (ABA)

Year	Win	Loss	%	Playoffs
1967-68	29	49	.372	
1968-69	23	55	.295	
1969-70 - team moved to North Carolina to become the Cougars				

Houston Rockets (NBA)

The National Basketball Association first came to Texas in 1971 when the Rockets franchise moved from San Diego.

The San Diego Rockets franchise had been an expansion team in 1967 when they entered the NBA along with the Seattle Super-Sonics. The Rockets name derived from the San Diego slogan, "A City in Motion."

The Houston Rockets have been in the NBA finals four times, winning the national championship twice, in 1994 and 1995.

Since 2003, the team has played in the Toyota Center in downtown Houston, following several years at The Summit.

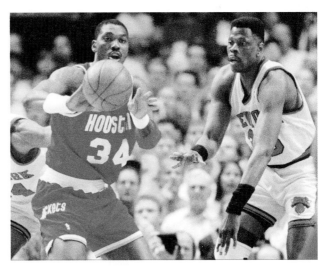

Rockets center Hakeem Olajuwon and New York Knicks center Patrick Ewing in the NBA finals in 1994. File photo.

Year	Win	Loss	%	Playoffs
- 1971 Rockets team relocates to **Houston** from San Diego				
1971-72	34	48	.415	
1972-73	33	49	.402	
1973-74	32	50	.390	
1974-75	41	41	.500	lost conference semifinals to Philadelphia 76ers 4-1
1975-76	40	42	.488	
1976-77	49	33	.598	lost conference finals to Philadelphia 76ers 4-2
1977-78	28	54	.341	
1978-79	47	35	.573	lost first round to Atlanta Hawks 2-0
1979-80	41	41	.500	lost conference semifinals to Boston Celtics 4-0
1980-81	40	42	.488	lost **NBA finals** to Boston Celtics 4-2
1981-82	46	36	.561	lost first round to Seattle SuperSonics 2-1
1982-83	14	68	.171	
1983-84	29	53	.354	
1984-85	48	34	.585	lost first round to Utah Jazz 3-2
1985-86	51	31	.622	lost **NBA finals** to Boston Celtics 4-2
1986-87	42	40	.512	lost conference semifinals to Seattle SuperSonics 4-2
1987-88	46	36	.561	lost first round to Dallas Mavericks 3-1
1988-89	45	37	.549	lost first round to Seattle SuperSonics 3-1
1989-90	41	41	.500	lost first round to Los Angeles Lakers 3-0
1990-91	52	30	.634	lost first round to Los Angeles Lakers 3-0
1991-92	42	40	.512	
1992-93	55	27	.671	lost conference semifinals to Seattle SuperSonics 4-3
1993-94	58	24	.707	won **NBA finals** over New York Knicks 4-3
1994-95	47	35	.573	won **NBA finals** over Orlando Magic 4-0
1995-96	48	34	.585	lost conference semifinals to Seattle SuperSonics 4-0
1996-97	57	25	.695	lost conference finals to Utah Jazz 4-2
1997-98	41	41	.500	lost first round to Utah Jazz 3-2
1998-99	31	19	.620	lost first round to Los Angeles Lakers 3-1
1999-00	34	48	.415	
2000-01	45	37	.550	
2001-02	28	54	.341	
2002-03	43	39	.524	
2003-04	45	37	.550	lost first round to Los Angeles Lakers 4-1
2004-05	51	31	.622	lost first round to Dallas Mavericks 4-3
2005-06	34	48	.415	
2006-07	52	30	.634	lost first round to Utah Jazz 4-3
2007-08	55	27	.671	lost first round to Utah Jazz 4-2
2008-09	53	29	.646	lost conference semifinals to Los Angeles Lakers 4-3

The Toyota Center in Houston. Robert Plocheck photo.

Dallas fans celebrate at the American Airlines Center before Game 1 of the NBA finals in 2006. File photo.

Dallas Mavericks (NBA)

In 1980, the NBA awarded an expanison franchise to Dallas and millionaire Don Carter, who named the team the Mavericks.

After the 1995-96 sesaon, Carter sold the team to a group of investors led by Ross Perot Jr. In January 2000, the Perot group sold the Mavericks to internet entrepreneur Mark Cuban, who became one of the best-known professional team owners in sports.

Year	Win	Loss	%	Playoffs
1980-81	15	67	.183	
1981-82	23	54	.341	
1982-83	38	44	.463	
1983-84	43	39	.524	lost conference semifinals to Los Angeles Lakers 4-1
1984-85	44	38	.537	lost first round to Portland Trailblazers 3-1
1985-86	44	38	.537	lost conference semifinals to Los Angeles Lakers 4-2
1986-87	55	27	.671	lost first round to Seattle SuperSonics 3-1
1987-88	53	29	.646	lost conference finals to Los Angeles Lakers 4-3
1988-89	38	44	.463	
1989-90	47	35	.573	lost first round to Portland Trailblazers 3-0
1990-91	28	54	.341	
1991-92	22	60	.268	
1992-93	11	71	.134	
1993-94	13	69	.159	
1994-95	36	46	.439	
1995-96	26	56	.317	
1996-97	24	58	.293	
1997-98	20	62	.244	
1998-99	14	36	.280	
1999-00	40	42	.488	
2000-01	53	29	.646	lost conference semifinals to San Antonio Spurs 4-1
2001-02	57	25	.695	lost conference semifinals to Sacramento Kings 4-1
2002-03	60	22	.732	lost conference finals to San Antonio Spurs 4-2
2003-04	52	30	.634	lost first round to Sacramento Kings 4-1
2004-05	58	24	.707	lost conference semifinals to Phoenix Suns 4-2
2005-06	60	22	.732	lost **NBA finals** to Miami Heat 4-2
2006-07	67	15	.817	lost first round to Golden State Warriors 4-2
2007-08	51	31	.622	lost first round to New Orleans Hornets 4-1
2008-09	50	32	.610	lost conference semifinals to Denver Nuggets 4-1

Prosper players and fans celebrate victory in their 2008 AAA championship game. Louis DeLuca photo.

STATE: High School Football Championships

The University Interscholastic League, which governs literary and athletic competition among schools in Texas, was organized in 1910 as a division of the University of Texas extension service. Initially, it sponsored forensic competition.

By 1920, the UIL organized the structure of the high school football game in response to the growing popularity of the sport in Texas. Town football teams had begun competing around the state in the early 1890s.

From 1920 until 1947, the UIL named only one state football champion for the larger schools. Smaller schools were limited to regional titles.

Beginning in 1948, champions were named by divisions based on school enrollment, with the introduction of City, AA and A divisions.

Over the years, other adjustments have been made in determining the divisions, so that today the divisions range from 6-Man competition for the smaller schools to the largest 5A schools.

In the 1990s, subdivisions were added within 2A-5A divisions, with the larger schools included in the Division I. Subdivisions were added to the two other divisions for the season competition in 2006.

Following are listed the champions by UIL division, along with the runner up, and the points scored by each team in the championship game. Included in years 1940-68 are the teams competing in the Prairie View Interscholastic League (PVIL, first called the Interscholastic League of Colored Schools). Between 1965 and 1968, the schools were integrated into the UIL. (OT refers to overtime.) *Source: The University Interscholastic League at www.uil.utexas.edu.*

2008

6-Man Division I
Strawn 58
Follett 29

6-Man Division II
Borden County 54
Woodson 8

A Division I
Canadian 38
Mart 7

A Division II
Stratford 24
Cayuga 13

AA Division I
Muleshoe 48
Kirbyville 26

AA Division II
Daingerfield 26
Cisco 8

AAA Division I
Prosper 17
Waco La Vega 10

AAA Division II
Carthage 49
Celina 37

AAAA Division I
Lake Travis 48
Longview 23

AAAA Division II
Sulphur Springs 69
Dayton 49

AAAAA Division I
Allen 21
Fort Bend Hightower 14

AAAAA Division II
Katy 17
Wylie 3

2007

6-Man Division I
Richland Springs 98
Rule 54

6-Man Division II
Motley County 44
Woodson 38

A Division I
Munday 26
Bremond 6

A Division II
Alto 22
Seymour 0

AA Division I
Farmersville 27
Tatum 24

AA Division II
Canadian 40
Elysian Fields 25

AAA Division I
Liberty Hill 38
Gilmer 13

AAA Division II
Celina 21
China Spring 14

AAAA Division I
Lamar Consolidated 20
Copperas Cove 14

AAAA Division II
Lake Travis 36
Highland Park (Dallas) 34

AAAAA Division I
Euless Trinity 13
Converse Judson 10

AAAAA Division II
Katy 28
Pflugerville 7

2006

6-Man Division I
Richland Springs 78
Rule 58

6-Man Division II
Vernon Northside 60
Jayton 41

UIL football championships

A Division I
Alto 42
McCamey 13

A Division II
Chilton 20
Windthorst 10

AA Division I
Tatum 32
Littlefield 14

AA Division II
Mart 23
Cisco 13

AAA Division I
Texarkana
Liberty-Eylau 35
Robinson 34

AAA Division II
Liberty Hill 22
Celina 19

AAAA Division I
Alamo Heights 40
Copperas Cove 28

AAAA Division II
La Marque 34
Waco 14

AAAAA Division I
Southlake Carroll 43
Austin Westlake 29

AAAAA Division II
Cedar Hill 51
Cypress Falls 17

2005

6-Man
Throckmorton 68
Turkey Valley 22

A
Stratford 21
Big Sandy 20

AA Division I
Newton 28
Argyle 20

AA Division II
Celina 28
Omaha Paul Pewitt 12

AAA Division I
Wimberley 21
Gainsville 7

AAA Division II
Tatum 38
Hutto 34

AAAA Division I
Highland Park (Dallas) 59
Marshall 0

AAAA Division II
Lewisville Hebron 28
Calallen (Corpus Christi) 0

AAAAA Division I
Euless Trinity 28
Converse Judson 14

AAAAA Division II
Southlake Carroll 34
Katy 20

2004

6-Man
Richland Springs 58
Turkey Valley 38

A
Shiner 33
Stratford 19

AA Division I
Boyd 17
Newton 14

AA Division II
Crawford 28
Troup 14

AAA Division I
Wylie (Abilene) 17
Cuero 14

AAA Division II
Gilmer 49
Jasper 47

AAAA Division I
Ennis 23
Marshall 21

AAAA Division II
(OT2) Kilgore 33
Dallas Lincoln 27

AAAAA Division I
Tyler Lee 28
Spring Westfield 21

AAAAA Division II
Southlake Carroll 27
Smithson Valley 24

2003

6-Man
Strawn 67
Fort Davis 62

A
Windthorst 28
Shiner 27

AA Division I
San Augustine 28
Tuscola Jim Ned 7

AA Division II
Garrison 27
Bangs 0

AAA Division I
Gainsville 35
Burnet 24

AAA Division II
Atlanta 34
Marlin 0

AAAA Division I
North Crowley 20
Bay City 6

AAAA Division II
(OT 3) La Marque 43
Denton Ryan 35

AAAAA Division I
Galena Park
North Shore 23
Conroe The Woodlands 7

AAAAA Division II
Katy 16
Southlake Carroll 15

2002

6-Man
Calvert 51
Sanderson 46

A
Petrolia 39
Celeste 18

AA Division I
Corrigan-Camden 33
Bangs 14

AA Division II
Rosebud-Lott 34
Cisco 0

AAA Division I
Everman 35
Burnet 14

AAA Division II
(OT 2) Bandera 27
Greenwood 24

AAAA Division I
Texarkana 42
New Braunfels 11

AAAA Division II
Denton Ryan 38
Brenham 8

AAAAA Division I
Converse Judson 33
Midland 32

AAAAA Division II
Southlake Carroll 45
Smithson Valley 14

2001

6-Man
Whitharral 27
Richland Springs 20

A
Burkeville 27
Celeste 8

AA Division I
Blanco 16
Van Alstyne 0

AA Division II
Celina 41
Garrison 35

AAA Division I
Everman 25
Sinton 14

AAA Division II
Commerce 14
La Grange 11

AAAA Division I
(OT) Denton Ryan 42
Smithson Valley 35

AAAA Division II
Ennis 21
Bay City 0

AAAAA Division I
Mesquite 14
San Antonio Taft 13

AAAAA Division II
Lufkin 38
Westlake (Austin) 24

2000

6-Man
Panther Creek 42
Highland 36

A
Stratford 49
Burkeville 14

AA Division I
Sonora 27
Blanco 24

AA Division II
Celina 21
Mart 17

AAA Division I
Gatesville 14
Wylie (Abilene) 10

AAA Division II
La Grange 20
Forney 17

AAAA Division I
Bay City 24
Denton Ryan 2

AAAA Division II
Ennis 38
West Orange-Stark 24

AAAAA Division I
Midland Lee 33
Westlake (Austin) 21

AAAAA Division II
Katy 35
Tyler John Tyler 20

1999

6-Man
Gordon 54
Groom 34

A
Bartlett 35
Aspermont 6

AA Division I
Mart 40
Boyd 7

AA Division II
Celina 38
Elysian Fields 7

AAA Division I
Liberty Eylau 49
Mathis 6

AAA Division II
Commerce 17
Sealy 10

AAAA Division I
Texas City 27
Hereford 14

AAAA Division II
Stephenville 28
Port Neches-Groves 18

AAAAA Division I
Midland Lee 42
Aldine Eisenhower 21

AAAAA Division II
Garland 37
Katy 25

1998

6-Man
Trinidad 62
Borden County 16

A
Tenaha 20
Wheeler 13

AA Division I
Omaha Paul Pewitt 28
Brookshire-Royal 26

AA Division II
Celina 21
Elysian Fields 0

AAA Division I
Aledo 14
Cuero 7

AAA Division II
Newton 21
Daingerfield 0

AAAA Division I
Grapevine 22
Bay City 0

AAAA Division II
Stephenville 34
La Marque 7

AAAAA Division I
Duncanville 24

UIL football championships

Converse Judson 21
AAAAA Division II
Midland Lee 54
San Antonio MacArthur 0

1997

6-Man
Borden County 48
Panther Creek 16
A
Granger 40
Wheeler 0
AA
Stanton 33
Rogers 7
AAA
Sealy 28
Commerce 21
AAAA Division I
Texas City 37
Corsicana 34
AAAA Division II
La Marque 17
Denison 0
AAAAA Division I
Katy 24
Longview 3
AAAAA Division II
Flower Mound Marcus 59
Alief Hastings 20

1996

6-Man
Gordon 51
Whitharral 50
A
Windthorst 41
Tenaha 12
AA
Iraan 14
Groveton 7
AAA
Sealy 36
Tatum 27
AAAA Division I
Grapevine 34
Hays Consolidated 19
AAAA Division II
La Marque 34
Denison 3
AAAAA Division I
Lewisville 58
Converse Judson 34
AAAAA Division II
Westlake (Austin) 55
Abilene Cooper 15

1995

6-Man
Amherst 78
Milford 42
A
Thorndale 14
Roscoe 7
AA
Celina 32
Alto 28
AAA
Sealy 21
Commerce 20
AAAA
La Marque 31

Denison 8
AAAAA Division I
Converse Judson 31
Odessa Permian 28
AAAAA Division II
San Antonio Roosevelt 17
Flower Mound Marcus 10

1994

6-Man
Amherst 30
Milford 20
A
Thorndale 36
Crawford 13
AA
Goldthwaite 20
Schulenburg 16
AAA
Sealy 36
Atlanta 15
AAAA
Stephenville 32
La Marque 17
AAAAA Division I
Plano 28
Katy 7
AAAAA Division II
Tyler John Tyler 35
Westlake (Austin) 24

1993

6-Man
Panther Creek 56
Dell City 28
A
Sudan 54
Bremond 0
AA
Goldthwaite 21
Omaha Paul Pewitt 8
AAA
Southlake Carroll 14
Cuero 6
AAAA
Stephenville 26
La Marque 13
AAAAA Division I
Converse Judson 36
Plano 13
AAAAA Division II
Lewisville 43
Aldine MacArthur 37

1992

6-Man
Panther Creek 54
Fort Hancock 26
A
Bartlett 33
Sudan 26
AA
Schulenburg 35
Goldthwaite 20
AAA
Southlake Carroll 48
Coldspring 0
AAAA
Waxahachie 28
A&M Consolidated 24
AAAAA Division I
Converse Judson 52

Euless Trinity 0
AAAAA Division II
Temple 38
Houston Yates 20

1991

6-Man
Fort Hancock 64
Christoval 14
A
Memphis 21
Oakwood 14
AA
Schulenburg 21
Albany 0
AAA
Groesbeck 7
Burnet 0
AAAA
A&M Consolidated 35
Carthage 16
AAAAA Division I
Killeen 14
Sugar Land Dulles 10
AAAAA Division II
Odessa Permian 27
San Antonio Marshall 14

1990

6-Man
Fort Hancock 66
Christoval 17
A
Bartlett 36
Munday 28
AA
Groveton 25
De Leon 19
AAA
Vernon 41
Crockett 20
AAAA
Wilmer-Hutchins 19
Westlake (Austin) 7
AAAAA Division I
Marshall 21
Converse Judson 19
AAAAA Division II
Aldine 27
Arlington Lamar 10

1989

6-Man
Fort Hancock 48
Jayton-Girard 24
A
Thorndale 42
Sudan 24
AA
Groveton 20
Lorena 13
AAA
Mexia 22
Vernon 21
AAAA
Chapel Hill (Tyler) 14
A&M Consolidated 0
AAAAA
Odessa Permian 28
Aldine 14

1988

6-Man

Fort Hancock 76
Zephyr 30
A
White Deer 14
Flatonia 13
AA
Corrigan-Camden 35
Quanah 14
AAA
Southlake Carroll 42
Navasota 8
AAAA
Paris 31
West Orange-Stark 13
AAAAA
Converse Judson 1
Dallas Carter 0
*(On-field score:
Dallas Carter 31, Converse
Judson 14. Dallas Carter
stripped of title.)*

1987

6-Man
Lohn 58
Wellman 30
A
Wheeler 23
Bremond 21
AA
Lorena 8
Refugio 7
AAA
Cuero 14
McGregor 6
AAAA
West Orange-Stark 17
Rockwall 7
AAAAA
Plano 28
Houston Stratford 21

1986

6-Man
Fort Hancock 50
Christoval 36
A
Burkeville 33
Throckmorton 7
AA
Shiner 18
Mart 0
AAA
Jefferson 24
Cuero 0
AAAA
West Orange-Stark 21
McKinney 9
AAAAA
Plano 24
La Marque 7

1985

6-Man
Jayton 64
Christoval 14
A
Goldthwaite 24
Runge 7
AA
Electra 29
Groveton 13
AAA

UIL football championships

Daingerfield 47
Cuero 22
AAAA
Sweetwater 17
Tomball 7
AAAAA
Houston Yates 37
Odessa Permian 0
1984
6-Man
Jayton 44
May 28
A
Munday 13
Union Hill 0
AA
Groveton 38
Panhandle 7
AAA
Medina Valley 21
Daingerfield 13
AAAA
Denison 27
Tomball 13
AAAAA Co-Champions
Odessa Permian 21
Beaumont French 21
1983
6-Man
Highland 67
Mozella 50
A
Knox City 27
Bremond 20
AA
Boyd 16
Groveton 8
AAA
Daingerfield 42
Sweeny 0
AAAA
Bay City 30
Lubbock Estacado 0
AAAAA
Converse Judson 25
Midland Lee 21
1982
6-Man
Highland 60
Mullin 13
A
Union Hill 13
Roscoe 0
AA
Eastland 28
East Bernard 6
AAA
Refugio 22
Littlefield 21
AAAA
Sugar LandWillowridge 22
Corsicana 17
AAAAA
Beaumont West Brook 21
Hurst Bell 10
1981
6-Man
Whitharral 56
Mullin 36

A
Bremond 12
Wink 9
AA
Pilot Point 32
Garrison 0
AAA
Cameron 26
Gilmer 3
AAAA
Brownwood 24
Sugar Land Willowridge 9
AAAAA
Richardson
Lake Highlands 19
Houston Yates 6
1980
6-Man
Milford 36
Highland 16
A
Valley View 7
Rankin 6
AA Co-Champions
Pilot Point 0
Tidehaven 0
AAA
Pittsburg 13
Van Vleck 2
AAAA
Huntsville 19
Paris 0
AAAAA
Odessa Permian 28
Port Arthur Jefferson 19
1979
6-Man
Milford 53
Cotton Center 34
A
Wheeler 33
High Island 21
AA
Hull-Daisetta 28
China Spring 18
AAA
Van 25
McGregor 0
AAAA
McKinney 20
Bay City 7
AAAAA
Temple 28
Houston Memorial 6
1978
6-Man
Cherokee 29
Cotton Center 27
A
Union Hill 14
Wheeler 7
AA
China Spring 42
Lexington 3
AAA
Sealy 42
Wylie 20
AAAA

Brownwood 21
Gainesville 12
AAAAA
Houston Stratford 29
Plano 13
1977
6-Man
May 42
Marathon 35
B
Wheeler 35
Lone Oak 13
A
East Bernard 27
Seagraves 10
AA
Wylie 22
Bellville 14
AAA
Dickinson 40
Brownwood 28
AAAA
Plano 13
Port Neches-Groves 10
1976
6-Man
Marathon 62
May 16
B
Gorman 18
Ben Bolt 6
A
Barbers Hill 17
De Leon 8
AA
Rockdale 23
Childress 6
AAA
Beaumont Hebert 35
Gainesville 7
AAAA
San Antonio Churchill 10
Temple 0
1975
6-Man
Cherokee 40
Marathon 26
8-Man
Leakey 32
Follett 14
B
Big Sandy 26
Groom 2
A
De Leon 28
Schulenburg 15
AA
La Grange 27
Childress 6
AAA
Ennis 13
Cuero 10
AAAA
Port Neches-Groves 20
Odessa Permian 10
1974
6-Man
Marathon 60
Cherokee 58

8-Man
Follett 28
La Pryor 22
B Co-Champions
Big Sandy 0
Celina 0
A
Grapeland 19
Aledo 18
AA
Newton 56
Spearman 26
AAA
Cuero 19
Gainsville 7
AAAA
Brazoswood (Clute) 22
Mesquite 12
1973
6-Man
Cherokee 43
Marathon 12
8-Man
Goree 52
La Pryor 22
B
Big Sandy 25
Rule 0
A
Troup 28
Vega 7
AA
Friendswood 28
Hooks 15
AAA
Cuero 21
Mount Pleasant 7
AAAA
Tyler John Tyler 21
Austin Reagan 14
1972
6-Man
O'Brien 60
Jarrell 14
8-Man
Goree 28
Harold 24
B
Chilton 6
Windthorst 0
A
Schulenburg 14
Clarendon 10
AA
Boling 20
Rockwall 0
AAA
Uvalde 33
Lewisville 27
AAAA
Odessa Permian 37
Baytown Sterling 7
1971
A
Co-Champions
Barbers Hill 3
Sonora 3
AA
Jacksboro 20
Rosebud-Lott 14

UIL football championships

AAA
Plano 21
Gregory-Portland 20

AAAA
San Antonio Lee 28
Wichita Falls 27

1970

A
Sonora 45
Pflugerville 6

AA Co-Champions
Refugio 7
Iowa Park 7

AAA
Brownwood 14
Cuero 0

AAAA
Austin Reagan 21
Odessa Permian 14

1969

A
Mart 28
Sonora 0

AA
Iowa Park 31
Klein 14

AAA
Brownwood 34
West Columbia 16

AAAA
Wichita Falls 28
San Antonio Lee 20

1968

A
Sonora 9
Poth 0

AA
Daingerfield 7
Lufkin Dunbar 6

AAA
Lubbock Estacado 14
Refugio 0

AAAA
Austin Reagan 17
Odessa Permian 11

PVIL AAA
Corsicana Jackson 31
Galdewater Weldon 6

1967

A
Tidehaven 7
Clifton 6

AA
Plano 27
San Antonio Randolph 8

AAA
Brownwood 36
El Campo 12

AAAA
Austin Reagan 20
Abilene Cooper 19

PVIL AA
Jasper Rowe 55
Hallsville Gallilee 12

PVIL AAA
Lufkin Dunbar 44
Texarkana Dunbar 24

1966

A
Sonora 40
Schulenburg 14

AA
Sweeny 29
Granbury 7

AAA
Bridge City 30
McKinney 6

AAAA
San Angelo Central 21
Spring Branch 14

PVIL AA
Bay City Hilliard 42
Denton Moore 0

PVIL AAA
Lufkin Dunbar 14
Wichita Falls Washington 7

PVIL AAAA
Beaumont Hebert 14
Dallas Madison 3

1965

A
Wills Point 14
White Deer 0

AA
Plano 20
Edna 17

AAA
Brownwood 14
Bridge City 0

AAAA
Odessa Permian 11
San Antonio Lee 6

PVIL A
Sweeny Carver 21
Cameron Price 14

PVIL AA
Conroe Washington 33
Sherman Douglas 12

PVIL AAA
Wichita Falls Washington 31
Nacogdoches Campbell 0

PVIL AAAA
Houston Yates 18
Fort Worth Terrell 0

1964

A
Archer City 13
Ingleside 6

AA
Palacios 12
Marlin 0

AAA
Palestine 24
San Marcos 15

AAAA
Garland 26
Galena Park 21

PVIL A
Bartlett Washington 8
Garland Carver 6

PVIL AA
Sherman Douglas 32
Conroe Washington 18

PVIL AAA
Lufkin Dunbar 20
Marlin Washington 7

PVIL AAAA
Waco Moore 16
Houston Yates 14

1963

A
Petersburg 20
George West 12

AA
Rockwall 7
Sugar Land Dulles 6

AAA
Corsicana 7
Pharr-San Juan-Alamo 0

AAAA
Garland 17
Corpus Christi Miller 0

PVIL A
Smithville Brown 38
Mineola McFarland 6

PVIL AA
Lubbock Dunbar 19
Conroe Washington 14

PVIL AAA
Fort Worth Kirkpatrick 46
Gladewater Weldon 14

PVIL AAAA
Galveston Central 34
Dallas Madison 14

1962

A
Rotan 39
Ingleside 6

AA
Jacksboro 52
Rockdale 0

AAA
Dumas 14
Pharr-San Juan-Alamo 3

AAAA
San Antonio Brackenridge 30
Borger 26

PVIL A
Taylor Price 42
Dayton Colbert 6

PVIL AA
Wharton Training 40
Lubbock Dunbar 6

PVIL AAA
Fort Worth Kirkpatrick 6
Houston Fidelity Manor 0

PVIL AAA
Houston Yates 18
Fort Worth Dunbar 15

1961

A
Albany 18
Hull-Daisetta 12

AA
Donna 28
Quanah 21

AAA
Dumas 6
Nederland 0

AAAA
Wichita Falls 21
Galena Park 14

PVIL A

Richardson
Hamilton Park 24
Sweeny Carver 0

PVIL AA
Midland Carver 42
Conroe Washington 16

PVIL AAA
Baytown Carver 21
Fort Worth Kirkpatrick 6

PVIL AAAA
Austin Anderson 20
Houston Yates 13

1960

A
Albany 20
Crosby 0

AA
Denver City 26
Bellville 21

AAA
Brownwood 26
Port Lavaca 6

AAAA
Corpus Christi Miller 13
Wichita Falls 6

PVIL A
Freeport Lanier 28
West Dunbar 24

PVIL AA
Conroe Washington 16
Midland Carver 6

PVIL AAA
Corpus Christi Coles 38
Wichita Falls Washington 21

PVIL AAAA Co-Champions
Houston Washington 6
Waco Moore 6

1959

A
Katy 16
Sundown 6

AA
Brady 1
Stamford 0
(On-field score: Stamford 19, Brady 14. Stamford stripped of title.)

AAA Co-Champions
Breckenridge 20
Cleburne 20

AAAA
Corpus Christi Ray 20
Wichita Falls 6

PVIL A
West Dunbar 42
Livingston Dunbar 12

PVIL AA
Bay City Hilliard 22
Fort Worth Kirkpatrick 14

PVIL AAA
Beaumount Hebert 37
Dallas Lincoln 0

1958

A
White Deer 44
Elgin 22

AA
Stamford 23

UIL football championships

	Angleton 0
AAA	
	Breckenridge 42
	Kingsville 14
AAAA	
	Wichita Falls 48
	Pasadena 6
PVIL A	
	Livingston Dunbar 26
Grand Prairie Dal-Worth 24	
PVIL AA	
	Baytown Carver 17
	Denton Moore 14
PVIL AAA	
	Dallas Washington 35
	Houston Washington 0

1957

A	Co-Champions
	Mart 7
	White Oak 7
AA	
	Terrell 41
	Brady 6
AAA	
	Nederland 20
	Sweetwater 7
AAAA	
Highland Park (Dallas) 21	
	Port Arthur 9
PVIL A	
	Galena Park
	Fidelity Manor 29
	Vernon Washington 6
PVIL AA	
	Corsicana Jackson 46
	Denton Moore 0
PVIL AAA	
	Austin Anderson 22
	Dallas Washington 14

1956

A	
	Stinnett 35
	Hondo 13
AA	
	Stamford 26
	Brady 13
AAA	
	Garland 3
	Nederland 0
AAAA	
	Abilene 14
	Corpus Christi Ray 0
PVIL A	
	Sealy County Austin 19
	Kaufman Pyle 18
PVIL AA	
	Corsicana Jackson 18
	Denton Moore 0
PVIL AAA	
	Austin Anderson 26
	Dallas Washington 7

1955

A	
	Deer Park 7
	Stinnett 0
AA	
	Stamford 34
	Hillsboro 7
AAA	

	Port Neches 20
	Garland 14
AAAA	
	Abilene 33
	Tyler 13
PVIL A	
	Rockdale Aycock 21
	West Dunbar 7
PVIL AA	
	Baytown Carver 33
	Gladewater Weldon 13
PVIL AAA	
	Port Arthur Lincoln 9
	Dallas Lincoln 6

1954

A	
	Deer Park 26
	Albany 6
AA	
	Phillips 21
	Killeen 13
AAA	
	Breckenridge 20
	Port Neches 7
AAAA	
	Abilene 14
	Houston S.F. Austin 7
PVIL A	
	Livingston Dunbar 25
College Station Lincoln 20	
PVIL AA	
	Orange Wallace 39
	Greenville Carver 0
PVIL AAA	
	Houston Wheatley 13
	Waco Moore 0

1953

A	
	Ranger 34
	Luling 21
AA	
	Huntsville 40
	Ballinger 6
AAA	
	Port Neches 24
	Big Spring 13
AAAA	
	Houston Lamar 33
	Odessa 7
PVIL A	
Livingston Dunbar (winner)	
West Columbia Brown	
(No Score Available.)	
PVIL AA	
	Corsicana Jackson 19
	Abilene Woodson 0
PVIL AAA	
	Port Arthur Lincoln 38
	Dallas Washington 7

1952

A	
	Wink 26
	Deer Park 20
AA	
	Terrell 61
	Yoakum 13
AAA	
	Breckenridge 28
	Temple 20

AAAA	
	Lubbock 12
	Baytown Lee 7
PVIL A	
	Arp Industrial (winner)
	Lockhart Carver
(No Score Available.)	
PVIL AA	
	Amarillo Carver 7
	Palestine Lincoln 0
PVIL AAA	
	Waco Moore 14
	Corpus Christi Coles 0

1951

A	
	Giddings 25
	Newcastle 9
AA	
	Arlington 7
	La Vega (Waco) 0
AAA	
	Breckenridge 20
	Temple 14
AAAA	
	Lubbock 14
	Baytown Lee 12
PVIL A	
Huntsville Sam Houston 7	
	Hillsboro Peabody 6
PVIL AA	Co-Champions
	Houston Yates 6
	Waco Moore 6

1950

A	
	Wharton 13
	Kermit 9
AA	
	Wichita Falls 14
	Austin 13
City	
	Dallas Sunset 14
	Houston Reagan 6
PVIL A	
San Angelo Blackshear 32	
Huntsville Sam Houston 0	
PVIL AA	
	Dallas Washington 24
	Houston Yates 21

1949

A	
	Littlefield 13
	Mexia 0
AA	
	Wichita Falls 34
	Austin 13
City	
San Antonio Jefferson 31	
	Dallas Sunset 13
PVIL A	
	Orange Wallace 34
	Victoria Gross 13
PVIL AA	Co-Champions
	Dallas Lincoln 13
Port Arthur Lincoln 13	

1948

A	
	Monahans 14
	New Braunfels 0
AA	

	Waco 21
	Amarillo 0
City	
	Fort Worth
	Arlington Heights 20
	Houston Lamar 0
PVIL A	
	Denison Terrell 13
	Orange Wallace 0
PVIL AA	
	Corpus Christi Coles 6
	Dallas Washington 0

1947

	San Antonio
	Brackenridge 22
Highland Park (Dallas) 13	
PVIL A	Co-Champions
	Denison Terrell 6
	Taylor Price 6
PVIL AA	
	Fort Worth Terrell 13
	Corpus Christi Coles 6

1946

	Odessa 21
San Antonio Jefferson 14	
PVIL	Co-Champions
	Dallas Washington 19
	Galveston Central 19

1945

	Co-Champions
Highland Park (Dallas) 7	
	Waco 7
PVIL	
	Wichita Falls
	Washington 12
	Austin Anderson 2

1944

	Port Arthur 20
Highland Park (Dallas) 7	
PVIL	
	Houston Wheatley 7
	Fort Worth Terrell 6

1943

	San Angelo 26
	Lufkin 13
PVIL	
Wichita Falls Washington 7	
	Houston Yates 7

1942

	Austin 20
	Dallas Sunset 7
PVIL	
	Austin Anderson 20
	Paris Gibbons 0

1941

	Wichita Falls 13
	Temple 0
PVIL	
	Dallas Washington 12
	Houston Wheatley 0

1940

	Amarillo 20
	Temple 7
PVIL	
	Fort Worth Terrell 26
	Austin Anderson 0

1939

	Lubbock 20

UIL football championships

Waco 14	**1933**	**1929**	**1924**
1938	Greenville 21	Co-Champions	Dallas Oak Cliff 31
Corpus Christi 20	Dallas Tech 0	Port Arthur 0	Waco 0
Lubbock 6	**1932**	Breckenridge 0	**1923**
1937	Corsicana 0	**1928**	Abilene 3
Longview 19	Fort Worth	Abilene 38	Waco 0
Wichita Falls 12	Masonic Home 0	Port Arthur 0	**1922**
1936	*(Corsicana awarded title on*	**1927**	Waco 13
Amarillo 10	*penetrations, 3-0.)*	Waco 21	Abilene 10
Kerrville 6	**1931**	Abilene 14	**1921**
1935	Abilene 13	**1926**	Bryan 35
Amarillo 13	Beaumont 0	Waco 20	Dallas Oak Cliff 13
Greenville 7	**1930**	Dallas Oak Cliff 7	**1920**
1934	Tyler 25	**1925**	Co-Champions
Amarillo 48	Amarillo 13	Waco 20	Houston Heights 0
Corpus Christi 0		Dallas Forest Avenue 7	Cleburne 0

Boys High School Basketball Champions

The University Interscholastic League basketball championships began in 1921 when El Paso High School, coached by Luther Coblentz, won over the Brackenridge team from San Antonio.

The Prairie View Interscholastic League began basketball championships in 1940 when Houston Yates defeated Houston Wheatley. The PVIL began to merge with the UIL at the start of the 1967-68 school year and disbanded at the end of the 1969-70 school year.

Today, the UIL has divisions determined by the school size from 1A to 5A. Girls basketball championships have been awarded by the UIL since 1951.

Following are the champions by UIL division, along with the runner up, and the points scored by each team in the championship game. Included in years 1940-70 are the teams competing in the Prairie View Interscholastic League (PVIL, first called the Interscholastic League of Colored Schools). (OT refers to overtime.) *Sources: The University Interscholastic League at www.uil.utexas.edu, and The Dallas Morning News.*

2009
A Division I
Roscoe 52
Plains 48
A Division II
Elkhart Slocum 45
Nazareth 27
AA
Ponder 51
New Waverly 39
AAA
Dallas Madison 68
Lubbock Estacado 66
AAAA
Houston Yates 94
Dallas Kimball 78
AAAAA
DeSoto 59
Cedar Hill 47

2008
A Division I
Thorndale 53
Big Sandy 42
A Division II
Laneville 56
Goodrich 50
AA
Ponder 72
Tuscola Jim Ned 51
AAA
Kennedale 61
Burkburnett 59
AAAA
Dallas South Oak Cliff 80
Fort Worth Southwest 77
AAAAA

North Crowley 73
Fort Bend Dulles 67

2007
A Division I
Thorndale 39
Martins Mill 37
A Division II
Nazareth 52
Laneville 43
AA
Kountze 71
Shallowater 57
AAA
Sour Lake
Hardin-Jefferson 56
Wylie (Abilene) 44
AAAA
Dallas South Oak Cliff 54
Beaumont Ozen 42
AAAAA
Duncanville 60
Humble Kingwood 46

2006
A Division I
Bogata Rivercrest 57
Gruver 49
A Division II
Nazareth 53
Lipan 48
AA
Arp 65
Ponder 49
AAA
Dallas Roosevelt 61
Carrollton Ranchview 46
AAAA

Fort Worth Dunbar 2
Dallas South Oak Cliff 0
(Game score: South Oak Cliff 76, Dunbar 58. South Oak Cliff stripped of title.)
AAAAA
(OT)   Plano 60
Humble Kingwood 58

2005
A (Texas Cup)
Morton 69
Lipan 53
AA
Kountze 77
Tuscola Jim Ned 64
AAA
Van 62
Graham 41
AAAA
Dallas South Oak Cliff 64
San Antonio Houston 43
AAAAA
Humble Kingwood 54
DeSoto 52

2004
A (Texas Cup)
Normangee 50
Lenorah Grady 37
AA
(OT)   Shallowater 47
Argyle 45
AAA
Kountze 73
Greenwood (Midland) 54
AAAA
Houston Jones 63
Dallas Lincoln 61

AAAAA
Houston Milby 72
Cedar Hill 67

2003
A (Texas Cup)
Nazareth 51
Tenaha 47
AA
Brock 81
Hitchcock 52
AAA
Everman 72
Tatum 44
AAAA
Fort Worth Dunbar 66
Beaumount Ozen 54
AAAAA
DeSoto 94
Corpus Christi Ray 73

2002
A (Texas Cup)
Brock 70
Nazareth 50
AA
Little River-Academy 49
Frankston 48
AAA
Gainesville 79
Kountze 62
AAAA
Dallas Lincoln 71
Beaumount Ozen 51
AAAAA
San Antonio Jay 54
Dallas Kimball 53

UIL boys basketball championships

2001
A (Texas Cup)
Evadale 66
Goodrich 60
AA
Ponder 50
Danbury 49
AAA
Mexia 74
Corpus Christi West Oso 49
AAAA
Beaumount Ozen 58
San Antonio Lanier 42
AAAAA
Sugar Land Willowridge 65
Bryan 58

2000
A
Brookeland 63
Moulton 53
AA
Peaster 67
Van Vleck 58
AAA
Waco La Vega 60
Gainesville 47
AAAA
Denton Ryan 80
Madison 69
AAAAA
Sugar Land Willowridge 59
Klein Forest 52

1999
A
Moulton 54
Brookeland 49
AA
(OT) Peaster 66
Wellington 62
AAA
(OT) Mexia 77
Seminole 71
AAAA
Crowley 60
Port Arthur Lincoln 51
AAAAA
Duncanville 78
Dallas Kimball 61

1998
A
Moulton 67
Goodrich 44
AA
Krum 64
Little River-Academy 52
AAA
Clarksville 90
Crockett 83
AAAA
Houston Waltrip 67
Highland Park (Dallas) 60
AAAAA
Midland 63
San Antonio Taft 51

1997
A
Wortham 50
Nazareth 42

AA
Italy 71
Vanderbilt Industrial 63
AAA
Dallas Madison 64
Tulia 58
AAAA
San Antonio Fox Tech 68
Dallas Lincoln 59
AAAAA
Dallas Kimball 64
Galena Park NorthShore 53

1996
A
Avinger 51
Anderson-Shiro 48
AA
Krum 53
Winnie East Chambers 39
AAA
Sinton 66
Graham 59
AAAA
Pampa Arthur 82
Dallas Madison 68
AAAAA
Dallas Kimball 72
Euless Trinity 64

1995
A
Sudan 74
Calvert 71
AA
Larue La Poynor 60
Maypearl 56
AAA
Clarksville 87
Madisonville 69
AAAA
Port Arthur Lincoln 57
Austin Anderson 56
AAAAA
SanAntonio EastCentral 108
Dallas Carter 86

1994
A
Lipan 62
Nazareth 60
AA
Krum 56
Troup 45
AAA
Ferris 84
Littlefield 66
AAAA
Plainview 54
Austin Anderson 52
AAAAA
Suger Land Willowridge 50
Plano East 44

1993
A
Laneville 77
Brock 68
AA
Troup 69
Amarillo Highland Park 49
AAA
Southlake Carroll 66

Ferris 56
AAAA
Dallas Lincoln 46
Port Arthur Lincoln 45
AAAAA
Fort Worth Dunbar 74
Converse Judson 64

1992
A
Laneville 51
Petersburg 49
AA
Troup 60
Krum 40
AAA
Stafford 73
Groesbeck 72
AAAA
Dallas South Oak Cliff 73
Georgetown 60
AAAAA
(OT) Longview 71
Victoria 67

1991
A
Moulton 53
Bronte 44
AA
Abernathy 55
Troup 46
AAA
Sour Lake
Hardin-Jefferson 75
Clarksville 68
AAAA
Port Arthur Lincoln 77
SA Alamo Heights 68
AAAAA
Duncanville 65
San Antonio Jay 38

1990
A
Santo 67
Moulton 64
AA
Ingram Moore 73
Troup 72
AAA
Navasota 71
Lamesa 54
AAAA
Dallas Lincoln 87
Boerne 77
AAAAA
Dallas Kimball 59
League City ClearLake 56

1989
A
Ladonia Fannindel 75
Moulton 58
AA
Edgewood 48
Tidehaven 46
AAA
San Antonio Cole 66
Clarksville 60
AAAA
Port Arthur Lincoln 86
Austin Travis 72

AAAAA
League City ClearLake 86
San Antonio Jay 69

1988
A
Paducah 99
Dallardsville Big Sandy 61
AA
Archer City 80
Liberty Hill 69
AAA
Sweeny 59
Corpus Christi West Oso 50
AAAA
Port Arthur Lincoln 66
Wichita Falls Hirschi 59
AAAAA
Houston Sam Houston 73
Fort Worth Dunbar 68

1987
A
Paducah 71
Bronte 39
AA
Morton 84
Liberty Hill 72
AAA
Sweeny 66
Hughes Springs 64
AAAA
Dallas Hillcrest 54
Cleburne 42
AAAAA
La Porte 64
San Antonio Holmes 58

1986
A
Nazareth 53
Archer City 49
AA
Morton 73
Dripping Springs 59
AAA
Cleveland 57
Dimmitt 56
AAAA
Port Arthur Lincoln 55
Mansfield 39
AAAAA
Amarillo 68
Dallas Kimball 63

1985
A
Larue La Poynor 47
Nazareth 41
AA
Grapeland 63
Morton 56
AAA
Sweeny 55
Brownsboro 43
AAAA
Bay City 65
Lamesa 63
AAAAA
Houston Madison 86
Conroe 69

1984
A

UIL boys basketball championships

Snook 39
Nazareth 30
AA
Shelbyville 73
Somerville 67
AAA
New Boston 76
Sour Lake
Hardin-Jefferson 65
AAAA
Port Arthur Lincoln 61
Flour Bluff (Corpus Christi) 52
AAAAA
Bryan 68
Houston Memorial 56

1983
A
Snook 76
Nacogdoches Central Heights 40
AA
Morton 91
Bartlett 69
AAA
Dimmitt 81
Van Vleck 54
AAAA
Waxahachie 79
Borger 66
AAAAA
Bryan 71
Fort Worth Paschal 54

1982
A
Snook 52
Greenwood (Midland) 45
AA
Shelbyville 46
Nixon 39
AAA
Dimmitt 60
Linden Kildare 59
AAAA
Beaumont Hebert 76
Waxahachie 71
AAAAA
San Antonio Churchill 75
Galveston Ball 74

1981
A
Snook 41
Henrietta Midway 33
AA
Liberty City Sabine 62
Shallowater 42
AAA
Altair Rice 56
Paris North Lamar 52
AAAA
Beaumont Hebert 59
Canyon 57
AAAAA
Port Arthur Lincoln 92
San Antonio Marshall 84

1980
B
Snook 59
Petty West Lamar 58
A

Liberty City Sabine 69
Bartlett 68
AA
Abernathy 64
Boling 58
AAA
Beaumont Hebert 88
Snyder 53
AAAA
Houston Kashmere 70
Plano 69

1979
B
Snook 57
Krum 56
A
Vega 52
Larue La Poynor 44
AA
Seminole 47
Altair Rice 42
AAA
Huntsville 48
Mineral Wells 45
AAAA
Lufkin 75
Fort Worth Dunbar 74

1978
B
Krum 69
Avinger 68
A
Snook 63
Coppell 62
AA
Whitehouse 60
Dimmitt 59
AAA
Huntsville 55
Mineral Wells 49
AAAA
Houston Wheatley 84
San Antonio Fox Tech 83

1977
B
Avinger 68
Hedley 62
A
Broaddus 84
Whitewright 71
AA
Morton 63
Kountze 60
AAA
Daingerfield 72
Borger 68
AAAA
Dallas South Oak Cliff 78
Fort Worth Dunbar 71

1976
B
Richards 57
Brookeland 47
A
Broaddus 57
Crowell 46
AA
Mart 57
Moulton 52

AAA
Odessa Ector 78
Waxahachie 75
AAAA
El Paso Eastwood 74
Tyler 62

1975
B
Larue La Poynor 52
Spade 42
A
Brookshire Royal 62
Whitewright 57
AA
Dimmitt 49
Van Vleck 43
AAA
Lamesa 59
South Grand Prairie 55
AAAA
Houston Kashmere 60
Fort Worth Paschal 58

1974
B
Huckabay 49
Larue La Poynor 48
A
Huntington 41
Snook 39
AA
Bowie 76
Friona 66
AAA
Gonzales 77
Crosby 62
AAAA
Houston Kashmere 91
Dallas South Oak Cliff 87

1973
B
Larue La Poynor 72
Brock 52
A
Kennard 77
Petrolia 67
AA
San Augustine 60
Grand Saline 58
AAA
Longview Pine Tree 45
Lamesa 38
AAAA
Houston Wheatley 84
Midland 78

1972
B
Larue La Poynor 53
Snook 44
A
Pottsboro 61
Garrison 60
AA
Morton 62
Whitehouse 59
AAA
Odessa Ector 71
Henderson 64
AAAA
Dallas Roosevelt 68

San Antonio Jefferson 63

1971
B
Krum 52
Snook 51
A
Van Horn 68
Pottsboro 67
AA
Hughes Spring 64
Friendswood 60
AAA
Dumas 65
Fort Worth Como 59
AAAA
Cypress-Fairbanks 70
Houston Wheatley 58

1970
B
Chester 75
Henrietta Midway 53
A
Kennard 72
Clarendon 64
AA
Kountze 75
Taft 73
AAA
Kerrville Tivy 81
Cypress-Fairbanks 68
AAAA
Houston Wheatley 108
Carrollton R.L. Turner 80
PVIL AAA
Jacksonville Douglass 88
Kilgore Dansby 69

1969
B
Snook 50
Brookeland 41
A
Friendswood 51
Pineland West Sabine 49
AA
Fort Worth Kirkpatrick 63
Spring Klein 54
AAA
Kerrville Tivy 55
Perryton 54
AAAA
Houston Wheatley 52
Houston Memorial 47
PVIL A
Carverdale Houston 78
Madisonville Marion 66
PVIL AAA
Jacksonville Douglass 69
Crockett Bunch 45

1968
B
Kennard 64
Friendswood 49
A
Aspermont 52
Louise 50
AA
Kirbyville 57
Mexia 52
AAA

UIL boys basketball championships

Richardson
Lake Highlands 51
Lubbock Dunbar 49
AAAA
Houston Wheatley 85
Dallas Jefferson 80
PVIL A
East Liberty Center 67
Mount Enterprise Concord 56
PVIL AA
Crockett Bunch 67
Texarkana Macedonia 62
PVIL AAA
Tyler Emmett 114
Carthage Turner 90

1967
B
Kennard 51
Krum 47
A
Brownsboro 68
Archer City 59
AA
Sour Lake
Hardin-Jefferson 59
Dimmitt 51
AAA
Lamesa 60
South San Antonio 56
AAAA
San Antonio Lee 70
Houston Memorial 69
PVIL A
Mount Enterprise Concord 61
West Kirbyville 39
PVIL AA
San Augustine Lincoln 87
Mexia Dunbar 77
PVIL AAA
Fort Worth Kirkpatrick 68
Galena Park Fidelity Manor 66
PVIL AAAA
Fort Worth Terrell 92
Houston Yates 67

1966
B
Snook 64
Channing 40
A
Gruver 63
Honey Grove 62
AA
FW Lake Worth 60
Crane 42
AAA
San Antonio Marshall 64
League City Clear Creek 60
AAAA
Houston Memorial 73
Dallas Samuell 68
PVIL A
Center Daniels (winner)
Taylor Hughes
(No Score Available.)
PVIL AA

Cypress-Fairbanks Carverdale 70
Gilmer Valley View 67
PVIL AAA
Galena Park Fidelity Manor 61
Bryan Kemp 45
PVIL AAAA
Houston Wheatley 87
Fort Worth Terrell 74

1965
B
Snook 48
Deweyville 44
A
Pineland West Sabine 51
Woodsboro 48
AA
FW Lake Worth 60
Port Arthur Austin 49
AAA
San Marcos 87
Waxahachie 63
AAAA
Houston Jones 64
Dallas Jefferson 59
PVIL A
Arp Industrial 63
Sweeny Carver 38
PVIL AA
Cypress-Fairbanks Carverdale 75
Grand Prairie Dal-Worth 72
PVIL AAA
Lubbock Dunbar 82
Carthage Turner 66
PVIL AAAA
Fort Worth Terrell 81
Houston Worthing 80

1964
B
McAdoo 66
Hutto 65
A
Talco 75
Henrietta 60
AA
Canyon 52
Lancaster 51
AAA
Graham 60
League City Cleark Creek 50
AAAA
Houston Austin 50
Dallas Adamson 42
PVIL A
Commerce Norris 51
Larue Central 46
PVIL AA
Daingerfield Rhoads 57
Midland Carver 55
PVIL AAA
Fort Worth Kirkpatrick 65
Galena Park Fidelity Manor 61
PVIL AAAA
Beaumont Pollard 58
Houston Kashmere 55

1963
B
McAdoo 53
Nocona Prairie Valley 35
A
Pineland West Sabine 66
Woodsboro 51
AA
Buna 47
Canyon 41
AAA
League City Clear Creek 62
Seminole 57
AAAA
San Angelo 62
Houston Spring Branch 49
PVIL A
West Kirbyville 64
Smithville Brown 45
PVIL AA
Midland Carver 47
Fairfield Dogan 36
PVIL AAA
Carthage Turner 68
Bryan Kemp 48
PVIL AAAA
(OT2) Ft. Worth Terrell 87
Galveston Central 83

1962
B
Huntington 60
Roxton 56
A
White Deer 59
Woodsboro 39
AA
Buna 49
Jacksboro 30
AAA
Dumas 58
Waxahachie 38
AAAA
Dallas Jefferson 69
Houston Jeff Davis 46
PVIL A
Colorado City Wallace 70
Brucesville Sunset 56
PVIL AA
Lubbock Dunbar 63
Galena Park Fidelity Manor 52
PVIL AAA
Fort Worth Como 75
Carthage Turner 56
PVIL AAAA
(OT) Houston Worthing 62
Dallas Madison 56

1961
B
Frankston 60
Hutto 44
A
Simms Bowie 53
Brownsboro 52
AA
Buna 60
Dimmitt 36
AAA

South San Antonio 67
League City Clear Creek 54
AAAA
Houston Austin 68
Amarillo Palo Duro 60
PVIL A
Prairie View 75
Neches Clemons 48
PVIL AA
Galena Park Fidelity Manor 63
Daingerfield Rhoads 48
PVIL AAA
Fort Worth Kirkpatrick 67
Corpus Christi Coles 45
PVIL AAAA
Houston Wheatley 98
Dallas Madison 48

1960
B
McAdoo 58
Henrietta Midway 42
A
Huntington 61
Sunray 46
AA
Linden-Kildare 52
Dimmitt 44
AAA
Lamesa 56
South San Antonio 54
AAAA
Beaumont South Park 41
Austin S.F. Austin 36
PVIL A
College Station Lincoln 69
Ladonia Clark 56
PVIL AA
Lubbock Dunbar 74
Houston Elmore 71
PVIL AAAA Co-Champions
Houston Kashmere
Dallas Madison
(Game called off.)

1959
B
Henrietta Midway 65
Kyle 58
A
Huntington 63
Plains 43
AA
Buna 53
Bowie 48
AAA
Houston Smiley 58
Hereford 42
AAAA
Pampa 65
Dallas Jefferson 52
PVIL A
Center Daniels (winner)
Linden Fairview
(No Score Available.)
PVIL AAA
Navasota Carver 66
Amarillo Carver 58
PVIL AAAA
Houston Wheatley 70

UIL boys basketball championships

Dallas Madison	55

1958

B

Blossom	67
Dallardsville Big Sandy	61

A

Simms Bowie	48
Brownsboro	47

AA

Belton	58
New London	56

AAA

Waxahachie	77
South San Antonio	63

AAAA

Pampa	48
Port Arthur	47

PVIL A

Woodville Scott	67
Fairfield Dogan	40

PVIL AAA

Temple Dunbar	66
Aldine Carver	45

PVIL AAAA

Houston Wheatley	63
Beaumont Hebert	39

1957

B

Dallardsville Big Sandy	80
Meadows	59

A

White Oak	66
McGregor	51

AA

Buna	74
Seminole	45

AAA

Houston Smiley	52
Pecos	35

AAAA

Port Arthur	67
Pampa	51

PVIL A

Woodville Scott	75
Fairfield Dogan	54

PVIL AAA

Lubbock Dunbar	98
Baytown Carver	79

PVIL AAAA

Fort Worth Terrell	73
Houston Wheatley	69

1956

B

Pollok Central	74
Krum	68

A

Buna	52
Troup	42

AA

Jacksonville	70
Phillips	68

AAA

Amarillo Palo Duro	59
Beaumont French	51

AAAA

Laredo	65
North Dallas	54

PVIL A

Rockdale Aycock	53
Daingerfield Rhoads	51

PVIL AAA

Orange Wallace	49
Lufkin Dunbar	46

PVIL AAAA

Port Arthur Lincoln	76
Galveston Central	64

1955

B

Avoca	47
Dallardsville Big Sandy	41

A

Buna	58
Dickinson	49

AA

Seminole	50
San Marcos	49

AAA

Victoria	60
Beaumont French	51

AAAA

Dallas Crozier Tech	59
Waco	57

PVIL A

Palestine Green Bay	64
Daingerfield Rhoads	48

PVIL AAA

Victoria Goss	71
Odessa Blackshear	48

PVIL AAAA

Houston Wheatley	58
Houston Yates	45

1954

B

Cayuga	79
Dallardsville Big Sandy	54

A

Sweeny	92
Sundown	67

AA

Bowie	70
Houston Spring Branch	40

AAA

SA Alamo Heights	67
Galena Park	60

AAAA

Pampa	47
Dallas Crozier Tech	44

PVIL A

Palestine Green Bay	80
Tyler Stanton	48

PVIL AAA

Paris Gibbons	62
Odessa Blackshear	60

PVIL AAAA

Houston Wheatley	63
Beaumont Charlton	47

1953

B

Cayuga	66
Dallardsville Big Sandy	50

A

White Oak	69
Denver City	53

AA

Bowie	81
Dumas	44

AAA

Beaumont South Park	83
San Antonio Edison	54

AAAA

Pampa	61
Austin	47

PVIL A

Center Daniels	55
Palestine Green Bay	33

PVIL AAA

Lubbock Dunbar	67
Odessa Blackshear	55

PVIL AAAA

Houston Wheatley	62
Fort Worth Terrell	43

1952

B

Dallardsville Big Sandy	62
Laneville	41

A

Dimmitt	62
Plano	40

AA

Bowie	65
Levelland	59

AAA

SA Alamo Heights	49
Gladewater	45

AAAA

Fort Worth Polytechnic	56
Borger	51

Division I (4A vs. 3A)

SA Alamo Heights	54
Fort Worth Polytechnic	46

Division II (2A vs 1A)

Dimmitt	59
Bowie	54

PVIL A

West Columbia Brown	(winner)
Livingston Dunbar	
(No Score Available.)	

PVIL AAA

Houston Wheatley	56
Houston Washington	50

1951

B

Cayuga	44
Dallardsville Big Sandy	38

A

Bowie	54
Brenham	34

AA

Lubbock	44
Austin	43

City

Houston Lamar	78
SA Alamo Heights	52

PVIL A

Huntsville S. Houston	58
Atlanta Pruitt	56

PVIL AAAA

Houston Wheatley	61
Austin Anderson	51

1950

B

Gruver	43
Waelder	34

A

Canyon	49
South San Antonio	25

AA

Corpus Christi	40
Vernon	34

City

Houston Milby	40
Dallas Crozier Tech	39

PVIL A

West Columbia Brown	72
Hallsville Galilee	34

PVIL AAAA

Houston Wheatley	54
Houston Yates	47

1949

B

Martin's Mill	39
Dallardsville Big Sandy	33

A

Memphis	27
Beaumont French	25

AA

Texas City	30
Brownwood	28

City

Fort Worth Paschal	41
Houston Milby	40

PVIL A

Arp Industrial	59
Wharton	38

PVIL AAAA

Houston Yates (winner)	
San Antonio Wheatley	
(No Score Available.)	

1948

B

Maydelle	35
Johnson City	22

A

Mount Vernon	44
East Mountain	43

AA

Dallas Crozier Tech	29
Lufkin	28

PVIL A

West Columbia Brown	65
Hallsville Galilee	42

PVIL AAAA

Houston Wheatley	46
Dallas Lincoln	26

1947

B

Johnson City	16
Marfa	14

A

East Mountain	35
Bowie	22

AA

El Paso	27
San Antonio Jefferson	22

PVIL AAAA

Houston Yates	40
Beaumont Hebert	33

1946

B

Stratford	29
Perrin	18

A

Pasadena	50
Levelland	35

AA

Dallas Crozier Tech	32
Houston Jeff Davis	28

PVIL AAAA

UIL boys basketball championships

Houston Washington 40
Galveston Central 31
1945
B
Prairie Lea 35
Mount Enterprise 33
A
San Antonio Lanier 30
Quitman 24
AA
Fort Worth Paschal 43
Lufkin 29
PVIL AAAA
Houston Yates 42
Beaumont Hebert 16
1944
B
Prairie Lea 30
Blossom 26
A
Nocona 33
Mount Vernon 22
AA
Sunset 29
Childress 20
PVIL AAAA
Galveston Central 40
Dallas Lincoln 29
1943
B
Slidell 36
Sidney 23

A
San Antonio Lanier 30
Beaumont French 18
AA
Houston Jeff Davis 40
Austin 27
PVIL AAAA
Houston Yates 35
Beaumont Hebert 15
1942
B
Slidell 32
Fayetteville 22
A
Van 35
Nederland 27
AA
Houston Jeff Davis 55
Lufkin 35
PVIL AAAA
Houston Wheatley 31
Houston Yates 30
1941
El Paso 27
Abilene 20
PVIL AAAA
Dallas Washington 26
Houston Wheatley 25
1940
San Marcos 22
El Paso 21
PVIL AAAA

Houston Yates 32
Houston Wheatley 19
1939
Livingston 37
San Antonio Lanier 35
1938
Dallas Wilson 41
Abilene 27
1937
Carey 26
Gober 18
1936
Cushing 33
El Paso 29
1935
Denton 38
Lamesa 23
1934
Athens 28
Lamesa 22
1933
Athens 36
Houston Davis 20
1932
Temple 30
Houston San Jacinto 23
1931
Athens 25
Houston San Jacinto 22
1930
Denton 30

Estelline 11
1929
Athens 22
Denton 11
1928
Austin 33
Temple 13
(Austin disqualified.)
1927
Athens 23
Denton 14
1926
San Antonio
Brackenridge 29
Corsicana 23
1925
Beaumont 14
San Antonio 12
1924
Dallas Oak Cliff 29
El Paso 18
1923
Dallas Oak Cliff 17
El Paso 15
1922
Lindale 27
El Paso 15
(Lindale disqualified.)
1921
El Paso 25
San Antonio
Brackenridge 11

Girls High School Basketball Champions

Following are listed the champions by UIL division, along with the runner up, and the points scored by each team in the championship game. (OT refers to overtime.) *Sources: The University Interscholastic League at* www.uil.utexas. edu, *and* The Dallas Morning News.

2009
A Division I
Sudan 71
Roscoe 38
A Division II
Roby 44
Neches 34
AA
Brock 61
Woodville 32
AAA
Robinson 49
Argyle 33
AAAA
Waco Midway 50
Mansfield Timberview 27
AAAAA
Mansfield Summit 52
Houston Nimitz 43
2008
A Division I
Martin's Mill 48
Sudan 43
A Division II
Follett 71
Kennard 51
AA
Tuscola Jim Ned 65

Poth 49
AAA
Canyon 59
Kennedale 43
AAAA
Dallas Lincoln 50
Dickinson 47
AAAAA
Cypress-Fairbanks 50
DeSoto 33
2007
A Division I
Lindsay 43
Sundown 36
A Division II
Nazareth 61
Garden City 31
AA
(OT2)   Poth 72
Winnsboro 70
AAA
Canyon 53
Crockett 38
AAAA
Forth Worth Dunbar 62
Dickinson 51
AAAAA
(OT)   Rockwall 59
Cypress-Fairbanks 54

2006
A Division I
Martin's Mill 61
Elkhart Slocum 30
A Division II
Kennard 44
Springlake-Earth 26
AA
Argyle 51
Wall 33
AAA
China Spring 57
Wylie (Abilene) 54
AAAA
Waxahachie 52
Kerrville Tivy 48
AAAAA
Plano West 54
Rockwall 47
2005
A (Texas Cup)
Seagraves 56
Nazareth 51
AA
Brock 64
Canadian 30
AAA
Canyon 66

Cleveland 46
AAAA
Fort Worth Dunbar 56
Angleton 50
AAAAA
Arlington Bowie 69
Humble 62
2004
A (Texas Cup)
Archer City 59
Fayetteville 47
AA
Shallowater 44
Aubrey 37
AAA
Canyon 63
Winnsboro 33
AAAA
Dallas Lincoln 57
Plainview 35
AAAAA
Spring Westfield 66
Duncanville 49
2003
A (Texas Cup)
Priddy 66
La Poynor 63
AA

Brock 55
Shallowater 36
AAA
Canyon 76
Kountze 45
AAAA
Plainview 50
Dallas Lincoln 42
AAAAA
Duncanville 47
Georgetown 27

2002

A Division I
Brock 58
Larue La Poynor 26
A Division II
Nazareth 67
Dodd City 42
AA
Buffalo 48
Abernathy 43
AAA
Llano 67
Texarkana
Liberty-Eylau 51
AAAA
Plainview 68
Dallas Lincoln 40
AAAAA
Mansfield 47
San Antonio Taft 42

2001

A
Nazareth 61
Kennard 44
AA
Nacogdoches
Central Heights 57
Boyd 56
AAA
Winnsboro 51
Wylie (Abilene) 48
AAAA
Plainview 51
Dallas Lincoln 40
AAAAA
Mansfield 62
Spring Westfield 49

2000

A
Nazareth 72
Valley View 56
AA
Farwell 47
Brock 35
AAA
Winnsboro 54
Smithville 51
AAAA
Canyon 74
Waxahachie 54
AAAAA
Mansfield 69
Plano 43

1999

A
Vega 70
Valley View 64
AA
Hughes Springs 61
Salado 33

Rockwall shows their 5A championship trophy in 2007. Erich Schlegel photo.

AAA
Winnsboro 56
Lufkin Hudson 48
AAAA
Dallas Lincoln 52
Canyon 49
AAAAA
Mansfield 65
Corpus Christi Carroll 46

1998

A
Karnack 69
Nazareth 45
AA
Hamilton 54
Ozona 45
AAA
Comanche 65
Winnsboro 56
AAAA
Canyon Randall 52
Bay City 23
AAAAA
Alief Elsik 58
Amarillo Palo Duro 38

1997

A
Whiteface 59
Celeste 39
AA
Poth 54
Shallowater 50
AAA
Barbers Hill 66
Dripping Springs 45
AAAA

Levelland 36
Cedar Hill 33
AAAAA
Duncanville 44
Alief Elsik 33

1996

A
Nazareth 43
Celeste 30
AA
Ozona 45
Gunter 39
AAA
Groesbeck 63
Slaton 61
AAAA
Canyon 60
Cedar Hill 34
AAAAA
(OT2) Westlake (Austin) 64
Alief Elsik 60

1995

A
Sudan 66
Alvord 42
AA
Ozona 61
Cooper 47
AAA
Bowie 65
Dripping Springs 50
AAAA
Cleburne 55
Silsbee 50
AAAAA
(OT) Westlake (Austin) 59

Duncanville 56

1994

A
Sudan 40
Jayton 36
AA
Tuscola Jim Ned 31
Hemphill 29
AAA
Dripping Springs 64
Waco La Vega 56
AAAA
Waco Midway 52
Dallas Lincoln 40
AAAAA
Amarillo 62
Conroe 46

1993

A
Celeste 63
Muenster 38
AA
Marion 69
Hamilton 63
AAA
Dimmitt 59
Dripping Springs 51
AAAA
Westlake (Austin) 48
Levelland 40
AAAAA
Amarillo 68
Corpus Christi King 65

1992

A
Celeste 70

UIL girls basketball championships

	Brock	57
AA		
	Panhandle	52
	Marion	49
AAA		
	Canyon	49
	Winnsboro	29
AAAA		
	Canyon Randall	43
	Georgetown	42
AAAAA		
	San Marcos	45
	Duncanville	43
1991		
A		
	Nazareth	50
	Moulton	30
AA		
	Abernathy	37
	Honey Grove	32
AAA		
	Tulia	58
	Winnsboro	39
AAAA		
	Levelland	51
	Lincoln	30
AAAAA		
	Amarillo Tascosa	54
	Victoria	41
1990		
A		
	Nazareth	53
	Moulton	34
AA		
	Tatum	61
	Marion	50
AAA		
	Wylie (Abilene)	51
	Edna	37
AAAA		
	Corpus Chrisit Calallen	46
	Waco Midway	39
AAAAA		
	Duncanville	74
	Houston Yates	51
1989		
A		
	Nazareth	57
	La Poynor	33
AA		
	Grapeland	54
	Abernathy	47
AAA		
	Hardin-Jefferson	46
	Canyon	44
AAAA		
	Levelland	45
	West Orange-Stark	24
AAAAA		
	Duncanville	42
	Victoria	38
1988		
A		
	Nazareth	64
	La Poynor	28
AA		
	Godley	60
	Grapeland	58
AAA		

	Brownfield	49
	Hardin-Jefferson	40
AAAA		
	Levelland	38
	Corpus Christi Calallen	35
AAAAA		
	Duncanville	60
	North Mesquite	46
1987		
A		
	Sudan	55
	Moulton	26
AA		
	Morton	68
	Paris	53
AAA		
	Slaton	43
	Sweeny	40
AAAA		
	Levelland	41
	Corpus Christi Calallen	30
AAAAA		
	Plainview	59
	Austin Lanier	47
1986		
A		
	Snook	36
	Nazareth	33
AA		
	Abernathy	51
	Rogers	42
AAA		
	Hardin-Jefferson	72
	Ingleside	53
AAAA		
	Levelland	44
	A&M Consolidated	43
AAAAA		
	Victoria	57
	Tyler Lee	44
1985		
A		
	Nazareth	56
	Priddy	48
AA		
	Troy	80
	Abernathy	72
AAA		
	Vernon	52
	Sweeny	51
AAAA		
	Waco Richfield	44
	Sweetwater	35
AAAAA		
	Dallas South Oak Cliff	60
	Victoria	46
1984		
A		
	Nazareth	64
	Petty West Lamar	32
AA		
	Pollock Central	37
	Hale Center	36
AAA		
	Abernathy	67
	Groesbeck	57
AAAA		
	Waco Richfield	56
	Levelland	43

AAAAA		
	Longview	72
	Houston Yates	52
1983		
A		
	Sudan	46
	La Poynor	34
AA		
	Hardin	41
	Hale Center	39
AAA		
	Barbers Hill	86
	Sweeny	81
AAAA		
	Levelland	41
	Corpus Christi Calallen	28
AAAAA		
	Houston Yates	58
	Victoria	56
1982		
A		
	Nazareth	64
	Dime Box	37
AA		
	Hardin	69
	Phillips	61
AAA		
	Barbers Hill	68
	Sweeny	53
AAAA		
	Del Valle (Austin)	76
	Carthage	64
AAAAA		
	Victoria	46
	Dallas South Oak Cliff	45
1981		
A		
	Nazareth	84
	Colmesneil	39
AA		
	Hardin	61
	New Deal	46
AAA		
	Abernathy	61
	Sweeny	59
AAAA		
	Canyon	64
	Bay City	53
AAAAA		
	Lubbock Monterey	71
	Duncanville	70
1980		
B		
	Nazareth	56
	Brock	50
A		
	Bogata Rivercrest	68
	Panhandle	41
AA		
	Slaton	75
	Kyle Hays	44
AAA		
	Duman	53
	Flour Bluff (Corpus Christi)	43
AAAA		
	Dallas South Oak Cliff	74
	Lubbock Monterey	49
1979		

B		
	Nazareth	46
	Brock	43
A		
	Hale Center	46
	Bogata Rivercrest	29
AA		
	Slaton	68
	Pflugerville	54
AAA		
	Georgetown	41
	Sweeny	49
AAAA		
	Victoria	43
	Dallas South Oak Cliff	41
1978		
B		
	Nazareth	47
	Graford	39
A		
	Robert Lee	44
	Cushing	41
AA		
	Slaton	55
	Granbury	45
AAA		
	Canyon	59
	Corpus Christi Tuloso Midway	37
AAAA		
	Dallas South Oak Cliff	70
	Victoria	62
1977		
B		
	Nazareth	73
	May	54
A		
	Cooper	85
	Deweyville	69
AA		
	Spearman	61
	Waco Robinson	58
AAA		
	Canyon	58
	Waco Midway	54
AAAA		
	Dallas South Oak Cliff	79
	Schertz Clemens	65
1976		
B		
	Neches	53
	Crawford	49
A		
	Stratford	60
	Archer City	57
AA		
	Phillips	83
	Bellville	69
AAA		
	Waco Midway	64
	Canyon	59
AAAA		
	Duncanville	70
	Victoria	69
1975		
B		
	Crawford	45
	Neches	44
A		

UIL girls basketball championships

Southlake Carroll 50
Vega 48

AA
George West 52
Bellville 51

AAA
Waco Midway 60
Canyon 52
1974

B
Poolville 60
Lamesa Klondike 54

A
Grandview 52
Shiner 36

AA
Slaton 51
Comanche 45

AAA
Canyon 65
Conroe 41
1973

B
Neches 49
Poolville 45

A
Grandview 39
Turkey Valley 37

AA
Waco Midway 65
Comanche 46

AAA
Angleton 57
Canyon 55
1972

B
Round Top-Carmine 54
Huckabay 48

A
Claude 57
Southlake Carroll 55

AA
Spearman 50
Waco Robinson 49

AAA
Canyon 59
Rockdale 36
1971

B
Round Top-Carmine 48
Grandview 33

A
Claude 46
Glen Rose 33

AA
Spearman 52
Buna 47

AAA
Victoria 55
Canyon 51
1970

B
Follett 59
Trent 50

A
Wylie (Abilene) 80
Grandview 57

AA
Waco Robinson 57

Spearman 49

AAA
Corpus Christi
Tuloso Midway 66
Canyon 54
1969

B
Lamesa Klondike 62
High Island 48

A
Stratford 42
Deweyville 37

AA
Waco Midway 66
Spearman 55

AAA
Canyon 59
Angleton 42
1968

B
High Island 53
Lamesa Klondike 40

A
Springlake-Earth 75
George West 65

AA
Bogata Rivercrest 56
Gregory-Portland 54

AAA
Stephenville 39
West Orange 27
1967

B
High Island 48
Quitaque 39

A
Springlake-Earth 105
Cross Plains 52

AA
Little Cypress
(Orange) 52
Spearman 43

AAA
Tulia 70
Victoria 57
1966

B
Round Top-Carmine 57
Deport 32

A
Jourdanton 79
Springlake-Earth 74

AA
Spearman 50
Little Cypress
(Orange) 46

AAA
Tulia 76
Victoria 75
1965

B
Trent 69
Round Top-Carmine 65

A
Lubbock Roosevelt 77
Jourdanton 71

AA
Edna 60
Friona 57

AAA
Victoria 63
Weslaco 46
1964

B
Trent 76
Burkeville 27

A
Baird 85
Jourdanton 68

AA
Friona 50
Clear Creek 45
1963

B
Slidell 71
Wells 65

A
Sundown 51
Moulton 48

AA
West 49
Little Cypress (Orange) 42
1962

B
Claude 55
Wells 41

A
Sundown 51
Ladonia
Fannindel 46

AA
Devine 38
Tulia 37
1961

B
Henrietta Midway 54
Claude 48

A
Sundown 50
Moulton 46

AA
Buna 66
Spearman 47
1960

B
North Hopkins
(Sulphur Springs) 42
Claude 38

A
Cooper 60
Moulton 51

AA
Buna 66
Friona 63
1959

B
North Hopkins 64
Bovina 47

A
Pollok Central 58
Sudan 57

AA
Abernathy 59
Buna 57
1958

B
North Hopkins
(Sulphur Springs) 86

Collinsville 28

A
Cooper 59
Moulton 53

AA
Abernathy 64
Fort Worth Brewer 53
1957

B
Lubbock
Roosevelt 56
Hawley 40

A
Ropesville 64
Cooper 51

AA
Buna 69
Seagoville 31
1956

B
Collinsville 83
North Hopkins
(Sulphur Springs) 75

A
Buna 54
New Deal 44

AA
Angleton 51
Seagoville 48
1955

B
Waco Midway 58
Cotton Center 50

A
Dimmitt 62
Granbury 44

AA
Bowie 54
Angleton 52
1954

B
Winnie East Chambers 46
Claude 45

A
Dimmitt 66
Granbury 60
1953

B
New Deal 58
Whitesboro 44

A
Claude 40
Bryson 30
1952

B
Claude 47
Duncanville 42

A
Hamilton 27
Morton 19
1951

B
Claude 42
Clyde
Denton Valley 40

A
Comanche 50
McLean 49

Counties

The Anderson County Courthouse in Palestine. Robert Plocheck photo.

History

Maps

Vital Statistics

Recreation

Population

Cities and Towns

Climate

Counties of Texas

These pages describe Texas' 254 counties and hundreds of towns. Descriptions are based on reports from chambers of commerce, the Texas Cooperative Extension, federal and state agencies, the *New Handbook of Texas* and other sources. Consult the index for other county information.

County maps are based on those of the Texas Department of Transportation and are copyrighted, 2009, as are the entire contents.

Physical Features: Descriptions are from U.S. Geological Survey and local sources.

Economy: From information provided by local chambers of commerce and county extension agents.

History: From Texas statutes, *Fulmore's History and Geography of Texas as Told in County Names*, WPA Historical Records Survey, Texas Centennial Commission Report and the *New Handbook of Texas*.

Ethnicity: Percentage estimates of 2007 from the Texas State Data Center, University of Texas at San Antonio. **Anglo** refers to non-Hispanic whites; **Black** refers to non-Hispanic blacks; **Hispanic** refers to Hispanics of all races; **Other** is composed of persons from all other racial groups who are non-Hispanic.

Vital Statistics, 2006: From the Texas Department of State Health Services Annual Report 2006, except for births, which are from 2004.

Recreation: From information provided by local chambers of commerce and county extension agents. Attempts were made to note activities unique to the area or that point to ethnic or cultural heritage.

Minerals: From county extension agents.

Agriculture: Condensed from information provided to the Texas Almanac by county extension agents in 2006. Market value (total cash receipts) of agricultural products sold is from the **2007 Census of Agriculture** of the U.S. Department of Agriculture for that year.

Cities: The county seat, incorporated cities and towns with post offices are listed. Population figures for incorporated towns are estimates from the State Data Center published Jan. 1, 2008. Population estimates for other towns are from local officials. (NA) means a population estimate was not available. When figures for a small part of a city are given, such as **part [45,155] of Dallas** in Collin County, they are from the 2000 U.S. census because more recent estimates are not available.

Sources of DATA LISTS

Population (of county): The county population estimate as of July 1, 2008, U.S. Census Bureau. The line following gives the percentage of increase or decrease from the 2000 U.S. census count.

Area: Total area in square miles, including water surfaces, as determined in the 2000 U.S. census.

Land Area: The land area in square miles as determined by the U.S. Census Bureau in 2000.

Altitude (ft.): Principally from U.S. Geological Survey topographic maps, including **revisions available in 2008**. Not all of the surface of Texas has been precisely surveyed for elevation; in some cases data are from the Texas Railroad Commission or the Texas Department of Transportation.

Climate: Provided by the National Oceanic and Atmospheric Administration state climatologist, College Station. Data are revised at 10-year intervals to cover the previous three decades. Listed are the latest compilations, as of Jan. 1, 2003, and pertain to a particular site within the county (usually the county seat). The data include: **Rainfall** (annual mean in inches); **Temperature** (in degrees Fahrenheit); January mean minimum and July mean maximum.

Workforce/Wages: Prepared by the Texas Workforce Commission, Austin, in cooperation with the Bureau of Labor Statistics of the U.S. Department of Labor. The data are computed from reports by all establishments subject to the Texas Unemployment Compensation Act.

(Agricultural employers are subject to the act if they employ as many as three workers for 20 weeks or pay cash wages of $6,250 in a quarter. Employers who pay $1,000 in wages in a quarter for domestic services are subject also. Still not mandatorily covered are self-employed, unpaid family workers, and those employed by churches and some small nonprofit organizations.)

The work/wage data include (state total, lowest county and highest county included here):

Civilian labor force as of December 2008. Texas, 11,833,270; Loving County, 45; Harris County, 1,987,913.

Unemployed: The unemployment rate (percentage of workforce) as of December 2008. Texas, 5.7; Reagan Counties,1.9; Starr County, 15.2.

Total Wages paid in the third quarter of 2008. Texas, $115,295,781,275; Loving County $762,359; Harris County, $28,120,465,067.

Average Weekly Wage as of the third quarter of 2008. Texas, $851; Kent County, $397; Carson County, $1,338.

Property Values: Appraised gross market value of real and personal property in each county appraisal district in 2007 as reported to the State Property Tax Board.

Retail Sales: Figures for 2007 as reported to the state Comptroller of Public Accounts.

Anderson County

Physical Features: Forested, hilly East Texas county, slopes to Trinity and Neches rivers; sandy, clay, black soils; pines, hardwoods.

Economy: Manufacturing, distribution, agribusiness, tourism; hunting and fishing leases; prison units.

History: Comanche, Waco, other tribes. Anglo-American settlers arrived in 1830s. Antebellum slaveholding area. County created from Houston County in 1846; named for K.L. Anderson, last vice president of the Republic of Texas.

Race/Ethnicity, 2007: (In percent) Anglo, 61.8; Black, 23.1; Hispanic, 14.2; Other, 0.9.

Vital Statistics, 2006: Births, 670; deaths, 594; marriages, 404; divorces, 159.

Recreation: Fishing, hunting, streams, lakes; dogwood trails; historic sites; railroad park; museums.

Minerals: Oil and gas.

Agriculture: Cattle, hay, truck vegetables, melons, pecans, peaches. Market value $39.4 million. Timber sold.

PALESTINE (17,882), county seat; clothing, metal, wood products; transportation and agribusiness center; scientific balloon station; historic bakery; library; vocational-technical facilities; hospitals; community college; dulcimer festival in March, hot pepper festival in October.

Other towns include: **Cayuga** (137); **Elkhart** (1,332); **Frankston** (1,251), tourism, packaging industry, oil and gas, commuters to Tyler; depot museum, Square Fair in October; **Montalba** (110); **Neches** (175); and **Tennessee Colony** (300) site of state prisons.

Population	56,838
Change fm 2000	3.1
Area (sq. mi.)	1,077.95
Land Area (sq. mi.)	1,070.79
Altitude (ft.)	174-773
Rainfall (in.)	46.38
Jan. mean min.	37.4
July mean max.	93.9
Civ. Labor	20,693
Unemployed	6.2
Wages	$162,495,645
Av. Weekly Wage	$693
Prop. Value	$2,615,483,021
Retail Sales	$3,070,306,614

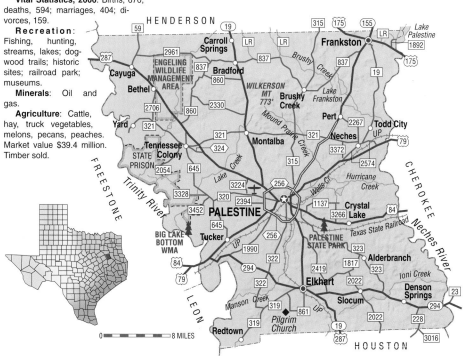

Railroad Abbreviations

AAT	Austin Area Terminal Railroad
AGC	Alamo Gulf Coast Railway
ATK	AMTRAK
ANR	Angelina & Neches River Railroad
ATCX	Austin & Texas Central Railroad
BLR	Blacklands Railroad
BNSF	BNSF Railroad
BOP	Border Pacific Railroad
BRG	Brownsville & Rio Grande Int'l Railway
CMC	CMC Railroad
DART	Dallas Area Rapid Transit
DGNO	Dallas, Garland & Northeastern Railroad
FWWR	Fort Worth & Western Railroad/Tarantula
GCSR	Gulf, Colorado & San Saba RailwayCorp.
GRR	Georgetown Railroad
GVSR	Galveston Railroad
KCS	Kansas City Southern Railway
KRR	Kiamichi Railroad Company
MCSA	Moscow, Camden & San Augustine RR
PCN	Point Comfort & Northern Railway
PNR	Panhandle Northern Railroad Company
PTRA	Port Terminal Railroad Association
PVS	Pecos Valley Southern Railway
RSS	Rockdale, Sandow & Southern Railroad
RVSC	Rio Valley Switching
SAW	South Plains Switching LTD
SRN	Sabine River & Northern Railroad Company
SSC	Southern Switching (Lone Star Railroad)
SW	Southwestern Shortline Railroad
TCT	Texas City Terminal Railway
TIBR	Timber Rock Railroad
TM	The Texas Mexican Railway Company
TN	Texas & Northern Railway
TNER	Texas Northeastern Railroad
TNMR	Texas & New Mexico Railroad
TNW	Texas North Western Railway
TP	Texas Pacifico Transportation
TSE	Texas South-Eastern Railroad Company
TXGN	Texas, Gonzales & Northern Railway
TXR	Texas Rock Crusher Railway
TSSR	Texas State Railroad
UP	Union Pacific Railroad Company
WTJR	Wichita, Tillman & Jackson Railway
WTLR	West Texas & Lubbock Railroad

Andrews County

Population **13,645**
Change fm 2000 .... 4.9
Area (sq. mi.) 1,500.99
Land Area (sq. mi.) 1,500.64
Altitude (ft.) 2,862-3,570
Rainfall (in.) 15.15
Jan. mean min. 30.4
July mean max. 94.5
Civ. Labor 7,222
Unemployed 3.3
Wages $61,318,439
Av. Weekly Wage $867
Prop. Value $3,664,531,109
Retail Sales $130,350,432

Physical Features: South Plains, drain to playas; grass, mesquite, shin oak; red clay, sandy soils.

Economy: Natural resources/mining; manufacturing; trade, construction; government/services; agribusiness.

History: Apache, Comanche area until U.S. Army campaigns of 1875. Ranching developed around 1900. Oil boom in 1940s. County created 1876 from Bexar Territory; organized 1910; named for Texas Revolutionary soldier Richard Andrews.

Race/Ethnicity, 2007: (In percent) Anglo, 51.7; Black, 1.8; Hispanic, 45.1; Other, 1.4.

Vital Statistics, 2006: Births, 211; deaths, 124; marriages, 107; divorces, 82.

Recreation: Prairie dog town, wetlands, bird viewing; museum; camper facilities; Fall Fiesta in September.

Minerals: Oil and gas.

Agriculture: Beef, cotton, sorghums, grains, corn, hay; significant irrigation. Market value $15.9 million.

ANDREWS (9,845) county seat; trade center, amphitheatre, hospital.

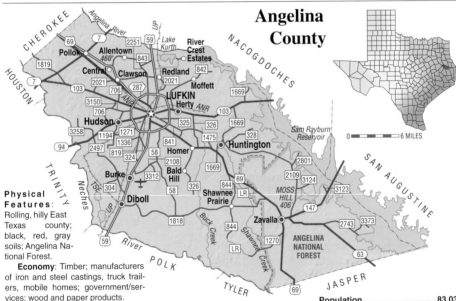

Angelina County

Physical Features: Rolling, hilly East Texas county; black, red, gray soils; Angelina National Forest.

Economy: Timber; manufacturers of iron and steel castings, truck trailers, mobile homes; government/services; wood and paper products.

History: Caddoan area. First land deed to Vicente Micheli 1801. Anglo-American setters arrived in 1820s. County created 1846 from Nacogdoches County; named for legendary Indian maiden Angelina.

Race/Ethnicity, 2007: (In percent) Anglo, 64.4; Black, 14.4; Hispanic, 20.0; Other, 1.2.

Vital Statistics, 2006: Births, 1,296; deaths, 783; marriages, 772; divorces, 421.

Recreation: Sam Rayburn Reservoir; national, state forests, parks; locomotive exhibit; Forest Festival, bike ride in fall.

Minerals: Limited output of natural gas and oil.

Agriculture: Poultry, beef, horticulture, limited fruits and vegetables. Market value $29.4 million. A leading timber-producing county.

LUFKIN (33,803) county seat; manufacturing; Angelina College; hospitals; U.S., Texas Forest centers; zoo; Expo Center and Texas Forestry Museum.

Other towns include: **Burke** (313); **Diboll** (5,882); **Hudson** (4,381); **Huntington** (2,141); **Pollok** (300); **Zavalla** (659).

Population **83,038**
Change from 2000 .... 3.6
Area (sq. mi.) 864.45
Land Area (sq. mi.) 801.56
Altitude (ft.) 102-460
Rainfall (in.) 46.62
Jan. mean min. 37.9
July mean max. 93.5
Civ. Labor 41,300
Unemployed 5.3
Wages $808,994,810
Av. Weekly Wage $637
Prop. Value $3,466,582,584
Retail Sales $1,274,609,008

For explanation of sources, abbreviations and symbols, see p. 210 and foldout map.

Aransas County

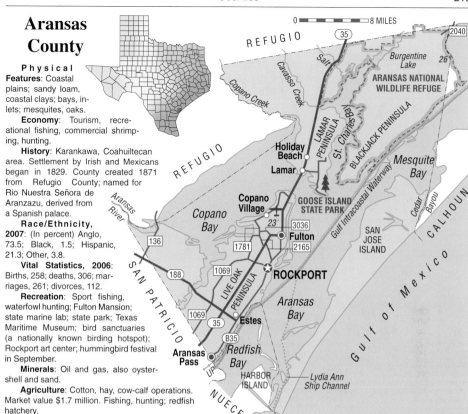

Physical Features: Coastal plains; sandy loam, coastal clays; bays, inlets; mesquites, oaks.

Economy: Tourism, recreational fishing, commercial shrimping, hunting.

History: Karankawa, Coahuiltecan area. Settlement by Irish and Mexicans began in 1829. County created 1871 from Refugio County; named for Rio Nuestra Señora de Aranzazu, derived from a Spanish palace.

Race/Ethnicity, 2007: (In percent) Anglo, 73.5; Black, 1.5; Hispanic, 21.3; Other, 3.8.

Vital Statistics, 2006: Births, 258; deaths, 306; marriages, 261; divorces, 112.

Recreation: Sport fishing, waterfowl hunting; Fulton Mansion; state marine lab; state park; Texas Maritime Museum; bird sanctuaries (a nationally known birding hotspot); Rockport art center; hummingbird festival in September.

Minerals: Oil and gas, also oystershell and sand.

Agriculture: Cotton, hay, cow-calf operations. Market value $1.7 million. Fishing, hunting; redfish hatchery.

ROCKPORT (9,141) county seat; tourism, commercial oyster and shrimp harvesting, sport fishing; commuting to Corpus Christi and Victoria, retirement residences; Festival of Wines in May.

Fulton (1,728) tourism, oyster and shrimp harvesting, Oysterfest in March.

Part [867] of **Aransas Pass**.

Population	**24,900**
Change fm 2000	10.7
Area (sq. mi.)	527.95
Land Area (sq. mi.)	251.86
Altitude (ft.)	sea level-26
Rainfall (in.)	35.96
Jan. mean min.	44.9
July mean max.	90.1
Civ. Labor	11,185
Unemployed	5.4
Wages	$42,360,765
Av. Weekly Wage	$543
Prop. Value	$2,767,704,163
Retail Sales	$225,205,900

Waterfowl and boats at Rockport-Fulton. Robert Plocheck photo.

Archer County

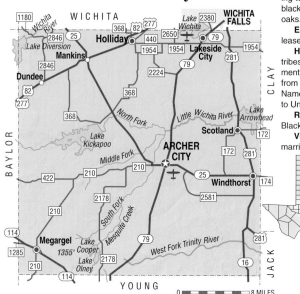

Population	9,119
Change fm 2000	3.0
Area (sq. mi.)	925.78
Land Area (sq. mi.)	909.70
Altitude (ft.)	900-1,355
Rainfall (in.)	29.78
Jan. mean min.	26.7
July mean max.	97.0
Civ. Labor	5,507
Unemployed	4.4
Wages	$17,373,278
Av. Weekly Wage	$612
Prop. Value	$559,127,893
Retail Sales	$71,313,345

Physical Features: Northwestern county, rolling to hilly, drained by Wichita, Trinity River forks; black, red loams, sandy soils; mesquites, post oaks.

Economy: Cattle, milk production, oil, hunting leases. Part of Wichita Falls metropolitan area.

History: Caddo, Comanche, Kiowas and other tribes in area until 1875; Anglo-American settlement developed soon afterward. County created from Fannin Land District, 1858; organized 1880. Named for Dr. B.T. Archer, Republic commissioner to United States.

Race/Ethnicity, 2007: (In percent) Anglo, 93.0; Black, 0.1; Hispanic, 6.1; Other, 0.7.

Vital Statistics, 2006: Births, 120; deaths, 73; marriages, 38; divorces, 32.

Recreation: Hunting of deer, turkey, dove, feral hog, coyote; fishing in area lakes, rodeo in June.

Minerals: Oil and natural gas.

Agriculture: Cow/calf, stocker cattle, dairy, wheat, hay, silage and horses. Market value $61 million.

ARCHER CITY (1,846) county seat; cattle, oil field service center; museum; book center; Royal Theatre productions; some manufacturing.

Other towns include: **Holliday** (1,739) Mayfest in spring; **Lakeside City** (1,022); **Megargel** (247); **Scotland** (440); **Windthorst** (477), biannual German sausage festival (also in Scotland).

Armstrong County

Physical Features: Partly on High Plains, broken by Palo Duro Canyon. Chocolate loam, gray soils.

Economy: Agribusiness, tourism, commuting to Amarillo.

History: Apache, then Comanche territory until U.S. Army campaigns of 1874-75. Anglo-Americans began ranching soon afterward. County created from Bexar District, 1876; organized 1890; name honors pioneer Texas family.

Race/Ethnicity, 2007: (In percent) Anglo, 93.4; Black, 0.2; Hispanic, 6.0; Other, 0.4.

Vital Statistics, 2006: Births, 24; deaths, 25; marriages, 11; divorces, 1.

Recreation: State park; Goodnight Ranch Home.

Minerals: Sand, gravel.

Agriculture: Stocker cattle, cow-calf operations; wheat, sorghum, cotton and hay; some irrigation. Market value $37.4 million.

CLAUDE (1,353) county seat; farm, ranch supplies; glass company; medical center; Caprock Roundup in July.

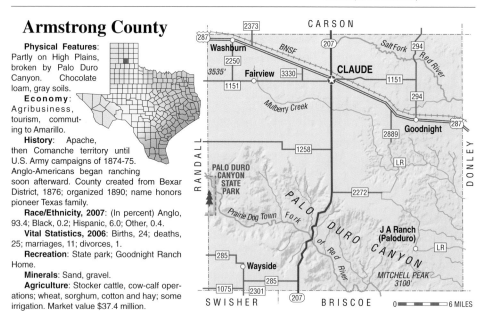

For explanation of sources, abbreviations and symbols, see p. 210 and foldout map.

Population	2,123
Change fm 2000	-1.2
Area (sq. mi.)	913.81
Land Area (sq. mi.)	913.63
Altitude (ft.)	2,300-3,535
Rainfall (in.)	22.39
Jan. mean min.	21.2
July mean max.	90.5
Civ. Labor	1,103
Unemployed	4.0
Wages	$3,218,072
Av. Weekly Wage	$653
Prop. Value	$129,589,910
Retail Sales	$4,430,344

Atascosa County

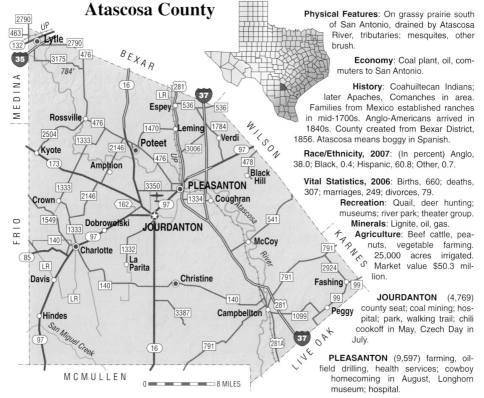

Physical Features: On grassy prairie south of San Antonio, drained by Atascosa River, tributaries; mesquites, other brush.

Economy: Coal plant, oil, commuters to San Antonio.

History: Coahuiltecan Indians; later Apaches, Comanches in area. Families from Mexico established ranches in mid-1700s. Anglo-Americans arrived in 1840s. County created from Bexar District, 1856. Atascosa means boggy in Spanish.

Race/Ethnicity, 2007: (In percent) Anglo, 38.0; Black, 0.4; Hispanic, 60.8; Other, 0.7.

Vital Statistics, 2006: Births, 660; deaths, 307; marriages, 249; divorces, 79.

Recreation: Quail, deer hunting; museums; river park; theater group.

Minerals: Lignite, oil, gas.

Agriculture: Beef cattle, peanuts, vegetable farming. 25,000 acres irrigated. Market value $50.3 million.

JOURDANTON (4,769) county seat; coal mining; hospital; park, walking trail; chili cookoff in May, Czech Day in July.

PLEASANTON (9,597) farming, oilfield drilling, health services; cowboy homecoming in August, Longhorn museum; hospital.

Other towns include: **Campbellton** (350); **Charlotte** (1,774); **Christine** (480); **Leming** (268); **Lytle** (2,815) greenhouse, peanuts processed; **Peggy** (22); **Poteet** (3,537) strawberry "capital," festival in April.

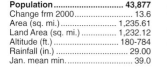

Population	43,877
Change frm 2000	13.6
Area (sq. mi.)	1,235.61
Land Area (sq. mi.)	1,232.12
Altitude (ft.)	180-784
Rainfall (in.)	29.00
Jan. mean min.	39.0
July mean max.	95.9
Civ. Labor	19,797
Unemployed	5.0
Wages	$76,895,573
Av. Weekly Wage	$620
Prop. Value	$1,862,504,273
Retail Sales	$378,264,831

Palo Duro Canyon stretches across Armstrong, Randall and Briscoe counties. Robert Plocheck photo.

Austin County

Physical Features: Level to hilly, drained by San Bernard, Brazos rivers; black prairie to sandy upland soils.

Economy: Agribusiness; tourism, government/services; metal, other manufacturing; commuting to Houston.

History: Tonkawa Indians; reduced by diseases. Birthplace of Anglo-American colonization, 1821, and German mother colony at Industry, 1831. County created 1837; named for Stephen F. Austin, father of Texas.

Race/Ethnicity, 2007: (In percent) Anglo, 68.7; Black, 10.8; Hispanic, 19.8; Other, 0.7.

Vital Statistics, 2006: Births, 344; deaths, 262; marriages, 190; divorces, 106.

Recreation: Fishing, hunting; state park, Pioneer Trail; Bellville Country Livin' festival in April; Lone Star Raceway Park.

Minerals: Oil and natural gas.

Agriculture: Beef production and hay. Also rice, corn, sorghum, nursery crops, grapes, pecans. Market value $30.9 million.

BELLVILLE (4,628) county seat; varied manufacturing; hospital; oil.

SEALY (6,841) oil-field and military vehicle manufacturing, varied industries; Blinn College branch; polka fest in March.

Other towns include: **Bleiblerville** (125); **Brazos Country** (291); **Cat Spring** (200); **Frydek** (900) Grotto celebration in April; **Industry** (368); **Kenney** (957); **New Ulm** (974) retail, art festival in April; **San Felipe** (966) colonial capital of Texas; **Wallis** (1,377).

Population	**26,851**
Change fm 2000	13.8
Area (sq. mi.)	656.37
Land Area (sq. mi.)	652.59
Altitude (ft.)	70-463
Rainfall (in.)	40.68
Jan. mean min.	40.7
July mean max.	94.9
Civ. Labor	13,452
Unemployed	4.7
Wages	$127,627,704
Av. Weekly Wage	$805
Prop. Value	$2,424,894,659
Retail Sales	$2,254,058,999

Bailey County

Physical Features: High Plains county, sandy loam soils; mesquite brush; drains to draws forming upper watershed of Brazos River, playas.

Economy: Farm supply manufacturing; electric generating plant; food-processing plants.

History: Settlement began after 1900. County created from Bexar District 1876, organized 1917. Named for Alamo hero Peter J. Bailey.

Race/Ethnicity, 2007: (In percent) Anglo, 45.5; Black, 1.3; Hispanic, 52.7; Other, 0.5.

Vital Statistics, 2006: Births, 128; deaths, 64; marriages, 64; divorces, 13.

Recreation: Muleshoe National Wildlife Refuge; "Old Pete," the national mule memorial; historical building park; museum; motorcycle rally; mule deer, sandhill crane, pheasant hunting.

Minerals: Insignificant.

Agriculture: Feedlot, dairy cattle; cotton, wheat, sorghum, corn, vegetables; 100,000 acres irrigated. Market value $234 million.

MULESHOE (4,502) county seat; agribusiness center; feed-corn milling; hospital; livestock show.

Other towns include: **Enochs** (80); **Maple** (75).

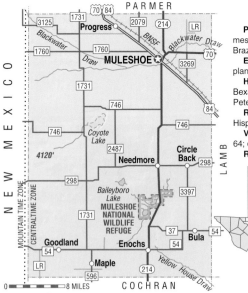

Population	**6,279**
Change fm 2000	–4.8
Area (sq. mi.)	827.38
Land Area (sq. mi.)	826.69
Altitude (ft.)	3,660-4,120
Rainfall (in.)	17.37
Jan. mean min.	20.2
July mean max.	91.9
Civ. Labor	3,434
Unemployed	4.8
Wages	$20,104,359
Av. Weekly Wage	$564
Prop. Value	$358,987,215
Retail Sales	$48,453,373

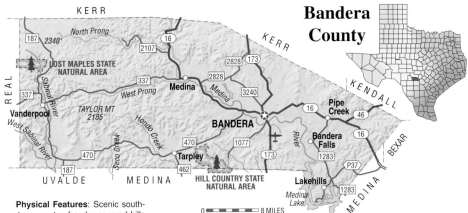

Bandera County

Physical Features: Scenic southwestern county of cedar-covered hills on the Edwards Plateau; Medina, Sabinal Rivers; limestone, sandy soils; species of oaks, walnuts, native cherry and Uvalde maple.

Economy: Tourism, hunting, fishing, ranching supplies, forest products.

History: Apache, then Comanche territory. White settlement began in early 1850s, including Mormons and Poles. County created from Bexar, Uvalde counties, 1856; named for Bandera (flag) Mountains.

Race/Ethnicity, 2007: (In percent) Anglo, 85.4; Black, 0.3; Hispanic, 13.4; Other, 0.9.

Vital Statistics, 2006: Births, 194; deaths, 180; marriages, 128; divorces, 111.

Recreation: RV parks, resort ranches; Lost Maples and Hill Country State Natural Areas; rodeo on Memorial Day weekend; Medina Lake.

Agriculture: Beef cattle, sheep, goats, horses, apples. Market value $7 million. Hunting and nature tourism important.

BANDERA (1,197) county seat; "cowboy capital of the world"; tourism, ranching, furniture making; Frontier Times Museum.

Other towns include: **Medina** (850) apple growing; **Pipe Creek** (130); **Tarpley** (30); **Vanderpool** (20). Also, the community of **Lakehills** (5,412) on Medina Lake, Cajun Fest in September.

Population	20,303
Change fm 2000	15.1
Area (sq. mi.)	797.54
Land Area (sq. mi.)	791.73
Altitude (ft.)	1,064-2,340
Rainfall (in.)	35.78
Jan. mean min.	33.3
July mean max.	93.9
Civ. Labor	10,097
Unemployed	5.0
Wages	$19,609,080
Av. Weekly Wage	$470
Prop. Value	$1,511,408,122
Retail Sales	$93,079,024

For explanation of sources, abbreviations and symbols, see p. 210 and foldout map.

A cypress-lined creek at the Bandera–Kerr county line along Texas 16. Robert Plocheck photo.

Physical Features: Rolling; alluvial, sandy, loam soils; varied timber, Lost Pines; bisected by Colorado River.

Economy: Government/services; tourism; agribusiness; bio-technology research; computer-related industries; commuters to Austin.

History: Tonkawa Indian area; Comanches also present. Spanish fort established 1804. County created 1836; named for Baron de Bastrop, who aided Moses and Stephen F. Austin in establishing colony in 1820s.

Race/Ethnicity, 2007: (In percent) Anglo, 61.9; Black, 7.9; Hispanic, 29.2; Other, 1.0.

Vital Statistics, 2006: Births, 871; deaths, 501; marriages, 394; divorces, 251.

Recreation: Fishing, hunting; state parks; Lake Bastrop; historic sites; museum; railroad park; natural science center; nature trails.

Minerals: Clay, oil, gas and lignite.

Agriculture: Hay, beef cattle, horses, goats, pecans. Market value $38.2 million. Pine for lumber, oak for firewood.

BASTROP (8,359) county seat; government/services, tourism, hospitals, University of Texas cancer research center, federal prison; riverwalk; River of Lights in December.

Elgin (9,133) sausage plants, brick plant; horse, cattle breeding; medical research; library; Western Days in June, Hogeye festival in October.

Smithville (4,953) government/services, railroad; environmental science park; hospital; model recycling center; jamboree on weekend after Easter.

Other towns: **Cedar Creek** (145); **Circle D-KC Estates** (2,220); **McDade** (345) watermelon festival in July; **Paige** (275); **Red Rock** (40); **Rosanky** (210) automotive museum; **Wyldwood** (2,623). Also, **Camp Swift** (5,353).

Population	**73,491**
Change fm 2000	27.3
Area (sq. mi.)	895.92
Land Area (sq. mi.)	888.35
Altitude (ft.)	300-729
Rainfall (in.)	38.04
Jan. mean min.	36.7
July mean max.	95.4
Civ. Labor	35,973
Unemployed	5.7
Wages	$111,520,631
Av. Weekly Wage	$620
Prop. Value	$4,078,784,650
Retail Sales	$765,090,506

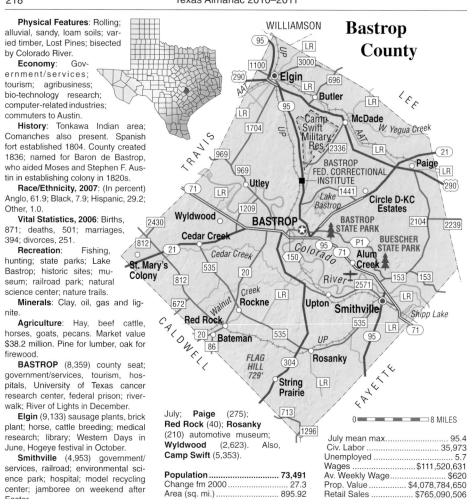

Bastrop County

For explanation of sources, abbreviations and symbols, see p. 210 and foldout map.

An abandoned church sits in an open field near Bomarton in Baylor County. Robert Plocheck photo.

Baylor County

Physical Features: Northwest county; level to hilly; drains to Brazos, Wichita rivers; sandy, loam, red soils; grassy, mesquites, cedars.

Economy: Agribusiness; retail/service; health services.

History: Comanches, with Wichitas and other tribes; removed in 1874-75. Anglo-Americans settled in the 1870s. County created from Fannin County 1858; organized 1879. Named for H.W. Baylor, Texas Ranger surgeon.

Race/Ethnicity, 2007: (In percent) Anglo, 85.1; Black, 3.7; Hispanic, 10.2; Other, 1.1.

Vital Statistics, 2006: Births, 47; deaths, 52; marriages, 40; divorces, 8.

Recreation: Lakes; hunting; settlers reunion, rodeo, go-cart races in July.

Minerals: Oil, gas produced.

Agriculture: Wheat, cattle, cow-calf operations, grain sorghum, cotton, hay. Market value $42.9 million.

SEYMOUR (2,911) county seat; agribusiness; hospital; dove hunters' breakfast in September.

Population		3,737
Change fm 2000		−8.7
Area (sq. mi.)		901.01
Land Area (sq. mi.)		870.77
Altitude (ft.)		1,053-1,537
Rainfall (in.)		27.79

Jan. mean min.	27.7
July mean max.	96.5
Civ. Labor	2,100
Unemployed	3.7

Wages	$8,462,003
Av. Weekly Wage	$492
Prop. Value	$186,028,910
Retail Sales	$27,569,869

Bee County

Physical Features: South Coastal Plain, level to rolling; black clay, sandy, loam soils; brushy.

Economy: Agriculture, government/services; hunting leases; oil and gas business.

History: Karankawa, Apache, Pawnee territory. First Spanish land grant, 1789. Irish settlers arrived 1826-29. County created from Karnes, Live Oak, Goliad, Refugio, San Patricio, 1857; organized 1858; named for Gen. Barnard Bee.

Race/Ethnicity, 2007: (In percent) Anglo, 33.1; Black, 9.2; Hispanic, 57.0; Other, 0.8.

Vital Statistics, 2006: Births, 370; deaths, 209; marriages, 162; divorces, 80.

Recreation: Hunting, birding, camping; historical sites, antiques; rodeo/roping events.

Minerals: Oil, gas produced.

Agriculture: Beef cattle, corn, cotton and grain sorghhum. Market value $39.2 million. Hunting leases.

BEEVILLE (14,228) county seat; aircraft maintenance, waste-bind manufacturing, retail center; Costal Bend College; hospital; art museum; Diez y Seis festival in September.

Other towns and places include: **Blue Berry Hill** (999); **Mineral** (65); **Normanna** (168); **Pawnee** (244); **Pettus** (736); **Skidmore** (1,162); **Tuleta** (408); **Tynan** (298).

Population		32,661
Change fm 2000		0.9
Area (sq. mi.)		880.31
Land Area (sq. mi.)		880.14
Altitude (ft.)		39-540

Rainfall (in.)	33.48
Jan. mean min.	43.1
July mean max.	94.6
Civ. Labor	11,632
Unemployed	6.9
Wages	$62,207,116
Av. Weekly Wage	$584
Prop. Value	$1,120,418,749
Retail Sales	$236,757,085

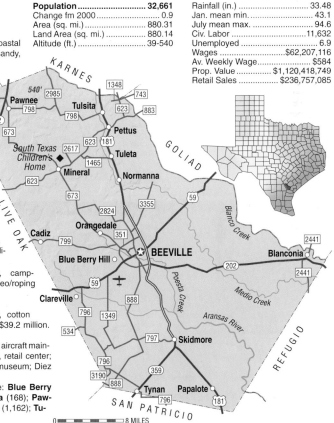

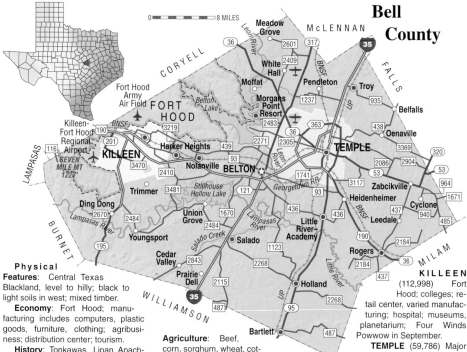

Bell
County

0 ▬▬ 8 MILES

Physical

Features: Central Texas Blackland, level to hilly; black to light soils in west; mixed timber.

Economy: Fort Hood; manufacturing includes computers, plastic goods, furniture, clothing; agribusiness; distribution center; tourism.

History: Tonkawas, Lipan Apaches; reduced by disease and advancing frontier by 1840s. Comanches raided into 1870s. Settled in 1830s as part of Robertson's colony. A few slaveholders in 1850s. County created from Milam County in 1850; named for Gov. P.H. Bell.

Race/Ethnicity, 2007: (In percent) Anglo, 51.4; Black, 22.9; Hispanic, 20.4; Other, 5.2.

Vital Statistics, 2006: Births, 4,916; deaths, 1,691; marriages, 4,125; divorces, 1,849.

Recreation: Fishing, hunting; lakes; historic sites; exposition center; Salado gathering of Scottish clans in November.

Minerals: Gravel.

Agriculture: Beef, corn, sorghum, wheat, cotton. Market value $61.7 million.

BELTON (16,953) county seat; University of Mary Hardin-Baylor; government/services; manufacturing; museum, nature center.

Population	285,084
Change fm 2000	19.8
Area (sq. mi.)	1,087.93
Land Area (sq. mi.)	1,059.72
Altitude (ft.)	390-1,227
Rainfall (in.)	35.81
Jan. mean min.	34.9
July mean max.	95.0
Civ. Labor	119,843
Unemployed	5.6
Wages	$888,456,021
Av. Weekly Wage	$659
Prop. Value	$12,399,355,279
Retail Sales	$4,698,372,568

KILLEEN (112,998) Fort Hood; colleges; retail center, varied manufacturing; hospital; museums, planetarium; Four Winds Powwow in September.

TEMPLE (59,786) Major medical center with two hospitals and VA hospital; diversified industries; rail, wholesale distribution center; retail center; Temple College; Czech museum; early-day tractor, engine show in October.

Other towns include: **Harker Heights** (25,160) Founder's Day in October; **Heidenheimer** (224); **Holland** (1,127) corn festival in June; **Little River-Academy** (1,718); **Morgan's Point Resort** (4,597); **Nolanville** (3,015); **Pendelton** (369); **Rogers** (1,145); **Salado** (3,786) tourism, civic center, amphitheathre, art fair in August; **Troy** (1,400). Also, part of **Bartlett** (1,974) is in Bell County.

Fort Hood has a population of 32,560.

The residence of the Spanish governors in San Antonio. Robert Plocheck photo.

Physical Features: On edge of Balcones Escarpment, Coastal Plain; heavy black to thin limestone soils; spring-fed streams; underground water; mesquite, other brush.

Economy: Medical/biomedical research and services; government center with large federal payroll, military bases; tourism; education center.

History: Coahuiltecan Indian area; also Lipan Apaches and Tonkawas present. Mission San Antonio de Valero (Alamo) founded in 1718. Canary Islanders arrived in 1731. Anglo-American settlers began arriving in late 1820s. County created 1836 from Spanish municipality named to honor the duke of Bexar; a colonial capital of Texas.

Race/Ethnicity, 2007: (In percent) Anglo, 31.5; Black, 7.8; Hispanic, 57.7; Other, 3.0.

Vital Statistics, 2006: Births, 25,398; deaths, 10,626; marriages, 12,625; divorces, 4,642.

Bexar County

Recreation: Historic sites include the Alamo, other missions, Casa Navarro, La Villita; Riverwalk, El Mercado (market), Tower of the Americas, Brackenridge Park, zoo, Seaworld, HemisFair Park, Institute of Texan Cultures; museums, symphony orchestra; hunting, fishing; NBA Spurs; Fiesta in April, Folklife Festival in June.

Minerals: Gravel, sand, limestone.

Agriculture: Nursery crops, beef cattle, grain sorghum, hay, corn. Market value $84.2 million.

Education: Fourteen colleges including Our Lady of the Lake, St. Mary's University, Trinity University and the University of Texas at San Antonio.

SAN ANTONIO (1,336,040) county seat; Texas' second largest city; varied manufacturing with emphasis on high-tech industries; other products include construction equipment, concrete and

dairy products; industrial warehousing. **Leon Spring**s is now part of San Antonio.

Other towns include: **Alamo Heights** (7,556); **Balcones Heights** (3,048); **Castle Hills** (4,075); **China Grove** (1,357); **Converse** (16,026); **Elmendorf** (863); **Fair Oaks Ranch** (6,175); **Grey Forest** (439) **Helotes** (7,245); **Hill Country Village** (1,083); **Hollywood Park** (3,341).

Also, **Kirby** (8,965); **Leon Valley** (10,481); **Live Oak** (12,519); **Macdona** (297); **Olmos Park** (2,408); **St. Hedwig** (2,174); **Selma** (3,445, parts in Guadalupe and Comal counties); **Shavano Park** (3,126); **Somerset** (1,826); **Terrell Hills** (5,558); **Universal City** (17,417); **Windcrest** (5,311).

Part [1,045] of **Schertz** (30,552).

Population	**1,622,899**
Change fm 2000	16.5
Area (sq. mi.)	1,256.66
Land Area (sq. mi.)	1,246.82
Altitude (ft.)	400-1,896
Rainfall (in.)	32.92
Jan. mean min.	38.6
July mean max.	94.6
Civ. Labor	754,848
Unemployed	5.4
Wages	$6,930,802,662
Av. Weekly Wage.......................	$734
Fed. Wages	$347,876,629
Prop. Value	$95,253,783,540
Retail Sales	$22,270,578,631

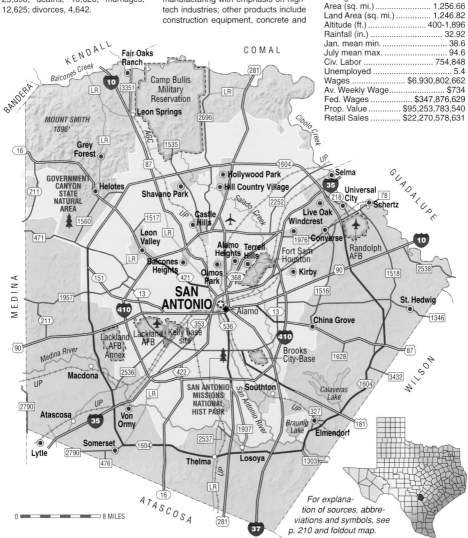

For explanation of sources, abbreviations and symbols, see p. 210 and foldout map.

Blanco County

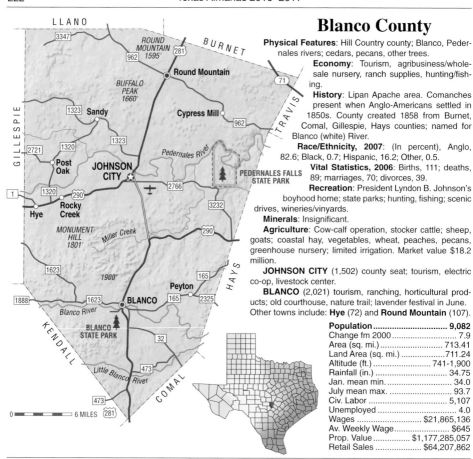

Physical Features: Hill Country county; Blanco, Pedernales rivers; cedars, pecans, other trees.

Economy: Tourism, agribusiness/wholesale nursery, ranch supplies, hunting/fishing.

History: Lipan Apache area. Comanches present when Anglo-Americans settled in 1850s. County created 1858 from Burnet, Comal, Gillespie, Hays counties; named for Blanco (white) River.

Race/Ethnicity, 2007: (In percent), Anglo, 82.6; Black, 0.7; Hispanic, 16.2; Other, 0.5.

Vital Statistics, 2006: Births, 111; deaths, 89; marriages, 70; divorces, 39.

Recreation: President Lyndon B. Johnson's boyhood home; state parks; hunting, fishing; scenic drives, wineries/vinyards.

Minerals: Insignificant.

Agriculture: Cow-calf operation, stocker cattle; sheep, goats; coastal hay, vegetables, wheat, peaches, pecans, greenhouse nursery; limited irrigation. Market value $18.2 million.

JOHNSON CITY (1,502) county seat; tourism, electric co-op, livestock center.

BLANCO (2,021) tourism, ranching, horticultural products; old courthouse, nature trail; lavender festival in June. Other towns include: **Hye** (72) and **Round Mountain** (107).

Population	9,082
Change fm 2000	7.9
Area (sq. mi.)	713.41
Land Area (sq. mi.)	711.24
Altitude (ft.)	741-1,900
Rainfall (in.)	34.75
Jan. mean min.	34.0
July mean max.	93.7
Civ. Labor	5,107
Unemployed	4.0
Wages	$21,865,136
Av. Weekly Wage	$645
Prop. Value	$1,177,285,057
Retail Sales	$64,207,862

Borden County

Physical Features: Rolling surface, broken by Caprock Escarpment; drains to Colorado River; sandy loam, clay soils.

Economy: Agriculture and hunting leases; oil; wind turbines.

History: Comanche area. Anglo-Americans settled in 1870s. County created 1876 from Bexar District, organized 1891; named for Gail Borden, patriot, inventor, editor.

Race/Ethnicity, 2007: (In percent) Anglo, 86.0; Black, 0.0; Hispanic, 13.7; Other, 0.3.

Vital Statistics, 2006: Births, 2; deaths, 5; marriages, 1; divorce, 3.

Recreation: Fishing; quail and deer hunting; Lake J.B. Thomas; museum; Coyote Opry in September; junior livestock show in January, ranch horse competition in September.

Minerals: Oil, gas, caliche, sand, gravel.

Agriculture: Beef cattle, cotton, wheat, hay, pecans, oats; some irrigation. Market value $13.2 million.

GAIL (200) county seat; museum, antique shop, ambulance service; "star" construction atop Gail Mountain.

Population	593	Jan. mean min.	29.8	Prop. Value	$706,291,982
Change fm 2000	-18.7	July mean max.	94.6	Retail Sales	$59,627
Area (sq. mi.)	906.04	Civ. Labor	366		
Land Area (sq. mi.)	898.80	Unemployed	4.4	*For explanation of sources, abbrevia-*
Altitude (ft.)	2,258-2,990	Wages	$868,437	*tions and symbols, see p. 210 and*
Rainfall (in.)	19.68	Av. Weekly Wage	$495	*foldout page.*

Bosque County

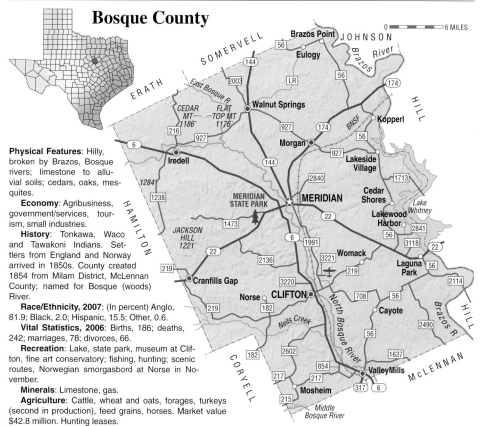

Physical Features: Hilly, broken by Brazos, Bosque rivers; limestone to alluvial soils; cedars, oaks, mesquites.

Economy: Agribusiness, government/services, tourism, small industries.

History: Tonkawa, Waco and Tawakoni Indians. Settlers from England and Norway arrived in 1850s. County created 1854 from Milam District, McLennan County; named for Bosque (woods) River.

Race/Ethnicity, 2007: (In percent) Anglo, 81.9; Black, 2.0; Hispanic, 15.5; Other, 0.6.

Vital Statistics, 2006: Births, 186; deaths, 242; marriages, 78; divorces, 66.

Recreation: Lake, state park, museum at Clifton, fine art conservatory; fishing, hunting; scenic routes, Norwegian smorgasbord at Norse in November.

Minerals: Limestone, gas.

Agriculture: Cattle, wheat and oats, forages, turkeys (second in production), feed grains, horses. Market value $42.8 million. Hunting leases.

MERIDIAN (1,564) county seat; distribution center, varied manufacturing; national championship barbecue cookoff in August.

CLIFTON (3,795) retirement/health care, limestone sales, light manufacturing; hospital, nursing school; library; Norwegian historic district; Norwegian Country Christmas.

Other towns include: **Cranfills Gap** (361) Lutefisk dinner in December; **Iredell** (388); **Kopperl** (225); **Laguna Park** (750); **Morgan** (539); **Valley Mills** (1,163); **Walnut Springs** (825).

Population **17,760**
Change fm 2000 .... 3.2
Area (sq. mi.) 1,002.63
Land Area (sq. mi.) 989.18

Altitude (ft.) 410-1,284
Rainfall (in.) 35.07
Jan. mean min. 32.7
July mean max. 96.2
Civ. Labor 8,441
Unemployed 5.4
Wages $28,225,254
Av. Weekly Wage....................... $576
Prop. Value $1,222,834,971
Retail Sales $86,867,225

Downtown De Kalb in Bowie County. Robert Plocheck photo.

Bowie County

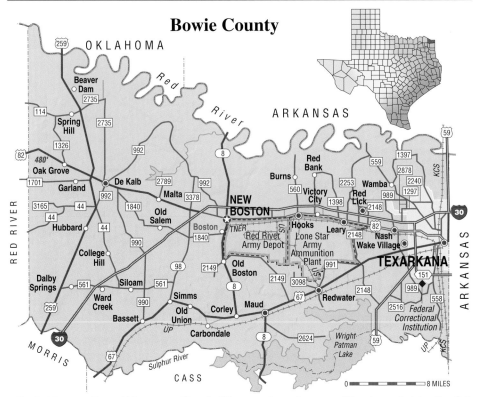

Physical Features: Forested hills at northeast corner of state; clay, sandy, alluvial soils; drained by Red and Sulphur rivers.

Economy: Government/services, lumber, manufacturing, agribusiness.

History: Caddo area, abandoned in 1790s after trouble with Osage tribe. Anglo-Americans began arriving 1815-20. County created 1840 from Red River County; named for Alamo hero James Bowie.

Race/Ethnicity, 2007: (In percent) Anglo, 67.5; Black, 25.1; Hispanic, 6.0; Other, 1.4.

Vital Statistics, 2006: Births, 1,127; deaths, 876; marriages, 665; divorces, 384.

Recreation: Lakes, Crystal Springs beach; hunting, fishing; historic sites; Four-States Fair in September, Oktoberfest.

Minerals: Oil, gas, sand, gravel.

Agriculture: Beef cattle, pecans, hay, corn, poultry, soybeans, dairy, nurseries, wheat, rice, horses, milo. Market value $48.4 million. Pine timber, hardwoods, pulpwood harvested.

NEW BOSTON (4,795) site of county courthouse; army depot, lumber mill, steel manufacture, agribusiness, state prison; Pioneer Days in August.

The area of **Boston**, officially designated as the county seat, has been annexed by New Boston.

TEXARKANA (36,596 in Texas, 29,624 in Arkansas) rubber company, paper manufacturing, distribution; hospitals; tourism; colleges; federal prison; Perot Theatre; Quadrangle Festival in September.

Other towns include: **De Kalb** (1,648) agriculture, government/services, commuting to Texarkana, Oktoberfest; **Hooks** (3,170); **Leary** (581); **Maud** (1,024); **Nash** (2,436); **Red Lick** (876); **Redwater** (905); **Simms** (240); **Wake Village** (5,621).

Population	**92,283**
Change fm 2000	3.3
Area (sq. mi.)	922.77
Land Area (sq. mi.)	887.87
Altitude (ft.)	200-480
Rainfall (in.)	51.24
Jan. mean min.	30.7
July mean max.	93.1
Civ. Labor	43,597
Unemployed	5.6
Wages	$379,325,896
Av. Weekly Wage	$666
Prop. Value	$4,530,757,020
Retail Sales	$1,303,951,711

The Gulf Intracoastal Waterway at the mouth of the San Bernard River in Brazoria County. Robert Plocheck photo.

Brazoria County

Physical Features: Flat Coastal Plain, coastal soils, drained by Brazos and San Bernard rivers.

Economy: Petroleum and chemical industry, fishing, tourism, agribusiness. Part of Houston metropolitan area.

History: Karankawa area. Part of Austin's "Old Three Hundred" colony of families arriving in early 1820s. County created 1836 from Municipality of Brazoria; name derived from Brazos River.

Race/Ethnicity, 2007: (In percent) Anglo, 60.2; Black, 9.1; Hispanic, 27.2; Other, 3.4.

Vital Statistics, 2006: Births, 4,288; deaths, 1,832; marriages, 1,764; divorces, 1,338.

Recreation: Beaches, water sports, fishing, hunting; wildlife refuges, historic sites; state and county parks; replica of the first capitol of the Republic of Texas at West Columbia.

Minerals: Oil, gas, sand, gravel.

Agriculture: Cattle, hay, rice, soybeans, sorghum, nurseries, corn, cotton, aquaculture, bees (second in number of colonies). 20,000 acres of rice irrigated. Market value $55.1 million.

ANGLETON (19,745) county seat; banking and distribution center for oil, chemical, agricultural area; fish-processing plant; hospital.

BRAZOSPORT (61,833) is a community of eight cities; chemical complex, deepwater seaport, commercial fishing, tourism; college; hospital; Bra-

For explanation of sources, abbreviations and symbols, see p. 210 and foldout page.

zosport cities include: **Clute** (11,481) mosquito festival in July, **Freeport** (13,427) blues festival in August, **Jones Creek** (2,259), **Lake Jackson** (28,773) museum, sea center, Gulf Coast Bird Observatory, **Oyster Creek** (1,411), **Quintana** (38) Neotropical Bird Sanctuary, **Richwood** (3,537), **Surfside Beach** (907).

ALVIN (24,135) petrochemical processing, agribusiness, rail, trucking; junior college; hospital; Crawfest and Shrimp Boil in April.

PEARLAND (85,701, partly in Harris County) rail, trucking, oilfield, chemical production; commuting to Houston, NASA; community college.

Other towns include: **Bailey's Prairie** (779); **Bonney** (420); **Brazoria** (3,056) government/services, retail, manufacturing; library; No-Name Festival in June, Santa Anna Ball in July; **Brookside Village** (2,160).

Also, **Damon** (572); **Danbury** (1,776); **Danciger** (357); **Hillcrest Village** (778); **Holiday Lakes** (1,186); **Iowa Colony** (982);

Liverpool (460); **Manvel** (4,966); **Old Ocean** (150); **Rosharon** (435); **Sandy Point** (250); **Sweeny** (3,894) petrochemicals, agriculture, grass farming, hospital, library, Pride Day in May, Levi Jordan Plantation; **West Columbia** (4,423) chemical industry, retail, cattle, rice farming, museum, historic sites, plantation, San Jacinto Festival in April, Stephen F. Austin funeral procession re-eactment in October.

Population	301,044
Change fm 2000	24.5
Area (sq. mi.)	1,597.44
Land Area (sq. mi.)	1,386.40
Altitude (ft.)	sea level-146
Rainfall (in.)	57.24
Jan. mean min.	43.7
July mean max.	91.8
Civ. Labor	143,732
Unemployed	6.0
Wages	$893,676,612
Av. Weekly Wage......................	$806
Prop. Value	$25,407,373,890
Retail Sales	$2,986,254,087

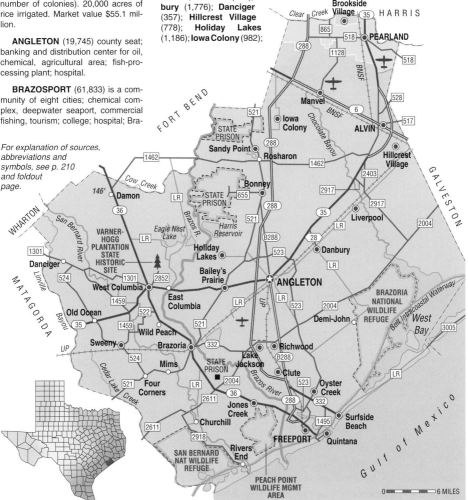

Brazos County

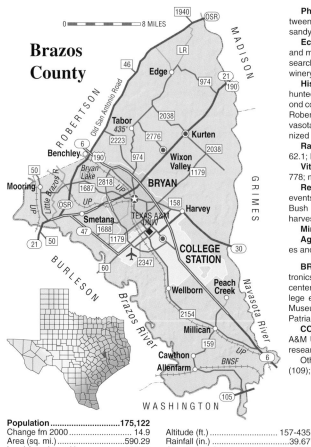

Physical Features: South central county between Brazos, Navasota rivers; rich bottom soils, sandy, clays on rolling uplands; oak trees.

Economy: Texas A&M University; market and medical center; agribusiness; computers, research and development; government/services; winery; industrial parks; tourism.

History: Bidais and Tonkawas; Comanches hunted in area. Part of Stephen F. Austin's second colony, late 1820s. County created 1841 from Robertson, Washington counties and named Navasota; renamed for Brazos River in 1842, organized 1843.

Race/Ethnicity, 2007: (In percent) Anglo, 62.1; Black, 11.4; Hispanic, 21.5; Other, 5.0.

Vital Statistics, 2006: Births, 2,383; deaths, 778; marriages, 1,391; divorces, 278.

Recreation: Fishing, hunting; raceway; many events related to Texas A&M activities; George Bush Presidential Library and Museum; winery harvest weekends in August.

Minerals: Sand and gravel, lignite, gas, oil.

Agriculture: Cattle, poultry, cotton, hay, horses and horticulture. Market value $54.5 million.

BRYAN (74,985) county seat; defense electronics, other varied manufacturing, agribusiness center; hospitals, psychiatric facilities; Blinn College extension; Brazos Valley African American Museum; steak & grape festival in June, Fiestas Patrias in September.

COLLEGE STATION (80,526) home of Texas A&M University, varied high-tech manufacturing, research; hospital.

Other towns include: **Kurten** (240); **Millican** (109); **Wellborn** (250); **Wixon Valley** (241).

July mean max.	95.6
Civ. Labor	89,987
Unemployed	3.8
Wages	$695,523,896
Av. Weekly Wage	$644
Prop. Value	$9,799,759,264
Retail Sales	$2,213,429,817

Population	175,122
Change fm 2000	14.9
Area (sq. mi.)	590.29
Land Area (sq. mi.)	585.78
Altitude (ft.)	157-435
Rainfall (in.)	39.67
Jan. mean min.	39.8

Chisos Mountains, Big Bend National Park, Brewster County. Robert Plocheck photo.

Brewster County

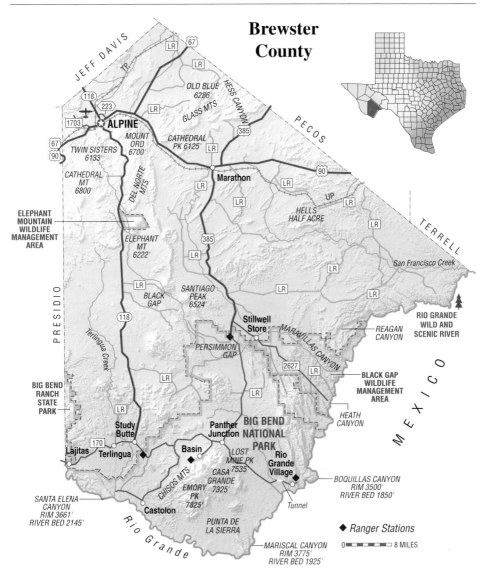

Ranger Stations

0 ▬▬▬▬▬ 8 MILES

Physical Features: Largest county, with area slightly less than that of Connecticut plus Rhode Island; mountains, canyons, distinctive geology, plant life, animals.

Economy: Tourism and retirement area, ranching, Sul Ross State University, government/services, hunting leases.

History: Pueblo culture had begun when Spanish explored in 1500s. Mescalero Apaches in Chisos; Comanches raided in area. Ranching developed in northern part 1880s; Mexican agricultural communites along river. County created 1887 from Presidio County; named for Henry P. Brewster, Republic secretary of war.

Race/Ethnicity, 2007: (In percent) Anglo, 50.8; Black, 1.1; Hispanic, 46.9; Other, 1.2.

Vital Statistics, 2006: Births, 120; deaths, 66; marriages, 31; divorces, 0.

Recreation: Big Bend National Park, Big Bend Ranch State Park, Rio Grande Wild and Scenic River; ghost towns, scenic drives; hunting; museum; rockhound areas; cavalry post, Barton Warnock Environmental Education Center at Lajitas; Terlingua chili cookoff in November.

Minerals: Bentonite.

Agriculture: Beef cattle, horses, pecans. Market value $9.6 million.

ALPINE (6,233) county seat; ranch trade center, tourism, varied manufacturing; Sul Ross State University; hospital.

Marathon (468) tourism, ranching center, Gage Hotel, Marathon Basin quilt show in October. Also, **Basin** (22) and **Study Butte-Terlingua** (297).

Population	9,331
Change fm 2000	5.2
Area (sq. mi.)	6,192.78
Land Area (sq. mi.)	6,192.61
Altitude (ft.)	1,400-7,825
Rainfall (in.) Alpine	17.19
Rainfall (in.) Big Bend	19.17
Jan. mean min. Alpine	31.3
Jan. mean min. Big Bend	36.1
July mean max. Alpine	88.7
July mean max. Big Bend	84.2
Civ. Labor	5,452
Unemployed	3.6
Wages	$32,243,903
Av. Weekly Wage	$528
Prop. Value	$505,442,664
Retail Sales	$78,058,243

For explanation of sources, abbreviations and symbols, see p. 210 and foldout map.

Briscoe County

Physical Features: Partly on High Plains, broken by Caprock Escarpment, fork of Red River; sandy, loam soils.

Economy: Agribusiness, government/services, banking.

History: Apaches, displaced by Comanches around 1700. Ranchers settled in 1880s. County created from Bexar District, 1876, organized 1892; named for Andrew Briscoe, Republic of Texas soldier.

Race/Ethnicity, 2007: (In percent) Anglo, 71.9; Black, 2.5; Hispanic, 25.3; Other, 0.3.

Vital Statistics, 2006: Births, 17; deaths, 17; marriages, 12; divorces, 6.

Recreation: Hunting, fishing; scenic drives; museum; state park, trailway, Clarity tunnel, Mackenzie Reservoir.

Minerals: Insignificant.

Agriculture: Cotton, cow-calf, stocker cattle, sorghum, wheat, hay. Some 32,000 acres irrigated. Market value $27.9 million.

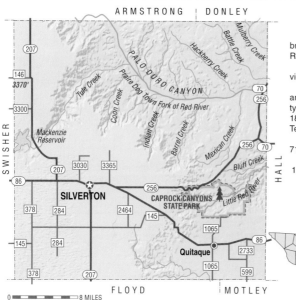

SILVERTON (722) county seat; agribusiness center, irrigation supplies manufactured; clinics.

Quitaque (374) trade center, agribusiness, nature tourism.

Population		**1,462**
Change fm 2000		–18.3
Area (sq. mi.)		901.59
Land Area (sq. mi.)		900.25
Altitude (ft.)		2,064-3,370
Rainfall (in.)		22.34
Jan. mean min.		21.6
July mean max.		90.9
Civ. Labor		778
Unemployed		4.2
Wages		$1,967,074
Av. Weekly Wage		$427
Prop. Value		$90,377,046
Retail Sales		$8,835,650

Brooks County

Physical Features: On Rio Grande plain; level to rolling; brushy; light to dark sandy loam soils.

Economy: Oil, gas, hunting leases, cattle, watermelons and hay.

History: Coahuiltecan Indians. Spanish land grants date to around 1800. County created from Hidalgo, Starr, Zapata counties, 1911. Named for J.A. Brooks, Texas Ranger and legislator.

Race/Ethnicity, 2007: (In percent) Anglo, 7.6; Black, 0.1; Hispanic, 92.1; Other, 0.3.

Vital Statistics, 2006: Births, 139; deaths, 85; marriages, 47; divorces, 35.

Recreation: Hunting, fishing; Heritage Museum, Don Pedrito shrine; Fiesta del Campo in October.

Minerals: Oil, gas production; uranium.

Agriculture: Beef cow-calf operations, stocker; crops include hay, squash, watermelons, habanero peppers. Market value $19.1 million.

FALFURRIAS (5,165) county seat; agricultural market center, government/services.

Other towns include: **Encino** (174).

Population		**7,549**
Change fm 2000		–5.4
Area (sq. mi.)		943.61
Land Area (sq. mi.)		943.28
Altitude (ft.)		46-431
Rainfall (in.)		25.42
Jan. mean min.		43.9
July mean max.		97.0
Civ. Labor		3,187
Unemployed		5.6
Wages		$20,751,657
Av. Weekly Wage		$606
Prop. Value		$939,244,879
Retail Sales		$64,135,315

For explanation of sources, abbreviations and symbols, see p. 210 and foldout map.

Brown County

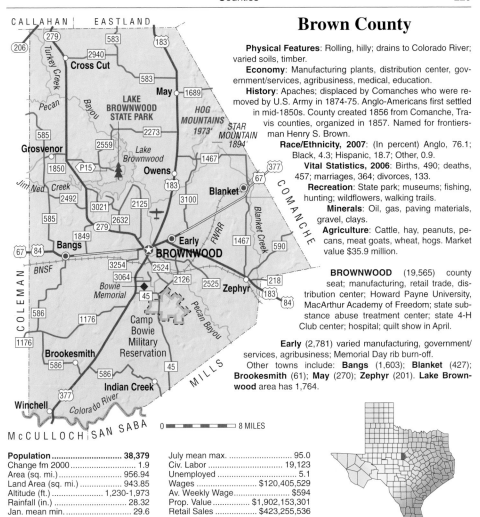

Physical Features: Rolling, hilly; drains to Colorado River; varied soils, timber.

Economy: Manufacturing plants, distribution center, government/services, agribusiness, medical, education.

History: Apaches; displaced by Comanches who were removed by U.S. Army in 1874-75. Anglo-Americans first settled in mid-1850s. County created 1856 from Comanche, Travis counties, organized in 1857. Named for frontiersman Henry S. Brown.

Race/Ethnicity, 2007: (In percent) Anglo, 76.1; Black, 4.3; Hispanic, 18.7; Other, 0.9.

Vital Statistics, 2006: Births, 490; deaths, 457; marriages, 364; divorces, 133.

Recreation: State park; museums; fishing, hunting; wildflowers, walking trails.

Minerals: Oil, gas, paving materials, gravel, clays.

Agriculture: Cattle, hay, peanuts, pecans, meat goats, wheat, hogs. Market value $35.9 million.

BROWNWOOD (19,565) county seat; manufacturing, retail trade, distribution center; Howard Payne University, MacArthur Academy of Freedom; state substance abuse treatment center; state 4-H Club center; hospital; quilt show in April.

Early (2,781) varied manufacturing, government/services, agribusiness; Memorial Day rib burn-off.

Other towns include: **Bangs** (1,603); **Blanket** (427); **Brookesmith** (61); **May** (270); **Zephyr** (201). **Lake Brownwood** area has 1,764.

Population	38,379
Change fm 2000	1.9
Area (sq. mi.)	956.94
Land Area (sq. mi.)	943.85
Altitude (ft.)	1,230-1,973
Rainfall (in.)	28.32
Jan. mean min.	29.6
July mean max.	95.0
Civ. Labor	19,123
Unemployed	5.1
Wages	$120,405,529
Av. Weekly Wage	$594
Prop. Value	$1,902,153,301
Retail Sales	$423,255,536

The red bluffs of Caprock Canyons State Park in Briscoe County. Robert Plocheck photo.

Physical Features: Rolling to hilly; drains to Brazos, Yegua Creek, Somerville Lake; loam and heavy bottom soils; oaks, other trees.

Economy: Oil and gas, tourism, commuters to Texas A&M University, agribusiness.

History: Tonkawas and Caddoes roamed the area. Mexicans and Anglo-Americans settled around fort in 1830. Black freedmen migration increased until 1910. Germans, Czechs, Italians migrated in 1870s-80s. County created 1846 from Milam, Washington counties; named for Edward Burleson, a hero of the Texas Revolution.

Race/Ethnicity, 2007: (In percent) Anglo, 67.6; Black, 15.1; Hispanic, 16.8; Other, 0.5.

Vital Statistics, 2006: Births, 231; deaths, 162; marriages, 60; divorces, 79.

Recreation: Fishing, hunting; lake recreation; historic sites; Czech heritage museum; Kolache Festival in September.

Minerals: Oil, gas, sand, gravel.

Agriculture: Cattle, cotton, corn, hay, sorghum, broiler production, soybeans; some irrigation. Market value $56.4 million.

CALDWELL (4,139) county seat; agribusiness, oil and gas, manufacturing, distribution center, tourism; hospital; civic center, museum.

Somerville (1,911) tourism, railroad center, some manufacturing.

Other towns include: **Chriesman**

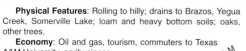

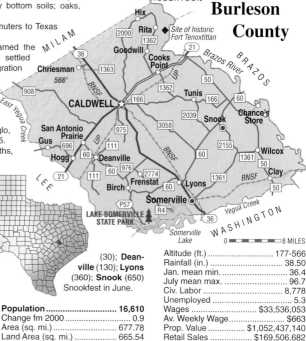

Burleson County

(30); **Deanville** (130); **Lyons** (360); **Snook** (650) Snookfest in June.

Population	16,610
Change fm 2000	0.9
Area (sq. mi.)	677.78
Land Area (sq. mi.)	665.54

Altitude (ft.)	177-566
Rainfall (in.)	38.50
Jan. mean min.	36.4
July mean max.	96.7
Civ. Labor	8,778
Unemployed	5.3
Wages	$33,536,053
Av. Weekly Wage	$663
Prop. Value	$1,052,437,140
Retail Sales	$169,506,682

Burnet County

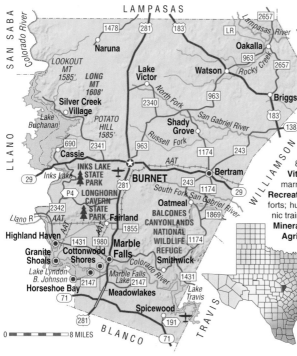

Physical Features: Scenic Hill Country county with lakes; caves; sandy, red, black waxy soils; cedars, other trees.

Economy: Tourism, manufacturing, stone processing, hunting leases.

History: Tonkawas, Lipan Apaches. Comanches raided in area. Frontier settlers arrived in the late 1840s. County created from Bell, Travis, Williamson counties, 1852; organized 1854; named for David G. Burnet, provisional president of the Republic.

Race/Ethnicity, 2007: (In percent) Anglo, 81.0; Black, 1.3; Hispanic, 17.0; Other, 0.8.

Vital Statistics, 2006: Births, 485; deaths, 388; marriages, 355; divorces, 225.

Recreation: Water sports on lakes; sites of historic forts; hunting; state parks; wildflowers; birding, scenic train ride.

Minerals: Granite capital of Texas, limestone.

Agriculture: Cattle, goats, horses, hay. Market value $12.3 million. Deer, wild hog and turkey hunting leases.

BURNET (5,907) county seat; tourism, government/services, varied industries, ranching; hospital; museums; vineyards; Bluebonnet festival in April.

Marble Falls (7,038) tourism, retail, manufacturing; granite, limestone quarries; August drag boat race.

Other towns include: **Bertram** (1,369) Oatmeal festival on Labor Day; **Briggs** (172); **Cottonwood Shores** (1,118); **Granite Shoals** (2,532); **Highland Haven** (592); **Meadowlakes** (1,972); **Spicewood** (2,000). Also, part of **Horseshoe Bay** (3,567).

Population	44,488
Change fm 2000	30.3
Area (sq. mi.)	1,020.96
Land Area (sq. mi.)	996.04
Altitude (ft.)	682-1,608
Rainfall (in.)	32.43
Jan. mean min.	33.3

July mean max.	93.6
Civ. Labor	22,952
Unemployed	4.5
Wages	$115,114,475
Av. Weekly Wage	$690
Prop. Value	$4,267,573,221
Retail Sales	$585,443,173

Caldwell County

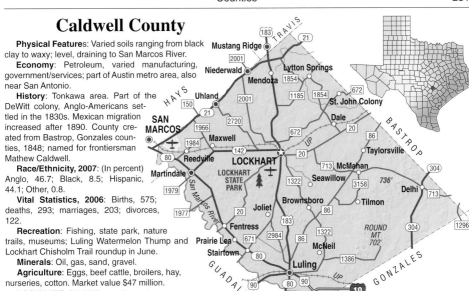

Physical Features: Varied soils ranging from black clay to waxy; level, draining to San Marcos River.

Economy: Petroleum, varied manufacturing, government/services; part of Austin metro area, also near San Antonio.

History: Tonkawa area. Part of the DeWitt colony, Anglo-Americans settled in the 1830s. Mexican migration increased after 1890. County created from Bastrop, Gonzales counties, 1848; named for frontiersman Mathew Caldwell.

Race/Ethnicity, 2007: (In percent) Anglo, 46.7; Black, 8.5; Hispanic, 44.1; Other, 0.8.

Vital Statistics, 2006: Births, 575; deaths, 293; marriages, 203; divorces, 122.

Recreation: Fishing, state park, nature trails, museums; Luling Watermelon Thump and Lockhart Chisholm Trail roundup in June.

Minerals: Oil, gas, sand, gravel.

Agriculture: Eggs, beef cattle, broilers, hay, nurseries, cotton. Market value $47 million.

LOCKHART (13,633) county seat; petroleum, agribusiness center, tourism, light manufacturing, prison.

Luling (5,658) oil, tourism, agriculture; oil museum; hospital, barbecue cook-off in April.

Population **36,899**
Change fm 2000 .... 14.6

Area (sq. mi.) 547.41
Land Area (sq. mi.) 545.73
Altitude (ft.) 315-736
Rainfall (in.) 36.86
Jan. mean min. 36.9
July mean max. 95.8

Civ. Labor 16,733
Unemployed 6.0
Wages $48,478,297
Av. Weekly Wage $542
Prop. Value $1,485,647,629
Retail Sales $284,142,150

Calhoun County

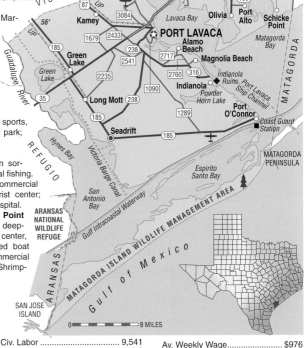

Physical Features: Sandy, broken by bays; partly on Matagorda Island.

Economy: Aluminum, plastics plants; marine construction; agribusinesses; petroleum; tourism; fish processing.

History: Karankawa area. Empresario Martín De León brought 41 families in 1825. County created from Jackson, Matagorda, Victoria counties, 1846. Named for John C. Calhoun, U.S. statesman.

Race/Ethnicity, 2007: (In percent) Anglo, 49.0; Black, 2.6; Hispanic, 44.1; Other, 4.3.

Vital Statistics, 2006: Births, 291; deaths, 199; marriages, 152; divorces, 47.

Recreation: Beaches, fishing, water sports, duck, goose hunting; historic sites, county park; La Salle Days in April.

Minerals: Oil, gas.

Agriculture: Cotton, cattle, corn, grain sorghum. Market value $29 million. Commercial fishing.

PORT LAVACA (12,002) county seat; commercial seafood operations, offshore drilling, tourist center; some manufacturing; convention center; hospital.

Other towns include: **Long Mott** (76); **Point Comfort** (720) aluminum, plastic plants, deepwater port; **Port O'Connor** (1,184) tourist center, seafood processing, manufacturing, lighted boat parade in December; **Seadrift** (1,438) commercial fishing, processing plants, Bayfront Park, Shrimpfest in June.

Population **20,406**
Change fm 2000 .... −1.2
Area (sq. mi.) 1,032.16
Land Area (sq. mi.) 512.31
Altitude (ft.) .... sea level-56
Rainfall (in.) 34.78
Jan. mean min. 47.9
July mean max. 88.2

Civ. Labor 9,541
Unemployed 6.3
Wages $121,035,055

Av. Weekly Wage $976
Prop. Value $4,285,950,977
Retail Sales $175,367,746

Callahan County

Physical Features: On divide between Brazos, Colorado rivers; level to rolling.

Economy: Manufacturing; feed and fertilizer business; many residents commute to Abilene; 200,000 acres in hunting leases.

History: Comanche territory until 1870s. Anglo-American settlement began around 1860. County created 1858 from Bexar, Bosque, Travis counties; organized 1877. Named for Texas Ranger J.H. Callahan.

Race/Ethnicity, 2007: (In percent) Anglo, 91.7; Black, 0.3; Hispanic, 6.9; Other, 1.1.

Vital Statistics, 2006: Births, 133; deaths, 156; marriages, 63; divorces, 66.

Recreation: Hunting, lakes; museums; Cross Plains Hunters' Feed at deer season.

Minerals: Oil and gas.

Agriculture: Cattle, wheat, dairy, hay, peanuts, sorghum, goats, horses. Market value $25.4 million.

BAIRD (1,664) county seat; ranching/agricultural trade center, antiques shops, some manufacturing, shipping; historic sites; Market Daze in June.

Clyde (3,770) steel water systems manufacturing, government/services; library; Pecan Festival in October.

Other towns include: **Cross Plains** (1,123) oil and gas, agriculture, government/services, home of creator of Conan the Barbarian, museum, Barbarian Festival in June; **Putnam** (91).

For explanation of sources, abbreviations and symbols, see p. 210 and foldout map.

Population	13,533
Change fm 2000	4.9
Area (sq. mi.)	901.26
Land Area (sq. mi.)	898.62
Altitude (ft.)	1,350-2,204
Rainfall (in.)	25.52
Jan. mean min.	31.1
July mean max.	94.9
Civ. Labor	7,064
Unemployed	4.3
Wages	$19,349,322
Av. Weekly Wage	$646
Prop. Value	$663,624,080
Retail Sales	$54,260,393

A couple strolls along the beach on South Padre Island. Robert Plocheck photo.

Cameron County

Physical Features: Southernmost county in rich Rio Grande Valley soils; flat landscape; semitropical climate.

Economy: Agribusiness, tourism, seafood processing, shipping, manufacturing, government/services.

History: Coahuiltecan Indian area. Spanish land grants date to 1781. County created from Nueces County, 1848; named for Capt. Ewen Cameron of Mier Expedition.

Race/Ethnicity, 2007: (In percent) Anglo, 12.2; Black, 0.3; Hispanic, 86.8; Other, 0.8.

Vital Statistics, 2006: Births, 8,665; deaths, 2,032; marriages, 2,742; divorces, 949.

Recreation: South Padre Island: year-round resort; fishing, hunting, water sports; historical sites, Palo Alto visitors center; gateway to Mexico, state parks; wildlife refuge; recreational vehicle center.

Minerals: Natural gas, oil.

Agriculture: Cotton, grain sorghums, vegetables. Ranked second in sugar cane acreage. Wholesale nursery plants raised. Small feedlot and cow-calf operations; 200,000 acres irrigated, mostly cotton and grain sorghums Market value $112.4 million. Ranked second in value of aquaculture.

BROWNSVILLE (172,609) county seat; international trade, varied indus-tries, shipping, tourism; college, hospitals, crippled children health center; Gladys Porter Zoo, historic Fort Brown; University of Texas at Brownsville.

Harlingen (69,359) health care, manufacturing, agribusiness, food processing, ecotourism, education; hospitals; nature center; greyhound races; birding festival in November.

San Benito (25,939) varied manufacturing, bottling; tourism; hospital; recreation facilities.

South Padre Island (3,022) beaches, tourism/convention center, Coast Guard station, Sand Castle Days in October.

Other towns include: **Bayview** (423); **Bluetown-Igle-**sia Antigua (712); **Cameron Park** (6,470); **Combes** (2,798); **Encantada-Ranchito El Calaboz** (2,278); **Indian Lake** (550); **La Feria** (7,714); **Laguna Heights** (2,123); **Laguna Vista** (3,848); **Laureles** (3,906); **Los Fresnos** (5,586) Little Graceland Museum, Butterfly Farm, library; **Los Indios** (1,334); **Olmito** (1,258); **Palm Valley** (1,314).

Also, **Port Isabel** (5,265) tourist center, fishing, museums, old lighthouse, Shrimp Cook-Off in November; **Primera** (4,036); **Rancho Viejo** (1,937); **Rangerville** (205); **Rio Hondo** (2,241); **Santa Maria** (874); **Santa Rosa** (3,122).

Population	**392,736**
Change fm 2000	17.2
Area (sq. mi.)	1,276.33
Land Area (sq. mi.)	905.76
Altitude (ft.)	sea level-67
Rainfall (in.)	27.55
Jan. mean min.	50.5
July mean max.	92.4
Civ. Labor	147,078
Unemployed	8.2
Wages	$866,499,628
Av. Weekly Wage	$541
Prop. Value	$14,925,594,095
Retail Sales	$3,501,342,491

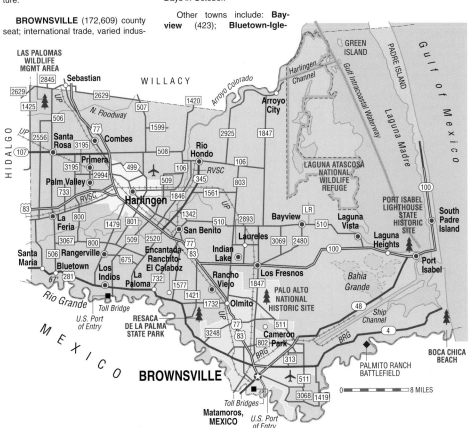

Population **12,666**
Change fm 2000 .... 9.7
Area (sq. mi.) 203.20
Land Area (sq. mi.) 197.51
Altitude (ft.) 236-538
Rainfall (in.) 45.10
Jan. mean min. 32.0
July mean max. 94.0
Civ. Labor 5,987
Unemployed 6.0
Wages $31,077,680
Av. Weekly Wage $559
Prop. Value $707,898,790
Retail Sales $112,267,914

Camp County

Physical Features: East Texas county with forested hills; drains to Cypress Creek on north; Lake O' the Pines, Lake Bob Sandlin; third smallest county in Texas.

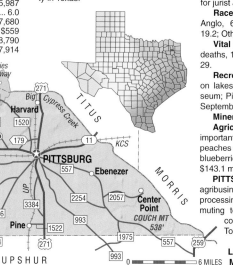

Economy: Agribusiness, chicken processing, timber industries, light manufacturing, retirement center.

History: Caddo area. Anglo-American settlers arrived in late 1830s. Antebellum slaveholding area. County created from Upshur County 1874; named for jurist J.L. Camp.

Race/Ethnicity, 2007: (In percent) Anglo, 62.4; Black, 17.9; Hispanic, 19.2; Other, 0.5.

Vital Statistics, 2006: Births, 193; deaths, 135; marriages, 103; divorces, 29.

Recreation: Water sports, fishing on lakes; farmstead and airship museum; Pittsburg hot links; Chickfest in September.

Minerals: Oil, gas, clays, coal.

Agriculture: Poultry and products important; beef, dairy cattle, horses; peaches (second in acreage), hay, blueberries, vegetables. Market value $143.1 million. Forestry.

PITTSBURG (4,609) county seat; agribusiness, timber, tourism, food processing, light manufacturing, commuting to Longview, Tyler; hospital; community college; Prayer Tower.

Other towns include: **Leesburg** (128) and **Rocky Mound** (102).

Physical Features: In center of Panhandle on level, some broken land; loam soils.

Economy: Pantex nuclear weapons assembly/disassembly facility (U.S. Department of Energy), commuting to Amarillo, petrochemical plants, agribusiness.

History: Apaches, displaced by Comanches. Anglo-American ranchers settled in 1880s. German, Polish

Carson County

farmers arrived around 1910. County created from Bexar District, 1876; organized 1888. Named for Republic secretary of state S.P. Carson.

Race/Ethnicity, 2007: (In percent) Anglo, 90.9; Black, 0.7; Hispanic, 7.4; Other, 0.9.

Vital Statistics, 2006: Births, 76;

deaths, 70; marriages, 28; divorces, 27.

Recreation: Museum, The Cross at Groom; Square House Barbecue in fall.

Minerals: Oil, gas production.

Agriculture: Cattle, cotton, wheat, sorghum, corn, hay, soybeans. Market value $93.7 million.

PANHANDLE (2,678) county seat; government/services, agribusiness, petroleum center, commuters to Amarillo; Veterans Day celebration, car show in June.

Other towns include: **Groom** (575) farming center, government/services, Groom Day festival in August; **Skellytown** (621); **White Deer** (1,019) Polish Sausage festival in November.

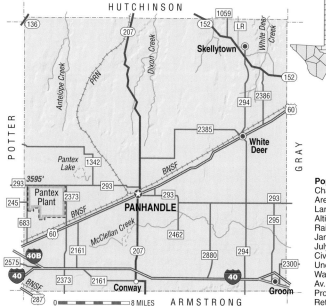

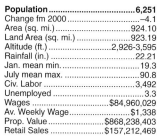

Population **6,251**
Change fm 2000 .... –4.1
Area (sq. mi.) 924.10
Land Area (sq. mi.) 923.19
Altitude (ft.) 2,926-3,595
Rainfall (in.) 22.21
Jan. mean min. 19.3
July mean max. 90.8
Civ. Labor 3,492
Unemployed 3.3
Wages $84,960,029
Av. Weekly Wage $1,338
Prop. Value $868,238,403
Retail Sales $157,212,469

Cass County

Physical Features: Forested Northeast county rolling to hilly; drained by Cypress Bayou, Sulphur River.

Economy: Timber, paper industries; varied manufacturing; agribusiness; government/services.

History: Caddoes, displaced by other tribes in 1790s. Anglo-Americans arrived in 1830s. Antebellum slaveholding area. County created 1846 from Bowie County; named for U.S. Sen. Lewis Cass.

Race/Ethnicity, 2007: (In percent) Anglo, 76.8; Black, 20.4; Hispanic, 2.1; Other, 0.7.

Vital Statistics, 2006: Births, 338; deaths, 361; marriages, 190; divorces, 148.

Recreation: Fishing, hunting, water sports; state, county parks; lake, wildflower trails.

Minerals: Oil, iron ore.

Agriculture: Poultry, cattle, nurseries, forage, watermelons. Market value $68.8 million. Timber important.

LINDEN (2,464) county seat, timber, agribusiness, tourism; oldest courthouse still in use as courthouse, hospital; Rock and Roll Hall of Fame.

ATLANTA (5,718) Paper and timber industries, government/services, varied manufacturing, hospital, library; Forest Festival in August.

Other towns include: **Avinger** (460) timber, paper industry, steel plant, early cemetery, Glory Days celebration in October; **Bivins** (215); **Bloomburg** (388); **Domino** (82); **Douglassville** (172); **Hughes Springs** (1,919) varied manufacturing, warehousing, truck-

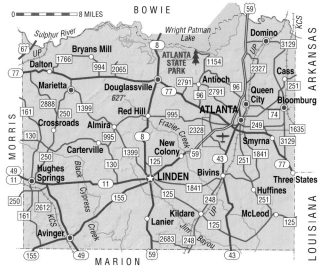

ing school, Pumpkin Glow in October; **Kildare** (104); **Marietta** (108); **McLeod** (600); **Queen City** (1,651) paper industry, commuters to Texarkana, government/services, historic sites.

Population	29,284
Change fm 2000	–3.8
Area (sq. mi.)	960.35
Land Area (sq. mi.)	937.35
Altitude (ft.)	167-627
Rainfall (in.)	48.20
Jan. mean min.	31.0
July mean max.	94.0
Civ. Labor	13,186
Unemployed	7.4
Wages	$59,361,122
Av. Weekly Wage	$581
Prop. Value	$1,901,347,468
Retail Sales	$209,341,585

For explanation of sources, abbreviations and symbols, see p. 210 and foldout map.

The Leaning Water Tower, built as a gimmick, west of Groom in Carson County. Robert Plocheck photo

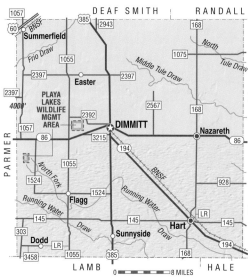

Castro County

Physical Features: Flat Panhandle county, drains to creeks, draws and playas; underground water.

Economy: Agribusiness.

History: Apaches, displaced by Comanches in 1720s. Anglo-American ranchers began settling in 1880s. Germans settled after 1900. Mexican migration increased after 1950. County created 1876 from Bexar District, organized 1891. Named for Henri Castro, Texas colonizer.

Race/Ethnicity, 2007: (In percent) Anglo, 41.2; Black, 2.5; Hispanic, 56.0; Other, 0.3.

Vital Statistics, 2006: Births, 142; deaths, 54; marriages, 40; divorces, 17.

Recreation: Pheasant hunting; Italian POW camp site; Dimmitt Harvest Days celebrated in August.

Minerals: Insignificant.

Agriculture: Beef cattle, dairies, corn, cotton, wheat, sheep. Market value $973.4 million; second in state.

DIMMITT (4,097) county seat; agribusiness center; library, hospital; quilt festival in April.

Other towns include: **Hart** (1,104) and **Nazareth** (345).

Population 7,129	Rainfall (in.) 19.71	
Change fm 2000 .... −14.0	Jan. mean min. 20.4	Wages $17,181,399
Area (sq. mi.) 899.32	July mean max. 90.1	Av. Weekly Wage....................... $534
Land Area (sq. mi.) 898.31	Civ. Labor 3,795	Prop. Value $471,453,540
Altitude (ft.) 3,565-4,000	Unemployed 3.7	Retail Sales $50,936,917

Chambers County

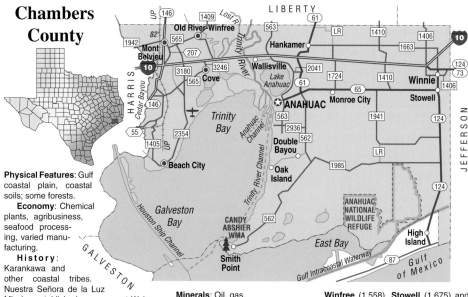

Physical Features: Gulf coastal plain, coastal soils; some forests.

Economy: Chemical plants, agribusiness, seafood processing, varied manufacturing.

History: Karankawa and other coastal tribes. Nuestra Señora de la Luz Mission established near present Wallisville in 1756. County created 1858 from Liberty, Jefferson counties. Named for Gen. T. J. Chambers, surveyor.

Race/Ethnicity, 2007: (In percent) Anglo, 75.3; Black, 9.4; Hispanic, 14.2; Other, 1.1.

Vital Statistics, 2006: Births, 360; deaths, 181; marriages, 156; divorces, 148.

Recreation: Fishing, hunting; water sports; camping; county parks; wildlife refuge; historic sites; Wallisville Heritage Museum; Texas Rice Festival and Texas Gatorfest in September.

Minerals: Oil, gas.

Agriculture: Rice, cattle and forage, soybeans, aquaculture, corn, grain sorghum, sugar cane; significant irrigation. Market value $17.6 million.

ANAHUAC (2,451) county seat; canal connects with Houston Ship Channel; agribusiness; hospital, library.

Winnie (3,195) fertilizer manufacturing; wholesale greenhouse; hospital; depot museum.

Other towns include: **Beach City** (2,032), **Cove** (333), **Hankamer** (226), **Mont Belvieu** (2,775), **Old River-** **Winfree** (1,558), **Stowell** (1,675) and **Wallisville** (452).

Population 28,356	
Change fm 2000 .... 12.8	
Area (sq. mi.) 871.99	
Land Area (sq. mi.) 599.31	
Altitude (ft.) .... sea level-82	
Rainfall (in.) 54.08	
Jan. mean min. 41.7	
July mean max. 91.9	
Civ. Labor 14,779	
Unemployed 6.6	
Wages $115,029,484	
Av. Weekly Wage....................... $852	
Prop. Value $5,677,206,490	
Retail Sales $1,514,728,806	

Cherokee County

Physical Features: East Texas county; hilly, partly forested; drains to Angelina, Neches rivers; many streams, lakes; sandy, clay soils.

Economy: Government/services, varied manufacturing, agribusiness.

History: Caddo tribes attracted Spanish missionaries around 1720. Cherokees began settling area around 1820, and soon afterward Anglo-Americans began to arrive. Cherokees forced to Indian Territory 1839. Named for Indian tribe; created 1846 from Nacogdoches County.

Race/Ethnicity, 2007: (In percent) Anglo, 65.9; Black, 15.6; Hispanic, 17.7; Other, 0.8.

Vital Statistics, 2006: Births, 695; deaths, 455; marriages, 333; divorces, 196.

Recreation: Water sports; fishing, hunting; historic sites and parks; Texas State Railroad; nature trails through forests; lakes.

Minerals: Gas, oil.

Agriculture: Nurseries (first in state in value of sales), hay, beef cattle, dairies, poultry. Market value $140.3 million. Timber, hunting income significant.

RUSK (5,228) county seat; agribusiness, tourism, state mental hospital, prison unit; heritage festival in October.

JACKSONVILLE (14,576) varied manufacturing, plastics, agribusiness, tourism, retail center; hospitals, junior colleges; Love's Lookout; Tomato Fest in June.

Other towns include: **Alto** (1,305) farming, timber, light manufacturing, pecan festival in November; **Cuney** (149); **Gallatin** (393); **Maydelle** (250); **New Summerfield** (1,119); **Reklaw** (361, partly in Rusk County); **Wells** (776). Part [53] of **Bullard** and part [40] of **Troup**.

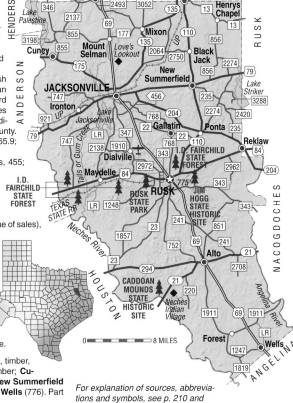

For explanation of sources, abbreviations and symbols, see p. 210 and foldout map.

Population	**48,321**	Altitude (ft.)	187-775
Change fm 2000	3.6	Rainfall (in.)	48.50
Area (sq. mi.)	1,061.93	Jan. mean min.	36.8
Land Area (sq. mi.)	1,052.22	uly mean max.	92.8
		Civ. Labor	21,038

Unemployed	7.4
Wages	$105,602,575
Av. Weekly Wage	$557
Prop. Value	$2,430,514,433
Retail Sales	$393,600,490

The Battleship Texas sits along the Houston Ship Channel. Robert Plocheck photo.

Childress County

Physical Features: Rolling prairie, at corner of Panhandle, draining to fork of Red River; mixed soils.

Economy: Government/services, retail trade, tourism, agriculture.

History: Apaches, displaced by Comanches. Ranchers arrived around 1880. County created 1876 from Bexar, Young districts; organized 1887; named for writer of Texas Declaration of Independence, George C. Childress.

Race/Ethnicity, 2007: (In percent) Anglo, 62.2; Black, 14.0; Hispanic, 23.1; Other, 0.7.

Vital Statistics, 2006: Births, 81; deaths, 79; marriages, 44; divorces, 29.

Recreation: Recreation on lakes and creek, fishing; hunting of deer, turkey, wild hog, quail, dove; parks; county museum.

Agriculture: Cotton, beef cattle, wheat, hay, sorghum, peanuts; 6,000 acres irrigated. Market value $25.9 million. Hunting leases.

CHILDRESS (6,832) county seat; agribusiness, hospital, prison unit; settlers reunion and rodeo in July. Other towns include: **Tell** (15).

Population	7,536
Change fm 2000	–2.0
Area (sq. mi.)	713.61
Land Area (sq. mi.)	710.34
Altitude (ft.)	1,560-2,060
Rainfall (in.)	22.65
Jan. mean min.	26.8
July mean max.	95.3
Civ. Labor	3,080
Unemployed	5.6
Wages	$16,583,453
Av. Weekly Wage	$525
Prop. Value	$320,064,530
Retail Sales	$70,665,533

Clay County

Physical Features: Hilly, rolling; Northwest county drains to Red, Trinity rivers, lake; sandy loam, chocolate soils; mesquites, post oaks.

Economy: Oil, agribusiness, varied manufacturing.

History: Wichitas arrived from north-central plains in mid-1700s, followed by Apaches and Comanches. Ranching attempts began in 1850s. County created from Cooke County, 1857; Indians forced disorganization, 1862; reorganized, 1873; named for Henry Clay, U.S. statesman.

Race/Ethnicity, 2007: (In percent) Anglo, 94.6; Black, 0.4; Hispanic, 3.9; Other, 1.1.

Vital Statistics, 2006: Births, 100; deaths, 101; marriages, 46; divorces, 50.

Recreation: Fishing, water sports; state park; pioneer reunion.

Minerals: Oil and gas, stone.

Agriculture: Beef and dairy cattle, horses raised; wheat, cotton, pecan, peaches. Market value $56.9 million. Oaks, cedar, elms sold to nurseries, mesquite cut for firewood.

HENRIETTA (3,300) county seat; agribusiness, government/services, manufacturing; hospital; museum; Turkey Fest in April.

Other towns include: **Bellevue** (386), **Bluegrove** (135), **Byers** (498), **Dean** (345), **Jolly** (180), **Petrolia** (757).

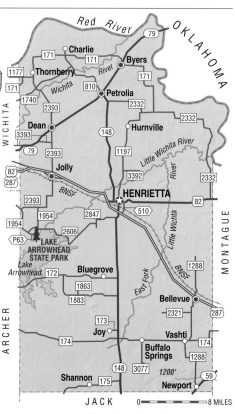

Population	10,888
Change fm 2000	–1.1
Area (sq. mi.)	1,116.17
Land Area (sq. mi.)	1,097.82
Altitude (ft.)	791-1,200
Rainfall (in.)	31.66
Jan. mean min.	26.8
July mean max.	95.0
Civ. Labor	6,504
Unemployed	4.6
Wages	$14,794,716
Av. Weekly Wage	$561
Prop. Value	$942,021,226
Retail Sales	$73,276,321

For explanation of sources, abbreviations and symbols, see p. 210 and foldout page.

Cochran County

Physical Features: South Plains bordering New Mexico with small lakes (playas); underground water; loam, sandy loam soils.

Economy: Farming, government/services, retail.

History: Hunting area for various Indian tribes. Ranches operated in 1880s but population in 1900 was still only 25. Farming began in 1920s. County created from Bexar, Young districts, 1876; organized 1924; named for Robert Cochran, who died at the Alamo.

Race/Ethnicity 2007: (In percent) Anglo, 47.4; Black, 5.1; Hispanic, 46.7; Other, 0.8.

Vital Statistics, 2006: Births, 67; deaths, 28; marriages, 19; divorces, 11.

Recreation: Museum; Last Frontier Trail Drive and Buffalo Soldier Day in June.

Minerals: Insignificant.

Agriculture: Cotton, grain sorghum, peanuts, sunflowers, peas. Crops 60 percent irrigated. Market value $91.7 million.

MORTON (2,081) county seat; oil, farm center, meat packing, light manufacture; hospital.

Other towns include: **Bledsoe** (126), **Whiteface** (450).

Population	2,977
Change fm 2000	−20.2
Area (sq. mi.)	775.31
Land Area (sq. mi.)	775.22
Altitude (ft.)	3,565-4,000
Rainfall (in.)	18.34
Jan. temp. min.	23.1
July temp. max.	91.4
Civ. Labor	1,687
Unemployed	4.1
Wages	$6,004,971
Av. Weekly Wage	$561
Prop. Value	$556,575,290
Retail Sales	$23,431,904

The farming community of Byers, Clay County, from FM 171 east of town. Robert Plocheck photo.

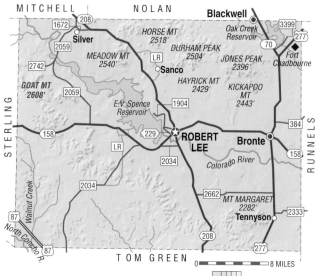

Coke County

Physical Features: West Texas prairie, hills, Colorado River valley; sandy loam, red soils; reservoirs.

Economy: Oil and gas, government/services, agriculture.

History: From 1700 to 1870s, Comanches roamed the area. Ranches began operating after the Civil War. County created 1889 from Tom Green County; named for Gov. Richard Coke.

Race/Ethnicity, 2007: (In percent) Anglo, 77.8; Black, 1.8; Hispanic, 19.4; Other,1.0.

Vital Statistics, 2006: Births, 30; deaths, 63; marriages, 16; divorces, 16.

Recreation: Hunting, fishing, Caliche Loop birdwatching trail; lakes; Sumac hiking trail; historic sites, Fort Chadbourne, county museum, Fort Chadbourne Days in May; amphitheater.

Minerals: Oil, gas.

Agriculture: Beef cattle, small grains, sheep and goats, hay. Market value $13.6 million.

ROBERT LEE (1,097) county seat; oil and gas, wind farms, ranching, government/services; old jail museum.

Bronte (1,054) ranching, oil.

Other towns include: **Silver** (34) and **Tennyson** (46). Also, a small part of **Blackwell** (330).

Population	**3,480**
Change fm 2000	–9.9
Area (sq. mi.)	927.97
Land Area (sq. mi.)	898.81
Altitude (ft.)	1,700-2,608
Rainfall (in.)	23.00
Jan. mean min.	29.0
July mean max.	96.4
Civ. Labor	1,366
Unemployed	7.2
Wages	$5,150,656
Av. Weekly Wage	$477
Prop. Value	$517,925,130
Retail Sales	$21,851,694

For explanation of sources, abbreviations and symbols, see p. 210 and foldout page.

Fort Chadbourne in northeast Coke County. Robert Plocheck photo.

The Santa Anna Mountains in Coleman County. Robert Plocheck photo.

Coleman County

Physical Features: Hilly, rolling; drains to Colorado River, Pecan Bayou; lakes; mesquite, oaks.

Economy: Agribusiness, petroleum, ecotourism, varied manufacturing.

History: Presence of Apaches and Comanches brought military outpost, Camp Colorado, before the Civil War. Settlers arrived after organization. County created 1858 from Brown, Travis counties; organized 1864; named for Houston's aide, R.M. Coleman.

Race/Ethnicity, 2007: (In percent), Anglo, 80.7; Black, 2.5; Hispanic, 16.1; Other, 0.7.

Vital Statistics, 2006: Births, 105; deaths, 158; marriages, 62; divorces, 49.

Recreation: Fishing, hunting; water sports; city park, historic sites; lakes; Santa Anna Peak; Santa Anna bison cook-off in May.

Minerals: Oil, gas, stone, clays.

Agriculture: Cattle, wheat, sheep, hay, grain sorghum, goats, oats, cotton. Market value $20 million. Mesquite for firewood and furniture.

COLEMAN (5,052) county seat; varied manufacturing; hospital, library, museums: Fiesta de la Paloma in October.

Santa Anna (1,009) agribusiness, some manufacturing, tourism.

Other towns include: **Burkett** (30), **Goldsboro** (30), **Gouldbusk** (70), **Novice** (136), **Rockwood** (80), **Talpa** (127), and **Valera** (80).

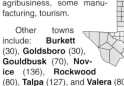

Population	**8,577**
Change fm 2000	−7.1
Area (sq. mi.)	1,281.45
Land Area (sq. mi.)	1,260.20

Altitude (ft.)	1,289-2,250
Rainfall (in.)	28.70
Jan. mean min.	30.0
July mean max.	93.7

Civ. Labor	4,639
Unemployed	4.7
Wages	$15,439,715
Av. Weekly Wage	$508
Prop. Value	$315,947,041
Retail Sales	$63,720,536

Collin County

Physical Features: Heavy, black clay soil; level to rolling; drains to Trinity, Lake Lavon.

Economy: Government/services, manufacturing plants, retail and wholesale center, many residents work in Dallas.

History: Caddo area until 1850s. Settlers of Peters colony arrived in early 1840s. County created from Fannin County 1846. Named for pioneer settler Collin McKinney.

Race/Ethnicity, 2007: (In percent) Anglo, 73.0; Black, 5.5; Hispanic, 12.0; Other, 8.6.

Vital Statistics, 2006: Births, 10,415; deaths, 2,475; marriages, 4,653; divorces, 2,371.

Recreation: Fishing, water sports; historic sites; old homes restoration, tours; natural science museum.

Minerals: Insignificant.

Agriculture: Landscape nurseries, corn, wheat, cattle. Market value $61.1 million.

McKINNEY (116,233) county seat; agribusiness, trade center, varied industry; hospital, community college; museums.

PLANO (279,607) telecommunications, manufacturing, newspaper printing, medical services, research center, commercial and financial center; community college; hospitals; balloon festival in September.

Frisco (89,905) technical, areospace industry, hospital, community college.

Other towns include: **Allen** (75,291) telecommunications, hospital, conservatory, natatorium, historic dam, Cinco de Mayo celebration; **Anna** (1,962); **Blue Ridge** (971); **Celina** (5,046) museum, historic town square, Fun Day in September; **Copeville** (243); **Fairview** (6,446) government/services, retail center, commuters, museum, old mill site, wildlife sanctuary; **Farmersville** (3,945) agriculture, light industries, Audie Murphy Day in June.

Also, **Josephine** (937); **Lavon** (585); **Lowry Crossing** (1,856); **Lucas** (4,456); **Melissa** (4,688); **Murphy** (13,080); **Nevada** (866); **New Hope** (758); **Parker** (2,594); **Princeton** (6,141) manufacturing, commuters, Spring Onion festival in April; **Prosper** (4,743); **St. Paul** (912); **Westminster** (470); **Weston** (683); **Wylie** (34,044) manufacturing, retail, hospital, historic sites, July Jubilee.

Also, part [45,155] of **Dallas**, part [20,873] of **Richardson** and part [1,660] of **Sachse**.

Population	762,010
Change fm 2000	55.0
Area (sq. mi.)	885.85
Land Area (sq. mi.)	847.56
Altitude (ft.)	434-810
Rainfall (in.)	41.01
Jan. mean min.	31.1
July mean max.	92.7
Civ. Labor	398,736
Unemployed	5.5
Wages	$3,814,899,867
Av. Weekly Wage	$992
Prop. Value	$78,722,521,468
Retail Sales	$11,312,744,296

For explanation of sources, abbreviations and symbols, see p. 210 and foldout page.

Collingsworth County

Physical Features: Panhandle county of rolling, broken terrain, draining to Red River forks; sandy and loam soils.

Economy: Agribusiness.

History: Apaches, displaced by Comanches. Ranchers from England arrived in late 1870s. County created 1876, from Bexar and Young districts, organized 1890. Named for Republic of Texas' first chief justice, James Collinsworth (name misspelled in law).

Race/Ethnicity, 2007: (In percent) Anglo, 67.4; Black, 6.0; Hispanic, 25.0; Other, 1.6.

Vital Statistics, 2006: Births, 44; deaths, 39; marriages, 22; divorces, 14.

Recreation: Deer, quail hunting; children's camp, county museum, pioneer park; Wellington peanut festival in September.

Minerals: Gas, oil production.

Agriculture: Cotton, peanuts (second in acreage), cow-calf operations, wheat, stocker cattle; 22,000 acres irrigated. Market value $50.3 million.

WELLINGTON (2,165) county seat; peanut-processing plants, varied manufacturing, agriculture; hospital, library; restored Ritz Theatre.

Other towns include: **Dodson** (114), **Quail** (32), **Samnorwood** (40).

Population	**2,985**
Change fm 2000	–6.9
Area (sq. mi.)	919.44
Land Area (sq. mi.)	918.80
Altitude (ft.)	1,750-2,840
Rainfall (in.)	22.80
Jan. mean min.	27.0
July mean max.	97.9
Civ. Labor	1,652
Unemployed	3.6
Wages	$5,667,709
Av. Weekly Wage	$498
Prop. Value	$157,386,940
Retail Sales	$13,,105,509

Colorado County

Physical Features: Located in three soil areas; level to rolling; bisected by Colorado River; oaks.

Economy: Agribusiness, oil-field services, ecotourism, mineral processing, gravel mining.

History: Karankawa and other tribes. Anglo settlers among Stephen F. Austin's Old Three Hundred families. First German settlers arrived around 1840. Antebellum slaveholding area. County created 1836, organized 1837; named for river.

Race/Ethnicity, 2007: (In percent) Anglo, 60.6; Black, 15.4; Hispanic, 23.5; Other, 0.5.

Vital Statistics, 2006: Births, 247; deaths, 229; marriages, 137; divorces, 81.

Recreation: Hunting, bicycling, canoeing; historic sites; prairie chicken refuge; opera house in Columbus.

Minerals: Gas, oil.

Agriculture: Rice (second in state in acres), cattle, corn, cotton, soybeans, nurseries, hay, poultry, sorghum; significant irrigation for rice. Market value $72 million.

COLUMBUS (3,903) county seat; mining, agribusiness center, tourism, oil-field servicing, timber-treating center; hospital; historical sites, homes, walking tour; Live Oak festival in May.

Eagle Lake (3,626) rice drying center; hospital; goose hunting; Prairie Edge museum.

Weimar (2,073) agriculture, feed mill, light industry, meat processing, retail; hospital, library; "Gedenke" (remember) celebration on Mother's Day; Babe Ruth World Series.

Other towns include: **Altair** (30), **Garwood** (975), **Nada** (165), **Oakland** (80), **Rock Island** (160), **Sheridan** (225).

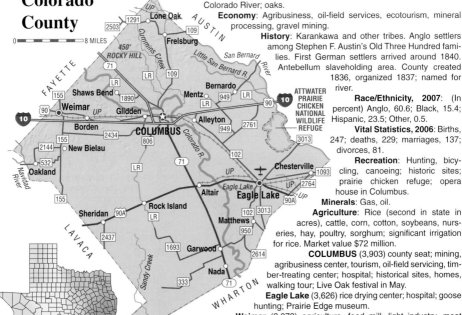

Population	**20,734**
Change fm 2000	1.8
Area (sq. mi.)	973.59
Land Area (sq. mi.)	962.95
Altitude (ft.)	125-450
Rainfall (in.)	44.72
Jan. mean min.	36.8
July mean max.	96.3
Civ. Labor	11,091
Unemployed	4.7
Wages	$56,008,118
Av. Weekly Wage	$616
Prop. Value	$1,732,376,157
Retail Sales	$268,631,720

Comal County

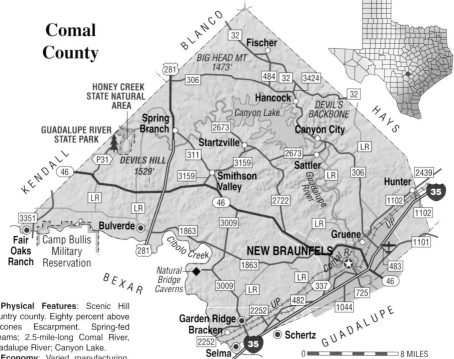

Physical Features: Scenic Hill Country county. Eighty percent above Balcones Escarpment. Spring-fed streams; 2.5-mile-long Comal River, Guadalupe River; Canyon Lake.

Economy: Varied manufacturing, tourism, government/services, agriculture; county in San Antonio metropolitan area.

History: Tonkawa, Waco Indians. A pioneer German settlement 1845. Mexican migration peaked during Mexican Revolution. County created from Bexar, Gonzales, Travis counties and organized in 1846; named for river, a name for Spanish earthenware or metal pan used for cooking tortillas.

Race/Ethnicity, 2007: (In percent) Anglo, 75.3; Black, 0.9; Hispanic, 22.8; Other, 1.0.

Vital Statistics, 2006: Births, 1,144; deaths, 759; marriages, 875; divorces, 316.

Recreation: Fishing, hunting; historic sites; scenic drives; lake facilities; Prince Solms Park, other county parks; Landa Park with 76 species of trees; Gruene historic area; caverns; river resorts; river tubing; Schlitterbahn water park; Wurstfest in November, Wasselfest in December.

Minerals: Stone, lime, sand and gravel.

Agriculture: Cattle, goats, sheep, hogs, horses; nursery, hay, corn, sorghum, wheat. Market value $6.6 million.

NEW BRAUNFELS (56,595) county seat; manufacturing, retail, distribution center; picturesque city, making it a tourist center; Conservation Plaza; rose garden; hospital; library; mental health and retardation center. **Gruene** is now part of New Braunfels.

Other towns include: **Bulverde** (4,895); **Garden Ridge** (3,168); the retirement and recreation community around **Canyon Lake** (19,508), which includes **Startzville, Sattler, Smithson Valley, Canyon City, Fischer** and **Spring Branch**.

Also in the county, parts of **Fair Oaks Ranch** (6,175), **Selma** (3,445) and **Schertz** (30,552).

Population	109,635
Change fm 2000	40.5
Area (sq. mi.)	574.59
Land Area (sq. mi.)	561.45
Altitude (ft.)	560-1,529
Rainfall (in.)	35.74
Jan. mean min.	35.5
July mean max.	94.7
Civ. Labor	53,082
Unemployed	4.8
Wages	$328,474,433
Av. Weekly Wage	$635
Prop. Value	$12,287,007,086
Retail Sales	$1,257,105,358

For explanation of sources, abbreviations and symbols, see p. 210 and foldout page.

Gruene Hall, one of the premier entertainment venues in the state. Emily Plocheck photo.

Comanche County

Physical Features: Rolling, hilly terrain; sandy, loam, waxy soils; drains to Leon River, Proctor Lake; pecans, oaks, mesquites, cedars.

Economy: Dairies, peanut-, pecan-shelling plants, manufacturing.

History: Comanche area. Anglo-American settlers arrived in 1854 on land granted earlier to Stephen F. Austin and Samuel May Williams. County created 1856 from Bosque, Coryell counties; named for Indian tribe.

Race/Ethnicity, 2007: (In percent) Anglo, 74.4; Black, 0.5; Hispanic, 24.6; Other, 0.5.

Vital Statistics, 2006: Births, 200; deaths, 193; marriages, 111; divorces, 39.

Recreation: Hunting, fishing, water sports, nature tourism; parks, community center, museums; Comanche Pow-Wow in September, rodeo in July.

Minerals: Limited gas, oil, stone, clay.

Agriculture: Dairies, beef cattle, pecans (first in state in acreage), hay, wildlife, melons. Market value $144.9 million.

COMANCHE (4,618) county seat; plants process feed, food; varied manufacturing; agribusiness; winery; hospital; Ranger College branch; library; state's oldest courthouse, "Old Cora," on display on town square.

De Leon (2,535) pecans, light manufacturing; hospital; car museum, Peach and Melon Festival in August.

Other towns include: **Energy** (70), **Gustine** (478), **Proctor** (228) and **Sidney** (148).

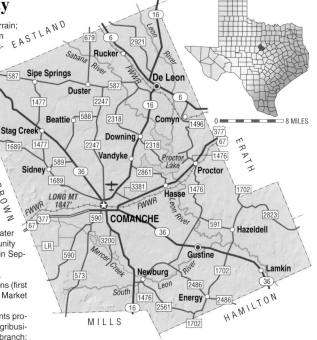

Population	13,483
Change fm 2000	–3.9
Area (sq. mi.)	947.67
Land Area (sq. mi.)	937.69
Altitude (ft.)	1,020-1,847
Rainfall (in.)	31.12
Jan. mean min.	30.6
July mean max.	95.5
Civ. Labor	6,716
Unemployed	4.3
Wages	$25,449,705
Av. Weekly Wage	$512
Prop. Value	$591,809,354
Retail Sales	$124,468,563

Concho County

Physical Features: On Edwards Plateau; rough, broken to south; level in north; sandy, loam and dark soils; drains to creeks and Colorado River.

Economy: Agribusiness, manufacturing.

History: Athabascan-speaking Plains Indians, then Jumanos in 1600s, absorbed by Lipan Apaches 1700s. Comanches raided after 1800. Anglo-Americans began ranching around 1850; farming after the Civil War. Mexican-Americans employed on sheep ranches 1920s-30s. County created from Bexar District, 1858, organized 1879; named for river.

Race/Ethnicity, 2007: (In percent) Anglo, 55.3; Black, 0.8; Hispanic, 43.6; Other, 0.3.

Vital Statistics, 2006: Births, 36; deaths, 26; marriages, 9; divorces, 4.

Recreation: Famed for 1,500 Indian pictographs; reservoir.

Minerals: Oil, gas, stone.

Agriculture: Sheep, cattle, goats; wheat, feed grains; 10,000 acres irrigated for cotton. Market value $21.2 million.

PAINT ROCK (306) county seat; named for Indian pictographs nearby; farming, ranching center.

EDEN (2,449) steel fabrication, detention center; hospital; fall fest.

Other towns include: **Eola** (215), **Lowake** (40) and **Millersview** (80).

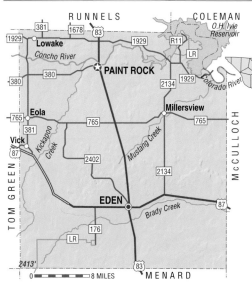

Population	3,610
Change fm 2000	–9.0
Area (sq. mi.)	993.69
Land Area (sq. mi.)	991.45
Altitude (ft.)	1,421-2,413
Rainfall (in.)	25.50
Jan. mean min.	31.9
July mean max.	97.4
Civ. Labor	1,406
Unemployed	5.5
Wages	$6,119,680
Av. Weekly Wage	$514
Prop. Value	$228,124,400
Retail Sales	$19,916,354

Cooke County

Physical Features: North Texas county; drains to Red, Trinity rivers, lakes; sandy, red, loam soils.

Economy: Oil, agribusiness, tourism, varied manufacturing, commuting to northern DFW metroplex.

History: Frontier between Caddoes and Comanches. Anglo-Americans arrived in late 1840s. Germans settled western part around 1890. County created 1848 from Fannin County; named for Capt. W.G. Cooke of the Texas Revolution.

Race/Ethnicity, 2007: (In percent) Anglo, 82.1; Black, 3.3; Hispanic, 13.2; Other, 1.4.

Vital Statistics, 2006: Births, 544; deaths, 382; marriages, 629; divorces, 166.

Recreation: Water sports; hunting, fishing, zoo; museum; park, Depot Day/car show in October.

Minerals: Oil, natural gas, sand, gravel.

Agriculture: Beef, horses, dairies, wheat, grain sorghum, corn, pecans. Market value $58.3 million. Hunting leases.

GAINESVILLE (17,058) county seat; tourism, plastics, agribusiness, aircraft and steel fabrication; Victorian homes, walking tours; hospital; community college, juvenile correction unit; Camp Sweeney for diabetic children.

Muenster (1,701) oil, food processing, tourism, varied manufacturing; hospital, Germanfest in April.

Other towns include: **Callisburg** (388), **Era** (150), **Lindsay** (956) 1919 Romanesque-style church, **Myra** (150), **Oak Ridge** (246), **Rosston** (75), **Valley View** (799) and the residential community around **Lake Kiowa** (1,888).

For explanation of sources, abbreviations and symbols, see p. 210 and foldout page.

Population 38,407
Change fm 2000 .... 5.6
Area (sq. mi.) 898.81
Land Area (sq. mi.) 873.64
Altitude (ft.) 617-1,217
Rainfall (in.) 36.90
Jan. mean min. 28.0
July mean max. 95.0
Civ. Labor 23,040
Unemployed 3.8
Wages $158,336,166
Av. Weekly Wage....................... $752
Prop. Value $2,523,745,751
Retail Sales $570,069,242

The hills and grasses near Bulcher in Cooke County. Robert Plocheck photo.

Physical Features: Leon Valley in center, remainder rolling, hilly.

Economy: Fort Hood, prisons, agribusiness, manufacturing.

History: Tonkawa area, later various other tribes. Anglo-Americans settled around Fort Gates in late 1840s. Permanent establishment of Fort Hood in 1950 changed cultural geography. County created from Bell County 1854; named for local pioneer James Coryell.

Race/Ethnicity, 2007: (In percent) Anglo, 58.5; Black, 22.4; Hispanic, 14.9; Other, 4.3.

Vital Statistics, 2006: Births, 796; deaths, 364; marriages, 512; divorces, 276.

Recreation: State park; deer hunting; fishing; lakes, Leon River; bluebonnet area; historic homes; log jail; Shivaree in June.

Minerals: Oil and gas.

Agriculture: Beef, forages, oats (second in acreage), wildlife, row crops. Market value $40.1 million. Hunting leases, timber.

GATESVILLE (16,233) county seat; prisons, varied manufacturing; hospital; refurbished courthouse; museum; branch Central Texas College.

COPPERAS COVE (32,365) business center for Fort Hood; industrial filters, other manufacturing; hospital, library; Central Texas College; Spurfest in September.

Other towns include: **Evant** (416, partly in Hamilton County), **Flat** (210), **Jonesboro** (125), **Mound** (125), **Oglesby** (444), **Purmela** (50), **South Mountain** (409). Part [16,429] of **Fort Hood**.

Coryell County

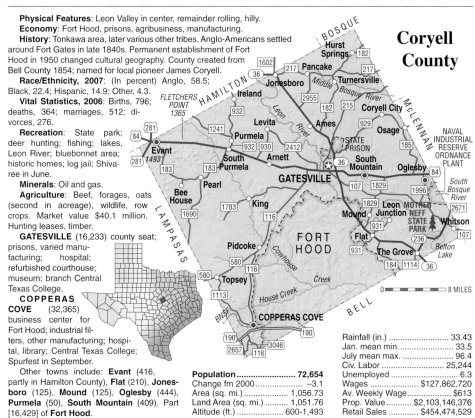

Population	72,654
Change fm 2000	–3.1
Area (sq. mi.)	1,056.73
Land Area (sq. mi.)	1,051.76
Altitude (ft.)	600-1,493

Rainfall (in.)	33.43
Jan. mean min.	33.5
July mean max.	96.4
Civ. Labor	25,244
Unemployed	6.3
Wages	$127,862,720
Av. Weekly Wage	$613
Prop. Value	$2,103,146,376
Retail Sales	$454,474,529

Cottle County

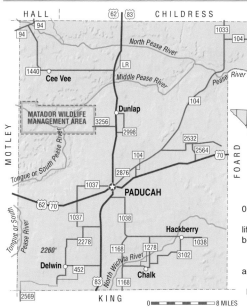

Physical Features: Northwest county below Caprock, rough in west, level in east; gray, black, sandy and loam soils; drains to Pease River.

Economy: Agribusiness, government/services.

History: Around 1700, Apaches were displaced by Comanches, who in turn were driven out by U.S. Army 1870s. Anglo-American settlers arrived in 1880s. County created 1876 from Fannin County; organized 1892; named for George W. Cottle, Alamo hero.

Race/Ethnicity, 2007: (In percent) Anglo, 66.4; Black, 10.9; Hispanic, 22.4; Other, 0.4.

Vital Statistics, 2006: Births, 14; deaths, 35; marriages, 0; divorces, 1.

Recreation: Hunting of quail, dove, wild hogs, deer; wildlife management area; museum, Fiestas Patrias in September, horse and colt show in April.

Minerals: Oil, natural gas.

Agriculture: Beef cattle, cotton, peanuts, wheat. 3,000 acres irrigated. Market value $17.5 million.

PADUCAH (1,286) county seat; government/services, library.

Other towns include: **Cee Vee** (45).

Population	1,617
Change fm 2000	–15.1
Area (sq. mi.)	901.59
Land Area (sq. mi.)	901.18
Altitude (ft.)	1,470-2,260
Rainfall (in.)	24.11

Jan. mean min.	26.2
July mean max.	96.8
Civ. Labor	856
Unemployed	4.3
Wages	$3,627,794
Av. Weekly Wage	$557

Prop. Value	$139,586,340
Retail Sales	$10,730,450

For explanation of sources, abbreviations and symbols, see p. 210 and foldout page.

Crane County

Physical Features: Rolling prairie, Pecos Valley, some hills; sandy, loam soils; Juan Cordona Lake (intermittent).

Economy: Oil and gas; agriculture; government/services.

History: Lipan Apache area. Ranching developed in 1890s. Oil discovered in 1926. County created from Tom Green County 1887, organized 1927; named for Baylor University president W. C. Crane.

Race/Ethnicity, 2007: (In percent) Anglo, 49.0; Black, 3.1; Hispanic, 47.3; Other, 0.6.

Vital Statistics, 2006: Births, 61; deaths, 39; marriages, 34; divorces, 6.

Recreation: Museum of the Desert Southwest; sites of pioneer trails and historic Horsehead Crossing on Pecos River; hunting of mule deer, quail; camping park; rodeo in May.

Minerals: Oil, gas production.

Agriculture: Cattle ranching, goats. Market value $1.7 million.

CRANE (3,144) county seat; oil-well servicing and production, foundry, steel, surfboard manufacturing; hospital.

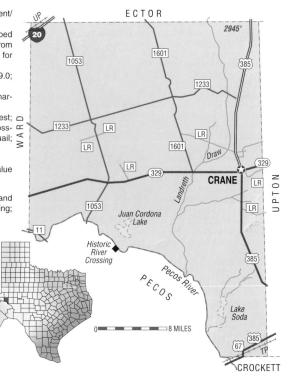

Population	4,017
Change fm 2000	0.5
Area (sq. mi.)	785.59
Land Area (sq. mi.)	785.56
Altitude (ft.)	2,290-2,945
Rainfall (in.)	15.38
Jan. mean min.	30.6
July mean max.	95.3
Civ. Labor	1,841
Unemployed	4.5
Wages	$19,892,711
Av. Weekly Wage	$1,007
Prop. Value	$1,958,340,250
Retail Sales	$46,840,909

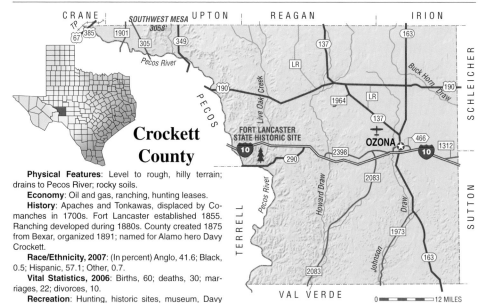

Crockett County

Physical Features: Level to rough, hilly terrain; drains to Pecos River; rocky soils.

Economy: Oil and gas, ranching, hunting leases.

History: Apaches and Tonkawas, displaced by Comanches in 1700s. Fort Lancaster established 1855. Ranching developed during 1880s. County created 1875 from Bexar, organized 1891; named for Alamo hero Davy Crockett.

Race/Ethnicity, 2007: (In percent) Anglo, 41.6; Black, 0.5; Hispanic, 57.1; Other, 0.7.

Vital Statistics, 2006: Births, 60; deaths, 30; marriages, 22; divorces, 10.

Recreation: Hunting, historic sites, museum, Davy Crockett statue in park; Davy Crockett festival in August, Deerfest in December.

Minerals: Oil, gas production.

Agriculture: Sheep (first in numbers), goats; beef cattle. Market value $13.6 million.

OZONA (3,697) county seat; trade center for ranching, hunting leases, tourism.

Population	3,802	July mean max.	93.0
Change fm 2000	−7.2	Civ. Labor	2,077
Area (sq. mi.)	2,807.43	Unemployed	3.2
Land Area (sq. mi.)	2,807.42	Wages	$11,200,497
Altitude (ft.)	1,720-3,058	Av. Weekly Wage	$562
Rainfall (in.)	18.95	Prop. Value	$2,054,083,260
Jan. mean min.	27.7	Retail Sales	$24,707,151

Crosby County

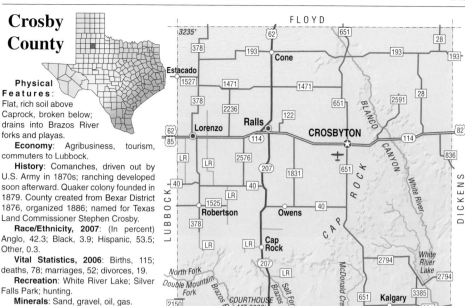

Physical Features: Flat, rich soil above Caprock, broken below; drains into Brazos River forks and playas.

Economy: Agribusiness, tourism, commuters to Lubbock.

History: Comanches, driven out by U.S. Army in 1870s; ranching developed soon afterward. Quaker colony founded in 1879. County created from Bexar District 1876, organized 1886; named for Texas Land Commissioner Stephen Crosby.

Race/Ethnicity, 2007: (In percent) Anglo, 42.3; Black, 3.9; Hispanic, 53.5; Other, 0.3.

Vital Statistics, 2006: Births, 115; deaths, 78; marriages, 52; divorces, 19.

Recreation: White River Lake; Silver Falls Park; hunting.

Minerals: Sand, gravel, oil, gas.

Agriculture: Cotton, beef cattle, sorghum; about 200,000 acres irrigated. Market value $92.7 million.

CROSBYTON (1,731) county seat; agribusiness center; hospital, Pioneer Museum, Prairie Ladies Multi-Cultural Center, library; Cowboy Gathering in October.

Other towns include: **Lorenzo** (1,304); **Ralls** (2,130) government/services, agribusiness, museums, Cotton Boll Fest in September.

Population	**6,192**
Change fm 2000	−12.4
Area (sq. mi.)	901.69
Land Area (sq. mi.)	899.51
Altitude (ft.)	2,250-3,235
Rainfall (in.)	22.95
Jan. mean min.	25.3
July mean max.	92.5
Civ. Labor	2,814
Unemployed	4.7

Wages	$9,978,831
Av. Weekly Wage	$508
Prop. Value	$271,041,510
Retail Sales	$120,942,039

For explanation of sources, abbreviations and symbols, see p. 210 and foldout map.

Ruins of Fort Lancaster in Crockett County. Robert Plocheck photo.

The Sierra Diablo Wildlife Management Area in Culberson County. Robert Plocheck photo.

Culberson County

Physical Features: Contains Texas' highest mountain; slopes toward Pecos Valley on east, Diablo Bolson on west; salt lakes; unique vegetation in canyons.

Economy: Tourism, government/services, talc mining and processing, agribusiness.

History: Apaches arrived about 600 years ago. U.S. military frontier after Civil War. Ranching developed after 1880. Mexican migration increased after 1920. County created from El Paso County 1911, organized 1912; named for D.B. Culberson, Texas congressman.

Race/Ethnicity, 2007: (In percent) Anglo, 24.5; Black, 0.5; Hispanic, 73.8; Other, 1.2.

Vital Statistics, 2006: Births, 25; deaths, 17; marriages, 0; divorces, 2.

Recreation: National park; Guadalupe and El Capitan, twin peaks; scenic canyons and mountains; classic car museum, antique saloon bar; frontier days in June, big buck tournament.

Minerals: Sulfur, talc, marble, oil.

Agriculture: Beef cattle; crops include cotton, vegetables, melons, pecans; 4,000 acres in irrigation. Market value $15.1 million.

VAN HORN (2,152) county seat; agribusiness, tourism, rock crushing, government/services; hospital.

Other towns: **Kent** (30).

Population	**2,431**
Change fm 2000	−18.3
Area (sq. mi.)	3,812.71
Land Area (sq. mi.)	3,812.46
Altitude (ft.)	2,900-8,749
Rainfall (in.)	11.98
Jan. mean min.	27.8
July mean max.	91.7
Civ. Labor	1,846
Unemployed	3.0
Wages	$8,478,262
Av. Weekly Wage	$564
Prop. Value	$298,403,330
Retail Sales	$103,717,657

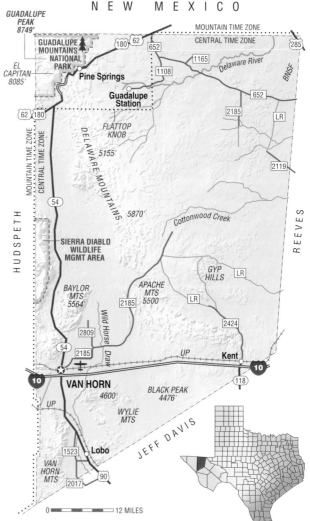

Dallam County

Physical Features: Prairie, broken by creeks; playas; sandy, loam soils; Rita Blanca National Grassland.

Economy: Agribusiness, dairies, cheese manufacturing, tourism.

History: Earliest Plains Apaches; displaced by Comanches and Kiowas. Ranching developed in late 19th century. Farming began after 1900. County created from Bexar District, 1876, organized 1891. Named for lawyer-editor James W. Dallam.

Race/Ethnicity, 2007: (In percent) Anglo, 65.8; Black, 1.6; Hispanic, 31.6; Other, 1.0.

Vital Statistics, 2006: Births, 107; deaths, 64; marriages, 78; divorces, 31.

Recreation: XIT museum, XIT rodeo in August, pheasant hunting, wildlife, grasslands.

Minerals: Petroleum.

Agriculture: First in production of grain (corn, wheat, sorghum). Cattle, hogs (second in number), dairies, potatoes, sunflowers, beans; substantial irrigation. Market value $552.9 million.

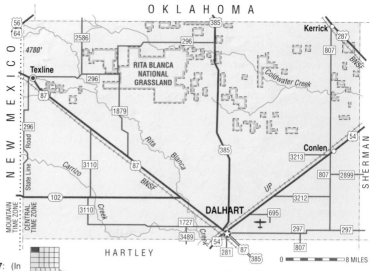

DALHART (7,495, partly in Hartley County) county seat; government/services; agribusiness center for parts of Texas, New Mexico, Oklahoma; railroad; cheese plant; grain operations; hospital; prison.

Other towns include: **Kerrick** (35) and **Texline** (525).

Population	6,267
Change fm 2000	0.7
Area (sq. mi.)	1,505.26
Land Area (sq. mi.)	1,504.69
Altitude (ft.)	3,655-4,780
Rainfall (in.)	18.57
Jan. mean min.	19.0
July mean max.	90.0
Civ. Labor	3,502
Unemployed	3.2
Wages	$31,455,379
Av. Weekly Wage	$627
Prop. Value	$673,288,795
Retail Sales	$88,974,128

For explanation of sources, abbreviations and symbols, see p. 210 and foldout map.

The Dallas-Fort Worth National Cemetery in southwestern Dallas County. Robert Plocheck photo.

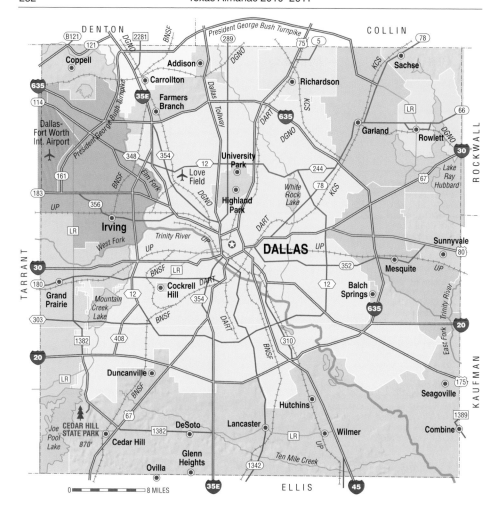

Dallas County

Physical Features: Mostly flat, heavy blackland soils, sandy clays in west; drains to Trinity River.

Economy: A national center for telecommunications, transportation, electronics manufacturing, data processing, conventions and trade shows; foreign-trade zone located at D/FW International Airport, U.S. Customs port of entry; government/services.

History: Caddoan area. Anglo-Americans began arriving in 1840. Antebellum slaveholding area. County created 1846 from Nacogdoches, Robertson counties; named for U.S. Vice President George Mifflin Dallas.

Race/Ethnicity, 2007: (In percent) Anglo, 34.9; Black, 20.5; Hispanic, 38.9; Other, 5.8.

Vital Statistics, 2006: Births, 42,524; deaths, 13,873; marriages, 14,460; divorces, 8,271.

Recreation: One of the state's top tourist destinations and one of the nation's most popular conven-

tion centers; State Fair, museums, zoo, West End shopping and tourist district, historical sites, including Sixth Floor museum in the old Texas School Book Depository, site of the assassination of President Kennedy.

Other important attractions include the Morton H. Meyerson Symphony Center; performing arts; professional sports; Texas broadcast museum; lakes; theme and amusement parks.

Minerals: Sand, gravel.

Population	**2,412,827**
Change fm 2000	8.7
Area (sq. mi.)	908.56
Land Area (sq. mi.)	879.60
Altitude (ft.)	350-870
Rainfall (in.)	37.05
Jan. mean min.	36.4
July mean max.	96.1
Civ. Labor	1,188,055
Unemployed	6.3
Wages	$19,887,202,877
Av. Weekly Wage	$1,026
Prop. Value	$196,288,494,958
Retail Sales	$51,251,521,018

Agriculture: Horticultural crops, wheat, hay, corn, soybeans (fourth in acreage), horses. Market value $35.2 million.

Education: Southern Methodist University, University of Dallas, Dallas Baptist University, University of Texas at Dallas, University of Texas Southwestern Medical Center and many other education centers.

DALLAS (1,248,184) county seat; center of state's largest consolidated metropolitan area and third-largest city in Texas; D/FW International Airport is one of the world's busiest; headquarters for the U.S. Army and Air Force Exchange Service; Federal Reserve Bank; a leader in fashions and in computer operations; hospitals; many hotels in downtown area offer adequate accommodations for most conventions.

Garland (222,007) varied manufacturing, community college branch, hospitals, performing arts center.

Irving (201,784) telecommunications; varied light manufacturing, food processing; distribution center; Boy Scout headquarters and museum; North Lake College; hospitals.

Other cities include: **Addison** (15,547) general aviation airport, theater center; **Balch Springs** (21,141); part [49,822] of **Carrollton** (129,329 total) residential community, distribution center, hospital; **Cedar Hill** (43,373) residential, light manufacturing, retail, Northwood University, state park, Country Day on the Hill

in October; **Cockrell Hill** (4,421); **Coppell** (39,806) distribution, varied manufacturing, office center, hike and bike trails; **DeSoto** (44,019) residential community, light industry and distribution, hospitals; Toad Holler Creekfest in June.

Also, **Duncanville** (36,540) varied manufacturing, many commuters to Dallas; Sandra Meadows Classic girls basketball tournament in December; **Farmers Branch** (28,234) distribution center, varied manufacturing, Brookhaven College, hospital.

Also, **Glenn Heights** (10,428, partly in Ellis County); most [99,760] of **Grand Prairie** (158,646 total) wholesale trade, aerospace, entertainment, hospital, library, Joe Pool Reservoir, Indian pow-wow in September, Lone Star horse-racing track; **Highland Park** (9,153).

Also, **Hutchins** (3,124) varied manufacturing; **Lancaster** (34,896) residential, industrial, distribution center, Cedar Valley College, Commemorative Air Force museum, Bear

Creek nature preserve, depot, historic town square, Musicfests monthly in the spring, Oktoberfest.

Also, **Mesquite** (131,685) varied industries; hospitals; championship rodeo, rodeo parade in spring; community college, historical parks; most [70,929] of **Richardson** (102,803 total) telecommunications, software development, financial services, hospital, library, Wildflower Music Festival in May; **Rowlett** (56,103) residential, manufacturing, government/services, hospital, library, park, hike and bike trails.

Also, **Sachse** (19,392, partly in Collin County) commuting to Dallas, government/services, Fallfest in October; **Seagoville** (12,223) rural/suburban setting, federal prison, Seagofest in October; **Sunnyvale** (4,533) tile manufacturing, hospital, Samuell Farm, Sunnyfest on July 4; **University Park** (23,576); **Wilmer** (3,755).

Part of **Combine** (2,084) and part of **Ovilla** (4,115).

Dawson County

Physical Features: South Plains county, broken on the east; loam and sandy soils.

Economy: Agriculture, farm and gin equipment manufacturing, peanut plant, government/services.

History: Comanche, Kiowa area. Ranching developed in 1880s. Farming began after 1900. Hispanic population increased after 1940. County created from Bexar District, 1876, organized 1905; named for Nicholas M. Dawson, San Jacinto veteran.

Race/Ethnicity, 2007: (In percent) Anglo, 38.9; Black, 8.3; Hispanic, 52.3; Other, 0.5.

Vital Statistics, 2006: Births, 186; deaths, 132; marriages, 92; divorces, 40.

Recreation: Parks, museum, campground; barbecue and chili cook-off in August, Fiestas Patrias in September.

Minerals: Oil, natural gas.

Agriculture: First in cotton acreage; peanuts, sorghums, watermelons, alfalfa, grapes. 70,000 acres irrigated. Market value $112.3 million.

LAMESA (9,225) county seat; agribusiness, food processing, oil-field services, some manufacturing, computerized cotton-classing office; hospital; Howard College branch; prison unit.

Other towns include: **Ackerly** (243, partly in Martin County), **Los Ybañez** (31) and **Welch** (95). Also, **O'Donnell** (915, mostly in Lynn County) bust of Dan Blocker.

For explanation of sources, abbreviations and symbols, see p. 210 and foldout map.

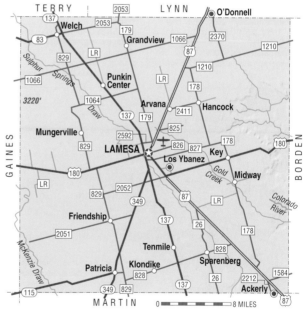

Population	13,692
Change fm 2000	−8.6
Area (sq. mi.)	902.12
Land Area (sq. mi.)	902.06
Altitude (ft.)	2,580-3,220
Rainfall (in.)	19.07
Jan. mean min.	26.0
July mean max.	92.9
Civ. Labor	5,150
Unemployed	5.5
Wages	$32,599,402
Av. Weekly Wage	$572
Prop. Value	$1,113,249,600
Retail Sales	$176,603,999

Deaf Smith County

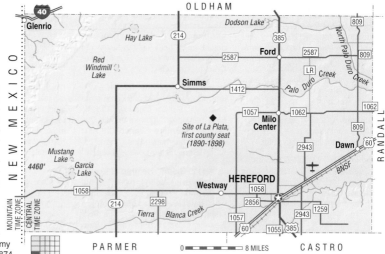

Physical Features: High Plains county, partly broken; chocolate and sandy loam soils; drains to Palo Duro and Tierra Blanca creeks.

Economy: Agriculture, varied industries, meat packing, offset printing.

History: Apaches, displaced by Comanches, Kiowas. Ranching developed after U.S. Army drove out Indians 1874-75. Farming began after 1900. Hispanic settlement increased after 1950. County created 1876, from Bexar District; organized 1890. Named for famed scout in Texas Revolution, Erastus (Deaf) Smith.

Race/Ethnicity, 2007: (In percent) Anglo, 35.4; Black, 1.4; Hispanic, 62.6; Other, 0.6.

Vital Statistics, 2006: Births, 355; deaths, 149; marriages, 137; divorces, 37.

Recreation: Museum, tours, POW camp chapel; Cinco de Mayo, Pioneer Days in May.

Minerals: Insignificant.

Agriculture: Leading agricultural county, dairies, feedlot operations, cotton, wheat, sorghum, corn; 50 percent irrigated. Market value $1.15 billion, first in state.

HEREFORD (15,031) county seat; cattle feeding, agribusiness, grain processing; hospital; Amarillo College branch; aquatic center.

Other towns include: **Dawn** (52).

Population	18,501
Change fm 2000	–0.3
Area (sq. mi.)	1,498.26
Land Area (sq. mi.)	1,497.34
Altitude (ft.)	3,650-4,460
Rainfall (in.)	18.65
Jan. mean min.	21.1
July mean max.	91.6
Civ. Labor	9,499
Unemployed	3.7
Wages	$52,628,637
Av. Weekly Wage	$581
Prop. Value	$898,314,795
Retail Sales	$270,682,068

Delta County

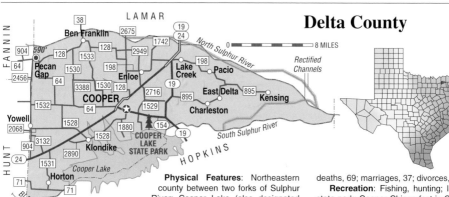

Population	5,458
Change fm 2000	2.5
Area (sq. mi.)	277.92
Land Area (sq. mi.)	277.08
Altitude (ft.)	322-590
Rainfall (in.)	45.00
Jan. mean min.	30.0
July mean max.	94.0
Civ. Labor	2,493
Unemployed	5.9
Wages	$7,530,273
Av. Weekly Wage	$465
Prop. Value	$194,391,005
Retail Sales	$10,080,773

Physical Features: Northeastern county between two forks of Sulphur River; Cooper Lake (also designated Jim Chapman Lake); black, sandy loam soils.

Economy: Agriculture, government/services, retirement location.

History: Caddo area, but disease, other tribes caused displacement around 1790. Anglo-Americans arrived in 1820s. County created from Lamar, Hopkins counties 1870. Greek letter delta origin of name, because of shape of the county.

Race/Ethnicity, 2007: (In percent) Anglo, 87.1; Black, 8.9; Hispanic, 3.1; Other, 0.9.

Vital Statistics, 2006: Births, 50; deaths, 69; marriages, 37; divorces, 18.

Recreation: Fishing, hunting; lake, state park; Cooper Chiggerfest in October.

Minerals: Insignificant.

Agriculture: Beef, hay, soybeans, wheat, corn, sorghum, cotton. Market value $17.2 million.

COOPER (2,147) county seat; industrial park, some manufacturing, agribusiness; museum.

Other towns include: **Ben Franklin** (60), **Enloe** (90), **Klondike** (175), **Lake Creek** (55) and **Pecan Gap** (210).

For explanation of sources, abbreviations and symbols, see p. 210 and foldout map.

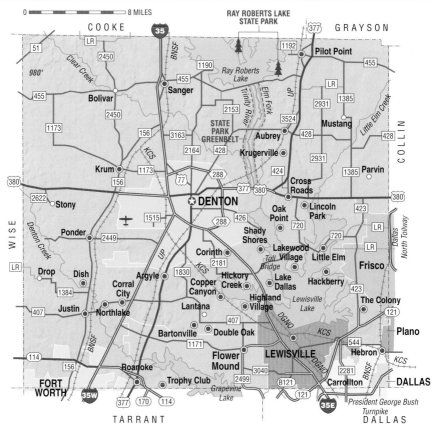

Denton County

Physical Features: North Texas county; partly hilly, draining to Elm Fork of Trinity River, lakes; Blackland and Grand Prairie soils and terrain.

Economy: Varied industries, colleges, horse industry, tourism, government/services; part of Dallas-Fort Worth metropolitan area.

History: Land grant from Texas Congress 1841 for Peters colony. County created out of Fannin County 1846; named for John B. Denton, pioneer Methodist minister.

Race/Ethnicity, 2007: (In percent) Anglo, 72.3; Black, 6.9; Hispanic, 15.3; Other, 5.5.

Vital Statistics, 2006: Births, 8,854; deaths, 2,187; marriages, 3,971; divorces, 2,367.

Recreation: Lake activities, parks; universities' cultural, athletic activities, including "Texas Women; A Celebration of History"; "First Ladies of Texas" collection of memorabilia; Little Chapel in the Woods; Texas Motor Speedway; Denton Jazz Festival in April.

Minerals: Natural gas.

Education: University of North Texas and Texas Woman's University.

Agriculture: Second in number of horses. Eggs, nurseries, turf, cattle; also, hay, sorghum, wheat, peanuts grown. Market value $79.2 million.

DENTON (114,456) county seat; universities, manufacturers of trucks (Peterbilt), medical, aviation; hospitals; historic courthouse square; storytelling festival in March.

LEWISVILLE (102,580) commuting to Dallas-Fort Worth, retail center, electronics and varied industries; hospital, library; Celtic Feis & Scottish Highland Games in March.

Flower Mound (67,413) residential community, library, mound of native grasses, bike classic in spring.

Carrollton (129,329, also in Dallas County), hospital.

Other towns include: **Argyle** (3,520) horse farms/training, bluegrass festival in March; **Aubrey** (2,494) horse farms/training, cabinet construction, peanut festival in October; **Bartonville** (1,558); **Copper Canyon** (1,507); **Corinth** (19,215); **Corral City** (109); **Cross Roads** (764); **Dish** (393); **Double Oak** (3,152); **Hackberry** (678); **Hebron** (234); **Hickory Creek** (3,426); **Highland Village** (16,511); **Justin** (3,067); **Krugerville** (1,605);

Krum (3,612) commuters, old grain mill; **Lake Dallas** (8,022) light manufacturing, marina, historic downtown.

Also, **Lakewood Village** (507); **Lincoln Park** (641); **Little Elm** (21,366) light manufacturing, lake activities, summer concert series; **Northlake** (1,816); **Oak Point** (2,707); **Pilot Point** (4,511) light manufacturing, horse ranches, Fireman's Fest in April; **Ponder** (1,313); **Roanoke** (4,613); **Sanger** (7,169) distribution center, commuters, government/services, lakes, Sellabration in September; **Shady Shores** (2,345); **The Colony** (36,621) tourism, IBM offices, chili cook-off in June, Las Vegas Night in April; and **Trophy Club** (8,215).

Part [22,273] of **Dallas**, part [44] of **Fort Worth**, part [3,402] of **Frisco**, part [2,140] of **Plano**.

Population	**636,557**
Change fm 2000	47.0
Area (sq. mi.)	957.88
Land Area (sq. mi.)	888.54
Altitude (ft.)	433-980
Rainfall (in.)	37.79
Jan. mean min.	32.0
July mean max.	94.1
Civ. Labor	338,134
Unemployed	5.2
Wages	$1,609,654,449
Av. Weekly Wage	$737
Prop. Value	$57,607,813,385
Retail Sales	$11,126,719,614

DeWitt County

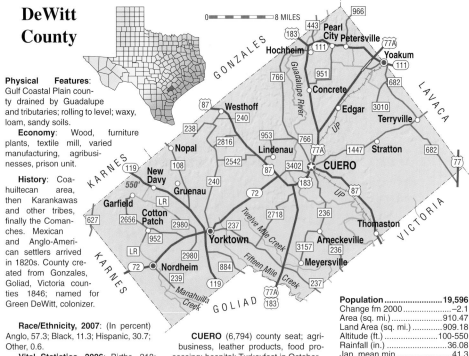

Physical Features: Gulf Coastal Plain county drained by Guadalupe and tributaries; rolling to level; waxy, loam, sandy soils.

Economy: Wood, furniture plants, textile mill, varied manufacturing, agribusinesses, prison unit.

History: Coahuiltecan area, then Karankawas and other tribes, finally the Comanches. Mexican and Anglo-American settlers arrived in 1820s. County created from Gonzales, Goliad, Victoria counties 1846; named for Green DeWitt, colonizer.

Race/Ethnicity, 2007: (In percent) Anglo, 57.3; Black, 11.3; Hispanic, 30.7; Other, 0.6.

Vital Statistics, 2006: Births, 218; deaths, 264; marriages, 128; divorces, 81.

Recreation: Hunting, fishing, historic homes, museums, wildflowers, German dance halls.

Minerals: Oil and natural gas.

Agriculture: Cattle, dairy products, poultry, swine, corn, sorghum, cotton, hay, pecans. Market value $41 million.

CUERO (6,794) county seat; agribusiness, leather products, food processing; hospital; Turkeyfest in October.

Yorktown (2,266) agribusiness, oil and gas; library, museum, park, hike/bike trail; Western Days in October.

Other towns include: **Hochheim** (70), **Meyersville** (110), **Nordheim** (315), **Thomaston** (45), **Westhoff** (410). Part [2,137] of **Yoakum** (5,804 total) cattle, leather, hospital, museum, Land of Leather in February.

Population	**19,596**
Change fm 2000	−2.1
Area (sq. mi.)	910.47
Land Area (sq. mi.)	909.18
Altitude (ft.)	100-550
Rainfall (in.)	36.08
Jan. mean min.	41.3
July mean max.	95.1
Civ. Labor	9,028
Unemployed	4.8
Wages	$50,586,547
Av. Weekly Wage	$590
Prop. Value	$1,148,997,955
Retail Sales	$155,906,743

For explanation of sources, abbreviations and symbols, see p. 210 and foldout map.

The oil field in Spur, Dickens County. Robert Plocheck photo.

Dickens County

Physical Features: West Texas county; broken land, Caprock in northwest; sandy, chocolate, red soils; drains to Croton, Duck creeks.

Economy: Services/prison unit, agribusiness, hunting leases.

History: Comanches driven out by U.S. Army 1874-75. Ranching and some farming began in late 1880s. County created 1876, from Bexar District; organized 1891; named for Alamo hero who is variously listed as James R. Demkins or Dimpkins and J. Dickens.

Race/Ethnicity, 2007: (In percent) Anglo, 65.2; Black, 8.3; Hispanic, 26.2; Other, 0.4.

Vital Statistics, 2005: Births, 25; deaths, 33; marriages, 21; divorces, 7.

Recreation: Hunting, fishing; Soldiers Mound site, Dickens Springs; downtown Spur.

Agriculture: Cattle, cotton, forages, small grains, horses. Some irrigation. Market value $21.1 million. Hunting leases important.

Minerals: Oil, gas.

DICKENS (329) county seat, market for ranching country.

SPUR (1,023) agribusiness and shipping center, oil and gas, state prison; homecoming in October.

Other towns include: **Afton** (15) and **McAdoo** (75).

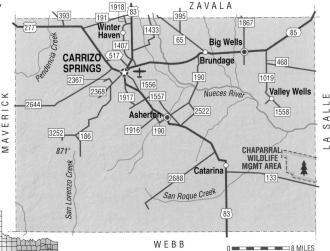

Population	2,450
Change fm 2000	−11.3
Area (sq. mi.)	905.21
Land Area (sq. mi.)	904.21
Altitude (ft.)	1,800-3,037
Rainfall (in.)	18.68
Jan. mean min.	25.5
July mean max.	95.4
Civ. Labor	1,262
Unemployed	5.7
Wages	$4,399,549
Av. Weekly Wage	$593
Prop. Value	$276,351,770
Retail Sales	$12,791,733

For explanation of sources, abbreviations and symbols, see p. 210 and foldout map.

Dimmit County

Physical Features: Southwest county; level to rolling; much brush; sandy, loam, red soils; drained by Nueces River.

Economy: Government/services, agribusiness, petroleum products, tourism.

History: Coahuiltecan area, later Comanches. John Townsend, a black man from Nacogdoches, led first attempt at settlement before the Civil War. Texas Rangers forced out Indians in 1877. Mexican migration increased after 1910. County created 1858 from Bexar, Maverick, Uvalde, Webb counties; organized 1880. Named for Philip Dimitt of Texas Revolution; law misspelled name.

Race/Ethnicity, 2007: (In percent) Anglo, 12.3; Black, 0.7; Hispanic, 86.1; Other, 0.9.

Vital Statistics, 2006: Births, 190; deaths, 83; marriages, 37; divorces, 2.

Recreation: Hunting, fishing, campsites, wildlife area; winter haven for tourists.

Minerals: Oil, natural gas.

Agriculture: Onions, pecans, cantaloupes, olives, tomatoes, tangerines, cattle, goats, horses, hay. Market value $21.7 million.

CARRIZO SPRINGS (5,560) county seat; agribusiness center, feedlot, food processing, oil, gas processing, hunting center; hospital; historic Baptist church; Brush Country Day in October.

Other towns include: **Asherton** (1,261), **Big Wells** (690) Cinco de Mayo, and **Catarina** (126) Camino Real festival in April.

Population	9,758
Change fm 2000	−4.8
Area (sq. mi.)	1,334.48
Land Area (sq. mi.)	1,330.91
Altitude (ft.)	410-871
Rainfall (in.)	20.21
Jan. mean min.	39.6
July mean max.	98.3
Civ. Labor	4,446
Unemployed	7.3
Wages	$22,738,862
Av. Weekly Wage	$612
Prop. Value	$501,722,128
Retail Sales	$68,154,274

Donley County

Physical Features: Panhandle county bisected by Red River Salt Fork; rolling to level; clay, loam, sandy soils.

Economy: Agribusiness, government/services, tourism.

History: Apaches displaced by Kiowas and Comanches, who were driven out in 1874-75 by U.S. Army. Methodist colony from New York settled in 1878. County created in 1876, organized 1882, out of Bexar District; named for Texas Supreme Court Justice S.P. Donley.

Race/Ethnicity, 2007: (In percent) Anglo, 86.9; Black, 5.2; Hispanic, 7.0; Other, 0.9.

Vital Statistics, 2006: Births, 31; deaths, 51; marriages, 23; divorces, 15.

Recreation: Lake, hunting, fishing, camping, water sports; Col. Goodnight Chuckwagon cook-off in September.

Minerals: Small amount of natural gas.

Agriculture: Cattle top revenue source; cotton, peanuts, alfalfa, wheat, hay, melons; 11,000 acres irrigated. Market value $85.8 million.

CLARENDON (2,127) county seat; agribusiness, tourism, medical center; Saints Roost museum, library, junior college.

Other towns include: **Hedley** (416) cotton festival in October, **Howardwick** (467) and **Lelia Lake** (71).

Population	**3,850**
Change fm 2000	0.6
Area (sq. mi.)	933.05
Land Area (sq. mi.)	929.77
Altitude (ft.)	2,080-3,268
Rainfall (in.)	23.89
Jan. mean min.	22.4
July mean max.	94.7
Civ. Labor	1,887
Unemployed	3.7
Wages	$5,847,250
Av. Weekly Wage	$465
Prop. Value	$188,576,069
Retail Sales	$20,989,394

Duval County

Physical Features: South Texas county; level to hilly, brushy in most areas; varied soils.

Economy: Ranching, petroleum, tourism, government/services.

History: Coahuiltecans, displaced by Comanche bands. Mexican settlement began in 1812. County created from Live Oak, Nueces, Starr counties, 1858, organized 1876; named for Burr H. Duval, a victim of Goliad massacre.

Race/Ethnicity, 2007: (In percent) Anglo, 10.9; Black, 0.4; Hispanic, 88.3; Other, 0.4.

Vital Statistics, 2006: Births, 226; deaths, 118; marriages, 47; divorces, 37.

Recreation: Hunting, tourist crossroads.

Minerals: Oil, gas, salt, sand, gravel, uranium.

Agriculture: Most income from beef cattle; grains, cotton, vegetables, hay, dairy. Market value $14.8 million.

SAN DIEGO (4,473, part [825] in Jim Wells County) county seat; ranching, oil field, tourist center; hospital.

Freer (3,060) oil and gas, construction, ranching and hunting; rattlesnake roundup in May.

Benavides (1,535) serves truck-farming area.

Other towns include: **Concepcion** (58) and **Realitos** (202).

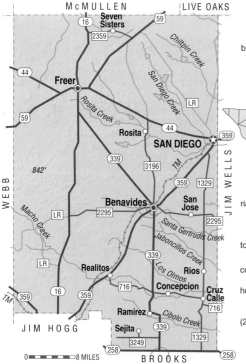

Population	**12,033**
Change fm 2000	–8.2
Area (sq. mi.)	1,795.67
Land Area (sq. mi.)	1,792.71
Altitude (ft.)	180-842
Rainfall (in.)	25.40
Jan. mean min.	42.5
July mean max.	97.3
Civ. Labor	5,338
Unemployed	6.2
Wages	$27,778,577
Av. Weekly Wage	$670
Prop. Value	$846,272,145
Retail Sales	$50,458,768

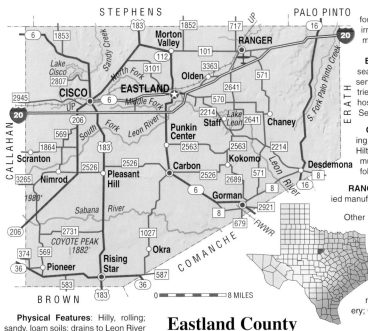

Eastland County

For explanation of sources, abbreviations and symbols, see p. 210 and foldout map.

Agriculture: Beef cattle, forage and hay. 20,000 acres irrigated. Market value $28 million.

EASTLAND (3,922) county seat; tourism, government/services, petroleum industries, varied manufacturing; hospital, library; Old Ripfest in September.

CISCO (3,851) manufacturing, oilfield services; Conrad Hilton's first hotel restored, museums; junior college; folklife festival in April.

RANGER (2,532) oil center, varied manufacturing, junior college.

Other towns include: **Carbon** (230) livestock equipment manufacturing; **Desdemona** (180); **Gorman** (1,240) peanut processing, agribusiness, hospital; **Olden** (113), and **Rising Star** (841) cap manufacturing, plant nursery; Octoberfest.

Physical Features: Hilly, rolling; sandy, loam soils; drains to Leon River forks.

Economy: Agribusiness, education, petroleum industries, varied manufacturing.

History: Plains Indian area. Frank Sánchez among first settlers in 1850s. County created from Bosque, Coryell, Travis counties, 1858, organized 1873; named for W.M. Eastland, Mier Expedition casualty.

Race/Ethnicity, 2007: (In percent) Anglo, 84.1; Black, 2.4; Hispanic, 12.9; Other, 0.6.

Vital Statistics, 2006: Births, 227; deaths, 237; marriages, 135; divorces, 78.

Recreation: Lakes, water sports; fishing, hunting; museums; historic sites and displays.

Minerals: Oil, natural gas.

Population	**18,186**
Change fm 2000	–0.6
Area (sq. mi.)	931.90
Land Area (sq. mi.)	926.01
Altitude (ft.)	960-1,980
Rainfall (in.)	27.53
Jan. mean min.	26.7
July mean max.	94.9
Civ. Labor	8,477
Unemployed	5.2
Wages	$52,966,615
Av. Weekly Wage	$598
Prop. Value	$971,913,650
Retail Sales	$279,190,163

The Presidential Museum and Leadership Library in Odessa. Robert Plocheck photo.

Ector County

Physical Features: West Texas county; level to rolling, some sand dunes; meteor crater; desert vegetation.

Economy: Center for Permian Basin oil field operations, plastics, electric generation plants.

History: First settlers in late 1880s. Oil boom in 1926. County created from Tom Green County, 1887; organized 1891; named for jurist M.D. Ector.

Race/Ethnicity, 2007: (In percent) Anglo, 43.2; Black, 4.7; Hispanic, 50.6; Other, 1.5.

Vital Statistics, 2006: Births, 2,312; deaths, 1,120; marriages, 1,125; divorces, 726.

Recreation: Globe Theatre replica; presidential museum and Bush childhood home; art institute; second-largest U.S. meteor crater; Stonehenge replica.

Minerals: More than 3 billion barrels of oil produced since 1926; gas, cement, stone.

Agriculture: Beef cattle, horses are chief producers; pecans, hay, poultry; minor irrigation. Market value $3.6 million.

Education: University of Texas of Permian Basin, Texas Tech University Health Sciences Center, Odessa (junior) College.

ODESSA (96,849, part [1,042] in Midland County) county seat; oil and gas, manufacturing, ranching; hospitals; cultural center; Permian Basin Fair and Expo in September.

Other towns include: **Gardendale** (1,282), **Goldsmith** (260), **Notrees** (20), **Penwell** (41), and **West Odessa** (19,130).

Population 131,941
Change fm 2000 .... 8.9
Area (sq. mi.) 901.68
Land Area (sq. mi.) 901.06

Altitude (ft.) 2,780-3,360
Rainfall (in.) 13.29
Jan. mean min. 28.7
July mean max. 96.0
Civ. Labor 68,986
Unemployed 3.9
Wages $682,057,251
Av. Weekly Wage $843
Prop. Value $8,979,672,626
Retail Sales $2,330,363,951

Edwards County

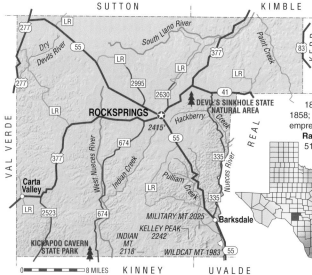

Physical Features: Rolling, hilly; caves; spring-fed streams; rocky, thin soils; drained by Llano, Nueces rivers; varied timber.

Economy: Hunting leases, tourism, oil, gas production, ranching.

History: Apache area. First land sold in 1876. County created from Bexar District, 1858; organized 1883; named for Nacogdoches empresario Hayden Edwards.

Race/Ethnicity, 2007: (In percent) Anglo, 51.8; Black, 0.2; Hispanic, 47.4; Other, 0.6.

Vital Statistics, 2006: Births, 28; deaths, 18; marriages, 1; divorces, 1.

Recreation: Hunting, fishing; scenic drives; Devil's Sinkhole, Kickapoo Cavern state parks.

Minerals: Gas.

Agriculture: Second in number of goats. Mohair-wool production, Angora goats, sheep, cattle, some pecans. Market value $8.8 million. Cedar for oil.

ROCKSPRINGS (1,218) county seat; ranching, tourism, Diez y Seis Festival in September.

Other towns include: **Barksdale** (100).

Population 1,952
Change fm 2000 .... –9.7
Area (sq. mi.) 2,119.95
Land Area (sq. mi.) 2,119.75
Altitude (ft.) 1,480-2,415
Rainfall (in.) 24.76
Jan. mean min. 34.3
July mean max. 91.6
Civ. Labor 1,056
Unemployed 4.3
Wages $3,346,513
Av. Weekly Wage $556
Prop. Value $375,627,696
Retail Sales $14,990,068

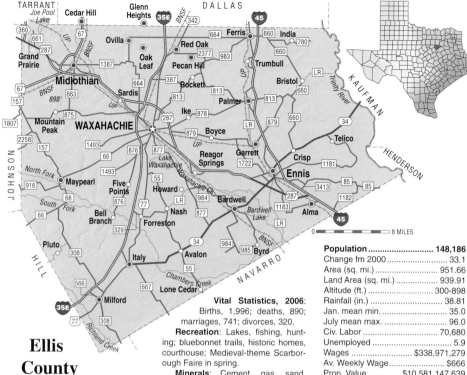

Population 148,186
Change fm 2000 .... 33.1
Area (sq. mi.) 951.66
Land Area (sq. mi.) 939.91
Altitude (ft.) 300-898
Rainfall (in.) 38.81
Jan. mean min. 35.0
July mean max. 96.0
Civ. Labor 70,680
Unemployed 5.9
Wages $338,971,279
Av. Weekly Wage........................ $666
Prop. Value $10,581,147,639
Retail Sales $1,233,470,450

Vital Statistics, 2006:
Births, 1,996; deaths, 890;
marriages, 741; divorces, 320.

Recreation: Lakes, fishing, hunting; bluebonnet trails, historic homes, courthouse; Medieval-theme Scarborough Faire in spring.

Minerals: Cement, gas, sand, gravel.

Agriculture: Cattle, cotton, corn, hay, nurseries. Market value $49.4 million.

Ellis County

Physical Features: Blackland soils; level to rolling; Chambers Creek, Trinity River.

Economy: Cement, steel production, warehousing and distribution, government/services; many residents work in Dallas.

History: Tonkawa area. Part of Peters colony settled in 1843. County created 1849, organized 1850, from Navarro County. Named for Richard Ellis, president of convention that declared Texas' independence.

Race/Ethnicity, 2007: (In percent) Anglo, 65.7; Black, 9.1; Hispanic, 24.1; Other, 1.1.

WAXAHACHIE (27,484) county seat; manufacturing, steel, aluminum, tourism; hospital; colleges, museums; hike/bike trail; Crape Myrtle festival in July.

Ennis (20,232) agribusiness, manufacturing, tourism; hospital; bluebonnet trails, National Polka Festival in May.

Midlothian (15,142) cement plants, steel plant, distribution center, manufacturing; heritage park, cabin; Scarecrow festival in October.

Other towns include: **Alma** (348); **Avalon** (400); **Bardwell** (615); **Ferris** (2,511); **Forreston** (400); **Garrett** (511); **Howard** (60); **Italy** (2,279); **Maypearl** (962); **Milford** (744); **Oak Leaf** (1,484); **Ovilla** (4,115); **Palmer** (2,209); **Pecan Hill** (713); and **Red Oak** (9,428) manufacturing, Founders Day in September.

Also, **Glenn Heights** (10,428, mostly in Dallas County).

And part of **Grand Prairie**.

For explanation of sources, abbreviations and symbols, see p. 210 and foldout map.

The Bhutanese-style architecture of the University of Texas at El Paso. Robert Plocheck photo.

Benjamin Franklin Coons

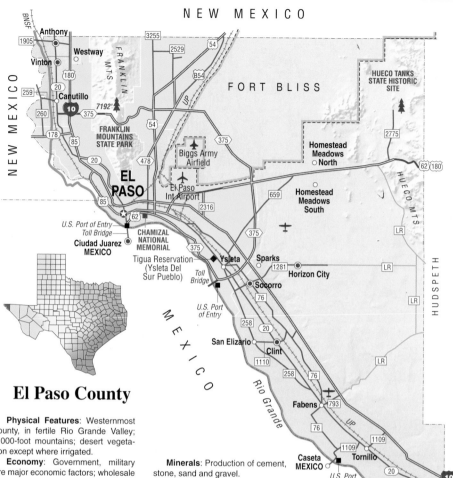

El Paso County

Physical Features: Westernmost county, in fertile Rio Grande Valley; 7,000-foot mountains; desert vegetation except where irrigated.

Economy: Government, military are major economic factors; wholesale and retail distribution center, education, tourism, maquiladora plants, varied manufacturing, oil refining, cotton, food processing.

History: Various Indian tribes inhabited the valley before Spanish civilization arrived in late 1650s. Agriculture in area dates to at least 100 A.D. Spanish along with Tigua and Piro tribes fleeing Santa Fe uprising of 1680 sought refuge in area. County created from Bexar District, 1849; organized 1850; named for historic pass (Paso del Norte), lowest all-weather pass through Rocky Mountains.

Race/Ethnicity, 2007: (In percent) Anglo, 12.7; Black, 2.7; Hispanic, 82.8; Other, 1.8.

Vital Statistics, 2006: Births, 14,414; deaths, 4,356; marriages, 6,391; divorces, 86.

Recreation: Gateway to Mexico; Chamizal Museum; major tourist center; December Sun Carnival with football game; state parks, mountain tramway, missions and other historic sites.

For explanation of sources, abbreviations and symbols, see p. 210 and foldout map.

Minerals: Production of cement, stone, sand and gravel.

Agriculture: Dairies, cattle, cotton, pecans (third in acreage), onions, forage, peppers. Third in colonies of bees. 50,000 acres irrigated, mostly cotton. Market value $47.5 million.

Education: University of Texas at El Paso, UT School of Nursing at El Paso, Texas Tech University Health Sciences Center, El Paso Community College.

EL PASO (609,327) county seat; Texas' sixth-largest city, fifth-largest metro area, largest U.S. city on Mexican border.

A center for government operations. Federal installations include Fort Bliss, William Beaumont General Hospital, La Tuna federal prison, and headquarters of the U.S. Army Air Defense Command.

Manufactured products include clothing, electronics, auto equipment, plastics; trade and distribution; refining; processing oil, food, cotton and other farm products.

Hospitals; museums; convention center; theater, symphony orchestra.

Other towns include: **Anthony** (12,174, partly in New Mexico); Ca-

nutillo (5,309); **Clint** (1,020); **Fabens** (8,526); **Homestead Meadows North** (4,205); **Homestead Meadows South** (6,862); **Horizon City** (9,812); **Prado Verde** (200); **San Elizario** (11,835); **Socorro** (32,708) settled in 1680; **Sparks** (3,153); **Tornillo** (1,669); **Vinton** (2,137); **Westway** (4,072), and **Ysleta** (now within El Paso) settled in 1680, called the oldest town in Texas.

And, **Fort Bliss** (8,150).

Population	742,062
Change fm 2000	9.2
Area (sq. mi.)	1,014.68
Land Area (sq. mi.)	1,013.11
Altitude (ft.)	3,520-7,192
Rainfall (in.)	9.43
Jan. mean min.	32.9
July mean max.	94.5
Civ. Labor	302,116
Unemployed	7.0
Wages	$2,093,881,827
Av. Weekly Wage	$602
Prop. Value	$35,016,283,497
Retail Sales	$8,183,603,275

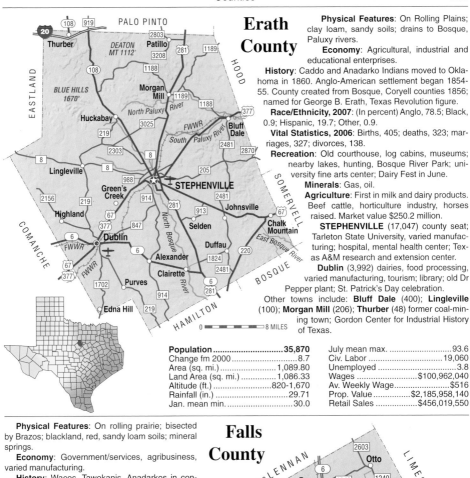

Erath County

Physical Features: On Rolling Plains; clay loam, sandy soils; drains to Bosque, Paluxy rivers.

Economy: Agricultural, industrial and educational enterprises.

History: Caddo and Anadarko Indians moved to Oklahoma in 1860. Anglo-American settlement began 1854-55. County created from Bosque, Coryell counties 1856; named for George B. Erath, Texas Revolution figure.

Race/Ethnicity, 2007: (In percent) Anglo, 78.5; Black, 0.9; Hispanic, 19.7; Other, 0.9.

Vital Statistics, 2006: Births, 405; deaths, 323; marriages, 327; divorces, 138.

Recreation: Old courthouse, log cabins, museums; nearby lakes, hunting, Bosque River Park; university fine arts center; Dairy Fest in June.

Minerals: Gas, oil.

Agriculture: First in milk and dairy products. Beef cattle, horticulture industry, horses raised. Market value $250.2 million.

STEPHENVILLE (17,047) county seat; Tarleton State University, varied manufacturing; hospital, mental health center; Texas A&M research and extension center.

Dublin (3,992) dairies, food processing, varied manufacturing, tourism; library; old Dr Pepper plant; St. Patrick's Day celebration.

Other towns include: **Bluff Dale** (400); **Lingleville** (100); **Morgan Mill** (206); **Thurber** (48) former coal-mining town; Gordon Center for Industrial History of Texas.

Population	35,870
Change fm 2000	8.7
Area (sq. mi.)	1,089.80
Land Area (sq. mi.)	1,086.33
Altitude (ft.)	820-1,670
Rainfall (in.)	29.71
Jan. mean min.	30.0
July mean max.	93.6
Civ. Labor	19,060
Unemployed	3.8
Wages	$100,962,040
Av. Weekly Wage	$516
Prop. Value	$2,185,958,140
Retail Sales	$456,019,550

Falls County

Physical Features: On rolling prairie; bisected by Brazos; blackland, red, sandy loam soils; mineral springs.

Economy: Government/services, agribusiness, varied manufacturing.

History: Wacos, Tawokanis, Anadarkos in conflict with Comanches. Cherokees alone in area 1830 until 1835 when Anglo-American settlement began. County created 1850 from Limestone, Milam counties; named for Brazos River falls.

Race/Ethnicity, 2007: (In percent) Anglo, 52.8; Black, 26.9; Hispanic, 19.8; Other, 0.5.

Vital Statistics, 2006: Births, 208; deaths, 247; marriages, 89; divorces, 33.

Recreation: Fishing, hunting, camping; Highland Mansion and Falls on the Brazos.

Minerals: Gravel, sand, oil.

Agriculture: Stocker cattle, cow-calf operations, corn, grain sorghum, soybeans, cotton, wheat, oats, goats, sheep, horses. Some cotton irrigated. Market value $126.8 million.

MARLIN (6,441) county seat; agriculture, prison; hospital; museum.

Other towns include: **Chilton** (274); **Golinda** (451); **Lott** (700); **Reagan** (208); **Rosebud** (1,404) feed, fertilizer processing, clothing manufactured; **Satin** (86). Part of **Bruceville-Eddy** (1,570).

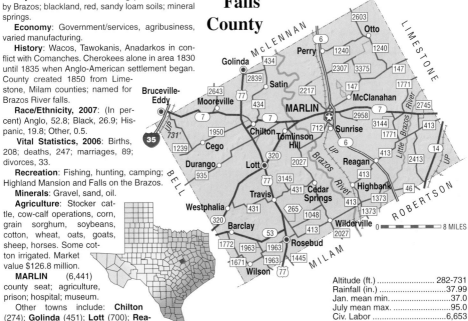

Population	16,900
Change fm 2000	-9.0
Area (sq. mi.)	773.81
Land Area (sq. mi.)	769.09
Altitude (ft.)	282-731
Rainfall (in.)	37.99
Jan. mean min.	37.0
July mean max.	95.0
Civ. Labor	6,653
Unemployed	6.9
Wages	$23,118,240
Av. Weekly Wage	$541
Prop. Value	$513,072,158
Retail Sales	$113,185,640

Fannin County

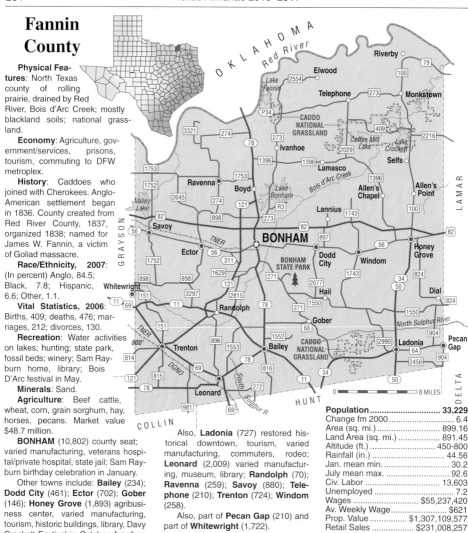

Physical Features: North Texas county of rolling prairie, drained by Red River, Bois d'Arc Creek; mostly blackland soils; national grassland.

Economy: Agriculture, government/services, prisons, tourism, commuting to DFW metroplex.

History: Caddoes who joined with Cherokees. Anglo-American settlement began in 1836. County created from Red River County, 1837, organized 1838; named for James W. Fannin, a victim of Goliad massacre.

Race/Ethnicity, 2007: (In percent) Anglo, 84.5; Black, 7.8; Hispanic, 6.6; Other, 1.1.

Vital Statistics, 2006: Births, 409; deaths, 476; marriages, 212; divorces, 130.

Recreation: Water activities on lakes; hunting; state park, fossil beds; winery; Sam Rayburn home, library; Bois D'Arc festival in May.

Minerals: Sand.

Agriculture: Beef cattle, wheat, corn, grain sorghum, hay, horses, pecans. Market value $48.7 million.

BONHAM (10,802) county seat; varied manufacturing, veterans hospital/private hospital, state jail; Sam Rayburn birthday celebration in January.

Other towns include: **Bailey** (234); **Dodd City** (461); **Ector** (702); **Gober** (146); **Honey Grove** (1,893) agribusiness center, varied manufacturing, tourism, historic buildings, library, Davy Crockett Festival in October; **Ivanhoe** (110).

Also, **Ladonia** (727) restored historical downtown, tourism, varied manufacturing, commuters, rodeo; **Leonard** (2,009) varied manufacturing, museum, library; **Randolph** (70); **Ravenna** (259); **Savoy** (880); **Telephone** (210); **Trenton** (724); **Windom** (258).

Also, part of **Pecan Gap** (210) and part of **Whitewright** (1,722).

Population	**33,229**
Change fm 2000	6.4
Area (sq. mi.)	899.16
Land Area (sq. mi.)	891.45
Altitude (ft.)	450-800
Rainfall (in.)	44.56
Jan. mean min.	30.2
July mean max.	92.6
Civ. Labor	13,603
Unemployed	7.2
Wages	$55,237,420
Av. Weekly Wage	$621
Prop. Value	$1,307,109,577
Retail Sales	$231,008,257

For explanation of sources, abbreviations and symbols, see p. 210 and foldout map.

Sportsmen on Lake Crockett in northeast Fannin County. Robert Plocheck photo.

Fayette County

Physical Features: South central county bisected by Colorado River; rolling to level; sandy loam, black waxy soils.

Economy: Agribusiness, production of electricity, mineral production, government/services, small manufacturing, tourism.

History: Lipan Apaches and Tonkawas. Austin's colonists arrived in 1822. Germans and Czechs began arriving in 1840s. County created from Bastrop, Colorado counties, 1837; organized, 1838; named for hero of American Revolution, Marquis de Lafayette.

Race/Ethnicity, 2007: (In percent) Anglo, 75.0; Black, 7.1; Hispanic, 17.3; Other, 0.6.

Vital Statistics, 2006: Births, 238; deaths, 308; marriages, 141; divorces, 72.

Recreation: Monument Hill, Kreische brewery, Faison Home Museum, other historic sites including "Painted Churches"; hunting, fishing, lake; German and Czech ethnic foods; Prazska Pout in August, Octoberfests.

Minerals: Oil, gas, sand, gravel, bentonite clay.

Agriculture: Beef cattle, corn, hay, sorghum, pecans, dairies. Market value $52.8 million. Firewood sold.

LA GRANGE (4,841) county seat; electric-power generation, varied manufacturing, food processing, retail trade, tourism; hospital, library, museum, archives; Czech heritage center; Texas Independence Day observance.

Schulenburg (2,947) varied manufacturing, food processing; Bluebonnet Festival in spring.

Round Top (87) music center, tourism; old Lutheran church, museums; International Festival Institute, July-August; Schuetzenfest in September, and **Winedale** (67), historic restorations including Winedale Inn.

Other towns include: **Carmine** (238); **Ellinger** (386) Tomato Festival in May; **Fayetteville** (282) tourism, antiques, old precinct courthouse, Lickskillet festival in October; **Flatonia** (1,436) farm market, varied manufacturing, antiques,

Czhilispiel in October; **Ledbetter** (83); **Muldoon** (95); **Plum** (145); **Warda** (121); **Warrenton** (186) antique Cadillac museum; **West Point** (213), and **Winchester** (232).

Population	22,698
Change fm 2000	4.0
Area (sq. mi.)	959.84
Land Area (sq. mi.)	950.03
Altitude (ft.)	200-590
Rainfall (in.)	40.31
Jan. mean min.	41.4
July mean max.	95.9
Civ. Labor	12,480
Unemployed	3.8
Wages	$75,937,078
Av. Weekly Wage	$653
Prop. Value	$2,176,801,032
Retail Sales	$274,052,813

Fisher County

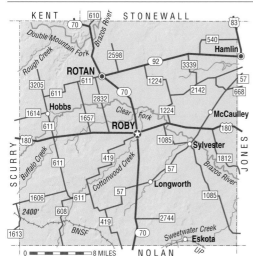

Physical Features: On rolling prairie; mesquite; red, sandy loam soils; drains to forks of Brazos River.

Economy: Agribusiness, hunting, gypsum.

History: Lipan Apaches, disrupted by Comanches and other tribes around 1700. Ranching began in 1876. County created from Bexar District, 1876; organized 1886; named for S.R. Fisher, Republic of Texas secretary of navy.

Race/Ethnicity, 2007: (In percent) Anglo, 72.6; Black, 2.9; Hispanic, 23.9; Other, 0.6.

Vital Statistics, 2006: Births, 32; deaths, 62; marriages, 28; divorces, 5.

Recreation: Quail, dove, turkey hunting; wildlife viewing; county fair, rodeo in August in Roby.

Minerals: Gypsum, oil.

Agriculture: Cattle, cotton, hay, wheat, sorghum, horses, sheep, goats. Irrigation for cotton and alfalfa. Market value $50.5 million.

ROBY (661) county seat; agribusiness, cotton gin; hospital between Roby and Rotan.

ROTAN (1,515) gypsum plant, oil mill, agribusiness.

Other towns include: **McCaulley** (96) and **Sylvester** (79). Part of **Hamlin** (2,153).

Population	3,912
Change fm 2000	−9.9
Area (sq. mi.)	901.74
Land Area (sq. mi.)	901.16
Altitude (ft.)	1,720-2,405
Rainfall (in.)	24.22
Jan. mean min.	27.2
July mean max.	94.2
Civ. Labor	2,032
Unemployed	3.9
Wages	$6,523,144
Av. Weekly Wage	$568
Prop. Value	$200,935,625
Retail Sales	$11,821,450

Floyd County

Physical Features: Flat High Plains, broken by Caprock on east, by White River on south; many playas; red, black loam soils.

Economy: Cotton, wind farm, varied manufacturing, government/services.

History: Plains Apaches and later Comanches. First white settlers arrived in 1884. County created from Bexar District, 1876; organized 1890. Named for Dolphin Ward Floyd, who died at Alamo.

Race/Ethnicity, 2007: (In percent) Anglo, 45.4; Black, 3.6; Hispanic, 50.4; Other, 0.6.

Vital Statistics, 2006: Births, 114; deaths, 74; marriages, 32; divorces, 21.

Recreation: Hunting of pheasant, deer, quail; fishing; Blanco Canyon; Floydada Punkin Day in October; museum.

Minerals: Not significant.

Agriculture: Cotton, wheat, sorghum, corn; pumpkins (first in state in production). Some 260,000 acres irrigated. Market value $263 million.

FLOYDADA (3,394) county seat; agriculture, varied manufacturing; Texas A&M engineering extension.

Lockney (1,917) agriculture center; manufacturing; hospital.

Other towns include: **Aiken** (52), **Dougherty** (91), and **South Plains** (67).

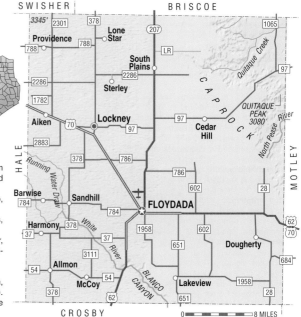

Population	6,455
Change fm 2000	−16.9
Area (sq. mi.)	992.51
Land Area (sq. mi.)	992.19
Altitude (ft.)	2,440-3,345
Rainfall (in.)	20.95
Jan. mean min.	23.2
July mean max.	92.3
Civ. Labor	3,237
Unemployed	5.5
Wages	$12,567,304
Av. Weekly Wage	$508
Prop. Value	$276,011,830
Retail Sales	$39,336,854

For explanation of sources, abbreviations and symbols, see p. 210 and foldout map.

Foard County

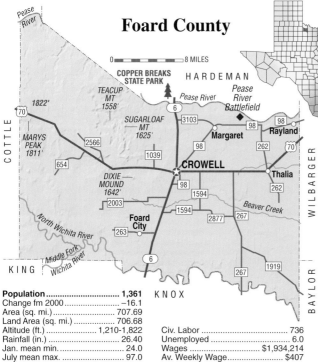

Population	1,361
Change fm 2000	−16.1
Area (sq. mi.)	707.69
Land Area (sq. mi.)	706.68
Altitude (ft.)	1,210-1,822
Rainfall (in.)	26.40
Jan. mean min.	24.0
July mean max.	97.0
Civ. Labor	736
Unemployed	6.0
Wages	$1,934,214
Av. Weekly Wage	$407

Physical Features: Northwest county drains to North Wichita, Pease rivers; sandy, loam soils, rolling surface.

Economy: Agribusiness, clothes manufacturing, government/service.

History: Comanches, Kiowas ranged the area until driven away in 1870s. Ranching began in 1880. County created out of Cottle, Hardeman, King, Knox counties, 1891; named for Maj. Robert L. Foard of Confederate army.

Race/Ethnicity, 2007: (In percent) Anglo, 77.2; Black, 3.6; Hispanic, 18.4; Other, 0.7.

Vital Statistics, 2006: Births, 13; deaths, 22; marriages, 2; divorces, 1.

Recreation: Three museums; hunting; astronomy and ecotourism foundation; wild hog cook-off in November.

Minerals: Natural gas, some oil.

Agriculture: Wheat, cattle, alfalfa, cotton, sorghum, dairies. Market value $17.6 million. Hunting leases important.

CROWELL (1,056) county seat; retail center, clothing manufacturing; library.

Prop. Value	$84,377,563
Retail Sales	$7,122,891

Physical Features: On Gulf Coastal Plain; drained by Brazos, San Bernard rivers; level to rolling; rich alluvial soils.

Economy: Agribusiness, petro-chemicals, technology, government/services; many residents work in Houston.

History: Karankawas retreated to Mexico by 1850s. Named for river bend where some of Austin's colonists settled 1824. Antebellum plantations made it one of six Texas counties with black majority in 1850. County created 1837 from Austin County; organized 1838.

Race/Ethnicity, 2007: (In percent) Anglo, 41.3; Black, 22.2; Hispanic, 22.7; Other, 13.8.

Vital Statistics, 2006: Births, 6,158; deaths, 1,941; marriages, 2,267; divorces, 1,473.

Recreation: Many historic sites, museums, memorials, parks; George Ranch historical park; state park with George Observatory; fishing, water-fowl hunting.

Minerals: Oil, gas, sulphur, salt, clays, sand and gravel.

Fort Bend County

Agriculture: Nursery crops, cotton, sorghum, corn, hay, cattle, horses; irrigation for rice. Market value $94.5 million.

RICHMOND (14,755) county seat; foundry; University of Houston branch, Wharton County Junior College branch; Richmond State School (for mentally retarded), hospital.

SUGAR LAND (91,805) government/services, prisons, commuting to Houston; hospitals; University of Houston branch; Museum of Southern History.

MISSOURI CITY (77,305, part [5,494] in Harris County) hospital.

ROSENBERG (35,087) varied industry.

Other towns include: **Arcola** (1,365); **Beasley** (745); **Cinco Ranch** (13,232); **Fairchilds** (849); **Fresno** (8,702); **Fulshear** (1,024); **Guy** (239); **Katy** (17,334, mostly in Harris County) hospital; **Kendleton** (599); **Meadows Place** (6,652); **Mission Bend** (36,437).

Also, **Needville** (3,632); **New Territory** (17,006); **Orchard** (528); **Pecan Grove** (17,387); **Pleak** (1,244); **Simonton** (936); **Stafford** (21,656, partly in Harris County); **Thompsons** (333); **Weston Lakes** (2,500).

Also, part [33,384] of **Houston**.

Population	**532,141**
Change fm 2000	50.1
Area (sq. mi.)	886.05
Land Area (sq. mi.)	874.64
Altitude (ft.)	46-158
Rainfall (in.)	49.34
Jan. mean min.	41.6
July mean max.	93.7
Civ. Labor	259,214
Unemployed	5.1
Wages	$1,451,333,379
Av. Weekly Wage	$870
Prop. Value	$40,859,538,307
Retail Sales	$6,660,314,380

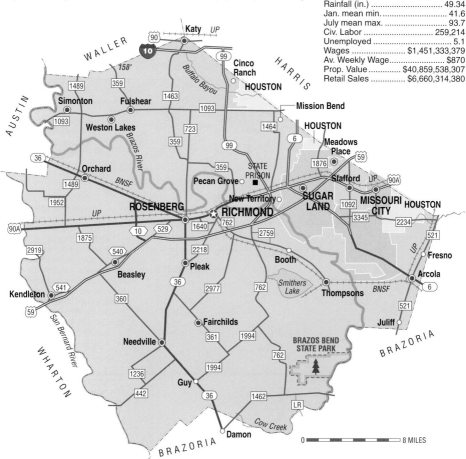

Franklin County

Physical Features: Small Northeast county with many wooded hills; drained by numerous streams; alluvial to sandy clay soils; two lakes.

Economy: Agribusiness, government/services, retirement area, distribution.

History: Caddoes abandoned the area in 1790s because of disease and other tribes. First white settlers arrived around 1818. County created 1875 from Titus County; named for jurist B.C. Franklin.

Race/Ethnicity, 2007: (In percent) Anglo, 84.2; Black, 4.2; Hispanic, 10.9; Other, 0.7.

Vital Statistics, 2006: Births, 123; deaths, 116; marriages, 83; divorces, 37.

Population	11,001
Change fm 2000	16.3
Area (sq. mi.)	294.77
Land Area (sq. mi.)	285.66
Altitude (ft.)	300-600
Rainfall (in.)	47.65
Jan. mean min.	32.2
July mean max.	92.8
Civ. Labor	5,882
Unemployed	4.5
Wages	$24,279,810
Av. Weekly Wage	$622
Prop. Value	$1,023,726,510
Retail Sales	$83,445,556

Recreation: Fishing, water sports; historic homes; wild hog hunting, horse stables; stew cook-off in October.

Minerals: Lignite coal, oil and gas.

Agriculture: Beef cattle, milk production, poultry, hay. Market value $85.8 million. Timber marketed.

MOUNT VERNON (2,573) county seat; distribution center, manufacturing, tourism, antiques; hospital; museum with Don Meredith exhibit; Labor Day rodeo.

Other towns include: **Scroggins** (150), and **Winnsboro** (4,210, mostly in Wood County) commercial center, Autumn Trails.

Freestone County

Physical Features: East central county bounded by the Trinity River; rolling Blackland, sandy, loam soils.

Economy: Natural gas, mining, electricity generating plants, agriculture.

History: Caddo and Tawakoni area. David G. Burnet received land grant in 1825. Seven Mexican citizens received grants in 1833. In 1860, more than half population was black. County created 1850 from Limestone County; organized 1851. Named for indigenous stone.

Race/Ethnicity, 2007: (In percent) Anglo, 70.3; Black, 18.5; Hispanic, 10.5; Other, 0.7.

Vital Statistics, 2006: Births, 213; deaths, 194; marriages, 165; divorces, 54.

Recreation: Fishing, hunting; lakes; historic sites; state park.

Minerals: Natural gas, oil and lignite coal.

Agriculture: Beef cattle, peaches (third in acreage), hay, blueberries, horticulture. First in number of ducks. Market value $33.9 million. Hunting leases.

FAIRFIELD (3,634) county seat; lignite mining, government/services, trade center; hospital, museum; wild game supper in July.

TEAGUE (5,112) railroad terminal, oil and gas, government/services, electric generating plant, agriculture; library, museum; Parkfest in October.

Other towns include: **Donie** (250), **Kirvin** (134), **Streetman** (212), **Wortham** (1,276) agribusiness, blues festival in September, Blind Lemon Jefferson gravesite.

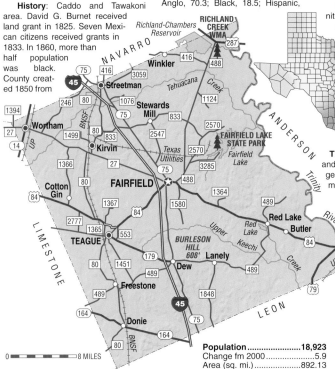

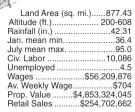

Population	18,923
Change fm 2000	5.9
Area (sq. mi.)	892.13
Land Area (sq. mi.)	877.43
Altitude (ft.)	200-608
Rainfall (in.)	42.31
Jan. mean min.	36.4
July mean max.	95.0
Civ. Labor	10,086
Unemployed	4.5
Wages	$56,209,876
Av. Weekly Wage	$704
Prop. Value	$4,853,324,045
Retail Sales	$254,702,662

Frio County

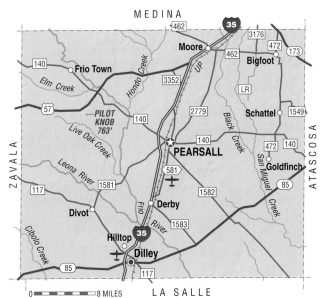

Physical Features: South Texas county of rolling terrain with much brush; bisected by Frio River; sandy, red sandy loam soils.

Economy: Agribusiness, oil-field services, hunting leases.

History: Coahuiltecans; many taken into San Antonio missions. Comanche hunters kept settlers out until after the Civil War. Mexican citizens recruited for labor after 1900. County created 1858 from Atascosa, Bexar, Uvalde counties, organized in 1871; named for Frio (cold) River.

Race/Ethnicity, 2007: (In percent) Anglo, 19.4; Black, 4.2; Hispanic, 75.7; Other, 0.7.

Vital Statistics, 2006: Births, 233; deaths, 128; marriages, 82; divorces, 24.

Recreation: Hunting, Big Foot Wallace Museum, Winter Garden area, Pearsall potato fest in May.

Minerals: Oil, natural gas, stone.

Agriculture: Peanuts, potatoes, sorghum, cotton, corn, spinach, cucumbers, watermelons. Second in vegetables harvested. Market value $70.3 million. Hunting leases.

PEARSALL (7,905) county seat; agriculture center, oil and gas, food processing, shipping; old jail museum; hospital; Pioneer Days in April.

Dilley (4,069) shipping center for melons and peanuts; hospital.

Other towns include: **Bigfoot** (319), **Hilltop** (283); **Moore** (653) and **North Pearsall** (510).

Population	**16,163**
Change fm 2000	–0.5
Area (sq. mi.)	1,134.28
Land Area (sq. mi.)	1,133.02
Altitude (ft.)	400-763
Rainfall (in.)	25.73
Jan. mean min.	37.9
July mean max.	97.5
Civ. Labor	6,880
Unemployed	6.3
Wages	$29,968,797
Av. Weekly Wage	$542
Prop. Value	$545,564,560
Retail Sales	$95,554,830

For explanation of sources, abbreviations and symbols, see p. 210 and foldout map.

The main thoroughfare in Streetman, Freestone County. Robert Plocheck photo.

Gaines County

Physical Features: On South Plains, drains to draws; playas; underground water.

Economy: Oil and gas, cotton, peanuts.

History: Comanche country until U.S. Army campaigns of 1875. Ranchers arrived in 1880s; farming began around 1900. County created from Bexar District, 1876; organized 1905; named for James Gaines, signer of Texas Declaration of Independence.

Race/Ethnicity, 2007: (In percent) Anglo, 57.4; Black, 2.2; Hispanic, 39.9; Other, 0.5.

Vital Statistics, 2006: Births, 312; deaths, 107; marriages, 171; divorces, 28.

Recreation: Cedar Lake one of largest alkali lakes on Texas plains.

Minerals: Oil, gas.

Agriculture: Cotton (third in acreage), peanuts (first in acreage), small grains, pecans, paprika, rosemary; cattle, sheep, hogs; substantial irrigation. Market value $193.2 million.

SEMINOLE (6,134) county seat; oil and gas, market center, biodiesel fuel plant; hospital, library, museum; county airport; Ag and Oil Day in September.

Seagraves (2,478) market for three-county area; cotton, peanut farming; library, museum; Celebrate Seagraves in July.

Other towns include: **Loop** (315). Also, part of **Denver City** (3,934).

Population	**15,081**
Change fm 2000	4.2
Area (sq. mi.)	1,502.84
Land Area (sq. mi.)	1,502.35
Altitude (ft.)	2,935-3,695
Rainfall (in.)	18.20
Jan. mean min.	26.7
July mean max.	94.1
Civ. Labor	6,858
Unemployed	3.8
Wages	$44,607,510
Av. Weekly Wage	$669
Prop. Value	$4,665,238,494
Retail Sales	$174,161,220

Sacred Heart Church in Galveston, built in 1903-04. Robert Plocheck photo.

Galveston County

Physical Features: Partly island, partly coastal; flat, artificial drainage; sandy, loam, clay soils; broken by bays.

Economy: Port activities dominate economy; insurance and finance center, petrochemical plants, varied manufacturing, tourism, medical education, oceanographic research, ship building, commercial fishing.

History: Karankawa and other tribes roamed the area until 1850. French, Spanish and American settlement began in 1815 and reached 1,000 by 1817. County created from Brazoria County 1838; organized 1839; named for Spanish governor of Louisiana Count Bernardo de Gálvez.

Race/Ethnicity, 2007: (In percent) Anglo, 59.2; Black, 15.0; Hispanic, 22.7; Other, 3.7.

Vital Statistics, 2006: Births, 3,957; deaths, 2,348; marriages, 1,999; divorces, 994.

Recreation: One of Texas' most historic cities; popular tourist and convention center; fishing, surfing, boating, sailing and other water sports; state park; historic homes tour in spring, Moody Gardens; Mardi Gras celebration; Rosenberg Library; museums; restored sailing ship, "Elissa," railroad museum; Dickens on the Strand in early December.

Minerals: Oil, gas, clays, sand and gravel.

Agriculture: Cattle, aquaculture, nursery crops, rice, hay, horses, soybeans, grain sorghum. Market value $8.3 million.

GALVESTON (59,186) county seat; tourist center, shipyard, other industries, insurance, port container facility; University of Texas Medical Branch; National Maritime Research Center; Texas A&M University at Galveston; Galveston College; hospitals.

League City (68,836) residential community, commuters to Houston, hospital.

Texas City (44, 391) refining, petrochemical plants, port, rail shipping; College of the Mainland; hospital, library; dike; Cinco de Mayo, Shrimp Boil in August.

Bolivar Peninsula (3,746) includes: **Port Bolivar** (800) lighthouse, free ferry; **Crystal Beach** (1,200) seafood industry, sport fishing, tourism, Fort Travis Seashore Park, shorebird sanctuary, Crab Festival in May; **Gilchrist** (600) and **High Island** (300).

Other towns include: **Bacliff** (7,425); **Bayou Vista** (1,764); **Clear Lake Shores** (1,296).

Also, **Dickinson** (22,655) manufacturing, commuters, strawberry festival in May; **Friendswood** (33,106, partly [7,800] in Harris County); **Hitchcock** (7,265) residential community, tourism, fishing and shrimping, Good Ole Days in August, WWII blimp base, museum.

Also, **Jamaica Beach** (1,293); **Kemah** (2,620) tourism, boating, commuters, museum, Blessing of Fleet in August; **La Marque** (14,435) refining, greyhound racing, farming, hospital, library, Gulf Coast Grill-off in October; **San Leon** (4,790); **Santa Fe** (10,750); **Tiki Island** (1,222).

Population	288,239
Change fm 2000	15.2
Area (sq. mi.)	872.93
Land Area (sq. mi.)	398.47
Altitude (ft.)	sea level-40
Rainfall (in.)	43.84
Jan. mean min.	49.7
July mean max.	88.7
Civ. Labor	148,848
Unemployed	7.5
Wages	$1,008,115,022
Av. Weekly Wage	$804
Prop. Value	$33,562,794,221
Retail Sales	$2,780,998,907

For explanation of sources, abbreviations and symbols, see p. 210 and foldout map.

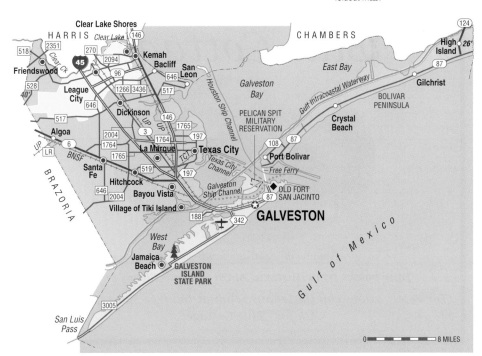

Garza County

Physical Features: On edge of Caprock; rough, broken land, with playas, gullies, canyons, Brazos River forks, lake; sandy, loam, clay soils.

Economy: Agriculture, oil & gas, trade, government/services, hunting leases.

History: Kiowas and Comanches yielded to U.S. Army in 1875. Ranching began in 1870s, farming in the 1890s. C.W. Post, the cereal millionaire, established enterprises in 1906. County created from Bexar District, 1876; organized 1907; named for early Texas family.

Race/Ethnicity, 2007: (In percent) Anglo, 53.8; Black, 5.1; Hispanic, 40.6; Other, 0.6.

Vital Statistics, 2006: Births, 64; deaths, 43; marriages, 46; divorces, 17.

Recreation: Scenic areas, lake activities, Post-Garza Museum, Founders Day in September.

Minerals: Oil, gas, sand, gravel.

Agriculture: Cotton, beef cattle, hay; 12,800 acres irrigated. Market value $27.4 million. Hunting leases.

POST (3,960) county seat; founded by C.W. Post; agriculture, tourism, government/services, prisons; Garza Theatre.

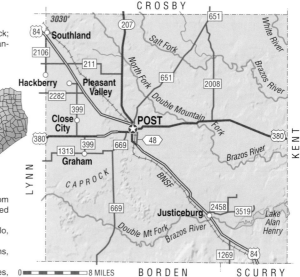

Population	**4,628**
Change fm 2000	−5.0
Area (sq. mi.)	896.19
Land Area (sq. mi.)	895.56
Altitude (ft.)	2,140-3,030
Rainfall (in.)	21.29
Jan. mean min.	27.8
July mean max.	94.0
Civ. Labor	2,546

Unemployed	3.7
Wages	$13,616,227
Av. Weekly Wage	$612
Prop. Value	$713,156,870
Retail Sales	$33,942,374

For explanation of sources, abbreviations and symbols, see p. 210 and foldout map.

Gillespie County

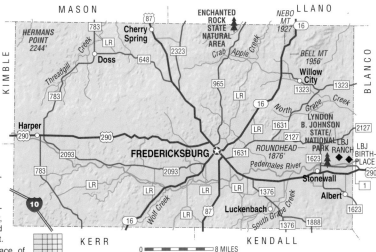

Physical Features: Picturesque Edwards Plateau area with hills, broken by spring-fed streams.

Economy: Tourism, government/services, agriculture, wine and specialty foods, hunting leases.

History: German settlement founded 1846 in heart of Comanche country. County created 1848 from Bexar, Travis counties; named for Texas Ranger Capt. R.A. Gillespie. Birthplace of President Lyndon B. Johnson and Fleet Admiral Chester W. Nimitz.

Race/Ethnicity, 2007: (In percent) Anglo, 81.7; Black, 0.2; Hispanic, 17.6; Other, 0.5.

Vital Statistics, 2006: Births, 249; deaths, 270; marriages, 195; divorces, 82.

Recreation: Among leading deer-hunting areas; numerous historic sites and tourist attractions include LBJ Ranch, Nimitz Hotel and Pacific war museum; Pioneer Museum Complex, Enchanted Rock.

Minerals: Sand, gravel, gypsum, limestone rock.

Agriculture: Beef cattle, peaches (first in acreage), grapes, sheep and goats, hay, grain sorghum, oats, wheat. Market value $28.6 million. Hunting leases important.

FREDERICKSBURG (10,872) county seat; agribusiness, tourism, wineries, food processing; museum; tourist attractions; hospital; Easter Fires, Oktoberfest.

Other towns include: **Doss** (100); **Harper** (1,119) ranching, deer hunting, Dachshund Hounds Downs race and Trades Day in October; **Luckenbach** (25) saloon, general store and dance hall; **Stonewall** (521) agribusiness, wineries, tourism, hunting, Peach Jamboree in June, and **Willow City** (22) scenic drive.

Population	23,782
Change fm 2000	14.3
Area (sq. mi.)	1,061.48
Land Area (sq. mi.)	1,061.06
Altitude (ft.)	1,040-2,244
Rainfall (in.)	31.65
Jan. mean min.	36.1
July mean max.	93.1
Civ. Labor	13,462
Unemployed	3.5
Wages	$66,303,271
Av. Weekly Wage	$562
Prop. Value	$2,685,333,428
Retail Sales	$376,291,037

Glasscock County

Physical Features: Western county on rolling plains, broken by small streams; sandy, loam soils.

Economy: Farming, ranching, hunting leases, oil and gas, quarries.

History: Hunting area for Kickapoos and Lipan Apaches. Anglo-American sheep ranchers and Mexican-American shepherds or pastores moved into the area in 1880s. County created 1887 from Tom Green County; organized, 1893; named for Texas pioneer George W. Glasscock.

Race/Ethnicity, 2007: (In percent) Anglo, 68.0; Black, 0.5; Hispanic, 31.4; Other, 0.1.

Vital Statistics, 2006: Births, 7; deaths, 4; marriages, 3; divorces, 2.

Recreation: Hunting of deer, quail, turkey, fox, bobcat, coyote; St. Lawrence Fall Festival in October.

Minerals: Oil, gas, stone/rock.

Agriculture: Cotton, watermelons, wheat, sorghum, hay; 60,000 acres irrigated. Cattle, goats, sheep, hogs raised. Market value $46.3 million.

GARDEN CITY (293), county seat; serves sparsely settled ranching, oil area.

Population	1,212
Change fm 2000	−13.8
Area (sq. mi.)	900.93
Land Area (sq. mi.)	900.75
Altitude (ft.)	2,470-2,785
Rainfall (in.)	17.32
Jan. mean min.	26.7
July mean max.	94.0
Civ. Labor	677
Unemployed	3.4
Wages	$2,441,586
Av. Weekly Wage	$528
Prop. Value	$797,226,950
Retail Sales	$3,166,197

Physical Features: Coastal Plain county; rolling, brushy; bisected by San Antonio River; sandy, loam, alluvial soils.

Economy: Government/services, oil/gas, agriculture, electricity-generating plant, tourism.

History: Karankawas, Comanches and other tribes in area in historic period. La Bahía presidio/mission established 1749. County created 1836 from Spanish municipality; organized 1837; name is anagram of (H)idalgo. Birthplace of Gen. Ignacio Zaragoza, hero of Battle of Puebla (Mexico).

Race/Ethnicity, 2007: (In percent) Anglo, 58.6; Black, 4.4; Hispanic, 36.7; Other, 0.3.

Vital Statistics, 2006: Births, 72; deaths, 78; marriages, 39; divorces, 18.

Recreation: Missions, restored Presidio La Bahía, Fannin Battleground; Old Market House museum; lake, fishing, hunting (deer, quail, dove, hogs), camping, canoeing, birding.

Minerals: Production of oil, gas.

Agriculture: Beef cattle, stocker operations and fed cattle are top revenue producers; corn, grain sorghum, cotton, hay; minor irrigation for pasture. Market value $20 million. Hunting leases.

GOLIAD (2,008) county seat; one of state's oldest towns; oil, gas center; agriculture; tourism; library; Zaragoza Birthplace State Historic Site, statue; Goliad Massacre re-enactment in March, Diez y Seis in September.

Other towns include: **Berclair** (253), **Fannin** (359) and **Weesatche** (411).

Goliad County

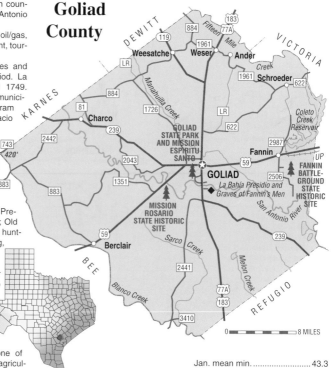

Population	7,152
Change fm 2000	3.2
Area (sq. mi.)	859.35
Land Area (sq. mi.)	853.52
Altitude (ft.)	50-420
Rainfall (in.)	38.58

Jan. mean min.	43.3
July mean max.	95.5
Civ. Labor	3,470
Unemployed	4.6
Wages	$10,804,427
Av. Weekly Wage	$565
Prop. Value	$1,150,863,400
Retail Sales	$30,832,953

Mission Espíritu Santo in Goliad is a replica of the original built in 1749. Robert Plocheck photo.

Gonzales County

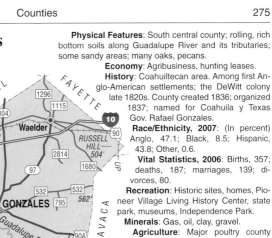

Physical Features: South central county; rolling, rich bottom soils along Guadalupe River and its tributaries; some sandy areas; many oaks, pecans.

Economy: Agribusiness, hunting leases.

History: Coahuiltecan area. Among first Anglo-American settlements; the DeWitt colony late 1820s. County created 1836; organized 1837; named for Coahuila y Texas Gov. Rafael Gonzales.

Race/Ethnicity, 2007: (In percent) Anglo, 47.1; Black, 8.5; Hispanic, 43.8; Other, 0.6.

Vital Statistics, 2006: Births, 357; deaths, 187; marriages, 139; divorces, 80.

Recreation: Historic sites, homes, Pioneer Village Living History Center, state park, museums, Independence Park.

Minerals: Gas, oil, clay, gravel.

Agriculture: Major poultry county (leader in turkeys sold); cattle, hogs; hay, corn, sorghum, pecans. Market value $404 million.

GONZALES (7,306) county seat; first shot in Texas Revolution fired here; shipping, processing center, manufacturing; hospital; "Come and Take It" festival in October.

Other towns include: **Belmont** (55); **Cost** (84) First Shot monument; **Harwood** (118); **Leesville** (152); **Nixon** (2,362) poultry-processing plant, Feather Fest in September; **Ottine** (80); **Smiley** (446); **Waelder** (1,004) Guacamole Fest in September; **Wrightsboro** (10).

For explanation of sources, abbreviations and symbols, see p. 210.

M.O. NEASLONEY WILDLIFE MANAGEMENT AREA

Population	19,155
Change fm 2000	2.8
Area (sq. mi.)	1,069.82
Land Area (sq. mi.)	1,067.75
Altitude (ft.)	200-562
Rainfall (in.)	36.02
Jan. mean min.	38.7
July mean max.	93.9
Civ. Labor	10,327
Unemployed	4.4
Wages	$47,975,366
Av. Weekly Wage	$577
Prop. Value	$916,130,213
Retail Sales	$464,610,606

Gray County

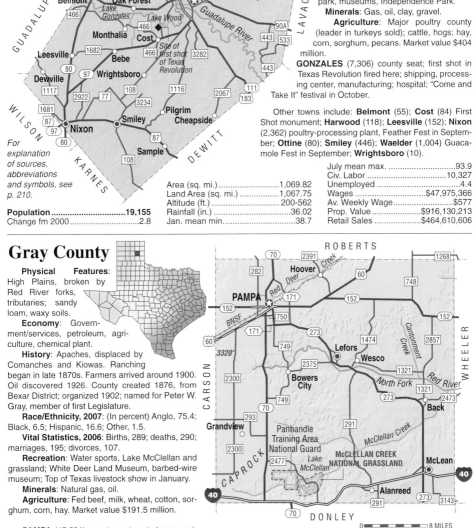

Physical Features: High Plains, broken by Red River forks, tributaries; sandy loam, waxy soils.

Economy: Government/services, petroleum, agriculture, chemical plant.

History: Apaches, displaced by Comanches and Kiowas. Ranching began in late 1870s. Farmers arrived around 1900. Oil discovered 1926. County created 1876, from Bexar District; organized 1902; named for Peter W. Gray, member of first Legislature.

Race/Ethnicity, 2007: (In percent) Anglo, 75.4; Black, 6.5; Hispanic, 16.6; Other, 1.5.

Vital Statistics, 2006: Births, 289; deaths, 290; marriages, 195; divorces, 107.

Recreation: Water sports, Lake McClellan and grassland; White Deer Land Museum, barbed-wire museum; Top of Texas livestock show in January.

Minerals: Natural gas, oil.

Agriculture: Fed beef, milk, wheat, cotton, sorghum, corn, hay. Market value $191.5 million.

PAMPA (17,591) county seat; petroleum, agriculture, chemical plant; hospital; college; prison; Woody Guthrie museum; Mud Bog in June.

Other towns include: **Alanreed** (48); **Lefors** (569); **McLean** (901) commercial center for southern part of county.

Population	22,248
Change fm 2000	-2.2
Area (sq. mi.)	929.25
Land Area (sq. mi.)	928.28
Altitude (ft.)	2,450-3,320
Rainfall (in.)	22.74
Jan. mean min.	21.9
July mean max.	92.0
Civ. Labor	11,629
Unemployed	3.7
Wages	$91,976,122
Av. Weekly Wage	$789
Prop. Value	$1,515,260,615
Retail Sales	$393,673,424

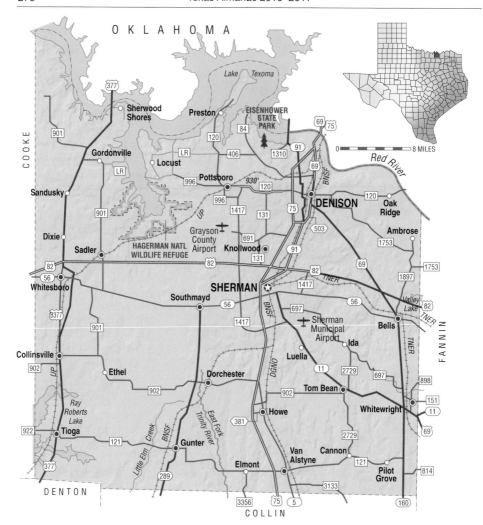

Grayson County

Physical Features: North Texas county; level, some low hills; sandy loam, blackland soils; drains to Red River and tributaries of Trinity River.

Economy: A manufacturing, distribution and trade center for northern Texas and southern Oklahoma; nature tourism, mineral production, prisons.

History: Caddo and Tonkawa area. Preston Bend trading post established 1836-37. Peters colony settlers arrived in 1840s. County created 1846 from Fannin County; named for Republic Atty. Gen. Peter W. Grayson.

Race/Ethnicity, 2007: (In percent) Anglo, 81.4; Black, 6.2; Hispanic, 9.8; Other, 2.7.

Vital Statistics, 2006: Births, 1,659; deaths, 1,281; marriages, 974; divorces, 509.

Recreation: Lakes, fishing, pheasant hunting, water sports, state park,

For explanation of sources, abbreviations and symbols, see p. 210 and foldout map.

cultural activities, wildlife refuge, Pioneer Village, railroad museum.

Minerals: Oil, gas, gravel, sand.

Agriculture: Wheat, corn, hay, beef cattle, horses (third in number). Market value $52.8 million.

Education: Austin College in Sherman and Grayson County College located between Sherman and Denison.

SHERMAN (38,885) county seat; varied manufacturing, processors and distributors for major companies; Austin College; hospital.

DENISON (24,678) manufacturing, food processing, medical servies, tourism; hospital; Eisenhower birthplace; Arts & Wine Renaissance in May, Main Street Fall festival in October.

Other towns include: **Bells** (1,317); **Collinsville** (1,616); **Dorchester** (126); **Gordonville** (165); **Gunter** (1,819); **Howe** (2,937) distribution, varied manufacturing, museum, Founders' Day

in May; **Knollwood** (412); **Pottsboro** (2,268) lake activities, marinas, Frontier Days in September; **Sadler** (423); **Southmayd** (1,085); **Tioga** (942) Gene Autry museum, festival in September; **Tom Bean** (1,025); **Van Alstyne** (2,780) window screen, electronics, saddle, tack manufacturing; **Whitesboro** (4,219) agribusiness, tourism, manufacturing, library, Peanut Festival in October; **Whitewright** (1,722) agribusiness, tourism, manufacturing, museum, Wine & Rose tour in May.

Population	118,804
Change fm 2000	7.4
Area (sq. mi.)	979.19
Land Area (sq. mi.)	933.51
Altitude (ft.)	500-930
Rainfall (in.)	42.04
Jan. mean min.	32.2
July mean max.	92.7
Civ. Labor	57,937
Unemployed	6.0
Wages	$375,155,909
Av. Weekly Wage	$670
Prop. Value	$6,661,659,643
Retail Sales	$1,490,508,489

Physical Features: A populous, leading petroleum county, heart of the famed East Texas oil field; bisected by the Sabine River; hilly, timbered; with sandy, clay, alluvial soils.

Economy: Oil but with significant other manufacturing; tourism, conventions, agribusiness and lignite coal production.

History: Caddoes; later Cherokees, who were driven out in 1838 by President Lamar. First land grants issued in 1835 by Republic of Mexico. County created and organized in 1873 from Rusk, Upshur counties; named for Confederate Gen. John Gregg. In U.S. censuses 1880-1910, blacks were more numerous than whites. Oil discovered in 1931.

Race/Ethnicity, 2007: (In percent) Anglo, 63.3; Black, 20.6; Hispanic, 14.5; Other, 1.7.

Vital Statistics, 2006: Births, 1,879; deaths, 1,163; marriages, 1,158; divorces, 465.

Recreation: Water activities on lakes, hunting, varied cultural events, East Texas Oil Museum in Kilgore.

Minerals: Leading oil-producing county with more than 3 billion barrels produced since 1931; also, sand, gravel and natural gas.

Agriculture: Cattle, horses, hay, nursery crops. Market value $3.8 million. Timber sales.

LONGVIEW (76,885, small part [1,598] in Harrison County) county seat; chemical manufacturing, oil industry, distribution and retail center; hospitals; LeTourneau University, UT-Tyler Longview center; convention center; balloon race in July.

Kilgore (12,341, part [2,580] in Rusk County), oil center; manufacturing; Kilgore College (junior), Rangerette museum; Shakespeare festival in summer.

Gladewater (6,453, part [2,454] in Upshur County) oil, manufacturing, tourism, antiques, agriculture; library; airport, skydiving; Gusher Days in April; daffodils in February-March.

Other towns include: **Clarksville City** (882); **Easton** (578, partly in Rusk County); **Judson** (1,057); **Lakeport** (972); **Liberty City** (2,175) oil, tourism, government/services, Honor America Night in November; **Warren City** (375); **White Oak** (6,182) oil &

gas, industrial park, commuting to Longview, Tyler; Roughneck Days in spring.

Population	**117,528**
Change fm 2000	5.5
Area (sq. mi.)	276.37
Land Area (sq. mi.)	274.03
Altitude (ft.)	240-530
Rainfall (in.)	49.06
Jan. mean min.	33.7
July mean max.	94.5
Civ. Labor	64,438
Unemployed	4.4
Wages	$712,952,639
Av. Weekly Wage	$734
Prop. Value	$9,059,404,630
Retail Sales	$2,545,054,205

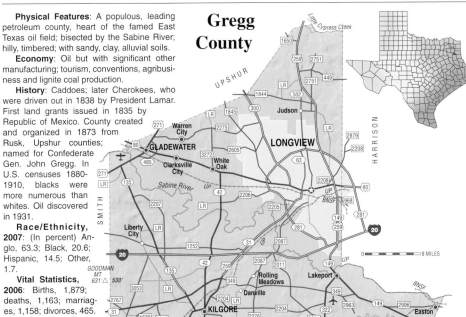

Gregg County

The birthplace of President Dwight Eisenhower in Denison, Grayson County. Robert Plocheck photo.

Grimes County

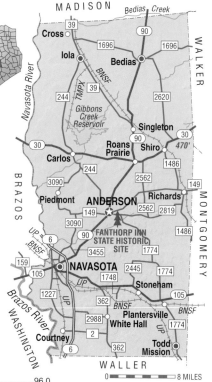

Physical Features: Rich bottom soils along Brazos, Navasota rivers; remainder hilly, partly forested.

Economy: Varied manufacturing, agribusiness, tourism.

History: Bidais (customs similar to the Caddoes) lived peacefully with Anglo-American settlers who arrived in 1820s, but tribe was removed to Indian Territory. Planter agriculture reflected in 1860 census, which listed 77 persons owning 20 or more slaves. County created from Montgomery County 1846; named for Jesse Grimes, who signed Texas Declaration of Independence.

Race/Ethnicity, 2007: (In percent) Anglo, 63.1; Black, 18.7; Hispanic,17.7; Other, 0.6.

Vital Statistics, 2006: Births, 343; deaths, 187; marriages, 139; divorces, 63.

Recreation: Hunting, fishing; Gibbons Creek Reservoir; historic sites; fall Renaissance Festival at Plantersville.

Minerals: Lignite coal, natural gas.

Agriculture: Cattle, forage, horses, poultry; berries, pecans, honey sales significant. Market value $49.9 million. Some timber sold, Christmas tree farms.

ANDERSON (283) county seat; rural center; Fanthorp Inn historic site; Go-Texan weekend in February.

NAVASOTA (7,791) agribusiness center for parts of three counties; varied manufacturing; food, wood processing; hospital; prisons; La Salle statue; Blues Fest in August.

Other towns include: **Bedias** (431); **Iola** (350); **Plantersville** (260); **Richards** (300); **Roans Prairie** (64); **Shiro** (210); **Todd Mission** (172).

Population	**25,895**
Change fm 2000	9.9
Area (sq. mi.)	801.16
Land Area (sq. mi.)	793.60
Altitude (ft.)	150-470
Rainfall (in.)	44.70
Jan. mean min.	40.0

July mean max.	96.0
Civ. Labor	11,018
Unemployed	5.9
Wages	$71,438,670

Av. Weekly Wage	$788
Prop. Value	$1,803,102,114
Retail Sales	$203,524,539

The Brazos River where ferries crossed to Grimes County from Washington County. Robert Plocheck photo.

Guadalupe County

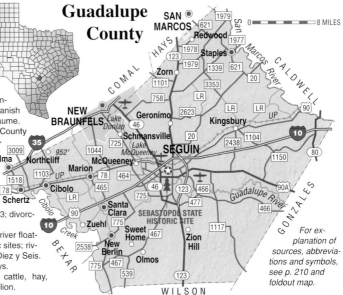

Physical Features: South central county bisected by Guadalupe River; level to rolling surface; sandy, loam, blackland soils.

Economy: Varied manufacturing, commuting to San Antonio, agribusiness, tourism.

History: Karankawas, Comanches, other tribes until 1850s. Spanish land grant in 1806 to José de la Baume. DeWitt colonists arrived in 1827. County created 1846 from Bexar, Gonzales counties; named for river.

Race/Ethnicity, 2007: (In percent) Anglo, 56.4; Black, 5.2; Hispanic, 36.6; Other, 1.8.

Vital Statistics, 2006: Births, 1,352; deaths, 733; marriages, 543; divorces, 378.

Recreation: Fishing, hunting, river floating; Sebastopol site, other historic sites; river drive; Freedom Fiesta in July, Diez y Seis.

Minerals: Oil, gas, gravel, clays.

Agriculture: Nursery crops, cattle, hay, row crops. Market value $41.2 million.

For explanation of sources, abbreviations and symbols, see p. 210 and foldout map.

SEGUIN (28,346) county seat; electronics, steel, manufacturing, government/services; hospital, museums; Texas Lutheran University.

Other towns include: **Cibolo** (14,056), **Geronimo** (706), **Kingsbury** (760), **Marion** (1,306), **McQueeney** (3,020), **New Berlin** (559), **Northcliff** (2,024); **Redwood** (4,116); **Santa Clara** (1,016); **Schertz** (30,552, parts in Bexar and Comal counties), **Staples** (396).

Also, part [1,166] of **New Braunfels**, part [50] of **Selma**, and a small part of **San Marcos**.

Population	**117,172**
Change fm 2000	31.6
Area (sq. mi.)	714.17
Land Area (sq. mi.)	711.14
Altitude (ft.)	350-952
Rainfall (in.)	34.50
Jan. mean min.	35.5
July mean max.	94.7
Civ. Labor	56,178
Unemployed	5.0
Wages	$256,685,685
Av. Weekly Wage	$677
Prop. Value	$8,225,502,398
Retail Sales	$933,427,530

Hale County

Physical Features: High Plains; fertile sandy, loam soils; playas; large underground water supply.

Economy: Agribusiness, food processing/ distribution, manufacturing, government/services.

History: Comanche hunters driven out by U.S. Army in 1875. Ranching began in 1880s. First motor-driven irrigation well drilled in 1911. County created from Bexar District, 1876; organized 1888; named for Lt. J.C. Hale, who died at San Jacinto.

Race/Ethnicity, 2007: (In percent), Anglo, 41.2; Black, 5.9; Hispanic, 52.1; Other, 0.8.

Vital Statistics, 2006: Births, 628; deaths, 301; marriages, 266; divorces, 94.

Recreation: Llano Estacado Museum; art gallery, antiques stores; pheasant hunting; Plainview Cattle Drive in September.

Minerals: Some oil.

Agriculture: Cotton, fed beef, sorghum, dairies, corn, vegetables, wheat. Market value $364.4 million. Irrigation of 448,000 acres.

PLAINVIEW (21,324) county seat; distribution center, food processing; Wayland Baptist University; hospital, library, mental health center; state prisons.

Hale Center (2,133) trade center; farm museum, library, parks, murals, cacti gardens.

Abernathy (2,791, part [708] in Lubbock County) government/services, farm supplies, textile plant, gins.

Other towns include: **Cotton Center** (300), **Edmonson** (127), **Petersburg** (1,187), **Seth Ward** (1,966).

Population	**35,234**
Change fm 2000	–3.7
Area (sq. mi.)	1,004.77
Land Area (sq. mi.)	1,004.65
Altitude (ft.)	3,180-3,620
Rainfall (in.)	19.90
Jan. mean min.	24.4
July mean max.	91.0
Civ. Labor	16,624
Unemployed	4.6
Wages	$102,253,788
Av. Weekly Wage	$551
Prop. Value	$1,767,581,806
Retail Sales	$2,413,641,856

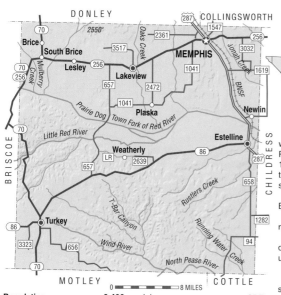

Hall County

Physical Features: Rolling to hilly, broken by Red River forks, tributaries; red and black sandy loam.

Economy: Agriculture, farm, ranch supplies, marketing for large rural area.

History: Apaches displaced by Comanches, who were removed to Indian Territory in 1875. Ranching began in 1880s. Farming expanded after 1910. County created 1876 from Bexar, Young districts; organized 1890; named for Republic of Texas secretary of war W.D.C. Hall.

Race/Ethnicity, 2007: (In percent) Anglo, 57.9; Black, 8.4; Hispanic, 33.2; Other, 0.5.

Vital Statistics, 2006: Births, 41; deaths, 52; marriages, 20; divorces, 8.

Recreation: Hunting of deer, wild hog, turkey, quail, dove; Rails to Trails system; Bob Wills museum; Memphis Old Settlers reunion in September.

Minerals: None.

Agriculture: Cotton, cattle, peanuts, wheat, sorghum, alfalfa hay. Market value $43.5 million. Hunting leases.

MEMPHIS (2,345) county seat; cotton gins, peanut processing; historic buildings.

Other towns include: **Estelline** (154), motorcycle rally/chili cookoff in August, **Lakeview** (144), **Turkey** (451) Bob Wills Day in April.

Population	3,400
Change fm 2000	–10.1
Area (sq. mi.)	904.08
Land Area (sq. mi.)	903.09
Altitude (ft.)	1,750-2,550
Rainfall (in.)	22.51
Jan. mean min.	25.5
July mean max.	95.7
Civ. Labor	1,509
Unemployed	6.6
Wages	$5,212,640
Av. Weekly Wage	$428
Prop. Value	$187,638,091
Retail Sales	$28,224,824

Hamilton County

Physical Features: Hilly north central county broken by scenic valleys; loam soils.

Economy: Varied manufacturing, agribusiness, hunting leases, tourism.

History: Waco and Tawakoni Indian area. Anglo-American settlers arrived in mid-1850s. County created, organized 1858, from Bosque, Comanche, Lampasas counties; named for South Carolina Gov. James Hamilton, who aided Texas Revolution and Republic.

Race/Ethnicity, 2007: (In percent) Anglo, 90.4; Black, 0.2; Hispanic, 8.8; Other, 0.7.

Vital Statistics, 2006: Births, 76; deaths, 132; marriages, 62; divorces, 40.

Recreation: Deer, quail, duck hunting; Linear Pecan Creek park in Hamilton; Hamilton dove festival on Labor Day.

Minerals: Limited oil, gas.

Agriculture: Dairies, beef cattle top revenue sources. Oats (first in acreage), hay, wheat, sorghum. Also, pecans, sheep, horses. Market value $51.4 million.

HAMILTON (3,130) county seat; varied manufacturing; hospital; Central Texas College branch; historical homes.

Hico (1,383) tourism, agriculture, varied manufacturing; antiques shops, Billy the Kid museum; steak cookoff in May.

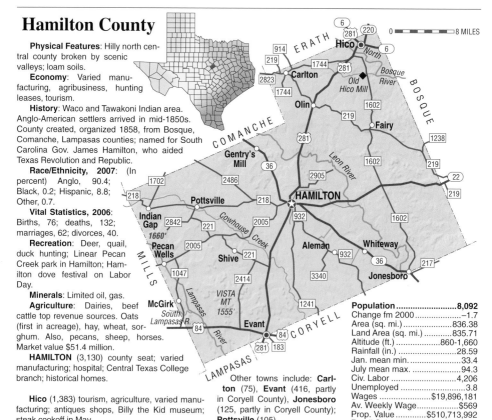

Other towns include: **Carlton** (75), **Evant** (416, partly in Coryell County), **Jonesboro** (125, partly in Coryell County); **Pottsville** (105).

Population	8,092
Change fm 2000	–1.7
Area (sq. mi.)	836.38
Land Area (sq. mi.)	835.71
Altitude (ft.)	860-1,660
Rainfall (in.)	28.59
Jan. mean min.	33.4
July mean max.	94.3
Civ. Labor	4,206
Unemployed	3.8
Wages	$19,896,181
Av. Weekly Wage	$569
Prop. Value	$510,713,992
Retail Sales	$84,059,200

Hansford County

Physical Features: High Plains, many playas, creeks, draws; sandy, loam, black soils; underground water.

Economy: Agribusinesses; oil, gas operations.

History: Apaches, pushed out by Comanches around 1700. U.S. Army removed Comanches in 1874-75 and ranching began soon afterward. Farmers, including Norwegians, moved in around 1900. County created 1876, from Bexar, Young districts; organized 1889; named for jurist J.M. Hansford.

Race/Ethnicity, 2007: (In percent) Anglo, 60.7; Black, 0.1; Hispanic, 38.5; Other, 0.7.

Vital Statistics, 2006: Births, 112; deaths, 45; marriages, 24; divorces, 12.

Recreation: Stationmasters House Museum, hunting, lake activities, ecotourism.

Minerals: Production of gas, oil.

Agriculture: Large cattle-feeding operations; corn, wheat (second in acreage), sorghum; hogs. Substantial irrigation. Market value $589.8 million.

SPEARMAN (2,981) county seat; farming, cattle production, oil and gas, wind energy, biofuels; hospital, library, windmill collection; Heritage Days in June.

Other towns include: **Gruver** (1,153) farm-ranch market, natural gas production, Fourth of July barbecue; **Morse** (192).

For explanation of sources, abbreviations and symbols, see p. 210 and foldout map.

Population	5,280
Change fm 2000	−1.7
Area (sq. mi.)	920.40
Land Area (sq. mi.)	919.80
Altitude (ft.)	2,750-3,378
Rainfall (in.)	20.30
Jan. mean min.	22.4
July mean max.	95.5
Civ. Labor	2,693
Unemployed	3.1
Wages	$16,339,505
Av. Weekly Wage	$658
Prop. Value	$1,020,522,127
Retail Sales	$28,823,495

St. Paul's Lutheran Church in Aleman, Hamilton County, dates from 1886. Robert Plocheck photo.

Grasses surround a pier at Copper Breaks State Park in Hardeman County. Robert Plocheck photo.

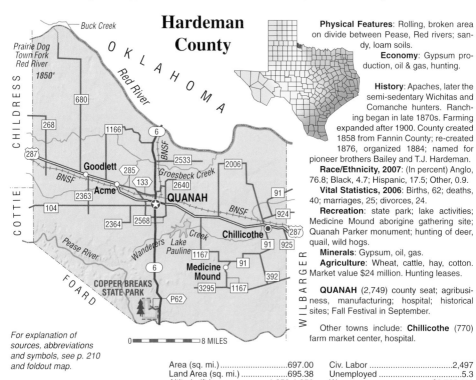

Hardeman County

Physical Features: Rolling, broken area on divide between Pease, Red rivers; sandy, loam soils.

Economy: Gypsum production, oil & gas, hunting.

History: Apaches, later the semi-sedentary Wichitas and Comanche hunters. Ranching began in late 1870s. Farming expanded after 1900. County created 1858 from Fannin County; re-created 1876, organized 1884; named for pioneer brothers Bailey and T.J. Hardeman.

Race/Ethnicity, 2007: (In percent) Anglo, 76.8; Black, 4.7; Hispanic, 17.5; Other, 0.9.

Vital Statistics, 2006: Births, 62; deaths, 40; marriages, 25; divorces, 24.

Recreation: state park; lake activities; Medicine Mound aborigine gathering site; Quanah Parker monument; hunting of deer, quail, wild hogs.

Minerals: Gypsum, oil, gas.

Agriculture: Wheat, cattle, hay, cotton. Market value $24 million. Hunting leases.

QUANAH (2,749) county seat; agribusiness, manufacturing; hospital; historical sites; Fall Festival in September.

Other towns include: **Chillicothe** (770) farm market center, hospital.

For explanation of sources, abbreviations and symbols, see p. 210 and foldout map.

Population	**3,984**
Change fm 2000	–15.7

Area (sq. mi.)	697.00	Civ. Labor	2,497
Land Area (sq. mi.)	695.38	Unemployed	5.3
Altitude (ft.)	1,250-1,850	Wages	$9,795,113
Rainfall (in.)	26.76	Av. Weekly Wage	$537
Jan. mean min.	24.6	Prop. Value	$333,952,880
July mean max.	96.5	Retail Sales	$24,524,462

Hardin County

Physical Features: Southeast county; timbered; many streams; sandy, loam soils; Big Thicket covers much of area.

Economy: Paper manufacturing, wood processing, minerals, food processing, oil and gas; county in Beaumont-Port Arthur-Orange metropolitan area.

History: Lorenzo de Zavala received first land grant in 1829. Anglo-American settlers arrived in 1830. County created 1858 from Jefferson, Liberty counties. Named for Texas Revolutionary leader William Hardin.

Race/Ethnicity, 2007: (In percent) Anglo, 88.7; Black, 7.4; Hispanic, 3.2; Other, 0.6.

Vital Statistics, 2006: Births, 705; deaths, 485; marriages, 557; divorces, 317.

Recreation: Big Thicket with rare plant, animal life; national preserve; Red Cloud Water Park in Silsbee; hunting, fishing; state park; Cajun Country Music Festival in October in Kountze.

Minerals: Oil, gas, sand, gravel.

Agriculture: Beef cattle, hay, blueberries (first in acreage), bees (first in number of colonies) and rice; market value $6.3 million. Timber provides most income; more than 85 percent of county forested. Hunting leases.

KOUNTZE (2,202) county seat; government/services, retail center, commuting to Beaumont; library, museum.

SILSBEE (6,685) forest products, rail center, oil, gas; library, Ice House museum; Dulcimer Festival in fall.

LUMBERTON (10,745) construction, government/services, tourism; library; Village Creek Festival in April.

Other towns and places include: **Batson** (140); **Pinewood Estates** (1,730); **Rose Hill Acres** (485); **Saratoga** (1,000) Big Thicket Museum; **Sour Lake** (1,780) oil, lumbering; Old Timer's Day in September; **Thicket** (306); **Village Mills** (1,700); **Votaw** (160).

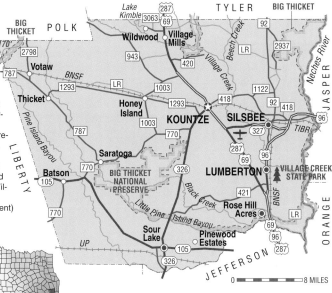

Population	**52,143**
Change fm 2000	8.5
Area (sq. mi.)	897.37
Land Area (sq. mi.)	894.33
Altitude (ft.)	7-170
Rainfall (in.)	56.50
Jan. mean min.	37.0
July mean max.	93.0
Civ. Labor	25,729
Unemployed	5.9
Wages	$97,832,279
Av. Weekly Wage	$616
Prop. Value	$2,982,004,150
Retail Sales	$528,953,398

For explanation of sources, abbreviations and symbols, see p. 210 and foldout map.

The skyline of Houston, Harris County. Robert Plocheck photo.

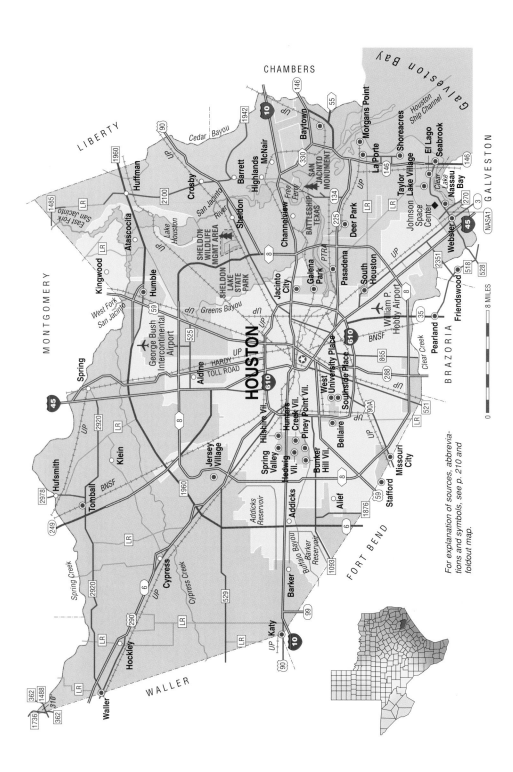

Physical Features: Largest county in eastern half of state; level; typically coastal surface and soils; many bayous, lakes, canals for artificial drainage; partly forested.

Economy: Highly industrialized county with largest population; more than 80 foreign governments maintain offices in Houston; corporate management center; nation's largest concentration of petrochemical plants; largest U.S. wheat-exporting port, among top U.S. ports in the value of foreign trade and total tonnage.

Petroleum refining, chemicals, food, fabricated metal products, nonelectrical machinery, primary metals, scientific instruments; paper and allied products, printing and publishing; center for energy, space and medical research; center of international business.

History: Orcoquiza villages visited by Spanish authorities in 1746. Pioneer settlers arrived by boat from Louisiana in 1822. Antebellum planters brought black slaves. Mexican migration increased after Mexican Revolution. County created 1836, organized 1837; named for John R. Harris, founder of Harrisburg (now part of Houston) in 1824.

Race/Ethnicity, 2007: (In percent) Anglo, 33.6; Black, 18.7; Hispanic, 40.7; Other, 7.0.

Vital Statistics, 2006: Births, 67,131; deaths, 20,573; marriages, 30,333; divorces, 13,618.

Recreation: Professional baseball, basketball, football, soccer; rodeo and livestock show; Jones Hall for the Performing Arts; Nina Vance Alley Theatre; Convention Center; Toyota Center, a 19,000-seat sports and entertainment center; Reliant Stadium and downtown ballpark.

Sam Houston Park, with restored early Houston homes, church, stores; Museum of Fine Arts, Contemporary Arts Museum, Rice Museum; Wortham Theater; Hobby Center for Performing Arts; museum of natural science, planetarium, zoo in Hermann Park.

San Jacinto Battleground, Battleship Texas; Johnson Space Center.

Fishing, boating, other freshwater and saltwater activities.

Minerals: Among leading oil, gas, petrochemical areas; production of petroleum, cement, natural gas, salt, lime, sulfur, sand and gravel, clays, stone.

Agriculture: Nursery crops, grass (third in acreage of sod), cattle, hay, horses, vegetables, Christmas trees, goats, rice, corn. Market value $62.5 million. Substantial income from forest products.

Education: Houston is a major center of higher education, with more

Harris County

than 300,000 students enrolled in 28 colleges and universities in the county. Among these are Rice University, the University of Houston, Texas Southern University, University of St. Thomas, Houston Baptist University.

Medical schools include Houston Baptist University School of Nursing, University of Texas Health Science Center, Baylor College of Medicine, Institute of Religion and Human Development, Texas Chiropractic College, Texas Woman's University-Houston Center.

The Sam Houston Momument at Hermann Park. Robert Plocheck photo.

HOUSTON (2,149,948) county seat; largest Texas city; fourth-largest in nation.

A leading center for manufacture of petroleum equipment, agricultural chemicals, fertilizers, pesticides, oil and gas pipeline transmission; a leading scientific center; manufacture of machinery, fabricated metals; a major distribution, shipping center; engineering and research center; food processing; hospitals.

Plants make apparel, lumber and wood products; furniture, paper, chemical, petroleum and coal products; publishing center; one of the nation's largest public school systems; prominent corporate center; Go Texan Days (rodeo) in February/March; international festival in April.

Pasadena (152,168) residential city with large industrial area manufacturing petrochemicals and other petroleum-related products; civic center; San Jacinto College, Texas Chiropractic College; hospitals; historical museum; Strawberry Festival in May.

Baytown (71,523) refining, petrochemical center; commuters to Houston; Lee College; hospital, museum,

library; historical homes; Chili When It's Chilly cookoff in January.

Bellaire (17,578) residential city with several major office buildings.

The **Clear Lake Area** — which includes **El Lago** (3,004); **Nassau Bay** (4,152); **Seabrook** (11,577); **Taylor Lake Village** (5,563); **Webster** (10,738) — tourism, Johnson Space Center, University of Houston-Clear Lake, commuting to Houston; Bayport Industrial Complex includes Port of Bayport; 12 major marinas; hospitals; Christmas lighted boat parade.

Other towns include: **Aldine** (14,788); **Atascocita** (36,263); **Barrett** (2,795); **Bunker Hill Village** (3,803); **Channelview** (31,036) hospital; **Crosby** (1,796); **Deer Park** (30,401) ship-channel industries, Totally Texas celebration in April; **Galena Park** (11,466); **Hedwig Village** (2,230); **Highlands** (7,206), heritage museum, Jamboree in October; **Hilshire Village** (724); **Hockley** (400); **Huffman** (15,000); **Humble** (16,528) oil-field equipment manufactured, retail center, hospital; **Hunters Creek Village** (4,638); **Jacinto City** (10,693); **Jersey Village** (7,584).

Also, **Katy** (17,334, partly in Fort Bend, Waller counties) corporate headquarters, distribution center, hospitals; museums, park; Rice Harvest festival in October; **Klein** (45,000); **La Porte** (34,091) petrochemical industry; Sylvan Beach Festival in April; Galveston Bay; **Morgan's Point** (343); **Piney Point Village** (3,428); **Sheldon** (1,879); **Shoreacres** (1,635); **South Houston** (16,751).

Also, **Southside Place** (1,679); **Spring** (37,947); **Spring Valley** (3,789); **Tomball** (11,076) computers, oil equipment, retail center, antiques, hospital, sports medical center, museum, junior college, parks, Germanfest in March; **West University Place** (15,431).

Parts of **Friendswood, Missouri City, Pearland, Stafford** and **Waller**.

Addicks, Alief and **Kingwood** are now within the city limits of Houston.

Population	3,984,349
Change fm 2000	17.2
Area (sq. mi.)	1,777.69
Land Area (sq. mi.)	1,728.83
Altitude (ft.)	sea level-310
Rainfall (in.)	53.96
Jan. mean min.	45.2
July mean max.	93.6
Civ. Labor	1,987,913
Unemployed	5.4
Wages	$28,120,465,067
Av. Weekly Wage	$1,050
Prop. Value	$306,512,928,828
Retail Sales	$55,931,031,110

Harrison County

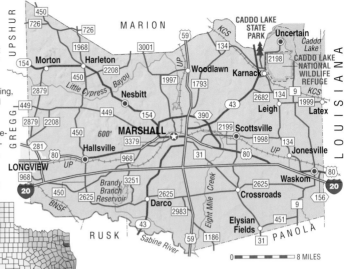

Physical Features: East Texas county; hilly, rolling; over half forested; Sabine River; Caddo Lake.

Economy: Oil, gas processing, lumbering, pottery, other varied manufacturing.

History: Agriculturist Caddo Indians whose numbers were reduced by disease. Anglo-Americans arrived in 1830s. In 1850, the county had more slaves than any other in the state. County created 1839 from Shelby County; organized 1842. Named for eloquent advocate of Texas Revolution, Jonas Harrison.

Race/Ethnicity, 2007: (In percent) Anglo, 67.4; Black, 23.3; Hispanic, 8.5; Other, 0.8.

Vital Statistics, 2006: Births, 807; deaths, 569; marriages, 462; divorces, 122.

Recreation: Fishing, other water activities on Caddo and other lakes; hunting; plantation homes, historic sites; Stagecoach Days in May; Old Courthouse Museum; Old World Store; state park, performing arts; Fire Ant festival in October.

Minerals: Oil, gas, lignite coal, clays, sand and gravel.

Agriculture: Cattle, hay. Also, poultry, nursery plants, horses, vegetables, watermelons. Market value $14.1 million. Hunting leases important. Substantial timber industry.

MARSHALL (24,332) county seat; petroleum and lumber processing, varied manufacturing; civic center; historic sites, including Starr Family State Historic Site; hospital; Wiley College, East Texas Baptist University; Wonderland of Lights in December.

Other towns include: **Elysian Fields** (500); **Hallsville** (3,076) Western Days in October, museum; **Harleton** (390); **Jonesville** (70); **Karnack** (350); **Nesbitt** (297); **Scottsville** (257); **Uncertain** (150) tourism, fishing, hunting, Mayhaw Festival in May; **Waskom** (2,170) oil, gas, ranching, Armadillo Daze in April; **Woodlawn** (550). Also, part [1,598] of **Longview**.

Population	63,594
Change fm 2000	2.4
Area (sq. mi.)	915.09
Land Area (sq. mi.)	898.71
Altitude (ft.)	168-600
Rainfall (in.)	51.22
Jan. mean min.	33.4
July mean max.	92.4
Civ. Labor	33,663
Unemployed	5.3
Wages	$220,473,899
Av. Weekly Wage	$725
Prop. Value	$6,689,429,900
Retail Sales	$695,617,913

For explanation of sources, abbreviations and symbols, see p. 210 and foldout map.

East Texas hay field in Rusk County. Robert Plocheck photo.

Hartley County

Physical Features: Panhandle High Plains; drains to Canadian River tributaries, playas; sandy, loam, chocolate soils; lake.

Economy: Agriculture, dairies, gas production.

History: Apaches, pushed out by Comanches around 1700. U.S. Army removed Indians in 1875. Pastores (Hispanic sheepmen) in area until 1880s. Cattle ranching began in 1880s. Farming expanded after 1900. County created 1876 from Bexar, Young districts; organized 1891; named for Texas pioneers O.C. and R.K. Hartley.

Race/Ethnicity, 2007: (In percent) Anglo, 78.3; Black, 7.5; Hispanic, 13.7; Other, 0.5.

Vital Statistics, 2006: Births, 65; deaths, 57; marriages, 3; divorces, 13.

Recreation: Rita Blanca Lake activities; ranch museum; XIT Rodeo and Reunion at Dalhart in August.

Minerals: Sand, gravel, natural gas.

Agriculture: Cattle, corn (second in acreage), wheat, hay, dairy cows, vegetables. 110,000 acres irrigated. Market value $724.5 million. Hunting leases.

CHANNING (380) county seat, Roundup.

DALHART (7,495, mostly in Dallam County), feedlots; feed, meat processing, cheese plant; hospital.
Also, **Hartley** (436).

Population	5,162
Change fm 2000	−6.8
Area (sq. mi.)	1,463.20
Land Area (sq. mi.)	1,462.25
Altitude (ft.)	3,340-4,465
Rainfall (in.)	17.20
Jan. mean min.	20.0
July mean max.	90.9
Civ. Labor	2,542
Unemployed	3.6
Wages	$10,465,511
Av. Weekly Wage	$548
Prop. Value	$587,316,523
Retail Sales	$28,511,483

Haskell County

Physical Features: Northwest county; rolling; broken areas; drained by Brazos tributaries; lake; sandy loam, gray, black soils.

Economy: Agribusiness, oil-field operations.

History: Apaches until 1700, then Comanche area. Ranching began in late 1870s after Indians removed. Farming expanded after 1900. County created 1858, from Milam, Fannin counties; recreated 1876; organized 1885; named for Goliad victim C.R. Haskell.

Race/Ethnicity, 2007: (In percent) Anglo, 72.0; Black, 3.1; Hispanic, 24.3; Other, 0.6.

Vital Statistics, 2006: Births, 65; deaths, 76; marriages, 37; divorces, 19.

Recreation: Lake Stamford activities, bass tournament in August; Haskell arts & crafts show in November; hunting of deer, geese, wild hog.

Minerals: Oil and gas.

Agriculture: Wheat, cotton, peanuts; 28,000 acres irrigated. Beef cattle raised. Market value $67.7 million.

HASKELL (2,835) county seat; farming center; hospital; city park; Wild Horse Prairie Days in June.

Other towns include: **O'Brien** (120), **Rochester** (342), **Rule** (629), **Weinert** (192).

Also, **Stamford** (3,527, mostly in Jones County).

Population	5,216
Change fm 2000	−14.4
Area (sq. mi.)	910.25
Land Area (sq. mi.)	902.97
Altitude (ft.)	1,340-1,795
Rainfall (in.)	24.93
Jan. mean min.	28.8
July mean max.	96.1
Civ. Labor	3,231
Unemployed	3.7
Wages	$14,813,647
Av. Weekly Wage	$550
Prop. Value	$237,081,329
Retail Sales	$54,860,157

Physical Features: Hilly in west, blackland in east; on edge of Balcones Escarpment.

Economy: Education, tourism, retirement area, some manufacturing; part of Austin metropolitan area.

History: Tonkawa area, also Apache and Comanche presence. Spanish authorities attempted first permanent settlement in 1807. Mexican land grants in early 1830s to Juan Martín Veramendi, Juan Vicente Campos and Thomas Jefferson Chambers. County created 1843 from Travis County; named for Capt. Jack Hays, famous Texas Ranger.

Race/Ethnicity, 2007: (In percent) Anglo, 63.8; Black, 3.5; Hispanic, 31.2; Other, 1.5.

Vital Statistics, 2006: Births, 1,700; deaths, 656; marriages, 858; divorces, 359.

Recreation: Fishing, hunting; college cultural, athletic events; African-American museum, LBJ museum; Cypress Creek and Blanco River resorts, guest ranches, Wonder World park, Aquarena center.

Minerals: Sand, gravel, cement produced.

Agriculture: Beef cattle, goats, exotic wildlife; greenhouse nurseries; hay, corn, sorghum, wheat and cotton. Market value $11.4 million.

SAN MARCOS (52,705) county seat; Texas State University, Gary Job Corps Training Center; government/services, distribution center, outlet center; hospital, sports medicine, physical therapy center; Scheib Center for mentally handicapped; San Marcos River; Cinco de Mayo festival.

Other towns include: **Bear Creek** (417); **Buda** (6,347); **Driftwood** (100); **Dripping Springs** (1,981); **Hays** (249); **Kyle** (24,518); **Mountain City** (796); **Niederwald** (533, partly in Caldwell County; **Uhland** (457, partly in Caldwell County); **Wimberley** (4.513) tourism, retirement community, artists, concert series, Country Pie Social and Fair in April; **Woodcreek** (1,656).

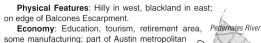

Hays County

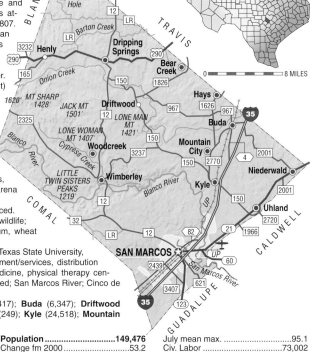

Population 149,476	July mean max. 95.1
Change fm 2000 .... 53.2	Civ. Labor 73,002
Area (sq. mi.) 679.79	Unemployed 4.9
Land Area (sq. mi.) 677.87	Wages $365,778,864
Altitude (ft.) 550-1,620	Av. Weekly Wage $602
Rainfall (in.) 37.19	Prop. Value $10,230,704,494
Jan. mean min. 38.6	Retail Sales $1,926,118,817

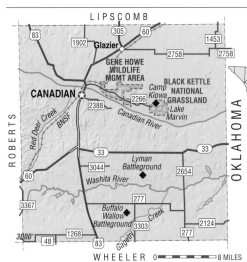

Population 3,472	July mean max. 93.9
Change fm 2000 .... 3.6	Civ. Labor 2,994
Area (sq. mi.) 912.06	Unemployed 2.2
Land Area (sq. mi.) 909.68	Wages $28,403,146
Altitude (ft.) 2,170-3,000	Av. Weekly Wage $876
Rainfall (in.) 21.68	Prop. Value $1,913,112,630
Jan. mean min. 18.8	Retail Sales $29,291,587

Hemphill County

Physical Features: Panhandle county; sloping surface, broken by Canadian, Washita rivers; sandy, red, dark soils.

Economy: Oil and gas, agriculture, tourism and hunting, government/services.

History: Apaches, who were pushed out by Comanches, Kiowas. Tribes removed to Indian Territory in 1875. Ranching began in late 1870s. Farmers began to arrive after 1900. County created from Bexar, Young districts, 1876; organized 1887; named for Republic of Texas Justice John Hemphill.

Race/Ethnicity, 2007: Anglo, 78.4; Black, 1.4; Hispanic, 19.1; Other, 1.1.

Vital Statistics, 2006: Births, 47; deaths, 39; marriages, 21; divorces, 13.

Recreation: Lake Marvin; fall foliage tour; hunting, fishing; Indian Battleground, wildlife management area; museum; 4th of July rodeo; prairie chicken viewing in April.

Minerals: Oil, natural gas, caliche.

Agriculture: Beef cattle, wheat, horses, hay, alfalfa, avocados; some irrigation. Market value $117.7 million. Hunting leases, nature tourism.

CANADIAN (2,414) county seat; oil, gas production; hospital.

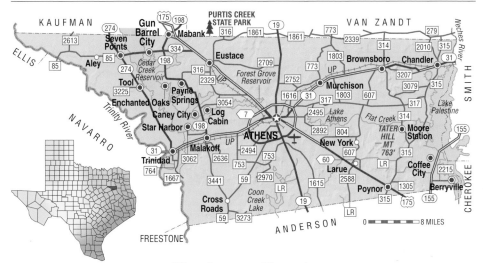

Henderson County

Physical Features: East Texas county bounded by Neches, Trinity rivers; hilly, rolling; one-third forested; sandy, loam, clay soils; commercial timber; Cedar Creek, other lakes.

Economy: Agribusiness, retail trade, varied manufacturing, minerals, recreation, tourism.

History: Caddo area. Cherokee, other tribes migrated into the area in 1819-20 ahead of white settlement. Cherokees forced into Indian Territory in 1839. Anglo-American settlers arrived in 1840s. County created 1846 from Nacogdoches, Houston counties and named for Gov. J. Pinckney Henderson.

Race/Ethnicity, 2007: (In percent) Anglo, 82.9; Black, 6.5; Hispanic, 9.8; Other, 0.9.

Vital Statistics, 2006: Births, 938; deaths, 894; marriages, 561; divorces, 165.

Recreation: Cedar Creek Reservoir, Lake Palestine, other lakes; Purtis Creek State Park; hunting, fishing, birdwatching; East Texas Arboretum.

Minerals: Oil, gas, clays, lignite, sulfur, sand and gravel.

Agriculture: Nurseries, cattle, hay, horses, rabbits. Market value $44.5 million. Hunting leases and fishing.

ATHENS (12,380) county seat; agribusiness center, varied manufacturing, tourism, state fish hatchery and museum; hospital, mental health center; Trinity Valley Community College; Texas Fiddlers' Contest in May.

Gun Barrel City (5,880) recreation, retirement, retail center.

Malakoff (2,398) brick factory, varied industry, tourism, library, Cornbread Festival in April.

Other towns include: **Berryville** (983); **Brownsboro** (990); **Caney City** (264); **Chandler** (2,546) retail trade, tourism, commuting to Tyler, Pow Wow Festival in October; **Coffee City** (201); **Enchanted Oaks** (419); **Eustace** (919); **Larue** (250); **Log Cabin** (825);

Moore Station (187); **Murchison** (627); **Payne Springs** (719); **Poynor** (357); **Seven Points** (1,320) agribusiness, retail trade, recreation, Monte Carlo celebration in November; **Star Harbor** (465); **Tool** (2,488), and **Trinidad** (1,142).

Also, **Mabank** (2,821, mostly in Kaufman County).

Population	**78,814**
Change fm 2000	7.6
Area (sq. mi.)	949.00
Land Area (sq. mi.)	874.24
Altitude (ft.)	256-763
Rainfall (in.)	42.03
Jan. mean min.	35.2
July mean max.	93.4
Civ. Labor	35,107
Unemployed	6.5
Wages	$116,146,675
Av. Weekly Wage	$554
Prop. Value	$5,390,043,986
Retail Sales	$673,612,352

For explanation of sources, abbreviations and symbols, see p. 210 and foldout map.

Horses graze east of Mabank in Henderson County. Robert Plocheck photo.

Physical Features: Rich alluvial soils along Rio Grande; sandy, loam soils in north; semitropical vegetation.

Economy: Food processing and shipping, other agribusinesses, tourism, mineral operations.

History: Coahuiltecan and Karankawa area. Comanches forced Apaches southward into valley in 1700s; Comanches arrived in valley in 1800s. Spanish settlement occurred 1750-1800. County created 1852 from Cameron, Starr counties; named for leader of Mexico's independence movement, Father Miguel Hidalgo y Costillo.

Race/Ethnicity, 2007: (In percent) Anglo, 7.9; Black, 0.3; Hispanic, 90.9; Other, 0.9.

Vital Statistics, 2006: Births, 16,540; deaths, 3,303; marriages, 4,629; divorces, 136.

Recreation: Winter resort, retirement area; fishing, hunting; gateway to Mexico; historical sites; Bentsen-Rio Grande Valley State Park; museums; All-Valley Winter Vegetable Show at Pharr.

Minerals: Oil, gas, stone, sand and gravel.

Agriculture: Ninety percent of farm cash receipts from crops (ranked first in state), principally from sugar cane (first in acreage), grain, vegetables (first in acreage), citrus, cotton; livestock includes cattle; 270,000 acres irrigated. Market value $314.3 million.

EDINBURG (71,174) county seat; vegetable processing and packing, petroleum operations, tourism, clothing; planetarium; the University of Texas-Pan American; hospitals; behavorial health center; museum; Texas Cook'em High Steaks July 4 weekend, Fiesta Edinburg in February.

Hidalgo County

Population	726,604
Change fm 2000	27.6
Area (sq. mi.)	1,582.66
Land Area (sq. mi.)	1,569.75
Altitude (ft.)	28-376
Rainfall (in.)	22.61
Jan. mean min.	48.2
July mean max.	95.5
Civ. Labor	289,883
Unemployed	9.1
Wages	$1,522,655,134
Av. Weekly Wage	$550
Prop. Value	$25,819,962,192
Retail Sales	$7,791,749,970

McALLEN (128,888) government/services; food processing and shipping, varied manufacturing, tourism; community college; hospitals; Palmfest in October.

Mission (67,082) citrus groves, agricultural processing and distribution; hospital; community college; international butterfly park; Citrus Fiesta in January.

Pharr (65,967) agriculture, trading center; trucking; tourism; old clock, juke box museums; folklife festival in February.

Other towns include: **Abram-Perezville** (5,824); **Alamo** (19,654) live steam museum; **Alton** (9,967); **Alton North** (5,410); **Doffing** (4,574); **Donna** (17,903) citrus center, varied manufacturing; lamb, sheep show; **Edcouch** (4,393); **Elsa** (6,794); **Granjeno** (324); **Hargill** (1,349); **Hidalgo** (11,582) trade zone, shipping, winter resort, agribusiness, historical sites, library, Borderfest in March; **La Blanca** (2,555); **La Homa** (11,683); **La Joya** (4,391); **La Villa** (1,404); **Los Ebanos** (425).

Also, **Mercedes** (16,129) "boot capital," citrus, and vegetable center, food processing, tourism, recreation vehicle show in January, Hispanic Fest July 4; **Mila Doce** (5,481); **Monte Alto** (1,718); **North Alamo** (2,178); **Nurillo** (5,432); **Palmhurst** (5,341); **Palmview** (5,358); **Palmview South** (6,484); **Peñitas** (2,307); **Progreso** (5,910); **Progreso Lakes** (273); **San Carlos** (2,824); **San Juan** (34,431) retirement area, trucking, Shrine of Our Lady of San Juan, Spring Fiesta in February; **San Manuel-Linn** (987); **South Alamo** (3,315); **Sullivan City** (4,560); **Weslaco** (32,893) agriculture, nature tourism, South Texas College, hospital, Dragonfly Days in May.

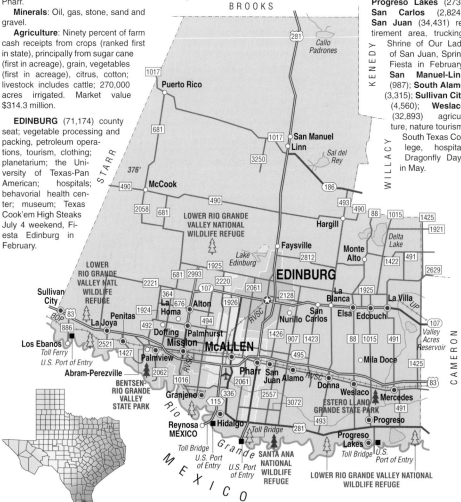

Hill County

Physical Features: North central county; level to rolling; blackland soils, some sandy loams; drains to Brazos; lakes.

Economy: Agri-business, tourism, varied manufacturing.

History: Waco and Tawakoni area, later Comanches. Believed to be Indian "council spot," a place of safe passage without evidence of raids. Anglo-Americans of the Robertson colony arrived in early 1830s. Fort Graham established in 1849. County created from Navarro County 1853; named for G.W. Hill, Republic of Texas official.

Race/Ethnicity, 2007: (In percent) Anglo, 74.4; Black, 7.5; Hispanic, 17.6; Other, 0.6.

Vital Statistics, 2006: Births, 453; deaths, 441; marriages, 235; divorces, 145.

Recreation: Lake activities; excursion boat on Lake Whitney; Texas Heritage Museum including Confederate and Audie Murphy exhibits, historic structures, rebuilt frontier fort barracks; motorcycle track.

Minerals: Gas, limestone.

Agriculture: Corn, cattle, sorghum, wheat, cotton, dairies, turkeys. Market value $74.2 million. Some firewood marketed.

HILLSBORO (9,176) county seat; agribusiness, varied manufacturing, retail, outlet center, tourism, antiques malls; Hill College; hospital; Cell Block museum, restored courthouse; Cotton Pickin Fair in September.

Whitney (2,020) tourist center, hospital, varied manufacturing.

Other towns include: **Abbott** (302); **Aquilla** (147); **Blum** (452); **Brandon** (75); **Bynum** (256); **Carl's Corner** (153); **Covington** (323); **Hubbard** (1,769) agriculture, antiques shops, museums, Magnolias & Mistletoe Victorian Christmas celebration; **Irene** (170); **Itasca** (1,701); **Malone** (296); **Mertens** (157); **Mount Calm** (332); **Penelope** (221).

Population	35,637
Change fm 2000	10.3
Area (sq. mi.)	985.65
Land Area (sq. mi.)	962.36
Altitude (ft.)	417-897
Rainfall (in.)	37.15
Jan. mean min.	35.2
July mean max.	95.2
Civ. Labor	16,121
Unemployed	6.0
Wages	$65,8860,284
Av. Weekly Wage	$538
Prop. Value	$1,736,069,855
Retail Sales	$415,377,864

For explanation of sources, abbreviations and symbols, see p. 210 and foldout map.

The approach to Bentsen–Rio Grande Valley State Park, Hidalgo County, on FM 2062. Robert Plocheck photo.

Hockley County

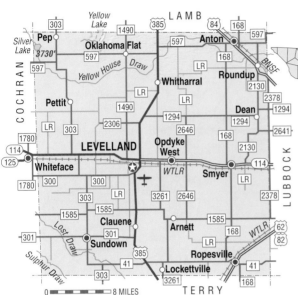

Physical Features: South Plains, numerous playas, drains to Yellow House Draw; loam, sandy loam soils.

Economy: Extensive oil, gas production and services; manufacturing; varied agribusiness.

History: Comanches displaced Apaches in early 1700s. Large ranches of 1880s brought few residents. Homesteaders arrived after 1900. County created 1876, from Bexar, Young districts; organized 1921. Named for Republic of Texas secretary of war Gen. G.W. Hockley.

Race/Ethnicity, 2007: Anglo, 53.8; Black, 4.1; Hispanic, 41.5; Other, 0.6.

Vital Statistics, 2006: Births, 363; deaths, 202; marriages, 173; divorces, 75.

Recreation: Early Settlers' Day in July; Marigolds Arts, Crafts Festival in November.

Minerals: Oil, gas, stone; one of leading oil counties with more than 1 billion barrels produced.

Agriculture: Cotton, grain sorghum; cattle, hogs raised; substantial irrigation. Market value $107.7 million.

LEVELLAND (12,628) county seat; oil, cotton, cattle center; government/services; hospital; South Plains College; Hot Burrito & Bluegrass Music Festival in July.

Other towns include: **Anton** (1,162); **Opdyke West** (204); **Pep** (3); **Ropesville** (523); **Smyer** (483); **Sundown** (1,472); **Whitharral** (158).

Population	22,205
Change fm 2000	–2.2
Area (sq. mi.)	908.55
Land Area (sq. mi.)	908.28
Altitude (ft.)	3,300-3,730
Rainfall (in.)	19.58
Jan. mean min.	23.7
July mean max.	92.7
Civ. Labor	11,783
Unemployed	4.0
Wages	$81,394,887
Av. Weekly Wage	$697
Prop. Value	$3,571,881,441
Retail Sales	$212,463,218

The Hood County Courthouse in Granbury. Robert Plocheck photo.

Hood County

Physical Features: Hilly; broken by Paluxy, Brazos rivers; sandy loam soils.

Economy: Tourism, commuting to Fort Worth, nuclear power plant, agriculture.

History: Lipan Apache and Comanche area. Anglo-American settlers arrived in late 1840s. County created 1866 from Johnson and Erath counties; named for Confederate Gen. John B. Hood.

Race/Ethnicity, 2007: (In percent) Anglo, 88.6; Black, 0.3; Hispanic, 10.1; Other, 1.0.

Vital Statistics, 2006: Births, 537; deaths, 540; marriages, 414; divorces, 228.

Recreation: Lakes, fishing, scenic areas; summer theater; Gen. Granbury's Bean & Rib cookoff in March; Acton historic site.

Minerals: Oil, gas, stone.

Agriculture: Hay, turfgrass, beef cattle, nursery crops, pecans, peaches; some irrigation. Market value $18.9 million.

GRANBURY (8,198) county seat; tourism, real estate, power plants; historic downtown area, opera house; hospital; library; Civil War re-enactment in October.

Other towns include: **Acton** (1,129)

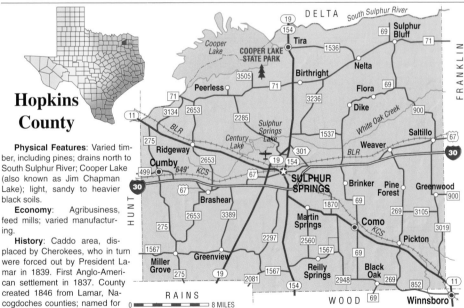

grave of Elizabeth Crockett, wife of Davy; **Brazos Bend** (66); **Cresson** (718); **DeCordova** (3,030); **Lipan** (539); **Oak Trail Shores** (2,733); **Paluxy** (76); **Pecan Plantation** (3,744); **Tolar** (644).

Population 50,573
Change fm 2000 .... 23.0

Area (sq. mi.) 436.80
Land Area (sq. mi.) 421.61
Altitude (ft.) 600-1,230
Rainfall (in.) 33.10
Jan. mean min. 33.0
July mean max. 97.0
Civ. Labor 24,622
Unemployed 5.2
Wages $105,983,808
Av. Weekly Wage $625
Prop. Value $4,349,127,070
Retail Sales $561,455,862

Hopkins County

Physical Features: Varied timber, including pines; drains north to South Sulphur River; Cooper Lake (also known as Jim Chapman Lake); light, sandy to heavier black soils.

Economy: Agribusiness, feed mills; varied manufacturing.

History: Caddo area, displaced by Cherokees, who in turn were forced out by President Lamar in 1839. First Anglo-American settlement in 1837. County created 1846 from Lamar, Nacogdoches counties; named for pioneer Hopkins family.

Race/Ethnicity, 2007: (In percent) Anglo, 78.8; Black, 8.3; Hispanic, 12.0; Other, 1.0.

Vital Statistics, 2006: Births, 431; deaths, 310; marriages, 325; divorces, 201.

Recreation: Fishing, hunting; lake activities; dairy museum; dairy festival in June; stew contest in September.

Minerals: Lignite coal.

Agriculture: Forage (first in acreage), dairies, beef cattle, horses, poul-

try. Market value $208.3 million. Firewood and hardwood lumber marketed.

SULPHUR SPRINGS (15,501) county seat; dairy farming, equine center, food processing and distribution, varied manufacturing, tourism; hospital; library, heritage park, music box gallery, civic center.

Other towns include: **Brashear** (280), **Como** (673), **Cumby** (668), **Dike** (170), **Pickton** (300), **Saltillo** (200), **Sulphur Bluff** (280), **Tira** (256).

Population 33,804
Change fm 2000 .... 5.8
Area (sq. mi.) 792.74
Land Area (sq. mi.) 782.40
Altitude (ft.) 340-649
Rainfall (in.) 47.69
Jan. mean min. 31.1
July mean max. 94.8
Civ. Labor 17,332
Unemployed 4.7
Wages $90,129,796
Av. Weekly Wage $588
Prop. Value $1,692,524,990
Retail Sales $452,521,111

Houston County

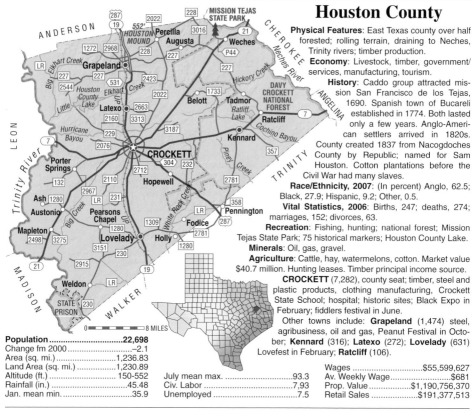

Physical Features: East Texas county over half forested; rolling terrain, draining to Neches, Trinity rivers; timber production.

Economy: Livestock, timber, government/ services, manufacturing, tourism.

History: Caddo group attracted mission San Francisco de los Tejas, 1690. Spanish town of Bucareli established in 1774. Both lasted only a few years. Anglo-American settlers arrived in 1820s. County created 1837 from Nacogdoches County by Republic; named for Sam Houston. Cotton plantations before the Civil War had many slaves.

Race/Ethnicity, 2007: (In percent) Anglo, 62.5; Black, 27.9; Hispanic, 9.2; Other, 0.5.

Vital Statistics, 2006: Births, 247; deaths, 274; marriages, 152; divorces, 63.

Recreation: Fishing, hunting; national forest; Mission Tejas State Park; 75 historical markers; Houston County Lake.

Minerals: Oil, gas, gravel.

Agriculture: Cattle, hay, watermelons, cotton. Market value $40.7 million. Hunting leases. Timber principal income source.

CROCKETT (7,282), county seat; timber, steel and plastic products, clothing manufacturing, Crockett State School; hospital; historic sites; Black Expo in February; fiddlers festival in June.

Other towns include: **Grapeland** (1,474) steel, agribusiness, oil and gas, Peanut Festival in October; **Kennard** (316); **Latexo** (272); **Lovelady** (631) Lovefest in February; **Ratcliff** (106).

Population	22,698
Change fm 2000	–2.1
Area (sq. mi.)	1,236.83
Land Area (sq. mi.)	1,230.89
Altitude (ft.)	150-552
Rainfall (in.)	45.48
Jan. mean min.	35.9

July mean max.	93.3
Civ. Labor	7,93
Unemployed	7.5

Wages	$55,599,627
Av. Weekly Wage	$681
Prop. Value	$1,190,756,370
Retail Sales	$191,377,513

Howard County

Physical Features: On edge of Llano Estacado; sandy loam soils.

Economy: Government/services, agribusiness, oil, gas, varied manufacturing including clothing.

History: Pawnee and Comanche area. Anglo-American settlement began in 1870. Oil boom in mid-1920s. County named for V.E. Howard, legislator; created 1876 from Bexar, Young districts; organized 1882.

Race/Ethnicity, 2007: (In percent) Anglo, 52.6; Black, 4.7; Hispanic, 41.5; Other, 1.1.

Vital Statistics, 2006: Births, 465; deaths, 369; marriages, 236; divorces, 44.

Recreation: Lakes, state park; campground in Comanche Trail Park, Native Plant Trail, museum, historical sites, Pow Wow in April, Pops in the Park in July.

Minerals: Oil, gas, sand, gravel and stone.

Agriculture: Cotton, beef, hay, beans. Market value $40.9 million.

BIG SPRING (25,529) county seat; agriculture, petrochemicals, varied manufacturing; hospitals including a state institution and Veterans Administration hospital; federal prison; Howard College; railroad plaza.

Other towns include: **Coahoma** (923), **Forsan** (211), **Knott** (200).

Population	32,537
Change fm 2000	–3.2
Area (sq. mi.)	904.19
Land Area (sq. mi.)	902.84
Altitude (ft.)	2,180-2,800
Rainfall (in.)	20.12
Jan. mean min.	29.6
July mean max.	94.3

Civ. Labor	14,604
Unemployed	5.1
Wages	$111,395,286
Av. Weekly Wage	$666
Prop. Value	$2,083,447,057
Retail Sales	$323,274,535

Hudspeth County

Physical Features: Plateau, basin terrain, draining to salt lakes; Rio Grande; mostly rocky, alkaline, clay soils and sandy loam soils, except alluvial along Rio Grande; desert, mountain vegetation. Fertile agricultural valley.

Economy: Agribusiness, mining, tourism, hunting leases.

History: Mescalero Apache area. Fort Quitman established in 1858 to protect routes to west. Railroad in 1881 brought Anglo-American settlers. Political turmoil in Mexico (1912-29) brought more settlers from Mexico. County named for Texas political leader Claude B. Hudspeth; created 1917 from El Paso County.

Race/Ethnicity, 2007: (In percent) Anglo, 21.9; Black, 0.1; Hispanic, 76.9; Other, 1.0.

Vital Statistics, 2006: Births, 51; deaths, 17; marriages, 0; divorces, 0.

Recreation: Scenic drives; fort ruins; hot springs; salt basin; white sands; hunting; birding; part of Guadalupe Mountains National Park, containing unique plant life, canyons.

Minerals: Talc, stone, gypsum.

Agriculture: Most income from cotton, vegetables, hay, alfalfa; beef cattle raised; 35,000 acres irrigated. Market value $31.1 million.

SIERRA BLANCA (578) county seat; ranching center, tourist stop on interstate highway; adobe courthouse; 4th of July fair, livestock show in January.

Other towns include: **Dell City** (420) feedlots, vegetable packing, gypsum processing, trade center, airport, some of largest water wells in state, Wild West Chili Fest in September; and **Fort Hancock** (1,811).

Map labels

NEW MEXICO
GUADALUPE MTS NATIONAL PARK
EL PASO
CORNUDAS MTS 5500'
5500'
2249
Dell City
1576
SIERRA TINAJA PINTA 5303'
1437
Salt Basin
62
180
LR
Cornudas
2317
Eight Mile Draw
Salt Flat
62
180
Antelope Draw
South Well Draw
BLACK MTS 5561'
APACHE CANYON
MOUNTAIN TIME ZONE
CENTRAL TIME ZONE
RIM ROCK
10
20
Acala
FORT HANCOCK SITE
Fort Hancock
1088
McNary
U.S. Port of Entry
1111
SIERRA BLANCA 6950'
UP
LR
SIERRA DIABLO WILDLIFE MANAGEMENT AREA
SIERRA DIABLO MTS
LR
CULBERSON
SIERRA BLANCA
2217
Esperanza
34
FORT QUITMAN SITE
192
LR
5683'
1111
DEVIL RIDGE
UP
Allamoore
UP
10
QUITMAN MTS
Red Light Draw
LR
MEXICO
Rio Grande
INDIAN HOT SPRINGS
EAGLE PEAK 7484'
Green River
0 ▬▬▬ 12 MILES
JEFF DAVIS

Population....................**3,137**	Jan. mean min. 25.1	Prop. Value $305,902,238
Change fm 2000 ....–6.2	July mean max. 92.0	Retail Sales $8,990,083
Area (sq. mi.) 4,571.93	Civ. Labor 1,775	*For explanation of sources, abbreviations and symbols, see p. 210 and foldout map.*
Land Area (sq. mi.) 4,571.00	Unemployed 3.0	
Altitude (ft.) 3,117-7,484	Wages $9,877,331	
Rainfall (in.) 11.93	Av. Weekly Wage........................$715	

Big Spring, Howard County. Robert Plocheck photo.

Hunt County

Physical Features: Level to rolling surface; Sabine, Sulphur rivers; Lake Tawakoni; mostly heavy Blackland soil, some loam, sandy loams.

Economy: Education, varied manufacturing, agribusiness; several Fortune 500 companies in county; many residents employed in Dallas area.

History: Caddo Indians gone by 1790s. Kiowa bands in the area when Anglo-American settlers arrived in 1839. County named for Memucan Hunt, Republic secretary of navy; created 1846 from Fannin, Nacogdoches counties.

Race/Ethnicity, 2007: (In percent) Anglo, 75.5; Black, 10.5; Hispanic, 12.1; Other, 1.9.

Vital Statistics, 2006: Births, 1,053; deaths, 791; marriages, 604; divorces, 282.

Recreation: Lake Tawakoni sports, catfish tournament in August; Texas A&M University-Commerce events.

Minerals: Sand and white rock, gas, oil.

Agriculture: Cattle, forage, greenhouse crops, top revenue sources; horses, wheat, oats, cotton, grain sorghum. Market value $40.5 million. Some firewood sold.

GREENVILLE (25,357) county seat; varied manufacturing, government/services, commuters to Dallas; hospital; branch of Paris Junior College; cotton museum, Audie Murphy exhibit; Native American Pow-wow in January.

Commerce (9,188) Texas A&M University-Commerce, varied manufacturing, tourism; hospital; children's museum; Bois d'Arc Bash in September.

Other towns include: **Caddo Mills** (1,269); **Campbell** (791); **Celeste** (907); **Hawk Cove** (465); **Lone Oak** (570); **Merit** (225); **Neylandville** (57); **Quinlan** (1,468); **West Tawakoni** (1,685) tourist center, light industry, Lakefest in October; **Wolfe City** (1,634) manufacturing, antiques shops, commuters to Dallas, museum, library, car and truck show in October.

For explanation of sources, abbreviations and symbols, see p. 210 and foldout map.

Population	**82,805**
Change fm 2000	8.1
Area (sq. mi.)	882.02
Land Area (sq. mi.)	841.16
Altitude (ft.)	437-730
Rainfall (in.)	43.70
Jan. mean min.	31.2
July mean max.	93.3
Civ. Labor	39,682
Unemployed	6.0
Wages	$247,718,000
Av. Weekly Wage	$735
Prop. Value	$3,709,289,205
Retail Sales	$1,000,408,629

A refinery on a hillside at Borger, Hutchinson County. Robert Plocheck photo.

Hutchinson County

Physical Features: High Plains, broken by Canadian River and tributaries, Lake Meredith; fertile valleys along streams.

Economy: Oil, gas, petrochemicals, agribusiness, varied manufacturing, tourism.

History: Antelope Creek Indian area. Later Comanches were driven out in U.S. cavalry campaigns of 1874-75. Adobe Walls site of two Indian attacks, 1864 and 1874. Ranching began in late 1870s. Oil boom in early 1920s. County created 1876 from Bexar Territory; organized 1901; named for pioneer jurist Anderson Hutchinson.

Race/Ethnicity, 2007: (In percent) Anglo, 77.4; Black, 2.8; Hispanic, 18.0; Other, 1.8.

Vital Statistics, 2006: Births, 316; deaths, 256; marriages, 185; divorces, 103.

Recreation: Lake activities, fishing, camping; Adobe Walls, historic Indian battle site.

Minerals: Gas, oil, sand, gravel.

Agriculture: Cattle, corn, wheat, grain sorghum; about 45,000 acres irrigated. Market value $49.6 million.

STINNETT (1,836) county seat; petroleum refining, farm center.

BORGER (13,618) petroleum refining, petrochemicals, carbon-black production, oil-field servicing, varied manufacturing, retail center; Frank Phillips College; museum; hospital; downtown beach bash in June.

Other cities include: **Fritch** (2,168), **Sanford** (199).

Population	**21,512**
Change fm 2000	–9.8
Area (sq. mi.)	894.95

Land Area (sq. mi.)	887.37
Altitude (ft.)	2,600-3,380
Rainfall (in.)	21.98
Jan. mean min.	23.4
July mean max.	92.6
Civ. Labor	11,692
Unemployed	4.3
Wages	$116,113,485
Av. Weekly Wage	$975
Prop. Value	$2,602,274,460
Retail Sales	$175,876,081

Map labels: HANSFORD, TNW, 136, 281, 207, 281, 281, LR, LR, South Palo Duro Creek, 1598, Pringle, Adobe Walls, Bugby Creek, Moore Creek, Canadian River, ROBERTS, MOORE, 3380', 1923, 152, STINNETT, 1526, White Deer Creek, 1319, 687, 2277, Big Creek, LAKE MEREDITH NATIONAL REC AREA, Spring Creek, 3395, Dixon Ck, 280, Lake Meredith, Sanford, 119, LR, BORGER, Fritch, 1319, 1559, 2171, 687, 136, 1551, 246, 1059, 207, Texroy, 152, PNWR, CARSON, 0 — 8 MILES

Irion County

Physical Features: West Texas county with hilly surface, broken by Middle Concho, tributaries; clay, sandy soils.

Economy: Ranching, oil, gas production, wildlife recreation, commuters.

History: Tonkawa Indian area. Anglo-American settlement began in late 1870s. County named for Republic leader R.A. Irion; created 1889 from Tom Green County.

Race/Ethnicity, 2007: (In percent) Anglo, 75.3; Black, 0.2; Hispanic, 24.4; Other, 0.2.

Vital Statistics, 2006: Births 9; deaths, 13; marriages, 10; divorces, 10.

Recreation: Hunting; historic sites, including Dove Creek battlefield and stagecoach stops, old Sherwood courthouse built 1900; hunters appreciation dinner in November.

Minerals: Oil, gas.

Agriculture: Beef cattle, sheep, goats; wheat, cotton, hay. Market value $6.1 million.

MERTZON (818) county seat; farm center. wool warehousing.

Other towns include: **Barnhart** (110).

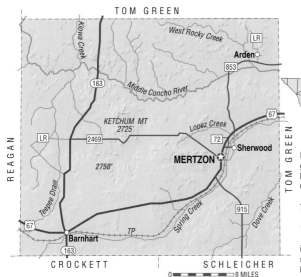

Map labels: TOM GREEN, Kiowa Creek, West Rocky Creek, LR, Arden, 853, 163, Middle Concho River, 67, KETCHUM MT 2725', Lopez Creek, 72, Sherwood, REAGAN, LR, 2469, MERTZON, TOM GREEN, 2750', Teepee Draw, 67, Barnhart, TP, Spring Creek, 915, Dove Creek, 163, CROCKETT, SCHLEICHER, 0 — 8 MILES

Population	**1,699**
Change fm 2000	–4.1
Area (sq. mi.)	1,051.59
Land Area (sq. mi.)	1,051.48
Altitude (ft.)	2,000-2,750
Rainfall (in.)	19.90
Jan. mean min.	32.0
July mean max.	95.0

Civ. Labor	977
Unemployed	4.0
Wages	$5,960,856
Av. Weekly Wage	$791
Prop. Value	$497,358,850
Retail Sales	$7,045,474

Jack County

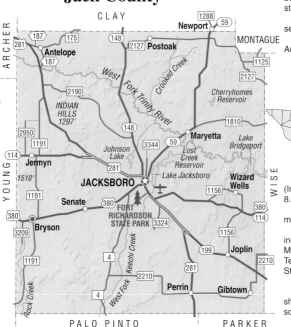

Physical Features: Rolling Cross Timbers, broken by West Fork of the Trinity, other streams; sandy, dark brown, loam soils; lakes.

Economy: Petroleum production, oil-field services, livestock, manufacturing, tourism.

History: Caddo and Comanche borderland. Anglo-American settlers arrived in 1855, part of Peters Colony. County named for brothers P.C. and W.H. Jack, leaders in Texas' independence effort; created 1856 from Cooke County; organized 1857 with Mesquiteville (orginal name of Jacksboro) as county seat.

Race/Ethnicity, 2007: (In percent) Anglo, 85.4; Black, 5.0; Hispanic, 8.8; Other, 0.9.

Vital Statistics, 2006: Births, 90; deaths, 97; marriages, 65; divorces, 24.

Recreation: Hunting, wildlife leases; fishing; lake activities; Fort Richardson, Texas 4-H Museum (county is birthplace of 4-H clubs in Texas), other historic sites; Lost Creek Reservoir State Trailway.

Minerals: Oil, gas.

Agriculture: Cattle, hay, wheat, goats, sheep. Market value $18.3 million. Firewood sold.

JACKSBORO (4,700) county seat; agribusiness, varied manufacturing, tourism; petroleum production and services; hospital, hospice; library; Old Mesquiteville Festival in fall.

Other towns include: **Bryson** (522), **Jermyn** (75), **Perrin** (300).

Population	**8,793**
Change fm 2000	0.3
Area (sq. mi.)	920.11
Land Area (sq. mi.)	916.61
Altitude (ft.)	836-1,510
Rainfall (in.)	31.44
Jan. mean min.	29.7
July mean max.	94.4
Civ. Labor	5,281
Unemployed	3.8
Wages	$31,508,032
Av. Weekly Wage	$808
Prop. Value	$974,654,470
Retail Sales	$48,441,134

A statue of French explorer La Salle faces Matagorda and Lavaca bays. His group took refuge probably along Garcitas Creek, which separates Jackson and Victoria counties. Robert Plocheck photo.

Physical Features: South coastal county of prairie and motts of trees; loam, clay, black soils; drains to creeks, rivers, bays.

Economy: Petroleum production, plastics manufacturing, agribusinesses.

History: Karankawa area. Lipan Apaches and Tonkawas arrived later. Six of Austin's Old Three Hundred families settled in the 1820s. Mexican municipality, created 1835, became original county the following year; named for U.S. President Andrew Jackson. Oil discovered in 1934.

Race/Ethnicity, 2007: (In percent) Anglo, 63.7; Black, 7.7; Hispanic, 27.8; Other, 0.8.

Vital Statistics, 2006: Births, 194; deaths, 159; marriages, 115; divorces, 40.

Recreation: Hunting, fishing, birding (southern bald eagle in area); historic sites; Texana Museum; Lake Texana, Brackenridge Plantation campground, state park; Chili Spill in November at Lake Texana, county fair, rodeo in April.

Minerals: Oil and natural gas.

Agriculture: Beef cattle, corn, rice, sorghum, cotton; 13,000 acres of rice irrigated. Market value $62.6 million.

EDNA (6,042) county seat; oil and gas, chemical plants, agriculture; hospital, library, museums.

Other towns include: **Francitas** (125); **Ganado** (2,009) oil and gas, agriculture, historic movie theater, Crawfish Festival in May; **LaSalle** (110); **La Ward** (220); **Lolita** (553); **Vanderbilt** (419).

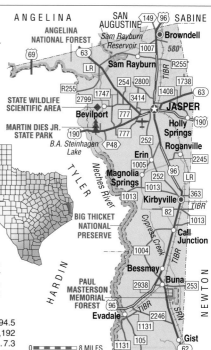

Jackson County

Population	14,146
Change fm 2000	–1.7
Area (sq. mi.)	857.03
Land Area (sq. mi.)	829.49
Altitude (ft.)	sea level-155

Rainfall (in.)	42.10
Jan. mean min.	42.0
July mean max.	94.0
Civ. Labor	6,974
Unemployed	4.8

Wages	$43,056,491
Av. Weekly Wage	$621
Prop. Value	$1,332,572,616
Retail Sales	$176,355,647

Jasper County

Physical Features: East Texas county; hilly to level; national forest; lakes; Neches River.

Economy: Timber industries; oil; tourism; fishing; aircraft manufacturer; agriculture.

History: Caddo and Atakapa Indian area. Land grants to John R. Bevil and Lorenzo de Zavala in 1829. County created 1836, organized 1837, from Mexican municipality; named for Sgt. William Jasper of American Revolution.

Race/Ethnicity, 2007: (In percent) Anglo, 76.6; Black, 17.9; Hispanic, 4.7; Other, 0.8.

Vital Statistics, 2006: Births, 489; deaths, 369; marriages, 346; divorces, 197.

Recreation: Lake activities; hunting, fishing; state park, Big Thicket.

Minerals: Oil, gas produced.

Agriculture: Cattle, hogs, major revenue source; vegetables, fruit, pecans. Market value $6.7 million. Timber is major income producer.

JASPER (7,683) county seat; timber, government/services, manufacturing; hospital; prison; museum; Azalea Festival in March, October Fest.

Other towns include: **Browndell** (228); **Buna** (2,237) timber, oil, polka dot house, redbud festival in March; **Evadale** (1,458); **Kirbyville** (2,123) government/services, retail, commuters, museum, Calaboose museum, Magnolia Festival in April; **Sam Rayburn** (600).

Population	34,374
Change fm 2000	–3.5
Area (sq. mi.)	969.62
Land Area (sq. mi.)	937.40
Altitude (ft.)	10-580
Rainfall (in.)	60.57
Jan. mean min.	35.2

July mean max.	94.5
Civ. Labor	16,192
Unemployed	7.3
Wages	$84,978,453
Av. Weekly Wage	$610
Prop. Value	$1,871,280,392
Retail Sales	$326,215,836

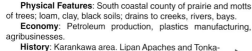

For explanation of sources, abbreviations and symbols, see p. 210 and foldout map.

The Davis Mountains, including Sawtooth Mountain, along Texas 166 in Jeff Davis County. Robert Plocheck photo.

Jeff Davis County

Physical Features: Highest average elevation in Texas; peaks (Mt. Livermore, 8,378 ft.), canyons, plateaus; intermountain wash, clay, loam soils; cedars, oaks in highlands.

Economy: Tourism, ranching, greenhouse/nurseries.

History: Mescalero Apaches in area when Antonio de Espejo explored in 1583. U.S. Army established Fort Davis in 1854 to protect routes to west. Civilian settlers followed, including Manuel Músquiz, a political refugee from Mexico. County named for Jefferson Davis, U.S. war secretary, Confederate president; created 1887 from Presidio County.

Race/Ethnicity, 2007: (In percent) Anglo, 62.8; Black, 0.8; Hispanic, 35.9; Other, 0.5.

Vital Statistics, 2006: Births, 21; deaths, 15; marriages, 0; divorces, 0.

Recreation: Scenic drives including loop along Limpia Creek, Mt. Livermore, Blue Mountain; hunting; Fort Davis National Historic Site; state park; McDonald Observatory on Mt.

Locke; solar power park; Chihuahuan Desert Research Institute; hummingbird festival in August.

Minerals: Bentonite.

Agriculture: Greenhouse nurseries, beef cattle, apples, grapes, pecans. Market value $10.4 million.

FORT DAVIS (1,500), county seat; ranch center, trade, tourism, government/services; library; "Coolest July 4th in Texas."

Other town: **Valentine** (218).

Population	2,275
Change fm 2000	3.1
Area (sq. mi.)	2,264.60
Land Area (sq. mi.)	2,264.43
Altitude (ft.)	3,162-8,378
Rainfall (in.) Fort Davis	15.86
Rainfall (in.) Mt. Locke	20.37
Jan. mean min. Fort Davis	28.4
Jan. mean min. Mt. Locke	32.4
July mean max. Fort Davis	89.5
July mean max. Mt. Locke	84.5
Civ. Labor	1,185
Unemployed	3.7
Wages	$6,829,519
Av. Weekly Wage	$551
Prop. Value	$203,535,820
Retail Sales	$7,948,590

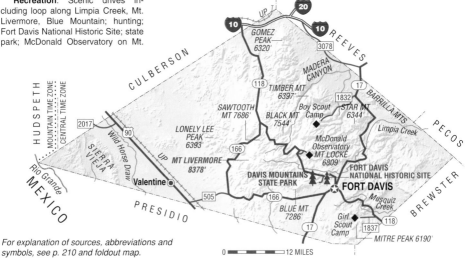

0 ▬▬▬▬▬ 12 MILES

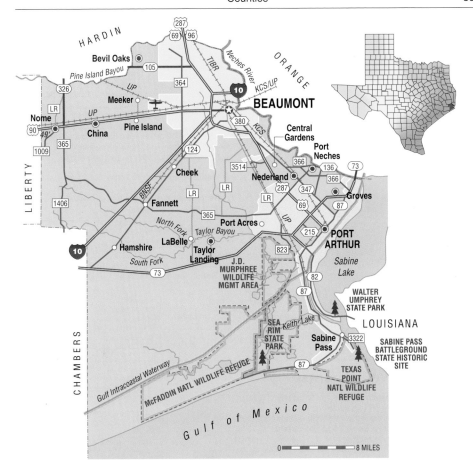

Jefferson County

Physical Features: Gulf Coast grassy plain, with timber in northwest; beach sands, sandy loams, black clay soils; drains to Neches River, Gulf of Mexico.

Economy: Government/services, petrochemical and other chemical plants, shipbuilding, steel mill, port activity, oil-field supplies.

History: Atakapas and Orcoquizas, whose numbers were reduced by epidemics or migration before Anglo-American settlers arrived in 1820s. Cajuns arrived in 1840s; Europeans in 1850s. Antebellum slaveholding area. County created 1836 from Mexican municipality; organized 1837; named for U.S. President Thomas Jefferson.

Race/Ethnicity, 2007: (In percent) Anglo, 45.4; Black, 34.8; Hispanic, 15.1; Other, 4.7.

Vital Statistics, 2006: Births, 3,447; deaths, 2,501; marriages, 2,196; divorces, 1,043.

Recreation: Beaches, fresh and saltwater fishing; duck, goose hunting; water activities; Dick Dowling Monument and Park; Spindletop site, museums; saltwater lake; wildlife refuge; Lamar University events; historic sites; South Texas Fair in October.

Minerals: Large producer of oil, gas, sulfur, salt, sand and gravel.

Agriculture: Rice, soybeans; crawfish; beef cattle; hay; considerable rice irrigated. Market value $26.8 million. Timber sales significant.

BEAUMONT (111,528) county seat; petrochemical production, shipbuilding, port activities, rice milling, government/services; Lamar University; hospitals; entertainment district; Neches River Festival in April.

PORT ARTHUR (55,702) oil, chemical activities, shrimping and crawfishing, shipping, offshore marine, tourism; hospitals; museum; prison; Asian New Year Tet, Janis Joplin Birthday Bash in January. **Sabine Pass** and **Port Acres** are now within the city limits of Port Arthur.

Other towns include: **Bevil Oaks** (1,277); **Central Gardens** (3,911); **China** (1,052); **Fannett** (1,877); **Groves** (15,049) retail center, some manufacturing, government/services, tourism; hospital, pecan festival in September; **Hamshire** (759).

Also, **Nederland** (17,208) manufacturing, transportation, petrochemical refining; Windmill and French museum; hospital; Tex Ritter memorial and park, heritage festival in March (city founded by Dutch immigrants in 1898).

Also, **Nome** (541); **Port Neches** (13,184) chemical and synthetic rubber industry, manufacturing, library, river-front park with La Maison Beausoleil, RiverFest in May; **Taylor Landing** (211).

Population	**243,090**
Change fm 2000	–3.6
Area (sq. mi.)	1,111.26
Land Area (sq. mi.)	903.55
Altitude (ft.)	sea level-49
Rainfall (in.)	59.89
Jan. mean min.	42.9
July mean max.	91.6
Civ. Labor	115,171
Unemployed	8.2
Wages	$1,328,716,768
Av. Weekly Wage	$820
Prop. Value	$23,151,020,515
Retail Sales	$3,433,404,508

For explanation of sources, symbols and abbreviations, see p. 210 and foldout map.

Jim Hogg County

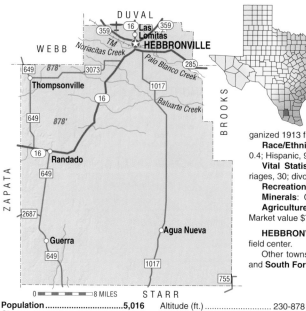

Physical Features: South Texas county on rolling plain, with heavy brush cover; white blow sand and sandy loam; hilly, broken.

Economy: Oil, cattle operations.

History: Coahuiltecan area, then Lipan Apache. Spanish land grant in 1805 to Xavier Vela. County named for Gov. James Stephen Hogg; created, organized 1913 from Brooks, Duval counties.

Race/Ethnicity, 2007: (In percent) Anglo, 8.7; Black, 0.4; Hispanic, 90.3; Other, 0.6.

Vital Statistics, 2006: Births, 84; deaths, 43; marriages, 30; divorces, 0.

Recreation: White-tailed deer and bobwhite hunting.

Minerals: Oil and gas.

Agriculture: Cattle, hay, milk goats; some irrigation. Market value $7.4 million.

HEBBRONVILLE (4,305) county seat; ranching, oil-field center.

Other towns include: **Guerra** (8), **Las Lomitas** (266) and **South Fork Estates** (46).

Population	5,016
Change fm 2000	–5.0
Area (sq. mi.)	1,136.16
Land Area (sq. mi.)	1,136.11
Altitude (ft.)	230-878
Rainfall (in.)	23.75
Jan. mean min.	43.8
July mean max.	97.5
Civ. Labor	2,975
Unemployed	4.3
Wages	$13,416,793
Av. Weekly Wage	$525
Prop. Value	$469,837,591
Retail Sales	$31,262,199

Jim Wells County

Physical Features: South Coastal Plains; level to rolling; sandy to dark soils; grassy with mesquite brush.

Economy: Oil and gas production, agriculture, nature tourism.

History: Coahuiltecans, driven out by Lipan Apaches in 1775. Tomás Sánchez established settlement in 1754. Anglo-American settlement in 1878. County created 1911 from Nueces County; organized 1912; named for developer J.B. Wells Jr.

Race/Ethnicity, 2007: (In percent) Anglo, 21.3; Black, 0.5; Hispanic, 77.5; Other, 0.7.

Vital Statistics, 2006: Births, 665; deaths, 340; marriages, 264; divorces, 180.

Recreation: Hunting; fiestas; Tejano Roots hall of fame; South Texas museum.

Minerals: Oil, gas, caliche.

Agriculture: Cattle, sorghum, corn, cotton, dairies, goats, wheat, watermelons, sunflowers, peas, hay. Market value $61 million.

ALICE (20,312) county seat; oil-field service center, agribusiness, government/services; hospital; Bee County College extension; Fiesta Bandana (from original name of city) in May.

Other towns include: **Alfred-South La Paloma** (511); **Ben Bolt** (1,600); **Orange Grove** (1,432); **Pernitas Point** (274, partly in Live Oak County); **Premont** (2,877) wildflower tour in spring; **Rancho Alegre** (1,848); **Sandia** (458).

Also, a small part of **San Diego** (4,473).

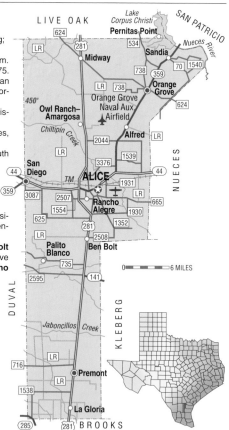

Population	41,069
Change fm 2000	4.4
Area (sq. mi.)	868.22
Land Area (sq. mi.)	864.52
Altitude (ft.)	50-450
Rainfall (in.)	27.52
Jan. mean min.	44.1
July mean max.	96.1
Civ. Labor	22,189
Unemployed	4.5
Wages	$175,990,355
Av. Weekly Wage	$744
Prop. Value	$1,605,062,192
Retail Sales	$431,231,594

For explanation of sources, symbols and abbreviations, see p. 210 and foldout map.

Johnson County

Physical Features: North central county drained by tributaries of Trinity, Brazos rivers; lake; hilly, rolling, many soil types.

Economy: Agribusiness, railroad shops; manufacturing, distribution, lake activities, many residents employed in Fort Worth; part of Fort Worth-Arlington metropolitan area.

History: No permanent Indian villages existed in area. Anglo-American settlers arrived in 1840s. County named for Col. M.T. Johnson of Mexican War, Confederacy; created, organized 1854. Formed from McLennan, Hill, Navarro counties.

Race/Ethnicity, 2007: (In percent) Anglo, 78.4; Black, 2.7; Hispanic, 17.0; Other, 1.8.

Vital Statistics, 2006: Births, 2,057; deaths, 1,072; marriages, 1,223; divorces, 542.

Recreation: Bird, deer hunting; water activities on Lake Pat Cleburne; state park; sports complex; museum; Chisholm Trail; Goatneck bike ride in July.

Minerals: Limestone, sand and gravel.

Agriculture: Cattle, hay, horses (fourth in numbers), dairies, cotton, sorghum, wheat, oats, hogs. Market value $62 million.

CLEBURNE (29,603) county seat; manufacturing, oil and gas; hospital, library, museum; Hill College campus; Whistle Stop Christmas.

BURLESON (34,467, part [3,462] in Tarrant County) agriculture, retail center; hospital.

Other towns include: **Alvarado** (4,415) County Pioneer Days; **Briaroaks** (511); **Cross Timber** (313); **Godley** (1,061); **Grandview** (1,595); **Joshua** (5,592) many residents work in Fort Worth; **Keene** (6,299) Southwestern Adventist University; **Lillian** (1,160); **Rio Vista** (781), and **Venus** (2,518).

Also, part of **Cresson** (718); and part of **Mansfield** (44,957 total, mostly in Tarrant County).

Population	153,630
Change fm 2000	21.1
Area (sq. mi.)	734.46
Land Area (sq. mi.)	729.42
Altitude (ft.)	500-1,065
Rainfall (in.)	36.25
Jan. mean min.	34.0
July mean max.	97.0
Civ. Labor	75,528
Unemployed	5.3
Wages	$356,727,509
Av. Weekly Wage	$674
Prop. Value	$9,849,464,897
Retail Sales	$2,815,823,589

Old downtown Venus, Johnson County. Robert Plocheck photo.

Jones County

Physical Features: West Texas Rolling Plains; drained by Brazos River fork, tributaries; Lake Fort Phantom Hill.

Economy: Agribusiness; government/services; varied manufacturing.

History: Comanches and other tribes hunted in area. Military presence began in 1851. Ranching established in 1870s. County named for the last president of the Republic, Anson Jones; created 1858 from Bexar, Bosque counties; re-created 1876; organized 1881.

Race/Ethnicity, 2007: (In percent) Anglo, 64.6; Black, 11.4; Hispanic, 23.0; Other, 1.0.

Vital Statistics, 2006: Births, 191; deaths, 182; marriages, 76; divorces, 38.

Recreation: Lake activities, hunting, Fort Phantom Hill, Cowboy Reunion July 4 in Stamford.

Minerals: Oil, gas, sand and gravel, stone.

Agriculture: Cotton, wheat, sesame and peanuts; cattle. Some 10,000 acres irrigated for peanuts and hay. Market value $59.2 million.

ANSON (2,503) county seat; farming center, government/services, trailer and furniture manufacturing; hospital; old courthouse, opera house, museums; Mesquite Daze festivals in April and October.

STAMFORD (3,527) trade center for three counties, hospital, historic homes, cowboy museum.

HAMLIN (2,153) farm and ranching, feed mill, oil/gas, electricity/steam plant using mesquite trees; hospital; museums; dove cookoff in October.

Other towns include: **Hawley** (633), **Lueders** (281) limestone quarries.

Part [5,488] of **Abilene**.

Population **19,197**
Change fm 2000 .... –7.6
Area (sq. mi.) 937.13

Land Area (sq. mi.) 930.99
Altitude (ft.) 1,480-1,970
Rainfall (in.) 26.00
Jan. mean min. 30.7
July mean max. 96.3
Civ. Labor 7,924
Unemployed 5.5
Wages $31,905,935
Av. Weekly Wage $571
Prop. Value $564,515,487
Retail Sales $176,510,344

Karnes County

Physical Features: Sandy loam, dark clay, alluvial soils in rolling terrain; traversed by San Antonio River; mesquite, oak trees.

Economy: Agribusiness; government/services.

History: Coahuiltecan Indian area. Spanish ranching began around 1750. Anglo-Americans arrived in 1840s; Polish in 1850s. County created 1854 from Bexar, Goliad, San Patricio counties; named for Texas Revolutionary figure Henry W. Karnes.

Race/Ethnicity, 2007: (In percent) Anglo, 39.9; Black, 9.3; Hispanic, 50.1; Other, 0.6.

Vital Statistics, 2006: Births, 170; deaths, 154; marriages, 17; divorces, 19.

Recreation: Panna Maria, nation's oldest Polish settlement, founded 1854; Old Helena restored courthouse, museum; hunting, nature tourism, guest ranches.

Minerals: Oil, gas.

Agriculture: Beef cattle, feed grain, hay, cotton. Market value $24.6 million.

KARNES CITY (3,484) county seat; agribusiness, tourism, processing center, oil-field servicing, manufacturing; library; Lonesome Dove Fest in September.

KENEDY (3,678) farm and oil center, library, dove/quail hunting, prison, hospital; Bluebonnet Days in April.

Other towns include: **Falls City** (636) ranching, sausage making, library, city park on river; **Gillett** (120); **Hobson** (135); **Panna Maria** (45); **Runge** (1,228) oil and gas services, farming, museum, library; cowboy breakfast in December.

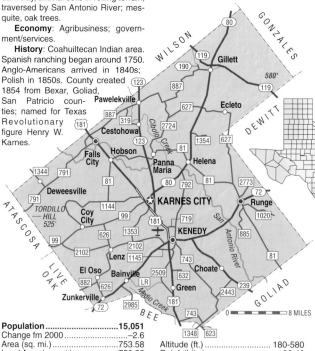

Population **15,051**
Change fm 2000 .... –2.6
Area (sq. mi.) 753.58
Land Area (sq. mi.) 750.32
Altitude (ft.) 180-580
Rainfall (in.) 28.40

Jan. mean min. 41.0
July mean max. 95.0
Civ. Labor 5,178
Unemployed 6.5
Wages $27,335,942
Av. Weekly Wage $556
Prop. Value $469,140,344
Retail Sales $90,93,005

Kaufman County

Physical Features: North Blackland prairie, draining to Trinity River, Cedar Creek and Lake.

Economy: varied manufacturing, trade center, government/services, antiques center, commuting to Dallas.

History: Caddo and Cherokee Indians; removed by 1840 when Anglo-American settlement began. County created from Henderson County and organized, 1848; named for member of Texas and U.S. congresses D.S. Kaufman.

Race/Ethnicity, 2007: (In percent) Anglo, 73.1; Black, 10.1; Hispanic, 15.5; Other, 1.2.

Vital Statistics, 2006: Births, 1,257; deaths, 763; marriages, 767; divorces, 351.

Recreation: Lake activities; Porter Farm near Terrell is site of origin of U.S.-Texas Agricultural Extension program; antique centers near Forney; historic homes at Terrell.

Minerals: Oil, gas, stone, sand.

Agriculture: Nursery crops; beef cattle, horses, goats, hogs, sheep; wheat, hay, sorghum, oats, cotton, peaches. Market value $43.7 million.

KAUFMAN (9,032) county seat; government/services, manufacturing and distribution, commuters to Dallas; hospital; Caboodle Fest in October.

TERRELL (18,366) agribusiness, varied manufacturing, outlet center; private hospital, state hospital; community college, Southwestern Christian College.

Other towns include: **Combine** (2,084, partly in Dallas County); **Cottonwood** (234); **Crandall** (3,630); **Elmo** (300); **Forney** (13,977) important antiques center, light manufacturing, historic homes, Jackrabbit Stampede bike race in September; **Grays Prairie** (354); **Kemp** (1,427); **Lawrence** (259); **Mabank** (2,821, partly in Henderson County) varied manufacturing, tourism, retail trade, Western Week in June; **Oak Grove** (948); **Oak Ridge** (546); **Post Oak Bend** (581); **Rosser** (428); **Scurry** (712); **Talty** (1,335).

Population	100,527
Change fm 2000	41.0
Area (sq. mi.)	806.81
Land Area (sq. mi.)	786.04
Altitude (ft.)	300-611
Rainfall (in.)	38.90
Jan. mean min.	32.3
July mean max.	94.6
Civ. Labor	46,151
Unemployed	6.5
Wages	$209,228,173
Av. Weekly Wage	$617
Prop. Value	$6,107,242,352
Retail Sales	$1,579,670,627

For explanation of sources, abbreviations and symbols, see p. 210 and foldout map.

A field near Prairieville, Kaufman County. Robert Plocheck photo.

Kendall County

Physical Features: Hill Country, plateau, with springfed streams; caves; scenic drives.

Economy: Government/services, agribusiness, commuters to San Antonio, tourism, retirement area, some manufacturing.

History: Lipan Apaches, Kiowas and Comanches in area when German settlers arrived in 1840s. County created from Blanco, Kerr counties 1862; named for pioneer journalist-sheepman and early contributor to Texas Almanac, George W. Kendall.

Race/Ethnicity, 2007: (In percent) Anglo, 81.0; Black, 0.2; Hispanic, 18.2; Other, 0.6.

Vital Statistics, 2006: Births, 349; deaths, 303; marriages, 360; divorces, 74.

Recreation: Hunting, fishing, exotic wildlife, state park; Cascade Cavern, Cave Without a Name; historic sites.

Minerals: Limestone rock, caliche.

Agriculture: Cattle, goats, sheep, hay. Market value $7.6 million. Cedar posts, firewood sold.

BOERNE (9,217) county seat; tourism, antiques, some manufacturing, ranching, commuting to San Antonio; library; Berges Fest on Father's Day weekend.

Other towns include: **Comfort** (2,779) tourism, ranching, Civil War monument honoring Unionists, library, mountain bike trail; **Kendalia** (149); **Sisterdale** (110); **Waring** (73). Part of **Fair Oaks Ranch** (6,175).

Population **32,886**	July mean max. 91.9
Change fm 2000 ....38.5	Civ. Labor 15,545
Area (sq. mi.) 663.04	Unemployed 4.3
Land Area (sq. mi.) 662.44	Wages $101,827,444
Altitude (ft.) 1,000-2,080	Av. Weekly Wage...............$735
Rainfall (in.) 37.36	Prop. Value $4,806,865,723
Jan. mean min. 34.3	Retail Sales $842,064,367

The Treüe der Union Monument in Comfort honors German immigrants killed in 1862 at the Nueces River. They were trying to flee to Mexico rather than fight in the Civil War against their adopted homeland. Robert Plocheck photo.

Kenedy County

Physical Features: Gulf coastal county; flat, sandy terrain; some loam soils; motts of live oaks.

Economy: Oil, ranching, hunting leases, nature tourism.

History: Coahuiltecan Indians who assimilated or were driven out by Lipan Apaches. Spanish ranching began in 1790s. Anglo-Americans arrived after Mexican War. Among last counties created, organized 1921, from Cameron, Hidalgo, Willacy counties; named for pioneer steamboat operator and cattleman, Capt. Mifflin Kenedy.

Race/Ethnicity, 2007: (In percent) Anglo, 18.7; Black, 0.0; Hispanic, 80.2; Other, 1.1.

Vital Statistics, 2006: Births, 3; deaths, 2; marriages, 2; divorces, 1.

Recreation: Hunting, fishing, bird watching.

Minerals: Oil, gas.

Agriculture: Beef cattle. Market value $19 million. Hunting leases.

SARITA (185) county seat; cattle-shipping point, ranch headquarters, gas processing; one of state's least populous counties.

Also, **Armstrong** (4).

Population **388**
Change fm 2000 .... –6.3

Area (sq. mi.) 1,945.60	Civ. Labor 254
Land Area (sq. mi.) 1,456.77	Unemployed 3.1
Altitude (ft.) .... sea level-115	Wages $5,638,396
Rainfall (in.) 27.90	Av. Weekly Wage.....................$883
Jan. mean min. 45.0	Prop. Value $758,434,849
July mean max. 95.0	Retail Sales $5,007

Kent County

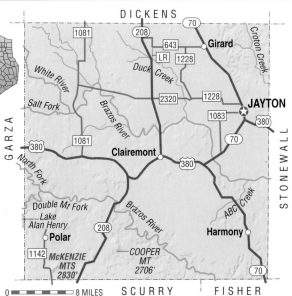

Physical Features: Rolling, broken terrain; lake; drains to Salt and Double Mountain forks of Brazos River; sandy, loam soils.

Economy: Agribusiness, oil and gas operations, government/services, hunting leases.

History: Comanches driven out by U.S. Army in 1870s. Ranching developed in 1880s. County created 1876 from Bexar, Young territories; organized 1892. Name honors Andrew Kent, one of 32 volunteers from Gonzales who died at the Alamo.

Race/Ethnicity, 2007: (In percent) Anglo, 89.8; Black, 0.2; Hispanic, 9.8; Other, 0.1.

Vital Statistics, 2006: Births, 5; deaths, 18; marriages, 7; divorces, 5.

Recreation: Hunting, fishing; scenic croton breaks and salt flat; Winterfest in December.

Minerals: Oil, gas.

Agriculture: Cattle, cotton, wheat, sorghum. Market value $6.8 million.

JAYTON (484) county seat; oil-field services, farming center; Summerfest in August.

Other towns include: **Girard** (67).

For explanation of symbols, sources and abbreviations, see p. 210 and foldout map.

Population **708**
Change fm 2000 .... –17.6

Area (sq. mi.) 902.91	July mean max. 95.7
Land Area (sq. mi.) 902.33	Civ. Labor 449
Altitude (ft.) 1,740-2,830	Unemployed 4.2
Rainfall (in.) 22.94	Wages $1,555,379
Jan. mean min. 24.9	Av. Weekly Wage................. $397
	Prop. Value $567,436,470
	Retail Sales $13,265,878

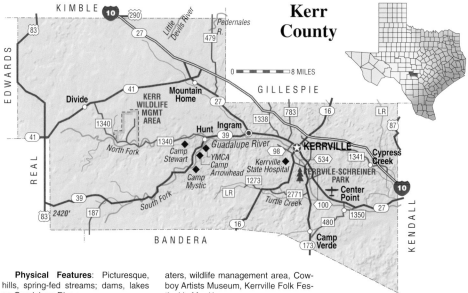

Kerr County

0 ▬▬▬▬ 8 MILES

Physical Features: Picturesque, hills, spring-fed streams; dams, lakes on Guadalupe River.

Economy: Tourism, medical services, agribusiness, hunting leases.

History: Lipan Apaches, Kiowas and Comanches in area. Anglo-American settlers arrived in late 1840s. County created 1856 from Bexar County; named for member of Austin's Colony, James Kerr.

Race/Ethnicity, 2007: (In percent) Anglo, 75.6; Black, 1.7; Hispanic, 21.6; Other, 1.0.

Vital Statistics, 2006: Births, 514; deaths, 661; marriages, 408; divorces, 210.

Recreation: Youth camps, dude ranches, park, Cailloux and Point the-aters, wildlife management area, Cowboy Artists Museum, Kerrville Folk Festival in May/June.

Minerals: none.

Agriculture: Cattle, hay, goats, horses; deer (first in numbers as livestock). Market value $13.4 million. Hunting leases important.

KERRVILLE (22,402) county seat; tourist center, youth camps, agribusiness, aircraft and parts, varied manufacturing; Schreiner University; state hospital, veterans hospital, private hospital; retirement center; retail trade; state arts, crafts show in May.

Other towns include: **Camp Verde** (41); **Center Point** (800); **Hunt** (708) youth camps, hospital; **Ingram** (1,904) camps, cabins; **Mountain Home** (96).

Population	48,269
Change fm 2000	10.6
Area (sq. mi.)	1,107.66
Land Area (sq. mi.)	1,106.12
Altitude (ft.)	1,400-2,420
Rainfall (in.)	32.60
Jan. mean min.	32.0
July mean max.	92.0
Civ. Labor	22,781
Unemployed	5.0
Wages	$152,683,925
Av. Weekly Wage	$642
Prop. Value	$3,503,831,222
Retail Sales	$802,576,735

For explanation of symbols, sources and abbreviations, see p. 210 and foldout map.

The red soil and rolling hills on the 6666 Ranch at Guthrie, King County. Robert Plocheck photo.

Kimble County

Population 4,432
Change fm 2000 .... −0.8
Area (sq. mi.) 1,250.92
Land Area (sq. mi.) 1,250.70
Altitude (ft.) 1,476-2,460
Rainfall (in.) 23.24
Jan. mean min. 29.3
July mean max. 94.8
Civ. Labor 2,413
Unemployed 4.0
Wages $9,582,060
Av. Weekly Wage $466
Prop. Value $337,915,047
Retail Sales $60,579,071

Physical Features: Picturesque Edwards Plateau; rugged, broken by numerous streams; drains to Llano River; sandy, gray, chocolate loam soils.

Economy: Livestock production and market, tourism, cedar oil and wood products, metal building materials.

History: Apache, Kiowas and Comanche stronghold until 1870s. Military outposts protected first Anglo-American settlers in 1850s. County created from Bexar County 1858; organized 1876. Named for George C. Kimble, a Gonzales volunteer who died at the Alamo.

Race/Ethnicity, 2007: (In percent) Anglo, 76.1; Black, 0.1; Hispanic, 23.1; Other, 0.7.

Vital Statistics, 2006: Births, 42; deaths, 73; marriages, 22; divorces, 15.

Recreation: Hunting, fishing in spring-fed streams, nature tourism; among leading deer counties; state park; Kimble Kounty Kow Kick on Labor Day, Wild Game dinner on Thanksgiving Saturday.

Minerals: gravel.

Agriculture: Cattle, meat goats, sheep, Angora goats, pecans. Market value $8.4 million. Hunting leases important. Firewood, cedar sold.

JUNCTION (2,663) county seat; tourism, varied manufacturing, livestock production; two museums; Texas Tech University center; hospital; library, airport.

Other towns include: **London** (180); **Roosevelt** (14).

[County map: MENARD to north; SUTTON to west; EDWARDS and KERR to south; MASON, GILLESPIE to east. Features include JUNCTION, Cleo, Roosevelt, Telegraph, Segovia, Noxville, London; Llano River, North Llano River, South Llano River, Bear Creek, Red Creek, Copperas Creek, Cedar Creek, James River, Little Devils River, Pedernales R.; SOUTH LLANO RIVER STATE PARK & WILDLIFE MGMT AREA; highways 10, 377, 83, 377, 385, 481, 73, 291, 479, 2169, 1871, 1221, 3480, 1674, 2291, 2460', 2100', 1674', 290. 0—8 MILES]

King County

Physical Features: Hilly, broken by Wichita, Brazos tributaries; extensive grassland; dark loam to red soils.

Economy: Oil and gas, ranching, government/services, horse sales, hunting leases.

History: Apache area until Comanches moved in about 1700. Comanches removed by U.S. Army in 1874-75 after which ranching began. County created 1876 from Bexar District; organized 1891; named for William P. King, a volunteer from Gonzales who died at the Alamo.

Race/Ethnicity, 2007: (In percent) Anglo, 90.7; Black, 0.00; Hispanic, 8.4; Other, 0.8.

Vital Statistics, 2006: Births, 1; deaths, 1; marriages, 3; divorces, 0.

Recreation: 6666 Ranch visits, hunting, roping and ranch horse competitions.

Minerals: Oil, gas.

Agriculture: Cattle, horses, wheat, hay, cotton. Market value $17.9 million. Hunting leases important.

GUTHRIE (125) county seat; ranch-supply center, government/services; community center complex, library; Thanksgiving community supper.

Population 281
Change fm 2000 .... −21.1
Area (sq. mi.) 913.33
Land Area (sq. mi.) 912.29
Altitude (ft.) 1,450-2,250
Rainfall (in.) 25.00
Jan. mean min. 23.9
July mean max. 96.7
Civ. Labor 218
Unemployed 4.1
Wages $3,052,286
Av. Weekly Wage $1,285
Prop. Value $280,475,168
Retail Sales $620,210

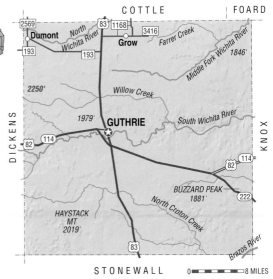

[County map: COTTLE and FOARD to north; DICKENS to west; KNOX to east; STONEWALL to south. Features include GUTHRIE, Dumont, Grow; North Wichita River, South Wichita River, Middle Fork Wichita River, Farrer Creek, Willow Creek, North Croton Creek, Brazos River; BUZZARD PEAK 1881', HAYSTACK MT 2019'; highways 82, 83, 114, 193, 222, 2569, 1168, 3416; altitudes 2250', 1979', 1846'. 0—8 MILES]

Kinney County

Physical Features: Hilly, broken by Rio Grande tributaries; Anacacho Mountains; Nueces Canyon.

Economy: Agribusiness, government/services, hunting leases.

History: Coahuiltecans, Apaches, Comanches in area. Spanish Franciscans established settlement in late 1700s. English empresarios John Beales and James Grant established English-speaking colony in 1834. Black Seminoles served as army scouts in 1870s. County created from Bexar County 1850; organized 1874; named for H.L. Kinney, founder of Corpus Christi.

Race/Ethnicity, 2007: (In percent) Anglo, 43.9; Black, 1.4; Hispanic, 54.4; Other, 0.3.

Vital Statistics, 2006: Births, 33; deaths, 32; marriages, 23; divorces, 2.

Recreation: Hunting; replica of Alamo; old Fort Clark Springs; state park; Cinco de Mayo, Juneteenth.

Minerals: Not significant.

Agriculture: Cattle, goats, hay, grain sorghum, cotton, corn, oats, wheat. Market value $6.4 million.

BRACKETTVILLE (1,868) county seat; agriculture, tourism; museum.

Other towns include: **Fort Clark Springs** (1,300); **Spofford** (73).

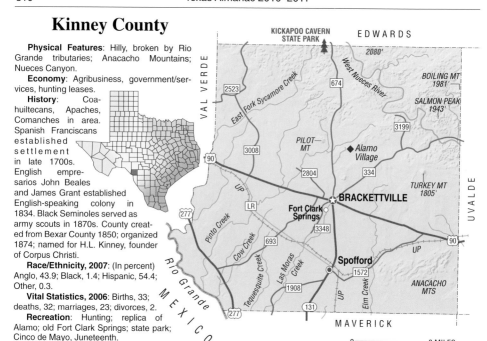

Population	**3,233**
Change fm 2000	–4.3
Area (sq. mi.)	1,365.31
Land Area (sq. mi.)	1,363.44
Altitude (ft.)	790-2,080
Rainfall (in.)	22.79
Jan. mean min.	37.3
July mean max.	95.5
Civ. Labor	1,447

Unemployed	5.5
Wages	$5,906,348
Av. Weekly Wage	$583
Prop. Value	$173,459,448
Retail Sales	$10,905,917

For explanation of sources, symbols and abbreviations, see p. 210 and foldout map.

Texas A & M University – Kingsville, Kleberg County. Robert Plocheck photo.

Kleberg County

Physical Features: Coastal plain, broken by bays; sandy, loam, clay soils; tree motts.

Economy: Oil and gas, Naval air station, chemicals and plastics, agriculture, Texas A&M University-Kingsville.

History: Coahuiltecan and Karankawa area. Spanish land grants date to 1750s. In 1853 Richard King purchased Santa Gertrudis land grant. County created 1913 from Nueces County; named for San Jacinto veteran and rancher Robert Kleberg.

Race/Ethnicity, 2007: (In percent) Anglo, 26.6; Black, 3.9; Hispanic, 67.3; Other, 2.3.

Vital Statistics, 2006: Births, 495; deaths, 202; marriages, 243; divorces, 106.

Recreation: Fishing, hunting, water sports, park Baffin Bay; wildlife sanctuary; winter bird watching; university events, museum; King Ranch headquarters, tours; La Posada celebration in November.

Minerals: Oil, gas, uranium.

Agriculture: Cotton, beef cattle, grain sorghum. Market value $65 million. Hunting leases/eco-tourism.

KINGSVILLE (24,477) county seat; government/services, oil, gas, agribusiness, tourism, chemical plant, university, Coastal Bend College branch; hospital; ranching heritage festival in February.

Other towns include: **Riviera** (1,064).

Population		**30,739**
Change fm 2000		–2.6
Area (sq. mi.)		1,090.29
Land Area (sq. mi.)		870.97
Altitude (ft.)	sea level-165	
Rainfall (in.)		29.03
Jan. mean min.		43.4
July mean max.		95.5
Civ. Labor		16,805
Unemployed		4.5
Wages		$97,360,235
Av. Weekly Wage		$599
Prop. Value		$1,386,809,159
Retail Sales		$478,427,475

Knox County

Physical Features: Eroded breaks on West Texas Rolling Plains; Brazos, Wichita rivers; sandy, loam soils.

Economy: Oil, agriculture, government/services.

History: Indian conscripts used during Spanish period to mine copper deposits along the Brazos. Ranching, farming developed in 1880s. German colony settled in 1895. County created from Bexar, Young territories 1858; re-created 1876; organized 1886; named for U.S. Secretary of War Henry Knox.

Race/Ethnicity, 2007: (In percent) Anglo, 63.0; Black, 7.9; Hispanic, 28.5; Other, 0.7.

Vital Statistics, 2006: Births, 46; deaths, 51; marriages, 0; divorces, 3.

Recreation: Lake activities, fishing, hunting; Knox City seedless watermelon festival in July.

Minerals: Oil, gas.

Agriculture: Wheat, cattle, cotton. Some cotton irrigated. Market value $38.4 million.

BENJAMIN (253) county seat; ranching, farm center; veterans memorial.

MUNDAY (1,447) portable buildings, other manufacturing; A&M vegetable research station.

KNOX CITY (1,114) agribusiness, petroleum center; USDA plant materials research center; hospital.

Other towns include: **Goree** (297); **Rhineland** (120) old church established by German immigrants.

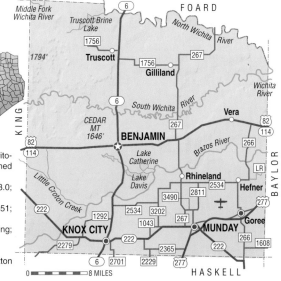

Population		**3,393**
Change fm 2000		–20.2
Area (sq. mi.)		855.43
Land Area (sq. mi.)		849.00
Altitude (ft.)		1,200-1,794
Rainfall (in.)		26.36
Jan. mean min.		28.1
July mean max.		96.5
Civ. Labor		1,985
Unemployed		3.8
Wages		$10,774,635
Av. Weekly Wage		$640
Prop. Value		$165,225,251
Retail Sales		$35,773,568

Lamar County

Physical Features: North Texas county on divide between Red, Sulphur rivers; soils chiefly blackland, except along Red; pines, hardwoods.

Economy: Varied manufacturing, agribusiness, medical, government/services.

History: Caddo Indian area. First Anglo-American settlers arrived about 1815. County created 1840 from Red River County; organized 1841; named for second president of Republic, Mirabeau B. Lamar.

Race/Ethnicity, 2007: (In percent) Anglo, 79.8; Black, 14.4; Hispanic, 4.0; Other, 1.8.

Vital Statistics, 2006: Births, 688; deaths, 563; marriages, 436; divorces, 323.

Recreation: Lake activities; Gambill goose refuge; hunting, fishing; state park; Trail de Paris rail-to-trail; Sam Bell Maxey Home; State Sen. A.M. Aikin Archives, other museums.

Minerals: Negligible.

Agriculture: Beef, hay (second in acreage), dairy, soybeans (second in acreage), wheat, corn, sorghum, cotton. Market value $60.4 million.

PARIS (26,324) county seat; varied manufacturing, food processing, government/services; hospitals; junior college; museums; Tour de Paris bicycle rally in July; archery pro-am tournament in March.

Other towns include: **Arthur City** (180), **Blossom** (1,462), **Brookston** (130), **Chicota** (150), **Cunningham** (110), **Deport** (672, partly in Red River

County), **Pattonville** (180), **Petty** (130), **Powderly** (185), **Reno** (3,137), **Roxton** (718), **Sumner** (95), **Sun Valley** (63), **Toco** (83).

Population	**49,286**
Change fm 2000	1.6
Area (sq. mi.)	932.47
Land Area (sq. mi.)	916.81
Altitude (ft.)	335-670
Rainfall (in.)	47.82

Jan. mean min.	29.9
July mean max.	94.3
Civ. Labor	25,277
Unemployed	6.0
Wages	$164,818,516
Av. Weekly Wage	$628
Prop. Value	$2,566,201,064
Retail Sales	$614,334,884

For explanation of sources, symbols and abbreviations, see p. 210 and foldout map.

Old gasoline pumps are collected in front of the store at Nix, Lampasas County. Robert Plocheck photo.

Lamb County

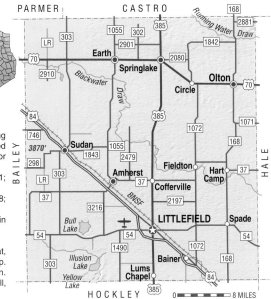

Physical Features: Rich, red, brown soils on the High Plains; some hills; drains to upper Brazos River tributaries; numerous playas.

Economy: Agribusiness; distribution center; denim textiles.

History: Apaches, displaced by Comanches around 1700. U.S. Army pushed Comanches into Indian Territory in 1875. Ranching began in 1880s; farming after 1900. County created 1876 from Bexar District; organized 1908; named for Lt. G.A. Lamb, who died in battle of San Jacinto.

Race/Ethnicity, 2007: (In percent) Anglo, 46.1; Black, 4.6; Hispanic, 48.9; Other, 0.5.

Vital Statistics, 2006: Births, 248; deaths, 168; marriages, 70; divorces, 35.

Recreation: Waylon Jennings Birthday Bash in June at Littlefield, museums.

Minerals: Oil, stone, gas.

Agriculture: Fed cattle; cotton, corn, wheat, grain sorghum, vegetables, soybeans, hay; sheep. 385,000 acres irrigated. Market value $406.3 million.

LITTLEFIELD (6,514) county seat; textile mill, agribusiness, manufacturing; hospital, prison.

Olton (2,333) agribusiness, retail center; Sandcrawl museum; pheasant hunt in winter; Sandhills Celebration in August.

Other towns include: **Amherst** (825); **Earth** (1,082) farming center, manufacturing, feed lot, supplies; **Fieldton** (20); **Spade** (99); **Springlake** (137); **Sudan** (1,032) farming center, government/services, Homecoming Day in fall.

Population 13,585	July mean max. 92.0
Change fm 2000 .... −7.6	Civ. Labor 7,292
Area (sq. mi.) 1,017.73	Unemployed 4.7
Land Area (sq. mi.) 1,016.21	Wages $33,848,598
Altitude (ft.) 3,390-3,870	Av. Weekly Wage $545
Rainfall (in.) 18.69	Prop. Value $888,675,739
Jan. mean min. 22.7	Retail Sales $80,804,298

Lampasas County

Physical Features: Central Texas on edge of Hill Country; Colorado, Lampasas rivers; cedars, oaks, pecans.

Economy: Many employed at Fort Hood, several industrial plants, agribusinesses, tourism.

History: Mineral springs attracted first Anglo-Americans in 1853. Frontier confrontations between settlers, Comanches continued into 1870s. County created 1856 from Bell, Travis counties. Named for river. Some have speculated that an early expedition named river for city of Lampazos in Mexico.

Race/Ethnicity, 2007: (In percent) Anglo, 79.2; Black, 3.0; Hispanic, 16.5; Other, 1.3.

Vital Statistics, 2006: Births, 239; deaths, 182; marriages, 135; divorces, 88.

Recreation: Scenic drives; state park; deer hunting, fishing in streams; Hancock Springs free-flow swim area at Lampasas.

Minerals: Sand and gravel, building stone.

Agriculture: Beef cattle, hay, goats, exotic animals. Market value $14 million. Hunting leases, ecotourism.

LAMPASAS (8,031) county seat; varied manufacturing, government/services, ranching, hunting center; historic downtown; hospital; museum; Spring Ho in July.

Other towns include: **Bend** (115, partly in San Saba County); **Izoro** (17); **Kempner** (1,143); **Lometa** (871) market and shipping point; Diamondback Jubilee in March.

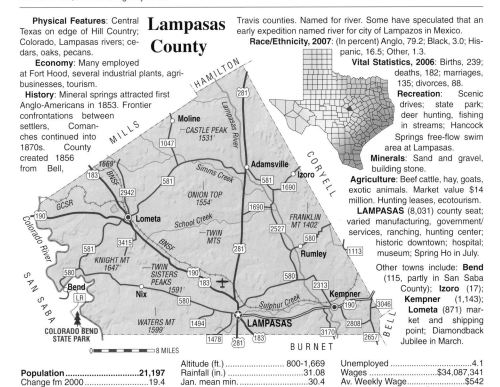

Population 21,197	Altitude (ft.) 800-1,669	Unemployed 4.1
Change fm 2000 .... 19.4	Rainfall (in.) 31.08	Wages $34,087,341
Area (sq. mi.) 713.96	Jan. mean min. 30.4	Av. Weekly Wage $542
Land Area (sq. mi.) 712.04	July mean max. 94.1	Prop. Value $1,099,630,780
	Civ. Labor 10,833	Retail Sales $180,632,005

La Salle County

Physical Features: Brushy plain, broken by Nueces, Frio rivers and their tributaries; chocolate, dark gray, sandy loam soils.

Economy: Agribusiness, hunting leases, tourism, government services.

History: Coahuiltecans, squeezed out by migrating Apaches. U.S. military outpost in 1850s; settlers of Mexican descent established nearby village. Anglo-American ranching developed in 1870s. County created from Bexar District 1858; organized 1880; named for Robert Cavelier Sieur de La Salle, French explorer who died in Texas.

Race/Ethnicity, 2007: (In percent) Anglo, 16.7; Black, 2.9; Hispanic, 79.9; Other, 0.4.

Vital Statistics, 2006: Births, 85; deaths, 51; marriages, 13; divorces, 4.

Recreation: Nature trails; school where Lyndon B. Johnson taught; wildlife management area; deer, bird, javelina hunting, fishing; wild hog cookoff in March.

Minerals: Oil, gas.

Agriculture: Beef cattle, peanuts, watermelons, grain sorghum. Market value $31 million.

COTULLA (3,593) county seat; livestock, state prison; hunting center; Brush Country museum; Cinco de Mayo celebration.

Other towns include: **Encinal** (701), **Fowlerton** (63).

Population	5,861	July mean max.	98.9
Change fm 2000	–0.1	Civ. Labor	3,114
Area (sq. mi.)	1,494.23	Unemployed	6.3
Land Area (sq. mi.)	1,488.85	Wages	$17,395,679
Altitude (ft.)	255-650	Av. Weekly Wage	$768
Rainfall (in.)	22.56	Prop. Value	$462,130,046
Jan. mean min.	39.1	Retail Sales	$78,640,734

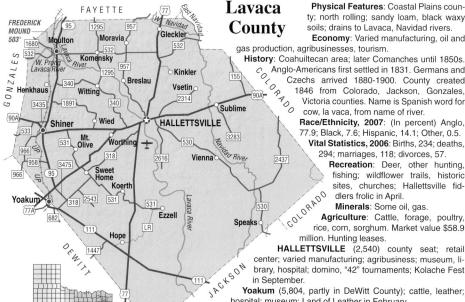

Lavaca County

Physical Features: Coastal Plains county; north rolling; sandy loam, black waxy soils; drains to Lavaca, Navidad rivers.

Economy: Varied manufacturing, oil and gas production, agribusinesses, tourism.

History: Coahuiltecan area; later Comanches until 1850s. Anglo-Americans first settled in 1831. Germans and Czechs arrived 1880-1900. County created 1846 from Colorado, Jackson, Gonzales, Victoria counties. Name is Spanish word for cow, la vaca, from name of river.

Race/Ethnicity, 2007: (In percent) Anglo, 77.9; Black, 7.6; Hispanic, 14.1; Other, 0.5.

Vital Statistics, 2006: Births, 234; deaths, 294; marriages, 118; divorces, 57.

Recreation: Deer, other hunting, fishing; wildflower trails, historic sites, churches; Hallettsville fiddlers frolic in April.

Minerals: Some oil, gas.

Agriculture: Cattle, forage, poultry, rice, corn, sorghum. Market value $58.9 million. Hunting leases.

HALLETTSVILLE (2,540) county seat; retail center; varied manufacturing; agribusiness; museum, library, hospital; domino, "42" tournaments; Kolache Fest in September.

Yoakum (5,804, partly in DeWitt County); cattle, leather; hospital; museum; Land of Leather in February.

Shiner (2,054) Spoetzl brewery, varied manufacturing; museum; clinic; Half Moon Holidays in July.

Other towns include: **Moulton** (949) agribusiness, Town & Country Jamboree in July; **Sublime** (75); **Sweet Home** (360).

Population	18,652	Land Area (sq. mi.)	969.90
Change fm 2000	–2.9	Altitude (ft.)	85-503
Area (sq. mi.)	970.35	Rainfall (in.)	42.23
		Jan. mean min.	41.8
		July mean max.	94.4
		Civ. Labor	10,451
		Unemployed	3.8
		Wages	$48,473,315
		Av. Weekly Wage	$536
		Prop. Value	$1,611,208,999
		Retail Sales	$188,245,551

Lee County

Physical Features: Rolling terrain, broken by Yegua and its tributaries; red to black soils, sandy to heavy loams.

Economy: Varied manufacturing, agribusiness, lignite coal operations, government/services.

History: Tonkawas; removed in 1855 to Brazos Reservation. Most Anglo-American settlement occurred after Texas Revolution. Slaveholding area. Germans, Wends, other Europeans began arriving in 1850s. County created from Bastrop, Burleson, Fayette, Washington counties and organized in 1874; named for Confederate Gen. Robert E. Lee.

Race/Ethnicity, 2007: (In percent) Anglo, 64.6; Black, 11.7; Hispanic, 23.1; Other, 0.7.

Vital Statistics, 2006: Births, 200; deaths, 162; marriages, 103; divorces, 54.

Recreation: Fishing, hunting; state park; pioneer village; historic sites; Giddings food/wine fest in March.

Minerals: Lignite coal, iron ore, gravel.

Agriculture: Beef cattle, hay, nurseries, poultry, peanuts, goats, horses, aquaculture, corn; 25,000 acres irrigated. Market value $40.9 million. Firewood.

GIDDINGS (5,743) county seat; agriculture, oil-field services, light manufacturing, hospital.

Other towns include: **Dime Box** (381); **Lexington** (1,334) livestock-marketing center; **Lincoln** (336); **Serbin** (109) Wendish museum.

Population	16,400
Change fm 2000	4.7
Area (sq. mi.)	634.03
Land Area (sq. mi.)	628.50
Altitude (ft.)	238-762
Rainfall (in.)	36.02
Jan. mean min.	37.3
July mean max.	93.6
Civ. Labor	9,317
Unemployed	4.6
Wages	$48,473,315
Av. Weekly Wage	$668
Prop. Value	$1,262,909,932
Retail Sales	$263,766,336

For explanation of sources, symbols and abbreviations, see p. 210 and foldout map.

Leon County

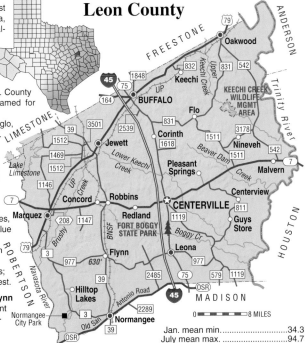

Physical Features: Hilly, rolling, almost half covered by timber; drains to Navasota, Trinity rivers and tributaries; sandy, dark, alluvial soils.

Economy: Oil, gas, agribusiness.

History: Bidais band, absorbed into Kickapoos and other groups. Permanent settlement by Anglo-Americans occurred after Texas Revolution; Germans in 1870s. County created 1846 from Robertson County; named for founder of Victoria, Martín de León.

Race/Ethnicity, 2007: (In percent) Anglo, 79.9; Black, 10.0; Hispanic, 9.5; Other, 0.6.

Vital Statistics, 2006: Births, 198; deaths, 191; marriages, 108; divorces, 70.

Recreation: Lake Limestone resort area; sites of Camino Real, Fort Boggy State Park; deer hunting.

Minerals: Oil, gas, iron ore, lignite.

Agriculture: Cow-calf production, hogs, poultry. Hay, watermelons, vegetables, small grains. Christmas trees. Market value $85.8 million. Hardwoods, pine marketed.

CENTERVILLE (929) county seat; farm center, hunting, tourism, oil, gas, timber.

BUFFALO (1,909) coal mining, oil/gas; library; May Spring Fest with fiddlers' contest.

Other towns include: **Concord** (28); **Flynn** (81); **Hilltop Lakes** (500) resort, retirement center; **Jewett** (960) electricity-generating plant, steel mill, strip mining, civic center, museum, library, Classic Coon Hunt in January; **Leona** (179) candle factory; **Marquez** (221); **Normangee** (762, partly in Madison County) farming, tourism; library, museum, city park; **Oakwood** (483).

Population	16,859
Change fm 2000	9.9
Area (sq. mi.)	1,080.38
Land Area (sq. mi.)	1,072.04
Altitude (ft.)	150-630
Rainfall (in.)	43.08
Jan. mean min.	34.3
July mean max.	94.7
Civ. Labor	7,732
Unemployed	4.9
Wages	$56,462,287
Av. Weekly Wage	$783
Prop. Value	$2,123,075,951
Retail Sales	$175,491,735

Liberty County

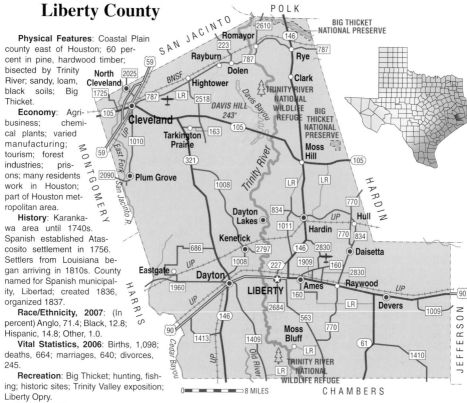

Physical Features: Coastal Plain county east of Houston; 60 percent in pine, hardwood timber; bisected by Trinity River; sandy, loam, black soils; Big Thicket.

Economy: Agribusiness; chemical plants; varied manufacturing; tourism; forest industries; prisons; many residents work in Houston; part of Houston metropolitan area.

History: Karankawa area until 1740s. Spanish established Atascosito settlement in 1756. Settlers from Louisiana began arriving in 1810s. County named for Spanish municipality, Libertad; created 1836, organized 1837.

Race/Ethnicity, 2007: (In percent) Anglo, 71.4; Black, 12.8; Hispanic, 14.8; Other, 1.0.

Vital Statistics, 2006: Births, 1,098; deaths, 664; marriages, 640; divorces, 245.

Recreation: Big Thicket; hunting, fishing; historic sites; Trinity Valley exposition; Liberty Opry.

Minerals: Oil, gas.

Agriculture: Beef cattle; rice is principal crop. Also nursery crops, corn, hay, sorghum. Market value $25.1 million. Some lumbering.

LIBERTY (8,548) county seat; petroleum-related industry, agribusiness; library, museum, regional historical resource depository; Liberty Bell; hospital; Jubilee in March.

Cleveland (8,624) forest products processed, shipped; tourism; library; museum; hospital.

Dayton (7,028) rice, oil center.

Other towns include: **Ames** (1,389); **Daisetta** (1,086); **Dayton Lakes** (93); **Devers** (483); **Hardin** (771); **Hull** (800); **Kenefick** (699); **North Cleveland** (254); **Plum Grove** (986); **Raywood** (231); **Romayor** (135); **Rye** (150).

For explanation of sources, symbols and abbreviations, see p. 210 and foldout map.

Population 75,333
Change fm 2000 .... 7.4
Area (sq. mi.) 1,176.22
Land Area (sq. mi.) 1,159.68
Altitude (ft.) 3-243
Rainfall (in.) 60.52
Jan. mean min. 40.3
July mean max. 92.2
Civ. Labor 32,848
Unemployed 7.1
Wages $148,178,236
Av. Weekly Wage................. $650
Prop. Value $4,425,335,365
Retail Sales $1,121,459,014

The Panhandle landscape at the Ochiltree-Lipscomb county line south of Booker. Robert Plocheck photo.

Limestone County

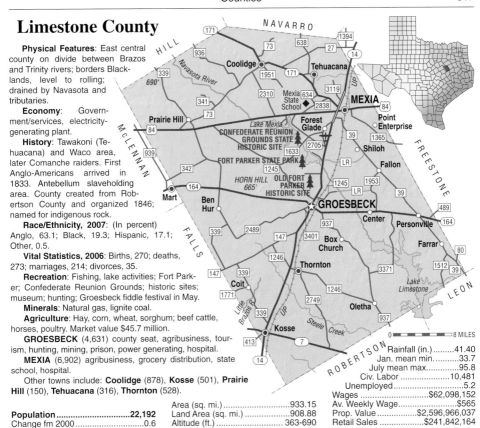

Physical Features: East central county on divide between Brazos and Trinity rivers; borders Blacklands, level to rolling; drained by Navasota and tributaries.

Economy: Government/services, electricity-generating plant.

History: Tawakoni (Tehuacana) and Waco area, later Comanche raiders. First Anglo-Americans arrived in 1833. Antebellum slaveholding area. County created from Robertson County and organized 1846; named for indigenous rock.

Race/Ethnicity, 2007: (In percent) Anglo, 63.1; Black, 19.3; Hispanic, 17.1; Other, 0.5.

Vital Statistics, 2006: Births, 270; deaths, 273; marriages, 214; divorces, 35.

Recreation: Fishing, lake activities; Fort Parker; Confederate Reunion Grounds; historic sites; museum; hunting; Groesbeck fiddle festival in May.

Minerals: Natural gas, lignite coal.

Agriculture: Hay, corn, wheat, sorghum; beef cattle, horses, poultry. Market value $45.7 million.

GROESBECK (4,631) county seat, agribusiness, tourism, hunting, mining, prison, power generating, hospital.

MEXIA (6,902) agribusiness, grocery distribution, state school, hospital.

Other towns include: **Coolidge** (878), **Kosse** (501), **Prairie Hill** (150), **Tehuacana** (316), **Thornton** (528).

Population	22,192
Change fm 2000	0.6

Area (sq. mi.)	933.15
Land Area (sq. mi.)	908.88
Altitude (ft.)	363-690

Rainfall (in.)	41.40
Jan. mean min.	33.7
July mean max.	95.8
Civ. Labor	10,481
Unemployed	5.2
Wages	$62,098,152
Av. Weekly Wage	$565
Prop. Value	$2,596,966,037
Retail Sales	$241,842,164

Lipscomb County

Physical Features: High Plains, broken in east; drains to tributaries of Canadian, Wolf Creek; sandy loam, black soils.

Economy: Oil, gas operations, agribusinesses, government/services.

History: Apaches, later Kiowas and Comanches who were driven into Indian Territory in 1875. Ranching began in late 1870s. County created 1876 from Bexar District; organized 1887; named for A.S. Lipscomb, Republic of Texas leader.

Race/Ethnicity, 2007: (In percent) Anglo, 74.0; Black, 0.4; Hispanic, 24.2; Other, 1.4.

Vital Statistics, 2006: Births, 41; deaths, 30; marriages, 42; divorces, 12.

Recreation: Hunting; Wolf Creek museum.

Minerals: Oil, natural gas.

Agriculture: Cattle, corn, wheat, silage, grain sorghum, hay, sunflowers. Some 19,000 acres irrigated. Market value $80.5 million.

LIPSCOMB (46), county seat; livestock center.

BOOKER (1,332, partly in Ochiltree County) trade center, library.

Other towns include: **Darrouzett** (296) Deutsches Fest in July; **Follett** (399); **Higgins** (423) library, Will Rogers Day in August.

Population	2,981
Change fm 2000	−2.5
Area (sq. mi.)	932.22
Land Area (sq. mi.)	932.11
Altitude (ft.)	2,220-2,892
Rainfall (in.)	22.57
Jan. mean min.	16.2

July mean max.	94.2
Civ. Labor	2,091
Unemployed	3.2
Wages	$13,782,276
Av. Weekly Wage	$764
Prop. Value	$941,310,029
Retail Sales	$26,335,740

Live Oak County

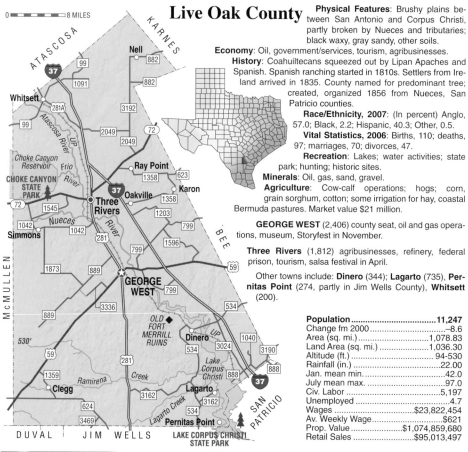

Physical Features: Brushy plains between San Antonio and Corpus Christi, partly broken by Nueces and tributaries; black waxy, gray sandy, other soils.

Economy: Oil, government/services, tourism, agribusinesses.

History: Coahuiltecans squeezed out by Lipan Apaches and Spanish. Spanish ranching started in 1810s. Settlers from Ireland arrived in 1835. County named for predominant tree; created, organized 1856 from Nueces, San Patricio counties.

Race/Ethnicity, 2007: (In percent) Anglo, 57.0; Black, 2.2; Hispanic, 40.3; Other, 0.5.

Vital Statistics, 2006: Births, 110; deaths, 97; marriages, 70; divorces, 47.

Recreation: Lakes; water activities; state park; hunting; historic sites.

Minerals: Oil, gas, sand, gravel.

Agriculture: Cow-calf operations; hogs; corn, grain sorghum, cotton; some irrigation for hay, coastal Bermuda pastures. Market value $21 million.

GEORGE WEST (2,406) county seat, oil and gas operations, museum, Storyfest in November.

Three Rivers (1,812) agribusinesses, refinery, federal prison, tourism, salsa festival in April.

Other towns include: **Dinero** (344); **Lagarto** (735), **Pernitas Point** (274, partly in Jim Wells County), **Whitsett** (200).

Population	**11,247**
Change fm 2000	–8.6
Area (sq. mi.)	1,078.83
Land Area (sq. mi.)	1,036.30
Altitude (ft.)	94-530
Rainfall (in.)	22.00
Jan. mean min.	42.0
July mean max.	97.0
Civ. Labor	5,197
Unemployed	4.7
Wages	$23,822,454
Av. Weekly Wage	$621
Prop. Value	$1,074,859,680
Retail Sales	$95,013,497

Cropland along U.S. 281 south of George West. Robert Plocheck photo.

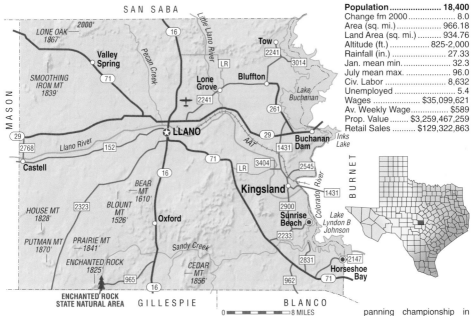

Population 18,400
Change fm 2000 .... 8.0
Area (sq. mi.) 966.18
Land Area (sq. mi.) 934.76
Altitude (ft.) 825-2,000
Rainfall (in.) 27.33
Jan. mean min. 32.3
July mean max. 96.0
Civ. Labor 8,632
Unemployed 5.4
Wages $35,099,621
Av. Weekly Wage............... $589
Prop. Value $3,259,467,259
Retail Sales $129,322,863

Llano County

Physical Features: Central county drains to Colorado, Llano rivers; rolling to hilly; Highland lakes.

Economy: Tourism, retirement, ranch trading center, vineyards.

History: Tonkawas, later Comanches. Anglo-American and German settlers arrived in 1840s. County name is Spanish for plains; created, organized 1856 from Bexar District, Gillespie County.

Race/Ethnicity, 2007: (In percent) Anglo, 93.1; Black, 0.3; Hispanic, 5.9; Other, 0.8.

Vital Statistics, 2006: Births, 144; deaths, 289; marriages, 115; divorces, 72.

Recreation: Leading deer-hunting county; fishing, lake activities, major tourist area, Enchanted Rock, bluebonnet festival, Hill Country Wine Trail in spring.

Minerals: Granite, vermiculite, llanite.

Agriculture: Beef cattle, sheep, goats. Market value $11.8 million. Deer-hunting, wildlife leases.

LLANO (3,840) county seat; agriculture, hunting, tourism; hospital; historic district; museum; Texas gold panning championship in September.

Kingsland (5,249) tourism, retirement community, recreaton, ranching, vineyards; library; archaeological center; AquaBoom on July 4.

Other towns include: **Bluffton** (75); **Buchanan Dam** (1,785) hydroelectric industry, tourism, fishing, water sports; **Castell** (72); **Horseshoe Bay** (3,567, partly in Burnet County); **Sunrise Beach** (790); **Tow** (305); **Valley Spring** (50).

For explanation of sources, symbols and abbreviations, see p. 210 and foldout map.

Loving County

Physical Features: Flat desert terrain with a few low-rolling hills; slopes to Pecos River; Red Bluff Reservoir; sandy, loam, clay soils.

Economy: Petroleum operations; cattle.

History: Land developers began operations in late 19th century. Oil discovered in 1925. County created 1887 from Tom Green County; organized 1931, last county organized. Named for Oliver Loving, trail driver. Loving is Texas' least populous county.

Race/Ethnicity, 2007: (In percent) Anglo, 86.9; Black, 0.0; Hispanic, 13.1; Other, 0.0.

Vital Statistics, 2006: Births, 0; deaths, 0; marriages, 1; divorces, 0.

Recreation: NA.

Minerals: Oil, gas.

Agriculture: Some cattle. Market value not available.

MENTONE (20) county seat, oil-field supply center; only town.

Population 42
Change fm 2000 .... −37.3
Area (sq. mi.) 676.85
Land Area (sq. mi.) 673.08
Altitude (ft.) 2,660-3,374
Rainfall (in.) 9.10
Jan. mean min. 28.0
July mean max. 96.0
Civ. Labor 45
Unemployed 11.1
Wages $762,359
Av. Weekly Wage............... $669
Prop. Value $770,050,980
Retail Sales $0

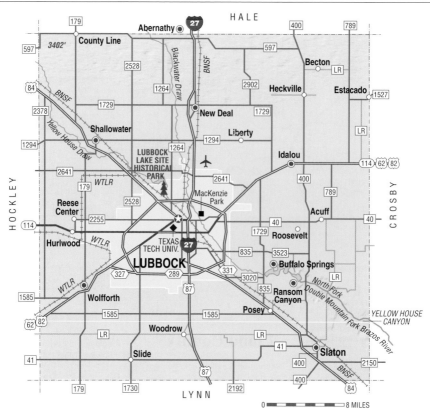

Physical Features: South Plains, broken by 1,500 playas, upper Brazos River tributaries; rich soils with underground water.

Economy: Among world's largest cottonseed processing centers, a leading agribusiness center, cattle feedlots, varied manufacturing, higher education center, medical center, government/services.

History: Evidence of human habitation for 12,000 years. In historic period, Apache Indians, followed by Comanche hunters. Sheep raisers from Midwest arrived in late 1870s. Cotton farms brought in Mexican laborers in 1940s-60s. County named for Col. Tom S. Lubbock, an organizer of Confederate Terry's Rangers; county created 1876 from Bexar District; organized 1891.

Race/Ethnicity, 2007: (In percent) Anglo, 58.1; Black, 7.9; Hispanic, 31.7; Other, 2.3.

Vital Statistics, 2006: Births, 4,049; deaths, 2,031; marriages, 1,988; divorces, 1,122.

Recreation: Lubbock Lake archaeological site; Texas Tech events; civic center; Buddy Holly

Lubbock County

statue, Walk of Fame, festival in September; planetarium; Ranching Heritage Center; Panhandle-South Plains Fair; wine festivals; Buffalo Springs Lake.

Minerals: Oil, gas, stone, sand and gravel.

Agriculture: The leading cotton-producing county. Fed beef, cow-calf operations; poultry; eggs; hogs. Other crops, nursery, grain sorghum, wheat, sunflowers, soybeans, hay, vegetables; more than 230,000 acres irrigated, mostly cotton. Market value $209 million.

Education: Texas Tech University with law and medical schools; Lubbock Christian University; South Plains College branch; Wayland Baptist University off-campus center.

LUBBOCK (218,327) county seat; center for large agricultural area; manufacturing includes electronics, earth-moving equipment, food containers, fire-protection

equipment, clothing, other products; distribution center for South Plains; feedlots; museum; government/services; hospitals, psychiatric hospital; state school for retarded; wind power center.

Other towns include: **Buffalo Springs** (506); **Idalou** (2,247); **New Deal** (975); **Ransom Canyon** (1,143); **Shallowater** (2,362); **Slaton** (6,155) agribusiness, government/services, varied manufacturing, railroad, Harvey House museum, sausagefest in October; **Wolfforth** (3,579) retail, government/services, harvest festival in September.

Also, part of **Abernathy** (2,791).

Population	264,418
Change fm 2000	9.0
Area (sq. mi.)	900.70
Land Area (sq. mi.)	899.49
Altitude (ft.)	2,821-3,402
Rainfall (in.)	18.69
Jan. mean min.	24.4
July mean max.	91.9
Civ. Labor	136,996
Unemployed	3.8
Wages	$1,034,696,751
Av. Weekly Wage	$641
Prop. Value	$13,616,159,864
Retail Sales	$4,220,654,945

For explanation of sources, abbreviations and symbols, see p. 210 and foldout map.

Lynn County

Physical Features: South Plains, broken by Caprock Escarpment, playas, draws; sandy loam, black, gray soils.

Economy: Agribusiness.

History: Apaches, ousted by Comanches who were removed to Indian Territory in 1875. Ranching began in 1880s. Farming developed after 1900. County created 1876 from Bexar District; organized 1903; named for Alamo victim W. Lynn.

Race/Ethnicity, 2007: (In percent) Anglo, 48.0; Black, 2.8; Hispanic, 48.0; Other, 0.8.

Vital Statistics, 2006: Births, 86; deaths, 55; marriages, 30; divorces, 16.

Recreation: Pioneer museum in Tahoka; Dan Blocker museum in O'Donnell; sandhill crane migration in winter.

Minerals: Oil, natural gas.

Agriculture: Cotton produces largest income (second in acreage); 77,000 acres irrigated. Also, ranching, grain sorghum. Market value $98.9 million.

TAHOKA (2,663) county seat; agricultural center, electric/telephone cooperatives; hospital; museum; Harvest Festival in the fall.

O'Donnell (915, partly in Dawson County) commercial center.

Other towns include: **New Home** (337); **Wilson** (483).

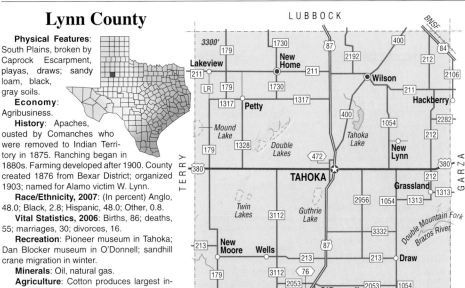

Population	5,783
Change fm 2000	–11.7
Area (sq. mi.)	893.46
Land Area (sq. mi.)	891.88
Altitude (ft.)	2,660-3,300
Rainfall (in.)	20.48
Jan. mean min.	25.1
July mean max.	92.2
Civ. Labor	2,844
Unemployed	4.8
Wages	$8,808,833
Av. Weekly Wage	$500
Prop. Value	$318,697,410
Retail Sales	$19,628,140

Madison County

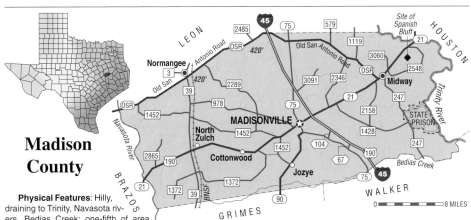

Physical Features: Hilly, draining to Trinity, Navasota rivers, Bedias Creek; one-fifth of area timbered; alluvial, loam, sandy soils.

Economy: Prison, government/services, varied manufacturing, agribusiness, oil production.

History: Caddo, Bidai Indian area; Kickapoos migrated from east. Spanish settlements established in 1774 and 1805. Anglo-Americans arrived in 1829. Census of 1860 showed 30 percent of population was black. County named for U.S. President James Madison; created from Grimes, Leon, Walker counties 1853; organized 1854.

Race/Ethnicity, 2007: (In percent) Anglo, 60.5; Black, 21.7; Hispanic, 17.2; Other, 0.6.

Vital Statistics, 2006: Births, 145; deaths, 136; marriages, 87; divorces, 37.

Recreation: Fishing, hunting; Spanish Bluff where survivors of the Gutiérrez-Magee expedition were executed in 1813; other historic sites.

Minerals: sand, oil.

Agriculture: Nursery crops, cattle, horses, poultry raised; forage for livestock. Market value $83.3 million.

MADISONVILLE (4,481) county seat; farm-trade center, varied manufacturing; hospital, library; Spring Fling in April.

Other towns, **Midway** (297); **Normangee** (762, mostly in Leon County); **North Zulch** (150).

Population	13,382
Change fm 2000	3.4
Area (sq. mi.)	472.44
Land Area (sq. mi.)	469.65
Altitude (ft.)	131-420
Rainfall (in.)	44.00
Jan. mean min.	35.8
July mean max.	96.0
Civ. Labor	5,374
Unemployed	5.2
Wages	$25,974,073
Av. Weekly Wage	$522
Prop. Value	$643,698,901
Retail Sales	$172,052,643

Marion County

Physical Features: Northeastern county; hilly, three-quarters forested with pines, hardwoods; drains to Caddo Lake, Lake O' the Pines, Cypress Bayou.

Economy: Tourism, forestry, food processing.

History: Caddoes forced out in 1790s. Kickapoo in area when settlers arrived from Deep South around 1840. Antebellum slaveholding area. County created 1860 from Cass County; named for Gen. Francis Marion of American Revolution.

Race/Ethnicity, 2007: (In percent) Anglo, 73.4; Black, 23.1; Hispanic, 2.4; Other, 1.1.

Vital Statistics, 2006: Births, 121; deaths, 164; marriages, 100; divorces, 58.

Recreation: Lake activities, hunting, Excelsior Hotel, 84 medallions on historic sites including Jay Gould railroad car, museum, historical homes tour in May, Spring Festival.

Minerals: Iron ore, natural gas, oil.

Agriculture: Hay, beef cattle. Market value $4.2 million. Forestry is most important industry.

JEFFERSON (2,019) county seat; tourism, forestry, recreation; museum, library; historical sites.

Other towns include: **Lodi** (175).

Population	10,544
Change fm 2000	–3.6
Area (sq. mi.)	420.36
Land Area (sq. mi.)	381.21
Altitude (ft.)	168-523
Rainfall (in.)	49.26
Jan. mean min.	31.4
July mean max.	93.1
Civ. Labor	5,464
Unemployed	6.6
Wages	$13,648,309
Av. Weekly Wage	$536
Prop. Value	$658,788,550
Retail Sales	$56,303,909

Martin County

Physical Features: South Plains; sandy, loam soils, broken by playas, creeks.

Economy: Oil and gas production, agribusiness.

History: Apaches, ousted by Comanches who in turn were forced out by U.S. Army 1875. Farming began in 1881. County created from Bexar District 1876; organized 1884; named for Wylie Martin, senator of Republic of Texas.

Race/Ethnicity, 2007: (In percent) Anglo, 54.4; Black, 1.7; Hispanic, 43.6; Other, 0.3.

Vital Statistics, 2006: Births, 66; deaths, 51; marriages, 41; divorces, 22.

Recreation: Museum, settlers reunion.

Minerals: Oil, gas.

Agriculture: Cotton, beef cattle, milo, wheat, horses, meat goats. Market value $52.9 million.

STANTON (2,558) county seat; farm, ranch, oil center; varied manufacturing; electric co-op; commuting to Midland, Big Spring; hospital; restored monastery, other historic buildings; Old Sorehead trade days April, June, October.

Other towns include: **Ackerly** (243, partly in Dawson County); **Lenorah** (83); **Tarzan** (30). A small part of **Midland**.

Population	4,513
Change fm 2000	–4.9
Area (sq. mi.)	915.62
Land Area (sq. mi.)	914.78
Altitude (ft.)	2,470-2,976
Rainfall (in.)	18.20
Jan. mean min.	30.0
July mean max.	94.0
Civ. Labor	2,270
Unemployed	3.5
Wages	$11,121,997
Av. Weekly Wage	$673
Prop. Value	$1,176,010,571
Retail Sales	$48,018,957

Mason County

Physical Features: Central county; hilly, draining to Llano and San Saba rivers and their tributaries; limestone, red soils; varied timber.

Economy: Hunting, nature tourism, agriculture.

History: Lipan Apaches, driven south by Comanches around 1790. German settlers arrived in mid-1840s, followed by Anglo-Americans. Mexican immigration increased after 1930. County created from Bexar, Gillespie counties 1858; named for Mexican War victim U.S. Army Lt. G.T. Mason.

Race/Ethnicity, 2007: (In percent) Anglo, 76.4; Black, 0.3; Hispanic, 22.8; Other, 0.6.

Vital Statistics, 2006: Births, 33; deaths, 44; marriages, 32; divorces, 24.

Recreation: Hunting of deer, turkey, hogs, dove; river fishing; camping; historic homes of stone; prehistoric Indian artifacts exhibit; Fort Mason, where Robert E. Lee served; bat cave; wildflower drives in spring, Old Yeller Day in October.

Minerals: Topaz, sand.

Agriculture: Hay, beef cattle, meat goats, peanuts. Market value $48 million. Hunting leases important.

MASON (2,168) county seat; agriculture, hunting, nature tourism; museums, historical district, homes, rock fences built by German settlers; wild game dinner in November.

Other towns include: **Art** (14), **Fredonia** (55), **Pontotoc** (125).

Population	3,882
Change fm 2000	3.8
Area (sq. mi.)	932.18
Land Area (sq. mi.)	932.07
Altitude (ft.)	1,180-2,217
Rainfall (in.)	27.95
Jan. mean min.	30.8
July mean max.	94.9
Civ. Labor	2,449
Unemployed	3.1
Wages	$6,720,195
Av. Weekly Wage	$466
Prop. Value	$257,785,865
Retail Sales	$22,268,289

For explanation of sources, symbols and abbreviations, see p. 210 and foldout map.

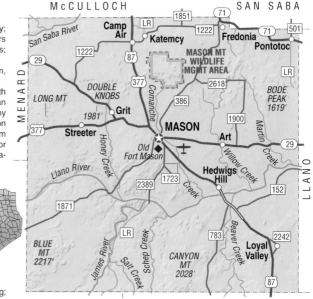

The Carmelite monastery built in 1884 in Stanton and abandoned in 1938. Robert Plocheck photo.

Matagorda County

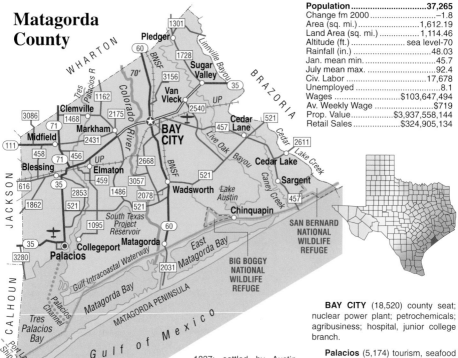

Population	37,265
Change fm 2000	–1.8
Area (sq. mi.)	1,612.19
Land Area (sq. mi.)	1,114.46
Altitude (ft.)	sea level-70
Rainfall (in.)	48.03
Jan. mean min.	45.7
July mean max.	92.4
Civ. Labor	17,678
Unemployed	8.1
Wages	$103,647,494
Av. Weekly Wage	$719
Prop. Value	$3,937,558,144
Retail Sales	$324,905,134

Physical Features: Gulf Coastal Plain; flat, broken by bays; many different soils; drains to Colorado River, creeks, coast.

Economy: Nuclear power plant, petrochemicals, agribusiness.

History: Karankawa Indian area, Tonkawas later. Anglo-Americans arrived in 1822. Mexican immigration increased after 1920. An original county, created 1836 from Spanish municipality, named for canebrake; organized 1837; settled by Austin colonists.

Race/Ethnicity, 2007: (In percent) Anglo, 48.2; Black, 12.4; Hispanic, 35.8; Other, 3.5.

Vital Statistics, 2006: Births, 587; deaths, 326; marriages, 247; divorces, 130.

Recreation: Fishing, water sports, hunting, birding; historic sites, museums; Bay City rice festival in October.

Minerals: Oil and gas.

Agriculture: Cattle, cotton, rice (third in acreage), sorghum, soybeans; 24,000 acres irrigated for rice. Market value $106.8 million. First in value of aquaculture.

BAY CITY (18,520) county seat; nuclear power plant; petrochemicals; agribusiness; hospital, junior college branch.

Palacios (5,174) tourism, seafood industry; hospital; Marine Education Center; public fishing piers; Bay Festival on Labor Day.

Other towns include: **Blessing** (871) historic sites; **Cedar Lane** (300); **Collegeport** (80); **Elmaton** (160); **Markham** (1,074); **Matagorda** (710); **Midfield** (305); **Pledger** (265); **Sargent** (900) retirement community, fishing, birding, commercial fishing, barbecue cookoff in April; **Van Vleck** (1,338); **Wadsworth** (160).

For explanation of sources, symbols and abbreviations, see p. 210 and foldout map.

Youngsters at Matagorda prepare to board a boat that offers educational workshops. Robert Plocheck photo.

The Maverick County Courthouse in Eagle Pass. Robert Plocheck photo.

Maverick County

Physical Features: Southwestern county on Rio Grande; broken, rolling surface, with dense brush; clay, sandy, alluvial soils.

Economy: Oil, government/services, agribusiness, tourism.

History: Coahuiltecan Indian area; later Comanches in area. Spanish ranching began in 1760s. First Anglo-Americans arrived in 1834. County named for Sam A. Maverick, whose name is now a synonym for unbranded cattle; created 1856 from Kinney County; organized 1871.

Race/Ethnicity, 2007: (In percent) Anglo, 3.1; Black, 0.1; Hispanic, 95.4; Other, 1.4.

Vital Statistics, 2006: Births, 1,093; deaths, 300; marriages, 521; divorces, 40.

Recreation: Tourist gateway to Mexico; white-tailed deer, bird hunting; fishing; historic sites, Fort Duncan museum.

Minerals: Oil, gas, sand, gravel.

Agriculture: Cattle feedlots; pecans, vegetables, sorghum, wheat; goats, sheep. Some irrigation from Rio Grande. Market value $26.1 million.

EAGLE PASS (25,859) county seat; government/services, retail center, tourism; hospital; junior college, Sul Ross college branch; entry point to Piedras Negras, Mex., Nacho Festival in Piedras Negras in October.

Other communities include: **Eidson Road** (9,956), **El Indio** (284), **Las Quintas Fronterizas** (2,164), **Rosita North** (3,625); **Rosita South** (2,951), all immediately south of Eagle Pass.

Also, **Elm Creek** (2,233) and **Quemado** (264).

Population	52,279
Change fm 2000	10.5
Area (sq. mi.)	1,291.74
Land Area (sq. mi.)	1,280.08
Altitude (ft.)	550-975
Rainfall (in.)	21.48

Jan. mean min.	40.1
July mean max.	98.1
Civ. Labor	21,472
Unemployed	12.6
Wages	$100,517,381
Av. Weekly Wage	$499

Prop. Value	$1,646,668,172
Retail Sales	$549,827,218

McCulloch County

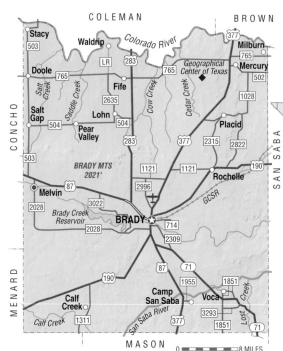

Physical Features: Hilly and rolling; drains to Colorado, Brady Creek and Lake, San Saba River; black loams to sandy soils.

Economy: Agribusiness, manufacturing, tourism, hunting leases.

History: Apache area. First Anglo-American settlers arrived in late 1850s, but Comanche raids delayed further settlement until 1870s. County created from Bexar District 1856; organized 1876; named for San Jacinto veteran Gen. Ben McCulloch.

Race/Ethnicity, 2007: (In percent) Anglo, 69.0; Black, 1.5; Hispanic, 29.0; Other, 0.5.

Vital Statistics, 2006: Births, 93; deaths, 100; marriages, 13; divorces, 49.

Recreation: Hunting; lake activities; museum, restored Santa Fe depot, goat cookoff on Labor Day, muzzle-loading rifle association state championship; rodeos; golf, tennis tournaments.

Minerals: Sand, gravel, gas and oil.

Agriculture: Beef cattle provide most income; wheat, sheep, goats, hay, cotton, sorghum, hogs, dairy cattle; some irrigation for peanuts. Market value $18.1 million.

BRADY (5,519) county seat; silica sand, oilfield equipment, ranching, tourism, other manufacturing; hospital; Heart of Texas car show in April, Cinco de Mayo.

Other towns: **Doole** (74), **Lohn** (149), **Melvin** (149), **Mercury** (166), **Rochelle** (163) and **Voca** (56).

Population 7,943	July mean max. 94.5
Change fm 2000 .... –3.2	Civ. Labor 4,070
Area (sq. mi.) 1,073.35	Unemployed 4.3
Land Area (sq. mi.) 1,069.31	Wages $22,590,499
Altitude (ft.) 1,280-2,021	Av. Weekly Wage $559
Rainfall (in.) 27.63	Prop. Value $386,895,390
Jan. mean min. 32.3	Retail Sales $80,468,150

The site of the Spanish presidio along the San Saba River in Menard County. In 1936 this portion of the walls was reconstructed using an 1847 description as a guide. Robert Plocheck photo.

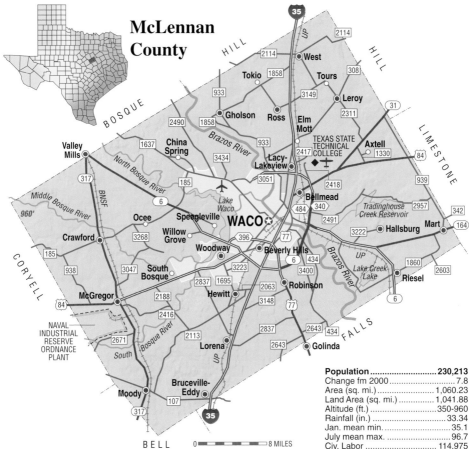

McLennan County

Population 230,213
Change fm 2000 .... 7.8
Area (sq. mi.) 1,060.23
Land Area (sq. mi.) 1,041.88
Altitude (ft.) 350-960
Rainfall (in.) 33.34
Jan. mean min. 35.1
July mean max. 96.7
Civ. Labor 114,975
Unemployed 4.8
Wages $919,285,500
Av. Weekly Wage...................... $685
Prop. Value $11,332,509,778
Retail Sales $2,995,101,910

Physical Features: Central Texas county of mostly Blackland prairie, but rolling hills in west; drains to Bosque, Brazos rivers and Lake Waco; heavy, loam, sandy soils.

Economy: A leading distribution, government center for Central Texas; diversified manufacturing; agribusiness; education; aerospace; health care.

History: Tonkawas, Wichitas and Wacos in area. Anglo-American settlers arrived in 1840s. Indians removed to Brazos reservations in 1854. County created from Milam County in 1850; named for settler, Neil McLennan Sr.

Race/Ethnicity, 2007: (In percent) Anglo, 58.5; Black, 15.5; Hispanic, 24.0; Other, 2.0.

Vital Statistics, 2006: Births, 3,264; deaths, 2,023; marriages, 1,850; divorces, 915.

Recreation: Texas Ranger Hall of Fame; Texas Sports Hall of Fame; Dr Pepper Museum; Cameron Park; drag boat races April and May; zoo; historic sites, homes; museums; libraries, art center; symphony; civic theater; Baylor University events; Heart o' Texas Fair in October.

Minerals: Sand and gravel, limestone, oil, gas.

Agriculture: Poultry, beef cattle, corn, wheat, hay, grain sorghum, soybeans, dairy cattle. Market value $104.7 million.

Education: Baylor University; community college; Texas State Technical College.

WACO (120,577) county seat; higher education, government/services, varied manufacturing; hospitals; riverside park; zoo.

Hewitt (13,634) iron works, other manufacturing; hamburger cookoff in September.

West (2,780) famous for Czech foods; varied manufacturing; Westfest Labor Day weekend.

Other towns include: **Axtell** (300); **Bellmead** (9,367); **Beverly Hills** (2,059); **Bruceville-Eddy** (1,570, partly in Falls County); **China Spring** (1,000); **Crawford** (751); **Elm Mott** (300); **Gholson** (971); **Hallsburg** (528); **Lacy-Lakeview** (6,104); **Leroy** (338); **Lorena** (1,621); **Mart** (2,446) agricultural center, some manufacturing, museum, juvenile correction facility; **McGregor** (4,786) agriculture, manufacturing, distribution; private telephone museum; Frontier Founders Day in September; **Moody** (1,441) agriculture, commuting to Waco, Temple; library; Cotton Harvest fest in September; **Riesel** (1,003); **Robinson** (10,570); **Ross** (232); **Woodway** (9,013).

Part of **Golinda** (451, mostly in Falls County) and part of **Valley Mills** (1,163, mostly in Bosque County).

For explanation of sources, abbreviations and symbols, see p. 210 and foldout map.

McMullen County

Physical Features: Southern county of brushy plain, sloping to Frio, Nueces rivers and tributaries; saline clay soils.

Economy: Government/services, retail, agriculture.

History: Coahuiltecans, squeezed out by Lipan Apaches and other tribes. Anglo-American settlers arrived in 1858. Sheep ranching of 1870s attracted Mexican laborers. County created from Atascosa, Bexar, Live Oak counties 1858; organized 1862, reorganized 1877; named for Nueces River pioneer-empresario John McMullen.

Race/Ethnicity, 2007: (In percent) Anglo, 64.5; Black, 1.5; Hispanic, 33.6; Other, 0.3.

Vital Statistics, 2006: Births, 7; deaths, 8; marriages, 4; divorces, 1.

Recreation: Hunting, wildlife viewing; lake activities, state park; Labor Day rodeo.

Minerals: Gas, oil, lignite coal, caliche, kaolinite.

Agriculture: Beef cattle, grain sorghum. Market value $8.8 million. Wildlife enterprises important.

TILDEN (300), county seat; oil, gas, lignite mining, ranch center, government/services. Other towns include: **Calliham** (100).

Population		837
Change fm 2000		–1.6
Area (sq. mi.)		1,142.60
Land Area (sq. mi.)		1,113.00
Altitude (ft.)		150-642
Rainfall (in.)		23.87

Jan. mean min.	40.1
July mean max.	98.7
Civ. Labor	350
Unemployed	7.4

Wages	$1,871,880
Av. Weekly Wage	$707
Prop. Value	$409,777,296
Retail Sales	$5,780,572

Medina County

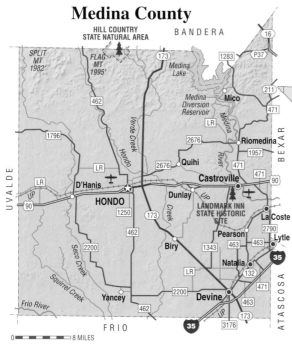

Physical Features: Southwestern county with scenic hills in north; south has fertile valleys, rolling surface; Medina River, Lake.

Economy: Agribusiness, tourism, varied manufacturing, commuters to San Antonio, government/services.

History: Lipan Apaches and Comanches. Settled by Alsatians led by Henri Castro in 1844. Mexican immigration increased after 1900. County created 1848 from Bexar; named for river, probably for Spanish engineer Pedro Medina.

Race/Ethnicity, 2007: (In percent) Anglo, 50.2; Black, 1.7; Hispanic, 47.2; Other, 0.9.

Vital Statistics, 2006: Births, 574; deaths, 331; marriages, 228; divorces, 135.

Recreation: A leading deer area; scenic drives, camping, fishing, historic buildings, museum, market trail days most months.

Minerals: Oil, gas, clay, sand, gravel.

Agriculture: Cattle, corn, grains, cotton, hay, vegetables; 40,000 acres irrigated. Market value $80.9 million.

HONDO (9,142) county seat; Air Force screening center, aerospace industry, agribusiness, varied manufacturing, hunting leases; hospital; prisons.

Castroville (2,997) farming; tourism; commuting to San Antonio; Landmark Inn, museum; St. Louis Day celebration in August.

Devine (4,423) commuters, shipping for truck crop-livestock; fall festival in October.

Other towns: **D'Hanis** (575), **La Coste** (1,392), **Natalia** (1,931), **Riomedina** (60), **Yancey** (209). Also, **Lytle** (2,815, mostly in Atascosa County).

Population	44,275
Change fm 2000	12.6
Area (sq. mi.)	1,334.53
Land Area (sq. mi.)	1,327.76
Altitude (ft.)	570-1,995
Rainfall (in.)	26.30
Jan. mean min.	38.0
July mean max.	95.0
Civ. Labor	20,489

Unemployed	5.4
Wages	$55,591,456
Av. Weekly Wage	$517
Prop. Value	$1,966,643,564
Retail Sales	$327,519,880

For explanation of sources, abbreviations and symbols, see p. 210 and foldout map.

Menard County

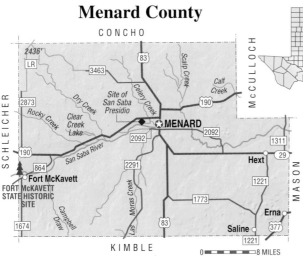

CONCHO

SCHLEICHER

McCULLOCH

MASON

KIMBLE

0 ▬▬▬▬ 8 MILES

Physical Features: West central county of rolling topography, draining to San Saba River and tributaries; limestone soils.

Economy: Agribusiness, tourism, oil, gas production.

History: Apaches, followed by Comanches in 18th century. Mission Santa Cruz de San Sabá established in 1757. A few Anglo-American and German settlers arrived in 1840s. County created from Bexar County in 1858, organized 1871; named for Galveston's founder, Michel B. Menard.

Race/Ethnicity, 2007: (In percent) Anglo, 65.6; Black, 0.3; Hispanic, 33.2; Other, 1.0.

Vital Statistics, 2006: Births, 26; deaths, 39; marriages, 7; divorces, 2.

Recreation: Hunting, fishing; historic sites, including Spanish presidio, mission, irrigation ditches; U.S. fort; museum; Jim Bowie days in September.

Minerals: Oil, gas.

Agriculture: Cattle, wildlife, goats, sheep, pecans. Market value $7.9 million.

MENARD (1,617) county seat; ranching center, tourism. Other towns include: **Fort McKavett** (50); **Hext** (75).

Population	2,138
Change fm 2000	–9.4
Area (sq. mi.)	902.25
Land Area (sq. mi.)	901.91
Altitude (ft.)	1,690-2,436
Rainfall (in.)	24.90
Jan. mean min.	30.7
July mean max.	94.8
Civ. Labor	1,226
Unemployed	3.7
Wages	$2,967,751
Av. Weekly Wage	$420
Prop. Value	$121,650,830
Retail Sales	$12,924,616

St. Louis Church, built in 1870, in Castroville, Medina County. Robert Plocheck photo.

Midland County

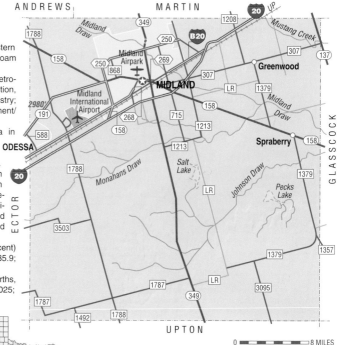

Physical Features: Flat western county, broken by draws; sandy, loam soils with native grasses.

Economy: Among leading petroleum-producing counties; distribution, administrative center for oil industry; varied manufacturing; government/services.

History: Comanches in area in 19th century. Sheep ranching developed in 1880s. Permian Basin oil boom began in 1920s. County created from Tom Green County 1885; name came from midway location on railroad between El Paso and Fort Worth. Chihuahua Trail and Emigrant Road were pioneer trails that crossed county.

Race/Ethnicity, 2007: (In percent) Anglo, 55.2; Black, 7.1; Hispanic, 35.9; Other, 1.8.

Vital Statistics, 2006: Births, 1,918; deaths, 912; marriages, 1,025; divorces, 603.

Recreation: Permian Basin Petroleum Museum, Library, Hall of Fame; Museum of Southwest; Commemorative Air Force and Museum; community theater; metropolitan events; homes of Presidents Bush.

Minerals: Oil, natural gas.

Agriculture: Beef cattle, horses, sheep and goats; cotton, hay, pecans; 20,000 acres irrigated. Market value $15.4 million.

MIDLAND (102,691) county seat; petroleum, petrochemical center; varied manufacturing; livestock sale center; hospitals; cultural activities; community college; polo club, Texas League baseball; Celebration of the Arts in May.

Part [1,042] of **Odessa**.

Population	129,494
Change fm 2000	11.6
Area (sq. mi.)	901.97
Land Area (sq. mi.)	900.25

Altitude (ft.)	2,550-2,980
Rainfall (in.)	14.80
Jan. mean min.	29.6
July mean max.	94.3
Civ. Labor	72,405
Unemployed	3.1
Wages	$882,592,624
Av. Weekly Wage	$984
Prop. Value	$9,956,264,750
Retail Sales	$2,375,981,797

For explanation of sources, abbreviations and symbols, see p. 210 and foldout map.

The skyline of Midland. Robert Plocheck photo.

Milam County

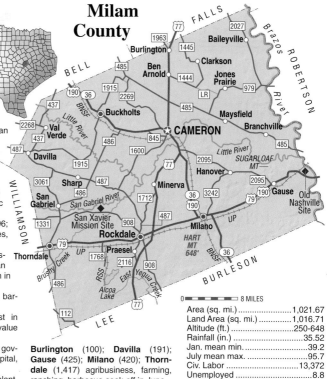

Physical Features: East central county of partly level Blackland; southeast rolling to Post Oak Belt; Brazos, Little rivers.

Economy: Lignite mining, aluminum, other manufacturing, agribusiness.

History: Lipan Apaches, Tonkawas and Comanches in area. Mission San Francisco Xavier established in 1745-48. Anglo-American settlers arrived in 1834. County created 1836 from municipality named for Ben Milam, a leader who died at the battle for San Antonio in December 1835; organized 1837.

Race/Ethnicity, 2007: (In percent) Anglo, 65.9; Black, 11.4; Hispanic 22.0; Other, 0.7.

Vital Statistics, 2006: Births, 396; deaths, 335; marriages, 186; divorces, 114.

Recreation: Fishing, hunting; historic sites include Fort Sullivan, Indian battlegrounds, mission sites; museum in old jail at Cameron.

Minerals: Large lignite deposits, barite, limited oil and gas production.

Agriculture: Cattle, poultry (first in number of turkeys), corn. Market value $105.3 million.

CAMERON (6,275) county seat; government/services, manufacturing; hospital, library; dewberry festival in April.

ROCKDALE (5,872) aluminum plant, government/services; hospital, juvenile detention center.

Other towns include: **Buckholts** (448); **Burlington** (100); **Davila** (191); **Gause** (425); **Milano** (420); **Thorndale** (1,417) agribusiness, farming, ranching, barbecue cook-off in June.

Population 24,892
Change fm 2000 .... 2.7

Area (sq. mi.)	1,021.67
Land Area (sq. mi.)	1,016.71
Altitude (ft.)	250-648
Rainfall (in.)	35.52
Jan. mean min.	39.2
July mean max.	95.7
Civ. Labor	13,372
Unemployed	8.8
Wages	$62,517,994
Av. Weekly Wage	$707
Prop. Value	$1,522,193,580
Retail Sales	$167,398,344

Mills County

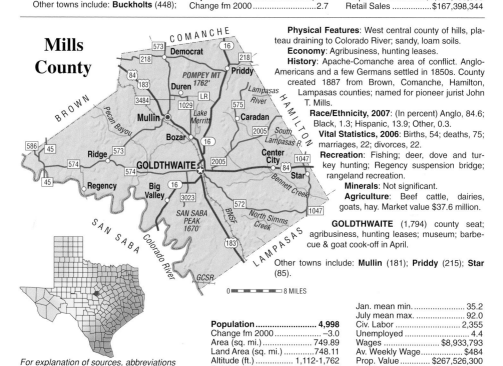

Physical Features: West central county of hills, plateau draining to Colorado River; sandy, loam soils.

Economy: Agribusiness, hunting leases.

History: Apache-Comanche area of conflict. Anglo-Americans and a few Germans settled in 1850s. County created 1887 from Brown, Comanche, Hamilton, Lampasas counties; named for pioneer jurist John T. Mills.

Race/Ethnicity, 2007: (In percent) Anglo, 84.6; Black, 1.3; Hispanic, 13.9; Other, 0.3.

Vital Statistics, 2006: Births, 54; deaths, 75; marriages, 22; divorces, 22.

Recreation: Fishing; deer, dove and turkey hunting; Regency suspension bridge; rangeland recreation.

Minerals: Not significant.

Agriculture: Beef cattle, dairies, goats, hay. Market value $37.6 million.

GOLDTHWAITE (1,794) county seat; agribusiness, hunting leases; museum; barbecue & goat cook-off in April.

Other towns include: **Mullin** (181); **Priddy** (215); **Star** (85).

For explanation of sources, abbreviations and symbols, see p. 210 and foldout map.

Population 4,998
Change fm 2000 .... −3.0
Area (sq. mi.) 749.89
Land Area (sq. mi.) 748.11
Altitude (ft.) 1,112-1,762
Rainfall (in.) 28.78

Jan. mean min.	35.2
July mean max.	92.0
Civ. Labor	2,355
Unemployed	4.4
Wages	$8,933,793
Av. Weekly Wage	$484
Prop. Value	$267,526,300
Retail Sales	$88,621,402

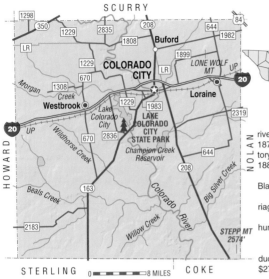

Mitchell County

Physical Features: Rolling, draining to Colorado and tributaries; sandy, red, dark soils; Lake Colorado City and Champion Creek Reservoir.

Economy: Government/services, agribusiness, oil, some manufacturing.

History: Jumano Indians in area; Comanches arrived about 1780. Anglo-American settlers arrived in late 1870s after Comanches were forced into Indian Territory. County created 1876 from Bexar District; organized 1881; named for pioneer brothers Asa and Eli Mitchell.

Race/Ethnicity, 2007: (In percent) Anglo, 52.8; Black, 12.6; Hispanic, 33.8; Other, 0.8.

Vital Statistics, 2006: Births, 96; deaths, 88; marriages, 47; divorces, 29.

Recreation: Lake activities, state park, museums, hunting, Colorado City playhouse.

Minerals: Oil.

Agriculture: Cotton principal crop, grains also produced. Cattle, sheep, goats, hogs raised. Market value $27.3 million.

COLORADO CITY (4,359) county seat; prisons, manufacturing, tourism, electric service center; hospital; boar goat cook-off in October.

Other towns include: **Loraine** (636) and **Westbrook** (202), trade centers.

Population	9,230
Change fm 2000	–4.8
Area (sq. mi.)	915.90
Land Area (sq. mi.)	910.04
Altitude (ft.)	1,930-2,574
Rainfall (in.)	19.43
Jan. mean min.	27.0
July mean max.	95.9
Civ. Labor	3,362
Unemployed	5.6
Wages	$17,376,320
Av. Weekly Wage	$591
Prop. Value	$627,974,253
Retail Sales	$37,640,495

Montague County

Physical Features: Rolling, draining to tributaries of Trinity, Red rivers; sandy loams, red, black soils; Lake Nocona, Lake Amon G. Carter.

Economy: Agribusiness, oil, varied manufacturing, government/services.

History: Kiowas and Wichitas who allied with Comanches. Anglo-American settlements developed in 1850s. County created from Cooke County 1857, organized 1858; named for pioneer Daniel Montague.

Race/Ethnicity, 2007: (In percent) Anglo, 92.0; Black, 0.1; Hispanic, 6.8; Other, 1.0.

Vital Statistics, 2006: Births, 253; deaths, 233; marriages, 130; divorces, 95.

Recreation: Lake activities; quail, turkey, deer hunting; scenic drives; museums; historical sites.

Minerals: Oil, rock, limestone.

Agriculture: Beef, hay, wheat, dairies, pecans, peaches, melons. Market value $36.6 million.

MONTAGUE (400) county seat.

BOWIE (5,516) varied manufacturing, livestock, hospital, library; Jim Bowie Days in June.

NOCONA (3,412) athletic goods, boot manufacturing; hospital; Fun Day each May, Chisholm Trail rodeo in September.

Other towns include: **Forestburg** (50); **Ringgold** (100); **Saint Jo** (1,001) farm center, saloon, Pioneer Days in May; **Sunset** (349).

Population	19,716
Change fm 2000	3.2
Area (sq. mi.)	938.44
Land Area (sq. mi.)	930.66
Altitude (ft.)	715-1,318
Rainfall (in.)	33.72
Jan. mean min.	28.3
July mean max.	94.7
Civ. Labor	10,953
Unemployed	3.9
Wages	$41,758,049
Av. Weekly Wage	$610
Prop. Value	$1,156,852,630
Retail Sales	$183,810,606

Montgomery County

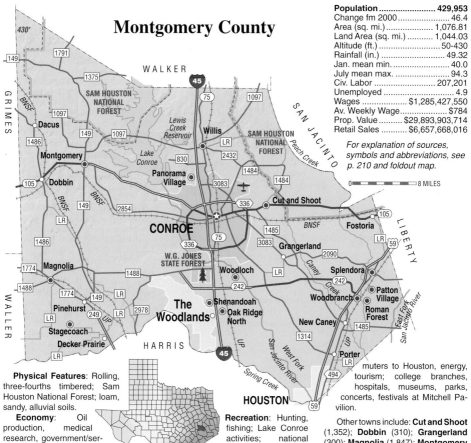

Population	429,953
Change fm 2000	46.4
Area (sq. mi.)	1,076.81
Land Area (sq. mi.)	1,044.03
Altitude (ft.)	50-430
Rainfall (in.)	49.32
Jan. mean min.	40.0
July mean max.	94.3
Civ. Labor	207,201
Unemployed	4.9
Wages	$1,285,427,550
Av. Weekly Wage	$784
Prop. Value	$29,893,903,714
Retail Sales	$6,657,668,016

For explanation of sources, symbols and abbreviations, see p. 210 and foldout map.

Physical Features: Rolling, three-fourths timbered; Sam Houston National Forest; loam, sandy, alluvial soils.

Economy: Oil production, medical research, government/services, many residents work in Houston.

History: Orcoquisacs and Bidais, removed from area by 1850s. Anglo-Americans arrived in 1820s as part of Austin's colony. County created 1837 from Washington County; named for Richard Montgomery, American Revolution general.

Race/Ethnicity, 2007: (In percent) Anglo, 78.3; Black, 3.7; Hispanic, 16.1; Other, 1.9.

Vital Statistics, 2006: Births, 5,169; deaths, 2,566; marriages, 2,777; divorces, 1,582.

Recreation: Hunting, fishing; Lake Conroe activities; national and state forests; hiking, boating, horseback riding; historic sites.

Minerals: Natural gas.

Agriculture: Greenhouse crops, forage, horses, beef cattle, goats. Market value $42.6 million. Timber is primary industry.

CONROE (55,129) county seat; retail/wholesale center, government/services, manufacturing, commuters to Houston; hospitals, community college, museum; Cajun catfish festival in October.

The Woodlands (67,971) commuters to Houston, energy, tourism; college branches, hospitals, museums, parks, concerts, festivals at Mitchell Pavilion.

Other towns include: **Cut and Shoot** (1,352); **Dobbin** (310); **Grangerland** (300); **Magnolia** (1,847); **Montgomery** (867) commuters to Houston and Conroe, antiques stores, pioneer museum, historic homes tour in April; **New Caney** (6,800); **Oak Ridge North** (3,842); **Panorama Village** (2,472); **Patton Village** (1,695); **Pinehurst** (5,319); **Porter** (4,200); **Porter Heights** (1,754); **Roman Forest** (3,627); **Shenandoah** (2,295); **Splendora** 1,654; **Stagecoach** (602); **Willis** (4,799) commuters to Conroe and Houston; **Woodbranch** (1,523); **Woodloch** (287).

Also, part [458] of **Houston** [Kingwood], hospital.

The business district in Forestburg, Montague County. Robert Plocheck photo.

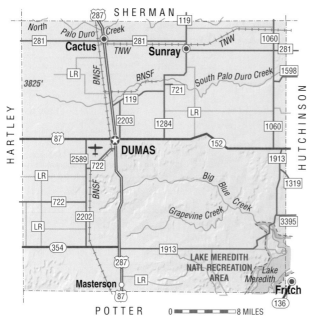

Moore County

Physical Features: Flat to rolling, broken by creeks; sandy loams; lake.

Economy: Varied agribusiness, petroleum, natural gas.

History: Comanches, removed to Indian Territory in 1874-75; ranching began soon afterward. Farming developed after 1910. Oil boom in 1920s. County created 1876 from Bexar District; organized 1892; named for Republic of Texas navy commander E.W. Moore.

Race/Ethnicity, 2007: (In percent) Anglo, 44.7; Black, 0.5; Hispanic, 53.4; Other, 1.4.

Vital Statistics, 2006: Births, 437; deaths, 144; marriages, 151; divorces, 92.

Recreation: Lake Meredith activities; pheasant, deer, quail hunting; historical museum; arts center; free overnight RV park; Dogie Days in June.

Minerals: Oil and gas.

Agriculture: Fed beef, corn, wheat, stocker cattle, sorghum, cotton, soybeans, sunflowers. Market value $463.2 million. Irrigation of 162,000 acres.

DUMAS (13,669) county seat; tourism, retail trade, varied agribusiness; hospital, hospice, retirement complex.

Other towns include: **Cactus** (2,804), **Sunray** (1,897). Small part of **Fritch**.

For explanation of sources, symbols and abbreviations, see p. 210 and foldout map.

Population	20,308
Change fm 2000	0.9
Area (sq. mi.)	909.61
Land Area (sq. mi.)	899.66
Altitude (ft.)	2,915-3,825
Rainfall (in.)	17.75
Jan. mean min.	20.8

July mean max.	91.7
Civ. Labor	10,904
Unemployed	3.4
Wages	$84,452,280
Av. Weekly Wage	$643
Prop. Value	$2,382,067,574
Retail Sales	$363,724,116

Prairie and hills of Motley County. Robert Plocheck photo.

Morris County

Physical Features: East Texas county of forested hills; drains to streams, lakes.

Economy: Steel manufacturing, agriculture, timber, government/services.

History: Caddo Indians until 1790s. Kickapoo and other tribes in area 1820s-30s. Anglo-American settlement began in mid-1830s. Antebellum slaveholding area. County named for legislator-jurist W.W. Morris; created from Titus County and organized in 1875.

Race/Ethnicity, 2007: (In percent) Anglo, 69.6; Black, 25.1; Hispanic, 4.4; Other, 0.9.

Vital Statistics, 2006: Births, 162; deaths, 180; marriages, 110; divorces, 71.

Recreation: Activities on Lake O' the Pines, small lakes; fishing, hunting; state park.

Minerals: Iron ore.

Agriculture: Beef cattle, broiler production, hay. Market value $38.6 million. Timber industry significant.

DAINGERFIELD (2,589) county seat; varied manufacturing; library, museum, city park, historic theater; Northeast Texas Community College; Daingerfield Days in October.

Other towns include: **Cason** (173); **Lone Star** (1,695) oil-field equipment manufactured, catfish farming, Starfest in September; **Naples** (1,445) trailer manufacturing, livestock, watermelon festival in July; **Omaha** (1,133), retail center, government/services, commuters.

Population	**12,915**
Change fm 2000	–1.0
Area (sq. mi.)	258.64
Land Area (sq. mi.)	254.51
Altitude (ft.)	228-614
Rainfall (in.)	46.76
Jan. mean min.	33.7
July mean max.	95.0
Civ. Labor	6,349
Unemployed	7.2
Wages	$54,688,161
Av. Weekly Wage	$881
Prop. Value	$944,180,280
Retail Sales	$67,416,016

For explanation of sources, symbols and abbreviations, see p. 210 and foldout map.

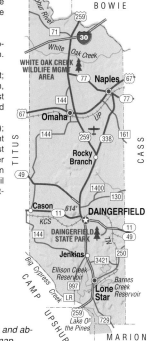

Motley County

Physical Features: Western county just below Caprock; rough terrain, broken by Pease tributaries; sandy to red clay soils.

Economy: Government/services, ranching and farming, light manufacturing.

History: Comanches, removed to Indian Territory by U.S. Army in 1874-75. Ranching began in late 1870s. County created out of Bexar District 1876; organized 1891; named for Dr. J.W. Mottley, signer of Texas Declaration of Independence (name misspelled in statute).

Race/Ethnicity, 2007: (In percent) Anglo, 82.2; Black, 3.8; Hispanic, 13.3; Other, 0.8.

Vital Statistics, 2006: Births, 12; deaths, 23; marriages, 7; divorces, 1.

Recreation: Quail, dove, turkey, deer hunting; Matador Ranch headquarters; spring-fed pool at Roaring Springs; Motley-Dickens settlers reunion in August at Roaring Springs.

Minerals: Minimal.

Agriculture: Beef cattle, cotton, wheat, hay, sorghum. Some irrigation. Market value $16.4 million. Hunting leases important.

MATADOR (767) county seat; farm trade center; museum, historic oil-derrick gas station; motorcycle race in March.

Other towns include: **Flomot** (181) bluegrass festival in May, and **Roaring Springs** (272).

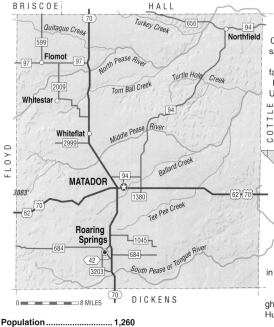

Population	**1,260**
Change fm 2000	–11.6
Area (sq. mi.)	989.81
Land Area (sq. mi.)	989.38
Altitude (ft.)	1,800-3,083
Rainfall (in.)	22.90
Jan. mean min.	27.3
July mean max.	94.8
Civ. Labor	757
Unemployed	4.0
Wages	$2,239,477
Av. Weekly Wage	$439
Prop. Value	$77,632,897
Retail Sales	$5,260,936

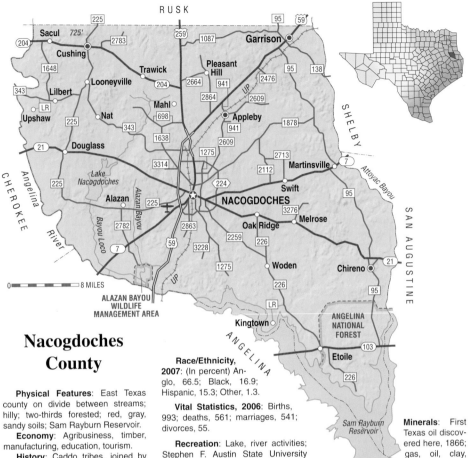

Nacogdoches County

Physical Features: East Texas county on divide between streams; hilly; two-thirds forested; red, gray, sandy soils; Sam Rayburn Reservoir.

Economy: Agribusiness, timber, manufacturing, education, tourism.

History: Caddo tribes, joined by displaced Cherokees in 1820s. Indians moved west of Brazos by 1840. Spanish missions established in 1716. Spanish settlers in mid-1700s. Anglo-Americans arrived in 1820s. Original county of Republic 1836, organized 1837.

Race/Ethnicity, 2007: (In percent) Anglo, 66.5; Black, 16.9; Hispanic, 15.3; Other, 1.3.

Vital Statistics, 2006: Births, 993; deaths, 561; marriages, 541; divorces, 55.

Recreation: Lake, river activities; Stephen F. Austin State University events; Angelina National Forest; historic sites; tourist attractions include the Old Stone Fort, pioneer homes, museums, Millard's Crossing Historic Village, Piney Woods Native Plant Center; Azalea Trail in March, Blueberry Festival in June.

Minerals: First Texas oil discovered here, 1866; gas, oil, clay, stone.

Agriculture: A leading poultry-producing county (second in number of broilers); beef cattle raised. Market value $317.2 million. Substantial timber sold.

NACOGDOCHES (32,028) county seat; varied manufacturing, lumber mills, wood products, trade center; hospitals; Stephen F. Austin University; Nine Flags Festival in November/December.

Other towns include: **Appleby** (435), **Chireno** (408), **Cushing** (676), **Douglass** (380), **Etoile** (700), **Garrison** (835), **Martinsville** (350), **Sacul** (150), **Woden** (400).

Population	**62,768**
Change fm 2000	6.0
Area (sq. mi.)	981.33
Land Area (sq. mi.)	946.77
Altitude (ft.)	164-725
Rainfall (in.)	48.40
Jan. mean min.	36.0
July mean max.	94.0
Civ. Labor	30,403
Unemployed	4.5
Wages	$171,854,661
Av. Weekly Wage	$574
Prop. Value	$3,275,609,431
Retail Sales	$750,325,519

The Old Stone Fort in Nacogdoches is a replica that was built using original stones from the 1779 structure. Robert Plocheck photo

Navarro County

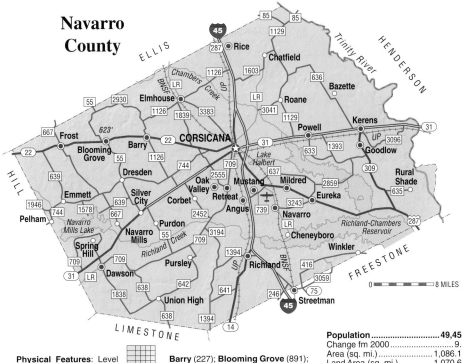

Rice · Chatfield · Bazette · Roane · Elmhouse · Powell · Kerens · Frost · Barry · CORSICANA · Goodlow · Blooming Grove · Lake Halbert · Dresden · Rural Shade · Oak Valley · Mildred · Emmett · Silver City · Mustang · Eureka · Pelham · Corbet · Retreat · Angus · Navarro · Purdon · Cheneyboro · Navarro Mills Lake · Navarro Mills · Richland-Chambers Reservoir · Spring Hill · Richland Creek · Winkler · Dawson · Pursley · Richland · Union High · Streetman

0 — 8 MILES

Physical Features: Level Blackland, some rolling; drains to creeks, Trinity River; Navarro Mills Lake, Richland-Chambers Reservoir.

Economy: Diversified manufacturing, agribusinesses, oil-field operations, distribution.

History: Kickapoo and Comanche area. Anglo-Americans settled in late 1830s. Antebellum slaveholding area. County created from Robertson County, organized in 1846; named for Republic of Texas leader José Antonio Navarro.

Race/Ethnicity, 2007: (In percent) Anglo, 60.4; Black, 16.1; Hispanic, 22.3; Other, 1.2.

Vital Statistics, 2006: Births, 619; deaths, 524; marriages, 436; divorces, 202.

Recreation: Lake activities; Pioneer Village; historic buildings; youth exposition, Derrick Days in April.

Minerals: Longest continuous Texas oil flow; more than 200 million barrels produced since 1895; natural gas, sand and gravel also produced.

Agriculture: Beef cattle, cotton, sorghum, corn, wheat, herbs, horses, dairies. Market value $52.4 million.

CORSICANA (26,602) county seat; major distribution center, pecans, candy, fruitcakes; varied manufacturing; agribusiness; hospital; Navarro College; Texas Youth Commission facility.

Other towns include: **Angus** (404);

Barry (227); **Blooming Grove** (891); **Chatfield** (40); **Dawson** (919); **Em-house** (169); **Eureka** (361); **Frost** (725); **Goodlow** (262).

Also, **Kerens** (1,933) some manufacturing, nature tourism, Cotton Harvest Festival in October; **Mildred** (469); **Mustang** (51); **Navarro** (206); **Oak Valley** (456); **Powell** (119); **Purdon** (133); **Retreat** (365); **Rice** (941); **Richland** (327).

Population	49,456
Change fm 2000	9.6
Area (sq. mi.)	1,086.17
Land Area (sq. mi.)	1,070.66
Altitude (ft.)	250-623
Rainfall (in.)	39.48
Jan. mean min.	34.0
July mean max.	94.5
Civ. Labor	21,173
Unemployed	6.1
Wages	$119,560,407
Av. Weekly Wage	$571
Prop. Value	$2,356,855,583
Retail Sales	$499,200,019

For explanation of sources, symbols and abbreviations, see p. 210 and foldout map.

The Navarro County Courthouse in Corsicana. Elizabeth Alvarez photo.

Newton County

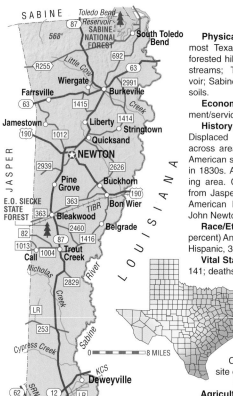

Physical Features: Eastern-most Texas county of densely forested hills, valleys; spring-fed streams; Toledo Bend Reservoir; Sabine River; mostly sandy soils.

Economy: Forestry, government/services, tourism.

History: Caddo Indian area. Displaced Coushattas moved across area from South. Anglo-American settlement established in 1830s. Antebellum slaveholding area. County created 1846 from Jasper County; named for American Revolutionary soldier John Newton.

Race/Ethnicity, 2007: (In percent) Anglo, 74.5; Black, 21.0; Hispanic, 3.6; Other, 0.9.

Vital Statistics, 2006: Births, 141; deaths, 166; marriages, 97; divorces, 79.

Recreation: Toledo Bend Reservoir, water sports, fishing, hunting, birding, tourism, state forest, Azalea Canyons; Belgrade, site of early town.

Minerals: Oil, gas.

Agriculture: Cattle, hay, nursery crops, vegetables, goats, hogs. Market value $2 million. Hunting leases. Major forestry area.

NEWTON (2,502) county seat; lumber manufacturing, plywood mill, private prison unit, tourist center; genealogical library, museum; Wild Azalea festival in March.

Deweyville (1,257) power plant, commercial center for forestry, farming area.

Other towns include: **Bon Wier** (375); **Burkeville** (603); **Call** (493); **South Toledo Bend** (477); **Wiergate** (350).

Population	**13,752**
Change fm 2000	–8.8
Area (sq. mi.)	939.51
Land Area (sq. mi.)	932.69
Altitude (ft.)	10-568
Rainfall (in.)	54.90
Jan. mean min.	35.0
July mean max.	94.0
Civ. Labor	5,994
Unemployed	8,0
Wages	$12,835,062
Av. Weekly Wage	$519
Prop. Value	$887,958,508
Retail Sales	$38,698,000

For explanation of sources, symbols and abbreviations, see p. 210 and foldout map.

Nolan County

Physical Features: On divide between Brazos, Colorado watersheds; mostly red sandy loams, some waxy, sandy soils; lakes.

Economy: Farms/ranches, oil/gas, wind energy, government/services.

History: Anglo-American settlement began in late 1870s. County created from Bexar, Young districts 1876; organized 1881; named for adventurer Philip Nolan, who was killed near Waco.

Race/Ethnicity, 2007: (In percent) Anglo, 63.1; Black, 5.2; Hispanic, 31.2; Other, 0.4.

Vital Statistics, 2006: Births, 227; deaths, 179; marriages, 131; divorces, 51.

Recreation: Lakes, hunting, pioneer museum; rattlesnake roundup in March, Soap Box Derby in June.

Minerals: Oil, gas.

Agriculture: Beef cattle, cotton, sorghum. Market value $37.1 million. Twenty percent irrigated.

SWEETWATER (10,723) county seat; wind energy, varied manufacturing, gypsum; hospital; Texas State Technical College; WWII museum.

Other towns include: **Blackwell** (330, partly in Coke County), Oak Creek Reservoir to south; **Maryneal** (61); **Nolan** (47); **Roscoe** (1,297).

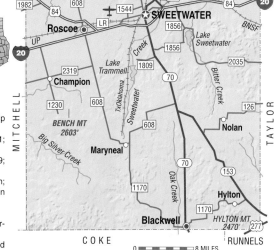

Population	**14,879**
Change fm 2000	–5.8
Area (sq. mi.)	913.93
Land Area (sq. mi.)	911.98
Altitude (ft.)	1,896-2,603
Rainfall (in.)	23.54
Jan. mean min.	28.9
July mean max.	93.8
Civ. Labor	7,727
Unemployed	4.5
Wages	$49,945,238
Av. Weekly Wage	$604
Prop. Value	$1,801,790,617
Retail Sales	$191,787,770

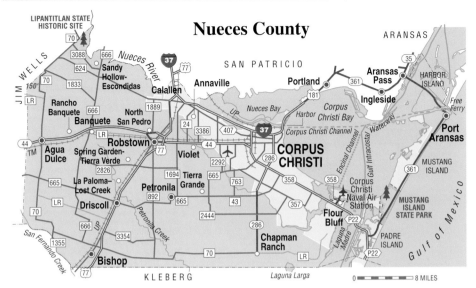

Nueces County

Physical Features: Southern Gulf Coast county; flat, rich soils, broken by bays, Nueces River, Petronila Creek; includes Mustang Island, north tip of Padre Island.

Economy: Petroleum processing, deepwater port facility, agriculture, tourism.

History: Coahuiltecan, Karankawa and other tribes who succumbed to disease or fled by 1840s. Spanish settlers arrived in 1760s. Settlers from Ireland arrived around 1830. County name is Spanish for nuts; county named for river; created 1846 out of San Patricio County.

Race/Ethnicity, 2007: (In percent) Anglo, 32.3; Black, 4.1; Hispanic, 61.4; Other, 2.2.

Vital Statistics, 2006: Births, 5,023; deaths, 2,477; marriages, 2,268; divorces, 1,530.

Recreation: Major resort area; beaches, fishing, water sports, birding; Padre Island National Seashore, Mustang Island State Park, Lipantitlan State Historic Site; Art Museum of South Texas, Corpus Christi Museum of Science and History; Texas State Aquarium; professional baseball, hockey; greyhound race track.

Minerals: Oil, gas, sand, gravel.

Agriculture: Grain sorghum (first in acreage), cotton, cattle, wheat, hay, nurseries/turfgrass. Market value $110.9 million.

CORPUS CHRISTI (285,600) county seat; seaport, naval bases, varied manufacturing, petroleum processing, tourism; hospitals; museums; Army depot; Texas A&M University-Corpus Christi, Del Mar College; replica of Columbus' ship on display, USS Lexington museum, Harbor Lights; Buccaneer Days in late April.

Port Aransas (3,826) deepwater port, tourism, birding, Coast Guard base, fishing industry; University of Texas Marine Science Institute; museum; Celebration of Whooping Cranes in February; Texas Sand Fest in April.

Robstown (13,316) market center for oil, farm area; regional fairgrounds; Cottonfest in November, Fiesta Mexicana in March.

Other towns include: **Agua Dulce** (744); **Banquete** (582); **Bishop** (3,322) petrochemicals, agriculture, pharmaceuticals, plastics, nature trail, Old Tyme Faire in April; **Chapman Ranch** (200); **Driscoll** (825); **La Paloma-Lost Creek** (275); **North San Pedro** (829); **Petronila** (81); **Rancho Banquete** (444); **Sandy Hollow-Escondidas** (377); **Spring Garden-Tierra Verde** (627); **Tierra Grande** (360).

Annaville, Calallen and **Flour Bluff** are now part of Corpus Christi.

Population	322,077
Change fm 2000	2.7
Area (sq. mi.)	1,166.42
Land Area (sq. mi.)	835.82
Altitude (ft.)	sea level-150
Rainfall (in.)	32.26
Jan. mean min.	46.2
July mean max.	93.2
Civ. Labor	159,453
Unemployed	5.3
Wages	$1,465,471,565
Av. Weekly Wage	$728
Prop. Value	$18,948,863,687
Retail Sales	$3,895,351,291

The Corpus Christi Municipal Marina and city skyline. Robert Plocheck photo.

Ochiltree County

Physical Features: Panhandle county bordering Oklahoma; level, broken by creeks; deep loam, clay soils.

Economy: Oil/gas, agribusiness, center of large feedlot and swine operations.

History: Apaches, pushed out by Comanches in late 1700s. Comanches removed to Indian Territory in 1874-75. Ranching developed in 1880s; farming after 1900. Created from Bexar District 1876, organized 1889; named for Republic of Texas leader W.B. Ochiltree.

Race/Ethnicity, 2007: (In percent) Anglo, 59.4; Black, 0.1; Hispanic, 39.5; Other, 1.1.

Vital Statistics, 2006: Births, 182; deaths, 74; marriages, 97; divorces, 40.

Recreation: Wolf Creek park; Museum of the Plains; Prehistoric settlement site of "Buried City"; pheasant hunting, also deer and dove; Wheatheart of the Nation celebration in August.

Minerals: Oil, natural gas, caliche.

Agriculture: Cattle, swine (first in numbers), wheat (first in acreage), corn, sorghum, cotton; 80,000 acres irrigated. Market value $395.1 million.

PERRYTON (8,255) county seat; oil/gas, cattle feeding, grain center; hospital; college.

Other towns include: **Farnsworth** (130); **Waka** (65). Also, **Booker** (1,332, mostly in Lipscomb County).

Population	9,613
Change fm 2000	6.7
Area (sq. mi.)	918.07
Land Area (sq. mi.)	917.56
Altitude (ft.)	2,550-3,120
Rainfall (in.)	20.88
Jan. mean min.	18.4
July mean max.	91.4
Civ. Labor	5,692
Unemployed	2.7
Wages	$48,106,735
Av. Weekly Wage	$785
Prop. Value	$923,573,279
Retail Sales	$135,865,494

Oldham County

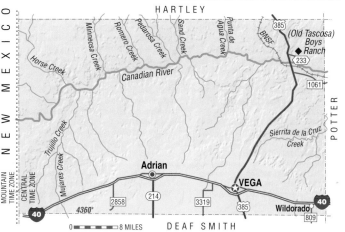

Physical Features: Northwestern Panhandle county; level, broken by Canadian River and tributaries.

Economy: Agriculture, wind energy, sand and gravel.

History: Apaches; followed later by Comanches, Kiowas. U.S. Army removed Indians in 1875. Anglo ranchers and Spanish pastores (sheep men) from New Mexico were in area in 1870s. County created 1876 from Bexar District; organized 1880; named for editor-Confederate senator W.S. Oldham.

Race/Ethnicity, 2007: (In percent) Anglo, 84.6; Black, 2.4; Hispanic, 11.5; Other, 1.6.

Vital Statistics, 2006: Births, 34; deaths, 14; marriages, 8; divorces, 3.

Recreation: Old Tascosa, Cal Farley's Boys Ranch, Boot Hill Cemetery, museums; midway point on old Route 66; County Roundup in August, Boys Ranch rodeo Labor Day weekend.

Minerals: Sand and gravel, oil, natural gas, stone.

Agriculture: Beef cattle; crops include wheat, grain sorghum. Market value $119.4 million.

VEGA (1,011) county seat; ranch trade center; museums.

Other towns: **Adrian** (150); **Wildorado** (210). Also, Cal Farley's **Boys Ranch** (470).

Population	2,062
Change fm 2000	−5.6
Area (sq. mi.)	1,501.42
Land Area (sq. mi.)	1,500.63
Altitude (ft.)	3,140-4,360
Rainfall (in.)	18.18
Jan. mean min.	20.5
July mean max.	92.3
Civ. Labor	962
Unemployed	4.6
Wages	$4,866,263
Av. Weekly Wage	$520
Prop. Value	$553,451,504
Retail Sales	$13,785,923

For explanation of sources, symbols and abbreviations, see p. 210 and foldout map.

Orange County

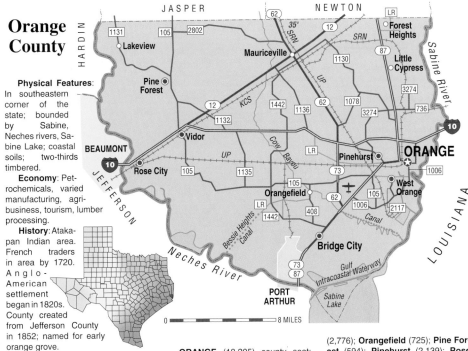

JASPER

NEWTON

HARDIN

LR

1131   Lakeview   105   2802   62   35'   12   Forest Heights
SRN   SRN

Mauriceville   1130   87   Little Cypress

Pine Forest   12   KCS   1442   1136   62   1078   3274   736   3274

1132   Vidor   Cow Bayou   LR

BEAUMONT   Rose City   105   UP   1135   Pinehurst   ORANGE   1006

JEFFERSON   Orangefield   LR   1442   408   73   62   105   1006   West Orange   2117   Canal

Bessie Heights Canal   Bridge City   73   87   Gulf Intracoastal Waterway

Neches River   PORT ARTHUR   Sabine Lake

LOUISIANA

0 ▭▭▭▭ 8 MILES

Physical Features: In southeastern corner of the state; bounded by Sabine, Neches rivers, Sabine Lake; coastal soils; two-thirds timbered.

Economy: Petrochemicals, varied manufacturing, agribusiness, tourism, lumber processing.

History: Atakapan Indian area. French traders in area by 1720. Anglo-American settlement began in 1820s. County created from Jefferson County in 1852; named for early orange grove.

Race/Ethnicity, 2007: (In percent) Anglo, 83.7; Black, 9.4; Hispanic, 5.0; Other, 2.0.

Vital Statistics, 2006: Births, 1,079; deaths, 831; marriages, 703; divorces, 323.

Recreation: Fishing, hunting, water sports, birding, county park, museums; historical homes, crawfish and crab festivals in spring.

Minerals: Salt, oil, gas, clays, sand and gravel.

Agriculture: Cattle, hay, Christmas trees and rice are top revenue sources; honey a significant revenue producer; fruits, berries, vegetables. Also, crawfishing. Market value not available. Hunting leases. Timber important.

ORANGE (18,205) county seat; seaport, petrochemical plants, varied manufacturing, food and timber processing shipping; hospital, theater, museums; Lamar State College-Orange; Mardi Gras/gumbo festival in February.

Bridge City (8,657) varied manufacturing, ship repair yard, steel fabrication, fish farming, government/services; library; tall bridge and newer suspension bridge over Neches; stop for Monarch butterfly in fall during its migration to Mexico.

Vidor (11,451) steel processing, railroad-car refinishing; library; barbecue festival in April.

Other towns include: **Mauriceville** (2,776); **Orangefield** (725); **Pine Forest** (594); **Pinehurst** (2,139); **Rose City** (493); **West Orange** (3,776).

Population	**83,022**
Change fm 2000	–2.3
Area (sq. mi.)	379.54
Land Area (sq. mi.)	356.40
Altitude (ft.)	sea level-35
Rainfall (in.)	59.00
Jan. mean min.	41.0
July mean max.	91.0
Civ. Labor	42,276
Unemployed	8.3
Wages	$225,871,974
Av. Weekly Wage	$754
Prop. Value	$5,336,489,299
Retail Sales	$818,327,322

For explanation of sources, symbols and abbreviations, see p. 210 and foldout map.

Trucks on Interstate 20 pass the smokestack, part of the remains of the once-thriving mining town of Thurber, on the Palo Pinto-Erath county line. Robert Plocheck photo.

Physical Features: **Palo Pinto County**
North central county; broken, hilly, wooded in parts; Possum Kingdom Lake, Lake Palo Pinto; sandy, gray, black soils.

Economy: Varied manufacturing, tourism, petroleum, agribusiness.

History: Anglo-American ranchers arrived in 1850s. Conflicts between settlers and numerous Indian tribes who had sought refuge on Brazos resulted in Texas Rangers removing Indians in 1856. County created 1856 from Bosque, Navarro counties; organized 1857; named for creek (in Spanish name means painted stick).

Race/Ethnicity, 2007: (In percent) Anglo, 77.8; Black, 2.6; Hispanic, 18.4; Other, 1.2.

Vital Statistics, 2006: Births, 388; deaths, 314; marriages, 167; divorces, 138.

Recreation: Lake activities, hunting, fishing, state park, Rails to Trails hiking, biking.

Minerals: Oil, gas, clays.

Agriculture: Cattle, dairy products, nursery crops, hay, wheat. Market value $23.5 million. Cedar posts marketed.

PALO PINTO (411) county seat; government center.

MINERAL WELLS (17,513, part [2,176] in Parker County) manufacturing, oil-field services/exploration, tourism; hospital, Weatherford College branch; art center; state park east of city in Parker County; Crazy Water Festival in October.

Other towns include: **Gordon** (445); **Graford** (601) retirement/recreation area, Possum Fest in October; **Mingus** (260); **Santo** (445), and **Strawn** (769).

Population	27,486
Change fm 2000	1.7
Area (sq. mi.)	985.50
Land Area (sq. mi.)	952.93
Altitude (ft.)	782-1,530
Rainfall (in.)	31.79
Jan. mean min.	33.4
July mean max.	97.3
Civ. Labor	14,707
Unemployed	5.2
Wages	$75,371,382
Av. Weekly Wage	$672
Prop. Value	$2,185,994,593
Retail Sales	$308,403,679

Panola County

Physical Features: East Texas county; sixty percent forested, rolling plain; broken by Sabine, Murvaul Creek, Toledo Bend Reservoir.

Economy: Gas processing, oil-field operation, agribusiness, food processing.

History: Caddo area. Anglo-American settlement established in 1833. Antebellum slaveholding area. County name is Indian word for cotton; created from Harrison, Shelby counties 1846.

Race/Ethnicity, 2007: (In percent) Anglo, 76.0; Black, 18.7; Hispanic, 4.6; Other, 0.7.

Vital Statistics, 2006: Births, 286; deaths, 278; marriages, 230; divorces, 84.

Recreation: Lake fishing, water activities, hunting; Jim Reeves memorial, Tex Ritter museum and Texas Country Music Hall of Fame.

Minerals: Oil, gas.

Agriculture: Broilers, cattle, forages. Market value $63.4 million. Timber sales significant.

CARTHAGE (6,951) county seat; petroleum processing, poultry, sawmills; hospital, junior college; Oil & Gas Blast in October.

Other towns include: **Beckville** (777), **Clayton** (125), **DeBerry** (200), **Gary** (318), **Long Branch** (150), **Panola** (305). Also, **Tatum** (1,173, mostly in Rusk County).

Population	23,084
Change fm 2000	1.4
Area (sq. mi.)	821.34
Land Area (sq. mi.)	800.92
Altitude (ft.)	172-548
Rainfall (in.)	51.51
Jan. mean min.	33.9
July mean max.	93.7
Civ. Labor	13,167
Unemployed	4.7
Wages	$86,588,659
Av. Weekly Wage	$752
Prop. Value	$4,596,972,387
Retail Sales	$217,759,769

Parker County

Physical Features: Hilly, broken by Brazos, Trinity tributaries, lakes; varied soils.

Economy: Agribusiness, varied manufacturing, government/services, commuting to Fort Worth; part of Dallas-Fort Worth-Arlington metropolitan area.

History: Comanche and Kiowa area in late 1840s when Anglo-American settlers arrived. County named for pioneer legislator Isaac Parker; created 1855 from Bosque, Navarro counties.

Race/Ethnicity, 2007: (In percent) Anglo, 86.8; Black, 2.1; Hispanic, 9.9; Other, 1.2.

Vital Statistics, 2006: Births, 1,163; deaths, 799; marriages, 781; divorces, 466.

Recreation: Water sports; state park and trailway; nature trails; hunting; Peach Festival in July and frontier rodeo days in June; first Monday trade days monthly.

Minerals: Natural gas, oil, stone, sand and gravel, clays.

Agriculture: Beef cattle, hay, greenhouse horticultural, horses (first in number), dairies, peaches, pecans. Market value $60 million.

WEATHERFORD (27,210) county seat; commuting to Fort Worth, retail center, government/services, equine industry; hospital, Weatherford College; museums, gardens.

Other towns include: **Aledo** (2,396); **Annetta** (1,307), **Annetta North** (513)

and **Annetta South** (646); **Cool** (173); **Dennis** (300); **Hudson Oaks** (1,875); **Millsap** (406); **Peaster** (102); **Poolville** (520); **Reno** (2,722); **Sanctuary** (604); **Springtown** (2,729) commuters, government/services, Wild West Festival in September; **Whitt** (38); **Willow Park** (3,847).

Also, part of **Azle** (10,904); **Briar** (5,861); **Cresson** (718) and part [2,176] of **Mineral Wells**. Also, part of **Fort Worth**.

Population	111,776
Change fm 2000	26.3
Area (sq. mi.)	910.09
Land Area (sq. mi.)	903.51
Altitude (ft.)	700-1,362
Rainfall (in.)	34.70
Jan. mean min.	29.0
July mean max.	95.2
Civ. Labor	53,859
Unemployed	5.1
Wages	$227,565,742
Av. Weekly Wage	$663
Prop. Value	$8,216,999,310
Retail Sales	$1,652,266,512

The Rails-to-Trails route for hikers and bikers runs between Weatherford and Mineral Wells. Robert Plocheck photo.

Parmer County

Physical Features: Western High Plains, broken by draws, playas; sandy, clay, loam soils.

Economy: Cattle feeding, grain elevators, meat-packing plant, other agribusiness.

History: Apaches, pushed out in late 1700s by Comanches, Kiowas. U.S. Army removed Indians in 1874-75. Anglo-Americans arrived in 1880s. Mexican migration increased after 1950. County named for Republic figure Martin Parmer; created from Bexar District 1876, organized 1907.

Race/Ethnicity, 2007: (In percent) Anglo, 44.1; Black, 0.9; Hispanic, 54.4; Other, 0.6.

Vital Statistics, 2006: Births, 198; deaths, 79; marriages, 31; divorces, 20.

Recreation: Hunting, Border Town Days in July at Farwell.

Minerals: Not significant.

Agriculture: Beef cattle (third in numbers), dairies (second in value of sales); crops include wheat, corn, cotton, grain sorghum, alfalfa; apples and potatoes also raised; 190,000 acres irrigated. Market value $937.7 million, third in state.

FARWELL (1,323) county seat; agribusiness center, grain storage, plants make farm equipment.

FRIONA (3,827) feedlots, grain elevators, meat packing; hospital; museum;

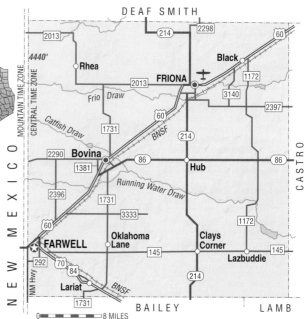

Cheeseburger Festival in July.

Other towns include: **Bovina** (1,874) farm trade center; **Lazbuddie** (248).

Population	**9,224**
Change fm 2000	–7.9
Area (sq. mi.)	885.17
Land Area (sq. mi.)	881.66
Altitude (ft.)	3,785-4,440
Rainfall (in.)	18.38

Jan. mean min.	21.7
July mean max.	89.8
Civ. Labor	4,634
Unemployed	3.3
Wages	$36,741,846
Av. Weekly Wage	$565
Prop. Value	$585,435,244
Retail Sales	$32,363,805

For explanation of sources, symbols and abbreviations, see p. 210 and foldout map.

The Pecos River Valley between Pecos and Crockett counties. Robert Plocheck photo.

Pecos County

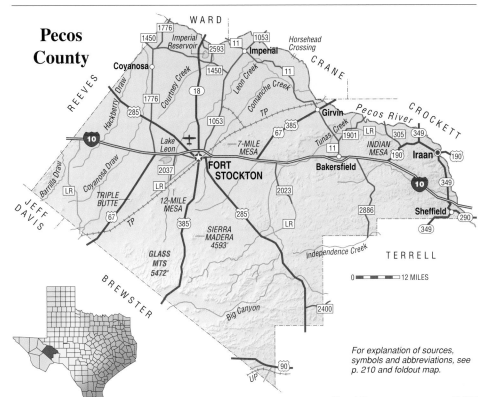

For explanation of sources, symbols and abbreviations, see p. 210 and foldout map.

Physical Features: Second largest county; high, broken plateau in West Texas; draining to Pecos and tributaries; sandy, clay, loam soils.

Economy: Oil, gas, agriculture, government/services, wind turbines.

History: Comanches in area when military outpost established in 1859. Settlement began after Civil War. Created from Presidio County 1871; organized 1872; named for Pecos River, name origin uncertain.

Race/Ethnicity, 2007: (In percent) Anglo, 31.4; Black, 3.9; Hispanic, 64.0; Other, 0.7.

Vital Statistics, 2006: Births, 269; deaths, 111; marriages, 102; divorces, 24.

Recreation: Old Fort Stockton, Annie Riggs Museum, stagecoach stop, scenic drives, Dinosaur Track Roadside Park, cattle-trail sites, archaeological museum with oil and ranch-heritage collections; Comanche Springs Water Carnival in summer.

Minerals: Natural gas, oil, gravel, caliche.

Agriculture: Cattle, alfalfa, pecans, sheep, goats, onions, peppers, melons. Market value $27.5 million. Aquaculture firm producing shrimp. Hunting leases.

FORT STOCKTON (7,557) county seat, distribution center for petroleum industry, government/services, agri-culture, tourism, varied manufacturing, winery, prison units, spaceport launching small satellites; hospital; historical tours.

Iraan (1,213) oil and gas center, tourism, ranching, meat processing; hospital; Alley Oop park.

Other towns include: **Coyanosa** (140); **Girvin** (20); **Imperial** (399) center for irrigated farming; **Sheffield** (322) oil, gas center.

Population	16,307
Change fm 2000	–3.0
Area (sq. mi.)	4,764.73
Land Area (sq. mi.)	4,763.66
Altitude (ft.)	2,040-5,472
Rainfall (in.)	14.06
Jan. mean min.	31.4
July mean max.	95.8
Civ. Labor	6,713
Unemployed	5.3
Wages	$36,790,098
Av. Weekly Wage	$623
Prop. Value	$3,302,954,143
Retail Sales	$130,269,739

Fort Stockton's roadrunner. Robert Plocheck photo.

Polk County

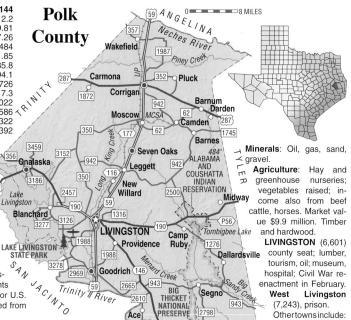

Population 46,144
Change fm 2000 .... 12.2
Area (sq. mi.) 1,109.81
Land Area (sq. mi.) 1,057.26
Altitude (ft.) 68-484
Rainfall (in.) 51.85
Jan. mean min. 35.8
July mean max. 94.1
Civ. Labor 16,726
Unemployed 7.3
Wages $77,984,022
Av. Weekly Wage.................. $586
Prop. Value $2,263,454,322
Retail Sales $447,002,392

Physical Features: Rolling; densely forested, with Big Thicket, unique plant, animal life; Neches, Trinity rivers, tributaries.

Economy: Timber, lumber production, tourism, manufacturing.

History: Caddo area; Alabama and Coushatta Indians arrived from Louisiana in late 1700s. Anglo-American and Hispanic families received land grants in early 1830s. County named for U.S. President James K. Polk; created from Liberty County, organized 1846.

Race/Ethnicity, 2007: (In percent) Anglo, 75.3; Black, 12.1; Hispanic, 10.5; Other, 2.2.

Vital Statistics, 2006: Births, 508; deaths, 627; marriages, 372; divorces, 140.

Recreation: Lake and state park, water activities, fishing, hunting, Alabama-Coushatta Reservation, museum, Big Thicket, woodland trails, champion trees, historic homes.

Minerals: Oil, gas, sand, gravel.

Agriculture: Hay and greenhouse nurseries; vegetables raised; income also from beef cattle, horses. Market value $9.9 million. Timber and hardwood.

LIVINGSTON (6,601) county seat; lumber, tourism, oil; museum, hospital; Civil War reenactment in February. **West Livingston** (7,243), prison. Other towns include: **Ace** (40); **Camden** (1,200); **Corrigan** (1,863) plywood plant; **Dallardsville** (350); **Goodrich** (264); **Leggett** (500); **Moscow** (170) historic sites; **Onalaska** (1,415); **Seven Oaks** (136).

Potter County

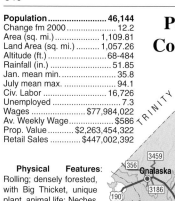

Physical Features: Panhandle county; mostly level, part rolling; broken by Canadian River and tributaries; sandy, sandy loam, chocolate loam, clay soils; Lake Meredith.

Economy: Transportation and distribution hub for large area, manufacturing, agribusiness, tourism, government/services, petrochemicals, gas processing.

History: Apaches, pushed out by Comanches in 1700s. Comanches removed to Indian Territory in 1874-75. Ranching began in late 1870s. Oil boom in 1920s. County named for Robert Potter, Republic leader; created 1876 from Bexar District; organized 1887.

Race/Ethnicity, 2007: (In percent) Anglo, 50.9; Black, 9.9; Hispanic, 35.1; Other, 4.0.

Vital Statistics, 2006: Births, 2,406; deaths, 1,174; marriages, 1,519; divorces, 423.

Recreation: Lake activities, Alibates Flint Quarries National Monument, hunting, fishing, Wildcat Bluff nature center, Cadillac Ranch, professional sports events, Tri-State Fair in September.

Minerals: Natural gas, oil, helium.

Agriculture: Beef cattle production and processing; wheat, sorghum, cotton. Market value $29.9 million.

AMARILLO (189,861 total, part [73,794] in Randall County) county seat; hub for northern Panhandle oil and ranching, distribution and marketing center, tourism, manufacturing, food processing, prison; hospitals; Amarillo College, Texas Tech University medical, engineering, pharmacy schools; Quarter Horse Hall of Fame, museum.

Other towns include: **Bishop Hills** (200) and **Bushland** (1,485).

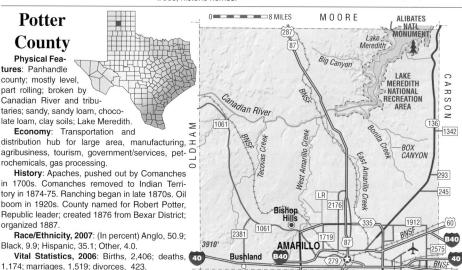

Population 120,918
Change fm 2000 .... 6.5

Area (sq. mi.) 921.98
Land Area (sq. mi.) 909.24
Altitude (ft.) 2,915-3,910
Rainfall (in.) 19.71
Jan. mean min. 22.6
July mean max. 91.0
Civ. Labor 57,486
Unemployed 4.4
Wages $733,707,077
Av. Weekly Wage....................... $726
Prop. Value $6,297,697,155
Retail Sales $2,70,517,509

Flowers along Texas 170 south of Presidio. Robert Plocheck photo.

Presidio County

Physical Features: Rugged, some of Texas' tallest mountains; clays, loams, sandy loams on uplands; intermountain wash; timber sparse; Capote Falls, state's highest.

Economy: Government/services, ranching, hunting leases, tourism.

History: Presidio area has been cultivated farmland since at least 1200 A.D. Spanish explorers of 1500s encountered villages along Rio Grande. Jumanos, Apaches and Comanches in area when Spanish missions began in 1680s. Anglo-Americans arrived in 1840s. County created 1850 from Bexar District; organized 1875; named for Spanish Presidio del Norte (fort of the north).

Race/Ethnicity, 2007: (In percent) Anglo, 13.5; Black, 0.2; Hispanic, 85.9; Other, 0.4.

Vital Statistics, 2006: Births, 159; deaths, 44; marriages, 96; divorces, 1.

Recreation: Hunting; scenic drives along Rio Grande, in mountains; ghost towns, mysterious Marfa Lights; Fort D.A. Russell; Big Bend Ranch State Park; hot springs; Cibolo Creek Ranch Resort; Chinati Foundation art festival in fall. (Chinati Mountains State Natural Area not yet open to public.)

Minerals: Sand, gravel, silver, zeolite.

Agriculture: Cattle, tomatoes, hay, onions, melons. 5,500 acres irrigated near Rio Grande. Market value not available.

MARFA (2,134) county seat; ranching supply, Border Patrol headquarters, tourism, art center, gateway to mountainous area; Paisano Hotel, headquarters for movie, *Giant*; Old Timers Roping on Memorial Day weekend.

PRESIDIO (5,133) international bridge to Ojinaga, Mex., gateway to Mexico's West Coast by rail; Fort Leaton historic site; asado cook-off in February.

Other towns include: **Redford** (129); **Shafter** (57) old mining town.

Population	**7,467**
Change fm 2000	2.2
Area (sq. mi.)	3,856.26
Land Area (sq. mi.)	3,855.51
Altitude (ft.)	2,400-7,728
Rainfall (in.) Marfa	15.79
Rainfall (in.) Presidio	10.76
Jan. mean min. Marfa	23.9
Jan. mean min. Presidio	34.5
July mean max. Marfa	88.9
July mean max. Presidio	100.8
Civ. Labor	3,348
Unemployed	13.2
Wages	$15,146,566
Av. Weekly Wage	$569
Prop. Value	$246,072,706
Retail Sales	$45,329,477

For explanation of sources, symbols, see p. 210 and foldout map.

Rains County

Physical Features: Northeastern county; rolling; partly Blackland, sandy loams, sandy soils; Sabine River, Lake Tawakoni.

Economy: Agribusiness, some manufacturing.

History: Caddo area. In 1700s, Tawakoni Indians entered the area. Anglo-Americans arrived in 1840s. County, county seat named for Emory Rains, Republic leader; created 1870 from Hopkins, Hunt and Wood counties; birthplace of National Farmers Union, 1902.

Race/Ethnicity, 2007: (In percent) Anglo, 90.7; Black, 2.5; Hispanic, 5.7; Other, 1.1.

Vital Statistics, 2006: Births, 115; deaths, 113; marriages, 76; divorces, 49.

Recreation: Lake Tawakoni and Lake Fork Reservoir activities; birding, Eagle Fest in February.

Minerals: Gas, oil.

Agriculture: Beef, forages, dairies, vegetables (second in sweet potato acreage), fruits, nurseries. Market value $13.9 million.

EMORY (1,882) county seat; local trade, tourism, government/services, commuting to Greenville and Dallas; African-American museum.

Other towns include: **East Tawakoni** (947) and **Point** (936), manufacturing, tourism, tamale fest on July 4. Part of **Alba** (473), mostly in Wood County.

Population	11,204	
Change fm 2000	22.6	
Area (sq. mi.)	258.87	
Land Area (sq. mi.)	232.05	
Altitude (ft.)	340-570	
Rainfall (in.)	43.50	

Jan. mean min.	31.6
July mean max.	92.4
Civ. Labor	5,294
Unemployed	6.1
Wages	$10,958,434
Av. Weekly Wage	$489
Prop. Value	$533,605,011
Retail Sales	$99,018,560

Randall County

Randal (name misspelled in statute).

Physical Features: Panhandle county; level, but broken by scenic Palo Duro Canyon, Buffalo Lake; silty clay, loam soils.

Economy: Agribusiness, education, tourism, part of Amarillo metropolitan area.

History: Comanche Indians removed in mid-1870s; ranching began soon afterward. County created 1876 from Bexar District; organized 1889; named for Confederate Gen. Horace Randal.

Race/Ethnicity, 2007: (In percent) Anglo, 82.7; Black, 1.8; Hispanic, 13.4; Other, 2.1.

Vital Statistics, 2006: Births, 1,365; deaths, 825; marriages, 388; divorces, 431.

Recreation: State park, with *Texas* outdoor musical drama each summer; Panhandle-Plains Historical Museum; West Texas A&M University events; aoudad sheep, migratory waterfowl hunting in season; Buffalo Lake National Wildlife Refuge; cowboy breakfasts at ranches.

Minerals: Not significant.

Agriculture: Grain sorghum, beef cattle, wheat, silage, cotton, dairies, hay. Market value $393.4 million.

CANYON (14,014) county seat; West Texas A&M University, tourism, commuting to Amarillo, ranching, farm center, light manufacturing, gateway to state park.

AMARILLO (189,861 total, mostly [111,851] in Potter County) hub for northern Panhandle oil and ranching, distribution and marketing center, manufacturing; hospitals.

Other towns include: **Lake Tanglewood** (965); **Palisades** (374); **Timbercreek Canyon** (461); **Umbarger** (327) German sausage festival in November. Part of **Happy** (653, mostly in Swisher County).

Population	114,546
Change fm 2000	9.8
Area (sq. mi.)	922.42
Land Area (sq. mi.)	914.43
Altitude (ft.)	2,700-3,890
Rainfall (in.)	19.19
Jan. mean min.	23.7
July mean max.	92.6
Civ. Labor	66,548
Unemployed	3.3
Wages	$219,280,618
Av. Weekly Wage	$599
Prop. Value	$6,804,004,479
Retail Sales	$1,161,327,235

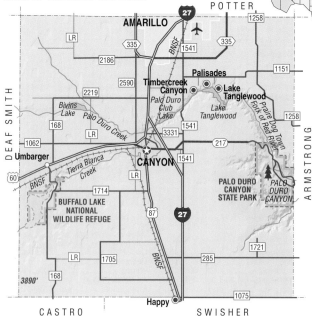

Reagan County

Physical Features: Western county; level to hilly, broken by draws, Big Lake (intermittent); sandy, loam, clay soils.

Economy: Oil production, natural gas, ranching.

History: Comanches in area until mid-1870s. Ranching began in 1880s. Hispanic migration increased after 1950. County named for Sen. John H. Reagan, first chairman, Texas Railroad Commission; county created 1903 from Tom Green County.

Race/Ethnicity, 2007: (In percent) Anglo, 43.5; Black, 2.9; Hispanic, 53.0; Other, 0.5.

Vital Statistics, 2006: Births, 47; deaths, 26; marriages, 16; divorces, 2.

Recreation: Site of 1923 discovery well Santa Rita No. 1 on University of Texas land, Texon reunion in June.

Minerals: Gas, oil.

Agriculture: Cotton, cattle, sheep, goats; cotton, grains principal crops; 36,000 acres irrigated. Market value $16.5 million.

BIG LAKE (2,932) county seat; center for oil activities, farming, ranching; hospital; Spring Bluegrass Festival.

Population		3,086
Change fm 2000		–7.2
Area (sq. mi.)		1,175.98
Land Area (sq. mi.)		1,175.30
Altitude (ft.)		2,370-2,960
Rainfall (in.)		18.79
Jan. mean min.		29.1
July mean max.		93.4
Civ. Labor		2,805
Unemployed		1.9
Wages		$24,789,507
Av. Weekly Wage		$885
Prop. Value		$1,318,991,469
Retail Sales		$14,693,653

For explanation of sources, abbreviations and symbols, see p. 210 and foldout map.

Real County

Physical Features: Hill Country, spring-fed streams, scenic canyons; Frio, Nueces rivers; cedars, pecans, walnuts, many live oaks.

Economy: Ranching, tourism, government/services, cedar cutting.

History: Tonkawa area; Lipan Apaches arrived in early 1700s; later, Comanche hunters in area. Spanish mission established 1762. Anglo-Americans arrived in 1850s. County created 1913 from Bandera, Edwards, Kerr counties; named for legislator-ranchman Julius Real.

Race/Ethnicity, 2007: (In percent) Anglo, 75.3; Black, 0.3; Hispanic, 23.9; Other, 0.6.

Vital Statistics, 2006: Births, 34; deaths, 44; marriages, 27; divorces, 2.

Recreation: Tourist and hunting center, birding, fishing, camping, scenic drives, state natural area.

Minerals: Not significant.

Agriculture: Goats, sheep, beef cattle produce most income. Market value $2.8 million. Cedar posts processed.

LEAKEY (398) county seat; tourism, ranching; museums; July Jubilee.

Population		2,875
Change fm 2000		–5.6
Area (sq. mi.)		700.04
Land Area (sq. mi.)		699.91
Altitude (ft.)		1,400-2,400
Rainfall (in.)		27.99
Jan. mean min.		33.1
July mean max.		94.2
Civ. Labor		1,346
Unemployed		4.5
Wages		$3,999,978
Av. Weekly Wage		$412
Prop. Value		$299,723,132
Retail Sales		$14,574,285

CAMP WOOD (885) tourist and ranching hub for parts of three counties; San Lorenzo de la Santa Cruz mission site; museum; settlers reunion in August.

Other towns include: **Rio Frio** (50).

The main square of Clarksville, Red River County. Robert Plocheck photo.

Red River County

Physical Features: On Red-Sulphur rivers' divide; 39 different soil types; half timbered.

Economy: Agribusinesses, lumbering, manufacturing.

History: Caddo Indians abandoned area in 1790s. One of the oldest counties; settlers were moving in from the United States in 1810s. Kickapoo and other tribes arrived in 1820s. Antebellum slaveholding area. County created 1836 as original county of the Republic; organized 1837; named for Red River, its northern boundary.

Race/Ethnicity, 2007: (In percent) Anglo, 74.7; Black, 18.4; Hispanic, 6.1; Other, 0.7.

Vital Statistics, 2006: Births, 145; deaths, 201; marriages, 74; divorces, 61.

Recreation: Historical sites include pioneer homes, birthplace of John Nance Garner; water activities; hunting of deer, turkey, duck, small game.

Minerals: Small oil flow.

Agriculture: Beef cattle, hay, corn. Market value $35.9 million. Timber sales substantial. Hunting leases important.

CLARKSVILLE (3,690) county seat; varied manufacturing; hospital, library; Historical Society bazaar in October.

Other towns include: **Annona** (255); **Avery** (441); **Bagwell** (150); **Bogata** (1,340); **Detroit** (754) commercial center in west. Part of **Deport** (672).

Population	12,955
Change fm 2000	–9.5
Area (sq. mi.)	1,057.61
Land Area (sq. mi.)	1,050.18
Altitude (ft.)	260-560
Rainfall (in.)	47.83
Jan. mean min.	29.7
July mean max.	92.2
Civ. Labor	6,466
Unemployed	6.9
Wages	$18,777,313
Av. Weekly Wage	$503
Prop. Value	$539,990,740
Retail Sales	$51,913,123

Reeves County

MOUNTAIN TIME ZONE
CENTRAL TIME ZONE

N E W   M E X I C O

Population	11,062
Change fm 2000	–15.8
Area (sq. mi.)	2,641.95
Land Area (sq. mi.)	2,635.88
Altitude (ft.)	2,460-5,115
Rainfall (in.) Pecos	11.61
Rainfall (in.) Balmorhea	14.19
Jan. mean min. Pecos	28.1
Jan. mean min. Balmorhea	30.1
July mean max. Pecos	98.5
July mean max. Balmorhea	94.7
Civ. Labor	4,249
Unemployed	6.8
Wages	$29,324,285
Av. Weekly Wage	$594
Prop. Value	$916,339,370
Retail Sales	$111,124,896

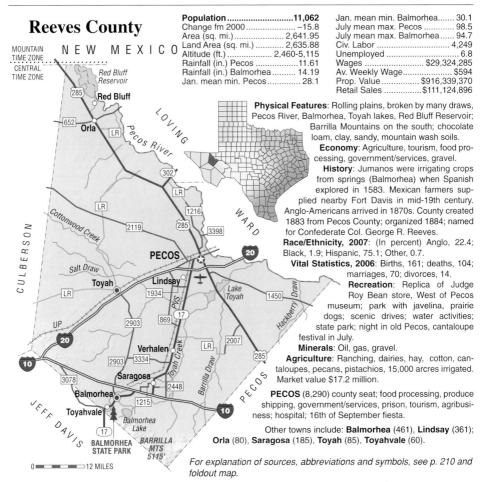

Physical Features: Rolling plains, broken by many draws, Pecos River, Balmorhea, Toyah lakes, Red Bluff Reservoir; Barrilla Mountains on the south; chocolate loam, clay, sandy, mountain wash soils.

Economy: Agriculture, tourism, food processing, government/services, gravel.

History: Jumanos were irrigating crops from springs (Balmorhea) when Spanish explored in 1583. Mexican farmers supplied nearby Fort Davis in mid-19th century. Anglo-Americans arrived in 1870s. County created 1883 from Pecos County; organized 1884; named for Confederate Col. George R. Reeves.

Race/Ethnicity, 2007: (In percent) Anglo, 22.4; Black, 1.9; Hispanic, 75.1; Other, 0.7.

Vital Statistics, 2006: Births, 161; deaths, 104; marriages, 70; divorces, 14.

Recreation: Replica of Judge Roy Bean store, West of Pecos museum; park with javelina, prairie dogs; scenic drives; water activities; state park; night in old Pecos, cantaloupe festival in July.

Minerals: Oil, gas, gravel.

Agriculture: Ranching, dairies, hay, cotton, cantaloupes, pecans, pistachios, 15,000 arcres irrigated. Market value $17.2 million.

PECOS (8,290) county seat; food processing, produce shipping, government/services, prison, tourism, agribusiness; hospital; 16th of September fiesta.

Other towns include: **Balmorhea** (461), **Lindsay** (361); **Orla** (80), **Saragosa** (185), **Toyah** (85), **Toyahvale** (60).

For explanation of sources, abbreviations and symbols, see p. 210 and foldout map.

The Barrilla Mountains, southern Reeves County. Robert Plocheck photo.

Refugio County

Physical Features: Coastal plain, broken by streams, bays; sandy, loam, black soils; mesquite, oak, huisache motts.

Economy: Petroleum, petrochemical production, agribusinesses, tourism, commuting to Corpus Christi, Victoria.

History: Karankawa area. Spanish mission, for which the county is named, Our Lady of Refuge, established in 1793. Colonists from Ireland and United States arrived in 1830s. Original county of the Republic created 1836, organized 1837.

Race/Ethnicity, 2007: (In percent) Anglo, 44.3; Black, 6.9; Hispanic, 47.9; Other, 0.9.

Vital Statistics, 2006: Births, 94; deaths, 88; marriages, 36; divorces, 24.

Recreation: Water activities, hunting, fishing, historic sites, wildlife refuge, home of the whooping crane; chili cook-off in August, Festival of Flags in October.

Minerals: Oil, natural gas.

Agriculture: Cotton, beef cattle, sorghum, corn, soybeans, horses. Market value $29.4 million. Hunting leases.

REFUGIO (2,807) county seat; petroleum, agribusiness center; hospital; museum, historic homes.

Other towns include: **Austwell** (177);

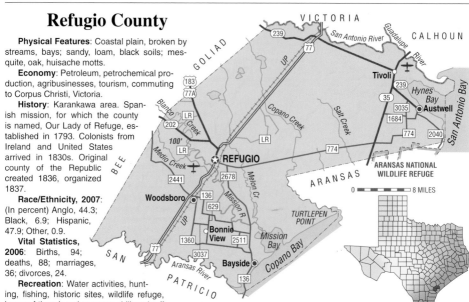

Bayside (339) resorts; **Tivoli** (550); **Woodsboro** (1,607) commercial center.

Population	7,350
Change fm 2000	–6.1
Area (sq. mi.)	818.64
Land Area (sq. mi.)	770.21
Altitude (ft.)	sea level-100
Rainfall (in.)	40.10
Jan. mean min.	45.0
July mean max.	94.0

Civ. Labor	3,898
Unemployed	4.6
Wages	$18,093,547
Av. Weekly Wage	$631
Prop. Value	$1,030,612,660
Retail Sales	$64,031,673

For explanation of sources, symbols and abbreviations, see p. 210 and foldout map.

Roberts County

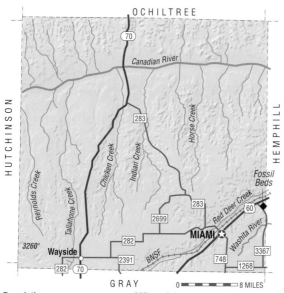

Physical Features: Rolling, broken by Canadian and tributaries; Red Deer Creek; black, sandy loam, alluvial soils.

Economy: Oil-field operations, agribusiness.

History: Apaches; pushed out by Comanches who were removed in 1874-75 by U.S. Army. Ranching began in late 1870s. County created 1876 from Bexar District; organized 1889; named for Texas leaders John S. Roberts and Gov. O.M. Roberts.

Race/Ethnicity, 2007: (In percent) Anglo, 96.1; Black, 0.4; Hispanic, 3.3; Other, 0.2.

Vital Statistics, 2006: Births, 9; deaths, 9; marriages, 11; divorces, 1.

Recreation: Scenic drives, hunting, museum; national cow-calling contest in June.

Minerals: Production of gas, oil.

Agriculture: Beef cattle; wheat, sorghum, corn, soybeans, hay; 10,000 acres irrigated. Market value $16.7 million.

MIAMI (557) county seat; ranching, oil center, some manufacturing.

Population	833
Change fm 2000	–6.1
Area (sq. mi.)	924.19
Land Area (sq. mi.)	924.09
Altitude (ft.)	2,380-3,260
Rainfall (in.)	23.30
Jan. mean min.	20.6

July mean max.	92.4
Civ. Labor	590
Unemployed	2.5
Wages	$4,911,994
Av. Weekly Wage	$1,074
Prop. Value	$724,398,471
Retail Sales	$2,666,827

Robertson County

Physical Features: Rolling in north and east, draining to bottoms along Brazos, Navasota rivers; sandy soils, heavy in bottoms.

Economy: Agribusiness, government/services, oil and gas.

History: Tawakoni, Waco, Comanche and other tribes. Anglo-Americans arrived in 1820s. Antebellum slaveholding area. County created 1837, organized 1838, subdivided into many others later; named for pioneer Sterling Clack Robertson.

Race/Ethnicity, 2007: (In percent) Anglo, 58.6; Black, 23.6; Hispanic, 17.3; Other, 0.6.

Vital Statistics, 2006: Births, 216; deaths, 191; marriages, 108; divorces, 33.

Recreation: Hunting, fishing; historic sites; dogwood trails, wildlife preserves.

Minerals: Gas, oil, lignite coal.

Agriculture: Poultry, beef cattle, cotton, hay, corn; 20,000 acres of cropland irrigated. Market value $116 million.

FRANKLIN (1,530) county seat; oil and gas, power plants, mining, agriculture; Carnegie library.

HEARNE (4,755) agribusiness, varied manufacturing; depot museum; music festival in October.

Other towns include: **Bremond** (793) power plant, coal mining, Polish Days in June; **Calvert** (1,362) agriculture, tourism, antiques, Maypole festival, tour of homes; **Mumford** (170); **New Baden** (150); **Wheelock** (225).

Population	15,693
Change fm 2000	–1.9
Area (sq. mi.)	865.67
Land Area (sq. mi.)	854.56
Altitude (ft.)	230-610
Rainfall (in.)	39.03
Jan. mean min.	38.2
July mean max.	95.1
Civ. Labor	7,828
Unemployed	5.9
Wages	$31,961,912
Av. Weekly Wage	$624
Prop. Value	$2,468,163,720
Retail Sales	$91,142,727

Grasses along Copano Bay, which separates Refugio and Aransas counties. Robert Plocheck photo.

Rockwall County

Physical Features: Rolling prairie, mostly Blackland soil; Lake Ray Hubbard. Texas' smallest county.

Economy: Industrial employment in local plants and in Dallas; in Dallas metropolitan area; residential development around Lake Ray Hubbard.

History: Caddo area. Cherokees arrived in 1820s. Anglo-American settlers arrived in 1840s. County created 1873 from Kaufman; named for wall-like rock formation.

Race/Ethnicity, 2007: (In percent) Anglo, 80.0; Black, 3.5; Hispanic, 14.6; Other, 1.9.

Vital Statistics, 2006: Births, 855; deaths, 381; marriages, 1,318; divorces, 276.

Recreation: Lake activities; proximity to Dallas; unusual rock outcrop.

Minerals: Not significant.

Agriculture: Small grains, cattle, horticulture, horses. Market value $3.9 million.

ROCKWALL (33,078) county seat; commuters, varied manufacturing; hospital; harbor retail/enterainment district; Founders Day in April.

Other towns include: **Fate** (4,409); **Heath** (7,129); **McLendon-Chisholm** (1,225) chili cookoff in October; **Mobile City** (253); **Royse City** (8,707) government/services, varied manufacturing, agribusiness, museum, library, Funfest in October.

Part [7,041] of **Rowlett**, hospital, and a small part [315] of **Wylie**.

Population	**77,633**
Change fm 2000	80.2
Area (sq. mi.)	148.70
Land Area (sq. mi.)	128.79
Altitude (ft.)	430-624
Rainfall (in.)	39.40
Jan. mean min.	33.0

July mean max.	96.0
Civ. Labor	36,395
Unemployed	5.5
Wages	$167,492,911
Av. Weekly Wage	$644
Prop. Value	$6,662,900,848
Retail Sales	$891,603,823

For explanation of sources, abbreviations and symbols, see p. 210 and foldout map.

Runnels County

Physical Features: Level to rolling; bisected by Colorado and tributaries; sandy loam, black waxy soils.

Economy: Agribusiness, oil, government/services, manufacturing.

History: Spanish explorers found Jumanos in area in 1650s; later, Apaches and Comanches driven out in 1870s by U.S. military. First Anglo-Americans arrived in 1850s; Germans, Czechs around 1900. County named for planter-legislator H.G. Runnels; created 1858 from Bexar, Travis counties; organized 1880.

Race/Ethnicity, 2007: (In percent) Anglo, 64.6; Black, 1.6; Hispanic, 33.1; Other, 0.7.

Vital Statistics, 2006: Births, 145; deaths, 137; marriages, 79; divorces, 39.

Recreation: Deer, dove and turkey hunting; O.H. Ivie Reservoir; fishing; antique car museum; historical markers in county.

Minerals: Oil, gas, sand.

Agriculture: Cattle, cotton, wheat, sorghum, dairies, sheep and goats. Market value $53.8 million.

BALLINGER (4,075) county seat; varied manufacturing, oil-field services, meat processing; Carnegie Library, hospital, Western Texas College extension; the Cross, 100-ft. tall atop hill south of city; Festival of Ethnic Cultures in April.

Other towns include: **Miles** (821); **Norton** (50); **Rowena** (349); **Wingate** (100); **Winters** (2,737) manufacturing, museum, hospital.

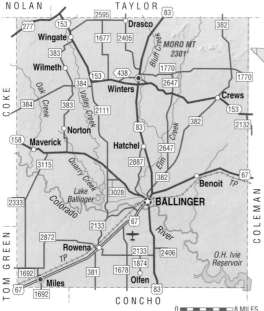

Population	**10,273**
Change fm 2000	−10.6
Area (sq. mi.)	1,057.13
Land Area (sq. mi.)	1,050.73
Altitude (ft.)	1,915-2,301
Rainfall (in.)	23.76
Jan. mean min.	28.5

July mean max.	94.3
Civ. Labor	4,504
Unemployed	4.9
Wages	$21,760,542
Av. Weekly Wage	$560
Prop. Value	$524,618,960
Retail Sales	$66,727,307

Rusk County

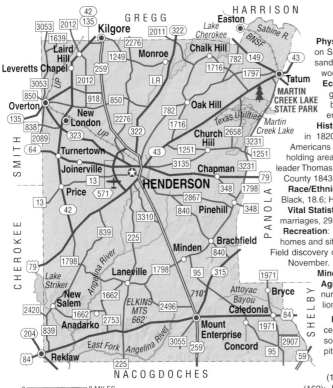

Physical Features: East Texas county on Sabine-Angelina divide; varied deep, sandy soils; over half in pines, hardwoods; lakes.

Economy: Lignite mining, electricity generation, oil and gas, lumbering, brick production, agribusiness, government/services.

History: Caddo area. Cherokees settled in 1820s; removed in 1839. First Anglo-Americans arrived in 1829. Antebellum slaveholding area. County named for Republic, state leader Thomas J. Rusk; created from Nacogdoches County 1843.

Race/Ethnicity, 2007: (In percent) Anglo, 69.0; Black, 18.6; Hispanic, 11.8; Other, 0.7.

Vital Statistics, 2006: Births, 618; deaths, 507; marriages, 291; divorces, 215.

Recreation: Water sports, state park, historic homes and sites, scenic drives, site of East Texas Field discovery oil well; Henderson syrup festival in November.

Minerals: Oil, natural gas, lignite, clays.

Agriculture: Beef cattle, hay, broilers, nursery plants. Market value $56.1 million. Timber income substantial.

HENDERSON (12,866) county seat; center for agribusiness, oil activities, some manufacturing, state jails; hospital, museum.

Other towns include: **Joinerville** (140); **Laird Hill** (300); **Laneville** (169); **Minden** (150); **Mount Enterprise** (553); **New London** (993) site of 1937 school explosion that killed 293 students and faculty; **Overton** (2,407, partly in Smith County) oil, lumbering center, petroleum processing, prison, A&M research center, blue grass festival in July; **Price** (275); **Tatum** (1,173, partly in Panola County); **Turnertown-Selman City** (271).

Also, part of **Easton** (578, mostly in Gregg County), part of **Reklaw** (361, mostly in Cherokee County) and part [2,580] of **Kilgore** (12,341 total).

Population	48,887
Change fm 2000	3.2
Area (sq. mi.)	938.62
Land Area (sq. mi.)	923.55
Altitude (ft.)	250-710
Rainfall (in.)	48.22
Jan. mean min.	33.1
July mean max.	93.1
Civ. Labor	24,045
Unemployed	4.6
Wages	$148,262,609
Av. Weekly Wage	$782
Prop. Value	$5,184,665,380
Retail Sales	$358,765,969

A plant nursery on Texas 42 near Price, Rusk County. Robert Plocheck photo.

Sabine County

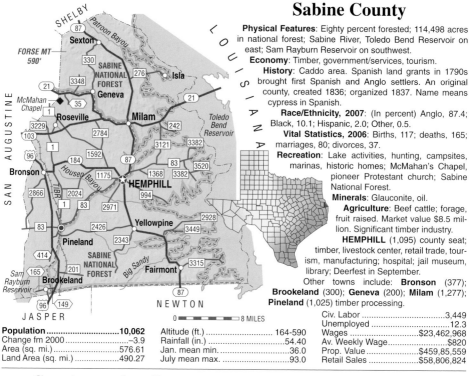

Physical Features: Eighty percent forested; 114,498 acres in national forest; Sabine River, Toledo Bend Reservoir on east; Sam Rayburn Reservoir on southwest.

Economy: Timber, government/services, tourism.

History: Caddo area. Spanish land grants in 1790s brought first Spanish and Anglo settlers. An original county, created 1836; organized 1837. Name means cypress in Spanish.

Race/Ethnicity, 2007: (In percent) Anglo, 87.4; Black, 10.1; Hispanic, 2.0; Other, 0.5.

Vital Statistics, 2006: Births, 117; deaths, 165; marriages, 80; divorces, 37.

Recreation: Lake activities, hunting, campsites, marinas, historic homes; McMahan's Chapel, pioneer Protestant church; Sabine National Forest.

Minerals: Glauconite, oil.

Agriculture: Beef cattle; forage, fruit raised. Market value $8.5 million. Significant timber industry.

HEMPHILL (1,095) county seat; timber, livestock center, retail trade, tourism, manufacturing; hospital; jail museum, library; Deerfest in September.

Other towns include: **Bronson** (377); **Brookeland** (300); **Geneva** (200); **Milam** (1,277); **Pineland** (1,025) timber processing.

Population	10,062
Change fm 2000	–3.9
Area (sq. mi.)	576.61
Land Area (sq. mi.)	490.27
Altitude (ft.)	164-590
Rainfall (in.)	54.40
Jan. mean min.	36.0
July mean max.	93.0
Civ. Labor	3,449
Unemployed	12.3
Wages	$23,462,968
Av. Weekly Wage	$820
Prop. Value	$459,85,559
Retail Sales	$58,806,824

San Augustine County

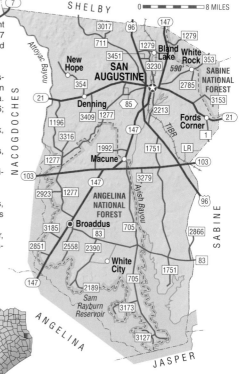

Physical Features: Hilly East Texas county, 80 percent forested with 66,799 acres in Angelina National Forest, 4,317 in Sabine National Forest; Sam Rayburn Reservoir; varied soils, sandy to black alluvial.

Economy: Lumbering, poultry, varied manufacturing.

History: Presence of Ais Indians attracted Spanish mission in 1717. First Anglos and Indians from U.S. southern states arrived around 1800. Antebellum slaveholding area. County created and named for Mexican municipality in 1836; an original county; organized 1837.

Race/Ethnicity, 2007: (In percent) Anglo, 65.6; Black, 29.8; Hispanic, 4.2; Other, 0.4.

Vital Statistics, 2006: Births, 106; deaths, 119; marriages, 16; divorces, 4.

Recreation: Lake activities, historic homes, tourist facilities in national forests; sassafras festival in October.

Minerals: Small amount of oil.

Agriculture: Poultry, cattle, horses; watermelons, peas, corn, truck crops. Market value $55.7 million. Timber sales significant.

SAN AUGUSTINE (2,542) county seat; poultry, timber, livestock center; Deep East Texas Electric Cooperative; hospital; Mission Dolores museum.

Other towns include: **Broaddus** (186).

Population	8,576
Change fm 2000	–4.1
Area (sq. mi.)	592.21
Land Area (sq. mi.)	527.87
Altitude (ft.)	164-590
Rainfall (in.)	51.10
Jan. mean min.	35.0
July mean max.	93.0
Civ. Labor	3,594
Unemployed	7.7
Wages	$11,442,026
Av. Weekly Wage	$528
Prop. Value	$258,768,798
Retail Sales	$59,968,619

For explanation of sources, abbreviations and symbols, see p. 210 and foldout map.

San Jacinto County

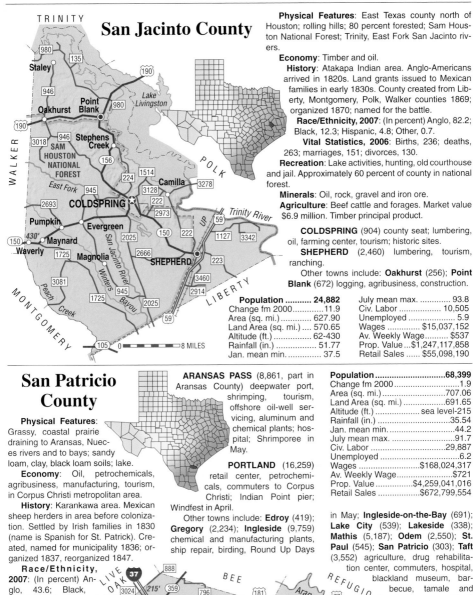

Physical Features: East Texas county north of Houston; rolling hills; 80 percent forested; Sam Houston National Forest; Trinity, East Fork San Jacinto rivers.

Economy: Timber and oil.

History: Atakapa Indian area. Anglo-Americans arrived in 1820s. Land grants issued to Mexican families in early 1830s. County created from Liberty, Montgomery, Polk, Walker counties 1869; organized 1870; named for the battle.

Race/Ethnicity, 2007: (In percent) Anglo, 82.2; Black, 12.3; Hispanic, 4.8; Other, 0.7.

Vital Statistics, 2006: Births, 236; deaths, 263; marriages, 151; divorces, 130.

Recreation: Lake activities, hunting, old courthouse and jail. Approximately 60 percent of county in national forest.

Minerals: Oil, rock, gravel and iron ore.

Agriculture: Beef cattle and forages. Market value $6.9 million. Timber principal product.

COLDSPRING (904) county seat; lumbering, oil, farming center, tourism; historic sites.

SHEPHERD (2,460) lumbering, tourism, ranching.

Other towns include: **Oakhurst** (256); **Point Blank** (672) logging, agribusiness, construction.

Population 24,882	July mean max. 93.8
Change fm 2000............11.9	Civ. Labor 10,505
Area (sq. mi.)............. 627.90	Unemployed 5.9
Land Area (sq. mi.) 570.65	Wages $15,037,152
Altitude (ft.) 62-430	Av. Weekly Wage......... $537
Rainfall (in.) 51.77	Prop. Value...$1,247,117,858
Jan. mean min. 37.5	Retail Sales $55,098,190

San Patricio County

Physical Features: Grassy, coastal prairie draining to Aransas, Nueces rivers and to bays; sandy loam, clay, black loam soils; lake.

Economy: Oil, petrochemicals, agribusiness, manufacturing, tourism, in Corpus Christi metropolitan area.

History: Karankawa area. Mexican sheep herders in area before colonization. Settled by Irish families in 1830 (name is Spanish for St. Patrick). Created, named for municipality 1836; organized 1837, reorganized 1847.

Race/Ethnicity, 2007: (In percent) Anglo, 43.6; Black, 3.1; Hispanic, 51.8; Other, 1.5.

Vital Statistics, 2006: Births, 1,215; deaths, 493; marriages, 335; divorces, 267.

Recreation: Water activities, hunting, Corpus Christi Bay, state park, Welder Wildlife Foundation and Park, birdwatching.

Minerals: Oil, gas, gravel, caliche.

Agriculture: Cotton, grain sorghum, beef cattle, corn. Market value $109.2 million. Fisheries income significant.

SINTON (5,705) county seat; oil, agribusiness, tourism; Go Texan Days in October.

ARANSAS PASS (8,861, part in Aransas County) deepwater port, shrimping, tourism, offshore oil-well servicing, aluminum and chemical plants; hospital; Shrimporee in May.

PORTLAND (16,259) retail center, petrochemicals, commuters to Corpus Christi; Indian Point pier; Windfest in April.

Other towns include: **Edroy** (419); **Gregory** (2,234); **Ingleside** (9,759) chemical and manufacturing plants, ship repair, birding, Round Up Days in May; **Ingleside-on-the-Bay** (691); **Lake City** (539); **Lakeside** (338); **Mathis** (5,187); **Odem** (2,550); **St. Paul** (545); **San Patricio** (303); **Taft** (3,552) agriculture, drug rehabilitation center, commuters, hospital, blackland museum, barbecue, tamale and hot sauce cook-off in December; **Taft Southwest** (1,579).

Population.............................68,399	
Change fm 2000............................1.9	
Area (sq. mi.).........................707.06	
Land Area (sq. mi.) 691.65	
Altitude (ft.) .... sea level-215	
Rainfall (in.) 35.54	
Jan. mean min. 44.2	
July mean max. 91.7	
Civ. Labor 29,887	
Unemployed 6.2	
Wages $168,024,317	
Av. Weekly Wage.......................$721	
Prop. Value $4,259,041,016	
Retail Sales $672,799,554	

San Saba County

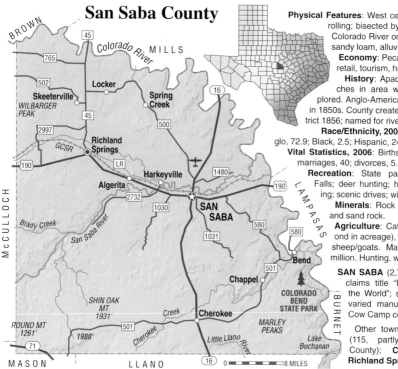

Physical Features: West central county; hilly, rolling; bisected by San Saba River; Colorado River on east; black, gray sandy loam, alluvial soils.

Economy: Pecan processing and retail, tourism, hunting leases.

History: Apaches and Comanches in area when Spanish explored. Anglo-American settlers arrived in 1850s. County created from Bexar District 1856; named for river.

Race/Ethnicity, 2007: (In percent) Anglo, 72.9; Black, 2.5; Hispanic, 24.1; Other, 0.6.

Vital Statistics, 2006: Births, 58; deaths, 76; marriages, 40; divorces, 5.

Recreation: State park with Gorman Falls; deer hunting; historic sites; fishing; scenic drives; wildflower trail.

Minerals: Rock quarry, limestone and sand rock.

Agriculture: Cattle, pecans (second in acreage), wheat, hay, some sheep/goats. Market value $28.6 million. Hunting, wildlife leases.

SAN SABA (2,706) county seat; claims title "Pecan Capital of the World"; stone processing, varied manufacturing, prison; Cow Camp cookoff in May.

Other towns include: **Bend** (115, partly in Lampasas County); **Cherokee** (175); **Richland Springs** (350).

Population	5,881
Change fm 2000	–4.9
Area (sq. mi.)	1,138.25
Land Area (sq. mi.)	1,134.47
Altitude (ft.)	1,020-1,980
Rainfall (in.)	27.72
Jan. mean min.	33.4
July mean max.	95.8
Civ. Labor	2,366
Unemployed	5.5
Wages	$11,389,373
Av. Weekly Wage	$489
Fed. Wages	$193,542
Prop. Value	$271,967,891
Retail Sales	$31,981,610

Schleicher County

Physical Features: West central county on edge of Edwards Plateau, broken by Devils, Concho, San Saba tributaries; part hilly; black soils.

Economy: Oil, ranching, hunting.

History: Jumanos in area in 1630s. Later, Apaches and Comanches; removed in 1870s. Ranching began in 1870s. Census of 1890 showed third of population from Mexico. County named for Gustav Schleicher, founder of German colony; county created from Crockett County 1887, organized 1901.

Race/Ethnicity, 2007: (In percent) Anglo, 50.0; Black, 1.3; Hispanic, 48.1; Other, 0.6.

Vital Statistics, 2006: Births, 39; deaths, 36; marriages, 22; divorces, 5.

Recreation: Hunting, livestock show in January, youth and open rodeos, mountain bike events.

Minerals: Oil, natural gas.

Agriculture: Beef cattle, sheep, goats, cotton, hay. Market value $13.6 million. Hunting leases important.

ELDORADO (2,006) county seat; oil activities, center for livestock, mohair marketing, woolen mill, government/services; hospital.

For explanation of sources, abbreviations and symbols, see p. 210 and foldout map.

Population	2,819
Change fm 2000	–4.0
Area (sq. mi.)	1,310.65
Land Area (sq. mi.)	1,310.61
Altitude (ft.)	2,070-2,600
Rainfall (in.)	19.00
Jan. mean min.	28.0
July mean max.	93.0
Civ. Labor	1,551
Unemployed	3.8
Wages	$6,604,676
Av. Weekly Wage	$610
Prop. Value	$372,312,869
Retail Sales	$10,041,059

Scurry County

Physical Features: Plains county below Caprock, some hills; drained by Colorado, Brazos tributaries; lake; sandy, loam soils.

Economy: Oil, government/services, agribusiness, manufacturing.

History: Apaches; displaced later by Comanches who were relocated to Indian Territory in 1875. Ranching began in late 1870s. County created from Bexar District 1876; organized 1884; named for Confederate Gen. W.R. Scurry.

Race/Ethnicity, 2007: (In percent) Anglo, 61.2; Black, 6.6; Hispanic, 31.7; Other, 0.5.

Vital Statistics, 2006: Births, 219; deaths, 145; marriages, 111; divorces, 62.

Recreation: Lake J.B. Thomas water recreation; Towle Memorial Park; museums, community theater, White Buffalo Days and Bikefest in October.

Minerals: Oil, gas.

Agriculture: Cotton, wheat, cattle, hay. Market value $43.4 million.

SNYDER (10,790) county seat; textiles, brick plant, cotton, oil center; Western Texas College, hospital, museum; Western Swing days in July.

Other towns include: **Dunn** (75); **Fluvanna** (180); **Hermleigh** (406); **Ira** (250).

Population	15,973
Change fm 2000	−2.4
Area (sq. mi.)	907.53
Land Area (sq. mi.)	902.50
Altitude (ft.)	1,800-2,840
Rainfall (in.)	22.51
Jan. mean min.	26.7
July mean max.	94.6
Civ. Labor	7,609
Unemployed	4.3
Wages	$65,812,861
Av. Weekly Wage	$797
Prop. Value	$2,699,144,657
Retail Sales	$182,664,304

The San Saba County Courthouse in San Saba. Robert Plocheck photo.

Shackelford County

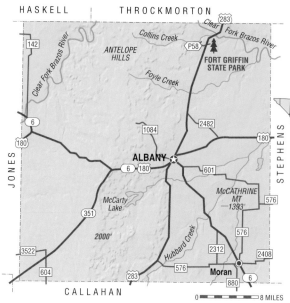

Physical Features: Rolling, hilly, drained by tributaries of Brazos; sandy and chocolate loam soils; lake.

Economy: Oil and ranching, some manufacturing, hunting leases.

History: Apaches; driven out by Comanches. First Anglo-American settlers arrived soon after establishment of military outpost in 1850s. County created from Bosque County 1858; organized 1874; named for Dr. Jack Shackelford (sometimes referred to as John), Texas Revolutionary hero.

Race/Ethnicity, 2006: (In percent) Anglo, 90.9; Black, 0.2; Hispanic, 8.4; Other, 0.4.

Vital Statistics, 2004: Births, 35; deaths, 32; marriages, 20; divorces, 15.

Recreation: Fort Griffin State Park, courthouse historical district, hunting, lake, outdoor activities, June Fandangle musical about area history.

Minerals: Oil, natural gas.

Agriculture: Beef cattle, wheat, hay, cotton. Market value $16.1 million. Hunting leases.

ALBANY (1,948) county seat; tourism, hunting, oil, ranching; historical district, Old Jail art center.

Other town: **Moran** (236).

Population	3,105
Change fm 2000	–6.0
Area (sq. mi.)	915.54
Land Area (sq. mi.)	913.95
Altitude (ft.)	1,150-2,000
Rainfall (in.)	28.45
Jan. mean min.	28.4
July mean max.	95.4
Civ. Labor	2,066
Unemployed	2.8
Wages	$10,016,816
Av. Weekly Wage	$664
Prop. Value	$321,707,053
Retail Sales	$14,602,145

For explanation of sources, abbreviations and symbols, see p. 210 and foldout map.

The old Shelby County Courthouse in Center. Robert Plocheck photo.

Shelby County

Physical Features: East Texas county; partly hills, much bottomland; well-timbered, 67,762 acres in national forest; Attoyac Bayou and Toledo Bend, other streams; sandy, clay, alluvial soils.

Economy: Poultry, timber, cattle, tourism.

History: Caddo Indian area. First Anglo-Americans settled in 1810s. Antebellum slaveholding area. Original county of Republic, created 1836; organized 1837; named for Isaac Shelby of American Revolution.

Race/Ethnicity, 2007: (In percent) Anglo, 66.0; Black, 19.9; Hispanic, 13.5; Other, 0.6.

Vital Statistics, 2006: Births, 406; deaths, 284; marriages, 218; divorces, 55.

Recreation: Toledo Bend Reservoir activities; Sabine National Forest; hunting, fishing; camping; historic sites, restored 1885 courthouse.

Minerals: Natural gas, oil.

Agriculture: First in poultry and egg production. Cattle; hay, vegetables, watermelons. Second in acreage of Christmas trees. Market value $403.1 million. Timber sales significant.

CENTER (5,957) county seat; poultry, lumber, varied manufacturing, tourism; hospital, Shelby College Center, museum; poultry festival in October.

Other towns: **Huxley** (312); **Joaquin** (991); **Shelbyville** (600); **Tenaha** (1,039); **Timpson** (1,110) livestock, timber, farming, commuters, genealogy library, So-So Festival in fall.

Population	26,529
Change fm 2000	5.2
Area (sq. mi.)	834.53
Land Area (sq. mi.)	794.11
Altitude (ft.)	174-630
Rainfall (in.)	53.01
Jan. mean min.	34.9
July mean max.	93.9
Civ. Labor	12,820
Unemployed	5.2
Wages	$58,581,953
Av. Weekly Wage	$544
Prop. Value	$1,246,129,428
Retail Sales	$300,756,665

Sherman County

Physical Features: A northern Panhandle county; level, broken by creeks, playas; sandy to dark loam soils; underground water.

Economy: Agribusiness, tourism.

History: Apaches; pushed out by Comanches in 1700s. Comanches removed to Indian Territory in 1875. Ranching began around 1880; farming after 1900. County named for Texas Gen. Sidney Sherman; created from Bexar District 1876; organized 1889.

Race/Ethnicity, 2007: (In percent) Anglo, 69.3; Black, 0.4; Hispanic, 29.8; Other, 0.5.

Vital Statistics, 2006: Births, 34; deaths, 26; marriages, 16; divorces, 8.

Recreation: Depot museum; pheasant, pronghorn hunting, jamboree and rodeo in July, carriage driving event in September.

Minerals: Natural gas, oil.

Agriculture: Beef and stocker cattle, wheat, corn, milo, cotton; 145,000 acres irrigated. Market value $448.9 million.

STRATFORD (2,061) county seat; agribusiness, petroleum, tourism, birdseed packaging; VA clinic; science and art museum.

Texhoma (1,251 [with 324 in Texas]) other principal town.

Population	2,930
Change fm 2000	–8.0
Area (sq. mi.)	923.20
Land Area (sq. mi.)	923.03
Altitude (ft.)	3,200-3,805
Rainfall (in.)	17.89
Jan. mean min.	18.5
July mean max.	91.1
Civ. Labor	1,467
Unemployed	3.7
Wages	$5,542,056
Av. Weekly Wage	$543
Prop. Value	$710,837,692
Retail Sales	$15,255,054

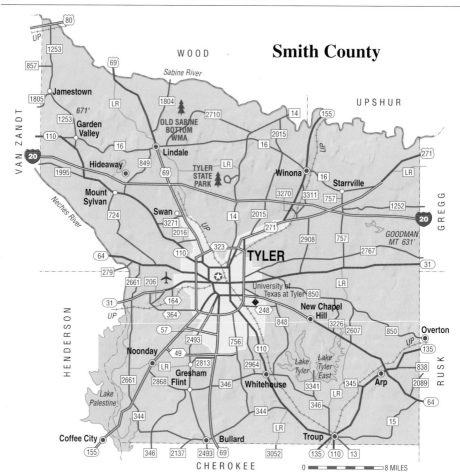

Smith County

Physical Features: Populous East Texas county of rolling hills, many timbered; Sabine, Neches, other streams; Tyler, Palestine lakes; alluvial, gray, sandy loam, clay soils.

Economy: Medical facilities, education, government/services, agribusiness, petroleum production, manufacturing, distribution center, tourism.

History: Caddoes of area reduced by disease and other tribes in 1790s. Cherokees settled in 1820s; removed in 1839. In late 1820s, first Anglo-American settlers arrived. Antebellum slaveholding area. County named for Texas Revolutionary Gen. James Smith; county created 1846 from Nacogdoches County.

Race/Ethnicity, 2007: (In percent) Anglo, 62.8; Black, 18.8; Hispanic, 16.7; Other, 1.7.

Vital Statistics, 2006: Births, 2,876; deaths, 1,675; marriages, 1,847; divorces, 512.

Recreation: Activities on Palestine, Tyler lakes; Rose Garden; state park; Goodman Museum; Caldwell Zoo; collegiate events; Juneteenth celebration, Rose Festival in October, Azalea Trail, East Texas Fair in Sept./Oct.

Minerals: Oil, gas.

Agriculture: Horticultural crops and nurseries, beef cattle, forages, fruits and vegetables, horses, Christmas trees (first in acreage). Market value $68 million. Timber sales substantial.

TYLER (98,493) county seat; claims title, "Rose Capital of the Nation"; administrative center for oil production, varied manufacturing; University of Texas at Tyler, Tyler Junior College, Texas College, University of Texas Health Center; hospitals, nursing school.

Other towns include: **Arp** (1,019) Strawberry Festival in April; **Bullard** (1,717, part in Cherokee County); **Flint** (2,500); **Hideaway** (2,906); **Lindale** (4,862) distribution center, foundry, varied manufacturing, Country Fest in October; **New Chapel Hill** (605); **Noonday** (567) Sweet Onion festival in June; **Troup** (2,144, part in Cherokee County); **Whitehouse** (6,989) commuters to Tyler, government/services, Yesteryear festival in June; **Winona** (653).

Part of **Overton** (2,407, mostly in Rusk County).

Population 201,277
Change fm 2000 .... 15.2
Area (sq. mi.) 949.45
Land Area (sq. mi.) 928.38
Altitude (ft.) 275-671
Rainfall (in.) 45.40
Jan. mean min. 38.0
July mean max. 94.0
Civ. Labor 98,361
Unemployed 5.6
Wages $911,000,270
Av. Weekly Wage $741
Prop. Value $13,594,893,135
Retail Sales $3,139,520,054

For explanation of sources, symbols and abbreviations, see p. 210 and foldout map.

Somervell County

Physical Features: Hilly terrain southwest of Fort Worth; Brazos, Paluxy rivers; gray, dark, alluvial soils; second-smallest county.

Economy: Tourism, nuclear power plant, government/services, commuters, natural gas.

History: Wichita, Tonkawa area; Comanches later. Anglo-Americans arrived in 1850s. County created as Somerville County 1875 from Hood County. Spelling was changed 1876; named for Republic of Texas Gen. Alexander Somervell.

Race/Ethnicity, 2007: (In percent) Anglo, 83.6; Black, 0.3; Hispanic, 15.4; Other, 0.8.

Vital Statistics, 2006: Births, 93; deaths, 75; marriages, 82; divorces, 34.

Recreation: Fishing, hunting; unique geological formations; dinosaur tracks in state park; Glen Rose Big Rocks Park; Fossil Rim Wildlife Center; nature trails, museums; exposition center; Paluxy Pedal bicycle ride in October.

Minerals: Sand, gravel, silica, natural gas.

Agriculture: Cattle, hay, horses, nuseries. Market value $4.5 million. Hunting leases important.

GLEN ROSE (2,658) county seat; nuclear power plant, tourism, farm trade center; hospital; Hill College branch.

Other towns include: **Nemo** (56); **Rainbow** (121).

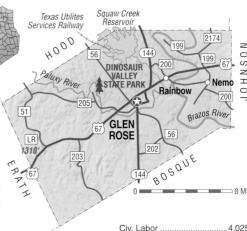

Population	**7,942**
Change fm 2000	16.6
Area (sq. mi.)	191.90
Land Area (sq. mi.)	187.17
Altitude (ft.)	550-1,310
Rainfall (in.)	34.82
Jan. mean min.	28.9
July mean max.	97.3

Civ. Labor	4,025
Unemployed	5.4
Wages	$73,009,168
Av. Weekly Wage	$1,031
Prop. Value	$2,893,827,137
Retail Sales	$45,502,989

For explanation of sources, symbols and abbreviations, see p. 210 and foldout map.

The East Texas Medical Center in Tyler. Robert Plocheck photo.

Starr County

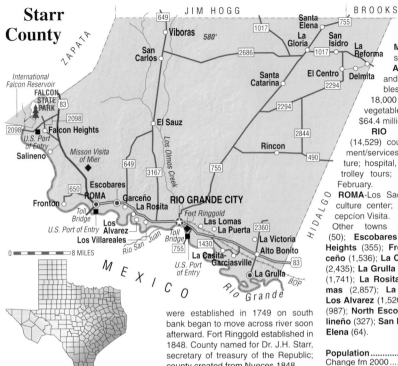

JIM HOGG

Viboras 580'

San Carlos

International Falcon Reservoir

FALCON STATE PARK 83

2098

2098 Falcon Heights
U.S. Port of Entry
Salineño
Misson Visita of Mier

El Sauz

649

3167

650 Escobares
Fronton ROMA Garceño
La Rosita RIO GRANDE CITY
Toll Bridge Los Fort Ringgold
U.S. Port of Entry Alvarez Las Lomas
Los Villareales La Puerta 2360
Toll Bridge 755
1430 La Victoria
La Casita-
U.S. Port Garciasville 83
of Entry La Grulla
Alto Bonito
Rio San Juan

0 ⬛⬛⬛ 8 MILES

Santa Elena 755
La Gloria San Isidro
2686 1017 La Reforma
Santa Catarina El Centro Delmita
2294
2294
2844
Rincon
490

Rio Grande

BROOKS

HIDALGO

BOP

MEXICO

Physical Features: Rolling, some hills; dense brush; clay, loam, sandy soils, alluvial on Rio Grande; Falcon Reservoir.

Economy: Vegetable packing, other agribusiness, oil processing, tourism, government/services.

History: Coahuiltecan Indian area. Settlers from Spanish villages that were established in 1749 on south bank began to move across river soon afterward. Fort Ringgold established in 1848. County named for Dr. J.H. Starr, secretary of treasury of the Republic; county created from Nueces 1848.

Race/Ethnicity, 2007: (In percent) Anglo, 1.8; Black, 0.0; Hispanic, 97.9; Other, 0.3.

Vital Statistics, 2006: Births, 1,492; deaths, 276; marriages, 371; divorces, 35.

Recreation: Falcon Reservoir activities; deer, white-wing dove hunting; access to Mexico; historic houses, Lee House at Fort Ringgold; grotto at Rio Grande City; Roma Fest in November.

Minerals: Oil, gas, sand, gravel.

Agriculture: Beef and fed cattle; vegetables, cotton, sorghum; 18,000 acres irrigated for vegetables. Market value $64.4 million.

RIO GRANDE CITY (14,529) county seat; government/services, tourism, agriculture; hospital, college branches; trolley tours; Vaquero Days in February.

ROMA-Los Saenz (11,707) agriculture center; La Purísima Concepcíon Visita.

Other towns include: **Delmita** (50); **Escobares** (2,029); **Falcon Heights** (355); **Fronton** (643); **Garceño** (1,536); **La Casita-Garciasville** (2,435); **La Grulla** (1,807); **La Puerta** (1,741); **La Rosita** (1,829); **Las Lomas** (2,857); **La Victoria** (1,797); **Los Alvarez** (1,520); **Los Villareales** (987); **North Escobares** (1,800); **Salineño** (327); **San Isidro** (281); **Santa Elena** (64).

Population	62,249
Change fm 2000	16.1
Area (sq. mi.)	1,229.28
Land Area (sq. mi.)	1,223.02
Altitude (ft.)	125-580
Rainfall (in.)	21.61
Jan. mean min.	44.5
July mean max.	99.1
Civ. Labor	23,188
Unemployed	15.2
Wages	$81,163,982
Av. Weekly Wage	$470
Prop. Value	$1,920,927,530
Retail Sales	$463,809,641

A ranch entrance along Texas 158 near the Sterling–Coke county line. Robert Plocheck photo.

Stephens County

Physical Features: West central county; broken, hilly; Hubbard Creek Reservoir, Possum Kingdom, Daniel lakes; Brazos River; loam, sandy soils.

Economy: Oil, agribusiness, manufacturing, recreation.

History: Comanches, Tonkawas in area when Anglo-American settlement began in 1850s. County created as Buchanan 1858 from Bosque; renamed 1861 for Confederate Vice President Alexander H. Stephens; organized 1876.

Race/Ethnicity, 2007: (In percent) Anglo, 78.3; Black, 3.0; Hispanic, 18.2; Other, 0.5.

Vital Statistics, 2006: Births, 123; deaths, 97; marriages, 90; divorces, 54.

Recreation: Lakes activities, hunting, campsites, historical points, Swenson Museum, Sandefer Oil Museum, aviation museum, festival and car show in fall.

Minerals: Oil, natural gas, stone.

Agriculture: Beef cattle, hogs, goats, sheep; wheat, oats, hay, peanuts, grain sorghums, cotton, pecans. Market value $12.4 million.

BRECKENRIDGE (5,834) county seat; oil, agriculture, oil-field equipment, aircraft parts; hospital, prison, Texas State Technical College branch, library.

Other towns include: **Caddo** (70) gateway to Possum Kingdom State Park.

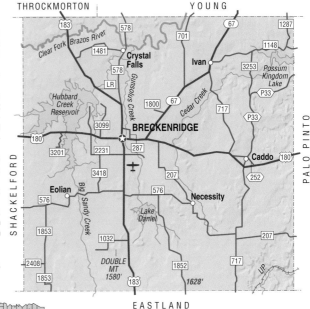

Population	9,585
Change fm 2000	−0.9
Area (sq. mi.)	921.48
Land Area (sq. mi.)	894.64
Altitude (ft.)	995-1,628
Rainfall (in.)	27.04
Jan. mean min.	30.9
July mean max.	96.8
Civ. Labor	4,724
Unemployed	4.4
Wages	$26,772,503
Av. Weekly Wage	$600
Prop. Value	$676,296,650
Retail Sales	$109,470,199

For explanation of sources, symbols and abbreviations, see p. 210 and foldout map.

Sterling County

Physical Features: Central prairie, surrounded by hills, broken by Concho River and tributaries; sandy to black soils.

Economy: Ranching, oil and gas, hunting leases.

History: Ranching began in late 1870s after Comanches, Kickapoos and other tribes removed by U.S. Army. County named for buffalo hunter W.S. Sterling; created 1891 from Tom Green County.

Race/Ethnicity, 2007: (In percent) Anglo, 67.0; Black, 0.0; Hispanic, 32.7; Other, 0.3.

Vital Statistics, 2006: Births, 6; deaths, 12; marriages, 10; divorces, 3.

Recreation: Hunting of deer, quail, turkey, dove; hunters appreciation dinner in November; junior livestock show in January.

Minerals: Oil, natural gas.

Agriculture: Meat goats, sheep, beef cattle, wheat, hay; about 1,000 acres irrigated. Market value not available.

STERLING CITY (978) county seat; farm, ranch trade center, oil-field services.

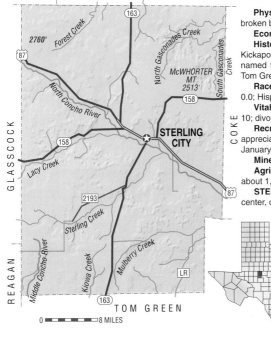

Population	1,257
Change fm 2000	−9.8
Area (sq. mi.)	923.49
Land Area (sq. mi.)	923.36
Altitude (ft.)	2,000-2,760
Rainfall (in.)	19.40
Jan. mean min.	27.4
July mean max.	94.7
Civ. Labor	808
Unemployed	2.8
Wages	$5,144,935
Av. Weekly Wage	$670
Prop. Value	$576,218,296
Retail Sales	$3,381,244

Physical Features: Western county on Rolling Plains below Caprock, bisected by Brazos forks; sandy loam, sandy, other soils; some hills.

Economy: Agribusiness, light fabrication, government/services.

History: Anglo-American ranchers arrived in 1870s after Comanches and other tribes removed by U.S. Army. German farmers settled after 1900. County named for Confederate Gen. T.J. (Stonewall) Jackson; created from Bexar District 1876, organized 1888.

Race/Ethnicity, 2007: (In percent) Anglo, 83.0; Black, 3.6; Hispanic, 12.8; Other, 0.6.

Vital Statistics, 2006: Births, 17; deaths, 25; marriages, 11; divorces, 8.

Recreation: Deer, quail, feral hog, turkey hunting; rodeos in June, September.

Minerals: Gypsum, gravel, oil.

Agriculture: Beef cattle, wheat, cotton, peanuts, hay. Also, grain sorghum, meat goats and swine. Market value $13.7 million.

ASPERMONT (875) county seat; oil field and ranching center, light fabrication; hospital; livestock show in February, Springfest.

Other towns include: **Old Glory** (100) farming center.

For explanation of sources, symbols and abbreviations, see p. 210 and foldout map.

Stonewall County

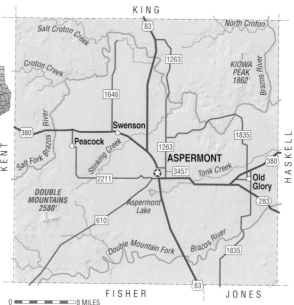

Population	1,440
Change fm 2000	–14.9
Area (sq. mi.)	920.23
Land Area (sq. mi.)	918.67
Altitude (ft.)	1,450-2,580
Rainfall (in.)	23.24
Jan. mean min.	27.2
July mean max.	97.4
Civ. Labor	877
Unemployed	3.4
Wages	$4,318,000
Av. Weekly Wage	$542
Prop. Value	$173,652,832
Retail Sales	$8,634,327

The Sutton County Courthouse in Sonora. Robert Plocheck photo.

Sutton County

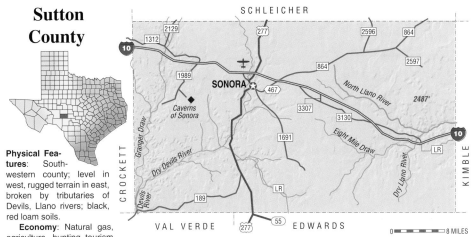

Physical Features: Southwestern county; level in west, rugged terrain in east, broken by tributaries of Devils, Llano rivers; black, red loam soils.

Economy: Natural gas, agriculture, hunting, tourism.

History: Lipan Apaches drove out Tonkawas in 1600s. Comanches, military outpost and disease forced Apaches south. Anglo-Americans settled in 1870s. Mexican immigration increased after 1890. County created from Crockett 1887; organized 1890; named for Confederate Col. John S. Sutton.

Race/Ethnicity, 2007: (In percent) Anglo, 45.5; Black, 0.4; Hispanic, 53.6; Other, 0.5.

Vital Statistics, 2006: Births, 71; deaths, 30; marriages, 30; divorces, 20.

Recreation: Hunting, Meirs Museum, Caverns of Sonora, wildlife santuary, Cinco de Mayo.

Minerals: Oil, natural gas.

Agriculture: Meat goats, sheep, cattle, Angora goats (first in number of goats). Exotic wildlife. Wheat and oats raised for grazing, hay; minor irrigation. Market value $9.6 million. Hunting leases important.

SONORA (3,101) county seat; oil and gas production, ranching, tourism; hospital; wool, mohair show in June.

Population	**4,270**
Change fm 2000	4.7
Area (sq. mi.)	1,454.40
Land Area (sq. mi.)	1,453.76
Altitude (ft.)	1,840-2,487
Rainfall (in.)	22.40
Jan. mean min.	27.2
July mean max.	94.7
Civ. Labor	3,326
Unemployed	2.3
Wages	$47,298,206
Av. Weekly Wage	$1,229
Prop. Value	$1,429,677,986
Retail Sales	$37,110,970

Swisher County

Physical Features: High Plains; level, broken by Tule Canyon and Creek; playas; large underground water supply; rich soils.

Economy: Feedlots, grain storage, manufacturing, tourism, prison.

History: Apaches; displaced by Comanches around 1700. U.S. Army removed Comanches in 1874. Ranching began in late 1870s. Farming developed after 1900. County named for J.G. Swisher of Texas Revolution; county created from Bexar, Young territories 1876; organized 1890.

Race/Ethnicity, 2007: (In percent) Anglo, 54.9; Black, 6.2; Hispanic, 38.5; Other, 0.5.

Vital Statistics, 2006: Births, 141; deaths, 83; marriages, 52; divorces, 25.

Recreation: Mackenzie battle site, county picnic in July, Ozark Trail marker.

Minerals: Not significant.

Agriculture: Stocker cattle, feedlots. Cotton, corn, wheat, sorghum. Some 400,000 acres irrigated. Market value $453.7 million.

TULIA (4,975) county seat; cattle feeding, cotton processing, manufacturing, prison; hospital, library, museum; Music on the Square in July.

Other towns include: **Happy** (653, partly in Randall County); **Kress** (806); **Vigo Park** (36).

Population	**7,654**
Change fm 2000	–8.6
Area (sq. mi.)	900.68
Land Area (sq. mi.)	900.43
Altitude (ft.)	3,160-3,735
Rainfall (in.)	20.71
Jan. mean min.	22.2
July mean max.	91.1
Civ. Labor	3,608
Unemployed	4.3
Wages	$14,496,302
Av. Weekly Wage	$525
Prop. Value	$300,010,263
Retail Sales	$37,770,611

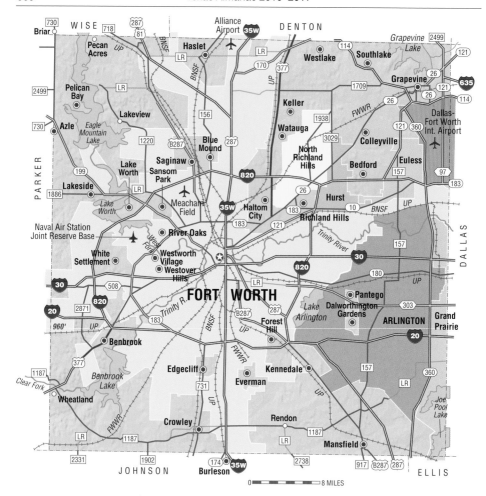

Tarrant County

Physical Features: Part Blackland, level to rolling; drains to Trinity; Worth, Grapevine, Eagle Mountain, Benbrook lakes.

Economy: Tourism, planes, helicopters, foods, mobile homes, electronic equipment, chemicals, plastics among products of more than 1,000 factories, large federal expenditure, D/FW International Airport, economy closely associated with Dallas urban area.

History: Caddoes in area. Comanches, other tribes arrived about 1700. Anglo-Americans settled in 1840s. Named for Gen. Edward H. Tarrant, who helped drive Indians from area. County created 1849 from Navarro County; organized 1850.

Race/Ethnicity, 2007: (In percent) Anglo, 53.6; Black, 13.8; Hispanic, 26.5; Other, 6.0.

Vital Statistics, 2006: Births, 27,592; deaths, 10,028; marriages, 12,905; divorces, 7,264.

Recreation: Scott Theatre; Amon G. Carter Museum; Kimbell Art Museum; Modern Art Museum; Museum of Science and History; Casa Manana; Botanic Gardens; Fort Worth Zoo; Log Cabin Village, all in Fort Worth.

Also, Six Flags Over Texas at Arlington; Southwestern Exposition, Stock Show; Convention Center; Stockyards Historical District; Texas Rangers and Dallas Cowboys at Arlington, other athletic events.

Minerals: Production of cement, sand, gravel, stone, gas.

Agriculture: Hay, beef cattle, wheat, horses, horticulture. Market value $61.4 million. Firewood marketed.

Education: Texas Christian University, University of Texas at Arlington, Texas Wesleyan University, Southwestern Baptist Theological Seminary and several other academic centers including a junior college system with five campus and various centers.

FORT WORTH (688,222, parts in Denton and Parker counties) county seat; a major mercantile, commercial and financial center; airplane, helicopter and other plants.

A cultural center with renowned art museums, Bass Performance Hall; many conventions held in downtown center; agribusiness center for wide area with grain-storage and feed-mill operations; adjacent to D/FW International Airport; hospitals.

ARLINGTON (374,943) tourist center with Six Flags Over Texas, the Texas Rangers baseball team, Dallas Cowboys football stadium, restaurants, retail, industrial and distribution center for automobiles, food products, electronic components, aircraft and parts, rubber and plastic products; hospitals, colleges, museums; Scottish festival in June.

Other towns include: **Hurst** (38,661); **Euless** (52,809); **Bedford** (49,960) helicopter plant, hospital, Celtic festival in fall; **North Richland Hills** (65,702) hospital.

Azle (10,904, partly in Parker County) government/services, varied industries, natural gas, hospital, commuters to Fort Worth, Jumpin' Jack Jamboree in September; **Benbrook** (22,363) varied manufacturing, hospitals; **Blue Mound** (2,535); **Briar** (5,861, parts in Wise and Parker counties).

Also, **Colleyville** (23,138) major residential development, some retail, manufacturing; **Crowley** (11,770) varied manufacturing, government/services, hospital; **Dalworthington Gardens** (2,439); **Edgecliff** (2,613); **Everman** (6,027); **Forest Hill** (14,137).

Also, **Grapevine** (49,150) manufacturing, distribution, near the D/FW International Airport, tourist center, hospital, Grapefest in September; **Haltom City** (41,918) light manufacturing, food processing, medical center; library; **Haslet** (1,442); **Keller** (37,386) Bear Creek Park, Wild West Fest.

Largest U.S. Media Markets

Rank	TV Homes
1. New York	7.43 million
2. Los Angeles	5.65 million
3. Chicago	3.49 million
4. Philadelphia	2.95 million
5. Dallas/Fort Worth	2.49 million
6. San Francisco	2.48 million
7. Boston	2.41 million
8. Atlanta	2.37 million
9. Washington, D.C.	2.32 million
10. Houston	2.11 million

Source: Nielsen Media Research, 2009.

Also, **Kennedale** (7,016) commuters, printing, manufacturing, library, drag strip, custom car show in May; **Lakeside** (1,231); **Lake Worth** (4,793) retail, government/services, Bullfrog festival in April; **Mansfield** (44,957, partly in Johnson County) varied manufacturing, retail, government/services, commuters, hospital, community college, library, museum, parks, Pecan festival in September; **Pantego** (2,351); **Pelican Bay** (1,763); **Rendon** (9,670); **Richland Hills** (8,277).

Also, **River Oaks** (7,206); **Saginaw** (20,929) grain milling, manufacturing, distribution, library, aquatic center; **Sansom Park** (4,410); **Southlake**

(25,859) technology, financial, retail center, hospital, parks, Oktoberfest; **Watauga** (24,030); **Westlake** (227); **Westover Hills** (690); **Westworth Village** (2,800).

Also, **White Settlement** (15,814) aircraft manufacturing, drilling equipment, technological services, museums, parks, historical sites; industrial park; White Settlement Day parade in fall.

Also, part [3,462] of **Burleson** (34,467); part [27,621] of **Grand Prairie** (158,646), and part of **Pecan Acres** (2,555).

Population	1,750,091
Change fm 2000	21.0
Area (sq. mi.)	897.48
Land Area (sq. mi.)	863.42
Altitude (ft.)	420-960
Rainfall (in.)	34.01
Jan. mean min.	31.4
July mean max.	96.6
Civ. Labor	897,820
Unemployed	5.7
Wages	$8,414,892,170
Av. Weekly Wage	$841
Prop. Value	$150,150,277,565
Retail Sales	$24,153,051,454

For explanation of sources, abbreviations and symbols, see p. 210 and foldout map.

The marina on Joe Pool Lake, which is in Tarrant, Dallas and Ellis counties. Robert Plocheck photo.

Taylor County

Physical Features: Prairies, with Callahan Divide, draining to Colorado tributaries, Brazos forks; Lakes Abilene, Kirby; mostly loam soils.

Economy: Agribusiness, oil and gas, education, Dyess Air Force Base.

History: Comanches in area about 1700. Anglo-American settlers arrived in 1870s. Named for Alamo heroes Edward, James and George Taylor, brothers; county created from Bexar, Travis counties 1858; organized 1878.

Race/Ethnicity, 2007: (In percent) Anglo, 68.8; Black, 7.6; Hispanic, 21.0; Other, 2.6.

Vital Statistics, 2006: Births, 2,055; deaths, 1,169; marriages, 1,345; divorces, 650.

Recreation: Abilene State Park, lake activities, Nelson Park Zoo, college events, Buffalo Gap historical tour and arts festival in April, Western Heritage ranch rodeo in May and West Texas Fair in September at Abilene.

Minerals: Oil, natural gas.

Agriculture: Beef cattle, small grain, cotton, milo. Market value $50.6 million.

Education: Abilene Christian University, Hardin-Simmons University, McMurry University, Texas Tech University pharmacy school and branch campus, Cisco Junior College branch.

ABILENE (117,028, a small part in Jones County) county seat; distribution center, manufacturing, wind energy, meat and dairy processing, oil-field service center; hospitals, Abilene State School, West Texas Rehabilitation Center; Fort Phantom Hill (in Jones County). **Wylie** is now part of Abilene.

Other communities include: **Buffalo Gap** (450) historic sites; **Impact** (42); **Lawn** (348); **Merkel** (2,650) agribusiness center, clothing manufacturing, oil-field services; **Ovalo** (225); **Potosi** (1,697); **Trent** (309); **Tuscola** (763); **Tye** (1,200).

Population	**126,791**
Change fm 2000	0.2
Area (sq. mi.)	919.25
Land Area (sq. mi.)	915.63
Altitude (ft.)	1,640-2,490
Rainfall (in.)	23.78
Jan. mean min.	31.8
July mean max.	94.8
Civ. Labor	65,862
Unemployed	4.1
Wages	$479,229,022
Av. Weekly Wage	$626
Prop. Value	$6,659,368,143
Retail Sales	$1,977,207,569

For explanation of sources, abbreviations and symbols, see p. 210 and foldout map.

Terrell County

Physical Features: Trans-Pecos southwestern county; semi-mountainous, many canyons; rocky, limestone soils.

Economy: Ranching, hunting leases, oil and gas exploration, tourism.

History: Coahuiltecans, Jumanos and other tribes left many pictographs in area caves. Sheep ranching began in 1880s. Named for Confederate Gen. A.W. Terrell; county created 1905 from Pecos County.

Race/Ethnicity, 2007: (In percent) Anglo, 47.7; Black, 0.00; Hispanic, 50.1; Other, 2.2.

Vital Statistics, 2006: Births, 11; deaths, 11; marriages, 5; divorces, 0.

Recreation: Nature tourism, hunting, especially white-tailed and mule deer, Rio Grande Wild and Scenic River, varied wildlife; Cinco de Mayo, Prickly Pear Pachanga in October.

Minerals: Gas, oil, limestone.

Agriculture: Goats (meat, Angora); sheep (meat, wool); some beef cattle. Market value $4 million. Wildlife leases important.

SANDERSON (798) county seat; ranching, petroleum center, tourism; museum.

Other town: **Dryden** (13).

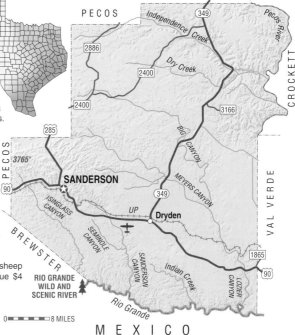

Population **924**	Unemployed 8.0
Change fm 2000 ....–14.5	Wages $2,086,912
Area (sq. mi.) 2,357.75	Av. Weekly Wage........................$587
Land Area (sq. mi.) 2,357.72	Prop. Value $937,529,804
Altitude (ft.) 1,180-3,765	Retail Sales $2,771,117
Rainfall (in.) 14.94	
Jan. mean min. 30.5	
July mean max. 91.9	
Civ. Labor 376	

U.S. 90 between Sanderson, Terrell County, and Marathon, Brewster County. Robert Plocheck photo.

Terry County

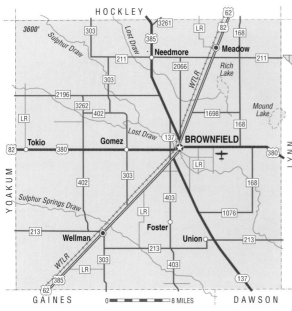

Physical Features: South Plains, broken by draws, playas; sandy, sandy loam, loam soils.

Economy: Agribusiness, government/services, trade, commuting to Lubbock.

History: Comanches removed in 1870s by U.S. Army. Ranching developed in 1890s; farming after 1900. Oil discovered in 1940. County named for Confederate Col. B.F. Terry, head of the Eighth Texas Cavalry (Terry's Texas Rangers). Created from Bexar District 1876; organized 1904.

Race/Ethnicity, 2007: (In percent), Anglo, 46.1; Black, 5.0; Hispanic, 48.2; Other, 0.6.

Vital Statistics, 2006: Births, 182; deaths, 104; marriages, 88; divorces, 39.

Recreation: Museum, aquatic center, quilt show in April, harvest festival in October.

Minerals: Oil, gas, salt mining.

Agriculture: Cotton is principal crop; peanuts (third in acreage), grain sorghum, guar, wheat, melons, cucumbers, sesame. 170,000 acres irrigated. Market value $124.8 million.

BROWNFIELD (9,170) county seat; oil-field services, wind energy, agribusiness, minerals and peanut processing; hospital; prison.

Other towns include: **Meadow** (660); **Tokio** (5); **Wellman** (188).

Population	12,135
Change fm 2000	–4.9
Area (sq. mi.)	890.93
Land Area (sq. mi.)	889.88
Altitude (ft.)	3,080-3,600
Rainfall (in.)	18.89
Jan. mean min.	26.1
July mean max.	92.5
Civ. Labor	6,245
Unemployed	4.2
Wages	$33,397,803
Av. Weekly Wage	$638
Prop. Value	$916,027,520
Retail Sales	$134,648,272

Throckmorton County

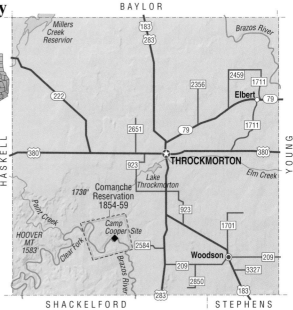

Physical Features: Northwest county southwest of Wichita Falls; rolling, between Brazos forks; red to black soils.

Economy: Oil, agribusiness, hunting.

History: Site of Comanche Indian Reservation 1854-59. Ranching developed after Civil War. County named for Dr. W.E. Throckmorton, father of Gov. J.W. Throckmorton; county created from Fannin 1858; organized 1879.

Race/Ethnicity, 2007: (In percent) Anglo, 88.8; Black, 0.01; Hispanic, 10.6; Other, 0.5.

Vital Statistics, 2006: Births, 14; deaths, 19; marriages, 8; divorces, 4.

Recreation: Hunting, fishing; historic sites include Camp Cooper, site of former Comanche reservation, restored ranch home; Millers Creek Reservoir; wild game dinner in January.

Minerals: Natural gas, oil.

Agriculture: Beef cattle, horses, wheat, hay. Market value $21.9 million. Mesquite firewood sold. Hunting leases important.

THROCKMORTON (833) county seat; varied manufacturing, oil-field services; hospital; Old Jail museum.

Other towns include: **Elbert** (57), **Woodson** (305).

Population	1,667
Change fm 2000	–9.9
Area (sq. mi.)	915.47
Land Area (sq. mi.)	912.34
Altitude (ft.)	1,100-1,730
Rainfall (in.)	26.60
Jan. mean min.	28.0
July mean max.	97.0
Civ. Labor	992
Unemployed	2.8
Wages	$3,432,843
Av. Weekly Wage	$565
Prop. Value	$150,832,541
Retail Sales	$7,049,553

Titus County

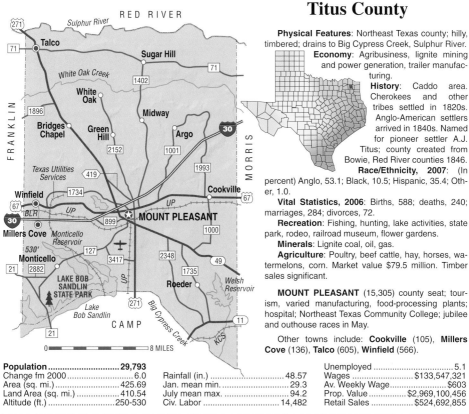

Physical Features: Northeast Texas county; hilly, timbered; drains to Big Cypress Creek, Sulphur River.

Economy: Agribusiness, lignite mining and power generation, trailer manufacturing.

History: Caddo area. Cherokees and other tribes settled in 1820s. Anglo-American settlers arrived in 1840s. Named for pioneer settler A.J. Titus; county created from Bowie, Red River counties 1846.

Race/Ethnicity, 2007: (In percent) Anglo, 53.1; Black, 10.5; Hispanic, 35.4; Other, 1.0.

Vital Statistics, 2006: Births, 588; deaths, 240; marriages, 284; divorces, 72.

Recreation: Fishing, hunting, lake activities, state park, rodeo, railroad museum, flower gardens.

Minerals: Lignite coal, oil, gas.

Agriculture: Poultry, beef cattle, hay, horses, watermelons, corn. Market value $79.5 million. Timber sales significant.

MOUNT PLEASANT (15,305) county seat; tourism, varied manufacturing, food-processing plants; hospital; Northeast Texas Community College; jubilee and outhouse races in May.

Other towns include: **Cookville** (105), **Millers Cove** (136), **Talco** (605), **Winfield** (566).

Population		29,793
Change fm 2000		6.0
Area (sq. mi.)		425.69
Land Area (sq. mi.)		410.54
Altitude (ft.)		250-530
Rainfall (in.)		48.57
Jan. mean min.		29.3
July mean max.		94.2
Civ. Labor		14,482
Unemployed		5.1
Wages		$133,547,321
Av. Weekly Wage		$603
Prop. Value		$2,969,100,456
Retail Sales		$524,692,855

Fall foliage in Northeast Texas, here in Red River County, north of the Sulphur River. Robert Plocheck photo.

Tom Green County

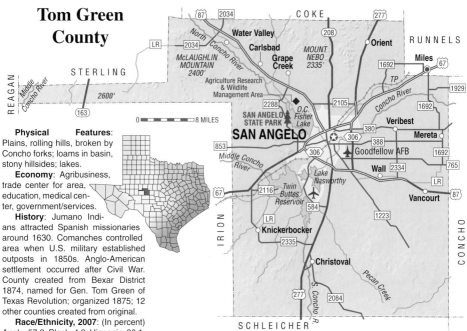

Physical Features: Plains, rolling hills, broken by Concho forks; loams in basin, stony hillsides; lakes.

Economy: Agribusiness, trade center for area, education, medical center, government/services.

History: Jumano Indians attracted Spanish missionaries around 1630. Comanches controlled area when U.S. military established outposts in 1850s. Anglo-American settlement occurred after Civil War. County created from Bexar District 1874, named for Gen. Tom Green of Texas Revolution; organized 1875; 12 other counties created from original.

Race/Ethnicity, 2007: (In percent) Anglo, 57.8; Black, 4.3; Hispanic, 36.1; Other, 1.8.

Vital Statistics, 2006: Births, 1,590; deaths, 933; marriages, 1,094; divorces, 447.

Recreation: Water sports, hunting, Fort Concho museum, symphony, hockey, baseball teams, Christmas at Old Fort Concho, February rodeo.

Minerals: Oil, natural gas.

Agriculture: Cotton, cattle, goats, sheep, small grains, milo. About 30,000 acres irrigated. Market value $133 million; first in sheep and goat production.

SAN ANGELO (89,343) county seat; government/services, retail, transportation, education; hospitals, Angelo State University, Howard Junior College branch; riverwalk; Museum of Fine Arts, drag boat races in June.

Other towns include: **Carlsbad** (236); **Christoval** (419); **Grape Creek** (3,025); **Knickerbocker** (94); **Mereta** (131); **Vancourt** (131); **Veribest** (115); **Wall** (329); **Water Valley** (203).

Population	107,864
Change fm 2000	3.7
Area (sq. mi.)	1,540.54
Land Area (sq. mi.)	1,522.10
Altitude (ft.)	1,675-2,600
Rainfall (in.)	20.91
Jan. mean min.	31.8
July mean max.	94.4
Civ. Labor	51,222
Unemployed	4.5
Wages	$356,716,669
Av. Weekly Wage	$621
Prop. Value	$4,135,272,129
Retail Sales	$1,465,169,382

For explanation of sources, symbols and abbreviations, see p. 210 and foldout map.

The University of Texas Tower and Littlefield Memorial Fountain in Austin. Robert Plocheck photo.

Travis County

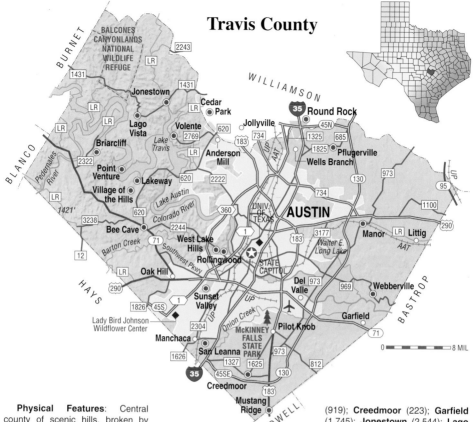

BALCONES CANYONLANDS NATIONAL WILDLIFE REFUGE

BURNET

2243

1431

LR

Jonestown

1431

Cedar Park

WILLIAMSON

35 Round Rock

Jollyville

45N

LR

Lago Vista

Volente

620

734

1325

685

Briarcliff

BLANCO

2769

183

1825 Pflugerville

Lake Travis

Anderson Mill

Wells Branch

2322

Point Venture

Lakeway

620

2222

130

973

Village of the Hills

Lake Austin

734

95

LR

1421'

Colorado River

UNIV. OF TEXAS

AUSTIN

1100

3238

620

360

290

Bee Cave

2244

1

183

3177

Manor

LR Littig

12

Barton Creek

West Lake Hills

Walter E. Long Lake

AAT

71

Southwest Pkwy

Rollingwood

STATE CAPITOL

LR

Oak Hill

HAYS

290

1

Sunset Valley

Del Valle

973

969

Webberville

BASTROP

1826

45S

Lady Bird Johnson Wildflower Center

2304

Garfield

71

Manchaca

McKINNEY FALLS STATE PARK

Pilot Knob

0 ⊏⊐⊏⊐⊐ 8 MIL

San Leanna

1626

1327

1625

973

812

35

45SE

130

Creedmoor

183

Mustang Ridge

CALDWELL

Physical Features: Central county of scenic hills, broken by Colorado River and lakes; cedars, pecans, other trees; diverse soils, mineral deposits.

Economy: Government/services, education, technology, research and industry.

History: Tonkawa and Lipan Apache area; Comanches, Kiowas arrived about 1700. Spanish missions from East Texas temporarily relocated near Barton Springs in 1730 before removing to San Antonio. Anglo-Americans arrived in early 1830s. County created 1840, when Austin became Republic's capital, from Bastrop County; organized 1843; named for Alamo commander Col. William B. Travis; many other counties created from its original area.

Race/Ethnicity, 2007: (In percent) Anglo, 50.2; Black, 9.3; Hispanic, 34.4; Other, 6.1.

Vital Statistics, 2006: Births, 14,930; deaths, 4,339; marriages, 7,775; divorces, 3,025.

Recreation: Colorado River lakes, hunting, fishing; McKinney Falls State Park; Lady Bird Johnson Wildflower Center; collegiate, metropolitan, governmental events;

official buildings and historic sites; museums; Sixth St. restoration area; scenic drives; many city parks; South by Southwest film, music festival in March.

Minerals: Production of lime, stone, sand, gravel, oil and gas.

Agriculture: Cattle, nursery crops, hogs; sorghum, corn, cotton, small grains, pecans. Market value $22.8 million.

Education: University of Texas main campus, St. Edward's University, Concordia Lutheran University, Huston-Tillotson College, Austin Community College, Episcopal and Presbyterian seminaries.

AUSTIN (736,172, part [11,810] in Williamson County) county seat and state capital; state and federal payrolls, IRS center, tourism, Lyndon B. Johnson Library, research, high-tech industries; hospitals, including state institutions for blind, deaf, mental illnesses; popular retirement area. **Del Valle** is now part of Austin.

Other towns include: **Bee Cave** (1,910) retail, tourism; **Briarcliff**

(919); **Creedmoor** (223); **Garfield** (1,745); **Jonestown** (2,544); **Lago Vista** (6,328); **Lakeway** (11,399) residential real estate, retail, tourism, lake activities, SpringFest in April; **Manchaca** (2,259) **Manor** (3,399); **Mustang Ridge** (996, partly in Caldwell County).

Also, **Pflugerville** (33,392) high-tech industries, agriculture, government/services, Deutchenfest in May; **Point Venture** (473); **Rollingwood** (1,357); **San Leanna** (527); **Sunset Valley** (575); **The Hills** (1,910) residential community; **Volente** (398); **Webberville** (318); **Wells Branch** (11,867); **West Lake Hills** (3,259).

Also, part of **Anderson Mill**, part of **Cedar Park**, part of **Jollyville** and part of **Round Rock**, all mostly in Williamson County.

Population	998,543
Change fm 2000	22.9
Area (sq. mi.)	1,022.06
Land Area (sq. mi.)	989.30
Altitude (ft.)	400-1,421
Rainfall (in.)	33.65
Jan. mean min.	40.0
July mean max.	95.0
Civ. Labor	541,874
Unemployed	5.0
Wages	$6,939,960,073
Av. Weekly Wage	$927
Prop. Value	$102,396,525,760
Retail Sales	$14,187,297,018

Trinity County

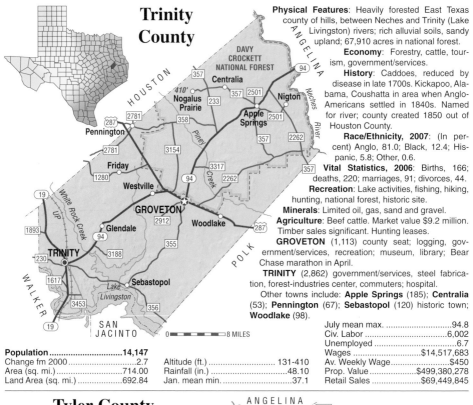

Physical Features: Heavily forested East Texas county of hills, between Neches and Trinity (Lake Livingston) rivers; rich alluvial soils, sandy upland; 67,910 acres in national forest.

Economy: Forestry, cattle, tourism, government/services.

History: Caddoes, reduced by disease in late 1700s. Kickapoo, Alabama, Coushatta in area when Anglo-Americans settled in 1840s. Named for river; county created 1850 out of Houston County.

Race/Ethnicity, 2007: (In percent) Anglo, 81.0; Black, 12.4; Hispanic, 5.8; Other, 0.6.

Vital Statistics, 2006: Births, 166; deaths, 220; marriages, 91; divorces, 44.

Recreation: Lake activities, fishing, hiking, hunting, national forest, historic site.

Minerals: Limited oil, gas, sand and gravel.

Agriculture: Beef cattle. Market value $9.2 million. Timber sales significant. Hunting leases.

GROVETON (1,113) county seat; logging, government/services, recreation; museum, library; Bear Chase marathon in April.

TRINITY (2,862) government/services, steel fabrication, forest-industries center, commuters; hospital.

Other towns include: **Apple Springs** (185); **Centralia** (53); **Pennington** (67); **Sebastopol** (120) historic town; **Woodlake** (98).

Population	**14,147**
Change fm 2000	2.7
Area (sq. mi.)	714.00
Land Area (sq. mi.)	692.84
Altitude (ft.)	131-410
Rainfall (in.)	48.10
Jan. mean min.	37.1
July mean max.	94.8
Civ. Labor	6,002
Unemployed	6.7
Wages	$14,517,683
Av. Weekly Wage	$450
Prop. Value	$499,380,278
Retail Sales	$69,449,845

Tyler County

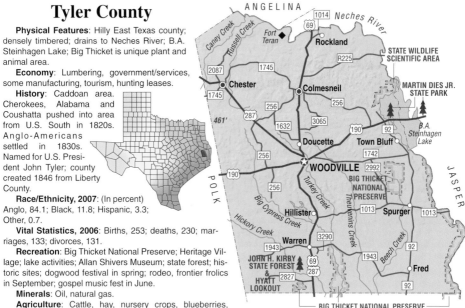

Physical Features: Hilly East Texas county; densely timbered; drains to Neches River; B.A. Steinhagen Lake; Big Thicket is unique plant and animal area.

Economy: Lumbering, government/services, some manufacturing, tourism, hunting leases.

History: Caddoan area. Cherokees, Alabama and Coushatta pushed into area from U.S. South in 1820s. Anglo-Americans settled in 1830s. Named for U.S. President John Tyler; county created 1846 from Liberty County.

Race/Ethnicity, 2007: (In percent) Anglo, 84.1; Black, 11.8; Hispanic, 3.3; Other, 0.7.

Vital Statistics, 2006: Births, 253; deaths, 230; marriages, 133; divorces, 131.

Recreation: Big Thicket National Preserve; Heritage Village; lake activities; Allan Shivers Museum; state forest; historic sites; dogwood festival in spring; rodeo, frontier frolics in September; gospel music fest in June.

Minerals: Oil, natural gas.

Agriculture: Cattle, hay, nursery crops, blueberries, horses. Market value $21.8 million. Timber sales significant.

WOODVILLE (2,345) county seat; lumber, cattle market, varied manufacturing, tourism; hospital, prison.

Other towns include: **Chester** (259) **Colmesneil** (666), **Doucette** (160), **Fred** (299), **Hillister** (250), **Spurger** (590), **Warren** (310).

Population	**20,470**
Change fm 2000	–1.9
Area (sq. mi.)	935.71
Land Area (sq. mi.)	922.90
Altitude (ft.)	50-461
Rainfall (in.)	54.79
Jan. mean min.	38.3
July mean max.	92.1
Civ. Labor	8,282
Unemployed	7.3
Wages	$29,397,997
Av. Weekly Wage	$549
Prop. Value	$1,246,106,531
Retail Sales	$102,900,963

Upshur County

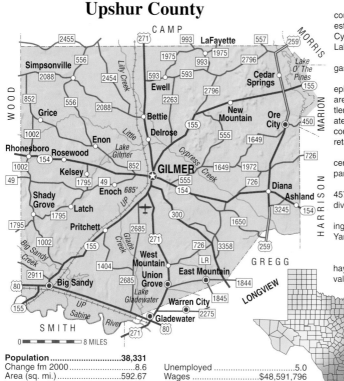

Physical Features: East Texas county; rolling to hilly, over half forested; drains to Sabine River, Little Cypress Creek, Lake O' the Pines, Lake Gilmer, Lake Gladewater.

Economy: Manufacturing, oil, gas, agribusiness, timber.

History: Caddoes; reduced by epidemics in 1700s. Cherokees in area in 1820s. Anglo-American settlement in mid-1830s. County created from Harrison, Nacogdoches counties 1846; named for U.S. Secretary of State A.P. Upshur.

Race/Ethnicity, 2007: (In percent) Anglo, 82.9; Black, 10.1; Hispanic, 6.1; Other, 1.0.

Vital Statistics, 2006: Births, 457; deaths, 381; marriages, 269; divorces, 227.

Recreation: Scenic trails, hunting, fishing, fall foliage, East Texas Yamboree in October.

Minerals: Oil, gas, sand, gravel.

Agriculture: Dairies, beef cattle, hay, vegetable crops, poultry. Market value $48.9 million. Timber a major product.

GILMER (5,094) county seat; manufacturing, petroleum, agribusiness, timber; hospital; museums.

Other towns include: **Big Sandy** (1,375); **Diana** (585); **East Mountain** (600); **Ore City** (1,264); **Union Grove** (383). Part [2,454] of **Gladewater** (6,453).

Population	38,331
Change fm 2000	8.6
Area (sq. mi.)	592.67
Land Area (sq. mi.)	587.64
Altitude (ft.)	228-685
Rainfall (in.)	47.08
Jan. mean min.	31.4
July mean max.	93.4
Civ. Labor	19,856

Unemployed	5.0
Wages	$48,591,796
Av. Weekly Wage	$568
Prop. Value	$2,547,198,533
Retail Sales	$275,001,836

For explanation of sources, symbols and abbreviations, see p. 210 and foldout map.

An early-morning pastoral scene along U.S. 80 in Upshur County. Robert Plocheck photo.

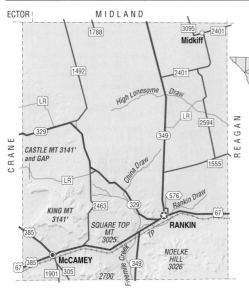

Upton County

Physical Features: Western county; north flat, south rolling, hilly; limestone, sandy loam soils, drains to creeks.

Economy: Oil, wind turbines, farming, ranching.

History: Apache and Comanche area until tribes removed by U.S. Army in 1870s. Sheep, cattle ranching developed in 1880s. Oil discovered in 1925. County created in 1887 from Tom Green County; organized 1910; name honors brothers John and William Upton, Confederate colonels.

Race/Ethnicity, 2007: (In percent) Anglo, 51.4; Black, 1.6; Hispanic, 46.1; Other, 0.8.

Vital Statistics, 2006: Births, 51; deaths, 35; marriages, 9; divorces, 15.

Recreation: Historic sites, Mendoza Trail museum, scenic areas; McCamey chili cookoff in October, pecan show in November.

Minerals: Oil, natural gas.

Agriculture: Cotton, sheep, goats, cattle, watermelons, pecans. Extensive irrigation. Market value $8.6 million.

Population	3,149	July mean max.	95.6
Change fm 2000	–7.5	Civ. Labor	1,834
Area (sq. mi.)	1,241.83	Unemployed	3.3
Land Area (sq. mi.)	1,241.68	Wages	$14,990,589
Altitude (ft.)	2,310-3,141	Av. Weekly Wage	$786
Rainfall (in.)	14.45	Prop. Value	$2,847,680,973
Jan. mean min.	33.1	Retail Sales	$14,843,392

RANKIN (744) county seat, oil, ranching, farming; hospital; Barbados cookoff in May, All Kid rodeo in June.

McCAMEY (1,703) oil, gas, wind; hospital; Wind Energy bluegrass festival in September.

Other town: **Midkiff** (182).

Uvalde County

Physical Features: Edwards Plateau, rolling hills below escarpment; spring-fed Sabinal, Frio, Leona, Nueces rivers; cypress, cedar, other trees, including maple groves.

Economy: Agribusinesses, hunting leases, light manufacturing, tourism.

History: Spanish mission Nuestra Señora de la Candelaria founded in 1762 for Lipan Apaches near present-day Montell; Comanches harassed mission. U.S. military outpost established in 1849. County created from Bexar 1850; re-created, organized 1856; named for 1778 governor of Coahuila, Juan de Ugalde, with name Anglicized.

Race/Ethnicity, 2007: (In percent) Anglo, 29.9; Black, 0.3; Hispanic, 69.2; Other, 0.7.

Vital Statistics, 2006: Births, 471; deaths, 206; marriages, 153; divorces, 71.

Recreation: Deer, turkey hunting; Garner State Park; water activities on rivers; John Nance Garner museum; Uvalde Memorial Park; scenic trails, historic sites.

Minerals: Asphalt, stone, sand, gravel.

Agriculture: Cattle, vegetables, corn, cotton, sorghum, sheep, goats, hay, wheat. Substantial irrigation. Market value $77.7 million.

UVALDE (16,053) county seat; vegetable, wool, mohair processing, tourism; opera house; junior college, A&M research center; hospital; Fort Inge Day in April.

Sabinal (1,755) farm, ranch center, tourism, retirement area.

Other towns include: **Concan** (225); **Knippa** (788); **Utopia** (306) resort; **Uvalde Estates** (1,806).

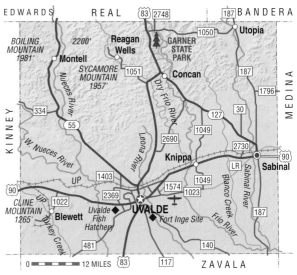

Population	26,461
Change fm 2000	2.1
Area (sq. mi.)	1,558.60
Land Area (sq. mi.)	1,556.55
Altitude (ft.)	650-2,200
Rainfall (in.)	23.30
Jan. mean min.	37.0
July mean max.	96.0
Civ. Labor	11,259
Unemployed	6.5
Wages	$62,223,479
Av. Weekly Wage	$517
Prop. Value	$1,352,281,916
Retail Sales	$336,064,013

Val Verde County

Physical Features: Southwestern county bordering Mexico, rolling, hilly; brushy; Devils, Pecos rivers, Rio Grande and Amistad Reservoir; limestone, alluvial soils.

Economy: Agribusiness, tourism, trade center, military, Border Patrol, hunting leases, fishing.

History: Apaches, Coahuiltecans, Jumanos present when Spanish came through in late 1500s. Comanches arrived later. U.S. military outposts established in 1850s to protect settlers. Only county named for Civil War battle; Val Verde means green valley. Created 1885 from Crockett, Kinney, Pecos counties.

Race/Ethnicity, 2007: (In percent) Anglo, 20.3; Black, 1.4; Hispanic, 77.2; Other, 1.1.

Vital Statistics, 2006: Births, 998; deaths, 315; marriages, 402; divorces, 65.

Recreation: Gateway to Mexico; deer hunting, fishing; Amistad lake activities; two state parks; Langtry restoration of Judge Roy Bean's saloon; ancient pictographs; San Felipe Springs; winery.

Minerals: Production sand and gravel, gas, oil.

Agriculture: Sheep (second in numbers), Angora and meat goats (third in numbers); cattle; minor irrigation. Market value $12 million.

DEL RIO (36,582) county seat; tourism and trade with Mexico, government/services including federal agencies and military, varied manufacturing, winery; hospital, extension colleges; Fiesta de Amistad in October.

Laughlin Air Force Base (2,318).

Other towns and places include: **Cienegas Terrace** (3,233); **Comstock** (344); **Langtry** (30); **Val Verde Park** (2,176).

Population	48,053
Change fm 2000	7.1
Area (sq. mi.)	3,232.40
Land Area (sq. mi.)	3,170.38
Altitude (ft.)	845-2,343
Rainfall (in.)	18.80
Jan. mean min.	39.7
July mean max.	96.2
Civ. Labor	21,228
Unemployed	6.5
Wages	$130,192,371
Av. Weekly Wage	$580
Prop. Value	$1,646,308,187
Retail Sales	$475,820,284

For explanation of sources, symbols and abbreviations, see p. 210 and foldout map.

The Baptist church in Langtry, Val Verde County. Robert Plocheck photo.

Van Zandt County

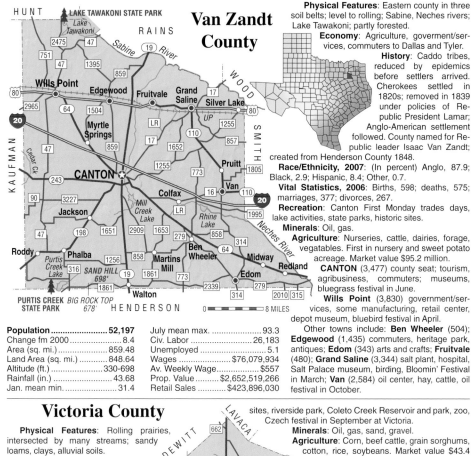

Physical Features: Eastern county in three soil belts; level to rolling; Sabine, Neches rivers; Lake Tawakoni; partly forested.

Economy: Agriculture, goverment/services, commuters to Dallas and Tyler.

History: Caddo tribes, reduced by epidemics before settlers arrived. Cherokees settled in 1820s; removed in 1839 under policies of Republic President Lamar; Anglo-American settlement followed. County named for Republic leader Isaac Van Zandt; created from Henderson County 1848.

Race/Ethnicity, 2007: (In percent) Anglo, 87.9; Black, 2.9; Hispanic, 8.4; Other, 0.7.

Vital Statistics, 2006: Births, 598; deaths, 575; marriages, 377; divorces, 267.

Recreation: Canton First Monday trades days, lake activities, state parks, historic sites.

Minerals: Oil, gas.

Agriculture: Nurseries, cattle, dairies, forage, vegatables. First in nursery and sweet potato acreage. Market value $95.2 million.

CANTON (3,477) county seat; tourism, agribusiness, commuters; museums; bluegrass festival in June.

Wills Point (3,830) government/services, some manufacturing, retail center, depot museum, bluebird festival in April.

Other towns include: **Ben Wheeler** (504); **Edgewood** (1,435) commuters, heritage park, antiques; **Edom** (343) arts and crafts; **Fruitvale** (480); **Grand Saline** (3,344) salt plant, hospital, Salt Palace museum, birding, Bloomin' Festival in March; **Van** (2,584) oil center, hay, cattle, oil festival in October.

Population	52,197	
Change fm 2000	8.4	
Area (sq. mi.)	859.48	
Land Area (sq. mi.)	848.64	
Altitude (ft.)	330-698	
Rainfall (in.)	43.68	
Jan. mean min.	31.4	
July mean max.	93.3	
Civ. Labor	26,183	
Unemployed	5.1	
Wages	$76,079,934	
Av. Weekly Wage	$557	
Prop. Value	$2,652,519,266	
Retail Sales	$423,896,030	

Victoria County

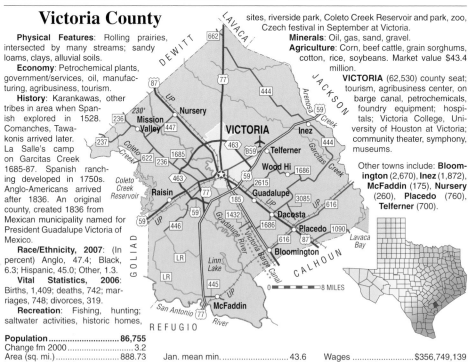

Physical Features: Rolling prairies, intersected by many streams; sandy loams, clays, alluvial soils.

Economy: Petrochemical plants, government/services, oil, manufacturing, agribusiness, tourism.

History: Karankawas, other tribes in area when Spanish explored in 1528. Comanches, Tawakonis arrived later. La Salle's camp on Garcitas Creek 1685-87. Spanish ranching developed in 1750s. Anglo-Americans arrived after 1836. An original county, created 1836 from Mexican municipality named for President Guadalupe Victoria of Mexico.

Race/Ethnicity, 2007: (In percent) Anglo, 47.4; Black, 6.3; Hispanic, 45.0; Other, 1.3.

Vital Statistics, 2006: Births, 1,409; deaths, 742; marriages, 748; divorces, 319.

Recreation: Fishing, hunting; saltwater activities, historic homes, sites, riverside park, Coleto Creek Reservoir and park, zoo, Czech festival in September at Victoria.

Minerals: Oil, gas, sand, gravel.

Agriculture: Corn, beef cattle, grain sorghums, cotton, rice, soybeans. Market value $43.4 million.

VICTORIA (62,530) county seat; tourism, agribusiness center, on barge canal, petrochemicals, foundry equipment; hospitals; Victoria College, University of Houston at Victoria; community theater, symphony, museums.

Other towns include: **Bloomington** (2,670), **Inez** (1,872), **McFaddin** (175), **Nursery** (260), **Placedo** (760), **Telferner** (700).

Population	86,755	
Change fm 2000	3.2	
Area (sq. mi.)	888.73	
Land Area (sq. mi.)	882.50	
Altitude (ft.)	sea level-230	
Rainfall (in.)	40.10	
Jan. mean min.	43.6	
July mean max.	93.4	
Civ. Labor	44,658	
Unemployed	4.6	
Wages	$356,749,139	
Av. Weekly Wage	$704	
Prop. Value	$4,893,707,279	
Retail Sales	$1,333,425,640	

Physical Features: South central county north of Houston of rolling hills; more than 70 percent forested; national forest; San Jacinto, Trinity rivers.

Economy: State employment in prison system, education.

History: Coahuiltecans, Bidais in area when Spanish explored around 1690. Later, area became trading ground for many Indian tribes. Anglo-Americans settled in 1830s. Antebellum slaveholding area. County created 1846 from Montgomery County; first named for U.S. Secretary of Treasury R.J. Walker; renamed 1863 for Texas Ranger Capt. S.H. Walker.

Race/Ethnicity, 2007: (In percent) Anglo, 60.0; Black, 23.3; Hispanic, 15.3; Other, 1.4.

Vital Statistics, 2006: Births, 589; deaths, 423; marriages, 436; divorces, 180.

Recreation: Fishing, hunting, lake activities; Sam Houston museum, homes, grave; prison museum; other historic sites, state park, Sam Houston National Forest; Sam Houston folk festival in spring.

Minerals: Clays, natural gas, oil, sand and gravel, stone.

Agriculture: Cattle, nursery plants, poultry, cotton, hay. Market value $26.9 million. Timber sales substantial; Christmas trees.

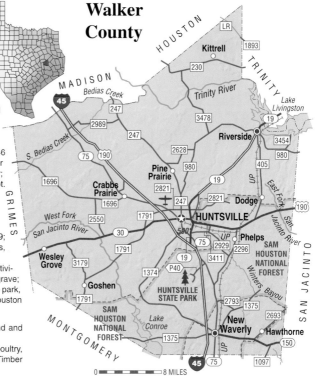

Walker County

HUNTSVILLE (37,790) county seat; state prison system, Sam Houston State University, forest products, varied manufacturing; hospital; museums, arts center.

Other towns include: **Dodge** (150), **New Waverly** (825), **Riverside** (467).

Population	**64,212**
Change fm 2000	4.0
Area (sq. mi.)	801.44
Land Area (sq. mi.)	787.45
Altitude (ft.)	131-500
Rainfall (in.)	48.51
Jan. mean min.	39.0
July mean max.	93.8
Civ. Labor	26,011

Unemployed	5.4
Wages	$182,314,173
Av. Weekly Wage	$610
Prop. Value	$2,083,025,336
Retail Sales	$710,240,198

For explanation of sources, symbols and abbreviations, see p. 210 and foldout map.

Monahans Sandhills State Park, which is in Ward and Winkler counties. Robert Plocheck photo.

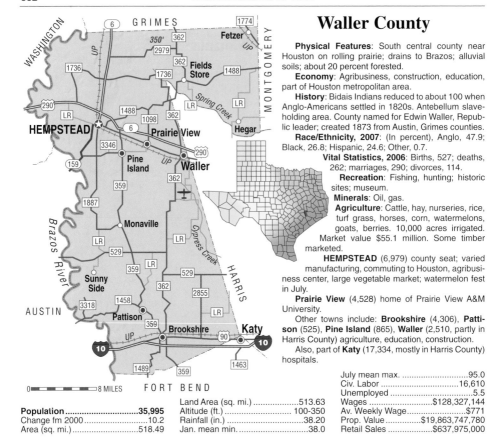

Waller County

Physical Features: South central county near Houston on rolling prairie; drains to Brazos; alluvial soils; about 20 percent forested.

Economy: Agribusiness, construction, education, part of Houston metropolitan area.

History: Bidais Indians reduced to about 100 when Anglo-Americans settled in 1820s. Antebellum slave-holding area. County named for Edwin Waller, Republic leader; created 1873 from Austin, Grimes counties.

Race/Ethnicity, 2007: (In percent), Anglo, 47.9; Black, 26.8; Hispanic, 24.6; Other, 0.7.

Vital Statistics, 2006: Births, 527; deaths, 262; marriages, 290; divorces, 114.

Recreation: Fishing, hunting; historic sites; museum.

Minerals: Oil, gas.

Agriculture: Cattle, hay, nurseries, rice, turf grass, horses, corn, watermelons, goats, berries. 10,000 acres irrigated. Market value $55.1 million. Some timber marketed.

HEMPSTEAD (6,979) county seat; varied manufacturing, commuting to Houston, agribusiness center, large vegetable market; watermelon fest in July.

Prairie View (4,528) home of Prairie View A&M University.

Other towns include: **Brookshire** (4,306), **Pattison** (525), **Pine Island** (865), **Waller** (2,510, partly in Harris County) agriculture, education, construction.

Also, part of **Katy** (17,334, mostly in Harris County) hospitals.

July mean max.	95.0
Civ. Labor	16,610
Unemployed	5.5
Wages	$128,327,144
Av. Weekly Wage	$771
Prop. Value	$19,863,747,780
Retail Sales	$637,975,000

Population	35,995
Change fm 2000	10.2
Area (sq. mi.)	518.49
Land Area (sq. mi.)	513.63
Altitude (ft.)	100-350
Rainfall (in.)	38.20
Jan. mean min.	38.0

Ward County

Physical Features: Western county on Pecos River; plain covered by grass, brush; sandy, loam soils.

Economy: Oil, gas, sand and gravel produced, government/services, retail.

History: Jumano Indians in area when Spanish explored in 1580s. Comanches arrived later. Railroad stations established in 1880s. Oil discovered in 1920s. County named for Republic leader Thomas W. Ward; county created from Tom Green 1887; organized 1892.

Race/Ethnicity, 2007: (In percent) Anglo, 49.3; Black, 4.8; Hispanic, 45.0; Other, 0.9.

Vital Statistics, 2006: Births, 156; deaths, 115; marriages, 65; divorces, 35.

Recreation: Sandhills state park, camel treks, Million Barrel museum, county park, Butterfield stagecoach festival in July.

Minerals: Oil, gas, caliche, sand, gravel.

Agriculture: Beef cattle, horses, alfalfa, goats, cotton. Market value $1.5 million.

MONAHANS (6,663) county seat; oil and gas, ranching, tourism; hospital; Juneteenth.

Other towns: **Barstow** (383); **Grandfalls** (376); **Pyote** (153) West Texas Children's Home, Rattlesnake bomber base museum; **Thorntonville** (412); **Wickett** (427).

Population	10,549
Change fm 2000	−3.3
Area (sq. mi.)	835.74
Land Area (sq. mi.)	835.49
Altitude (ft.)	2,400-2,880
Rainfall (in.)	13.23
Jan. mean min.	26.5
July mean max.	98.6
Civ. Labor	5,225
Unemployed	4.2
Wages	$43,764,926
Av. Weekly Wage	$857
Prop. Value	$1,648,451,508
Retail Sales	$88,495,321

The remains of the original campus of Baylor University at Independence. Robert Plocheck photo.

Washington County

Physical Features: South central county in Brazos valley; rolling prairie of sandy loam, alluvial soils.

Economy: Agribusiness, oil, tourism, manufacturing, government/services.

History: Coahuiltecan tribes and Tonkawas in area when Anglo-American settlers arrived in 1821. Antebellum slaveholding area. Germans arrived around 1870. County named for George Washington; an original county, created 1836, organized 1837.

Race/Ethnicity, 2007: (In percent), Anglo, 68.5; Black, 18.4; Hispanic, 11.5; Other, 1.6.

Vital Statistics, 2006: Births, 429; deaths, 337; marriages, 280; divorces, 117.

Recreation: Many historic sites, including Washington-on-the-Brazos, Texas Baptist Historical Museum, Star of Republic Museum; Somerville Lake, fishing, hunting, birding; antique rose nursery, miniature horse farm.

Minerals: Oil, gas and stone.

Agriculture: Cattle, poultry, dairy products, hogs, horses; hay, corn, sorghum, cotton, small grains, nursery crops. Market value $44.8 million.

BRENHAM (15,002) county seat; manufacturing, education, retail, Blue Bell creamery, tourism; hospital; Blinn College, Brenham State School; Maifest, Juneteenth.

Other towns include: **Burton** (374) agriculture, tourism, national landmark cotton gin, festival in April; **Chappell Hill** (750) sausage production, tourism, historic homes, Scarecrow festival in October; **Washington** (100) site of signing of Texas Declaration of Independence.

Population	32,244
Change fm 2000	6.2
Area (sq. mi.)	621.35
Land Area (sq. mi.)	609.22
Altitude (ft.)	150-560
Rainfall (in.)	44.15
Jan. mean min.	39.3
July mean max.	96.7
Civ. Labor	16,767
Unemployed	4.1
Wages	$117,020,804
Av. Weekly Wage	$627
Prop. Value	$2,383,687,989
Retail Sales	$389,408,369

For explanation of sources, abbreviations and symbols, see p. 210 and foldout map.

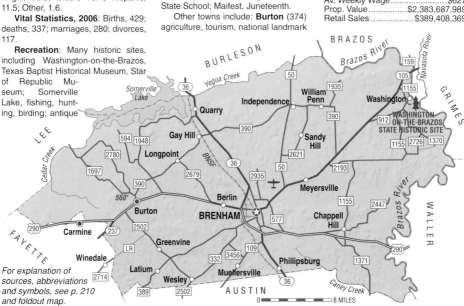

Webb County

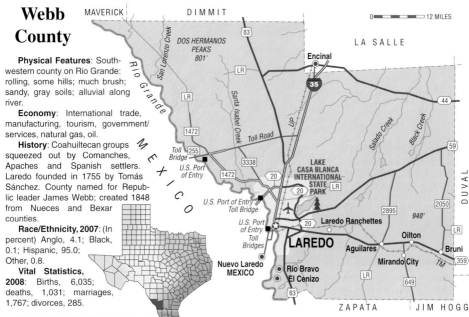

Physical Features: Southwestern county on Rio Grande: rolling, some hills; much brush; sandy, gray soils; alluvial along river.

Economy: International trade, manufacturing, tourism, government/services, natural gas, oil.

History: Coahuiltecan groups squeezed out by Comanches, Apaches and Spanish settlers. Laredo founded in 1755 by Tomás Sánchez. County named for Republic leader James Webb; created 1848 from Nueces and Bexar counties.

Race/Ethnicity, 2007: (In percent) Anglo, 4.1; Black, 0.1; Hispanic, 95.0; Other, 0.8.

Vital Statistics, 2008: Births, 6,035; deaths, 1,031; marriages, 1,767; divorces, 285.

Recreation: Tourist gateway to Mexico; hunting, fishing; Lake Casa Blanca park, water recreation; historic sites; Museum of Republic of the Rio Grande; Fort McIntosh; minor league baseball, hockey; Washington's Birthday celebration.

Minerals: Natural gas, oil, coal.

Agriculture: Onions, melons, nursery crops, cattle, horses, goats. About 4,500 acres irrigated. Market value $24.7 million. Mesquite sold. Hunting leases important.

LAREDO (222,482) county seat; international trade, government/ser-

vices, retail center; rail; highway gateway to Mexico; junior college, Texas A&M International University, community college; hospitals; entertainment/sports arena; "El Grito" on Sept. 15; Jalapeño festival in February.

Other towns and places include: **Bruni** (466); **El Cenizo** (3,805); **Laredo Ranchettes** (1,890); **Mirando City** (585); **Oilton** (368); **Rio Bravo** (5,941).

Population	**236,941**
Change fm 2000	22.7
Area (sq. mi.)	3,375.53
Land Area (sq. mi.)	3,356.83
Altitude (ft.)	310-940
Rainfall (in.)	21.53
Jan. mean min.	43.7
July mean max.	101.6
Civ. Labor	91,795
Unemployed	6.0
Wages	$637,544,740
Av. Weekly Wage	$562
Prop. Value	$12,908,742,169
Retail Sales	$3,194,349,462

For explanation of sources, abbreviations and symbols, see p. 210 and foldout map.

A cattle feedlot in Wheeler County. Robert Plocheck photo.

Wharton County

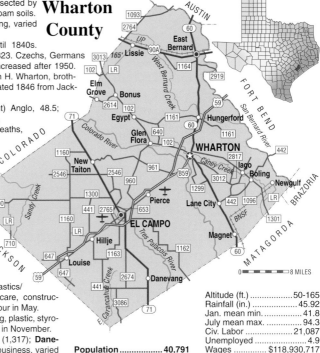

Physical Features: Gulf prairie; bisected by Colorado River; alluvial, black, sandy loam soils.

Economy: Oil, agribusiness, hunting, varied manufacturing, government/services.

History: Karankawas in area until 1840s. Anglo-American colonists settled in 1823. Czechs, Germans arrived in 1880s. Mexican migration increased after 1950. County named for John A. and William H. Wharton, brothers active in the Texas Revolution; created 1846 from Jackson, Matagorda counties.

Race/Ethnicity, 2007: (In percent) Anglo, 48.5; Black, 14.8; Hispanic, 36.1; Other, 0.6.

Vital Statistics, 2006: Births, 663; deaths, 371; marriages, 278; divorces, 139.

Recreation: Waterfowl hunting, fishing, big-game, birding; art, historical museums; river-front park at Wharton; historic sites; Fiesta Hispano Americana in September at Wharton.

Minerals: Oil, gas.

Agriculture: Top rice-producing county; cotton, milo, corn, sorghum, soybeans (first in acreage); 130,000 acres irrigated. Also, eggs, turfgrass, cattle, aquaculture. Market value $240.2 million.

WHARTON (9,264) county seat; plastics/rubber, government/services, health care, construction; hospitals, junior college; garden tour in May.

EL CAMPO (11,065) rice processing, plastic, styrofoam processing; hospital; Polka Expo in November.

Other towns include: **Boling-Iago** (1,317); **Danevang** (61); **East Bernard** (2,261) agribusiness, varied manufacturing; **Egypt** (26); **Glen Flora** (210); **Hungerford** (651); **Lane City** (111); **Lissie** (72); **Louise** (979); **Pierce** (51).

Altitude (ft.)	50-165
Rainfall (in.)	45.92
Jan. mean min.	41.8
July mean max.	94.3
Civ. Labor	21,087
Unemployed	4.9
Wages	$118,930,717
Av. Weekly Wage	$594
Prop. Value	$2,660,316,646
Retail Sales	$532,041,131

Population	40,791
Change fm 2000	–1.0
Area (sq. mi.)	1,094.43
Land Area (sq. mi.)	1,090.13

Wheeler County

Physical Features: Panhandle county adjoining Oklahoma. Plain, on edge of Caprock; Red River, Sweetwater Creek; some canyons; red sandy loam, black clay soils.

Economy: Oil, gas, agribusiness, tourism.

History: Apaches, displaced by Kiowas, Comanches around 1700. Military outpost established in 1875 after Indians forced into Oklahoma. Ranching began in late 1870s. Oil boom in 1920s. County named for pioneer jurist R.T. Wheeler; county created from Bexar, Young districts 1876; organized 1879.

Race/Ethnicity, 2007: (In percent) Anglo, 80.3; Black, 3.2; Hispanic, 15.0; Other, 1.5.

Vital Statistics, 2006: Births, 61; deaths, 70; marriages, 145; divorces, 8.

Recreation: Pioneer West museum at Shamrock; historic sites; Old Mobeetie jail, trading post, Fort Elliott; ostrich depot.

Minerals: Oil, natural gas.

Agriculture: Fed beef, cow-calf and stocker cattle, swine, horses; wheat, rye (second in acreage), grain sorghum, cotton. Market value $129.5 million.

WHEELER (1,339) county seat; agribusiness, petroleum center, tourism, slaughter plant; hospital, library.

SHAMROCK (1,946) tourism, agribusiness; hospital, library, old Route 66 sites; St. Patrick's Day event.

Other towns include: **Allison** (135); **Briscoe** (135); **Mobeetie** (107).

Land Area (sq. mi.)	914.26
Altitude (ft.)	2,005-3,000
Rainfall (in.)	24.32
Jan. mean min.	22.9
July mean max.	93.3
Civ. Labor	3,302
Unemployed	2.8
Wages	$23,377,762
Av. Weekly Wage	$694
Prop. Value	$2,141,692,554
Retail Sales	$52,698,779

Population	4,772
Change fm 2000	–9.7
Area (sq. mi.)	915.34

Wichita County

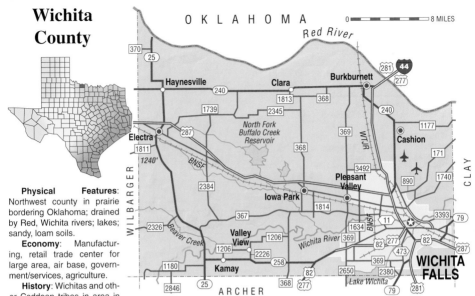

Physical Features: Northwest county in prairie bordering Oklahoma; drained by Red, Wichita rivers; lakes; sandy, loam soils.

Economy: Manufacturing, retail trade center for large area, air base, government/services, agriculture.

History: Wichitas and other Caddoan tribes in area in 1700s; Comanches, Apaches also present until 1850s. Anglo-American settlement increased after 1870. County named for tribe; created from Young Territory 1858; organized 1882.

Race/Ethnicity, 2007: (In percent) Anglo, 69.5; Black, 11.1; Hispanic, 15.6; Other, 3.9.

Vital Statistics, 2006: Births, 1,961; deaths, 1,282; marriages, 1,945; divorces, 719.

Recreation: Museums; historic sites; Texas-Oklahoma High School Oil Bowl football game; collegiate activities; water sports on lakes; Fiestas Patrias parade, Ranch Round-up in August.

Minerals: Oil.

Agriculture: Beef cattle, horticulture, wheat, hay. Seventy-five percent of hay irrigated; 10 percent of wheat/cotton. Market value $27.2 million.

WICHITA FALLS (103,202) county seat; distribution center for large area of Texas and Oklahoma, government/services, varied manufacturing, oil-field services; hospitals, including North Texas state hospital; Midwestern State University, vocational-technical training center; hiking trails; Hotter'n Hell bicycle race in August.

Sheppard Air Force Base.

Other cities include: **Burkburnett** (10,944) some manufacturing, Trails and Tales of Boomtown USA display and tours; **Cashion** (338); **Electra** (3,055) oil, agriculture, manufacturing, commuters to Wichita Falls; hospital; goat barbecue in May; **Iowa Park** (6,590) manufacturing, prison, Whoop-t-do homecoming in September; **Kamay** (640); **Pleasant Valley** (392).

Population	**127,321**
Change fm 2000	–3.3
Area (sq. mi.)	633.01
Land Area (sq. mi.)	627.66
Altitude (ft.)	912-1,240
Rainfall (in.)	28.83
Jan. mean min.	28.9
July mean max.	97.2
Civ. Labor	63,509
Unemployed	5.7
Wages	$479,232,434
Av. Weekly Wage	$661
Prop. Value	$6,378,964,129
Retail Sales	$1,617,578,825

For explanation of sources, abbreviations and symbols, see p. 210 and foldout map.

An open-air store along U.S. 77 south of Raymondville, Willacy County. Robert Plocheck photo.

Wilbarger County

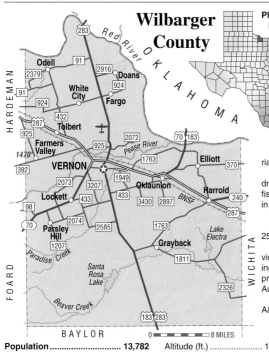

Physical Features: Gently rolling prairie draining to Red, Pease rivers, tributaries; sandy, loam, waxy soils; Santa Rosa Lake.

Economy: Agribusiness, electricity generating plant, government/services.

History: Anglo-American settlement developed after removal of Comanches into Indian Territory in 1875. County named for pioneers Josiah and Mathias Wilbarger; created from Bexar District 1858; organized 1881.

Race/Ethnicity, 2007: (In percent) Anglo, 64.5; Black, 9.6; Hispanic, 24.5; Other, 1.4.

Vital Statistics, 2006: Births, 228; deaths, 177; marriages, 236; divorces, 38.

Recreation: Doan's Crossing, on route of cattle drives; Waggoner Ranch, other historic sites; hunting, fishing; Red River Valley Museum; Santa Rosa roundup in May.

Minerals: Oil.

Agriculture: Wheat, cattle, cotton, alfalfa, peanuts; 25,000 acres irrigated. Market value $42.9 million.

VERNON (11,579) county seat; government/services, agribusiness, manufacturing, electricity-generating plant; college; state hospital/mental health center, private hospital, prison; museums; vintage car show in August.

Other towns include: **Harrold** (200); **Lockett** (150) A&M extension center; **Odell** (100); **Oklaunion** (138).

Population	13,782
Change fm 2000	–6.1
Area (sq. mi.)	978.10
Land Area (sq. mi.)	971.06
Altitude (ft.)	1,030-1,470
Rainfall (in.)	28.55
Jan. mean min.	25.7
July mean max.	97.2
Civ. Labor	7,985
Unemployed	3.6
Wages	$52,136,855
Av. Weekly Wage	$588
Prop. Value	$970,265,630
Retail Sales	$111,176,522

Willacy County

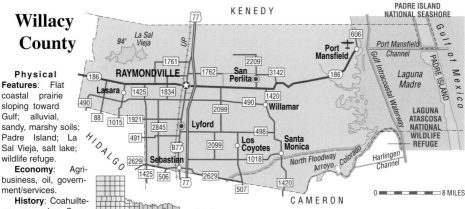

Physical Features: Flat coastal prairie sloping toward Gulf; alluvial, sandy, marshy soils; Padre Island; La Sal Vieja, salt lake; wildlife refuge.

Economy: Agribusiness, oil, government/services.

History: Coahuiltecan area when Spanish explored in 1500s. Spanish ranching began in 1790s. County named for Texas legislator John G. Willacy; created 1911 from Cameron, Hidalgo counties; reorganized 1921.

Race/Ethnicity, 2007: (In percent) Anglo, 10.2; Black, 1.8; Hispanic, 87.7; Other, 0.3.

Vital Statistics, 2006: Births, 411; deaths, 117; marriages, 95; divorces, 20.

Recreation: Fresh and saltwater fishing, hunting of deer, turkey, dove; mild climate attracts many winter tourists.

Minerals: Oil, natural gas.

Agriculture: Cotton, sorghum, corn, vegetables, sugar cane; 20 percent of cropland irrigated. Livestock includes cattle, horses, goats, hogs. Market value $51.2 million.

RAYMONDVILLE (9,852) county seat; agribusiness, oil center, food processing, tourism, enterprise zone, prison; museum; Boot Fest in October.

Other towns include: **Lasara** (1,139); **Lyford** (2,453); **Port Mansfield** (415) popular sport-fishing port; tourism, fishing tournament in late July; **San Perlita** (727); **Sebastian** (1,889).

Population	20,600
Change fm 2000	2.6
Area (sq. mi.)	784.23
Land Area (sq. mi.)	596.68
Altitude (ft.)	sea level-94
Rainfall (in.)	27.97
Jan. mean min.	47.5
July mean max.	95.3
Civ. Labor	8,159
Unemployed	9.8
Wages	$29,281,193
Av. Weekly Wage	$628
Prop. Value	$685,316,449
Retail Sales	$105,993,938

For explanation of sources, abbreviations and symbols, see p. 210 and foldout map.

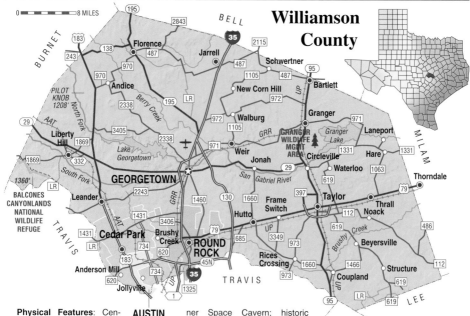

Williamson County

Physical Features: Central county near Austin. Level to rolling; mostly Blackland soil, some loam, sand; drained by San Gabriel River and tributaries.

Economy: Agribusinesses, varied manufacturing, education center, government/services; the county is part of Austin metropolitan area.

History: Tonkawa area; later, other tribes. Comanches raided until 1860s. Anglo-American settlement began in late 1830s. County named for Robert M. Williamson, pioneer leader; created from Milam and organized in 1848.

Race/Ethnicity, 2007: (In percent) Anglo, 70.5; Black, 5.8; Hispanic, 20.2; Other, 3.5.

Vital Statistics, 2006: Births, 5,409; deaths, 1,550; marriages, 1,939; divorces, 786.

Recreation: Lake recreation; Inner Space Cavern; historic sites; deer hunting, fishing; Gov. Dan Moody Museum at Taylor; San Gabriel Park; old settlers park; walking tours, rattlesnake sacking, barbecue cookoff, frontier days in summer; Round Rock minor league baseball.

Minerals: Building stone, sand and gravel.

Agriculture: Corn, cattle, sorghum, cotton, wheat, hay, nusery crops. Market value $190.4 million.

GEORGETOWN (47,066) county seat; education, health, government/services, manufacturing, retail; hospital; Southwestern University; Red Poppy festival in April.

ROUND ROCK (100,596, part [1,076] in Travis County) semiconductor, varied manufacturing, tourism and distribution center; hospital; Texas Baptist Children's Home.

Cedar Park (52,809, part in Travis County) oil production/services, varied manufacturing, commuting to Austin, hospital, steam-engine train.

Taylor (17,663) agribusiness, publishing center, varied manufacturing including cottonseed and meat processing; hospital.

Other towns include: **Andice** (300); **Bartlett** (1,974, partly in Bell County) cotton, corn production, commuters, prison, first rural electrification in nation in 1933, clinic, library, Friendship Fest in September; **Brushy Creek** (19,059); **Coupland** (280); **Florence** (1,370).

Also, **Granger** (1,620); **Hutto** (13,498) agriculture, manufacturing, government/services, commuters to Austin, museum, Olde Tyme Days in October; **Jarrell** (1,419); **Jollyville** (17,934, partly in Travis County); **Leander** (24,135); **Liberty Hill** (1,838) artisans center; **Schwertner** (175); **Thrall** (998); **Walburg** (277); **Weir** (764).

Also, the residential community of **Anderson Mill** (10,280), which extends into Travis County, and part [11,810] of **Austin**.

Population	394,193
Change fm 2000	57.7
Area (sq. mi.)	1,134.74
Land Area (sq. mi.)	1,122.77
Altitude (ft.)	400-1,360
Rainfall (in.)	35.11
Jan. mean min.	35.8
July mean max.	95.3
Civ. Labor	199,536
Unemployed	5.7
Wages	$1,260,096,955
Av. Weekly Wage	$807
Prop. Value	$41,176,255,895
Retail Sales	$5,324,970,929

The Williamson County Courthouse in Georgetown. Robert Plocheck photo.

Wilson County

Physical Features: Upper Coastal Plains; mostly sandy soils, some heavier; San Antonio River, Cibolo Creek.

Economy: Agribusiness, commuters to San Antonio; part of San Antonio metropolitan area.

History: Coahuiltecan Indians in area when Spanish began ranching around 1750. Anglo-American settlers arrived in 1840s. Germans, Polish settled in 1850s. County created from Bexar, Karnes counties 1860; named for James C. Wilson, member of the Mier Expedition.

Race/Ethnicity, 2007: (In percent) Anglo, 60.2; Black, 1.0; Hispanic, 38.2; Other, 0.6.

Vital Statistics, 2006: Births, 302; deaths, 301; marriages, 242; divorces, 98.

Recreation: Mission ranch ruins, historic homes; Stockdale watermelon jubilee in June; Floresville peanut festival in October.

Minerals: Oil, gas, clays.

Agriculture: Cattle, dairies, hogs, poultry; peanuts, sorghum, corn, small grains, vegetables, watermelons, fruit. Market value $52.9 million.

FLORESVILLE (7,381) county seat; agribusiness; hospital, veterans home; Heritage Days in spring.

Other towns include: **La Vernia** (1,220); **Pandora** (110); **Poth** (2,210) agriculture, commuting to San Antonio; Mayfest; **Stockdale** (1,600) agriculture, commuting to San Antonio, nature center; **Sutherland Springs** (420). Part of **Nixon** (2,362, mostly in Gonzales County).

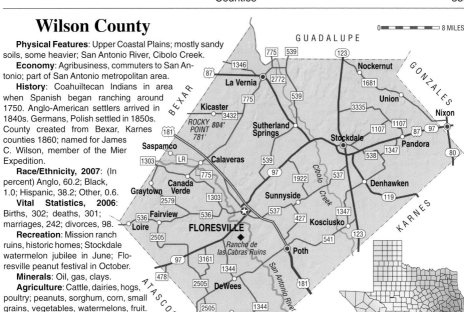

For explanation of sources, abbreviations and symbols, see p. 210 and foldout map.

Population 40,398	July mean max. 95.7
Change fm 2000 .... 24.7	Civ. Labor 18,846
Area (sq. mi.) 808.57	Unemployed 5.0
Land Area (sq. mi.) 806.99	Wages $42,081,246
Altitude (ft.) 300-804	Av. Weekly Wage.................. $501
Rainfall (in.) 27.60	Prop. Value $1,942,772,136
Jan. mean min. 38.4	Retail Sales $333,296,529

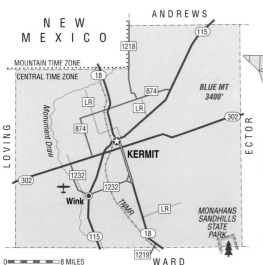

Winkler County

Physical Features: Western county adjoining New Mexico on plains, partly sandy hills.

Economy: Oil, natural gas, ranching, prison, some farming.

History: Apache area until arrival of Comanches in 1700s. Anglo-Americans began ranching in 1880s. Oil discovered 1926. Mexican migration increased after 1960. County named for Confederate Col. C.M. Winkler; created from Tom Green County 1887; organized 1910.

Race/Ethnicity, 2007: (In percent) Anglo, 49.5; Black, 1.9; Hispanic, 48.1; Other, 0.5.

Vital Statistics, 2006: Births, 101; deaths, 83; marriages, 47; divorces, 25.

Recreation: Monahans Sandhills State Park; museum; zoo; wooden oil derrick; Roy Orbison festival in June at Wink; Wink Sink, large sinkhole.

Minerals: Oil, gas.

Agriculture: Major producer of chip potatoes; meat goats, beef cattle. Market value $3.3 million.

KERMIT (5,424) county seat; oil, gas, ranching, some farming; hospital; Celebration Days in August.

Wink (889) oil, gas, ranching.

Population 6,675	July mean max. 96.1
Change fm 2000 .... −6.9	Civ. Labor 3,657
Area (sq. mi.) 841.24	Unemployed 4.4
Land Area (sq. mi.) 841.05	Wages $31,273,479
Altitude (ft.) 2,665-3,400	Av. Weekly Wage....................... $936
Rainfall (in.) 12.92	Prop. Value $1,137,123,390
Jan. mean min. 27.8	Retail Sales $48,585,160

Wise County

Physical Features: Northwest county of rolling prairie, some oaks; clay, loam, sandy soils; lakes.

Economy: Petroleum, sand and gravel, agribusiness, many residents work in Fort Worth.

History: Caddo Indian groups. Delaware tribe present when Anglo-Americans arrived in 1850s. County created 1856 from Cooke County; named for Virginian, U.S. Sen. Henry A. Wise, who favored annexation of Texas.

Race/Ethnicity, 2007: (In percent) Anglo, 84.7; Black, 1.1; Hispanic, 13.2; Other, 0.9.

Vital Statistics, 2006: Births, 684; deaths, 433; marriages, 417; divorces, 291.

Recreation: Lake activities, hunting, exotic deer preserve, historical sites, Lyndon B. Johnson National Grassland, heritage museum; Decatur Chisholm trail days in June, Bridgeport Butterfield stage days in July.

Minerals: Gas, oil, sand, gravel.

Agriculture: Beef cattle, hay, dairies, horses, wheat, goats. Market value $41.1 million.

DECATUR (6,298) county seat; petroleum center, dairying, cattle marketing, some manufacturing; hospital.

BRIDGEPORT (5,943) trade center for lake resort, oil and gas production, manufacturing, prison release facility; time-share housing, art community.

Other towns include: **Alvord** (1,279); **Aurora** (1,153) sand and gravel, manufacturing, equestrian center, "alien crash" site; **Boyd** (1,307) chili cookoff in May; **Briar** (5,861, mostly in Tarrant County); **Chico** (1,091); **Greenwood** (76); **Lake Bridgeport** (437); **Newark** (1,076); **New Fairview** (1,144); **Paradise** (525); **Pecan Acres** (2,555, partly in Tarrant County); **Rhome** (1,271); **Runaway Bay** (1,304) tourism, fishing, boating, Spring Fest at Easter; **Slidell** (175).

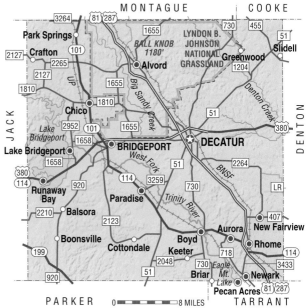

Population	58,506
Change fm 2000	19.9
Area (sq. mi.)	922.77
Land Area (sq. mi.)	904.61
Altitude (ft.)	649-1,180
Rainfall (in.)	34.02
Jan. mean min.	30.5
July mean max.	98.0
Civ. Labor	28,972
Unemployed	5.0
Wages	$215,935,170
Av. Weekly Wage	$804
Prop. Value	$6,648,719,550
Retail Sales	$620,060,112

For explanation of sources, abbreviations and symbols, see p. 210 and foldout map.

The area of the Lyndon B. Johnson National Grassland in Wise County. Robert Plocheck photo.

Wood County

Physical Features: Hilly northeastern county almost half forested; sandy to alluvial soils; drained by Sabine and tributaries; many lakes.

Economy: Agribusiness, oil, gas, tourism.

History: Caddo Indians, reduced by disease. Anglo-American settlement developed in 1840s. County created from Van Zandt County 1850; named for Gov. George T. Wood.

Race/Ethnicity, 2007: (In percent) Anglo, 86.5; Black, 5.8; Hispanic, 7.1; Other, 0.7.

Vital Statistics, 2006: Births, 453; deaths, 511; marriages, 268; divorces, 118.

Recreation: Autumn trails; lake activities; hunting, bass fishing, birding; Gov. Hogg shrine and museum; historic sites; scenic drives; Mineola Choo Choo, Chili & Bean Fest in May; autumn trails.

Minerals: Gas, oil, sand, gravel.

Agriculture: Cattle, dairies, poultry, forages, vegetables, nurseries. Market value $104 million. Timber production significant.

QUITMAN (2,392) county seat; tourism, food processing, some manufacturing; hospital; Light Crust Doughboy museum; Dogwood Fiesta.

MINEOLA (5,187) agribusiness, some manufacturing, railroad center, antiques shops; museum, library; nature preserve; Ironhorse Fall Fest.

Winnsboro (4,210, partly in Franklin County) chicken-raising, dairies, distribution, prison; hospital.

Other towns include: **Alba** (473, partly in

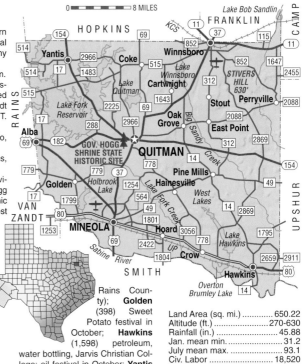

Rains County); **Golden** (398) Sweet Potato festival in October; **Hawkins** (1,598) petroleum, water bottling, Jarvis Christian College; oil festival in October; **Yantis** (400).

Population **42,461**
Change fm 2000 .... 15.5
Area (sq. mi.) 695.80

Land Area (sq. mi.) 650.22
Altitude (ft.) 270-630
Rainfall (in.) 45.88
Jan. mean min. 31.2
July mean max. 93.1
Civ. Labor 18,520
Unemployed 6.1
Wages $69,760,956
Av. Weekly Wage................... $560
Prop. Value $2,889,455,062
Retail Sales $353,915,394

Yoakum County

Physical Features: Western county is level to rolling; playas, draws; sandy, loam, chocolate soils.

Economy: Oil, gas, cotton.

History: Comanche hunting area. Anglo-Americans began ranching in 1890s. Oil discovered 1936. Mexican migration increased in 1950s. County named for Henderson Yoakum, pioneer historian; created from Bexar District 1876; organized 1907.

Race/Ethnicity, 2007: (In percent) Anglo, 47.2; Black, 1.2; Hispanic, 51.1; Other, 0.5.

Vital Statistics, 2006: Births, 138; deaths, 43; marriages, 57; divorces, 30.

Recreation: Tsa Mo Ga museum at Plains; Denver City roughneck rodeo and farmboy jamboree in May; Plains watermelon roundup on Labor Day weekend.

Minerals: Oil, natural gas.

Agriculture: Cotton, peanuts (second in acreage), sorghum, watermelons, wheat, cattle. 100,000 acres irrigated. Market value $90.1 million.

PLAINS (1,502) county seat; oil, agribusiness center.

DENVER CITY (3,934) center for oil, agriculture activities in two counties; hospital, library, museum.

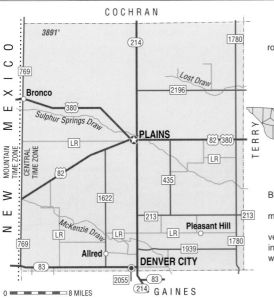

Population 7,571
Change fm 2000 ....3.4
Area (sq. mi.) 799.76
Land Area (sq. mi.) 799.75
Altitude (ft.) 3,400-3,891
Rainfall (in.) 18.41
Jan. mean min. 25.1

July mean max. 91.7
Civ. Labor 4,498
Unemployed 3.2
Wages $42,125,808
Av. Weekly Wage...................$907
Prop. Value $3,431,746,277
Retail Sales $69,245,396

Young County

Physical Features: Hilly, broken; drained by Brazos and tributaries; Possum Kingdom Lake, Lake Graham.

Economy: Oil, agribusiness, tourism, hunting leases.

History: U.S. military outpost established 1851. Site of Brazos Indian Reservation 1854-59 with Caddoes, Wacos, other tribes. Anglo-American settlers arrived in 1850s. County named for early Texan, Col. W.C. Young; created 1856 from Bosque, Fannin counties; reorganized 1874.

Race/Ethnicity, 2007: (In percent) Anglo, 83.8; Black, 1.4; Hispanic, 14.0; Other, 0.8.

Vital Statistics, 2006: Births, 213; deaths, 280; marriages, 163; divorces, 82.

Recreation: Lake activities; hunting; Fort Belknap; marker at oak tree in Graham where ranchers formed forerunner of Texas and Southwestern Cattle Raisers Association.

Minerals: Oil, gas, sand, gravel.

Agriculture: Beef cattle; wheat chief crop, also hay, cotton, pecans, nursery plants. Market value $21.2 million.

GRAHAM (8,805) county seat; oil, gas, agriculture, tourism, government/services; hospital; old post office museum/art center; Western heritage days in September.

Other towns include: **Loving**

(300); **Newcastle** (615) old coal-mining town; **Olney** (3,494) aluminum, varied manufacturing, hospital; One-Arm Dove Hunt in September; **South Bend** (140).

Population 17,579
Change fm 2000 .... –2.0
Area (sq. mi.) 930.84

Land Area (sq. mi.) 922.33
Altitude (ft.) 995-1,522
Rainfall (in.) 31.35
Jan. mean min. 27.1
July mean max. 96.6
Civ. Labor 10,000
Unemployed 4.0
Wages $61,893,722
Av. Weekly Wage $665
Prop. Value $921,275,218
Retail Sales $209,953,148

The old bridge over the Brazos River at U.S. 380 west of Newcastle, Young County. Robert Plocheck photo.

Zapata County

Physical Features: South Texas county of rolling, brushy topography; broken by tributaries of Rio Grande; Falcon Reservoir.

Economy: Natural gas, oil, ranching, Falcon Reservoir activities, government/services.

History: Coahuiltecan Indians in area when the ranch settlement of Nuestra Señora de los Dolores was established in 1750. Anglo-American migration increased after 1980. County named for Col. Antonio Zapata, pioneer rancher; created 1858 from Starr, Webb counties.

Race/Ethnicity, 2007: (In percent) Anglo, 11.2; Black, 0.2; Hispanic, 88.4; Other, 0.3.

Vital Statistics, 2006: Births, 297; deaths, 64; marriages, 19; divorces, 2.

Population	**13,847**
Change fm 2000	13.7
Area (sq. mi.)	1,058.10
Land Area (sq. mi.)	996.76
Altitude (ft.)	301-860
Rainfall (in.)	19.53
Jan. mean min.	45.4
July mean max.	98.0
Civ. Labor	5,155
Unemployed	6.0
Wages	$34,295,468
Av. Weekly Wage	$726
Prop. Value	$3,220,585,717
Retail Sales	$67,964,515

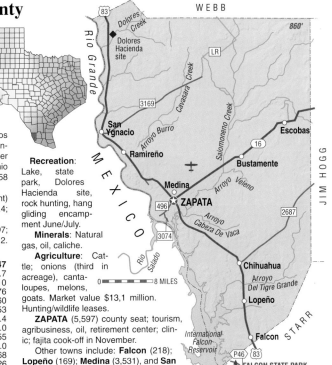

Recreation: Lake, state park, Dolores Hacienda site, rock hunting, hang gliding encampment June/July.

Minerals: Natural gas, oil, caliche.

Agriculture: Cattle; onions (third in acreage), cantaloupes, melons, goats. Market value $13,1 million. Hunting/wildlife leases.

ZAPATA (5,597) county seat; tourism, agribusiness, oil, retirement center; clinic; fajita cook-off in November.

Other towns include: **Falcon** (218); **Lopeño** (169); **Medina** (3,531), and **San Ygnacio** (1,000) historic buildings, museum.

Zavala County

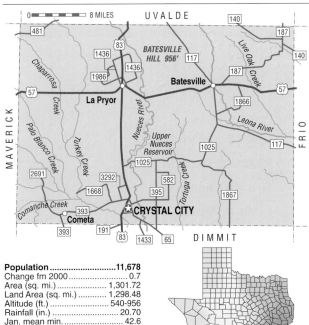

Physical Features: Southwestern county near Mexican border; rolling plains broken by much brush; Nueces, Leona, other streams.

Economy: Agribusiness, food packaging, leading county in Winter Garden truck-farming area, government/services.

History: Coahuiltecan area; Apaches, Comanches arrived later. Ranching developed in late 1860s. County created from Maverick, Uvalde counties 1858; organized 1884; named for Texas Revolutionary leader Lorenzo de Zavala.

Race/Ethnicity, 2007: (In percent) Anglo, 7.7; Black, 0.4; Hispanic, 91.7; Other, 0.2.

Vital Statistics, 2006: Births, 241; deaths, 94; marriages, 33; divorces, 0.

Recreation: Hunting, fishing; spinach festival in November.

Minerals: Oil, natural gas.

Agriculture: Cattle, grains, vegetables, cotton, pecans. About 50,000 acres irrigated. Market value $59.8 million. Hunting leases important.

CRYSTAL CITY (7,455) county seat; agribusiness, food processing, oil-field services; site of Japanese detention center. Home of Popeye statue.

Other towns include: **Batesville** (1,316) and **La Pryor** (1,550).

Population	**11,678**
Change fm 2000	0.7
Area (sq. mi.)	1,301.72
Land Area (sq. mi.)	1,298.48
Altitude (ft.)	540-956
Rainfall (in.)	20.70
Jan. mean min.	42.6
July mean max.	97.1
Civ. Labor	4,140
Unemployed	11.9
Wages	$15,513,575
Av. Weekly Wage	$452
Prop. Value	$357,741,701
Retail Sales	$35,186,531

For explanation of sources, abbreviations and symbols, see p. 210 and foldout map.

Population

Visitors outside the Capitol in Austin with Congress Ave. in the background. Robert Plocheck photo.

2008 Estimates

2000 U.S. Census

Growth Analysis

Metro Areas

Population Center

Recent Population Growth in Texas

By Karl Eschbach

The population of Texas on July 1, 2008, was estimated by the U.S. Census Bureau to be 24,326,974, an increase of 3.48 million persons from the 2000 census.

Estimated population growth in Texas between 2000 and 2008 was the largest of any state in raw numbers, and was the sixth largest in percentage terms (16.67%).

The population of Texas grows rapidly through both natural increase (the excess of births over deaths) and in-migration. The crude birth rate in Texas in 2005 was 16.8 births per 1,000 persons, compared to 14.0 births per 1,000 persons in the United States as a whole, second highest of any state.

The crude death rate in Texas in 2005 was 6.8 per 100,000 persons compared to 8.3 per 100,000 in the United States as a whole, and was fifth lowest among states. The birth rate is high and the death rate is low in Texas in part because the state's population is young, with a median age in 2008 of 33.2 years, compared to 36.8 years for the United States as a whole.

Texas also has a relatively high total fertility rate: 2.34 children per woman in 2005, compared to 2.05 children per women in the United States as a whole. Texas was the fourth highest among all states on this measure in 2005.

For the past two decades, in-migration from other states and other countries has contributed approximately half of the state's population growth in any given year. Estimated net in-migration from other states to Texas between 2000 and 2008 was 710,000, and net international migration to the state was 850,000. Between 2000 and 2005, net in-migration to Texas from other states was relatively slow, reflecting the economic slowdown that slowed the pace of job creation in the state in the early years in the decade.

The displacement of population from Gulf Coast states by Hurricane Katrina in 2005 together with a more robust pace of job growth in the state has sustained much higher rates of in-migration between 2005 and 2008.

A large majority of population growth in the state occurs in its four largest metropolitan areas: Dallas-Fort Worth-Arlington, Houston-Baytown-Sugar Land, Austin-Round Rock, and San Antonio. The 35 counties that make up these areas accounted for 62 percent of the state's population at the 2000 census, but 83 percent of population growth in Texas between 2000 and 2008.

Location of growth

Within these metropolitan areas, five counties grew by more than 50 percent of their 2000 population: Rockwall (80%), Williamson (58%), Collin (55%), Hays (53%) and Fort Bend (50%). Growth in these counties has been fueled primarily by suburbanizing out-migration from nearby central cities.

Growth has been slower in the largest of the core metropolitan counties in the state. Dallas County grew by 8.75%. The pace of growth in Travis County (22.9%), Tarrant County (21.0%) and Harris County (17.2%) was faster than for the state as a whole, while slower than most adjacent counties.

Metropolitan counties on the Texas-Mexico border have grown more quickly than the state as a whole since 2000. Hidalgo County in the McAllen-Edinburg-Mission metropolitan area has experienced the most rapid growth (28%) between 2000 and 2008, and is a net in-migration area for both domestic and international migrants.

All other border counties experienced net domestic out-migration, offset by international migration and a high birth rate.

Population growth in smaller metropolitan areas in Texas outside the immediate border area has generally lagged behind the state's overall growth rate. As a group, both the smaller metropolitan areas and non-metropolitan counties have been net out-migration

Population change, 1850–2008

Year	Total Population		Percent change	
	Texas	U.S.	Texas	U.S.
1850	212,592	23,191,876	...	...
1860	604,215	31,443,321	184.2	35.6
1870	818,579	39,181,449	35.5	26.6
1880	1,591,749	50,155,783	94.5	26.0
1890	2,235,527	62,947,714	40.4	25.5
1900	3,048,710	75,994,575	36.4	20.7
1910	3,896,542	91,972,266	27.8	21.0
1920	4,663,228	105,710,620	19.7	14.9
1930	5,824,715	122,775,046	24.9	16.1
1940	6,414,824	131,669,275	10.1	7.2
1950	7,711,194	150,697,361	20.2	14.5
1960	9,579,677	179,323,175	24.2	19.0
1970	11,196,730	203,302,031	16.9	13.4
1980	14,229,191	226,545,805	27.1	11.4
1990	16,986,510	248,709,873	19.4	9.8
2000	20,851,820	281,421,906	22.8	13.2
2008	**24,326,974**	**304,059,724**	**16.7**	**8.0**

Source: U.S. Census, compiled by Texas State Data Center, University of Texas at San Antonio.

Rank	METRO AREA	2008 Population
1.	New York	19,006,798
2.	Los Angeles	12,872,808
3.	Chicago	9,569,624
4.	**Dallas-Fort Worth**	**6,300,006**
5.	Philadelphia	5,838,471
6.	**Houston**	**5,728,143**
7.	Miami	5,414,772
8.	Atlanta	5,376,285
9.	Washington, D.C.	5,358,130
10.	Boston	4,522,858

Source: U.S. Census.

areas between 2000 and 2008. The Census Bureau estimates that 119 counties in Texas lost population between 2000 and 2008, including 107 of the state's 177 non-metropolitan counties.

Changing Racial and Ethnic Composition

Texas has no majority racial or ethnic population. Non-Hispanic whites decreased from 52.4 percent in 2000 to 47.4 percent in 2008.

The Hispanic share increased from 32.0 percent to 36.5 percent. African-Americans were 11.3 percent of the state's population in 2008, and Asian-Americans were 3.3 percent.

Non-Hispanic whites contributed less than one-sixth of the population growth in the state between 2000 and 2008 — fewer than 500,000 persons. By contrast, the Hispanic population accounted for more than three-fifths of the growth — nearly 2 million persons.

The Hispanic population is growing more rapidly than the non-Hispanic white population because of both natural increase and immigration. In 1990, births to non-Hispanic white mothers (150,461) substantially exceeded births to Hispanic mothers (115,576).

Hispanic births first exceeded non-Hispanic white births in 1996. By 2004, Hispanic mothers accounted for 49 percent of all births in the state, compared to 36 percent for non-Hispanic white mothers, 11 percent for African-American mothers, and 4 percent for Asian-American mothers.

The Hispanic share of births in the state is high and increasing because Hispanics are young, with a median age of 27.7 compared to 40.1 for non-Hispanic whites, 30.6 years for African-Americans, and 34.4 years for Asian-Americans in 2008.

The total fertility rate in 2005 was also substantially higher for Hispanic women (2.94 children per woman) compared to all other groups: non-Hispanic whites (1.91), African-Americans (2.02) and Asian-American (1.88).

Immigration also contributed significantly to Hispanic population growth. The Hispanic foreign-born population increased from 2.1 million in 2000 to 2.8 million in 2007.

Dr. Eschbach is state demographer and director of the Texas State Data Center at the University of Texas at San Antonio.

Counties of Significant Population Change: 2000 to 2008

Fastest Growing by Percent Gain			Fastest Growing by Most Persons Gained		
Rank, County	Largest cities	Percent	Rank, County	Largest cities	Number
1. Rockwall	Rockwall	80.2	1. Harris	Houston	583,759
2. Williamson	Round Rock-Georgetown	57.7	2. Tarrant	Fort Worth-Arlington	303,867
3. Collin	Plano-McKinney-Frisco	55.0	3. Collin	Plano-McKinney-Frisco	270,234
4. Hays	San Marcos	53.2	4. Bexar	San Antonio	229,963
5. Fort Bend	Sugar Land-Missouri City	50.1	5. Denton	Denton-Lewisville	203,589
6. Denton	Denton-Lewisville	47.0	6. Dallas	Dallas	194,035
7. Montgomery	The Woodlands-Conroe	46.4	7. Travis	Austin	186,261
8. Kaufman	Terrell-Kaufman	41.0	8. Fort Bend	Sugar Land-Missouri City	177,689
9. Comal	New Braunfels	40.5	9. Hidalgo	McAllen-Edinburg-Mission	157,141
10. Kendall	Boerne	38.5	10. Williamson	Round Rock-Georgetown	144,211

Chart shows Rockwall County increased in population by 80.2 percent since 2000, while Harris County (Houston) gained 583,759 people, etc. Source: U.S. Bureau of the Census.

Fastest Declining by Percent Loss			Fasting Declining by Most Persons Lost		
Rank, County	Largest towns	Percent	Rank, County	Largest cities	Number
1. Loving	Mentone	−37.3	1. Jefferson	Beaumont-Port Arthur	−8,961
2. King	Guthrie	−21.1	2. Wichita	Wichita Falls	−4,343
3. Knox	Munday-Knox City	−20.2	3. Hutchinson	Borger-Stinnett	−2,345
3. Cochran	Morton-Whiteface	−20.2	4. Coryell	Gatesville	−2,324
5. Borden	Gail	−18.7	5. Reeves	Pecos-Balmorhea	−2,075
6. Briscoe	Silverton-Quitaque	−18.3	6. Orange	Orange	−1,944
6. Culberson	Van Horn	−18.3	7. Falls	Marlin-Rosebud	−1,676
8. Kent	Jayton	−17.6	8. Jones	Anson-Stamford	−1,588
9. Floyd	Floydada	−16.9	9. Hale	Plainview	−1,368
10. Foard	Crowell	−16.1	10. Red River	Clarksville	−1,359

Chart shows Loving County declined in population by 37.3 percent (from 67 to 42) since the 2000 census according to estimates, while Jefferson County declined by 8,961 people, etc. Source: U.S. Bureau of the Census.

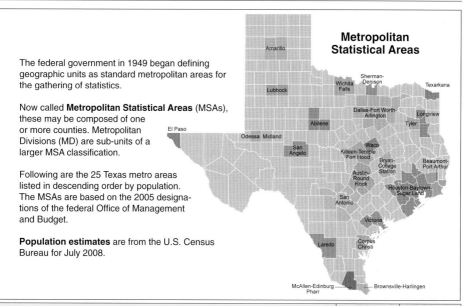

The federal government in 1949 began defining geographic units as standard metropolitan areas for the gathering of statistics.

Now called **Metropolitan Statistical Areas** (MSAs), these may be composed of one or more counties. Metropolitan Divisions (MD) are sub-units of a larger MSA classification.

Following are the 25 Texas metro areas listed in descending order by population. The MSAs are based on the 2005 designations of the federal Office of Management and Budget.

Population estimates are from the U.S. Census Bureau for July 2008.

Metropolitan Statistical Areas

Metropolitan Statistical Areas	2008 Population estimate	Percent change 2000-2008
1. **Dallas-Fort Worth-Arlington** (Dallas-Plano-Irving MD and Fort Worth-Arlington MD) Dallas-Plano-Irving MD (Collin, Dallas, Delta, Denton, Ellis, Hunt, Kaufman, Rockwall counties) Fort Worth-Arlington MD (Johnson, Parker, Tarrant, Wise counties)	6,300,006	22.1
2. **Houston-Baytown-Sugar Land** (Austin, Brazoria, Chambers, Fort Bend, Galveston, Harris, Liberty, Montgomery, San Jacinto, Waller counties)	5,728,143	21.5
3. **San Antonio** (Atascosa, Bandera, Bexar, Comal, Guadalupe, Kendall, Medina, Wilson counties)	2,031,445	18.7
4. **Austin-Round Rock** (Bastrop, Caldwell, Hays, Travis, Williamson counties)	1,652,602	32.2
5. **El Paso** (El Paso County)	742,062	9.2
6. **McAllen-Edinburg-Pharr** (Hidalgo County)	726,604	27.6
7. **Corpus Christi** (Aransas, Nueces, San Patricio counties)	415,376	3.0
8. **Brownsville-Harlingen** (Cameron County)	392,736	17.2
9. **Killeen-Temple-Fort Hood** (Bell, Coryell, Lampasas counties)	378,935	14.6
10. **Beaumont-Port Arthur** (Hardin, Jefferson, Orange counties)	378,255	−1.8
11. **Lubbock** (Crosby, Lubbock counties)	270,610	8.4
12. **Amarillo** (Armstrong, Carson, Potter, Randall counties)	243,838	7.6
13. **Laredo** (Webb County)	236,941	22.7
14. **Waco** (McLennan County)	230,213	7.8
15. **Bryan-College Station** (Brazos, Burleson, Robertson counties)	207,425	12.2
16. **Longview** (Gregg, Rusk, Upshur counties)	204,746	5.5
17. **Tyler** (Smith County)	201,277	15.2
18. **Abilene** (Callahan, Jones, Taylor counties)	159,521	−0.4
19. **Wichita Falls** (Archer, Clay, Wichita counties)	147,328	−2.8
20. **Texarkana** (Bowie County, TX, and Miller County, AR)	135,509	4.4
21. **Odessa** (Ector County)	131,941	8.9
22. **Midland** (Midland County)	129,494	11.6
23. **Sherman-Denison** (Grayson County)	118,804	7.4
24. **Victoria** (Calhoun, Goliad, Victoria counties)	114,313	2.4
25. **San Angelo** (Irion, Tom Green counties)	109,563	3.6

Population 2000 and 2008

Population: Numbers in parentheses are from the 2000 U.S. census. The Census Bureau counts only incorporated cities and a few unincorporated towns called Census Designated Places.

Population figures at the far right for incorporated cities are Texas State Data Center estimates as of Jan. 1, 2008. Names of the incorporated cities are in capital letters, e.g., "ABBOTT".

The population figure given for all other towns is an estimate received from local officials through a Texas Almanac survey.

When no 2000 census was conducted for a city newly incorporated, these places show "(nc)" for "not counted" in place of a 2000 population figure.

Location: The county in which the town is located follows the name of town. If more than one county is listed, the town is principally in the first-named county, e.g., "ABERNATHY, Hale-Lubbock".

Businesses: For incorporated cities, the number following the county name indicates the number of business in the city as of January 2008 as reported by the state comptroller. For unincorporated towns, it is the number of businesses within the postal zip code as reported by the U.S. Bureau of the Census for 2006.

For example, "ABBOTT, Hill, 28" means Abbott in Hill County had 28 businesses.

Post Offices: Places with post offices, as of Nov. 2006, are marked with an asterisk (*), e.g., "*Afton".

Town, County ....Pop. 2008	Town, County ....Pop. 2008	Town, County ....Pop. 2008
*ABBOTT, Hill, 28, (300)..............302	*ALAMO, Hidalgo, 452,	*Altair, Colorado, 11......................30
*ABERNATHY, Hale-Lubbock, 73,	(14,760)............................19,654	*ALTO, Cherokee, 64,
(2,839)................................2,791	Alamo Alto, El Paso.......................19	(1,190)................................1,305
*ABILENE, Taylor-Jones, 3,938,	Alamo Beach, Calhoun.................100	Alto Bonito, Starr, (569)...............610
(115,930)........................117,028	ALAMO HEIGHTS, Bexar, 341,	Altoga, Collin..............................137
Ables Springs, Kaufman.................20	(7,319)...............................7,556	*ALTON, Hidalgo, 298,
Abner, Kaufman..............................75	*Alanreed, Gray, 3..........................48	(4,384)................................9,967
Abram-Perezville, Hidalgo,	Alazan, Nacogdoches...................100	Alton North, Hidalgo, (5,051).....5,410
(5,444)................................5,824	*ALBA, Wood-Rains, 57,	Alum Creek, Bastrop.......................70
*ACADEMY [Little River-], Bell,	(430)....................................473	*ALVARADO, Johnson, 199,
26, (1,645).........................1,718	*ALBANY, Shackelford, 107,	(3,288)................................4,415
Acala, Hudspeth.............................25	(1,921)................................1,948	*ALVIN, Brazoria, 996,
*Ace, Polk......................................40	Albert, Gillespie.............................25	(21,413)..........................24,135
*ACKERLY, Dawson-Martin, 16,	Albion, Red River...........................52	*ALVORD, Wise, 57, (1,007).....1,279
(245)...................................243	Alderbranch, Anderson....................5	Amargosa [Owl Ranch-], Jim Wells,
Acme, Hardeman............................14	Aldine, Harris, (13,979)...........14,788	(527)...................................555
Acton, Hood...............................1,129	*ALEDO, Parker, 249,	*AMARILLO, Potter-Randall,
Acuff, Lubbock.............................152	(1,726)...............................2,396	6,542, (173,627).............189,861
Acworth, Red River.........................50	Aleman, Hamilton...........................50	Ambia, Lamar................................16
Adams Gardens, Cameron...........200	Alexander, Erath.............................40	Ambrose, Grayson..........................90
Adams Store, Panola.....................12	Aley, Henderson.............................45	Ames, Coryell................................10
Adamsville, Lampasas....................41	Alfred-South La Paloma,	AMES, Liberty, 10, (1,079)........1,389
Addicks, Harris........[part of Houston]	Jim Wells, (451)....................511	Amherst, Lamar............................125
Addielou, Red River........................31	Algerita, San Saba.........................48	*AMHERST, Lamb, 16, (791)........825
*ADDISON, Dallas, 1,868,	Algoa, Galveston..........................135	Amistad [Box Canyon-],
(14,166).............................15,547	*ALICE, Jim Wells, 798,	Val Verde, (76)......................88
Adell, Parker..................................40	(19,010)............................20,312	Ammannsville, Fayette.................137
*Adkins, Bexar, 89........................241	Alice Acres, Jim Wells, (491)........528	Amphion, Atascosa.........................26
Admiral, Callahan...........................18	*Alief, Harris.............[part of Houston]	Amsterdam, Brazoria....................193
Adobes, Presidio..............................5	Allamoore, Hudspeth......................25	Anadarko, Rusk..............................30
*ADRIAN, Oldham, 12, (159)........150	*ALLEN, Collin, 2,415,	*ANAHUAC, Chambers, 83,
Advance, Parker..............................10	(43,554).............................75,291	(2,210)................................2,451
*Afton, Dickens, 1...........................15	Allenfarm, Brazos...........................35	*ANDERSON, Grimes, 48,
Agnes, Parker.................................60	Allenhurst, Matagorda.....................72	(257)....................................283
*AGUA DULCE, Nueces, 27	Allen's Chapel, Fannin....................41	Anderson Mill, Williamson-Travis,
(737).....................................744	Allen's Point, Fannin.......................76	(8,953)..............................10,280
Agua Dulce, El Paso, (738)..........711	Allentown, Angelina......................110	Ander-Weser-Kilgore, Goliad.......322
Agua Nueva, Jim Hogg.....................5	Alleyton, Colorado, 17..................165	*Andice, Williamson.....................300
Aguilares, Webb.............................37	*Allison, Wheeler, 3......................135	*ANDREWS, Andrews, 393,
*Aiken, Floyd, 1..............................52	Allmon, Floyd.................................24	(9,652)................................9,845
Aiken, Shelby...............................150	Allred, Yoakum..............................90	*ANGLETON, Brazoria, 596,
Aikin Grove, Red River....................15	ALMA, Ellis, 8, (302)....................348	(18,130)...........................19,745
Airport Road Addition, Brooks,	Almira, Cass..................................30	ANGUS, Navarro, 18, (334)..........404
(132)...................................137	*ALPINE, Brewster, 360,	*ANNA, Collin, 168, (1,225).......1,962
Airville, Bell...................................65	(5,786)................................6,233	Annaville, Nueces
Alabama-Coushatta, Polk, (480)..480	Alsa, Van Zandt.............................30	..............[part of Corpus Christi]

Town, County ....Pop. 2008	Town, County ....Pop. 2008	Town, County ....Pop. 2008

ANNETTA, Parker, 28,
(1,108) 1,307
ANNETTA NORTH, Parker, 18,
(467) 513
ANNETTA SOUTH, Parker, 8,
(555) 646
*ANNONA, Red River, 8,
(282) 255
*ANSON, Jones, 106,
(2,556) 2,503
Antelope, Jack 65
*ANTHONY, El Paso-
(Dona Ana Co., N.M.), 290,
(11,754) 12,174
Antioch, Cass 45
Antioch, Delta 10
Antioch, Madison 15
Antioch Colony, Hays 25
*ANTON, Hockley, 17,
(1,200) 1,162
APPLEBY, Nacogdoches,
(444) 435
*Apple Springs, Trinity, 13 185
*AQUILLA, Hill, 11, (136) 147
*ARANSAS PASS, San Patricio-
Aransas, 398, (8,138) 8,861
Arbala, Hopkins 41
Arcadia, Shelby 35
*ARCHER CITY, Archer, 77,
(1,848) 1,846
ARCOLA, Fort Bend, 44,
(1,048) 1,365
Arden, Irion 1
Argo, Titus 200
*ARGYLE, Denton, 212,
(2,365) 3,520
*ARLINGTON, Tarrant, 10,606,
(332,969) 374,943
Armstrong, Bell 25
*Armstrong, Kenedy, 1 4
Arneckeville, DeWitt 50
Arnett, Coryell 5
Arnett, Hockley 5
*ARP, Smith, 69, (901) 1,019
Arroyo Alto, Cameron, (320) 337
Arroyo City, Cameron 250
Arroyo Colorado Estates, Cameron,
(755) 780
Arroyo Gardens-La Tina Ranch,
Cameron, (732) 750
*Art, Mason, 2 14
Artesia Wells, La Salle, 2 35
*Arthur City, Lamar, 10 180
Arvana, Dawson 25
Asa, McLennan 46
Ash, Houston 19
Ashby, Matagorda 60
*ASHERTON, Dimmit, 15,
(1,342) 1,261
Ashland, Upshur 45
Ashtola, Donley 25
Ashwood, Matagorda 132
Asia, Polk 83
*ASPERMONT, Stonewall, 62,
(1,021) 875
Atascocita, Harris, (35,757) 36,263
*Atascosa, Bexar, 31 600
Ater, Coryell 12
*ATHENS, Henderson, 607,
(11,297) 12,380
*ATLANTA, Cass, 254,
(5,745) 5,718

Atlas, Lamar 28
Atoy, Cherokee 50
*AUBREY, Denton, 116,
(1,500) 2,494
Augusta, Houston 40
AURORA, Wise, 14, (853) 1,153
*AUSTIN, Travis-Williamson,
31,607, (656,562) 736,172
Austonio, Houston 37
*AUSTWELL, Refugio, 4,
(192) 177
Authon, Parker 15
*Avalon, Ellis, 6 400
*AVERY, Red River, 18, (462) 441
*AVINGER, Cass, 25, (464) 460
*Avoca, Jones, 4 121
*Axtell, McLennan, 23 300
*AZLE, Tarrant-Parker, 531
(9,600) 10,904

B

Back, Gray 6
*Bacliff, Galveston, 82,
(6,962) 7,425
*Bagwell, Red River, 3 150
*BAILEY, Fannin, 8, (213) 234
BAILEY'S PRAIRIE, Brazoria, 12,
(694) 779
Baileyville, Milam 32
Bainer, Lamb 10

Bainville, Karnes 8
*BAIRD, Callahan, 71,
(1,623) 1,664
Baker, Floyd 28
Bakersfield, Pecos 11
*BALCH SPRINGS, Dallas, 528,
(19,375) 21,141
BALCONES HEIGHTS, Bexar,
137, (3,016) 3,048
Bald Hill, Angelina 100
Bald Prairie, Robertson 40
*BALLINGER, Runnels, 211,
(4,243) 4,075
*BALMORHEA, Reeves, 18,
(527) 461
Balsora, Wise 50
*BANDERA, Bandera, 282,
(957) 1,197
Bandera Falls, Bandera 90
*BANGS, Brown, 45,
(1,620) 1,603
*Banquete, Nueces, 4 582
Barbarosa, Guadalupe 46
Barclay, Falls 58
*BARDWELL, Ellis, 9, (583) 615
*Barker, Harris 2,500
*Barksdale, Edwards, 5 100
Barnes, Polk 75
*Barnhart, Irion, 6 110

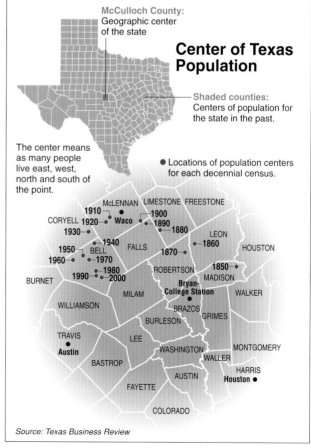

McCulloch County:
Geographic center
of the state

**Center of Texas
Population**

Shaded counties:
Centers of population for
the state in the past.

The center means
as many people
live east, west,
north and south of
the point.

● Locations of population centers
for each decennial census.

Source: Texas Business Review

Town, County	Pop. 2008

Barnum, Polk 50
*Barrett, Harris, (2,872) 2,795
*BARRY, Navarro, 7, (209) 227
*BARSTOW, Ward, 1, (406) 383
*BARTLETT, Williamson-Bell, 65,
   (1,675) 1,974
Barton Corners, Lipscomb 4
Barton Creek, Travis, (1,589) 1,606
BARTONVILLE, Denton, 73,
   (1,093) 1,558
Barwise, Floyd 16
*Basin, Brewster, 5 22
Bassett, Bowie 373
*BASTROP, Bastrop, 628,
   (5,340) 8,359
Bateman, Bastrop 12
Batesville, Red River 14
*Batesville, Zavala, 10,
   (1,298) 1,316
*Batson, Hardin, 13 140
Battle, McLennan 100
Bausell-Ellis, Willacy, (112) 124
Baxter, Henderson 150
*BAY CITY, Matagorda, 600,
   (18,667) 18,520
Baylor Lake, Childress 27
BAYOU VISTA, Galveston, 24,
   (1,644) 1,764
*BAYSIDE, Refugio, 9, (360) 339
*BAYTOWN, Harris, 1,852,
   (66,430) 71,523
BAYVIEW, Cameron, 10,
   (323) 423
Bazette, Navarro 30
BEACH CITY, Chambers, 0,
   (1,645) 2,032
Bear Creek, Dallas 1,000
BEAR CREEK, Hays, 0,
   (360) 417
*BEASLEY, Fort Bend, 11,
   (590) 745
Beattie, Comanche 48
*BEAUMONT, Jefferson, 4,164,
   (113,866) 111,528
Beaver Dam, Bowie 55
Bebe, Gonzales 42
Becker, Kaufman 300
*BECKVILLE, Panola, 31,
   (752) 777
Becton, Lubbock 62
*BEDFORD, Tarrant, 1,544,
   (47,152) 49,960
*BEDIAS, Grimes, 30, (nc) 431
BEE CAVE, Travis, 258,
   (656) 1,910
Bee House, Coryell 15
*BEEVILLE, Bee, 483,
   (13,129) 14,228
Belcherville, Montague 25
Belfalls, Bell 30
Belgrade, Newton 20
Belk, Lamar 58
*BELLAIRE, Harris, 865,
   (15,642) 17,578
Bell Branch, Ellis 125
*BELLEVUE, Clay, 13, (386) 386
*BELLMEAD, McLennan, 248,
   (9,214) 9,367
*BELLS, Grayson, 33,
   (1,190) 1,317
*BELLVILLE, Austin, 332,
   (3,794) 4,628

Belmena, Milam 15
*Belmont, Gonzales, 2 55
Belott, Houston 101
*BELTON, Bell, 707,
   (14,623) 16,953
Ben Arnold, Milam 100
*BENAVIDES, Duval, 22,
   (1,686) 1,535
*Ben Bolt, Jim Wells, 2 1,600
*BENBROOK, Tarrant, 746,
   (20,208) 22,363
Benchley, Robertson 110
*Bend, San Saba-Lampasas, 3 115
*Ben Franklin, Delta 60
Ben Hur, Limestone 100
*BENJAMIN, Knox, 11, (264) 253
Bennett, Parker 40
Benoit, Runnels 10
Bentonville, Jim Wells 15
*Ben Wheeler, Van Zandt, 61 504
*Berclair, Goliad, 1 253
Berea, Houston 41
Berea, Marion 200
Bergheim, Kendall, 17 1,213
Berlin, Washington 40
Bernardo, Colorado 155
BERRYVILLE, Henderson, 11,
   (891) 983
*BERTRAM, Burnet, 81,
   (1,122) 1,369
Bessmay, Jasper 400
Best, Reagan 2
Bethany, Panola 50
Bethel, Anderson 50
Bethel, Ellis 100
Bethel, Henderson 125
Bethel, Runnels 20
Bethlehem, Upshur 75
Bettie, Upshur 110
Beulah, Limestone 12
BEVERLY HILLS, McLennan,
   99, (2,113) 2,059
BEVIL OAKS, Jefferson, 19,
   (1,346) 1,277
Bevilport, Jasper 12
Beyersville, Williamson 80
Biardstown, Lamar 75
*Bigfoot, Frio, 2, (304) 319
Big Hill, Limestone 9
*BIG LAKE, Reagan, 141,
   (2,885) 2,932
*BIG SANDY, Upshur, 108,
   (1,288) 1,375
*BIG SPRING, Howard, 668,
   (25,233) 25,529
Big Valley, Mills 35
*BIG WELLS, Dimmit, 15, (704) ... 690
Biloxi, Newton 75
Birch, Burleson 200
Birome, Hill 30
Birthright, Hopkins 40
Biry, Medina 24
*BISHOP, Nueces, 69,
   (3,305) 3,322
BISHOP HILLS, Potter, 0, (210) ... 200
*Bivins, Cass, 11 215
Bixby, Cameron, (356) 366
Black, Parmer 100
Blackfoot, Anderson 35
Black Hill, Atascosa 60
Black Hills, Navarro 80
Black Jack, Cherokee 47

Black Jack, Robertson 45
Black Oak, Hopkins 150
*BLACKWELL, Nolan-Coke, 14,
   (360) 330
Blair, Taylor 25
Blanchard, Polk 500
*BLANCO, Blanco, 245,
   (1,505) 2,021
Blanconia, Bee 40
Bland Lake, San Augustine 80
*BLANKET, Brown, 21,
   (402) 427
Blanton, Hill 5
Bleakwood, Newton 450
*Bledsoe, Cochran, 3 126
*Bleiblerville, Austin, 5 125
*Blessing, Matagorda, 23,
   (861) 871
Blevins, Falls 36
Blewett, Uvalde 10
Blodgett, Titus 60
*BLOOMBURG, Cass, 11,
   (375) 388
*BLOOMING GROVE, Navarro,
   24, (833) 891
*Bloomington, Victoria, 10,
   (2,562) 2,670
*BLOSSOM, Lamar, 40,
   (1,439) 1,462
Blue, Lee 75
Blue Berry Hill, Bee, (982) 999
*Bluegrove, Clay, 2 135
BLUE MOUND, Tarrant, 38,
   (2,388) 2,535
*BLUE RIDGE, Collin, 30,
   (672) 971
Bluetown-Iglesia Antigua,
   Cameron, (692) 712
*Bluff Dale, Erath, 19 400
Bluff Springs, Travis 200
*Bluffton, Llano, 5 75
*BLUM, Hill, 16, (399) 452
Bluntzer, Nueces 150
*BOERNE, Kendall, 1,239,
   (6,178) 9,217
*BOGATA, Red River, 36,
   (1,396) 1,340
Bois d'Arc, Anderson 10
Bois d'Arc, Rains 10
Bold Springs, Polk 100
*Boling-Iago, Wharton, 25,
   (1,271) 1,317
Bolivar, Denton 140
Bolivar Peninsula, Galveston,
   (3,853) 3,746
Bomarton, Baylor 15
Bonami, Jasper 12
Bonanza, Hopkins 26
*BONHAM, Fannin, 378,
   (9,990) 10,802
Bonita, Montague 25
BONNEY, Brazoria, (384) 420
Bonnie View, Refugio 97
Bonus, Wharton 44
*Bon Wier, Newton, 10 375
*BOOKER, Lipscomb-Ochiltree,
   46, (1,315) 1,332
Boonsville, Wise 52
Booth, Fort Bend 118
Borden, Colorado 60
*BORGER, Hutchinson, 471,
   (14,302) 13,618

Town, County ....Pop. 2008	Town, County ....Pop. 2008	Town, County ....Pop. 2008

Bosqueville, McLennan 200
Boston, Bowie.... [part of New Boston]
Botines, Webb, (132).................... 144
*BOVINA, Parmer, 24,
  (1,874) 1,874
Bowers City, Gray 26
*BOWIE, Montague, 338,
  (5,219) 5,516
Bowman, Archer 200
Bowser, San Saba 20
Box Canyon-Amistad, Val Verde,
  (76) 88
Box Church, Limestone 45
Boxelder, Red River..................... 100
Boxwood, Upshur 20
Boyce, Ellis 125
Boyd, Fannin 40
*BOYD, Wise, 130,
  (1,099) 1,307
*Boys Ranch, Oldham, 3 470
Bozar, Mills 9
Brachfield, Rusk 40
Bracken, Comal 95
*BRACKETTVILLE, Kinney,
  77, (1,876) 1,868
Brad, Palo Pinto............................ 16
Bradford, Anderson........................ 30
Bradshaw, Taylor 61
*BRADY, McCulloch, 266,
  (5,523) 5,519
Branch, Collin 530
Branchville, Milam 127
*Brandon, Hill, 1............................ 75
*Brashear, Hopkins, 7................. 280
*BRAZORIA, Brazoria, 210,
  (2,787) 3,056
Brazos, Palo Pinto 97
BRAZOS BEND, Hood, 0, (nc) 66
BRAZOS COUNTRY, Austin, 9,
  (nc) 291
Brazos Point, Bosque 20
Brazosport, Brazoria,
  (59,440) 61,833
*BRECKENRIDGE, Stephens,
  306, (5,868) 5,834
*BREMOND, Robertson, 44,
  (876) 793
*BRENHAM, Washington,
  962, (13,507) 15,002
Breslau, Lavaca............................ 65

Briar, Tarrant-Wise-Parker,
  (5,350) 5,861
BRIARCLIFF, Travis, 41, (895) 919
BRIAROAKS, Johnson, 7,
  (493) 511
Brice, Hall 20
*BRIDGE CITY, Orange, 264,
  (8,651) 8,657
*BRIDGEPORT, Wise, 285,
  (4,309) 5,943
Bridges Chapel, Titus 90
*Briggs, Burnet, 8 172
Bright Star, Rains......................... 592
Brinker, Hopkins 100
*Briscoe, Wheeler, 6 135
Bristol, Ellis 250
*BROADDUS, San Augustine,
  27, (189) 186
Broadway, Lamar........................... 25
Brock, Parker............................ 2,000
Brock Junction, Parker 100
Bronco, Yoakum 30
*Bronson, Sabine, 6..................... 377
*BRONTE, Coke, 48,
  (1,076) 1,054
*Brookeland, Sabine, 27.............. 300
*Brookesmith, Brown, 3 61
Brooks, Panola 40
Brookshier, Runnels 15
*BROOKSHIRE, Waller, 170,
  (3,450) 4,306
BROOKSIDE VILLAGE, Brazoria,
  38, (1,960) 2,160
*Brookston, Lamar, 16................. 130
Broom City, Anderson.................... 20
BROWNDELL, Jasper, 2, (219).... 228
*BROWNFIELD, Terry, 269,
  (9,488) 9,170
Browning, Smith 25
Brownsboro, Caldwell.................... 50
*BROWNSBORO, Henderson,
  50, (796) 990
*BROWNSVILLE, Cameron,
  4,220, (139,722) 172,609
*BROWNWOOD, Brown, 784,
  (18,813) 19,565
Broyles Chapel, Anderson 40
*BRUCEVILLE-EDDY, McLennan-
  Falls, 27, (1,490) 1,570
Brumley, Upshur 75

Brundage, Dimmit, (31) 33
*Bruni, Webb, 8, (412)................. 466
Brushie Prairie, Navarro 35
Brushy Creek, Anderson................ 50
Brushy Creek, Williamson,
  (15,371) 19,059
*BRYAN, Brazos, 2,286,
  (65,660) 74,985
Bryans Mill, Cass........................ 150
Bryarly, Red River........................... 3
Bryce, Rusk 15
*BRYSON, Jack, 17, (528) 522
*Buchanan Dam, Llano, 42,
  (1,688) 1,785
Buchel, DeWitt............................. 45
Buckeye, Matagorda....................... 16
*BUCKHOLTS, Milam, 19,
  (387) 448
Buckhorn, Austin.......................... 50
Buckhorn, Newton 80
Buckner, Parker 10
*BUDA, Hays, 406, (2,404)........ 6,347
*BUFFALO, Leon, 148,
  (1,804) 1,909
*BUFFALO GAP, Taylor, 48,
  (463) 450
Buffalo Mop, Limestone................. 21
Buffalo Springs, Clay 45
BUFFALO SPRINGS, Lubbock, 0,
  (493) 506
Buford, Mitchell............................ 30
Bula, Bailey.................................. 35
Bulcher, Cooke 3
*BULLARD, Smith-Cherokee,
  172, (1,150) 1,717
Bull Run, Newton........................... 90
*BULVERDE, Comal, 428,
  (3,761) 4,895
*Buna, Jasper, 88, (2,269)......... 2,237
Buncombe, Panola 95
Bunger, Young 40
BUNKER HILL VILLAGE, Harris,
  65, (3,654) 3,803
Bunyan, Erath............................... 20
*BURKBURNETT, Wichita, 251,
  (10,927) 10,944
BURKE, Angelina, (315)............... 313
*Burkett, Coleman, 2 30
*Burkeville, Newton, 14 603
Burleigh, Austin........................... 150

Barstow, Ward County. Robert Plocheck photo.

Town, County .... Pop. 2008	Town, County .... Pop. 2008	Town, County .... Pop. 2008
*BURLESON, Johnson-Tarrant, 1,223, (20,976) 34,467	Cantu Addition, Brooks, (217) 227	Cedar Springs, Upshur 100
*Burlington, Milam, 7 100	*Canutillo, El Paso, 111, (5,129) 5,309	Cedarvale, Kaufman 50
*BURNET, Burnet, 391, (4,735) 5,907	*CANYON, Randall, 379, (11,775) 14,014	Cedar Valley, Bell 14
Burns, Bowie 400	Canyon City, Comal 300	*Cee Vee, Cottle, 1 45
Burns City, Cooke 45	*Canyon Lake, Comal, 247, (16,870) 19,508	Cego, Falls 42
Burrantown, Houston 70	Caplen, Galveston 60	Cele, Travis 20
*BURTON, Washington, 55, (359) 374	Capps Corner, Montague 30	*CELESTE, Hunt, 39, (817) 907
*Bushland, Potter, 10 1,485	Cap Rock, Crosby 6	*CELINA, Collin, 176, (1,861) 5,046
Bustamante, Zapata 15	Caps, Taylor 300	Center, Limestone 76
Busterville, Hockley 6	Caradan, Mills 20	*CENTER, Shelby, 366, (5,678) 5,957
Butler, Bastrop 67	Carancahua, Jackson 375	Center City, Mills 15
Butler, Freestone 67	*CARBON, Eastland, 8, (224) 230	Center Grove, Houston 39
Butterfield, El Paso, (61) 63	Carbondale, Bowie 30	Center Grove, Titus 65
*BYERS, Clay, 16, (517) 498	Carey, Childress 15	Center Hill, Houston 105
*BYNUM, Hill, 4, (225) 256	Carlisle, Trinity 68	Center Plains, Swisher 20
Byrd, Ellis 30	Carlos, Grimes 60	Center Point, Camp 41
Byrdtown, Lamar 22	*Carlsbad, Tom Green, 7 236	*Center Point, Kerr, 45 800
C	CARL'S CORNER, Hill, 3, (134) 153	Center Point, Upshur 50
*CACTUS, Moore, 33, (2,538) 2,804	Carlson, Travis 20	Centerview, Leon 20
*Caddo, Stephens, 4 70	*Carlton, Hamilton, 2 75	*CENTERVILLE, Leon, 88, (903) 929
*CADDO MILLS, Hunt, 100, (1,149) 1,269	*CARMINE, Fayette, 39, (228) 238	Centerville, Trinity 60
Cade Chapel, Navarro 25	Carmona, Polk 50	Central, Angelina 200
Cadiz, Bee 15	Caro, Nacogdoches 70	Central Gardens, Jefferson, (4,106) 3,911
Calallen, Nueces .... [part of Corpus Christi]	Carricitos, Cameron 147	Central High, Cherokee 30
Calaveras, Wilson 100	Carrizo Hill, Dimmit, (548) 573	*Centralia, Trinity 53
*CALDWELL, Burleson, 305, (3,449) 4,139	*CARRIZO SPRINGS, Dimmit, 158, (5,655) 5,560	Cesar Chavez, Hidalgo, (1,469) 1,510
Caledonia, Rusk 75	Carroll, Smith 60	Cestohowa, Karnes 110
Calf Creek, McCulloch 23	Carroll Springs, Anderson 20	Chalk, Cottle 17
Calina, Limestone 10	*CARROLLTON, Dallas-Denton, 5,120, (109,576) 129,329	Chalk Hill, Rusk 200
*Call, Newton, 3 493	Carson, Fannin 22	Chalk Mountain, Erath 25
*Calliham, McMullen, 2 100	Carta Valley, Edwards 12	Chambersville, Collin 103
CALLISBURG, Cooke, (365) 388	Carterville, Cass 39	Chambliss, Collin 29
Call Junction, Jasper 50	*CARTHAGE, Panola, 360, (6,664) 6,951	Champion, Nolan 8
*CALVERT, Robertson, 71, (1,426) 1,362	Cartwright, Wood 144	Champions, Harris 21,250
*Camden, Polk, 2 1,200	Casa Piedra, Presidio 8	Chances Store, Burleson 15
*CAMERON, Milam, 223, (5,634) 6,275	Cash, Hunt 56	*CHANDLER, Henderson, 137, (2,099) 2,546
Cameron Park, Cameron, (5,961) 6,470	CASHION, Wichita, 0, (346) 338	Chaney, Eastland 35
Camilla, San Jacinto 200	*Cason, Morris, 2 173	*Channelview, Harris, 387 (29,685) 31,036
Camp Air, Mason 12	Cass, Cass 100	*CHANNING, Hartley, 13, (356) 380
*CAMPBELL, Hunt, 45, (734) 791	Cassie, Burnet 496	Chapman, Rusk 20
*Campbellton, Atascosa, 4 350	Cassin, Bexar 200	*Chapman Ranch, Nueces, 3 200
Camp Creek Lake, Robertson 350	*Castell, Llano, 1 72	Chappel, San Saba 25
Campo Alto, Hidalgo 500	CASTLE HILLS, Bexar, 338, (4,202) 4,075	*Chappell Hill, Washington, 35 750
Camp Ruby, Polk 35	Castolon, Brewster 8	Charco, Goliad 96
Camp San Saba, McCulloch 36	*CASTROVILLE, Medina, 241, (2,664) 2,997	Charleston, Delta 150
Camp Seale, Polk 53	*Catarina, Dimmit, 6, (135) 126	Charlie, Clay 70
Camp Springs, Scurry 10	*Cat Spring, Austin, 17 200	*CHARLOTTE, Atascosa, 36, (1,637) 1,774
Camp Swift, Bastrop, (4,731) 5,353	Cavazos, Cameron 282	*Chatfield, Navarro, 2 40
Camp Switch, Gregg 70	Caviness, Lamar 90	Cheapside, Gonzales 5
Campti, Shelby 25	Cawthon, Brazos 75	Cheek, Jefferson 1,096
*Camp Verde, Kerr 41	Cayote, Bosque 75	Cheneyboro, Navarro 100
*CAMP WOOD, Real, 48, (822) 885	*Cayuga, Anderson, 4 137	*Cherokee, San Saba, 12 175
Canada Verde, Wilson 40	Cedar Bayou, Harris 1,555	Cherry Spring, Gillespie 75
*CANADIAN, Hemphill, 143, (2,233) 2,414	*Cedar Creek, Bastrop, 98 145	*CHESTER, Tyler, 20, (265) 259
Candelaria, Presidio 55	*CEDAR HILL, Dallas-Ellis, 1,183, (32,093) 43,373	Chesterville, Colorado 50
CANEY CITY, Henderson, 11, (236) 264	Cedar Hill, Floyd 24	*CHICO, Wise, 67, (947) 1,091
Cannon, Grayson 50	Cedar Lake, Matagorda 160	*Chicota, Lamar, 1 150
*CANTON, Van Zandt, 812, (3,292) 3,477	*Cedar Lane, Matagorda, 3 300	Chihuahua, Zapata, 95 109
	*CEDAR PARK, Williamson-Travis, 1,667, (26,049) 52,809	*CHILDRESS, Childress, 195, (6,778) 6,832
	Cedar Shores, Bosque 270	*CHILLICOTHE, Hardeman, 17, (798) 770
	Cedar Springs, Falls 90	*Chilton, Falls, 13 274

Town, County .... Pop. 2008	Town, County .... Pop. 2008	Town, County .... Pop. 2008
*CHINA, Jefferson, 52, (1,112) 1,052	Cleo, Kimble 3	Cone, Crosby 50
CHINA GROVE, Bexar, 50, (1,247) 1,357	Cleveland, Austin 125	Conlen, Dallam 14
China Grove, Scurry 15	*CLEVELAND, Liberty, 459, (7,605) 8,624	Connor, Madison 20
*China Spring, McLennan, 54.... 1,000	Cliffside, Potter 206	*CONROE, Montgomery, 2,587, (36,811) 55,129
Chinati, Presidio 8	*CLIFTON, Bosque, 227, (3,542) 3,795	Content, Bell 25
Chinquapin, Matagorda 6	Climax, Collin 82	*CONVERSE, Bexar, 492, (11,508) 16,026
*CHIRENO, Nacogdoches, 22, (405) 408	Cline, Uvalde 15	Conway, Carson 20
CHISHOLM [McLendon-], Rockwall, 3, (914) 1,225	*CLINT, El Paso, 56, (980) 1,020	Cooks Point, Burleson 60
Chita, Trinity 81	Clinton, Hunt 150	*Cookville, Titus, 14 105
Choate, Karnes 20	Close City, Garza 94	COOL, Parker, 9, (162) 173
Chocolate Bayou, Brazoria 60	Cloverleaf, Harris, (23,508) 25,061	*COOLIDGE, Limestone, 13, (848) 878
Choice, Shelby 35	*CLUTE, Brazoria, 376, (10,424) 11,481	*COOPER, Delta, 74, (2,150)... 2,147
*Chriesman, Burleson 30	*CLYDE, Callahan, 141, (3,345) 3,770	Cooper, Houston 27
*CHRISTINE, Atascosa, 0, (436) 480	*COAHOMA, Howard, 27, (932)... 923	Copano Village, Aransas 210
*Christoval, Tom Green, 19, (422) 419	Coble, Hockley 11	*Copeville, Collin, 6 243
Chula Vista-Orason, Cameron, (394) 408	Cochran, Austin 200	*COPPELL, Dallas-Denton, 1,339, (35,958) 39,806
Chula Vista-River Spur, Zavala, (400) 424	COCKRELL HILL, Dallas, 84, (4,443) 4,421	*COPPERAS COVE, Coryell, 616, (29,592) 32,365
Church Hill, Rusk 20	COFFEE CITY, Henderson, 12, (193) 201	COPPER CANYON, Denton, 45, (1,216) 1,507
Churchill, Brazoria 90	Coffeeville, Upshur 50	Corbet, Navarro 80
*CIBOLO, Guadalupe, 307, (3,035) 14,056	Cofferville, Lamb 4	Cordele, Jackson 51
Cienegas Terrace, Val Verde, (2,878) 3,233	Coit, Limestone 25	CORINTH, Denton, 527, (11,325) 19,215
Cinco Ranch, Fort Bend-Harris, (11,196) 13,232	Coke, Wood 53	Corinth, Jones 10
Cipres, Hidalgo 20	*COLDSPRING, San Jacinto, 122, (691) 904	Corinth, Leon 50
Circle, Lamb 6	*COLEMAN, Coleman, 209, (5,127) 5,052	Corley, Bowie 35
Circle Back, Bailey 10	Colfax, Van Zandt 94	Cornersville, Hopkins 200
Circle D-KC Estates, Bastrop, (2,010) 2,220	Colita, Polk 50	Cornett, Cass 30
Circleville, Williamson 50	College Hill, Bowie 116	Cornudas, Hudspeth 19
*CISCO, Eastland, 152, (3,851) 3,851	College Mound, Kaufman 500	*CORPUS CHRISTI, Nueces, 9,562, (277,454) 285,600
Cistern, Fayette 137	*Collegeport, Matagorda, 1 80	CORRAL CITY, Denton, 4, (89) 109
Citrus City, Hidalgo, (941).......... 1,013	*COLLEGE STATION, Brazos, 2,059, (67,890) 80,526	*CORRIGAN, Polk, 77, (1,721) 1,863
Citrus Grove, Matagorda 30	*COLLEYVILLE, Tarrant, 1,049, (19,636) 23,138	*CORSICANA, Navarro, 974, (24,485) 26,602
Clairemont, Kent 12	*COLLINSVILLE, Grayson, 50, (1,235) 1,616	Coryell City, Coryell 70
Clairette, Erath 55	*COLMESNEIL, Tyler, 42, (638)... 666	*Cost, Gonzales, 4 84
Clara, Wichita 100	Colony, Rains 70	Cotton Center, Fannin 5
Clardy, Lamar 160	*COLORADO CITY, Mitchell, 180, (4,281) 4,359	*Cotton Center, Hale, 5 300
*CLARENDON, Donley, 102, (1,974) 2,127	Coltharp, Houston 40	Cottondale, Wise 300
Clareville, Bee 25	Colton, Travis 50	Cotton Gin, Freestone 28
Clark, Liberty 75	*COLUMBUS, Colorado, 324, (3,916) 3,903	Cotton Patch, DeWitt 11
Clarkson, Milam 10	*COMANCHE, Comanche, 196, (4,482) 4,618	Cottonwood, Callahan 65
*CLARKSVILLE, Red River, 144, (3,883) 3,690	*COMBES, Cameron, 36, (2,553) 2,798	COTTONWOOD, Kaufman, 0, (181) 234
CLARKSVILLE CITY, Gregg, 18, (806) 882	COMBINE, Kaufman-Dallas, 44, (1,788) 2,084	Cottonwood, Madison 40
*CLAUDE, Armstrong, 47, (1,313) 1,353	Cometa, Zavala 10	Cottonwood, McLennan 150
Clauene, Hockley 10	*Comfort, Kendall, 123, (2,358) 2,779	Cottonwood, Somervell-Erath......... 24
Clawson, Angelina 195	*COMMERCE, Hunt, 227, (7,669) 9,188	COTTONWOOD SHORES, Burnet, 22, (877) 1,118
Clay, Burleson 61	*COMO, Hopkins, 20, (621).......... 673	*COTULLA, La Salle, 111, (3,614) 3,593
Clays Corner, Parmer 15	*Comstock, Val Verde, 3 344	Couch, Karnes 10
*Clayton, Panola, 3 125	Comyn, Comanche 30	Coughran, Atascosa 20
Claytonville, Swisher 85	*Concan, Uvalde, 28 225	County Acres [Falman-], San Patricio, (289) 279
Clear Creek, Burnet 78	*Concepcion, Duval, 2, (61)............ 58	County Line, Lubbock 59
CLEAR LAKE SHORES, Galveston, 86, (1,205) 1,296	Concord, Cherokee 50	County Line, Rains 40
*CLEBURNE, Johnson, 1,116, (26,005) 29,603	*Concord, Leon, 3 28	*Coupland, Williamson, 25 280
Clegg, Live Oak 125	Concord, Madison 50	Courtney, Grimes 60
Clemville, Matagorda 25	Concord, Rusk 23	COVE, Chambers, 15, (323) 333
	Concrete, DeWitt 46	Cove Springs, Cherokee 40
		*COVINGTON, Hill, 17, (282) 323
		Cox, Upshur 30
		*Coyanosa, Pecos, 6, (138).......... 140
		Coy City, Karnes 30

Town, County ....Pop. 2008	Town, County ....Pop. 2008	Town, County ....Pop. 2008
Coyote Acres, Jim Wells, (389) 417	Croton, Dickens 7	*DAISETTA, Liberty, 16,
Crabbs Prairie, Walker................. 240	Crow, Wood 178	(1,034) 1,086
Craft, Cherokee 21	*CROWELL, Foard, 46,	Dalby Springs, Bowie 141
Crafton, Wise................................. 60	(1,141) 1,056	*Dale, Caldwell, 29 500
*CRANDALL, Kaufman, 92,	*CROWLEY, Tarrant, 358,	*DALHART, Dallam-Hartley,
(2,774) 3,630	(7,467) 11,770	299, (7,237) 7,495
*CRANE, Crane, 105,	Crown, Atascosa............................ 10	*Dallardsville, Polk, 1 350
(3,191) 3,144	Cruz Calle, Duval........................... 12	*DALLAS, Dallas-Collin-Denton,
*CRANFILLS GAP, Bosque,	Cryer Creek, Navarro 15	43,037, (1,188,580) 1,248,184
19, (335) 361	Crystal Beach, Galveston 1,200	Dalton, Cass................................. 50
*CRAWFORD, McLennan, 47,	*CRYSTAL CITY, Zavala,	DALWORTHINGTON GARDENS,
(705) 751	109, (7,190) 7,455	Tarrant, 142, (2,186)......... 2,439
Creath, Houston 20	Crystal Falls, Stephens.................. 10	*Damon, Brazoria, 23, (535)........ 572
Crecy, Trinity................................. 15	Crystal Lake, Anderson 20	*DANBURY, Brazoria, 35,
CREEDMOOR, Travis, 21,	Cuadrilla, El Paso 67	(1,611) 1,776
(211) 223	*CUERO, DeWitt, 290,	*Danciger, Brazoria...................... 357
Crescent Heights, Henderson 180	(6,571) 6,794	*Danevang, Wharton, 6 61
*CRESSON, Hood-Johnson-Parker,	Cuevitas, Hidalgo, (37) 39	Daniels, Panola 75
69, (nc) 718	*CUMBY, Hopkins, 50, (616) 668	Danville, Gregg............................ 200
Crews, Runnels 30	Cumings, Fort Bend, (683) 853	Darby Hill, San Jacinto 50
Crisp, Ellis.................................. 115	Cundiff, Jack................................. 45	Darco, Harrison 10
*CROCKETT, Houston, 316,	*CUNEY, Cherokee, 10,	Darden, Polk................................ 320
(7,141) 7,282	(145) 149	*DARROUZETT, Lipscomb,
*Crosby, Harris, 341, (1,714) 1,796	*Cunningham, Lamar.................... 110	19, (303) 296
*CROSBYTON, Crosby, 53,	Currie, Navarro 25	Datura, Limestone 2
(1,874) 1,731	Curtis, Jasper 150	*Davilla, Milam, 1........................ 191
Cross, Grimes................................ 53	*CUSHING, Nacogdoches,	Davis, Atascosa............................... 8
Cross, McMullen............................ 25	40, (637) 676	Davis Prairie, Limestone............... 17
Cross Cut, Brown 22	Cusseta, Cass 30	*Dawn, Deaf Smith, 3 52
Cross Mountain, Bexar,	*CUT AND SHOOT, Montgomery,	*DAWSON, Navarro, 21,
(1,524) 1,630	53, (1,158) 1,352	(852) 919
*CROSS PLAINS, Callahan, 64,	Cuthand, Red River 116	*DAYTON, Liberty, 345,
(1,068) 1,123	Cyclone, Bell................................. 47	(5,709) 7,028
Crossroads, Cass 60	Cypress, Franklin........................... 20	DAYTON LAKES, Liberty, 0,
Crossroads, Delta.......................... 20	Cypress Creek, Kerr 200	(101) 93
CROSS ROADS, Denton, 41,	*Cypress [-Fairbanks] , Harris,	Deadwood, Panola 106
(603) 764	1,029 27,000	DEAN, Clay, 2, (341) 345
Crossroads, Harrison.................... 100	Cypress Mill, Blanco 200	Dean, Hockley 20
Cross Roads, Henderson 160	**D**	*Deanville, Burleson, 6 130
Crossroads, Hopkins 50	Dacosta, Victoria 89	*DeBerry, Panola, 23 200
Cross Roads, Madison 75	Dacus, Montgomery 190	*DECATUR, Wise, 464,
Cross Roads, Milam 35	Daffan, Travis 500	(5,201) 6,298
CROSS TIMBER, Johnson, 0,	*DAINGERFIELD, Morris, 104,	Decker Prairie, Montgomery...... 2,000
(277) 313	(2,517) 2,589	DeCORDOVA, Hood, 0, (nc) 3,030

Downtown Del Rio, Val Verde County. Robert Plocheck photo.

Town, County ....Pop. 2008	Town, County ....Pop. 2008	Town, County ....Pop. 2008
*DEER PARK, Harris, 994, (28,520) 30,401	Ding Dong, Bell............................. 301	*DUNCANVILLE, Dallas, 1,215, (36,081) 36,540
*DE KALB, Bowie, 88, (1,769) 1,648	Direct, Lamar 85	Dundee, Archer................................. 12
*DE LEON, Comanche, 102, (2,433) 2,535	Dirgin, Rusk 50	Dunlap, Cottle 10
Delhi, Caldwell............................ 300	DISH, Denton, 0, (nc) 393	Dunlap, Travis................................. 80
Delia, Limestone........................... 20	Divide, Kerr................................... 250	Dunlay, Medina............................ 145
*DELL CITY, Hudspeth, 16, (413) 420	Divot, Frio 9	*Dunn, Scurry 75
Del Mar Heights, Cameron, (259) 263	Dixie, Grayson 17	Duplex, Fannin 25
*Delmita, Starr, 2 50	Dixon, Hunt...................................... 31	Durango, Falls 54
Delray, Panola 45	Dixon-Hopewell, Houston 10	Duren, Mills.................................... 15
*DEL RIO, Val Verde, 978, (33,867) 36,582	Doak Springs, Lee 50	Duster, Comanche........................ 25
Delrose, Upshur............................. 35	Doans, Wilbarger............................ 20	Dye, Montague 30
Del Sol-Loma Linda, San Patricio, (726) 709	*Dobbin, Montgomery, 7 310	Hopewell [Dixon-], Houston 10
*Del Valle, Travis, 93 ... [part of Austin]	Dobrowolski, Atascosa 10	**E**
Delwin, Cottle 12	Dodd, Castro 12	Eagle, Chambers........................... 50
Demi-John, Brazoria.................... 300	*DODD CITY, Fannin, 23, (419) ... 461	*EAGLE LAKE, Colorado, 130, (3,664) 3,626
Democrat, Mills................................ 8	*Dodge, Walker, 1 150	Eagle Mountain, Tarrant, (6,599) 6,954
Denhawken, Wilson 52	*DODSON, Collingsworth, 0, (115) 114	*EAGLE PASS, Maverick, 798, (22,413) 25,859
*DENISON, Grayson, 956 (22,773) 24,678	Dodson Prairie, Palo Pinto 18	*EARLY, Brown, 172, (2,588) 2,781
Denning, San Augustine 100	Doffing, Hidalgo, (4,256)............. 4,574	*EARTH, Lamb, 23, (1,109) 1,082
*Dennis, Parker, 3........................ 300	Dog Ridge, Bell............................ 215	East Afton, Dickens 13
Denson Springs, Anderson........... 100	Dogwood City, Smith 800	*EAST BERNARD, Wharton, 99, (1,729) 2,261
Denton, Callahan............................. 6	Dolen, Liberty 75	East Caney, Hopkins 100
*DENTON, Denton, 3,370, (80,537) 114,456	DOMINO, Cass, 3, (52) 82	East Columbia, Brazoria................ 95
*DENVER CITY, Yoakum, 172, (3,985) 3,934	*Donie, Freestone, 6................... 250	East Delta, Delta............................ 60
*DEPORT, Lamar-Red River, 10, (718) 672	*DONNA, Hidalgo, 432, (14,768) 17,903	East Direct, Lamar......................... 48
Derby, Frio 50	*Doole, McCulloch 74	Easter, Castro 26
*Desdemona, Eastland, 7............. 180	Doolittle, Hidalgo, (2,358)........... 2,533	Easterly, Robertson 61
Desert, Collin 35	DORCHESTER, Grayson, 0, (109) 126	Eastgate, Liberty.......................... 200
*DESOTO, Dallas, 1,156, (37,646) 44,019	Dorras, Stonewall 20	East Hamilton, Shelby 25
*DETROIT, Red River, 30, (776) 754	Doss, Cass 15	*EASTLAND, Eastland, 269, (3,769) 3,922
*DEVERS, Liberty, 20, (416) 483	*Doss, Gillespie, 8 100	EAST MOUNTAIN, Upshur, 8, (580) 600
*DEVINE, Medina, 224, (4,140) 4,423	Dot, Falls 17	*EASTON, Gregg-Rusk, 3, (524) 578
Dew, Freestone 150	Dotson, Panola 35	East Point, Wood............................ 40
DeWees, Wilson 60	Double Bayou, Chambers 400	East Sweden, McCulloch................ 40
Deweesville, Karnes 12	DOUBLE OAK, Denton, 109, (2,179) 3,152	EAST TAWAKONI, Rains, 17, (775) 947
*Deweyville, Newton, 17, (1,190) 1,257	*Doucette, Tyler, 4 160	Ebenezer, Camp............................. 55
Dewville, Gonzales 30	*Dougherty, Floyd, 1 91	Ebenezer, Jasper........................... 50
Dexter, Cooke................................ 12	Dougherty, Rains 342	Echo, Coleman 16
*D'Hanis, Medina, 20.................... 575	*Douglass, Nacogdoches, 19 380	Ecleto, Karnes 22
Dial, Fannin 76	*DOUGLASSVILLE, Cass, 9, (175) 172	*ECTOR, Fannin, 22, (600) 702
Dialville, Cherokee....................... 200	Downing, Comanche 30	*EDCOUCH, Hidalgo, 49, (3,342) 4,393
*Diana, Upshur, 41 585	Downsville, McLennan.................. 150	*EDDY [Bruceville-], McLennan-Falls, 30, (1,490) 1,570
*DIBOLL, Angelina, 135, (5,470) 5,882	Doyle, Limestone............................ 50	*EDEN, Concho, 47, (2,561) 2,449
Dicey, Parker 8	Doyle, San Patricio, (285)............ 276	Eden, Nacogdoches 100
*DICKENS, Dickens, 16, (332) 329	Dozier, Collingsworth........................ 4	Edgar, DeWitt 8
*DICKINSON, Galveston, 534, (17,093) 22,655	Drane, Navarro 16	Edge, Brazos 100
*Dike, Hopkins, 3........................ 170	Drasco, Runnels 15	EDGECLIFF, Tarrant, 0, (2,550) 2,613
*DILLEY, Frio, 64, (3,674).......... 4,069	Draw, Lynn 18	Edgewater-Paisano, San Patricio, (182) 183
Dilworth, Gonzales 18	Dreka, Shelby 30	*EDGEWOOD, Van Zandt, 97, (1,348) 1,435
Dilworth, Red River........................ 22	Dresden, Navarro 25	Edgeworth, Bell 15
*Dime Box, Lee, 20....................... 381	Dreyer, Gonzales 20	Edhube, Fannin 25
*DIMMITT, Castro, 132, (4,375) 4,097	*Driftwood, Hays, 32..................... 100	*EDINBURG, Hidalgo, 1,463, (48,465) 71,174
Dimple, Red River 60	*DRIPPING SPRINGS, Hays, 428, (1,548) 1,981	*EDMONSON, Hale, 5, (123) 127
*Dinero, Live Oak, 2 344	*DRISCOLL, Nueces, 11, (825) 825	*EDNA, Jackson, 271, (5,899) 6,042
	Drop, Denton 90	
	*Dryden, Terrell, 3........................... 13	
	Dubina, Fayette 272	
	*DUBLIN, Erath, 162, (3,754) 3,992	
	Dudley, Callahan 25	
	Duffau, Erath 76	
	*DUMAS, Moore, 383, (13,747) 13,669	
	Dumont, King.................................. 19	
	Dunbar, Rains................................. 40	

Town, County .... Pop. 2008	Town, County .... Pop. 2008	Town, County .... Pop. 2008
Edna Hill, Erath............................ 32	Encantada-Ranchito El Calaboz,	Fairview, Wilson............................ 95
EDOM, Van Zandt, 14, (322) 343	Cameron, (2,100) 2,278	Fairy, Hamilton.............................. 40
*Edroy, San Patricio, 3, (420) 419	ENCHANTED OAKS, Henderson,	Falcon, Zapata, (184) 218
Egan, Johnson............................. 133	0, (357) 419	*Falcon Heights, Starr, (335) 355
*Egypt, Wharton, 2 26	*ENCINAL, La Salle, 16, (629) 701	Falcon Lake Estates, Zapata,
Eidson Road, Maverick,	*Encino, Brooks, 8, (177)............. 174	(830) 988
(9,348) 9,956	*Energy, Comanche, 1................... 70	Falcon Mesa, Zapata, (506) 578
Elam Springs, Upshur.................... 50	Engle, Fayette 141	Falcon Village, Starr, (78) 82
El Arroyo, Starr 500	English, Red River....................... 100	*FALFURRIAS, Brooks, 159,
Elbert, Throckmorton, (56).............. 57	*Enloe, Delta, 4............................. 90	(5,297) 5,165
Elbow, Howard.............................. 10	*ENNIS, Ellis, 669,	Fallon, Limestone 100
El Camino Angosto, Cameron,	(16,045) 20,232	*FALLS CITY, Karnes, 39,
(254) 261	Enoch, Upshur............................... 25	(591) 636
*EL CAMPO, Wharton, 567,	*Enochs, Bailey 80	Falman-County Acres, San Patricio,
(10,945) 11,065	Enon, Upshur.............................. 204	(289) 279
EL CENIZO, Webb, 25,	*Eola, Concho, 3.......................... 215	Famuliner, Cochran 5
(3,545) 3,805	Eolian, Stephens 9	Fannett, Jefferson...................... 1,877
El Centro, Starr............................. 10	*Era, Cooke, 7............................ 150	*Fannin, Goliad, 4........................ 359
*ELDORADO, Schleicher, 80,	Ericksdahl, Jones 35	Fargo, Wilbarger......................... 169
(1,951) 2,006	Erin, Jasper 70	Farmers Academy, Titus 75
Eldorado Center, Navarro.............. 20	Erna, Menard................................ 27	*FARMERS BRANCH, Dallas,
Eldridge, Colorado........................ 20	Erwin, Grimes................................ 52	1,844, (27,508) 28,234
*ELECTRA, Wichita, 82,	ESCOBARES, Starr, (1,954) 2,029	Farmers Valley, Wilbarger.............. 30
(3,168) 3,055	Escobas, Zapata.............................. 3	*FARMERSVILLE, Collin, 176,
Elevation, Milam 12	Escondidas [Sandy Hollow-],	(3,118) 3,945
*ELGIN, Bastrop, 367,	Nueces, (433) 377	Farmington, Grayson..................... 40
(5,700) 9,133	Eskota, Fisher................................ 20	*Farnsworth, Ochiltree, 6............. 130
Eliasville, Young.......................... 150	Esperanza, Hudspeth 75	Farrar, Limestone 51
*El Indio, Maverick, 2, (263) 284	Espey, Atascosa 55	Farrsville, Newton 152
Elk, McLennan............................ 150	Estacado, Lubbock-Crosby 32	*FARWELL, Parmer, 46,
*ELKHART, Anderson, 69,	*ESTELLINE, Hall, 6, (168) 154	(1,364) 1,323
(1,215) 1,332	Estes, Aransas.............................. 50	Fashing, Atascosa 35
EL LAGO, Harris, 77, (3,075) 3,004	Ethel, Grayson.............................. 40	*FATE, Rockwall, 87, (497)........ 4,409
*Ellinger, Fayette, 4 386	*Etoile, Nacogdoches, 10 700	Faught, Lamar 25
Elliott, Robertson 55	Eula, Callahan 125	Faulkner, Lamar 48
Elliott, Wilbarger 50	*EULESS, Tarrant, 1,422,	Fawil, Newton 183
Ellis [Bausell-], Willacy, (112)........ 124	(46,005) 52,809	*FAYETTEVILLE, Fayette, 53,
*Elmaton, Matagorda, 2................ 160	Eulogy, Bosque 10	(261) 282
Elm Creek, Maverick, (1,928) 2,233	Eureka, Franklin 18	Faysville, Hidalgo, (348) 364
*ELMENDORF, Bexar, 72,	EUREKA, Navarro, 12, (340)........ 361	Fedor, Lee 92
(664) 863	*EUSTACE, Henderson, 41,	*Fentress, Caldwell, 8.................. 291
Elm Grove, Cherokee.................... 50	(798) 919	*FERRIS, Ellis, 78, (2,175) 2,511
Elm Grove, San Saba.................... 15	*Evadale, Jasper, 18, (1,430) 1,458	Fetzer, Waller.............................. 150
Elm Grove, Wharton 76	*EVANT, Coryell-Hamilton, 32,	Fields Store, Waller 500
Elm Grove Camp, Guadalupe 88	(393) 416	*Fieldton, Lamb, 4 20
*Elm Mott, McLennan, 68 300	Evergreen, San Jacinto 150	Fife, McCulloch 32
*Elmo, Kaufman, 3........................ 300	EVERMAN, Tarrant, 128,	Fifth Street, Fort Bend,
Elmont, Grayson........................... 15	(5,836) 6,027	(2,059) 2,450
Elm Ridge, Milam 25	Ewell, Upshur............................... 20	Files Valley, Hill............................ 60
Elmwood, Anderson...................... 25	Ezzell, Lavaca 55	Fincastle, Henderson..................... 75
Eloise, Falls 29		Finney, Hale.................................. 18
El Oso, Karnes 35	**F**	*Fischer, Comal, 12 200
*EL PASO, El Paso, 15,525,	*Fabens, El Paso, 76,	Fisk, Coleman................................ 40
(563,662) 609,327	(8,043) 8,526	Five Points, Ellis 25
El Refugio, Starr, (221) 239	FAIRCHILDS, Fort Bend,	Flaccus, Karnes 15
Elroy, Travis 125	(678) 849	Flagg, Castro 26
*ELSA, Hidalgo, 117,	*FAIRFIELD, Freestone, 233,	*Flat, Coryell, 2 210
(5,549) 6,794	(3,094) 3,634	Flat Fork, Shelby 10
El Sauz, Starr 50	Fairland, Burnet............................ 340	*FLATONIA, Fayette, 94,
El Tacalote, Jim Wells.................. 100	Fairlie, Hunt 80	(1,377) 1,436
Elton, Dickens................................ 4	Fairmount, Sabine 1,500	Flat Prairie, Trinity......................... 33
El Toro, Jackson.......................... 136	Fair Oaks, Limestone 15	Flats, Rains 646
El Venadito, Cameron.................. 207	*FAIR OAKS RANCH, Bexar-Comal-	Flat Top, Stonewall 5
Elwood, Fannin............................. 31	Kendall, 120, (4,695) 6,175	*Flint, Smith, 146 2,500
Elwood, Madison 50	Fair Play, Panola 80	Flo, Leon...................................... 12
*Elysian Fields, Harrison, 5 500	Fairview, Armstrong....................... 75	*Flomot, Motley, 2 181
Emberson, Lamar 80	Fairview, Cass 20	Flora, Hopkins 20
Emerald Bay, Smith 616	FAIRVIEW, Collin, 177,	*FLORENCE, Williamson, 67,
EMHOUSE, Navarro, 3, (159) 169	(2,644) 6,446	(1,054) 1,370
Emmett, Navarro 100	Fairview, Gaines.......................... 160	*FLORESVILLE, Wilson, 324,
*EMORY, Rains, 170,	Fairview, Hockley........................... 10	(5,868) 7,381
(1,021), ... 1,882	Fairview, Hood............................... 30	Florey, Andrews 25
	Fairview, Howard............................. 5	

State Street in Fort Davis, Jeff Davis County. Robert Plocheck photo.

Town, County ....Pop. 2008	Town, County ....Pop. 2008	Town, County ....Pop. 2008

Flour Bluff, Nueces,
.................[part of Corpus Christi]
Flowella, Brooks, (134)................129
Flower Hill, Colorado 20
*FLOWER MOUND, Denton,
2,280, (50,702) 67,413
Floyd, Hunt 90
*FLOYDADA, Floyd, 102,
(3,676) 3,394
*Fluvanna, Scurry, 3 180
*Flynn, Leon, 5 81
Foard City, Foard...........................10
Fodice, Houston 49
*FOLLETT, Lipscomb, 26,
(412) 399
Folsom, Shelby..............................30
Ford, Deaf Smith 25
Fords Corner, San Augustine 30
Fordtran, Victoria 18
Forest, Cherokee...........................85
*Forestburg, Montague, 4...............50
Forest Chapel, Lamar..................105
Forest Glade, Limestone 340
Forest Grove, Milam 60
Forest Heights, Orange 250
Forest Hill, Lamar...........................50
FOREST HILL, Tarrant, 317,
(12,949) 14,137
Forest Hill, Wood 30
*FORNEY, Kaufman, 601,
(5,588) 13,977
*Forreston, Ellis, 3 400
*FORSAN, Howard, 9,
(226) 211
Fort Bliss, El Paso, (8,264)........8,150
Fort Clark Springs, Kinney.........1,300
*Fort Davis, Jeff Davis, 63,
(1,050) 1,501
*Fort Hancock, Hudspeth, 14,
(1,713) 1,811
Fort Hood, Bell-Coryell,
(33,711) 32,560
*Fort McKavett, Menard, 1.............50
Fort Parker, Limestone 2
Fort Parker State Park, Limestone . 30
Fort Spunky, Hood..........................15

*FORT STOCKTON, Pecos,
280, (7,846) 7,557
*FORT WORTH, Tarrant-Denton-
Parker-Wise, 18,883,
(534,694) 688,222
Foster, Terry.....................................6
Fostoria, Montgomery...................586
Fouke, Wood 30
Four Corners, Brazoria 30
Four Corners, Chambers...............18
Four Corners, Fort Bend,
(2,954) 3,648
Four Corners, Montgomery 500
*Fowlerton, La Salle, 2, (62)...........63
Frame Switch, Williamson 25
*Francitas, Jackson 125
Frankel City, Andrews......................2
Frankell, Stephens............................8
*FRANKLIN, Robertson, 83,
(1,470) 1,530
*FRANKSTON, Anderson,
102, (1,209) 1,251
*Fred, Tyler, 8 299
*FREDERICKSBURG, Gillespie,
1,148, (8,911) 10,872
*Fredonia, Mason, 3 55
Freedom, Rains 60
*FREEPORT, Brazoria, 321,
(12,708) 13,427
*FREER, Duval, 91,
(3,241) 3,060
Freestone, Freestone 100
Frelsburg, Colorado.......................75
Frenstat, Burleson 50
Fresno, Collingsworth....................10
*Fresno, Fort Bend, 78,
(6,603) 8,702
Freyburg, Fayette 148
Friday, Trinity 99
Friendship, Dawson 5
Friendship, Smith.........................200
Friendship, Upshur 25
Friendship Village, Bowie 200
*FRIENDSWOOD, Galveston-Harris,
1,229, (29,037) 33,106
Frio Town, Frio.................................9

*FRIONA, Parmer, 97,
(3,854) 3,827
*FRISCO, Collin-Denton, 2,855,
(55,635) 89,905
*FRITCH, Hutchinson-Moore, 81,
(2,235) 2,168
Frog, Kaufman...............................90
Fronton, Starr, (599) 643
*FROST, Navarro, 26, (648) 725
Fruitland, Montague.......................20
*FRUITVALE, Van Zandt, 9,
(418) 480
Frydek, Austin...............................900
Fulbright, Red River......................150
*FULSHEAR, Fort Bend, 111,
(716) 1,024
*FULTON, Aransas, 99,
(1,553) 1,728
Funston, Jones 26
Furrh, Panola 40

G

Gadston, Lamar.............................35
*Gail, Borden, 3 200
*GAINESVILLE, Cooke, 859,
(15,538) 17,058
Galena, Smith................................50
*GALENA PARK, Harris, 168,
(10,592) 11,466
Galilee, Smith 150
*GALLATIN, Cherokee, 2,
(378) 393
Galloway, Panola...........................71
*GALVESTON, Galveston, 1,744,
(57,247) 59,186
*GANADO, Jackson, 87,
(1,915) 2,009
Garceño, Starr, (1,438)..............1,536
*Garciasville [La Casita-], Starr,
5, (2,177) 2,435
*Garden City, Glasscock, 19........293
*Gardendale, Ector, 18,
(1,197) 1,282
Gardendale, La Salle.....................40
GARDEN RIDGE, Comal, 119,
(1,882) 3,168
Garden Valley, Smith 150

Town, County .... Pop. 2008	Town, County .... Pop. 2008	Town, County .... Pop. 2008
Garfield, DeWitt, ... 16	*GOLDSMITH, Ector, 18,	Green, Karnes 35
Garfield, Travis, (1,660) 1,745	(253) 260	Green Hill, Titus 150
Garland, Bowie 125	*GOLDTHWAITE, Mills, 106,	Green Lake, Calhoun 51
*GARLAND, Dallas, 6,650,	(1,802) 1,794	Greenpond, Hopkins 150
(215,768) 222,007	*GOLIAD, Goliad, 131,	Green's Creek, Erath 75
Garner, Parker 196	(1,975) 2,008	Green Valley, Denton 55
Garner State Park, Uvalde 50	GOLINDA, Falls-McLennan, 12,	Green Valley Farms, Cameron,
GARRETT, Ellis, 7, (448) 511	(423) 451	(720) 748
Garrets Bluff, Lamar 25	Golly, DeWitt 41	Greenview, Hopkins 25
*GARRISON, Nacogdoches, 46,	Gomez, Terry 6	*GREENVILLE, Hunt, 931,
(844) 835	*GONZALES, Gonzales, 368,	(23,960) 25,357
*Garwood, Colorado, 20 975	(7,202) 7,306	Greenvine, Washington 35
*GARY, Panola, 14, (303) 318	Goober Hill, Shelby 30	Greenwood, Hopkins 100
Gastonia, Kaufman 100	Goodland, Bailey 10	Greenwood, Midland 2,000
*GATESVILLE, Coryell, 407,	Goodlett, Hardeman 80	Greenwood, Red River 20
(15,591) 16,223	GOODLOW, Navarro, 4, (264) 262	*Greenwood, Wise, 5....................... 76
*Gause, Milam, 6 425	Good Neighbor, Hopkins 40	*GREGORY, San Patricio, 35,
Gay Hill, Washington 40	Goodnight, Armstrong..................... 18	(2,318) 2,234
*Geneva, Sabine 200	Goodnight, Navarro 25	Gresham, Smith......................... 1,000
Geneview, Stonewall 3	*GOODRICH, Polk, 26, (243) 264	GREY FOREST, Bexar, 16,
Gentry's Mill, Hamilton 20	Goodsprings, Rusk 40	(418) 439
George's Creek, Somervell 43	Goodwill, Burleson 12	Grice, Upshur 20
*GEORGETOWN, Williamson,	Goodwin, San Augustine 70	Griffith, Cochran 12
1,831, (28,339) 47,066	*GORDON, Palo Pinto, 30,	Grigsby, Shelby 15
*GEORGE WEST, Live Oak, 155,	(451) 445	Grit, Mason 15
(2,524) 2,406	*Gordonville, Grayson, 21 165	*GROESBECK, Limestone, 161,
Georgia, Lamar................................ 55	*GOREE, Knox, 5, (321)............... 297	(4,291) 4,631
Germany, Houston.......................... 23	*GORMAN, Eastland, 43,	*GROOM, Carson, 37,
*Geronimo, Guadalupe, 4,	(1,236) 1,240	(587) 575
(619) 706	Goshen, Walker 250	Grosvenor, Brown........................... 24
GHOLSON, McLennan, 18,	Gould, Cherokee 20	*GROVES, Jefferson, 362,
(922) 971	*Gouldbusk, Coleman, 2................. 70	(15,733) 15,049
Gibtown, Jack 20	Graceton, Upshur 100	*GROVETON, Trinity, 44,
*GIDDINGS, Lee, 331,	*GRAFORD, Palo Pinto, 34,	(1,107) 1,113
(5,105) 5,743	(578) 601	Grow, King 9
*Gilchrist, Galveston, 12 600	Graham, Garza 139	Gruenau, DeWitt............................. 18
*Gillett, Karnes, 4.......................... 120	*GRAHAM, Young, 587,	Gruene, Comal,
Gilliland, Knox................................. 20	(8,716) 8,805	.... [part of New Braunfels]
*GILMER, Upshur, 388,	*GRANBURY, Hood, 1,083,	Grulla, Starr .... (see La Grulla)
(4,799) 5,094	(5,718,) 8,198	*GRUVER, Hansford, 47,
Gilpin, Dickens................................. 2	Grand Acres, Cameron, (203) 208	(1,162) 1,153
Ginger, Rains 96	Grand Bluff, Panola 115	Guadalupe, Victoria 106
*Girard, Kent, (62) 67	*GRANDFALLS, Ward, 6,	Guadalupe Station, Culberson 10
Girlstown USA, Cochran.................. 98	(391) 376	*Guerra, Jim Hogg, (8) 8
*Girvin, Pecos................................. 20	*GRAND PRAIRIE, Dallas-Tarrant,	Gum Springs, Cass 50
Gist, Jasper 20	4,220, (127,427) 158,646	*GUN BARREL CITY, Henderson,
Givens, Lamar 135	*GRAND SALINE, Van Zandt,	294, (5,145) 5,880
*GLADEWATER, Gregg-Upshur,	149, (3,028) 3,344	Gunsight, Stephens 6
354, (6,078) 6,453	Grandview, Dawson........................ 12	*GUNTER, Grayson, 64,
Glaze City, Gonzales 10	Grandview, Gray............................. 13	(1,230) 1,819
Glazier, Hemphill 48	*GRANDVIEW, Johnson, 82,	Gus, Burleson................................. 50
Glecker, Lavaca.............................. 78	(1,358) 1,595	*GUSTINE, Comanche, 15,
Glen Cove, Coleman 40	*GRANGER, Williamson, 53,	(457) 478
Glendale, Trinity............................ 175	(1,299) 1,620	*Guthrie, King, 1 125
Glenfawn, Rusk 100	Grangerland, Montgomery........... 300	*Guy, Fort Bend, 8 239
*Glen Flora, Wharton, 3................ 210	*GRANITE SHOALS, Burnet, 75,	Guys Store, Leon............................ 20
Glenn, Dickens................................. 4	(2,040) 2,532	**H**
GLENN HEIGHTS, Dallas-Ellis,	GRANJENO, Hidalgo, 2, (313) 324	Haciendito, Presidio........................ 10
159, (7,224) 10,428	Grape Creek, Tom Green,	Hackberry, Cottle 30
Glenrio, Deaf Smith 5	(3,138) 3,025	HACKBERRY, Denton, 4,
*GLEN ROSE, Somervell, 193,	*GRAPELAND, Houston, 90,	(544) 678
(2,122) 2,658	(1,451) 1,474	Hackberry, Edwards 3
Glenwood, Upshur......................... 150	*GRAPEVINE, Tarrant, 2,601,	Hackberry, Garza 5
Glidden, Colorado, 2..................... 255	(42,059) 49,150	Hackberry, Lavaca 40
Globe, Lamar.................................. 60	Grassland, Lynn 40	Hagansport, Franklin 40
Glory, Lamar................................... 30	Gray, Marion 12	Hagerville, Houston 70
*Gober, Fannin 146	Grayback, Wilbarger....................... 10	Hail, Fannin 30
*GODLEY, Johnson, 51,	GRAYS PRAIRIE, Kaufman, 5,	Hainesville, Wood 95
(879) 1,061	(296) 354	*HALE CENTER, Hale, 45,
*Golden, Wood, 6 398	Graytown, Wilson, ... 85	(2,263) 2,133
Goldfinch, Frio 35	Greatwood, Fort Bend,	Halfway, Hale.............................. 165
*Goldsboro, Coleman 30	(6,640) 8,267	Hall, San Saba............................... 15

Town, County ....Pop. 2008	Town, County ....Pop. 2008	Town, County ....Pop. 2008

*HALLETTSVILLE, Lavaca,
  209, (2,345) 2,540
Hall's Bluff, Houston 67
HALLSBURG, McLennan, 4,
  (518) 528
*HALLSVILLE, Harrison, 105,
  (2,772) 3,076
*HALTOM CITY, Tarrant, 1,411,
  (39,018) 41,918
Hamby, Taylor 100
*HAMILTON, Hamilton, 206,
  (2,977) 3,130
*HAMLIN, Jones-Fisher, 78,
  (2,248) 2,153
Hammond, Robertson 44
Hamon, Gonzales 20
*Hamshire, Jefferson, 9 759
Hancock, Comal 200
Hancock, Dawson 30
*Hankamer, Chambers, 8 226
Hannibal, Erath..............................25
Hanover, Milam..............................25
*HAPPY, Swisher-Randall, 17,
  (647) 653
Happy Union, Hale 25
Happy Valley, Taylor 10
Harbin, Erath 21
*HARDIN, Liberty, 18, (755) 771
Hare, Williamson 60
*Hargill, Hidalgo, 7....................1,349
*HARKER HEIGHTS, Bell, 492,
  (17,308) 25,160
Harkeyville, San Saba 12
*Harleton, Harrison, 16 390
*HARLINGEN, Cameron, 2,099,
  (57,564) 69,359
Harmon, Lamar 12
Harmony, Floyd 42
Harmony, Grimes............................12
Harmony, Kent 10
Harmony, Nacogdoches 50
*Harper, Gillespie, 39,
  (1,006) 1,119
Harpersville, Stephens 5
Harrison, McLennan 100
*Harrold, Wilbarger, 2 200
*HART, Castro, 34, (1,198)........1,104
Hartburg, Newton 893
Hart Camp, Lamb 4
*Hartley, Hartley, 16, (441)...........436
Harvard, Camp 48
Harvey, Brazos 1,000
Harwell Point, Burnet....................138
*Harwood, Gonzales, 9................118
*HASKELL, Haskell, 122,
  (3,106) 2,835
Haslam, Shelby 100
*HASLET, Tarrant, 155,
  (1,134) 1,442
Hasse, Comanche 50
Hatchel, Runnels 6
Hatchetville, Hopkins 20
Havana, Hidalgo, (452)................485
HAWK COVE, Hunt, 6,
  (457) 465
*HAWKINS, Wood, 99,
  (1,331) 1,598
*HAWLEY, Jones, 34, (646)..........633
Hawthorne, Walker 100
Haynesville, Wichita 65
HAYS, Hays, 3, (233) 249
Hazeldell, Comanche 12

*HEARNE, Robertson, 142,
  (4,690) 4,755
HEATH, Rockwall, 217,
  (4,149) 7,129
*Hebbronville, Jim Hogg, 108,
  (4,498) 4,305
HEBRON, Denton, 34, (874) 234
Heckville, Lubbock..........................91
*HEDLEY, Donley, 7, (379) 416
Hedwigs Hill, Mason 12
HEDWIG VILLAGE, Harris, 245,
  (2,334) 2,230
Hefner, Knox....................................3
Hegar, Waller 100
Heidelberg, Hidalgo, (1,586)......1,679
*Heidenheimer, Bell, 8 224
Helena, Karnes..............................35
Helmic, Trinity 86
*HELOTES, Bexar, 483,
  (4,285) 7,245
*HEMPHILL, Sabine, 114,
  (1,106) 1,095
*HEMPSTEAD, Waller, 247,
  (4,691) 6,979
*HENDERSON, Rusk, 559,
  (11,273) 12,866
Henkhaus, Lavaca..........................88
Henly, Hays 140
*HENRIETTA, Clay, 134,
  (3,264) 3,300
Henry's Chapel, Cherokee 75
*HEREFORD, Deaf Smith, 459,
  (14,597) 15,031
Hermits Cove, Rains......................40
*Hermleigh, Scurry, 8, (393) 406
Herty, Angelina 605
Hester, Navarro 35
*HEWITT, McLennan, 397,
  (11,085) 13,634
*Hext, Menard..............................75
HICKORY CREEK, Denton, 98,
  (2,078) 3,426
Hickory Creek, Houston..................31
Hickory Creek, Hunt 40
*HICO, Hamilton, 132,
  (1,341) 1,383
*HIDALGO, Hidalgo, 434,
  (7,322) 11,582
Hidden Acres [Lakeshore Gardens-],
  San Patricio, (720)................701
HIDEAWAY, Smith, (2,619)........2,906
Higginbotham, Gaines 21
*HIGGINS, Lipscomb, 16, (425) ...423
High, Lamar 14
Highbank, Falls..............................68
High Hill, Fayette 176
*High Island, Galveston, 3............300
Highland, Erath..............................60
HIGHLAND HAVEN, Burnet, 0,
  (450) 592
HIGHLAND PARK, Dallas, 388,
  (8,842) 9,153
*Highlands, Harris, 122,
  (7,089) 7,206
HIGHLAND VILLAGE, Denton,
  449, (12,173) 16,511
Hightower, Liberty 225
HILL COUNTRY VILLAGE, Bexar,
  99, (1,028) 1,083
Hillcrest, Colorado 25
HILLCREST VILLAGE, Brazoria, 0,
  (722) 778

*Hillister, Tyler, 10 250
Hillje, Wharton 51
Hills, Lee......................................20
*HILLSBORO, Hill, 416,
  (8,232) 9,176
Hilltop, Frio, (300) 283
*Hilltop Lakes, Leon......................500
HILSHIRE VILLAGE, Harris, 22,
  (720) 724
Hinckley, Lamar 40
Hindes, Atascosa............................14
Hinkles Ferry, Brazoria 35
Hiram, Kaufman 75
*HITCHCOCK, Galveston, 173,
  (6,386) 7,265
Hitchland, Hansford 15
Hix, Burleson 35
Hoard, Wood 45
Hobbs, Fisher 32
*Hobson, Karnes, 8 135
*Hochheim, DeWitt 70
*Hockley, Harris, 97 400
Hodges, Jones..............................150
Hogansville, Rains........................200
Hogg, Burleson..............................20
Holiday Beach, Aransas 1,000
HOLIDAY LAKES, Brazoria, 5,
  (1,095) 1,186
*HOLLAND, Bell, 50, (1,102)...1,127
Holland Quarters, Panola 40
*HOLLIDAY, Archer, 66,
  (1,632) 1,739
Holly, Houston 95
Holly Grove, Polk............................20
HOLLYWOOD PARK, Bexar, 106,
  (2,983) 3,341
Holman, Fayette 101
Homer, Angelina 360
Homestead Meadows North, El Paso,
  (4,232) 4,205
Homestead Meadows South, El Paso,
  (6,807) 6,862
*HONDO, Medina, 327,
  (7,897) 9,142
*HONEY GROVE, Fannin, 72,
  (1,746) 1,893
Honey Island, Hardin 401
Hood, Cooke................................13
Hooker Ridge, Rains 250
*HOOKS, Bowie, 66, (2,973) 3,170
Hoover, Gray 5
Hoover, Lamar 20
Hope, Lavaca 45
Hopewell, Franklin 50
Hopewell, Houston 22
Hopewell, Red River 152
Hopewell [Dixon-], Houston............10
HORIZON CITY, El Paso, 177,
  (5,233) 9,812
Hornsby Bend, Travis 200
HORSESHOE BAY, Llano-Burnet,
  134, (3,337) 3,567
Hortense, Polk................................20
Horton, Delta 40
Horton, Panola..............................200
*HOUSTON, Harris-Fort Bend-
  Montgomery, 82,866,
  (1,953,631)..................2,149,948
Howard, Ellis................................60
HOWARDWICK, Donley, 13,
  (437) 467
*HOWE, Grayson, 75, (2,478) ...2,937

Town, County	Pop. 2008
Howland, Lamar	65
Hoxie, Williamson	60
Hoyte, Milam	20
Hub, Parmer	25
Hubbard, Bowie	269
*HUBBARD, Hill, 68, (1,586)	1,769
Huber, Shelby	15
Huckabay, Erath	150
HUDSON, Angelina, 67, (3,792)	4,381
Hudson Bend, Travis, (2,369)	2,324
HUDSON OAKS, Parker, 103, (1,637)	1,875
Huffines, Cass	140
*Huffman, Harris, 133	15,000
Hufsmith, Harris	500
*HUGHES SPRINGS, Cass, 68, (1,856)	1,919
*Hull, Liberty, 17	800
*HUMBLE, Harris, 2,027, (14,579)	16,528
*Hungerford, Wharton, 11, (645)	651
*Hunt, Kerr, 46	708
Hunter, Comal	40
HUNTERS CREEK VILLAGE, Harris, 109, (4,374)	4,638
*HUNTINGTON, Angelina, 110, (2,068)	2,141
Huntoon, Ochiltree	22
*HUNTSVILLE, Walker, 1,061, (26,531)	37,790
Hurley, Wood	30
Hurlwood, Lubbock	115
Hurnville, Clay	10
*HURST, Tarrant, 1,709, (36,273)	38,661
Hurstown, Shelby	20
Hurst Springs, Coryell	10
*HUTCHINS, Dallas, 105, (2,805)	3,124
*HUTTO, Williamson, 269, (1,250)	13,498

Town, County	Pop. 2008
HUXLEY, Shelby, 4, (298)	312
*Hye, Blanco, 4	72
Hylton, Nolan	6

I

Town, County	Pop. 2008
*Iago [Boling-], Wharton, 25, (1,271)	1,317
Ida, Grayson	30
*IDALOU, Lubbock, 78, (2,157)	2,247
Iglesia Antigua [Bluetown-], Cameron, (692)	712
Ike, Ellis	50
Illinois Bend, Montague	40
IMPACT, Taylor, (39)	42
*Imperial, Pecos, 4, (428)	399
Inadale, Scurry	8
Independence, Washington	140
India, Ellis	30
Indian Creek, Brown	28
Indian Creek, Smith	300
Indian Gap, Hamilton	35
Indian Hill, Newton	7
Indian Hills, Hidalgo, (2,036)	2,183
INDIAN LAKE, Cameron, (541)	550
Indianola, Calhoun	200
Indian Rock, Upshur	45
Indian Springs, Polk	250
Indio, Presidio	5
*INDUSTRY, Austin, 30, (304)	368
*Inez, Victoria, 34, (1,787)	1,872
*INGLESIDE, San Patricio, 212, (9,388)	9,759
INGLESIDE-ON-THE-BAY, San Patricio, 11, (659)	691
*INGRAM, Kerr, 161, (1,740)	1,904
*IOLA, Grimes, 13	350
IOWA COLONY, Brazoria, 21, (804)	982
*IOWA PARK, Wichita, 183, (6,431)	6,590
*Ira, Scurry, 13	250

Town, County	Pop. 2008
*IRAAN, Pecos, 62, (1,238)	1,213
*IREDELL, Bosque, 22, (360)	388
Ireland, Coryell	60
*Irene, Hill	170
Ironton, Cherokee	110
*IRVING, Dallas, 6,651, (191,615)	201,784
Isla, Sabine	350
Israel, Polk	25
*ITALY, Ellis, 54, (1,993)	2,279
*ITASCA, Hill, 45, (1,503)	1,701
Ivan, Stephens	15
*Ivanhoe, Fannin, 9	110
Izoro, Lampasas	17

J

Town, County	Pop. 2008
*JACINTO CITY, Harris, 215, (10,302)	10,693
*JACKSBORO, Jack, 175, (4,533)	4,700
Jackson, Shelby	50
Jackson, Van Zandt	25
*JACKSONVILLE, Cherokee, 740, (13,868)	14,576
Jacobia, Hunt	60
Jakes Colony, Guadalupe	95
JAMAICA BEACH, Galveston, 39, (1,075)	1,293
James, Shelby	75
Jamestown, Newton	196
Jamestown, Smith	75
*JARRELL, Williamson, 84, (1,319)	1,419
*JASPER, Jasper, 471, (7,657)	7,683
*JAYTON, Kent, 18, (513)	484
Jean, Young	110
*JEFFERSON, Marion, 257, (2,024)	2,019
Jenkins, Morris	350
Jennings, Lamar	85
*Jermyn, Jack, 4	75

The old church at Bluetown-Iglesia Antigua, Cameron County. Robert Plocheck photo.

Town, County .... Pop. 2008	Town, County .... Pop. 2008	Town, County .... Pop. 2008

JERSEY VILLAGE, Harris, 263,
(6,880) 7,584
*JEWETT, Leon, 78, (861) 960
Jiba, Kaufman 50
*JOAQUIN, Shelby, 25, (925) 991
Joe Lee, Bell 8
*JOHNSON CITY, Blanco,
159, (1,191) 1,502
Johnsville, Erath 25
Johntown, Red River 175
*Joinerville, Rusk 140
Joliet, Caldwell 192
JOLLY, Clay, 2, (188) 180
Jollyville, Williamson-Travis,
(15,813) 17,934
Jonah, Williamson 60
*Jonesboro, Coryell-Hamilton, 6 ... 125
JONES CREEK, Brazoria,
26, (2,130) 2,259
Jones Prairie, Milam 20
JONESTOWN, Travis, 97,
(1,681) 2,544
*Jonesville, Harrison, 4 70
Joplin, Jack 15
Joppa, Burnet 84
Jordans Store, Shelby 20
*JOSEPHINE, Collin, 18,
(594) 937
*JOSHUA, Johnson, 245,
(4,528) 5,592
Josserand, Trinity 29
Jot-Em-Down, Delta 8
*JOURDANTON, Atascosa, 123,
(3,732) 4,769
Joy, Clay 110
Jozye, Madison 36
Juarez [Las Palmas-], Cameron,
(1,666) 1,944
Jud, Haskell 60
*Judson, Gregg, 8 1,057
Juliff, Fort Bend 250
Jumbo, Panola 60
*JUNCTION, Kimble, 167,
(2,618) 2,663
Justiceburg, Garza, 1 76
*JUSTIN, Denton, 205,
(1,891) 3,067

K

Kalgary, Crosby 2
*Kamay, Wichita, 7 640
Kamey, Calhoun 25
Kanawha, Red River 90
*Karnack, Harrison, 21 350
Karon, Live Oak 25
Katemcy, Mason 80
*KATY, Harris-Waller-Fort Bend,
2,241, (11,775) 17,334
*KAUFMAN, Kaufman, 303,
(6,490) 9,032
K-Bar Ranch, Jim Wells, (350) 362
Keechi, Leon 15
*KEENE, Johnson, 120,
(5,003) 6,299
Keeter, Wise 250
Keith, Grimes 50
*KELLER, Tarrant, 1,614,
(27,345) 37,386
Kellers Corner, Cameron 123
Kellerville, Wheeler 50
Kellogg, Hunt 20

Kellyville, Marion 75
Kelsey, Upshur 50
Kelton, Wheeler 20
*KEMAH, Galveston, 282,
(2,330) 2,620
*KEMP, Kaufman, 98,
(1,133) 1,427
Kemper City, Victoria 16
*KEMPNER, Lampasas, 80,
(1,004) 1,143
*Kendalia, Kendall, 6 149
*KENDLETON, Fort Bend, 5,
(466) 599
*KENEDY, Karnes, 112,
(3,487) 3,678
KENEFICK, Liberty, 6, (667) 699
*KENNARD, Houston, 19,
(317) 316
*KENNEDALE, Tarrant, 328,
(5,850) 7,016
*Kenney, Austin, 2 957
Kenser, Hunt 100
Kensing, Delta 30
Kent, Culberson 30
Kentucky Town, Grayson 20
*KERENS, Navarro, 62,
(1,681) 1,933
*KERMIT, Winkler, 182,
(5,714) 5,424
*Kerrick, Dallam, 1 35
*KERRVILLE, Kerr, 1,537,
(20,425) 22,402
Kerrville South, Kerr 6,600
Key, Dawson 20
Kiam, Polk 24
Kicaster, Wilson 190
*Kildare, Cass, 1 104
Kilgore, Goliad .... (see Ander)
*KILGORE, Gregg-Rusk, 826,
(11,301) 12,341
*KILLEEN, Bell, 2,319,
(86,911) 112,998
King, Coryell 30
King Ranch Headquarters, Kleberg,
.... 191
*Kingsbury, Guadalupe, 20,
(652) 760
*Kingsland, Llano, 152,
(4,584) 5,249
Kingston, Hunt 140
*KINGSVILLE, Kleberg, 643,
(25,575) 24,477
Kingtown, Nacogdoches 300
Kingwood, Harris ..... [part of Houston]
Kinkler, Lavaca 75
Kiomatia, Red River 50
KIRBY, Bexar, 137, (8,673) 8,965
*KIRBYVILLE, Jasper, 141,
(2,085) 2,123
Kirk, Limestone 10
Kirkland, Childress 25
Kirtley, Fayette 93
*KIRVIN, Freestone, 6, (122) 134
Kittrell, Walker 126
Klein, Harris 45,000
Klondike, Dawson 50
*Klondike, Delta, 3 175
Klump, Washington 20
Knapp, Scurry 10
*Knickerbocker, Tom Green 94
*Knippa, Uvalde, 15, (739) 788
Knobbs Springs, Lee 20

KNOLLWOOD, Grayson, 4,
(375) 412
*Knott, Howard 200
*KNOX CITY, Knox, 55,
(1,219) 1,114
Koerth, Lavaca 45
Kokomo, Eastland 25
Komensky, Lavaca 75
Kopernik Shores, Cameron 34
*Kopperl, Bosque, 9 225
Kosciusko, Wilson 390
*KOSSE, Limestone, 22,
(497) 501
*KOUNTZE, Hardin, 115,
(2,115) 2,202
*KRESS, Swisher, 20, (826) 806
KRUGERVILLE, Denton, 39,
(903) 1,605
*KRUM, Denton, 127,
(1,979) 3,612
*KURTEN, Brazos, 2, (227) 240
*KYLE, Hays, 524,
(5,314) 24,518
Kyote, Atascosa 34

L

LaBelle, Jefferson 40
*La Blanca, Hidalgo, 12,
(2,351) 2,555
La Casita-Garciasville, Starr,
5, (2,177) 2,435
Laceola, Madison 10
Lackland Air Force Base, Bexar,
(7,123) 6,953
*LA COSTE, Medina, 44,
(1,255) 1,392
Lacy, Trinity 44
LACY-LAKEVIEW, McLennan,
126, (5,764) 6,104
*LADONIA, Fannin, 25,
(667) 727
LaFayette, Upshur 80
*LA FERIA, Cameron, 183,
(6,435) 7,714
La Feria North, Cameron, (168) ... 170
Lagarto, Live Oak 735
La Gloria, Jim Wells 70
La Gloria, Starr 102
Lago, Cameron, (246) 256
*LAGO VISTA, Travis, 299,
(4,507) 6,328
*LA GRANGE, Fayette, 424,
(4,478) 4,841
*LA GRULLA, Starr, 9,
(1,211) 1,807
Laguna, Uvalde 20
Laguna Heights, Cameron
(1,990) 2,123
*Laguna Park, Bosque 750
Laguna Seca, Hidalgo, (251) 263
Laguna Vista, Burnet 94
LAGUNA VISTA, Cameron, 51,
(1,658) 3,848
La Homa, Hidalgo, (10,433) 11,683
*Laird Hill, Rusk, 4 300
La Isla, El Paso 27
Lajitas, Brewster 75
*LA JOYA, Hidalgo, 67,
(3,303) 4,391
La Junta, Parker 300
Lake Arrowhead, Clay 250
LAKE BRIDGEPORT, Wise, 6,
(372) 437

Town, County ....Pop. 2008	Town, County ....Pop. 2008	Town, County ....Pop. 2008
Lake Brownwood, Brown, (1,694) 1,764	La Puerta, Starr, (1,636) 1,741	Leon Springs, Bexar, ... [part of San Antonio]
Lake Cisco, Eastland................... 300	*LAREDO, Webb, 5,443, (176,576) 222,482	*LEON VALLEY, Bexar, 503, (9,239) 10,481
LAKE CITY, San Patricio, 0, (526) 539	Laredo Ranchettes, Webb, (1,845) 1,890	*LEROY, McLennan, 10, (335) 338
*Lake Creek, Delta, 4 55	La Reforma, Starr 45	Lesley, Hall 25
*LAKE DALLAS, Denton, 276, (6,166) 8,022	Larga Vista, Webb, (742).............. 765	*LEVELLAND, Hockley, 454, (12,866) 12,628
Lake Dunlap, Guadalupe........... 1,370	Lariat, Parmer............................. 100	Leverett's Chapel, Rusk 400
Lakehills, Bandera, (4,668)........ 5,412	La Rosita, Starr, (1,729) 1,829	Levi, McLennan 50
*LAKE JACKSON, Brazoria, 759, (26,386) 28,773	*Larue, Henderson, 20 250	Levita, Coryell 70
Lake Kiowa, Cooke, (1,883) 1,888	*LaSalle, Jackson 110	*LEWISVILLE, Denton, 3,436, (77,737) 102,580
Lake Leon, Eastland...................... 75	Lasana, Cameron, (135).............. 138	*LEXINGTON, Lee, 74, (1,178) 1,334
Lake Nueces, Uvalde 60	*Lasara, Willacy, 3, (1,024)........ 1,139	*LIBERTY, Liberty, 441, (8,033) 8,548
LAKEPORT, Gregg, 14, (861) 972	Las Colonias, Zavala, (283).......... 315	Liberty, Lubbock 228
Lakeshore Gardens-Hidden Acres, San Patricio, (720)................. 701	Las Escobas, Starr 10	Liberty, Milam 40
LAKESIDE, San Patricio, (333) 338	Las Lomas, Starr, (2,684).......... 2,857	Liberty, Newton 128
LAKESIDE, Tarrant, 42, (1,040) 1,231	Las Lomitas, Jim Hogg, (267)...... 266	Liberty City, Gregg, (1,935) 2,175
LAKESIDE CITY, Archer, 19, (984) 1,022	Las Palmas-Juarez, Cameron, (1,666) 1,944	Liberty Hill, Houston 73
Lakeside Village, Bosque 226	Las Quintas Fronterizas, Maverick, (2,030) 2,164	Liberty Hill, Milam 25
LAKE TANGLEWOOD, Randall, 17, (825) 965	Las Rusias, Cameron 225	*LIBERTY HILL, Williamson, 269, (1,409) 1,838
Lake Victor, Burnet 265	Lassater, Marion 60	Lilbert, Nacogdoches.................. 100
Lakeview, Floyd 39	Las Yescas, Cameron 221	*Lillian, Johnson, 10 1,160
*LAKEVIEW, Hall, 4, (152) 144	Latch, Upshur 50	*Lincoln, Lee, 13........................ 336
Lakeview, Lynn 15	Latex, Harrison 75	LINCOLN PARK, Denton, 5, (517) 641
Lakeview, Orange.......................... 75	*LATEXO, Houston, 8, (272) 272	*LINDALE, Smith, 377, (2,954) 4,862
Lake View, Val Verde, (167) 174	La Tina Ranch [Arroyo Gardens-], Cameron, (732)..................... 750	*LINDEN, Cass, 88, (2,256) 2,464
LAKEVIEW [Lacy-], McLennan, 126, (5,764) 6,104	Latium, Washington 30	Lindenau, DeWitt........................... 50
*LAKEWAY, Travis, 584, (8,002) 11,399	Laughlin Air Force Base, Val Verde, (2,225) 2,318	Lindendale, Kendall 70
Lakewood Harbor, Bosque 250	Laurel, Newton 357	*LINDSAY, Cooke, 31, (788)........ 956
LAKEWOOD VILLAGE, Denton, 0, (342) 507	Laureles, Cameron, (3,285)....... 3,906	Lindsay, Reeves, (394)................ 361
*LAKE WORTH, Tarrant, 258, (4,618) 4,793	Lavender, Limestone 30	*Lingleville, Erath, 1 100
Lamar, Aransas......................... 1,600	*LA VERNIA, Wilson, 151, (931) 1,220	Linn Flat, Nacogdoches................ 60
*LA MARQUE, Galveston, 414, (13,682) 14,435	La Victoria, Starr, (1,683).......... 1,797	*Linn [San Manuel-], Hidalgo, 11, (958) 987
Lamasco, Fannin 32	*LA VILLA, Hidalgo, 15, (1,305) 1,404	Linwood, Cherokee....................... 40
*LAMESA, Dawson, 342, (9,952) 9,225	*LAVON, Collin, 67, (387)............ 585	*LIPAN, Hood, 42, (425) 539
Lamkin, Comanche........................ 87	*LA WARD, Jackson, 15, (200) 220	Lipscomb, Lipscomb, 2, (44)........ 46
*LAMPASAS, Lampasas, 379, (6,786) 8,031	*LAWN, Taylor, 17, (353) 348	*Lissie, Wharton, 4 72
Lanark, Cass 30	Lawrence, Kaufman...................... 259	Littig, Travis 37
*LANCASTER, Dallas, 708, (25,894) 34,896	*Lazbuddie, Parmer, 8................ 248	Little Cypress, Orange................. 900
Landrum Station, Cameron 125	*LEAGUE CITY, Galveston-Harris, 2,025, (45,444) 68,836	*LITTLE ELM, Denton, 472, (3,646) 21,366
*Lane City, Wharton, 4..................111	Leagueville, Henderson................. 50	*LITTLEFIELD, Lamb, 214, (6,507) 6,514
Lanely, Freestone 27	*LEAKEY, Real, 61, (387)............. 398	Little Hope, Wood 25
Laneport, Williamson 40	*LEANDER, Williamson, 794, (7,596) 24,135	Little Midland, Burnet.................... 82
*Laneville, Rusk, 11 169	LEARY, Bowie, 10, (555) 581	Little New York, Gonzales.............. 15
*Langtry, Val Verde 30	*Ledbetter, Fayette, 14 83	*LITTLE RIVER-ACADEMY, Bell, 30, (1,645) 1,718
Lanier, Cass 80	Leedale, Bell 24	Lively, Kaufman 50
Lannius, Fannin 79	*Leesburg, Camp, 16.................. 128	LIVE OAK, Bexar, 379, (9,156) 12,519
Lantana, Cameron 137	*Leesville, Gonzales, 3 152	*LIVERPOOL, Brazoria, 18, (404) 460
Lantana, Denton 1,000	*LEFORS, Gray, 18, (559)............ 569	*LIVINGSTON, Polk, 540, (5,433) 6,601
La Paloma, Cameron, (354) 363	*Leggett, Polk, 6 500	*LLANO, Llano, 277, (3,325) 3,840
La Paloma-Lost Creek, Nueces, (323) 275	Lehman, Cochran 6	Llano Grande, Hidalgo, (3,333) 3,474
La Parita, Atascosa........................ 48	Leigh, Harrison 60	Lobo, Culberson 15
*LA PORTE, Harris, 916, (31,880) 34,091	Lela, Wheeler 135	Locker, San Saba 16
La Presa, Webb, (508) 528	*Lelia Lake, Donley, 2.................... 71	Lockett, Wilbarger 150
*La Pryor, Zavala, 13, (1,491) 1,550	*Leming, Atascosa, 7 268	Lockettville, Hockley...................... 20
	*Lenorah, Martin, 3 83	*LOCKHART, Caldwell, 424, (11,615) 13,633
	Lenz, Karnes 20	
	Leo, Cooke 20	
	Leo, Lee 10	
	*LEONA, Leon, 11, (181) 179	
	*LEONARD, Fannin, 93, (1,846) 2,009	
	Leon Junction, Coryell................... 50	

Marfa, Presidio County. Robert Plocheck photo.

Town, County ....Pop. 2008	Town, County ....Pop. 2008	Town, County ....Pop. 2008
*LOCKNEY, Floyd, 65, (2,056) 1,917	*Los Ebanos, Hidalgo, 1, (403)..... 425	Mabelle, Baylor................................. 9
Locust, Grayson 118	Los Escondidos, Burnet................. 80	Mabry, Red River............................ 60
*Lodi, Marion 175	*LOS FRESNOS, Cameron, 133, (4,512) 5,586	*Macdona, Bexar, 3 297
Loebau, Lee..................................... 35	*LOS INDIOS, Cameron, 19, (1,149) 1,334	Macon, Franklin 21
Logan, Panola 40	Losoya, Bexar............................... 500	Macune, San Augustine.................. 50
LOG CABIN, Henderson, 5, (733) 825	Los Saenz [ROMA-], Starr, 265, (9,617) 11,707	*MADISONVILLE, Madison, 202, (4,159) 4,481
*Lohn, McCulloch 149	Lost Creek, Travis, (4,729) 4,743	Madras, Red River.......................... 61
Loire, Wilson.................................... 50	Lost Creek [La Paloma-], Nueces, (323) 275	Magnet, Wharton 42
Lois, Cooke..................................... 10	Lost Prairie, Limestone.................... 2	*MAGNOLIA, Montgomery, 445, (1,111)................................ 1,847
*Lolita, Jackson, 8, (548) 553	Los Villareales, Starr, (930) 987	Magnolia, San Jacinto 330
Loma Alta, McMullen 25	LOS YBANEZ, Dawson, 2, (32)...... 31	Magnolia Beach, Calhoun 250
Loma Alta, Val Verde 30	*LOTT, Falls, 52, (724) 700	Magnolia Springs, Jasper.............. 20
Loma Linda [Del Sol-], San Patricio, (726) 709	*Louise, Wharton, 32, (977).......... 979	Maha, Travis 200
Loma Linda East, Jim Wells, (214) 226	Lovelace, Hill 30	Mahl, Nacogdoches....................... 150
Lomax, Howard 25	*LOVELADY, Houston, 28, (608) 631	Mahomet, Burnet............................ 97
*LOMETA, Lampasas, 42, (782)... 871	*Loving, Young, 1.......................... 300	Majors, Franklin 13
*London, Kimble, 6 180	*Lowake, Concho, 2 40	*MALAKOFF, Henderson, 113, (2,257) 2,398
Lone Camp, Palo Pinto................ 110	LOWRY CROSSING, Collin, 37, (1,229) 1,856	Mallard, Montague.......................... 12
Lone Cedar, Ellis 18	Loyal Valley, Mason........................ 52	*MALONE, Hill, 19, (278).............. 296
Lone Grove, Llano 50	Loyola Beach, Kleberg 195	Malta, Bowie 297
Lone Oak, Colorado 50	*Lozano, Cameron, 1, (324) 335	Malvern, Leon................................. 12
*LONE OAK, Hunt, 45, (521)........ 570	*LUBBOCK, Lubbock, 7,376, (199,564) 218,327	Mambrino, Hood.............................. 74
Lone Pine, Houston 81	LUCAS, Collin, 124, (2,890) 4,456	*Manchaca, Travis, 92 2,259
Lone Star, Cherokee....................... 20	Luckenbach, Gillespie 25	Manchester, Red River................. 185
Lone Star, Floyd 42	*LUEDERS, Jones, 9, (300) 281	Mangum, Eastland.......................... 15
Lone Star, Lamar............................ 35	Luella, Grayson 639	Manheim, Lee................................. 50
*LONE STAR, Morris, 53, (1,631) 1,695	*LUFKIN, Angelina, 1,714, (32,709) 33,803	Mankin, Henderson 30
*Long Branch, Panola, 4.............. 150	*LULING, Caldwell, 261, (5,080) 5,658	Mankins, Archer 10
Long Lake, Anderson...................... 15	*LUMBERTON, Hardin, 386, (8,731) 10,745	*MANOR, Travis, 174, (1,204) 3,399
Long Mott, Calhoun 76	Lums Chapel, Lamb 6	*MANSFIELD, Tarrant-Johnson, 1,684, (28,031) 44,957
Longpoint, Washington.................... 30	Luther, Howard 3	*MANVEL, Brazoria, 213, (3,046) 4,966
*LONGVIEW, Gregg-Harrison, 3,581, (73,344) 76,885	Lutie, Collingsworth 10	*Maple, Bailey, 1 75
Longworth, Fisher 47	Lydia, Red River 109	Maple, Red River............................ 30
Looneyville, Nacogdoches.............. 50	*LYFORD, Willacy, 36, (1,973) 2,453	Maple Springs, Titus 25
*Loop, Gaines, 5........................... 315	Lyford South, Willacy, (172).......... 176	Mapleton, Houston 32
*Lopeno, Zapata, 2, (140)............. 169	Lynn Grove, Grimes........................ 25	*Marathon, Brewster, 15, (455) 468
Lopezville, Hidalgo, (4,476)....... 4,998	*Lyons, Burleson, 9 360	*MARBLE FALLS, Burnet, 673, (4,959) 7,038
*LORAINE, Mitchell, 17, (656)...... 636	*LYTLE, Atascosa-Medina-Bexar, 164, (2,383) 2,815	*MARFA, Presidio, 130, (2,121) 2,134
*LORENA, McLennan, 142, (1,433) 1,621	Lytton Springs, Caldwell 500	Margaret, Foard.............................. 50
*LORENZO, Crosby, 20, (1,372) 1,304	**M**	Marie, Runnels 10
Los Alvarez, Starr, (1,434) 1,520	*MABANK, Kaufman-Henderson, 208, (2,151) 2,821	*MARIETTA, Cass, 4, (112)......... 108
Los Angeles, La Salle..................... 20		*MARION, Guadalupe, 97, (1,099) 1,306
Los Angeles Subdivision, Willacy, (86) 95		*Markham, Matagorda, 14, (1,138) 1,074
Los Barreras, Starr 75		
Los Coyotes, Willacy 4		

Town, County ....Pop. 2008

Markley, Young 50
*MARLIN, Falls, 172, (6,628)..... 6,441
Marlow, Milam.................................. 45
*MARQUEZ, Leon, 32, (220)........ 221
Mars, Van Zandt 20
*MARSHALL, Harrison, 915,
   (23,935)........................... 24,332
Marston, Polk.................................. 25
*MART, McLennan, 66,
   (2,273) 2,446
*MARTINDALE, Caldwell, 47,
   (953) 1,192
Martins Mill, Van Zandt 158
Martin Springs, Hopkins 200
*Martinsville, Nacogdoches, 2 350
Marvin, Lamar.................................. 48
Maryetta, Jack 7
*Maryneal, Nolan, 3 61
Marysville, Cooke 12
*MASON, Mason, 198,
   (2,134) 2,168
Massey Lake, Anderson 30
Masterson, Moore, 1.......................... 2
*MATADOR, Motley, 38, (740)...... 767
*Matagorda, Matagorda, 23.......... 710
*MATHIS, San Patricio, 133,
   (5,034) 5,187
Matthews, Colorado......................... 25
*MAUD, Bowie, 41, (1,028) 1,024
*Mauriceville, Orange, 16,
   (2,743) 2,776
Maverick, Runnels 35
Maxdale, Bell 25
Maxey, Lamar.................................. 70
*Maxwell, Caldwell, 29..................500
*May, Brown, 17 270
*Maydelle, Cherokee, 1 250
Mayfield, Hale.................................. 26
Mayfield, Hill 25
Mayflower, Newton 50
Maynard, San Jacinto................... 150
*MAYPEARL, Ellis, 31, (746)........ 962
Maysfield, Milam........................... 140
*McAdoo, Dickens, 2...................... 75
*McALLEN, Hidalgo, 4,862,
   (106,414) 128,888
*McCAMEY, Upton, 61,
   (1,805) 1,703

*McCaulley, Fisher, 1 96
McClanahan, Falls.......................... 42
McCook, Hidalgo 50
McCoy, Atascosa 30
McCoy, Floyd.................................. 20
McCoy, Kaufman 20
McCoy, Panola 30
McCoy, Red River......................... 175
*McDade, Bastrop, 13 345
*McFaddin, Victoria, 1 175
McGirk, Hamilton 9
*McGREGOR, McLennan, 206,
   (4,727) 4,786
*McKINNEY, Collin, 3,617,
   (54,369) 116,233
McKinney Acres, Andrews 197
*McLEAN, Gray, 33,(830) 901
McLENDON-CHISHOLM,
   Rockwall, 3, (914)............... 1,225
*McLeod, Cass, 4 600
McMahan, Caldwell 125
McMillan, San Saba....................... 15
McNair, Harris............................ 2,039
McNary, Hudspeth 250
McNeil, Caldwell 200
*McQueeney, Guadalupe, 36,
   (2,527) 3,020
*MEADOW, Terry, 13, (658).......... 660
Meadow Grove, Bell 20
MEADOWLAKES, Burnet, 19,
   (1,293) 1,972
MEADOWS PLACE, Fort Bend,
   97, (4,912) 6,652
Mecca, Madison 48
Medicine Mound, Hardeman 50
Medill, Lamar.................................. 50
*Medina, Bandera, 32................... 850
Medina, Zapata,(2,960) 3,531
Meeker, Jefferson 2,280
Meeks, Bell 6
*MEGARGEL, Archer, 10,
   (248) 247
*MELISSA, Collin, 103,
   (1,350) 4,688
Melrose, Nacogdoches................. 400
*MELVIN, McCulloch, 6, (155)...... 149
*MEMPHIS, Hall, 80,
   (2,479) 2,345

*MENARD, Menard, 75,
   (1,653) 1,617
Mendoza, Caldwell 100
Menlow, Hill 12
*Mentone, Loving, 2....................... 20
Mentz, Colorado 100
*MERCEDES, Hidalgo, 467,
   (13,649) 16,129
Mercury, McCulloch 166
*Mereta, Tom Green, 4 131
*MERIDIAN, Bosque, 79,
   (1,491) 1,564
*Merit, Hunt, 3.............................225
*MERKEL, Taylor, 114,
   (2,637) 2,650
Merle, Burleson 10
Merriman, Eastland 14
*MERTENS, Hill, 6, (146) 157
*MERTZON, Irion, 66,
   (839) 818
*MESQUITE, Dallas, 3,481,
   (124,523) 131,685
Metcalf Gap, Palo Pinto.................. 6
*MEXIA, Limestone, 308,
   (6,563) 6,902
*Meyersville, DeWitt, 10 110
Meyersville, Washington................ 15
*MIAMI, Roberts, 23, (588).......... 557
Mico, Medina 107
Midcity, Lamar 50
Middleton, Leon 26
*Midfield, Matagorda, 6................ 305
*Midkiff, Upton, 9 182
*MIDLAND, Midland-Martin,
   4,312, (94,996) 102,691
*MIDLOTHIAN, Ellis, 593,
   (7,480) 15,142
Midway, Bell.................................. 140
Midway, Dawson............................. 20
Midway, Fannin................................. 7
Midway, Jim Wells 24
Midway, Limestone 9
*MIDWAY, Madison, 15, (288) 297
Midway, Red River.......................... 40
Midway, Titus 110
Midway, Upshur 20
Midway, Van Zandt 31
Midway, Polk................................. 525

Winter residents at Mission, Hidalgo County. Robert Plocheck photo.

Town, County .... Pop. 2008	Town, County .... Pop. 2008	Town, County .... Pop. 2008
Midway North, Hidalgo, (3,946) 4,220	Moore's Crossing, Travis 25	MURPHY, Collin, 386, (3,099) 13,080
Midway South, Hidalgo, (1,711) 1,823	MOORE STATION, Henderson, 0, (184) 187	Murray, Young 45
Midyett, Panola 150	Mooreville, Falls 96	Murvaul, Panola 150
Mikeska, Live Oak 10	Mooring, Brazos 80	Mustang, Denton 25
Mila Doce, Hidalgo, (4,907) 5,481	Morales, Jackson 72	MUSTANG, Navarro, 0, (47) 51
*Milam, Sabine, 7, (1,329) 1,277	*MORAN, Shackelford, 10, (233) 236	Mustang Mott, DeWitt 20
*MILANO, Milam, 30, (400) 420	Moravia, Lavaca 165	MUSTANG RIDGE, Travis-Caldwell, 19, (785) 996
Milburn, McCulloch 8	*MORGAN, Bosque, 15, (485) 539	*Myra, Cooke, 2 150
MILDRED, Navarro, 4, (405) 469	Morgan Creek, Burnet 126	Myrtle Springs, Van Zandt 165
*MILES, Runnels, 52, (850) 821	Morgan Farm Area, San Patricio, (484) 510	**N**
*MILFORD, Ellis, 14, (685) 744	*Morgan Mill, Erath, 6 206	*NACOGDOCHES, Nacogdoches, 1,365, (29,914) 32,028
Mill Creek, Washington 40	MORGAN'S POINT, Harris, 17, (336) 343	*Nada, Colorado, 10 165
Miller Grove, Hopkins 115	MORGAN'S POINT RESORT, Bell, 55, (2,989) 4,597	*NAPLES, Morris, 65, (1,410) 1,445
MILLERS COVE, Titus, 3, (120) 136	Morning Glory, El Paso, (627) 631	Naruna, Burnet 95
*Millersview, Concho, 2 80	*Morse, Hansford, 4, (172) 192	*NASH, Bowie, 79, (2,169) 2,436
Millett, La Salle 40	*MORTON, Cochran, 48, (2,249) 2,081	Nash, Ellis 40
Millheim, Austin 170	Morton, Harrison 75	NASSAU BAY, Harris, 175, (4,170) 4,152
*Millican, Brazos, 8, (108) 109	Morton Valley, Eastland 46	Nat, Nacogdoches 50
*MILLSAP, Parker, 51, (353) 406	*Moscow, Polk, 10 170	*NATALIA, Medina, 70, (1,663) 1,931
Milo Center, Deaf Smith 5	Mosheim, Bosque 75	NAVARRO, Navarro, 0, (191) 206
Milton, Lamar 50	Moss Bluff, Liberty 65	Navarro Mills, Navarro 90
Mims, Brazoria 90	Moss Hill, Liberty 180	*NAVASOTA, Grimes, 345, (6,789) 7,791
*Minden, Rusk, 3 150	Mostyn, Montgomery 90	Navidad, Jackson 227
*MINEOLA, Wood, 424, (4,550) 5,187	*MOULTON, Lavaca, 71, (944) 949	*NAZARETH, Castro, 14, (356) 345
Mineral, Bee 65	*Mound, Coryell, 2 125	Necessity, Stephens 10
*MINERAL WELLS, Palo Pinto-Parker, 613, (16,946) 17,513	Mound City, Anderson-Houston 60	Nechanitz, Fayette 57
Minerva, Milam 100	MOUNTAIN CITY, Hays, 24, (671) 796	*Neches, Anderson, 8 175
Mings Chapel, Upshur 50	*Mountain Home, Kerr, 16 96	*NEDERLAND, Jefferson, 679, (17,422) 17,208
*MINGUS, Palo Pinto, 18, (246) 260	Mountain Peak, Ellis 300	Needmore, Bailey 45
Minter, Lamar 78	Mountain Springs, Cooke 600	Needmore, Terry 7
*Mirando City, Webb, 15, (493) 585	Mount Bethel, Panola 65	*NEEDVILLE, Fort Bend, 126, (2,609) 3,632
*MISSION, Hidalgo, 1,623, (45,408) 67,082	*MOUNT CALM, Hill, 18, (310) 332	Negley, Red River 136
Mission Bend, Fort Bend-Harris, (30,831) 36,437	*MOUNT ENTERPRISE, Rusk, 49, (525) 553	Neinda, Jones 21
Mission Valley, Victoria 225	Mount Haven, Cherokee 30	Nell, Live Oak 60
*MISSOURI CITY, Fort Bend-Harris, 1,723, (52,913) 77,305	Mount Hermon, Shelby 80	Nelson City, Kendall 50
Mixon, Cherokee 50	Mount Olive, Lavaca 50	Nelsonville, Austin 200
*MOBEETIE, Wheeler, 9, (107) 107	*MOUNT PLEASANT, Titus, 704, (13,935) 15,305	Nelta, Hopkins 36
MOBILE CITY, Rockwall, 2, (196) 253	Mount Rose, Falls 26	*Nemo, Somervell, 13 56
Moffat, Bell 1,406	Mount Selman, Cherokee 325	Nesbitt, Harrison, (302) 297
Moffett, Angelina 100	Mount Sylvan, Smith 181	Neuville, Shelby 65
Moline, Lampasas 12	*MOUNT VERNON, Franklin, 151, (2,286) 2,573	*NEVADA, Collin, 40, (563) 866
*MONAHANS, Ward, 223, (6,821) 6,663	Mount Vernon, Houston 43	*NEWARK, Wise, 50, (887) 1,076
Monaville, Waller 180	Mozelle, Coleman 15	*New Baden, Robertson, 4 150
Monkstown, Fannin, ... 35	Muellersville, Washington 20	NEW BERLIN, Guadalupe, 10, (467) 559
Monroe, Rusk 96	*MUENSTER, Cooke, 139, (1,556) 1,701	New Bielau, Colorado 75
Monroe City, Chambers 11	Mulberry, Fannin 17	New Birthright, Hopkins 80
Mont, Lavaca 30	*Muldoon, Fayette, 3 95	*NEW BOSTON, Bowie, 195, (4,808) 4,795
*Montague, Montague, 13 400	*MULESHOE, Bailey, 200, (4,530) 4,502	*NEW BRAUNFELS, Comal-Guadalupe, 2,591, (36,494) 56,595
*Montalba, Anderson, 16 110	*MULLIN, Mills, 9, (175) 181	New Bremen, Austin 125
*MONT BELVIEU, Chambers, 159, (2,324) 2,775	Mullins Prairie, Fayette 107	Newburg, Comanche 32
Monte Alto, Hidalgo, (1,611) 1,718	*Mumford, Robertson 170	Newby, Leon 40
Monte Grande, Cameron 97	*MUNDAY, Knox, 47, (1,527) 1,447	*New Caney, Montgomery, 185 6,800
Montell, Uvalde 20	Munger, Limestone 5	*NEWCASTLE, Young, 21, (575) 615
*MONTGOMERY, Montgomery, 431, (489) 867	Mungerville, Dawson 25	NEW CHAPEL HILL, Smith, 9, (553) 605
Monthalia, Gonzales 32	Muniz, Hidalgo, (1,106) 1,191	New Colony, Bell 12
Monticello, Titus 20	*MURCHISON, Henderson, 34, (592) 627	
*MOODY, McLennan, 72, (1,400) 1,441		
*Moore, Frio, 11, (644) 653		

Town, County .... Pop. 2008	Town, County .... Pop. 2008	Town, County .... Pop. 2008
New Colony, Cass 65	North Alamo, Hidalgo, (2,601) ... 2,178	OAK RIDGE NORTH, Montgomery,
New Corn Hill, Williamson 475	NORTH CLEVELAND, Liberty,	182, (2,991) 3,842
New Davy, DeWitt........................... 20	2, (263) 254	Oak Trail Shores, Hood,
*NEW DEAL, Lubbock, 17,	Northcliff, Guadalupe, (1,819) ... 2,024	(2,475) 2,733
(708) 975	North Escobares, Starr,	OAK VALLEY, Navarro, 3, (401) ... 456
NEW FAIRVIEW, Wise, 14,	(1,692) 1,800	Oakville, Live Oak, 4.................... 260
(877) 1,144	Northfield, Motley.......................... 15	*OAKWOOD, Leon, 23, (471)....... 483
Newgulf, Wharton 10	NORTHLAKE, Denton, 18,	Oatmeal, Burnet 76
New Harmony, Shelby 40	(921) 1,816	*O'BRIEN, Haskell, 1, (132) 120
New Harmony, Smith.................... 350	North Pearsall, Frio, (561) 510	Ocee, McLennan 84
*NEW HOME, Lynn, 7, (320) 337	*NORTH RICHLAND HILLS,	Odds, Limestone 24
New Hope, Cherokee 50	Tarrant, 1,970, (55,635).... 65,702	*Odell, Wilbarger 100
NEW HOPE, Collin, 18, (662)....... 758	Northrup, Lee.................................. 86	*ODEM, San Patricio, 71,
New Hope, Jones 9	North San Pedro, Nueces, (920) .. 829	(2,499) 2,550
New Hope, San Augustine.............. 75	North Star, Archer, ... 10	*ODESSA, Ector-Midland,
New Hope, Smith............................ 75	*North Zulch, Madison, 14............ 150	3,772, (90,943,) 96,849
New Hope, Wood 15	*Norton, Runnels............................ 50	*O'DONNELL, Lynn-Dawson,
Newlin, Hall.................................... 27	*Notrees, Ector, 2 20	15, (1,011) 915
*NEW LONDON, Rusk, 16,	*NOVICE, Coleman, 5, (142)......... 136	Oenaville, Bell.............................. 108
(987) 993	Novice, Lamar 35	O'Farrell, Cass............................... 20
New Lynn, Lynn 4	Noxville, Kimble 3	Ogburn, Wood 10
New Moore, Lynn............................ 10	Nugent, Jones 41	*OGLESBY, Coryell, 20, (458)...... 444
New Mountain, Upshur 20	Nunelee, Fannin 25	*Oilton, Webb, 2, (310) 368
Newport, Clay-Jack 75	Nurillo, Hidalgo, (5,056)............. 5,432	Oklahoma, Montgomery 800
New Salem, Palo Pinto 89	*Nursery, Victoria, 5 260	Oklahoma Flat, Hockley 4
New Salem, Rusk 55	**O**	Oklahoma Lane, Parmer 25
Newsome, Camp 113	Oakalla, Burnet............................... 99	*Oklaunion, Wilbarger, 4.............. 138
*NEW SUMMERFIELD, Cherokee,	Oakdale, Polk 25	Okra, Eastland................................ 20
22, (998) 1,119	Oak Forest, Gonzales..................... 24	Ola, Kaufman................................. 65
New Sweden, Travis....................... 60	Oak Grove, Bowie 294	Old Boston, Bowie 100
New Taiton, Wharton 10	Oak Grove, Colorado...................... 40	Old Center, Panola 83
New Territory, Fort Bend,	OAK GROVE, Kaufman, 0,	Old Dime Box, Lee 225
(13,861) 17,006	(710) 948	*Olden, Eastland, 6...................... 113
*NEWTON, Newton, 82,	Oak Grove, Wood.......................... 140	Oldenburg, Fayette......................... 92
(2,459) 2,502	Oak Hill, Hood 247	*Old Glory, Stonewall, 3.............. 100
*New Ulm, Austin, 37................... 974	Oak Hill, Rusk 200	Old Midway, Leon 12
*NEW WAVERLY, Walker, 88,	*Oakhurst, San Jacinto, 11,	*Old Ocean, Brazoria, 15............. 150
(950) 825	(230) 256	OLD RIVER-WINFREE, Chambers,
New Wehdem, Austin 414	Oak Island, Chambers.................. 255	17, (1,364) 1,558
New Willard, Polk 160	Oakland, Cherokee......................... 50	Old Salem, Bowie 50
New York, Henderson..................... 60	*Oakland, Colorado........................ 80	Old Union, Bowie 238
NEYLANDVILLE, Hunt, 1, (56)....... 57	Oakland, Van Zandt....................... 26	Old Union, Limestone 25
NIEDERWALD, Hays-Caldwell,	OAK LEAF, Ellis, 27, (1,209) ... 1,484	Oletha, Limestone 53
22, (584) 533	OAK POINT, Denton, 90,	Olfen, Runnels................................ 35
Nigton, Trinity................................. 87	(1,747) 2,707	Olin, Hamilton 15
Nimrod, Eastland............................ 45	OAK RIDGE, Cooke, (224)........... 246	Olivarez, Hidalgo, (2,445)......... 2,608
Nineveh, Leon 50	Oak Ridge, Grayson 161	Olivia, Calhoun 215
Nix, Lampasas................................. 6	OAK RIDGE, Kaufman, 11,	Ollie, Polk 5
*NIXON, Gonzales-Wilson, 64,	(400) 546	*Olmito, Cameron, 50, (1,198)... 1,258
(2,186) 2,362	Oak Ridge, Nacogdoches............. 225	Olmos, Guadalupe.......................... 65
Noack, Williamson 70		
Nobility, Fannin 21		
Noble, Lamar 14		
Nockernut, Wilson 20		
*NOCONA, Montague, 161,		
(3,198) 3,412		
Nogalus Prairie, Trinity 109		
*Nolan, Nolan, 2 47		
*NOLANVILLE, Bell, 37,		
(2,150) 3,015		
*NOME, Jefferson, 22, (515) 541		
Noodle, Jones................................. 40		
NOONDAY, Smith, 46, (515)........ 567		
Nopal, DeWitt 25		
*NORDHEIM, DeWitt, 13,		
(323) 315		
Norman, Williamson 40		
Normandy, Maverick..................... 114		
*NORMANGEE, Leon-Madison,		
53, (719) 762		
*Normanna, Bee, (121)................. 168		
Norse, Bosque.............................. 110		

The harbor at Palacios, Matagorda County. Robert Plocheck photo.

Town, County ....Pop. 2008	Town, County ....Pop. 2008	Town, County ....Pop. 2008

OLMOS PARK, Bexar, 112,
  (2,343) 2,408
*OLNEY, Young, 137,
  (3,396) 3,494
*OLTON, Lamb, 57, (2,288)....... 2,333
*OMAHA, Morris, 30, (999)........ 1,133
Omen, Smith.............................. 150
*ONALASKA, Polk, 106,
  (1,174) 1,415
Onion Creek, Travis, (2,116)...... 2,083
Opdyke, Hockley 20
OPDYKE WEST, Hockley, 3,
  (188) 204
Oplin, Callahan............................ 75
O'Quinn, Fayette 191
Oran, Palo Pinto 61
*ORANGE, Orange, 719,
  (18,643) 18,205
Orangedale, Bee 40
*Orangefield, Orange, 9............... 725
*ORANGE GROVE, Jim Wells,
  90, (1,288) 1,432
Oranson [Chula Vista-], Cameron,
  (394) 408
*ORCHARD, Fort Bend, 20,
  (408) 528
*ORE CITY, Upshur, 59,
  (1,106) 1,264
Orient, Tom Green 57
*Orla, Reeves, 2 80
Osage, Colorado 50
Osage, Coryell............................. 30
Oscar, Bell 58
Osceola, Hill 95
Otey, Brazoria............................ 318
*Ottine, Gonzales, 1 80
Otto, Falls 48
*Ovalo, Taylor, 2 225
*OVERTON, Rusk-Smith, 96,
  (2,350) 2,407
*OVILLA, Ellis-Dallas, 121,
  (3,405) 4,115
Owens, Brown 16
Owens, Crosby 4
Owentown, Smith 100
Owl Creek, Bell........................... 130
Owl Ranch-Amargosa, Jim Wells,
  (527) 555
Oxford, Llano 18
OYSTER CREEK, Brazoria, 35,
  (1,192) 1,411
*Ozona, Crockett, 122,
  (3,436) 3,697

P

Pacio, Delta 35
Padgett, Young 28
*PADUCAH, Cottle, 48,
  (1,498) 1,286
*Paige, Bastrop, 24...................... 275
Paint Creek, Haskell 150
*PAINT ROCK, Concho, 13,
  (320) 306
Paisano [Edgewater-], San Patricio,
  (182) 183
*PALACIOS, Matagorda, 158,
  (5,153) 5,174
*PALESTINE, Anderson, 812,
  (17,598) 17,882
PALISADES, Randall, 0, (352) 374
Palito Blanco, Jim Wells 750
*PALMER, Ellis, 59,
  (1,774) 2,209

PALMHURST, Hidalgo, 77,
  (4,872) 5,341
PALM VALLEY, Cameron, 13,
  (1,298) 1,314
PALMVIEW, Hidalgo, 186,
  (4,107) 5,358
Palmview South, Hidalgo,
  (6,219) 6,484
Paloduro, Armstrong..................... 10
*Palo Pinto, Palo Pinto, 15 411
*Paluxy, Hood 76
*PAMPA, Gray, 616,
  (17,887) 17,591
Pancake, Coryell 11
Pandale, Val Verde 25
*Pandora, Wilson, 2 110
*PANHANDLE, Carson, 72,
  (2,589) 2,678
*Panna Maria, Karnes, 5 45
*Panola, Panola, 3....................... 305
PANORAMA VILLAGE, Montgomery,
  30, (1,965) 2,472
*PANTEGO, Tarrant, 408,
  (2,318) 2,351
Panther Junction, Brewster 112
Papalote, Bee 75
*PARADISE, Wise, 49, (459)........ 525
*PARIS, Lamar, 1,167,
  (25,898) 26,324
Park, Fayette 25
PARKER, Collin, 78, (1,379)...... 2,594
Parker, Johnson............................ 93
Park Springs, Wise 90
Parsley Hill, Wilbarger 25
Parvin, Denton............................. 44
*PASADENA, Harris, 3,249,
  (141,674) 152,168
Patillo, Erath 10
Patman Switch, Cass 40
Patonia, Polk 15
Patricia, Dawson.......................... 40
Patroon, Shelby 25
*PATTISON, Waller, 35, (447) 525
Pattonfield, Upshur....................... 20
PATTON VILLAGE, Montgomery,
  10, (1,391) 1,695
*Pattonville, Lamar, 6.................. 180
Pawelekville, Karnes 105
*Pawnee, Bee, 3, (201) 244
Paxton, Shelby 50
Paynes Corner, Gaines 18
PAYNE SPRINGS, Henderson,
  15, (683) 719
Peach Creek, Brazos.................... 150
Peacock, Stonewall 100
Peadenville, Palo Pinto 15
Pearl, Coryell.............................. 50
*PEARLAND, Brazoria-Harris,
  2,632, (37,640) 85,701
Pearl City, DeWitt 4
*PEARSALL, Frio, 196,
  (7,506) 7,905
Pearson, Medina 24
Pearsons Chapel, Houston............. 95
Pear Valley, McCulloch................. 37
*Peaster, Parker, 1...................... 102
Pecan Acres, Tarrant-Wise,
  (2,289) 2,555
*PECAN GAP, Delta-Fannin, 8,
  (214) 210
Pecan Grove, Fort Bend,
  (13,551) 17,387

PECAN HILL, Ellis, 8, (672).......... 713
Pecan Plantation, Hood,
  (3,544) 3,744
Pecan Wells, Hamilton 6
*PECOS, Reeves, 239,
  (9,501) 8,290
Peeltown, Kaufman 75
Peerless, Hopkins......................... 90
*Peggy, Atascosa, 2..................... 22
Pelham, Navarro........................... 75
PELICAN BAY, Tarrant, 8,
  (1,505) 1,763
*Pendleton, Bell, 1 369
*PENELOPE, Hill, 6, (211)........... 221
*PEÑITAS, Hidalgo, 68,
  (1,167) 2,307
*Pennington, Trinity-Houston, 5...... 67
*Penwell, Ector, 4 41
Peoria, Hill 105
*Pep, Hockley 3
Percilla, Houston 95
Perezville [Abram-], Hidalgo,
  (5,444) 5,824
Pernitas Point, Live Oak-Jim Wells,
  0, (269).............................. 274
*Perrin, Jack, 9 300
Perry, Falls.................................. 76
*PERRYTON, Ochiltree, 372,
  (7,774) 8,255
Perryville, Wood 35
Personville, Limestone 50
Pert, Anderson............................. 20
Peters, Austin 150
*PETERSBURG, Hale-Floyd,
  36, (1,262) 1,187
Peter's Prairie, Red River............. 40
Petersville, DeWitt 38
*PETROLIA, Clay, 21, (782) 757
PETRONILA, Nueces, 2, (83)........ 81
Petteway, Robertson 25
Pettibone, Milam.......................... 25
Pettit, Hockley............................. 15
*Pettus, Bee, 14, (608) 736
*Petty, Lamar, 2 130
Petty, Lynn 8
Peyton, Blanco 30
*PFLUGERVILLE, Travis, 1,169,
  (16,335) 33,392
Phalba, Van Zandt 73
*PHARR, Hidalgo, 1,404,
  (46,660) 65,967
Phelps, Walker............................. 98
Phillipsburg, Washington 75
Pickens, Henderson 20
Pickett, Navarro........................... 30
*Pickton, Hopkins, 4 300
Pidcoke, Coryell........................... 50
Piedmont, Grimes......................... 50
Piedmont, Upshur......................... 20
*Pierce, Wharton, 3 51
Pike, Collin 47
Pilgrim, Gonzales 22
Pilgrim Rest, Rains....................... 72
Pilot Grove, Grayson 48
Pilot Knob, Travis....................... 500
*PILOT POINT, Denton, 195,
  (3,538) 4,511
Pine, Camp.................................. 78
Pine Branch, Red River................. 40
Pine Forest, Hopkins 100
PINE FOREST, Orange, 8,
  (632) 594

Town, County .... Pop. 2008	Town, County .... Pop. 2008	Town, County .... Pop. 2008
Pine Grove, Cherokee 30	Poole, Rains 50	Pringle, Hutchinson 20
Pine Grove, Newton 180	*Poolville, Parker, 24 520	Pritchett, Upshur.......................... 125
Pinehill, Rusk................................ 70	Port Acres, Jefferson	*Proctor, Comanche, 6 228
*Pinehurst, Montgomery, 109,	.... [part of Port Arthur]	*PROGRESO, Hidalgo, 50,
(4,266) 5,319	Port Alto, Calhoun........................ 45	(4,851) 5,910
PINEHURST, Orange, 161,	*PORT ARANSAS, Nueces,	PROGRESO LAKES, Hidalgo,
(2,274) 2,139	369, (3,370,) 3,826	11, (234) 273
Pine Island, Jefferson 350	*PORT ARTHUR, Jefferson,	Progress, Bailey 49
PINE ISLAND, Waller, 0, (849) 865	1,185, (57,755) 55,702	Prospect, Rains 40
*PINELAND, Sabine, 32,	*Port Bolivar, Galveston, 82.......... 800	*PROSPER, Collin, 220,
(980) 1,025	*Porter, Montgomery, 290.......... 4,200	(2,097) 4,743
Pine Mills, Wood............................ 75	Porter Heights, Montgomery,	Providence, Floyd........................... 78
Pine Prairie, Walker 450	(1,490) 1,754	Providence, Polk.......................... 350
Pine Springs, Culberson................. 20	Porter Springs, Houston 50	Pruitt, Cass................................... 25
Pine Springs, Smith 150	*PORT ISABEL, Cameron, 251,	Pruitt, Van Zandt........................... 45
Pineview, Wood 10	(4,865) 5,265	Puerto Rico, Hidalgo...................... 50
Pinewood Estates, Hardin,	*PORTLAND, San Patricio, 441,	Pullman, Potter............................. 31
(1,633) 1,730	(14,827) 16,259	Pumphrey, Runnels 15
Piney, Austin 60	*PORT LAVACA, Calhoun, 445,	Pumpkin, San Jacinto................... 150
PINEY POINT VILLAGE, Harris,	(12,035) 12,002	Pumpville, Val Verde...................... 25
65, (3,380) 3,428	*Port Mansfield, Willacy, 9,	Punkin Center, Dawson.................. 30
Pioneer, Eastland 40	(415) 415	Punkin Center, Eastland................ 12
*Pipe Creek, Bandera, 124........... 130	*PORT NECHES, Jefferson,	*Purdon, Navarro, 9..................... 133
Pitner Junction, Rusk..................... 20	389, (13,601) 13,184	Purley, Franklin........................... 100
*PITTSBURG, Camp, 243,	*Port O'Connor, Calhoun, 39 1,184	*Purmela, Coryell, 4..................... 50
(4,347) 4,609	Port Sullivan, Milam....................... 15	Pursley, Navarro 40
*Placedo, Victoria, 6 760	Porvenir, Presidio 3	Purves, Erath................................. 50
Placid, McCulloch 32	Posey, Hopkins 12	*PUTNAM, Callahan, 5,
Plain, Houston 30	Posey, Lubbock 225	(88) 91
*PLAINS, Yoakum, 52,	*POST, Garza, 202, (3,708)....... 3,960	*PYOTE, Ward, 8, (131) 153
(1,450) 1,502	Post Oak, Blanco........................... 10	**Q**
*PLAINVIEW, Hale, 782,	Postoak, Jack................................ 79	*Quail, Collingsworth, 1, (33)......... 32
(22,336) 21,324	Postoak, Lamar 65	*QUANAH, Hardeman, 99,
*PLANO, Collin-Denton, 10,423,	Post Oak, Lee.............................. 100	(3,022) 2,749
(222,030) 279,607	POST OAK BEND, Kaufman,	Quarry, Washington, ... 60
*Plantersville, Grimes, 37 260	9, (404) 581	Quarterway, Hale 24
Plaska, Hall.................................. 20	Post Oak Point, Austin 60	*QUEEN CITY, Cass, 63,
PLEAK, Fort Bend, 29,	*POTEET, Atascosa, 114,	(1,613) 1,651
(947) 1,244	(3,305) 3,537	*Quemado, Maverick, 11,
Pleasant Farms, Ector................. 800	*POTH, Wilson, 48, (1,850)....... 2,210	(243) 264
Pleasant Grove, Falls 35	Potosi, Taylor, (1,664)................. 1,697	Quicksand, Newton 50
Pleasant Grove, Limestone 20	*POTTSBORO, Grayson, 114,	Quihi, Medina 125
Pleasant Grove, Upshur, ... 35	(1,579) 2,268	*QUINLAN, Hunt, 197,
Pleasant Grove, Wood 30	*Pottsville, Hamilton, 1................ 105	(1,370) 1,468
Pleasant Hill, Eastland 15	*Powderly, Lamar, 37................... 185	QUINTANA, Brazoria, 1, (38) 38
Pleasant Hill, Nacogdoches.......... 250	*POWELL, Navarro, 13, (105) 119	*QUITAQUE, Briscoe, 16,
Pleasant Hill, Yoakum.................... 40	*POYNOR, Henderson, 19,	(432) 374
*PLEASANTON, Atascosa, 439,	(314) 357	*QUITMAN, Wood, 197,
(8,266) 9,597	Prado Verde, El Paso, (200)........ 200	(2,030) 2,392
Pleasant Valley, Garza.................... 5	Praesel, Milam............................ 115	**R**
PLEASANT VALLEY, Wichita, 0,	Praha, Fayette 90	Rabbs Prairie, Fayette.................... 79
(408) 392	Prairie Chapel, McLennan 35	Raccoon Bend, Austin 775
*Pledger, Matagorda, 1................ 265	Prairie Dell, Bell 34	Rachal, Brooks 36
Pluck, Polk.................................... 53	*Prairie Hill, Limestone, 2 150	Radar Base, Maverick, (162)........ 172
*Plum, Fayette, 5.......................... 145	Prairie Hill, Washington 20	Radium, Jones.............................. 10
PLUM GROVE, Liberty, 2, (930)... 986	*Prairie Lea, Caldwell, 10 255	Ragtown, Lamar 30
Pluto, Ellis.................................... 30	Prairie Point, Cooke....................... 22	*Rainbow, Somervell, 10 121
Poetry, Kaufman 90	*PRAIRIE VIEW, Waller, 27,	Raisin, Victoria.............................. 50
*POINT, Rains, 43, (792) 936	(4,410) 4,528	Raleigh, Navarro............................ 40
*POINT BLANK, San Jacinto,	Prairieville, Kaufman...................... 75	*RALLS, Crosby, 58, (2,252) 2,130
5, (559) 672	*PREMONT, Jim Wells, 71,	Ramireno, Zapata........................... 25
*POINT COMFORT, Calhoun,	(2,772) 2,877	Ramirez, Duval 40
40, (781) 720	*PRESIDIO, Presidio, 99,	Ranchette Estates, Willacy,
Point Enterprise, Limestone 200	(4,167) 5,133	(133) 139
POINT VENTURE, Travis, 24,	Preston, Grayson.......................... 325	Ranchito El Calaboz [Encantada-],
(nc) 473	*Price, Rusk, 5............................ 275	Cameron,(2,100) 2,273
Polar, Kent.................................... 15	*Priddy, Mills, 11 215	Ranchitos Las Lomas, Webb,
*Pollok, Angelina, 27..................... 300	PRIMERA, Cameron, 30,	(334) 371
*PONDER, Denton, 59,	(2,723) 4,036	Rancho Alegre, Jim Wells,
(507) 1,313	Primrose, Van Zandt...................... 26	(1,775) 1,848
Ponta, Cherokee............................ 50	*PRINCETON, Collin, 149,	Rancho Banquete, Nueces,
*Pontotoc, Mason, 4 125	(3,477) 6,141	(469) 444

Town, County ....Pop. 2008	Town, County ....Pop. 2008	Town, County ....Pop. 2008

Rancho Chico, San Patricio,
  (309) 314
Rancho Penitas West, Webb,
  (520) 529
RANCHO VIEJO, Cameron, 38,
  (1,754) 1,937
Rand, Kaufman.............................. 70
Randado, Jim Hogg.......................... 6
*Randolph, Fannin, 2...................... 70
*RANGER, Eastland, 95,
  (2,584) 2,532
RANGERVILLE, Cameron, 0,
  (203) 205
Rankin, Ellis.................................... 10
*RANKIN, Upton, 34, (800)........... 744
RANSOM CANYON, Lubbock,
  21, (1,011) 1,143
Ratamosa, Cameron, (218) 223
*Ratcliff, Houston, 3..................... 106
Ratibor, Bell 22
Rattan, Delta................................... 10
*RAVENNA, Fannin, 9, (215)........ 259
Rayburn, Liberty 60
Rayland, Foard................................ 30
*RAYMONDVILLE, Willacy, 186,
  (9,733) 9,852
Ray Point, Live Oak...................... 200
*Raywood, Liberty, 11 231
Razor, Lamar 20
*Reagan, Falls, 2 208
Reagan Wells, Uvalde 20
Reagor Springs, Ellis 250
*Realitos, Duval, 2, (209)............. 202
Red Bank, Bowie 125
Red Bluff, Jackson.......................... 45
Red Bluff, Reeves........................... 40
Red Cut Heights, Bowie 563
*Redford, Presidio, (132) 129
Red Hill, Cass................................. 28
Red Hill, Limestone 20
Red Lake, Freestone 50
Redland, Angelina 250

Redland, Leon 35
Redland, Van Zandt........................ 45
RED LICK, Bowie, 0, (853)........... 876
*RED OAK, Ellis, 420,
  (4,301) 9,428
Red Ranger, Bell 30
*Red Rock, Bastrop, 17.................. 40
Red Springs, Baylor........................ 42
Red Springs, Smith....................... 350
Redtown, Anderson 30
Redtown, Angelina.......................... 50
*REDWATER, Bowie, 23,
  (872) 905
Redwood, Guadalupe,
  (3,586) 4,116
Reeds Settlement, Red River 50
Reedville, Caldwell 432
Reese, Cherokee............................ 75
Reese Center, Lubbock, (42).......... 44
Refuge, Houston............................. 20
*REFUGIO, Refugio, 122,
  (2,941) 2,807
Regency, Mills 25
Rehburg, Washington..................... 20
Reid Hope King, Cameron,
  (802) 825
Reilly Springs, Hopkins.................. 75
Rek Hill, Fayette 168
*REKLAW, Cherokee-Rusk, 8,
  (327) 361
Relampago, Hidalgo, (104)........... 110
Rendon, Tarrant, (9,022) 9,670
*RENO, Lamar, 4, (2,767) 3,137
RENO, Parker, 4, (2,441) 2,722
Retreat, Grimes 25
RETREAT, Navarro, 0, (339) 365
Retta, Tarrant-Johnson 780
Reynard, Houston........................... 75
Rhea, Parmer 98
Rhea Mills, Collin........................... 25
Rhineland, Knox 120
*RHOME, Wise, 68, (551) 1,271

Rhonesboro, Upshur 40
Ricardo, Kleberg........................ 1,641
*RICE, Navarro, 47, (798) 941
Rice's Crossing, Williamson 130
*Richards, Grimes, 8 300
*RICHARDSON, Dallas-Collin,
  5,026, (91,802) 102,803
*RICHLAND, Navarro, 11,
  (291) 327
Richland, Rains 100
*RICHLAND HILLS, Tarrant,
  411, (8,132) 8,277
*RICHLAND SPRINGS, San Saba,
  8, (350) 350
*RICHMOND, Fort Bend, 602,
  (11,081) 14,755
RICHWOOD, Brazoria, 72,
  (3,012) 3,537
Riderville, Panola............................ 50
Ridge, Mills 25
Ridge, Robertson............................ 67
Ridgeway, Hopkins 54
Ridings, Fannin............................... 10
*RIESEL, McLennan, 45,
  (973) 1,003
Rincon .... Starr, 5
*Ringgold, Montague 100
RIO BRAVO, Webb, 46,
  (5,553) 5,941
*Rio Frio, Real, 5 50
*RIO GRANDE CITY, Starr,
  351, (11,923) 14,529
Rio Grande Village, Brewster 9
*RIO HONDO, Cameron, 55,
  (1,942) 2,241
*Riomedina, Medina, 10 60
Rios, Duval 75
*RIO VISTA, Johnson, 36,
  (656) 781
*RISING STAR, Eastland,
  39, (835) 841
Rita, Burleson 50

Rio Grande City, with the Starr County Courthouse at the top of the hill. Robert Plocheck photo.

Town, County	Pop. 2008
Riverby, Fannin	15
River Crest Estates, Angelina	250
River Hill, Panola	125
RIVER OAKS, Tarrant, 149, (6,985)	7,206
Rivers End, Brazoria	90
*RIVERSIDE, Walker, 33, (425)	467
River Spur [Chula Vista-], Zavala, (400)	424
*Riviera, Kleberg, 28	1,064
Riviera Beach, Kleberg	155
Roach, Cass	50
Roane, Navarro	120
*ROANOKE, Denton, 381, (3,241)	4,613
*Roans Prairie, Grimes, 4	64
*ROARING SPRINGS, Motley, 15, (265)	272
Robbins, Leon	20
*ROBERT LEE, Coke, 45, (1,171)	1,097
Robertson, Crosby	10
ROBINSON, McLennan, 352, (7,845)	10,570
*ROBSTOWN, Nueces, 371, (12,727)	13,316
*ROBY, Fisher, 20, (673)	661
*Rochelle, McCulloch, 5	163
*ROCHESTER, Haskell, 11, (378)	342
Rock Bluff, Burnet	90
Rock Creek, Somervell	70
*ROCKDALE, Milam, 258, (5,439)	5,872
Rockett, Ellis	300
Rockford, Lamar	30
Rockhouse, Austin	100
*Rock Island, Colorado, 1	160
Rockland, Tyler	98
Rockne, Bastrop	190
*ROCKPORT, Aransas, 620, (7,385)	9,141
*ROCKSPRINGS, Edwards, 55, (1,285)	1,218
*ROCKWALL, Rockwall, 1,630, (17,976)	33,078
*Rockwood, Coleman, 2	80
Rocky Branch, Morris	135
Rocky Creek, Blanco	20
ROCKY MOUND, Camp, 0, (93)	102
Rocky Point, Burnet	152
Roddy, Van Zandt	29
Rodney, Navarro	15
Roeder, Titus	110
Roganville, Jasper	70
*ROGERS, Bell, 42, (1,117)	1,145
Rogers, Taylor	151
Rolling Hills, Potter	1,000
Rolling Meadows, Gregg	362
ROLLINGWOOD, Travis, 118, (1,403)	1,357
*ROMA-Los Saenz, Starr, 237, (9,617)	11,707
Roma Creek, Starr, (610)	649
ROMAN FOREST, Montgomery, 0, (1,279)	3,627
*Romayor, Liberty, 4	135
*Roosevelt, Kimble, 2	14
Roosevelt, Lubbock	362
*ROPESVILLE, Hockley, 14, (517)	523
Rosalie, Red River	100

Town, County	Pop. 2008
*Rosanky, Bastrop, 13	210
*ROSCOE, Nolan, 29, (1,378)	1,297
*ROSEBUD, Falls, 67, (1,493)	1,404
ROSE CITY, Orange, 29, (519)	493
Rose Hill, Harris	3,500
Rose Hill, San Jacinto	30
ROSE HILL ACRES, Hardin, 0, (480)	485
*ROSENBERG, Fort Bend, 916, (24,043)	35,087
Rosevine, Sabine	50
Rosewood, Upshur	100
*Rosharon, Brazoria, 101	435
Rosita, Duval	25
Rosita North, Maverick, (3,400)	3,625
Rosita South, Maverick, (2,574)	2,951
*ROSS, McLennan, 11, (228)	232
*ROSSER, Kaufman, 7, (379)	428
*Rosston, Cooke, 1	75
Rossville, Atascosa	200
*ROTAN, Fisher, 54, (1,611)	1,515
Rough Creek, San Saba	15
Round House, Navarro	40
*ROUND MOUNTAIN, Blanco, 6, (111)	107
Round Mountain, Travis	59
Round Prairie, Navarro	40
*ROUND ROCK, Williamson-Travis, 3,266, (61,136)	100,596
Round Timber, Baylor	2
*ROUND TOP, Fayette, 66, (77)	87
Roundup, Hockley	20
Rowden, Callahan	30
*Rowena, Runnels, 8	349
*ROWLETT, Dallas-Rockwall, 1,673, (44,503)	56,103
*ROXTON, Lamar, 20, (694)	718
Royalty, Ward	27
*ROYSE CITY, Rockwall-Collin, 321, (2,957)	8,707
Rucker, Comanche	28
Rucker's Bridge, Lamar	20
Rugby, Red River	24
Ruidosa, Presidio	18
*RULE, Haskell, 16, (698)	629
Rumley, Lampasas	8
RUNAWAY BAY, Wise, 30, (1,104)	1,304
*RUNGE, Karnes, 29, (1,080)	1,228
Rural Shade, Navarro	30
Rushing, Navarro	10
*RUSK, Cherokee, 183, (5,085)	5,228
Russell, Leon	27
Rutersville, Fayette	137
Ruth Springs, Henderson	120
*Rye, Liberty, 4	150
S	
Sabanno, Eastland	12
*SABINAL, Uvalde, 65, (1,586)	1,755
*Sabine Pass, Jefferson, 21,	[part of Port Arthur]
*SACHSE, Dallas-Collin, 469, (9,751)	19,392

Town, County	Pop. 2008
*Sacul, Nacogdoches, 2	150
*SADLER, Grayson, 12, (404)	423
Sagerton, Haskell	171
*SAGINAW, Tarrant, 509, (12,374)	20,929
St. Francis, Potter	39
*ST. HEDWIG, Bexar, 88, (1,875)	2,174
*SAINT JO, Montague, 37, (977)	1,001
St. John Colony, Caldwell	150
St. Lawrence, Glasscock	90
St. Mary's Colony, Bastrop	50
ST. PAUL, Collin, 37, (630)	912
St. Paul, San Patricio, (542)	545
*SALADO, Bell, 301, (3,475)	3,786
Salem, Cherokee	20
Salem, Grimes	54
Salem, Newton	218
Salesville, Palo Pinto	88
Saline, Menard	70
*Salineño, Starr, 1, (304)	327
Salmon, Anderson	20
*Salt Flat, Hudspeth, 1	35
Salt Gap, McCulloch	25
*Saltillo, Hopkins, 6	200
Samaria, Navarro	90
*Samnorwood, Collingsworth, (39)	40
Sample, Gonzales	16
Sam Rayburn, Jasper	600
*SAN ANGELO, Tom Green, 3,393, (88,439)	89,343
*SAN ANTONIO, Bexar, 40,738, (1,150,535)	1,336,040
San Antonio Prairie, Burleson	20
*SAN AUGUSTINE, San Augustine, 135, (2,475)	2,542
*SAN BENITO, Cameron, 588, (23,444)	25,939
San Carlos, Hidalgo, (2,650)	2,824
San Carlos, Starr	10
Sanco, Coke	15
SANCTUARY, Parker, 22, (256)	604
Sandbranch, Dallas	400
*Sanderson, Terrell, 19, (861)	798
Sand Flat, Johnson	133
Sand Flat, Rains	100
Sand Flat, Smith	100
Sand Flat, Leon	32
Sandhill, Floyd	33
Sand Hill, Upshur	75
*Sandia, Jim Wells, 38, (431)	458
*SAN DIEGO, Duval-Jim Wells, 89, (4,753)	4,473
Sandlin, Stonewall	3
Sandoval, Williamson	60
Sand Springs, Howard	1,000
Sandusky, Grayson	15
Sandy, Blanco	150
Sandy, Limestone	5
Sandy Harbor, Llano	85
Sandy Hill, Washington	50
Sandy Hollow-Escondidas, Nueces, (433)	377
SANDY POINT, Brazoria, (nc)	250
*San Elizario, El Paso, 41, (11,046)	11,835

Town, County ....Pop. 2008	Town, County ....Pop. 2008	Town, County ....Pop. 2008

*SAN FELIPE, Austin, 21,
  (868) 966
*SANFORD, Hutchinson, 8,
  (203) 199
San Gabriel, Milam 70
*SANGER, Denton, 259,
  (4,534) 7,169
*San Isidro, Starr, 7, (270) 281
San Jose, Duval 15
*SAN JUAN, Hidalgo, 535,
  (26,229) 34,431
SAN LEANNA, Travis, 0, (384) 527
San Leon, Galveston,
  (4,365) 4,790
*San Manuel-Linn, Hidalgo,
  11, (958) 987
*SAN MARCOS, Hays-Caldwell,
  1,728, (34,733) 52,705
SAN PATRICIO, San Patricio,
  (318) 303
San Pedro, Cameron, (668) 694
*SAN PERLITA, Willacy, 3,
  (680) 727
San Roman, Starr 5
*SAN SABA, San Saba, 148,
  (2,637) 2,706
SANSOM PARK, Tarrant, 96,
  (4,181) 4,410
*SANTA ANNA, Coleman, 54,
  (1,081) 1,009
Santa Anna, Starr 20
Santa Catarina, Starr 15
SANTA CLARA, Guadalupe,
  20, (889) 1,016
Santa Cruz, Starr, (630) 681
*Santa Elena, Starr, 1 64
*SANTA FE, Galveston, 359,
  (9,548) 10,750

*Santa Maria, Cameron, 3, (846) .. 874
Santa Monica, Willacy, (78) 77
*SANTA ROSA, Cameron, 42,
  (2,833) 3,122
*Santo, Palo Pinto, 23 445
*San Ygnacio, Zapata, 4,
  (853) 1,000
*Saragosa, Reeves, 2 185
*Saratoga, Hardin, 11 1,000
Sardis, Ellis 60
Sargent, Matagorda 900
*Sarita, Kenedy, 2 185
Saron, Trinity 5
Saspamco, Wilson 300
*Satin, Falls, 1 86
Sattler, Comal 1,000
Saturn, Gonzales 15
*SAVOY, Fannin, 39, (850) 880
Scenic Oaks, Bexar, (3,279) 3,523
Schattel, Frio 30
*SCHERTZ, Guadalupe-Comal-
  Bexar, 912, (18,694) 30,552
Schicke Point, Calhoun 70
Schroeder, Goliad 347
*SCHULENBURG, Fayette, 228,
  (2,699) 2,947
Schumansville, Guadalupe 678
Schwab City, Polk 120
*Schwertner, Williamson, 3 175
Scissors, Hidalgo, (2,805) 3,130
*SCOTLAND, Archer, 11,
  (438) 440
*SCOTTSVILLE, Harrison,
  10, (263) 257
Scranton, Eastland 40
*Scroggins, Franklin, 18 150
*SCURRY, Kaufman, 37,
  (nc) 712

*SEABROOK, Harris, 486,
  (9,443) 11,577
*SEADRIFT, Calhoun, 46,
  (1,352) 1,438
*SEAGOVILLE, Dallas, 367,
  (10,823) 12,223
*SEAGRAVES, Gaines, 59,
  (2,334) 2,478
Seale, Robertson 60
*SEALY, Austin, 354,
  (5,248) 6,841
Seaton, Bell 60
Seawillow, Caldwell 100
*Sebastian, Willacy, 15,
  (1,864) 1,889
Sebastopol, Trinity 120
Seco Mines, Maverick 692
Security, Montgomery 200
Sedalia, Collin 24
Segno, Polk 80
Segovia, Kimble 12
*SEGUIN, Guadalupe, 1,176,
  (22,011) 28,346
Sejita, Duval 22
Selden, Erath 55
Selfs, Fannin 30
SELMA, Bexar-Guadalupe-Comal,
  242, (788) 3,445
*Selman City [Turnertown-],
  Rusk, 8 271
*SEMINOLE, Gaines, 232,
  (5,910) 6,134
Sempronius, Austin 25
Senate, Jack 14
Serbin, Lee 109
Serenada, Williamson,
  (1,847) 2,166
Seth Ward, Hale, (1,926) 1,966

Seadrift's city park on the shore of San Antonio Bay in Calhoun County. Robert Plocheck photo.

Town, County ....Pop. 2008	Town, County ....Pop. 2008	Town, County ....Pop. 2008

SEVEN OAKS, Polk, 3, (131) 136
Seven Pines, Gregg-Upshur........... 50
*SEVEN POINTS, Henderson,
  100, (1,145) 1,320
Seven Sisters, Duval 60
Sexton, Sabine 29
*SEYMOUR, Baylor, 129,
  (2,908) 2,911
Shady Grove , Burnet.................... 114
Shady Grove, Cherokee 30
Shady Grove, Houston 83
Shady Grove, Panola 45
Shady Grove, Smith 250
Shady Grove, Upshur 40
Shady Hollow, Travis, (5,140).... 5,082
Shady Oaks, Henderson 300
SHADY SHORES, Denton,
  69, (1,461) 2,345
Shafter, Presidio 57
*SHALLOWATER, Lubbock, 89,
  (2,086) 2,362
*SHAMROCK, Wheeler, 100,
  (2,029) 1,946
Shangri La, Burnet....................... 108
Shankleville, Newton 35
Shannon, Clay 20
Sharp, Milam 52
SHAVANO PARK, Bexar, 105,
  (1,754) 3,126
Shawnee Prairie, Angelina 20
Shaws Bend, Colorado................ 100
*Sheffield, Pecos, 10 322
Shelby, Austin 300
*Shelbyville, Shelby, 23 600
Sheldon, Harris, (1,831) 1,879
SHENANDOAH, Montgomery,
  208, (1,503) 2,295
Shep, Taylor 60
*SHEPHERD, San Jacinto,
  89, (2,029) 2,460
*Sheridan, Colorado, 15 225
*SHERMAN, Grayson, 1,627,
  (35,082) 38,885
Sherry, Red River 15
Sherwood, Irion 170
Sherwood Shores, Bell 774
Sherwood Shores, Burnet 920
Sherwood Shores, Grayson 1,590
Shields, Coleman 13
Shiloh, Leon 30
Shiloh, Limestone 250
*SHINER, Lavaca, 150,
  (2,070) 2,054
Shirley, Hopkins 20
*Shiro, Grimes, 3 210
Shive, Hamilton 60
SHOREACRES, Harris, 34,
  (1,488) 1,635
Short, Shelby 15
Shovel Mountain, Burnet 148
*Sidney, Comanche, 4 148
Sienna Plantation, Fort Bend,
  (1,896) 2,337
*Sierra Blanca, Hudspeth, 12,
  (533) 578
Siesta Shores, Zapata, (890)..... 1,041
Silas, Shelby 75
Siloam, Bowie 50
*SILSBEE, Hardin, 310,
  (6,393) 6,685
*Silver, Coke, 2 34
Silver City, Milam 25

Silver City, Navarro 100
Silver City, Red River..................... 25
Silver Creek Village, Burnet......... 300
Silver Lake, Van Zandt 42
*SILVERTON, Briscoe, 37,
  (771) 722
Silver Valley, Coleman 20
Simmons, Live Oak 65
*Simms, Bowie, 9 240
Simms, Deaf Smith 10
*SIMONTON, Fort Bend, 32,
  (718) 936
Simpsonville, Matagorda 6
Simpsonville, Upshur................... 100
Sinclair City, Smith........................ 50
Singleton, Grimes 47
*SINTON, San Patricio, 207,
  (5,676) 5,705
Sipe Springs, Comanche................ 70
Sisterdale, Kendall...................... 110
Sivells Bend, Cooke 36
Six Mile, Calhoun......................... 300
Skeeterville, San Saba 10
*SKELLYTOWN, Carson, 15,
  (610) 621
*Skidmore, Bee, 11, (1,013) 1,162
Slate Shoals, Lamar 10
*SLATON, Lubbock, 187,
  (6,109) 6,155
Slayden, Gonzales 10
Slide, Lubbock 245
*Slidell, Wise, 4........................... 175
Sloan, San Saba 30
Slocum, Anderson 250
Smetana, Brazos 80
*SMILEY, Gonzales, 12,
  (453) 446
Smithland, Marion....................... 179
Smith Point, Chambers................ 180
Smithson Valley, Comal 1,000
*SMITHVILLE, Bastrop, 282,
  (3,901) 4,953
Smithwick, Burnet........................ 102
*SMYER, Hockley, 5, (480) 483
Smyrna, Cass 215
Smyrna, Rains 25
*SNOOK, Burleson, 25, (568)...... 650
Snow Hill, Collin............................ 23
Snow Hill, Upshur.......................... 75
*SNYDER, Scurry, 469,
  (10,783) 10,790
*SOCORRO, El Paso, 575,
  (27,152) 32,708
Soldier Mound, Dickens................. 10
Solis, Cameron, (545).................. 555
*SOMERSET, Bexar, 75,
  (1,550) 1,826
*SOMERVILLE, Burleson, 92,
  (1,704) 1,911
Sommer's Mill, Bell........................ 27
*SONORA, Sutton, 188,
  (2,924) 3,101
*SOUR LAKE, Hardin, 112,
  (1,667) 1,780
South Alamo, Hidalgo, (3,101)... 3,315
*South Bend, Young, 2 140
South Bosque, McLennan 1,523
South Brice, Hall........................... 10
South Fork Estates, Jim Hogg,
  (47) 46
*SOUTH HOUSTON, Harris,
  656, (15,833) 16,751

*SOUTHLAKE, Tarrant-Denton,
  1,550, (21,519) 25,859
Southland, Garza......................... 157
South La Paloma [Alfred-],
  Jim Wells, (451) 511
*SOUTHMAYD, Grayson, 20,
  (992) 1,085
SOUTH MOUNTAIN, Coryell, 0,
  (412) 409
*SOUTH PADRE ISLAND, Cameron,
  315, (2,422) 3,022
*South Plains, Floyd 67
South Point, Cameron,
  (1,118) 1,169
South Purmela, Coryell.................. 10
South Shore, Bell.......................... 80
SOUTHSIDE PLACE, Harris, 67,
  (1,547) 1,679
South Sulphur, Hunt 60
South Toledo Bend, Newton,
  (576) 477
Southton, Bexar........................... 113
*Spade, Lamb, 4, (100) 99
Spanish Fort, Montague 50
Sparenberg, Dawson..................... 20
Sparks, Bell 40
Sparks, El Paso, (2,974)............ 3,153
Speaks, Lavaca 60
*SPEARMAN, Hansford, 120,
  (3,021) 2,981
Speegleville, McLennan 1,655
*Spicewood, Burnet, 187 2,000
Spider Mountain, Burnet................ 92
*SPLENDORA, Montgomery,
  135, (1,275) 1,654
SPOFFORD, Kinney, 0, (75) 73
Spraberry, Midland 46
*Spring, Harris, 444,
  (36,385) 37,947
*Spring Branch, Comal, 213...... 4,000
Spring Creek, Hutchinson............. 139
Spring Creek, San Saba................ 20
Springdale, Cass 55
Springfield, Anderson 30
Spring Garden-Tierra Verde,
  Nueces, (693)...................... 627
Spring Hill, Bowie 209
Spring Hill, Navarro 60
Spring Hill, San Jacinto 38
*SPRINGLAKE, Lamb, 13,
  (135) 137
*SPRINGTOWN, Parker, 280,
  (2,062) 2,729
SPRING VALLEY, Harris, 101,
  (3,611) 3,789
Spring Valley, McLennan 400
*SPUR, Dickens, 52,
  (1,088) 1,023
*Spurger, Tyler, 11 590
Stacy, McCulloch 20
Staff, Eastland 65
*STAFFORD, Fort Bend-Harris,
  1,480, (15,681) 21,656
Stag Creek, Comanche 45
STAGECOACH, Montgomery, 15,
  (455) 602
Stairtown, Caldwell 35
Staley, San Jacinto 55
*STAMFORD, Jones-Haskell,
  117, (3,636) 3,527
Stampede, Bell 6
Stamps, Upshur 45

Town, County ....Pop. 2008	Town, County ....Pop. 2008	Town, County ....Pop. 2008
*STANTON, Martin, 79, (2,556) 2,558	*Study Butte-Terlingua, Brewster, 35, (267) 297	Swenson, Stonewall 80
*STAPLES, Guadalupe, 6.............396	Sturgeon, Cooke...........................10	Swift, Nacogdoches......................210
*Star, Mills, 1....................................85	Styx, Kaufman 50	Swiss Alp, Fayette 17
STAR HARBOR, Henderson, 6, (416) 465	*Sublime, Lavaca...........................75	Sylvan, Lamar................................68
Star Route, Cochran......................15	*SUDAN, Lamb, 25, (1,039) 1,032	*Sylvester, Fisher, 2.......................79
Starrville, Smith 75	Sugar Hill, Titus 150	**T**
Steele Hill, Dickens...........................4	*SUGAR LAND, Fort Bend, 3,175, (63,328) 91,805	Tabor, Brazos...............................150
Stephens Creek, San Jacinto 385	Sugar Valley, Matagorda.................47	Tadmor, Houston 67
*STEPHENVILLE, Erath, 778, (14,921) 17,047	*SULLIVAN CITY, Hidalgo, 67, (3,998) 4,560	*TAFT, San Patricio, 85, (3,396) 3,552
Sterley, Floyd.................................31	*Sulphur Bluff, Hopkins, 4.............280	Taft Southwest, San Patricio, (1,721) 1,579
*STERLING CITY, Sterling, 33, (1,081) 978	*SULPHUR SPRINGS, Hopkins, 781, (14,551) 15,501	*TAHOKA, Lynn, 66, (2,910)......2,663
Stewards Mill, Freestone...............22	Summerfield, Castro.......................48	*TALCO, Titus, 27, (570) 605
Stewart, Rusk 15	Summerville, Gonzales...................45	*Talpa, Coleman, 2 127
Stiles, Reagan 4	*Sumner, Lamar, 30.......................95	TALTY, Kaufman, 28, (1,028).....1,335
Stillwell Store, Brewster...................2	*SUNDOWN, Hockley, 57, (1,505) 1,472	Tamina, Montgomery....................900
*STINNETT, Hutchinson, 43, (1,936) 1,836	Sunnyside, Castro 64	Tanglewood, Lee 60
Stith, Jones.....................................50	Sunny Side, Waller 120	Tarkington Prairie, Liberty............300
*STOCKDALE, Wilson, 60, (1,398) 1,600	Sunnyside, Wilson 100	*Tarpley, Bandera, 3 30
Stockman, Shelby...........................55	SUNNYVALE, Dallas, 212, (2,693) 4,533	*Tarzan, Martin, 3 30
Stoneburg, Montague.....................51	*SUNRAY, Moore, 50, (1,950) 1,897	Tascosa Hills, Potter, ...90
Stoneham, Grimes.........................15	Sunrise, Falls 845	*TATUM, Rusk-Panola, 59, (1,175) 1,173
*Stonewall, Gillespie, 28, (469) 521	*SUNRISE BEACH, Llano, 26, (704) 790	*TAYLOR, Williamson, 487, (13,575) 17,663
Stony, Denton 25	*SUNSET, Montague, 16, (339)....349	TAYLOR LAKE VILLAGE, Harris, 57, (3,694) 5,563
Stout, Wood..................................302	Sunset Oaks, Burnet 198	TAYLOR LANDING, Jefferson, 0, (nc) 211
*Stowell, Chambers, 9, (1,572) 1,675	SUNSET VALLEY, Travis, 131, (365) 575	Taylorsville, Caldwell 20
Stranger, Falls 27	SUN VALLEY, Lamar, 4, (51).........63	Taylor Town, Lamar 40
*STRATFORD, Sherman, 78, (1,991) 2,061	SURFSIDE BEACH, Brazoria, 17, (763) 907	Tazewell, Hopkins..........................20
Stratton, DeWitt 25	*Sutherland Springs, Wilson, 4.....420	*TEAGUE, Freestone, 117, (4,557) 5,112
*STRAWN, Palo Pinto, 37, (739) 769	Swamp City, Gregg...........................8	Teaselville, Smith.........................150
Streeter, Mason 85	Swan, Smith 150	*TEHUACANA, Limestone, 2, (307) 316
*STREETMAN, Freestone, 14, (203) 212	*SWEENY, Brazoria, 97, (3,624) 3,894	Telegraph, Kimble, 1.........................3
String Prairie, Bastrop 40	Sweet Home, Guadalupe 294	*Telephone, Fannin, 11.................210
Stringtown, Newton 20	*Sweet Home, Lavaca, 7..............360	*Telferner, Victoria, 8 700
Structure, Williamson.....................50	Sweet Home, Lee 30	Telico, Ellis..................................115
Stuart Place, Cameron 990	Sweet Union, Cherokee..................40	*Tell, Childress, 2............................15
Stubblefield, Houston 15	*SWEETWATER, Nolan, 428, (11,415) 10,723	*TEMPLE, Bell, 1,965, (48,465) 59,786
Stubbs, Kaufman 50		*TENAHA, Shelby, 35, (1,046) 1,039
		Tenmile, Dawson 30

Residences of Terlingua, Brewster County. Robert Plocheck photo.

CITIES & TOWNS

Town, County .... Pop. 2008

*Tennessee Colony, Anderson,
12 300
*Tennyson, Coke, 1 46
*Terlingua [Study Butte-], Brewster,
35, (267) 297
*TERRELL, Kaufman, 756,
(13,606) 18,366
TERRELL HILLS, Bexar, 118,
(5,019) 5,558
Terry Chapel, Falls 30
Terryville, DeWitt 40
*TEXARKANA, Bowie-(Miller Co.,
Ark.), 2,321, (61,230) 66,220
*TEXAS CITY, Galveston,
1,005, (41,512) 44,391
TEXHOMA, Sherman-(Texas Co.,
Okla.), 22, (1,306) 1,251
*TEXLINE, Dallam, 26, (511) 525
Texroy, Hutchinson 30
Thalia, Foard, ... 50
*THE COLONY, Denton, 866,
(26,531) 36,621
Thedford, Smith 65
The Grove, Coryell 100
THE HILLS, Travis, 0,
(1,492) 1,910
Thelma, Bexar 150
Thelma, Limestone 20
Theon, Williamson 30
Thermo, Hopkins 56
*The Woodlands, Montgomery,
538, (55,649) 67,971
*Thicket, Hardin, 7 306
*Thomaston, DeWitt, 2 45
*THOMPSONS, Fort Bend, 4,
(236) 333
Thompsonville, Gonzales 30
Thompsonville, Jim Hogg 55
Thornberry, Clay 75
*THORNDALE, Milam, 63,
(1,278) 1,417
*THORNTON, Limestone, 17,
(525) 528
THORNTONVILLE, Ward, 9,
(442) 412
Thorp Spring, Hood 222
*THRALL, Williamson, 29,
(710) 998
Three Oaks, Wilson 150
*THREE RIVERS, Live Oak,
116, (1,878) 1,812
Three States, Cass 45
*THROCKMORTON, Throckmorton,
45, (905) 833
Thurber, Erath 48
Tidwell, Hunt 50
Tierra Bonita, Cameron, (160) 163
Tierra Grande, Nueces, (362) 360
Tierra Verde [Spring Garden-],
Nueces, (693) 627
Tigertown, Lamar 400
TIKI ISLAND VILLAGE, Galveston,
30, (1,016) 1,222
*Tilden, McMullen, 15 300
Tilmon, Caldwell 117
TIMBERCREEK CANYON, Randall,
0, (406) 461
Timberwood, Bexar, (5,889) 6,327
*TIMPSON, Shelby, 49,
(1,094) 1,110
Tin Top, Parker 500
*TIOGA, Grayson, 35, (754) 942

Town, County .... Pop. 2008

TIRA, Hopkins, 0, (248) 256
*Tivoli, Refugio, 7 550
TOCO, Lamar, 2, (89) 83
Todd City, Anderson 10
TODD MISSION, Grimes, 57,
(146) 172
Tokio, McLennan 250
*Tokio, Terry 5
*TOLAR, Hood, 46, (504) 644
Tolbert, Wilbarger 15
Tolette, Lamar 40
Tolosa, Kaufman 65
*TOMBALL, Harris, 1,281,
(9,089) 11,076
*TOM BEAN, Grayson, 28,
(941) 1,025
Tomlinson Hill, Falls 64
TOOL, Henderson, 32,
(2,275) 2,488
Topsey, Coryell 35
*Tornillo, El Paso, 20, (1,609) 1,669
Tours, McLennan 130
*Tow, Llano, 7 305
Town Bluff, Tyler 429
*TOYAH, Reeves, 2, (100) 85
*Toyahvale, Reeves, 1 60
Tradewinds, San Patricio,
(163) 164
Travis, Falls 48
Trawick, Nacogdoches 375
*TRENT, Taylor, 7, (318) 309
*TRENTON, Fannin, 39,
(662) 724
Trickham, Coleman 12
Trimmer, Bell 390
*TRINIDAD, Henderson, 31,
(1,091) 1,142
*TRINITY, Trinity, 151,
(2,721) 2,862
TROPHY CLUB, Denton, 211,
(6,350) 8,215
*TROUP, Smith-Cherokee, 110,
(1,949) 2,144
Trout Creek, Newton 70
*TROY, Bell, 78, (1,378) 1,400
Truby, Jones 26
Trumbull, Ellis 100
Truscott, Knox 50
Tucker, Anderson 304
*Tuleta, Bee, 7, (292) 408
*TULIA, Swisher, 150,
(5,117) 4,975
Tulip, Fannin 10
Tulsita, Bee, (20) 25
Tundra, Van Zandt 34
Tunis, Burleson 150
.*TURKEY, Hall, 17, (494) 451
Turlington, Freestone 27
Turnersville, Coryell 125
Turnersville, Travis 90
*Turnertown-Selman City, Rusk,
8 271
Turtle Bayou, Chambers 42
*TUSCOLA, Taylor, 49, (714) 763
Tuxedo, Jones 42
Twichell, Ochiltree 22
Twitty, Wheeler 12
*TYE, Taylor, 46, (1,158) 1,200
*TYLER, Smith, 4,566,
(83,650) 98,493
*Tynan, Bee, 4, (301) 298
Type, Williamson 40

Town, County .... Pop. 2008

U

UHLAND, Hays-Caldwell, 17,
(386) 457
*Umbarger, Randall, 6 327
UNCERTAIN, Harrison, 9, (150) ... 150
Union, Scurry 20
Union, Terry 8
Union, Wilson 22
Union Grove, Bell 12
UNION GROVE, Upshur, 5,
(346) 383
Union High, Navarro 30
Union Hill, Denton 25
UNION VALLEY, Hunt 226
Unity, Lamar 60
*UNIVERSAL CITY, Bexar, 628,
(14,849) 17,417
UNIVERSITY PARK, Dallas, 790,
(23,324) 23,576
Upper Meyersville, DeWitt 33
Upshaw, Nacogdoches 400
Upton, Bastrop 25
Urbana, San Jacinto 25
Utley, Bastrop 30
*Utopia, Uvalde, 32, (241) 306
*UVALDE, Uvalde, 554,
(14,929) 16,053
Uvalde Estates, Uvalde,
(1,972) 1,806

V

Valdasta, Collin 82
*VALENTINE, Jeff Davis, 1,
(187) 218
*Valera, Coleman, 3 80
Valley Creek, Fannin 12
*VALLEY MILLS, Bosque-McLennan,
78, (1,123) 1,163
*Valley Spring, Llano 50
*VALLEY VIEW, Cooke, 62,
(737) 799
Valley View, Runnels 10
Valley View, Upshur 75
Valley View, Wichita 210
Valley Wells, Dimmit 21
Val Verde, Milam 25
Val Verde Park, Val Verde,
(1,945) 2,176
*VAN, Van Zandt, 103,
(2,362) 2,584
*VAN ALSTYNE, Grayson, 156,
(2,502) 2,780
Vance, Real 20
*Vancourt, Tom Green, 1 131
Vandalia, Red River 35
*Vanderbilt, Jackson, 7, (411) 419
*Vanderpool, Bandera, 2 20
Vandyke, Comanche 20
*VAN HORN, Culberson, 91,
(2,435) 2,152
*Van Vleck, Matagorda, 27,
(1,411) 1,338
Vasco, Delta 20
Vashti, Clay 70
Vattmann, Kleberg 25
Vaughan, Hill 75
Veach, San Augustine 12
Vealmoor, Howard 5
*VEGA, Oldham, 31, (936) 1,011
*VENUS, Johnson, 44,
(1,892) 2,518
Vera, Knox 30
Verdi, Atascosa 110

Town, County ....Pop. 2008	Town, County ....Pop. 2008	Town, County ....Pop. 2008
Verhalen, Reeves 12	*WAKE VILLAGE, Bowie, 101,	Wayne, Cass 15
*Veribest, Tom Green, 3 115	(5,129) 5,621	Wayside, Armstrong, 2...................35
*VERNON, Wilbarger, 378,	*Walburg, Williamson, 4................277	Wayside, Roberts 105
(11,660) 11,579	Waldeck, Fayette 34	Wealthy, Leon,...............................12
Verona, Collin 34	Waldrip, McCulloch........................15	*WEATHERFORD, Parker,
Vessey, Red River 15	Walhalla, Fayette 38	1,424, (19,000) 27,210
Viboras, Starr..................................22	*Wall, Tom Green, 10....................329	Weatherly, Hall................................8
Vick, Concho 20	*WALLER, Waller-Harris, 210,	Weaver, Hopkins 35
Victoria, Limestone 25	(2,092) 2,510	WEBBERVILLE, Travis, 8,
*VICTORIA, Victoria, 2,819,	*WALLIS, Austin, 65,	(nc) 318
(60,603) 62,530	(1,172) 1,377	Webbville, Coleman........................50
Victory City, Bowie 250	*Wallisville, Chambers, 11 452	*WEBSTER, Harris, 792,
*VIDOR, Orange, 501,	Walnut Bend, Cooke.......................45	(9,083) 10,738
(11,440) 11,451	Walnut Grove, Collin.......................40	Weches, Houston 46
Vienna, Lavaca...............................40	Walnut Grove, Panola...................125	Weedhaven, Jackson 35
View, Taylor 350	Walnut Hills, Potter 60	Weeping Mary, Cherokee 85
Vigo Park, Swisher 36	*WALNUT SPRINGS, Bosque,	*Weesatche, Goliad, 3.................411
Villa del Sol, Cameron,	22, (755) 825	*WEIMAR, Colorado, 178,
(132) 134	Walton, Van Zandt 35	(1,981) 2,073
*Village Mills, Hardin, 11 1,700	Wamba, Bowie...............................430	*WEINERT, Haskell, 6,
Villa Nueva North, Cameron........374	Waneta, Houston 19	(177) 192
Villa Nueva South, Cameron 402	Waples, Hood 155	*WEIR, Williamson, 15,
Villa Pancho, Cameron, (386) 404	*Warda, Fayette, 7........................121	(591) 764
Villa Verde, Hidalgo, (891)............954	Ward Creek, Bowie.......................164	Weiss Bluff, Jasper 60
Vincent, Howard 10	*Waring, Kendall, 11 73	*Welch, Dawson, 8 95
VINTON, El Paso, 81,	*Warren, Tyler, 15 310	Welcome, Austin...........................300
(1,892) 2,137	WARREN CITY, Gregg-Upshur,	Weldon, Houston 131
Violet, Nueces 160	3, (343) 375	Welfare, Kendall 10
Vistula, Houston 21	*Warrenton, Fayette, 3.................186	*Wellborn, Brazos, 7....................250
*Voca, McCulloch, 3 56	Warsaw, Kaufman 100	*WELLINGTON, Collingsworth,
VOLENTE, Travis, 28, (nc) 398	Washburn, Armstrong 120	80, (2,275) 2,165
Volga, Houston 9	*Washington, Washington, 17 100	*WELLMAN, Terry, 2, (203) 188
*Von Ormy, Bexar, 68 500	*WASKOM, Harrison, 81,	*WELLS, Cherokee, 16,
Voss, Coleman, 1 20	(2,068) 2,170	(769) 776
*Votaw, Hardin, 4..........................160	Wastella, Nolan................................4	Wells, Lynn 10
Vsetin, Lavaca................................45	*WATAUGA, Tarrant, 610,	Wells Branch, Travis,
W	(21,908) 24,030	(11,271) 11,867
*WACO, McLennan, 4,412,	Waterloo, Williamson....................70	Wesco, Gray....................................7
(113,726) 120,577	Waterman, Shelby 40	Weser, Goliad ....(see Ander)
*Wadsworth, Matagorda, 12 160	*Water Valley, Tom Green, 2.........203	*WESLACO, Hidalgo, 886,
*WAELDER, Gonzales, 23,	Watson, Burnet.............................148	(26,935) 32,893
(947) 1,004	Watt, Limestone.............................25	Wesley, Washington 65
Wagner, Hunt...................................75	Waverly, San Jacinto 200	Wesley Grove, Walker....................25
*Waka, Ochiltree, 2..........................65	*WAXAHACHIE, Ellis, 1,018,	*WEST, McLennan, 175,
Wakefield, Polk...............................25	(21,426) 27,484	(2,692) 2,780

Vattmann, Kleberg County. Robert Plocheck photo.

Town, County ....Pop. 2008	Town, County ....Pop. 2008	Town, County ....Pop. 2008
*WESTBROOK, Mitchell, 11, (203) 202	*WHITEWRIGHT, Grayson-Fannin, 93, (1,740) 1,722	*Woden, Nacogdoches, 3.............400
*WEST COLUMBIA, Brazoria, 166, (4,255) 4,423	*Whitharral, Hockley 158	*WOLFE CITY, Hunt, 54, (1,566) 1,634
Westcott, San Jacinto....................25	Whitman, Washington.....................25	*WOLFFORTH, Lubbock, 125, (2,554) 3,579
Westdale, Jim Wells, (295)..........317	*WHITNEY, Hill, 219, (1,833) 2,020	Womack, Bosque 25
*Westhoff, DeWitt, 4 410	*Whitsett, Live Oak, 3 200	Woodbine, Cooke 250
WESTLAKE, Tarrant-Denton, 51, (207) 227	Whitson, Coryel 50	WOODBRANCH, Montgomery, 0, (1,305) 1,523
*WEST LAKE HILLS, Travis, 427, (3,116) 3,259	*Whitt, Parker 38	Woodbury, Hill...............................45
West Livingston, Polk, (6,612) 7,243	Whon, Coleman 15	WOODCREEK, Hays, 37, (1,274) 1,656
West Mineola, Wood 20	*WICHITA FALLS, Wichita, 3,204, (104,197) 103,202	Wooded Hills, Johnson.................580
*Westminster, Collin, 3, (390) 470	*WICKETT, Ward, 22, (455)..........427	Wood Hi, Victoria 35
West Mountain, Upshur 325	Wied, Lavaca 65	*Woodlake, Trinity, 1 98
West Odessa, Ector, (17,799) 19,130	Wiedeville, Washington 35	Woodland, Red River 128
*WESTON, Collin, 14, (635) 683	*Wiergate, Newton, 2....................350	*Woodlawn, Harrison, 6...............550
WESTON LAKES, Fort Bend 2,500	Wigginsville, Montgomery.............100	WOODLOCH, Montgomery, 0, (247) 287
WEST ORANGE, Orange, 96, (4,111).................................3,776	Wilcox, Burleson.............................39	Woodrow, Lubbock 2,034
Westover, Baylor 18	Wilderville, Falls.............................45	Woods, Panola 65
WESTOVER HILLS, Tarrant, 0, (658) 690	*Wildorado, Oldham, 9 210	*WOODSBORO, Refugio, 54, (1,685) 1,607
Westphalia, Falls 186	Wild Peach, Brazoria, (2,498) 2,631	*WOODSON, Throckmorton, 15, (296) 305
*West Point, Fayette, 6 213	Wildwood, Hardin 499	Wood Springs, Smith....................200
West Sharyland, Hidalgo, (2,947) 3,151	Wilkins, Upshur..............................75	Woodville, Cherokee 20
West Sinton, San Patricio.............318	Willamar, Willacy, 15......................20	*WOODVILLE, Tyler, 186, (2,415) 2,345
WEST TAWAKONI, Hunt, 54, (1,462) 1,685	William Penn, Washington..............40	Woodward, La Salle 10
WEST UNIVERSITY PLACE, Harris, 294, (14,211).........15,431	*WILLIS, Montgomery, 288, (3,985) 4,799	WOODWAY, McLennan, 298, (8,733)..............................9,013
Westville, Trinity............................46	Willow City, Gillespie, 3 22	Woosley, Rains...............................47
Westway, Deaf Smith.....................15	Willow Grove, McLennan..............100	*WORTHAM, Freestone, 39, (1,082) 1,276
Westway, El Paso, (3,829).........4,072	WILLOW PARK, Parker, 147, (2,849) 3,847	Worthing, Lavaca 55
WESTWORTH VILLAGE, Tarrant, 39, (2,124) 2,800	Willow Springs, Fayette 74	Wright City, Smith 172
*WHARTON, Wharton, 364, (9,237) 9,264	Willow Springs, Rains....................50	*Wrightsboro, Gonzales.................10
Wheatland, Tarrant 175	*WILLS POINT, Van Zandt, 240, (3,496) 3,830	Wyldwood, Bastrop, (2,310) 2,623
*WHEELER, Wheeler, 56, (1,378) 1,339	*WILMER, Dallas, 45, (3,393) 3,755	*WYLIE, Collin-Rockwall-Dallas, 949, (15,132) 34,044
Wheeler Springs, Houston.............89	Wilmeth, Runnels 15	Wylie, Taylor ....[part of Abilene]
*Wheelock, Robertson, 7..............225	Wilson, Falls 42	**Y**
White City, San Augustine 20	*WILSON, Lynn, 16, (532)............483	*Yancey, Medina, 7 209
White City, Wilbarger 40	*WIMBERLEY, Hays, 627, (3,797) 4,513	*YANTIS, Wood, 49, (321)............400
*WHITE DEER, Carson, 36, (1,060) 1,019	Winchell, Brown 20	Yard, Anderson 18
*WHITEFACE, Cochran, 20, (465) 450	Winchester, Fayette.....................232	Yarrellton, Milam 35
Whiteflat, Motley 4	WINDCREST, Bexar, 217, (5,105) 5,311	Yellowpine, Sabine 97
White Hall, Bell 262	Windemere, Travis, (6,868) 7,190	*YOAKUM, Lavaca-DeWitt, 247, (5,731) 5,804
White Hall, Grimes.........................30	*WINDOM, Fannin, 14, (245) 258	*YORKTOWN, DeWitt, 108, (2,271) 2,266
*WHITEHOUSE, Smith, 287, (5,346) 6,989	*WINDTHORST, Archer, 37, (440) 477	Youngsport, Bell 49
*WHITE OAK, Gregg, 255, (5,624) 6,182	Winedale, Fayette...........................67	Yowell, Delta-Hunt 30
White Oak, Titus 100	*WINFIELD, Titus, 24, (499) 566	*Ysleta del Sur Pueblo, El Paso ... 421
White River Lake, Crosby...............83	WINFREE [Old River-], Chambers, 17, (1,364) 1,558	Yznaga, Cameron, (103) 102
White Rock, Hunt...........................80	*Wingate, Runnels, 4....................100	**Z**
White Rock, Red River 90	*WINK, Winkler, 25, (919) 889	Zabcikville, Bell..............................79
White Rock, Robertson...................80	Winkler, Navarro-Freestone...........26	*Zapata, Zapata, 164, (4,856) 5,597
White Rock, San Augustine 60	*Winnie, Chambers, 137, (2,914) 3,195	Zapata Ranch, Willacy, (88) 95
*WHITESBORO, Grayson, 177, (3,760) 4,219	*WINNSBORO, Wood-Franklin, 291, (3,584) 4,210	*ZAVALLA, Angelina, 32, (647) 659
*WHITE SETTLEMENT, Tarrant, 304, (14,831) 15,814	*WINONA, Smith, 53, (582).........653	*Zephyr, Brown, 11 201
White Star, Motley 6	Winter Haven, Dimmit.................123	Zimmerscheidt, Colorado 50
Whiteway, Hamilton 8	*WINTERS, Runnels, 94, (2,880) 2,737	Zion Hill, Guadalupe 595
	Witting, Lavaca 90	Zipperlandville, Falls......................22
	WIXON VALLEY, Brazos, 13, (235) 241	Zorn, Guadalupe...........................287
	Wizard Wells, Jack 69	Zuehl, Guadalupe, (346)...............398
		Zunkerville, Karnes........................15

Elections

"Election Day in Balmorhea in 1938" by Jerry Bywaters. Texas Almanac.

2008 General Election

2008 Primaries

Party Leaders

Political Analysis

Legislative Session

Presidential Race Changes Texas Politics

By Carolyn Barta

Texas has been a reliably red state in recent years and remained so in 2008, favoring John McCain for president. But the Lone Star State was less red than usual.

Obama-mania restored some political equilibrium, boosting local Democratic candidates and giving Democrats hope that they might become more competitive in statewide races long dominated by Republicans.

Among the highlights of the election year: Texas had a fierce fight in the Democratic presidential primary between Hillary Clinton and Barack Obama, and the eight-year era of George W. Bush ended with the ultimate election of Obama as president, leaving Texas with a diminished sphere of influence in Washington.

The election of Obama leaves Texas with a diminished sphere of influence in Washington

Voters nationally reacted to the worst economic crisis since the Great Depression and fatigue with wars in Iraq and Afghanistan by accepting Obama's message of change.

Still, Texas remained the most populous state to go Republican. The John McCain-Sarah Palin ticket won 55 percent to the Democrats' 43.7 percent. But the 11-point margin was only half that of Bush's Texas win in 2004 by 23 points, and less than the former governor's initial win with 59 percent in 2000. Changing demographics contributed to the Democratic surge, including urban growth, the creeping urbanization of suburbs, and more Hispanic and minority voters.

Obama carried five of six major urban areas and drew more voters than normal for Democrats in suburban counties around Dallas, Houston and Austin.

Democrats swept countywide races in Dallas County and made major inroads in formerly Republican Harris County. In other notable outcomes, the Republican advantage in the Texas House was cut to 76-74, down from 79-71 two years before and an 88-62 GOP advantage after the 2002 election.

But Republicans continued to dominate among rural, white and suburban voters. The GOP widened its control of the Texas congressional delegation to 20-12 by winning back Congressional District 22 once held by former House Majority Leader Tom DeLay. And Republicans won the few statewide offices on the off-year ballot for state races.

Voters also returned Republican John Cornyn to the U.S. Senate. Cornyn, the former Texas Supreme Court justice and attorney general, won re-election comfortably over Rick Noriega, an underfunded and little known Texas House member from Houston.

Primary Interests

But it was the huge turnout in the Texas primary that had political tongues wagging. The March 4, 2008, primary occurred at the height of competition between Hillary Clinton and Obama. Both campaigned in Tex-

Barack Obama campaigning in Austin during the Democratic primary. Erich Schlegel photo.

as, attracting large crowds and building organizations.

The Republican primary was only nominally a contest between McCain and Mike Huckabee, a minister and former governor of Arkansas, as McCain virtually had the nomination wrapped up nationally, though Huckabee attracted Texas' religious conservatives.

The biggest surprise was that 2.8 million voted in the Democratic primary – more than double the Republican primary vote of 1.3 million. And that in a state where Democrats had not won a statewide election since 1994.

The Obama-Clinton contest energized thousands of new Democrats. Party involvement was mandated by the convoluted Texas "Two-Step" system. After voting in the primary, Texas Democrats had to return to precinct caucuses when polls closed to elect more delegates. Party leaders were unprepared for the number of people who stormed the caucuses but welcomed the new activists.

Roughly two-thirds of national convention delegates were chosen by the primary and one-third through the caucus system. Clinton won the primary vote by 50.8 percent to Obama's 47.3 percent, but Obama ended up getting slightly more delegates to the national convention because of the caucuses.

Jockeying for the Future

As for the future, the highlight of the 2010 election is projected to be a Republican primary scrap for the gubernatorial nomination between Gov. Rick Perry and U.S. Sen. Kay Bailey Hutchison. Perry, who succeeded Bush as governor, will be the longest-serving chief executive in state history with 10 years at the end of his second term. If re-elected in 2010, he would serve 14 years.

That's too long, according to Hutchison, arguably the state's most popular political personality. Having first been elected to the Senate in a 1993 special election, she has been re-elected three times, with more than 60 percent of the vote every time.

The outcome could determine whether big-tent conservatives and new voters, who would favor Hutchison, or the party's social issues core, Perry's base, will shape its future.

The first Democrat to announce for governor was Tom Schieffer, who served in the Legislature in the 1970s. Schieffer was Bush's partner in the Texas Rangers baseball team and his ambassador to Japan and Australia. Several Republicans and Democrats were lining up in anticipation of an open Senate seat.

Bush Exit

Meanwhile, George W. and Laura Bush returned to Dallas where they bought a home and began preparations for the $300 million George W. Bush presidential library, museum and public policy center at Southern Methodist University, scheduled to break ground in 2010 and be completed by 2013.

Despite waning clout in Washington with the Team Bush exit, Texas Republicans grabbed two political leadership positions. Sen. Cornyn was named head of the National Republican Senatorial Committee to lead Republican efforts to regain a Senate majority in 2010. Rep.

Pete Sessions (R-Dallas) will head the National Republican Congressional Committee, which will try to overcome an 80-seat Democratic advantage in the U.S. House.

As for Democrats in the Obama administration, the president named former Dallas mayor Ron Kirk, an early supporter, as U.S Trade Ambassador.

Carolyn Barta, a retired political writer for The Dallas Morning News, teaches journalism at Southern Methodist University.

Texas Election Turnout by Voting Age Population

Year	2008	2004	2000	1996	1992	1988	1984	1980	1976	1972
Major Candidates	Obama McCain	Bush Kerry	Bush Gore	Clinton Dole	Clinton Bush Perot	Bush Dukakis	Reagan Mondale	Reagan Carter	Carter Ford	Nixon McGovern
Percent of VAP that voted	45.6	46.1	44.3	41.0	47.6	44.3	47.6	45.6	46.1	44.9
Percent of registered voters that voted	59.5	56.6	51.8	53.2	72.9	66.2	68.3	68.4	64.8	66.6

The **voting age population (VAP)** refers to the total number of persons of voting age regardless of citizenship, military status, felony conviction or mental state. The Bureau of the Census is the source for the VAP estimates.

Since the National Voter Registration Act of 1993, non-voters cannot be removed from registration rolls of a county until two federal elections have been held. So, for instance, if a person moved in December 2004 from one county to another, that person could be counted as a non-voter in the previous county of residence through the general election of November 2008.

These are called "suspense voters" on county rolls and have affected the statistical reports of the percentage of registered voters participating in elections.

In the early 1970s, various election reforms were enacted by the Legislature, including eliminating the requirement for an annual registration and allowing for a continuing voter registration system.

The presidential elections have a larger voter turnout than off-year and state elections. — RP

Sources: Federal Election Commission and the Texas Secretary of State office.

2008 Election Results for President, Senate

Below are the official results by county in the races for U.S. president and senator. The Democratic Party candidate for president was Sen. Barack Obama of Illinois. The Republican Party candidate for president was Sen. John McCain of Arizona.

The Republican candidate for the U.S. Senate was incumbent John Cornyn. The Democratic challenger was Rick Noriega.

The total number of votes, **8,077,795**, was 59.50 percent of the registered voters. The voting age population was estimated at 17,735,442.

The statewide turnout in the previous presidential election in 2004 was 56.57 percent of the registered voters. *Source: Texas Secretary of State.*

COUNTY	Registered Voters	Turnout %	PRESIDENT				SENATOR			
			McCain	%	Obama	%	Cornyn	%	Noriega	%
Statewide	**13,575,062**	**59.50**	4,479,328	55.45	3,528,633	43.68	4,337,469	54.82	3,389,365	42.83
Anderson	27,627	60.3	11,884	71.4	4,630	27.8	11,093	67.7	5,027	30.7
Andrews	8,463	54.7	3,816	82.4	790	17.1	3,658	81.3	734	16.3
Angelina	48,860	59.7	19,569	67.1	9,379	32.2	18,508	64.8	9,623	33.7
Aransas	16,354	59.8	6,693	68.4	3,006	30.7	6,449	67.3	2,793	29.5
Archer	6,482	67.3	3,595	82.4	740	17.0	3,378	80.3	761	18.1
Armstrong	1,466	67.5	856	86.5	128	12.9	821	84.6	130	13.4
Atascosa	24,557	40.5	5,462	55.0	4,415	44.4	5,012	51.6	4,518	46.5
Austin	18,035	65.0	8,786	75.0	2,821	24.1	8,403	72.8	2,947	25.5
Bailey	3,868	59.9	1,618	69.9	682	29.4	1,586	70.4	627	27.8
Bandera	14,944	62.2	6,935	74.6	2,250	24.2	6,709	73.1	2,175	23.7
Bastrop	40,871	63.4	13,817	53.3	11,687	45.1	13,478	52.6	11,094	43.3
Baylor	2,764	59.4	1,262	76.8	366	22.3	1,173	74.4	367	23.3
Bee	15,809	51.6	4,471	54.8	3,645	44.7	4,042	50.7	3,746	47.0
Bell	162,177	55.7	49,242	54.5	40,413	44.7	50,118	56.7	35,936	40.7
Bexar	931,118	56.5	246,275	46.8	275,527	52.4	233,983	45.5	265,311	51.6
Blanco	6,935	71.2	3,418	69.2	1,467	29.7	3,390	69.4	1,324	27.1
Borden	438	82.4	316	87.5	40	11.1	300	85.0	48	13.6
Bosque	12,626	60.6	5,762	75.4	1,797	23.5	5,400	71.6	1,977	26.2
Bowie	60,017	58.6	24,162	68.7	10,815	30.7	22,471	65.6	11,252	32.8
Brazoria	172,083	61.0	67,515	64.3	36,480	34.8	63,342	61.5	36,993	35.9
Brazos	92,984	63.1	37,465	63.9	20,502	34.9	37,818	66.3	17,701	31.0
Brewster	6,484	60.1	1,855	47.6	1,970	50.5	1,809	47.5	1,861	48.9
Briscoe	1,255	66.1	617	74.3	205	24.7	586	74.6	187	23.8
Brooks	6,456	35.8	556	24.1	1,747	75.7	408	18.1	1,817	80.5
Brown	24,884	60.3	12,052	80.3	2,822	18.8	11,457	77.5	2,973	20.1
Burleson	11,234	59.3	4,547	68.2	2,053	30.8	4,377	67.0	2,003	30.7
Burnet	26,474	63.8	12,059	71.4	4,608	27.3	11,964	71.3	4,288	25.6
Caldwell	21,265	54.8	6,107	52.4	5,403	46.4	5,932	51.5	5,244	45.5
Calhoun	13,096	52.5	4,106	59.7	2,729	39.7	3,825	56.3	2,806	41.3
Callahan	9,228	61.9	4,589	80.3	1,063	18.6	4,410	79.0	1,039	18.6
Cameron	174,428	43.4	26,671	35.6	48,480	64.1	24,233	32.7	48,020	64.8
Camp	7,453	61.3	2,798	61.3	1,734	38.0	2,705	60.6	1,695	38.0
Carson	4,615	64.6	2,548	85.5	406	13.6	2,467	83.8	409	13.9
Cass	18,563	63.8	8,279	69.9	3,490	29.5	7,466	65.1	3,816	33.3
Castro	4,350	52.7	1,562	68.2	719	31.4	1,526	68.6	671	30.1
Chambers	22,660	58.7	9,988	75.1	3,188	24.0	9,053	71.0	3,416	26.8
Cherokee	28,347	57.9	11,695	71.2	4,610	28.1	11,324	70.3	4,569	28.4
Childress	3,526	65.1	1,782	77.6	497	21.6	1,668	76.0	475	21.6
Clay	8,027	66.5	4,213	78.9	1,085	20.3	3,837	75.2	1,158	22.7
Cochran	1,957	54.0	758	71.7	284	26.9	750	72.8	259	25.1
Coke	2,512	62.5	1,252	79.8	299	19.1	1,194	81.1	231	15.7
Coleman	6,321	58.6	3,011	81.3	643	17.4	2,858	80.0	651	18.2
Collin	425,091	69.8	184,897	62.3	109,047	36.8	184,000	64.1	96,094	33.5
Collingsworth	1,977	60.4	943	78.9	234	19.6	864	77.1	234	20.9
Colorado	13,709	60.9	5,795	69.4	2,508	30.0	5,389	66.2	2,628	32.3
Comal	73,281	65.7	35,233	73.2	12,384	25.7	34,392	72.9	11,373	24.1
Comanche	9,341	55.9	3,813	73.1	1,334	25.6	3,498	68.7	1,509	29.6
Concho	1,804	59.7	807	74.9	257	23.9	794	75.0	248	23.4

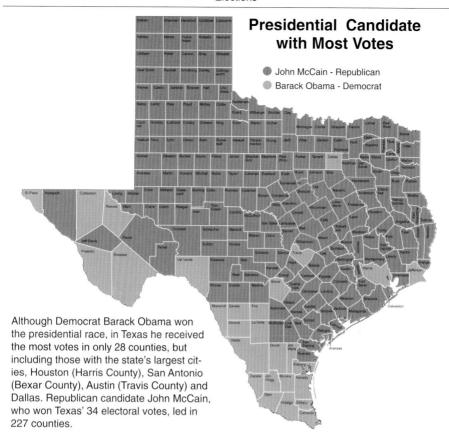

Presidential Candidate with Most Votes

● John McCain - Republican
● Barack Obama - Democrat

Although Democrat Barack Obama won the presidential race, in Texas he received the most votes in only 28 counties, but including those with the state's largest cities, Houston (Harris County), San Antonio (Bexar County), Austin (Travis County) and Dallas. Republican candidate John McCain, who won Texas' 34 electoral votes, led in 227 counties.

COUNTY	Registered Voters	Turnout %	PRESIDENT				SENATOR			
			McCain	%	Obama	%	Cornyn	%	Noriega	%
Cooke	24,646	61.0	11,871	79.0	3,051	20.3	11,259	76.1	3,239	21.9
Coryell	39,244	46.7	11,550	63.0	6,619	36.1	11,642	64.6	5,914	32.8
Cottle	1,252	56.3	509	72.2	187	26.5	440	68.8	182	28.4
Crane	2,606	55.8	1,119	77.0	319	21.9	990	73.1	319	23.6
Crockett	2,683	57.6	1,026	66.4	512	33.1	877	60.0	569	38.9
Crosby	3,988	48.0	1,221	63.8	684	35.7	1,184	64.5	638	34.7
Culberson	1,982	38.3	257	33.9	492	64.8	239	35.9	401	60.3
Dallam	3,235	49.1	1,269	79.9	302	19.0	1,245	80.1	259	16.7
Dallas	1,206,543	61.2	310,000	42.0	422,989	57.3	312,781	43.2	396,354	54.8
Dawson	8,062	50.8	2,906	70.9	1,152	28.1	2,742	70.6	1,064	27.4
Deaf Smith	9,317	50.9	3,466	73.1	1,247	26.3	3,382	73.0	1,175	25.4
Delta	3,586	61.0	1,580	72.2	589	26.9	1,409	66.2	684	32.1
Denton	366,830	66.3	149,935	61.6	91,160	37.5	150,389	63.0	81,939	34.3
DeWitt	12,324	53.8	4,888	73.8	1,716	25.9	4,767	73.4	1,619	24.9
Dickens	1,473	66.0	730	75.1	234	24.1	699	76.6	202	22.1
Dimmit	7,487	47.9	874	24.4	2,692	75.0	751	21.8	2,651	76.9
Donley	2,549	66.3	1,374	81.3	291	17.2	1,333	80.9	270	16.4
Duval	9,345	47.2	1,076	24.4	3,298	74.8	773	18.2	3,386	79.7
Eastland	10,719	60.7	5,165	79.4	1,271	19.5	4,859	76.1	1,360	21.3
Ector	70,039	50.8	26,199	73.6	9,123	25.6	25,356	72.1	8,933	25.4
Edwards	1,520	68.1	673	65.0	346	33.4	635	66.4	305	31.9
Ellis	85,541	63.0	38,078	70.7	15,333	28.5	36,186	68.1	15,491	29.2
El Paso	388,498	47.7	61,783	33.4	122,021	65.9	56,692	31.5	118,284	65.8
Erath	21,503	65.2	10,768	76.8	3,128	22.3	10,374	74.8	3,198	23.1
Falls	9,653	58.0	3,328	59.4	2,225	39.7	3,253	59.7	2,115	38.8
Fannin	19,835	59.0	8,092	69.2	3,464	29.6	7,345	63.9	3,925	34.1

COUNTY	Registered Voters	Turnout %	PRESIDENT				SENATOR			
			McCain	%	Obama	%	Cornyn	%	Noriega	%
Fayette	15,569	68.8	7,582	70.8	3,014	28.1	7,311	69.6	2,971	28.3
Fisher	2,960	60.3	1,083	60.7	687	38.5	1,037	59.4	684	39.2
Floyd	4,567	55.2	1,784	70.8	730	29.0	1,700	71.4	654	27.5
Foard	1,047	51.4	327	60.8	198	36.8	283	56.7	203	40.7
Fort Bend	299,110	67.8	103,206	50.9	98,368	48.5	101,563	50.9	94,909	47.5
Franklin	6,747	66.6	3,392	75.5	1,036	23.1	3,315	75.8	964	22.0
Freestone	11,589	62.9	5,205	71.4	2,034	27.9	4,808	67.5	2,170	30.5
Frio	10,528	38.6	1,644	40.5	2,405	59.2	1,500	38.2	2,369	60.4
Gaines	7,372	55.2	3,385	83.2	650	16.0	3,184	81.6	653	16.7
Galveston	189,357	55.5	62,258	59.3	41,805	39.8	57,291	55.8	43,107	42.0
Garza	2,976	58.8	1,356	77.5	375	21.4	1,308	74.3	421	23.9
Gillespie	17,519	70.4	9,563	77.5	2,576	20.9	9,612	78.7	2,256	18.5
Glasscock	739	75.4	502	90.1	52	9.3	481	89.6	46	8.6
Goliad	5,694	64.2	2,298	62.9	1,329	36.4	2,157	61.8	1,233	35.3
Gonzales	12,424	50.6	4,076	64.8	2,167	34.5	3,799	62.3	2,187	35.8
Gray	14,312	56.8	6,924	85.1	1,153	14.2	6,777	84.4	1,085	13.5
Grayson	75,689	60.1	31,136	68.5	13,900	30.6	30,180	67.8	13,377	30.1
Gregg	73,555	57.9	29,203	68.5	13,166	30.9	29,176	69.5	12,211	29.1
Grimes	14,872	56.0	5,562	66.8	2,704	32.5	5,234	63.8	2,803	34.2
Guadalupe	73,892	64.2	30,869	65.0	16,156	34.0	29,752	64.4	15,293	33.1
Hale	21,247	46.8	7,171	72.1	2,708	27.2	6,905	71.1	2,632	27.1
Hall	2,138	59.1	930	73.6	324	25.6	847	70.8	327	27.3
Hamilton	5,711	66.2	2,876	76.1	863	22.8	2,688	72.5	945	25.5
Hansford	3,178	66.1	1,847	87.9	240	11.4	1,806	88.4	207	10.1
Hardeman	3,031	52.6	1,199	75.2	373	23.4	1,116	72.0	397	25.6
Hardin	35,160	58.9	16,603	80.2	3,939	19.0	15,534	76.8	4,361	21.5
Harris	1,959,284	59.8	571,883	48.8	590,982	50.4	544,857	47.3	583,782	50.7
Harrison	42,829	61.1	17,103	65.4	8,887	34.0	16,310	64.9	8,465	33.7
Hartley	2,897	68.5	1,711	86.2	250	12.6	1,695	86.3	243	12.4
Haskell	3,869	54.7	1,388	65.6	699	33.0	1,311	63.7	709	34.5
Hays	97,390	60.6	29,638	50.2	28,431	48.1	30,071	51.8	25,688	44.2
Hemphill	2,245	69.9	1,345	85.7	216	13.8	1,294	84.3	218	14.2
Henderson	49,829	58.2	20,857	71.9	7,913	27.3	19,699	68.8	8,384	29.3
Hidalgo	305,316	42.8	39,668	30.3	90,261	69.0	35,720	28.3	88,539	70.0
Hill	22,524	58.6	9,264	70.2	3,811	28.9	8,640	66.5	4,112	31.6
Hockley	13,989	54.7	5,795	75.8	1,797	23.5	5,771	76.9	1,587	21.2
Hood	34,728	65.1	17,299	76.6	5,087	22.5	16,523	74.1	5,239	23.5
Hopkins	21,920	58.9	9,299	72.0	3,530	27.3	8,380	66.9	3,876	30.9
Houston	15,040	57.3	5,872	68.1	2,656	30.8	5,513	66.2	2,677	32.2
Howard	17,787	54.5	7,029	72.5	2,545	26.3	6,562	69.5	2,609	27.6
Hudspeth	1,631	55.1	458	51.0	430	47.9	392	47.4	393	47.5
Hunt	50,602	58.3	20,573	69.7	8,594	29.1	19,752	68.0	8,592	29.6
Hutchinson	15,262	57.4	7,361	84.0	1,322	15.1	7,245	83.9	1,191	13.8
Irion	1,280	63.8	644	78.8	164	20.1	623	78.6	150	18.9
Jack	4,983	60.7	2,528	83.6	470	15.5	2,333	79.0	567	19.2
Jackson	9,073	55.7	3,723	73.6	1,301	25.7	3,420	71.0	1,320	27.4
Jasper	21,541	59.3	9,022	70.6	3,658	28.6	8,170	66.1	3,961	32.1
Jeff Davis	1,835	67.4	749	60.6	468	37.9	645	55.1	480	41.0
Jefferson	151,569	58.2	42,905	48.6	44,888	50.8	40,800	47.6	43,820	51.1
Jim Hogg	3,897	46.6	472	26.0	1,336	73.6	308	17.3	1,456	81.6
Jim Wells	26,513	43.8	4,841	41.7	6,706	57.8	4,117	36.4	6,948	61.4
Johnson	82,260	60.8	36,685	73.3	12,912	25.8	34,512	69.7	13,830	27.9
Jones	10,257	56.6	4,203	72.4	1,528	26.3	4,013	70.9	1,495	26.4
Karnes	8,121	55.7	2,736	60.4	1,760	38.9	2,581	58.8	1,709	38.9
Kaufman	58,408	60.2	23,735	67.5	11,161	31.8	22,527	64.9	11,499	33.1
Kendall	23,704	70.6	12,971	77.5	3,599	21.5	12,765	77.6	3,224	19.6
Kenedy	353	57.2	94	46.5	108	53.5	90	46.9	101	52.6
Kent	678	66.1	342	76.3	99	22.1	317	74.9	98	23.2
Kerr	34,361	65.6	16,752	74.3	5,570	24.7	16,249	73.2	5,391	24.6
Kimble	2,969	62.1	1,487	80.7	342	18.6	1,436	79.6	328	18.2

COUNTY	Registered Voters	Turnout %	PRESIDENT				SENATOR			
			McCain	%	Obama	%	Cornyn	%	Noriega	%
King	202	80.7	151	92.6	8	4.9	121	91.0	10	7.5
Kinney	2,376	65.3	907	58.5	633	40.8	868	57.8	615	40.9
Kleberg	18,905	52.2	4,540	46.0	5,256	53.2	3,896	40.2	5,569	57.4
Knox	2,530	54.1	986	72.1	367	26.8	923	69.1	399	29.9
Lamar	31,700	57.9	12,952	70.5	5,243	28.6	11,612	64.6	6,027	33.5
Lamb	9,155	49.4	3,344	73.9	1,156	25.5	3,262	74.2	1,060	24.1
Lampasas	12,979	58.8	5,651	74.0	1,903	24.9	5,616	74.5	1,699	22.5
La Salle	4,122	43.1	714	40.2	1,052	59.2	592	35.4	1,055	63.0
Lavaca	13,470	61.0	6,293	76.5	1,869	22.7	5,769	72.6	2,044	25.7
Lee	9,498	67.1	4,312	67.6	2,000	31.4	4,088	67.3	1,838	30.3
Leon	11,400	61.8	5,566	79.1	1,418	20.1	5,251	77.0	1,442	21.2
Liberty	45,526	47.5	15,448	71.4	5,991	27.7	13,903	65.8	6,770	32.0
Limestone	14,302	53.5	5,079	66.4	2,516	32.9	4,831	64.4	2,552	34.0
Lipscomb	1,961	64.0	1,093	87.0	155	12.3	1,060	86.2	150	12.2
Live Oak	7,499	55.7	3,095	74.1	1,048	25.1	2,864	70.4	1,086	26.7
Llano	14,489	66.5	7,281	75.6	2,250	23.4	7,163	75.1	2,102	22.0
Loving	119	66.4	67	84.8	12	15.2	55	75.3	16	21.9
Lubbock	163,745	59.6	66,304	68.0	30,486	31.3	67,267	70.3	26,246	27.4
Lynn	4,071	52.0	1,473	69.6	627	29.6	1,488	70.9	578	27.5
Madison	7,063	57.7	2,891	71.0	1,146	28.1	2,680	67.3	1,226	30.8
Marion	7,718	55.1	2,567	60.4	1,644	38.7	2,436	59.4	1,584	38.6
Martin	2,913	58.9	1,389	81.0	314	18.3	1,252	76.7	343	21.0
Mason	2,954	71.8	1,544	72.8	546	25.7	1,516	74.6	451	22.2
Matagorda	21,703	57.0	7,835	63.3	4,440	35.9	7,142	59.0	4,676	38.6
Maverick	27,050	40.4	2,316	21.2	8,554	78.2	1,849	18.9	7,759	79.1
McCulloch	5,297	56.8	2,263	75.2	728	24.2	2,207	74.9	676	22.9
McLennan	134,780	59.1	49,044	61.6	29,998	37.7	48,995	62.4	28,197	35.9
McMullen	719	74.7	400	74.5	132	24.6	347	73.7	109	23.1
Medina	26,613	59.1	10,480	66.6	5,147	32.7	10,120	65.1	5,095	32.8
Menard	1,861	54.7	712	70.9	295	29.0	695	71.9	245	25.4
Midland	74,440	62.1	36,155	78.2	9,691	21.0	35,514	78.1	8,798	19.3
Milam	14,652	57.0	5,217	62.4	3,044	36.4	5,012	61.0	3,054	37.2
Mills	3,407	63.9	1,753	80.5	398	18.3	1,620	77.1	414	19.7
Mitchell	4,786	50.8	1,815	74.7	586	24.1	1,657	70.8	628	26.8
Montague	13,132	60.5	6,245	78.6	1,597	20.1	5,751	74.4	1,765	22.8
Montgomery	243,539	64.8	119,884	75.9	36,703	23.3	116,003	74.4	36,699	23.5
Moore	9,887	55.0	4,282	78.8	1,123	20.7	4,154	78.1	1,078	20.3
Morris	9,283	56.5	3,158	60.2	2,055	39.2	2,885	56.6	2,134	41.9
Motley	904	65.7	522	87.9	67	11.3	494	85.8	76	13.2
Nacogdoches	33,644	69.5	14,828	63.4	8,393	35.9	14,493	63.7	7,845	34.5
Navarro	28,485	57.3	10,810	66.2	5,400	33.1	9,996	62.8	5,658	35.5
Newton	9,236	57.0	3,446	65.5	1,751	33.3	2,986	58.3	2,007	39.2
Nolan	9,162	55.3	3,485	68.8	1,521	30.0	3,359	68.0	1,481	30.0
Nueces	198,850	50.9	52,391	51.8	47,912	47.3	48,179	48.6	48,299	48.7
Ochiltree	5,093	61.0	2,851	91.7	243	7.81	2,768	90.8	243	8.0
Oldham	1,465	62.8	813	88.4	102	11.1	777	87.5	85	9.6
Orange	52,145	56.4	21,509	73.1	7,646	26.0	19,885	68.5	8,593	29.6
Palo Pinto	17,386	56.9	7,264	73.4	2,499	25.3	6,714	69.3	2,782	28.7
Panola	16,562	61.7	7,582	74.2	2,586	25.3	7,123	71.8	2,661	26.8
Parker	73,422	65.3	36,974	77.1	10,502	21.9	35,486	74.4	11,132	23.3
Parmer	4,995	74.3	2,969	80.0	719	19.4	2,894	80.0	667	18.4
Pecos	8,103	49.5	2,480	61.8	1,476	36.8	2,268	59.1	1,467	38.2
Polk	38,390	52.5	13,731	68.1	6,230	30.9	12,254	63.7	6,502	33.8
Potter	56,449	53.2	20,761	69.2	8,939	29.8	20,361	69.2	8,197	27.9
Presidio	5,218	33.7	489	27.8	1,252	71.3	396	25.6	1,132	73.1
Rains	6,734	62.9	3,146	74.3	1,048	24.7	2,820	68.2	1,220	29.5
Randall	78,794	65.8	41,948	80.9	9,468	18.5	41,718	81.1	8,501	16.5
Reagan	1,994	49.8	795	80.0	197	19.8	752	79.1	179	18.8
Real	2,523	64.5	1,238	76.0	375	23.0	1,192	75.2	346	21.8
Red River	8,117	62.2	3,461	68.5	1,539	30.5	3,000	62.2	1,750	36.3

COUNTY	Registered Voters	Turnout %	PRESIDENT				SENATOR			
			McCain	%	Obama	%	Cornyn	%	Noriega	%
Reeves	6,464	47.6	1,445	47.0	1,606	52.2	1,171	40.5	1,651	57.1
Refugio	5,540	58.9	1,855	56.9	1,382	42.4	1,643	53.7	1,353	44.3
Roberts	724	71.5	477	92.1	41	7.9	471	92.5	31	6.1
Robertson	12,389	54.2	3,980	59.3	2,675	39.9	3,758	57.3	2,677	40.7
Rockwall	45,470	70.5	23,300	72.7	8,492	26.5	22,875	72.4	8,002	25.3
Runnels	6,969	55.5	3,118	80.6	720	18.6	2,952	79.4	683	18.4
Rusk	31,794	58.9	13,646	72.9	4,983	26.6	13,159	72.4	4,752	26.5
Sabine	7,776	62.7	3,749	76.9	1,077	22.1	3,300	70.4	1,266	27.0
SanAugustine	6,537	56.8	2,342	63.0	1,328	35.7	2,114	60.2	1,332	37.9
San Jacinto	15,859	56.5	6,151	68.7	2,721	30.4	5,418	62.0	3,091	35.4
San Patricio	46,865	45.7	12,404	58.0	8,854	41.4	11,277	54.3	8,956	43.1
San Saba	3,767	65.2	1,941	79.0	487	19.8	1,849	78.4	458	19.4
Schleicher	2,030	64.2	970	74.4	324	24.8	838	68.8	346	28.4
Scurry	10,180	54.7	4,414	79.3	1,088	19.5	4,210	77.7	1,086	20.1
Shackelford	2,486	60.5	1,284	85.3	208	13.8	1,227	84.2	210	14.4
Shelby	14,961	61.6	6,630	71.9	2,548	27.6	6,146	69.3	2,598	29.3
Sherman	1,488	68.5	884	86.7	127	12.5	849	85.9	113	11.4
Smith	130,132	61.1	55,187	69.4	23,726	29.8	54,25	69.4	22,613	28.9
Somervell	5,883	60.1	2,677	75.8	799	22.6	2,433	70.8	920	26.8
Starr	27,474	35.6	1,492	15.2	8,274	84.5	1,220	13.2	7,910	85.8
Stephens	5,796	60.8	2,869	81.4	626	17.8	2,668	77.6	706	20.5
Sterling	906	68.3	520	84.0	97	15.7	482	83.7	86	14.9
Stonewall	1,095	67.1	524	71.3	206	28.0	472	67.4	212	30.3
Sutton	2,708	58.3	1,189	75.3	381	24.1	1,113	71.6	417	26.8
Swisher	4,621	54.9	1,683	66.4	813	32.1	1,580	63.4	861	34.6
Tarrant	965,232	65.1	348,420	55.4	274,880	43.7	341,772	55.3	262,870	42.5
Taylor	79,667	59.5	34,317	72.3	12,690	26.8	34,144	73.3	11,392	24.4
Terrell	831	62.5	323	62.2	186	35.8	283	58.7	183	38.0
Terry	7,571	56.5	2,879	67.3	1,379	32.2	2,852	69.2	1,181	28.6
Throckmorton	1,237	67.7	671	80.1	166	19.8	593	77.7	162	21.2
Titus	15,828	58.4	6,028	65.2	3,145	34.0	5,619	61.9	3,308	36.4
Tom Green	64,400	60.3	27,362	70.4	11,158	28.7	27,296	71.3	9,937	26.0
Travis	611,367	65.1	136,981	34.4	254,017	63.9	145,520	37.3	228,620	58.6
Trinity	11,353	53.5	4,095	67.4	1,925	31.7	3,637	61.8	2,114	35.9
Tyler	13,480	58.7	5,644	71.4	2,166	27.4	5,102	66.7	2,336	30.6
Upshur	26,374	57.5	11,222	74.0	3,790	25.0	10,677	71.7	3,920	26.3
Upton	2,180	54.9	898	75.0	288	24.1	830	74.8	255	23.0
Uvalde	16,506	53.1	4,590	52.4	4,126	47.1	4,206	48.8	4,281	49.6
Val Verde	26,590	44.8	5,752	44.9	6,982	54.5	5,170	41.4	7,062	56.6
Van Zandt	33,897	60.1	15,734	77.1	4,505	22.1	14,601	72.8	5,086	25.3
Victoria	53,404	56.0	19,878	66.4	9,832	32.8	19,590	67.0	9,036	30.9
Walker	30,998	61.8	11,623	60.7	7,334	38.3	11,080	58.9	7,235	38.4
Waller	29,623	52.4	8,265	53.3	7,153	46.1	7,995	52.0	7,167	46.6
Ward	6,412	56.2	2,667	74.0	899	25.0	2,466	70.7	912	26.2
Washington	21,766	66.1	10,176	70.8	4,034	28.1	9,894	70.0	3,960	28.0
Webb	105,448	44.4	13,119	28.0	33,452	71.4	9,626	20.9	35,802	77.7
Wharton	25,002	57.7	9,431	65.4	4,937	34.2	8,681	61.5	5,215	37.0
Wheeler	3,797	59.1	1,918	85.4	314	14.0	1,800	83.4	327	15.2
Wichita	84,161	54.6	31,731	69.0	13,868	30.2	30,354	68.4	12,946	29.2
Wilbarger	8,396	53.7	3,283	72.8	1,196	26.5	3,032	70.5	1,178	27.4
Willacy	11,278	43.5	1,456	29.7	3,409	69.5	1,358	29.0	3,242	69.1
Williamson	232,642	68.1	88,323	55.8	67,691	42.7	91,115	58.6	58,250	37.5
Wilson	26,752	61.2	10,904	66.6	5,362	32.8	10,431	64.6	5,322	33.0
Winkler	3,843	52.9	1,529	75.2	477	23.5	1,452	73.8	464	23.6
Wise	35,953	57.4	15,973	77.4	4,471	21.7	15,035	73.5	4,974	24.3
Wood	27,030	65.8	13,658	76.8	4,010	22.5	13,280	75.7	3,928	22.4
Yoakum	4,396	55.9	1,989	80.9	450	18.3	1,877	78.5	474	19.8
Young	11,581	63.1	5,942	81.3	1,303	17.8	5,598	78.7	1,368	19.2
Zapata	7,224	39.7	919	32.1	1,939	67.7	626	22.8	2,082	76.0
Zavala	8,124	47.7	596	15.4	3,263	84.2	506	14.0	3,064	84.7

General Election, 2008

Below are the voting results for the general election held November 4, 2008, for all statewide races and for contested congressional, state senate, courts of appeals and state board of education races. These are official returns as canvassed by the State Canvassing Board. Abbreviations used are (Dem.) Democrat, (Rep.) Republican, (Lib.) Libertarian, (Ind.) Independent and (W-I) Write-in.

President
John McCain (Rep.)	4,479,328	55.45%
Barack Obama (Dem.)	3,528,633	43.68%
Bob Barr (Lib.)	56,116	0.69%
Ralph Nader (W-I)	5,214	0.06%
Chuck Baldwin (W-I)	5,052	0.06%
Brian Moore (W-I)	910	0.01%
Alan Keyes (W-I)	895	0.01%
Thaddaus Hill (W-I)	876	0.01%
Cynthia McKinney (W-I)	671	0.00%
Jonathan Allen (W-I)	100	0.00%
Total vote	8,077,795	

U.S. Senator
John Cornyn (Rep.)	4,337,469	54.82%
Richard J. "Rick" Noriega (Dem.)	3,389,365	42.83%
Yvonne Adams Schick (Lib.)	185,241	2.34%
Total Vote	7,912,075	

U.S. HOUSE OF REPRESENTATIVES
(See map of districts on p. 530.)

District 1
Louie Gohmert (Rep.)	189,012	87.57%
Roger L. Owen (Ind.)	26,814	12.42%
Total Vote	215,826	

District 2
Ted Poe (Rep.)	175,101	88.92%
Craig Wolfe (Lib.)	21,813	11.07%
Total Vote	196,914	

District 3
Sam Johnson (Rep.)	170,742	59.74%
Tom Daley (Dem.)	108,693	38.03%
Christopher J. Claytor (Lib.)	6,348	2.22%
Total Vote	285,783	

District 4
Ralph M. Hall (Rep.)	206,906	68.79%
Glenn Melancon (Dem.)	88,067	29.28%
Fred Annett (Lib.)	5,771	1.91%
Total Vote	300,744	

District 5
Jeb Hensarling (Rep.)	162,894	83.59%
Ken Ashby (Lib.)	31,967	16.40%
Total Vote	194,861	

District 6
Joe Barton (Rep.)	174,008	62.01%
Ludwig Otto (Dem.)	99,919	35.61%
Max W. Koch III (Lib.)	6,655	2.37%
Total Vote	280,582	

District 7
John Culberson (Rep.)	162,635	55.90%
Michael Skelly (Dem.)	123,242	42.36%
Drew Parks (Lib.)	5,057	1.73%
Total Vote	290,934	

District 8
Kevin Brady (Rep.)	207,128	72.56%
Kent Hargett (Dem.)	70,758	24.78%
Brian Stevens (Lib.)	7,565	2.65%
Total Vote	285,451	

District 9
Al Green (Dem.)	143,868	93.64%
Brad Walters (Lib.)	9,760	6.35%
Total Vote	153,628	

District 10
Michael T. McCaul (Rep.)	179,493	53.88%
Larry Joe Doherty (Dem.)	143,719	43.14%
Matt Finkel (Lib.)	9,871	2.96%
Total Vote	333,083	

District 11
Mike Conaway (Rep.)	189,625	88.33%
John R. Strohm (Lib.)	25,051	11.66%
Total Vote	214,676	

District 12
Kay Granger (Rep.)	181,662	67.59%
Tracey Smith (Dem.)	82,250	30.60%
Shiloh Sidney Shambaugh (Lib.)	4,842	1.80%
Total Vote	268,754	

District 13
Mac Thornberry (Rep.)	180,078	77.64%
Roger James Waun (Dem.)	51,841	22.35%
Total Vote	231,919	

District 15
Eddie Zamora (Rep.)	52,303	31.94%
Rubén Hinojosa (Dem.)	107,578	65.71%
Gricha Raether (Lib.)	3,827	2.33%
Total Vote	163,708	

District 16
Silvestre Reyes (Dem.)	130,375	82.13%
Mette A. Baker (Lib.)	12,000	7.56%
Benjamin Eloy "Ben" Mendoza (Ind.)	16,348	10.29%
Total Vote	158,723	

District 17
Rob Curnock (Rep.)	120,250	47.50%
Chet Edwards (Dem.)	128,082	50.60%
Gardner C. Osborne (Lib.)	4,780	1.88%
Total Vote	253,112	

District 18
John Faulk (Rep.)	39,095	20.34%
Sheila Jackson Lee (Dem.)	148,617	77.32%
Mike Taylor (Lib.)	4,486	2.33%
Total Vote	192,198	

District 19
Randy Neugebauer (Rep.)	168,501	72.43%
Dwight Fullingim (Dem.)	58,030	24.94%
Richard "Chip" Peterson (Lib.)	6,080	2.61%
Total Vote	232,611	

District 20
Robert Litoff (Rep.)	44,585	25.18%
Charles A. Gonzalez (Dem.)	127,298	71.89%
Michael Idrogo (Lib.)	5,172	2.92%
Total Vote	177,055	

District 21
Lamar Smith (Rep.)	243,471	79.99%
James Arthur Strohm (Lib.)	60,879	20.00%
Total Vote	304,350	

District 22
Pete Olson (Rep.)	161,996	52.42%
Nick Lampson (Dem.)	140,160	45.35%
John Wieder (Lib.)	6,839	2.21%
Total Vote	308,995	

District 23
Lyle Larson (Rep.)	100,799	41.91%
Ciro D. Rodriguez (Dem.)	134,090	55.76%
Lani Connolly (Lib.)	5,581	2.32%
Total Vote	240,470	

District 24
Kenny E. Marchant (Rep.)	151,434	55.98%

Tom Love (Dem.) .... 111,089 ...... 41.06%
David A. Casey (Lib.) .... 7,972 .... 2.94%
   Total Vote 270,495

District 25
George L. Morovich (Rep.) .... 88,693 ...... 30.44%
Lloyd Doggett (Dem.) .... 191,755 ..... 65.82%
Jim Stutsman (Lib.) .... 10,848 .... 3.72%
   Total Vote 291,296

District 26
Michael C. Burgess (Rep.) .... 195,181 ...... 60.17%
Ken Leach (Dem.) .... 118,167 ...... 36.42%
Stephanie B. Weiss (Lib.) .... 11,028 .... 3.39%
   Total Vote 324,376

District 27
William Willie Vaden (Rep.) .... 69,458 ...... 38.38%
Solomon P. Ortiz (Dem.) .... 104,864 ..... 57.95%
Robert E. Powell (Lib.) .... 6,629 .... 3.66%
   Total Vote 180,951

District 28
Jim Fish (Rep.) .... 52,524 ...... 29.22%
Henry Cuellar (Dem.) .... 123,494 ..... 68.70%
Ross Lynn Leone (Lib.) .... 3,722 .... 2.07%
   Total Vote 179,740

District 29
Eric Story (Rep.) .... 25,512 ...... 23.88%
Gene Green (Dem.) .... 79,718 ...... 74.64%
Joel Grace (Lib.) .... 1,564 .... 1.46%
   Total Vote 106,794

District 30
Fred Wood (Rep.) .... 32,361 ...... 15.86%
Eddie Bernice Johnson (Dem.) .... 168,249 ...... 82.48%
Jarrett Woods (Lib.) .... 3,366 .... 1.65%
   Total Vote 203,976

District 31
John Carter (Rep.) .... 175,563 ...... 60.26%
Brian P. Ruiz (Dem.) .... 106,559 ...... 36.57%
Barry N. Cooper (Lib.) .... 9,182 .... 3.15%
   Total Vote 291,304

District 32
Pete Sessions (Rep.) .... 116,283 ...... 57.25%
Eric Roberson (Dem.) .... 82,406 ...... 40.57%
Alex Bischoff (Lib.) .... 4,421 .... 2.17%
   Total Vote 203,110

STATE RACES
Railroad Commissioner
Michael L. Williams (Rep.) .... 4,003,789 ...... 52.13%
Mark Thompson (Dem.) .... 3,406,174 ...... 44.35%
David Floyd (Lib.) .... 270,078 .... 3.51%
   Total vote 7,680,041

Chief Justice, Supreme Court
Wallace B. Jefferson (Rep.) .... 4,092,181 ...... 53.10%
Jim Jordan (Dem.) .... 3,374,433 ...... 43.79%
Tom Oxford (Lib.) .... 239,063 .... 3.10%
   Total Vote 7,705,677

Justice, Supreme Court, Place 7
Dale Wainwright (Rep.) .... 3,926,015 ...... 50.99%
Sam Houston (Dem.) .... 3,525,158 ..... 45.78%
David G. Smith (Lib.) .... 247,512 .... 3.21%
   Total Vote 7,698,685

Justice, Supreme Court, Place 8
Phil Johnson (Rep.) .... 4,018,396 ...... 52.31%
Linda Reyna Yañez (Dem.) .... 3,428,179 ...... 44.63%
Drew Shirley (Lib.) .... 234,092 .... 3.04%
   Total Vote 7,680,667

Judge, Court of Criminal Appeals, Place 3
Tim Price (Rep.) .... 3,949,722 ..... 51.64%
Susan Strawn (Dem.) .... 3,482,718 ..... 45.53%
Matthew E. Eilers (Lib.) .... 216,060 .... 2.82%
   Total Vote 7,648,500

Judge, Court of Criminal Appeals, Place 4
Paul Womack (Rep.) .... 4,044,788 ...... 52.96%
J.R. Molina (Dem.) .... 3,340,754 ...... 43.74%
Dave Howard (Lib.) .... 250,672 .... 3.28%
   Total Vote 7,636,214

Judge, Court of Criminal Appeals, Place 9
Cathy Cochran (Rep.) .... 4,719,538 ...... 81.89%
William Bryan Strange III (Lib.) .... 1,043,642 ...... 18.10%
   Total Vote 5,763,180

COURTS OF APPEALS
Chief Justice, Third District
Ken Law (Rep.) .... 407,243 ...... 47.59%
Woodie Jones (Dem.) .... 448,373 ...... 52.40%
   Total Vote 855,616

Chief Justice, Fourth District
Ann Comerio (Rep.) .... 338,988 ...... 44.18%
Catherine Stone (Dem.) .... 428,283 ...... 55.81%
   Total Vote 767,271

Chief Justice, Fourteenth District
Adele Hedges (Rep.) .... 798,272 ...... 50.96%
Joe W. Beverly (Dem.) .... 768,045 ...... 49.03%
   Total Vote 1,566,317

Justice, First District, Place 3
Ed Hubbard (Rep.) .... 776,587 ...... 49.42%
Jim Sharp (Dem.) .... 794,759 ...... 50.57%
   Total Vote 1,571,346

Justice, First District, Place 5
Laura Carter Higley (Rep.) .... 802,668 ...... 51.23%
Leslie C. Taylor (Dem.) .... 763,840 ...... 48.76%
   Total Vote 1,566,508

Justice, Fifth District, Place 3
Mary Murphy (Rep.) .... 587,728 ...... 53.55%
Don B. Chae (Dem.) .... 509,619 ...... 46.44%
   Total Vote 1,097,347

Justice, Fifth District, Place 6
David L. Bridges (Rep.) .... 569,570 ...... 52.05%
David Hanschen (Dem.) .... 524,637 ...... 47.94%
   Total Vote 1,094,207

Justice, Fifth District, Place 8
Kerry Fitzgerald (Rep.) .... 578,233 ...... 52.73%
Tina Yoo (Dem.) .... 518,339 ...... 47.26%
   Total Vote 1,096,572

Justice, Eighth District, Place 3
Kenneth R. "Kenn" Carr (Rep.) .... 68,432 ...... 33.51%
Guadalupe "Lupe" Rivera (Dem.) .... 135,725 ...... 66.48%
   Total Vote 204,157

Justice, Tenth District, Place 2
Rex Davis (Rep.) .... 221,291 ...... 63.92%
Richard Ferguson (Dem.) .... 124,879 ...... 36.07%
   Total Vote 346,170

Justice, Thirteenth District, Place 6
Caroline Bertuzzi (Rep.) .... 179,848 ...... 41.41%
Dori Contreras Garza (Dem.) .... 254,433 ...... 58.58%
   Total Vote 434,281

Justice, Fourteenth District, Place 4
Jeff Brown (Rep.) .... 806,648 ...... 51.61%
Bert Moser (Dem.) .... 756,035 ...... 48.38%
   Total Vote 1,562,683

Justice, Fourteenth District, Place 6
Bill Boyce (Rep.) .... 793,829 ...... 50.82%
Mary M. Markantonis (Dem.) .... 768,014 ...... 49.17%
   Total Vote 1,561,843

Justice, Fourteenth District, Place 7
Kem Thompson Frost (Rep.) .... 790,831 ...... 50.64%
Martin J. Siegel (Dem.) .... 770,586 ...... 49.35%
   Total Vote 1,561,417

STATE BOARD OF EDUCATION
District 2
Peter H. Johnston (Rep.)....................152,165 ...... 40.50%
Mary Helen Berlanga (Dem.)..............223,465.......59.49%
Total Vote 375,630

District 6
Terri Leo (Rep.)...............................332,910 ....79.27%
Mary Ann Bryan (Lib.)..........................87,056 ....20.72%
Total Vote 419,966

District 7
David Bradley (Rep.) ....287,175 ....53.66%
Laura Ewing (Dem.)..........................233,238 ....43.58%
Richard R. Johnson (Lib.)....................14,667 ....2.74%
Total Vote 535,080

District 8
Barbara Cargill (Rep.).........................401,363 ...... 85.32%
Kim B. Stroman (Lib.) ....65,105 ..... 13.84%
Linda Ellis (W-I) ....3,908 .... 0.83%
Total Vote 470,376

District 11
Patricia "Pat" Hardy (Rep.) ....446,231 ....84.29%
Bruce Beckman (Lib.) ....83,121 ....15.70%
Total Vote 529,352

District 13
Cindy Werner (Rep.)............................95,706 ....25.54%
Mavis Best Knight (Dem.)...................278,896 ....74.45%
Total Vote 374.602

District 14
Gail Lowe (Rep.)...............................376,415 ....64.99%
Edra Bogie (Dem.)............................181,405 ....31.32%
John E. Shuey (Lib.) ....21,352 ....3.68%
Total Vote 579,172

STATE SENATE
District 6
Gilbert Pena (Rep.)...............................27,751 ....26.63%
Mario V. Gallegos Jr. (Dem.)................72,960 ....70.01%
Susan Delgado (Lib.)..............................3,496 ....3.35%
Total Vote 104,207

District 9
Chris Harris (Rep.)............................125,443 ...... 54.08%
Melvin Willms (Dem.).........................100,509 ...... 43.33%
Carl Nulsen (Lib.)..................................5,991 .... 2.58%
Total Vote 231,943

District 10
Kim Brimer (Rep.)..............................140,737 ....47.52%
Wendy R. Davis (Dem.).....................147,832 ....49.91%
Richard A. Cross (Lib.) ....7,591 ....2.56%
Total Vote 296,160

District 11
Mike Jackson (Rep.)...........................155,772 ....56.48%
Joe Jaworski (Dem.)...........................113,567 ....41.18%
Cliff Messina (Lib.)................................6,419 ....2.32%
Total Vote 275,758

District 16
John Carona (Rep.)............................122,439 ....56.26%
Rain Levy Minns (Dem.).......................89,346 ....41.05%
Paul E. Osborn (Lib.)............................5,825 ....2.67%
Total Vote 217,610

District 17 (unexpired term)
*(After Republican Kyle Janek resigned, the governor
called a special election to coincide with the general
election to fill the vacant seat.)*
Chris Bell (Dem.) ....85,725 ....38.39%
Austen Furse (Rep.) ....22,588 ....10.11%
Grant Harpold (Rep.) ....9,056 ....4.05%
Joan Huffman (Rep.) ....58,359 ....26.13%
Ken Sherman (Rep.)............................16,728 ....7.49%
Stephanie E. Simmons (Dem.).............30,839 ....13.81%
Total Vote 223,295

Runoff for District 17 (held Dec. 16)
Chris Bell (Dem.) ....19,176 ....43.90%
Joan Huffman (Rep.) ....24,497 ....56.09%
Total Vote 43,673

District 20
Juan "Chuy" Hinojosa (Dem.).............124,456 ....81.40%
Billy "Bill" Parker (Lib.) ....28,429 ....18.59%
Total Vote 152,885

District 21
Louis H. Bruni (Rep.)...........................55,480 ....29.15%
Judith Zaffirini (Dem.) ....129,802 ....68.22%
Barry L. Allison (Lib.) ....4,980 ....2.61%
Total Vote 190,262

District 23
Royce West (Dem.) ....176,451 ....92.40%
Jim Renfro (Lib.) ....14,503 ....7.59%
Total Vote 190,954

District 24
Troy Fraser (Rep.) ....197,125 ....85,46%
Bill Oliver (Lib.) ....33,518 ....14.53%
Total Vote 230,643

District 26
Leticia Van de Putte (Dem.)...............136,913 ....81.44%
Steve Lopez (Lib.) ....31,194 ....18.55%
Total Vote 168,107

District 28
Robert Duncan (Rep.) ....179,059 ....88.17%
M.J. "Smitty" Smith (Lib.)....................24,022 ....11.82%
Total Vote 203,081

District 31
Kel Seliger (Rep.) ....180,267 ....90.20%
Lauren Poindexter (Lib.).......................19,569 ....9.79%
Total Vote 199,836

Texas Primary Elections, 2008

Below are the official returns for the contested races only in the Republican and Democratic Party primaries held March 4, 2008. Included are statewide races and selected district races. The runoffs were held on April 8.

DEMOCRATIC PRIMARY

President
Hillary Clinton ....1,462,734 ....50.87%
Barack Obama...............................1,362,476 ....47.39%
John Edwards.....................................29,936 ....1.04%
Bill Richardson.....................................10,773 ....0.37%
Joe Biden..5,290 ....0.18%
Christopher J. Dodd..............................3,777 ....0.13%
Total vote....................................2,874,986

U.S. Senator
Richard J. "Rick" Noriega ....1,110,579 ....51.00%
Gene Kelly..584,966 ....26.86%
Ray McMurrey ....269,402 ....12.37%
Rhett R. Smith ....212,305 ....9.75%
Total Vote....................................2,177,252

U.S. HOUSE OF REPRESENTATIVES
District 3
Tom Daley..33,529 ....71.62%

Ronald E. "Ron" Minkow...................... 13,305 .... 28.37%
    Total Vote...................................... 46,897

District 4
VaLinda Hathcox .... 27,766 .... 42.59%
Glenn Melancon .... 37,416 ...... 57.40%
    Total Vote...................................... 65,182

District 6
Steve Bush .... 31,959 .... 49.18%
Ludwig Otto .... 33,021 .... 50.81%
    Total Vote...................................... 64,980

District 10
Larry Joe Doherty .... 51,977 .... 61.11%
Dan Grant... 33,072 .... 38.88%
    Total Vote...................................... 85,049

District 16
Silvestre Reyes.................................. 75,058 .... 80.42%
Jorge Artalejo...................................... 18,274 .... 19.57%
    Total Vote...................................... 93,332

District 19
Dwight Fullingim .... 26,966 .... 61.63%
Rufus Mark .... 16,786 .... 38.36%
    Total Vote...................................... 43,752

District 32
Dennis Burns....................................... 9,705 .... 21.72%
Steve Love... 14,929 .... 33.41%
Eric Roberson.................................... 20,043 .... 44.86%
    Total Vote...................................... 44,677

RAILROAD COMMISSIONER
Art Hall... 467,794 .... 23.97%
Dale Henry....................................... 540,175 .... 27.68%
Mark Thompson................................. 943,326 .... 48.34%
    Total Vote.................................. 1,951,295

STATE SUPREME COURT
Justice, Place 7
Baltasar D. Cruz .... 899,365 .... 44.05%
Sam Houston.................................. 1,133,077 .... 55.94%
    Total Vote.................................. 2,025,442

Justice, Place 8
Susan Criss .... 975,699 .... 48.56%
Linda Reyna Yañez .... 1,033,218 .... 51.43%
    Total Vote.................................. 2,008,917

COURTS OF APPEALS
Justice, Eighth District, Place 3
David C. Guaderrama........................... 37,864 .... 38.43%
Guadalupe "Lupe" Rivera .... 60,813 .... 61.56%
    Total Vote...................................... 98,777

STATE BOARD OF EDUCATION
District 2
Mary Helen Berlanga........................... 94,343 .... 56.29%
Lupe A. Gonzalez .... 73,246 .... 43.70%
    Total Vote.................................... 167,589

STATE SENATE
District 11
Bryan Hermann .... 23,880 .... 40.95%
Joe Jaworski....................................... 34,433 .... 59.04%
    Total Vote...................................... 58,313

District 21
Judith Zaffirini .... 85,168 .... 78.60%
Rene Barrientos.................................. 23,179 .... 21.39%
    Total Vote.................................... 108,347

DEMOCRATIC RUNOFF

U.S. HOUSE OF REPRESENTATIVES
District 32
Steve Love.. 753 .... 27.54%

Eric Roberson...................................... 1,981 .... 72.45%
    Total Vote.. 2,734

RAILROAD COMMISSIONER
Dale Henry....................................... 76,582 .... 40.79%
Mark Thompson................................ 111,126 .... 59.20%
    Total Vote.................................... 187,708

REPUBLICAN PRIMARY
President
John McCain...................................... 697,767 .... 51.21%
Mike Huckabee.................................. 518,002 .... 38.02%
Ron Paul... 66,360 .... 4.87%
Mitt Romney .... 27,264 .... 2.00%
Fred Thompson .... 11,503 .... 0.84%
Alan Keyes .... 8,260 .... 0.60%
Duncan Hunter .... 8,222 .... 0.60%
Rudy Giuliani .... 6,038 .... 0.44%
Hugh Cort .... 728 .... 0.05%
Hoa Tran .... 604 .... 0.04%
Uncommitted .... 17,574 .... 1.29%
    Total vote.................................. 1,362,322

U.S. Senator
John Cornyn .... 997,216 .... 81.48%
Larry Kilgore .... 226,649 .... 18.51%
    Total Vote.................................. 1,223,865

U.S. HOUSE OF REPRESENTATIVES
District 3
Sam Johnson..................................... 36,050 .... 86.93%
Wayne Avellanet.................................. 1,952 .... 4.70%
Harry Pierce... 3,466 .... 8.35%
    Total Vote...................................... 41,468

District 4
Ralph M. Hall...................................... 41,764 .... 73.38%
Gene Christensen................................. 5,492 .... 9.65%
Kevin George.. 2,965 .... 5.21%
Joshua Kowert.. 852 .... 1.49%
Kathy Seel .... 5,836 .... 10.25%
    Total Vote...................................... 56,908

District 14
Ron Paul... 37,777 .... 70.43%
W. Chris Peden.................................. 15,859 .... 29.56%
    Total Vote...................................... 53,636

District 18
John Faulk.. 5,638 .... 78.55%
TJ Baker Holm...................................... 1,539 .... 21.44%
    Total Vote.. 7,177

District 22
Shelley Sekula Gibbs .... 16,697 .... 29.72%
Kevyn Bazzy... 880 .... 1.56%
Cynthia Dunbar..................................... 2,116 .... 3.76%
Dean Hrbacek....................................... 5,864 .... 10.44%
Brian Klock... 992 .... 1.76%
John Manlove .... 8,399 .... 14.95%
Pete Olson .... 11,634 .... 20.71%
Ryan Rowley .... 424 .... 0.75%
Jim Squier... 989 .... 1.76%
Robert Talton .... 8,163 .... 14.54%
    Total Vote...................................... 56,164

District 23
Lyle Larson .... 18,681 .... 61.54%
Quico Canseco .... 11,671 .... 38.45%
    Total Vote...................................... 30,352

District 27
George Benavidez................................. 7,236 .... 43.78%
William Willie Vaden .... 9,292 .... 56.21%
    Total Vote...................................... 16,528

STATE COURTS
Judge, Court of Criminal Appeals, Place 4
Paul Womack .... 678,726 .... 68.63%
Robert Frances................................... 310,108 .... 31.36%
Total Vote..................................... 988,834

STATE BOARD OF EDUCATION
District 11
Patricia "Pat" Hardy .... 59,016 .... 59.06%
Barney Maddox .... 40,896 .... 40.93%
Total Vote..................................... 99,912

STATE SENATE
District 4
Tommy Williams.................................... 26,677 .... 60.50%
Michael Galloway .... 17,415 .... 39.49%
Total Vote..................................... 44,092

District 30
Craig Estes... 41,106 .... 70.07%
Charles R. Stafford .... 18,838 .... 29.92%
Total Vote..................................... 62,944

COURTS OF APPEALS
Chief Justice, Ninth District
Steve McKeithen .... 25,785 .... 52.93%

Jay M. Wright....................................... 22,925 .... 47.06%
Total Vote..................................... 48,710

Justice, First District, Place 3
Sam Nuchia .... 82,156 .... 42.67%
Ed Hubbard .... 110,358 ...... 57.32%
Total Vote..................................... 192,514

Justice, Second District, Place 2
Deeia Beck .... 27,922 .... 20.25%
Barcus "Barc" Hunter.......................... 25,018 .... 18.15%
Bill Meier.. 84,899 ...... 61.59%
Total Vote..................................... 137,839

Justice, Fourteenth District, Place 6
Bill Boyce... 104,909 .... 58.54%
James "Jim" C. Holland Jr. .... 74,276 .... 41.45%
Total Vote..................................... 179,185

REPUBLICAN RUNOFF

U.S. HOUSE OF REPRESENTATIVES
District 22
Shelley Sekula Gibbs .... 7,125 .... 31.47%
Pete Olson.. 15,511 .... 68.52%
Total Vote..................................... 22,636

2008 Presidential Primaries: Results by County

Below are the results by county in the presidential party primaries that were held March 4. This table lists the principal candidates still in the presidential race at the time of the Texas primary.

The candidates in the Democratic primary were: New York Sen. Hillary Clinton and Illinois Sen. Barack Obama. In the Republican primary were: Ari-zona Sen. John McCain, former Arkansas Gov. Mike Huckabee, and U.S. Rep. Ron Paul of Texas.

Beside the number of votes received by each candidate is listed the percent of the total vote received by each candidate. When no votes are reported, no primary was held in that county by the party. *Source: Texas Secretary of State.*

DEMOCRATIC PRIMARY				County	REPUBLICAN PRIMARY					
Clinton	%	Obama	%		McCain	%	Huckabee	%	Paul	%
1,462,734	50.9	1,362,476	47.4	Statewide	697,767	51.2	518,002	38.0	66,360	4.9
2,975	56.1	2,182	41.1	Anderson	2,101	50.0	1,816	43.2	156	3.7
674	53.8	448	35.8	Andrews	480	48.8	446	45.4	15	1.5
7,714	61.3	4,329	34.4	Angelina	2,254	45.2	2,389	47.9	146	2.9
1,402	57.0	1,018	41.4	Aransas	2,667	63.6	882	21.0	300	7.2
785	68.7	296	25.9	Archer	742	57.6	458	35.5	26	2.0
0	-	0	-	Armstrong	194	37.0	226	43.0	59	11.2
3,451	61.7	1,971	35.3	Atascosa	923	51.7	740	41.5	54	3.0
1,745	58.3	1,218	40.7	Austin	1,413	48.2	1,166	39.8	159	5.4
306	60.4	175	34.5	Bailey	376	55.1	266	39.0	13	1.9
954	54.0	783	44.3	Bandera	2,312	56.8	1,155	28.4	241	5.9
5,573	49.5	5,409	48.0	Bastrop	2,085	44.5	1,759	37.6	613	13.1
613	67.4	186	20.4	Baylor	82	62.1	45	34.1	3	2.3
2,724	61.7	1,429	32.4	Bee	513	56.1	326	35.6	34	3.7
9,837	40.6	14,193	58.5	Bell	10,451	58.4	5,639	31.5	803	4.5
114,391	56.0	87,583	42.9	Bexar	39,329	56.5	23,971	34.4	2,763	4.0
675	48.5	698	50.1	Blanco	483	45.6	418	39.5	93	8.8
93	66.9	32	23.0	Borden	0	-	0	-	0	-
1,901	61.2	949	30.6	Bosque	744	51.5	599	41.5	33	2.3
6,224	62.8	3,237	32.7	Bowie	1,850	24.5	5,458	72.2	134	1.8
14,636	50.1	14,209	48.7	Brazoria	10,683	45.4	8,030	34.1	3,612	15.3
5,863	42.4	7,835	56.6	Brazos	6,348	48.1	5,405	41.0	712	5.4
989	44.0	1,168	51.9	Brewster	470	51.3	286	31.2	117	12.8
164	59.9	90	32.8	Briscoe	132	48.2	120	43.8	4	1.5
2,294	72.0	763	24.0	Brooks	0	-	0	-	0	-
1,717	65.8	803	30.8	Brown	2,860	55.2	1,902	36.7	146	2.8

Barack Obama led in only 24 counties, including Houston (Harris County) and its western suburbs, and Fort Worth (Tarrant County) and Dallas and their northern suburbs. He also led in the counties north and southwest of Austin (Travis County).

Democratic Primary

- ● Obama
- ○ Clinton

In Coryell County, the vote was tied.

No Democratic primary was held in the counties in white.

DEMOCRATIC PRIMARY				County	REPUBLICAN PRIMARY					
Clinton	%	Obama	%		McCain	%	Huckabee	%	Paul	%
1,335	60.2	826	37.3	**Burleson**	648	49.4	544	41.4	66	5.0
2,453	56.8	1,807	41.8	**Burnet**	3,318	57.6	1,829	31.8	298	5.2
2,738	53.4	2,252	44.0	**Caldwell**	730	43.6	663	39.6	197	11.8
2,222	59.9	1,252	33.7	**Calhoun**	428	52.3	271	33.1	91	11.1
848	59.6	527	37.1	**Callahan**	556	42.7	659	50.6	39	3.0
32,824	67.6	14,836	30.6	**Cameron**	2,910	60.3	1,238	25.7	283	5.9
953	51.0	847	45.3	**Camp**	360	48.9	329	44.7	20	2.7
399	69.5	148	25.8	**Carson**	436	44.5	467	47.7	29	3.0
3,692	66.9	1,463	26.5	**Cass**	425	28.6	961	64.8	69	4.6
581	61.8	303	32.2	**Castro**	200	49.9	183	45.6	6	1.5
1,958	57.8	1,339	39.5	**Chambers**	1,640	48.6	1,260	37.3	265	7.8
2,950	56.4	2,121	40.6	**Cherokee**	2,052	51.2	1,684	42.0	101	2.5
433	68.1	173	27.2	**Childress**	178	51.9	151	44.0	4	1.2
1,436	69.3	459	22.1	**Clay**	644	57.2	398	35.4	33	2.9
184	55.9	116	35.3	**Cochran**	121	43.1	151	53.7	1	0.4
405	53.4	226	29.8	**Coke**	65	48.9	57	42.9	2	1.5
503	71.4	164	23.3	**Coleman**	956	53.8	645	36.3	30	1.7
32,064	44.2	40,113	55.3	**Collin**	24,606	47.7	21,777	42.2	2,095	4.1
332	60.4	156	28.4	**Collingsworth**	85	44.0	94	48.7	5	2.6
1,693	57.4	1,190	40.3	**Colorado**	947	51.0	685	36.9	132	7.1
5,047	50.7	4,817	48.4	**Comal**	8,026	53.7	5,199	34.8	727	4.9
1,345	66.6	553	27.4	**Comanche**	420	47.2	400	44.9	37	4.2
214	62.9	111	32.6	**Concho**	173	53.6	117	36.2	8	2.5
1,738	62.4	987	35.4	**Cooke**	3,128	53.4	2,090	35.7	247	4.2
2,434	49.1	2,434	49.1	**Coryell**	2,007	57.7	1,161	33.4	114	3.3

DEMOCRATIC PRIMARY				County	REPUBLICAN PRIMARY					
Clinton	%	Obama	%		McCain	%	Huckabee	%	Paul	%
276	58.6	113	24.0	Cottle	0	-	0	-	0	-
282	48.4	235	40.3	Crane	172	53.8	119	37.2	8	2.5
566	48.5	414	35.5	Crockett	0	-	0	-	0	-
641	55.7	373	32.4	Crosby	49	35.0	83	59.3	0	0.0
312	59.3	175	33.3	Culberson	0	-	0	-	0	-
135	57.7	88	37.6	Dallam	306	47.9	273	42.7	18	2.8
113,460	38.1	182,619	61.3	Dallas	47,245	51.3	36,521	39.7	3,856	4.2
777	62.4	402	32.3	Dawson	749	52.6	562	39.5	33	2.3
604	62.4	336	34.7	Deaf Smith	992	53.6	687	37.1	19	1.0
656	69.7	219	23.3	Delta	269	41.4	304	46.8	18	2.8
24,103	44.0	30,468	55.6	Denton	17,266	44.7	17,166	44.5	1,766	4.6
996	57.5	699	40.4	DeWitt	1,058	56.5	542	28.9	183	9.8
335	54.7	194	31.7	Dickens	0	-	0	-	0	-
2,149	67.7	886	27.9	Dimmit	10	55.6	7	38.9	1	5.6
297	64.4	119	25.8	Donley	208	47.2	192	43.5	12	2.7
3,913	77.4	988	19.6	Duval	0	-	0	-	0	-
1,104	71.7	374	24.3	Eastland	954	44.4	1,047	48.7	34	1.6
5,347	65.3	2,717	33.2	Ector	5,755	55.4	3,708	35.7	287	2.8
175	54.5	131	40.8	Edwards	146	53.9	99	36.5	10	3.7
7,086	54.7	5,725	44.2	Ellis	6,151	46.1	6,198	46.4	445	3.3
71,298	69.1	30,019	29.1	El Paso	12,494	66.7	4,040	21.6	535	2.9
1,696	62.4	971	35.7	Erath	1,474	45.2	1,499	46.0	110	3.4
1,335	50.8	1,188	45.2	Falls	469	55.0	295	34.6	36	4.2
2,976	70.6	1,115	26.4	Fannin	1,361	48.5	1,179	42.0	116	4.1
3,068	55.1	2,087	37.5	Fayette	830	54.7	460	30.3	156	10.3
751	64.3	304	26.0	Fisher	29	33.7	51	59.3	3	3.5
345	59.8	213	36.9	Floyd	455	49.0	393	42.3	20	2.2
264	61.1	108	25.0	Foard	0	-	0	-	0	-
25,670	36.8	43,893	62.9	Fort Bend	18,652	53.0	11,521	32.8	1,950	5.5
798	68.9	313	27.0	Franklin	548	47.0	539	46.2	31	2.7
1,551	55.4	1,100	39.3	Freestone	599	48.4	553	44.7	41	3.3
2,650	62.7	1,348	31.9	Frio	17	31.5	26	48.1	6	11.1
373	62.6	197	33.1	Gaines	837	48.6	690	40.1	29	1.7
20,435	51.7	18,522	46.8	Galveston	7,606	48.9	5,726	36.8	1,326	8.5
316	50.2	226	35.9	Garza	222	48.4	197	42.9	10	2.2
953	46.6	1,067	52.2	Gillespie	3,445	59.9	1,409	24.5	471	8.2
11	57.9	8	42.1	Glasscock	250	56.6	105	23.8	40	9.0
722	57.3	509	40.4	Goliad	459	55.8	212	25.8	111	13.5
1,563	51.5	1,254	41.3	Gonzales	534	51.7	372	36.0	90	8.7
738	60.9	421	34.7	Gray	1,539	48.9	1,412	44.8	48	1.5
7,431	62.0	4,359	36.4	Grayson	5,332	51.3	4,230	40.7	294	2.8
4,580	40.9	6,503	58.1	Gregg	5,893	52.5	4,542	40.4	395	3.5
1,546	54.7	1,206	42.7	Grimes	849	46.0	809	43.8	88	4.8
5,943	47.4	6,468	51.6	Guadalupe	5,836	53.6	3,858	35.4	562	5.2
1,317	58.5	875	38.9	Hale	1,094	46.5	1,121	47.7	41	1.7
493	60.6	205	25.2	Hall	0	-	0	-	0	-
800	56.2	507	35.6	Hamilton	385	50.6	314	41.3	26	3.4
0	-	0	-	Hansford	654	52.9	459	37.1	22	1.8
640	58.9	246	22.7	Hardeman	0	-	0	-	0	-
6,045	68.1	2,090	23.5	Hardin	1,210	47.7	1,104	43.5	98	3.9
176,268	43.3	228,610	56.2	Harris	87,567	51.7	57,945	34.2	9,153	5.4
4,744	51.7	4,057	44.2	Harrison	1,731	39.4	2,309	52.5	192	4.4
215	66.8	87	27.0	Hartley	375	48.5	361	46.7	17	2.2
897	69.1	293	22.6	Haskell	60	42.9	67	47.9	10	7.1
8,595	42.9	11,256	56.2	Hays	3,594	44.9	2,782	34.8	1,310	16.4
81	64.3	37	29.4	Hemphill	593	57.7	352	34.2	17	1.7
5,260	63.7	2,815	34.1	Henderson	5,003	52.8	3,685	38.9	212	2.2
61,581	72.5	21,978	25.9	Hidalgo	3,163	55.0	1,914	33.3	265	4.6
2,861	67.7	1,264	29.9	Hill	1,813	50.2	1,513	41.9	90	2.5
810	60.4	503	37.5	Hockley	1,439	52.1	1,141	41.3	36	1.3

Mike Huckabee led in 50 counties, including many in Northeast Texas and several in the Panhandle-Plains region. No Republican primary was held in 21 counties.

Republican Primary

● **Huckabee**
○ **McCain**

In Stephens County, the vote was tied.

No Republican primary was held in the counties in white.

DEMOCRATIC PRIMARY				County	REPUBLICAN PRIMARY					
Clinton	%	Obama	%		McCain	%	Huckabee	%	Paul	%
3,070	63.1	1,694	34.8	**Hood**	4,205	56.0	2,614	34.8	226	3.0
2,898	65.4	1,385	31.3	**Hopkins**	1,040	40.9	1,328	52.3	78	3.1
1,486	49.2	1,379	45.6	**Houston**	1,407	55.3	956	37.5	72	2.8
1,459	64.0	751	32.9	**Howard**	1,641	52.5	1,209	38.7	64	2.0
291	61.0	140	29.4	**Hudspeth**	0	-	0	-	0	-
4,664	61.0	2,839	37.1	**Hunt**	3,652	43.9	3,905	46.9	285	3.4
1,015	66.0	482	31.3	**Hutchinson**	1,588	50.1	1,411	44.5	52	1.6
230	44.9	205	40.0	**Irion**	43	55.8	28	36.4	1	1.3
492	63.6	241	31.2	**Jack**	254	45.1	264	46.9	18	3.2
1,106	57.8	697	36.4	**Jackson**	439	46.9	350	37.4	106	11.3
4,086	57.9	2,208	31.3	**Jasper**	435	43.3	494	49.2	38	3.8
312	45.8	300	44.1	**Jeff Davis**	99	49.3	64	31.8	24	11.9
17,262	40.4	24,744	57.9	**Jefferson**	4,061	53.1	2,772	36.2	376	4.9
1,726	75.7	470	20.6	**Jim Hogg**	5	41.7	7	58.3	0	0.0
7,033	71.1	2,502	25.3	**Jim Wells**	242	53.8	176	39.1	17	3.8
4,857	68.7	2,142	30.3	**Johnson**	4,579	43.8	4,937	47.2	407	3.9
1,452	70.6	523	25.4	**Jones**	460	41.7	556	50.4	37	3.4
1,615	54.9	1,101	37.4	**Karnes**	130	46.8	109	39.2	29	10.4
5,462	56.2	4,176	42.9	**Kaufman**	3,604	44.6	3,885	48.1	181	2.2
1,294	44.8	1,577	54.6	**Kendall**	3,507	55.8	2,058	32.7	276	4.4
121	65.4	50	27.0	**Kenedy**	7	70.0	2	20.0	0	0.0
152	60.8	52	20.8	**Kent**	0	-	0	-	0	-
2,196	48.2	2,303	50.5	**Kerr**	5,096	58.8	2,458	28.4	411	4.7
167	58.8	111	39.1	**Kimble**	614	62.0	273	27.5	35	3.5
36	42.9	27	32.1	**King**	8	40.0	10	50.0	0	0.0

DEMOCRATIC PRIMARY				County	REPUBLICAN PRIMARY					
Clinton	%	Obama	%		McCain	%	Huckabee	%	Paul	%
502	51.4	412	42.2	Kinney	103	51.2	83	41.3	7	3.5
3,815	64.0	1,915	32.1	Kleberg	482	58.0	268	32.3	42	5.1
366	67.4	151	27.8	Knox	111	46.4	115	48.1	4	1.7
5,566	61.6	2,801	31.0	Lamar	993	42.5	1,172	50.1	82	3.5
807	61.4	421	32.0	Lamb	508	42.0	643	53.2	22	1.8
900	56.1	673	41.9	Lampasas	1,479	58.6	748	29.7	125	5.0
845	60.7	467	33.5	La Salle	0	-	0	-	0	-
2,541	61.1	1,231	29.6	Lavaca	509	50.2	324	32.0	136	13.4
1,535	52.3	1,197	40.8	Lee	343	44.5	318	41.3	78	10.1
1,300	64.0	624	30.7	Leon	989	52.2	760	40.1	66	3.5
5,172	61.3	2,837	33.6	Liberty	1,365	38.7	1,881	53.3	151	4.3
1,932	50.5	1,537	40.1	Limestone	572	49.6	493	42.8	38	3.3
146	69.2	57	27.0	Lipscomb	211	45.9	221	48.0	6	1.3
902	63.1	485	33.9	Live Oak	428	57.8	268	36.2	18	2.4
1,206	57.6	856	40.9	Llano	2,785	61.8	1,186	26.3	206	4.6
5	20.8	7	29.2	Loving	0	-	0	-	0	-
12,638	52.8	10,965	45.8	Lubbock	12,722	54.3	8,856	37.8	563	2.4
431	66.6	178	27.5	Lynn	226	48.4	209	44.8	11	2.4
796	56.7	535	38.1	Madison	341	46.8	313	42.9	38	5.2
1,204	52.6	889	38.9	Marion	158	40.8	194	50.1	20	5.2
284	62.0	148	32.3	Martin	298	48.1	257	41.5	14	2.3
201	48.8	198	48.1	Mason	669	59.0	316	27.9	57	5.0
3,353	52.6	2,639	41.4	Matagorda	861	47.3	701	38.5	194	10.7
6,970	72.1	1,387	14.4	Maverick	0	-	0	-	0	-
523	66.5	239	30.4	McCulloch	529	56.8	314	33.7	30	3.2
12,277	50.1	11,862	48.4	McLennan	9,935	54.4	7,141	39.1	489	2.7
170	47.4	140	39.0	McMullen	22	57.9	11	28.9	1	2.6
2,654	61.1	1,610	37.1	Medina	2,674	57.5	1,484	31.9	152	3.3
188	62.0	105	34.7	Menard	217	60.3	94	26.1	9	2.5
3,868	51.0	3,603	47.5	Midland	7,189	54.9	4,669	35.7	474	3.6
2,749	56.6	1,668	34.4	Milam	360	49.9	287	39.8	33	4.6
460	59.6	232	30.1	Mills	242	49.7	173	35.5	29	6.0
665	61.9	280	26.0	Mitchell	196	56.0	137	39.1	12	3.4
1,647	69.1	616	25.8	Montague	1,178	53.5	824	37.4	83	3.8
17,299	55.8	13,443	43.4	Montgomery	20,874	50.6	15,995	38.8	1,791	4.3
549	64.4	278	32.6	Moore	1,214	48.2	1,066	42.3	28	1.1
1,637	57.1	967	33.7	Morris	124	37.5	196	59.2	4	1.2
97	64.7	44	29.3	Motley	76	42.9	80	45.2	1	0.6
3,005	51.1	2,788	47.4	Nacogdoches	3,650	55.4	2,392	36.3	249	3.8
3,289	56.2	2,395	40.9	Navarro	1,924	51.6	1,553	41.7	85	2.3
1,641	59.4	818	29.6	Newton	132	42.7	145	46.9	20	6.5
1,746	57.3	885	29.0	Nolan	137	47.7	134	46.7	7	2.4
32,125	65.6	16,252	33.2	Nueces	8,139	63.4	3,604	28.1	555	4.3
72	59.0	44	36.1	Ochiltree	1,176	57.7	686	33.6	37	1.8
125	54.6	70	30.6	Oldham	76	39.2	108	55.7	4	2.1
10,317	66.0	4,143	26.5	Orange	1,487	48.2	1,327	43.0	134	4.3
2,148	69.8	807	26.2	Palo Pinto	999	50.1	778	39.0	80	4.0
2,887	59.5	1,440	29.7	Panola	312	36.4	494	57.6	33	3.8
6,006	65.6	2,998	32.8	Parker	7,076	46.3	6,373	41.7	794	5.2
367	58.1	248	39.2	Parmer	395	48.6	386	47.5	9	1.1
1,119	59.1	624	32.9	Pecos	276	52.8	192	36.7	23	4.4
4,004	63.4	2,078	32.9	Polk	2,398	53.9	1,647	37.0	154	3.5
4,080	56.4	2,994	41.4	Potter	4,558	51.1	3,656	41.0	201	2.3
977	57.4	636	37.3	Presidio	17	48.6	9	25.7	6	17.1
1,095	70.5	399	25.7	Rains	385	46.0	398	47.6	27	3.2
5,894	60.8	3,672	37.9	Randall	6,948	46.1	7,218	47.9	287	1.9
44	61.1	26	36.1	Reagan	444	57.3	195	25.2	13	1.7
125	62.2	75	37.3	Real	545	58.1	299	31.9	49	5.2
2,045	64.1	854	26.8	Red River	70	33.5	113	54.1	21	10.0
1,448	65.0	628	28.2	Reeves	0	-	0	-	0	-

DEMOCRATIC PRIMARY				County	REPUBLICAN PRIMARY					
Clinton	%	Obama	%		McCain	%	Huckabee	%	Paul	%
1,178	56.2	815	38.9	Refugio	166	60.1	73	26.4	26	9.4
0	-	0	-	Roberts	137	52.5	101	38.7	9	3.4
1,744	49.3	1,579	44.6	Robertson	352	47.1	340	45.5	19	2.5
3,982	50.3	3,885	49.1	Rockwall	3,678	47.7	3,439	44.6	219	2.8
686	61.0	393	34.9	Runnels	472	56.4	323	38.6	16	1.9
2,550	49.9	2,398	47.0	Rusk	2,577	49.5	2,311	44.4	123	2.4
1,762	64.9	668	24.6	Sabine	540	57.3	351	37.2	22	2.3
1,498	53.4	972	34.7	SanAugustine	76	42.7	82	46.1	12	6.7
2,475	58.7	1,462	34.7	San Jacinto	691	46.9	653	44.3	60	4.1
6,320	67.7	2,791	29.9	San Patricio	1,830	60.4	940	31.0	127	4.2
351	68.3	143	27.8	San Saba	156	53.6	105	36.1	17	5.8
185	53.2	140	40.2	Schleicher	138	52.9	100	38.3	13	5.0
643	66.8	292	30.3	Scurry	1,270	58.9	693	32.2	50	2.3
451	62.7	156	21.7	Shackelford	65	43.6	77	51.7	2	1.3
2,418	65.8	1,044	28.4	Shelby	722	41.6	912	52.6	57	3.3
118	60.5	66	33.8	Sherman	227	48.8	206	44.3	6	1.3
7,401	39.7	11,125	59.6	Smith	12,290	54.4	8,721	38.6	565	2.5
704	63.7	348	31.5	Somervell	355	47.0	349	46.2	27	3.6
7,360	82.6	1,454	16.3	Starr	52	50.5	37	35.9	10	9.7
709	62.3	326	28.6	Stephens	271	48.0	271	48.0	4	0.7
64	76.2	17	20.2	Sterling	141	65.6	60	27.9	4	1.9
303	62.7	108	22.4	Stonewall	0	-	0	-	0	-
298	66.5	132	29.5	Sutton	189	62.0	97	31.8	9	3.0
851	63.4	336	25.0	Swisher	39	27.5	94	66.2	1	0.7
90,417	45.3	108,105	54.1	Tarrant	48,104	47.7	42,854	42.5	4,489	4.5
6,350	58.7	4,302	39.7	Taylor	6,405	49.7	5,535	43.0	386	3.0
125	59.5	69	32.9	Terrell	31	44.3	32	45.7	5	7.1
1,115	50.5	756	34.3	Terry	160	50.3	135	42.5	6	1.9
401	67.3	131	22.0	Throckmorton	0	-	0	-	0	-
2,712	56.8	1,565	32.8	Titus	333	33.4	600	60.2	23	2.3
5,874	57.2	4,239	41.3	Tom Green	5,221	59.2	2,892	32.8	229	2.6
68,303	36.8	116,314	62.6	Travis	7,191	48.3	4,054	27.2	3,070	20.6
2,528	57.9	1,275	29.2	Trinity	162	50.2	137	42.4	15	4.6
2,772	65.7	1,047	24.8	Tyler	507	51.2	401	40.5	42	4.2
3,545	60.9	1,915	32.9	Upshur	1,219	41.3	1,438	48.7	152	5.1
373	45.7	308	37.7	Upton	0	-	0	-	0	-
2,772	60.3	1,590	34.6	Uvalde	719	52.1	522	37.8	48	3.5
3,503	64.0	1,856	33.9	Val Verde	669	54.8	435	35.6	33	2.7
4,407	71.4	1,580	25.6	Van Zandt	2,353	43.4	2,711	50.1	156	2.9
5,621	58.8	3,622	37.9	Victoria	3,106	53.7	1,429	24.7	973	16.8
2,772	48.2	2,861	49.8	Walker	2,468	50.8	1,842	37.9	264	5.4
1,567	32.1	3,272	67.0	Waller	1,722	49.6	1,447	41.7	222	6.4
1,189	53.7	647	29.2	Ward	77	51.3	59	39.3	9	6.0
1,285	40.8	1,827	58.1	Washington	3,098	56.2	1,810	32.8	251	4.6
32,383	77.3	8,615	20.6	Webb	833	67.6	231	18.8	64	5.2
2,692	53.5	2,197	43.7	Wharton	1,914	53.6	1,161	32.5	357	10.0
460	58.4	192	24.4	Wheeler	160	28.4	232	41.2	2	0.4
7,468	58.7	4,934	38.8	Wichita	6,417	62.4	3,095	30.1	267	2.6
1,084	58.3	559	30.1	Wilbarger	322	51.8	265	42.6	21	3.4
3,024	62.5	1,568	32.4	Willacy	29	74.4	8	20.5	1	2.6
21,289	43.0	27,906	56.4	Williamson	14,720	50.9	9,799	33.9	2,907	10.1
3,486	60.7	2,170	37.8	Wilson	1,684	52.3	1,299	40.4	111	3.5
262	71.6	98	26.8	Winkler	477	58.0	262	31.9	5	0.6
3,186	70.8	1,204	26.7	Wise	2,647	45.2	2,630	44.9	253	4.3
2,559	63.4	1,412	35.0	Wood	3,451	52.3	2,647	40.1	227	3.4
367	62.7	179	30.6	Yoakum	376	56.5	261	39.2	12	1.8
1,161	66.6	505	29.0	Young	1,223	54.5	864	38.5	49	2.2
2,448	76.6	638	20.0	Zapata	0	-	0	-	0	-
2,626	70.6	968	26.0	Zavala	0	-	0	-	0	-

The state Senate during the 81st session at the Capitol. Robert Plocheck photo.

Legislature Voter ID Fight Leaves Unfinished Business

By Carolyn Barta

The election of a new speaker and a narrow 76–74 Republican majority in the Texas House of Representatives defined the 2009 legislative session – one that featured less rancor than two years before but ended with a meltdown in the final days leaving unfinished business.

Democratic House members conducted a five-day talk-a-thon late in the 81st session to kill a Republican-backed voter identification bill, stranding hundreds of bills and causing senators to scramble to attach their bills to existing legislation.

Senators blamed the House for not taking care of business and, irritated, adjourned without reauthorizing the Texas Department of Transportation and the Department of Insurance, agencies that are scheduled to sunset in September 2010. Gov. Rick Perry called a special session to reconstitute these and three other agencies.

Lawmakers did pass a $182.3 billion budget, accomplishing the one task required of the 140-day session. While revenues were down, $12 billion in federal economic stimulus money allowed them to craft a budget without a tax increase.

A big story of the session was the election of Joe

Critics claimed the session only worked at the margins, rather than addressing major issues

Straus of San Antonio, a little-known, four-year Republican legislator, as Speaker of the House – one of the state's most powerful positions. Three-term Speaker Tom Craddick, a Midland Republican and 40-year House member, staved off near mutiny at the end of the 2007 session that left lingering resentment over the level of his control.

Eleven Republicans known as the ABCs, for "Anybody But Craddick," gathered before the session's January opening and unexpectedly picked Straus as their alternative candidate. With heavy Democrat support, Straus was able to cement enough pledges to force the sitting speaker to withdraw, and he was elected unanimously.

An easy-going moderate Republican, Strauss was unbloodied by past battles and not one of the dominant GOP social conservatives. He promised to follow House rules and return the reins to the members. The result was a more moderate chamber – but some thought it rudderless.

The Texas Senate, under the steady hand of Republican Lt. Gov. David Dewhurst, was solidly Republican with a 19–13 majority, and dispatched its bills in business-like fashion, while the House, working at a slower pace, spent most of its time on the budget.

The Senate suspended its rules early to pass the

controversial voter identification bill that would require voters to show a photo ID or two alternative non-photo IDs. Democrats fought the bill, claiming it would deter minority and elderly voters, while Republicans called it necessary to prevent voter fraud.

The bill was scheduled for House debate late in the session but Democrats raised inconsequential and time-consuming questions on local and non-controversial measures until the deadline passed for the bill's consideration. Other legislation also died, producing calls for greater leadership to focus legislators on major issues.

Critics also blamed the political ambitions of Gov. Rick Perry and Lt. Gov. Dewhurst for the leadership deficiency. Perry was accused of being distracted by his 2010 race for the Republican nomination for governor, and Dewhurst was thinking about a possible U.S. Senate run.

Perry repeatedly railed against the federal government, calling it intrusive and spendthrift and, in highly publicized remarks, launched a veiled threat that Texas could secede from the union.

His intent appeared to some to be to run against the federal government and to brand Sen. Kay Bailey Hutchison, his expected primary opponent, as part of the Beltway bunch. Perry demanded that his priority projects not be funded by federal stimulus money. The Legislature complied, and he called the session successful.

He was pleased that lawmakers replenished the Texas Windstorm Insurance fund that provides insurance coverage to property owners in 14 coastal counties hit hard by storms. Lawmakers also passed a tax break for 40,000 small businesses, raising the exemption to the franchise tax from $300,000 in revenues to $1 million.

They also agreed to a 5-year, $112-million settlement with the Justice Department to make improvements in Texas' state schools for people with disabilities.

Responding to a federal investigation and media reports of abuse and neglect, legislators voted to hire 1,000 more workers, improve health care and install monitors to oversee conditions.

Legislators also provided the University of Texas relief from the rule that requires state universities to admit students from the top 10 percent of their high school class. The rule was designed to increase diversity on state campuses, but UT was overwhelmed by automatic admissions.

The new law allows UT to limit its freshman class to 75 percent from the top-10 field. Also on higher education, seed money was authorized to create more first-tier state universities.

Other education bills that passed included a new school accountability bill that no longer requires third-graders to pass the Texas Assessment of Knowledge and Skills test but requires high school seniors to pass English, math, science and social studies tests to receive a diploma.

Lawmakers made it illegal for a driver to operate a cell phone in a school zone without a hand-held device and raised the age for children who must be secured in a car booster seat from 4 to those under 8 who are less than four-feet, nine-inches tall.

Proposed laws that failed included: Concealed handguns on college campuses, a statewide smoking ban, legalized gambling casinos, "Choose Life" license plates, a public health needle exchange program, expansion of the state's unemployment program and the so-called "pork-chopper bill" that would allow landowners to lease property to hunters using helicopters to control the feral hog population.

Critics claimed the session only worked at the margins, rather than addressing major issues such as high property taxes, the highest home insurance rates in the nation, more children without health insurance than any other state, and the overhaul of TxDOT and the state's growing transportation problems.

Carolyn Barta, a veteran political reporter, is a senior lecturer in journalism at Southern Methodist University.

People make their way to the Capitol during the 81st session of the Legislature. Robert Plocheck photo.

Political Party Organizations

REPUBLICAN State Executive Committee
www.texasgop.org

Chairman, Tina Benkiser, 900 Congress Ave. Ste. 300, Austin 78701; **Vice Chairman**, Robin Armstrong; **Secretary**, Kathy Haigler; **Treasurer**, Wayne Tucker; **General Counsel**, Dennis Donley; **Associate General Counsel**, Quico Canseco; **Parliamentarian**, Butch Davis; **Finance Chairman**, Urve Kiik; **Sergeant-at-Arms**,

John Larrison; **Chaplain**, Bob Long.
National Committee members: Bill Crocker, Austin; Cathie Adams, Dallas.

District — Member and Hometown

1. Steve Findley, Marshall; Brenda Patterson, Gilmer.
2. Cindy Burkett, Mesquite; John Cook, Terrell.
3. Dianne Caron, Tyler; James Wiggins, Conroe.

4. Rosemary Roe, The Woodlands; Michael J. Truncale, Beaumont.
5. Bernice Lewis, College Station; Hal Talton, Round Rock.
6. Rex Teter, Pasadena; Glenda Bowles, Houston.
7. Valoree Swanson, Spring; Clint Moore, Spring.
8. Mandy Tschoepe, Plano; Neal J. Katz, Plano.
9. Timothy Hoy, Dallas; Jane Burch, Grand Prairie.
10. Clifford M. Hayes, Mansfield; Leslie Recine, Pantego.
11. Sheryl Berg, Houston; Dennis Paul, Houston.
12. Tom Quinones, Haltom City; Jean McIver, Frisco.
13. Rex Lamb, Houston; Bonnie Lugo, Houston.
14. Brian Russell, Austin; Davida Stike, Pflugerville.
15. Nelda Eppes, Houston; Josh Flynn, Houston.
16. Daniel Pickens, Garland; Chris B. Davis, Richardson.
17. Bruce Campbell, Houston; Terese Raia, Sugar Land.
18. Mark McCaig, Katy; Phyllis Worsham, Sugar Land.
19. Gayla Gabro Miller, Rio Frio; James Barnes, San Antonio.
20. Robert Jones, Corpus Christi; Luann Caudle, Mission.
21. John Larrison, La Vernia; Amy Clark, Floresville.
22. Peggy Thompson, Copperas Cove; Christopher DeCluitt, Waco.
23. Michael Flusche, DeSoto; Angie King, Dallas.
24. Rebecca Williamson, Hunt; Skipper Wallace, Lampasas.
25. Curt Nelson, San Antonio; Jan Koehne, Seguin.
26. Johnny E. Lovejoy II; Marian K. Stanko, San Antonio.
27. Humberto Zamora, Harlingen; Norma I. Tovar, Brownsville.
28. Cheri Isett, Lubbock; Russ Duerstine, San Angelo.
29. Cindy S. Facker, El Paso; Carlos Garza, El Paso.
30. Ashlea J. Quinonez, Celina; Clyde Siebman, Sherman.
31. Jason Moore; Benona Love, Amarillo.

Statewide Auxiliary Organizations
Texas College Republicans: txcollegerepublicans.com
Texas Republican County Chairmen's Association: www.trcca.org
Texas Federation of Republican Women: www.tfrw.org
Texas Young Republican Federation: www.tyrf.org
Texas Federation for Republican Outreach: www.txblackgop.org
Texas Republican Assembly: www.texasra.org

DEMOCRATIC State Executive Committee
www.txdemocrats.org
Chair, Boyd Richie, Graham, 707 Rio Grande, Austin 78701; **Vice Chair**, Lenora Sorola-Pohlman, Houston; **Vice Chair for Finance**, Dennis Speight, Austin; **Secretary**, Ruby Jensen, Houston; **Treasurer**, Amber Goodwin, Austin; **Parliamentarians**, Ed Cogburn, Houston; Corinne Sabo, San Antonio; Albert G. Gonzales, Houston; J.B. Hall, San Angelo; **Sergeant-at-Arms**, Bruce Elfant, Austin.

National Committee members: Rick Cofer, Austin; Yvonne Davis, Dallas; Gilberto Hinojosa, Brownsville; Eddie Bernice Johnson, Arlington; Sue Lovell, Houston; Choco G. Meza, San Antonio; John Patrick, Baytown; Betty Richie, Graham; Bob Slagle, Sherman; Senfronia Thompson, Houston; Royce West, Dallas; David Hardt, Dallas; Linda Chavez-Thompson, San Antonio, Robert G. Martinez Jr., Dallas; Mary Alice Cisneros, San Antonio..

District — Member and Hometown
1. Norma Narramore, Winfield; Johnny Weaver, Henderson.
2. Martha Williams, Terrell; Steve Tillery, Garland.
3. Kathleen Hawkins, Buna; Dennis Teal, Livingston.
4. Sylvia McDuffie, Nederland; Mark Carter, Orange.
5. Kay Sweat, Lexington; Brian Hamon, Round Rock.
6. Rose A. Salas, Houston; Allan Jamail, Houston.
7. Joy Demark, Houston; Farrukh Shamsi, Houston.
8. Barbara Oldenburg, Plano; David Griggs, Addison.
9. Susan Culp, Grand Prairie; Kennedy Barnes, Plano.
10. Vonda L. Harden, Fort Worth; Dee Jay Johanneson, Arlington.
11. Loretta Davis, San Leon; Joe Parra, Pearland.
12. Charles K. Yarbough, Frisco; Joe Pierce, Euless.
13. Mary Seymore, Houston; John Robert Behrman, Houston.
14. Susan Shelton, Austin; Garry Brown, Austin.
15. Monica Flores, Houston; Ken Yarbrough, Houston.
16. Theresa Daniel, Dallas; David Bailey, Dallas.
17. Carol Wright, Katy; Alan Blakley, Surfside.
18. Donald Bankston, Richmond; Vickie Vogel, La Grange.
19. Diana Salgado, Del Rio; Albert C. Lopez, San Antonio.
20. John D. Bell, Corpus Christi; Rosalie Weisfeld, McAllen.
21. Tom Walker, Tilden; Judith A. Solis, Rio Grande City.
22. JoAnn Jenkins, Ovilla; Danny Trull, Waxahachie.
23. Kenneth Molberg, Dallas; Natesha Wyrick-Cathey, Dallas.
24. Dian Cuellar Ruud, Temple; Guy Lyndon Stuart, Burnet.
25. Zada True-Courage, San Antonio; Michael Wilson, Austin.
26. Celina Peña, San Antonio; Joshua Bailey, San Antonio.
27. Israel Rocha Jr., Elsa; Veronica de Lafuente, Harlingen.
28. Tommy Jones, Lubbock; Carolyn Salsberry, Amherst.
29. Yolanda Clay, El Paso; Michael Apodaca, El Paso.
30. Hal R. Ray Jr., Aledo; Cindy J. Crain, Weatherford.
31. Roberta Hicks, Amarillo; Chris McCormack, Midland.

Asian American Democrats: AJ Durrani, Katy; Mini Timmaraju, Houston.
House Democratic Caucus: Roberto Alonzo, Dallas.
Senate Democratic Caucus: Leticia Van de Putte, San Antonio.
Coalition of Black Democrats: Daniel Davis Clayton, Dallas; Almeda Dento, Houston.
County Chairs Assn.: Eddie Pevehouse, Wortham; Bill Holcomb, Crockett.
Democrats with Disablilities: Jacqueline Acquistapace, Houston; David Frye, Austin.
Environmental Democrats: Blair Dancy, Austin; Donna Bryant, Houston.
Non-Urban/Ag Caucus: Bill Brannon, Sulphur Springs; Alieca Hux, Sulphur Springs.
Stonewall Democrats: Erin Moore, Dallas; Daniel Graney, San Antonio.
Hispanic Caucas: Gloria M. Carillo, Grand Prairie; Victor M. Garza, McAllen.
Texas Democratic Women: Gloria Caceres, Corpus Christi; Susie Blackmon, Rusk.
Young Democrats: Shondra Wygal, Houston; Kris Banks, Houston.

Statewide Organizations
Asian American Democrats: aadt.us
Coalition of Black Democrats: texascbd.org
Caucus on Computers/Communications
Democrats with Disabilities: democratswithdisabilities.org
Mexican American Democrats
Progressive Populist Caucus: texaspopulists.com
Small Business Caucus
Stonewall Democrats: stonewalldemocratsofdallas.org/texas/
Texas Environmental Democrats: texasenvironmentaldemocrats.org
Texas Democratic Veterans: texasdemocraticveterans.org
Texas Democratic Women: tdw.org.
Texas Young Democrats: www.texasyds.org. ☆

TEXAS STATE HISTORICAL ASSOCIATION BOOKS

PEG LEG: The Improbable Life of a Texas Hero, Thomas William Ward, 1807–1852

David C. Humphrey

This warts-and-all biography of one of the Texas Revolution's most intriguing heroes details "Peg Leg" Ward's extraordinary record of service to Texas. "Rich in high drama and exceptionally well written—one of the most compelling and forceful pieces of research I have read in years."—Jerry Thompson. 340 pp, color illus. $39.95 cloth

SACRED MEMORIES: The Civil War Monument Movement in Texas

Kelly McMichael

Sacred Memories takes the reader on a tour of Civil War monuments throughout Texas, and in doing so tells the story of each monument and its creation. 116 pp, maps and photographs. $9.95 paper.

GENERAL VICENTE FILISOLA'S ANALYSIS OF JOSÉ URREA'S MILITARY DIARY: A Forgotten 1838 Publication by an Eyewitness to the Texas Revolution

Gregg J. Dimmick

NOW IN PAPERBACK! This long-forgotten eyewitness account of the Texas Revolution has been translated into English for the first time. 350 pp, bibliography, index. $24.95 paper

AT THE HEART OF TEXAS: 100 Years of the Texas State Historical Association, 1897–1997

Richard B. McCaslin

In this history of the TSHA's first 100 years, McCaslin details the forces that have accorded the association a character and suppleness that continues to ensure its long endurance. 333 pp, photographs. $39.95

PIGSKIN PULPIT: A Social History of Texas High School Football Coaches

Ty Cashion

"*Pigskin Pulpit* is an important book—a must-read for any fan of Texas high school football. . . . With good stories and some seventy photographs, *Pigskin Pulpit* is a pleasure to read."—Blackie Sherrod, Dallas *Morning News*. 320 pp, $22.95 paper

THE PORTABLE HANDBOOK OF TEXAS

Edited By Roy R. Barkley And Mark F. Odintz

Now available for the special price of $5, *The Portable Handbook* brings together more historical information about Texas than can be found in any other single volume. It is the most useful and reliable one-volume reference work ever published on Texas—ideal for the home and office, the student, teacher, and traveler. 1,072 pp, illustrations, cloth.

To order visit www.tshaonline.org or call 940-369-5200.

Government

The State Capitol in Austin, March 2009. Elizabeth Alvarez photo.

Historical Documents

Constitutional Amendments, 2007 & 2009

Chief Government Officials, 1691–2009

State Government

Local Government

Federal Government

Crime in Texas, 2008

Declaration of Independence of the Republic of Texas

The Declaration of Independence of the Republic of Texas was adopted in general convention at Washington-on-the-Brazos, March 2, 1836.

Richard Ellis, president of the convention, appointed a committee of five to write the declaration for submission to the convention. However, there is much evidence that George C. Childress, one of the members, wrote the document with little or no help from the other members. Childress is therefore generally accepted as the author.

The text of the declaration is followed by the names of the signers of the document. The names are presented here as the signers actually signed the document.

Our thanks to the staff of the Texas State Archives for furnishing a photocopy of the signatures.

UNANIMOUS

DECLARATION OF INDEPENDENCE,

BY THE

DELEGATES OF THE PEOPLE OF TEXAS,

IN GENERAL CONVENTION,

AT THE TOWN OF WASHINGTON,

ON THE SECOND DAY OF MARCH, 1836.

When a government has ceased to protect the lives, liberty and property of the people from whom its legitimate powers are derived, and for the advancement of whose happiness it was instituted; and so far from being a guarantee for the enjoyment of those inestimable and inalienable rights, becomes an instrument in the hands of evil rulers for their oppression; when the Federal Republican Constitution of their country, which they have sworn to support, no longer has a substantial existence, and the whole nature of their government has been forcibly changed without their consent, from a restricted federative republic, composed of sovereign states, to a consolidated central military despotism, in which every interest is disregarded but that of the army and the priesthood — both the eternal enemies of civil liberty, and the ever-ready minions of power, and the usual instruments of tyrants; When long after the spirit of the Constitution has departed, moderation is at length, so far lost, by those in power that even the semblance of freedom is removed, and the forms, themselves, of the constitution discontinued; and so far from their petitions and remonstrances being regarded, the agents who bear them are thrown into dungeons; and mercenary armies sent forth to force a new government upon them at the point of the bayonet. When in consequence of such acts of malfeasance and abdication, on the part of the government, anarchy prevails, and civil society is dissolved into its original elements: In such a crisis, the first law of nature, the right of self-preservation — the inherent and inalienable right of the people to appeal to first principles and take their political affairs into their own hands in extreme cases — enjoins it as a right towards themselves and a sacred obligation to their posterity, to abolish such government and create another in its stead, calculated to rescue them from impending dangers, and to secure their future welfare and happiness.

Nations, as well as individuals, are amenable for their acts to the public opinion of mankind. A statement of a part of our grievances is, therefore, submitted to an impartial world, in justification of the hazardous but unavoidable step now taken of severing our political connection with the Mexican people, and assuming an independent attitude among the nations of the earth.

The Mexican government, by its colonization laws, invited and induced the Anglo-American population of Texas to colonize its wilderness under the pledged faith of a written constitution, that they should continue to enjoy that constitutional liberty and republican government to which they had been habituated in the land of their birth, the United States of America. In this expectation they have been cruelly disappointed, inasmuch as the Mexican nation has acquiesced in the late changes made in the government by General Antonio Lopez de Santa Anna, who, having overturned the constitution of his country, now offers us the cruel alternative either to abandon our homes, acquired by so many privations, or submit to the most intolerable of all tyranny, the combined despotism of the sword and the priesthood.

It has sacrificed our welfare to the state of Coahuila, by which our interests have been continually depressed, through a jealous and partial course of legislation carried on at a far distant seat of government, by a hostile majority, in an unknown tongue; and this too, notwithstanding we have petitioned in the humblest terms, for the establishment of a separate state government, and have, in accordance with the provisions of the national constitution, presented the general Congress, a republican constitution which was without just cause contemptuously rejected.

It incarcerated in a dungeon, for a long time, one of our citizens, for no other cause but a zealous endeavor to procure the acceptance of our constitution and the establishment of a state government.

It has failed and refused to secure on a firm basis, the right of trial by jury; that palladium of civil liberty, and only safe guarantee for the life, liberty, and property of the citizen.

It has failed to establish any public system of education, although possessed of almost boundless resources (the public domain) and, although, it is an axiom, in political science, that unless a people are educated and enlightened it is idle to expect the continuance of civil liberty, or the capacity for self-government.

It has suffered the military commandants stationed among us to exercise arbitrary acts of oppression and tyranny; thus trampling upon the most sacred rights of the citizen and rendering the military superior to the civil power.

It has dissolved by force of arms, the state Congress of Coahuila and Texas, and obliged our representatives to fly for their lives from the seat of government; thus depriving us of the fundamental political right of representation.

It has demanded the surrender of a number of our citizens, and ordered military detachments to seize and carry them into the Interior for trial; in contempt of the civil authorities, and in defiance of the laws and constitution.

It has made piratical attacks upon our commerce; by commissioning foreign desperadoes, and authorizing them to seize our vessels, and convey the property of our citizens to far distant ports of confiscation.

It denies us the right of worshipping the Almighty according to the dictates of our own consciences, by the support of a national religion calculated to promote the temporal interests of its human functionaries rather than the glory of the true and living God.

It has demanded us to deliver up our arms; which are essential to our defense, the rightful property of freemen, and formidable only to tyrannical governments.

It has invaded our country, both by sea and by land, with intent to lay waste our territory and drive us from our homes; and has now a large mercenary army advancing to carry on against us a war of extermination.

It has, through its emissaries, incited the merciless savage, with the tomahawk and scalping knife, to massacre the inhabitants of our defenseless frontiers.

It hath been, during the whole time of our connection with it, the contemptible sport and victim of successive military revolutions and hath continually exhibited every characteristic of a weak, corrupt and tyrannical government.

These, and other grievances, were patiently borne by the people of Texas until they reached that point at which forbearance ceases to be a virtue. We then took up arms in defense of the national constitution. We appealed to our Mexican brethren for assistance. Our appeal has been made in vain. Though months have elapsed, no sympathetic response has yet been heard from the Interior. We are, therefore, forced to the melancholy conclusion that the Mexican people have acquiesced in the destruction of their liberty, and the substitution therefor of a military government — that they are unfit to be free and incapable of self-government.

The necessity of self-preservation, therefore, now decrees our eternal political separation.

We, therefore, the delegates, with plenary powers, of the people of Texas, in solemn convention assembled, appealing to a candid world for the necessities of our condition, do hereby resolve and DECLARE that our political connection with the Mexican nation has forever ended; and that the people of Texas do now constitute a FREE, SOVEREIGN and INDEPENDENT REPUBLIC, and are fully invested with all the rights and attributes which properly belong to the independent nations; and, conscious of the rectitude of our intentions, we fearlessly and confidently commit the issue to the decision of the Supreme Arbiter of the destinies of nations.

RICHARD ELLIS, president of the convention and Delegate from Red River.	Wm B Scates	Thomas Jefferson Rusk
	M.B. Menard	Chas. S. Taylor
	A.B. Hardin	John S. Roberts
	J.W. Bunton	
Charles B Stewart	Thos J. Gasley	Robert Hamilton
	R. M. Coleman	Collin McKinney
Thos Barnett	Sterling C. Robertson	Albert H Latimer
John S.D. Byrom	Benj Briggs Goodrich	James Power
	G.W. Barnett	
Franco Ruiz	James G. Swisher	Sam Houston
J. Antonio Navarro	Jesse Grimes	David Thomas
Jesse B. Badgett	S. Rhoads Fisher	
Wm D. Lacey	John W. Moore	Edwd Conrad
William Menefee	John W. Bower	Martin Parmer
Jno Fisher	Saml A Maverick from Bejar	Edwin O. LeGrand
Mathew Caldwell	Sam P. Carson	Stephen W. Blount
William Mottley	A. Briscoe	Jas Gaines
Lorenzo de Zavala	J.B. Woods	Wm Clark, Jr
Stephen H. Everitt	Jas Collinsworth	Sydney O. Penington
Geo W Smyth	Edwin Waller	Wm Carrol Crawford
	Asa Brigham	Jno Turner
Elijah Stapp	Geo. C. Childress	
Claiborne West	Bailey Hardeman	
	Rob. Potter	Test. H.S. Kimble, Secretary

Documents Concerning the Annexation
of Texas to the United States

(For an overview of the subject, please see these discussions: *The New Handbook of Texas,* Texas State Historical Association, Austin, 1996; Vol. 1, pages 192–193. On the Web: **www.tshaonline.org/handbook/online/articles/AA/ mga2.html**. Also see the Texas State Library and Archives Web site: **www.tsl.state.tx.us/ref/abouttx/annexation/index.html** and the *Texas Almanac* Web site: **www.texasalmanac.com/history/timeline/annexation/**.)

Joint Resolution for Annexing

Texas to the United States

Resolved

by the Senate and House of Representatives of the United States of America in Congress assembled, That Congress doth consent that the territory properly included within and rightfully belonging to the Republic of Texas, may be erected into a new State to be called the State of Texas, with a republican form of government adopted by the people of said Republic, by deputies in convention assembled, with the consent of the existing Government in order that the same may by admitted as one of the States of this Union.

2. And be it further resolved, That the foregoing consent of Congress is given upon the following conditions, to wit: First, said state to be formed, subject to the adjustment by this government of all questions of boundary that may arise with other government, --and the Constitution thereof, with the proper evidence of its adoption by the people of said Republic of Texas, shall be transmitted to the President of the United States, to be laid before Congress for its final action on, or before the first day of January, one thousand eight hundred and forty-six. Second, said state when admitted into the Union, after ceding to the United States all public edifices, fortifications, barracks, ports and harbors, navy and navy yards, docks, magazines and armaments, and all other means pertaining to the public defense, belonging to the said Republic of Texas, shall retain funds, debts, taxes and dues of every kind which may belong to, or be due and owing to the said Republic; and shall also retain all the vacant and unappropriated lands lying within its limits, to be applied to the payment of the debts and liabilities of said Republic of Texas, and the residue of said lands, after discharging said debts and liabilities, to be disposed of as said State may direct; but in no event are said debts and liabilities to become a charge upon the Government of the United States. Third — New States of convenient size not exceeding four in number, in addition to said State of Texas and

having sufficient population, may, hereafter by the consent of said State, be formed out of the territory thereof, which shall be entitled to admission under the provisions of the Federal Constitution; and such states as may be formed out of the territory lying south of thirty-six degrees thirty minutes north latitude, commonly known as the Missouri Compromise Line, shall be admitted into the Union, with or without slavery, as the people of each State, asking admission shall desire; and in such State or States as shall be formed out of said territory, north of said Missouri Compromise Line, slavery, or involuntary servitude (except for crime) shall be prohibited.

3. And be it further resolved, That if the President of the United States shall in his judgment and discretion deem it most advisable, instead of proceeding to submit the foregoing resolution of the Republic of Texas, as an overture on the part of the United States for admission, to negotiate with the Republic; then,

Be it resolved, That a State, to be formed out of the present Republic of Texas, with suitable extent and boundaries, and with two representatives in Congress, until the next appointment of representation, shall be admitted into the Union, by virtue of this act, on an equal footing with the existing States, as soon as the terms and conditions of such admission, and the cession of the remaining Texian territory to the United States shall be agreed upon by the governments of Texas and the United States: And that the sum of one hundred thousand dollars be, and the same is hereby, appropriated to defray the expenses of missions and negotiations, to agree upon the terms of said admission and cession, either by treaty to be submitted to the Senate, or by articles to be submitted to the two houses of Congress, as the President may direct.

Approved, March 1, 1845.

Source: Peters, Richard, ed., The Public Statutes at Large of the United States of America, v.5, pp. 797–798, Boston, Chas. C. Little and Jas. Brown, 1850.

Twenty-Ninth Congress:
Session 1 -- Resolutions
[No. 1.] Joint Resolution for the Admission of the State of Texas into the Union.

Whereas

the Congress of the United States, by a joint resolution approved March the first, eighteen hundred and forty-five, did consent that the territory properly included within, and rightfully belonging to, the Republic of Texas, might be erected into a new State, to be called _The State of Texas,_ with a republican form of government, to be adopted by the people of said republic, by deputies in convention assembled, with the consent of the existing government, in order that the same might be admitted as one of the States of the Union; which consent of Congress was given upon certain conditions specified in the first and second sections of said joint resolution; and whereas the people of the said Republic of Texas, by deputies in convention assembled, with the consent of the existing government, did adopt a constitution, and erect a new State with a republican form of government, and, in the name of the people of Texas, and by their authority, did ordain and declare that they assented to and accepted the

proposals, conditions, and guaranties contained in said first and second sections of said resolution: and whereas the said constitution, with the proper evidence of its adoption by the people of the Republic of Texas, has been transmitted to the President of the United States and laid before Congress, in conformity to the provisions of said joint resolution:

Therefore—

Resolved by the Senate and House of Representatives of the United States of America in Congress assembled, That the State of Texas shall be one, and is hereby declared to be one, of the United States of America, and admitted into the Union on an equal footing with the original States in all respects whatever.

Sec. 2. And be it further resolved, That until the representatives in Congress shall be apportioned according to an actual enumeration of the inhabitants of the United States, the State of Texas shall be entitled to choose two representatives.

Approved, December 29, 1845.

SOURCE: Minot, Geo., ed., Statutes at Large and Treaties of the United States of America from Dec. 1, 1845 to March 3, 1851, V. IX, p. 108

Constitution of Texas

The complete official text of the Constitution of Texas, including the original document, which was adopted on Feb. 15, 1876, plus all amendments approved since that time, is available on the State of Texas Web page at this address: **http://www.constitution.legis.state.tx.us/**. An index at that site points you to the Article and Section of the Constitution that deals with a particular subject.

For election information, upcoming elections, amendment or other election votes and voter registration information, go to: **www.sos.state.tx.us/elections/index.shtml**.

According to the **Legislative Reference Library of Texas**: "The Texas Constitution is one of the longest in the nation and is still growing. As of 2007 (80th Legislature), the Texas Legislature has passed a total of 632 amendments. Of these, 456 have been adopted and 176 have been defeated by Texas voters. Thus, **the Texas Constitution has been amended 456 times since its adoption in 1876**."

Amendment of the Texas Constitution requires a two-thirds favorable vote by both the Texas House of Representatives and the Texas Senate, followed by a majority vote of approval by voters in a statewide election.

Prior to 1973, amendments to the constitution could not be submitted by a special session of the Legislature. But the constitution was amended in 1972 to allow submission of amendments if the special session was opened to the subject by the governor.

Constitutional amendments are not subject to a gubernatorial veto. Once submitted, voters have the final decision on whether to change the constitution as proposed.

The following table lists the total number of amendments submitted to voters by the Texas Legislature and shows the year in which the Legislature approved them for submission to voters; e.g., the 70th Legislature in 1987 approved 28 bills proposing amendments to be submitted to voters — 25 in 1987 and 3 in 1988.

For more information on bills and constitutional amendments, see the Legislative Reference Library of Texas Web site at: **www.lrl.state.tx.us/legis/lrlhome.cfm**.

Amendments, 2007

The following amendment was submitted to the voters by the 80th Legislature in an election on May 12, 2007:

SJR 13 — Authorizing the legislature to provide for a reduction of the limitation on the total amount of ad valorem taxes that may be imposed for public school purposes on the residence homesteads of the elderly or disabled to reflect any reduction in the rate of those taxes for the 2006 and 2007 tax years. **Passed:** 815,596 for; 113,983 against.

The following 16 amendments were submitted to the voters by the 80th Legislature in an election on Nov. 6, 2007:

HJR 6 — Authorizing the denial of bail to a person who violates certain court orders or conditions of release in a felony or family violence case. **Passed:** 916,173 for; 176,189 against.

HJR 19 — Requiring that a record vote be taken by a house of the legislature on final passage of any bill, other than certain local bills, of a resolution proposing or ratifying a constitutional amendment, or of any other nonceremonial resolution, and to provide for public access on the Internet to those record votes. **Passed:** 893,686 for; 163,553 against.

Constitutional Amendments Submitted to Voters by the Texas Legislature

Year	No.	Year	No.	Year	No.
1879	1	1927	8	1973	9
1881	2	1929	7	1975	12
1883	5	1931	9	1977	15
1887	6	1933	12	1978	1
1889	2	1935	13	1979	12
1891	5	1937	7	1981	10
1893	2	1939	4	1982	3
1895	2	1941	5	1983	19
1897	5	1943	3	1985	17
1899	1	1945	8	1986	1
1901	1	1947	9	1987	28
1903	3	1949	10	1989	21
1905	3	1951	7	1990	1
1907	9	1953	11	1991	15
1909	4	1955	9	1993	18
1911	5	1957	12	1995	14
1913	7	1959	4	1997	15
1915	7	1961	14	1999	17
1917	3	1963	7	2001	20
1919	13	1965	27	2003	22
1921	5	1967	20	2005	9
1923	2	1969	16	2007	17
1925	4	1971	18	2009	11

HJR 30 — Allowing governmental entities to sell property acquired through eminent domain back to the previous owners at the price the entities paid to acquire the property. **Passed:** 867,973 for; 212,555 against.

HJR 36 — Permitting a justice or judge who reaches the mandatory retirement age while in office to serve the remainder of the justice's or judge's current term. **Passed:** 814,148 for; 271,245 against.

HJR 40 — Authorizing the legislature to provide that the maximum appraised value of a residence homestead for ad valorem taxation is limited to the lesser of the most recent market value of the residence homestead as determined by the appraisal entity or 110 percent, or a greater percentage, of the appraised value of the residence homestead for the preceding tax year. **Passed:** 769,908 for; 306,830 against.

HJR 54 — Authorizing the legislature to exempt from ad valorem taxation one motor vehicle owned by an individual and used in the course of the owner's occupation or profession and also for personal activities of the owner. **Passed:** 800,005 for; 285,537 against.

HJR 69 — Abolishing the constitutional authority for the office of inspector of hides and animals. **Passed:** 806,652 for; 246,914 against.

HJR 72 — Clarifying certain provisions relating to the making of a home equity loan and use of home equity loan proceeds. **Passed:** 823,189 for; 238,136 against.

HJR 90 — Requiring the creation of the Cancer Prevention and Research Institute of Texas and authorizing the issuance of up to $3 billion in bonds payable from the general revenues of the state for research in Texas to find the causes of and cures for cancer. **Passed:** 673,763 for; 422,647 against.

HJR 103 — Providing for the continuation of the constitutional appropriation for facilities and other capital items at Angelo State University on a change in the governance of the university. **Passed:** 696,426 for; 353,922 against.

SJR 20 — Providing for the issuance of additional general obligation bonds by the Texas Water Development Board in an amount not to exceed $250 million to provide assistance to economically distressed areas. **Passed:** 650,533 for; 419,914 against.

SJR 29—Authorizing the legislature to exempt all or part of the residence homesteads of certain totally disabled veterans from ad valorem taxation and authorizing a change in the manner of determining the amount of the existing exemption from ad valorem taxation to which a disabled veteran is entitled. **Passed:** 932,418 for; 149,275 against.

SJR 44—Authorizing the legislature to permit the voters of a municipality having a population of less than 10,000 to authorize the governing body of the municipality to enter into

The top portion of a monument dedicated to "The Heroes of the Alamo" on the grounds of the State Capitol. Elizabeth Alvarez photo.

an agreement with an owner of real property in or adjacent to an area in the municipality that has been approved for funding under certain programs administered by the Texas Department of Agriculture under which the parties agree that all ad valorem taxes imposed on the owner's property may not be increased for the first five tax years after the tax year in which the agreement is entered into. **Passed:** 690,650 for; 355,583 against.

SJR 57 — Providing for the issuance of $500 million in general obligation bonds to finance educational loans to students and authorizing bond enhancement agreements with respect to general obligation bonds issued for that purpose. **Passed:** 718,282 for; 372,659 against.

SJR 64 — Providing for the issuance of general obligation bonds by the Texas Transportation Commission in an amount not to exceed $5 billion to provide funding for highway improvement projects. **Passed:** 670,186 for; 400,383 against.

SJR 65 — Authorizing the issuance of up to $1 billion in bonds payable from the general revenues of the state for maintenance, improvement, repair, and construction projects and for the purchase of needed equipment. **Passed:** 627,609 for; 451,440 against.

Amendments, 2009

The following 11 amendments were submitted to the voters by the 81st Legislature in an election on **Nov. 3, 2009:**

HJR 7 — Authorizing the state to contribute money, property, and other resources for the establishment,

maintenance, and operation of veterans hospitals in this state.

HJR 14 — Prohibiting the taking, damaging, or destroying of private property for public use unless the action is for the ownership, use, and enjoyment of the property by the State, a political subdivision of the State, the public at large, or entities granted the power of eminent domain under law or for the elimination of urban blight on a particular parcel of property, but not for certain economic development or enhancement of tax revenue purposes, and to limit the legislature's authority to grant the power of eminent domain to an entity.

HJR 14 — Establishing the national research university fund to enable emerging research universities in this state to achieve national prominence as major research universities and transferring the balance of the higher education fund to the national research university fund.

HJR 36 — Authorizing the legislature to provide for the ad valorem taxation of a residence homestead solely on the basis of the property's value as a residence homestead.

HJR 36 — Authorizing the legislature to authorize a single board of equalization for two or more adjoining appraisal entities that elect to provide for consolidated equalizations.

HJR 36 — Providing for uniform standards and procedures for the appraisal of property for ad valorem tax purposes.

HJR 85 — Providing that elected members of the governing boards of emergency services districts may serve terms not to exceed four years."

HJR 102 — Protecting the right of the public, individually and collectively, to access and use the public beaches bordering the seaward shore of the Gulf of Mexico.

HJR 116 — Authorizing the Veterans' Land Board to issue general obligation bonds in amounts equal to or less than amounts previously authorized.

HJR 127 — Allowing an officer or enlisted member of the Texas State Guard or other state militia or military force to hold other civil offices.

HJR 132 — Authorizing the financing, including through tax increment financing, of the acquisition by municipalities and counties of buffer areas or open spaces adjacent to a military installation for the prevention of encroachment or for the construction of roadways, utilities, or other infrastructure to protect or promote the mission of the military installation. ☆

A view of the rotunda in the State Capitol. Elizabeth Alvarez photo.

Texas' Chief Governmental Officials

On this and following pages are lists of the principal administrative officials who have served the Republic and State of Texas with dates of their tenures of office. In a few instances there are disputes as to the exact dates of tenures. Dates listed here are those that appear the most authentic.

★ ★ ★ ★ ★ ★ ★

Governors and Presidents
*Spanish Royal Governors

Domingo Terán de los Rios	1691–1692
Gregorio de Salinas Varona	1692–1697
Francisco Cuerbo y Valdés	1698–1702
Mathías de Aguirre	1703–1705
Martín de Alarcón	1705–1708
Simón Padilla y Córdova	1708–1712
Pedro Fermin de Echevers y Subisa	1712–1714
Juan Valdéz	1714–1716
Martín de Alarcón	1716–1719
José de Azlor y Virto de Vera, Marqués de San Miguel de Aguayo	1719–1722
Fernando Pérez de Almazán	1722–1727
Melchor de Mediavilla y Azcona	1727–1731
Juan Antonio Bustillo y Ceballos	1731–1734
Manuel de Sandoval	1734–1736
Carlos Benites Franquis de Lugo	1736–1737
Joseph Fernández de Jáuregui y Urrutia	1737–1737
Prudencio de Orobio y Basterra	1737–1741
Tomás Felipe Winthuisen (or Winthuysen)	1741–1743
Justo Boneo y Morales	1743–1744
Francisco García Larios	1744–1748
Pedro del Barrio Junco y Espriella	1748–1750
Jacinto de Barrios y Jáuregui	1751–1759

Angel de Martos y Navarrete	1759–1767
Hugo Oconór	1767–1770
Juan María Vicencio, Barón de Ripperdá	1770–1778
Domingo Cabello y Robles	1778–1786
Rafael Martínez Pacheco	1787–1790
Manuel Muñoz	1790–1799
Juan Bautista de Elguezábal	1799–1805
Antonio Cordero y Bustamante	1805–1808
Manuel María de Salcedo	1808–1813
Juan Bautista de las Casas (revolutionary gov.)	1811–1811
Cristóbal Domínguez, Benito de Armiñan, Mariano Varela, Juan Ignacio Pérez, Manuel Pardo	1813–1817
Antonio María Martínez	1817–1821

*Some authorities would include Texas under administrations of several earlier Spanish Governors. The late Dr. C.E. Castañeda, Latin-American librarian of The University of Texas and authority on the history of Texas and the Southwest, would include the following four: Francisco de Garay, 1523–26; Pánfilo de Narváez, 1526–28; Nuño de Guzmán, 1528–30; Hernando de Soto, 1538–43.

Governors Under Mexican Rule

The first two Governors under Mexican rule, Trespalacios and García, were of Texas only as Texas was then constituted. Beginning with Gonzáles, 1824, the Governors were for the joint State of Coahuila y Texas.

José Felix Trespalacios	1822–1823
Luciano García	1823–1824
Rafael Gonzáles	1824–1826

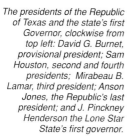

The presidents of the Republic of Texas and the state's first Governor, clockwise from top left: David G. Burnet, provisional president; Sam Houston, second and fourth presidents; Mirabeau B. Lamar, third president; Anson Jones, the Republic's last president; and J. Pinckney Henderson the Lone Star State's first governor.

Victor Blanco 1826–1827
José María Viesca 1827–1830
Ramón Eca y Músquiz 1830–1831
José María Letona 1831–1832
Ramón Eca y Músquiz 1832–1832
Juan Martín de Veramendi 1832–1833
Juan José de Vidáurri y Villasenor 1833–1834
Juan José Elguezábal 1834–1835
José María Cantú 1835–1835
Agustín M. Viesca 1835–1835
Marciel Borrego 1835–1835
Ramón Eca y Músquiz 1835–1835

Provisional Colonial Governor, Before Independence

Henry Smith (Impeached) 1835

James W. Robinson served as acting Governor just prior to March 2, 1836, after Smith was impeached.

Presidents of the Republic of Texas

David G. Burnet .... Mar. 16, 1836–Oct. 22, 1836
(provisional President)
Sam Houston .... Oct. 22, 1836–Dec. 10, 1838
Mirabeau B. Lamar .... Dec. 10, 1838–Dec. 13, 1841
Sam Houston .... Dec. 13, 1841–Dec. 9, 1844
Anson Jones .... Dec. 9, 1844–Feb. 19, 1846

Governors Since Annexation

J. Pinckney Henderson.... Feb. 19, 1846–Dec. 21, 1847

(Albert C. Horton served as acting Governor while Henderson was away in the Mexican War.)

George T. Wood .... Dec. 21, 1847–Dec. 21, 1849
Peter Hansbrough Bell .... Dec. 21, 1849–Nov. 23, 1853
J. W. Henderson .... Nov. 23, 1853–Dec. 21, 1853
Elisha M. Pease .... Dec. 21, 1853–Dec. 21, 1857
Hardin R. Runnels .... Dec. 21, 1857–Dec. 21, 1859

Sam Houston (resigned because of state's secession from the Union) ....Dec. 21, 1859–Mar. 16, 1861
Edward Clark .... Mar. 16, 1861–Nov. 7, 1861
Francis R. Lubbock (resigned to enter Confederate Army) ....Nov. 7, 1861–Nov. 5, 1863
Pendleton Murrah (administration terminated by fall of Confederacy) ..... Nov. 5, 1863–June 17, 1865
Fletcher S. Stockdale (Lt. Gov. performed some duties of office on Murrah's departure, but is sometimes included in list of Governors. Hamilton's appointment was for immediate succession, as shown by the dates.)
Andrew J. Hamilton (Provisional, appointed by President Johnson) .....June 17, 1865–Aug. 9, 1866
James W. Throckmorton ...... Aug. 9, 1866–Aug. 8, 1867
Elisha M. Pease (appointed July 30, 1867, under martial law) .... Aug. 8, 1867–Sept. 30, 1869

Interregnum

Pease resigned and vacated office Sept. 30, 1869; no successor was named until Jan. 8, 1870. Some historians extend Pease's term until Jan. 8, 1870, but in reality Texas was without a head of its civil government from Sept. 30, 1869, until Jan. 8, 1870.

Edmund J. Davis (appointed provisional Governor after being elected) ...... Jan. 8, 1870–Jan. 15, 1874
Richard Coke (resigned to enter United States Senate) ....Jan. 15, 1874–Dec. 1, 1876
Richard B. Hubbard ....Dec. 1, 1876–Jan. 21, 1879
Oran M. Roberts .... Jan. 21, 1879–Jan. 16, 1883
John Ireland .... Jan. 16, 1883–Jan. 18, 1887
Lawrence Sullivan Ross .... Jan. 18, 1887–Jan. 20, 1891
James Stephen Hogg .... Jan. 20, 1891–Jan. 15, 1895
Charles A. Culberson .... Jan. 15, 1895–Jan. 17, 1899
Joseph D. Sayers .... Jan. 17, 1899–Jan. 20, 1903
S. W. T. Lanham .... Jan. 20, 1903–Jan. 15, 1907

Thos. Mitchell Campbell ....Jan. 15, 1907–Jan. 17, 1911	
Oscar Branch Colquitt ....Jan. 17, 1911–Jan. 19, 1915	
James E. Ferguson	
(impeached) ....Jan. 19, 1915–Aug. 25, 1917	
William Pettus Hobby ....Aug. 25, 1917–Jan. 18, 1921	
Pat Morris Neff.................. Jan. 18, 1921–Jan. 20, 1925	
Miriam A. Ferguson .... Jan. 20, 1925–Jan. 17, 1927	
Dan Moody .... Jan. 17, 1927–Jan. 20, 1931	
Ross S. Sterling................ Jan. 20, 1931–Jan. 17, 1933	
Miriam A. Ferguson .... Jan. 17, 1933–Jan. 15, 1935	
James V. Allred................. Jan. 15, 1935–Jan. 17, 1939	

W. Lee O'Daniel (*resigned to enter United States*
Senate*) ....Jan. 17, 1939–Aug. 4, 1941
Coke R. Stevenson.............Aug. 4, 1941–Jan. 21, 1947
Beauford H. Jester.............Jan. 21, 1947–July 11, 1949
Allan Shivers (*Lt. Governor succeeded on death of
Governor Jester. Elected in 1950 and re-elected
in 1952 and 1954*).......July 11, 1949–Jan. 15, 1957
Price Daniel .... Jan. 15, 1957–Jan. 15, 1963
John Connally................... Jan. 15, 1963–Jan. 21, 1969
Preston Smith .... Jan. 21, 1969–Jan. 16, 1973
*Dolph Briscoe................. Jan. 16, 1973–Jan. 16, 1979
**William P. Clements .... Jan. 16, 1979–Jan. 18, 1983
Mark White .... Jan. 18, 1983–Jan. 20, 1987
**William P. Clements .... Jan. 20, 1987–Jan. 15, 1991
Ann W. Richards............... Jan. 15, 1991–Jan. 17, 1995
**George W. Bush ....Jan. 17, 1995–Dec. 21, 2000
**Rick Perry (*Lt. Gov. succeeded on inauguration of
Bush as U.S. President*) ....Dec. 21, 2000–present

*Effective in 1975, term of office was raised to 4
years, according to a constitutional amendment approved by Texas voters in 1972. See introduction to
State Government chapter in this edition for other state
officials whose terms were raised to four years.*
***Republicans.*

★ ★ ★ ★ ★ ★ ★

Vice Presidents and Lieutenant Governors
Vice Presidents of the Republic

	Date Elected
Lorenzo de Zavala (*provisional Vice President*)	
Mirabeau B. Lamar	Sept. 5, 1836
David G. Burnet	Sept. 3, 1838
Edward Burleson	Sept. 6, 1841
Kenneth L. Anderson	Sept. 2, 1844

State Lieutenant Governors

Albert C. Horton..1846–1847	
John A. Greer 1847–1851	
J. W. Henderson...Aug. 4, 1851	
D. C. Dickson...1853–1855	
H. R. Runnels...Aug. 6, 1855	
F. R. Lubbock...Aug. 4, 1857	
Edward Clark...Aug. 1, 1859	
John M. Crockett 1861–1863	
Fletcher S. Stockdale 1863–1866	
George W. Jones..1866	

(*Jones was removed by General Sheridan.*)
J. W. Flanagan...1869
(*Flanagan was appointed U.S. Senator and was
never inaugurated as Lt. Gov.*)

R. B. Hubbard...1873–1876	
J. D. Sayers 1878–1880	
L. J. Storey 1880–1882	
Marion Martin 1882–1884	
Barnett Gibbs...1884–1886	
T. B. Wheeler...1886–1890	
George C. Pendleton....................................1890–1892	
M. M. Crane .... Jan. 17, 1893–Jan. 25, 1895	
George T. Jester...1895–1898	
J. N. Browning 1898–1902	

George D. Neal..1902–1906	
A. B. Davidson...1906–1912	
Will H. Mayes..1912–1914	
William Pettus Hobby 1914–1917	

W. A. Johnson (*served Hobby's unexpired
term and until*...Jan. 1920)

Lynch Davidson 1920–1922	
T. W. Davidson...1922–1924	
Barry Miller 1924–1931	
Edgar E. Witt 1931–1935	
Walter Woodul 1935–1939	
Coke R. Stevenson.......................................1939–1941	
John Lee Smith............................. 1943–Jan. 21, 1947	
Allan Shivers.....................Jan. 21, 1947–July 11, 1949	

(*Shivers succeeded to the governorship on death of
Governor Beauford H. Jester.*)
Ben Ramsey 1951–Sept. 18, 1961
(*Ben Ramsey resigned to become a member of the
State Railroad Commission.*)

Preston Smith 1963–1969	
Ben Barnes 1969–1973	
William P. Hobby Jr. 1973–1991	
Robert D. Bullock...1991–1999	
Rick Perry 1999–Dec. 21, 2000	
*Bill Ratliff ....Dec. 28, 2000–Jan. 21, 2003	
David Dewhurst .... Jan. 21, 2003–present	

*Elected by Senate when Rick Perry succeeded to
governorship on election of George W. Bush as U.S.
President.*

★ ★ ★ ★ ★ ★ ★

Secretaries of State
Of the Republic

*Raines Yearbook for Texas, 1901, gives the follow-
ing record of Secretaries of State during the era of the
Republic of Texas:*

Under David G. Burnet — Samuel P. Carson,
James Collingsworth and W. H. Jack.

Under Sam Houston (first term) — Stephen F. Austin, 1836. J. Pinckney Henderson and Dr. Robert A. Irion,
1837–38.

Under Mirabeau B. Lamar — Bernard Bee appointed Dec. 16, 1838; James Webb appointed Feb. 6, 1839;
D. G. Burnet appointed Acting Secretary of State, May
31, 1839; N. Amory appointed Acting Secretary of State,
July 23, 1839; D. G. Burnet appointed Acting Secretary
of State, Aug. 5, 1839; Abner S. Lipscomb appointed
Secretary of State, Jan. 31, 1840, and resigned Jan.
22, 1841; Joseph Waples appointed Acting Secretary
of State, Jan. 23, 1841, and served until Feb. 8, 1841;
James S. Mayfield appointed Feb. 8, 1841; Joseph
Waples appointed April 30, 1841, and served until May
25, 1841; Samuel A. Roberts appointed May 25, 1841;
reappointed Sept. 7, 1841.

Under Sam Houston (second term) — E. Lawrence
Stickney, Acting Secretary of State until Anson Jones
appointed Dec. 13, 1841. Jones served as Secretary
of State throughout this term except during the summer
and part of this term of 1842, when Joseph Waples filled
the position as Acting Secretary of State.

Under Anson Jones — Ebenezer Allen served from
Dec. 10, 1844, until Feb. 5, 1845, when Ashbel Smith
became Secretary of State. Allen was again named Acting Secretary of State, March 31, 1845, and later named
Secretary of State.

(In addition to the above, documents in theTexas
State Archives indicate that Joseph C. Eldredge, Chief
Clerk of the State Department during much of the Re-
public's existence, signed a number of documents in the
absence of the office-holder in the capacity of "Acting
Secretary of State.")

State Secretaries of State

Charles Mariner .... Feb. 20, 1846–May 4, 1846
David G. Burnet .... May 4, 1846–Jan. 1, 1848
Washington D. Miller .... Jan. 1, 1848–Jan. 2, 1850
James Webb .... Jan. 2, 1850–Nov. 14, 1851
Thomas H. Duval .... Nov. 14, 1851–Dec. 22, 1853
Edward Clark .... Dec. 22, 1853–Dec. 1857
T. S. Anderson .... Dec. 1857–Dec. 27, 1859
E. W. Cave .... Dec. 27, 1859–Mar. 16, 1861
Bird Holland .... Mar. 16, 1861–Nov. 1861
Charles West .... Nov. 1861–Sept. 1862
Robert J. Townes .... Sept. 1862–May 2, 1865
Charles R. Pryor .... May 2, 1865–Aug, 1865
James H. Bell .... Aug. 1865–Aug. 1866
John A. Green .... Aug. 1866–Aug. 1867
D. W. C. Phillips .... Aug. 1867–Jan. 1870
J. P. Newcomb .... Jan. 1, 1870–Jan. 17, 1874
George Clark .... Jan. 17, 1874–Jan. 27, 1874
A. W. DeBerry .... Jan. 27, 1874–Dec. 1, 1876
Isham G. Searcy .... Dec. 1, 1876–Jan. 23, 1879
J. D. Templeton .... Jan. 23, 1879–Jan. 22, 1881
T. H. Bowman .... Jan. 22, 1881–Jan. 18, 1883
J. W. Baines .... Jan. 18, 1883–Jan. 21, 1887
John M. Moore .... Jan. 21, 1887–Jan. 22, 1891
George W. Smith .... Jan. 22, 1891–Jan. 17, 1895
Allison Mayfield .... Jan. 17, 1895–Jan. 5, 1897
J. W. Madden .... Jan. 5, 1897–Jan. 18, 1899
D. H. Hardy .... Jan. 18, 1899–Jan. 19, 1901
John G. Tod .... Jan. 19, 1901–Jan., 1903
J. R. Curl .... Jan. 1903–April 1905
O. K. Shannon .... April 1905–Jan. 1907
L. T. Dashiel .... Jan. 1907–Feb. 1908
W. R. Davie .... Feb. 1908–Jan. 1909
W. B. Townsend .... Jan. 1909–Jan. 1911
C. C. McDonald .... Jan. 1911–Dec. 1912
J. T. Bowman .... Dec. 1912–Jan. 1913
John L. Wortham .... Jan. 1913–June 1913
F. C. Weinert .... June 1913–Nov. 1914
D. A. Gregg .... Nov. 1914–Jan. 1915
John G. McKay .... Jan. 1915–Dec. 1916
C. J. Bartlett .... Dec. 1916–Nov. 1917
George F. Howard .... Nov. 1917–Nov. 1920
C. D. Mims .... Nov. 1920–Jan. 1921
S. L. Staples .... Jan. 1921–Aug. 1924
J. D. Strickland .... Sept. 1924–Jan. 1, 1925
Henry Hutchings .... Jan. 1, 1925–Jan. 20, 1925
Mrs. Emma G. Meharg .... Jan. 20, 1925–Jan. 1927
Mrs. Jane Y. McCallum .... Jan. 1927–Jan. 1933
W. W. Heath .... Jan. 1933–Jan. 1935
Gerald C. Mann .... Jan. 1935–Aug. 31, 1935
R. B. Stanford .... Aug. 31, 1935–Aug. 25, 1936
B. P. Matocha .... Aug. 25, 1936–Jan. 18, 1937
Edward Clark .... Jan. 18, 1937–Jan. 1939
Tom L. Beauchamp .... Jan. 1939–Oct. 1939
M. O. Flowers .... Oct. 26, 1939–Feb. 25, 1941
William J. Lawson .... Feb. 25, 1941–Jan. 1943
Sidney Latham .... Jan. 1943–Feb. 1945
Claude Isbell .... Feb. 1945–Jan. 1947
Paul H. Brown .... Jan. 1947–Jan. 19, 1949
Ben Ramsey .... Jan. 19, 1949–Feb. 9, 1950
John Ben Shepperd .... Feb. 9, 1950–April 30, 1952
Jack Ross .... April 30, 1952–Jan. 9, 1953
Howard A. Carney .... Jan. 9, 1953–Apr. 30, 1954
C. E. Fulgham .... May 1, 1954–Feb. 15, 1955
Al Muldrow .... Feb. 15, 1955–Nov. 1, 1955
Tom Reavley .... Nov. 1, 1955–Jan. 16, 1957
Zollie Steakley .... Jan. 16, 1957–Jan. 2, 1962
P. Frank Lake .... Jan. 2, 1962–Jan. 15, 1963
Crawford C. Martin .... Jan. 15, 1963–March 12, 1966
John L. Hill .... March 12, 1966–Jan. 22, 1968
Roy Barrera .... March 7, 1968–Jan. 23, 1969
Martin Dies Jr. .... Jan. 23, 1969–Sept. 1, 1971
Robert D. (Bob) Bullock .... Sept. 1, 1971–Jan. 2, 1973

V. Larry Teaver Jr. .... Jan. 2, 1973–Jan. 19, 1973
Mark W. White Jr. .... Jan. 19, 1973–Oct. 27, 1977
Steven C. Oaks .... Oct. 27, 1977–Jan. 16, 1979
George W. Strake Jr. .... Jan. 16, 1979–Oct. 6, 1981
David A. Dean .... Oct. 22, 1981–Jan. 18, 1983
John Fainter .... Jan. 18, 1983–July 31, 1984
Myra A. McDaniel .... Sept. 6, 1984–Jan. 26, 1987
Jack Rains .... Jan. 26, 1987–June 15, 1989
George Bayoud Jr. .... June 19, 1989–Jan. 15, 1991
John Hannah Jr. .... Jan. 17, 1991–March 11, 1994
Ronald Kirk .... April 4, 1994–Jan. 10, 1995
Antonio O. "Tony" Garza Jr. Jan. 18, 1995–Dec. 2, 1997
Alberto R. Gonzales .... Dec. 2, 1997–Jan. 10, 1999
Elton Bomer .... Jan. 11, 1999–Dec. 31, 2000
Henry Cuellar .... Jan. 2, 2001–Oct. 5, 2001
Gwyn Shea .... Jan. 2, 2002–Aug. 4, 2003
Geoff Connor .... Sept. 26, 2003–Jan. 1, 2005
J. Roger Williams .... Jan. 1, 2005–July 1, 2007
Phil Wilson .... July 1, 2007–July 6, 2008
Esperanza (Hope) Andrade ...... July 23, 2008–present

★ ★ ★ ★ ★ ★ ★

Attorneys General
Of the Republic

David Thomas and
   Peter W. Grayson .... Mar. 2–Oct. 22, 1836
J. Pinckney Henderson, Peter W. Grayson,
   John Birdsall, A. S. Thurston 1836–1838
J. C. Watrous .... Dec. 1838–June 1, 1840
Joseph Webb and F. A. Morris 1840–1841
George W. Terrell, Ebenezer Allen 1841–1844
Ebenezer Allen 1844–1846

*Of the State

Volney E. Howard .... Feb. 21, 1846–May 7, 1846
John W. Harris .... May 7, 1846–Oct. 31, 1849
Henry P. Brewster .... Oct. 31, 1849–Jan. 15, 1850
A. J. Hamilton .... Jan. 15, 1850–Aug. 5, 1850
Ebenezer Allen .... Aug. 5, 1850–Aug. 2, 1852
Thomas J. Jennings .... Aug. 2, 1852–Aug. 4, 1856
James Willie .... Aug. 4, 1856–Aug. 2, 1858
Malcolm D. Graham .... Aug. 6, 1858–Aug. 6, 1860
George M. Flournoy .... Aug. 6, 1860–Jan. 15, 1862
N. G. Shelley .... Feb. 3, 1862–Aug. 1, 1864
B. E. Tarver .... Aug. 1, 1864–Dec. 11, 1865
Wm. Alexander .... Dec. 11, 1865–June 25, 1866
W. M. Walton .... June 25, 1866–Aug. 27, 1867
Wm. Alexander .... Aug. 27, 1867–Nov. 5, 1867
Ezekiel B. Turner .... Nov. 5, 1867–July 11, 1870
Wm. Alexander .... July 11, 1870–Jan. 27, 1874
George Clark .... Jan. 27, 1874–Apr. 25, 1876
H. H. Boone .... Apr. 25, 1876–Nov. 5, 1878
George McCormick .... Nov. 5, 1878–Nov. 2, 1880
J. H. McLeary .... Nov. 2, 1880–Nov. 7, 1882
John D. Templeton .... Nov. 7, 1882–Nov. 2, 1886
James S. Hogg .... Nov. 2, 1886–Nov. 4, 1890
C. A. Culberson .... Nov. 4, 1890–Nov. 6, 1894
M. M. Crane .... Nov. 6, 1894–Nov. 8, 1898
Thomas S. Smith .... Nov. 8, 1898–Mar. 15, 1901
C. K. Bell .... Mar. 20, 1901–Jan., 1904
R. V. Davidson .... Jan. 1904–Dec. 31, 1909
Jewel P. Lightfoot .... Jan. 1, 1910–Aug. 31, 1912
James D. Walthall .... Sept. 1, 1912–Jan. 1, 1913
B. F. Looney .... Jan. 1, 1913–Jan., 1919
C. M. Cureton .... Jan. 1919–Dec. 1921
W. A. Keeling .... Dec. 1921–Jan. 1925
Dan Moody .... Jan. 1925–Jan. 1927
Claude Pollard .... Jan. 1927–Sept. 1929
R. L. Bobbitt (Apptd.) .... Sept. 1929–Jan. 1931
James V. Allred .... Jan. 1931–Jan. 1935
William McCraw .... Jan. 1935–Jan. 1939
Gerald C. Mann (resigned) .... Jan. 1939–Jan. 1944

Grover Sellers................................. Jan. 1944–Jan. 1947
Price Daniel .... Jan. 1947–Jan. 1953
John Ben Shepperd.................. Jan. 1953–Jan. 1, 1957
Will Wilson .... Jan. 1, 1957–Jan. 15, 1963
Waggoner Carr .... Jan. 15, 1963–Jan. 1, 1967
Crawford C. Martin ....Jan. 1, 1967–Dec. 29, 1972
John Hill................................Jan. 1, 1973–Jan. 16, 1979
Mark White .... Jan. 16, 1979–Jan. 18, 1983
Jim Mattox .... Jan. 18, 1983–Jan. 15, 1991
Dan Morales .... Jan. 15, 1991–Jan. 13, 1999
John Cornyn .... Jan. 13, 1999–Dec. 2, 2002
Greg Abbott................................Dec. 2, 2002–present

The first few Attorneys General held office by appointment of the Governor. The office was made elective in 1850 by constitutional amendment. Ebenezer Allen was the first elected Attorney General.

★ ★ ★ ★ ★ ★ ★

Treasurers
Of the Republic

Asa Brigham... 1838–1840
James W. Simmons...................................... 1840–1841
Asa Brigham... 1841–1844
Moses Johnson 1844–1846

Of the State

James H. Raymond........... Feb. 24, 1846–Aug. 2, 1858
*C. H. Randolph........................Aug. 2, 1858–June 1865
*Samuel Harris ....Oct. 2, 1865–June 25, 1866
W. M. Royston ....June 25, 1866–Sept. 1, 1867
John Y. Allen ....Sept. 1, 1867–Jan. 1869
**George W. Honey .... Jan. 1869–Jan. 1874
**B. Graham (short term) ....beginning May 27, 1872
A. J. Dorn.. Jan. 1874–Jan. 1879
F. R. Lubbock................................. Jan. 1879–Jan. 1891
W. B. Wortham .... Jan. 1891–Jan. 1899
John W. Robbins .... Jan. 1899–Jan. 1907
Sam Sparks.................................... Jan. 1907–Jan. 1912
J. M. Edwards................................. Jan. 1912–Jan. 1919
John W. Baker .... Jan. 1919–Jan. 1921
G. N. Holton .... July 1921–Nov. 21, 1921
C. V. Terrell .... Nov. 21, 1921–Aug. 15, 1924
S. L. Staples ....Aug. 16, 1924–Jan. 15, 1925
W. Gregory Hatcher............ Jan. 16, 1925–Jan. 1, 1931
Charley Lockhart ....Jan. 1, 1931–Oct. 25, 1941
Jesse James....................Oct. 25, 1941–Sept. 29, 1977
Warren G. Harding................Oct. 7, 1977–Jan. 3, 1983
Ann Richards .... Jan. 3, 1983–Jan. 2, 1991
Kay Bailey Hutchison................ Jan. 2, 1991–June 1993
†Martha Whitehead ....June 1993–Aug. 1996

Randolph fled to Mexico upon collapse of Confederacy. No exact date is available for his departure from office or for Harris' succession to the post. It is believed Harris took office Oct. 2, 1865.
**Honey was removed from office for a short period in 1872 and B. Graham served in his place.*
† The office of Treasurer was eliminated by constitutional amendment in an election Nov. 7, 1995, effective the last day of August 1996.

★ ★ ★ ★ ★ ★ ★

Railroad Commission of Texas

(After the first three names in the following list, each commissioner's name is followed by a surname in parentheses. The name in parentheses is the name of the commissioner whom that commissioner succeeded.)

John H. Reagan............... June 10, 1891–Jan. 20, 1903
L. L. Foster ....June 10, 1891–April 30, 1895
W. P. McLean.................. June 10, 1891–Nov. 20, 1894
L. J. Storey (McLean) ....Nov. 21, 1894–Mar. 28,1909
N. A. Stedman (Foster)......... May 1, 1895–Jan. 4, 1897
Allison Mayfield (Stedman). Jan. 5, 1897–Jan. 23, 1923

O. B. Colquitt (Reagan) .....Jan. 21, 1903–Jan. 17, 1911
William D. Williams (Storey)April 28, 1909–Oct. 1, 1916
John L. Wortham (Colquitt)..Jan. 21, 1911–Jan. 1, 1913
Earle B. Mayfield (Wortham)
....Jan. 2, 1913–March 1, 1923
Charles Hurdleston (Williams)
...................................Oct. 10, 1916–Dec. 31,1918
Clarence Gilmore (Hurdleston)
.... Jan. 1, 1919–Jan. 1, 1929
N. A. Nabors (A. Mayfield)March 1, 1923–Jan. 18, 1925
William Splawn (E. Mayfield)
....March 1, 1923–Aug. 1, 1924
C. V. Terrell (Splawn) ....Aug. 15, 1924–Jan. 1, 1939
Lon A. Smith (Nabors) .... Jan. 29, 1925–Jan. 1, 1941
Pat M. Neff (Gilmore)........... Jan. 1, 1929–Jan. 1, 1933
Ernest O. Thompson (Neff) .. Jan. 1, 1933–Jan. 8, 1965
G. A. (Jerry) Sadler (Terrell).. Jan. 1, 1939–Jan. 1, 1943
Olin Culberson (Smith) ...... Jan. 1, 1941–June 22, 1961
Beauford Jester (Sadler) .... Jan. 1, 1943–Jan. 21, 1947
William J. Murray Jr. (Jester)
....................................Jan. 21, 1947–Apr. 10, 1963
Ben Ramsey (Culberson)Sept. 18, 1961–Dec. 31, 1976
Jim C. Langdon (Murray)..May 28, 1963–Dec. 31, 1977
Byron Tunnell (Thompson)
...................................Jan. 11, 1965–Sept. 15, 1973
Mack Wallace (Tunnell) . Sept. 18, 1973–Sept. 22, 1987
Jon Newton (Ramsey) .... Jan. 10, 1977–Jan. 4, 1979
John H. Poerner (Langdon).. Jan. 2, 1978–Jan. 1, 1981
James E. Nugent (Newton) ... Jan. 4, 1979–Jan. 3,1995
Buddy Temple (Poerner).... Jan. 2, 1981–March 2, 1986
Clark Jobe (Temple) .... March 3, 1986–Jan. 5, 1987
John Sharp (Jobe .... Jan. 6, 1987–Jan. 2, 1991
Kent Hance (Wallace)........Sept. 23, 1987–Jan. 2, 1991
*Robert Krueger (Hance)..... Jan. 3, 1991–Jan. 22, 1993
Lena Guerrero (Sharp) ....Jan. 23, 1991–Sept. 25, 1992
James Wallace (Guerrero).....Oct. 2, 1992–Jan. 4, 1993
Barry Williamson (Wallace)... Jan. 5, 1993–Jan. 4, 1999
Mary Scott Nabers (Krueger)Feb. 9, 1993–Dec. 9, 1994
Carole K. Rylander (Nabers)
....................................Dec. 10, 1994–Jan. 4, 1999
Charles Matthews (Nugent) Jan. 3, 1995–Jan. 31, 2005
Antonio Garza (Williamson) Jan. 4, 1999–Nov. 18, 2002
Michael L. Williams (Rylander)... Jan. 4, 1999–present
Victor G. Carrillo (Garza)..........Feb. 19, 2003–present
Elizabeth A. Jones (Matthews) ...Feb. 2, 2005–present

* *Robert Krueger resigned when Gov. Ann Richards appointed him interim U.S. Senator on the resignation of Sen. Lloyd Bentsen.*

★ ★ ★ ★ ★ ★ ★

Comptroller of Public Accounts
Of the Republic

John H. Money .... Dec. 30, 1835–Jan. 17, 1836
H. C. Hudson ....Jan. 17, 1836–Oct. 22, 1836
E. M. Pease ....June 1837–Dec. 1837
F. R. Lubbock...............................Dec. 1837–Jan. 1839
Jas. W. Simmons.............Jan. 15, 1839–Sept. 30, 1840
Jas. B. Shaw................... Sept. 30, 1840–Dec. 24, 1841
F. R. Lubbock.................Dec. 24, 1841–Jan. 1, 1842
Jas. B. Shaw......................... Jan. 1, 1842–Jan. 1, 1846

Of the State

Jas. B. Shaw...................... Feb. 24, 1846–Aug. 2, 1858
Clement R. Johns................ Aug. 2, 1858–Aug. 1, 1864
Willis L. Robards.................Aug. 1, 1864–Oct. 12, 1865
Albert R. Latimer.............. Oct. 12, 1865–Mar. 27, 1866
Robert H. Taylor.............. Mar. 27, 1866–June 25, 1866
Willis L. Robards.............June 25, 1866–Aug. 27, 1867
Morgan C. Hamilton............Aug. 27, 1867–Jan. 8, 1870
A. Bledsoe........................ Jan. 8, 1870–Jan. 20, 1874
Stephen H. Darden............Jan. 20, 1874–Nov. 2, 1880
W. M. Brown .... Nov. 2, 1880–Jan. 16, 1883
W. J. Swain....................... Jan. 16, 1883–Jan. 18, 1887

John D. McCall .... Jan. 18, 1887–Jan. 15, 1895
R. W. Finley .... Jan. 15, 1895–Jan. 15, 1901
R. M. Love .... Jan. 15, 1901–Jan. 1903
J. W. Stephen ....Jan. 1903–Jan. 1911
W. P. Lane ....Jan. 1911–Jan. 1915
H. B. Terrell .... Jan. 1915–Jan. 1920
M. L. Wiginton............................... Jan. 1920–Jan. 1921
Lon A. Smith .... Jan. 1921–Jan. 1925
S. H. Terrell .... Jan. 1925–Jan. 1931
Geo. H. Sheppard................. Jan., 1931–Jan. 17, 1949
Robert S. Calvert.................. Jan. 17, 1949–Jan., 1975
Robert D. (Bob) Bullock............ Jan. 1975–Jan. 3, 1991
John Sharp .... Jan. 3, 1991–Jan. 2, 1999
Carole Keeton Strayhorn ...... Jan. 2, 1999–Jan. 1, 2007
Susan Combs.............................Jan. 1, 2007–present

★ ★ ★ ★ ★ ★ ★

U.S. Senators from Texas

U.S. Senators were selected by the legislatures of the states until the U.S. Constitution was amended in 1913 to require popular elections. In Texas, the first senator chosen by the voters in a general election was Charles A. Culberson in 1916. Because of political pressures, however, the rules of the Democratic Party of Texas were changed in 1904 to require that all candidates for office stand before voters in the primary. Consequently, Texas' senators faced voters in 1906, 1910 and 1912 before the U.S. Constitution was changed.

Following is the succession of Texas representatives in the United States Senate since the annexation of Texas to the Union in 1845:

Houston Succession

Sam Houston......................Feb. 21, 1846–Mar. 4, 1859
John Hemphill......................Mar. 4, 1859–July 11, 1861

Louis T. Wigfall and W. S. Oldham took their seats in the Confederate Senate, Nov. 16, 1861, and served until the Confederacy collapsed. After that event, the State Legislature on Aug. 21, 1866, elected David G. Burnet and Oran M. Roberts to the United States Senate, anticipating immediate readmission to the Union, but they were not allowed to take their seats.

†Morgan C. Hamilton.........Feb. 22, 1870–Mar. 3, 1877
Richard Coke........................Mar. 4, 1877–Mar. 3, 1895
Horace Chilton......................Mar. 3, 1895–Mar. 3, 1901
Joseph W. Bailey................. Mar. 3, 1901–Jan. 8, 1913
Rienzi Melville Johnston ....Jan. 8, 1913–Feb. 3, 1913
‡Morris Sheppard (died)..... Feb. 13, 1913–Apr. 9, 1941
Andrew J. Houston ....June 2–26, 1941
W. Lee O'Daniel....................Aug. 4, 1941–Jan. 3, 1949
Lyndon B. Johnson .... Jan. 3, 1949–Jan. 20, 1961
William A. Blakley .... Jan. 20, 1961–June 15, 1961
†John G. Tower .... June 15, 1961–Jan. 21, 1985
†Phil Gramm.......................Jan. 21, 1985–Dec. 2, 2002
†**John Cornyn** ....Dec. 2, 2002–present

Rusk Succession

Thomas J. Rusk (*died*) ...... Feb 21, 1846–July 29, 1857
J. Pinckney Henderson (*died*) ......Nov. 9, 1857–June 4, 1858
Matthias Ward (*appointed interim*) .... Sept. 29, 1858–Dec. 5, 1859
Louis T. Wigfall ....Dec. 5, 1859–March 23, 1861

Succession was broken by the expulsion of Texas Senators following secession of Texas from Union. See note above under "Houston Succession" on Louis T. Wigfall, W. S. Oldham, Burnet and Roberts.

†James W. Flanagan.........Feb. 22, 1870–Mar. 3, 1875
Samuel B. Maxey ....Mar. 3, 1875–Mar. 3, 1887
John H. Reagan (*resigned*)Mar. 3, 1887–June 10, 1891

Horace Chilton (*filled vacancy on appointment*)..................Dec. 7, 1891–Mar. 30,1892
Roger Q. Mills....................Mar. 30, 1892–Mar. 3, 1899
‡Charles A. Culberson.........Mar. 3, 1899–Mar. 4, 1923
Earle B. Mayfield ....Mar. 4, 1923–Mar. 4, 1929
Tom Connally.......................Mar. 4, 1929–Jan. 3, 1953
Price Daniel .... Jan. 3, 1953–Jan. 15, 1957
William A. Blakley ....Jan. 15, 1957–Apr. 27, 1957
Ralph W. Yarborough ....Apr. 27, 1957–Jan. 12, 1971
§Lloyd Bentsen .... Jan. 12, 1971–Jan. 20, 1993
Robert Krueger............... Jan. 20, 1993–June 14, 1993
†**Kay Bailey Hutchison**............ June 14, 1993–present

† Republicans
‡ First election to U.S. Senate held in 1916. Prior to that time, senators were appointed by the Legislature.
§ Resigned from Senate when appointed U.S. Secretary of Treasury by Pres. Bill Clinton.

★ ★ ★ ★ ★ ★ ★

Commissioners of the General Land Office
Of the Republic

John P. Borden .... Aug. 23, 1837–Dec. 12, 1840
H. W. Raglin .... Dec. 12, 1840–Jan. 4, 1841
*Thomas William Ward ...... Jan. 4, 1841–Mar. 20, 1848

Of the State

George W. Smyth ....Mar. 20, 1848–Aug. 4, 1851
Stephen Crosby....................Aug. 4, 1851–Mar. 1, 1858
Francis M. White.................Mar. 1, 1858–Mar. 1, 1862
Stephen Crosby..................Mar. 1, 1862–Sept. 1, 1865
Francis M. White................ Sept. 1, 1865–Aug. 7, 1866
Stephen Crosby................. Aug. 7, 1866–Aug. 27, 1867
Joseph Spence ....Aug. 27, 1867–Jan. 19, 1870
Jacob Kuechler................. Jan. 19, 1870–Jan. 20, 1874
J. J. Groos .... Jan. 20, 1874–June 15, 1878
W. C. Walsh.......................July 30, 1878–Jan. 10, 1887
R. M. Hall .... Jan. 10, 1887–Jan. 16, 1891
W. L. McGaughey .... Jan. 16, 1891–Jan. 26, 1895
A. J. Baker .... Jan. 26, 1895–Jan. 16, 1899
George W. Finger .... Jan. 16, 1899–May 4, 1899
Charles Rogan..................May 11, 1899–Jan. 10, 1903
John J. Terrell ....Jan. 10, 1903–Jan. 11, 1909
J. T. Robison..........................Jan, 1909–Sept. 11, 1929
J. H. Walker ....Sept. 11, 1929–Jan., 1937
William H. McDonald .... Jan 1937–Jan. 1939
Bascom Giles .... Jan. 1939–Jan. 5, 1955
J. Earl Rudder....................Jan. 5, 1955–Feb. 1, 1958
Bill Allcorn ....Feb. 1, 1958–Jan. 1, 1961
Jerry Sadler .... Jan. 1, 1961–Jan. 1, 1971
Bob Armstrong..................... Jan. 1, 1971–Jan. 1, 1983
Garry Mauro .... Jan. 1, 1983–Jan. 7, 1999
David Dewhurst .... Jan. 7, 1999–Jan. 3, 2003
Jerry Patterson .... Jan. 3, 2003–present

Part of term after annexation.

★ ★ ★ ★ ★ ★ ★

Speaker of the Texas House

The Speaker of the Texas House of Representatives is the presiding officer of the lower chamber of the State Legislature. The official is elected at the beginning of each regular session by a vote of the members of the House.

Speaker, Residence	Year Elected	Legis- lature
William E. Crump, Bellville	1846	1st
William H. Bourland, Paris	1846	1st
James W. Henderson, Houston	1847	2nd
Charles G. Keenan, Huntsville	1849	3rd
David C. Dickson, Anderson	1851	4th
Hardin R. Runnels, Boston	1853	5th
Hamilton P. Bee, Laredo	1855	6th
William S. Taylor, Larissa	1857	7th

Matt F. Locke, Lafayette	1858	7th
Marion DeKalb Taylor, Jefferson	1859	8th
Constantine W. Buckley, Richmond	1861	9th
Nicholas H. Darnell, Dallas	1861	9th
Constantine W. Buckley, Richmond	1863	9th
Marion DeKalb Taylor, Jefferson	1863	10th
Nathaniel M. Burford, Dallas	1866	11th
Ira H. Evans, Corpus Christi	1870	12th
William H. Sinclair, Galveston	1871	12th
Marion DeKalb Taylor, Jefferson	1873	13th
Guy M. Bryan, Galveston	1874	14th
Thomas R. Bonner, Tyler	1876	15th
John H. Cochran, Dallas	1879	16th
George R. Reeves, Pottsboro	1881	17th
Charles R. Gibson, Waxahachie	1883	18th
Lafayette L. Foster, Groesbeck	1885	19th
George C. Pendleton, Belton	1887	20th
Frank P. Alexander, Greenville	1889	21st
Robert T. Milner, Henderson	1891	22nd
John H. Cochran, Dallas	1893	23rd
Thomas Slater Smith, Hillsboro	1895	24th
L. Travis Dashiell, Jewett	1897	25th
J. S. Sherrill, Greenville	1899	26th
Robert E. Prince, Corsicana	1901	27th
Pat M. Neff, Waco	1903	28th
Francis W. Seabury, Rio Grande City	1905	29th
Thomas B. Love, Lancaster	1907	30th
Austin M. Kennedy, Waco	1909	31st
John W. Marshall, Whitesboro	1909	31st
Sam Rayburn, Bonham	1911	32nd
Chester H. Terrell, San Antonio	1913	33rd
John W. Woods, Rotan	1915	34th
Franklin O. Fuller, Coldspring	1917	35th
R. Ewing Thomason, El Paso	1919	36th
Charles G. Thomas, Lewisville	1921	37th
Richard E. Seagler, Palestine	1923	38th
Lee Satterwhite, Amarillo	1925	39th
Robert L. Bobbitt, Laredo	1927	40th
W. S. Barron, Bryan	1929	41st
Fred H. Minor, Denton	1931	42nd
Coke R. Stevenson, Junction	1933	43rd
"	1935	44th
Robert W. Calvert, Hillsboro	1937	45th
R. Emmett Morse, Houston	1939	46th
Homer L. Leonard, McAllen	1941	47th
Price Daniel, Liberty	1943	48th
Claud H. Gilmer, Rocksprings	1945	49th
William O. Reed, Dallas	1947	50th
Durwood Manford, Smiley	1949	51st
Reuben Senterfitt, San Saba	1951	52nd
"	1953	53rd
Jim T. Lindsey, Texarkana	1955	54th
Waggoner Carr, Lubbock	1957	55th
"	1959	56th
James A. Turman, Gober	1961	57th
Byron M. Tunnell, Tyler	1963	58th
Ben Barnes, DeLeon	1965	59th
"	1967	60th
Gus F. Mutscher, Brenham	1969	61st
"	1971	62nd
Rayford Price, Palestine	1972	62nd
Price Daniel Jr., Liberty	1973	63rd
Bill Clayton, Springlake	1975	64th
"	1977	65th
"	1979	66th
"	1981	67th
Gibson D. Lewis, Fort Worth	1983	68th
"	1985	69th
"	1987	70th
"	1989	71st
"	1991	72nd
James M. (Pete) Laney, Hale Center	1993	73rd
"	1995	74th
"	1997	75th
"	1999	76th
"	2001	77th
Tom Craddick	2003	78th
"	2005	79th
"	2007	80th
Joe Straus	2009	81st

★ ★ ★ ★ ★ ★ ★

Chief Justice of the Supreme Court
Republic of Texas

James Collinsworth .... Dec. 16, 1836–July 23, 1838
John Birdsall .... Nov. 19–Dec. 12, 1838
Thomas J. Rusk................. Dec. 12, 1838–Dec. 5, 1840
John Hemphill.................... Dec. 5, 1840–Dec. 29, 1845

Under the Constitutions of 1845 and 1861

John Hemphill..................... Mar. 2, 1846–Oct. 10, 1858
Royall T. Wheeler .... Oct. 11, 1858–April 1864
Oran M. Roberts ....Nov. 1, 1864–June 30, 1866

Under the Constitution of 1866
(Presidential Reconstruction)

*George F. Moore .... Aug. 16, 1866–Sept. 10, 1867

Removed under Congressional Reconstruction by military authorities who appointed members of the next court.

Under the Constitution of 1866
(Congressional Reconstruction)

Amos Morrill...................... Sept. 10, 1867–July 5, 1870

Under the Constitution of 1869

Lemuel D. Evans .... July 5, 1870–Aug. 31, 1873
Wesley Ogden ....Aug. 31, 1873–Jan. 29, 1874
Oran M. Roberts ....Jan. 29, 1874–Apr. 18, 1876

Under the Constitution of 1876

Oran M. Roberts .... Apr. 18, 1876–Oct. 1, 1878
George F. Moore...................Nov. 5, 1878–Nov. 1, 1881
Robert S. Gould................. Nov. 1, 1881–Dec. 23, 1882
Asa H. Willie ....Dec. 23, 1882–Mar. 3, 1888
John W. Stayton ....Mar. 3, 1888–July 5, 1894
Reuben R. Gaines ....July 10, 1894–Jan. 5, 1911
Thomas J. Brown................Jan. 7, 1911–May 26, 1915
Nelson Phillips ....June 1, 1915–Nov. 16, 1921
C. M. Cureton .... Dec. 2, 1921–Apr. 8, 1940
†Hortense Sparks Ward ..... Jan. 8, 1925–May 23, 1925
W. F. Moore ....Apr. 17, 1940–Jan. 1, 1941
James P. Alexander .... Jan. 1, 1941–Jan. 1, 1948
J. E. Hickman .... Jan. 5, 1948–Jan. 3, 1961
Robert W. Calvert ....Jan. 3, 1961–Oct. 4, 1972
Joe R. Greenhill...................Oct. 4, 1972–Oct. 25, 1982
Jack Pope...........................Nov. 29, 1982–Jan. 5, 1985
John L. Hill Jr. .... Jan. 5, 1985–Jan. 4, 1988
Thomas R. Phillips...............Jan. 4, 1988–Sept. 3 2004
Wallace B. Jefferson...............Sept. 14, 2004–present

†Mrs. Ward served as Chief Justice of a special Supreme Court to hear one case in 1925.

Presiding Judges, Court of Appeals (1876–1891) and Court of Criminal Appeals (1891–present)

Mat D. Ector........................May 6, 1876–Oct. 29, 1879
John P. White.................... Nov. 9, 1879–Apr. 26, 1892
James M. Hurt ....May 4, 1892–Dec. 31, 1898
W. L. Davidson .... Jan. 2, 1899–June 27, 1913
A. C. Prendergast............June 27, 1913–Dec. 31, 1916
W. L. Davidson .... Jan. 1, 1917–Jan. 25, 1921
Wright C. Morrow................ Feb. 8, 1921–Oct. 16, 1939
Frank Lee Hawkins..............Oct. 16, 1939–Jan. 2, 1951
Harry N. Graves.................Jan. 2, 1951–Dec. 31, 1954

W. A. Morrison .... Jan. 1, 1955–Jan. 2, 1961
Kenneth K. Woodley............. Jan. 3, 1961–Jan. 4, 1965
W. T. McDonald .... Jan. 4, 1965–June 25, 1966
W. A. Morrison .... June 25, 1966–Jan. 1, 1967
Kenneth K. Woodley............. Jan. 1, 1967–Jan. 1, 1971
John F. Onion Jr.................... Jan. 1, 1971–Jan. 1, 1989
Michael J. McCormick .... Jan. 1, 1989–Jan. 1, 2001
Sharon Keller .... Jan. 1, 2001–present

★ ★ ★ ★ ★ ★ ★

Administrators of Public Education
Superintendents of Public Instruction

Pryor Lea .... Nov. 10, 1866–Sept. 12, 1867
Edwin M. Wheelock ....Sept. 12, 1867–May 6, 1871
Jacob C. DeGress .... May 6, 1871–Jan. 20, 1874
O. H. Hollingsworth............. Jan. 20, 1874–May 6, 1884
B. M. Baker......................... May 6, 1884–Jan. 18, 1887
O. H. Cooper ....Jan 18, 1887–Sept. 1, 1890
H. C. Pritchett .... Sept. 1, 1890–Sept. 15, 1891
J. M. Carlisle....................Sept. 15, 1891–Jan. 10, 1899
J. S. Kendall ....Jan. 10, 1899–July 2, 1901
Arthur Lefevre......................July 2, 1901–Jan. 12, 1905
R. B. Cousins..................... Jan. 12, 1905–Jan. 1, 1910
F. M. Bralley..........................Jan. 1, 1910–Sept. 1, 1913

W. F. Doughty .... Sept. 1, 1913–Jan. 1, 1919
Annie Webb Blanton........... Jan. 1, 1919–Jan. 16, 1923
S. M. N. Marrs ....Jan. 16, 1923–April 28, 1932
C. N. Shaver....................... April 28, 1932–Oct. 1, 1932
L. W. Rogers.......................Oct. 1, 1932–Jan. 16, 1933
L. A. Woods ....Jan. 16, 1933–*1951

State Commissioner of Education

J. W. Edgar...................... May 31, 1951–June 30, 1974
Marlin L. Brockette............... July 1, 1974–Sept. 1, 1979
Alton O. Bowen...................Sept. 1, 1979–June 1, 1981
Raymon Bynum ....June 1, 1981–Oct. 31, 1984
W. N. Kirby.......................... April 13, 1985–July 1, 1991
Lionel R. Meno ....July 1, 1991–March 1, 1995
Michael A. Moses ....March 9, 1995–Aug. 18, 1999
Jim Nelson....................Aug. 18, 1999–March 25, 2002
Felipe Alanis ....March 25, 2002–July 31, 2003
Shirley J. Neeley..................Jan. 12, 2004–July 1, 2007
Robert Scott................................July 1, 2007–present

*The office of State Superintendent of Public In-
struction was abolished by the Gilmer-Aikin act of 1949
and the office of Commissioner of Education created,
appointed by a new State Board of Education elected by
the people.

First Ladies of Texas

Martha Evans Gindratt Wood................. 1847–49
† Bell Administration 1849–53
Lucadia Christiana Niles Pease1853-57; 1867–69
‡ Runnels Administration 1857–59
Margaret Moffette Lea Houston 1859–61
Martha Evans Clark 1861
Adele Barron Lubbock 1861–1863
Susie Ellen Taylor Murrah 1863–1865
Mary Jane Bowen Hamilton 1865–1866
Annie Rattan Throckmorton 1866–1867
Ann Elizabeth Britton Davis 1870–1874
Mary Home Coke............................... 1874–1876
Janie Roberts Hubbard 1876–1879
Frances Wickliff Edwards Roberts 1879–1883
Anne Maria Penn Ireland 1883–1887
Elizabeth Dorothy Tinsley Ross 1887–1891
Sarah Stinson Hogg........................... 1891–1895
Sally Harrison Culberson 1895–1899
Orlene Walton Sayers......................... 1899–1903
Sarah Beona Meng Lanham............... 1903–1907
Fannie Brunner Campbell................... 1907–1911
Alice Fuller Murrell Colquitt................. 1911–1915
§ Miriam A. Wallace Ferguson 1915–1917
Willie Cooper Hobby 1917–1921
Myrtle Mainer Neff.............................. 1921–1925
Mildred Paxton Moody 1927–1931
Maud Gage Sterling............................ 1931–1933
Jo Betsy Miller Allred.......................... 1935–1939
Merle Estella Butcher O'Daniel 1939–1941
**Fay Wright Stevenson...................... 1941–1942
**Edith Will Scott Stevenson............... 1942–1946
Mabel Buchanan Jester 1946–1949
Marialice Shary Shivers 1949–1957
Jean Houston Baldwin Daniel............. 1957–1963
Idanell Brill Connally 1963–1969
Ima Mae Smith................................... 1969–1973
Betty Jane Slaughter Briscoe............. 1973–1979
Rita Crocker Bass Clements............... 1979–1983
Linda Gale Thompson White 1983–1987
Rita Crocker Bass Clements............... 1987–1991
Laura Welch Bush.............................. 1995–2000
Anita Thigpen Perry..................... 2000–present

*First Lady Anita Perry. Photo courtesy of the Office
of the First Lady.*

†*Gov. Peter Hansbrough Bell was not married
while in office*

‡*Gov. Hardin R. Runnels never married.*

§*Miriam A. Wallace Ferguson was Mistress of the
Mansion while her husband, James E. Ferguson,
was governor, 1915–1917. She served as both
Governor and Mistress of the Mansion, 1925–
1927 and 1933–1935.*

**Mrs. Coke R. (Fay Wright) Stevenson, the gov-
ernor's wife, died in the Governor's Mansion Jan.
3, 1942. His mother, Edith Stevenson, served as
Mistress of the Mansion thereafter.*

*During Ann Richards' term as governor, 1991–
1995, she was not married. ☆*

State Government

Texas state government is divided into executive, legislative and judicial branches under the Texas Constitution adopted in 1876.

The chief executive is the Governor, whose term is for four years. Other elected state officials with executive responsibilities include the Lieutenant Governor, Attorney General, Comptroller of Public Accounts, Commissioner of the General Land Office and Commissioner of Agriculture. The terms of those officials are also four years.

The Secretary of State and the Commissioner of Education are appointed by the Governor.

Except for making numerous appointments and calling special sessions of the Legislature, the Governor's powers are limited in comparison with those in most states.

Current state executives "not-to-exceed" salaries are for the 2008–2009 biennium (maximum possible salaries; actual salaries can be lower); salaries for the 2010–2011 biennium were not available from the State Auditor at press time.

The Governor's office welcomes comments and concerns, which are relayed to government officials who may offer assistance. Send a message at: http://www2.governor.state.tx.us/contact/ or call the **Citizen's Opinion Hotline (1-800-252-9600).**

Governor Rick Perry
P.O. Box 12428, Austin 78711
512-463-2000
www.governor.state.tx.us
Salary: $150,000

Lt. Governor David Dewhurst
P.O. Box 12068, Austin 78711
512-463-0001
www.senate.state.tx.us
Salary: Same as Senator
when serving as President of
the Senate; same as Governor
when serving as Governor

**Attorney General
Greg Abbott**
P.O. Box 12548, Austin 78711
512-463-2100
www.oag.state.tx.us
Salary: $150,000

**Comptroller of Public
Accounts Susan Combs**
PO Box 13528, Austin 78774
512-463-4000
www.windows.state.tx.us
Salary: $150,000

**Land Office Commissioner
Jerry Patterson**
P.O. Box 12873, Austin 78711
512-463-5001
www.glo.state.tx.us
Salary: $137,500

Agriculture Commissioner
Todd Staples
P.O. Box 12847, Austin 78711
512-463-7476
www.agr.state.tx.us
Salary: $137,500

Secretary of State
Esperanza (Hope) Andrade
P.O. Box 12887, Austin 78711
512-463-5770
www.sos.state.tx.us
Salary: $117,516

Education Commissioner
Robert Scott
1701 N. Congress Ave.
Austin 78701
(512) 463-9734
www.tea.state.tx.us
Salary: $164,748

State Government Income and Expenditures

Taxes are the state government's primary source of income. On this and the following pages are summaries of state income and expenditures, percent change from previous year, tax collections, tax revenue by type of tax, a summary of the state budget for the 2010–2011 biennium, Texas Lottery income and expenditures and the amount of federal payments to state agencies. Totals may not sum due to rounding.

State Revenues by Source and Expenditures by Function
Amounts (in Millions) and Percent Change from Previous Year

Revenues by Source	2008	%	2007	%	2006	%	2005	%	2004	%
Tax Collections	$41,358	11.9	$36,956	10.2	$33,544	12.4	$29,838	6.9	$27,913	6.8
Federal Income	26,238	7.6	24,376	−1.4	24,726	8.4	22,810	4.0	21,938	4.6
Licenses, Fees, Permits, Fines, Penalties	10,228	47.9	6,914	15.3	5,999	−2.5	6,155	11.0	5,546	15.9
Interest & Other Investment Income	2,309	−2.7	2,373	21.7	1,949	27.5	1,529	8.8	1,406	−10.7
Net Lottery Proceeds	1,597	2.9	1,552	−2.1	1,585	0.0	1,584	−0.8	1,597	13.6
Sales of Goods & Services	496	−8.0	539	9.4	492	43.1	344	4.5	329	−5.1
Settlements of Claims	548	2.0	538	−1.4	545	−1.1	552	8.2	510	−8.0
Land Income	1,050	39.8	751	−12.7	861	31.6	654	31.3	498	27.8
Contributions to Employee Benefits	15	−93.7	238	7.7	221	12.0	197	10.7	178	11.3
Other Revenues	3,143	6.4	2,953	18.3	2,497	16.4	2,146	−0.6	2,158	8.4
Total Net Revenues	**$86,983**	**12.7**	**$77,189**	**6.6**	**$72,421**	**10.0**	**$65,810**	**6.0**	**$62,073**	**6.5**
Expenditures by Function	**2008**	**%**	**2007**	**%**	**2006**	**%**	**2005**	**%**	**2004**	**%**
General Government – Total	$2,514	8.1	$2,325	−3.6	$2,412	8.9	$2,215	8.6	$2,040	1.8
Executive	2,146	8.9	1,970	−5.9	2,094	9.7	1,908	8.5	1,759	3.0
Legislative	123	−4.9	129	11.2	116	−4.4	122	9.0	112	−7.5
Judicial	245	8.8	225	11.9	201	9.1	185	9.6	169	−3.6
Education	30,776	16.9	26,324	13.5	23,185	6.1	21,844	5.4	20,734	−0.5
Employee Benefits	2,980	5.1	2,836	4.7	2,709	−1.3	2,745	2.2	2,685	−14.7
Health and Human Services	29,681	6.4	27,895	9.6	25,458	4.7	24,308	5.8	22,966	0.4
Public Safety and Corrections	4,048	7.1	3,778	−10.4	4,218	27.8	3,301	0.8	3,276	−3.4
Transportation	7,668	0.8	7,609	4.0	7,316	10.2	6,641	26.6	5,248	6.4
Natural Resources/Recreational Services	2,103	10.8	1,898	16.2	1,634	−2.3	1,672	−12.7	1,915	38.1
Regulatory Agencies	301	29.3	233	1.6	229	−16.1	273	−12.0	310	28.4
Lottery Winnings Paid*	423	8.5	390	−18.1	476	6.1	448	−13.3	517	25.0
Debt Service – Interest	973	16.1	837	6.6	785	25.6	625	8.7	575	−8.1
Capital Outlay	468	25.0	375	−8.6	410	−33.7	618	36.9	452	10.2
Total Net Expenditures	**$81,936**	**10.0**	**$74,501**	**8.2**	**$68,833**	**6.4**	**$64,693**	**6.5**	**$60,719**	**0.7**

* Does not include payments made by retailers. All amounts rounded. Expenditures exclude trust funds. Fiscal years end August 31.
Source: 2008 State of Texas Annual Cash Report, Revenue and Expenditures of State Funds for the Year Ending August 31, 2008, Comptroller of Public Accounts' Office.

State Government Budget Summary
2010–2011 Biennium

Source: Legislative Budget Board; *www.lbb.state.tx.us.*

The Legislative Budget Board's (LBB) recommended baseline appropriations for state government operations for the 2010–2011 biennium total $170.8 billion from all fund sources. The recommendations provide a $1 billion, or 0.6 percent, increase from the 2008–2009 biennial level.

General Revenue Funds, including funds dedicated within the General Revenue Fund, total $89.7 billion for the 2010–2011 biennium, an increase of $1.1 billion, or 1.2 percent, over the anticipated 2008–2009 biennial spending level.

The LBB recommended appropriations for the 2010–2011 biennium are within the Comptroller's 2010–2011 Biennial Revenue Estimate. ☆

Article (Governmental Division) (all funds in millions)	Estimated/ Budgeted for 2008–2009*	Recommended 2010–2011 Budget	Biennial Change	Percentage Change
Art. I, General Government	$ 3,845.1	$ 3,481.0	$ −364.1	−9.5
Art. II, Health and Human Services	54,542.0	57,207.9	2,665.9	4.9
Art. III, Education	74,151.9	74,743.6	591.7	0.8
Public Education**	52,977.5	52,622.4	−355.1	−0.7
Higher Education	21,174.3	22,121.1	946.8	4.5
Art. IV, The Judiciary	624.2	637.0	12.8	2.0
Art. V, Public Safety & Criminal Justice	10,625.4	10,246.4	−379.0	−3.6
Art. VI, Natural Resources	3,344.0	3,359.8	15.8	0.5
Art. VII, Business & Economic Dev.	21,510.3	19,967.2	−1,543.1	−7.2
Art. VIII, Regulatory	767.3	785.3	18.0	2.3
Art. IX, General Provisions	0.0	0.0	0.0	NA
Art. X, The Legislature	344.0	355.4	11.5	3.3
Total	**$ 169,754.0**	**$ 170,783.5**	**$1,029.5**	**0.6**

All funds in millions.
*Estimated/budgeted amounts in the 2008–2009 biennium include $1,487.6 million to cover the cost of a 25th month of Foundation School Program payments, reversing the deferral of the August payment into the following fiscal year. This is a one-time cost and no appropriation is necessary in the 2010–2011 biennium.

State Tax Collections 1994–2008

Fiscal Year‡	State Tax Collections	Resident Population*	Per Capita Tax Collections	Taxes as % of Personal Income
1994	$18,105,950,592	18,340,852	$ 987.19	4.9
1995	18,858,790,042	18,693,032	1,008.87	4.8
1996	19,762,504,350	18,966,000	1,042.00	4.7
1997	21,187,868,237	19,312,000	1,097.13	4.7
1998	22,634,019,740	20,104,000	1,126.00	4.4
1999	23,614,611,235	20,507,000	1,152.00	4.4
2000	25,283,768,842	20,904,000	1,210.00	4.4
2001	27,230,212,416	21,317,000	1,277.00	4.5
2002	26,279,146,493	21,673,000	1,213.00	4.2
2003	26,126,675,424	22,052,000	1,185.00	4.1
2004	27,913,001,645	22,409,000	1,246.00	4.1
2005	29,838,277,614	22,808,000	1,308.00	4.0
2006	33,544,497,547	23,379,000	1,435.00	4.2
2007	36,955,629,884	23,841,000	1,550.00	4.2
2008	41,357,928,953	24,306,000	1,702.00	4.4

‡ Fiscal years end August 31.
* Revised fiscal year estimates

Sources: Tax collection data, Texas Comptroller of Public Accounts, Annual Financial Reports of various years. Population and personal income figures, 2004 to 2007: U.S. Dept. of Commerce (Bureau of the Census and Bureau of Economic Analysis), adjusted to Texas fiscal years by Comptroller of Public Accounts. Data for 2008 include partial estimates by the Texas Comptroller of Public Accounts.

Tax Revenues 2007–2008

Below are listed the major taxes and the amounts each contributed to the state in fiscal years 2007 and 2008.

Type of Tax	FY 2007	FY 2008
Sales	$20,270,476,222	$21,604,090,350
Motor Vehicle Sales and Rentals*	3,325,596,670	3,341,588,813
Motor Fuels	3,053,812,019	3,101,526,779
Franchise	3,144,059,392	4,451,325,736
Insurance	1,346,576,684	1,450,184,267
Natural Gas Production	1,895,487,909	2,684,647,510
Cigarette &Tobacco	1,334,038,617	1,446,894,671
Alcoholic Beverages	731,677,225	784,068,675
Oil Production	835,025,116	1,436,879,156
Inheritance	5,291,127	5,580,142
Utility	506,069,409	503,878,555
Hotel	340,634,147	370,979,724
Other Taxes	166,885,345	176,284,575
Totals	**$36,955,629,884**	**$41,357,928,953**

*Includes tax on manufactured housing sales and taxes on interstate motor carriers.

Source: 2008 State of Texas Annual Cash Report, Revenue and Expenditures of State Funds for the Year Ending August 31, 2008, Texas Comptroller of Public Accounts.

Federal Revenue by State Agency

Source: Texas Comptroller of Public Accounts, 2008 State of Texas Annual Cash Report, Revenue and Expenditures of State Funds for the Year Ending August 31, 2008.

Texas received $26.2 billion in federal funds during fiscal 2008, an increase of 7.6 percent from fiscal 2007. Federal funds are second only to tax collections as a source of revenue for the state accounting for 30.2 percent of total net revenue.

State Agency	2008	2007	2006	2005
Health and Human Services Commission	$14,943,839,631	$14,035,890,889	$12,776,549,811	$12,148,742,005
Texas Education Agency	4,268,435,111	4,342,879,281	4,247,418,741	3,834,814,130
Texas Department of Transportation	2,690,057,920	1,974,299,512	3,090,574,205	3,250,361,011
Department of State Health Services*	1,066,202,614	978,045,778	1,028,932,697	913,038,794
Texas Workforce Commission	881,300,645	961,052,202	939,632,616	876,996,803
Department of Assistive and Rehabilitative Services	410,578,731	378,867,613	346,265,781	302,975,841
Department of Family and Protective Services	345,358,433	366,446,983	342,709,315	330,138,905
Texas Department of Public Safety	321,177,791	378,228,787	969,835,174	155,148,088
Department of Agriculture	277,766,746	32,973,604	9,255,355	10,470,766
Attorney General	202,161,262	214,241,329	232,055,291	234,031,957
Texas Department of Housing and Community Affairs	164,054,834	165,741,641	158,572,570	151,228,941
Department of Aging and Disability Services	107,734,327	107,533,280	102,936,327	103,051,688
Office of Rural Community Affairs	106,691,789	99,845,076	76,785,273	83,837,810
Texas Higher Education Coordinating Board	85,016,320	14,954,678	8,255,869	5,489,315
All Other Agencies	367,951,531	325,051,848	396,674,915	417,769,958
Total All Agencies	**$ 26,238,327,684**	**$ 24,376,052,502**	**$ 24,726,453,940**	**$ 22,809,751,233**

*As of Sept. 1, 2004, several agencies were incorporated into the Dept.of State Health Services, including the Dept. of Human Services, Texas Dept. of Health, Texas Rehabilitation Commission and Texas Commission on Alcohol and Drug Abuse.

Texas Lottery

Source: Texas Lottery Commission; www.txlottery.org/

The State Lottery Act was passed by the Texas Legislature in July 1991. Texas voters approved a constitutional amendment authorizing a state lottery in an election on Nov. 5, 1991, by a vote of 1,326,154 to 728,994. Sales — since the first ticket was sold on May 29, 1992, through 2008 — totaled more than $51 billion. During the same period, more than $29.5 billion was paid out in prizes.

The Texas Lottery® offers players a wide range of choices, including about 80 instant ticket scratch-off games and online games.

About 27 percent of all lottery revenue is transferred to the Foundation School Fund, which supports public education in Texas. Before September 1997, revenues were deposited in the General Revenue Fund.

Texas Lottery transfers to the state from May 1992 to August 2008 totaled $16,110,443,611, with $10,673,963,036 going to the Foundation School Fund and $5,135,464,610 to the General Revenue Fund.

Who Plays the Texas Lottery

The Texas Lottery Commission executive director is required to conduct a biennial demographic survey of lottery players to determine the income, age, sex, race, education and frequency of participation of players. The following information is drawn from the survey, conducted in August and September 2008 by the Center for Public Policy at the University of Houston. A total of 1,695 usable interviews were completed with Texans ages 18 and older. All demographic information and participation rates were self-reported and not independently verified. The data has a +2.4 percent margin of error at a confidence level of 95 percent.

The percentage of Texans who reported purchasing at least one Texas Lottery ticket in 12 months preceding the survey was 38.8 percent. Of those, 68.9 percent played Lotto Texas®; 54 percent, "scratch off" or instant games; 45.3 percent, Mega Millions®; 20 percent, Cash Five®; 9.7 percent, Texas Two Step®; 22 percent, Pick 3™ day draw; 1.8 percent, Pick 3 night draw; and 1.8 percent, Daily 4™.

Age: The 25–34, 45–54 and 55–64 age groups had the highest participation rates. The 45–54 age group

Texas Lottery Financial Data

Start-up to Aug. 31, 2008

All dollar amounts in millions

Period	Sales	Value of Prizes Won	Retailer Comm- issions	Admin- istration	To State of Texas
Start-up– FY 1993	$2,448	$1,250	$122	$170	$812
FY 1994	2,760	1,529	138	167	869
FY 1995	3,037	1,689	152	188	927
FY 1996	3,432	1,951	172	217	1,158
FY 1997	3,745	2,152	187	236	1,189
FY 1998	3,090	1,648	155	198	1,157
FY 1999	2,572	1,329	129	169	969
FY 2000	2,657	1,509	133	172	918
FY 2001	2,825	1,643	141	173	865
FY 2002	2,966	1,715	148	167	957
FY 2003	3,131	1,845	157	158	955
FY 2004	3,488	2,069	174	181	1,044
FY 2005	3,662	2,228	183	179	1,077
FY 2006	3,775	2,311	189	185	1,085
FY 2007	3,774	2,315	189	183	1,091
FY 2008	3,671	2,281	184	167	1,037

All figures accrued.

reported spending more on average than those in other age categories.

Educational Level: Respondents with some college education were somewhat more likely to play than other groups; this group also spent the most on lottery products, averaging $16.50 per month.

Income Level: Respondents in the $60,000 to $74,999 and $75,000 to $100,000 annual income ranges were somewhat more likely to play than other groups.

Ethnic Background: Residents who self-identified as Hispanic, black or "other" were slightly more likely to participate, and Asian lottery players spent more per month than members of other racial/ethnic groups.

Sex: Males were more likely than females to play the lottery and averaged $15 per month. Females reported spending $10 per month on average. ☆

Texas Legislature

The Texas Legislature has **181 members: 31 in the Senate** and **150 in the House of Representatives**. Regular sessions convene on the second Tuesday of January in odd-numbered years, but the governor may call special sessions. Article III of the Texas Constitution deals with the legislative branch. On the Web: **www.capitol.state.tx.us**.

The following lists are of members of the **81st Legislature**, which convened for its Regular Session on Jan. 13, 2009, and adjourned on June 1, 2009. The **82nd Legislature** is scheduled to convene on Jan. 11, 2011, and adjourn May 30, 2011.

State Senate

Thirty-one members of the State Senate are elected to four-year, overlapping terms. Salary: The salary of all members of the Legislature, both Senators and Representatives, is $7,200 per year and $124 per diem during legislative sessions; mileage allowance at same rate provided by law for state employees. The per diem payment applies during each regular and special session of the Legislature.

Senatorial Districts include one or more whole counties and some counties have more than one Senator.

The **address of Senators** is Texas Senate, P.O. Box 12068, Austin 78711-2068; phone 512-463-0200; Fax: 512-463-0326. On the Web: **www.senate.state.tx.us**.

President of the Senate: Lt. Gov. David Dewhurst; **President Pro Tempore:** Robert Duncan; **Secretary of the Senate:** Patsy Spaw; **Sergeant-at-Arms:** Rick De-Leon.

Texas State Senators

District, Member, Party-Hometown, Occupation

1. Kevin P. Eltife, R-Tyler; businessman.
2. Robert F. Deuell, R-Greenville; family physician.
3. Robert Nichols, R-Jacksonville; engineer.
4. Tommy Williams, R-The Woodlands; businessman.
5. Steve Ogden, R-Bryan; oil and gas producer.
6. Mario Gallegos Jr., D-Houston; retired firefighter.
7. Dan Patrick, R-Houston; broadcasting.
8. Florence Shapiro, R-Plano; former small business owner.
9. Chris Harris, R-Arlington; attorney.
10. Wendy R. Davis, D-Fort Worth; attorney.
11. Mike Jackson, R-La Porte; businessman.
12. Jane Nelson, R-Lewisville; businesswoman.
13. Rodney Ellis, D-Houston; attorney, investment banker.
14. Kirk Watson, D-Austin; attorney.
15. John Whitmire, D-Houston; attorney (**Dean of the Senate**).
16. John J. Carona, R-Dallas; CEO.
17. Joan Huffman, R-Houston; attorney, former judge.
18. Glenn Hegar Jr., R-Katy; farmer.
19. Carlos I. Uresti, D-San Antonio; attorney.
20. Juan (Chuy) Hinojosa, D-McAllen; attorney.
21. Judith Zaffirini, D-Laredo; communications specialist, former educator.
22. Kip Averitt, R-Waco; CPA, tax consultant.
23. Royce West, D-Dallas; attorney.
24. Troy Fraser, R-Horseshoe Bay; businessman.
25. Jeff Wentworth, R-San Antonio; attorney, Realtor.
26. Leticia Van de Putte, D-San Antonio; pharmacist.
27. Eddie Lucio Jr., D-Brownsville; advertising executive.
28. Robert Duncan, R-Lubbock; attorney.
29. Eliot Shapleigh, D-El Paso; attorney, businessman.
30. Craig Estes, R-Wichita Falls; businessman.
31. Kel Seliger, R-Amarillo; business owner.

Lt. Gov. David Dewhurst presides over the Texas Senate. Harry Cabluck/AP photo.

Spectators watch the proceedings in the Texas House during the 81st Legislative session in March 2009. Robert Plocheck photo.

House of Representatives

This is a list of the 150 members of the House of Representatives in the 81st Legislature. They were elected for two-year terms from the districts shown below. Representatives and senators receive the same salary (see State Senate). The **address of all Representatives** is House of Representatives, P.O. Box 2910, Austin, 78768-2910; phone: 512-463-1000; Fax: 512-463-6337. On the Web: **www.house.state.tx.us/**

This is a list of the 150 members of the House of Representatives in the 81st Legislature. They were elected for two-year terms from the districts shown below. Representatives and senators receive the same salary (see State Senate). The **address of all Representatives** is House of Representatives, P.O. Box 2910, Austin, 78768-2910; phone: 512-463-1000; Fax: 512-463-6337. On the Web: **www.house.state.tx.us/**

Speaker Joe Straus

Speaker, Joe Straus III (R-San Antonio). **Speaker Pro Tempore**, Craig Eiland (D-Galveston). **Chief Clerk**, Robert Haney. **Sergeant-at-Arms**, Rod Welsh.

Texas State Representatives

District, Member, Party-Hometown, Occupation
1. Stephen J. Frost, D-Atlanta, attorney.
2. Dan Flynn, R-Van; businessman, rancher.
3. Mark S. Homer, D-Paris; small business owner.
4. Betty Brown, R-Terrell; homemaker, rancher.
5. Bryan Hughes, R-Mineola; attorney.
6. Leo Berman, R-Tyler; retired U.S. Army Lt. Col. and oil and gas executive.
7. Tommy Merritt, R-Longview; small business owner.
8. Byron C. Cook, R-Corsicana; businessman, rancher.
9. Wayne Christian, R-Center; investment sales.
10. Jim Pitts, R-Waxahachie; attorney.
11. Charles L. (Chuck) Hopson, D-Jacksonville; pharmacist.
12. Jim McReynolds, D-Lufkin; petroleum landman.
13. Lois W. Kolkhorst, R-Brenham; business owner, investor.
14. Fred H. Brown, R-College Station; healthcare.
15. Rob Eissler, R-The Woodlands; executive recruiter.
16. Brandon Creighton, R-Conroe; attorney, real estate development.
17. Tim Kleinschmidt, R-Lexington; attorney, rancher.
18. John C. Otto, R-Dayton; CPA.
19. Mike Hamilton, R-Mauriceville; catering.
20. Dan Gattis, R-Georgetown; attorney, rancher.
21. Allan B. Ritter, D-Nederland; business owner.
22. Joseph (Joe) Deshotel, D-Beaumont; attorney, businessman.
23. Craig Eiland, D-Galveston; attorney (**Speaker Pro Tempore).**
24. Larry Taylor, R-Friendswood; insurance agency owner.
25. Dennis H. Bonnen, R-Angleton; banking.
26. Charlie Howard, R-Sugar Land; Realtor, investor.
27. Dora F. Olivo, D-Rosenberg; attorney.
28. John Zerwas, R-Richmond; physician.
29. Randy Weber, R-Pearland; small business owner.
30. Geanie W. Morrison, R-Victoria; legislator.
31. Ryan Guillen, D-Rio Grande City; rancher, small businessman.

32. Todd Hunter, R-Corpus Christi; attorney.
33. Solomon P. Ortiz Jr., D-Corpus Christi; businessman.
34. Abel Herrero, D-Robstown; attorney.
35. Yvonne Gonzalez Toureilles, D-Alice; attorney.
36. Ismael (Kino) Flores, D-Palmview; business manager.
37. Rene O. Oliveira, D-Brownsville; attorney.
38. Eddie Lucio III, D-Brownsville; attorney.
39. Armando A. (Mando) Martinez, D-Weslaco; firefighter, paramedic.
40. Aaron Peña, D-Edinburg; attorney.
41. Veronica Gonzales, D-McAllen; attorney.
42. Richard Peña Raymond, D-Laredo; businessman.
43. Tara Rios Ybarra, D-South Padre Island; dentist.
44. Edmund Kuempel, R-Seguin; salesman.
45. Patrick M. Rose, D-Dripping Springs; attorney, Realtor.
46. Dawnna M. Dukes, D-Austin; business consultant.
47. Valinda Bolton, D-Austin; non-profit consultant.
48. Donna Howard, D-Austin; nursing, public health.
49. Elliott Naishtat, D-Austin; attorney.
50. Mark Strama, D-Austin; technology executive.
51. Eddie Rodriguez, D-Austin; legislator, law student.
52. Diane M. Maldonado, D-Round Rock; legislator.
53. Harvey Hilderbran, R-Kerrville; businessman.
54. Jimmie Don Aycock, R-Killeen; veterinarian, rancher.
55. Ralph Sheffield, R-Temple; restaurant owner.
56. Charles (Doc) Anderson, R-Waco; veterinarian.
57. Jim Dunnam, D-Waco; attorney.
58. Rob D. Orr, R-Burleson; real estate broker.
59. Sid Miller, R-Stephenville; nurseryman, rancher.
60. James L. Keffer, R-Eastland; businessman.
61. Phil S. King, R-Weatherford; attorney.
62. Larry Phillips, R-Sherman, attorney.
63. Tan Parker, R-Flower Mound; businessman.
64. Myra Crownover, R-Denton; ranching, businesswoman.
65. Burt R. Solomons, R-Carrollton; attorney.
66. Brian McCall, R-Plano; businessman.
67. Jerry Madden, R-Richardson; insurance agent.
68. Richard (Rick) L. Hardcastle, R-Vernon; rancher.
69. David Farabee, D-Wichita Falls; insurance agent.
70. Ken Paxton, R-McKinney; attorney.
71. Susan King, R-Abilene; surgical nurse.
72. Drew Darby, R-San Angelo; attorney, business owner.
73. Doug Miller, R-New Braunfels; insurance agent.
74. Pete P. Gallego, D-Alpine; attorney.
75. Inocente (Chente) Quintanilla, D-Tornillo; retired assistant superintendent, educator.
76. Norma Chávez, D-El Paso; business manager.
77. Marisa Marquez, D-El Paso; manager.
78. Joseph E. Moody, D-El Paso; assistant district attorney.
79. Joseph (Joe) C. Pickett, D-El Paso; real estate.
80. Tracy O. King, D-Batesville; hearing aid specialist.
81. Tryon D. Lewis, R-Odessa; attorney.
82. Tom Craddick, R-Midland; investor, sales representative.
83. Delwin Jones, R-Lubbock; businessman (**Senior House Member**).
84. Carl H. Isett, R-Lubbock; CPA.
85. Joe Heflin, D-Crosbyton; attorney.
86. John T. Smithee, R-Amarillo; attorney.
87. David A. Swinford, R-Dumas; businessman.
88. Warren D. Chisum, R-Pampa; oil and gas producer, rancher.
89. Jodie Laubenberg, R-Parker; legislator.
90. Lon Burnam, D-Fort Worth; Dallas Peace Center director.
91. Kelly G. Hancock, R-North Richland Hills; business owner.
92. Todd Smith, R-Euless; attorney.
93. Paula Pierson, D-Arlington; businesswoman.
94. Diane Patrick, R-Arlington; university professor.
95. Marc Veasey, D-Fort Worth; real estate.
96. Chris Turner, D-Burleson; business consultant.
97. Mark M. Shelton, R-Fort Worth; physician.
98. Vicki Truitt, R-Keller; small business owner.
99. Charlie L. Geren, R-Fort Worth; restaurant owner, real estate broker, rancher.
100. Terri Hodge, D-Dallas; legislator.
101. Robert Miklos, D-Mesquite; attorney.
102. Carol Kent, D-Dallas; legislator.
103. Rafael Anchiá, D-Dallas; attorney.
104. Roberto R. Alonzo, D-Dallas; attorney.
105. Linda Harper-Brown, R-Irving; CEO.
106. Kirk T. England, D-Grand Prairie; insurance agent.
107. Allen Vaught, D-Dallas; attorney.
108. Dan Branch, R-Dallas; attorney.
109. Helen Giddings, D-Dallas; small business owner.
110. Barbara Mallory Caraway, D-Dallas; small business owner.
111. Yvonne Davis, D-Dallas; small business owner.
112. Angie Button Chen, R-Garland; marketing executive.
113. Joe Driver, R-Garland; insurance agent.
114. Will Hartnett, R-Dallas; probate attorney, businessman.
115. Jim L. Jackson, R-Carrollton; legislator.
116. Trey Martinez Fischer, D-San Antonio; attorney.
117. David M. Leibowitz, D-San Antonio; attorney.
118. Joe Farias, D-San Antonio; legislator.
119. Roland Gutierrez, D-San Antonio; attorney.
120. Ruth Jones McClendon, D-San Antonio; businesswoman.
121. Joe Straus III, R-San Antonio; insurance, investments (**Speaker of the House**).
122. Frank J. Corte Jr., R-San Antonio; real estate, property management.
123. Michael (Mike) Villarreal, D-San Antonio; small business owner, investment banker.
124. Jose Menendez, D-San Antonio; marketing VP.
125. Joaquin Castro, D-San Antonio; attorney.
126. Patricia F. Harless, R-Spring; automobile dealer.
127. Joe Crabb, R-Atascocita; minister, attorney, rancher.
128. Wayne Smith, R-Baytown; civil engineer.
129. John E. Davis, R-Houston; roofing sales.
130. Allen Fletcher, R-Tomball; businessman.
131. Alma A. Allen, D-Houston; educator.
132. William A. Callegari, R-Katy; professional engineer.
133. Kristi Thibaut, D-Houston; public service, non-profit fundraising.
134. Ellen R. Cohen, D-Houston; CEO.
135. Gary Elkins, R-Houston; businessman, consultant.
136. Beverly Woolley, R-Houston; small business owner.
137. Scott Hochberg, D-Houston; software consultant.
138. Dwayne Bohac, R-Houston; businessman.
139. Sylvester Turner, D-Houston; attorney.
140. Armando Lucio Walle, D-Houston; county commissioner staff.
141. Senfronia Thompson, D-Houston; attorney.
142. Harold V. Dutton Jr., D-Houston; attorney.
143. Ana E. Hernandez, D-Houston; attorney.
144. Ken Legler, R-Pasadena; business owner.
145. Carol Alvarado, D-Houston; legislator.
146. Al Edwards, D-Houston; real estate broker.
147. Garnet Coleman, D-Houston; business consultant.
148. Jessica Farrar, D-Houston; architect.
149. Hubert Vo, D-Houston; Realtor.
150. Debbie Riddle, R-Tomball; horse breeder. ☆

The Tyler Rose Garden stretches out in front of the Texas Supreme Court Building. The Texas Pioneer Woman statue is at left. Ron Billings photo; Texas Forest Service.

Texas State Judiciary

The judiciary of the state consists of 9 members of the State Supreme Court; 9 members of the Court of Criminal Appeals; 80 of the Courts of Appeals; 443 of the State District Courts, including 13 Criminal District Courts; 494 County Court judges; 821 Justices of the Peace; and 1,412 Municipal Courts judges.

In addition to its system of formal courts, the State of Texas has established 17 **Alternative Dispute Resolution Centers**. The centers help ease the caseload of Texas courts by using mediation, arbitration, negotiation and moderated settlement conferences to handle disputes without resorting to more costly, time-consuming court actions.

Centers are located in Amarillo, Austin, Beaumont, Bryan, Conroe, Corpus Christi, Dallas, Denton, El Paso, Fort Worth, Houston, Kerrville, Lubbock, Paris, Richmond, San Antonio and Waco. For the fiscal year ending Aug. 31, 2005, the mediation sections of the centers had closed 18,292 cases and had 2,997 cases pending.

(The list of U.S. District Courts in Texas can be found in the Federal Government section, page 538.)

State Higher Courts

The state's higher courts are listed below and are current as of July 2009. Notations in parentheses indicate dates of expiration of terms of office. Judges of the Supreme Court, Court of Criminal Appeals and Courts of Appeals are elected to 6-year, overlapping terms. District Court judges are elected to 4-year terms.

The salaries for judges fiscal years 2008–2009 were as follows: Chief Justice of the Supreme Court and the Presiding Judge of the Court of Criminal Appeals: each $152,500; Justices, $150,000; Chief Justices of the Courts of Appeals, $140,000; justices, $137,500 from the state. A supplemental amount may be paid by counties, not to exceed $15,000 per year, and total salary must be at least $1,000 less than that received by Supreme Court justices. District Court judges receive $137,500 from the state, plus supplemental pay from various subdivisions. Their total salary must be $1,000 less than that received by justices of the Court of Appeals in which the district court is located.

Below is information on the Supreme Court, Court of Criminal Appeals and Courts of Appeals. The information was furnished by each court as of July 2009. Elsewhere in this section are names of county court judges by counties, District Court judges by district number, and the district numbers of the District Court(s) in each county.

Supreme Court

Chief Justice, Wallace B. Jefferson (12/31/08). **Associate Justices**: Scott A. Brister (12/31/10); Paul W. Green (12/31/10); Nathan L. Hecht (12/31/12); Phil Johnson (12/31/08); David M. Medina (12/31/12); Harriet O'Neill (12/31/10); Dale Wainwright (12/31/08); and Don R. Willett (12/31/12).

Clerk of Court, Blake A. Hawthorne. Location of court, Austin. Web: **www.supreme.courts.state.tx.us.**

Court of Criminal Appeals

Presiding Judge, Sharon Keller (12/31/12). **Judges**: Cathy Cochran (12/31/08); Barbara P. Hervey (12/31/12); Charles R. Holcomb (12/31/12); Cheryl Johnson (12/31/10); Michael E. Keasler (12/31/10); Lawrence E. Meyers (12/31/10); Tom Price (12/31/08); Paul Womack (12/31/08). State Prosecuting Attorney, Matthew Paul.

Clerk of Court, Louise Pearson. Location of court, Austin. Web: **www.cca.courts.state.tx.us.**

Courts of Appeals

These courts have jurisdiction within their respective supreme judicial districts. A constitutional amendment approved in 1978 raised the number of associate justices for Courts of Appeals where needed. Judges are elected from the district for 6-year terms. An amendment adopted in 1980 changed the name of the old Courts of Civil Appeals to the Courts of Appeals and changed the jurisdiction of the courts. Web: **www.courts.state.tx.us/courts/coa.asp.**

First District — Houston:* Chief Justice Sherry Radack (12/31/10). **Justices**: Elsa Alcala (12/31/12); Jane Bland (12/31/12); George C. Hanks Jr. (12/31/12); Laura Carter Higley (12/31/08); Terry Jennings (12/31/12); Evelyn Keyes (12/31/10); Sam Nuchia (12/31/08); and Michael C. Massengale (12/31/12). **Clerk of Court**, M Karinne McCullough. Counties in the First District: Austin, Brazoria, Chambers, Colorado, Fort Bend, Galveston, Grimes, Harris, Waller, Washington.

Second District — Fort Worth: Chief Justice John H. Cayce (12/31/12). **Justices**: Lee Ann Dauphinot (12/31/12); Anne L. Gardner (12/31/10); Dixon W. Holman (12/31/08); Terrie Livingston (12/31/08); Bob McCoy (12/31/12); and Sue Walker (12/31/12). **Clerk of Court**, Stephanie Robinson. Counties in Second District: Archer, Clay, Cooke, Denton, Hood, Jack, Montague, Parker, Tarrant, Wichita, Wise, Young.

Third District — Austin: Chief Justice W. Kenneth Law (12/31/08). **Justices**: Diane Henson (12/31/12); Jan P. Patterson (12/31/10); Bob Pemberton (12/31/12); David Puryear (12/31/12); Alan Waldrop (12/31/12). **Clerk of Court**, Diane O'Neal. Counties in the Third District: Bastrop, Bell, Blanco, Burnet, Caldwell, Coke, Comal, Concho, Fayette, Hays, Irion, Lampasas, Lee, Llano, McCulloch, Milam, Mills, Runnels, San Saba, Schleicher, Sterling, Tom Green, Travis, Williamson.

Fourth District — San Antonio: Chief Justice Alma L. Lopez (12/31/08). **Justices**: Karen Anne Angelini (12/31/12); Marialyn Barnard (12/31/12); Steve Hilbig (12/31/12); Sandee Bryan Marion (12/31/10); Rebecca Simmons (12/31/12); and Phylis J. Speedlin (12/31/12). **Clerk of Court**, Dan E. Crutchfield. Counties in the Fourth District: Atascosa, Bandera, Bexar, Brooks, Dimmit, Duval, Edwards, Frio, Gillespie, Guadalupe, Jim Hogg, Jim Wells, Karnes, Kendall, Kerr, Kimble, Kinney, La Salle, Mason, Maverick, McMullen, Medina, Menard, Real, Starr, Sutton, Uvalde, Val Verde, Webb, Wilson, Zapata, Zavala.

Fifth District — Dallas: Chief Justice Linda Thomas (12/31/12). **Justices**: David L. Bridges (12/31/08); Kerry P. FitzGerald, (12/31/08); Molly Meredith Francis (12/31/12); Douglas S. Lang (11/4/12); Elizabeth Lang-Miers (12/31/12); Robert M. Fillmore (12/31/10); Joseph B. Morris (12/31/12); Jim A. Moseley (12/31/12); Michael J. O'Neill (12/31/10); Martin E. Richter (12/31/12); Mark Whittington (12/31/08); Carolyn I. Wright (12/31/10). **Clerk of Court**, Lisa Matz. Counties in the Fifth District: Collin, Dallas, Grayson, Hunt, Kaufman, Rockwall.

Sixth District — Texarkana: Chief Justice Josh R. Morris III (12/31/10). **Justices**: Jack Carter (12/31/08) and Bailey C. Moseley (12/31/12). **Clerk of Court**, Debbie Autrey. Counties in the Sixth District: Bowie, Camp, Cass, Delta, Fannin, Franklin, Gregg, Harrison, Hopkins, Hunt, Lamar, Marion, Morris, Panola, Red River, Rusk, Titus, Upshur, Wood.

Seventh District — Amarillo: Chief Justice Brian P. Quinn (12/31/08). **Justices**: James T. Campbell (12/31/10); Mackey Hancock (12/31/12); and Patrick A. Pirtle (12/31/12). **Clerk of Court**, Peggy Culp. Counties in the Seventh District: Armstrong, Bailey, Briscoe, Carson, Castro, Childress, Cochran, Collingsworth, Cottle,

Crosby, Dallam, Deaf Smith, Dickens, Donley, Floyd, Foard, Garza, Gray, Hale, Hall, Hansford, Hardeman, Hartley, Hemphill, Hockley, Hutchinson, Kent, King, Lamb, Lipscomb, Lubbock, Lynn, Moore, Motley, Ochiltree, Oldham, Parmer, Potter, Randall, Roberts, Sherman, Swisher, Terry, Wheeler, Wilbarger, Yoakum.

Eighth District — El Paso: Chief Justice David Wellington Chew (12/31/08). **Justices**: Ann Crawford McClure (12/31/12); and Kenneth R. Carr (12/31/08). **Clerk of Court**, Denise Pacheco. Counties in the Eighth District: Andrews, Brewster, Crane, Crockett, Culberson, El Paso, Hudspeth, Jeff Davis, Loving, Pecos, Presidio, Reagan, Reeves, Terrell, Upton, Ward, Winkler.

Ninth District — Beaumont: Chief Justice Steve McKeithen (12/31/08). **Justices**: David B. Gaultney (12/31/12); Henry Hollis Horton (12/31/12); and Charles Kreger (12/31/10). **Clerk of Court**, Carol Anne Flores. Counties in the Ninth District: Hardin, Jasper, Jefferson, Liberty, Montgomery, Newton, Orange, Polk, San Jacinto, Tyler.

Tenth District — Waco: Chief Justice Thomas W. Gray (12/31/12). **Justices**: Felipe Reyna (12/31/10) and Bill Vance (12/31/08). **Clerk of Court**, Sharri Roessler. Counties in the Tenth District: Bosque, Brazos, Burleson, Coryell, Ellis, Falls, Freestone, Hamilton, Hill, Johnson, Leon, Limestone, Madison, McLennan, Navarro, Robertson, Somervell, Walker.

Eleventh District — Eastland: Chief Justice Jim R. Wright (12/31/12). **Justices**: Terry McCall (12/31/10); and Rick Strange (12/31/08). **Clerk of Court**, Sherry Williamson. Counties in the Eleventh District: Baylor, Borden, Brown, Callahan, Coleman, Comanche, Dawson, Eastland, Ector, Erath, Fisher, Gaines, Glasscock, Haskell, Howard, Jones, Knox, Martin, Midland, Mitchell, Nolan, Palo Pinto, Scurry, Shackelford, Stephens, Stonewall, Taylor, Throckmorton.

Twelfth District — Tyler: Chief Justice Jim Worthen (12/31/08). **Justices**: Sam Griffith (12/31/12) and Brian Hoyle (12/31/12). **Clerk of Court**, Cathy S. Lusk. Counties in the Twelfth District: Anderson, Angelina, Cherokee, Gregg, Henderson, Houston, Nacogdoches, Rains, Rusk, Sabine, San Augustine, Shelby, Smith, Trinity, Upshur, Van Zandt, Wood.

Thirteenth District — Corpus Christi: Chief Justice Rogelio Valdez (12/31/12). **Justices**: Gina M. Benavides (12/31/12); Dori Contreras Garza (12/31/08); Nelda V. Rodriguez (12/31/12); Rose Vela (12/31/12) and Linda Reyna Yañez (12/31/10). **Clerk of Court**, Cathy Wilborn. Counties in the Thirteenth District: Aransas, Bee, Calhoun, Cameron, DeWitt, Goliad, Gonzales, Hidalgo, Jackson, Kenedy, Kleberg, Lavaca, Live Oak, Matagorda, Nueces, Refugio, San Patricio, Victoria, Wharton, Willacy.

Fourteenth District—Houston†: Chief Justice Adele Hedges (12/31/08). **Justices**: John S. Anderson (12/31/12); Richard H. Edelman (12/31/12); Kent C. Sullivan (12/31/12); Kem Thompson Frost (12/31/08); Eva M. Guzman (12/31/10); J. Harvey Hudson (12/31/12); Charles W. Seymore (12/31/12); and Leslie Brock Yates (12/31/10). **Clerk of Court**, Ed Wells. Counties in the Fourteenth District: Austin, Brazoria, Chambers, Colorado, Fort Bend, Galveston, Grimes, Harris, Waller, Washington. ☆

*The location of the First Court of Appeals was changed from Galveston to Houston by the 55th Legislature, with the provision that all cases originated in Galveston County be tried in that city and with the further provision that any case may, at the discretion of the court, be tried in either city.

†Because of the heavy workload of the Houston area Court of Appeals, the 60th Legislature in 1967 provided for the establishment of a Fourteenth Appeals Court in Houston.

District Judges in Texas

Below are the names of all district judges in Texas, as of July 2009, listed in district court order. To determine which judges have jurisdiction in specific counties, refer to the table on pages 476–477.

Source: Texas Judicial System Directory 2009, Office of Court Administration.

Court	Judge	Court	Judge	Court	Judge
1	Gary H. Gatlin (D)	61	Alfred (Al) Bennett (D)	123	Guy William Griffin (D)
1A	Jerome P. Owens Jr. (D)	62	Robert Scott McDowell (D)	124	Alvin G. Khoury (R)
2	Dwight L. Phifer (D)	63	Fred Hernandez (D)	125	Kyle Carter (D)
3	Mark A. Calhoon (R)	64	Robert W. Kinkaid Jr. (R)	126	Darlene Byrne (D)
4	J. Clay Gossett (D)	65	Alfredo Chavez (D)	127	R.K. Sandill (D)
5	Ralph K. Burgess (R)	66	F.B. (Bob) McGregor Jr. (D)	128	Patrick Allen Clark (D)
6	Eric S. Clifford (R)	67	Donald J. Cosby (R)	129	Michael Paul Gomez (D)
7	Kerry L. Russell (R)	68	Martin J. Hoffman (D)	130	Craig Estlinbaum (D)
8	Robert E. Newsom (D)	69	Ronald E. Enns (R)	131	John D. Gabriel Jr. (D)
9	Frederick E. Edwards (R)	70	W. Denn Whalen (D)	132	Ernie B. Armstrong (R)
10	David Edward Garner (D)	71	William Todd Hughley (R)	133	Jaclanel McFarland (D)
11	Mike Miller (D)	72	Ruben Gonzales Reyes (R)	134	James M. Stanton (R)
12	Donald L. Kraemer (R)	73	Andy Mireles (D)	135	K. Stephen Williams (R)
13	James Lagomarsino (R)	74	Gary Coley (R)	136	Milton G. Shuffield (D)
14	Mary Murphy (R)	75	C.T. (Rusty) Hight (D)	137	Cecil G. Puryear (R)
15	Jim Patrick Fallon (R)	76	Jimmy L. White (D)	138	Arturo Cisneros Nelson (D)
16	Carmen Rivera-Worley (R)	77	Patrick (Pat) Simmons (D)	139	Jose Roberto Flores (D)
17	Melody Wilkinson (R)	78	Roy T. Sparkman (R)	140	Jim Bob Darnell (D)
18	John Edward Neill (R)	79	Richard Clark Terrell (D)	141	John P. Chupp
19	Ralph T. Strother (R)	80	Larry Weiman (D)	142	George David Gilles (R)
20	Edward Pierre Magre (D)	81	Donna S. Rayes (D)	143	Bob Parks (D)
21	Terry Flenniken (D)	82	Robert Miller Stem (D)	144	Catherine Torres-Stahl (D)
22	Charles R. Ramsay (R)	83	Carl Pendergrass (R)	145	Campbell Cox II (R)
23	Ben Hardin (R)	84	William D. Smith (R)	146	Jack R. (Rick) Morris (R)
24	Joseph Patrick Kelly (D)	85	J.D. Langley (R)	147	Wilford (Wil) Flowers (D)
25	Dwight E. Peschel (R)	86	Howard Tygrett (R)	148	Marisela Saldaña (D)
25A	Wm. C. (Bud) Kirkendall (R)	87	Deborah Oakes Evans (R)	149	Robert E. May (R)
26	Billy Ray Stubblefield (R)	88	Earl B. Stover III (D)	150	Janet P. Littlejohn (R)
27	Joe Carroll (R)	89	Mark Thomas Price (R)	151	Mike Engelhart (D)
28	Nanette Hasette (D)	90	Stephen O. Crawford (D)	152	Robert Schaffer (D)
29	Jerry D. Ray (R)	91	Steven R. Herod (R)	153	Kenneth Charles Curry (R)
30	Robert P. Brotherton (R)	92	Ricardo P. Rodriguez Jr. (D)	154	Felix Klein (R)
31	Steven R. Emmert (R)	93	Rodolfo (Rudy) Delgado (D)	155	Daniel Raymond Beck (D)
32	Glen N. Harrison (R)	94	Bobby Galvan (D)	156	Joel B. Johnson (D)
33	Guilford (Gil) L. Jones III (R)	95	Ken Molberg (D)	157	Randall William Wilson (R)
34	William E. Moody (D)	96	Roger J. (Jeff) Walker (R)	158	Jake Collier (R)
35	William Stephen Ellis (D)	97	Roger E. Towery (D)	159	Paul E. White (R)
36	Michael E. Welborn (D)	98	Rhonda Hurley (D)	160	Jim Jordan (D)
37	David A. Berchelmann Jr. (R)	99	William Charles Sowder (R)	161	John W. Smith (R)
38	Camile G. DuBose (R)	100	Stuart M. Messer (R)	162	Lorraine A. Raggio (D)
39	Shane Hadaway (D)	101	Martin (Marty) Lowy (D)	163	Dennis Robert Powell (D)
40	Gene Knize (R)	102	John F. Miller Jr. (D)	164	Alexandra Smoots-Hogan (D)
41	Mary Anne Bramblett (D)	103	Janet L. Leal (D)	165	Josefina Muniz Rendon (D)
42	John Wilson Weeks (R)	104	Lee Hamilton (R)	166	Martha B. Tanner (D)
43	Don M. Chrestman (R)	105	J. Manuel Bañales (D)	167	Mike F. Lynch (R)
44	Carlos Cortez (D)	106	Carter T. Schildknecht (R)	168	Christopher A. Antcliff (R)
45	Barbara H. Nellermoe (D)	107	Benjamin Euresti Jr. (D)	169	Gordon G. Adams (R)
46	Dan Mike Bird (D)	108	Douglas Woodburn (R)	170	Jim Meyer (R)
47	Hal Miner (R)	109	James L. Rex (D)	171	Bonnie Rangel (D)
48	David Lettimore Evans (R)	110	William P. Smith (R)	172	Donald J. Floyd (D)
49	Jose (Joe) A. Lopez (D)	111	Raul Vasquez (D)	173	Willis Daniel Moore (R)
50	William Hawkins Heatly (D)	112	Pedro (Pete) Gomez Jr. (D)	174	Ruben Guerrero (D)
51	Barbara Lane Walther (R)	113	Patricia Ann Hancock (R)	175	Mary D. Roman (D)
52	Trent D. Farrell (R)	114	Christi Kennedy (R)	176	Shawna L. Reagin (D)
53	Scott H. Jenkins (D)	115	Lauren L. Parish (D)	177	Kevin Fine (D)
54	Matt E. Johnson (R)	116	Bruce Priddy (D)	178	David Mendoza (D)
55	Dion Ramos (D)	117	Sandra L. Watts (D)	179	Randy Roll (D)
56	Lonnie Cox (R)	118	Robert H. Moore III (R)	180	Debbie Mantooth-Stricklin (D)
57	Antonia (Toni) Arteaga (D)	119	Garland (Ben) Woodward (R)	181	John Boyd Board (R)
58	Robert J. Wortham (D)	120	Maria A. Salas-Mendoza (D)	182	Jeannie S. Barr (R)
59	Rayburn (Rim) M. Nall Jr. (R)	121	Kelly Glen Moore (R)	183	Vanessa Velasquez (R)
60	James Gary Sanderson (D)	122	John A. Ellisor (R)	184	Jan Krocker (R)

Court	Judge	Court	Judge	Court	Judge
185	Susan Brown (R)	253	Chap B. Cain III (D)	321	Carole W. Clark (R)
186	Maria Teresa Herr (D)	254	David Hanschen (D)	322	Nancy L. Berger (R)
187	Raymond C. Angelini (R)	255	Lori Chrisman Hockett (D)	323	Jean Hudson Boyd (R)
188	David Scott Brabham (R)	256	Davis Lopez (D)	324	Jerome Scott Hennigan (R)
189	William Rambo Burke Jr. (R)	257	Judy Lynne Warne (R)	325	Judith G. Wells (R)
190	Patricia J. Kerrigan (R)	258	Elizabeth E. Coker (D)	326	Aleta Hacker (D)
191	Gena Slaughter (D)	259	Brooks H. Hagler (D)	327	Linda Yee Chew (D)
192	Craig Smith (D)	260	Buddie J. Hahn (D)	328	Ronald R. Pope (R)
193	Carl H. Ginsberg (D)	261	Lora J. Livingston (D)	329	Randy M. Clapp (D)
194	Ernest B. White (D)	262	Mike Anderson (R)	330	Marilea Whatley Lewis (R)
195	Fred Tinsley (D)	263	Jim Wallace (R)	331	Robert A. Perkins (D)
196	Joe M. Leonard (D)	264	Martha Jane Trudo (R)	332	Mario E. Ramirez Jr. (D)
197	Migdalia Lopez (D)	265	Mark C. Stoltz (D)	333	Joseph J. Halbach Jr. (R)
198	Emil Karl Prohl (R)	266	Donald Richard Jones (D)	334	Sharon McCally (R)
199	Robert T. Dry Jr. (R)	267	Juergen (Skipper) Koetter (R)	335	Reva L. Towslee-Corbett (R)
200	Gisela D. Triana (R)	268	Brady Gifford Elliott (R)	336	Laurine Jean Blake (R)
201	Suzanne Covington (D)	269	Daniel E. Hinde (R)	337	Herb Ritchie (D)
202	Leon F. Pesek Jr. (D)	270	Brent G. Gamble (R)	338	Hazel B. Jones (D)
203	Lana R. McDaniel (R)	271	John H. Fostel (D)	339	Maria T. (Terri) Jackson (D)
204	Lena Levario (D)	272	Travis B. Bryan III (R)	340	Jay Weatherby (R)
205	Kathleen H. Olivares (D)	273	Charles Ramsey Mitchell (D)	341	Elma Salinas Ender (D)
206	Rose Guerra Reyna (D)	274	Gary L. Steel (R)	342	Bob McGrath (R)
207	Jack Hollis Robison (R)	275	Juan R. Partida (D)	343	Janna K. Whatley (D)
208	Denise M. Collins (R)	276	William Reed Porter (D)	344	Carroll E. Wilborn Jr. (R)
209	Michael T. McSpadden (R)	277	Ken Anderson (R)	345	Stephen A. Yelenosky (D)
210	Gonzalo Garcia (D)	278	Kenneth H. Keeling (R)	346	Angie Juarez Barill (D)
211	L. Dee Shipman Jr. (R)	279	Jeffrey Randall Shelton (D)	347	Nelva Gonzales-Ramos (D)
212	Susan Elizabeth Criss (D)	280	Tony D. Lindsay (R)	348	Dana Michelle Womack (R)
213	Louis E. Sturns (R)	281	Sylvia A. Matthews (R)	349	Pamela Foster Fletcher (R)
214	José Longoria (D)	282	Andy Chatham (D)	350	Thomas Michael Wheeler (R)
215	Steven E. Kirkland (D)	283	Rick Magnis (D)	351	Mark Kent Ellis (R)
216	N. Keith Williams (R)	284	Cara Cordell Wood (R)	352	Bonnie Sudderth (R)
217	Barry Randolph Bryan (R)	285	Michael Parker Peden (R)	353	Scott Ozmun (D)
218	Stella H. Saxon (D)	286	Jay Michael (Pat) Phelan (R)	354	Richard (Rick) Beacom (D)
219	Curt B. Henderson (R)	287	Gordon Houston Green (R)	355	Ralph H. Walton Jr. (R)
220	James Edward Morgan (D)	288	Solomon (Sol) Casseb III (R)	356	Britton Edward Plunk (R)
221	Suzanne Stovall (R)	289	Carmen Kelsey (D)	357	Leonel Alejandro (D)
222	Roland Saul (R)	290	Sharon Sands MacRae (R)	358	Bill McCoy (D)
223	Leland W. Waters (D)	291	Susan Lynn Hawk (R)	359	Kathleen A. Hamilton (R)
224	Gloria Saldana (D)	292	Larry Mitchell (D)	360	Debra H. Lehrmann (R)
225	Peter Sakai (D)	293	Cynthia L. Muniz (D)	361	Steve Lee Smith (R)
226	Sid L. Harle (R)	294	Teresa Drum (R)	362	R. Bruce McFarling (R)
227	Philip A. Kazen Jr. (D)	295	Tracy E. Christopher (R)	363	Tracy F. Holmes (D)
228	Marc Christopher Carter (R)	296	John R. Roach Jr. (R)	364	Bradley S. Underwood (R)
229	Alex William Gabert (D)	297	Leo Everett Young Jr. (R)	365	Amado Jose Abascal III (D)
230	Belinda Joy Hill (R)	298	Emily G. Tobolowsky (D)	366	Gregory Brewer (R)
231	Randy Catterton (R)	299	Charlie F. Baird (D)	367	E. Lee Gabriel (R)
232	Mary Lou Keel (R)	300	K. Randall Hufstetler (R)	368	Alfred B. (Burt) Carnes (R)
233	William Wren Harris (R)	301	Lynn Cherry (D)	369	Bascom W. Bentley III (R)
234	Mauricio (Reece) Rondon (R)	302	Tena T. Callahan (D)	370	Noe Gonzalez (D)
235	Janelle M. Haverkamp (R)	303	Dennise Garcia (D)	371	Mollee Bennett Westfall (R)
236	Thomas Wilson Lowe III (R)	304	William A. Mazur Jr. (D)	372	David Scott Wisch (R)
237	Sam Medina (R)	305	Cheryl Lee Shannon (R)	377	Robert C. Cheshire (R)
238	John Gary Hyde (R)	306	Janis L. Yarbrough (D)	378	Al Scoggins Jr. (R)
239	Patrick Edward Sebesta (R)	307	Robin D. Sage (D)	379	Ron Rangel (D)
240	Thomas R. Culver III (R)	308	Georgia Dempster (R)	380	Suzanne H. Wooten (R)
241	Jack M. Skeen Jr. (R)	309	B. Frank Rynd (R)	381	Jose Luis Garza (D)
242	Edward L. Self (R)	310	Lisa Ann Millard (R)	382	Brett Hall (R)
243	David C. Guaderrama (D)	311	Doug Warne (R)	383	Mike Herrera (D)
244	William Stacy Trotter (R)	312	Arthur Robert Hinojosa (D)	384	Patrick Michael Garcia (D)
245	Annette Galik (R)	313	Patrick Scott Shelton (R)	385	Robin Malone Darr (R)
246	Jim York (R)	314	John Franklin Phillips (R)	386	Laura Lee Parker (R)
247	Bonnie Crane Hellums (R)	315	Michael H. Schneider Jr. (R)	387	Robert J. Kern (R)
248	Joan Campbell (R)	316	John W. LaGrone (R)	388	Patricia A. Macias (D)
249	Dennis Wayne Bridewell (R)	317	Larry Edward Thorne III (D)	389	Leticia (Letty) Lopez (D)
250	John K. Dietz (D)	318	Dean Rucker (R)	390	Julie Harris Kocurek (D)
251	Ana E. Estevez (R)	319	Thomas F. Greenwell (R)	391	Thomas J. Gossett (R)
252	Layne W. Walker (D)	320	Don R. Emerson (R)	392	Carter William Tarrance (R)

Court	Judge
393	Doug Robison (R)
394	Kenneth Daly DeHart (D)
395	Michael Paul Jergins (R)
396	George W. Gallagher (R)
397	Brian Keith Gary (R)
398	Aida Salinas Flores (D)
399	Juanita Vasquez-Gardner (R)
400	Clifford James Vacek (R)
401	Mark Joseph Rusch (R)
402	George Timothy Boswell (R)
403	Brenda P. Kennedy (D)
404	Elia Cornejo-Lopez (D)
405	Wayne Mallia (D)
406	Oscar (O.J.) Hale Jr. (D)
407	Karen Pozza (D)
408	Larry E. Noll (D)
409	Sam Medrano Jr. (D)
410	K. Michael Mayes (R)
411	Robert Hill Trapp (D)
412	W. Edwin Denman (R)
413	William C. Bosworth Jr. (R)

Court	Judge
414	Vicki Lynn Menard (R)
415	Graham Quisenberry (R)
416	John Christopher Oldner (R)
417	Cynthia M. Wheless (R)
418	Tracy A. Gilbert (R)
419	Orlinda L. Naranjo (D)
420	Edwin Allen Klein (R)
421	Todd Alexander Blomerth (R)
422	B. Michael Chitty (R)
423	Chris Duggan (D)
424	Daniel H. Mills (R)
425	Mark J. Silverstone (R)
426	Fancy H. Jezek (R)
427	Jim Coronado (D)
428	William R. Henry (R)
429	Jill R. Willis (R)
430	Israel Ramon Jr. (D)
433	Dibrell (Dib) Waldrip (R)
434	James H. Shoemake (R)
435	Michael Thomas Seiler (R)
444	David A. Sanchez (D)

Court	Judge
445	J. Rolando Olvera (D)
448	Regina B. Arditti (D)
449	Jesse Contreras (D)
506	Albert (Buddy) McCaig Jr. (R)

Criminal District Courts	
Dallas 1	Robert D. Burns III (D)
Dallas 2	Don Adams (D)
Dallas 3	Gracie Lewis (D)
Dallas 4	John Coleman Creuzot (D)
Dallas 5	Carter Thompson (D)
Dallas 6	Jeanine L. Howard (D)
Dallas 7	Michael Reuss Snipes (D)
El Paso	Manuel Baranza (D)
Jefferson	John B. Stevens Jr. (D)
Tarrant 1	Sharen Wilson (R)
Tarrant 2	Wayne Francis Salvant (R)
Tarrant 3	Elizabeth Berry (R)
Tarrant 4	Michael R. Thomas (R)

Administrative Judicial Districts of Texas

There are **nine administrative judicial districts** in the state for administrative purposes. An active or retired district judge or an active or retired appellate judge with judicial experience in a district court serves as the Presiding Judge upon appointment by the Governor. They receive extra compensation of $5,000, paid by counties in that administrative district.

The Presiding Judge convenes an annual conference of the judges in the administrative district to consult on the state of business in the courts. This conference is empowered to adopt rules for the administration of cases in the district.

The Presiding Judge may assign active or retired district judges residing within the administrative district to any of the district courts within the administrative district. The Presiding Judge of one administrative district may request the Presiding Judge of another administrative district to assign a judge from that district to sit in a district court located in the administrative district of the Presiding Judge making the request.

The Chief Justice of the Supreme Court of Texas convenes an annual conference of the nine Presiding Judges to determine the need for assignment of judges and to promote the uniform administration of the assignment of judges.

The Chief Justice is empowered to assign judges of one administrative district for service in another whenever necessary for the prompt and efficient administration of justice.

First District — John David Ovard, Dallas (2/1/13): Anderson, Bowie, Camp, Cass, Cherokee, Collin, Dallas, Delta, Ellis, Fannin, Franklin, Grayson, Gregg, Harrison, Henderson, Hopkins, Houston, Hunt, Kaufman, Lamar, Marion, Morris, Nacogdoches, Panola, Rains, Red River, Rockwall, Rusk, Shelby, Smith, Titus, Upshur, Van Zandt and Wood.

Second District — Olen Underwood, Willis (4/3/13): Angelina, Bastrop, Brazoria, Brazos, Burleson, Chambers, Fort Bend, Freestone, Galveston, Grimes, Hardin, Harris, Jasper, Jefferson, Lee, Leon, Liberty, Limestone, Madison, Matagorda, Montgomery, Newton, Orange, Polk, Robertson, Sabine, San Augustine, San Jacinto, Trinity, Tyler, Walker, Waller, Washington and Wharton.

Third District — B.B. Schraub, Seguin (2/1/10): Austin, Bell, Blanco, Bosque, Burnet, Caldwell, Colorado, Comal, Comanche, Coryell, Falls, Fayette, Gonzales, Guadalupe, Hamilton, Hays, Hill, Johnson, Lampasas, Lavaca, Llano, McLennan, Mason, Milam, Navarro, San Saba, Travis and Williamson.

Fourth District — David Peeples, San Antonio (10/8/12): Aransas, Atascosa, Bee, Bexar, Calhoun, DeWitt, Dimmit, Frio, Goliad, Jackson, Karnes, LaSalle, Live Oak, Maverick, McMullen, Refugio, San Patricio, Victoria, Webb, Wilson, Zapata and Zavala.

Fifth District — J. Manuel Bañales, Corpus Christi (1/5/11): Brooks, Cameron, Duval, Hidalgo, Jim Hogg, Jim Wells, Kenedy, Kleberg, Nueces, Starr and Willacy.

Sixth District — Stephen B. Ables, Kerrville (11/10/12): Bandera, Brewster, Crockett, Culberson, Edwards, El Paso, Gillespie, Hudspeth, Jeff Davis, Kendall, Kerr, Kimble, Kinney, Mason, Medina, Pecos, Presidio, Reagan, Real, Sutton, Terrell, Upton, Uvalde and Val Verde.

Seventh District — Dean Rucker, Midland: Andrews, Borden, Brown, Callahan, Coke, Coleman, Concho, Crane, Dawson, Ector, Fisher, Gaines, Garza, Glasscock, Haskell, Howard, Irion, Jones, Kent, Loving, Lynn, Martin, McCulloch, Menard, Midland, Mills, Mitchell, Nolan, Reeves, Runnels, Schleicher, Scurry, Shackelford, Sterling, Stonewall, Taylor, Throckmorton, Tom Green, Ward and Winkler.

Eighth District — Roger Jeffrey Walker, Fort Worth: Archer, Clay, Cooke, Denton, Eastland, Erath, Hood, Jack, Johnson, Montague, Palo Pinto, Parker, Somervell, Stephens, Tarrant, Wichita, Wise and Young.

Ninth District — Kelly G. Moore, Brownfield (11/10/12): Armstrong, Bailey, Baylor, Briscoe, Carson, Castro, Childress, Cochran, Collingsworth, Cottle, Crosby, Dallam, Deaf Smith, Dickens, Donley, Floyd, Foard, Gray, Hale, Hall, Hansford, Hardeman, Hartley, Hemphill, Hockley, Hutchinson, King, Knox, Lamb, Lipscomb, Lubbock, Moore, Motley, Ochiltree, Oldham, Parmer, Potter, Randall, Roberts, Sherman, Swisher, Terry, Wheeler, Wilbarger and Yoakum. ☆

Texas Courts by County

Below are listed the state district court or courts, court of appeals district, administrative judicial district and U.S. judicial district for each county in Texas as of July 2009. For the names of the district court judges, see table by district number on page 473. Lists of other judges in the Texas court system begin on page 471.

County	State Dist. Court(s)	Ct. of App'ls Dist.	Adm. Jud. Dist.	U.S. Jud. Dist.
Anderson	3, 87, 349, 369	12	1	E-Tyler
Andrews	109	8	7	W-Midland
Angelina	159, 217	9	2	E-Lufkin
Aransas	36, 156, 343	13	4	S-C.Christi
Archer	97	2	8	N-W. Falls
Armstrong	47	7	9	N-Amarillo
Atascosa	81, 218	4	4	W-San Ant.
Austin	155	1, 14	3	S-Houston
Bailey	287	7	9	N-Lubbock
Bandera	216	4	6	W-San Ant.
Bastrop	21, 335, 423	3	2	W-Austin
Baylor	50	11	9	N-W. Falls
Bee	36, 156, 343	13	4	S-C.Christi
Bell	27, 146, 169, 264, 426	3	3	W-Waco
Bexar	37, 45, 57, 73, 131, 144, 150, 166, 175, 186, 187, 224, 225, 226, 227, 285, 288, 289, 290, 379, 386, 399, 407, 408	4	4	W-San Ant.
Blanco	33, 424	3	3	W-Austin
Borden	132	11	7	N-Lubbock
Bosque	220	10	3	W-Waco
Bowie	5, 102, 202	6	1	E-Texark.
Brazoria	23, 149, 239, 300, 412	1, 14	2	S-Galves.
Brazos	85, 272, 361	1, 10, 14	2	S-Houston
Brewster	394	8	6	W-Pecos
Briscoe	110	7	9	N-Amarillo
Brooks	79	4	5	S-C.Christi
Brown	35	11	7	N-S. Ang.
Burleson	21, 335	1, 14	2	W-Austin
Burnet	33, 424	3	3	W-Austin
Caldwell	22, 207, 421	3	3	W-Austin
Calhoun	24, 135, 267	13	4	S-Victoria
Callahan	42	11	7	N-Abilene
Cameron	103, 107, 138, 197, 357, 404, 444, 445	13	5	S-Brownsville
Camp	76, 276	6	1	E-Marshall
Carson	100	7	9	N-Amarillo
Cass	5	6	1	E-Marshall
Castro	64, 242	7	9	N-Amarillo
Chambers	253, 344	1, 14	2	S-Galves.
Cherokee	2, 369	12	1	E-Tyler
Childress	100	7	9	N-Amarillo
Clay	97	2	8	N-W. Falls
Cochran	286	7	9	N-Lubbock
Coke	51	3	7	N-S. Ang.
Coleman	42	11	7	N-S. Ang.
Collin	199, 219, 296, 366, 380, 401, 416, 417, 429	5	1	E-Sherman
Collingsworth	100	7	9	N-Amarillo
Colorado	25, 25-A	1, 14	3	S-Houston
Comal	22, 207, 274, 433	3	3	W-San Ant.
Comanche	220	11	3	N-Ft. Worth
Concho	119	3	7	N-S. Ang.
Cooke	235	2	8	E-Sherman
Coryell	52	10	3	W-Waco
Cottle	50	7	9	N-W. Falls
Crane	109	8	7	W-Midland
Crockett	112	8	6	N-S. Ang.
Crosby	72	7	9	N-Lubbock
Culberson	205, 394	8	6	W-Pecos
Dallam	69	7	9	N-Amarillo
Dallas	14, 44, 68, 95, 101, 116, 134, 160, 162, 191, 192, 193, 194,195, 203, 204, 254, 255, 256, 265, 282, 283, 291, 292, 298, 301, 302, 303,	5	1	N-Dallas
Dallas continued	304, 305, 330, 363, Cr.1, Cr.2, Cr.3, Cr.4, Cr.5, Cr.6, Cr.7	5	1	N-Dallas
Dawson	106	11	7	N-Lubbock
Deaf Smith	222	7	9	N-Amarillo
Delta	8, 62	6	1	E-Paris
Denton	16, 158, 211, 362, 367, 393	2	8	E-Sherman
DeWitt	24, 135, 267	13	4	S-Victoria
Dickens	110	7	9	N-Lubbock
Dimmit	293, 365	4	4	W-San Ant.
Donley	100	7	9	N-Amarillo
Duval	229	4	5	S-C.Christi
Eastland	91	11	8	N-Abilene
Ector	70, 161, 244, 358	8	7	W-Midland
Edwards	63	4	6	W-Del Rio
Ellis	40, 378	10	1	N-Dallas
El Paso	34, 41, 65, 120, 168, 171, 205, 210, 243, 327, 346, 383, 384, 388, 409, 448	8	6	W-El Paso
Erath	266	11	8	N-Ft. Worth
Falls	82	10	3	W-Waco
Fannin	336	6	1	E-Paris
Fayette	155	3	3	S-Houston
Fisher	32	11	7	N-Abilene
Floyd	110	7	9	N-Lubbock
Foard	46	7	9	N-W. Falls
Fort Bend	240, 268, 328, 387, 400, 434	1, 14	2	S-Houston
Franklin	8, 62	6	1	E-Texark.
Freestone	77, 87	10	2	W-Waco
Frio	81, 218	4	4	W-San Ant.
Gaines	106	8	7	N-Lubbock
Galveston	10, 56, 122, 212, 306, 405	1, 14	2	S-Galves.
Garza	106	7	7	N-Lubbock
Gillespie	216	4	6	W-Austin
Glasscock	118	8	7	N-S. Ang.
Goliad	24, 135, 267	13	4	S-Victoria
Gonzales	25, 25-A	13	3	W-San Ant.
Gray	31, 223	7	9	N-Amarillo
Grayson	15, 59, 397	5	1	E-Sherman
Gregg	124, 188, 307	6, 12	1	E-Tyler
Grimes	12, 506	1, 14	2	S-Houston
Guadalupe	25, 25-A, 274	4	3	W-San Ant.
Hale	64, 242	7	9	N-Lubbock
Hall	100	7	9	N-Amarillo
Hamilton	220	10	3	W-Waco
Hansford	84	7	9	N-Amarillo
Hardeman	46	7	9	N-W. Falls
Hardin	88, 356	9	2	E-B'mont.
Harris	11, 55, 61, 80, 113, 125, 127, 129, 133, 151, 152, 157, 164, 165, 174, 176, 177, 178, 179, 180, 182, 183, 184, 185, 189, 190, 208, 209, 215, 228, 230, 232, 234, 245, 246, 247, 248, 257, 262, 263, 269, 270, 280, 281, 295, 308, 309, 310, 311, 312, 313, 314, 315, 333, 334, 337, 338, 339, 351	1, 14	2	S-Houston
Harrison	71	6	1	E-Marshall
Hartley	69	7	9	N-Amarillo
Haskell	39	11	7	N-Abilene
Hays	22, 207, 274, 428	3	3	W-Austin
Hemphill	31	7	9	N-Amarillo
Henderson	3, 173, 392	12	1	E-Tyler

County	Numbers			District
Hidalgo	92, 93, 139, 206, 275, 332, 370, 389, 398, 430, 449	13	5	S-McAllen
Hill	66	10	3	W-Waco
Hockley	286	7	9	N-Lubbock
Hood	355	2	8	N-Ft. Worth
Hopkins	8, 62	6, 12	1	E-Paris
Houston	3, 349	12	1	E-Lufkin
Howard	118	11	7	N-Abilene
Hudspeth	205, 394	8	6	W-Pecos
Hunt	196, 354	5, 6	1	N-Dallas
Hutchinson	84, 316	7	9	N-Amarillo
Irion	51	3	7	N-S. Ang.
Jack	271	2	8	N-Ft. Worth
Jackson	24, 135, 267	13	4	S-Victoria
Jasper	1, 1-A	9	2	E-B'mont.
Jeff Davis	394	8	6	W-Pecos
Jefferson	58, 60, 136, 172, 252, 279, 317, Cr.1	9	2	E-B'mont.
Jim Hogg	229	4	5	S-Laredo
Jim Wells	79	4	5	S-C.Christi
Johnson	18, 249, 413	10	3	N-Dallas
Jones	259	11	7	N-Abilene
Karnes	81, 218	4	4	W-San Ant.
Kaufman	86, 422	5, 12	1	N-Dallas
Kendall	216	4	6	W-San Ant.
Kenedy	105	13	5	S-C.Christi
Kent	39	7	7	N-Lubbock
Kerr	198, 216	4	6	W-San Ant.
Kimble	198	4	6	W-Austin
King	50	7	9	N-W. Falls
Kinney	63	4	6	W-Del Rio
Kleberg	105	13	5	S-C.Christi
Knox	50	11	9	N-W. Falls
Lamar	6, 62	6	1	E-Paris
Lamb	154	7	9	N-Lubbock
Lampasas	27	3	3	W-Austin
La Salle	81, 218	4	4	S-Laredo
Lavaca	25, 25-A	13	3	S-Victoria
Lee	21, 335	3	2	W-Austin
Leon	12, 87, 278	10	2	W-Waco
Liberty	75, 253	9	2	E-B'mont.
Limestone	77, 87	10	2	W-Waco
Lipscomb	31	7	9	N-Amarillo
Live Oak	36, 156, 343	13	4	S-C.Christi
Llano	33, 424	3	3	W-Austin
Loving	143	8	7	W-Pecos
Lubbock	72, 99, 137, 140, 237, 364	7	9	N-Lubbock
Lynn	106	7	9	N-Lubbock
Madison	12, 278	10	2	S-Houston
Marion	115, 276	6	1	E-Marshall
Martin	118	8	7	W-Midland
Mason	198	4	6	W-Austin
Matagorda	23, 130	13	2	S-Galves.
Maverick	293, 365	4	4	W-Del Rio
McCulloch	198	3	7	W-Austin
McLennan	19, 54, 74, 170, 414	10	3	W-Waco
McMullen	36, 156, 343	4	4	S-Laredo
Medina	38	4	6	W-San Ant.
Menard	198	4	7	N-S. Ang.
Midland	142, 238, 318, 385	8	7	W-Midland
Milam	20	3	3	W-Waco
Mills	35	3	7	N-S. Ang.
Mitchell	32	11	7	N-Abilene
Montague	97	2	8	N-W. Falls
Montgomery	9, 221, 284, 359, 410, 418, 435	9	2	S-Houston
Moore	69	7	9	N-Amarillo
Morris	76, 276	6	1	E-Marshall
Motley	110	7	9	N-Lubbock
Nacogdoches	145, 420	12	1	E-Lufkin
Navarro	13	10	3	N-Dallas
Newton	1, 1-A	9	2	E-B'mont.
Nolan	32	11	7	N-Abilene
Nueces	28, 94, 105, 117, 148, 214, 319, 347	13	5	S-C.Christi
Ochiltree	84	7	9	N-Amarillo
Oldham	222	7	9	N-Amarillo
Orange	128, 163, 260	9	2	E-B'mont.
Palo Pinto	29	11	8	N-Ft. Worth
Panola	123	6, 12	1	E-Tyler
Parker	43, 415	2	8	N-Ft. Worth
Parmer	287	7	9	N-Amarillo
Pecos	83, 112	8	6	W-Pecos
Polk	258, 411	9	2	E-Lufkin
Potter	47, 108, 181, 251, 320	7	9	N-Amarillo
Presidio	394	8	6	W-Pecos
Rains	8, 354	12	1	E-Tyler
Randall	47, 181, 251	7	9	N-Amarillo
Reagan	112	8	6	N-S. Ang.
Real	38	4	6	W-San Ant.
Red River	6, 102	6	1	E-Paris
Reeves	143	8	7	W-Pecos
Refugio	24, 135, 267	13	4	S-Victoria
Roberts	31	7	9	N-Amarillo
Robertson	82	10	2	W-Waco
Rockwall	382	5	1	N-Dallas
Runnels	119	3	7	N-S. Ang.
Rusk	4	6, 12	1	E-Tyler
Sabine	1, 273	12	2	E-Lufkin
San Augustine	1, 273	12	2	E-Lufkin
San Jacinto	258, 411	9	2	S-Houston
San Patricio	36, 156, 343	13	4	S-C.Christi
San Saba	33, 424	3	3	W-Austin
Schleicher	51	3	7	N-S. Ang.
Scurry	132	11	7	N-Lubbock
Shackelford	259	11	7	N-Abilene
Shelby	123, 273	12	1	E-Lufkin
Sherman	69	7	9	N-Amarillo
Smith	7, 114, 241, 321	12	1	E-Tyler
Somervell	18, 249	10	3	W-Waco
Starr	229, 381	4	5	S-McAllen
Stephens	90	11	8	N-Abilene
Sterling	51	3	7	N-S. Ang.
Stonewall	39	11	7	N-Abilene
Sutton	112	4	6	N-S. Ang.
Swisher	64, 242	7	9	N-Amarillo
Tarrant	17, 48, 67, 96, 141, 153, 213, 231, 233, 236, 297, 322, 323, 324, 325, 342, 348, 352, 360, 371, 372, 396, Cr.1, Cr.2, Cr.3, Cr.4	2	8	N-Ft. Worth
Taylor	42, 104, 326, 350	11	7	N-Abilene
Terrell	63, 83	8	6	W-Del Rio
Terry	121	7	9	N-Lubbock
Throckmorton	39	11	7	N-Abilene
Titus	76, 276	6	1	E-Texark.
Tom Green	51, 119, 340, 391	3	7	N-S. Ang.
Travis	53, 98, 126, 147, 167, 200, 201, 250, 261, 299, 331, 345, 353, 390, 403, 419, 427	3	3	W-Austin
Trinity	258, 411	1, 14	2	E-Lufkin
Tyler	1-A, 88	9	2	E-Lufkin
Upshur	115	6, 12	1	E-Marshall
Upton	112	8	6	W-Midland
Uvalde	38	4	6	W-Del Rio
Val Verde	63, 83	4	6	W-Del Rio
Van Zandt	294	5, 12	1	E-Tyler
Victoria	24, 135, 267, 377	13	4	S-Victoria
Walker	12, 278	1, 14	2	S-Houston
Waller	155, 506	1, 14	2	S-Houston
Ward	143	8	7	W-Pecos
Washington	21, 335	1, 14	2	W-Austin
Webb	49, 111, 341, 406	4	4	S-Laredo
Wharton	23, 329	13	2	S-Houston
Wheeler	31	7	9	N-Amarillo
Wichita	30, 78, 89	2	8	N-W. Falls
Wilbarger	46	7	9	N-W. Falls
Willacy	197	13	5	S-Browns-ville
Williamson	26, 277, 368, 395, 425	3	3	W-Austin
Wilson	81, 218	4	4	W-San Ant.
Winkler	109	8	7	W-Pecos
Wise	271	2	8	N-Ft. Worth
Wood	402	6, 12	1	E-Tyler
Yoakum	121	7	9	N-Lubbock
Young	90	2	8	N-W. Falls
Zapata	49	4	4	S-Laredo
Zavala	293, 365	4	4	W-Del Rio

Texas State Agencies

On the following pages is information about several of the many state agencies in Texas. Information was supplied to the Texas Almanac by the agencies, their Web sites and from news reports. The Web address for more information about state agencies, boards and commissions is: www2.tsl.state.tx.us/trail/agencies.jsp.

Texas Commission on Environmental Quality

Source: Texas Commission on Environmental Quality; www.tceq.state.tx.us

The Texas Commission on Environmental Quality (TCEQ) is the state's leading environmental agency. Known as the Texas Natural Resource Conservation Commission until September 2002, this agency works to protect Texas' human and natural resources in a manner consistent with sustainable economic development.

The TCEQ has about 2,900 employees; of those, about 1,000 work in the 16 regional offices. The operating budget for the 2007 fiscal year was $480.7 million, of which 85 percent ($409.8 million) was generated by program fees. The remaining revenues came from federal funds ($45.7 million or 10 percent); state general revenue ($5 million or 1 percent); and other sources ($20.2 million or 4 percent).

One of the TCEQ's major functions is issuing permits and other authorizations for the control of air pollution, the safe operation of water and wastewater utilities, and the management of hazardous and non-hazardous waste. More than 8,000 environmental permit applications are received annually.

A TCEQ employee conducts an inspection at an industrial facility. Photo courtesy of TCEQ.

The agency promotes voluntary compliance with environmental laws through pollution prevention programs, regulatory workshops, and assistance to businesses and local governments. But when environmental laws are violated, the TCEQ has the authority to levy penalties as much as $10,000 a day per violation for administrative cases and $25,000 a day per violation in civil judicial cases. In a typical year, the agency investigates more than 70,000 regulated entities for compliance with state and federal laws and responds to about 6,000 complaints.

In 2006, the TCEQ issued 1,531 administrative orders, which yielded $9.9 million in fines and directed another $3.2 million to supplemental environmental projects benefitting some of the communities in which the environmental violations occurred.

Air Quality

Texas is home to some of the largest U.S. cities, and therefore faces air quality challenges that are among the most difficult in the country. The state has a fast-growing population and a large industrial base, especially along the Gulf Coast. The TCEQ has worked with the U.S. Environmental Protection Agency and local municipalities to craft a state implementation plan to bring metropolitan areas into compliance with federal ozone standards. The leading areas of concern are Houston, Dallas-Fort Worth and Beaumont-Port Arthur.

Water Quality

Surface water bodies in Texas are routinely monitored to determine whether they support their designated uses. The TCEQ coordinates a comprehensive sampling program to collect water quality data. The agency also conducts special studies to determine sources of pollution and the appropriateness of water quality standards. The TCEQ also is responsible for most of the state and federal regulatory programs that protect groundwater, and for state and federal storm water permits. It is the primary Texas agency authorized to enforce the federal Safe Drinking Water Act, and administers the supervision program for the state's 6,660 public water systems.

Waste Management

Waste management projects at the TCEQ include Superfund projects, pesticide collections and waste tire recycling. In 2006, there were 103 sites in the state and federal Superfund programs. Another major clean-up program focuses on leaking petroleum storage tanks. From 1988 to 2008, more than 21,000 such sites were corrected, and work continues at another 3,400 sites. The TCEQ also issues permits for municipal landfill operations and monitors landfill capacity.

Pollution Prevention

The TCEQ offers services to anyone interested in environmental stewardship. Staff members host workshops on recycling and disposal opportunities, and on regulatory and pollution prevention topics. They also offer free on-site technical assistance for regulatory compliance. Contact the TCEQ at PO Box 13087, Austin TX 78711; phone: 512-239-1000; www.tceq.state.tx.us. ☆

Health and Human Services Commission

Source: Texas Health and Human Services Commission; www.hhs.state.tx.us

The Texas Health and Human Services Commission (HHSC) is the oversight agency for the state's health and human services system. HHSC also administers state and federal programs that provide financial, health and social services to Texans.

In 2003, the 78th Texas Legislature mandated an unprecedented transformation of the state's health and human services system to create an integrated, effective and accessible health and human services enterprise that protects public health and brings high-quality services and support to Texans in need. The transformation blends 12 agencies into 5 to create a system that is client-centered, efficient in its use of public resources and focused on accountability.

The Health and Human Services Commission coordinates administrative functions across the system, determines eligibility for its programs, and administers Medicaid, Children's Health Insurance Program, Temporary Assistance for Needy Families (TANF), food stamps, family violence and disaster assistance, refugee resettlement and special nutrition programs.

The HHSC executive commissioner is Albert Hawkins. The executive commissioner is appointed by the governor and confirmed by the Senate.

The state's health and human services agencies spend nearly $20 billion per year to administer more than 200 programs, employ approximately 46,000 state workers, and operate from more than 1,000 locations. The HHSC includes four departments, which operate under the oversight of HHSC. The four new departments under HHSC are:

The Department of Family and Protective Services includes the programs previously administered by the Department of Protective and Regulatory Services. DFPS began services Feb. 1, 2004.

The Department of Assistive and Rehabilitative Services combines the programs of the Texas Rehabilitation Commission, Commission for the Blind, Commission for the Deaf and Hard of Hearing, and Interagency Council on Early Childhood Intervention. DARS began services March 1, 2004.

The Department of Aging and Disability Services consolidates mental retardation and state school programs of the Department of Mental Health and Mental Retardation, community care and nursing home services programs of the Department of Human Services, and aging services programs of the Texas Department of Aging. DADS began services Sept. 1, 2004. Commissioner Adelaide (Addie) Horn. Consumer Rights and Services, 800-458-9858; State Long-Term Care Ombudsman, 800-252-2412.

The Department of State Health Services includes the programs provided by the Texas Department of Health, the Texas Commission on Alcohol and Drug Abuse and the Health Care Information Council, plus mental-health community services and state hospital programs operated by the Department of Mental Health and Mental Retardation. DSHS began services on Sept. 1, 2004.

Major HHSC Programs at a Glance

The **Medicaid** program provides healthcare coverage for one out of every three children in Texas, pays for half of all births and accounts for 27 percent of the state's total budget. In 2004, an average of 2.68 million Texans received healthcare coverage through Medicaid.

The **Children's Health Insurance Program (CHIP)** is designed for families who earn too much money to qualify for Medicaid health care, yet cannot afford private insurance.

The **Temporary Assistance for Needy Families (TANF)** program provides basic financial assistance for needy children and the parents or caretakers with whom they live. As a condition of eligibility, caretakers must sign and abide by a personal-responsibility agreement. Time limits for benefits have been set by both state and federal welfare-reform legislation. In fiscal year 2004, a monthly average of 255,081 individuals received TANF benefits.

The **Food Stamp** program is a federally funded program that assists low-income families, the elderly and single adults to obtain a nutritionally adequate diet. Those eligible for food stamps include households receiving TANF or federal Supplemental Security Income benefits and non-public assistance households having incomes below 130 percent of the poverty level.

Food stamp and TANF benefits are delivered through the electronic benefit transfer (EBT) system, through which clients access benefits at about 12,000 retail locations statewide with the Lone Star debit card. In 2006, the monthly average number of recipients (individuals) who received food stamps benefits was 2,266,240. The average monthly food stamp benefit per individual was $81 per month or $213 per household.

Information about Medicaid, CHIP and other health and human services programs can be found at www.hhsc.state.tx.us, www.211texas.org/211/home.do or by calling 2-1-1, a toll-free local resource for information on health and human service programs.

Other HHSC programs

The Family Violence program educates the public about domestic violence and offers emergency shelter and services to victims and their children.

The Disaster Assistance program processes grant applications for victims of presidentially declared disasters, such as tornados, floods and hurricanes.

The Refugee Resettlement program is federally funded and provides cash, health care and social services to eligible refugees to help them become self-sufficient as soon as possible after arriving in the United States.

Eight **Special Nutrition programs,** funded by the U.S. Dept. of Agriculture, provide meals to eligible recipients, including elderly or functionally impaired adults, children and low-income families. ☆

The General Land Office

Source: General Land Office of Texas. On the Web: www.glo.state.tx.us

History of the General Land Office

The Texas General Land Office (GLO) is one of the oldest governmental entities in the state, dating back to the Republic of Texas. The first General Land Office was established in 1836 in the Republic's constitution, and the first Texas Congress enacted the provision into law in 1837. The GLO was established to oversee distribution of public lands, register titles, issue patents on land and maintain records of land granted.

In the early years of statehood, beginning in 1845, Texas established the precedent of using its vast public domain for public benefit. The first use was to sell or trade land to eliminate the huge debt remaining from Texas' War for Independence and early years of the Republic.

Texas also gave away land to settlers as homesteads; to veterans as compensation for service; for internal improvements, including building railroads, shipbuilding and improving rivers for navigation; and to build the state Capitol.

The public domain was closed in 1898 when the Texas Supreme Court declared there was no more vacant and unappropriated land in Texas. In 1900, all remaining unappropriated land was set aside by the Texas Legislature to benefit public schools.

Today, 19.9 million acres of land and minerals, owned by the Permanent School Fund, the Permanent University Fund, various other state agencies or the Veterans Land Board, are managed by the General Land Office and the Commissioner of the Texas General Land Office. This includes over 4 million acres of submerged coastal lands, which consist of bays, inlets and the area from the Texas shoreline to the three-marine-league line (10.36 miles) in the Gulf of Mexico. It is estimated that more than 1 million acres make up the public domain of the state's riverbeds and another 1.7 million acres are excess lands belonging to the Permanent School Fund.

The General Land Office is the steward of the Texas Gulf Coast, serving as the premier state agency for protecting and renourishing the coast and fighting coastal erosion. In 1999, the legislature created the Coastal Erosion Planning and Response Act and put the GLO in charge of facilitating restoration and preservation of eroding beaches, dunes, wetlands and other bay shorelines along the Texas coast.

The Permanent University Fund holds title to 2.1 million fee acres, and other state agencies or special schools hold title to another 2.3 million acres. The Permanent School Fund owns mineral rights alone in almost 7.4 million acres covered under the Relinquishment Act, the Free Royalty Act and the various sales acts, and it has outright ownership to about 747,522 upland acres, mostly west of the Pecos River.

Veterans Land Board Programs

Veterans Land Program

In 1946, the Texas Legislature created a bond program to aid veterans in purchasing land. Up to $1.5 billion in bonding authority has been authorized over the

Distribution of the Public Lands of Texas

PURPOSE	ACRES
Settlers	**68,027,108**
Spain and Mexico	24,583,923
Spanish and Mexican Grants south of the Nueces River, recognized by Act of Feb. 10, 1852	3,741,241
Headrights	30,360,002
Republic colonies	4,494,806
Preemption land	4,847,136
Military	**9,874,262**
Bounty 5,354,250	
Battle donations	1,162,240
Veterans donations	1,377,920
Confederate	1,979,852
Improvements	**37,155,714**
Road	27,716
Navigation	4,261,760
Irrigation	584,000
Ships	17,000
Manufacturing	111,360
Railroads	32,153,878
Education	**52,329,168**
University, public school and eleemosynary institutions	52,329,168
Total of distributed lands	**167,386,252**

years in a series of constitutional amendments.

The Veterans Land Board has liens on more than 557,511 acres of land in active veterans accounts.

Veterans Housing Assistance Program

The 68th Legislature created the Veterans Housing Assistance Program, which also is funded through bond proceeds. Over the years, Texans have passed constitutional amendments authorizing the sale of up to $2.5 billion in bonds to finance this program.

Veterans Home Improvement Program

In 1986, the Veterans Land Board implemented the Veterans Home Improvement Program, which is funded through the Veterans Housing Assistance Program. It allows Texas veterans to borrow up to $25,000 to make substantial home repairs and improvements.

Texas State Veterans Homes

In 1997, the 75th Legislature approved legislation authorizing the Veterans Land Board to construct and operate Texas State Veterans Homes under a cost-sharing program with the U.S. Department of Veterans Affairs. The homes provide affordable, quality, long-term care for Texas' veterans.

Texas State Veterans Cemeteries

The Veterans Land Board owns and operates several cemeteries under USDVA guidelines. The USDVA funds the design and construction of the cemeteries, but the land must be donated.

For more information on any of these veterans programs, call 1-800-252-VETS (8387), or visit the Texas Veterans Land Board Web site at www.texasveterans.com.

Voices of Veterans Oral History Program

The Voices of Veterans oral history program seeks to record the stories of Texas veterans and archive the transcripts in the Office of Veterans Records for future researchers and historians. Any veteran interested in including his or her story in the Voices of Veterans program should contact the Veterans Land Board at 1-800-252-VETS. ☆

Texas Historical Commission

The Texas Historical Commission protects and preserves the state's historic and prehistoric resources. The Texas State Legislature established the Texas State Historical Survey Committee in 1953 to identify important historic sites across the state.

The Texas Legislature changed the agency's name to the Texas Historical Commission in 1973 and increased its mission and its protective powers. Today the agency's concerns include archaeology, architecture, history, economic development, heritage tourism, public administration and urban planning. The commission:

• Provides leadership, training and preservation planning through its Visionaries in Preservation Program for county historical commissions, heritage organizations and museums in Texas' 254 counties;

• Assists citizens in obtaining historical designations for buildings, cemeteries, sites and other properties important to the state's historic and prehistoric past;

• Works with communities to help protect Texas' diverse architectural heritage, including historic county courthouses and other public buildings;

• Administers the historical marker program. There are more than 11,000 historical markers across Texas;

• Assists cities in the revitalization of their historic downtowns through the Texas Main Street Program;

• Promotes travel to historic and cultural sites though its award-winning Texas Heritage Trails Program;

• Works with property owners to save archaeological sites on private land;

• Ensures that archaeological sites are protected when land is developed for highways and projects.

Mailing address: PO Box 12276, Austin 78711-2276; phone: 512-463-6100; fax: 512-463-8222; www.thc. state.tx.us.

Railroad Commission of Texas

The Railroad Commission of Texas has primary regulatory jurisdiction over the oil and natural gas industry, pipeline transporters, the natural gas and hazardous liquid pipeline industry, natural gas utilities, the liquefied petroleum gas (LP-gas) industry, rail industry, and coal and uranium surface mining operations. It also promotes the use of LP-gas as an alternative fuel in Texas through research and education.

The commission exercises its statutory responsibilities under provisions of the Texas Constitution, the Texas Natural Resources Code, the Texas Water Code, the Texas Utilities Code, the Coal and Uranium Surface Mining and Reclamation Acts, the Pipeline Safety Acts, and the Railroad Safety Act.

The commission has regulatory and enforcement responsibilities under federal law, including the Federal Railroad Safety Act, the Local Rail Freight Assistance Act, the Surface Coal Mining Control and Reclamation Act, Safe Drinking Water Act, the Pipeline Safety Acts, the Resource Conservation Recovery Act, and the Clean Water Act.

The Railroad Commission was established by the Texas Legislature in 1891 and given jurisdiction over rates and operations of railroads, terminals, wharves and express companies. In 1917, the legislature declared pipelines to be common carriers and gave the commission regulatory authority over them. It was also given the responsibility to administer conservation laws relating to oil and natural gas production.

The Railroad Commission exists to protect the environment, public safety, and the rights of mineral interest owners; to prevent waste of natural resources, and to assure fair and equitable utility rates in those industries over which it has authority. Mailing address: PO Box 12967, Austin 78711-2967; phone: 512-463-7288; www. rrc.state.tx.us.

Texas Workforce Commission

The Texas Workforce Commission (TWC) is the state government agency charged with overseeing and providing workforce development services to employers and job seekers of Texas.

For employers, TWC offers recruiting, retention, training and retraining, outplacement services and information on labor law and labor market statistics.

For job seekers, TWC offers career development information, job search resources, training programs, and, as appropriate, unemployment benefits. While targeted populations receive intensive assistance to overcome barriers to employment, all Texans can benefit from the services offered by TWC and our network of workforce partners.

The Texas Workforce Commission is part of a local and state network dedicated to developing the workforce of Texas. The network is composed of the statewide efforts of the commission coupled with planning and service provision on a regional level by 28 local workforce boards. This network gives customers access to local workforce solutions and statewide services in a single location—Texas Workforce Centers.

Primary services of the Texas Workforce Commission and our network partners are funded by federal tax revenue and are generally free to all Texans. Mailing address: 101 E. 15th Street, Austin 78778; 512-463-2222; www.twc.state.tx.us.

Texas Youth Commission

The Texas Youth Commission operates correctional facilities and halfway houses to provide for the care, custody and rehabilitation of chronically delinquent or serious youth offenders.

In 2007, however, widespread sexual and physical abuse was uncovered at many of the TYC facilities. After a number of supervisors were dismissed, the entire TYC board resigned on March 15, 2007, and their powers were transferred to a conservator. The 80th Texas Legislature approved a bill to overhaul the troubled agency. The legislation:

• Authorizes the governor to appoint an executive commissioner once the agency is out of conservatorship, and to appoint an ombudsman;

• Establishes an advisory board to the commission consisting of 9 members, with the governor, lieutenant governor and speaker each appointing 3 members;

• Requires TYC to maintain a ratio of one correctional officer for every 12 youth;

• Controls size of future population by requiring misdemeanor offenders to be held in local county probation detention centers instead of TYC;

• Requires TYC to evaluate lengths of stay unique to each offense and to discharge youths at age 19;

• Establishes inspector generals, who must be peace officers, to investigate allegations of criminal conduct in the agency and all contract facilities;

• Requires ombudsman and the TYC chief inspector general to submit reports on investigations to the executive commissioner, advisory board, governor, lieutenant governor, speaker, Texas Department of Criminal Justice Special Prosecution Unit, state auditor, and appropriate legislative committees with TYC oversight;

• Requires TYC to implement strict guidelines to separate and group committed youth by age; and

• Authorizes TDCJ Special Prosecution Unit for crimes that occur in the agency or contract facilities.

In 2009, Gov. Rick Perry appointed Cheryln K. Townsend executive commissioner of TYC. Although TYC has an advisory board, a board of directors has not yet been appointed.

Mailing address: PO Box 4260, Austin 78765; phone: 512-424-6130; www.tyc.state.tx.us. ☆

Texas Department of Criminal Justice

Source: Texas Department of Criminal Justice. On the Web: www.tdcj.state.tx.us

The Texas Board of Criminal Justice (TBCJ or Board) is headquartered in Huntsville and is composed of nine non-salaried members who are appointed by the Governor for staggered six-year terms. The Board governs primarily by employing the Executive Director, setting rules and policies that guide the Agency, and by considering other Agency actions at its regularly scheduled meetings.

The Board members serve in a separate capacity as Board of Trustees for the Windham School District by hiring a Superintendent and providing similar oversight. The Windham School District is a separate entity whose primary funding source comes from the Texas Education Agency (TEA). In addition to the TDCJ Executive Director, the Board is responsible for appointing an Inspector General, a Director of Internal Audits, a Director of State Counsel for Offenders and a Prison Rape Elimination Act Ombudsman.

The Executive Director is appointed by the Board of Criminal Justice and is responsible for the administration and enforcement of the statutes relative to the criminal justice system.

The Correctional Institutions Division, Private Facility Contract Monitoring/Oversight Division, Parole Division and Community Justice Assistance Division are most involved in the everyday confinement/supervision of convicted felons. The actual supervision of probationers is the responsibility of local community supervision and corrections departments (CSCD). Victim Services coordinates a central mechanism for crime victims to participate in the criminal justice process.

The remaining divisions (Office of the General Counsel, Administrative Review and Risk Management, Business and Finance, Information Technology, Manufacturing and Logistics, Facilities, Rehabilitation and Reentry Programs, Health Services, Human Resources, and Texas Correctional Office on Offenders with Medical or Mental Impairments) support the overall operation of the Agency.

The Correctional Institutions Division (CID) is responsible for the confinement of adult felony and state jail offenders who are sentenced to incarceration in a secure state-operated correctional facility. Institutional facilities house offenders convicted of first, second, and third degree felonies. State jail facilities house offenders convicted of a state jail felony, which consists of certain felonies previously considered non-violent third degree felonies or Class C misdemeanors. Punishment can be up to two years incarceration in a state jail facility and a fine not to exceed $10,000, with possible community supervision following release from the state jail.

The division encompasses 96 state operated prisons and jails, which include 52 prison facilities, four pre-release facilities, three psychiatric facilities, one Mentally Retarded Offender Program (MROP) facility, two medical facilities, 14 transfer facilities, 15 state jail facilities, and five substance abuse facilities. There are five expansion cellblock facilities, additional medical facilities, boot camps, and work camps co-located within several of the facilities mentioned above.

Private Facility Contract Monitoring/Oversight Division is responsible for oversight and monitoring of contracts for privately operated secure facilities as well as community based facilities, which includes substance abuse treatment services.

There are seven privately operated correctional centers that house CID general population level 1 & 2 offenders, five privately operated state jails that house state jail felons as well as CID transfer offenders, three

privately operated Pre-Parole Transfer facilities, three privately operated Intermediate Sanctions Facilities (ISFs), two multi-use facilities and seven privately operated halfway house facilities. SAFPF/IPTC treatment programs are provided on 13 secure facilities and there are currently 20 residential Transitional Treatment Centers. Additionally, TDCJ contracts for 500 Driving While Intoxicated (DWI) treatment beds.

The Parole Division supervises all offenders released on parole or mandatory supervision; conducts release and transition planning; and verifies compliance with statutory provisions of release.

Additionally, the division contracts for electronic monitoring and processing responses to violations as well as other services. The division administers rehabilitation and reintegration programs and services through District Resource Centers and Parole Offices and coordinates the Interstate Compact for Adult Offender Supervision.

The Community Justice Assistance Division (CJAD) administers community supervision, also known as adult probation in Texas. CJAD is responsible for the distribution of formula and grant funds, the development of standards (including best-practice treatment standards), approval of Community Justice Plans and budgets, conducting program and fiscal audits, and providing training and certification of Community Supervision Officers.

Inmate Profile
As of Fiscal Year 2008

AGE - SEX - ETHNICITY
92% are male
Average age: 37
37.3% are black
31.4% are white
30.9% are Hispanic

AVERAGE SENTENCES
Prison: 19.2 years   State jail: 1 year

AVERAGE PART OF SENTENCE SERVED
Prison: 60.1%   State jail: 99.6%

EDUCATION
Average IQ: 90.5
About 44.3% lack a high school diploma or GED
Average education achievement score: 7.99

On-Hand Population
As of May 31, 2009

PRISONERS	
Correctional Institutions Division	139,248
State Jails	12,598
SAFPF (Substance Abuse)	3,483
TOTAL:	**155,329**
(Total Includes 17,127 housed in privately-operated facilities.)	
PAROLE	
Mandatory Supervision	78,878
(As of April 30, 2009)	
PROBATION	
Felony and Misdemeanor	426,923
(As of Feb. 28, 2009)	

Correctional Institutions Division

The town listed is the nearest one to the facility, although the unit may actually be in another county. For instance, the Middleton Transfer Unit is in Jones County, but the nearest city is Abilene, which is in Taylor County. Data is current as of July 31, 2006. **SAFPF** = Substance Abuse Felony Punishment Facilities; **MROP** = Mentally Retarted Offender Program.

COUNTY	UNIT	NEAREST TOWN	INMATES	GENDER	EMPLOYEES	TYPE
Anderson	Beto	Tennessee Colony	3,391	Male	701	Prison
Anderson	Coffield	Tennessee Colony	4,077	Male	838	Prison
Anderson	Gurney	Tennessee Colony	2,025	Male	441	Transfer Unit
Anderson	Michael	Tennessee Colony	3,143	Male	815	Prison
Anderson	Powledge	Palestine	1,092	Male	307	Prison
Angelina	Diboll	Diboll	517	Male	155	Private Prison
Angelina	Duncan	Diboll	592	Male	129	Transfer Unit
Bee	Garza East	Beeville	2,177	Male	486	Transfer Unit
Bee	Garza West	Beeville	2,214	Male	468	Transfer Unit
Bee	McConnell	Beeville	2,818	Male	709	Prison
Bexar	Dominguez	San Antonio	2,042	Male	397	State Jail
Bowie	Bowie County	Texarkana	239 143	Female Male	176	Contract Leased Beds
Bowie	Telford	New Boston	2,808	Male	723	Prison
Brazoria	Clemens	Brazoria	1,066	Male	367	Prison
Brazoria	Darrington	Rosharon	1,807	Male	533	Prison
Brazoria	Ramsey	Rosharon	1,740	Male	480	Prison
Brazoria	Scott	Angleton	1,039	Male	305	Prison
Brazoria	Stringfellow	Rosharon	1,136	Male	333	Prison
Brazoria	C.T. Terrell	Rosharon	1,584	Male	465	Prison
Brazos	Hamilton	Bryan	1,158	Male	270	Prison
Brown	Havins	Brownwood	533	Male	173	State Jail
Burnet	Halbert	Burnet	596	Female	145	SAFPF
Caldwell	Lockhart	Lockhart	499 500	Female Male	208	Private Prison/ Work Program
Cherokee	Hodge	Rusk	955	Male	336	MROP
Cherokee	Skyview	Rusk	60 462	Female Male	428	Psychiatric
Childress	Roach	Childress	1,446	Male	330	Prison
Coryell	Gatesville	Gatesville	1,977	Female	764	Prison
Coryell	Hilltop	Gatesville	517	Female	274	Prison
Coryell	Hughes	Gatesville	2,894	Male	776	Prison
Coryell	Mountain View	Gatesville	585	Female	321	Prison
Coryell	Murray	Gatesville	1,248	Female	369	Prison
Coryell	Woodman	Gatesville	843	Female	270	State Jail
Dallas	Dawson	Dallas	1,107 1,076	Female Male	413	Private State Jail
Dallas	Hutchins	Dallas	2,088	Male	403	State Jail
Dawson	Smith	Lamesa	2,072	Male	534	Prison
DeWitt	Stevenson	Cuero	1,334	Male	308	Prison
Duvall	Glossbrenner	San Diego	591	Male	134	SAFPF
El Paso	Sanchez	El Paso	1,026	Male	295	State Jail
Falls	Hobby	Marlin	1,293	Female	334	Prison
Fannin	Cole	Bonham	842	Male	239	State Jail
Fannin	C. Moore	Bonham	1,208	Male	257	Transfer Unit
Fort Bend	Central	Sugar Land	976	Male	310	Prison
Fort Bend	Jester I	Richmond	305	Male	127	SAFPF
Fort Bend	Jester III	Richmond	1,131	Male	309	Prison
Fort Bend	Jester IV	Richmond	500	Male	442	Psychiatric

The Hilltop Unit at Gatesville in Coryell County houses female inmates. Robert Plocheck photo.

COUNTY	UNIT	NEAREST TOWN	INMATES	GENDER	EMPLOYEES	TYPE
Fort Bend	Vance	Richmond	315	Male	112	Prison
Freestone	Boyd	Fairfield	1,324	Male	318	Prison
Frio	Briscoe	Dilley	1,308	Male	316	Prison
Galveston	Hospital Galveston	Galveston	23 116	Female Male	565	Medical
Galveston	Young	Galveston	304 99	Female Male	297	Medical
Gray	Baten	Pampa	394	Male	79	Parole Unit
Gray	Jordan	Pampa	982	Male	253	Prison
Grimes	Luther	Navasota	1,294	Male	324	Prison
Grimes	Pack	Navasota	1,453	Male	348	Prison
Hale	Formby	Plainview	1,016	Male	284	State Jail
Hale	Wheeler	Plainview	558	Male	127	State Jail
Harris	Kegans	Houston	610	Male	154	State Jail
Harris	Lychner	Humble	2,110	Male	439	State Jail
Hartley	Dalhart	Dalhart	1,338	Male	267	Prison
Hays	Kyle	Kyle	515	Male	154	Private Prison
Hidalgo	Lopez	Edinburg	1,048	Male	252	State Jail
Hidalgo	Segovia	Edinburg	1,187	Male	243	Pre-Release
Houston	Eastham	Lovelady	2,444	Male	636	Prison
Jack	Lindsey	Jacksboro	1,031	Male	217	Private State Jail
Jasper	Goodman	Jasper	592	Male	155	Transfer Unit
Jefferson	Gist	Beaumont	2,086	Male	392	State Jail
Jefferson	Jefferson County	Beaumont	321	Male	101	Contract Leased Beds
Jefferson	Leblanc	Beaumont	1,019	Male	262	Pre-Release
Jefferson	Stiles	Beaumont	2,854	Male	746	Prison
Johnson	Estes	Venus	997	Male	217	Private Prison
Jones	Middleton	Abilene	1,995	Male	536	Transfer Unit
Jones	Robertson	Abilene	2,843	Male	784	Prison
Karnes	Connally	Kenedy	2,846	Male	629	Prison
La Salle	Cotulla	Cotulla	580	Male	124	Transfer Unit
Liberty	Cleveland	Cleveland	518	Male	134	Private Prison
Liberty	Henley	Dayton	550	Female	127	State Jail
Liberty	Hightower	Dayton	1,294	Male	343	Prison
Liberty	Plane	Dayton	2,096	Female	433	State Jail

COUNTY	UNIT	NEAREST TOWN	INMATES	GENDER	EMPLOYEES	TYPE
Limestone	Limestone County	Groesbeck	348	Male	164	Contract Leased Beds
Lubbock	Montford	Lubbock	900	Male	810	Psychiatric
Madison	Ferguson	Midway	2,347	Male	600	Prison
Medina	Ney	Hondo	560	Male	136	State Jail
Medina	Torres	Hondo	1,329	Male	308	Prison
Mitchell	Wallace	Colorado City	1,372	Male	309	Prison
Mitchell	Ware	Colorado City	901	Male	199	Transfer Unit
Newton	Newton County	Newton	848	Male	207	Contract Leased Beds
Pecos	Fort Stockton	Fort Stockson	585	Male	123	Transfer Unit
Pecos	Lynaugh	Fort Stockton	1,366	Male	306	Prison
Polk	Polunsky	Livingston	2,845	Male	775	Prison
Potter	Clements	Amarillo	3,671	Male	1,174	Prison
Potter	Neal	Amarillo	1,669	Male	389	Prison
Rusk	Bradshaw	Henderson	1,962	Male	318	Private State Jail
Rusk	B. Moore	Overton	497	Male	146	Private Prison
Scurry	Daniel	Snyder	1,322	Male	333	Prison
Stephens	Sayle	Breckenridge	615	Male	165	SAFPF
Swisher	Tulia	Tulia	582	Male	133	Transfer Unit
Terry	Rudd	Brownfield	578	Male	157	Prison
Travis	Travis County	Austin	1,115	Male	267	State Jail
Tyler	Lewis	Woodville	2,135	Male	551	Prison
Walker	Byrd	Huntsville	935	Male	311	Prison
Walker	Ellis	Huntsville	2,401	Male	617	Prison
Walker	Estelle	Huntsville	3,127	Male	1,016	Prison
Walker	Goree	Huntsville	1,109	Male	365	Prison
Walker	Holliday	Huntsville	2,037	Male	463	Transfer Unit
Walker	Huntsville	Huntsville	1,596	Male	483	Prison
Walker	Wynne	Huntsville	2,579	Male	800	Prison
Wichita	Allred	Iowa Park	3,631	Male	1,000	Prison
Willacy	Willacy County	Raymondville	1,063	Male	211	Private State Jail
Williamson	Bartlett	Bartlett	1,001	Male	245	Private State Jail
Wise	Bridgeport	Bridgeport	516	Male	134	Private Prison
Wise	Bridgeport	Bridgeport	204	Female	60	Parole Unit
Wood	Johnston	Winnsboro	575	Male	176	SAFPF

TEXAS' 12 OLDEST PRISONS

UNIT	COUNTY	DATE ESTABLISHED	TYPE
Huntsville	Walker	1849	Prison
Wynne	Walker	1883	Prison
Jester I	Fort Bend	1885	SAFPF
Vance	Fort Bend	1885	Prison
Clemens	Brazoria	1893	Prison
Goree	Walker	1907	Prison
Ramsey	Brazoria	1908	Prison
Stringfellow	Brazoria	1908	Prison
Central	Fort Bend	1909	Prison
Darrington	Brazoria	1917	Prison
Eastham	Houston	1917	Prison
Scott	Brazoria	1919	Prison

Texas State Boards and Commissions

Following is a list of appointees to state boards and commissions, as well as names of other state officials, revised to **July 15, 2009**. Information includes, where available, (1) date of creation; (2) whether the position is elective or appointive; (3) length of term; (4) compensation, if any; (5) number of members; (6) names of appointees, their hometowns and expiration of terms. In some instances the date of term expiration has passed; in such cases, no new appointment had been made by press time, and the official is continuing to fill the position until a successor can be named. Most positions marked "apptv." are appointed by the Governor. Where otherwise, appointing authority is given. Most advisory boards are not listed. Salaries for commissioners and administrators are those that were authorized by the appropriations bill passed by the 80th Legislature for the 2008–2009 biennium (2010–2011 salaries were not available from the State Auditor at press time). They are "not-to-exceed" salaries: maximum authorized salaries for the positions. Actual salaries may be less than those stated here.

Accountancy, Texas State Board of Public – (1945 with 2-yr. terms; reorganized 1959 as 9-member board with 6-yr. overlapping terms; number of members increased to 12 in 1979; increased to 15 in 1989); per diem and expenses: Chair Gregory Lee Bailes, Bee Cave (1/31/11); A. Carlos Barrera, Brownsville (1/31/13); John W. (Jay) Dunbar, El Paso (1/31/11); Ray Ferguson, Abilene (1/31/15); James Calvin Flagg, College Station (1/31/15); Dorothy M. Fowler, Corpus Christi (1/31/11); Jon R. Keeney, Taylor Lake Village (1/31/15); David King, San Antonio (1/31/13); Evelyn M. Martinez, San Antonio (1/31/13); Maribess L. Miller, Dallas (1/31/15); Stephen Peña, Georgetown (1/31/13); James W. Pollard, Canadian (1/31/11); Thomas G. Prothro, Tyler (1/31/15); Catherine Rodewald, Dallas (1/31/11); John W. Steinberg, Converse (1/31/13). Exec. Dir. William Treacy ($70,000), 333 Guadalupe, Suite 3-900, Austin 78701-3900; (512) 305-7800.

Acupuncture Examiners, Texas State Board of – (1993); apptv.; 6-yr.; per diem; 9 members: Chair Allen Cline, Austin (1/31/13); Chung-Hwei Chernly, Hurst (1/31/11); Suehing (Sue) Chiang, Sugar Land (1/31/15); Linda Wynn Drain, Lucas (1/31/15); Raymond J. Graham, Dallas (1/31/11); Terry Glenn Rascoe, Temple (1/31/13); Karen Siegel, Houston (1/31/11); Rachelle Webb, Austin (1/31/13); Rey Ximenes, Austin (1/31/15). Exec. Dir. Donald W. Patrick, 333 Guadalupe, Tower III, #610, Austin 78768; (512) 305-7010.

Ad Valorem Tax Rate, Board to Calculate the – Est. 1907 with 3 ex-officio members: Governor, State Comptroller of Public Accounts and State Treasurer; consolidated in 1973 with State Tax Board; abolished by 66th Legislature (SB 621, which created the Property Tax Code), effective 1/1/82, and replaced by the Texas State Property Tax Board.

Adjutant General's Dept. – (1836 by Republic of Texas; present office established 1905); apptv.: Adjutant General, Gen. Jose S. Mayorga (2/1/11); ($115,000); Assistant for Army, Brig. Gen. Joyce L. Stevens, Tomball; Assistant for Air, Col. John F. Nichols, Spring Branch; Deputy Assistant for Army, Col. Jeffrey L. Lewis, Cedar Park. Assistants each serve a term at the pleasure of the Gov.; c/o Camp Mabry, PO Box 5218, Austin 78763-5218; (512) 782-5001.

Administrative Hearings, State Office of – Created in 1991 by 72nd Leg.; apptv.; 2-yr.; 1 member: Chief Admin. Law Judge Cathleen Parsley ($118,625). William P. Clements Building, 300 W. 15th St., Ste. 502, Austin 78701; (512) 475-4993.

Administrative Judicial Districts of Texas, Presiding Judges – Apptv.; term served concurrent with term as District Judge, subject to reappointment if re-elected to bench. No additional compensation. For names of judges, see Administrative Judicial Districts in index.

Aging and Disability Services Council, Department of (DADS) – (2004); apptv.; 6-yr.; 9 members: Chair Sharon Swift Butterworth, El Paso (2/1/11); Glyn S. Crane, Longview (2/1/11); John A. Cuellar, Dallas (2/1/11); Jean L. Freeman, Galveston (2/1/11); Carolyn Harvey, Tyler (2/1/15); Thomas E. Oliver, Houston, (2/01/13); Ann Schneider, Austin (2/1/15); J. Russell Shannon, Andrews (2/1/13); David E. Young, Dallas (2/1/13). Commissioner (vacant) ($160,000); John H. Winters Human Services Complex, 701 W. 51st St., PO Box 149030, Austin 78714-9030; (512) 438-3011.

Agricultural Finance Authority, Texas – (1987); apptv.; 2-yr.; expenses; 2 ex-officio members: Agriculture Commissioner and Director for Institute for International Agribusiness Studies at Prairie View A&M Univeristy; 7 appt'd. members: Lisa Birkman, Round Rock (1/1/10); Ted Conover, Tyler (1/1/11); Dal DeWees, San Angelo (2/1/11); Mike Golden, Lake Jackson (1/1/10); Stanley Ray, Georgetown (1/1/11); Victoria Salin, College Station (1/1/10); Larry Shafer, Granbury (1/1/10). Robert Wood, PO Box 12847, Austin 78711; (512) 936-0273.

Alcohol and Drug Abuse, Texas Commission on – (1953 as Texas Commission on Alcoholism); abolished by House Bill 2292 and functions merged into Department of State Health Services in January 2004.

Alcoholic Beverage Commission, Texas – (1935 as Liquor Control Board; name changed in 1970); apptv.; 6-yr; per diem and expenses; administrator apptd. by commission; 3 members: Chair Jose Cuevas Jr., Midland (11/15/09); Melinda S. Fredricks, Conroe (11/15/13); Steven M. Weinberg, Colleyville (11/15/11). Administrator Alan Steen ($105,000), PO Box 13127, Austin 78711-3127; (512) 206-3333.

Alzheimer's Disease & Related Disorders, Texas Council on – (1999); apptv.; 2-yr.; 19 members: Chair Debbie Hanna, Austin; Ronald Devere, Austin; Leon Douglas, Bertram; Carlos Escobar, San Angelo; Carolyn Frazier, Huffman (8/31/13); Grayson Hankins, Odessa; Clint Hackney, Austin; Rita Hortenstine, Dallas (8/31/13); Mary M. Kenan, Houston; Jack C. Kern, Austin; Margaret Krasovec, Austin; Ray Lewis, Arlington; Audrey Deckinga, Austin; Sam Shore, Austin; Jennifer Smith, Austin; Winnie Rutledge, Austin; Michael Wilson, Austin; Bobby D. Schmidt, Austin; Mary Somerville, Austin. Project Coor. Jim Hinds; (512) 263-1943.

Angelina and Neches River Authority Board of Directors – (1935 as Sabine-Neches Conservation Dist.; reorganized in 1950 and name changed to Neches River Conservation Dist.; changed to present name in 1977); apptv.; expenses; 6-yr.; 9 members: Jody Anderson, Lufkin (9/5/13); Karen Elizabeth Barber, Jasper (9/5/09); Louis A. Bronaugh, Lufkin (9/5/11); Dominick B. (Nick) Bruno, Jacksonville (9/5/09); Al Chavira, Jacksonville (9/5/11); Kenneth R. Darden, Livingston (9/5/09); Patricia E. Dickey, Crockett (9/5/11); Julie Dowell, Bullard, (9/5/11); David King, Nacogdoches (9/5/13). Gen. Mgr. Kenneth Reneau, PO Box 387, Lufkin 75902-0387; (936) 632-7795.

Animal Health Commission, Texas – (1893 as Texas Livestock Sanitary Commission; name changed in 1959; members increased to 9 in 1973; raised to 12 in 1983); apptv.; per diem and expenses; 6-yr.; 13 members: Chair Ernesto A. Morales, Devine (9/6/13); Rita Esther Baca, El Paso (9/6/09); Randy C. Brown, Lubbock (9/6/13); Reta K. Dyess, Jacksonville (9/6/11); William F. Edmiston Jr., Eldorado (9/6/13); Ken Jordan, San Saba (9/6/13); Thomas George Kezar, Dripping Springs (9/6/11); Coleman Hudgins Locke, Wharton (9/6/09); Charles E. Real, Marion (9/6/13); Ralph Simmons, Center (9/6/09); Michael Louis Vickers, Falfurrias, (9/6/11); Mark A. Wheelis, Victoria (9/6/13); R.W. (Dick) Winders Jr., Brady (9/6/13). Exec. Dir. Bob R. Hillman ($120,000), PO Box 12966, Austin 78711-2966; (512) 719-0700.

Appraiser Licensing and Certification Board, Texas – (1991); 2-yr.; apptv.; per diem on duty; 9 members; 1 ex officio: Exec. Sec. of Texas Veterans' Land Board; 8 appt'd.: Chair Clinton P. Sayers, Austin (1/31/10); Walker Beard, El Paso (1/31/11); Luis F. De La Garza Jr., Laredo (1/31/10); Robert Del Davis Jr., Fort Worth (1/31/10); Danny R. Perkins, Houston (1/31/11); James B. Ratliff, Garland (1/31/11); Bill F. Schneider, Austin (1/31/10); Donna L. Walz, Lubbock (1/31/11). Commissioner Timothy K. Irvine, PO Box 12188, Austin 78711-2188; (512) 459-2232.

Architectural Examiners, Texas Board of – (1937 as 3-member board; raised to 6 members in 1951 and to 9 in 1977); apptv.; 6-yr.; per diem and expenses; 9 members: Chair Alfred Vidaurri Jr., Aledo (1/31/15); Charles H. Anastos, Corpus Christi (1/31/13); Corbett (Chase) Bearden, Austin (1/31/15); Rosemary A. Gammon, Plano (1/31/11); H.L. (Bert) Mijares Jr., El Paso (1/31/15); Brandon Pinson, Midland (1/31/13); Linda (Diane) Steinbrueck, Driftwood (1/31/13); Peggy Lewene (Lew) Vassberg, Lyford (1/31/11); James S. Walker II, Houston (1/31/11). Exec. Dir. Cathy L. Hendricks, ($65,000), PO Box 12337, Austin 78711-2337; (512) 305-9000.

Arts, Texas Commission on the – (1965 as Texas Fine Arts Commission; name changed to Texas Commission on the Arts and Humanities and members increased to 18 in 1971; name changed to present form in 1979); apptv.; 6-yr.; expenses; 17 members: Chair Billye Proctor Shaw, Abilene (8/31/11); Nelson H. Balido, San Antonio (8/31/09); Patty A. Bryant, Amarillo (8/31/11); Dorothy E. Caram, Houston (8/31/09); William W. Collins Jr., Fort Worth (8/31/09); Alphonse A. Dotson, Voca (8/31/13); David C. Garza, Brownsville (8/31/11); Susan Howard-Chrane, Boerne (8/31/13);

The Lorenzo de Zavala State Archives and Library Building in Austin is headquarters to the Texas State Library and Archives Commission. The commission celebrated its 100th anniversary in 2009. Elizabeth Alvarez photo.

Molly Hipp Hubbard, Houston (8/31/13); Paul K. McCash Jr., Texarkana (8/31/13); Lee William McNutt, Dallas (8/31/13); Jeanne Parker, Austin (8/31/13); Cobie Russell, Abilene (8/31/09); George R. Snead, El Paso (8/31/09); Polly Sowell, Austin (8/31/11); Mary H. Teeple, Spicewood (8/31/09); Norma H. Webb, Midland (8/31/11). Exec. Dir. Gary Gibbs ($77,500), PO Box 13406, Austin 78711-3406; (512) 463-5535.

Assistive and Rehabilitative Services Council, Department of (DARS) – (2004) apptv.; 6-yr.; 9 members: Chair Timothy J. Flannery, Seabrook (2/1/11); Lee Chayes, El Paso (2/1/13); David Coco, Austin (2/1/13); Diego Demaya, Houston (2/1/15); Berkley Dyer, Austin (2/1/15); Lance L. Goetz, Dallas (2/1/11); Diane Marie Novy, Sugar Land (2/1/11); Donald D. Roy, Mount Pleasant (2/1/13); Mary (Jody) Unruh, Houston (2/1/15). Commissioner Terrell I. Murphy ($130,000), PO Box 12866, Austin 78711-2866; (512) 377-0800.

Athletic Trainers, Advisory Board of – (1971 as Texas Board of Athletic Trainers; name changed and members increased to 6 in 1975; expenses; 6-yr.; 5 members: Chair David J. Weir, College Station (1/31/09); Marty Akins, Austin (1/31/15); David R. Schmidt, San Antonio (1/31/13); Rebecca Spurlock, Keller (1/31/15); Michael Alan Waters, Lufkin (1/31/13); c/o Texas Dept. of State Health Services, 1100 W. 49th St., Austin 78756-3183; (512) 834-6615.

Attorney, State Prosecuting – (1923) apptd. by Court of Criminal Appeals: Jeffrey L. Van Horn (12/31/08); ($125,000); Price Daniel Sr. Building, PO Box 12405, Austin 78711-2405; (512) 463-1660.

Auditor's Office, State – (1929); 2-yr.; apptd. by Legislative Audit Committee, a joint Senate-House committee: State Auditor John Keel, PO Box 12067, Austin 78711-2067; (512) 936-9500.

Autism and Pervasive Developmental Disorders, Texas Council on – (1987); 2-yr.; expenses; 13 members: 6 ex officio; 7 appt'd. by Gov.: Chair Frank Christian McCamant, Austin (2/1/11); Mike Bernoski, Cedar Park (2/1/10); Rick L. Campbell, Center (2/1/11); Anna Penn Hundley, Dallas (2/1/11); Pamela Rollins, Dallas (2/1/10); Stephanie Sokolosky, Lubbock (2/1/10); Manuel (Manny) Vela, Harlingen (2/1/11); c/o Texas Dept. of Aging and Disability Services; Texas Council on Autism and PDD; Mail Code W-578, PO Box 149030, Austin 78714-9030; (512) 438-3512.

Banking Commissioner, State – (1923); 2-yr.; apptd. by State Finance Commission: Randall S. James ($136,191), 2601 N. Lamar Blvd., Austin 78705-4294; (512) 475-1300. (*See* also Finance Commission of Texas.)

Bar of Texas, State – (1939 as administrative arm of Supreme Court); 30 directors elected by membership; 3-yr. terms; expenses paid from dues collected from membership. Executive director, general counsel and immediate past chair serve as ex-officio members. Exec. Dir. John Edwards, PO Box 12487, Austin 78711; (512) 463-1463.

Barbering Advisory Board, State – (1929 as 3-member Texas Board of Barber Examiners; members increased in 1975; named changed to current in 2005 and functions transferred to Texas Dept. of Licensing and Regulation); 6-yr.; apptd. by department commissioners; 5 members: Chair Linda G. Connor, Austin; Ronald L. Brown, Dripping Springs; Joseph B. Grondin, Round Rock; Aldene (Dene) Hudson Jr., Arlington; Jimmy Johnson, Manor; c/o Texas Department of Licensing and Regulation, 920 Colorado, Austin 78711-2157; (512) 463-6599.

Blind and Severely Disabled Persons, Committee on Purchases of Products of – (*See* **Disabilities, Texas Council on Purchasing from People with.)**

Blind, Texas Commission for the – Now the Division for Blind Services within the Department of Assistive and Rehabilitative Services (DARS) of the Health and Human Services Commission as of 3/1/04.

Blind and Visually Impaired Board of Trustees, Texas School for the – (1979); apptv.; 6-yr.; expenses; 9 members: Mary K. Alexander, Valley View (1/31/15); Gene I. Brooks, Austin (1/31/15); Caroline K. Daley, Kingwood (1/31/11); Bobby Druesedow, Aledo (1/31/13); Cindy Phillips Finley, Lubbock (1/31/11); Michael E. Garrett, Missouri City (1/31/13); Michelle D. Goodwin, Fort Worth (1/31/13); Deborah Louder, San Angelo (1/31/11); Joseph Muñoz, Harlingen (1/31/15). Superintendent William Daugherty ($115,000), 1100 W. 45th St., Austin 78756-3494; (512) 454-8631.

Board of (Note: In most instances, state boards are alphabetized under key word, as **Accountancy, Texas State Board of Public.)**

Bond Review Board – (1987); composed of Governor, Lieutenant Governor, House Speaker and Comptroller of Public Accounts; oversees debt financing for Texas' infrastructure and other public purposes, debt issuance and debt management functions of state and local entities, and the state's private activity bond allocation; Exec. Dir. Bob Kline ($85,000); PO Box 13292, Austin 78711-3292; (512) 463-1741.

Brazos River Authority, Board of Directors – (1929 as Brazos River Conservation and Reclamation District; name changed to present form in 1953); apptv.; 6-yr; expenses; 21 members: Chair Christopher D. DeCluitt, Waco (2/1/11); Christopher Steve Adams Jr., Granbury (2/1/11); Richard L. Ball, Mineral Wells (2/1/13); Grady Barr, Abilene (2/1/13); F. LeRoy Bell, Tuscola (2/1/13); Kari Belt, Gatesville (2/1/15); Peter G. Bennis, Cleburne (2/1/13); John Brieden, Brenham (2/1/13); Robert M. Christian, Jewett (2/1/11); Carolyn H. Johnson, Freeport (2/1/11); Roberta Jean Killgore, Somerville (2/1/11); James F. Landtroop, Plainview (2/1/15); Sara Lowrey Mackie, Salado (2/1/15); Trent McKnight, Throckmorton (2/1/15); Nancy W. Porter, Sugar Land (2/1/15); G. Dave Scott, Richmond (2/1/13); Jon Sloan, Round Rock (2/1/11); John D. Steinmetz, Lubbock (2/1/15); Robert E. Tesch, Georgetown (2/1/15); Mary Ward, Granbury (2/1/11); Salvatore A. Zaccagnino, Caldwell (2/1/13). Gen. Mgr. Phillip J. Ford, PO Box 7555, Waco 76714-7555; (254) 761-3100.

Building and Procurement Commission, Texas – (1919; renamed Texas Facilities Commission in 2007 and some procurement duties transferred to the Comptroller of Public Accounts); *see* **Facilities Commission, Texas.**

Canadian River Compact Commissioner – (1951); apptv.; salary and expenses; (negotiates with New Mexico and Oklahoma regarding waters of the Canadian): Richard McDonald ($10,767), Amarillo (12/31/09), PO Box 1931, Amarillo 79101; (806) 372-7040.

Canadian River Municipal Water Authority – (1953); 2-yr; 17 members: Glenn Bickel, Plainview (7/31/08); Jerry Carlson, Pampa (7/31/07); James O. Collins, Lubbock (7/31/07); Tom Edmonds, Borger (7/31/08); Richard Ellis, Levelland (7/31/07); Larry Hagood, Tahoka (7/31/07); William Hallerberg, Amarillo (7/31/08); Benny Kirksey, Pampa (7/31/08); E.R. Moore, O'Donnell (7/31/07); Dale Newberry, Lamesa (7/31/09); L.J. Richardson, Brownfield (7/31/07); Robert Rodgers, Lubbock (7/31/08); George Sell, Amarillo (7/31/07); Carl Shamburger, Levelland (7/31/08); Steve Tucker, Slaton (7/31/07); JoAnn Wasicek, Borger (7/31/07); Norman Wright, Plainview (7/31/07); PO Box 9, Sanford 79078-0009; (806) 865-3325.

Cancer Prevention & Research Institute of Texas – (1985 as Texas Cancer Council; named changed in 2007); apptv.; 6-yr.; expenses; 11 members; 2 ex officio: Attorney General and Comptroller of Public Accounts; 3 apptd. by Gov.: Malcolm Gillis, Houston (12/4/11), Faith S. Johnson, DeSoto (2/1/11), Scott C. Sanders, Austin (12/4/11); 3 apptd. by Lt. Gov.: Chair James M. Mansour, Austin (12/4/11); Lionel Sosa, Floresville (12/4/11), Charles Tate, Houston (12/4/11); 3 apptd. by House Speaker: Joseph S. Bailes, Austin (12/4/11); Dee J. Kelly, Fort Worth (12/4/11), Cindy Brinker Simmons, Dallas (12/4/11). Interim Admin. Dir. Sandra Balderrama ($61,729) PO Box 12097, Austin 78711; (512) 463-3190.

Cardiovascular Disease and Stroke, Texas Council on – (1999); apptv.; 2-yr.; 15 members: 4 ex officio: Department of Assistive and Rehabilitative Services, Department of Aging and Disability Services, Texas Education Agency, Texas Department of State Health Services; 11 appt'd.: Chair Thomas E. Tenner Jr., Lubbock (2/1/15); Pamela R.W. Akins, Austin (2/1/15); Michael M. Hawkins, Austin (2/1/15); Melbert (Bob) C. Hillert Jr., Dallas (2/1/15); Deanna Hoelscher, Austin (2/1/11); Sue Pope, Willis (2/1/13); J. Neal Rutledge, Austin (2/1/11); Erica W. Swegler, Keller (2/1/11); Ann Quinn Todd, Houston (2/1/15); Louis West, Taylor (2/1/13); Clyde W. Yancy, DeSoto (2/1/15); c/o Texas Dept. of State Health Services, PO Box 149347, Austin 78714-9347; (512) 458-7200.

Cemetery Committee, Texas State – (1997); apptv.; 6-yr.; 3 members: Chair Scott P. Sayers Jr., Austin (2/1/15); James Coley Cowden, Austin (2/1/11); Deborah (Borah) Van Dormolen, Salado (2/1/13); 909 Navasota, Austin 78702; (512)463-0605.

Central Colorado River Authority (*See* **Colorado River Authority, Central.**)

Chemist, Office of State – (1911); ex officio, indefinite term: State Chemist Timothy J. Herrman, PO Box 3160, College Station 77841-3160; (979) 845-1121.

Childhood Intervention, Interagency Council on Early – Combined 3/1/04 into Department of Assistive and Rehabilitative Services (DARS) of the Health and Human Services Commission.

Chiropractic Examiners, Texas Board of – (1949); apptv.; 6-yr.; expenses; 9 members: Chair Kenneth Mack Perkins, Conroe (2/1/11); Armando Elizarde, Harlingen (2/1/13); Janette A. Kurban, Arlington (2/1/13); Larry R. Montgomery, Belton (2/1/15); Kathleen S. Summers, Andrews (2/1/11); Cynthia Tays, Austin (2/1/13); Patrick J. Thomas, Corpus Christi (2/1/15); Tom O. Turner, San Antonio (2/1/15); Kenya Scott Woodruff, Dallas (2/1/11). Exec.

Dir. Glenn Parker ($61,600), 333 Guadalupe, Ste. 3-825, Austin 78701; 512-305-6700.

Coastal Water Authority – (1967 as Coastal Industrial Water Authority; name changed in 1985); 2-yr.; per diem and expenses; 7 members; 4 apptd. by Houston mayor; 3 apptd. by Gov.: Pres. Dionel E. Avilés (3/31/09); Rick Cloutier (3/31/08); Tony L. Council (3/31/08); Kurt F. Metyko (3/31/09); Zebulun Nash, Houston (4/1/11); A.R. (Rusty) Senac (4/1/11); Ray Stoesser (4/1/10). Exec. Dir. Gary N. Oradat, 500 Dallas, One Allen Center, Ste. 2800, Houston 77002; (713) 658-9429.

Colorado River Authority, Central – (1935); apptv.; 6-yr.; per diem on duty; 9 members: Mathew K. Gaines, Coleman (2/1/11); Kimberly E. Horne, Valera (2/1/11); Patrick S. Justiss, Coleman (2/1/11); David (Lance) McWhorter, Coleman (2/1/11); Roger Nelson, Santa Anna (2/1/13); Bruce N. Pittard, Novice (2/1/11); Andrew Mark Young, Coleman (2/1/11); 2 vacancies. Operations Mgr. Lynn W. Cardinas, PO Box 964, Coleman 76834; (325) 625-4398.

Colorado River Authority, Lower – (1934 as 9-member board; members increased in 1951 and 1975); apptv.; 6-yr.; per diem on duty; 15 members: Chair Rebecca A. Klein, Bexar Co. (2/1/13); Steve K. Balas, Colorado Co. (2/1/11); Lori A. Berger, Flatonia (2/1/15); Ida A. Carter, Burnet Co. (2/1/11); John C. Dickerson III, Bay City (2/1/15); Tom Martine, Cypress Mill (2/1/13); Woodrow (Woody) McCasland, Llano Co. (2/1/11); Michael G. McHenry, San Saba (2/1/15); Linda Clapp Raun, Wharton Co. (2/1/11); Vernon E. (Buddy) Schrader, Horseshoe Bay (2/1/15); Richard (Dick) Scott, Wimberley (2/1/15); Franklin (Scott) Spears Jr., Travis Co. (2/1/13); Timothy Timmerman, Travis Co. (2/1/13); B.R. (Skipper) Wallace, Lampasas Co. (2/1/11); Kathleen H. White, Bastrop Co. (2/1/13). Gen. Man. Thomas A. Mason, PO Box 220, Austin 78767-0220; (512) 473-3200.

Colorado River Authority, Upper, Board of Directors – (1935 as 9-member board; reorganized in 1965); apptv.; 6-yr.; per diem and expenses; 9 members: Chair Jeffie Harmon Roberts, Robert Lee (2/1/11); Ronny Alexander, Paint Rock (2/1/15); Bill Holland, San Angelo (2/1/13); William R. Hood, Robert Lee (2/1/15); Hope Wilson Huffman, San Angelo (2/1/13); A.J. Jones, Bronte (2/1/11); Martin Lee, Bronte (2/1/13); John Nikolauk, Eldorado (2/1/13); Hyman Sauer, Eldorado (2/1/11); 512 Orient, San Angelo 76903; (325) 655-0565.

Commissioner of (*See* keyword, as **Agriculture, Commissioner of.**)

Concho River Water and Soil Conservation Authority, Lower – (1939); 6-yr.; 9 members: Chair Benjamin Orland Sims, Paint Rock (2/1/97); Joseph Beach, Millersview (2/1/97); Leroy Beach, Millersview (2/1/99); Howard Loveless, Eden (2/1/99); Billy J. Mikeska, Eola (2/1/99); Eugene R. Rodgers, Eden (2/1/97); Edwin T. Tickle, Eden (2/1/01); Harvey P. Williams, Eola (2/1/01); 1 vacancy; 425 N. Crozier, Paint Rock 76866; (325) 732-4371.

Consumer Credit Commissioner – Leslie L. Pettijohn ($100,000), 2601 N. Lamar, Austin 78705-4207; (512) 936-7600.

Cosmetology Advisory Board, Texas – (1935 as 3-member State Board of Hairdressers and Cosmetologists; name changed and members increased in 1971; named changed to current in 2005 and functions transferred to Texas Dept. of Licensing and Regulation); apptv.; per diem and expenses; 6-yr.; 6 members: Pres. Officer Clive Lamb, Addison (9/29/11); Kerin Haney, Georgetown (9/29/13); Glenda Jemison, Houston (9/29/09); Allison Leigh West, Carrollton (9/29/13); Zelda Zepeda, Cedar Park (9/29/09); ex officio, Diane Salazar, Austin; c/o Texas Dept. of Licensing and Regulation, PO Box 12157, Austin 78711; (512) 463-6599.

Counselors, Texas State Board of Examiners of Professional – (1981); apptv.; 6-yr.; expenses; 9 members: Chair Glenda Corley, Round Rock (2/1/11); Brenda (Brandi) Buckner, Weatherford (2/1/15); Karen R. Burke, Austin (2/1/15); Steven D. Christopherson, Pasadena (2/1/13); Brenda S. Compagnone, Carrizo Springs (2/1/15); Michelle A. Eggleston, Amarillo (2/1/15); Leslie F. Pohl, Austin (2/1/13); Jaa A. St. Julien, Houston (2/1/11); Maria F. Teran, El Paso (2/1/13). Exec. Dir. Bobbe Alexander, c/o Texas Dept. of State Health Services, 1100 W. 49th St., Austin 78756-3183; (512) 834-6658.

Court Reporters Certification Board – (1977 as 9-member Texas Reporters Committee; name changed to present form and members increased in 1983); 6-yr.; expenses: 13 members (6 apptd. by State Supreme Court): Chair Ben Woodward, San Angelo (12/31/12); Attorney members: Olan Boudreaux, Houston (12/31/08); Wendy Tolson Ross, Lubbock (12/31/07). Official reporters: Tammy Adams, Houston (12/31/11); LaVearn Ivey, Houston (12/31/12). Freelance reporter: John Foster, Henderson (12/31/11); Firm reps.: Audree Crutcher, Lubbock (12/31/08); Janice Eidd-Meadows, Dallas (12/31/12); Lay members: Michelle Herrera, San Antonio (12/31/07); Angeliza Lozano, Irving (12/31/08); Gilbert M. Martinez, Austin (12/31/08); Thomas Melton, Cross

Plains (12/31/11); Ly T. Nguyen, Austin (12/31/08). Dir. Michele L. Henricks, PO Box 13131, Austin 78711-3131; (512) 463-1630.

Credit Union Commission – (1949 as 3-member Credit Union Advisory Commission; name changed and members increased to 6 in 1969; increased to 9 in 1981); apptv.; 6-yr.; expenses; 9 members: Chair Gary L. Janacek, Belton (2/15/15); Thomas Felton Butler, La Porte (2/15/13); Manuel Cavazos IV, Austin (2/15/11); David J. Cibrian, San Antonio (2/15/15); Dale E. Kimble, Denton (2/15/13); Allyson Truax Morrow, Harlingen (2/15/13); Barbara K. Sheffield, Houston (2/15/11); Henry E. (Pete) Snow, Texarkana (2/15/11); A. John Yoggerst, San Antonio (2/15/15). Comm. Harold E. Feeney ($115,000), 914 E. Anderson Ln., Austin 78752-1699; (512) 837-9236.

Crime Stoppers Advisory Council – (1981); apptv.; 4-yr.; per diem and expenses; 6 members: Nelda L. Garcia, Ben Bolt (9/1/12); Jorge Gaytan, Houston (9/1/12); Emerson Frederick Lane Jr., Victoria (9/1/12); William R. McDaniel, Montgomery (9/1/13); Tina Alexander Sellers, Lufkin (9/1/08); Dorothy Spinks, Burnet County (9/1/09); c/o Office of Texas Governor, Criminal Justice Division, 1100 San Jacinto, Austin 78701; (512) 463-1919.

Crime Victims' Institute Advisory Council – (1995 as function of attorney general's office; transferred to Sam Houston State University in 2003); apptv.; 2-yr.; 3 ex-officio: Attorney General, 1 member of House, 1 member of Senate; 14 appt'd. members: Ben Crouch, College Station (1/31/10); Nancy Ghigna, The Woodlands (1/31/10);Terry Gilmour, Midland (1/31/09); Rodman Goode, Cedar Hill (1/31/10); Lori Kennedy, Austin (1/31/09); Darlene McLaughlin, Bastrop (1/31/10); Lana Myers, Coppell (1/31/09); Stephanie Pecora, Houston (1/31/09); Henry Porretto, Galveston (1/31/10); Sydney Kroll Register, Georgetown (1/31/10); Debbie Unruh, Amarillo (1/31/10); Michael Valdez, Conroe (1/31/09); Mary Anne Wiley, Austin (1/31/10); Anthony York, Pearland (1/31/09). Director Glen Kercher, Criminal Justice Center, Sam Houston State University, A-175A, Huntsville 77341; (936) 294-1642.

Criminal Justice, Texas Board of – (1989: assumed duties of former Board of Corrections, Adult Probation Commission and Board of Pardons and Paroles); apptv; 6-yr.; expenses; 9 members: Chair Oliver J. Bell, Horseshoe Bay (2/1/15); John (Eric) Gambrell, Dallas (2/1/13); C.L. Jackson, Houston (2/1/11); Janice Harris Lord, Arlington (2/1/15); R. Terrell McCombs, San Antonio (2/1/13); Tom Mechler, Claude (2/1/11); J. David Nelson, Lubbock (2/1/13); Leopoldo R. Vasquez III, Houston (2/1/11); Carmen Villanueva-Hiles, Palmhurst (2/1/15). Exec. Dir. Dept. of Criminal Justice: Brad Livingston ($181,500), PO Box 13084, Austin 78711-3084; (512) 475-3250.

Deaf, Texas School for the, Governing Board – (1979); apptv.; 6-yr.; expenses; 9 members: Chair Walter Camenisch III, Austin (1/31/15); Jean Andrews, Beaumont (1/31/11); Beatrice M. Burke, Temple (1/31/13); Nancy M. Carrizales, Katy (1/31/13); Shalia Cowan, Dripping Springs (1/31/11); Eric Hogue, Wylie (1/31/15); Susan K. Ridley, Sugar Land (1/31/13); Connie F. Sefcik-Kennedy, Austin (1/31/11); Angela O. Wolf, Austin (1/31/15). Superintendent Claire Bugen ($115,000), 1102 S. Congress, Austin 78704; (512) 462-5353.

Deaf and Hard of Hearing, Texas Commission for the – Combined into Department of Assistive and Rehabilitative Services (DARS) of the Health and Human Services Commission as of 3/1/04.

Dental Examiners, State Board of – (1919 as 6-member board; increased to 9 members in 1971; increased to 12 in 1981; increased to 15 in 1991; sunsetted in 1994; reconstituted with 18 members in 1995; reduced to 15 in 2005); apptv.; 6-yr.; per diem and expenses; 15 members: Chair Gary W. McDonald, Kingwood (2/1/09); Steven J. Austin, Amarillo (2/1/13); Mary L. Baty, Humble (2/1/15); William R. Birdwell, Bryan (2/1/15); Maxwell D. Finn, Dallas (2/1/13); Tamela L. Gough, Allen (2/1/11); Alicia Grant, Richardson (2/1/13); Whitney Hyde, Midland (2/1/15); Georgiana M. Matz, Harlingen (2/1/11); Ann G. Pauli, El Paso (2/1/11); William Lindsay Purifoy, Fort Worth (2/1/11); Jerry Romero, El Paso (2/1/13); Rodolfo (Rudy) G. Ramos Jr., Houston (2/1/15); Russel H. Schlattman II, Houston (2/1/11); Arthur Troilo III, Austin (2/1/13). Exec. Dir. Sherri Sanders Meek ($75,000), PO Box 13165, Austin 78711-3165; (512) 463-6400.

Depository Board, State – Abolished in May 1997.

Diabetes Council, Texas – (1983; with 5 ex officio and 6 public members serving 2-yr. terms; changed in 1987 to 3 ex officio and 8 public members; changed to present configuration in 1991; term length changed from 4 to 6 years effective 1997); 6-yr.; 16 members: 11 apptv.: Chair Victor Hugo Gonzalez, McAllen (2/1/15); Gene Fulton Bell, Lubbock (2/1/15); Neil Burrell, Beaumont (2/1/13); Timothy Cavitt, Spring (2/1/13); Maria Duarte-Gardea, El Paso (2/1/11); John Griffin, Victoria (2/1/11); Arthur E. Hernandez, Corpus Christi (2/1/15); Dora Rivas, Dallas (2/1/15); Curtis Triplitt, San Antonio (2/1/13); Melissa Wilson, Corpus Christi

(2/1/13); Don Yarbrough, Garland (2/1/11); 5 ex officio: reps. from DARS-Rehabilitative Services; Dept. of State Health Services; Texas Education Agency; DARS-Services for the Blind; Dept. of Aging and Disability Services. Dir. Cassandra DeLeon, c/o Texas Dept. of State Health Services, 1100 W. 49th St., Austin 78756; (512) 458-7490.

Dietitians, State Board of Examiners of – (1983); apptv.; 6-yr.; per diem and expenses; 9 members: Belinda Bazan-Lara, San Antonio (9/1/11); Linda W. Dickerson, Angleton (9/1/09); Georgiana S. Gross, San Antonio (9/1/09); Janet S. Hall, Georgetown (9/1/13); Brian Ions, Lubbock (9/1/13); Amy N. McLeod, Lufkin (9/1/13); Hawley Poinsett, Austin (9/1/11); D.A. Sharpe, Aurora (9/1/11); Mary Kate Weems, Waco (9/1/09). Exec. Dir. Bobbe Alexander, c/o Texas Dept. of State Health Services, 1100 W. 49th St., MC 1982, Austin 78756-3183; (512) 834-6601.

Disabilities, Governor's Committee on People with – (1949 as Gov.'s Committee on Employment of the Handicapped; recreated in 1983, as Gov.'s Committee for Disabled Persons; in 1991, given current name and expanded duties); 2-yr. and at pleasure of Gov.; 4 ex-officio members: officials from Texas Rehabilitation Comm., the Texas Comm. for the Blind, Texas Workforce Comm. and Texas Comm. for the Deaf and Hard of Hearing; 1 advisory member: rep. from Texas Dept. of Licensing and Regulation; 12 apptd. members: Chair Judy C. Scott, Dallas (2/1/10); Alan Babin Jr., Round Rock (2/1/11); Aaron Bangor, Austin (2/1/10); Rodolfo (Rudy) Becerra Jr., Nacogdoches (2/1/10); Joe Bontke, Houston (2/1/11); Daphne Brookins, Fort Worth (2/1/11); Peggy Cosner, Belton (2/1/09); David A. Fowler, Katy (2/1/11); Bobby Z. (Robby) Holcomb Jr., Mount Pleasant (2/1/11); Maureen F. McClain, Pharr (2/1/10); Brian D. Shannon, Lubbock (2/1/11); Kathy S. Strong, Garrison (2/1/10). Exec. Dir. Pat Pound, PO Box 12428, Austin 78711-2428; (512) 463-5739.

Disabilities, Texas Council for Developmental – (1971); apptv.; 6-yr.; 27 members: 19 apptv.: Chair Brenda K. Coleman-Beattie, Austin (2/1/13); Rebecca Hunter Adkins, Lakeway (2/1/15); Kristine Bissmeyer, San Antonio (2/1/11); Kimberley A. Blackmon, Fort Worth (2/1/15); Kristen L. Cox, El Paso (2/1/15); Andrew D. Crim, Fort Worth (2/1/13); Mateo Delgado, El Paso (2/1/13); Mary M. Durheim, McAllen (2/1/11); Marcia J. Dwyer, Plano (2/1/11); Cindy Johnston, Dallas (2/1/13); Diana Kern, Cedar Creek (2/1/15); John C. Morris, Leander (2/1/15); Dana S. Perry, Brownwood (2/1/15); Deneesa A. Rasmussen, Arlington (2/1/15); Rene Requenez, Edinburg (2/1/13); Joe Rivas, Denton (2/1/11); Lora T. Taylor, Houston (2/1/13); Richard A. Tisch, Spring (2/1/15); Susan Vardell, Sherman (2/1/13); 8 ex offico members: reps. from Advocacy Inc., Center for Disability Studies, Center on Disability and Development at TAMU, Texas Education Agency, Health & Human Services Commission, Dept. of Aging and Disability Services, Dept. of Assistive and Rehabilitative Services, Dept. of State Health Services. Exec. Dir. Roger A. Webb, 6201 E. Oltorf, Ste. 600, Austin 78741; (512) 437-5432.

Disabilities, Texas Council on Purchasing from People with – (1979 as 10-member Committee on Purchases of Products and Services of Blind and Severely Disabled Persons; name changed and members reduced to 9 in 1995); apptv.; expenses; 5-yr.; 9 members: Chair John W. Luna, Euless (1/31/15); Chuck Brewton, San Antonio (1/31/11); Scott D. Burford, Austin (1/31/11); Les Butler, Fort Worth (1/31/13); James Michael Daugherty, Irving (1/31/13); Kevin M. Jackson, Austin (1/31/13); Victor Kilman, Lubbock (1/31/15); Margaret (Meg) Pfluger, Lubbock (1/31/11); Wanda White Stovall, Fort Worth (1/31/15). Exec. Dir. Kelvin Moore, PO Box 13528, Austin 78711-3528; (512) 463-3244.

Disabilities, Texas Office for Prevention of Developmental – (1991) 6-yr.; apptv.; 9 members: Chair Rep. Vicki Truitt, Keller; Richard Garnett, Fort Worth; Ashley C. Givens, Dallas (2/1/15); Rep. Jim L. Jackson, Carrollton; Valerie Kiper, Amarillo (2/1/13); Joan Roberts-Scott, Austin; Marian Sokol, San Antonio (2/1/11); Mary S. Tijerina, San Marcos; 1 vacancy. Exec. Dir. Carolyn Smith, PO Box 12668, Austin 78711-2668; (512) 206-4544.

Disaster Recovery and Renewal, Governor's Commission for – (2008); apptv.; terms at pleasure of Gov.; 23 ex-officio members: County judges from the coastal counties of Aransas, Brazoria, Calhoun, Cameron, Chambers, Galveston, Harris, Hidalgo, Jackson, Jefferson, Kenedy, Kleberg, Liberty, Matagorda, Nueces, Orange, Refugio, San Patricio, Starr, Victoria, and Willacy along with the General Land Office Commissioner and the Agriculture Commissioner; 24 appt'd. members: Chair Robert Eckels, Houston; Ronnie Acosta, Pearland; William B. Claybar, Orange; Irma Diaz-Gonzalez, Houston; George (Trey) H. Henderson III, Lufkin; Gary L. Hockstra, Lake Jackson; Jo Ann Howard, Austin; Jerry Kane, Corpus Christi; Mary E. Kelly, Austin; William E. King, Houston; H. Thomas Kornegay, Houston; David L. Lakey, Austin; David S. Lopez, Houston; Ross D. Margraves Jr., Houston; Scott McClelland, Houston; Tracye McDaniel, Houston; Allan B. Polunsky, San Antonio; Penny Redington, Austin; Regina Rogers, Beaumont; Rolando Rubiano, Harlingen; Karen A. Sexton, Galveston; Wade E. Upton, Houston; Daniel J. Wolterman, Houston; H. Edwin Young, Houston. c/o Office of the Governor, PO Box 12428, Austin, 78711; (512) 463-2000.

Education Board, Southern Regional – (1969); apptv.; 4-yr.; 5 members: Gov. ex officio, 4 apptv.: Rep. Rob Eissler, The Woodlands (6/30/08); Rep. Geanie W. Morrison, Victoria (6/30/11); Robert P. Scott, Austin (6/30/10); Sen. Florence Shapiro, Plano (6/30/09); President Daivd Spence, 592 10th St. N.W., Atlanta, GA 30318-5790; (404) 875-9211.

Education, Commissioner of – (1866 as Superintendent of Public Instruction; 1949 changed to present name by Gilmer-Aiken Act); apptv. by Gov. since 1995; 4-yr.: Robert P. Scott ($164,748); 1701 N. Congress Ave., Austin 78701-1494; (512) 463-9734. (*See also* Education, State Board of.)

Education, State Board of – (1866; re-created in 1928 and re-formed in 1949 by Gilmer-Aikin Act to consist of 21 elective members from districts co-extensive with 21 congressional districts at that time; increased to 24 with congressional redistricting in 1971; increased to 27 with congressional redistricting in 1981; reorganized by special legislative session as 15-member apptv. board in 1984; become elective board again in 1988); expenses; 4-yr.; 15 members: **District 1:** Rene Nuñez, El Paso (1/1/11); **District 2:** Mary Helen Berlanga, Corpus Christi (1/1/13); **District 3:** Rick Agosto, San Antonio (1/1/11); **District 4:** Lawrence A. Allen Jr., Houston (1/1/11); **District 5:** Ken Mercer, San Antonio (1/1/11); **District 6:** Terri Leo, Spring (1/1/13); **District 7:** David Bradley, Beaumont (1/1/13); **District 8:** Barbara Cargill, The Woodlands (1/1/13); **District 9:** Don McLeroy, College Station (2/1/11); **District 10:** Cynthia Noland Dunbar, Richmond (1/1/11) **District 11:** Patricia Hardy, Fort Worth (1/1/13); **District 12:** Geraldine (Tincy) Miller, Dallas (1/1/11); **District 13:** Mavis B. Knight, Dallas (1/1/13); **District 14:** Chair Gail Lowe, Lampasas (1/1/11); **District 15:** Bob Craig, Lubbock (1/1/11). c/o Texas Education Agency, 1701 N. Congress Ave., Austin 78701-1494; (512) 463-9007.

Educator Certification, State Board for – (1995); apptv.; 6-yr.; expenses; 14 members; 3 ex officio: rep. of Comm. of Education; rep. of Comm. of Higher Education; 1 dean of a college of education; 11 apptv.: Chair Bonny L. Cain, Pearland (2/1/15); Bradley W. Allard, Burleson (2/1/15); Christopher Barbic, Houston (2/1/11); Janie Baszile, Houston (2/1/11); Sandra D. Bridges, Rockwall (2/1/13); Stefani D. Carter, Plano (2/1/15); Jill Harrison Druesedow, Haskell (2/1/13); Benny W. Morris, Cleburne (2/1/15); Christie Pogue, Buda (2/1/11); Judy Robinson, El Paso (2/1/15); Homer Dean Treviño, Waco (2/1/13). Dir. Roman Echazarreta,1701 N. Congress Ave., 5th floor, Austin 78701-1494; (512) 936-8400.

Edwards Aquifer Authority – (1993); 4-yr.; expenses; 17 members (2 apptv. and 15 elected from single-member districts). Elected members: Chair Doug Miller, Comal & Guadalupe Cos. (12/1/10); Ken Barnes, Hays Co. (12/1/08); Luana Buckner, Medina & Atascosa Cos. (12/1/10); Ramon Chapa Jr., Comal Co. (12/1/08); Mario H. Cruz, Uvalde Co. (12/1/08); Ron Ellis, Bexar Co. (12/1/10); Bruce Gilleland, Uvalde Co. (12/1/10); Susan Hughes, Bexar Co. (12/1/08); Byron Miller, Bexar Co. (12/1/08); Carol Patterson, Bexar Co. (12/1/10); George Rice, Bexar Co. (12/1/10); Hunter Schuehle, Medina Co. (12/1/08); Mark B. Taylor, Hays & Caldwell Cos. (12/1/10); Enrique Valdivia, Bexar Co. (12/1/10); Benjamin Franklin Youngblood, Bexar Co. (12/1/08). Apptv. members: Clay Binford, Medina & Uvalde Cos. (12/1/08); Jerry James, South Central Texas Water Advisory Committee (12/1/08). Gen. Mgr. Velma R. Danielson, 1615 N. St. Mary's St., San Antonio 78215; (210) 222-2204.

Egg Marketing Advisory Board – Abolished May 1997.

Election Commission, State – (1973); 9 members; 4 ex officio: Chmn. of Democratic State Executive Committee; Chmn. of Republican State Executive Committee; Chief Justice of Supreme Court; Court of Criminal Appeals Presiding Judge; 5 apptv.: 1 justice of the Court of Appeals apptd. by Chief Justice of Supreme Court, 1 District Judge apptd. by presiding judge of Court of Criminal Appeals; 2 county chairmen (1 Democrat, 1 Republican, named by their parties); Secretary of State.

Emergency Communications, Commission on State – (1985 as 17-member Advisory Commission on State Emergency Communications; name changed and members reduced to 12 in 2000); expenses; 6-yr., 12 members: 3 ex offico: reps. of Dept. of State Health Services, Public Utilities Comm. and Dept. of Information Resources; 9 apptd. members: 5 apptd. by Gov: 2 apptd. by Lt. Gov.; 2 apptd. by House Speaker. Gov.'s apptees.: Chair John L. deNoyelles, Flint (9/1/09); Heberto Gutierrez, San Antonio (9/1/09); David A. Levy, Archer (9/1/13); Gregory Parker, New Braunfels (9/1/11); Steve Mitchell, Richardson (9/1/11); Speaker's apptees.: Kay Alexander, Abilene (8/31/13); James Beauchamp,

Midland (8/31/13); 2 vacancies. Exec. Dir. Paul Mallett ($82,500), 333 Guadalupe St., Ste. 2-212, Austin 78701-3942; (512) 305-6911.

Emergency Services Personnel Retirement Fund, Texas Statewide – (*See* Retirement Fund, Texas Statewide Emergency Services Personnel.)

Emissions Reductions Plan Advisory Board, Texas – (2001); apptv.; 2-yr.; 22 members: 7 ex officio: Senate Natural Resources Comm., House Environmental Regulation Comm., Texas Commission on Environmental Quality, Texas General Land Office, Railroad Commission of Texas, Texas Comptroller of Public Accounts, Environmental Protection Agency.; 5 appt'd. by Gov.; 5 by Lt. Gov.; 5 by House Speaker. Gov's. apptees: Scott J. Boxer, Frisco (2/1/09); Elizabeth Gunter, Austin (2/1/09); Kenneth A. Pelt, Sour Lake (2/1/11); Danny R. Perkins, Houston (2/1/11); Mark L. Rhea, Fort Worth (2/1/09). c/o TCEQ, PO Box 13087, Austin 78711-3087; (800) 919-8377.

Employment Commission, Texas – (*See* Workforce Commission, Texas.)

Engineers, Texas Board of Professional – (1937 as 6-member Texas State Board of Registration for Professional Engineers; members increased to 9 in 1981; name changed to present in 1997); apptv.; per diem and expenses; 6-yr.; 9 members: Chair G. Kemble Bennett, College Station (at pleasure of Gov.); Jose F. Cardenas, El Paso (9/26/09); James Greer, Dallas (9/26/09); Govind Nadkarni, Corpus Christi (9/26/11); Shannon K. McClendon, Dripping Springs (9/26/09); Gary W. Raba, San Antonio (9/26/13); Elvira Reyna, Little Elm (9/26/13); Edward L. Summers, Austin (9/26/11); Daniel O. Wong, Houston (9/26/13). Exec. Dir. Dale Beebe Farrow ($75,000), 1917 IH-35 S, Austin 78741; (512) 440-7723.

Environmental Quality, Texas Commission on – (1913 as State Board of Water Engineers; name changed in 1962 to Texas Water Commission; reorganized and name changed in 1965 to Water Rights Commission; reorganized and name changed back to Texas Water Commission in 1977 to perform judicial function for the Texas Dept. of Water Resources; name changed to Texas Natural Resource Conservation Commission in 1993; changed to present form in 2002); apptv.; 6-yr.; 3 members full-time at $120,120–$122,971: Chair Buddy Garcia, Austin (8/31/11); Bryan Shaw, Bryan (8/31/13); Larry Ross Soward, Austin (8/31/09). Exec. Dir. Mark Vickery ($145,200), PO Box 13087, Austin 78711-3087; (512) 239-1000.

Ethics Commission, Texas – (1991); apptv.; 4-yr.; 8 members: 2 apptd. by House Speaker, 2 apptd. by Lt. Gov, 4 apptd. by Gov.: Chair Tom Harrison, Austin (11/19/07); Wilhelmina Delco, Austin (11/19/11); Ross Fischer, Kendalia (11/19/09); Jim Graham, Dallas (11/19/09); George (Trey) H. Henderson III, Lufkin (11/19/11); Paula M. Mendoza, Houston (11/19/07); David Montagne, Beaumont (11/19/09); Nicholas C. Taylor, Midland (11/19/09). Exec. Dir. David A. Reisman ($115,000), PO Box 12070, Austin 78711-2070; (512) 463-5800.

Facilities Commission, Texas – (2007; formerly Texas Building and Procurement Commission); apptv.; 6-yr.; 7 members: Chair Betty Reinbeck, Sealy (1/31/11); Malcolm Beckendorff, Katy (1/31/13); William Derek Darby, Houston (1/31/09); Virginia I. Hermosa, Austin (1/31/09); Victor E. Leal, Amarillo (1/31/09); Barkley J. Stuart, Dallas (1/31/11); 1 vacancies. Exec. Dir. Edward Johnson ($126,500) PO Box 13047, Austin 78711-3047; (512) 463-3446.

Family and Protective Services Advisory Council, Department of – (1991 as Dept. of Protective and Regulatory Services; reorganized to present form in 2004); apptv.; 6-yr.; 9 members: Chair Ommy Strauch, San Antonio (2/1/11); Gigi Edwards Bryant, Austin (2/1/13); Debbie Epperson, Austin (1/31/13); Theodore Paul Furukawa, San Antonio (2/1/11); Christina R. Martin, Mission (2/1/15); Imogen Papadopoulos, Houston (2/1/15); Linda Bell Robinson, Houston (2/1/13); Scott Rosenbach, Amarillo (2/1/15); Mamie Salazar-Harper, El Paso (2/1/11). Commissioner Anne Heiligenstein ($160,000), PO Box 149030, Austin 78714-9030; (512) 438-4800.

Finance Commission of Texas – (1923 as Banking Commission; reorganized as Finance Commission in 1943 with 9 members; members increased to 12 in 1983; changed back to 9 members in 1989); apptv.; 6-yr.; per diem and traveling expenses; 9 members: Chair William James White, Georgetown (2/1/12); Mike Bradford, Midland (2/1/12); Darby Ray Byrd Sr., Orange (2/1/12); Riley Couch III, Frisco (2/1/12); Stacy G. London, Houston (2/1/14); Cindy F. Lyons, El Paso (2/1/10); Lori B. McCool, Boerne (2/1/14); Jonathan B. Newton, Houston (2/1/10); Paul Plunket, Dallas (2/1/14). Banking Commissioner, Randall S. James ($136,191), 2601 N. Lamar Blvd., Austin 78705; (512) 936-7640; appointee of Finance Commission. (*See also* Banking Commissioner, State.)

Fire Fighters' Pension Commissioner – (1937); apptv.; 2-yr.: Lisa Ivie Miller, Austin (7/1/07) ($70,000), PO Box 12577, Austin 78711-2577; (512) 936-3372. (*See also* Retirement Fund, Texas Statewide Emergency Services Personnel.)

Fire Protection, Texas Commission on – (1991; formed by consolidation of Fire Dept. Emergency Board and Commission on Fire Protection Personnel Standards and Education); apptv.; 6-yrs.; expenses; 13 members: Chair Christopher Connealy, Cedar Park (2/1/11); Les Bunte, Bryan (2/1/15); Elroy Carson, Ransom Canyon (2/1/11); Rhea Cooper, Lubbock (2/1/13); Yusuf Elias Farran, El Paso (2/1/15); Carl (Gene) Giles, Carthage (2/1/15); John Kelly Gillette III, Frisco (2/1/11); Joseph (Jody) Gonzalez, Krugerville (2/1/13); John W. Green, San Leon (2/1/11); Michael L. Melton, Gilmer (2/1/13); Arthur Lee Pertile III, Katy (2/1/13); Kimberley Shambley, Dallas (2/1/15); Steven C. Tull, Valley Mills (2/1/15). Exec. Dir. Gary L. Warren Sr. ($90,000), PO Box 2286, Austin 78768-2286; (512) 936-3838.

Food and Fibers Commission, Texas – Abolished Jan. 1, 2006, and duties transferred to the Texas Dept. of Agriculture Food and Fibers Research Council; PO Box 12847, Austin 78711; (512) 936-2450.

Forensic Science Commission, Texas – (2005); apptv.: 2-yr.; 9 members: 4 apptd. by Gov., 3 apptd. by Lt. Gov. and 2 apptd. by Atty. Gen.: Chair Samuel E. Bassett, Austin (9/1/09); Garry Adams, College Station (9/1/07); Arthur Jay Eisenberg, Fort Worth (9/1/08); Stanley R. Hamilton, Houston (9/1/07); Jean Hampton, Houston (9/1/07); Sarah Kerrigan, Huntsville (9/1/09); Alan L. Levy, Fort Worth (9/1/09); Sridhar Natarajan, Boerne (9/1/09); Aliece B. Watts, Burleson (9/1/09). Dir. Leigh Tomlin, 816 17th St., Huntsville 77340; (936) 294-1640.

Funeral Service Commission, Texas – (1903 as State Board of Embalming; 1935 as State Board of Funeral Directors and Embalmers; name changed to present form in 1987); apptv.; per diem and expenses; 6-yr.; 7 members: Chair Sue Evenwel, Mt. Pleasant (2/1/15); Gene Allen, Kerrville (2/1/15); Carol M. Becker, Aledo (9/1/13); Doug Carmichael, Pampa (2/1/11); Jess A. Fields Sr., Kingwood (2/1/13); Joyce M. Odom, San Antonio (2/1/11); Norberto Salinas, Mission (2/1/13). Exec. Dir. O.C. (Chet) Robbins ($55,816), 333 Guadalupe St., Ste. 2-110, Austin 78701; (512) 936-2474.

General Services Commission – Abolished in February 2002, with most functions taken over by the newly created Texas Building and Procurement Commission, which was renamed Texas Facilities Commission in 2007.

Geoscientists, Texas Board of Professional – (2001); apptv.; expenses; 6-yr.; 9 members (6 professional geoscientists, 3 public members): Chair Yale Lynn Clark, Farmers Branch (2/1/11); Kelly Krenz-Doe, Houston (2/1/09); Charles T. (Tom) Hallmark, College Station (2/1/13); Ronald L. Kitchens, Harper (2/1/13); Glenn R. Lowenstein, Houston (2/1/11); Rene D. Peña, El Paso (2/1/09); Barbara O. Roeling, Austin (2/1/13); Gregory C. Ulmer, Houston (2/1/11); Gordon D. Ware, Corpus Christi (2/1/09). Exec. Dir. Vincent R. Houston ($57,400), PO Box 13225, Austin 78711-3225; (512) 936-4400.

Guadalupe River Authority Board of Directors, Upper – (1939); apptv.; 6-yr.; 9 members: Mike L. Allen, Kerrville (2/1/13); Lana M. Edwards, Hunt (2/1/11); Lester C. Ferguson, Kerrville (2/1/15); Claudell Kercheville, Kerrville (2/1/13); Stan R. Kubenka, Kerrville (2/1/15); Mike Boyd McKenzie, Kerrville (2/1/11); Scott S. Parker, Kerrville (2/1/13); Karol A. Schreiner, Hunt (2/1/11); Lucy Wilke, Kerrville (2/1/15). Gen. Mgr. Ray Buck Jr., 125 Lehman Dr., Ste. 100, Kerrville 78028-5908; (830) 896-5445.

Guadalupe-Blanco River Authority – (1935); apptv.; per diem and expenses on duty; 6-yr.; 9 members: Chair Oscar H. Fogle, Lockhart (2/1/14); Grace G. Kunde, Seguin (2/1/15); Arlene N. Marshall, Port Lavaca (2/1/11); Myrna P. McLeroy, Gonzales (2/1/13); Frank J. Pagel, Tivoli (2/1/13); Jim Powers, Dripping Springs (2/1/14); Michael D. Schultz, Fair Oaks Ranch (2/1/15); Clifton L. Thomas Jr., Victoria (2/1/15); Tilmon Lee (T.L.) Walker, New Braunfels (2/1/09). Gen. Mgr. William E. West, 933 E. Court St., Seguin 78155; (830) 379-9718.

Guaranteed Student Loan Corporation, Texas – (1979 as non-profit corp.); apptv.; 6-yr.; 1 ex-officio member (Comptroller of Public Accounts); 10 apptv.: Ivan A. Andarza, Austin (1/31/13); Yvonne Batts, Tuscola (1/31/11); F.H. (Skip) Landis, College Station (1/31/11); Richard M. Rhodes, El Paso (1/31/15); Michael J. Savoie, Justin (1/31/11); Connie S. Sitterly, Fort Worth (1/31/13); Dora Ann Verde, San Antonio (1/31/15); Welcome W. Wilson, Houston (1/31/15); Phil W. Worley, Bruni (1/31/13); student apptee.: Wroe Jackson, Austin (1/31/11). Pres. and CEO Sue McMillin, P.O. Box 83100, Round Rock 78683-3100; (800) 252-9743.

Guardianship Certification Board – (2006); apptd. by the Texas Supreme Court; 6-yr.; 15 members: Chair Judge Gladys Burwell, Galveston (2/1/11); Barry Anderson, Arlington (2/1/13);

Leah Cohen, Austin (2/1/09); Jason Armstrong, Lufkin (2/1/13); Garth Corbett, Austin (2/1/11); Raymond Costello, San Antonio (2/1/11); Carol Patrice Dabner, Dallas (2/1/009); Susan Eason, Austin (2/1/11); Don D. Ford III, Houston (2/1/11); Philip A. Grant, Round Rock (2/1/09); Marlane Meyer, McAllen (2/1/13); Gina D. Patterson, Houston (2/1/13); Kathy S. Strong, Nacogdoches (2/1/13); Patti Turner, Fort Worth (2/1/09); Robert Warach, El Paso (2/1/09). Dir. Lesley Martin Ondrechen, PO Box 12066, Austin 78711-2066; (512) 463-1635.

Gulf Coast Waste Disposal Authority – (1969); apptv.; 2-yr.; per diem and expenses on duty; 9 members: 3 apptv. by Gov., 3 by County Commissioners Courts of counties in district, 3 by Municipalities Waste Disposal Councils of counties in district. Chair Mark Schultz, Anahuac (8/31/08); Zoe Milian Barinaga, Houston (8/31/09); Ron Crowder, LaMarque (8/31/07); Randy Jarrell, Crystal Beach (8/31/08); Franklin Jones, Houston (8/31/09); James A. Matthews Jr., Texas City (8/31/07); Lamont Meaux, Stowell (8/31/08); Irvin Osborne-Lee, Houston (8/31/04); Rita Standridge, Beach City (8/31/08). Gen. Mgr. Charles Ganze, 910 Bay Area Blvd., Houston 77058; (281) 488-3331.

Gulf States Marine Fisheries Commission – (1949 with members from Texas, Alabama, Florida, Louisiana and Mississippi); apptv.; 3-yr.; 3 Texas members: 2 ex officio: Texas Parks and Wildlife Dept. exec. dir. and 1 member of House; 1 apptd. by Gov.: David A. McKinney, Cypress Mill (3/17/11). Exec. Dir. Larry B. Simpson, PO Box 726, Ocean Springs, MS 39566-0726; (228) 875-5912.

Health Coordinating Council, Statewide – (1977); apptv.; 6-yr.; 17 members (4 ex officio; 13 apptd. by Gov.): Chair Ben G. Raimer, Galveston (8/1/09); Richard L. Beard, Mesquite (8/1/09); Davidica Blum, Georgetown (8/1/13); Lourdes M. Cuellar, Houston (8/1/11); James A. Endicott Jr., Harker Heights (8/1/11); Karl Alonzo Floyd, Stafford (8/1/09); Eric W. Ford, Lubbock (8/1/13); Janie Martinez Gonzalez, San Antonio (8/1/09); John Q. Gowan, Dallas (8/1/11); Ayeez A. Lalji, Sugar Land (8/1/13); Elva C. LeBlanc, Galveston (8/1/13); Lorraine O'Donnell, El Paso (8/1/11); Richard Madsen Smith, Amarillo (8/1/09). Ex-officio members include 1 each from Texas Dept. of State Health Services, Texas Dept. of Aging and Disability Services, Texas Higher Education Coordinating Board and Texas Health and Human Services Commission. Proj. Dir. Connie Turney, PO Box 149347, Austin, TX 78714-9347; 512-458-7261.

Health and Human Services Commission Council – (1991); apptv.; 4-yr.; 9 members: Chair Jerry Kane, Corpus Christi (2/1/15); Kathleen O. Angel, Round Rock (2/1/11); Sharon J. Barnes, Lake Jackson (2/1/13); Maryann Choi, Georgetown (2/1/11); Rev. Manson B. Johnson, Houston (2/1/15); Leon J. Leach, Houston (2/1/13); Ronald Luke, Austin (2/1/13); Robert A. Valadez, San Antonio (2/1/11); Teresa (Terry) Wilkinson, Midland (2/1/15). Commissioner Albert Hawkins III ($200,000), PO Box 13247, Austin 78711-3247; (512) 424-6603.

Health and Human Services, Commissioner of – (1879 as State Health Officer; 1955 changed to Commissioner of Health; 1975 changed to Director, Texas Department of Health Resources; 1977 changed to Commissioner, Texas Dept. of Health; changed to present name in 2004); apptv.; 2-yr.: Albert Hawkins ($200,000), PO Box 13247, Austin 78711-3247; (512) 424-6603.

Health Professions Council – (1993); ex officio; 14 members: 1 from Gov.'s office and 1 each from the following 13 regulating agencies: Texas Board of Chiropractic Examiners, Texas State Board of Dental Examiners, Texas Medical Board, Texas Board of Nursing, Texas Optometry Board, Texas State Board of Pharmacy, Physical Therapy Examiners Board, Texas State Board of Podiatric Medical Examiners, Texas Board of Examiners of Psychologists, Occupational Therapy Examiners Board, Texas Board of Veterinary Medical Examiners, Texas Funeral Service Commission, Texas Department of State Health Services Professional Licensing and Certification Unit. Admin. Officer John Monk, 333 Guadalupe St., Ste. 2-220, Austin 78701; (512) 305-8550.

Health Services Authority, Texas – (2007); apptv.; 2-yr.; expenses; 2 ex officio plus 11 appt'd. members: Chair Manfred Sternberg, Houston (6/15/09); Alesha Adamson, San Antonio (6/15/09); Fred Buckwold, Houston (6/15/09); Raymond F. Davis, El Paso (6/15/09); David C. Fleeger, Austin (6/15/09); Matthew J. Hamlin, Argyle (6/15/09); Edward W. Marx, Euless (6/15/09); Kathleen K. Mechler, Fredericksburg (6/15/09); Donna Montemayor, San Antonio (6/15/09); J. Darren Rodgers, Dallas (6/15/09); Stephen Yurco, Austin (6/15/09); c/o Texas Health Care Policy Council, Stephen Palmer, Health Policy Advisor, PO Box 12428, Austin 78711; (512) 463-1778.

Health Services Council, Texas Department of State – (1975); apptv.; 4-yr.; 9 members: Chair Glenda R. Kane, Corpus Christi (2/1/15); Beverly Barron, Odessa (2/1/13); Kirk Aquilla Calhoun, Tyler (2/1/11); Graciela A. Cigarroa, San Antonio (2/1/11);

Lewis E. Foxhall, Houston (2/1/15); Jacinto P. Juarez, Laredo (2/1/13); Jeffrey A. Ross, Bellaire, (2/1/13); Nasruddin Rupani, Sugar Land (2/1/15); David Woolweaver, Harlingen (2/1/11). Exec. Dir. David L. Lakey ($175,000), PO Box 149347, Austin 78714-9347; (512) 458-7111.

Hearing Instruments, State Committee of Examiners in the Fitting and Dispensing of – (1969); apptv.; 6-yr.; expenses; 9 members: Richard R. Davila II, Lubbock (12/31/09); Robert J. Gebhard Jr., Pearland (12/31/11); V. Rosemary Geraci, Lufkin (12/31/09); Kenneth B. Haesly, Pasadena (12/31/11); James Leffingwell, Arlington (12/31/13); Benjamin Norris, Elm Mott (12/31/13); Melissa Kay Rodriguez, El Paso (12/31/11); Cindy M. Steinbart, Round Rock (12/31/09); Amy Trost, Seguin (12/31/13). Exec. Dir. Joyce N. Parsons, c/o Texas Dept. of State Health Services, 1100 W. 49th St., Austin 78756-3183; (512) 834-6784.

Higher Education Coordinating Board, Texas – (1953 as temporary board; 1955 as permanent 15-member Texas Commission on Higher Education; 1965 as Texas College and University Systems Coordinating Board; name and membership changed to present form in 1987); apptv.; 6-yr.; expenses; 9 members: Chair A.W. (Whit) Riter III, Tyler (8/31/11); Laurie Bricker, Houston (8/31/09); Fred W. Heldenfels IV, San Marcos (8/31/13); Joe B. Hinton, Crawford (8/31/11); Elaine Mendoza, San Antonio (8/31/11); Brenda Pejovich, Dallas (8/31/13); Lyn Bracewell Phillips, Bastrop (8/31/11); Robert W. Shepard, Harlingen (8/31/09); Robert V. Wingo, El Paso (8/31/09). Commissioner of Higher Education, Raymund A. Paredes, ($165,000) PO Box 12788, Austin 78711-2788; (512) 427-6101.

Higher Education Tuition Board, Texas Prepaid – (1995); apptv.; expenses; term at pleasure of Gov.; 6 members, plus 1 ex officio: State Comptroller; 2 apptd. by Gov. and 4 apptd. by Lt. Gov.: Johh C. Anderson, Plainview; Richard H. Collins, Weatherford; Joe Colonnetta, Dallas (2/1/11); Jack R. Hamilton, Houston; Harrison Keller, Austin; Stephen N. Mueller, Cypress (2/1/15); c/o Texas Guaranteed Tuition Plan, Comptroller of Public Accounts, PO Box 13407, Austin 78711-3407; (800) 445-4723.

Historian, Texas State – (2005); apptv.; 2-yr.; Light Townsend Cummins, Sherman (5/29/11); c/o Department of History, Austin College, 900 N. Grand Ave., Sherman 75090-4400; (903) 813-2359.

Historical Commission, Texas – (1953); apptv.; expenses; 6-yr.; 17 members: Chair Jon T. Hansen, El Paso (1/31/15); Thomas E. Alexander, Kerrville (2/1/15); Earl P. Broussard, Austin (2/1/11); Diane D. Bumpas, Dallas (2/1/11); Donna Dean Carter, Austin (2/1/11); Mario Castillo, San Angelo (1/31/13); John Crain, Dallas (1/31/13); Leslie (Kirk) Courson, Perryton (1/31/15); David A. Gravelle, Dallas (1/31/13); Lisa Hembry, Dallas (1/31/13); Steven L. Highlander, Austin (2/1/15); Sara (Sarita) Hixon, Armstrong (2/1/11); Sheri S. Krause, Austin (2/1/15); Gilbert E. Peterson, Alpine (1/31/13); Thomas R. Phillips, Bastrop (2/1/11); Nancy Steves, San Antonio (2/1/15); Marcus Warren Watson, Plano (2/1/11). Commissioner Emeritus T.R. Fehrenbach, San Antonio. Exec. Dir. F. Lawerence Oaks ($99,500) PO Box 12276, Austin 78711-2276; (512) 463-6100.

Historical Records Advisory Board, Texas – (1976); apptv.; 3-yr.; 9 members: State Archivist; 6 apptd. by Texas State Library and Archives Commission director and librarian; 2 apptd. by Gov.: Coordinator and State Archivist Chris LaPlante, Austin (2/1/15); Cynthia J. Beeman, Austin; Suzanne Campbell, San Angelo; Margaret Harris, Houston; Shelly Henley Kelly, Houston; J.P. (Pat) McDaniel, Midland (2/1/12); Houston McGaugh, Washington; Jennifer Boswell Pickens, Dallas; John Slate, Dallas. c/o Texas State Library, PO Box 12927, Austin 78711; (512) 463-5480.

Housing and Community Affairs, Board of Texas Dept. of – (1979 as Texas Housing Agency; merged with Department of Community Affairs and name changed in 1991); apptv.; expenses; 6-yr.; 7 members: Chair C. Kent Conine, Dallas (1/31/15); Leslie Bingham-Escareño, Brownsville (1/31/13); Tomas Cardenas, El Paso (1/31/13); Tom H. Gann, Lufkin (1/31/15); Juan Sanchez Muñoz, Lubbock (1/31/11); Gloria L. Ray, San Antonio (1/31/11); 1 vacancy. Exec. Dir. Michael Gerber ($117,516), PO Box 13941, Austin 78711-3941; (512) 475-3800.

Housing Corp., Texas State Affordable – (1994); 6 yrs.; 5 members: Chair Robert Jones, Corpus Christi (2/1/15); William H. Dietz Jr., Waco (2/1/15); Jo Van Hovel, Temple (2/1/13); A. Cynthia Leon, Mission (2/1/15); Raymond Carter Sanders, Austin (2/1/11). Pres. David Long, PO Box 12637, Austin 78711-2637; (512) 477-3555.

Human Rights Commission, Texas – (2004 as part of the Texas Workforce Commission's Civil Rights Division); apptv.; 6-yr.; 7 members: Chair Thomas M. Anderson, Richmond (2/1/13); Michelle H. Diggs, Cedar Park (2/1/15); John H. James, Midland (2/1/11); Shara Michalka, Dallas (2/1/11); Travis A. Morris, Austin (2/1/15); Danny L. Osterhout, Andrews (2/1/13); Veronica Vargas

Stidvent, Austin (2/1/15). Exec. Dir. Robert Gomez, 101 E. 15th St., Rm. 144T, Austin 78778-0001; (512) 463-2642.

Industrialized Building Code Council, Texas – (1973); apptv.; 2-yr.; 12 members: Chair Martin (Marty) J. Garza, San Antonio (2/1/10); Robert L. Bowling IV, El Paso (2/1/15); Joe D. Campos, Dallas (2/1/10); Randy Childers, Waco (2/1/10); Mark G. Delaney, Tomball (2/1/15); Amy Dempsey, Austin (2/1/10); Michael G. Mount, Plano (2/1/15); Mark Remmert, Liberty Hill (2/1/10); Jesse Rider, Tyler (2/01/10); Rolando R. Rubiano, Harlingen (2/1/15); Ravi Shah, The Colony (2/1/15); Larry E. Wilkinson, Friendswood (2/1/15); c/o Texas Dept. of Licensing and Regulation, PO Box 12157, Austin 78711; (512) 463-6599.

Information Resources, Department of – (1981 as Automated Information and Telecommunications Council; name changed to current in 1990); 6-yr.; expenses; 10 members: 3 ex officio, 7 apptv.: Chair Cliff P. Mountain, Austin (2/1/09); Charles Bacarisse, Houston (2/1/13); Ramon Baez, Southlake (2/1/15); Rosemary Martinez, Brownsville (2/1/11); Debra McCartt, Amarillo (2/1/11); Phillip (Keith) Morrow, Southlake (2/1/11); Robert E. Pickering Jr., Houston (2/1/15); ex-officio members are from Health and Human Services Commission, Texas Dept. of Insurance and Texas Dept. of Transportation. Chief Technology Officer, Brian Rawson ($175,000), PO Box 13564, Austin 78711-3564; (512) 475-4700.

Insurance Commissioner, Texas Dept. of – (1876 as Dept. of Insurance; 1887 as Dept. of Agriculture, Insurance, Statistics and History; 1907 as Dept. of Insurance and Banking; 1923 as Dept. of Insurance); apptv.; 2-yr.; Commissioner Mike Geeslin (2/1/11), ($163,800), PO Box 149104, Austin 78714-9104; (512) 463-6169.

Insurance Counsel, Office of Public – (*See* Public Insurance Counsel, Office of.)

Interstate Commission for Adult Offender Supervision – (1937 as Interstate Compact for the Supervision of Parolees and Probationers; 2000 as present name); 50 member states; apptv.: Linda L. White, Magnolia (2/1/15). Dep. Admin. for Texas: Regina Grimes, 8712 Shoal Creek Blvd., Austin 78757; (512) 406-5990.

Interstate Mining Compact Commission – (1970); 19 member states, plus 5 associate member states; ex officio or apptv., according to Gov's. choice; Texas reps. are appointed from the Texas Railroad Commission: Michael L. Williams and Melvin Hodgkiss. Exec. Dir. Gregory Conrad, 459B Carlisle Dr., Herndon, VA 22170-4802; (703) 709-8654.

Interstate Oil and Gas Compact Commission, Texas Rep. – (1935); 30 member states, plus 8 associate member states; ex officio or apptv. according to Gov's. choice; per diem and expenses. Official rep. for Texas: Victor G. Carrillo, Austin (12/31/10). Exec. Dir. Mike Smith, PO Box 53127, Oklahoma City, OK 73152; (405) 525-3556.

Jail Standards, Texas Commission on – (1975); apptv.; 6-yr.; expenses; 9 members: Chair Donna S. Klaeger, Horseshoe Bay (1/31/13); Irene Armendariz, El Paso (1/31/15); Albert L. Black, Austin (1/31/11); Stanley D. Egger, Abilene (1/31/11); Jerry W. Lowry, New Caney (1/31/13); Larry S. May, Sweetwater (1/31/13); Gary Painter, Midland (2/1/15); Michael M. Seale, Houston (1/31/11); Tam Terry, White Deer (1/31/15). Exec. Dir. Adan Munoz Jr. ($68,500), PO Box 12985, Austin 78711-2985; (512) 463-5505.

Judicial Compensation Commission – (2007); apptv.; 6-yr.; expenses; 9 members: Chair William Strawn, Austin (2/01/15); Wanda Chandler Rohm, San Antonio (2/01/11); Tommy Harwell, El Paso (2/01/13); Cruz G. Hernandez, Burleson (2/01/15); Harold Jenkins, Irving (2/01/11); Patrick Mizell, Houston (2/01/13); Paul Bane Phillippi, Cedar Creek (2/01/15); Linda Russell, Houston (2/01/13); Michael Slack, Austin (2/01/11); c/o Office of Court Administration, Tom C. Clark Building, 205 W. 14th St., Ste. 600, Austin 78701; (512) 463-1625.

Judicial Conduct, State Commission on – (1965 as 9-member Judicial Qualifications Commission; name changed to present in 1977); expenses; 6-yr.; 13 members: 6 apptd. by Supreme Court; 2 apptd. by State Bar; 5 apptd. by Gov.: Chair Sid L. Harle, San Antonio, (11/19/11); Ann Appling Bradford, Midland (11/19/09); Tom Cunningham, Houston (11/19/11); Michael R. Fields, Houston (11/19/09); Monica A. Gonzalez, San Antonio, (11/19/09); Ernie Houdashell, Canyon (11/19/11); Patti H. Johnson, Canyon Lake (11/19/11); Tom Lawrence, Humble (11/19/09); William C. Lawrence, Highland Village (11/19/09); Karry K. Matson, Georgetown (11/19/13); Jan P. Patterson, Austin (11/19/13); Jorge C. Rangel, Corpus Christi, (11/19/11); Janelle Shephard, Weatherford (11/19/11). Exec. Dir. Seana B. Willing ($110,000), PO Box 12265, Austin 78711-2265; (512) 463-5533.

Judicial Council, Texas – (1929 as Texas Civil Judicial Council; name changed in 1975); 6-yr.; expenses; 22 members: 16 ex officio and 6 apptd. from general public. Public members: Keely

Appleton, Arlington (6/30/10); Richard Battle, College Station (6/30/09); Fred E. Davis, Austin (6/30/11); Richard S. Figueroa, Houston (6/30/13); Allyson Ho, Dallas (6/30/13); Henry Nuss, Corpus Christi (6/30/09). Exec. Dir. Carl Reynolds ($104,500), PO Box 12066, Austin 78711; (512) 463-1625.

Judicial Districts Board – (1985); 12 ex-officio members (term in other office); 1 apptv. (4 yrs.); ex officio: Chief Justice of Texas Supreme Court; Presiding Judge, Court of Criminal Appeals; Presiding Judge of each of 9 Administrative Judicial Districts; Gov. apptee.: Craig Enoch, Austin (12/12/10).

Judicial Districts of Texas, Administrative, Presiding Judges of – (See Administrative Judicial Districts, Presiding Judges.)

Juneteenth Cultural and Historical Commission, Texas Emancipation – (1997); expenses; 6 yr.; 11 members; 5 ex officio, non-voting: 2 apptd. by Lt. Gov., 2 apptd. by Speaker of House, and exec. dir. of Texas Historical Comm.; 6 apptd by Gov.: Chair Rep. Al Edwards, Houston; Vicki D. Blanton, Dallas (2/1/11); Willie Belle Boone, Houston (2/1/15); Carmen Francis, Georgetown (2/1/11); Clarence E. Glover Jr., Dallas (2/1/13); William H. Watson, Lubbock (2/1/13); PO Box 2910, Austin 78768-2910; (512) 463-0518.

Juvenile Justice Advisory Board – (2001); per diem and expenses; terms at pleasure of the Gov.; 1 ex-officio member: exec. dir. of the Gov.'s Criminal Justice Division; 18 apptd. members: Glenn Brooks, Austin; Charles Brawner, Katy; Christopher Demerson, Missouri City; Milton Duntley, El Paso; Harold Gaither Jr., Quinlan; Elizabeth Godwin, Houston; David Gutierrez, Huntsville; Tammy Hawkins, Odessa; Jim Kester, Austin; Kevin Knight, Houston; Luke Lowenfield, Austin; Felix Mejia Jr., Fredericksburg; Magdalena Manzano, College Station; Matt Mims, Colleyville; Stacey Parker, Austin; James Smith, Austin; Vicki Spriggs, Austin; Mario Watkins, Pearland; Jane Wetzel, Dallas. Criminal Justice Division, 100 San Jacinto, Austin 78701; (512) 475-2440.

Juvenile Probation Commission, Texas – (1981); apptv.; 6-yr.; expenses; 9 members: 3 District Court judges and 6 private citizens: Chair Judge Ray West, Amarillo (8/31/11); Judge Jean H. Boyd, Fort Worth (8/31/13); Bob Ed Culver Jr., Canadian (8/31/09); Billy Wayne McClendon, Austin (8/31/13); Scott O'Grady, Dallas (8/31/09); Rene Ordonez, El Paso (8/31/11); Judge Cheryl Lee Shannon, Dallas (8/31/09); Robert Shults, Houston (8/31/13); Lea R. Wright, Amarillo (8/31/11). Exec. Dir. Vicki Spriggs ($109,112), PO Box 13547, Austin 78711-3547; (512) 424-6700.

Land Board, School – (1939); 2-yr.; per diem and expenses; 3 members: 1 ex officio: Comm. of General Land Office; 2 apptd.: 1 by Atty. Gen. and 1 by Gov.: Todd F. Barth, Houston (8/29/09); David S. Herrmann, San Antonio (8/31/07); c/o General Land Office, SFA Office Bldg., 1700 N. Congress Ave., Austin 78701-1495; (512) 463-5001.

Land Board, Veterans' – (Est. 1949 as 3-member ex-officio board; reorganized 1956); 4-yr.; per diem and expenses; 3 members: 1 ex officio: Comm. of General Land Office; 2 apptd.: Alan L. Johnson, Harlingen (12/29/12); Alan K. Sandersen, Missouri City (12/29/10). Exec. Sec. Paul E. Moore, PO Box 12873, Austin 78711-2873; (512) 463-5060.

Land Surveying, Texas Board of Professional – (1979; formed from consolidation of Board of Examiners of Licensed Land Surveyors, est. 1977, and State Board of Registration for Public Surveyors, est. 1955); apptv.; 6-yr.; 9 members: 1 ex officio: Comm. of General Land Office; 8 apptd.: Chair Nedra J. Foster, Silsbee (1/31/15); James A. Childress, San Saba (1/31/15); Jon Hodde, Brenham (1/31/13); Paul P. Kwan, Houston (1/31/11); Robert H. Price, Euless (1/31/15); David G. Smyth, Devine (1/31/13); Anthony Treviño Jr., Laredo (1/31/11); Douglas Turner, Houston (1/31/11). Exec. Dir. Sandy Smith ($55,000), 12100 Park 35 Circle, Bldg. A, Ste. 156, MC 230, Austin 78753; (512) 239-5263.

Lands, Board for Lease of University – (1929 as 3-member board; members increased to 4 in 1985); ex officio; term in other office; 4 members: Comm. of General Land Office, 2 members of Board of Regents of University of Texas, 1 member Board of Regents of University of Texas A&M University. Sec. Sharon Burks, The University of Texas System; (432) 684-4404.

Lavaca-Navidad River Authority, Board of Directors – (1954 as 7-member Jackson County Flood Control District; reorganized as 9-member board in 1959; name changed to present form in 1969); apptv.; 6-yr.; per diem and expenses; 9 members: President Ronald Edwin Kubecka, Palacios (5/1/15); Jon Bradford, Edna (5/1/13); John Alcus Cotten Jr., Ganado (5/1/15); Sherry Kay Frels, Edna (5/1/13); Olivia R. Jarratt, Edna (5/1/13); Paul Littlefield, La Ward (5/1/11); Nils P. Mauritz, Ganado (5/1/15); David Martin Muegge, Edna (5/1/11); Kay W. Simons, Edna (5/1/11). Gen. Mgr. Patrick Brzozowski, PO Box 429, Edna 77957; (361) 782-5229.

Law Enforcement Officer Standards & Education, Texas

Commission on – (1965); expenses; 14 members; 5 ex officio: Atty. Gen., Director of Public Safety, Comm. of Education, Exec. Dir. of Governor's Office Criminal Justice Division, and Comm. of Higher Education; 9 apptv. members: Chair Charles R. Hall, Midland (8/30/11); Allan D. Cain, Carthage (8/30/11); Romulo Chavez, Houston (8/30/09); Stephen M. Griffith, Sugar Land (8/10/13); Johnny E. Lovejoy II, San Antonio (8/30/13); Betty Harper Murphy, Fredericksburg (8/10/09); Joel W. Richardson, Canyon (8/30/13); Pat Scheckel-Hollingsworth, Arlington (8/30/11); Gary M. Swindle, Brownsboro (8/30/09). Exec. Dir. Timothy Braaten ($88,000), 6330 U.S. Hwy. 290 E, Ste. 200, Austin 78723; (512) 936-7700.

Law Examiners, Texas Board of – (1919); 9 attorneys apptd. by Supreme Court biennially for 2-year terms expiring Sept. 30 of odd-numbered years. Compensation set by Supreme Court not to exceed $20,000 per annum: Chair Jorge C. Rangel, Corpus Christi; U. Lawrence Boze, Houston; Jerry Grissom, Dallas; Jerry Nugent, Austin; Cynthia Olsen, Houston; E. Lee Parsley, Austin; Dan Pozza, San Antonio; John Simpson, Lubbock; Michael Sokolow, Houston. Exec. Dir. Julia Vaughan, PO Box 13486, Austin 78711-3486; (512) 463-1621.

Law Library Board, Texas State – (1971); ex officio; expenses; 3 members: Atty. Gen., Chief Justice State Supreme Court, Presiding Judge Court of Criminal Appeals. Dir. Dale Propp ($63,800), PO Box 12367, Austin 78711-2367; (512) 463-1722.

Legislative Budget Board – (1949); 10 members; 5 ex-officio: Lt. Gov.; House Speaker; Chmn., Senate Finance Comm.; Chmn., House Appropriations Comm.; Chmn., House Ways and Means Comm.; plus 5 other members of Legislature. Dir. John O'Brian, PO Box 12666, Austin 78711-2666; (512) 463-1200.

Legislative Council, Texas – (1949); 14 ex-officio members: Lt. Gov.; House Speaker; 6 senators apptd. by Lt. Gov.; 5 representatives apptd. by Speaker; Chmn., House Administration Committee. Exec. Dir. Milton Rister, PO Box 12128, Austin 78711-2128; (512) 463-1155.

Legislative Redistricting Board – (1951); 5 ex-officio members: Lt. Gov., House Speaker, Atty. Gen., Comptroller of Public Accounts and Comm. of General Land Office; PO Box 12128, Austin 78711-2128; (512) 463-6622.

Legislative Reference Library – See Library, Legislative Reference.

Librarian, State – (Originally est. in 1839; present office est. 1909); apptv., indefinite term: Peggy D. Rudd ($95,000), PO Box 12927, Austin 78711-2927; (512) 463-5455.

Library and Archives Commission, Texas State – (1909 as 5-member Library and State Historical Commission; name changed to present form in 1979); apptv.; per diem and expenses on duty; 6-yr.; 7 members: Chair Sandra Pickett, Liberty (9/28/09); Sharon T. Carr, El Paso (9/28/11); Diana Rae Hester Cox, Canyon (9/28/07); Martha Doty Freeman, Austin (9/28/09); Sandra Gunter Holland, Pleasanton (9/28/07); Larry G. Holt, College Station (9/28/09); Sally Ann Reynolds, Rockport (9/28/11). Dir. and Librarian Peggy D. Rudd ($95,000), PO Box 12927, Austin 78711-2927; (512) 463-5455.

Library, Legislative Reference – (1909); 3 ex-officio members: Lt. Gov., House Speaker, Chrm., House Appropriations Committee; 3 Legislative members; indefinite term. Dir. Mary Camp, Box 12488, Austin 78711-2488; (512) 463-1252.

Licensing and Regulation, Texas Department on – (1989); apptv.; 6-yr.; expenses; 7 members: Chair Frank S. Denton, Conroe (2/1/13); Mike Arismendez Jr., Shallowater (2/1/15); Lewis Benavides, Oak Point (2/1/11); LuAnn Roberts Morgan, Midland (2/1/15); Fred N. Moses, Plano (2/1/15); Lillian Norman-Keeney, Taylor Lake Village (2/1/11); Deborah A. Yurco, Austin (2/1/13). Exec. Dir. Wllliam H. Kuntz Jr. ($123,750); PO Box 12157, Austin 78711-2157.

Licensing Standards, Committee on– (2007); apptv.; 2-yr.; expenses; 7 members: Chair Karyn Purvis, Fort Worth (2/1/09); Dan Adams, Amarillo (2/1/09); Adriene J. Driggers, San Antonio (2/1/11); Kimberly B. Kofron, Round Rock (2/1/11); Sasha Rasco, Austin (2/1/11); Ann Stanley, Austin (2/1/11); Tivy Whitlock, Mico (2/1/11). Dept. of Family and Protective Services, PO Box 149030, Austin 78714-9030; (512) 438-4800.

Lottery Commission, Texas – (1993); 6-yrs.; apptv.; expenses; 3 members: Chair Mary Ann Williamson, Weatherford (2/1/11); J. Winston Krause, Austin (2/1/11); David J. Schenck, Dallas (2/1/13). Exec. Dir. (vacant) ($135,000), PO Box 16630, Austin 78761-6630; (512) 344-5000.

Lower Colorado River Authority – (See Colorado River Authority, Lower).

Lower Concho River Water and Soil Conservation Authority – (See Concho River Water and Soil Conservation, Lower).

Lower Neches Valley Authority – (See Neches Valley Authority, Lower).

Manufactured Housing Governing Board – (1995); apptv.; 6 yrs.; 5 members: Chair Michael H. Bray, El Paso (1/31/11); Devora Mitchell, Kermit (1/31/11); Pablo Schneider, Richardson (1/31/13); Sheila M. Vallés-Pankratz, Mission (1/31/15), Donnie W. Wisenbaker, Sulphur Springs (1/31/13). Exec. Dir. Joe Garcia, PO Box 12489, Austin 78711-2489; (512) 475-2200.

Marriage & Family Therapists, Texas State Board of Examiners of – (1991); apptv.; 6 yrs.; per diem and transportation expenses; 9 members: Chair Sandra L. DeSobe, Houston (2/1/13); Timothy Brown, Rowlett (2/1/11); Joe Ann Clack, Missouri City (2/1/15); Michael Miller, Belton (2/1/13); Kaye W. Nelson, Corpus Christi (2/1/11); Michael R. Puhl, McKinney (2/1/15); Edna Reyes-Wilson, El Paso (2/1/11); Jennifer Smothermon, Abilene (2/1/13); Beverly Walker Womack, Jacksonville (2/1/15). Exec. Dir. Charles Horton, Texas Dept. of Health Services, PO Box 149347, Austin 78714-9347; (512) 834-6657.

Medical Board, Texas – (1907 as 11-member Texas State Board of Medical Examiners; members increased to 12 in 1931, 15 in 1981,18 in 1993 and 19 in 2003; changed to present name in 2005 by Senate Bill 419); apptv.; 6-yr.; per diem on duty; 19 members: Chair Irvin E. Zeitler Jr., San Angelo (4/13/11); Michael Arambula, San Antonio (4/13/13); Julie Attebury, Amarillo (4/13/11); David Baucom, Sulphur Springs (4/13/15); Jose M. Benavides, San Antonio (4/13/11); Patricia S. Blackwell, Midland (4/13/13); Patrick J. Crocker, Austin (4/13/15); John D. Ellis Jr., Houston (4/13/15); Manuel G. Guajardo, Brownsville (4/13/15); Scott Holliday, University Park (4/13/13); Melinda C. McMichael, Austin (4/13/13); Margaret C. McNeese, Houston (4/13/13); Charles E. Oswalt III, Waco (4/13/13); Allan N. Shulkin, Dallas (4/13/15); Wynne M. Snoots, Dallas (4/13/15); Paulette B. Southard, Alice (4/13/11); Timothy J. Turner, Houston (4/13/15); Timothy Webb, Houston (4/13/13); George Willeford III, Austin (4/13/11). Exec. Dir. Mari Robinson ($110,000), PO Box 2018, Austin 78768-2018; (512) 305-7010. *Consumer Complaint Hotline: (800) 201-9353.*

Medical Physicists, Texas Board of Licensure for Professional – (1991); apptv.; 6-yrs.; 9 members: Chair Philip D. Bourland, Temple (2/1/11); Shannon D. Cox, Austin (2/1/09); Valerie Foreman, Frisco (2/1/15); Kumar Krishen, Houston (2/1/11); John R. Leahy, Austin (2/1/13); Adrian D. LeBlanc, Houston (2/1/07); Pamela M. Otto, San Antonio (2/1/15); Rebecca C. Middleton, De Soto (2/1/11); Richard E. Wendt III, Houston (2/1/13). Exec. Sec. Pam Kaderka, PO Box 149347, Austin 78714-9347; (512) 834-6655.

Midwestern State University, Board of Regents – (1959); apptv.; 6-yr.; 9 members: Charles Engleman, Wichita Falls (2/25/14); Charlye O. Farris, Wichita Falls (2/25/12); Fenton Lynwood Givens, Plano (2/25/12); Carol Carlson Gunn, Graford (2/25/12); Stephen A. Gustafson, Wichita Falls (2/25/10); Shawn G. Hessing, Fort Worth (2/25/14); Munir A. Lanani, Wichita Falls (2/25/10); Jane W. Spears, Wichita Falls (2/25/14); Ben F. Wible, Sherman (2/25/10). Pres. Dr. Jesse W. Rogers, 3410 Taft Blvd., Wichita Falls 76308; (940) 397-4010.

Midwifery Board, Texas – (1999); apptv. by Health and Human Services Comm.; 6-yr.; travel expenses; 9 members: Susan Chick (1/1/09); Connie Carlos (1/1/11); Janet Dirmeyer (1/1/11); Laurie Fremgen (1/1/13); Charleta Guillory (1/1/13); Thalia Hufton (1/1/09); Sylyna Kennedy (1/1/11); Andrew MacLaurin (1/1/13); Barry E. Schwarz (1/1/15). c/o Texas Dept. of Health Services, PO Box 149347, Austin 78714-9347; (512) 834-4523.

Military Facilities Commission, Texas – (1935 as 3-member Texas National Guard Armory Board; reorganized in 1981 as 6-member board; name changed to present in 1997; members increased to 7 in 2003); 6-yr.; 7 members: Chair Sandra Paret, Dallas (4/30/06); Regino J. Gonzales, Galena Park (4/30/09); Delores Ann Harper, San Antonio (4/30/07); Larry W. Jackson, Temple (4/30/09); Chao-Chiung Lee, Houston (4/30/09); Jorge Perez, McAllen (4/30/05); Michael G. Taylor, Lufkin (4/30/07). Exec. Dir. John A. Wells, 2200 W. 35th St., Bldg. 64, Austin 78703-1222; (512) 782-6971.

Military Preparedness Commission, Texas– (2003); apptv.; some terms at pleasure of Gov.; 2 ex-officio members (1 Senator, 1 House Representative); 13 apptv.: Chair Paul F. Paine, Fort Worth; Dora G. Alcala, Del Rio (2/1/15); William J. (Bill) Ehrie, Abilene; Ralph C. Gauer, Harker Heights (2/1/15); Howard C. Ham Jr., Lockhart; Ronald D. Henson, Texarkana; Alvin W. Jones, College Station (2/1/15); James P. Maloney, El Paso; Loyd Neal, Corpus Christi; Charles E. Powell, San Angelo; Josue Robles Jr., San Antonio (2/1/11); Eugene N. Tulich, Houston; Thomas Whaylen, Wichita Falls; PO Box 12428, Austin, 78711; (512) 463-8800.

Municipal Retirement System, Texas (*See* Retirement System, Texas Municipal).

National Guard Armory Board, Texas – (*See* Military Facilities Commission, Texas).

Natural Resource Conservation Commission, Texas (*See*

Environmental Quality, Texas Commission on).

Neches River Municipal Water Authority, Upper – (1953 as 9-member board; members decreased to 3 in 1959); apptv.; 6-yr.; 3 members: Jesse D. Hickman, Palestine (2/1/15); William Barry James, Palestine (2/1/13); Robert E. McKelvey, Palestine (2/1/11). Gen. Mgr. Monty D. Shank, PO Box 1965, Palestine 75802; (903) 876-2237.

Neches Valley Authority, Lower – (1933); apptv.; per diem and expenses on duty; 6-yr.; 9 members: Lonnie Arrington, Beaumont (7/28/13); Brian Babin, Woodville (7/28/13); Sue Cleveland, Lumberton (7/28/09); Jimmie Ruth Cooley, Woodville (7/28/09); Kathleen Thea Jackson, Beaumont (7/28/09); Steven M. McReynolds, Groves (7/28/13); Dade Phelan, Beaumont (7/28/11); Jordan Reese IV, Beaumont (7/28/11); James Olan Webb, Silsbee (7/28/11). Gen. Mgr. Robert Stroder, PO Box 5117, Beaumont 77726-5117; (409) 892-4011.

Nueces River Authority – (1953 as Nueces River Conservation and Reclamation District; name changed to present in 1971); apptv.; 6-yr.; per diem and expenses; 22 members: President Dan S. Leyendecker, Corpus Christi (2/1/13); W. Scott Bledsoe III, Oakville (2/1/15); Karen Bonner, Corpus Christi (2/1/11); Rebecca Bradford, Corpus Christi (2/1/13); Fernando Camarillo, Boerne (2/1/15); Manuel D. Cano, Corpus Christi (2/1/15); Joe M. Cantu, Pipe Creek (2/1/13); James T. Clancy, Portland (2/1/15); William I. Dillard, Uvalde (2/1/15); Robert M. Dullnig, San Antonio (2/1/13); John Galloway, Beeville (2/1/09); Gary Jones, Beeville (2/1/11); Yale Leland Kerby, Uvalde (2/1/11); Lindsey Alfred Koenig, Orange Grove (2/1/15); James Richard Marmion III, Carrizo Springs (2/1/11); Betty Ann Peden, Hondo (2/1/09); Scott James Petty, Hondo (2/1/13); Curtis Raabe, Poth (2/1/15); Thomas M. Reding Jr., Portland (2/1/15); Fidel R. Rul Jr., Alice (2/1/11); Roxana P. Tom, Campbellton (2/1/11); 1 vacancy. Exec. Dir. Con Mims, PO Box 349, Uvalde 78802-0349; (830) 278-6810.

Nursing, Texas Board of – (1909 as 5-member Texas Board of Nurse Examiners; members increased to 6 in 1931 and to 9 in 1981; name changed to present and members increased to 13 in 2007); apptv.; per diem and expenses; 6-yr.; 13 members: President Linda Rounds, Galveston (1/31/11); Deborah Hughes Bell, Abilene (1/31/11); Kristin K. Benton, Austin (1/31/13); Patricia Clapp, Dallas (1/31/13); Tamara Cowen, Harlingen (2/1/15); Sheri Crosby, Mesquite (2/1/15); Marilyn Davis, Sugar Land (1/31/13); Blanca Rosa (Rosie) Garcia, Corpus Christi (1/31/11); Richard Gibbs, Mesquite (1/31/13); Kathy Leader-Horn, Granbury (2/1/15); Josefina Lujan, El Paso (2/1/15); Beverly Jean Nutall, Bryan (1/31/11); Mary Jane Salgado, Eagle Pass (2/1/15). Exec. Dir. Katherine A. Thomas ($89,749), 333 Guadalupe, Suite 3-460, Austin 78701; (512) 305-7400.

Nursing Facility Administrators, Texas Board of – Abolished Sept. 1997 and responsibilities transferred to Texas Dept. of Human Services, which itself was abolished in 2004 and responsibilities transferred to Texas Dept. of Aging and Disability Services.

Occupational Therapy Examiners, Texas Board of – (1983 as 6-member board; increased to 9 in 1999); apptv.; 6-yr.; per diem and expenses; 9 members: Catherine Benavidez, Carrollton (2/1/15); Judith Ann Chambers, Austin (2/1/13); Dely De Guia Cruz, Houston (2/1/09); Kathleen Hill, Hutto (2/1/13); Stephanie Johnston, Houston (2/1/11); Pamela D. Nelon, Fort Worth (2/1/11); Todd Novosad, Austin (2/1/13); Angela Sieffert, Dallas (2/1/15); Bobby James Vasquez, Frisco (2/1/11). Exec. Dir. John Maline ($62,000), 333 Guadalupe St., Ste. 2-510, Austin 78701-3942; (512) 305-6900.

Offenders with Medical or Mental Impairments, Texas Correctional Office on – Apptv.; 6-yr.; 21 members: 11 ex officio from various state agencies; 10 apptd. by Gov.: Chair John Bradley, Georgetown (2/1/13); Ellen Cokinos, Houston (7/20/08); Joseph Gutheinz, Houston (7/20/08); Kevin E. Haynes, Ennis (2/1/11); Gabriel Holguin, San Antonio (2/1/11); Christopher C. Kirk, Bryan (10/21/11); Kathryn J. Kotria, Georgetown (2/1/13); Jan Krocker, Houston (7/20/08); John L. Moore, Denison (2/1/13); Eulon Ross Taylor, Austin (2/1/13). Dir. Dee Wilson, 8610 Shoal Creek Blvd., Austin 78757; (512) 406-5406.

Office of Injured Employee Counsel – (2005; represents the interests of workers' compensation claimants); apptv.; 2-yr.; 1 member: Public Counsel Norman Darwin ($105,000), 7551 Metro Center Dr., Ste. 100, Austin 78744-1609; (866) 393-6432.

One-Call Board of Texas – (1997; created by the Underground Facility Damage Prevention and Safety Act and serves as the board for the Texas Underground Facility Notification Corp.); apptv.; 3-yr.; 12 members: Christian A. Alvarado, Austin (8/31/11); Joseph F. Berry, Houston (8/31/07); Dean D. Bernal, Austin (8/31/09); Barry Calhoun, Grapevine (8/31/09); Bill Daugette Jr., Huntsville (8/31/09); Judith H. Devenport, Midland (8/31/07); John Linton, Fort Worth (8/31/10); Barbara J. Mathis, Lufkin (8/31/11);

John A. Menchaca II, Austin (8/31/09); Christopher J. Rourk, Dallas (8/31/09); Rodney J. Unruh, Spring Branch (8/31/11); James Wynn, Midland (8/31/11). Exec. Dir. Donald M. Ward, PO Box 9764, Austin 78766-9764; (512) 467-9764.

Optometry Board, Texas – (1921 as 6-member State Board of Examiners in Optometry; name changed to present in 1981 and members increased to 9); apptv.; per diem; 6-yr.; 9 members: Chair D. Dixon Golden, Center (1/31/15); Carolyn Carmen-Merrifield, Mansfield (1/31/11); Melvin Cleveland, Arlington (1/31/13); John Coble, Rockwall (1/31/11); James Dyess, Austin (1/31/13); Larry Fields, Carthage (1/31/11); Cynthia T. Jenkins, Irving (1/31/15); Randall N. Reichle, Houston (1/31/15); Virginia Sosa, Uvalde (1/31/13). Exec. Dir. Chris Kloeris ($68,250), 333 Guadalupe St., Ste. 2-420, Austin 78701; (512) 305-8501.

Orthotics and Prosthetics, Texas Board of – (1998 with 6 members; increased to 7 in 2003); apptv.; per diem and travel expenses; 6-yr.; 7 members: Chair Richard Michael Neider, Lubbock (2/1/13); Erin Elizabeth Berling, Coppell (2/1/13); Rebecca Hill Brou, Rockport (2/1/11); Leah F. Esparza, Austin (2/1/15); Roy McCoy, Round Rock (2/1/15); Miguel Mojica, Coppell (2/1/15); James C. Wendlandt, Austin (2/1/11). Exec. Dir. David D. Olvera, Texas Dept. of Health Services, PO Box 149347, Austin 78714-9347; (512) 834-4520.

Pardons and Paroles, Texas Board of – (1893 as Board of Pardon Advisers; changed in 1936 to Board of Pardons and Paroles with 3 members; members increased to 6 in 1983; made a division of the Texas Dept. of Criminal Justice in 1990); apptv.; 6-yr.; 7 members (chairman, $99,500; members, $93,500 each): Chair Rissie L. Owens, Huntsville (2/1/15); Charles Franklin Aycock, Amarillo (2/1/11); Conrith Davis, Sugar Land (2/1/13); Jackie DeNoyelles, Flint (2/1/11); Juanita M. Gonzalez, Round Rock (2/1/15); Brenda Lorraine, Angleton (2/1/13); 1 vacancy. *Parole Commissioners:* Tommy Fordyce, Huntsville; Pamela Freeman, Angleton; Roy Garcia, Huntsville; Elvis Hightower, Gatesville; Paul Kiel, Palestine; Edgar Morales, San Antonio; James Poland, Amarillo; Lynn Ruzicka, Angleton; Charles A. Shipman, Amarillo; Charles Speier, San Antonio; Howard Thrasher, Gatesville. Gen. Counsel Bettie L. Wells, PO Box 13401, Austin 78711-3401; (512) 406-5852.

Parks and Wildlife Commission, Texas – (1963 as 3-member board; members increased to 6 in 1971 and to 9 in 1983; apptv.; expenses; 6-yr.; 9 members: Chair Peter M. Holt, San Antonio (2/1/11); Mark E. Bivins, Amarillo (2/1/11); Rick L. Campbell, Center (2/1/15); Ralph H. Duggins, Fort Worth (2/1/13); Antonio Falcon, Rio Grande City (2/1/13); T. Dan Friedkin, Houston (2/1/11); Karen J. Hixon, San Antonio (2/1/13); Margaret Martin, Boerne (2/1/15); S. Reed Morian, Houston (2/1/15). Chairman-Emeritus Lee Marshall Bass, Fort Worth. Exec. Dir. Carter Smith ($130,000), 4200 Smith School Rd., Austin 78744; (512) 389-4800.

Pecos River Compact Commissioner – (1942); apptv.; 6-yr.; salary and expenses; (negotiates with New Mexico regarding waters of the Pecos): Julian W. Thrasher Jr. ($32,247), Monahans (1/23/11), PO Box 340, Monahans 79756; (432) 940-1753.

Pension Boards – For old age, blind and dependent children's assistance, *see* Health and Human Services Commission Council. *Also see,* listings under Retirement for state and municipal employee and teacher retirement systems.

Pension Review Board, State – (1979); apptv.; 6-yr.; 9 members (1 senator apptd. by Lt. Gov., 1 representative apptd. by Speaker, 7 apptd. by Gov.): Chair Richard Earl McElreath, Amarillo (1/31/13); Paul A. Braden, Dallas (1/31/15); Andrew Cable, Wimberley (1/31/13); Jerry R. Massengale, Lubbock (1/31/11); Norman W. Parrish, The Woodlands (1/31/13); Wayne R. Roberts, Austin (1/31/15); Scott D. Smith, Cedar Park (1/31/15). Exec. Dir. Paul Janssen Nicholson ($60,000), PO Box 13498, Austin 78711-3498; (512) 463-1736.

Perfusionists, Texas State Board of Examiners of – Abolished September 2005; responsibilities transferred to the Texas Dept. of Human Services, now part of the Health and Human Services Commission.

Pest Control Board, Texas Structural – Abolished August 2007; responsibilities transferred to the Texas Dept. of Agriculture, Structural Pest Control Service, Pesticide Program.

Pharmacy, Texas State Board of – (1907 as 6-member board; members increased to 9 in 1981; apptv.; 6-yr.; 9 members: Pres. Wilson Benjamin Fry, San Benito (8/31/09); Buford T. Abeldt, Lufkin (8/31/13); Kim A. Caldwell, Plano (8/31/09); Rosemary F. Combs, El Paso (8/31/11); Suzan Kedron, Dallas (8/31/13); Marcelo Laijas Jr., Floresville (8/31/09); Alice G. Mendoza, Kingsville (8/31/11); Jeanne D. Waggener, Waco (8/31/11); Dennis Wiesner, Austin (8/31/13). Exec. Dir. Gay Dodson ($105,000), 333 Guadalupe St., Ste. 3-600, Austin 78701-3943; (512) 305-8000. *Consumer complaints: (800) 821-3205.*

Physical Therapy Examiners, Texas Board of – (1971);

apptv.; 6-yr.; expenses; 9 members: Chair Karen Gordon, Port O'Connor (1/31/13); Frank Bryan Jr., Austin (1/31/13); Gary Gray, Midland (1/31/11); Kevin Lindsey, Mission (1/31/15); Phillip B. Palmer, Abilene (1/31/11); Rene Peña, El Paso (1/31/15); Daniel Reyna, Waco (1/31/11); Melinda A. Rodriguez, San Antonio (1/31/15); Shari Waldie, Fredericksburg (1/31/13). Exec. Dir. John Maline ($62,000), 333 Guadalupe St., Ste. 2-510, Austin 78701-3942; (512) 305-6900.

Physical Therapy and Occupational Therapy Examiners, Executive Council of – (1971); apptv.; 2-yr.; expenses; 5 members: Chair Arthur Roger Matson, Georgetown (2/1/11); Stephanie Johnston, Houston (2/1/11); Pamela D. Nelon, Fort Worth (2/1/11); Daniel Reyna, Waco (2/1/11); Melinda Rodriguez, San Antonio (2/1/09). Exec. Dir. John Maline ($62,000), 333 Guadalupe St., Ste. 2-510, Austin 78701-3942; (512) 305-6900.

Physician Assistant Examiners, Texas State Board of – (1993 as Physician Assistant Advisory Council; changed to present name in 1995); apptv.; 6-yr.; 9 members: Chair Margaret K. Bentley, DeSoto (2/1/09); Ron Bryce, Red Oak (2/1/15); Anna Arredondo Chapman, Del Rio (2/1/11); Teralea Davis Jones, Beeville (2/1/13); Felix Koo, McAllen (2/1/13); Michael Allen Mitchell, Henrietta (2/1/13); Richard R. Rahr, Galveston (2/1/11); Abelino (Abel) Reyna, Waco (2/1/13); Edward W. Zwanziger, Eustace (2/1/15). Exec. Dir. Donald W. Patrick ($110,000), P.O. Box 2018, Austin, TX 78768-2018; (512) 305-7010. *Consumer Complaint Hotline: (800) 201-9353.*

Plumbing Examiners, State Board of – (1947 as 6-member board; members increased to 9 in 1981); apptv.; expenses; 6-yr.; Chair Tammy Betancourt, Houston (9/05/09); Enrique Castro, El Paso (9/05/11); Ricardo Jose Guerra, Austin (9/05/09); Robert Franklin Jalnos, San Antonio (9/05/09); Dave Lilley, Wichita Falls (9/05/13); Richard Allen Lord, Pasadena (9/05/09); Carol Lynne McLemore, La Marque (9/05/11); Alex Meade III, Brownsville (9/05/13); Ed Thompson, Tyler (9/05/13). Exec. Dir. Robert L. Maxwell ($70,000), PO Box 4200, Austin 78765-4200; (800) 845-6584.

Podiatric Medical Examiners, Texas State Board of – (1923 as 6-member State Board of Chiropody Examiners; name changed to State Board of Podiatry Examiners in 1967; made 9-member board in 1981; name changed to present in 1996); apptv.; 6-yr.; expenses; 9 members: Pres. Dorris A. Couch, Burleson (7/10/11); Richard C. Adam, San Antonio (7/10/09); Paul Kinberg, Dallas (7/10/09); James Michael Lunsford, Katy (7/10/13); Joe E. Martin Jr., College Station (7/10/13); James Michael Miller, Aledo (7/10/13); Travis Motley, Fort Worth (7/10/11); Ana Urukalo, Austin (7/10/11); Matthew Washington, Missouri City (7/10/09). Exec. Dir. Hemant Makan ($55,000), PO Box 12216, Austin 78711-2216; (512) 305-7000. *Consumer Complaint Hotline: (800) 821-3205.*

Polygraph Examiners Board – (1965); apptv.; 6-yr.; 7 members: Chair Andy Sheppard, Fate (6/18/09); Elizabeth P. Bellegarde, El Paso (6/18/07); Priscilla Jane Kleinpeter, Amarillo (6/18/09); Gory Dean Loveday, Tyler (6/18/11); Lawrence D. Mann, Plano (6/18/09); Horacio Ortiz, Corpus Christi (6/18/07); Donald K. Schutte, Texarkana (6/18/11). Exec. Officer Frank Di Tucci ($49,080), PO Box 4087, Austin 78765-4087; (512) 424-2058.

Port Freeport Commission – Apptv.; 6-yr.; 6 members: James F. Brown, Lake Jackson (5/31/11); John W. Damon, West Columbia (5/31/09); J.M Lowrey, Brazosport (5/31/11); Thomas S. Perryman, Angleton (5/31/09); Ravi K. Singhania, Brazoria (5/31/13); Bill Terry, Brazosport (5/31/13). Exec. Dir. A.J. Reixach Jr., PO Box 615, Freeport 77542-0615; (800) 362-5743.

Preservation Board, State – (1983); 2-yr.; 6 members (3 ex officio: Gov., Lt. Gov., House Speaker); 3 apptv.: 1 apptd. by Gov.: Charlotte C. Foster, San Antonio (2/1/11); 1 senator apptd. by Lt. Gov.; 1 representative apptd. by Speaker. Exec. Dir. John Sneed ($115,000), PO Box 13286, Austin 78711-3286; (512) 463-5495.

Prison Board – (*See* Criminal Justice, Texas Dept. of)

Prison Industries Oversight Authority, Private Sector – (1997); 6-yr.; expenses; 6 ex officio: Senate member, House member, Dept. of Criminal Justice, Texas Youth Comm., Texas Work Force Comm., employer liaison; 8 apptd.: Chair Jeffery R. LaBroski, Richmond (2/1/13); Sarah Abraham, Sugar Land (2/1/13); Elaine (Anne) Boatright, Smithville (2/1/15); Burnis Brazil, Richmond (2/1/15); William B. Brod, Granbury (2/1/11); S. Roxanne Carter, Canyon (2/1/15); Suzanne C. Hart, San Antonio (2/1/11); Rigoberto Villarreal, Mission (2/1/13); Employer Liaison: Randall Henderson, Austin. Admin. Robert Carter, 8610 Shoal Creek, Austin 78757; (512) 406-5310.

Private Security Bureau, Texas – (1969 as Board of Private Investigators and Private Security Agencies; reorganized in 1998 as Texas Comm. on Private Security; reestablished in 2004 as a bureau of the Texas Dept. of Public Safety); apptv.; expenses; 6-yr.; 8 members (1 ex officio: Dir., Dept. of Public Safety); 7 apptd. members: Chair John E. Chism, Irving (1/31/15); Stella Caldera, Houston (1/31/11); Charles E. Crenshaw, Austin (1/31/13); Howard H. Johnsen, Dallas (1/31/11); Patrick A. Patterson, Boerne (1/31/15); Mark L. Smith, Dallas (1/31/11); Doris F. Washington, Arlington (1/31/13). Man. Capt. Leonard Hinojosa, PO Box 4087, Austin 78773-0001; (512) 424-7710.

Process Server Review Board – Apptv. by Texas Supreme Court; staggered terms; 9 members: Chair Carl Weeks, Austin (7/1/11); Mark P. Blenden, Bedford (7/1/11); Joe F. Brown Jr., San Antonio (7/1/09); Ron Hickman, Houston (7/1/09); Tony Lindsay, Houston (7/1/11); Connie Mayfield, Corsicana (7/1/09); Justiss Rasberry, El Paso (7/1/10); Lois Rogers, Tyler (7/1/10); Lee H. Russell, Dallas (7/1/10). Clerk Meredith Musick, PO Box 12248, Austin 78711-2248; (512) 463-2713.

Produce Recovery Fund Board – (1977 as 3-member board; members increased to 5 in 1981); apptv.; expenses; 6-yr.; 5 members: Chair Doyle (Neal) Newson III, Plains (1/31/15); Ralph Diaz, Corpus Christi (1/31/05); Steven Dexter Jones, Lubbock (1/31/01); Ly H. Nguyen, Lake Jackson (1/31/15); Byron Edward White, Arlington (1/31/01). Coor. Rick Garza, c/o Texas Dept. of Agriculture, PO Box 12847, Austin 78711-2847; (512) 936-2430.

Psychologists, Texas Board of Examiners of – (1969 as 6-member board; members increased to 9 in 1981); apptv.; 6-yr.; per diem and expenses; 9 members: Chair Carl E. Settles, Killeen (10/31/09); Donna L. Black, Houston (10/31/11); Timothy Branaman, Dallas (10/31/13); Jo Ann Campbell, Abilene (10/31/11); Carlos R. Chacón, El Paso (10/31/09); Angela A. Downes, Irving (10/31/13); Gary R. Elkins, Temple (10/31/09); Lou Ann Todd Mock, Bellaire (10/31/13); 1 vacancy. Exec. Dir. Sherry L. Lee ($68,250), 333 Guadalupe St., Ste. 2-450, Austin 78701; (512) 305-7700.

Public Finance Authority, Texas – (1984, assumed duties of Texas Building Authority); apptv.; per diem and expenses; 6-yr.; 7 members: Chair Gary E. Wood, Lakeway (2/1/15); Gerald Byron Alley, Arlington (2/1/13); Linda McKenna, Harlingen (2/1/11); D. Joseph Meister, Dallas (2/1/13); Rodney K. Moore, Lufkin (2/1/15); Robert Thomas Roddy, San Antonio (2/1/13); Ruth Schiermeyer, Lubbock (2/1/13). Exec. Dir. Kimberly K. Edwards ($120,000), PO Box 12906, Austin 78711-2906; (512) 463-5544.

Public Insurance Counsel, Office of – (1995); apptv.; 2-yr.; 1 member: Deeia Beck (2/1/11) ($99,000), 333 Guadalupe St., Ste. 3-120; Austin 78701; (512) 322-4143.

Public Safety Commission – (1935 with 3 members; members increased to 5 in 2007); apptv.; expenses; 6-yr.; 5 members: Chair Allan B. Polunsky, San Antonio (12/31/09); Carin Marcy Barth, Houston (12/31/13); Ada Brown, Dallas (12/31/11); C. Thomas Clowe Jr., Austin (1/1/10); John Thomas Steen Jr., San Antonio (1/1/12). Interim Dir. of Texas Dept. of Public Safety, Col. Lamar Beckworth ($157,500), PO Box 4087, Austin 78773-0001; (512) 424-2000.

Public Utility Commission – (1975); apptv.; 6-yr.; 3 members (chairman, $111,800; members, $109,200): Chair Barry Thomas Smitherman, Austin (9/1/13); Kenneth W. Anderson, Dallas (9/1/11); Donna L. Nelson, Austin (9/1/09). Exec. Dir. W. Lane Lanford ($115,500), PO Box 13326, Austin 78711-3326; (512) 936-7120.

Public Utility Counsel, Office of – (1983); apptv.; 2-yr.; 1 member: Don Ballard, Austin (2/1/11); ($99,000); PO Box 12397, Austin 78711-2397; (512) 936-7500.

Racing Commission, Texas – (1986); apptv.; 6-yr.; per diem and expenses; 9 members; 2 ex officio: Chmn., Public Safety Commission and Comptroller of Public Accounts; 7 apptv.: Chair Rolando B. Pablos, San Antonio (2/01/11); G. Kent Carter, Caldwell (2/1/09); Ronald F. Ederer, Fair Oaks Ranch (2/1/13); Gloria Hicks, Corpus Christi (2/1/13); Thomas Latham, Sunnyvale (2/1/15); Robert Schmidt, Fort Worth (2/1/11); Vicki Smith Weinberg, Colleyville (2/1/15). Exec. Dir. Charla Ann King ($85,536), PO Box 12080, Austin 78711-2080; (512) 833-6699.

Radiation Advisory Board, Texas – (1961); apptv.; 6-yr.; 18 members: Jesse Ray Adams, Longview (4/16/13); Bradley Bunn, Andrews (4/16/13); Bill Campbell, Fort Worth (4/16/13); Ana Cleveland, Denton (4/16/11); Michael S. Ford, Amarillo (4/16/09); John Hageman, San Antonio (4/16/11); Bobby J. Haley, Denton (4/16/11); W. Kim Howard, Longview (4/16/09); L.R. Jacobi Jr., Austin (4/16/09); Nora Anita Janjan, Houston (4/16/09); Mitch Lucas, Glen Rose (4/16/13); Troy Marceleno, Austin (4/16/09); Melanie Marshall, Burleson (4/16/09); Darlene Metter, San Antonio (4/16/13); Rosana G. Moreira, College Station (4/16/11); Jay Murphy, Houston (4/16/13); Kevin Raabe, Austin (4/16/11); Mark Silberman, Austin (4/16/11). Program Dir. Richard A. Ratliff, Radia-

tion Control MC 2835, Texas Dept. of State Health Services, PO Box 149347, Austin 78714-9347; (512) 834-6679.

Radioactive Waste Disposal Compact, Texas Low-Level – (1993); apptv.; 6-yr.; expenses; 6 Texas members, plus one member each from Maine and Vermont; Texas apptees.: Chair Michael Ford, Amarillo (11/25/14); Richard Dolgener, Andrews (11/25/14); Bob Gregory, Austin (11/25/14); Kenneth L. Peddicord, College Station (11/25/14); John White, Plano (11/25/14); Robert C. Wilson, Lockhart (11/25/14). Radioactive Materials Division MC-233, Texas Commission on Environmental Quality, PO Box 13087, Austin 78711-3087; (512) 239-6466.

Railroad Commission of Texas – (1891); elective; 6-yr.; 3 members, $037,500 each: Victor Carrillo (12/31/10); Michael L. Williams (12/31/08); Elizabeth Ames Jones (12/31/12). Dir. Richard A. Varela ($106,381), PO Box 12967, Austin 78711-2967; (512) 463-7288.

Real Estate Commission, Texas – (1949 as 6-member board; members increased to 9 in 1979); apptv.; per diem and expenses; 6-yr.; 9 members: Chairs John D. Eckstrum, Conroe (1/31/11) and Avis Wukasch, Goergetown (1/31/13); Troy C. Alley Jr., Arlington (1/31/11); Adrian A. Arriaga, McAllen (1/31/13); Robert C. (Chris) Day, Jacksonville (1/31/13); Jaime Blevins Hensley, Lufkin (1/31/15); Joanne Justice, Arlington (1/31/15); Tom C. Mesa Jr., Houston (1/31/11); Dona Scurry, El Paso (1/31/15). Admin. Timothy K. Irvine ($100,000), PO Box 12188, Austin 78711-2188; (512) 459-6544.

Real Estate Research Center Advisory Committee – (1971); apptv.; 6-yr.; 10 members; 1 ex officio: rep. of Texas Real Estate Commission; 9 apptv.: Chair D. Marc McDougal, Lubbock (1/31/11); Mona R. Bailey, North Richland Hills (1/31/13); James M. Boyd, Houston (1/31/15); Louis A. (Tony) Cortes, San Antonio (1/31/15); Jacquelyn K. Hawkins, Austin (1/31/11); Joe Bob McCartt, Amarillo (1/31/13); Kathleen McKenzie Owen, Pipe Creek (1/31/13); Barbara A. Russell, Denton (1/31/11); Ronald C. Wakefield, San Antonio (1/31/15). Dir. Gary Maler, Texas A&M University Real Estate Center, 2115 TAMU, College Station 77843-2115; (979) 845-0460.

Red River Authority of Texas – (1959); apptv.; 6-yr.; per diem and expenses; 9 members: Pres. Cliff A. Skiles Jr., Hereford (8/11/09); Nathan J. (Jim) Bell IV, Paris (8/11/11); Lisa Caldwell Brent, Amarillo (8/11/11); Cole Camp (8/11/13); Penny Cogdell Carpenter, Silverton (8/11/09); Jerry B. Daniel, Truscott (8/11/09); Mayfield McCraw Jr., Telephone (8/11/11); Wilson Scaling II, Henrietta (8/11/09); Clyde Siebman, Pottsboro (8/11/13). Gen. Mgr. Curtis W. Campbell, PO Box 240, Wichita Falls 76307-0240; (940) 723-8697.

Red River Compact Commissioner – (1949); apptv.; 4-yr.; salary and expenses; (negotiates with Oklahoma, Arkansas and Louisiana regarding waters of the Red): William A. Abney ($24,225), El Paso (2/1/11); PO Box 1386, Marshall 75671; (903) 938-4572.

Redistricting Board, Legislative – (*See* Legislative Redistricting Board.)

Rehabilitation Commission, Texas – Combined into Department of Assistive and Rehabilitative Services (DARS) of the Health and Human Services Commission as of 3/1/04.

Residential Construction Commission, Texas – apptv.; 6-yr.; expenses; 9 members: Chair J. Paulo Flores, Dallas (2/1/11); Lewis Brown, Trinity (2/1/11); Art Cuevas, Lubbock (2/1/11); Kenneth L. Davis, Weatherford (2/1/09); Gerardo M. (Jerry) Garcia, Corpus Christi (2/1/13); John R. Krugh, Houston (2/1/09); Steven Leipsner, Lakeway (2/1/09); Glenda C. Mariott, Bryan (2/1/13); Mickey R. Redwine, Ben Wheeler (2/1/13). Exec. Dir. A. Duane Waddill ($98,000), PO Box 13509, Austin 78711-3509; (512) 463-1040.

Retirement System of Texas, Employees – (1949); apptv.; 6-yr.; 6 members: 1 apptd. by Gov., 1 by Chief Justice of State Supreme Court, 1 by House Speaker; 3 elected by ERS members: Gov.'s apptee: Cydney Donnell, College Station (8/31/12); Chief Justice's apptee: I. Craig Hester, Austin (8/31/10); Speaker's apptee: Donald Wood, Odessa (8/31/14). Elected members: Don Green, Austin (8/31/13); Chair Yolanda (Yoly) Griego, El Paso (8/31/09); Owen Whitworth, Austin (8/31/11). Exec. Dir. Ann S. Fuelberg ($220,000), PO Box 13207, Austin 78711-3207; (512) 867-7711.

Retirement System of Texas, Teacher – (1937 as 6-member board; members increased to 9 in 1973); 6-yr.; expenses; 9 members: 2 apptd. by State Board of Education, 3 apptd. by Gov., 4 apptd. by Gov. after being nominated by popular ballot of retirement system members: Chair Linus D. Wright, Dallas (8/31/11); Charlotte Renee Clifton, Snyder (8/31/13); Robert P. Gauntt, Houston (8/31/13); John Graham Jr., Fredericksburg (8/31/09); Mark Henry, Galena Park (8/31/09); R. David Kelly,

Dallas (8/31/11); Eric C. McDonald, Lubbock (8/31/13); Phillip M. Mullins, Austin (8/31/11); Dory A. Wiley, Dallas (8/31/09). Exec. Dir. Ronnie Jung ($225,000), 1000 Red River, Austin 78701; (512) 542-6400.

Retirement System, Texas County and District – (1967); apptv.; 6-yr.; 9 members: Chair Robert Eckels, Houston (12/31/07); Jerry Bigham, Canyon (12/31/09); H.C. (Chuck) Cazalas, Corpus Christi (12/31/11); Daniel R. Haggerty, El Paso (12/31/09); Jan Kennady, New Braunfels (12/31/09); Bridget McDowell, Baird (12/31/07); Eddie J. Miles Jr., San Antonio (12/31/11); Robert C. Willis, Livingston (12/31/07); Gerald (Buddy) Winn, Bryan (12/31/11). Exec. Dir. Gene Glass, PO Box 2034, Austin 78768-2034; (512) 328-8889.

Retirement System, Texas Municipal, – (1947); apptv.; 6-yr.; expenses; 6 members: Ben Gorzell Jr., San Antonio (2/1/13); Patricia Hernandez, Plainview (2/1/11); Carolyn M. Linér, San Marcos (2/1/13); April Nixon, Arlington (2/1/09); Roel Rodriguez, McAllen (2/1/11); H. Frank Simpson, Missouri City (2/1/09). Exec. Dir. Eric Henry, PO Box 149153, Austin 78714-9153; (512) 476-7577.

Retirement Fund, Texas Emergency Services Personnel – (1977; formerly the Fire Fighters' Relief and Retirement Fund); apptv.; expenses; 6-yr.; 9 members: Chair Francisco R. Torres, Raymondville (9/1/11); Kyle A. Donaldson, Sonora (9/1/09); Graciela G. Flores, Corpus Christi (9/1/09); Patrick Hull, Yoakum (9/1/11); Dan Key, Friendswood (9/1/13); Rex W. Klesel, Alvin (9/1/09); Ronald V. Larson, Horizon City (9/1/13); Maxie L. Patterson, Spring (9/1/13); Don R. Shipman, Colleyville (9/1/13). Commissioner Lisa Ivie Miller ($70,000), PO Box 12577, Austin 78711-2577; (512) 936-3372. (*See also* Fire Fighters' Pension Commissioner.)

Rio Grande Compact Commissioner of Texas – (1929); apptv.; 6-yr.; salary and expenses; (negotiates with Colorado and New Mexico regarding waters of the Rio Grande): Patrick R. Gordon ($41,195), El Paso (6/9/13); PO Box 1917, El Paso 79950-1917; (915) 834-7075.

Rio Grande Regional Water Authority – (2003); apptv.; 4-yr.; 18 members: 12 appt'd. by Gov.; 6 appt'd. by member counties. Gov.'s apptees.: Joe A. Barrera III, Brownsville (2/1/13); Dario (D.V.) Guerra Jr., Edinburg (2/1/13); Wayne Halbert, Harlingen (2/1/09); Paul Glenn Heller, Mission (2/1/11); Sonny Hinojosa, Edinburg (2/1/13); Sonia Kaniger, San Benito (2/1/13); Brian Macmanus, Rio Hondo (2/1/09); Joe Pennington, Raymondville (2/1/13); Roel Rodriguez, McAllen (2/1/11); Bobby Sparks, Valley Acres (2/1/09); Jimmie Steidinger, Donna (2/1/13); Frank (JoJo) White, Progreso Lakes (2/1/13). County apptees.: John Bruciak, Cameron Co.; Jim Darling, Hidalgo Co.; Ricardo Gutierrez, Starr Co.; Fitzgerald G. Sanchez, Webb Co.; Frank Torres, Willacy Co.; Karran Westerman, Zapata Co. Exec. Dir. Kenneth N. Jones Jr., 311 N. 15th St., McAllen 78501-4705; (956) 682-3481.

Risk Management, State Office of – apptv.; 2-yr.; 5 members: Chair Ernest C. Garcia, Austin (2/1/09); Lloyd M. Garland, Lubbock (2/1/09); Ruben W. Hope, Montgomery (2/1/13); Kenneth N. Mitchell, El Paso (2/1/09); Ronald James Walenta, Quitman (2/1/11). Exec. Dir. Jonathan D. Bow ($95,000), PO Box 13777 Austin 78711-3777; (512) 475-1440.

Rural Community Affairs, Office of – (2001); apptv.; 6-yr.; 11 members: 1 ex officio, Agriculture Commissioner; 10 appt'd.: Chair Wallace Klussmann, Fredericksburg (2/1/13); Dora G. Alcala, Del Rio (2/1/15); David Alders, Nacogdoches (2/1/13); Woodrow Anderson, Colorado City (2/1/15); Mackie Bobo, Bedias (2/1/13); Charles N. Butts Sr., Lampasas (2/1/13); Remelle Farrar, Crowell (2/1/11); Charles W. Graham, Elgin (2/1/15); Joaquin L. Rodriguez, Eagle Pass (2/1/13); Patrick Wallace, Athens (2/1/11). Exec. Dir. Charles S. (Charlie) Stone ($99,000), PO Box 12877, Austin 78711-2877; (512) 936-6701.

Sabine River Authority of Texas – (1949); apptv.; per diem and expenses; 6-yr.; 9 members: Pres. J.D. Jacobs Jr., Rockwall (7/06/13); Don O. Covington, Orange (7/06/11); David W. Koonce, Center (7/06/13); Richard A. (Link) Linkenauger, Greenville (7/06/09); Stanley N. Mathews, Pinehurst (7/6/11); Cliff R. Todd, Marshall (7/6/11); Connie J. Wade, Longview (7/06/09); Constance Moore Ware, Marshall (7/06/09); Clarence Earl Williams, Orange (7/06/13). Gen. Mgr. Jerry L. Clark, PO Box 579, Orange 77630; (409) 746-2192.

Sabine River Compact Commission – (1953); apptv.; 6-yr.; salary ($8,487) and expenses; (negotiates with Louisiana regarding the waters of the Sabine); 5 members — the chairman, who does not vote, is appointed by the President of United States; Texas and Louisiana each have 2 members. Texas members: Gary E. Gagnon, Mauriceville (7/12/07), Jerry F. Gipson, Longview (7/12/10); c/o P.O. Box 13087, Austin 78711; (512) 239-4707.

San Antonio River Authority – (1937); apptv., 6 yr., 12 members: Terry E. Baiamonte, Goliad Co. (11/1/09); Sara (Sally) Buchanan, Bexar Co. (11/1/11); John Flieller, Wilson Co. (11/1/09); Alois (Al) Kollodziej Jr., Wilson Co. (11/1/13); Hector Morales, Bexar Co. (11/1/11); Jeffrey Neathery, Bexar Co. (11/1/09); Gaylon J. Oehlke, Karnes Co. (11/1/13); Nazirite Ruben Perez, Bexar Co. (11/1/13); Roberto G. Rodriguez, Bexar Co. (11/1/13); H.B. (Trip) Ruckman III, Karnes Co. (11/1/09); Adair Ramsey Sutherland, Goliad Co. (11/1/13); Thomas G. Weaver, Bexar Co. (11/1/09). Gen. Mgr. Suzanne B. Scott, PO Box 839980, San Antonio 78283-9980; (210) 227-1373.

San Jacinto River Authority, Board of Directors – (1937); apptv.; expenses while on duty; 6-yr.; 6 members: Pres. R. Gary Montgomery, The Woodlands (10/16/13); David Kleimann, Willis (10/16/13); Mary L. Rummell, Spring (10/16/09); John H. Stibbs, The Woodlands (10/16/09); Lloyd B. Tisdale, Conroe (10/16/11); Joseph V. Turner, Conroe (10/16/11). Gen. Mgr. H. Reed Eichelberger, PO Box 329, Conroe 77305; (936) 588-1111.

Savings and Mortgage Lending Commissioner – (1961); apptd. by State Finance Commission: Douglas B. Foster ($100,000), 2601 N. Lamar, Ste. 201, Austin 78705; (512) 475-1350. *Consumer Complaint Hotline:* 877-276-5550.

School Land Board – (*See* Land Board, School).

School Safety Center, Texas – (2001); apptv.; 2-yr.; 6 ex-officio members from the Texas Commissioner of Higher Education, Texas Youth Commission, Texas Education Agency, Dept. of State Health Services, Attorney General's office, and the Texas Juvenile Probation Commission; 10 appt'd. members: Chair Carl A. Montoya, Brownsville (2/1/10); Eric J. Cedarstrom, Palo Pinto (2/1/11); Amy L. Clapper, Georgetown (2/1/11); Dawn DuBose, Houston (2/1/09); Garry Eoff, Brownwood (2/1/10); Daniel R. Griffith Jr., Pflugerville (2/1/10); James R. Pendell, Clint (2/1/09); Ruben Reyes, Lubbock (2/1/09); Severita Sanchez, Laredo (2/1/90); Jane A. Wetzel, Dallas (2/1/10); Associate Director Billy Jacobs, 350 N. Guadalupe Suite 140, PMB 164, San Marcos 78666; (877) 304-2727.

Securities Board, State – (Est. 1957, the outgrowth of several amendments to the Texas Securities Act, originally passed in 1913); act is administered by the Securities Commissioner, who is appointed by the board members; expenses; 6-yr.; 5 members: Chair Beth Ann Blackwood, Dallas (1/20/13); Bryan K. Brown, Pearland (1/20/11); Edward Escudero, El Paso (1/20/11); E. Wally Kinney, Dripping Springs (1/20/13); Derrick M. Mitchell, Houston (1/20/15). Commissioner Denise Voigt Crawford ($130,000), PO Box 13167, Austin 78711-3167; (512) 305-8300.

Seed and Plant Board, State – (1959); apptv.; 2-yr.; 6 members: Chair A. James Allison, Buchanan Dam (10/6/09); David Baltensperger, College Station (10/6/09); Nick Bamert, Muleshoe (10/6/10); Kelly A. Book, Bastrop (10/6/10); Robert Wright, Shallowater (10/6/09); James Wahrmund, Fredericksburg (10/6/10). Regulatory Branch Chief Ed Price, Texas Dept. of Agriculture, PO Box 12847, Austin 78711; (512) 463-7607.

Sex Offender Treatment, Council on – (1983); apptv.; expenses; 6-yr.; 7 members: Chair Frederick Liles Arnold, Plano (2/1/15); Ronnie Fanning, Woodway (2/1/11); Joseph Gutheinz, Houston (2/1/15); Alida S. Hernandez, McAllen (2/1/13); Holly A. Miller, The Woodlands (2/1/15); Aaron Paul Pierce, Rockdale (2/1/11); Dan Powers, Carrollton (2/1/13). Exec. Dir. Allison Taylor, c/o Texas Dept. of State Health Services, c/o Texas Dept. of State Health Services, PO Box 149347, Austin 78714-9347; (512) 834-4530

Skill Standards Board, Texas – (1995); apptv.; terms at pleasure of Gov.; 11 members: Chair Wayne J. Oswald, Freeport; Bruce Aumack, Austin; Gary Forrest Blagg, Grapevine; Carlos Chacón, El Paso; Andy Ellard, Dallas; Edward C. Foster Jr., Mansfield; Iria Ganious, Dallas; Erma Palmer, Houston; Linda Stegall, Houston; Whitney Wolf, San Antonio; 1 vacancy; PO Box 2241, Austin 78768-2241; (512) 936-8100.

Social Worker Examiners, Texas State Board of – (1993); apptv.; 6-yr.; per diem and travel expenses; 9 members: Chair Timothy M. Brown, Bryan (2/1/13); Jody Anne Armstrong, Abilene (2/1/15); Stewart Geise, Austin (2/1/15); Candace Guillen, La Feria (2/1/13); Kimberly Hernandez, El Paso (2/1/11); Dorinda N. Noble, San Marcos (2/1/11); Denise Pratt, Baytown (2/1/11); Nary Spears, Houston (2/1/15); Mark Talbot, McAllen (2/1/13). Exec. Dir. Charles Horton, c/o Texas Dept. of State Health Services, PO Box 149347 Austin 78714-9347; (512) 719-3521.

Soil and Water Conservation Board, Texas State – (1939); 2-yr.; 7 members: 2 apptd. by Gov.; 5 elected by district directors; **Gov.'s apptees:** Larry D. Jacobs, Montgomery (2/1/10); Joe L. Ward, Telephone (2/1/11); elected members: **Dist. 1:** Aubrey Russell, Panhandle (5/1/09); **Dist. 2:** Marty H. Graham, Rocksprings (5/1/10); **Dist. 3:** Jose Dodier Jr., Zapata (5/1/09); **Dist.**

4: Jerry D. Nichols, Nacogdoches (5/2/08); **Dist. 5:** Barry Mahler, Iowa Park (5/1/09). Exec. Dir. Rex Isom ($90,000), PO Box 658, Temple 76503; (254) 773-2250.

Special Education Continuing Advisory Committee, Texas – (1997); apptv.; 4 yr.; 17 members: Lené Al-Rashid, Austin (2/1/11); Ismael (Mel) Capelo, Pasadena (2/1/13); Rose Marie Cruz, Laredo (2/1/13); Debra B. Emerson, Austin (2/1/13); Julia W. Erwin, Montgomery (2/1/13); Kathy L. Grant, Houston (2/1/11); Sherri Hammack, Austin (2/1/11); Marjie Haynes, Huntsville (2/1/11); Candance L. Hawks, Belton (2/1/13); Teresa Hernandez, San Marcos (2/1/11); Drusilla Knight-Villarreal, Corpus Christi (2/1/11); Marnie L. Mast, Austin (2/1/11); Diane Taylor, Stephenville (2/1/13); Jennifer L. Taylor, Houston (2/1/13); Paul Watson, Flower Mound (2/1/13); Shewanda Williams, Houston (2/1/11); Pam Willson, Brookesmith (2/1/13); c/o Texas Education Agency, Division of IDEA Coordination, 1701 N. Congress Ave., Austin 78701-1494; (512) 463-9414; *Parent Information Line: 1-800-252-9668.*

Speech-Language Pathology and Audiology, State Board of Examiners for – (1983); apptv.; 6-yr.; per diem and expenses; 9 members: Chair Kerry Ormson, Amarillo (8/31/09); Patricia Elaine Brannon, San Antonio (8/31/11); Richard J. Caldwell, Houston (8/31/09); Tammy Camp, Lubbock (8/31/13); Kimberly M. Carlisle, Plano (8/31/09); Vickie B. Dionne, Nederland (8/31/11); Sonya Salinas, Mission (8/31/11); Leila Ramirez Salmons, Houston (8/31/13); Phillip Lee Wilson, Dallas (8/31/13). Exec. Dir. Joyce Parsons, PO Box 149347, Austin 78714-9347; (512) 834-6627.

Stephen F. Austin State University, Board of Regents – (1969); apptv.; expenses; 6-yr.; 9 members: Carlos Z. Amaral, Plano (1/31/13); Richard B. Boyer, The Colony (1/31/11); Scott Coleman, Houston (1/31/15); James Hinton Dickerson, New Braunfels (1/31/13); Valerie E. Ertz, Dallas (1/31/15); John R. (Bob) Garrett, Tyler (1/31/13); Steve D. McCarty, Alto (1/31/15); James A. Thompson, Sugar Land (1/31/11); Melvin R. White, Pflugerville (1/31/11). Pres. Baker Pattillo, PO Box 13026, SFA Station, Nacogdoches 75962-3026; (936) 468-4048.

Sunset Advisory Commission – (1977); 12 members: 5 members of House of Representatives, 5 members of Senate, 1 public member apptd. by Speaker, 1 public member apptd. by Lt. Gov.; 2-yr.; expenses. Public members: Charles McMahen, Houston (9/1/09); Ike Sugg, San Angelo (9/1/09). Dir. Joey Longley, PO Box 13066, Austin 78711-3066; (512) 463-1300.

Tax Board, State – Est. 1905; 3 ex-officio members: Comptroller, Secretary of State and State Treasurer; abolished by the 66th Legislature, effective 1/1/82, and replaced by the Texas State Property Tax Board.

Tax Professional Examiners, Texas Board of – (1977 as Board of Tax Assessor Examiners; name changed to present form 1983); apptv.; expenses; 6-yr.; 5 members: Chair Dorye Kristeen Roe, Bryan (3/1/13) James E. Childers, Canyon (3/1/11); P.H. (Fourth) Coates, Medina (3/1/11); Linda Lowes Hatchel, Woodway (3/1/15); Steve Mossman, Flower Mound (3/1/11). Exec. Dir. David E. Montoya ($60,000), 333 Guadalupe, Ste. 2-520 Austin 78701-3942; (512) 305-7300.

Teacher Retirement System – See, Retirement System, Teacher.

Texas A&M University System Board of Regents – (1875); apptv.; 6-yr.; expenses; 9 members: Chair Bill Jones, Austin (2/1/15); Phil Adams, Bryan (2/1/15); Richard Box, Austin (2/1/13); Morris E. Foster, Houston (2/1/13); Lupe Fraga, Houston (2/1/11); Jim Schwertner, Austin (2/1/15); Gene Stallings, Powderly (2/1/11); Ida Clement Steen, San Antonio (2/1/11); James P. Wilson, Sugar Land (2/1/13). Chancellor Michael D. (Mike) McKinney, PO Box C-1, College Station 77844-9021; (979) 845-9600.

Texas Southern University Board of Regents – (1947); expenses; 6-yr.; 9 members: Chair Glenn O. Lewis, Fort Worth (2/1/13); Gary Bledsoe, Austin (2/1/13); Samuel Lee Bryant, Austin (2/1/11); Dionicio (Don) Flores, El Paso (2/1/15); Richard C. Holland, Plano (2/1/13); Richard Knight Jr., Dallas (2/1/11); Curtistene McCowan, DeSoto (2/1/15); Tracye McDaniel, Houston (2/1/15); Richard Salwen, Austin (2/1/13). Pres. John M. Rudley. Exec. Dir. Karen A. Griffin 3100 Cleburne St., Hannah Hall, Rm. 104, Houston 77004; (713) 313-7992.

Texas State Technical College System Board of Regents – (1960 as Board of the Texas State Technical Institute; changed to present name in 1991); apptv.; expenses; 6-yr.; 9 members: Chair James Virgil Martin, Sweetwater (8/31/09); Nora Castañeda, Harlingen (8/31/09); Joe M. Gurecky, Rosenberg (8/31/11); Rolf R. Haberecht, Richardson (8/31/11); Joe K. Hearne, Richardson, (8/31/13); Mike Northcutt, Longview (8/31/13); Barbara N. Rusling, China Springs (8/31/09); Eugene Seaman, Corpus

Christi (8/31/13); Ellis Matthew Skinner II, Spicewood (8/31/13). Chancellor William Segura, TSTC System, 3801 Campus Dr., Waco 76705; (254) 867-4893.

Texas State University System Board of Regents – (1911 as Board of Regents of State Teachers Colleges; name changed in 1965 to Board of Regents of State Senior Colleges; changed to present form 1975); apptv.; per diem and expenses; 6-yr.; 9 members: Charlie Amato, San Antonio (2/1/13); Ron Blatchley, Bryan-College Station (2/1/11); Kevin J. Lilly, Houston (2/1/15); Ron Lynn Mitchell, Horseshoe Bay (2/1/15); James David Montagne, Beaumont (2/1/15); Trisha S. Pollard, Bellaire (2/1/13); Michael Truncale, Beaumont (2/1/13); Robert (Greg) Wilkinson, Dallas (2/1/11); Donna N. Williams, Arlington (2/1/11). Chancellor Charles R. Matthews, Thomas J. Rusk Bldg., 200 E. 10th Street, Ste. 600, Austin, 78701; (512) 463-1808.

Texas Tech University Board of Regents – (1923); apptv.; expenses; 6-yr.; 9 members: Larry Keith Anders, Dallas (1/31/11); L. Frederick (Rick) Francis, El Paso (1/31/13); Mark Griffin, Lubbock (1/31/11); John Huffaker, Amarillo (1/31/15); Mickey L. Long, Midland (1/31/15); Nancy Neal, Lubbock (1/31/15); John F. Scovell, Dallas (1/31/13); Daniel T. Serna, Arlington (1/31/11); Jerry Edward Turner, Blanco (1/31/13). Chancellor Kent Hance, P.O. Box 42011, Lubbock 79409-2011; (806) 742-2161.

Texas Woman's University Board of Regents – (1901); apptv.; expenses; 6-yr.; 9 members: Chair Harry L. Crumpacker II, Plano (2/1/09); Sue S. Bancroft, Argyle (2/1/15); Virginia Chandler Dykes, Dallas (2/1/11); Lola Chriss, Rowlett (2/1/15); P. Mike McCullough, Dallas (2/1/13); Ann Scanlon McGinity, Pearland (2/1/15); Cecilia May Moreno, Laredo (2/1/13); Lou Halsell Rodenberger, Baird (2/1/11); George R. Schrader, Dallas (2/1/13). Chancellor Ann Stuart, PO Box 425587, TWU Sta., Denton 76204-5587; (940) 898-3250.

Transportation Commission, Texas – (1917 as State Highway Commission; merged with Mass Transportation Commission and name changed to State Board of Highways and Public Transportation in 1975; merged with Texas Dept. of Aviation and Texas Motor Vehicle Commission and name changed to present form in 1991); apptv.; 6-yr.; 5 members ($15,914 each): Chair Deirdre Delisi, Austin (2/1/13); Ned S. Holmes, Houston (2/1/11); Ted Houghton, El Paso (2/1/15); William Meadows, Fort Worth (2/1/13); Fred Underwood, Lubbock (2/1/15). Exec. Dir. Amadeo Saenz Jr. ($192,500), 125 E. 11th St., Austin 78701-2483; (512) 305-9509.

Trinity River Authority – (1955); apptv.; per diem and expenses; 6-yr.; 25 members (3 from Tarrant County, 4 from Dallas County, 3 from area-at-large and 1 each from 15 other districts): Pres. Michael Cronin, Terrell (3/15/11); Harold L. Barnard, Waxahachie (3/15/11); Herschel Brannen III, Trinity (3/15/11); Karl R. Butler, Dallas (3/15/11); Patricia Carlson, Fort Worth (3/15/13); Steve Cronin, Shepherd (3/15/11); Amanda Davis, Buffalo (3/15/11); Ronald Goldman, Fort Worth (3/15/15); John W. Jenkins, Hankamer (3/15/15); Martha Hernandez, Burleson (3/15/11); Keith W. Kidd, Dallas (3/15/15); Jess Laird, Athens (3/15/11); Nancy E. Lavinski, Palestine (3/15/13); David Leonard, Liberty (3/15/13); Andrew Martinez, Huntsville (3/15/13); Kevin Maxwell, Crockett (3/15/15); Barbara Nash, Arlington (3/15/15); James W. Neale, Dallas (3/15/13); Manny Rachal, Livingston (3/15/15); Amir Rupani, Dallas (3/15/13); AnaLaura Saucedo, Dallas (3/15/15); Shirley K. Seale, Anahuac (3/15/15); J. Carol Spillars, Madisonville (3/15/11); Linda D. Timmerman, Streetman (3/15/15); K.C. Wyatt, Corsicana (3/15/15). Gen. Mgr. Danny F. Vance, PO Box 60, Arlington 76004-0060; (817) 467-4343.

Tuition Board, Prepaid Higher Education – (*See* Higher Education Tuition Board, Texas Prepaid).

Uniform State Laws, Commission on – (1941 as 5-member Commissioners to the National Conference on Uniform State Laws; name changed to present form, members increased to 6 and term of office raised to 6 years in 1977; members increased to 9 in 2001); apptv.; 6-yr.; 9 members: Rita Arneil, Austin (9/30/12); Levi J. Benton, Houston (9/30/10); Cullen M. Godfrey, Austin (9/30/10); Debra H. Lehrmann, Colleyville (9/30/10); Peter K. Munson, Pottsboro (9/30/14); Marilyn Phelan, Lubbock (9/30/12); Rodney Wayne Satterwhite, Midland (9/30/14); Karen R. Washington, Dallas (9/30/14); Earl L. Yeakel III, Austin (9/30/12). Life members, Patrick Guillot, Dallas; Stanley Plettman, Beaumont; Leonard Reece, Austin. Exec. Dir. John Sebert, 111 N. Washington Ave., Ste. 1010, Chicago, IL, 60602; (312) 450-6600.

University of Houston System Board of Regents – (1963); apptv.; expenses; 6-yr.; 9 members: Chair Welcome Wade Wilson Sr., Houston (8/31/11); Nelda Luce Blair, Houston (8/31/13); Dennis D. Golden, Carthage (8/31/09); Jacob Monty, Houston (8/31/13); Mica Mosbacher, Houston (8/31/13); Carroll Robertson Ray, Houston (8/31/11); Lynden B. Rose, Houston

Children play on a Civil War–era cannon on the grounds of the State Capitol in Austin. The 816-pound cannon was manufactured in 1862. Elizabeth Alvarez photo.

(8/31/09); Calvin W. Stephens, Dallas (8/31/09) Jim P. Wise, Houston (8/31/11). Chancellor Renu Khator; Exec. Admin. Gerry Mathisen, 4800 Calhoun, 128 E. Cullen Bldg., Houston 77204-6001; (832) 842-3446.

University of North Texas System Board of Regents – (1949); apptv.; 6-yr.; expenses; 9 members: Chair Gayle W. Strange, Denton (5/22/09); Don A. Buchholz, Dallas (5/22/13); Charles D. Mitchell, Dallas (5/22/11); Robert A. Nickell, Dallas (5/22/09); Gwyn Shea, Irving (5/22/13); Al Silva, San Antonio (5/22/11); C. Dan Smith, Plano (5/22/11); Rice M. Tilley Jr., Fort Worth (5/22/09); Jack A. Wall, Dallas (5/22/13). Chancellor Lee F. Jackson; Brd. Sec. Jana Dean, PO Box 311220, Denton 76203; (940) 565-4998.

University of Texas System Board of Regents – (1881); apptv.; expenses; 6-yr.: Chair James R. Huffines, Austin (2/1/15); James D. Dannenbaum, Houston (2/1/13); Paul Foster, El Paso (2/1/13); Printice L. Gary, Dallas (2/1/13); R. Steven Hicks, Austin (2/1/11); Janiece Longoria, Houston (2/1/11); Colleen McHugh, Corpus Christi (2/1/11); William (Gene) Powell, San Antonio (2/1/15); Robert L. Stillwell, Houston (2/1/15). Chancellor Francisco G. Cigarroa, 201 W. Seventh St., Ste. 820, Austin, 78701-4402; (512) 499-4402.

Utility Commission, Public – (*See* Public Utility Commission).

Veterans Commission, Texas – (1927 as Veterans State Service Office; reorganized as Veterans Affairs Commission in 1947 with 5 members; name changed to present in 1985; apptv.; 6-yr.; per diem while on duty and expenses; 5 members: Chair Karen S. Rankin, San Antonio (12/31/09); Eliseo Cantu Jr., Corpus Christi (12/31/13); John McKinney, El Paso (12/31/11); Terrence O'Mahoney, Dallas (12/31/11); Ezell Ware Jr. (12/31/11). Exec. Dir. James E. Nier ($115,000), PO Box 12277, Austin 78711-2277; (512) 463-6564.

Veterans' Land Board – (*See* Land Board, Veterans').

Veterinary Medical Examiners, Texas State Board of – (1911; revised 1953; made 9-member board in 1981); apptv.; expenses on duty; 9 members: Chair Bud E. Alldrege Jr., Sweetwater (8/26/09); Patrick M. Allen, Lubbock (8/26/09); Janie Allen Carpenter, Garland (8/26/11); John D. Clader, Jourdanton (8/26/13); Cynthia S. Diaz, San Antonio (8/26/11); David Wayne Heflin, Mission (8/26/11); David Kercheval, Fort Worth (8/26/13); Paul Martinez, Sonora (8/26/09); David Roseberg Jr., Mason (8/26/13). Exec. Dir. Dewey E. Helmcamp III ($65,000), 333 Guadalupe St., Ste. 3-810, Austin 78701-3942; (512) 305-7555.

Wastewater Treatment Research Council, Texas On-Site – (1987); apptv.; 2-yr.; 11 members: Janet R. Boone, North Zulch (9/1/10); Richard D. Gerard, Livingston (9/1/10); Susan R. Johnson, Austin (9/1/10); Sockalingam (Sam) Kannappan, Houston (9/1/09); Sarah E. Kirksey, Beaumont (9/1/09); Janet Dee Meyers, Aubrey (9/1/10); Brian L. Padden, Austin (9/1/09); Carl M. Russell Jr., Lubbock (9/1/09); William F. (Dubb) Smith III, Dripping Springs (9/1/09); Ronald J. Suchecki Jr., China Spring (9/1/10); Al Sulak, Orchard (9/1/09). Exec. Sec. Andy Gardner, TCEQ, Regulatory Compliance Section MC-178, PO Box 13087, Austin 78711-3087; (512) 239-1452.

Water Development Board, Texas – (1957; legislative function for the Texas Dept. of Water Resources, 1977); apptv.; per diem and expenses; 6-yr.; 6 members: Chair James Edward Herring, Amarillo (12/31/09); Joe M. Crutcher, Palestine (12/31/13); Jack Hunt, Houston (12/31/09); Thomas Weir Labatt III, San Antonio (12/31/11); Lewis McMahan, Dallas (12/31/11); Ed Vaughn, Boerne (12/31/13). Exec. Admin. J. Kevin Ward ($135,000), PO Box 13231, Austin 78711-3231; (512) 463-7847.

Women, Governor's Commission for – (1967); apptv.; 2-yr. term or at pleasure of Gov.; 14 members: Stephanie Cavender, San Antonio (12/31/09); Peggy Hairgrove, Haskell (12/31/09); Cynthia Tyson Jenkins, Irving (12/31/09); Christie M. Leedy, Abilene (12/31/09); Elisa Gonzales (Lisa) Lucero, Austin (12/31/09); Becky McKinley, Amarillo (12/31/09); Carmen Pagan, McAllen (12/31/09); Carol Foxhall Peterson, Alpine (12/31/09); Lisa Perini, Buffalo Gap (12/31/09); Sharon Pittman, College Station (12/31/09); Tresa Rockwell, Austin (12/31/09); Wendy Taylor, El Paso (12/31/09); Connie Weeks, Austin (12/31/09); Daisy Sloan White, Houston (12/31/09). Dir. Lesley Guthrie, PO Box 12428, Austin 78711; (800) 839-5323.

Workers' Compensation Commissioner, Texas – (1991); functions transferred to the Texas Dept. of Insurance Division of Workers' Compensation in 2005; apptv.; 2-yr.; Commissioner Rod A. Bordelon Jr., Austin, (2/1/11), PO Box 149104, Austin 78714-9104; (512) 463-6169.

Workforce Commission, Texas – (1936 as Texas Employment Commission; name changed 1995); apptv.; chairman, $125,000; commissioners, $115,000; 6-yr.; 3 members: Chair Tom Pauken, Dallas (2/1/15); Andres Alcantar, Austin (2/1/13), representing employers; Ronald G. Congleton, Rockwall (2/1/11), representing labor. Exec. Dir. Larry Temple ($140,000), 101 E. 15th St., Austin 78778-0001; (512) 463-2222.

Workforce Investment Council, Texas – (1993); apptv.; 19 members: 5 ex officio (directors from Economic Development and Tourism, Higher Education Coordinating Board, Texas Education Agency, Texas Health and Human Services Comm., Texas Workforce Comm.); 14 apptd.: Chair John W. Sylvester Jr., Houston (9/1/09); Karen Bonner, Corpus Christi (9/1/13); James Brookes, Amarillo (9/1/11); Steve Dement, Houston (9/1/09); Carmen Olivas Graham, El Paso (9/1/11); Richard Hatfield, Austin (9/1/09); Robert Hawkins, Bellmead (9/1/11); Sharla E. Hotchkiss, Midland (9/1/11); Larry Jeffus, Dallas (9/1/09); Wes Jurey, Arlington (9/1/13); Paul Mayer, Garland (9/1/13); Danny Prosperie, Bridge City (9/1/13); Joyce Delores Taylor, Houston (9/1/09); 1 vacancy. Dir. Cheryl Fuller, PO Box 2241, Austin 78768; (512) 936-8100.

Youth Commission, Texas – (1949 as 9-member advisory board; reorganized in 1957 and again in 1975; in March 2007, all board members resigned and the commission was placed under conservatorship; in October 2008, the Gov. removed TYC from conservatorship); terms expire at pleasure of Gov.; per diem on duty; 6 apptv. members: Chair Catherine Evans, Dallas; Scott W. Fisher, Bedford; Matthew J. Hay, Galveston; 3 vacancies. Independent Ombudsman Will Harrell, Austin (2/1/11); Exec. Comm. Cheryln K. (Cherie) Townsend ($125,000); PO Box 4260, Austin 78765; (512) 424-6004. ☆

The Austin skyline as seen from the Palmer Events Center. Elizabeth Alvarez photo.

Local Governments

Texas has **254 counties,** a number which has not changed since 1931 when Loving County was organized. Loving had a population of 42, according to the 2008 estimate by the State Data Center, compared with 164 in 1970 and a peak of 285 in 1940. It is the **least-populous county** in Texas. In contrast, Harris County has the **most residents** in Texas, with a 2008 population estimate of 3,984,349.

Counties range in area from Rockwall's 148.7 square miles to the 6,192.78 square miles in Brewster, which is equal to the combined area of the states of Connecticut and Rhode Island.

The Texas Constitution makes a county a legal subdivision of the state. Each county has a commissioners court. It consists of four commissioners, each elected from a commissioner's precinct, and a county judge elected from the entire county. In smaller counties, the county judge retains judicial responsibilities in probate and insanity cases. For names of county and district officials, see tables on pages 518–528.

There are **1210 incorporated municipalities** in Texas that range in size from 31 residents in Los Ybañez to Houston's 2,149,948, according to the State Data Center's 2008 estimate. More than 80 percent of the state's population lives in cities and towns, meeting the U.S. Census Bureau definition of urban areas.

Texas had 389 incorporated towns with more than 5,000 population, according to State Data Center estimates. Under law, these cities may adopt their own charters (called home rule) by a majority vote. Cities of less than 5,000 may be chartered only under the general law. Some home-rule cities may show fewer than 5,000 residents because population has declined since adopting home-rule charters. **Home-rule cities are marked in this list by a single-dagger symbol (†) after the name.** ☆

Mayors and City Managers of Texas Cities

This list was compiled from questionnaires sent out after the May 9, 2009, municipal elections. It includes the name of each city's mayor, as well as the name of the city manager, city administrator, city coordinator or other managing executive for munipalities having that form of government. If a town's mail goes to a post office in a different town, the mailing address is included. An asterisk (*) before the city name means the *Texas Almanac* received no response to the questionnaire and that the information is from the Texas State Directory 2009, 52nd edition. Home-rule cities are marked in this list by a single-dagger symbol (†) after the name.

— A —

Abbott .... Harry G. Nors
Abernathy .... Darrell Stephens
   City Mgr., Mike Cypert
Abilene (†) .... Norm Archibald
   City Mgr., Larry D. Gilley
*Ackerly .... Mary Schuelke
Addison (†) .... Joe Chow
   City Mgr., Ron Whitehead

Adrian .... Finis Brown
*Agua Dulce .... Carl Vajdos
Alamo (†) .... Rudy Villarreal
   City Mgr., Luciano Ozuna Jr.
Alamo Heights (†) (6116 Broadway, San
   Antonio 78209) .... Louis Cooper
   City Mgr., Rebecca Waldman
Alba .... Orvin Carroll
Albany .... Ed Tackett
   City Mgr., Bobby R. Russell

Aledo .... Kit Marshall
   City Admin., Ken Pfeifer
*Alice (†) .... Grace Saenz-Lopez.
   City Mgr., Pete Anaya
Allen (†) .... Stephen Terrell
   City Mgr., Peter H. Vargas
Alma .... Scot Shepherd
Alpine (†) .... Jerry Johnson
   City Mgr., Chuy Garcia
Alto, City of .... Carry Ann Walker

*Alton .... Salvador Vela
City Mgr., Jorge Arcaute
Alvarado .... Tom Durington
City Mgr., Don Ives
Alvin (†) .... Gary Appelt
City Mgr., Paul Horn
Alvord .... Frank Knittel
City Admin., John Cobb
Amarillo (†) .... Debra McCartt
City Mgr., Alan M. Taylor
*Ames .... John White
Amherst .... Joe A. Miller
Anahuac .... Guy R. Jackson
City Admin., Mary Chambers
Anderson .... Gail M. Sowell
Andrews (†) .... Robert Zap
City Mgr., Glen E. Hackler
*Angleton (†) .... J. Patrick Henry
City Admin., Michael Stoldt
Angus .... (6008 S. I-45 W, Corsicana
75109) .... Eben Dale Stover
Anna (†) .... Darren R. Driskell
City Mgr., Philip Sanders
*Annetta ...... (PO Box 1150, Aledo 76008)
.... Olan Usher
Annetta North .... (PO Box 1238, Aledo
76008) .... Robert Watson
*Annetta South .... (PO Box 61, Aledo
76008) .... Gerhard Kleinschmidt
*Annona .... George H. English
City Mgr., Garry L. Watkins
*Anson (†) .... Tom Isbell
City Mgr., Dowell Matthews
*Anthony .... Art Franco
Anton .... Karl Campbell
City Mgr., Larry Conkin
*Appleby (223 CR 257, Nacogdoches
75965) .... Gerald Herbert Sr.
*Aquilla .... James Hamner Sr.
*Aransas Pass (†) .... Tommy Knight
City Mgr., Mike Sullinger
Archer City .... David A. Levy
City Mgr., Kim Whitsitt
Arcola .... Mary Etta Anderson
*Argyle .... Greg Landrum
City Admin., Lyle Dresher
Arlington (†) .... Robert N. Cluck
City Mgr., Jim Holgersson
*Arp .... Vernon L. Bedair
*Asherton .... Gilberto Gonzalez Jr.
Aspermont .... Billie Carter
City Admin., Roger Parker
*Athens (†) .... Randy Daniel
City Mgr., Pam J. Burton
*Atlanta (†) .... Keith Crow
City Mgr., Michael Ahrens
Aubrey .... Gary Hammett
*Aurora .... (Box 558, Rhome 76078)
.... Barbara Brammer
City Admin., Toni Kelly-Richardson
Austin (†) .... Lee Leffingwell
City Mgr., Marc Ott
Austwell .... Mustafa Curtess
*Avery .... Bill Trimm
Avinger .... Marvin E. Parvino
*Azle (†) .... Russ Braudis
City Mgr., Craig Lemin

— B —

*Bailey .... John Robert Stephens
*Bailey's Prairie ... (PO Box 71, Angleton
77516) .... Randy Taylor
*Baird .... Jon E. Hardwick
City Mgr., Nancy Turnbow
Balch Springs (†) .... Carrie F. Gordon
City Mgr., (vacant)
Balcones Heights .... Suzanne de Leon
City Admin., Sean Pate
*Ballinger (†) .... Joe Selby
City Mgr., Tommy New
Balmorhea .... Joy E. Lewis
Bandera .... Horst Pallaske
City Admin., Gene R. Foerster

Bangs .... Martin Molotsky
Bardwell .... Clinton Ivy
*Barry .... John Wade Braly
Barstow .... James A. Collins
*Bartlett .... Arthur T. White
*Bartonville .... Ron Robertson
Bastrop (†) .... Terry Orr
City Mgr., Michael H. Talbot
Bay City (†) .... Richard Knapik
Bayou Vista .... Ed Flanagan
Bayside .... Billy P. Fricks
*Baytown (†) .... Stephen H. DonCarlos
City Mgr., Gary Jackson
Bayview .... (110 S. San Ramon, Los
Fresnos 78566) .... Dick Deason
*Beach City (12723 Tri City Beach Rd.,
Baytown 77520) .... Guido Persiani
*Bear Creek, Village of (6705 W. Hwy.
290, #502, Austin 78735) Bruce Upham
Beasley .... Kenneth Reid
*Beaumont (†) .... Becky Ames
City Mgr., Kyle Hayes
*Beckville .... Gene Mothershed
City Mgr., Peggy Harris
Bedias .... Mackie Bobo
*Bedford (†) .... Jim Story
City Mgr., Beverly Queen
Bee Cave, City of .... Caroline L. Murphy
City Admin., Frank L. Salvato
*Beeville (†) .... Kenneth Chesshir
City Mgr., Ford Patton
Bellaire (†) .... Cynthia Siegel
City Mgr., Bernard M. Satterwhite Jr.
*Bellevue .... Marvin Bigbie
Bellmead (†) .... Carl E. Swanson III
City Admin., S.G. (Scooter) Radcliff
Bells .... Shirley Mullinix
*Bellville .... Philip B. Harrison
City Admin., Lynn S. Roberts
Belton (†) .... Jim Covington
City Mgr., Sam A. Listi
Benavides .... Cynthia G. Canales
City Admin., Poncho Hernandez
Benbrook (†) .... Jerry B. Dittrich
City Mgr., Andy Waymon
Benjamin .... Sylinda Meinzer
City Mgr., Ronnie White
Berryville .... (PO Box 908, Frankston
75763) .... Roy Brown
City Mgr., Sharyn Harrison
Bertram .... JoAnn Stephens
*Beverly Hills (3418 Memorial Dr., Waco
76711) .... Douglas E. Woodward
Bevil Oaks ...... Rebecca (Becky) M. Ford
Big Lake .... Cindy O'Bryan
City Admin., Evelyn Ammons
Big Sandy .... Wayne Weese
Big Spring (†) .... Russ McEwen
City Mgr., Gary Fuqua
Big Wells .... Randall Matthews
City Admin., Charlene Greenhill
Bishop .... Victor Ramos
*Bishop Hills (#6 Manchester Rd., Ama-
rillo 79124) .... Betty Benham
Blackwell .... Laura Rozzelle
Blanco, City of .... Christina Gourley
Blanket .... John H. Jones
*Bloomburg .... Jerrell Ritchie
*Blooming Grove .... Alva L. Smith
Blossom .... Roger S. Johnson
Blue Mound ..... (301 S. Blue Mound Rd.,
Fort Worth 76131) .... Alan Hooks
Blue Ridge .... Dan Standeford
*Blum .... Elaine Edwards
Boerne (†) .... Dan Heckler
City Mgr., Ronald C. Bowman
Bogata .... Vincent Lum
Bonham (†) .... Roy V. Floyd
City Mgr., Corby D. Alexander
Bonney .... Raymond Cantu
Booker .... Jim Riggs
City Mgr., Donald R. Kerns
*Borger (†) .... Jeff Brain
City Mgr., Wanda Klause

Bovina .... Stan Miller
City Mgr., Jana Pitcock
Bowie (†) .... Larry Cox
City Mgr., James Cantwell
Boyd .... Brent Wilson
City Admin., John Hamilton
*Brackettville .... Eduardo Esparza
*Brady (†) .... Jesse McAnally
City Mgr., Merle Taylor
Brazoria, City of .... Ken Corley
City Mgr., Teresa Borders
*Brazos Bend .... Vernon E. Oechsle
Brazos Country (316 Pecan Grove Rd.,
Sealy 77474) .... Charles A. Kalkomey
Breckenridge (†) .... Jimmy McKay
City Mgr., Gary G. Ernest
Bremond .... Ricky Swick
Brenham (†) .... Milton Y. Tate Jr.
City Mgr., Terry K. Roberts
Briarcliff .... Robert Pigg
City Admin., Aaron Johnson
*Briaroaks .... (PO Box 816, Burleson
76097) .... James Dunn
*Bridge City (†) .... Kirk Roccaforte
City Mgr., Don Fields
Bridgeport .... Donald C. Majka
City Admin., Van James
*Broaddus .... William W. Barth
Bronte .... Gerald Sandusky
*Brookshire .... Keith A. Woods
Brookside Village .... Denise Ford
*Browndell (Box 430, Brookeland
75931) .... Monica Garrett
Brownfield (†) .... Glenn Waters
City Mgr., Eldon Jobe
*Brownsboro .... Ronny K. Harris
*Brownsville .... Pat M. Ahumada Jr.
City Mgr., Charlie Cabler
Brownwood (†) .... Bert V. Massey II
City Mgr., Bobby Rountree
Bruceville-Eddy ...... (143 Wilcox Dr., #A,
Eddy 76524) .... James Tomme
Bryan (†) .... D. Mark Conlee
City Mgr., David Watkins
*Bryson .... Kennith Boland
*Buckholts .... Angela Morgan
*Buda .... H. John Trube
City Admin., Robert Camareno
Buffalo .... Royce Dawkins
Buffalo Gap .... David L. Perry
Buffalo Springs (99-B Pony Express Trl.,
Lubbock 79404) .... Velvet Keys
*Bullard .... Connie R. Vaughan Sr.
City Mgr., Larry Morgan
*Bulverde .... Sarah Stevick
City Admin., Bob Hieronymus
Bunker Hill Village (11977 Memorial Dr.,
Houston 77024) .... Derry D. Essary
City Admin., Ruthie P. Sager
Burkburnett (†) .... Carl Law
City Mgr., Michael T. Slye
*Burke ..... (RR 3, Box 315, Diboll 75941)
.... John Thomas Jones
Burleson (†) .... Ken Shetter
City Mgr., Curtis E. Hawk
Burnet (†) .... Alan Smith
City Mgr., Michael T. Steele
Burton, City of .... Peggy A. Felder
Byers .... Robert Lawrence
*Bynum .... Lawana Jolene Custer

— C —

*Cactus .... Luiz Aguilar
City Mgr., Jeffrey G. Jenkins
Caddo Mills .... Dwayne Pattison
City Mgr., Manuel Leal
Caldwell .... Bernard E. Rychlik
City Admin., Billy Clemons
Callisburg, City of .... (59 Campbell St.,
Whitesboro 76273) .... Frances West
Calvert .... Marcus D. Greaves
Cameron (†) .... David Barkemeyer
City Mgr., Ricky Tow

*Campbell .... Geri Barnes
Camp Wood........................ Emma Dean
Canadian ....John Baker
   City Mgr., Colby Waters
Caney City ....Joe Barron
Canton ....William Wilson
   City Mgr., Andy McCuistion
*Canyon (†)...................Quinn Alexander
   City Mgr., Glen R. Metcalf
Carbon .... Dale Walker (pro tem)
Carl's Corner.................. Carl Cornelius
Carmine ....Justin Flasowski
Carrizo Springs (†) ....Ralph E. Salinas
   City Mgr., Mario A. Martinez
Carrollton (†)..............Ronald F. Branson
   City Mgr., Leonard Martin
*Carthage (†) ....Carson C. Joines
   City Mgr., Brenda Samford
Cashion Community (354 Baker Rd.,
   Wichita Falls 76305)......Robyn Murphy
*Castle Hills (209 Lemonwood Dr., San
   Antonio 78213).............. Marcy Harper
   City Mgr., Mchael R. Rietz
*Castroville............................Jesse Byars
   City Admin., Shawna Dowell
Cedar Hill (†) .... Rob Franke
   City Mgr., Alan Sims
Cedar Park (†) ....Bob Lemon
   City Mgr., Brenda Eivens
Celeste.................................... Mike Stout
Celina (†) .... Jim Lewis
   City Mgr., Jason Gray
Center (†)...................John D. Windham
   City Mgr., Chad D. Nehring
Centerville ..........................N.R. Goolsby
Chandler...............................Joye Rains
   City Admin., Jim Moffeit
Channing...........................Karen Schulz
*Charlotte ... Augustine (PeeWee) Munoz
Chester ...........................C.E. Lawrence
*Chico .... James Robinson
Childress........................Barbara Jones
   City Mgr., Bryan Tucker
*Chillicothe...................Wallace A. Clay
China, City of .... William T. Sanders
China Grove .... Dennis A. Dunk
*Chireno.........................Mike Metteauer
*Christine..........................Odel Vasquez
   City Admin., Calvin K. Howard
*Cibolo ....Johny Sutton
*Cisco (†) ....Hal Porter
   Interim City Mgr., Jim Baker
*Clarendon ....Mark White
Clarksville............................Ann Rushing
   City Mgr., Wayne Dial
Clarksville City ......(Box 1111, White Oak
   75693) .... Larry G. Allen
   City Mgr., Billy F. Silvertooth Jr.
Claude..................................Jim Hubbard
Clear Lake Shores .... Vern Johnson
   City Admin., Paul Shelley
*Cleburne (†) .... Ted Reynolds
   City Mgr., Chester Nolen
Cleveland (†) ....Jill B. Kirkonis
   City Mgr., Philip Cook
Clifton .... Fred Volcansek
   City Admin., Charles McLean
Clint .... Dale T. Reinhardt
*Clute (†)........................... Calvin Shiflet
   City Mgr., Kyle McCain
*Clyde ....Steve Livingston
   City Admin., Tim Atkinson
*Coahoma.................................Bill Read
*Cockrell Hill .....(4125 W. Clarendon Dr.,
   Dallas 75211) ....Luis D. Carrera
   City Admin., Bret Haney
*Coffee City .(Box 716, Frankston 75763)
   ....Frank Ross
*Coldspring ....Pat Eversole
Coleman (†)...................... Nick Poldrack
   City Mgr., Larry Weise
College Station (†).................Ben White
   City Mgr., Glenn Brown

Downtown Calvert, on State Highway 6 in Robertson County, is a destination for antique hunters. Elizabeth Alvarez photo.

Colleyville (†) .... David Kelly
   City Mgr., Jennifer Fadden
Collinsville....................Wayne McCorkle
Colmesneil .... Don Baird
*Colorado City (†) ....Jim Baum
   City Mgr., Paul Catoe
*Columbus..........................Richard Heffley
   City Mgr., David Meisell
Comanche .... Raymond W. Stepp
   City Admin., Bill Flannery
*Combes .... Silvestre (Silver) Garcia
   City Mgr., Lonnie Bearden
Combine .... Keith Taylor
*Commerce (†) ....Sheryl Zelhart
   City Mgr., Bill Shipp
Como ....James Carroll
Conroe (†)..................... Webb K. Melder
   City Admin., Jerry McGuire
*Converse (†) ....Al Suarez
   City Mgr., Sam Hughes
*Cool (†). (150 FM 113 S., Millsap 76066)
   .... Dorothy Hall
Coolidge ....Bobby Jacobs
Cooper................. Thomas Scotty Stegall
   City Admin., Margaret Eudy
Coppell (†).........................Jayne Peters
   City Mgr., Clay Phillips
Copperas Cove (†)...................John Hull
   City Mgr., Andrea M. Gardner
*Copper Canyon .... Sue Tejml
   Town Admin., Quentin Hix
Corinth (†) .... Paul Ruggiere
   Interim City Mgr., James Berzina
Corpus Christi (†) ....Joe Adame
   City Mgr., Angel R. Escobar
Corral City (14007 Corral City Dr., Argyle
   76226) .... Tim Gamblin
   Town Admin., Bob Blizzard
*Corrigan .... Grimes Fortune
   City Mgr., Mandy K. Risinger
Corsicana (†)...........C.L. (Buster) Brown
   City Mgr., Connie Standridge
Cottonwood...... (Box 293, Scurry 75158)
   ....Doug Harris
Cottonwood Shores .... Bentley Martin
   City Admin., Hans J. Schneider
Cotulla ....Joe Lozano
   Interim City Admin., Larry Dovalina
Cove.............(PO Box 529, Mont Belvieu
   77580) .... Lee Wiley
*Covington .... Tommy L. Elkins
Crandall ....Cody Frazier
   City Mgr., Heath Kaplan

Crane .... Kelly S. Nichols
   City Admin., Dru Gravens
Cranfills Gap, City of .....Ronald Hubbard
*Crawford ....David C. Posten
*Creedmoor.......(12108 FM 1625, Austin
   78747) ....Robert L. Wilhite
   City Admin. Richard L. Crandal Jr.
Cresson ....................W.R. (Bob) Cornett
Crockett (†)........................ Wayne Mask
   City Admin., Ronald M. Duncan
Crosbyton, City of ....Dusty Cornelius
   City Admin., Margot Hardin
Cross Plains.........................Ray Purvis
   City Admin., Debbie Gosnell
Cross Roads ....Harv Kitchens
   City Admin., Katherine M. Ritchie
Cross Timber .... Wava McCullough
Crowell................................Gayle Simpson
Crowley (†) ....Billy P. Davis
   City Mgr., Truitt Gilbreath
Crystal City (†) ....Benito C. Perez
   City Mgr., Diana Palacios
Cuero (†)..............................Randy Saenz
   City Mgr., Marie Gelles
Cumby ....Jeff Strickland
*Cuney .... Jessie Johnson
Cushing ....Don Bruce Richards
Cut and Shoot.............. Lang Thompson

— D —

Daingerfield (†) .... Lou Irvin
   City Mgr., Marty Byers
Daisetta.....................Edward Lynn Wells
*Dalhart (†) ....Kevin Caddell
   City Mgr., Greg Duggan
Dallas (†)............................. Tom Leppert
   City Mgr., Mary K. Suhm
*Dalworthington Gardens Michel Tedder
   City Admin., Melinda Brittain
Danbury, City of .... Fred Williamson
Darrouzett.......................Paul Laughead
Dawson...............................Linda Bryant
Dayton (†)................. Steve E. Stephens
   City Mgr., David Douglas
Dayton Lakes .... (Box 1476, Dayton
   77535) .... Jerry A. Ham
*Dean (6913 State Hwy. 79 N., Wichita
   Falls 76035)............... Steve L. Sicking
Decatur (†)......................Joe A. Lambert
   City Mgr., Brett Shannon
*De Cordova (PO Box 5905, Granbury
   76049) ....Dick Pruitt

Deer Park (†) ....Wayne Riddle
   City Mgr., Ronald V. Crabtree
*De Kalb......................Paul G. Meadows
   City Admin., Abbi Baker
De Leon (†) .... Danny Owen
   City Admin., Karen Wilkerson
*Dell City...........................Pamela Dean
   City Admin., Juanita R. Collier
*Del Rio (†) .... Efrain Valdez
   City Mgr., Rafael Castillo
Denison (†) ....Robert Brady
   City Mgr., Larry Cruise
Denton (†) ....Mark Burroughs
   City Mgr., George Campbell
Denver City (†) .... David Bruton
   City Mgr., Stan David
*Deport................................Edna Gifford
DeSoto (†)...................Bobby G. Waddle
   City Mgr., James (Jim) Baugh
*Detroit............................Travis Bronner
Devers..............................Edna Johnson
Devine................................Jerry Beck
   City Admin., Dora V. Rodriguez
Diboll (†) .... Bill Brown
   City Mgr., Dennis McDuffie
*Dickens .... Lena Penick
Dickinson (†)............Julie Dues Masters
   City Admin., Julie M. Johnson
Dilley, City of ....Mary Ann Obregon
   City Admin., Melissa L. Gonzalez
*Dimmitt (†) .... Wayne Collins
   City Mgr., David Denman
Dish...............................Calvin D. Tillman
Dodd City............................Jackie Lackey
*Dodson.............................Steve Kane
*Domino.......................Marvin Campbell
*Donna (†)....................Ricardo Morales
   City Mgr., Patricia Rene Avila
Dorchester...........................David Smith
Double Oak, Town of ....Mike Donnelly
Douglassville .... Douglass B. Heath
Dripping Springs .... Todd Purcell
   City Admin., Michelle Fischer
Driscoll ....John A. Aguilar
   City Admin., Sandra Martinez
Dublin .... Tom Gordon
   City Mgr., Jerry Guillory
*Dumas (†) .... Mike Milligan
   City Mgr., Vince DiPiazza
Duncanville (†)................David L. Green
   City Mgr., Kent Cagle

— E —

*Eagle Lake ....Mike Morales
   City Mgr., Ronald W. Holland
Eagle Pass (†) .... Chad Foster
   City Mgr., Daniel Valenzuela
Early........................ Robert G. Mangrum
   City Admin., Ken Thomas
Earth .... Brad Freeman
*East Bernard..................Buck Boettcher
Eastland (†) .... Mark Pipkin
   City Mgr., Ron Holliday
East Mountain (103 Municipal Dr., Gilmer
   75645).............................Ronnie Hill
   City Admin., Tammy Hazel
Easton, City of .... Walter Ward
East Tawakoni............James R. Thomas
*Ector ....Mary Dean Norris
*Edcouch ....Robert T. Schmalzried
   City Admin., Ernesto Ayala Jr.
Eden...................................Eugene Spann
   City Admin., Celina Hemmeter
*Edgecliff Village .... Tony Dauphinot
*Edgewood ....Charles Prater
Edinburg (†) ....Richard H. Garcia
   City Mgr., Juan Jose (J.J.) Rodriguez
*Edmonson.................Wendell Edmonson
Edna (†) ....Joe D. Hermes
   City Mgr., Kenneth Pryor
Edom ....Barbara Crow
*El Campo (†) ....Kenneth G. Martin
   City Mgr., John Steelman

*El Cenizo ....Raul L. Reyes
*Eldorado..........................John Nikolauk
Electra (†) .... Glen Branch
   City Admin., Stephen Giesbrecht
Elgin (†) ....Marc Holm
   City Mgr., Jeff Coffee
*Elkhart ....Joe B. Burris
El Lago...................................... Brad Emel
Elmendorf................... Thomas P. Hicks
   City Admin., Cody D. Dailey
El Paso (†) ....John F. Cook
   City Mgr., Joyce A. Wilson
*Elsa (†) ....Senovio Castillo
   City Mgr., Maria Hilda Ayala
*Emhouse (3825 Joe Johnson Dr., Corsi-
   cana 75110)................Johnny Pattison
*Emory ....Cay Frances B. House
   City Admin., Clyde Smith
*Enchanted Oaks (Box 5019, Mabank
   75147) .... Donald G. Warner III
*Encinal ....Javier Mancha
   City Admin., Matt Peter Olivera
Ennis (†) ....Russell R. Thomas
   City Mgr., Steve Howerton
Escobares ....Noel Escobar
*Estelline ....Rick Manley
Euless (†).........................Mary Lib Saleh
   City Mgr., Gary McKamie
Eureka...........(1305 FM 2859, Corsicana
   75109) .... R.B. (Barney) Thomas
*Eustace ....Laura R. Ward
Evant..........................Sterling Manning
*Everman (†)................ Jim Stephenson
   City Mgr., Donna Anderson

— F —

*Fairchilds (8713 Fairchilds Rd., Rich-
   mond 77469) .... Richard G. Vacek
*Fairfield ....Roy Hill
   City Admin., Mike Gokey
Fair Oaks Ranch .... Daniel E. Kasprowicz
   City Admin., Roy W. Thomas
Fairview (†).........................Sim Israeloff
   Town Mgr., John Godwin
Falfurrias ....Joe Garcia
Falls City......................Brent Houdmann
*Farmers Branch (†)..............Bob Phelps
   City Mgr., Gary D. Greer
*Farmersville ....Robbin H. Lamkin
   City Mgr., Alan Hein
Farwell ....Jimmie Mace
*Fate....................................Bill Broderick
*Fayetteville................Ronald Pflughaupt
   City Mgr., Billy J. Wasut
Ferris................................Jim E. Parks Jr.
   City Mgr., vacant
Flatonia ....Jeff M. Hairgrove
   City Mgr., Kenneth Knight
Florence.........................Mary Condon
Floresville (†) .... Daniel M. Tejada
   City Mgr., Gary Pelech
Flower Mound (†)..............Jody A. Smith
   Town Mgr., Harlan Jefferson
Floydada ....Bobby Gilliland
   City Mgr., Gary Brown
*Follett ....Lynn Blau
   City Mgr., Robert Williamson
Forest Hill (†) (6800 Forest Hill Dr., Fort
   Worth 76140)..................James Gosey
   City Mgr., David Miller
Forney (†) .... Darren Rozell
   City Mgr., Brian Brooks
Forsan............................. Roger Hudgins
Fort Stockton ....Ruben V. Falcon
   City Mgr., Rafael Castillo Jr.
Fort Worth (†)...................Mike Moncrief
   City Mgr., Dale A. Fisseler
Franklin...........................Charles Ellison
*Frankston.......................James Gouger
Fredericksburg (†).............Jeryl Hoover
   City Mgr., Gary Neffendorf
*Freeport (†).......James W. (Jim) Phillips
   City Mgr., Ron P. Bottoms

*Freer .... Arnoldo Cantu
*Friendswood (†) .... David J.H. Smith
   City Mgr., Roger Roecker
Friona...............................John C. Taylor
   City Mgr., Patricia Phipps
*Frisco (†) ....Mike Simpson
   City Mgr., George A. Purefoy
Fritch..........................Kevin R. Keener
   City Mgr., Ernest Terry
Frost....................................... Ken Reed
Fruitvale.............................Carl Waddell
Fulshear.........James (Jamie) W. Roberts
*Fulton ....Russel Cole

— G —

*Gainesville (†).....................Glenn Loch
   City Mgr., Mike Land
Galena Park (†) .... R.P. (Bobby) Barrett
   City Admin., John L. Cooper
*Gallatin ....Juanita Cotton
Galveston (†)............... Lyda Ann Thomas
   City Mgr., Steve LeBlanc
*Ganado.....................Clinton W. Tegeler
Garden Ridge.............Jay F. Feibelman
   City Admin., Nancy Cain
Garland (†).....................Ronald E. Jones
   City Mgr., William E. Dollar
Garrett................................Matt Newsom
*Garrison ....Patsy Nugent
Gary ....Jean L. Heaton
*Gatesville (†).................David K. Byrom
   City Mgr., Roger L. Mumby
Georgetown (†) .... George G. Garver
   City Mgr., Paul E. Brandenburg
George West (†) .... Sylvia Steele
   City Mgr., Jacquelyn Harborth
Gholson (155 Wesley Chapel Rd., Waco
   76705) ....Larry Binnion
Giddings (†)....................Charlie Brown
   City Mgr., Hector Forestier
Gilmer (†)................................R.D. Cross
   City Mgr., Jeff Ellington
Gladewater (†)................ Walter Derrick
   City Mgr., Jay Stokes
Glenn Heights (†).............Clark Choate
   City Mgr., Jacqueline L. Lee
Glen Rose...............................Pam Miller
*Godley..............................David Wallis
   City Admin., Stephanie Hodges
Goldsmith......................Billy Whittemore
   City Mgr., Vickie Emfinger
*Goldthwaite.................Mike McMahan
   City Mgr., Bobby Rountree
Goliad ....Jay Harvey
   City Admin., C.J. Snipes
*Golinda....................Mary Evelyn Hupp
Gonzales (†) ....Bobby G. O'Neal
   City Mgr., David Huseman
*Goodlow... Willie H. (Butch) Washington
*Goodrich ....Nita Gokey
Gordon.............................Pat M. Sublett
Goree ....Kent Trainham
   City Mgr., Tammie Trainham
Gorman (†) ....Robert Ervin
   City Admin., Tacy Warren
Graford ....Carl Walston
Graham (†)..................Wayne Christian
   City Mgr., Larry Fields
Granbury (†).................. David Southern
   City Mgr., Harold Sandel
*Grandfalls ....Mandy Brandenburg
   City Admin., Karen Thomas
Grand Prairie (†)...........Charles England
   City Mgr., Tom Hart
*Grand Saline .... Terry Tolar
   City Admin., Stephen G. Ashley
Grandview .... Travis Buck
   City Admin., Jerry McGlasson
*Granger ....Jerry Lalla
   City Admin., Kathleen Vrana
Granite Shoals (†).......... Frank M. Reilly
   City Mgr., John W. Gayle
Granjeno (6603 S. FM 494, Mission
   78572) ....Vincente Garza Jr.

*Grapeland ....Dan Walling
Grapevine (†).................. William D. Tate
    City Mgr., Bruno Rumbelow
Grayburg (17572 Grayburg Rd, Sour
    Lake 77659) .... J.W. Floyd
*Gray's Prairie (Box 116, Scurry 75158)
    .... Don Murray
Greenville (†)..... Thomas B. (Tom) Oliver
    City Mgr., Steven Alexander
Gregory...........................Victor P. Lara III
*Grey Forest ....Donald D. Darst
*Groesbeck...................Jackie Levingston
    City Admin., Martha Stanton
Groom................................Joe L. Homer
Groves (†)...........................Brad P. Bailey
    City Mgr., D.E. Sosa
Groveton.........................Troy W. Jones
*Gruver .... Mark K. Irwin
    City Mgr., Linda Weller
Gun Barrel City (†)................Paul Eaton
    City Mgr., Gary Boren
*Gunter .... Mark A. Millar
Gustine...............................Billy F. Kight

— H —

Hackberry (119 Maxwell Rd., Ste. B-7,
    Frisco 75034) ....Jeromy Cannon
    City Admin., Brenda Lewallen
Hale Center......................Eugene Carter
    City Mgr., Josh Jones
Hallettsville................Warren Grindeland
    City Admin., Tom Donnelly
*Hallsburg...........................Mike Glockzin
Hallsville ....Charles W. Dawson
Haltom City (†) .... Bill Lanford
    City Mgr., Tom Muir
Hamilton ....Roy Rumsey
    City Admin., Bill Funderburk
Hamlin...........................Jack W. Shields
*Happy ....Sara Tirey
Hardin.............................. W. Lee Miller
*Harker Heights (†) .... Ed Mullen
    City Mgr., Steve Carpenter
Harlingen (†).................... Chris Boswell
    City Mgr., Craig Lonon
*Hart......................................Stanley Dyer
*Haskell ....Bob N. Smith
    City Admin., Brandon Anderson
Haslet......................................Bob Golden
Hawk Cove ....Billy Cosby
*Hawkins..............................Sam Bradley
*Hawley.........................Ronnie Woodard
*Hays.................(Box 1285, Buda 78610)
    ....Joleen B. Brown
    City Admin., Wayne Ford
*Hearne (†).......................Ruben Gomez
    City Mgr., Wendell Hughey
*Heath .... John Ratcliffe
    City Mgr., Edward Thatcher
*Hebron.. (Box 118916, Carrollton 75011)
    ....Kelly Clem
Hedley.....................................Janie Hill
Hedwig Village ....Sue V. Speck
    City Admin., Beth Staton
Helotes......Thomas A. (Tom) Schoolcraft
    City Admin., Rick Schroder
Hemphill ....Robert Hamilton
    City Mgr., Donald P. Iles
*Hempstead..................Michael S. Wolfe
    City Admin. (vacancy)
Henderson (†) ....John W. Fullen
    City Mgr., Randall Freeman
Henrietta ....Tom Griffin
    City Mgr., Jeff Jenkins
*Hereford (†).......... Robert D. Josserand
    City Mgr., Rick L. Hanna
*Hewitt (†)...................Charles D. Turner
    City Mgr., Dennis H. Woodard
*Hickory Creek (Box 453, Lake Dallas
    75065) ....Jeff Price
Hico....................................Lavern Tooley
    City Admin., Lambert Little
Hidalgo (†)...................John David Franz

City Mgr., Joe Vera III
*Hideaway...........................Bill Kashouty
Higgins ....Gary Duncan
    City Mgr., Randy Immel
Highland Haven .... Peter E. Freehill
Highland Park (†)......William H. Seay Jr.
    City Admin., Bill Lindley
Highland Village (†) .... Dianne Costa
    City Mgr., Michael Leavitt
*Hill Country Village (116 Aspen Ln., San
    Antonio 78232).............Kirk W. Francis
*Hillcrest Village (Box 1172, Alvin 77512)
    ....Tom Wilson
*Hillsboro (†) ....John P. Erwin Jr.
    Acting City Mgr., Betty Harrell
*Hilshire Village (8301 Westview Dr.,
    Houston 77055)...........Robin S. Border
Hitchcock (†).............Anthony Matranga
Holiday Lakes (RR 4, Box 747, Angleton
    77515) .... Norman C. Schroeder
Holland ....Mae Smith
    City Admin., Kathleen Vrana
Holliday ....Allen Moore
Hollywood Park..... Richard W. McIlveen
Hondo (†)...............James W. Danner Sr.
    City Mgr., Robert T. Herrera
Honey Grove ....Harold Roberts
*Hooks ....Michael W. Babb
Horizon City (†).................. Walter Miller
*Horseshoe Bay ....Robert W. Lambert
    City Mgr., Stan R. Farmer
*Houston (†) .... Bill White
Howardwick ....Del Essary
*Howe..............................Michael Jones
    City Admin., Steven McKay
*Hubbard .... Terry F. Reddell
    City Mgr., Al Saldana
*Hudson .... Robert Smith
    City Admin., James M. Freeman
Hudson Oaks (150 N. Oakridge Dr.,
    Weatherford 76087) ....Par Deen
*Hughes Springs..............Reba Simpson
    City Mgr., George Fite
*Humble (†)........... Donald G. McMannes
    City Mgr., Darrell Boeske
Hunters Creek Village (1 Hunters Creek
    Pl., Houston 77024)... David A. Wegner
Huntington ....Herman Woolbright
    City Admin., Bruce Milstead
*Huntsville (†)...........................J. Turner
    City Mgr., Kevin Evans
Hurst (†)...........................Richard Ward
    City Mgr., W. Allan Weegar
Hutchins ....Artis Johnson
*Hutto ....Kenneth L. Love
    City Mgr., Edward Broussard
Huxley (11798 FM 2694, Shelbyville
    75973) ....Larry Vaughn

— I —

*Idalou..Jack Bush
    City Admin., Jeffrey Snyder
Impact ....Jack Sharp
Indian Lake (62 S. Aztec Cove Dr., Los
    Fresnos 78566) .... Barbara J. Collum
Industry .... Alan W. Kuehn
Ingleside (†)...................Stella Herrmann
    City Mgr., Jim Gray
Ingleside on the Bay (PO Box 309, Ingle-
    side 78362)...............Howard Gillespie
*Ingram ....Howard Jackson
Iola ....Christina Stover
*Iowa Colony (12003 County Rd. 65,
    Rosharon 77583)...............Robert Wall
Iowa Park ....Joe Ward
    City Admin., Michael C. Price
*Iraan...............................June Heck
Iredell............................. Royce P. Heath
Irving (†) ....Herbert A. Gears
    City Mgr., Tommy Gonzalez
Italy ....Frank Jackson
    City Admin., Terri Murdock
Itasca ....Matthew Fehnel

City Admin., Mark Gropp

— J —

*Jacinto City (†) (10301 Market St. Rd.,
    Houston 77029)..............Mike Jackson
    City Mgr., Jack D. Maner
Jacksboro.........................Tom Sessions
    City Admin., Shawna Dowell
*Jacksonville (†) ....Robert N. Haberle
    City Mgr., Mo Raissi
Jamaica Beach ....Victor Pierson
    City Admin., John Brick
*Jarrell .... Wayne E. Cavalier
Jasper (†)................................Mike Lout
    City Mgr., Alan Grindstaff
Jayton ....Kenneth McCurry
Jefferson ....Robert D. Avery
    City Admin., Jim Gibson
Jersey Village (†) .... Russell Hamley
    City Mgr., Mike Castro
Jewett ....Judi Kirkpatrick
*Joaquin ....Steve Hughes
Johnson City..............Kermit A. Roeder
    City Admin., David Dockery
Jolly .... (194 Milton St., Wichita Falls
    76310) ....Mary Y. Taylor
Jones Creek ....George Mitchell
Jonestown ....Deane Armstrong
    City Admin., Dan Dodson
*Josephine ....Cameron Brooks
Joshua (†).............. Merle M. Breitenstein
    City Mgr., Paulette Hartman
*Jourdanton .... Larry Pryor
    City Mgr., Daniel G. Nick
Junction...................Shannon R. Bynum
*Justin....................................Ed Trietsch
    City Admin., Mike Evans

— K —

*Karnes City ....Don Tymrak
    City Admin., Larry Pippen
Katy (†) .... Don Elder Jr.
    City Admin., Johnny Nelson
Kaufman (†)......................William Fortner
    City Mgr., Curtis Snow
*Keene (†)................... Roy W. Robinson
    City Admin., James Minor
Keller (†) .... Pat McGrail
    City Mgr., Dan O'Leary
*Kemah .... Greg Collins
    City Admin., R.W. (Bill) Kerber
Kemp.................................Matt Ganssle
    City Admin., James Stroman
Kempner ....Gene Isenhour
Kendleton ....Darryl K. Humphrey Sr.
Kenedy...............................Randy Garza
    City Mgr., Reggie H. Winters
*Kenefick (3564 FM 1008, Dayton
    77535) ....Keegan Johnson
Kennard ....Jesse Stephens
    City Admin., Mike Deckard
Kennedale (†) ....Bryan Lankhorst
    City Mgr., Bob Hart
*Kerens ....Jeffrey Saunders
    City Admin., Cindy Scott
*Kermit (†) .... Ted Westmoreland
    City Mgr., Sam Watson
Kerrville (†)...................... Todd A. Bock
    City Mgr., Todd Parton
Kilgore (†)...........................Joe T. Parker
    City Mgr., Jeffrey Howell
*Killeen (†)............... Timothy L. Hancock
    City Mgr., Connie J. Green
Kingsville (†)....................Sam R. Fugate
    City Mgr., Carlos R. Yerena
*Kirby (†)................................Ray Martin
    City Mgr., Zina Tedford
*Kirbyville.........................Giles Horn, Sr.
    City Admin., Paul Brister
*Kirvin.......................................(vacancy)
Knollwood (100 Collins Dr., Sherman
    75090) ....Richard R. Roelke

League Park in League City, Galveston County. Ron Billings photo; Texas Forest Service.

*Knox City .... Jeff Stanfield
City Mgr., Barbara Rector
Kosse......................................Ben Daniell
*Kountze ....Fred E. Williams
City Admin., Roderick Hutto
Kress....................................Esther Mount
City Admin., Kenny Hughes
*Krugerville ....Robert Cleversy
Krum .... Terri Wilson
*Kurten .... Ronnie Vitulli
Kyle (†)..........................Miguel Gonzalez
City Mgr., Thomas L. Mattis

— L —

La Coste ....Andy Keller
City Admin., C. George Salzman
Lacy-Lakeview (†).............Calvin Hodde
City Mgr., Michael Nicoletti
*Ladonia (†)...........................Leon Hurse
La Feria (†) ....Stephen Page Brewer
City Mgr., Sunny K. Philip
Lago Vista (†).....................Randy Kruger
City Mgr., Bill Angelo
La Grange (†) ....Janet Moerbe
City Mgr., Shawn Raborn
*La Grulla..................Oscar V. Gonzalez
Laguna Vista ....Susie Houston
City Mgr., Rolando Vela
*La Joya.................William R. (Billy) Leo
City Admin., Mike Alaniz
Lake Bridgeport .... Monty Slayton
Lake City ....Jake Hoskins
*Lake Dallas (†) ....Marjory Johnson
City Mgr., Earl Berner
Lake Jackson (†)....................Bob Sipple
City Mgr., William P. Yenne
Lakeport (207 Milam Rd., Longview 75603) .... Johnny Sammons
Lakeside (San Patricio Co.; Box 787, Mathis 78368)........E.H. (Ed) Gentry Jr.
Lakeside (Tarrant Co.) ....Patrick Jacob
City Admin., Dianna Buchanan
Lakeside City (Box 4287, Wichita Falls 76308) .... Steve Halloway
City Admin., Sam Bownds
*Lake Tanglewood (100 N. Shore Dr., Amarillo 79118) ....John Langford
Lakeview...................................Kelly Clark

Lakeway (†) .... Dave DeOme
City Mgr., Steve Jones
*Lakewood Village ....Frank Jaromin
City Mgr., Angela Rangel
Lake Worth (†)...................Walter Bowen
City Mgr., Brett McGuire
*La Marque (†)...................Larry E. Crow
City Mgr., Robert Ewart
*Lamesa (†) ....Kelvin Barkowsky
City Mgr., Fred Vera
Lampasas (†) ....Judith A. Hetherly
City Mgr., Michael Stoldt
Lancaster (†) ....Marcus E. Knight
City Mgr., Rickey Childers
La Porte (†) ....Barry Beasley
City Mgr., Ron Bottoms
*Laredo (†) ....Raul Salinas
City Mgr., Larry Dovalina
*Latexo...........................Deborah Bruner
La Vernia..........................Harold Schott
*La Villa..............................Rene Castillo
City Mgr., Jaime Gutierrez
Lavon....................Norma Cooper Martin
*La Ward ....Hunter A. Karl
Lawn ....Veronica Burleson
*League City (†) ....Jerry Shults
City Admin., Chris Reed
*Leakey ....Jesse Pendley
*Leander (†)................John D. Cowman
City Mgr., Anthony Johnson
*Leary........ (PO Box 1799, Hooks 75561)
.................................James Palma Sr.
Ledbetter ....(vacancy)
Lefors......................... Michael R. Young
*Leona.............................Travis J. Oden
Leonard ....Willaim J. Yoss
City Admin., George Henderson
Leon Valley............................Chris Riley
City Mgr., Lanny S. Lambert
Leroy....................................David Williams
Levelland (†)...............R.L. (Bo) Bowman
City Mgr., Richard A. Osburn
*Lewisville (†)....................Dean Ueckert
City Mgr., Claude King
Lexington .... Robert Willrich Sr.
*Liberty (†)............................Carl Pickett
Interim City Mgr., Michael Ramirez
Liberty Hill ....Connie Fuller
*Lincoln Park (110 Parker Pkwy., Aubrey

76227) ....Loretta Ray
City Mgr., Nat Parker III
*Lindale............................James Ballard
City Admin., Jim Cox
Linden........................Kenny R. Hamilton
Lindsay ....Steven K. Zwinggi
Lipan.......................................Mike Stowe
*Little Elm (†).......................Charles Platt
City Mgr., Ivan Langford
*Littlefield (†).....................Shirley Mann
City Mgr., Danny Davis
*Little River-Academy (Box 521, Little River 76554)............. Ronnie W. White
Live Oak (†)...............Joseph W. Painter
City Mgr., Matthew Smith
*Liverpool......................Michael Peters
Livingston ....Clarke Evans
City Mgr., Marilyn Sutton
*Llano...................................Mike Reagor
City Mgr., John T. Montgomery
Lockhart (†).....................James Bertram
City Mgr., Vance Rodgers
*Lockney.............................Rodger Stapp
City Admin., Ron Hall
Log Cabin (†) ....Billy Goodwin
*Lometa ....Mike McGarry
*Lone Oak...................Harold Slemmons
*Lone Star.........................Dinah Rushing
Longview (†)...............................Jay Dean
City Mgr., David Willard
*Loraine .... Ina Vay McAdams
*Lorena ....Stacy Garvin
City Mgr., John Moran
Lorenzo.........................Lester C. Bownds
City Mgr., Jim Lively
Los Fresnos (†)....David N. Winstead Sr.
City Mgr., Mark W. Milum
*Los Indios ....Diamantina Bennett
Los Ybañez....................Mary A. Ybañez
City Mgr., John Henry Castillo
*Lott ....Juanita Hogg
Lovelady ....Michael R. Broxson
Lowry Crossing (1405 S. Bridgefarmer Rd., McKinney 75069) Derek Stephens
Lubbock (†) ....Tom Martin
City Mgr., Lee Ann Dumbauld
Lucas (†) ....Bill Carmickle
City Mgr., Robert Patrick
Lueders..............................Danny Dillard

*Lufkin (†)...........................Jack Gorden
  City Mgr., Paul Parker
Luling (†) ....Mike Hendricks
  City Mgr., Robert W. Berger
*Lumberton ....Don Surratt
  City Mgr., Norman P. Reynolds
Lyford.........................Henry de la Paz Jr.
Lytle .... Mark L. Bowen
  City Admin., Josie Campa

— M —

Mabank .... Larry Teague
  City Admin., Louann Confer
Madisonville .... Don F. Dean
  City Mgr., Paul Catoe
*Magnolia........................ Jimmy Thornton
*Malakoff............................ Pat Isaacson
  City Admin., Glen Herriage, Ann Baker
Malone .... Ovie Kettler
Manor (†) .... Joe Sanchez
  City Mgr., Phil Tate
Mansfield (†).....................David L. Cook
  City Mgr., Clayton W. Chandler
Manvel ....Delores M. Martin
*Marble Falls (†)........Raymond Whitman
  City Mgr., (vacant)
Marfa...........................Daniel P. Dunlap
  City Admin., James R. Mustard Jr.
Marietta........................... Lynda Shaddix
Marion................................ Glenn A. Hild
*Marlin (†).............Norman D. Erskine
  City Mgr., Randall Holly
Marquez..................................Kim Smith
Marshall (†)..........William (Buddy) Power
  City Mgr., Frank Johnson
Marshall Creek (Box 1070, Roanoke
  76262) ....James Stimpson
Mart..............................Norman Hopping
Martindale.....................Cynthia Williams
Mason .... Brent Hinckley
  City Admin., (vacant)
*Matador ....Pat Smith
*Mathis (†) .... Mario Alonzo
  City Admin., Manuel Lara
Maud .... (vacant)
  City Mgr., Pat McCoy
Maypearl ....John Wayne Pruitt
McAllen (†) .... Richard F. Cortez
  City Mgr., Mike R. Perez

McCamey........................ Sherry Phillips
McGregor (†) ....James S. Hering
  City Mgr., Joseph Portugal
McKinney (†) .... Brian Loughmiller
  City Mgr., Frank Ragan
*McLean.............................Bobby Martin
*McLendon-Chisholm (1248 St Hwy 205
  S Rockwall 75032) ... Michael Donegan
  City Admin., David Butler
Meadow (†) ....Eloisa Cuellar
Meadowlakes ....John Aaron
  City Admin., Johnnie Thompson
Meadows Place..... Charles D. Jessup IV
Megargel..........................Danny Fails
Melissa................................. Reed Greer
  City Admin., Jason Little
*Melvin .... Ceth Holubec
  City Admin., Mike Hagan
*Memphis....................Robert C. Maddox
*Menard .... Johnny L. Brown
  City Admin., Sharon L. Key
*Mercedes (†) ....Joel Quintanilla
  City Mgr., Ricardo Garcia
Meridian...........................Jeffery Keese
  City Mgr., Marie Garland
*Merkel................................Rusty Watts
  City Mgr., Donnie Edwards
Mertens............................... Joey Watson
Mertzon.........................Arthur (Art) Uber
  Co-Admins., David Harris, Linda Harris
Mesquite (†)......................John Monaco
  City Mgr., Ted Barron
*Mexia (†)...........................Steve Brewer
  City Mgr., Carolyn Martin
Miami ....Chad Breeding
*Midland (†) .... Michael J. Canon
  City Mgr., Rick Menchaca
Midlothian (†) .... Boyce L. Whatley
  City Mgr., Don Hastings
Midway (†) .........................J.W. Williams
*Milano.................................Billy Barnett
Mildred.............(5417 FM 637, Corsicana
  75109) ....Robert Duane Carpenter
Miles...................................Juan Ornelas
Milford...................................John Knight
Miller's Cove (PO Box 300 Winfield
  75493) ....Grady Hughes
*Millsap .... Jamie French
Mineola .........................E.F. (Bo) Whitus

City Admin., David Stevenson
*Mineral Wells (†)....................Mike Allen
  City Mgr., Lance Howerton
Mingus ....Milo Moffit
*Mission (†) .... Norberto Salinas
  City Mgr., Julio Cerda
Missouri City (†)....................Allen Owen
  City Mgr., Frank Simpson
Mobeetie...........................Gordon Estes
Mobile City ..(824 Lilac, Rockwall 75087)
  .... Wanda Cooper
*Monahans (†)..............David B. Cutbirth
  City Mgr., David Mills
Mont Belvieu ....Nick Dixon
  City Admin., Bryan Easum
Montgomery .... Travis Mabry
  City Admin., Brant Gary
*Moody................................Michael Alton
  City Admin., Charleen Dowell
*Moore Station (4818 FM 314
  S, LaRue 75770) .... Arthur T. Earl
Moran .... Lisa Clopton
Morgan................. Jonathan W. Croom II
*Morgan's Point ....Patricia Grimes
  City Admin., Ken Bays
Morgan's Point Resort ... James Enyeart
  City Mgr., Stacy Wayne Hitchman
Morton .... Raymond G. Martinez
  City Mgr., Brenda Shaw
Moulton.......................... Cindy McIntosh
  City Admin., Deck Shaver Jr.
*Mountain City .... (Box 1494, Buda
  78610) .... Rick Tarr
  City Mgr., Jeff Radke
Mount Calm ....Jimmy Tucker
*Mount Enterprise.......... Harvey Graves
  City Mgr., Rosena J. Becker-Ross
Mount Pleasant (†)............Jerry Boatner
  City Mgr., Mike Ahrens
Mount Vernon.............J.D. Baumgardner
  City Admin., Lee Elliott
Muenster........................... Johnny Pagel
  City Admin., Stan Endres
Muleshoe (†)........................... Cliff Black
  City Mgr., David Brunson
*Mullin..................................Larry Reese
*Munday........................... Robert Bowen
  City Admin., Dwayne Bearden
Murchison ....Mike Hill

The Presidio County Courthouse in Marfa. Ron Billings photo; Texas Forest Service.

Murphy (†) ....Bret Baldwin
City Mgr., James Fisher
*Mustang ....(Box 325, Corsicana
75151) ....Jackie Bounds
Mustang Ridge ....Alfred Vallejo II

— N —

*Nacogdoches (†) .... Roger Van Horn
City Mgr., James P. Jeffers
*Naples ....John R. Anthony
Nash ....David H. Slaton
City Mgr., Elizabeth Lea
*Nassau Bay (†) (1800 NASA Rd. 1,
Houston 77058).........Donald C. Matter
City Mgr., John D. Kennedy
Natalia (†) ....Ruberta C. Vera
City Mgr., Beth Leonesio
Navarro (222 S. Harvard Ave., Corsicana
75109) ....Pam Chapman
Navasota (†) ....Bert Miller
City Mgr., Brad Stafford
*Nazareth ....Ralph Brockman
Nederland (†)..............R.A. (Dick) Nugent
City Mgr., Chris Duque
*Needville ....Delbert Wendt
*Nevada ....Christy Schell
Newark................................Matt Newby
New Berlin..............(275 FM 2538 Seguin
78155) ....Gilbert R. Merkle
New Boston...............Johnny L. Branson
*New Braunfels (†)..............Bruce Boyer
City Mgr., Michael Morrison
Newcastle ....Darlton Dyer
*New Chapel Hill (14039 Cty. Rd. 220,
Tyler 75707) ....Robert Whitaker
*New Deal ....Christopher Bruce
New Fairview ....Joe Max Wilson
*New Home ....Steve Lisemby
*New Hope (Box 562, McKinney 75070)
Johnny Hamm
New London ....Patrick Dailey
New Summerfield ....Jane Barrow
Newton...............................Rachel Martin
City Admin., Donald H. Meek
*New Waverly ....Dan Underwood
*Neylandville (2469 Cty. Rd. 4311, Green-
ville 75401) ....Kathy Wilson
Niederwald ....Reynell Smith
City Admin., Richard L. Crandal Jr.
*Nixon ....Don Chessher
City Admin., Marilyn Byrd
*Nocona ....Robert H. Fenoglio
City Mgr., Lynn Henley
Nolanville.........................James Cole Sr.
Noonday ....(Box 6425, Tyler 75711)
..................................J. Mike Turman
Nordheim........................Katherine Payne
*Normangee ....Tim Taylor
*North Cleveland (Box 1266, Cleveland
77327) ....Robert Bartlett
Northlake ....(Box 729, Justin 76247)
..................................Peter Dewing
City Admin., Drew Corn
North Richland Hills (†)....Oscar Trevino
City Mgr., Larry J. Cunningham
Novice...............................Wanda Motley

— O —

*Oak Grove ..(Box 309, Kaufman 75142)
..................................Jerry G. Holder
Oak Leaf ....Paul Klooster
*Oak Point ....Duane Olson
City Mgr., (vacant)
Oak Ridge (Cooke Co.; 129 Oak Ridge
Dr., Gainesville 76240).. Chad Ramsey
Oak Ridge (Kaufman Co.; Box 458,
Kaufman 75142)..........Roy W. Perkins
Oak Ridge North ....Fred R. O'Connor
City Mgr., Paul Mendes
Oak Valley (2211 Oak Valley, Corsicana
75110) ....Linda Bennett
*Oakwood ....Teresa Brewer
O'Brien.............................Richard Garcia

*Odem.....................Jessie Rodriguez Sr.
Odessa (†) ....Larry L. Melton
City Mgr., Richard N. Morton
*O'Donnell ....James E. Williams
Oglesby ....Melissa Wells
*Old River-Winfree ....Joe Landry
Olmos Park (119 W. El Prado Dr., San
Antonio 78212) .... Ronald G. Tefteller
City Mgr., Amy Buckert
Olney (†)......................Brenda Stennett
City Admin., Danny C. Parker
Olton ....Mark McFadden
City Mgr., Marvin Tillman
Omaha ....Greg Blair
Onalaska.................................Lew Vail
Opdyke West (Box 1179, Levelland
79336)..........................Wayne Riggins
*Orange (†) ....William Brown Claybar
City Mgr., Shawn Oubre
*Orange Grove ....Seale Brand
City Admin., Perry R. Young
Orchard.........................Rodney Pavlock
*Ore City ....Glenn Breazeale
Overton.......................John Edd Welch
City Mgr., B.J. Potts
*Ovilla ....Bill Turner
City Admin., Randall Whiteman
*Oyster Creek.....................Louis Guidry

— P —

*Paducah ....Henry Michael
Paint Rock ....Duane J. Schniers
*Palacios (†) ....Joseph Morton
City Mgr., Charles R. Winfield
Palestine (†) ....Robert Herrington
City Mgr., R. Dale Brown
*Palisades (115 Brentwood Rd., Amarillo
79118) ....Tommy Medlin
*Palmer ....Don Huskins
Palmhurst ....Ramiro J. Rodriguez Jr.
City Mgr., Lori A. Lopez
Palm Valley (1313 Stuart Place Rd., Har-
lingen 78552).......................Dean Hall
*Palmview ....Jorge G. García
City Mgr., John V. Alaniz
Pampa (†) ....Lonny Robbins
City Mgr., Richard Morris
*Panhandle.........................Dan Looten
City Mgr., Loren Brand
Panorama Village ......Howard L. Kravetz
*Pantego ....Dorothy Anderhult
City Mgr., Doug Davis
Paradise....................Nathan C. Cleveland
Paris (†) ....Jesse James Freelen
City Mgr., Kevin Carruth
*Parker ....Jerry Tartaglino
City Admin., Dina J. Daniel
*Pasadena (†).....................Joe Cordina
Pattison ....Bill Matthews
*Patton Village (16940 Main St., Splen-
dora 77372) .... Pamela (Vikki) Muñoz
Payne Springs ........................J.T. Noble
*Pearland (†)..........................Tom Reid
City Mgr., Bill Eisen
Pearsall (†) ....George Cabasos
City Mgr., José G. Treviño
*Pecan Gap...................Warner Cheney
Pecan Hill ....Howard Hobbs
Pecos (†)..................Richard L. Alligood
City Mgr., Joseph Torres
Pelican Bay ....Sandy Tolbert
*Penelope ....Inez Arriola
Peñitas.............................Marcos Ochoa
City Admin., Juan Ortiz
Perryton...........................David C. Hale
City Mgr., David Landis
Petersburg.........................Darin Greene
City Mgr., Marie Parr
*Petrolia ....Cindy Armour
Petronila (2475 Cty. Rd. 69, Robstown
78380).........................Dan Burkhardt
*Pflugerville (†) ....Jeff Coleman
Interim City Mgr., Lauri Gillam

*Pharr (†) ....Leopoldo (Leo) Palacios
City Mgr., Fred Sandoval
Pilot Point...........................Janet Groff
City Admin., J.C. Hughes
Pine Forest ....(305 Nagel Dr., Vidor
77662) ....Daniel J. Peno
Pinehurst (3640 Mockingbird, Orange
77630) ........................T.W. Permenter
City Admin., Robert Ewart
Pine Island (20005 Pine Island Rd.,
Hempstead 77445)...........Debra Ferris
Pineland.............................Randy Burch
City Admin., Chuck Corley
Piney Point Village (7676 Woodway Dr.,
#300, Houston 77063)
..............................Karen Bresenhan
City Admin., Terri J. Johnson
Pittsburg........................Shawn Kennington
Interim City Mgr., Margaret Jackson
*Plains...........................Pamela Redman
City Admin., Terry B. Howard
Plainview (†)..................John C. Anderson
City Mgr., Greg Ingham
*Plano (†) ....Phil Dyer
City Mgr., Thomas H. Muehlenbeck
Pleak, Village of (6621 FM 2218 S., Rich-
mond 77469) ....Margie Krenek
Pleasanton (†)......................Bill Carroll
City Mgr., Kathy Coronado
*Pleasant Valley (4006 Bs. 287 J, Iowa
Park 76367)...........Raymond Haynes
City Mgr., Norm Hodges
*Plum Grove (Box 1358, Splendora
77372) ............................T.W. Garrett
Point....................................Minda Painter
Point Blank.......................Steve Sasser
Point Comfort....................Pam Lambden
*Point Venture ....Richard Shinn
Ponder ....Jeff Vardell
Port Aransas (†)..............Claude Brown
City Mgr., Michael Kovacs
*Port Arthur (†)..............Oscar G. Ortiz
City Mgr., Steve Fitzgibbons
Port Isabel (†)....................Joe E. Vega
City Mgr., Edward Meza
Portland (†)......................David R. Krebs
City Mgr., Michael Tanner
Port Lavaca (†)................Jack Whitlow
City Mgr., Gary L. Broz
Port Neches (†) ....R. Glenn Johnson
City Mgr., André Wimer
Post ....Theressa Harp
City Mgr., Arbie Taylor
*Post Oak Bend (1175 Cty. Rd. 278,
Kaufman 75142).......Raymond Bedrick
*Poteet ....Lino Z. Donato
City Admin., Adolfo F. Rodriguez
Poth...................................Chrystal Eckel
Pottsboro.......................... Frank Budra
City Mgr., Kevin M. Farley
*Powell ....Dennis Bancroft
Poynor ....Dannie Smith
*Prairie View...............Frank D. Jackson
*Premont............................Norma Tullos
*Presidio ....Lorenzo P. Hernandez
City Admin., Brad Newton
Primera ....Rudy Garza Jr.
City Admin., Javier Mendez
*Princeton.................Steven Deffibaugh
City Admin., Lesia Thornhill
*Progreso ....Omar Vela
City Admin., Alfredo (Fred) Espinosa
Progreso Lakes (Box 760, Progreso
78579) ..................O.D. (Butch) Emery
Prosper (†) ....Charles E. Niswanger
Town Mgr., Mike Land
*Putnam ....Roy Petty
Pyote.................................. Willie Bates

— Q —

Quanah (†).......................Gary Newsom
City Admin., Danny Felty
Queen City.........................Harold Martin

*Quinlan .... Sharon Royal
Quintana .... Wallace Neeley
*Quitaque .... Clyde Dudley
City Mgr., Maria Cruz Merrell
Quitman .... Jerry Edwards

— R —

Ralls .... Kelly Wing
City Admin., J. Rhett Parker
Rancho Viejo .... Roberto Medrano
Town Admin., Cheryl J. Kretz
Ranger (†) .... John Casey
*Rangerville (31850 Rangerville Rd., San
Benito 78586) .... Wayne Halbert
Rankin .... Timothy Potter
Ransom Canyon ...... Robert G. Englund
City Admin., Murvat Musa
Ravenna .... Claude L. Lewis
Raymondville .... Orlando A. Correa
City Mgr., Eleazar Garcia Jr.
Red Lick .... (Box 870, Nash 75569)
.... Sheila K. Kegley
Red Oak (†) .... Alan Hugley
City Mgr., Tim Kelty
Redwater .... Beverly Phares
*Refugio .... Ray Jaso
Reklaw .... Gilbert Stafford
Reno (Lamar Co.) .... William Heuberger
Reno (Parker Co.; 195 W. Reno Rd., Azle
76020) .... Roen Cox
Retreat (621 N. Spikes Rd., Corsicana
75110) .... Janice Barfknecht
*Rhome .... Mark Lorance
*Rice .... Larry Bailey
*Richardson (†) .... Steve Mitchell
City Mgr., Bill Keffler
Richland .... Dolores Baldwin
*Richland Hills (†) .... David L. Ragan
City Mgr., James W. Quin
Richland Springs .... Jerry M. Benton
Richmond .... Hilmar G. Moore
City Mgr., R. Glen Gilmore
Richwood .... Michael Johnson
*Riesel .... David Guenat, Jr.
City Admin., Bill McLelland
*Rio Bravo (1402 Centeno Ln., Laredo
78046) .... Juan G. Gonzalez
Rio Grande City (†) ... Ruben O. Villarreal
City Admin., Juan F. Zuniga
*Rio Hondo .... Santiago A. Saldana Jr.
City Admin., Arturo F. Prida
*Rio Vista .... William Keith Hutchinson
Rising Star .... Mike McGinn
City Admin., Josh Constancio
River Oaks (†) .... Herman D. Earwood
City Admin., Marvin Gregory
*Riverside .... G. Frank Rich
City Mgr., Joan Harvey
*Roanoke .... Carl E. Gierisch Jr.
City Mgr., Jimmy Stathatos
Roaring Springs .... Corky Marshall
City Mgr., Robert Osborn
Robert Lee .... Joe V. White
*Robinson .... Bryan Ferguson
City Mgr., R.C. Fletcher
*Robstown (†) .... Rodrigo Ramon Jr.
Roby .... Eli Sepeda
City Mgr., Jack W. Brown
*Rochester .... Marvin Stegemoeller
City Mgr., Gregg Hearn
Rockdale (†) .... John C. Shoemake
City Mgr., Kelvin Knauf
Rockport (†) .... Todd W. Pearson
City Mgr., Thomas J. Blazek
Rocksprings .... LaWanda Goller
Rockwall (†) .... William R. Cecil
City Mgr., Julie Couch
*Rocky Mound .... (Box 795, Pittsburg
75686) .... Noble T. Smith
*Rogers .... Billy Ray Crow
Rollingwood .... Dale Dingley
City Admin., Vicky Rudy
Roma (†) .... Rogelio Ybarra
City Mgr., Crisanto Salinas

Roman Forest .... Floyd O. Jackson Jr.
*Ropesville .... Victor Marrett
Roscoe .... Frank S. (Pete) Porter
City Admin., Cody Thompson
Rosebud .... Ken Hensel
City Mgr., Eric Kuykendall
Rose City .... David E. Bush
Rose Hill Acres (100 Jordan Rd., Lum-
berton 77657) .... Rick Thomisee
*Rosenberg (†) .... Joe M. Gurecky
City Mgr., Jack S. Hamlett
Ross .... James L. Jaska Sr.
Rosser .... Shannon Rex Corder
Rotan .... Jerry A. Marshall
City Admin., Carla Thornton
*Round Mountain .... Alvin Gutierrez
Round Rock (†) .... Alan McGraw
City Mgr., Jim Nuse
Round Top .... Barnell Albers
Rowlett (†) .... John E. Harper
City Mgr., Lynda K. Humble
Roxton .... James (Jimmy) Cooper
*Royse City .... Jim Mellody
City Mgr., Karen Philippi
Rule .... James M. Marquis
Runaway Bay, City of .... A.L. (Len) Jowitt
City Admin., Mike Jump
Runge .... Homer Lott Jr.
Rusk (†) .... Angela Raiborn
City Mgr., Mike Murray

— S —

Sabinal .... Louis A. Landeros Jr.
Sachse (†) .... Mike J. Felix
City Mgr., Allen Barnes
Sadler .... Jaime Harris
*Saginaw (†) .... Gary Brinkley
City Mgr., Nan Stanford
Saint Hedwig .... Mary Jo Dylla
Saint Jo .... Tom Weger
Saint Paul .... Opie Walter
Salado .... Merle Stalcup
*San Angelo (†) .... (vacant)
City Mgr., Harold Dominguez
*San Antonio (†) .... Julián Castro
City Mgr., Sheryl L. Sculley
*San Augustine .... Leroy Hughes
City Mgr., James Duke Lyons Jr.
*San Benito (†) .... Joe Hernandez
City Mgr., Victor Trevino
*Sanctuary .... (Box 125, Azle 76098)
.... Cliff Scallan
San Diego .... Rupert Canales III
City Mgr., Ernesto Sanchez Jr.
*Sandy Point .... Curt Mowery
*San Felipe .... Bobby Byars
Sanford .... Rodney Ormon
Sanger (†) .... Joe Higgs
City Mgr., Mike Brice
San Juan (†) .... Pedro Contreras
City Mgr., Antonio (Tony) Garza
San Leanna (Box 1107, Manchaca
78652) .... Joel Chapa
City Admin., Kathleen Lessing
San Marcos (†) .... Susan Narvaiz
City Mgr., Rick Menchaca
*San Patricio (4615 Main, Mathis 78368)
.... Lonnie Glasscock III
*San Perlita .... Oscar de Luna
San Saba .... Kenneth Jordan
City Mgr., Stan Weik
*Sansom Park (5500 Buchanan St., Fort
Worth 76114) .... Robert Armstrong
Santa Anna .... Nancy Wylie
Santa Clara ...... (Box 429, Marion 78124)
.... David D. Mueller
Santa Fe (†) .... Ralph W. Stenzel Jr.
City Mgr., Joe Dickson
Santa Rosa .... America Gonzales
City Mgr., Rey Treviño
Savoy .... Charles Downs
Schertz (†) .... Harold D. (Hal) Baldwin
City Mgr., Don E. Taylor
Schulenburg .... Roger Moellenberndt

City Admin., Ronald Brossmann
Scotland .... Robert J. Krahl
*Scottsville .... Walter Johnson
Scurry .... Robert N. Stewart
Seabrook (†) .... Gary Renola
City Mgr., Chuck Pinto
*Seadrift .... Billy F. Ezell
City Mgr., Paula Moncrief
*Seagoville (†) .... Sydney Sexton Jr.
City Mgr., Denny Wheat
Seagraves .... Ovidio Martinez Jr.
Sealy (†) .... Nick Tirey
City Mgr., Chris Coffman
Seguin (†) .... Betty Ann Matthies
City Mgr., Douglas Faseler
Selma .... Jim Parma
City Admin., Kenneth Roberts
Seminole (†) .... Wayne Mixon
City Admin., Tommy Phillips
*Seven Oaks ... (Box 540, Leggett 77350)
.... Anna Wallace
*Seven Points .... Gerald E. Taylor
Seymour .... Ronald B. Reeves
City Admin., Joe Shephard
Shady Shores (Box 362, Lake Dallas
75065) .... Olive Stephens
Shallowater .... Robert Olmsted
*Shamrock .... Wendell Morgan
City Mgr., Johnny W. Rhodes
Shavano Park .... David Marne
City Mgr., Manuel Longoria Jr.
Shenandoah .... Garry B. Watts
City Admin., Chip VanSteenberg
Shepherd .... Pat A. Lunsford
*Sherman (†) .... Bill Magers
City Mgr., George Olson
Shiner .... Fred Henry Hilscher
*Shoreacres .... Jayo Washington
City Admin., David K. Stall
*Silsbee (†) .... Herbert Muckleroy
City Mgr., Tommy Barosh
*Silverton .... Lane B. Garvin
City Admin., Jerry Patton
Simonton .... Louis J. Boudreaux
*Sinton (†) .... Jessica Thomas Bates
City Mgr., Jackie Knox Jr.
Skellytown .... Randy Ruth
*Slaton (†) .... Laura Lynn Wilson
City Admin., Roger McKinney
*Smiley .... Donald Janicek
*Smithville .... Mark A. Bunte
City Mgr., Tex Middlebrook
Smyer .... Mary Beth Sims
*Snook .... John W. See III
Snyder (†) .... Francene Allen-Noah
City Mgr., Merle Taylor
Socorro (†) .... Trini Lopez
Interim City Mgr., Manny Soto
Somerset .... Paul G. Cuellar
City Admin., Miguel Cantu
*Somerville .... Tommy Thompson
City Admin., Barbara J. Pederson
*Sonora .... Gloria Lopez
City Mgr. JIm Polonis
*Sour Lake .... Bruce Robinson
City Mgr., Larry Saurage
*South Houston .... Joe Soto
Southlake (†) .... John Terrell
City Mgr., Shana Yelverton
Southmayd .... Daniel F. Pepe
*South Mountain (107 Barton Ln., Gates-
ville 76528) .... Billy Mayhew
*South Padre Island .... Bob Pinkerton
City Mgr., Dewey P. Cashwell Jr.
Southside Place (6309 Edloe St., Hous-
ton 77005) .... Richard L. Rothfelder
City Mgr., David N. Moss
Spearman .... Brian Gillispie
City Mgr., Edward Hansen
*Splendora .... Carol W. Carley
Spofford .... Alex Solis
*Springlake .... Harlon Watson
*Springtown .... Doug Hughes
City Admin., Mark Krey

Dusk falls at Town Center in Southlake, Tarrant County. Lamberto Alvarez photo.

*Spring Valley (1025 Campbell Rd., Houston 77055)..... T. Michael Andrews
City Admin., Richard Rockenbaugh
*Spur...........................Kenneth Gilcrease
Stafford (†) ....Leonard Scarcella
Stagecoach ....William Berger
*Stamford (†) .... Johnny Anders
City Mgr., Roy Rice
Stanton ....Lester Baker
City Admin., Danny Fryar
Staples.............................. Eddie Daffern
Star Harbor ... (Box 949, Malakoff 75148)
.... Duane Smith
Stephenville (†) ....Nancy A. Hunter
City Admin., Mark A. Kaiser
Sterling City ....Gregory Tatro
Stinnett ....Billy Murphy
City Mgr., Mike Lamberson
Stockdale...........................Johnny Stahl
City Mgr., Harry Grove
*Stratford ....David Brown
City Admin., Sean Hardman
Strawn.................................David G. Day
Streetman ....Johnny A. Robinson
Sudan.......................Robert K. Sisson Jr.
*Sugar Land (†) ....James A Thompson
City Mgr., Allen Bogard
*Sullivan City...........Rosendo Benavides
City Mgr., Rolando Gonzalez
Sulphur Springs (†) .... Gary Spraggins
City Mgr., Marc Maxwell
*Sundown .... Jim Winn
City Admin., T. Flemming
*Sunnyvale ....David Byrd
Town Mgr., Scott Campbell
*Sunray ....Casey Stone
City Mgr., Greg Smith
*Sunrise Beach Village......Patricia Frain
*Sunset .... Danny Russell
*Sunset Valley ....Jeff Mills
*Sun Valley (800 Shady Grove Rd., Paris 75462) ....Maria Z. Wagnon
*Surfside Beach ....Larry Davison
Sweeny (†)...........................Kenneth Lott
City Mgr., H.T. (Tim) Moss
Sweetwater (†) ....Gregory L. Wortham
City Mgr., Edward P. Brown

— T —

*Taft...................................Filberto Rivera
City Mgr., Dolores R. Topper
*Tahoka....................Michael R. Mensch
City Admin., Jerry W. Webster
*Talco ...........................K.M. (Mike) Sloan
Talty (9550 Helms Trail, Ste. 500, Forney 75126) .... Carla Milligan
Town Admin., Connie Goodwin
*Tatum..Phil Cory
Taylor (†)....................... Rod Hortenstine
City Mgr., Jim Dunaway
Taylor Lake Village ......Natalie S. O'Neill
*Taylor Landing..................John Durkay
*Teague.........................Jacqueline Utsey
City Admin., Don Doering
Tehuacana .... Doug East
Temple (†).................William A. Jones III
City Mgr., David A. Blackburn
Tenaha ....George N. Bowers
Terrell (†) ....Hal Richards
City Mgr., Torry L. Edwards
Terrell Hills (†).............J. Bradford Camp
City Mgr., James Mark Browne
Texarkana (†)...................Stephen A. Mayo
City Mgr., F. Larry Sullivan
Texas City (†) ....Matthew T. Doyle
*Texhoma................................ Mel Yates
Texline ....Brad Riley
City Mgr., G.A. (Buster) Poling Jr.
The Colony (†)...................Joe McCourry
City Mgr., Dale A. Cheatham
Thompsons .... Freddie Newsome Jr.
*Thorndale.........................Billy Simank
City Admin., Keith Kiesling
Thornton.............. James W. Jackson Jr.
Thorntonville (Box 740, Monahans 79756) ....David Mitchell
*Thrall .... Troy Marx
Three Rivers ....James Liska
City Admin., Marion R. Forehand
*Throckmorton.......................Will Carroll
Tiki Island ....Phillip Hopkins
Timbercreek Canyon (101 S. Timbercreek Dr., Amarillo 79118) .. Terri Welch
City Mgr., Jamie Allen

*Timpson ....Douglas McDonald
Tioga ....Stanley Kemp
Tira (801 Cty. Rd. 4612, Sulphur Springs 75482) ....Floyd Payton
*Toco (2103 Chestnut Dr., Brookston 75421) ....John Jason Waller
*Todd Mission (21718 FM 1774, Plantersville 77363) ....George Coulam
Tolar ....Terry R. Johnson
Tomball (†)....................Gretchen Fagan
City Mgr., Jan Belcher
*Tom Bean .... Tom Wilthers
Tool ....J. Mike Black
*Toyah ....Bart F. Sanchez
Trent...................................Leanna West
Trenton .... Tyler Bowman
Trinidad................................Larry Estes
City Admin., Terri R. Newhouse
Trinity .... Lyle Stubbs
City Mgr., Phil Patchett
Trophy Club (†) ....Connie White
Town Mgr., Brandon Emmons
Troup...................................John Whitsell
City Admin., Russ Obar
Troy .... Jeff Browning
Tulia (†) ....Pat George
City Mgr., Daniel R. Dible
Turkey .... Pat Carson
City Mgr., Jerry Landry
Tuscola ....Russell Bartlett
Tye ....Nancy Moore
Tyler (†)..............................Barbara Bass
City Mgr., Mark McDaniel

— U —

Uhland ....Daniel Heideman
*Uncertain............................ Sam Canup
*Union Grove (RR 2, Box 196-FF, Gladewater 75647)........Randy Simcox
Union Valley ....Chris Elliott
Universal City (†) ....John Williams
City Mgr., Ken Taylor
University Park (†)..James H. Holmes III
City Mgr., Bob Livingston
*Uvalde (†).........................Cody L. Smith
City Mgr., John H. Harrell

— V —

Valentine (†) .... Jesús Calderon
*Valley Mills .... Rodney Nichols
*Valley View .... Carl Kemplin
*Van .... Billy Wilson
   City Admin., Gary McDaniel
Van Alstyne .... Ruth Ann Collins
   City Mgr., Bill Harrington
Van Horn .... Ben Flanagan
*Vega .... Mark J. Groneman
Venus .... Charley Grimes
   City Admin., Jerry Reed
Vernon (†) .... Jeff Bearden
   City Mgr., Mitch Grant
*Victoria (†) .... Will Armstrong
   City Mgr., Charles E. Windwehen
Vidor (†) .... Ray Long
   City Mgr., Ricky Jorgensen
*Village of the Hills .... Virginia W. Jones
   City Admin., Dan Roark
Vinton .... Madeleine Praino
Volente .... Jan Paul Yenawine
Von Ormy .... Art Martinez de Vara

— W —

*Waco (†) .... Virginia DuPuy
   City Mgr., Larry D. Groth
Waelder .... Roy Tovar
Wake Village (†) .... Michael Huddleston
   City Admin., Mike Burke
Waller .... Paul A. Wood
Wallis .... Tony I. Salazar Jr.
Walnut Springs .... Benny Damron
Warren City (3004 George Richey Rd.,
   Gladewater 75647) ..... Ricky J. Wallace
Waskom .... Jesse Moore
Watauga (†) .... Henry J. Jeffries
   City Mgr., Kerry Lacy
Waxahachie (†) .... Ron Wilkinson
   City Mgr., Paul Stevens
Weatherford (†) .... Dennis E. Hooks
   City Mgr., Jerry Blaisdell
*Webberville .... Hector Gonzales
*Webster (†) .... Donna Rogers
   City Mgr., Michael W. Jez
*Weimar .... Bennie Kosler
   City Mgr., Randal W. Jones
*Weinert .... Julian Estrada
*Weir .... Charles Mervin Walker
*Wellington .... Gary Brewer
   City Mgr., Jon Sessions
Wellman .... Kent Davis
Wells .... Corbitt Doss
   City Coor., Lynette Duren
*Weslaco (†) .... Hector De La Rosa
   City Mgr., Anthony Covacevich
West .... Jerrel Bolton
*Westbrook .... Ramiro Fuentes
West Columbia .... Laurie Beal Kincannon
   City Mgr., Debbie Sutherland
*Westlake .... Laura Wheat
   Town Mgr., Tom Brymer
West Lake Hills .... Dave Claunch
   City Admin., Robert Wood
Weston .... Scott Morrissey
Weston Lakes .... Mary Rose Zdunkewicz
West Orange (†) .... Roy C. McDonald
Westover Hills (5824 Merrymount, Fort
   Worth 76107) .... Earle A. Shields Jr.
   City Admin., James Rutledge
West Tawakoni .... Pete Yoho
   City Admin., Cloy Richards
West University Place (†) .... Bob Kelly
   City Mgr., Michael Ross
*Westworth Village (311 Burton Hill Rd.,
   Fort Worth 76114) .... Ray Landy
   City Admin., Gary Robinson
Wharton (†) .... David W. Samuelson
   City Mgr., Andres Garza Jr.
*Wheeler .... Wanda Herd
*White Deer .... Dick Pierce
Whiteface .... Vernon Shellenberger
*Whitehouse (†) .... B.D. Jacobson

The historic suspension bridge in Waco was completed in 1869. Ron Billings photo. Texas Forest Service.

   City Mgr., Ronny Fite
*White Oak .... Tim Vaughn
   City Coor., Ralph J. Weaver
Whitesboro .... W.D. (Dee) Welch
   City Admin., Michael Marter
White Settlement (†) .... Jerry R. Burns
   City Mgr., Jimmy Burnett
Whitewright .... Bill Goodson
Whitney .... Gwen Evans
   City Admin., Chuck L. Upton
Wichita Falls (†) .... Lanham Lyne
   City Mgr., Darron Leiker
Wickett .... Harold Ferguson
Willis (†) .... Leonard Reed
   City Mgr., James H. McAlister
*Willow Park .... Brad Johnson
   City Admin., Claud Arnold
*Wills Point .... Scott McGriff
   City Mgr., Fred H. Hays
*Wilmer .... Don Hudson
   City Admin., Bobbie Jo Martinez
*Wilson .... Victor Steinhauser
Wimberley .... Tom Haley
   City Admin., Don Ferguson
*Windcrest .... Jack H. Leonhardt
   City Admin., Ronnie Cain
*Windom .... B.J.Stallings
*Windthorst .... Sue C. Steinberger
   City Mgr., Donald Frerich
Winfield .... John Walton
Wink .... Gregory J. Rogers
Winnsboro .... Carolyn S. Jones
   City Admin., Nina Browning
*Winona .... Rusty Smith

   City Admin., James Bixler
*Winters .... Nelan Bahlman
   City Mgr., Aref Hassan
Wixon Valley (9500 E. St. Hwy. 21, Bryan
   77808) .... Ruby Clara Andrews
Wolfe City .... Bryan Creed
Wolfforth .... L.C. Childers
   City Mgr., Frankie Pittman
*Woodbranch Village (58-A Woodbranch,
   New Caney 77357) ...... Chuch Cardoza
Woodcreek .... Eric Eskelund
   City Admin., Pieter Sybeswa
Woodloch .....(Box 1379, Conroe 77305)
   .... Diane L. Lincoln
Woodsboro .... George Hernandez Sr.
*Woodson .... Bobby Mathiews
*Woodville .... Tony Castillo
   City Admin., George K. Jones
Woodway (†) .... Donald J. Baker
   City Mgr., Yousry Zakhary
Wortham .... Kenneth Gibbs
Wylie (†) .... Eric Hogue
   City Mgr., Mindy Manson

— Y —

Yantis .... Jerry E. Miller
Yoakum (†) .... Anita R. Rodriguez
   City Mgr., Calvin Cook
*Yorktown .... Renee Hernandez

— Z —

*Zavalla .... Hulon Miller ☆

Regional Councils of Government

Source: Texas Association of Regional Councils; www.txregionalcouncil.org/

The concept of regional planning and cooperation, fostered by enabling legislation in 1965, has spread across Texas since organization of the North Central Texas Council of Governments in 1966.

Regional councils are voluntary associations of local governments that deal with problems and planning needs that cross the boundaries of individual local governments or that require regional attention.

These concerns include criminal justice, emergency communications, job-training programs, solid-waste management, transportation and water-quality management. The councils make recommendations to member governments and may assist in implementing the plans.

The Texas Association of Regional Councils is at 701 Brazos, Ste. 780, Austin 78701; (512) 478-4715. Financing is provided by local, state and federal governments.

Following is a list of the 24 regional councils, member counties, executive director and contact information. *See page 70 for a map of the 24 regions.*

1. Panhandle Regional Planning Commission: Armstrong, Briscoe, Carson, Castro, Childress, Collingsworth, Dallam, Deaf Smith, Donley, Gray, Hall, Hansford, Hartley, Hemphill, Hutchinson, Lipscomb, Moore, Ochiltree, Oldham, Parmer, Potter, Randall, Roberts, Sherman, Swisher and Wheeler. **Gary Pitner,** PO Box 9257, Amarillo 79105-9257; (806) 372-3381; www.prpc.cog.tx.us.

2. South Plains Association of Governments: Bailey, Cochran, Crosby, Dickens, Floyd, Garza, Hale, Hockley, King, Lamb, Lubbock, Lynn, Motley, Terry and Yoakum. **Tim Pierce,** PO Box 3730, Lubbock 79452-3730; (806) 762-8721; www.spag.org.

3. Nortex Regional Planning Commission: Archer, Baylor, Clay, Cottle, Foard, Hardeman, Jack, Montague, Wichita, Wilbarger and Young. **Dennis Wilde,** PO Box 5144, Wichita Falls 76307-5144; (940) 322-5281; www.nortexrpc.org.

4. North Central Texas Council of Governments: Collin, Dallas, Denton, Ellis, Erath, Hood, Hunt, Johnson, Kaufman, Navarro, Palo Pinto, Parker, Rockwall, Somervell, Tarrant and Wise. **R. Michael Eastland,** PO Box 5888, Arlington 76005-5888; (817) 640-3300; www.nctcog.org.

5. Ark-Tex Council of Governments: Bowie, Cass, Delta, Franklin, Hopkins, Lamar, Morris, Red River, Titus and Miller County, Ark. **L.D. Williamson,** 4808 Elizabeth St., Texarkana 75503; (903) 832-8636; www.atcog.org.

6. East Texas Council of Governments: Anderson, Camp, Cherokee, Gregg, Harrison, Henderson, Marion, Panola, Rains, Rusk, Smith, Upshur, Van Zandt and Wood. **David Cleveland,** 3800 Stone Rd., Kilgore 75662; (903) 984-8641; www.etcog.org.

7. West Central Texas Council of Governments: Brown, Callahan, Coleman, Comanche, Eastland, Fisher, Haskell, Jones, Kent, Knox, Mitchell, Nolan, Runnels, Scurry, Shackelford, Stephens, Stonewall, Taylor and Throckmorton. **Tom Smith,** PO Box 3195, Abilene 79601; (325) 672-8544; www.wctcog.org.

8. Rio Grande Council of Governments: Brewster, Culberson, El Paso, Hudspeth, Jeff Davis, Presidio and Doña Ana County, N.M. **Annette Gutierrez,** 1100 N. Stanton, Ste. 610, El Paso 79902; (915) 533-0998; www.riocog.org.

9. Permian Basin Regional Planning Commission: Andrews, Borden, Crane, Dawson, Ector, Gaines, Glasscock, Howard, Loving, Martin, Midland, Pecos, Reeves, Terrell, Upton, Ward and Winkler. **Terri Moore,** PO Box 60660, Midland 79711-0660; (432) 563-1061.

10. Concho Valley Council of Governments: Coke, Concho, Crockett, Irion, Kimble, Mason, McCulloch, Menard, Reagan, Schleicher, Sterling, Sutton and Tom Green. **Jeffrey Sutton,** Box 60050, San Angelo 76906-0050; (325) 944-9666; www.cvcog.org.

11. Heart of Texas Council of Governments: Bosque, Falls, Freestone, Hill, Limestone and McLennan. **Kenneth Simons,** PO Box 20847, Waco 76711; (254) 292-1800; www.hotcog.org.

12. Capital Area Council of Governments: Bastrop, Blanco, Burnet, Caldwell, Fayette, Hays, Lee, Llano, Travis and Williamson. **Betty Voights,** 6800 Burleson Rd., Bldg. 310, Ste. 165, Austin 78744-; (512) 916-6000; www.capcog.org.

13. Brazos Valley Council of Governments: Brazos, Burleson, Grimes, Leon, Madison, Robertson and Washington. **Tom Wilkinson Jr.,** 3991 E. 29th St., Bryan 77803; (979) 595-2800; www.bvcog.org.

14. Deep East Texas Council of Governments: Angelina, Houston, Jasper, Nacogdoches, Newton, Polk, Sabine, San Augustine, San Jacinto, Shelby, Trinity and Tyler. **Walter G. Diggles,** 210 Premier Dr., Jasper 75951; (409) 384-5704; www.detcog.org.

15. South East Texas Regional Planning Commission: Hardin, Jefferson and Orange. **Shaun P. Davis,** 2210 Eastex Fwy., Beaumont 77703; (409) 899-8444; www.setrpc.org.

16. Houston-Galveston Area Council: Austin, Brazoria, Chambers, Colorado, Fort Bend, Galveston, Harris, Liberty, Matagorda, Montgomery, Walker, Waller and Wharton. **Jack Steele,** PO Box 22777, Houston 77227-2777; (713) 627-3200; www.h-gac.com.

17. Golden Crescent Regional Planning Commission: Calhoun, DeWitt, Goliad, Gonzales, Jackson, Lavaca and Victoria. **Joe Brannan,** 568 Big Bend Dr., Victoria 77904; (361) 578-1587; www.gcrpc.org.

18. Alamo Area Council of Governments: Atascosa, Bandera, Bexar, Comal, Frio, Gillespie, Guadalupe, Karnes, Kendall, Kerr, Medina and Wilson. **Gloria C. Arriaga,** 8700 Tesoro Dr., Ste. 700, San Antonio 78217; (210) 362-5200; www.aacog.com.

19. South Texas Development Council: Jim Hogg, Starr, Webb and Zapata. **Amando Garza Jr.,** 1002 Dicky Lane, Laredo 78044-2187; (956) 722-3995; www.stdc.cog.tx.us.

20. Coastal Bend Council of Governments: Aransas, Bee, Brooks, Duval, Jim Wells, Kenedy, Kleberg, Live Oak, McMullen, Nueces, Refugio and San Patricio. **John P. Buckner,** PO Box 9909, Corpus Christi 78469-9909; (361) 883-5743; cbcog98.org.

21. Lower Rio Grande Valley Development Council: Cameron, Hidalgo and Willacy. **Kenneth N. Jones Jr.,** 311 N. 15th, McAllen 78501-4705; (956) 682-3481; www.lrgvdc.org.

22. Texoma Council of Governments: Cooke, Fannin and Grayson. **Susan B. Thomas,** 1117 Gallagher Dr., Ste. 100, Sherman 75090; (903) 893-2161; www.texoma.cog.tx.us.

23. Central Texas Council of Governments: Bell, Coryell, Hamilton, Lampasas, Milam, Mills and San Saba. **James Reed,** PO Box 729, Belton 76513-0729; (254) 770-2200; www.ctcog.org.

24. Middle Rio Grande Development Council: Dimmit, Edwards, Kinney, La Salle, Maverick, Real, Uvalde, Val Verde and Zavala. **Leodoro Martinez Jr.,** PO Box 1199, Carrizo Springs 78834-1199; (830) 876-3533; www.mrgdc.org. ☆

County Courts

*Each Texas county has one county court created by the Texas Constitution — a **constitutional county court** — which is presided over by the county judge (see table beginning on page 518 for a list of county judges). In more populated counties, the Legislature has created **statutory county courts,** including courts at law, probate courts, juvenile courts, domestic relations courts and criminal courts at law. Following is a list of statutory county courts and judges, as reported by county clerks as of July 2009. Other courts with jurisdiction in each county can be found on pages 470–476. Other county and district officials can be found on pages 518–528.*

Anderson — *Court at Law & Criminal Court at Law:* B. Jeffrey Doran. *Probate Courts No. 1:* Linda Bostick Ray; *No. 2:* B. Jeffrey Doran.

Aransas — *Court at Law:* William Adams.

Austin — *Court at Law, Criminal Court at Law, Probate, Domestic Relations and Juvenile courts:* Daniel W. Leedy.

Bailey — *Probate & Juvenile courts:* Sherri Harrison. *Domestic Relations Court:* Gordon H. Green.

Bastrop — *Court at Law:* Benton Eskew.

Baylor — *Probate Court:* Linda Rogers. *Juvenile Court:* William H. Heatly.

Bee — *Probate Court:* David Silva. *Juvenile Court:* Raul G. Casarez.

Bell — *Court at Law No. 1, Probate & Juvenile courts:* Edward S. Johnson. *Court at Law No. 2:* John Mischtian. *Court at Law No. 3:* Gerald Brown.

Bexar — *Courts at Law No. 1:* Al Alonso; *No. 2:* H. Paul Canales; *No. 3:* David J. Rodriguez; *No. 4:* Sarah E. Garrahan-Moulder; *No. 5:* Timothy F. Johnson; *No. 6:* Ray Olivarri; *No. 7:* Monica E. Guerrero; *No. 8:* Karen Crouch; *No. 9:* Laura Salinas; *No. 10:* Irene Rios; *No. 11:* Jo Ann De Hoyos; *No. 12:* Michael Mery. *Probate Courts No. 1:* Polly Jackson Spencer; *No. 2:* Tom Rickhoff.

Bowie — *Court at Law & Juvenile Court:* Jeff Addison. *Probate Court:* James M. Carlow.

Brazoria — *Courts at Law No. 1:* Jerri Lee Mills; *No. 2:* Marc W. Holder; *No. 3:* Jeremy Warren; *No. 4:* Lori Rickert.

Brazos — *Courts at Law No. 1:* Amanda Matzke; *No. 2:* Jim Locke.

Brooks — *Criminal Court at Law & Juvenile Court:* Joe B. Garcia.

Brown — *Court at Law:* Frank Griffin. *Juvenile Court:* E. Ray West III.

Burnet — *Court at Law:* W.R. Savage.

Caldwell — *Court at Law:* Edward L. Jarrett.

Calhoun — *All courts:* Alex R. Hernandez.

Cameron — *Court at Law No. 1:* Arturo McDonald; *No. 2:* Laura Betancourt; *No. 3:* T. Daniel Robles.

Carson — *Probate Court:* Lewis Powers.

Cass — *Court at Law:* Donald Dowd.

Chambers — *Probate & Juvenile courts:* Jimmy Sylvia. *Domestic Relations Court:* Carroll E. Wilborn Jr.

Cherokee — *Court at Law:* Daniel B. Childs.

Coke — *Probate Court:* Roy Blair. *Juvenile Court:* Barbara L. Walther.

Coleman — *Probate Court:* Jimmie Hobbs. *Juvenile Court:* John Weeks.

Collin — *Courts at Law No. 1:* Corinne Mason; *No. 2:* Jerry Lewis; *No. 3:* John Barry; *No. 4:* Raymond Wheless; *No. 5:* Gregory Brewer. *Probate Court:* Weldon Copeland. *Juvenile Court:* Cynthia Wheless.

Collingsworth — *Court at Law No. 1, Juvenile & Probate courts:* John James; *No. 2:* Jo Rita Henard; *Domestic Relations Court:* Stuart Messer.

Colorado — *Probate & Juvenile courts:* Al Jamison.

Comal — *Court at Law No. 1:* Randy Gray; *No. 2* Charles Stephens II.

Cooke — *Court at Law, Criminal Court at Law, Probate & Juvenile courts:* John H. Morris. *Domestic Relations Court:* Janelle Haverkamp.

Coryell — *Court at Law, Probate & Criminal Court at Law:* Susan Stephens. *Probate Court:* John Firth.

Dallas — *Courts at Law No. 1:* DeMetria Benson; *No. 2:* King Fifer; *No. 3:* Sally Montgomery; *No. 4:* Ken Tapscott; *No. 5:* Mark Greenberg. *County Criminal Courts No. 1:* Dan Patterson; *No. 2:* Lennox Bower; *No. 3:* Douglas Skemp; *No. 4:* Teresa Tolle; *No. 5:* Tom Fuller; *No. 6:* Angela King; *No. 7:* Elizabeth Crowder; *No. 8:* Jane Roden; *No. 9:* Peggy Hoffman; *No. 10:* Roberto Canas; *No. 11:* Elizabeth Frizell. *Probate Courts No. 1:* Nikki DeShazo; *No. 2:* Robert E. Price; *No. 3:* Michael Miller. *County Criminal Courts of Appeals No. 1:* Kristin Wade; *No. 2:* Jeff Rosenfield.

Delta — *Probate & Criminal Court at Law:* Ted Carrington. *Juvenile Court:* Robert. E. Newsom.

Denton — *Courts at Law No. 1 & Juvenile Court:* Darlene Whitten; *No. 2:* Margaret Barnes. *Probate Court:* Don Windle.

Ector — *Courts at Law No. 1 & Juvenile Court:* J.A. (Jim) Bobo; *No. 2:* Mark Owens.

Ellis — *Court at Law No. 1:* Bob Carroll; *No. 2:* A. Gene Calvert Jr. *Probate Court:* Bob Carroll. *Juvenile Court:* A. Gene Calvert Jr.

El Paso — *Courts at Law No. 1:* Ricardo Herrera; *No. 2:* Julie Gonzalez; *No. 3:* Javier Alvarez; *No. 4:* Alejandro Gonzalez; *No. 5:* Carlos Villa; *No. 6:* M. Sue Kurita; *No. 7:* Thomas Spieczny. *Probate Court No. 1:* Yvonne Rodrigueza; *No. 2:* Eduardo Gamboa. *Juvenile Court No. 1:* Richard Ainsa; *No. 2:* Maria T. Ligon. *Criminal Courts at Law No. 1:* Alma Trejo; *No. 2:* Robert Anchondo; *No. 3:* Carlos Carrasco; *No. 4:* Jesus R. Herrera.

Erath — *Court at Law:* Bart McDougal. *Domestic Relations Court:* Don Jones.

Fort Bend — *Courts at Law No. 1:* Bud Childers; *No. 2:* Walter S. McMeans; *No. 3:* Susan G. Lowery; *No. 4:* Sandy Bielstein.

Franklin — *Probate & Criminal courts:* Gerald Hubbell. *Juvenile Court:* Paul Lovier.

Galveston — *Courts at Law No. 1:* Mary Nell Crapitto; *No. 2:* C.G. Dibrell III; *No. 3:* Roy Quintanilla. *Probate Court:* Gladys B. Burwell.

Grayson — *Courts at Law No. 1:* James C. Henderson; *No. 2:* Carol Siebman.

Gregg — *Court at Law No. 1, Criminal Court at Law, Probate & Juvenile courts:* Rebecca Simpson. *Court at Law No. 2, Probate & Criminal Court at Law:* Alfonso Charles. *Domestic Relations:* Robin Sage.

Guadalupe — *Court at Law No. 1:* Linda Z. Jones; *No. 2 & Criminal Court at Law:* Frank Follis. *Probate & Juvenile courts:* Linda Z. Jones and Mike Wiggins.

Harris — *Courts at Law No. 1:* R. Jack Cagle; *No. 2:* Jacqueline Lucci Smith; *No. 3:* Linda Storey; *No. 4:* Roberta Lloyd. *County Criminal Courts at Law No. 1:* Reagan C. Helms; *No. 2:* Bill Harmon; *No. 3:* Don Jackson; *No. 4:* James E. Anderson; *No. 5:* Margaret Stewart Harris; *No. 6:* Larry Standley; *No. 7:* Pam Derbyshire; *No. 8:* Jay Karahan; *No. 9:* Analia Wilkerson; *No. 10:* Sherman A. Ross; *No. 11:* Diane Bull; *No. 12:* Robin Brown; *No. 13:* Mark Atkinson; *No. 14:* Mike Fields; *No. 15:* Jean Spradling Hughes. *Probate Courts No. 1:* Kathy Stone; *No. 2:* Mike Wood; *No. 3:* Rory Robert Olsen; *No. 4:* Wil-*

The Blanco County Courthouse in Johnson City. Ron Billings photo; Texas Forest Service.

liam C. McCulloch.

Harrison — *Court at Law & Juvenile Court:* Jim Ammerman II.

Hays — *Court at Law No. 1, Criminal Court at Law, Probate & Juvenile courts:* Howard S. Warner II. *Court at Law No. 2 & Criminal Court at Law:* Linda A. Rodriguez.

Henderson — *Court at Law & Criminal Court at Law, Probate & Juvenile:* D. Matt Livingston; *Court at Law & Criminal Court at Law, Probate & Juvenile:* Nancy Perryman. *Probate & Juvenile courts:* David Holstein.

Hidalgo — *Courts at Law No. 1:* Rodolfo (Rudy) Gonzalez; *No. 2:* Jaime (Jay) Palacios; *No. 3:* Homero Garza; *No. 4:* Fred Garza; *No. 5:* Arnoldo Cantu; *No. 6:* Albert Garcia. *Juvenile Court:* Jesse Contreras.

Hill — *Court at Law:* A. Lee Harris.

Hood — *Court at Law:* Vincent Messina.

Hopkins — *Court at Law:* Amy M. Smith.

Houston — *Court at Law:* Sarah Tunnell Clark.

Howard — *Probate & Juvenile courts:* Mark J. Barr. *Domestic Relations Court:* Robert H. Moore III.

Hunt — *Court at Law No. 1, Criminal Court at Law & Juvenile Court:* J. Andrew Bench; *Court at Law No. 2 & Criminal Court at Law:* R. Duncan Thomas.

Jeff Davis — *All courts:* George E. Grubb.

Jefferson — *Courts at Law No. 1:* Alfred S. Gerson; *No. 2:* G.R. (Lupe) Flores; *No. 3:* John Paul Davis.

Johnson — *Courts at Law No. 1:* Robert B. Mayfield III; *No. 2:* Jerry Webber.

Kaufman — *Court at Law No. 1 & Criminal Court at Law:* Erleigh Norville Wylie. *Court at Law No. 2:* David A. Lewis. *Probate Court:* Wayne Gent.

Kerr — *Court at Law & Criminal Court at Law:* Spencer W. Brown. *Probate & Juvenile courts:* Pat Tinley.

Klegerg — *Court at Law:* Martin J. Chiuminatto Jr..

Lamar — Court at Law: Deane A. Loughmiller. Juvenile Court: M.C. Superville Jr.

Lampasas — *Probate Court:* Wayne L. Boultinghouse. *Juvenile Court:* Joe Carroll.

Lamb — *Court at Law, Criminal Court at Law & Probate Court:* William A. Thompson Jr. *Juvenile & Domestic Relations courts:* Feliz Klein.

Lee — *Probate Court:* Evan Gonzales. *Juvenile Court:* Terry Flenniken.

Liberty — *Court at Law:* Don Taylor. *Probate & Juvenile courts:* Phil Fitzsgerald.

Lubbock — *Court at Law No. 1:* Larry B. (Rusty) Ladd; *No. 2:* Drue Farmer; *No. 3:* Judy Parker.

Lynn — *Court at Law & Domestic Relations Court:* Carter Schildnecht. *Criminal Court at Law, Probate & Juvenile courts:* H.G. Franklin.

Madison — *Probate & Juvenile courts:* Arthur M. Henson.

Marion — *Probate Court:* Phil A. Parker.

Mason — *Probate Court:* Jerry M. Bearden.

Matagorda — *Probate Court:* Nate McDonald. *Domestic Relations Court:* Ben Hardin and Craig Estlinbaum. *Juvenile Court:* Craig Estlinbaum.

McCulloch — *Juvenile Court:* Karl Prohl.

McLennan — *Courts at Law & Criminals Courts at Law No. 1:* Mike Freeman; *No. 2:* Michael B. Gassaway. *Probate Court:* Jim Lewis.

Medina — *Court at Law:* Vivian Torres.

Menard — *Probate Court:* Richard Cordes. *Domestic Relations & Juvenile courts:* Emil Prohl.

Midland — *Courts at Law No. 1:* Al Walvoord; *No. 2:* Marvin Moore. *Domestic Relations Court:* Dean Rucker.

Milam — *Probate Court:* Frank Summers. *Juvenile Court:* Ed P. Magre.

Montgomery — *Courts at Law No. 1:* Dennis Watson; *No. 2:* Jerry Winfree; *No. 3:* Patrice McDonald; *No. 4:* Mary Ann Turner.

Moore — *Court at Law, Domestic Relations, Juvenile & Criminal Court at Law:* Delwin McGee. *Probate:* J.E. (Rowdy) Rhoades.

Morris — *Probate Court:* J.C. Jennings.

Motley — *All courts:* Ed D. Smith.

Nacogdoches — *Court at Law & Criminal Court at Law:* John A. (Jack) Sinz.

Nolan — *Court at Law, Juvenile Court & Criminal Court*

at Law: Gary D. Harger. *Probate Court:* Tim D. Fambrough.

Nueces — *Courts at Law No. 1:* Robert J. Vargas; *No. 2:* Lisa Gonzales; *No. 3:* John Martinez; *No. 4:* James E. Klager; *No. 5:* Carl E. Lewis.

Orange — *Court at Law No. 1:* Michael W. Shuff; *No 2:*Troy Johnson. *Probate Court:* Michael W. Shuff. *Juvenile & Criminal Court at Law:* Michael W. Shuff and Troy Johnson.

Palo Pinto — *Probate & Juvenile courts:* Mike A. Smiddy. *Domestic Relations Court:* Jerry Ray.

Panola — *Court at Law:* Terry D. Bailey.

Parker — *Court at Law No. 1:* Deborah Dupont; *No. 2:*Ben Akers. *Probate Court:* Mark Riley. *Juvenile Court:* Mike Kidd. *Criminal Court at Law:* Don Crestman and Graham Quisenberry.

Parmer — *Juvenile Court:* Bonnie J. Heald.

Polk — *Court at Law:* Stephen Phillips.

Potter — *Court at Law No. 1 & Juvenile Court:* W.F. (Corky) Roberts; *Court at Law No. 2:* Pamela Cook Sirmon. *Probate Court:* Arthur Ware.

Rains — *Probate Court:* Joe Ray Dougherty.

Randall — *Court at Law No. 1:* James Anderson. *No. 2:* Ronnie Walker.

Reagan — *Probate Court:* Larry Isom.

Reeves — *All courts:* Walter M. Holcombe.

Rockwall — *Court at Law:* David E. Rakow.

Rusk — *Court at Law:* Chad Dean. *Probate Court:* Sandra Hodges.

Sabine — *Probate Court:* Charles Watson. *Domestic Relations & Juvenile courts:* Charles Watson and Joe Bob Golden.

San Augustine — *Probate Court:* Randy E. Williams.

San Jacinto — *Criminal Court at Law:* Fritz Faulkner.

San Patricio — *Court at Law:* Richard D. Hatch III.

Shackelford — *Probate & Juvenile courts:* Ross Montgomery.

Smith — *Courts at Law No. 1:* Thomas A. Dunn; *No. 2:* Randall L. Rogers. *Probate Court:* Joel Baker. *Juvenile Court:* Floyd Getz.

Somervell — *Probate & Juvenile courts:* Walter Maynard.

Starr — *Court at Law, Criminal Court at Law & Juvenile Court:* Romero Molina. *Probate Court:* Eloy Vera and Romero Molina. *Domestic Relations Court:* Eloy Vera.

Stephens — *Probate Court:* Gary L. Fuller.

Sterling — *Probate Court:* Ralph Sides. *Juvenile Court:* Barbara Walther.

Stonewall — *Court at Law & Probate Court:* Bobby McGough. *Domestic Relations & Juvenile courts:* Shane Hadaway.

Tarrant — *Courts at Law No. 1:* R. Brent Keis; *No. 2:* Jennifer Rymell; *No. 3:* Vince Sprinkle. *Criminal Courts at Law No. 1:* Sherry Hill; *No. 2:* Mike Mitchell; *No. 3:* Billy D. Mills; *No. 4:* Deborah Nekhom Harris; *No. 5:* Jamie Cummings; *No. 6:* Molly Jones; *No. 7:* Cheril S. Hardy; *No. 8:* Daryl Coffee; *No. 9:* Brent A. Carr; *No. 10:* Phil Sorrels. *Probate Courts No. 1:* Steve M. King; *No. 2:* Pat Ferchill.

Taylor — *Courts at Law and Criminal Courts at Law No. 1:* Robert Harper; *No. 2:* Barbara B. Rollins. *Probate Court:* George A. Newman. *Domestic Relations Court:* Aleta Hacker. *Juvenile Court:* Robert Harper and Barbara B. Rollins.

Terrell — *Court at Law:* Leo Smith.

Titus — *Probate & Criminal Court at Law:* Sam W. Russell.

Tom Green — *Court at Law No. 1:* Ben Nolan; *No. 2:*

The Lee County Courthouse in Giddings. Ron Billings. photo; Texas Forest Service.

Penny Roberts.

Travis — *Courts at Law No. 1:* J. David Phillips; *No. 2:* Eric Shepperd; *No. 3:* David Crain; *No. 4:* Mike Denton; *No. 5:* Nancy Hobengarten; *No. 6:* Jan Breland; *No. 7:* Elizabeth A. Earle. *Probate Court:* Guy Herman. *Juvenile Court:* Gardner Betts.

Trinity — *Probate & Criminal Court at Law:* Mark Evans.

Upshur — *Criminal Court at Law & Probate Court:* Dean Fowler. *Domestic Relations Court:* Lauren Parish.

Val Verde — *Court at Law:* Sergio J. Gonzalez.

Victoria — *Courts at Law No. 1:* Laura A. Weiser; *No. 2:* Juan Velasquez III.

Walker — *Court at Law & Criminal Court at Law:* Barbara W. Hale. *Probate Court:* Barbara W. Hale and Danny Pierce.

Waller — *Court at Law:* June Jackson.

Washington — *Court at Law:* Matthew Reue.

Webb — *Courts at Law, Probate & Juvenile courts:* Alvino (Ben) Morales and Jesús (Chuy) Garza.

Wharton — *Court at Law, Probate & Criminal Court at Law:* John W. Murrile. *Domestic Relations & Juvenile courts:* Daniel Sklar.

Wichita — *Courts at Law No. 1:* Jim Hogan; *No. 2:* Tom Bacus. *Probate, Domestic Relations & Juvenile courts:* Jim Hogan and Tom Bacus.

Willacy — *Court at Law, Probate & Criminal Court at Law:* Eliseo Barnhart.

Williamson — *Courts at Law No. 1:* Suzanne Brooks; *No. 2:* Tim Wright; *No. 3:* Don Higginbothom; No. 4: John McMaster.

Wilson — *Probate & Juvenile courts:* Marvin C. Quinney.

Winkler — *Criminal Court at Law, Probate & Juvenile courts:* Bonnie Leck. *Domestic Relations Court:* James L. Rex.

Wise — *Court at Law & Criminal Court at Law:* Melton D. Cude.

Wood — *Probate Court:* Bryan Jeanes. *Juvenile Court:* G. Timothy Boswell.

Young — *Probate & Juvenile courts:* Stanley H. Peavey III.

Zavala — *All courts:* Joe Luna. ☆

County Tax Appraisers

The following list of Chief Appraisers for Texas counties was furnished by the State Property Tax Division of the State Comptroller's office. It includes the mailing address for each appraiser and is current to July 2009.

Anderson—Carson Wages, PO Box 279, Palestine 75802

Andrews—Ron Huckabay, 600 N. Main, Andrews 79714

Angelina—Keith Kraemer, PO Box 2357, Lufkin 75902

Aransas—Jad Smith, 601 S. Church, Rockport 78382

Archer—Kimbra York, PO Box 1141, Archer City 76351

Armstrong—Deborah J. Sherman, Drawer 835, Claude 79019

Atascosa—Michelle L. Hons, PO Box 139, Poteet 78065

Austin—Richard Moring, 906 E. Amelia St., Bellville 77418

Bailey—Kaye Elliott, 302 Main St., Muleshoe 79347

Bandera—Ed Barnes, PO Box 1119, Bandera 78003

Bastrop—Mark Boehnke, Drawer 578, Bastrop 78602

Baylor—Ronnie Hargrove, 211 N. Washington, Seymour 76380

Bee—Ruth Sandoval, PO Box 1262, Beeville 78104

Bell—Marvin Hahn, PO Box 390, Belton 76513

Bexar—Michael Amezquita, PO Box 830248, San Antonio 78283

Blanco—Hollis Boatright, PO Box 338, Johnson City 78636

Borden—Jill Freeman, PO Box 298, Gail 79738

Bosque—F. Janice Henry, PO Box 393, Meridian 76665

Bowie—Dolores Baird, PO Box 6527, Texarkana 75505

Brazoria—Cheryl Evans, 500 N. Chenango, Angleton 77515

Brazos—Mark Price, 1673 Briarcrest Dr., A-101, Bryan 77802

Brewster—Matt White, 107 W. Avenue E, #2, Alpine 79830

Briscoe—Pat McWaters, PO Box 728, Silverton 79257

Brooks—Marylou Cantu, Drawer A, Falfurrias 78355

Brown—Doran E. Lemke, 403 Fisk Ave., Brownwood 76801

Burleson—Curtis Doss, PO Box 1000, Caldwell 77836

Burnet—Stan Hemphill, PO Box 908, Burnet 78611

Caldwell—Pete Islas, PO Box 900, Lockhart 78644

Calhoun—Phillip Gonzales, PO Box 49, Port Lavaca 77979

Callahan—Bun Barry, 132 W. 4th St., Baird 79504

Cameron—Frutoso Gomez Jr., PO Box 1010, San Benito 78586

Camp—Geraldine Hull, 143 Quitman St., Pittsburg 75686

Carson—Donita Davis, PO Box 970, Panhandle 79068

Cass—Ann Lummus, 502 N. Main St., Linden 75563

Castro—Jerry Heller, 204 S.E. 3rd (Rear), Dimmitt 79027

Chambers—Michael Fregia, PO Box 1520, Anahuac 77514

Cherokee—Lee Flowers, PO Box 494, Rusk 75785

Childress—Terry Holley, 100 Ave. E NW, Childress 79201

Clay—Gerald Holland, PO Box 108, Henrietta 76365

Cochran—JoAnn Dobson, 109 S.E. 1st, Morton 79346

Coke—Gayle Sisemore, PO Box 2, Robert Lee 76945

Coleman—Bill W. Jones, PO Box 914, Coleman 76834

Collin—Jimmie Honea, 2404 Ave. K, Plano 75074

Collingsworth—Ann Wauer, 800 W. Ave., Wellington, Rm. 104 79095

Colorado—Bill H. Mitchell, PO Box 10, Columbus 78934

Comal—Lynn E. Rodgers, PO Box 311222, New Braunfels 78131

Comanche—Rhonda Woods, PO Box 6, Comanche 76442

Concho—Scott Sutton, PO Box 68, Paint Rock 76866

Cooke—Doug Smithson, 201 N. Dixon St., Gainesville 76240

Coryell—Jerry Hogg, 705 Main St., Gatesville 76528

Cottle—Rue Young, PO Box 459, Paducah 79248

Crane—Janet Wilson, 511 W. 8th, Crane 79731

Crockett—Rhonda Shaw, PO Drawer H, Ozona 76943

Crosby—Kathy Harris, PO Box 505, Crosbyton 79322

Culberson—Sally Carrasco, PO Box 550, Van Horn 79855

Dallam—Edward G. Carter, PO Box 579, Dalhart 79022

Dallas—Ken Nolan, 2949 N. Stemmons Fwy., Dallas 75247

Dawson—Norma Brock, PO Box 797, Lamesa 79331

Deaf Smith—Danny Jones, PO Box 2298, Hereford 79045

Delta—Kim Gregory, PO Box 47, Cooper 75432

Denton—Joe Rogers, PO Box 2816, Denton 76202

DeWitt—Beverly Malone, PO Box 4, Cuero 77954

Dickens—Sherry Hill, PO Box 119, Dickens 79229

Dimmit—Gerri Renfroe, 404 W. Peña St., Carrizo Springs 78834

Donley—Paula Lowrie, PO Box 1220, Clarendon 79226

Duval—Ernesto Molina, PO Box 809, San Diego 78384

Eastland—Steve Thomas, PO Box 914, Eastland 76448

Ector—Karen McCord, 1301 E. 8th St., Odessa 79761

Edwards—Bruce Martin, PO Box 858, Rocksprings 78880

Ellis—Kathy Rodrigue, PO Box 878, Waxahachie 75165

El Paso—Jerry Griffin, 5801 Trowbridge, El Paso 79925

Erath—Jerry Lee, PO Box 94, Stephenville 76401

Falls—Edward Bridge, PO Box 430, Marlin 76661

Fannin—Mike Shannon, 831 W. State Hwy. 56, Bonham 75418

Fayette—Karen Schubert, PO Box 836, La Grange 78945

Fisher—Jacqueline Martin, PO Box 516, Roby 79543

Floyd—Jim Finley, PO Box 249, Floydada 79235

Foard—Jo Ann Vecera, PO Box 419, Crowell 79227

Fort Bend—Glen Whitehead, 2801 B.F. Terry Blvd., Rosenberg 77471

Franklin—Jamisson Griffith, PO Box 720, Mount Vernon 75457

Freestone—Bud Black, 218 N. Mount, Fairfield 75840

Frio—Irma Gonzalez, PO Box 1129, Pearsall 78061

Gaines—Betty Caudle, PO Box 490, Seminole 79360

Galveston—Ken Wright, 600 Gulf Fwy., Texas City 77591

Garza—Shirley A. Smith, PO Drawer F, Post 79356

Gillespie—David Oehler, 101 W. Main St., #11, Fredericksburg 78624

Glasscock—Royce Pruit, PO Box 89, Garden City 79739

Goliad—E.J. Bammert, PO Box 34, Goliad 77963

Gonzales—Glenda Strackbein, PO Box 867, Gonzales 78629

Gray—W. Pat Bagley, PO Box 836, Pampa 79066

Grayson—Teresa Parsons, 205 N. Travis, Sherman 75090

Gregg—Thomas Hays, 1333 E. Harrison Rd., Longview 75604

Grimes—Bill Sullivan, PO Box 489, Anderson 77830

Guadalupe—Jamie Osborne, 3000 N. Austin, Seguin 78155

Hale—Nikki Branscum, PO Box 29, Plainview 79073

Hall—Marlin D. Felts, 512 W. Main St., Memphis 79245

Hamilton—Doyle Roberts, 119 E. Henry St., Hamilton 76531

Hansford—Sonya Shieldknight, 709 W. 7th Ave., Spearman 79081

Hardeman—Twila Butler, PO Box 388, Quanah 79252

Hardin—Amador Reyna, PO Box 670, Kountze 77625

Harris—Jim Robinson, 13013 Northwest Fwy., Houston 77040

Harrison—Karen Jeans, PO Box 818, Marshall 75671

Hartley—Mary M. Thompson, PO Box 405, Hartley 79044

Haskell—Kenny Watson, PO Box 467, Haskell 79521

Hays—David G. Valle (interim), 21001 N. IH-35, Kyle 78640

Hemphill—Thomas Denney, PO Box 65, Canadian 79014

Henderson—Bill Jackson, PO Box 430, Athens 75751

Hidalgo—Rolando Garza, PO Box 208, Edinburg 78540

Hill—Mike McKibben, PO Box 416, Hillsboro 76645

Hockley—Greg Kelley, PO Box 1090, Levelland 79336

Hood—Jeff Law, PO Box 819, Granbury 76048

Hopkins—Cathy Singleton, PO Box 753, Sulphur Springs 75483

Houston—Kathryn Keith, PO Box 112, Crockett 75835

Howard—Brett McKibbin, PO Box 1151, Big Spring 79721

Hudspeth—Zedoch L. Pridgeon, Box 429, Sierra Blanca 79851

Hunt—Brent South, PO Box 1339, Greenville 75403

Hutchinson—Diana Hooks, PO Box 5065, Borger 79008

Irion—Byron Bitner, PO Box 980, Mertzon 76941

Jack—Kathy Conner, PO Box 958, Jacksboro 76458

Jackson—Damon D. Moore, 700 N. Wells, Ste. 204, Edna 77957

Jasper—David Luther, PO Box 1300, Jasper 75951

Jeff Davis—Zedoch L. Pridgeon, PO Box 373, Fort Davis 79734

Jefferson—Roland Bieber, PO Box 21337, Beaumont 77720

Jim Hogg—Jorge Arellano, PO Box 459, Hebbronville 78361

Jim Wells—J. Sidney Vela, PO Box 607, Alice 78333

Johnson—Jim Hudspeth, 109 N. Main, Cleburne 76033

Jones—Kim McLemore, PO Box 348, Anson 79501

Karnes—Kathey Barnhill, 915 S. Panna Maria, Karnes City 78118

Kaufman—Richard L. Mohundro, PO Box 819, Kaufman 75142

Kendall—Gary Eldridge, PO Box 788, Boerne 78006

Kenedy—Bill Fuller, PO Box 701085, San Antonio 78270

Kent—Kay Byrd, PO Box 68, Jayton 79528

Kerr—P.H. "Fourth" Coates IV, PO Box 294387, Kerrville 78029

Kimble—Kandy Dick, PO Box 307, Junction 76849

King—Sandy Burkett, PO Box 117, Guthrie 79236

Kinney—William F. Haenn, PO Box 1377, Brackettville 78832

Kleberg—Tina Flores, PO Box 1027, Kingsville 78364

Knox—Mitzi Welch, PO Box 47, Benjamin 79505

Lamar—Cathy Jackson, PO Box 400, Paris 75461

Lamb—Lesa Kloiber, PO Box 950, Littlefield 79339

Lampasas—Glenda January, Box 175, Lampasas 76550

La Salle—Domingo Paloma, PO Box O, Cotulla 78014

Lavaca—Pamela Lathrop, PO Box 386, Hallettsville 77964

Lee—Patricia Davis, 218 E. Richmond, Giddings 78942

Leon—Jeff Beshears, PO Box 536, Centerville 75833

Liberty—Alan Conner, PO Box 10016, Liberty 77575

Limestone—Karen Wietzikoski, PO Drawer 831, Groesbeck 76642

Lipscomb—Jerry Reynolds, PO Box 128, Darrouzett 79024

Live Oak—Bob Johanson, PO Box 2370, George West 78022

Llano—Cindy Cowan, 103 E. Sandstone, Llano 78643

Loving—Sherlene Burrows, PO Box 352, Mentone 79754

Lubbock—Dave Kimbrough, PO Box 10542, Lubbock 79408

Lynn—Marquita Scott, PO Box 789, Tahoka 79373

Madison—Larry Krumnow, PO Box 1328, Madisonville 77864

Marion—John Kirkland, PO Box 690, Jefferson 75657

Martin—Marsha Graves, PO Box 1349, Stanton 79782

Mason—Ted Smith, PO Box 1119, Mason 76856

Matagorda—Vince Maloney, 2225 Ave. G, Bay City 77414

Maverick—Victor Perry, 2243 Veterans Blvd., Eagle Pass 78852

McCulloch—Zane Brandenberger, 306 W. Lockhart, Brady 76825

McLennan—Andrew Hahn, PO Box 2297, Waco 76703

McMullen—Jesse Bryan, PO Box 37, Tilden 78072

Medina—James Garcia, 1410 Ave. K, Hondo 78861

Menard—Dianna Miller, PO Box 1008, Menard 76859

Midland—Jerry Bundick, PO Box 908002, Midland 79708

Milam—Patricia Moraw, PO Box 769, Cameron 76520

Mills—Carl Priddy, PO Box 565, Goldthwaite 76844

Mitchell—Kaye Cornutt, 2112 Hickory St., Colorado City 79512

Montague—June Deaton, PO Box 121, Montague 76251

Montgomery—Mark Castleschouldt, PO Box 2233, Conroe 77305

Moore—Diane Ball, PO Box 717, Dumas 79029

Morris—Rhonda Hall, PO Box 563, Daingerfield 75638

Motley—Brenda Osborn, PO Box 779, Matador 79244

Nacogdoches—Gary Woods, 216 W. Hospital, Nacogdoches 75961

Navarro—Karen Morris, PO Box 3118, Corsicana 75151

Newton—Margie Herrin, 109 Court St., Newton 75966

Nolan—Brenda Klepper, PO Box 1256, Sweetwater 79556

Nueces—Ollie Grant, 201 N. Chaparral, Corpus Christi 78401

Ochiltree—Terry Symons, 825 S. Main, #100, Perryton 79070

Oldham—Brenda Perkins, PO Box 310, Vega 79092

Orange—Michael Cedars, PO Box 457, Orange 77631

Palo Pinto—Donna Rhodes, PO Box 250, Palo Pinto 76484

Panola—Loyd Adams, 2 Ball Park Rd., Carthage 75633

Parker—Larry Hammonds, 1108 Santa Fe Dr., Weatherford 76086

Parmer—Curby Brantley, PO Box 56, Bovina 79009

Pecos—Sam Calderon Jr., PO Box 237, Fort Stockton 79735

Polk—Carolyn Allen, 114 W. Matthews, Livingston 77351

Potter—Jim Childers, PO Box 7190, Amarillo 79114

Presidio—Irma Salgado, PO Box 879, Marfa 79843

Rains—Carrol Houllis, PO Box 70, Emory 75440

Randall—Jim Childers, PO Box 7190, Amarillo 79114

Reagan—Byron Bitner, PO Box 8, Big Lake 76932

Real—Kelley Shultz, PO Box 158, Leakey 78873

Red River—Jan Raulston, PO Box 461, Clarksville 75426

Reeves—Carol King-Markman, PO Box 1229, Pecos 79772

Refugio—Connie Koonce, PO Box 156, Refugio 78377

Roberts—DeAnn Williams, PO Box 458, Miami 79059

Robertson—Dan Brewer, PO Box 998, Franklin 77856

Rockwall—Ray Helm, 841 Justin Rd., Rockwall 75087

Runnels—Patsy Dunn, PO Box 524, Ballinger 76821

Rusk—Terry Decker, PO Box 7, Henderson 75653

Sabine—Jim Nethery, PO Box 137, Hemphill 75948

San Augustine—Jamie Doherty, 122 N. Harrison, San Augustine 75972

San Jacinto—Clayton Adams, PO Box 1170, Coldspring 77331

San Patricio—Rufino H. Lozano, PO Box 938, Sinton 78387

San Saba—Randy Henderson, 423 E. Wallace, San Saba 76877

Schleicher—Scott Sutton, PO Box 936, Eldorado 76936

Scurry—Larry Crooks, 2612 College Ave., Snyder 79549

Shackelford—Teresa Peacock, PO Box 565, Albany 76430

Shelby—Robert Pigg, 724 Shelbyville St., Center 75935

Sherman—Teresa Edmond, PO Box 239, Stratford 79084

Smith—Michael Barnett, 245 South S.E. Loop 323, Tyler 75702

Somervell—Joseph W. Rollen, 112 Allen Dr., Glen Rose 76043

Starr—Humberto Saenz Jr., PO Box 137, Rio Grande City 78582

Stephens—Sherry Duggan, PO Box 351, Breckenridge 76424

Sterling—Linda Low, PO Box 28, Sterling City 76951

Stonewall—Ozella E. Warner, PO Box 308, Aspermont 79502

Sutton—Mary Bustamante, 300 E. Oak St., Sonora 76950

Swisher—Cindy McDowell, PO Box 8, Tulia 79088

Tarrant—John Marshall, 2500 Handley-Ederville Rd., Fort Worth 76118

Taylor—Richard Petree, PO Box 1800, Abilene 79604

Terrell—Blain Chriesman, PO Box 747, Sanderson 79848

Terry—Ronny Burran, PO Box 426, Brownfield 79316

Throckmorton—Francis Peacock, Box 788, Throckmorton 76483

Titus—Ronny Babcock, PO Box 528, Mount Pleasant 75456

Tom Green—Bill Benson, PO Box 3307, San Angelo 76902

Travis—Patrick Brown, PO Box 149012, Austin 78714

Trinity—Allen McKinley, PO Box 950, Groveton 75845

Tyler—Travis Chalmers, PO Drawer 9, Woodville 75979

Upshur—Sarah Pruit, 105 Diamond Loch, Gilmer 75644

Upton—Sheri Stephens, PO Box 1110, McCamey 79752

Uvalde—Elida Sanchez, 209 N. High, Uvalde 78801

Val Verde—Cherry T. Sheedy, PO Box 420487, Del Rio 78842

Van Zandt—Brenda Barnett, PO Box 926, Canton 75103

Victoria—John Haliburton, 2805 N. Navarro, Ste. 300, Victoria 77901

Walker—Grover Cook, PO Box 1798, Huntsville 77342

Waller—David Piwonka, PO Box 159, Katy 77492

Ward—Arlice Wittie, PO Box 905, Monahans 79756

Washington—Willy Dilworth, PO Box 681, Brenham 77834

Webb—Martin Villarreal, 3302 Clark Blvd., Laredo 78043

Wharton—Tylene Gamble, 2407 1/2 N. Richmond Rd., Wharton 77488

Wheeler—Kimberly Morgan, PO Box 1200, Wheeler 79096

Wichita—Eddie Trigg, PO Box 5172, Wichita Falls 76307

Wilbarger—Deborah Echols, PO Box 1519, Vernon 76385

Willacy—Agustin Lopez, Rt. 2, Box 256, Raymondville 78580

Williamson—Bill Carroll, 510 W. 9th St., Georgetown 78726

Wilson—Carlton R. Pape, Box 849, Floresville 78114

Winkler—Connie Carpenter, PO Box 1219, Kermit 79745

Wise—Mickey Hand, 400 E. Business 380, Decatur 76234

Wood—Tracy Nichols, PO Box 1706, Quitman 75783

Yoakum—Saundra Stephens, PO Box 748, Plains 79355

Young—Jerry Patton, PO Box 337, Graham 76450

Zapata—Amada Gonzalez, PO Box 2315, Zapata 78076

Zavala—Alberto Mireles, 323 W. Zavala, Crystal City 78839☆

Wet-Dry Counties

Source: Texas Alcoholic Beverage Commission; www.tabc.state.tx.us//

The list below shows the wet-or-dry status of counties in Texas as of July 2009.

An asterisk (*) indicates counties in which the sale of mixed beverages (liquor by the drink) is legal in all or part of the county.

In seven counties marked with a dagger (†), sale of mixed beverages in restaurants is permitted, but sale of distilled spirits for off-premise consumption is not permitted.

Wet / Dry Counties 2009

- ● Wet: Including distilled spirits
- ● Part wet: Including distilled spirits
- ● Wine/beer permitted in part or all
- ● Beer permitted in part or all
- ● Dry: No alcohol sales permitted

© Texas Almanac 2010 – 2011

When approved in local-option elections in "wet" precincts of counties, sale of liquor by the drink is permitted in Texas. This resulted from adoption of an amendment to the Texas Constitution in 1970 and subsequent legislation, followed by local-option elections. This amendment marked the first time in 50 years that the sale of liquor by the drink was legal in Texas.

In 2009, there were 31 counties wholly dry. In 1986, there were 62 counties wholly dry.

Counties (in part or all) in Which Distilled Spirits Are Legal (204): *Anderson, *†Angelina, *Aransas, Archer, Atascosa, *Austin, *Bandera, *Bastrop, *Bee, *Bell, *Bexar, *Blanco, *Bosque, *†Bowie, *Brazoria, *Brazos, *Brewster, Briscoe, *Brooks, *Brown, Burleson, *Burnet, *Caldwell, *Calhoun, Callahan, *Cameron, Camp, Carson, Cass, Castro, *Chambers, *Cherokee, *Childress, Coleman, *Collin, *Colorado, *Comal, Comanche, *Cooke, Coryell, *Cottle, Crane, Crockett, Culberson.

Also, Dallam, *Dallas, *Dawson, Deaf Smith, *Denton, *DeWitt, Dickens, *Dimmit, *Donley, *Duval, Eastland, *Ector, Edwards, *Ellis, *El Paso, Falls, Fannin, *Fayette, *Foard, *Fort Bend, Freestone, *Frio, *Galveston, Garza, *Gillespie, *Goliad, Gonzales, Gray, *Grayson, *Gregg, *Grimes, *Guadalupe, *Hale, Hall, Hamilton, *Hardeman, Hardin, *Harris, Harrison, Hartley, Haskell, *Hays, *Henderson, *Hidalgo, *Hill, *Hockley, *Hood, Hopkins, *†Houston, *Howard, *Hudspeth, *Hunt, Hutchinson, Jack, *Jackson, *Jasper, *Jeff Davis, *Jefferson, *Jim Hogg, *Jim Wells, *†Johnson.

Also, *Karnes, *Kaufman, *Kendall, *Kenedy, *Kerr, Kimble, King, *Kinney, *Kleberg, Knox, *Lamar, Lamb, *Lampasas, *La Salle, *Lavaca, *Lee, *Leon, *Liberty, Live Oak, *Llano, *Lubbock, *†Madison, *Marion, *Matagorda, *Maverick, *McCulloch, *McLennan, *Medina, Menard, *Midland, *†Milam, Mills, *Mitchell, *Montague, *Montgomery, *Moore, Nacogdoches, *Navarro, Newton, Nolan, *Nueces.

Also, *Orange, Palo Pinto, *Parker, *Pecos, *Polk, *Potter, *Presidio, *Rains, *Randall, Reagan, Red River, *Reeves, Refugio, *Robertson, *Rockwall, Runnels, Sabine, San Augustine, San Jacinto, *San Patricio, San Saba, Schleicher, *Scurry, Shackelford, Shelby, *†Smith, *Starr, Stonewall, *Sutton, Swisher, *Tarrant, *Taylor, Terrell, Titus, *Tom Green, *Travis, Trinity, Upshur, Upton, Uvalde, *Val Verde, *Victoria, *Walker, Waller, Ward, *Washington, *Webb, *Wharton, *Wichita, *Wilbarger, *Willacy, *Williamson, *Wilson, Winkler, *Wise, Young, *Zapata, *Zavala.

Counties in Which Only Beer Is Legal (6): Baylor, Concho, Irion, Mason, Oldham, Stephens.

Counties in Which Beer and Wine Are Legal (13): Clay, Cochran, Coke, Erath, Glasscock, Limestone, Lipscomb, Loving, McMullen, Real, Somervell, Terry, Van Zandt.

Counties Wholly Dry (31): Andrews, Armstrong, Bailey, Borden, Collingsworth, Crosby, Delta, Fisher, Floyd, Franklin, Gaines, Hansford, Hemphill, Jones, Kent, Lynn, Martin, Morris, Motley, Ochiltree, Panola, Parmer, Roberts, Rusk, Sherman, Sterling, Throckmorton, Tyler, Wheeler, Wood, Yoakum. ☆

Texas County and District Officials — Table No. 1

County Seats, County Judges, County Clerks, County Attorneys, County Treasurers, Tax Assessors-Collectors and Sheriffs.

See Table No. 2 on pages following this table for District Clerks, District Attorneys and County Commissioners. Judges in county courts at law, as well as probate courts, juvenile/domestic relations courts, county criminal courts and county criminal courts of appeal, can be found beginning on page 512. The officials listed here are elected by popular vote. An asterisk (*) before a county name marks a county whose county clerk failed to return our questionnaire; the names of officials for those counties are taken from most recent unofficial sources available to us.

County	County Seat	County Judge	County Clerk	County Attorney	County Treasurer	Assessor-Collector	Sheriff
Anderson	Palestine	Linda Bostick Ray	Wanda Burke	John L. Pool	Sharon Cook Peterson	Terri Garvey	Greg Taylor
Andrews	Andrews	Richard H. Dolgener	Kenda Heckler	Ed Jones	Office abolished 11-5-1985.	Robin Harper	Sam H. Jones
*Angelina	Lufkin	Wes Suiter	Jo Ann Chastain	Richard Bianchi	Deborah Huffman	Thelma Sherman	Kent Henson
Aransas	Rockport	C.H. (Burt) Mills Jr.	Peggy L. Friebele	R.B. (Burk) Morris	Marvine D. Wix	Jeri D. Cox	William (Bill) Mills
Archer	Archer City	Gary W. Beesinger	Karren Winter		Victoria Lear	Teresa K. Martin	Staci Williams Beesinger
*Armstrong	Claude	Hugh Reed	Connie Spiller		Sara Messer	Joe Reck	J.R. Walker
Atascosa	Jourdanton	Diana J. Bautista	Diane Gonzales	Lucinda A. Vickers	Ray Samson	Barbara Schorsch	Tommy Williams
Austin	Bellville	Carolyn Cerny Bilski	Carrie Gregor		Cathleen V. Frank	Janice Kokemor	R. DeWayne Burger
Bailey	Muleshoe	Sherri Harrison	Paula Benton	Jeanine Backus	Shonda Black	Melba Clark	Richard Wills
Bandera	Bandera	Richard A. Evans	Candy Wheeler	John D. Payne	Kay Welch	Mae Vion Meyer	Weldon Tucker
Bastrop	Bastrop	Ronnie McDonald	Rose Pietsch		Kathy Schroeder	Linda Harmon	Terry Pickering
Baylor	Seymour	Linda Rogers	Clara (Carrie) Coker	Susan Elliott	Kevin Hostas	Jeanette Holub	Bob Elliott
Bee	Beeville	David Silva	Mirella Escamilla Davis	Michael J. Knight	Office abolished 11-2-1982.	Linda Bridge	Carlos Carrizales Jr.
Bell	Belton	Jon H. Burrows	Shelley Coston	Richard J. Knight	Charles Jones	Sharon Long	Dan Smith
Bexar	San Antonio	Nelson W. Wolff	Gerald C. (Gerry) Rickhoff	Position abolished.	Office abolished 11-5-1985.	Sylvia S. Romo	Amadeo Ortiz
Blanco	Johnson City	Bill Guthrie	Karen Newman	Dean C. Myane	Camille Swift	Hollis Boatright	William (Bill) R. Elsbury
Borden	Gail	Van L. York	Joyce Herridge		Kenneth P. Bennett	Billy J. Gannaway	Billy J. Gannaway
Bosque	Meridian	Cole Word	Betty Spitzer Outlaw	Natalie Cobb Koehler	Diana Wellborn	Debbie Kibler	Anthony Malott
Bowie	New Boston	James M. Carlow	Velma Moore	Carol Dalby	Donna Bayns	Toni Barron	James Prince
Brazoria	Angleton	E.J. (Joe) King	Joyce Hudman		Sharon L. Reynolds	Ro'Vin Garrett	Charles S. Wagner
Brazos	Bryan	Randy Sims	Karen McQueen	Rob Anderson	Kay C. Hamilton	Kristeen (Kristy) Roe	Christopher C. (Chris) Kirk
Brewster	Alpine	Val Clark Beard	Berta Rios Martinez	Steve Houston	Carol Ofenstein	Betty Jo Rooney	Ronny D. Dodson
Briscoe	Silverton	Wayne Nance	Bena Hester	Emily Roy Teegardin	Mary Jo Brannon	Betty Ann Stephens	Gene Smith
*Brooks	Falfurrias	Raul M. Ramirez	Frutoso (Pepe) Garza	Homer Mora	Gilberto Vela	Rey Rodriguez	Rey Rodriguez
Brown	Brownwood	E. Ray West III	Sharon Ferguson	Shane Britton	Ann Krpoun	Cheryl Nelson	Bobby R. Grubbs
Burleson	Caldwell	Mike Sutherland	Anna L. Schielack	Joseph J. Skrivanek III	Beth Andrews Bills	Curtis Doss	A. Dale Stroud
*Burnet	Burnet	Donna Klaeger	Janet F. Parker	Eduardo (Eddie) Arredondo	Betty Trapp	Sherri Frazier	W.T. Smith
Caldwell	Lockhart	H.T. Wright	Nina S. Sells		Lori D. Rangel-Pompa	Mary Vicky Gonzales	Daniel C. Law
Calhoun	Port Lavaca	Michael J. Pfeifer	Anita Fricke		Rhonda Sikes Kokena	Gloria Ann Ochoa	Burnard B. Browning
Callahan	Baird	Roger Corn	Donna Bell	Shane Deel	Dianne Gunter	Tammy T. Walker	John Windham
*Cameron	Brownsville	Carlos H. Cascos	Joe G. Rivera	Armando Villalobos	David A. Betancourt	Antonio Yzaguirre Jr.	Omar Lucio
Camp	Pittsburg	Thomas Cravey	Elaine Young	Angela L. Hammonds	Judy Croley	Gale Burns	Alan D. McCandless
*Carson	Panhandle	Lewis Powers	Celeste Bichsel	Scott Sherwood	Denise Salzbrenner	Jackie Lewis	Tam Terry
Cass	Linden	Charles L. McMichael	Jannis Mitchell		Martha Fant Sheridan	Becky Watson	James D. (Troop) Estes
Castro	Dimmitt	William F. Sava	Joyce Marie Thomas	James R. Horton	Kristen M. Yorton	Pamala Rickert	Salvadore (Sal) Rivera Jr.
Chambers	Anahuac	Jimmy Sylvia	Heather H. Hawthorne	Scott Peal	Carren T. Sparks	Margie J. Henry	Joe LaRive
*Cherokee	Rusk	Chris Davis	Laverne Lusk	Craig D. Caldwell	Patsy J. Lassiter	Linda Little	James E. Campbell
Childress	Childress	Jay Mayden	Zona Prince	Greg Buckley	Jeanie Thomas	Kathy Dobbs	Michael Pigg
Clay	Henrietta	Kenneth Liggett	Kay Hutchison	Eddy Atkins	Debra Alexander	Linda Overstreet Sellers	K.R. (Kenny) Lemons Jr.
Cochran	Morton	James St. Clair	Rita Tyson	J.C. Adams Jr.	Doris Sealy	Linda Huckabee	R. Wallace Stalcup
Coke	Robert Lee	Roy Blair	Mary Grim	Nancy Arthur	Phelan Wrinkle	Josie Dean	Wayne McCutchen
Coleman	Coleman	Jimmie D. Hobbs	Stacey Mendoza	Joe Lee Rose	Kay LeMay	Jamie Trammell	Robert Wade Turner
*Collin	McKinney	Keith Self	Stacey Kemp			Kenneth L. Maun	Terry G. Box
Collingsworth	Wellington	John A. James	Jackie Johnson	G. Keith Davis	Yvonne Brewer	Generah Manuel	Joe Dale Stewart
*Colorado	Columbus	A.G. (Al) Jamison	Darlene Hayek	Ken Sparks	Diane Matus	Mary Jane Poenitzsch	R.H. (Curly) Wied

County	County Seat	County Judge	County Clerk	County Attorney	County Treasurer	Assessor-Collector	Sheriff
Comal	New Braunfels	Danny Scheel	Joy Streater	Craig Willingham	Renee Couch	Cathy Talcott	James R. (Bob) Holder
Comanche	Comanche	James R. (Bob) Arthur	Ruby Lesley	Bill Campbell	Billy Ruth Rust	Gay Horton Green	Jeff D. Lambert
Concho	Paint Rock	Allen Amos	Barbara K. Hoffman	Tanya S. Davis	Lisa J. Jost	Richard G. Doane	Richard G. Doane
Cooke	Gainesville	Bill Freeman	Rebecca Lawson	Brandon Belt	Donna Medford	Billie Jean Knight	Michael E. Compton
Coryell	Gatesville	John E. Firth	Barbara Simpson		Justin Carothers	Cathie Ross	Johnny Burks
Cottle	Paducah	D.N. Gregory Jr.	Jan Irons	John H. Richards	Kathy Biddy		Kenneth A. Burns
Crane	Crane	John Farmer	Judy Crawford	Susan Loyless	Cristy Tarin	Rebecca Gonzales	Robert DeLeon
*Crockett	Ozona	Fred Deaton	Debbi Puckett	Jody K. Upham	Burl J. Myers	Rhonda Shaw	Roy Glenn Sutton
Crosby	Crosbyton	Davey Abell	Linda S. Jones	C. Michael Ward	Debra Riley	Anna R. Rodriguez	David E. Barker
Culberson	Van Horn	Manuel Molinar	Linda McDonald	Stephen L. Mitchell	Susana R. Hinojos	Amalia Y. Hernandez	Oscar E. Carrillo
Dallam	Dalhart	David D. Field	Terri Banks	Jon King	Wes Ritchey	Kay Howell	Bruce Scott
Dallas	Dallas	Jim Foster	John F. Warren		Joe Wells	John R. Ames	Lupe Valdez
Dawson	Lamesa	Sam Saleh	Gloria Vera	Steven B. Payson	Julie Frizzell	Diane Hogg	Kent Parchman
Deaf Smith	Hereford	Tom Simons	David Ruland	Jim English	Paula B. Price	Teresa Garth	Brent Harrison
Delta	Cooper	Ted Carrington	Jane Jones	H. Michael Bartley	Phyllis London	Dawn Stewart	Gerald W. Teague
Denton	Denton	Mary Horn	Cynthia Mitchell		Cindy Yeatts Brown	Steve Mossman	Benny Parkey
DeWitt	Cuero	Ben E. Prause	Elva Petersen	Raymond H. Reese	Peggy Ledbetter	Susie Dreyer	Joe C. (Jode) Zavesky
Dickens	Dickens	Lesa Arnold	Winona Humphreys	Trey Poage	Sandy Vickrey	Sherry Hill	Jimmie Land
Dimmit	Carrizo Springs	Francisco G. Ponce	Mario N. Garcia	Daniel M. Gonzalez	Estanislado Z. Martinez	Melinda Vega Campos	Joel Gonzalez
Donley	Clarendon	Jack Hall	Fay Vargas	Landon Lambert	Wanda Smith	Linda Crump	Charles (Butch) Blackburn
Duval	San Diego	Abel Aragon	Oscar Garcia Jr.	Ricardo (Rocky) O. Carrillo	Lydia P. Molina	Carlos J. Montemayor Jr.	Romeo R. Ramirez
Eastland	Eastland	Rex Fields	Cathy Jentho	Cindy Weir-Nutter	Christina Dodrill	Sandra Cagle	Wayne Bradford
Ector	Odessa	Susan Redford	Linda Haney	Allen Ray Moody	Carolyn Sue Bowen	Barbara Horn	Mark Donaldson
Edwards	Rocksprings	Nick Gallegos	Dorothy R. Hatley	Joe F. Grubbs	Lupe Sifuentes-Enriquez	Lonna Fry	Donald G. Letsinger
*Ellis	Waxahachie	Chad Adams	Cindy Polley		Judy Burden	John Bridges	Johnny Brown
El Paso	El Paso	Anthoney Cobos	Delia Briones	José R. Rodriguez	Edward Dion	Victor A. Flores	Richard D. Wiles
*Erath	Stephenville	Tab Thompson	Gwinda Jones	Lisa Pence	Donna Kelly	Jennifer Carey	Tommy Bryant
Falls	Marlin	R. Steven Sharp	Frances Braswell	Jody Gilliam Morris	Sue Tacker	Bryant Hinson	Ben Kirk
Fannin	Bonham	Eileen Cox	Tammy Rich	Richard Glaser	Mike Towery	Pamela Sweet-Richardson	Kenneth L. Moore
Fayette	La Grange	Edward F. Janecka	Carolyn Kubos Roberts	Peggy S. Supak	Office abolished 11-3-87.	Carol Johnson	Keith K. Korenek
Fisher	Roby	Marshal J. Bennett	Pat Thomson	Rudy V. Hamric	Martha (Marty) Williamson	Jonnye Lu Gibson	Mickey A. Counts
Floyd	Floydada	Penny Golightly	Marilyn Holcomb	Lex S. Herrington	Elva Martinez	Delia G. Suarez	Paul Raissez
Foard	Crowell	Charlie Bell	Patricia Aydelott	Daryl Halencak	Esther Kajs	Mike Brown	Mike Brown
Fort Bend	Richmond	Robert E. Hebert	Dianne Wilson	Roy L. Cordes Jr.	Jeff Council	Patsy Schultz	Milton Wright
Franklin	Mount Vernon	Gerald Hubbell	Susan Winborne	Will Ramsay	Marla White	Sue Ann Harper	Paul B. Fletcher Jr.
Freestone	Fairfield	Linda K. Grant	Mary Lynn White	Chris Martin	Debra Kay Barger	Lisa Stephenson James	Ralph E. Billings
Frio	Pearsall	Carlos A. Garcia	Angie Tullis	Hector M. Lozano	Anna Luna Hernández	Anna Alaniz	Lionel G. Treviño
Gaines	Seminole	Tom N. Keyes	Vicki Phillips	Joe H. Nagy Jr.	Vicenta Munguia	Susan Shaw	Jon Key
Galveston	Galveston	James D. Yarbrough	Mary Ann Daigle	Harvey Bazaman	Kevin C. Walsh	Cheryl E. Johnson	Freddie L. Poor
Garza	Post	John Lee Norman	Jim Plummer	Mike Munk	Ruth Ann Young	Judy M. Bush	Cliff Laws
Gillespie	Fredericksburg	Mark Stroeher	Mary Lynn Rusche	Tamara Y.S. Keener	Laura Lindquist	Marissa Weinheimer	Buddy Mills
Glasscock	Garden City	Wilburn E. Bednar	Rebecca Batla	Hardy L. Wilkerson	Alan Dierschke	Nancy Hillger	Keith Burnett
Goliad	Goliad	Harold F. Gleinser	Mary Ellen Flores	Rob Baiamonte	June Bethke	Anna Lopez-Breen	Kirby Brumby
Gonzales	Gonzales	David Bird	Lee Riedel	Paul Watkins	Sheryl Barvorak	Norma Jean DuBose	Glen A. Sachtleben
Gray	Pampa	Richard Peet	Susan Winborne	Joshua Seabourn	Scott Hahn	Gaye Whitehead	Don Copeland
Grayson	Sherman	Drue Bynum	Wilma Blackshear Bush		Virginia Hughes	John W. Ramsey	J. Keith Gary
*Gregg	Longview	Bill Stoudt	Connie Wade		Office abolished 1-1-88.	William Kirk Shields	Maxey Cerliano
Grimes	Anderson	Betty Shiflett	David Pasket	Jon C. Fultz	Phillis Allen	Connie Perry	Donald G. Sowell
Guadalupe	Seguin	Mike Wiggins	Teresa Kiel	Elizabeth Murray-Kolb	Linda Douglass	Tavie Murphy	Arnold S. Zwicke
Hale	Plainview	Dwain Dodson	Latrice Kemp	James (Jim) Tirey	Ida A. Tyler	Kemp Hinch	David B. Mull
Hall	Memphis	Ray Powell	Raye Bailey	John M. Deaver II	Janet Bridges	Maribel C. Gonzales	Timothy K. Wiginton
Hamilton	Hamilton	Randy Mills	Debbie Rudolph	Mark C. Henkes	Debbie Eoff	Terry Payne Short	Gregg Bewley
Hansford	Spearman	Benny D. Wilson	Kim V. Vera	John L. Hutchison	Wanda Wagner	Linda Cummings	Gary Evans
*Hardeman	Quanah	Ronald Ingram	Linda Walker	Stanley R. Watson	Mary Ann Naylor	Darlene Gamble	Charles Mance Nelson
Hardin	Kountze	Billy Caraway	Glenda Alston	Rebecca R. Walton	Sharon Overstreet	Shirley Stephens	Ed J. Cain

County	County Seat	County Judge	County Clerk	County Attorney	County Treasurer	Assessor-Collector	Sheriff
Harris	Houston	Ed Emmett	Beverly B. Kaufman	Vince Ryan	Orlando Sanchez	Leo Vasquez	Adrian Garcia
Harrison	Marshall	Richard M. Anderson	Patsy Cox		James Noland Smith	Julie R. Cox	William T. (Tom) McCool
Hartley	Channing	Ronnie Gordon	Diane Thompson	M. Shane Turner	Dinkie Parman	Franky Scott	Franky Scott
Haskell	Haskell	David C. Davis	Rhonda Moeller	Kristen L. Fouts	Janis McDaniel	Bobbye Collins	David Halliburton
Hays	San Marcos	Elizabeth (Liz) Sumter	Linda C. Fritsche		Michele Tuttle	Luanne Caraway	Thomas Ratliff
Hemphill	Canadian	Steve Vandiver	Brenda Perrin	Ty M. Sparks	Cindy N. Bowen	Debra L. Ford	Gary S. Henderson
Henderson	Athens	David H. Holstein	Gwen Moffeit	Clint Davis	Michael Bynum	Milburn Chaney	Ray Nutt
Hidalgo	Edinburg	J.D. Salinas III	Arturo Guajardo Jr.	Steven Crain	Norma G. Garcia	Armando Barrera Jr.	Guadalupe (Lupe) Treviño
Hill	Hillsboro	Justin Lewis	Nicole Tanner	Mark Pratt	Becky Wilkins	Marchel Eubank	Jeffrey T. Lyon
Hockley	Levelland	Larry D. Sprowls	Irene Gonzalez Gumula	Christopher E. Dennis	Denise Bohannon	Christy Clevenger	David Kinney
*Hood	Granbury	Andy Rash	Sally Oubre	Kelton Conner	Kathy Davis	Teresa McCoy	Roger Deeds
Hopkins	Sulphur Springs	Cletis M. Millsap	Debbie Shirley	Dusty Hyde Rabe	Treva Watson	Debbie Pogue Jenkins	Charles (Butch) Adams
Houston	Crockett	Lonnie Hunt	Bridget Lamb	Daphne Session	Dina Herrera	Danette Millican	Darrel E. Bobbitt
Howard	Big Spring	Mark J. Barr	Donna Wright	Joshua Hamby	Teresa Thomas	Kathy A. Sayles	Stan Parker
Hudspeth	Sierra Blanca	Becky Dean-Walker	Abigail Ortega	C.R. (Kit) Bramblett	Jennifer Canaba	Yolanda Esparza	Arvin West
Hunt	Greenville	John L. Horn	Linda Brooks	Joel Littlefield	Delores Shelton	Barbara Wiggins	Randy Meeks
Hutchinson	Stinnett	Faye Blanks	Beverly Turner	Michael D. Milner	Kathy Sargent	Mary Lou Henderson	Guy D. Rowh
Irion	Mertzon	Leon Standard	Cori Manning	Kenneth Greer Jr.	Carolyn Huelster	Joyce Gray	Jimmy E. Martin
Jack	Jacksboro	Mitchell G. Davenport	Shelly Clayton	Michael G. Mask	Roger Sharp	Sharon Robinson	Danny R. Nash
*Jackson	Edna	Harrison Stafford II	Kenneth W. McElveen		Mary Horton	Donna Atzenhoffer	A.J. (Andy) Louderback
Jasper	Jasper	Mark Allen	Debbie Newman		Rene Kelley	Bobby Biscamp	Mitchell Newman
Jeff Davis	Fort Davis	George E. Grubb	Sue Blackley	Bart E. Medley	Geen Parrott	Rick McIvor	Rick McIvor
Jefferson	Beaumont	Ronald L. Walker	Carolyn L. Guidry		Linda Robinson	Miriam K. Johnson	G. Mitch Woods
Jim Hogg	Hebbronville	Guadalupe S. Canales	Noemi G. Salinas	Enrique A. Garza	Linda Jo G. Soliz	Norma Liza S. Hinojosa	Erasmo (Kiko) Alarcon Jr.
Jim Wells	Alice	L. Arnold Saenz	Ruben Sandoval	Jesusa Sánchez-Vera	Becky Dominguez	Mary Lozano	Oscar Lopez
Johnson	Cleburne	Roger Harmon	Curtis H. Douglas	Bill Moore	Barbara Robinson	Scott Porter	Bob L. Alford
Jones	Anson	Dale Spurgin	Julia McCray	Chad Cowan	Tish McIntire	Mary Ann Lovelady	Larry Moore
Karnes	Karnes City	Alger H. Kendall Jr.	Alva Jonas	Rober L. Busselman	Vida Swierc Malone	Ann Franke	David A. Jalufka
Kaufman	Kaufman	Wayne Gent	Laura Hughes		Johnny Countryman	Richard Murphy	David A. Byrnes
*Kendall	Boerne	Gaylan L. Schroeder	Darlene Herrin	Don Allee	Medana Crow	James A. Hudson Jr.	Roger Duncan
Kenedy	Sarita	J.A. Garcia Jr.	Veronica Vela	Jaime E. Tijerina	Cynthia M. Salinas	Eleuteria (Susie) Gonzalez	Ramon Salinas III
Kent	Jayton	Jim White	Richard Craig Harrison	Howard Freemyer	Margaret Linda McCurry	Brenda Long	William D. Scogin
Kerr	Kerrville	Pat Tinley	Jannett Pieper	Melvin (Rex) Emerson	Mindy Williams	Diane Bolin	Wm. R. (Rusty) Hierholzer
Kimble	Junction	Andrew S. Murr	Haydee Torres	Allen J. Ahlschwede	Jolene Williams	Hilaro Cantu	Hilaro Cantu
King	Guthrie	Duane Daniel	Jammye D. Timmons	Marshall Capps	Traci Butler	Sadie Spitzer	Gilbert Lee (Cotton) Elliott
Kinney	Brackettville	John Fritter	Dora Elia Sandoval	Robert Adams	Diane Gutierrez	Martha Peña Padron	Leland K. Burgess
*Kleberg	Kingsville	Pete DeLaGarza	Leo H. Alarcon	Delma Rios-Salazar	Priscilla Alaniz Cantu	Melissa Treviño DeLaGarza	Edward Mata Sr.
Knox	Benjamin	Travis Floyd	Annette Offutt	Bobby D. Burnett	Rosie Ake	Mitzi Welch	Dean W. Homstad
Lamar	Paris	Maurice C. Superville Jr.	Kathy Marlowe	Gary Young	Shirley Fults	Peggy Noble	Billy Joe (B.J.) McCoy
*Lamb	Littlefield	William A. Thompson Jr.	Jamee Long	Mark Yarbrough	Janice B. Wells	Brenda Goheen	Gary Maddox
Lampasas	Lampasas	Wayne L. Boultinghouse	Connie Hartmann	Larry Allison	Nelda DeRiso	Linda Crawford	David Whitis
La Salle	Cotulla	Joel Rodriguez Jr.	Margarita A. Esqueda	Elizabeth Martinez	Thelma R. Treviño	Elida A. Linares	Victor S. Villarreal
Lavaca	Hallettsville	Ronald L. Leck	Elizabeth A. Kouba	Stuart Fryer	Lois Henry	Margaret M. Kallus	Micah C. Harmon
Lee	Giddings	Paul Fischer	Sharon Blasig	Martin Placke	Melinda (Lyndy) Krause	Suzanne Kessler	Rodney W. Meyer
Leon	Centerville	Byron Ryder	Carla Neyland McEachern	James R. Witt Jr.	Phil Skelton	Louise Wilson	Jerry Wakefield
*Liberty	Liberty	Phil Fitzgerald	Delia Sellers	Wesley Hinch	Kim Harris	Mark McClelland	Henry Patterson
Limestone	Groesbeck	Daniel Burkeen	Peggy Beck	William Roy DeFriend	Carol Bostain	Charlene Black	Dennis D. Wilson
Lipscomb	Lipscomb	Willis V. Smith	Kim Blau	Matthew D. Bartosiewicz	Diana Schoenhals	Kathy Fry	James Robertson
Live Oak	George West	Jim Huff	Karen Irving	Gary Young	Peggy Benham	Virginia Horton	Larry R. Busby
Llano	Llano	Wayne Brascom	Bette Sue Hoy	Cheryll Mabray	Sandra Overstreet	Dexter Sagebiel	William Blackburn
Loving	Mentone	Skeet Jones	Beverly Hanson		Nicole Clark	Billy Burt Hopper	Billy Burt Hopper
Lubbock	Lubbock	Thomas V. Head	Kelly J. Pinion		Sharon Gossett	Ronnie Keister	David Gutierrez
Lynn	Tahoka	H.G. Franklin	Susan Tipton	Donnis M. Scott	Pam Miller	Sherry Pearce	Jerry Dee Franklin
Madison	Madisonville	Arthur M. Henson	Charlotte Barrett		Judy Weathers	Beverly Plumlee	Dan Douget
Marion	Jefferson	Phil A. Parker	Betty Smith	William K. Gleason	Terrie S. Neuville	Karen Jones	Bill McCay

County	County Seat	County Judge	County Clerk	County Attorney	County Treasurer	Assessor-Collector	Sheriff
Martin	Stanton	Charles T. (Corky) Blocker	Susie Hull	James L. McGilvray	H.D. Howard	Kathy Hull	John Woodward II
Mason	Mason	Jerry M. Bearden	Pam Beam	Shain V.H. Chapman	Polly McMillan	James (Buster) Nixon	James (Buster) Nixon
Matagorda	Bay City	Nate McDonald	Gail Denn	Jill Cornelius	Amy K. Perez	Cristyn Nixon	Gary Mathis
*Maverick	Eagle Pass	Jose A. Aranda Jr.	Sara Montemayor	Ricardo Ramos	Manuel Reyes Jr.	Isamari Villarreal	Tomas S. Herrera
McCulloch	Brady	Randy Young	Tina A. Smith	Mark Marshall	Donna Robinett	Treva A. Colen	Earl Howell
*McLennan	Waco	Jim Lewis	J.A. (Andy) Harwell		Bill Helton	A.F. (Buddy) Skeen	Larry Lynch
McMullen	Tilden	Linda Lee Henry	Dorairene Garza	Melaine Martin	Donald Haynes Jr.	Angel Bostwick	Bruce Thomas
Medina	Hondo	James E. Barden	Lisa J. Wernette	Kim Havel	Cynthia Alles Ivy	Loraine Neuman	Randy R. Brown
Menard	Menard	Richard Cordes	Polly Reeves	Ben Neel	Robert Bean	Tim Powell	Buck Miller
Midland	Midland	Mike Bradford	Cheryl Becker	Russell Malm	Mitzi Wohleking	Kathy Reeves	Gary Painter
Milam	Cameron	Frank Summers	Barbara Vansa	Kerry Spears	Danica Lara	Doug Bryan	David Greene
Mills	Goldthwaite	Kirkland A. Fulk	Carolyn Foster		Jane Toppert	Douglas Storey	Douglas Storey
Mitchell	Colorado City	Ray Mayo	Debby Carlock	Ty Wood	Sandra Ann Hallmark	Faye Lee	Patrick Toombs
Montague	Montague	Ted Winn	Glenda Henson	Jeb McNew	Linda McGaughey	Sydney Nowell	Paul Cunningham
*Montgomery	Conroe	Alan B. Sadler	Mark Turnbull	David Walker	Martha Gustavsen	J.R. Moore Jr.	Tommy Gage
Moore	Dumas	J.D. (Rowdy) Rhoades	Brenda McKanna	Scott Higginbotham	Pam Cox	Nikki McDonald	J.E. (Bo) DeArmond
Morris	Daingerfield	J.C. Jennings	Vicki Camp Falls	J. Stephen Cowan	Nita Beth Traylor	Kim Thomasson	Jack. D. Martin
Motley	Matador	Ed. D. Smith	Kate E. Hurt	Tom Edwards	Eva Barkley	Jo Elaine Hart	Michael K. Crutchley
Nacogdoches	Nacogdoches	Joe English	Carol Wilson	Jefferson Davis	Denise Baublet	Janie Weatherly	Thomas Kerss
Navarro	Corsicana	H.M. Davenport Jr.	Sherry Dowd		Ruby Coker	Russell P. Hudson	Leslie Cotten
Newton	Newton	Truman Dougharty	Mary Cobb		Karen Fuller Pousson	Melissa J. Burks	Joe A. Walker
*Nolan	Sweetwater	Tim D. Fambrough	Patricia (Pat) McGowan	Lisa W. Peterson	Gayle Biggerstaff	Kathy Boom	David Warren
*Nueces	Corpus Christi	Samuel L. (Loyd) Neal	Diana T. Barrera	Laura Garza Jimenez	Office abolished 11-3-87.	Ramiro (Ronnie) Canales	Jim Kaelin
Ochiltree	Perryton	Earl McKinley	Jane Hammerbeck	David Scott	Ginger Hays	Marsha Townsend	Terry L. Bouchard
Oldham	Vega	Don R. Allred	Becky Groneman	Kent Birdsong	Sherri Johnson	Cynthia Artho	David T. Medlin
Orange	Orange	Carl K. Thibodeaux	Karen Jo Vance	John D. Kimbrough	Vergie Moreland	Lynda Gunstream	Keith Merritt
Palo Pinto	Palo Pinto	Mike A. Smiddy	Bobbie Smith	Phil Garrett	Mary M. Motley	Linda Tuggle	Ira Mercer
Panola	Carthage	David L. Anderson	Clara Jones		Gloria Portman	Margaret Dyer	Jack Ellett
Parker	Weatherford	Mark Riley	Jeane Brunson	John Forrest	Jim Thorp	Margorie King	Larry Fowler
Parmer	Farwell	Bonnie J. Heald	Colleen Stover	Jeff Actkinson	Altha Herington	Bobbie Pierson	Randy Geries
Pecos	Fort Stockton	Joe Shuster	Judy Deerfield	Ori White	Barry McCallister	Santa Acosta	Cliff Harris
Polk	Livingston	John P. Thompson	Barbara Middleton		Nola Reneau	Marion A. (Bid) Smith	Kenneth Hammack
Potter	Amarillo	Arthur Ware	Julie Smith	C. Scott Brumley	Leann Renee Jennings	Robert Miller	Brian Thomas
Presidio	Marfa	Jerry C. Agan	Virginia Pallarez	John Fowlkes	Larry Skiles	Norma Arroyo	Danny C. Dominguez
Rains	Emory	Joe Ray Dougherty	Linda Wallace	Robert F. Vititow	Teresa Northcutt	David Traylor	David Traylor
Randall	Canyon	Ernie Houdashell	Sue Wicker Bartolino		Glenna Canada	Dianna Sharon Hollingsworth	Joel W. Richardson
Reagan	Big Lake	Larry Isom	Terri Pullig	J. Russell Ash	Nancy Ratliff	Cynthia Aguilar	Jeff N. Garner
Real	Leakey	W.B. (Sonny) Sansom Jr.	Bella A. Rubio	Garry A. Merritt	Kathy Brooks	Donna Brice	James Brice
Red River	Clarksville	Morris Harville	Lorie Taylor Moose	Val Varley	Kristy Gray	Tonya R. Martin	Robert Bridges
Reeves	Pecos	Sam Contreras	Dianne O. Florez	Alva E. Alvarez	Linda Clark	Rosemary Chabarria	Arnulfo (Andy) Gomez
Refugio	Refugio	Rene Mascorro	Ruby Garcia	Robert P. McGuill	Louise Null Adudell	Ida M. Turner	Robert Bolcik
Roberts	Miami	Vernon H. Cook	Toni Rankin	Leslie Breeding	Billie J. Lunsford	DeAnn Williams	Dana Miller
Robertson	Franklin	Jan Roe	Kathryn N. Brimhall	John C. Paschall	Mindy Turner	Carol D. Bielamowicz	Gerald Yezak
Rockwall	Rockwall	Chris Florance	Lisa Constant		William F.H. Sinclair	Barbara Barber	Harold Eavenson
Runnels	Ballinger	Marilyn Egan	Elesa Ocker	Stuart Holden	Margarette Smith	Robin M. Burgess	William A. Baird
Rusk	Henderson	Sandra Hodges	Joyce Lewis-Kugle	Micheal E. Jimerson	Karen Dobbs Vaughn	Matt B. Gabriel	Danny R. Pirtle
Sabine	Hemphill	Charles E. Watson	Janice McDaniel	Robert G. Neal Jr.	Tricia Woods Jacks	Martha Stone	Thomas N. Maddox
San Augustine	San Augustine	Randy E. Williams	Diana Kovar	Wesley Hoyt	Pamela Smith	Regina A. Barthol	David Smith
*San Jacinto	Coldspring	Fritz Faulkner	Angelia Steele		Charlene Everitt	Betty Davis	James L. Walters
San Patricio	Sinton	Terry Simpson	Gracie Alaniz-Gonzales	David Aken	Courtenay Dugat	Dalia Sanchez	Leroy Moody
San Saba	San Saba	Byron Theodosis	Kim Wells	Tim Inman	Gayla Hawkins	Allen Brown	Allen Brown
Schleicher	Eldorado	Charlie Bradley	Peggy Williams	Clint T. Griffin	Karen Henderson	Jeanne Snelson	David R. Doran
Scurry	Snyder	Rod Waller	Joan E. Bunch	Michael W. Hartman	Nelda Colvin	Jana Young	Darren Jackson
Shackelford	Albany	Ross Montgomery	Cathey Lee	Colton P. Johnson	Sherry Enloe	Edward Miller	Edward Miller
Shelby	Center	John Tomlin	Allison Harbison	Gary W. Rholes	Carolyn Bush Golden	Janie Graves	Newton Johnson Jr.

County	County Seat	County Judge	County Clerk	County Attorney	County Treasurer	Assessor-Collector	Sheriff
Sherman	Stratford	Terri Beth Carter	Gina Jones	Kimberly Allen	Doris Parsons	Valerie McAlister	Jack Haile
Smith	Tyler	Joel Baker	Judy Carnes		Kelli White	Gary Barber	J.B. Smith
Somervell	Glen Rose	Walter Maynard	Candace (Candy) Garrett	Ronald Hankins	Barbara Hudson	Darlene Chambers	Greg Doyle
Starr	Rio Grande City	Eloy Vera	Dennis D. Gonzalez	Victor Canales	Jaime V. Maldonado	Carmen A. Peña	Rene Fuentes
Stephens	Breckenridge	Gary L. Fuller	Helen Haddock	Gary D. Trammel	Sharon Trigg	Terry Simmons Sullivan	James D. (Jim) Reeves
Sterling	Sterling City	Ralph Sides	Susan Wyatt	William (Bill) Stroman	Wanda Foster	Joy Manning	Tim Sanders
Stonewall	Aspermont	Bobby McGough	Belinda Page	Melissa Morgan	Linda Messick	Jim B. Ward	William M. (Bill) Mullen
*Sutton	Sonora	Carla Garner	Veronica E. Hernandez	David W. Wallace	Joyce Hearn Chalk	Deedie McIntire	Joe M. Fincher
Swisher	Tulia	Harold Keeter	Brenda Hudson	J. Michael Criswell	Tricia Speed	Brenda Gunnels	Emmett Benavidez
Tarrant	Fort Worth	B. Glen Whitley	Suzanne Henderson		Office abolished 4-2-83.	Betsy Price	Dee B. Anderson
Taylor	Abilene	George A. Newman	Larry G. Bevill		Lesa Hart Crosswhite	Lavena Cheek	Les Bruce
Terrell	Sanderson	Leo C. Smith Jr.	Martha Allen	Marsha Monroe	Lynda Helmers	Clint McDonald	Clint McDonald
Terry	Brownfield	Alan D. Bayer	Kim Carter	Ramon Gallegos	Bobbye Jo Floyd	Rexann Turrentine	Larry Gilbreath
Throckmorton	Throckmorton	Trey Carrington	Mary Susie Walraven	Kristin L. Fouts	Brenda Rankin	John V. Riley	John V. Riley
Titus	Mount Pleasant	Sam W. Russell	Teresa Price	John M. Cobern	Debby E. Rhea	Judy Cook	Tim Ingram
Tom Green	San Angelo	Michael D. Brown	Elizabeth McGill	Chris Taylor	Dianna Spieker	Cindy Jetton	Joe B. Hunt
Travis	Austin	Samuel T. Biscoe	Dana DeBeauvoir	David Escamilla	Dolores Ortega-Carter	Nelda Wells Spears	Greg Hamilton
Trinity	Groveton	Mark Evans	Diane McCrory	Joe Warner Bell	Jo Bitner-Bartee	Kathy McCarty	Ralph Montemayor
*Tyler	Woodville	Jacques L. Blanchette	Donece Gregory		Sharon Fuller	Lynette Cruse	David Hennigan
Upshur	Gilmer	Dean Fowler	Peggy LaGrone		Myra Harris	Micheal L. Smith	Anthony Betterton
Upton	Rankin	Vikki Bradley	LaWanda McMurray	Melanie Spratt-Anderson	Nancy P. Poage	Dan W. Brown	Dan W. Brown
Uvalde	Uvalde	William R. Mitchell	Lucille C. Hutcherson	John P. Dodson	Joni Deorsam	Margarita (Maggie) Del Toro	Charles Mendeke
*Val Verde	Del Rio	Manuel (Mike) L. Fernandez	Generosa (Janie) Ramon	Ana Markowski-Smith	Morris L. Taylor	Beatriz I. (Bea) Muñoz	Joe Frank Martinez
Van Zandt	Canton	Rhita Koches	Charlotte Bledsoe	Leslie Poynter Dixon	Detra Janzen	J.J. Stubblefield	R.P. (Pat) Burnett Jr.
Victoria	Victoria	Donald R. Pozzi	Val D. Huvar		Sean K. Kennedy	Rena Scherer	T. Michael O'Connor
Walker	Huntsville	R.D. (Danny) Pierce	James D. Patton		Sharon Duke	Diana McRae	Clint McRae
Waller	Hempstead	Owen Ralston	Cheryl Peters		Susan Winfree	Ellen C. Shelburne	Glenn Smith
Ward	Monahans	Greg M. Holly	Natrell Cain	Hal Upchurch	Teresa Perry-Stoner	Vicki Heflin	Mikel Strickland
Washington	Brenham	Dorothy Morgan	Beth A. Rothermel	Julie Renken	Norman Draehn	Dot Borchgardt	J.W. Jankowski
Webb	Laredo	Danny Valdez	Margie Ramirez Ibarra	Greg Wilhelm	Delia Perales	Patricia Barrera	Martin Cuellar
Wharton	Wharton	John W. Murrile	Sandra K. Sanders	G.A. (Trey) Maffett	Donna Kocurek	Patrick L. Kubala	Jess Howell
Wheeler	Wheeler	Jerry Dan Hefley	Margaret Dorman	Misty L. Walker	Jauna Benefield	Lewis Scott Porter	Joel Finsterwald
Wichita	Wichita Falls	Woodrow (Woody) Gossom	Lori Bohannon		R.J. (Bob) Hampton	Lou H. Murdock	David Duke
Wilbarger	Vernon	Greg Tyra	Jana Kennon	Michael Baskerville	Joann Carr	Chris Quisenberry	Larry Lee
Willacy	Raymondville	Eliseo Barnhart	Terry Flores	Bernard Ammerman	Ruben Cavazos	Elizabeth Barnhard	Larry G. Spence
Williamson	Georgetown	Dan A. Gattis	Nancy E. Rister	Jana Duty	Vivian Wood	Deborah Hunt	James R. Wilson
Wilson	Floresville	Marvin C. Quinney	Eva S. Martinez	Russell H. Wilson	Jan Hartl	Anna D. Gonzales	Joe D. Tackitt Jr.
Winkler	Kermit	Bonnie Leck	Shethelia Reed	Scott M. Tidwell	Eulonda Everest	Patti Franks	Robert L. Roberts Jr.
Wise	Decatur	Bill McElhaney	Sherry Parker-Lemon	James Stainton	Katherine Canova	Monte Shaw	David Walker
Wood	Quitman	Bryan Jeanes	Brenda Taylor		Beckie Cannon	Carol Taylor	Bill Wansley
Yoakum	Plains	Jim Barron	Deborah L. Rushing	Richard Clark	Barbara Wright	Jan Parrish	Don Corzine
Young	Graham	Stanley H. Peavy III	Shirley Choate	Dayne Miller	Charlotte Farmer	Nancy Thomas	Bryan Walls
*Zapata	Zapata	Rosalva Guerra	Mary J. Villarreal-Bonoan	Said Alfonso Figueroa	Romeo Salinas	Luis Lauro Gonzalez	Sigifredo Gonzalez Jr.
Zavala	Crystal City	Joe Luna	Oralia G. Treviño	Eduardo Serna	Susie Perez	Florinda Perez	Eusevio E. Salinas Jr.

Texas County and District Officials — Table No. 2

District Clerks, District Attorneys and County Commissioners

See Table No. 1 on preceding pages for County Seats, County Judges, County Clerks, County Attorneys, County Treasurers, Tax Assessors-Collectors and Sheriffs. Judges in county courts at law, as well as probate courts, juvenile/domestic relations courts, county criminal courts and county criminal courts of appeal, can be found on page 512 An asterisk (*) before a county name marks a county whose county clerk failed to return our questionnaire; the names of officials for those counties are taken from the most recent unofficial sources available to us. If more than one district attorney is listed for a county, the district court number is noted in parentheses after each attorney's name. If no district attorney is listed, the county attorney, whose name is listed in Table No. 1, assumes the duties of that office.

County	District Clerk	District Attorney	Comm. Precinct 1	Comm. Precinct 2	Comm. Precinct 3	Comm. Precinct 4
Anderson	Janice Staples	Douglas E. Lowe	Joe W. Chaffin	Rashad Q. Mims I	Kenneth Dickson	Randy Watkins
Andrews	Cynthia Jones	John L. Pool	Randy Rowe	Brad Young	Hiram Hubert	Jim Waldrop
*Angelina	Reba Squyres	Clyde Herrington	Rick Harrison	Kenneth Timmons	Robert Louis Loggins	Lynn George
Aransas	Pam Heard	Patrick Flanigan	Jack Chaney	L.E. (Bubba) Casterline Jr.	Charles Smith	Howard Murph
Archer	Jane Ham	Jack McGaughey	Richard Shelley	Darin Wolf	Pat Martin III	Darryl Lightfoot
*Armstrong	Connie Spiller	Randall C. Sims	John Britten	Mike Baker	Tom Ferris	Todd R. Cagle
Atascosa	Jerome T. Brite	Rene M. Peña	Lon Gillespie	William Torans	Freddie Ogden	Weldon P. Cude
Austin	Sue Murphy	Travis J. Koehn	David Ottmer	Robert Wayne Rinn	Randy Reichardt	David Hubenak
Bailey	Elaine Parker	Kathryn Gurley	Floyd J. (Butch) Vandiver	C.E. Grant Jr.	Joey Kindle	Juan Chavez
Bandera	Tammy Kneuper	E. Bruce Curry	Bruce H. Eliker	Robert A. Harris	Richard Keese	Doug King
Bastrop	Cathy Smith	Bryan Goertz	William M. Piña	Clara Beckett	John Klaus	Lee Dildy
Baylor	Clara (Carrie) Coker	David W. Hajek	Travis Clark	John E. Nelson	Charles R. Morris	Charlie Piatt
Bee	Anna Marie Silvas	Martha Warner	Carlos Salazar Jr.	Susan C. Stasny	Eloy Rodriguez	Ronnie Olivares
Bell	Sheila Norman	Henry L. Garza	Richard Cortese	Tim Brown	Eddy Lange	John Fisher
Bexar	Margaret G. Montemayor	Susan D. Reed	Sergio (Chico) Rodriguez	Paul Elizondo	Kevin A. Wolff	Tommy Adkisson
Blanco	Debby Elsbury	Sam Oatman	John Wood	James Sultemeier	Chris Liesmann	Paul Granberg
Borden	Joyce Herridge	Dana W. Cooley	Monte Smith	Randy L. Adcock	Ernest Reyes	Joe T. Belew
Bosque	Sandra L. Woosley	B.J. Shepherd	Kent Harbison	Durwood Koonsman	Gary J. Arnold	Jimmy Schmidt
Bowie	Billy Fox	Bobby Lockhart	Jack Stone	John Addington	Kelly Blackburn	Carl Teel
Brazoria	Jerry Deere	Jeri Yenne	Donald W. (Dude) Payne	L.M. (Matt) Sebesta	Stacy L. Adams	Mary Ruth Rhodenbaugh
Brazos	Marc Hamlin	William R. (Bill) Turner	Lloyd Wassermann	E. Duane Peters	G. Kenny Mallard Jr.	Carey Cauley Jr.
Brewster	JoAnn Salgado	Jesse Gonzales Jr.	Asa (Cookie) Stone	Kathy Killingsworth	Ruben Ortega	Matilde Pallanez
Briscoe	Bena Hester	Becky B. McPherson	Jimmy Burson	Dale Smith	Larry Comer	John Burson
*Brooks	Noe Guerra	Armando Berrera	Gloria Garza	Luis Arevalo	Carlos Villarreal	Jose A. (Tony) Martinez
Brown	Jan Brown	Michael Brandon Murray	Steve Adams	Joel Kelton	Richard Gist	Larry Traweek
Burleson	Joy Brymer	William E. (Bill) Parham	Frank L. Kristof	Vincent Svec Jr.	David Hildebrand	John B. Landolt Jr.
*Burnet	Dana DeBerry	Sam Oatman	Bill Neve	Russell Graeter	Ronny Hibler	Joe Don Dockery
Caldwell	Tina Morgan	Richard R. (Trey) Hicks III	Tom D. Bonn	Charles C. Bullock	Neto Madrigal	Joe Ivan Roland
Calhoun	Pamela Martin Hartgrove	Dan W. Heard	Roger C. Galvan	Vernon Lyssy	Neil E. Fritsch	Kenneth W. Finster
Callahan	Sharon Owens	Shane Deel	Harold Hicks	Bryan Farmer	Tom Windham	Cliff Kirkham
*Cameron	Aurora De La Garza	Armando Villalobos	Sofia C. Benavidez	John Wood	David A. Garza	Edna Tamayo
Camp	Mignon Cook	Charles C. Bailey	Bart Townsend	Larry Frasier	Norman Townsend	Vernon Griffin
*Carson	Celeste Bichsel	Luke Inman	Mike Britten	Kenneth Ware	Paul Detten	Kevin Howell
Cass	Becky Wilbanks	Clint Allen	Brett Fitts	Danny Joe Shaddix	Paul Cothren	Max Bain
Castro	Joyce Marie Thomas	James R. Horton	Tom McLain	Larry Gonzales	W.A. (Bay) Baldridge	Dan Schmucker

County	District Clerk	District Attorney	Comm. Precinct 1	Comm. Precinct 2	Comm. Precinct 3	Comm. Precinct 4
Chambers	Patti L. Henry	Cheryl S. Lieck	Mark Huddleston	David (Bubba) Abernathy	Gary R. Nelson	W.O. (Bill) Wallace Jr.
*Cherokee	Janet Gates	Elmer C. Beckworth Jr.	Kelly Traylor	Kevin Pierce	Katherine Pinotti	Byron Underwood
Childress	Zona Prince	Luke Inman	Denzil Ray	Mark Ross	Lyall Foster	Don Ray Crook
Clay	Dan Slagle	Jack McGaughey	R.L. "Lindy" Choate	Johnny Gee	John McGregor	Brice Jackson
Cochran	Rita Tyson	Gary A. Goff	Donnie B. Simpson	Margaret Allen	Stacey Dunn	Jimmy Mullinax
Coke	Mary Grim	Stephen Lupton	Troy Gene Montgomery	Robert Feil	Gaylon L. Pitcock	Bobby Blaylock
Coleman	Jo Chapman	Heath Hemphill	Mark Williams	Billy Don McCrary	Mike Stephenson	Alan Davis
*Collin	Hannah Kunkle	John R. Roach	Matt Shaheen	Jerry Hoagland	Joe Jaynes	Kathy Ward
Collingsworth	Jackie Johnson	Luke Inman	Dan Langford	Mike Hughs	Eddie Orr	Kirby Campbell
*Colorado	Harvey Vornsand	Ken Sparks	Doug Wessels	Herbert Helmcamp	Tommy Hahn	Darrell Gertson
Comal	Katherine H. Faulkner	Geoffrey I. Barr	Donna Eccleston	Jay Millikin	Gregory Parker	Jan Kennady
Comanche	Brenda Dickey	B.J. Shepard	Gary D. (Corky) Underwood	Kenneth Feist	Sherman Sides	Jimmy Dale Johnson
Concho	Barbara K. Hoffman	George E. McCrea	Trey Bradshaw	Ralph Willberg	Ernest R. Gomez	Aaron (Sonny) Browning Jr.
Cooke	Patricia Payne	Janice Warder	Gary Hollowell	Stephen Key	Alan Smith	Leon Klement
Coryell	Janice M. Gray	David A. Castillo	Jack Wall	Daren Moore	Don Jones	Elizabeth Taylor
Cottle	Jan Irons	David W. Hajek	Jimmy W. Sweeney	Frank Taylor	Manuel Cruz Jr.	James A. Long
Crane	Judy Crawford	Michael L. Fostel	Tom Brown	Dennis Young	Domingo Escobedo	Roy Hodges
*Crockett	Debbi Puckett	Laurie K. English	Frank Tambunga	Pleas Childress III	Randy Branch	Alfredo Tobar
Crosby	Karla Isbell	C. Michael Ward	Gary V. Jordan	Frank Mullins	Larry Wampler	Billy Bob Wright
Culberson	Linda McDonald	Jaime Esparza	Cornelio Garibay	Duane Corrales	Lyndon C. McDonald	Adrian Norman
Dallam	Terri Banks	David M. Green	Glenn Reagan	Oscar Pzzilas	Don J. Bowers	Carl French
Dallas	Gary Fitzsimmons	Craig Watkins	Maurine Dickey	Mike Cantrell	John Wiley Price	Kenneth A. Mayfield
Dawson	Carolyn Turner	Brian L. Kingston	Ricky Minjarez	Gilbert Tejeda	Nicky Goode	Foy O'Brien
Deaf Smith	Jean Schumacher Coody	Jim English	Pat Smith	Jerry Roberts	Mike Brumley	Jerry O'Connor
Delta	Jane Jones	Martin Braddy	B.V. (Rip) Templeton	David Max Moody	Wayne Poole	Mark Brantley
Denton	Sherri Adelstein	Paul Johnson	Hugh Coleman	Ron Marchant	Bobbie J. Mitchell	Andrew Eads
DeWitt	Tabeth Gardner	Michael A. Sheppard	Curtis G. Afflerbach	Joe L. Machalec	John C. Oliver	Alfred Rangnow
Dickens	Winona Humphreys	Becky B. McPherson	Wayne Smith	Ricky West	Doc Edwards	Sheldon Parsons
Dimmit	Maricela G. Gonzalez	Roberto Serna	Mike Uriegas	Johnny Gloria	David W. Taylor	Rodrigo (Igo) Jaime
Donley	Fay Vargas	Luke Inman	Mark White	Don Hall	Andy Wheatly	Bob Trout
Duval	Richard M. Barton	Heriberto Silva	Alejo C. Garcia	Rene M. Perez	Nestor Garza Jr.	Gilberto Uribe Jr.
Eastland	Carol Ann Brittain	Russell D. Thomason	Wayne Honea	Norman Christian	Bill Underwood	Reggie Pittman
Ector	Janis Morgan	Robert Newton Bland IV	Freddie Gardner	Greg Simmons	Dale Childers	Armando S. Rodriguez
Edwards	Dorothy R. Hatley	Fred Hernandez	Terry Brooks	Steve Nance	Clifford Tuttle	Mike Grooms
*Ellis	Melanie P. Reed	Joe F. Grubbs	Dennis Robinson	Bill Dodson	Heath Sims	Ron Brown
El Paso	Gilbert Sanchez	Jaime E. Esparza	Anabel Perez	Veronica Escobar	Willie Gandara	Daniel R. Haggerty
*Erath	Wanda Pringle	Jason Cashon	Jim Pack	Lynn Tidwell	Joe Brown	Randy Lowe
Falls	Larry R. Hoelscher	Jody Gilliam Morris	Milton Albright	Robert Paul Sr.	Nelson Coker	Lester Whitt
Fannin	Nancy Young	Richard Glaser	Gary Whitlock	Stan Barker	Dewayne Strickland	Pat Hilliard
Fayette	Virginia Wied	Peggy S. Supak	Johns Saunders	Gary Weishuhn	James Kubecka	Tom Muras
Fisher	Tammy Haley	Ann Reed	Gordon Pippin	Rodney Tankersley	Preston Martin	Gene Terry
Floyd	Patty Davenport	William P. Smith	Mike Anderson	Linden Morris	Nathan Johnson	Jon Jones
Foard	Patricia Aydelott	Staley Heatly	W.N. Chatfield	Rockne Wisdom	Larry Wright	Edward Crosby
Fort Bend	Annie Rebecca Elliott	John Healey Jr.	Richard Morrison	Grady Prestage	W.A. (Andy) Meyers	James Patterson
Franklin	Ellen Jaggers	Martin Braddy	Danny Chitsey	Bobby R. Elbert	Deryl Carr	Sam Young

County	District Clerk	District Attorney	Comm. Precinct 1	Comm. Precinct 2	Comm. Precinct 3	Comm. Precinct 4
Freestone	Janet Chappell	Chris Martin	Luke Ward Sr.	Craig Oakes	Stanley Gregory	Clyde E. Ridge Jr.
Frio	Ramona B. Rodriguez	Rene M. Peña	Richard Hernandez	Robert Carrizales	Ruben Maldonado	Jose (Pepe) Flores
Gaines	Virginia Stewart	Brian L. Kingston	Danny Yocom	Craig Belt	Blair Tharp	Charlie Lopez
Galveston	Latonia Wilson	Kurt Sistrunk	Patrick F. Doyle	Bryan M. Lamb	Stephen W. Holmes	Kenneth F. Clark
Garza	Jim Plummer	Brian L. Kingston	Gary McDaniel	Charles Morris	Ted Brannon	Mike Sanchez
Gillespie	Barbara Meyer	E. Bruce Curry	Curtis Cameron	William A. Roeder	Calvin Ransleben	Donnie Schuch
Glasscock	Rebecca Batla	Hardy L. Wilkerson	Jimmy Strube	Mark Halfmann	Gary Jones	Michael Hoch
Goliad	Mary Ellen Flores	Michael A. Sheppard	Julian Flores	Jerry Rodriguez	Jim Kreneck	Ted Long
Gonzales	Sandra Baker	Heather Holub	Kenneth O. (Dell) Whiddon	Donnie R. Brzozowski	Kevin T. LaFleur	Otis S. (Bud) Wuest
Gray	Gaye Honderich	Lynn Switzer	Joe Wheeley	Gary Willoughby	John Mark Baggerman	James Hefley
Grayson	Tracy Powers	Joseph D. Brown	Johnny Waldrip	David Whitlock	Jackie Crisp	C.E. (Gene) Short
*Gregg	Barbara Duncan	Carl Dorrough	Charles W. Davis	R. Darryl Primo	Bob Barbee	John Mathis
Grimes	Gay Wells	Tuck Moody McLain	John Bertling	Bill Pendley	Julian Melchor Jr.	Pam Finke
Guadalupe	Debra Crow	Heather Hollub	Roger Baenziger	Cesareo Guadarrama III	Jim O. Wolverton	Judy Cope
Hale	Carla Cannon	Wally Hatch	Neal Burnett	Mario Martinez	Gary Koelder	Benny Cantwell
Hall	Raye Bailey	Luke Inman	Milton Beasley	Terry Lindsey	Buddy Logsdon	James Fuston
Hamilton	Leoma Larance	B.J. Shepherd	Jim D. Boatwright	Mike Lewis	Jon Bonner	Dickie Clary
Hansford	Kim V. Vera	Mark Snider	Ira G. (Butch) Reed	Joe T. Venneman	Tim Stedje	Danny Henson
*Hardeman	Linda Walker	Staley Heatly	Johnny Akers	Rodger Tabor	Barry Haynes	Rodney Foster
Hardin	Vicki Johnson	David Sheffield	Kenneth "Frank" Riedinger	Patricia McGallion	Ken Pelt	Bobby Franklin
Harris	Loren Jackson	Pat Lykos	El Franco Lee	Sylvia R. Garcia	Steve Radack	Jerry Eversole
Harrison	Sherry Griffis	Joe Black IV	Jeffrey L. Thompson	Emma Bennett	James Greer	Galen McBride
Hartley	Diane Thompson	David M. Green	David Vincent	Jim Hill	Jay Kuper	Robert (Butch) Owens
Haskell	Penny Anderson	Mike Fouts	Johnny Scoggins	Tiffen Mayfield	Kenny Thompson	Bobby Don Smith
Hays	Cecelia Adair	Sherri Tibbe	Debbie Gonzales Ingalsbe	Jefferson W. Barton	Will Conley	Karen Ford
Hemphill	Brenda Perrin	Lynn Switzer	Joe Schaef	Ed Culver	Mark Meek	Lynard G. Schafer
Henderson	Becky Hanks	Scott McKee	Joe D. Hall	Wade McKinney	Ronny Lawrence	Jerry West
Hidalgo	Laura L. Hinojosa	Rene A. Guerra	Sylvia Handy	Hector (Tito) Palacios	Joe M. Flores	Oscar L. Garza Jr.
Hill	Charlotte Barr	Dan V. Dent	Danny Bodeker	Steven Sulak	Larry Wright	Lee Harkins
Hockley	Dennis Price	Gary A. Goff	Curtis D. Thrash	Larry R. Carter	J.L. (Whitey) Barnett	Thomas R. Clevenger
*Hood	Tonna Trumble Hitt	Rob Christian	Mike Sympson	Dick Roan	Leonard Heathington	Steve Berry
Hopkins	Patricia Dorner	Martin Braddy	Beth B. Wisenbaker	Burke Bullock	Don Patterson	Danny Evans
Houston	Carolyn Rains	Donna Gordon Kaspar	Roger Dickey	Willie E. Kitchen	Pat Perry	Kennon Kellum
Howard	Colleen Barton	Hardy L. Wilkerson	Emma Puga Brown	Jerry D. Kilgore	Jimmie Long	Gary Simer
Hudspeth	Abigail Ortega	Jaime Esparza	Wayne West	Curtis Carr	Jim Ed Miller	James Kiehne
Hunt	Stacey Landrum	Noble Walker	Kenneth Thornton	Ralph Green	Larry Middlebrooks	Jim Latham
Hutchinson	Joan Carder	Mark Snider	Larry Coffman	Jerry D. Hefner	S.T. (Red) Isbell Jr.	Eddie Whittington
Irion	Cori Manning	Stephen Lupton	Wayne E. Smith	Jeff Davidson	John Nanny	Barbara Searcy
Jack	Tracie Pippin	Greg Lowery	James Logan	Bryson Sewell	James L. Cozart	Milton R. (Sonny) Pruitt
Jackson	Sharon Mathis	Robert E. (Bobby) Bell	Wayne Hunt	Wayne Bubela	Johnny E. Belicek	Larry Deyton
Jasper	Linda Ryall	Steve Hollis	Charles Shofner Jr.	Willie Stark	Roy Parker	Vance Moss
Jeff Davis	Sue Blackley	Jesse Gonzales Jr.	Larry Francell	Kathy Bencomo	Curtis Evans	Albert Miller
Jefferson	Lolita Ramos	Tom Maness	Eddie Arnold	Mark L. Domingue	Michael (Shane) Sinegal	Everette (Bo) Alfred
Jim Hogg	Noemi G. Salinas	Heriberto Silva	Antonio Flores	Abelardo Alaniz	Sandalio Ruiz	Ruben Rodriguez
Jim Wells	R. David Guerrero	Armando G. Barrera	Zenaida Sanchez	Ventura Garcia Jr.	Oswald (Wally) Alanis	Javier N. Garcia

County	District Clerk	District Attorney	Comm. Precinct 1	Comm. Precinct 2	Comm. Precinct 3	Comm. Precinct 4
Johnson	David Lloyd	Dale Hanna	Rick Bailey	John W. Matthews	Jerry D. Stringer	Don Beeson
Jones	Lacey Hansen	Billy John Edwards	James Clawson	Mike Polk	Gaite Taylor	Steve Lollar
Karnes	Robbie Shortner	Rene M. Peña	Carl Hummel	Jeffrey Wiatrek	James Rosales	Isidro D. Rossett Jr.
Kaufman	Sandra Featherston	Rick Harrison	Jerry Rowden	Ray Clark	James (J.C.) Jackson	Jim Deller
*Kendall	vacant	E. Bruce Curry	Anne Reissig	Gene Miertschin	Darrel L. Lux	Kenneth M. Rusch
Kenedy	Veronica Vela	John T. Hubert	Louis E. (Bud) Turcotte III	Roberto Salazar Jr.	Sarita Armstrong-Hixon	Gumecinda Gonzales
Kent	Richard Craig Harrison	Michael Fouts	Roy W. Chisum	Don Long	Tommy Stanaland	Robert Graham
Kerr	Linda Uecker	Amos Barton (198th) E. Bruce Curry (216th)	H.A. (Buster) Baldwin	William (Bill) Williams	Jonathan A. Letz	Bruce Oehler
Kimble	Haydee Torres	Amos L. Barton	Billy Braswell	Charles McGuire	Wylie Taff	Tooter Schulze
King	Jammye D. Timmons	William H. (Bill) Heatly	Reggie J. Hatfield	Larry Rush	Bobby J. Tidmore	Bob Burkett
Kinney	Dora Elia Sandoval	Enrique Fernandez	Woody Massengale	Joe Montalvo	Dennis Dodson	Pat Melancon
Kleberg	Martha I. Soliz	John T. Hubert	David Rosse	Norma Nelda Alvarez	Roy Cantu	Romeo L. Lomas
*Knox	Annette Offutt	David W. Hajek	Johnny McCowan	Dan Godsey	Jimmy Urbanczyk	Johnny Birkenfeld
Lamar	Marvin Ann Patterson	Gary Young	Lawrence Malone	Lonnie Layton	Kevin Jenkins	Jackie Wheeler
Lamb	Stephanie Chester	Mark Yarbrough	Rodney Smith	Kent Lewis	Danny Short	Jimmy Young
Lampasas	Terri Cox	Larry W. Allison	Robert L. Vincent Jr.	Alex Wittenburg	Lowell B. Ivey	Jack B. Cox
La Salle	Margarita A. Esqueda	René M. Peña	Chris Hinojosa III	Maria Teresa Adams	Rene Benavidez	Raul Ayala
Lavaca	Calvin J. Albrecht	Heather Hollub	Charles A. Netardus	Ronald Berckenhoff	David E. Wagner	Dennis W. Kocian
Lee	Lisa Teinert	Martin Placke	Maurice Pitts Jr.	Douglas Hartfield	Ronnie Bradshaw	Linda Kovar
Leon	Diane Oden Davis	Whitney Thompson Smith	Joey Sullivan	David Ferguson	Mark Ivey	Dean Player
*Liberty	Melody Gilmore	Michael R. (Mike) Little	Todd Fontenot	Lee Groce	Melvin Hunt	Norman Brown
Limestone	Carol Sue Jenkins	William Roy DeFriend	John McCarver	William (Pete) Kirven	Morris D. Beaver	Milton Carroll
Lipscomb	Kim Blau	Lynn Switzer	Juan Cantu	Stanley Born	Scotty Schilling	John Fritzlen
Live Oak	Lois Shannon	Martha Warner	Richard Lee	Donna K. Mills	Jim Bassett	Emilio Garza
Llano	Joyce Gillow	Sam Oatman	Johnnie B. Heck	Henry I. Parker	Thomas E. Duncan	Jerry Don Moss
Loving	Beverly Hanson	Randall W. Reynolds	Harlan Hopper	Joe R. Renteria	Tom Jones	William (Bill) Wilkinson
Lubbock	Barbara Sucsy	Matthew D. Powell	Bill McCay	Mark E. Heinrich	Gilbert Flores	Patti Jones
Lynn	Sandra Laws	Brian L. Kingston	Keith Wied	Mike Braddock	Don Blair	Brad Hammonds
Madison	Joyce Batson	William C. (Bill) Bennett	Ricky Driscoll	Phillip Grisham	Tommy Cornelius	Mary Andrus
Marion	Janie McCay	William K. Gleason	Bob Higgins	T. W. (Sam) Smith	C.E. (Cecil) Bourne	Charles W. Treadwell
Martin	Susie Hull	Hardy L. Wilkerson	Jesus Garza	Valentino Sotelo	Bobby Holland	Bryan Cox
Mason	Pam Beam	Amos Barton	Wayne Hofmann	John Dalton Fleming	Stanley Toeppich	Eldon Kothmann
Matagorda	Becky Denn	Steven E. Reis	Daniel Pustka	George Deshotels	James Gibson	David J. Woodson
*Maverick	Irene Rodriguez	Roberto Serna	Eliaz Maldonado	Rudy Heredia	David R. Saucedo	Cesar Flores
McCulloch	Mackye Johnson	Amos Barton	Jim Quinn	Jerry Bratton	J.P. Murray	Brent C. Deeds
*McLennan	Karen Matkin	John Segrest	Kelly Snell	Lester Gibson	Joe A. Mashek	Ray Meadows
McMullen	Dorairene Garza	Martha Warner	Tim Teal	Murray Swaim	Paul Koonce	Maximo G. Quintanilla Jr.
Medina	Maria Eva Soto	Daniel J. Kindred	Richard Saathoff	Beverly Keller	David Lynch	Kelly Carroll
Menard	Polly Reeves	Amos Barton	Boyd Murchison	James Taylor	Pete Crothers	Larry Burch
Midland	Vivian Wood	Teresa Clingman	Jimmy Smith	Robin Donnelly	Julius L. Brooks	Randy Prude
Milam	Cindy Fechner	Kerry Spears	George Tomek	Kenneth Hollas	C. Dale Jaecks	Burke Bauerschlag
Mills	Carolyn Foster	Michael Brandon Murray	John Mann	Jed Garren	William Crawford	Wayne Wilcox
Mitchell	Sharon Hammond	Ann Reed	Randy Anderson	Carl Guelker	Jesse Munoz	Billy H. Preston
Montague	Lesia Darden	Jack McGaughey	Jon Kernek	Jerry Clement	Steve Howard	Tommie Sappington

County	District Clerk	District Attorney	Comm. Precinct 1	Comm. Precinct 2	Comm. Precinct 3	Comm. Precinct 4
*Montgomery	Barbara Gladden Adamick	Brett W. Ligon	Mike Meador	Craig Doyal	Ed E. Chance	Ed Rinehart
Moore	Diane Hoefling	David M. Green	J. Daniel Garcia	Bobby Barker	Milton Pax	Lynn Cartrite
Morris	Gwen Oney	J. Stephen Cowan	Hubert L. Mitchell Jr.	Dearl Quarles	Michael Clair	Gary Camp
Motley	Kate E. Hurt	Becky B. McPherson	Roy G. Stephens	Donnie L. Turner	Franklin Jameson	Russell Alexander
Nacogdoches	Loretta Cammack	Stephanie K. Stephens	Tom Bush	Reggie L. Cotton Jr.	Charles W. Simmons	Tom Strickland
Navarro	Marilyn Greer	R. Lowell Thompson	Kit Herrington	Faith Holt	David (Butch) Warren	James Olson
Newton	Bree Allen	Misti Weeks Spacek	William L. Fuller	Thomas Gill	Prentiss L. Hopson	Leonard Powell
*Nolan	Patti Neill	Ann Reed	Terry Willman	Terry Locklar	Tommy White	Tony Lara
*Nueces	Patsy Perez	Carlos Valdez	Mike Pusley	Betty Jean Longoria	Oscar O. Ortiz	H.C. (Chuck) Cazalas
Ochiltree	Shawn Bogard	David Scott	Duane Pshigoda	Doug Barnes	Richard Burger	Larry Hardy
Oldham	Becky Groneman	Kent Birdsong	Quincy Taylor	Donnie Knox	Roger Morris III	Billy Don Brown
Orange	Vickie Edgerly	John D. Kimbrough	David Dubose	Owen Burton	John P. Dubose	Beamon Minton
Palo Pinto	Janie Glover	Michael K. Burns	Beth Ray	Ed Laney	George Nowak	Jeff Fryer
Panola	Debra Johnson	Danny Buck Davidson	Ronnie LaGrone	Douglas M. Cotton	Hermon E. Reed Jr.	Dale LaGrone
Parker	Elvera Johnson	Don Schnebly	George Conley	Joe Brinkley	John Roth	Jim Webster
Parmer	Sandra Warren	Kathryn Gurley	Kirk Frye	James Clayton	Ronald Byrd	Elvis Powell
Pecos	Gayle Henderson	Jesse Gonzales (83rd) / Laurie English (112th)	George Riggs	Juan Rodriguez	J.H. (Jay) Kent	Santiago Cantu Jr.
Polk	Kathy E. Clifton	Lee Hon	Robert C. (Bob) Willis	Ronnie Vincent	Milton (Milt) Purvis	Tommy Overstreet
Potter	Caroline Woodburn	Randall C. Sims	H.R. Kelly	Manuel Perez	Joe Kirkwood	Alphonso S. Vaughn
Presidio	Virginia Pallarez	Jesse Gonzales Jr.	Felipe A. Cordero	Eloy Aranda	Carlos Amendariz	Danny Watts
Rains	Deborah Traylor	Robert Vittow	Patsy Marshall	Robert M. Sisk	Gary Mike Bishop	Jimmie Painter
Randall	Jo Carter	James A. Farren	Robert (Bob) Karrh	Gene Parker	George E. (Skip) Huskey	Buddy DeFord
Reagan	Terri Pullig	Laurie English	Jim O'Bryan	Ron Galloway	Tommy Holt	Thomas Strube
Real	Bella A. Rubio	Daniel J. Kindred	Manuel Rubio	Wade Reagor	Gene Buckner	Joe W. Connell Sr.
Red River	Janice Gentry	Val Varley	Donnie Gentry	David Barnett	Richard Harvey	Josef Hausler
Reeves	Patricia Tarin	Randall W. Reynolds	Rojelio (Roy) Alvarado	Gabriel Martinez	Saul F. Herrera	Ramiro (Ram) Guerra
Refugio	Ruby Garcia	Michael A. Sheppard	Ann Lopez	Stanley Tuttle	Gary Bourland	Rodrigo Bernal
Roberts	Toni Rankin	Lynn Switzer	Cleve Wheeler	Ken R. Gill	Kelly V. Flowers	James F. Duvall Jr.
Robertson	Barbara Axtell	John C. Paschall	Keith Petitt	Donald Threadgill	Keith Nickelson	Robert Bielamowicz
Rockwall	Kay McDaniel	Kenda Culpepper	Jerry Wimpee	Lorie Grinnan	Dennis Bailey	David Magness
Runnels	Tammy Burleson	George McCrea	Robert Moore	Ronald Presley	James Thurman Self	Richard W. Strube
Rusk	Jean Hodges	Micheal E. Jimerson	W.D. (Bill) Hale	Michael Pepper	Freddy Swann	Harold Howell
Sabine	Tanya Walker	J. Kevin Dutton	Keith C. Clark	Jimmy McDaniel	Doyle Dickerson	Fayne Warner
San Augustine	Jean Steptoe	J. Kevin Dutton	Tommy Hunter	Edward Wilson	Dale Mixon	Rodney Ainsworth
*San Jacinto	Rebecca Capers	Bill Burnett	Laddie McAnally	Royce Wells	James (Butch) Moody	Mark Nettuno
San Patricio	Laura Miller	Patrick L. Flanigan	Nina G. Treviño	Fred P. Nardini	Alma V. Moreno	Jim Price Jr.
San Saba	Kim Wells	Sam Oatman	Otis Judkins	Rickey Lusty	Kenley Kroll	Roger McGehee
Schleicher	Peggy Williams	Stephen Lupton	Johnny F. Mayo Jr.	Lynn Meador	Kirk Griffin	Matt Brown
Scurry	Candace Jones	Dana Cooley	Terry D. Williams	Jerry House	Howard Limmer	Chloanne Lindsey
Shackelford	Cathey Lee	Billy John Edwards	David Everett	Larry Cauble	Jimmy T. Brooks	Stan West
Shelby	Lori Oliver	Lynda Kay Russell	Roscoe McSwain	Jimmy Lout	Travis Rodgers	Bradley Allen
Sherman	Gina Jones	David M. Green	Dana Buckles	Randy Williams	Jeff Crippen	Tommy Asher
Smith	Lois Rogers	D. Matt Bingham III	Jeff Warr	William A. (Bill) McGinnis	Terry Phillips	JoAnn Hampton
Somervell	Candace (Candy) Garrett	Dale Hanna	Zach Cummings	Mike Ford	Lloyd Wirt	James Barnard

County	District Clerk	District Attorney	Comm. Precinct 1	Comm. Precinct 2	Comm. Precinct 3	Comm. Precinct 4
Starr	Eloy R. Garcia	Heriberto Silva	Jaime M. Alvarez	Raul (Roy) Peña Jr.	Eloy Garza	Abel N. Gonzalez Jr.
Stephens	Christie Coapland	Brenda Gray	Jerry Toland	D.C. (Button) Sikes	Joe F. High	Rickie Ray Carr
Sterling	Susan Wyatt	Stephen Lupton	Terry Wojtek	Russell Noletubby	Deborah H. Horwood	Reed Stewart
Stonewall	Belinda Page	Michael Fouts	David Hoy	Kenny Spitzer	Billy Kirk Meador	Gary Myers
*Sutton	Veronica E. Hernandez	Laurie English	Miguel (Mike) Villanueva	John Wade	Milton Cavaness	Fred Perez
Swisher	Brenda Hudson	Wally Hatch	Lloyd Rahlfs	Joe Bob Thompson	Harvey N. Foster	Tim Reed
Tarrant	Thomas A. Wilder	Joe Shannon Jr.	Roy Brooks	Marti VanRavenswaay	Gary Fickes	J.D. Johnson
Taylor	Patricia Henderson	James M. Eidson	Randy Williams	Dwayne Tucker	Stan D. Egger	Charles (Chuck) Statler
Terrell	Martha Allen	Fred Hernandez	Yolanda G. Lopez	Della Fuentes	Charles Stegall	Kenn Norris
Terry	Paige Lindsey	Ramon Gallegos	Mike Swain	Dale Andrews	Shorty Martinez	Jessie Hartman
Throckmorton	Mary Susie Walraven	Michael Fouts	Casey Wells	Johnny Jones	Teddy Clark	Greg Scarlett
Titus	Debra Abston	Charles C. Bailey	Don Boggs	Mike Fields	Phillip Hinton	Thomas Hockaday
Tom Green	Sheri Woodfin	Stephen Lupton (51st) George McCrea (119th)	Ralph Hoelscher	Aubrey DeCordova	Steve Floyd	Richard S. Easingwood Jr.
Travis	Amalia Rodriguez-Mendoza	Rosemary Lehmberg	Ron Davis	Sarah Eckhardt	Karen Huber	Margaret Gómez
Trinity	Cheryl Cartwright	Joe Ned Dean	Grover Worsham	Jannette Hortman	Cecil Webb	Jimmy Brown
*Tyler	Melissie Evans	Joe R. Smith	Martin Nash	James (Rusty) Hughes	Mike Marshall	Jack Walston
Upshur	Carolyn Bullock	William (Billy) Byrd	James Crittenden	Joe (Buddy) Ferguson	Lloyd Crabtree	Glenn Campbell
Upton	LaWanda McMurray	Laurie English	Gary N. (Pete) Jackson	Tommy Owens	W.M. (Willie) Martinez	Leon Patrick
Uvalde	Lydia Steele	Daniel J. Kindred	Randy Scheide	Daniel Sanchez	Jerry W. Bates	Jesse R. Moreno
*Val Verde	Luz Clara Balderas	Fred Hernandez	Ramiro V. Ramon	Rogelio (Roy) H. Musquiz	Robert Beau Nettleton	Jesus E.(Cheo) Ortiz
Van Zandt	Karen Wilson	Leslie Poynter Dixon	Ricky LaPrade	Virgil Melton Jr.	Duanne Harvey	Ronald G. Carroll
Victoria	Cathy Stuart	Stephen B. Tyler	Kenny Spann	Kevin M. Janak	Gary E. Burns	Wayne D. Dierlam
Walker	Robyn Flowers	David P. Weeks	B.J. Gaines Jr.	Robert Earl Autery	Bobby Warren	Tim Paulsel
Waller	Patricia Spadachene	Elton Mathis	Odis Styers	Terry Harrison	Sylvia Cedillo	Glenn Beckendorff
Ward	Patricia Oyerbides	Randall W. Reynolds	Julian Florez	Larry Hanna	Dexter Nichols	Eddie Nelms
Washington	Vicki Lehmann	Bill Parham	Zeb Heckmann	Donald Ahrens	Kirk Hanath	Joy Fuchs
Webb	Manuel Gutierrez	Jose Rubio Jr.	Frank Sciaraffa	Rosaura (Wawi) Tijerina	Gerardo (Jerry) Garza	Sergio (Keko) Martinez
Wharton	Denice K. Malota	Josh McCown	Mickey Reynolds	D.C. (Chris) King	Philip Miller	James (Jimmy) Kainer
Wheeler	Sherri Jones	Lynn Switzer	Daryl G. Snelgrooes	Tom Puryear	Hubert C. Moore	John Walker
Wichita	Dorsey Ray Trapp	Barry Macha	Ray Gonzalez	Pat Norriss	Barry Mahler	William (Bill) Presson
Wilbarger	Brenda Peterson	Staley Heatly	Richard Jacobs	Phillip Graf	Rodney Johnston	Lenville Morris
Willacy	Gilbert Lozano	Bernard Ammerman	Eliberto Guerra	Erasmo (Eddie) Chapa	Alfredo Serrato	Aurelio Guerra
Williamson	Lisa David	John Bradley	Lisa Birkman	Cynthia Long	Valerie Covey	Ron Morrison
Wilson	Deborah Bryan	René M. Peña	Albert Gamez Jr.	Leonard Rotter Jr.	Robert (Bobby) H. Lynn	Larry A. Wiley
Winkler	Sherry Terry	Michael L. Fostel	J.R. Carpenter	James R. (Robbie) Wolf	Randy Neal	Billy Ray Thompson
Wise	Cristy Fuqua	Greg Lowery	Danny White	Kevin Burns	Mikel Richardson	Terry Ross
Wood	Jenica Turner	Jim Wheeler	Keith Gilbreath	Jerry Gaskill	Roger W. Pace	Jerry Galloway
Yoakum	Vicki Blundell	Richard Clark	Woody Lindsey	Ben Coston	Chris Blundell	Tim Addison
Young	Carolyn Collins	Brenda Gray	John Hawkins	John Charles Bullock	Stacey Rogers Spivey	Jimmy R. Wiley
*Zapata	Dora M. Ramos	Joe Rubio Jr.	Jose Emilio Vela	Gabriel Villarreal Jr.	Joseph Rathmell	Norberto Garza
Zavala	Rachel Ramirez	Roberto Serna	Alfredo Sanchez	Raul G. Gomez	David A. Lopez	Matthew McHazlett Jr.

Texans in Congress

Besides the two members of the U.S. Senate allocated to each state, Texas is allocated 32 members in the U.S. House of Representatives. The term of office for members of the House is two years; the terms of all members will expire on Jan. 1, 2011. Senators serve six-year terms. Sen. Kay Bailey Hutchison's term will end in 2013. Sen. John Cornyn's term will end in 2015.

Addresses and phone numbers of the lawmakers' Washington and district offices are below, as well as the committees on which they serve. Washington **zip codes** are **20515** for members of the House and **20510** for senators. The telephone area code for Washington is **202**. On the Internet, House members can be reached through **www.house.gov/writerep**. In 2009, members of Congress received a salary of $174,000. Members in leadership positions received $193,400.

U.S. Senate

CORNYN, John. Republican (Home: Austin); Washington Office: 517 HSOB, Washington, D.C. 20510; (202) 224-2934, Fax 228-2856. Web site, cornyn.senate.gov.

Texas Offices: 221 W. 6th Ste. 1530, **Austin** 78701, (512) 469-6034; 5005 LBJ Ste. 1150, **Dallas** 75244, (972) 239-1310; 222 E. Van Buren Ste. 404, **Harlingen**

John Cornyn.

78550, (956) 423-0162; 5300 Memorial Dr. Ste. 980, **Houston** 77007, (713) 572-3337; 3405 22nd Ste. 203, **Lubbock** 79410, (806) 472-7533; 600 Navarro Ste. 210, **San Antonio** 78205, (210) 224-7485; 100 E. Ferguson Ste. 1004, **Tyler** 75702, (903) 593-0905.

Committees: Budget, Finance, Judiciary.

HUTCHISON, Kay Bailey. Republican (Home: Dallas); Washington Of-

Kay Bailey Hutchison.

fice: 284 RSOB, Washington, D.C. 20510; (202) 224-5922, Fax 224-0776. Web site, hutchison.senate.gov.

Texas Offices: 961 Federal Bldg., 300 E. 8th St., **Austin** 78701, (512) 916-5834; 500 Chestnut Ste. 1570, **Abilene** 79602, (325) 676-2839; 10440 N. Central Expy. Ste. 1160, **Dallas** 75231, (214) 361-3500; 1906G

E. Tyler St., **Harlingen** 78550, (956) 425-2253; 1919 Smith Ste. 800, **Houston** 77002, (713) 653-3456; 3133 General Hudnell Dr., **San Antonio** 78226, (210) 340-2885.

Committees: Appropriations; Banking, Housing and Urban Affairs; Commerce, Science and Transportation; Rules and Administration.

U.S. House of Representatives

BARTON, Joe, R-Ennis, District 6; Washington Office: 2109 RHOB; (202) 225-2002; **District**

Offices: 6001 West I-20 Ste. 200, Arlington 76017, (817) 543-1000; 303 N. 6th, Crockett 75835, (936) 544-8488; 2106A W. Ennis Ave. Ennis 75119, (972) 875-8488. **Committee**: Energy and Commerce.

BRADY, Kevin, R-The Woodlands, District 8; Washington Office: 301 CHOB; (202) 225-4901, Fax 225-5524. **District Offices**: 200 River Pointe Ste. 304, Conroe 77304, (936) 441-5700; 1202 Sam Houston Ave. Ste. 8, Huntsville 77340, (936) 439-9542; 420 Green Ave., Orange 77630, (409) 883-4197. **Committee**: Ways and Means.

BURGESS, Michael, R-Lewisville, District 26; Washington Office: 229 CHOB; (202) 225-7772, Fax 225-2919. **District Offices**: 1660 S. Stemmons Fwy. Ste. 230, Lewisville 75067, (972) 434-9700; 1100 Circle Dr. Ste. 200, Fort Worth 76119, (817) 531-8454. **Committee**: Energy and Commerce.

CARTER, John, R-Round Rock, District 31; Washington Office: 408 CHOB; (202) 225-3864. District Offices: 1717 N. I-35 Ste. 303, Round Rock 78664, (512) 246-1600; 6544B S. General Bruce Dr., Temple 76502, (254) 933-1392. **Committee**: Appropriations.

CONAWAY, K. Michael, R-Midland, District 11; Washington Office: 1527 LHOB; (202) 225-3605. **District Offices**: 6 Desta Dr. Ste. 2000, Midland 79705, (432) 687-2390; 501 Center Ave. Brownwood 76801, (325) 646-1950; 104 W. Sandstone, Llano 78643, (325) 247-2826; 411 W. 8th, Odessa 79761, (866) 882-3811; 33 Twohig Ste. 307, San Angelo 76903, (325) 659-4010. **Committees**: Agriculture, Armed Services, Intelligence, Standards of Official Conduct.

CUELLAR, Henry, D-Laredo, District 28; Washington Office: 336 CHOB; (202) 225-1640, Fax 225-1641. **District Offices**: 602 E. Calton Rd., Laredo 78041, (956) 725-0639; 615 E. Houston Ste. 451, San Antonio 78205, (210) 271-2851; 320 N. Main Ste. 221, McAllen 78501, (956) 631-4826; 100 S. Austin, Seguin 78155, (830) 401-0457; 100 N. FM 3167, Rio Grande City 78582, (956) 488-0952. **Committees**: Agriculture, Homeland Security, Oversight and Government Reform.

CULBERSON, John Abney, R-Houston, District 7; Washington Office: 1514 LHOB; (202) 225-2571, Fax 225-4381; District Office: 10000 Memorial Dr. Ste. 620, Houston 77024, (713) 682-8828. **Committee**: Appropriations.

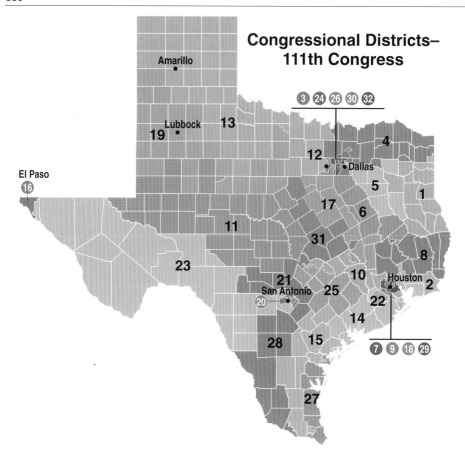

Congressional Districts–111th Congress

DOGGETT, Lloyd, D-Austin, District 25; Washington Office: 201 CHOB; (202) 225-4865; District Office: 300 E. 8th Ste. 763, Austin 78701, (512) 916-5921. Committees: Budget, Ways and Means.

EDWARDS, Chet, D-Waco, District 17; Washington Office: 2369 RHOB; (202) 225-6105, Fax 225-0350; District Offices: 600 Austin Ave. Ste. 29, Waco 76701, (254) 752-9600; 115 S. Main Ste. 202, Cleburne 76033, (817) 645-4743; 111 University Dr. East Ste. 216, College Station 77840, (979) 691-8787; 115 S. Main Ste. 202, Cleburne 76033, (817) 645-4796. Committees: Appropriations, Budget.

GOHMERT, Louie, R-Tyler, District 1; Washington Office: 510 CHOB; (202) 225-3035, Fax 226-1230; District Offices: 1121 ESE Loop 323 Ste. 206, Tyler 75701, (903) 561-6349; 101 E. Methvin Ste. 302, Longview 75601, (903) 236-8597; 300 E. Shepherd, Lufkin 75901, (866) 535-6302; 102 W. Houston, Marshall 75670, (866) 535-6302; 101 W. Main Ste. 160, Nacogdoches 75961, (866) 535-6302. Committees: Judiciary, Natural Resources, Small Business.

GONZALEZ, Charlie A., D-San Antonio, District 20; Washington Office: 303 CHOB; (202) 225-3236, Fax 225-1915; District Office: 124-B Federal Building, 727 East Durango, Federal Building, San Antonio 78206, (210) 472-6195. Committees: Energy and Commerce, House Administration, Judiciary.

GRANGER, Kay, R-Fort Worth, District 12; Washington Office: 320 CHOB; (202) 225-5071, Fax 225-5683; District Office: 1701 River Run Rd. Ste. 407, Fort Worth 76107, (817) 338-0909. Committee: Appropriations.

GREEN, Al, D-Houston, District 9; Washington Office: 236 CHOB; (202) 225-7508; District Office: 3003 South Loop West Ste. 460, Houston 77054, (713) 383-9234. Committees: Financial Services, Homeland Security.

GREEN, Gene, D-Houston, District 29; Washington Office: 2372 RHOB; (202) 225-1688, Fax 225-9903; District Offices: 256 N. Sam Houston Pkwy. E. Ste. 29, Houston 77060, (281) 999-5879; 11811 I-10 East Ste. 430, Houston 77029, (713) 330-0761; 909 Decker Dr. Ste. 124, Baytown 77520, (281) 420-0502. Committees: Energy and Commerce, Foreign Affairs.

HALL, Ralph M., R-Rockwall, District 4; Washington Office: 2405 RHOB; (202) 225-6673, Fax 225-3332; District Offices: 104 N. San Jacinto, Rockwall 75087, (972) 771-9118; 101 E. Pecan, Sherman 75090, (903) 892-1112; 710 James Bowie

Dr., New Boston 75570, (903) 628-8309; 1800 N. Graves Ste. 101, McKinney 75069, (214) 726-9949; 320 Church Ste. 132, Sulphur Springs 75482, (903) 885-8138; 4303 Texas Blvd. Ste. 2, Texarkana 75503, (903) 794-4445. **Committees**: Energy and Commerce, Science and Technology.

HENSARLING, Jeb, R-Dallas, District 5; Washington Office: 129 CHOB; (202) 225-3484, Fax 226-4888. **District Offices**: 6510 Abrams Rd. Ste. 243, Dallas 75231, (214) 349-9996; 702 E. Corsicana St., Athens 77571, (903) 675-8288. **Committees**: Budget, Financial Services.

HINOJOSA, Rubén, D-Mercedes, District 15; Washington Office: 2463 RHOB; (202) 225-2531, Fax 225-5688; **District Offices**: 2864 W. Trenton Rd., Edinburg 78539, (956) 682-5545; 107 S. St. Mary's St., Beeville 78102, (361) 358-8400. **Committees**: Education and Labor, Financial Services.

JACKSON LEE, Sheila, D-Houston, District 18; Washington Office: 2160 RHOB; (202) 225-3816, Fax 225-3317; **District Offices**: 1919 Smith Ste. 1180, Houston 77002, (713) 655-0050; 420 W. 19th St., Houston 77008, (713) 861-4070; 6719 W. Montgomery Ste. 204, Houston 77091; 3300 Lyons Ave. Ste. 301, Houston 77020, (713) 227-7740. **Committees**: Foreign Affairs, Homeland Security, Judiciary.

JOHNSON, Eddie Bernice, D-Dallas, District 30; Washington Office: 1511 LHOB; (202) 225-8885, Fax 225-1477; **District Office:** 3102 Maple Ave. Ste. 600, Dallas 75201, (214) 922-8885. **Committees**: Science and Technology, Transportation and Infrastructure.

JOHNSON, Sam, R-Plano, District 3; Washington Office: 1211 LHOB; (202) 225-4201, Fax 225-1485; **District Office**: 2929 N. Central Expressway, Ste. 240, Richardson 75080, (972) 470-0892. **Committee**: Ways and Means.

MARCHANT, Kenny, R-Coppell, District 24; Washington Office: 227 CHOB; (202) 225-6605, Fax 225-0074. **District Office**: 9901 E. Valley Ranch Parkway Ste. 3035, Irving 75063, (972) 556-0162. **Committees**: Financial Services.

McCAUL, Michael, R-Austin, District 10; Washington Office: 131 CHOB; (202) 225-2401, Fax 225-5955. **District Offices**: 5929 Balcones Dr. Ste. 305, Austin 78731, (512) 473-2357; 2000 S. Market Ste. 303, Brenham 77833, (979) 830-8497; [Katy] 1550 Foxlake Ste. 120, Houston 77084, (281) 398-1247; 990 Village Sq. Ste. B, Tomball 77375. **Committees**: Foreign Affairs, Homeland Security, Science and Technology.

NEUGEBAUER, Randy, R-Lubbock, District 19; Washington Office: 1424 LHOB; (202) 225-4005, Fax 225-9615. **District Offices**: 500 Chestnut Rm. 819, Abilene 79602, (325) 675-9779; 1510 Scurry Ste. B, Big Spring 79720, (432) 264-7592; 611 University Ave. Ste. 220, Lubbock 79401, (806) 763-1611. **Committees**: Agriculture, Financial Services, Science and Technology.

OLSON, Pete, R-Sugar Land, District 22; Washington Office: 514 CHOB; (202) 225-5951, Fax 225-5241. **District Office**: 1650 Hwy 6 Ste. 150, Sugar Land 77478, (281) 494-2690; 17225 El Camino Real Ste. 447, Houston 77058, (281) 486-1095. **Committee**: Homeland Security, Science and Technology, Transportation and Infrastructure..

ORTIZ, Solomon P., D-Corpus Christi, District 27; Washington Office: 2110 RHOB; (202) 225-7742, Fax 226-1134; **District Offices**: 3649 Leopard Ste. 510, Corpus Christi 78408, (361) 883-5868; 1805 Ruben Torres B-27, Brownsville 78526, (956) 541-1242. **Committees**: Armed Services, Transportation and Infrastructure.

PAUL, Ron, R-Lake Jackson, District 14; Washington Office: 203 CHOB; (202) 225-2831. **District Offices**: 122 West Way Ste. 301, Lake Jackson 77566, (979) 285-0231; 601 25th Ste. 216, Galveston 77550, (409) 766-7013; 1501 Mockingbird Lane Ste. 229, Victoria 77904, (361) 576-1231. **Committees**: Financial Services, Foreign Affairs.

POE, Ted, R-Humble, District 2; Washington Office: 430 CHOB; (202) 225-6565, Fax 225-5547. **District Offices**: 505 Orleans Ste. 100, Beaumont 77701, (409) 212-1997; 20202 U.S. Hwy 59 N. Ste. 105, Humble 77338, (281) 446-0242. **Committees**: Foreign Affairs, Judiciary.

REYES, Silvestre, D-El Paso, District 16; Washington Office: 2433 RHOB; (202) 225-4831, Fax 225-2016; **District Office**: 310 N. Mesa Ste. 400, El Paso 79901, (915) 534-4400. **Committees**: Armed Services, Intelligence (chairman).

RODRIGUEZ, Ciro, D-San Antonio, District 23; Washington Office: 2351 RHOB; (202) 225-4511. **District Offices**: 1313 SE Military Dr. Ste. 101, San Antonio 78221, (210) 992-1874; Pecos County Courthouse, 103 W. Callaghan, Fort Stockton 79735, (432) 336-3975; 100 S. Monroe, Eagle Pass 78852, (830) 757-8398; 208 E. Losoya, Del Rio 78840, (830) 774-5500. **Committees**: Appropriations, Veterans Affairs.

SESSIONS, Pete, R-Dallas, District 32; Washington Office: 2233 RHOB; (202) 225-2231, Fax 225-5878; **District Office**: 12750 Merit Dr. Ste. 1434, Dallas 75251, (972) 392-0505. **Committee**: Rules.

SMITH, Lamar S., R-San Antonio, District 21; Washington Office: 2409 RHOB; (202) 225-4236, Fax 225-8628; **District Offices**: 1100 NE Loop 410 Ste. 640, San Antonio 78209, (210) 821-5024; 3536 Bee Cave Rd. Ste. 212, Austin 78746, (512) 306-0439; 301 Junction Hwy. Ste. 346C, Kerrville 78028, (830) 896-0154. **Committees**: Homeland Security, Judiciary, Science and Technology.

THORNBERRY, William M. (Mac), R-Clarendon, District 13; Washington Office: 2209 RHOB; (202) 225-3706, Fax 225-3486; **District Offices**: 905 S. Fillmore Ste. 520, Amarillo 79101, (806) 371-8844; 4245 Kemp Ste. 506, Wichita Falls 76308, (940) 692-1700. **Committees**: Armed Services, Intelligence. ☆

Federal Funds to Texas by County, 2007

Texas received **$171,765,960,847** in 2007 from the federal government. Below, the distribution of funds is shown by county. The first figure after the county name represents **total direct** expenditures to the county for fiscal year 2007. The second and third figures are that part of the total that went directly for **individuals**, either in **retirement** payments, such as Social Security, or **other** direct payments, principally Medicare. In the last column are direct payments other than to individuals, principally **agricultural** programs such as crop insurance. *For a more complete explanation, see end of chart. *Source: Consolidated Federal Funds Report 2007, U.S. Department of Commerce.*

COUNTY	TOTAL	For INDIVIDUALS		other direct (ag., etc.)	COUNTY	TOTAL	For INDIVIDUALS		other direct (ag., etc.)
		retirement	other				retirement	other	
	(Thousands of dollars, 000)					(Thousands of dollars, 000)			
Anderson	$ 324,098	$ 152,477	$ 85,095	$ 123	Cooke	204,896	101,845	50,890	7,239
Andrews	63,319	29,434	18,155	5,127	Coryell	337,211	168,981	43,913	1,834
Angelina	511,560	245,943	133,263	1,660	Cottle	22,401	6,078	4,635	6,366
Aransas	141,823	90,837	33,667	327	Crane	16,528	7,427	6,581	267
Archer	64,990	34,598	8,347	2,941	Crockett	21,669	8,112	4,073	1,272
Armstrong	16, 231	6,079	3,330	4,307	Crosby	77,340	16,110	19,489	30,826
Atascosa	222,238	108,451	45,131	3,998	Culberson	23,804	5,050	4,799	924
Austin	1,831,265	73,248	38,565	1,832	Dallam	54,167	20,071	11,536	16,997
Bailey	55,804	14,870	12,061	18,424	Dallas	14,374,675	4,113,587	2,348,253	19,719
Bandera	135,634	79,753	16,031	200	Dawson	152,128	32,381	37,814	43,113
Bastrop	320,753	174,067	54,175	1,013	Deaf Smith	111,600	34,293	25,504	30,140
Baylor	40,901	15,300	11,165	5,285	Delta	44,772	16,970	11,665	1,878
Bee	184,008	67,850	50,234	4,597	Denton	1,870,544	704,037	226,624	5,349
Bell	5,043,939	921,703	224,125	6,823	DeWitt	135,519	51,157	38,421	1,718
Bexar	15,377,086	4,778,191	1,914,757	23,568	Dickens	32,711	7,762	10,743	5,910
Blanco	77,084	41,983	21,065	112	Dimmit	105,162	20,377	19,132	1,152
Borden	5,531	786	666	3,163	Donley	33,028	12,798	8,746	4,995
Bosque	132,537	64,700	30,012	992	Duval	130,128	32,154	33,503	2,429
Bowie	1,084,034	340,567	154,511	4,540	Eastland	156,142	64,935	46,443	4,774
Brazoria	1,008,270	563,522	225,598	15,647	Ector	566,876	272,300	178,417	823
Brazos	860,068	268,121	121,557	4,997	Edwards	21,569	6,787	9,418	373
Brewster	86,224	24,531	13,325	1,470	Ellis	551,483	298,517	124,127	9,202
Briscoe	26,882	5,341	4,969	8,129	El Paso	5,931,049	1,627,003	854,673	25,176
Brooks	78,025	18,505	16,926	849	Erath	178,988	83,236	51,487	1,915
Brown	269,988	126,617	78,058	2,242	Falls	142,390	50,865	32,198	6,832
Burleson	111,876	52,651	24,173	3,669	Fannin	265,932	110,439	53,083	8,045
Burnet	241,587	153,352	39,819	2,863	Fayette	173,277	81,696	43,562	1,287
Caldwell	185,037	83,543	44,465	2,227	Fisher	53,484	13,635	10,148	19,123
Calhoun	117,647	53,429	24,807	6,421	Floyd	86,521	16,863	15,023	36,102
Callahan	93,377	43,378	19,238	1,579	Foard	18,593	5,591	3,985	3,530
Cameron	2,029,808	639,652	446,509	24,294	Fort Bend	1,042,620	572,774	146,030	26,882
Camp	93,630	42,302	24,617	753	Franklin	52,761	27,909	14,933	299
Carson	43,626	16,942	10,141	10,592	Freestone	112,408	52,626	23,276	381
Cass	243,564	119,325	60,882	-856	Frio	103,413	30,816	21,149	7,053
Castro	61,415	14,448	10,922	27,151	Gaines	122,280	23,815	20,116	14,682
Chambers	155,045	45,651	30,857	6,085	Galveston	2,015,403	685,056	365,401	8,037
Cherokee	277,549	119,338	79,419	1,151	Garza	157,690	11,393	11,288	6,618
Childress	65,412	18,001	12,506	11,519	Gillespie	160,185	100,092	34,858	957
Clay	56,555	29,400	14,269	2,637	Glasscock	15,130	2,157	825	10,588
Cochran	38,918	8,091	6,514	19,040	Goliad	53,838	20,135	11,833	1,266
Coke	23,188	11,788	6,117	835	Gonzales	164,345	52,670	30,725	1,772
Coleman	87,893	34,290	29,311	2,191	Gray	148,206	66,759	54,070	5,779
Collin	3,341,516	941,288	205,930	7,804	Grayson	687,701	357,030	176,834	12,596
Collingsworth	41,689	9,950	8,069	15,246	Gregg	738,620	370,087	190,627	1,018
Colorado	140,587	60,708	33,644	7,767	Grimes	137,781	62,356	31,278	415
Comal	756,349	359,935	85,326	1,247	Guadalupe	566,275	385,416	82,320	4,743
Comanche	112,132	44,057	32,491	4,739	Hale	254,211	77,641	63,659	53,349
Concho	149,507	8,035	6,561	6,793	Hall	48,395	11,191	9,761	17,866

COUNTY	TOTAL	For INDIVIDUALS		other direct (ag., etc.)	COUNTY	TOTAL	For INDIVIDUALS		other direct (ag., etc.)
		retirement	other				retirement	other	
(Thousands of dollars, 000)					(Thousands of dollars, 000)				
Hamilton	68,702	25,731	20,754	882	Marion	84,186	34,331	16,752	155
Hansford	35,841	12,056	6,707	13,439	Martin	46,513	9,752	7,376	19,724
Hardeman	44,614	14,164	10,764	4,317	Mason	28,637	14,012	7,317	878
Hardin	279,265	143,241	75,669	7,506	Matagorda	251,207	96,191	50,612	13,367
Harris	21,152,659	6,086,947	3,608,070	68,661	Maverick	306,833	80,829	70,166	2,517
Harrison	407,265	153,548	86,572	1,258	McCulloch	68,585	25,324	19,143	3,670
Hartley	23,394	2,607	1,276	16,279	McLennan	1,503,698	651,666	250,642	13,927
Haskell	73,307	21,586	14,832	21,759	McMullen	9,040	2,525	759	435
Hays	503,195	253,723	80,953	1,751	Medina	238,026	117,172	43,800	5,836
Hemphill	15,809	7,057	5,149	1,012	Menard	18,512	7,744	5,703	348
Henderson	382,246	196,724	102,409	818	Midland	513,704	255,875	132,349	4,810
Hidalgo	2,870,374	929,932	717,072	48,642	Milam	168,435	76,873	34,344	6,056
Hill	243,391	117,726	58,343	12,031	Mills	37,137	17,212	11,314	546
Hockley	171,708	49,992	40,932	33,632	Mitchell	61,277	20,492	16,309	10,815
Hood	278,826	193,070	53,374	395	Montague	147,458	75,314	38,541	903
Hopkins	191,168	89,634	51,389	1,410	Montgomery	1,326,936	810,127	287,814	6,286
Houston	203,916	74,934	46,220	1,712	Moore	76,079	34,935	16,554	14,555
Howard	733,382	99,505	68,470	16,085	Morris	104,250	51,791	27,582	379
Hudspeth	48,209	5,728	3,494	2,785	Motley	17,763	5,044	3,720	4,056
Hunt	1,082,914	224,179	120,791	5,108	Nacogdoches	377,393	151,557	98,784	10,333
Hutchinson	131,328	65,179	37,797	4,153	Navarro	303,068	134,293	73,163	5,764
Irion	9,622	5,321	2,177	660	Newton	88,524	37,763	23,297	1,008
Jack	44,536	20,912	12,512	344	Nolan	146,623	46,345	32,555	10,099
Jackson	99,281	35,370	27,196	13,585	Nueces	2,391,389	858,654	466,924	28,674
Jasper	257,263	102,439	71,240	2,122	Ochiltree	40,608	16,531	8,806	11,097
Jeff Davis	15,657	7,104	2,517	166	Oldham	39,560	5,292	2,817	2,779
Jefferson	1,943,654	672,271	533,748	16,081	Orange	531,784	264,904	154,986	5,696
Jim Hogg	51,571	11,895	12,421	410	Palo Pinto	184,105	79,724	46,118	503
Jim Wells	303,440	102,234	79,006	7,264	Panola	138,519	63,850	38,973	81
Johnson	632,916	363,294	141,077	1,514	Parker	416,780	255,025	78,519	1,022
Jones	129,546	47,451	31,845	21,784	Parmer	71,251	18,123	11,134	32,339
Karnes	113,986	36,719	27,487	2,490	Pecos	80,096	27,106	16,343	5,972
Kaufman	488,176	266,539	127,744	1,755	Polk	426,420	278,191	91,943	1,325
Kendall	198,164	137,163	27,117	457	Potter	3,654,127	464,441	198,121	2,735
Kenedy	2,427	618	443	462	Presidio	80,991	15,047	9,466	342
Kent	9,397	2,932	1,707	2,285	Rains	57,175	35,179	11,698	141
Kerr	379,098	234,741	79,011	954	Randall	234,644	77,411	102,932	7,472
Kimble	41,157	15,808	7,278	252	Reagan	16,837	6,012	3,441	5,151
King	13,822	329	235	1,695	Real	38,197	15,209	5,719	38
Kinney	36,913	15,109	6,329	880	Red River	138,331	48,220	32,403	3,984
Kleberg	225,285	71,492	52,947	6,767	Reeves	283,391	26,027	19,317	4,409
Knox	43,602	12,350	11,133	10,372	Refugio	64,092	23,840	16,037	6,859
Lamar	353,151	157,882	81,348	544	Roberts	5,569	1,914	1,273	1,460
Lamb	137,227	35,622	30,970	38,969	Robertson	138,708	48,794	27,027	5,499
Lampasas	189,554	140,556	30,612	298	Rockwall	216,795	125,201	28,467	165
La Salle	57,629	14,054	11,888	1,726	Runnels	90,810	26,275	22,002	12,833
Lavaca	171,183	74,289	44,018	1,768	Rusk	247,940	116,144	65,858	401
Lee	74,638	39,448	17,266	415	Sabine	115,899	58,523	30,328	239
Leon	141,216	70,019	32,288	137	S. Augustine	79,052	32,724	19,708	256
Liberty	419,799	188,767	125,486	7,226	San Jacinto	122,164	60,153	31,402	84
Limestone	160,799	70,678	37,636	1,972	San Patricio	455,513	186,037	99,863	21,037
Lipscomb	19,188	7,341	4,715	3,224	San Saba	56,139	16.962	13,526	1,053
Live Oak	87,119	24,112	16,366	1,960	Schleicher	17,921	6,939	4,818	1,981
Llano	137,977	85,467	32,894	917	Scurry	107,843	39,570	28,629	12,475
Loving	797	237	17	293	Shackelford	24,117	10,394	5,511	1,340
Lubbock	1,453,129	581,078	403,255	46,182	Shelby	198,192	76,120	50,961	793
Lynn	74,442	15,234	12,910	35,197	Sherman	27,250	6,408	3,823	15,586
Madison	60,786	29,450	15,367	100	Smith	1,157,252	564,229	265,236	1,656

COUNTY	TOTAL	For INDIVIDUALS		other direct (ag., etc.)	COUNTY	TOTAL	For INDIVIDUALS		other direct (ag., etc.)
		retirement	other				retirement	other	
(Thousands of dollars, 000)					(Thousands of dollars, 000)				
Somervell	36,059	18,750	8,442	120	Van Zandt	300,984	154,662	82,635	1,124
Starr	292,713	76,198	67,998	6,726	Victoria	454,806	222,467	115,837	9,905
Stephens	58,003	26,522	19,37	607	Walker	266,331	115,932	66,636	874
Sterling	6,117	2,662	1,711	616	Waller	185,927	61,176	44,786	2,837
Stonewall	15,472	4,930	3,728	3,639	Ward	62,650	29,058	16,842	637
Sutton	16,382	7,404	4,538	617	Washington	205,668	97,334	45,311	698
Swisher	71,156	21,080	14,488	24,922	Webb	1,177,505	306,755	218,057	4,156
Tarrant	17,509,331	3,199,886	1,433,445	19,395	Wharton	278,638	101,589	70,438	27,323
Taylor	1,145,172	390,040	171,988	6,675	Wheeler	52,221	16,910	15,632	4,156
Terrell	10,575	3,629	1,806	708	Wichita	1,316,489	437,093	179,357	11,586
Terry	172,816	30,078	26,718	40,635	Wilbarger	119,881	40,779	32,468	11,857
Throckmrton	19,790	5,586	3,807	5,250	Willacy	134,248	37,244	31,380	17,059
Titus	161,991	66,943	45,512	242	Williamson	1,543,175	646,625	123,808	11,749
Tom Green	814,418	316,543	132,986	18,169	Wilson	194,918	104,144	29,190	2,696
Travis	9,038,425	1,892,525	649,998	71,483	Winkler	38,895	16,909	14,664	310
Trinity	118,386	58,517	34,388	104	Wise	211,834	122,292	41,881	745
Tyler	159,548	69,812	40,387	1,601	Wood	288,049	170,554	· 69,247	518
Upshur	225,093	113,841	56,932	554	Yoakum	54,047	15,203	9,665	22,305
Upton	20,737	8,667	6,147	2,533	Young	127,381	60,151	36,870	3,065
Uvalde	176,088	60,707	39,845	6,852	Zapata	66,863	19,848	21,930	105
Val Verde	440,038	109,659	43,991	1,608	Zavala	79,536	21,328	19,871	4,003

*__Total__ federal government expenditures include: grants, salaries and wages (Postal Service, Dept. of Defense, etc.), procurement contract awards, direct payments for individuals, and other direct payments other than for individuals, such as some agriculture programs.

__Retirement__ and disability programs include federal employee retirement and disability benefits, Social Security payments of all types, and veterans benefit payments.

__Other__ direct payments for individuals include Medicare, excess earned income tax credits, food stamps, unemployment compensation benefit payments and lower income housing assistance, but not salaries and wages.

__Other direct__ payments other than for individuals include crop insurance, wool and mohair loss assistance program, conservation reserve program, production flexibility payments for contract commodities and postal service funds other than salaries and procurements.

Source: Consolidated Federal Funds Report, Fiscal 2007, U.S. Department of Commerce, Bureau of the Census.

U.S. Tax Collections in Texas

*Fiscal Year	Individual Income and Employment Taxes	Corporation Income Taxes	Estate Taxes	Gift Taxes	Excise Taxes	TOTAL U.S. Taxes Collected in Texas
(1,000 of dollars) *Information for fiscal years, furnished by the Internal Revenue Service.*						
2007	$ 160,306,445	$ 41,823,425	$ 1,473,490	$ 218,194	$ 21,569,350	$ 225,390,904
2006	145,758,275	37,004,514	1,135,160	136,377	20,702,545	204,736,871
2005	125,816,805	29,186,478	1,196,362	118,231	13,074,838	169,392,715
2004	118,410,514	17,127,574	1,109,558	104,214	15,939,329	152,691,189
2003	116,353,959	11,487,059	958,791	147,351	12,987,394	141,934,554
2002	117,685,965	13,702,495	1,287,937	109,064	13,654,721	146,440,182
2001	127,738,858	17,598,181	1,242,130	248,892	14,350,268	161,178,329
2000	116,094,820	20,310,672	1,176,278	269,109	14,732,513	152,583,349
1999	104,408,504	13,098,033	968,736	446,168	16,729,589	135,651,029
1998	94,404,751	14,526,238	1,300,104	247,989	11,877,230	122,356,312
1997	90,222,786	13,875,653	933,616	159,111	12,185,271	117,376,440
1996	76,863,689	12,393,992	733,282	158,237	10,418,847	101,079,028
1995	69,706,333	10,677,881	869,528	152,683	11,135,857	92,342,282
1990	52,795,489	6,983,762	521,811	196,003	5,694,006	66,191,071
1985	41,497,114	5,637,148	528,106	41,560	6,058,110	53,762,038
1980	25,707,514	7,232,486	453,830	23,722	4,122,538	37,540,089
1970	6,096,961	1,184,342	135,694	20,667	843,724	8,281,389
1960	2,059,075	622,822	70,578	10,583	209,653	2,972,712

Beginning in 1976, the fiscal year ending date was changed to Sept. 30, from June 30.

Major Military Installations

Below are listed the major military installations in Texas in 2009. Data are taken from the U.S. Department of Defense *Base Structure Report 2008* and other sources. "Civilian" refers to Department of Defense personnel, and "other" refers to employees such as contractor personnel.

U.S. NAVY

Naval Air Station Corpus Christi
Location: Corpus Christi, in the Flour Bluff area (est. 1941).
Address: NAS Corpus Christi, 11001 D St., Corpus Christi 78419
Main phone number: (361) 961-2811
Personnel: 4,820 active-duty; 619 civilians.
Major units: Naval Air Training Command Headquarters; Training Air Wing Four; Commander of Mine Warfare Command; Coast Guard Air Group; Corpus Christi Army Depot (est. 1961).

Naval Air Station-Joint Reserve Base Fort Worth
Location: westside Fort Worth (est. 1994) [Carswell, est. 1942 as Fort Worth Army Air Field, closed 1993].
Address: NAS-JRB, 1215 Depot Ave., Fort Worth 76127
Main phone number: (817) 782-5000
Personnel: 4,658 active-duty; 33 civilians.
Major units: Fleet Logistics Support Squadron 46 and Squadron 59; 1; Marine Air Group 41; 14th Marine Regiment; 36th Airlift Wing, Texas Air National Guard; 301st Fighter Wing, Air Force Reserve; 10th Air Force.

Naval Station Ingleside
(the station is scheduled to close in April 2010.)
Location: Ingleside (est. 1990).
Address: 1455 Ticonderoga Rd., #W123, Ingleside 78362
Main phone number: (361) 776-4200
Personnel: 1,934 active-duty; 145 civilians.
Major units: Three Mine Countermeasures Squadrons with 6 mine warfare ships.

Naval Air Station Kingsville
Location: Kingsville (est. 1942).
Address: NAS Kingsville, Texas 78363
Main phone number: (361) 516-6136

Personnel: 500 active-duty; 350 civilians; 625 other.
Major units: Training Air Wing Two; Naval Auxiliary Landing Field Orange Grove; McMullen Target Range, Escondido Ranch.

U.S. ARMY

Fort Bliss
Location: El Paso (est. 1849).
Address: Fort Bliss, Texas 79916
Main phone number: (915) 568-2121
Personnel: 16,291 active-duty plus trainees; 2,423 civilians; 5,634 other.
Major units: 1st Armored Division; 32nd Air and Missile Defense Command; Air Defense Artillery School; 6th, 11th, 31st, and 108th Air Defense Artillery Brigades; 204th Military Intelligence Battalion; 76th Military Police Battalion; Biggs Army Airfield (est. 1916, originally called Bliss Field).

Fort Hood
Location: Killeen (est. 1942).
Address: Fort Hood, Texas 76544
Main phone number: (254) 287-2131
Personnel: 52,143 active-duty; 3,651 civilians; 11,065 other.
Major units: III Corps, Headquarters Command; 1st Cavalry Division; 4th Infantry Division; 13th Sustainment Command; 89th Military Police Brigade; 3rd Armored Cavalry Regiment; 504th Military Intelligence Brigade; 21st Cavalry Brigade (Air Combat); Army Operational Test Command; Darnell Army Medical Center.

Fort Sam Houston
Location: San Antonio (est. 1878).
Address: Fort Sam Houston, Texas 78234
Main phone number: (210) 221-1211
Personnel: 15,225 active-duty; 4,685 civilians; 5,517 other.
Major units: U.S. Army North; U.S. Army South;

Entrance to Sheppard Air Force Base at Wichita Falls. Robert Plocheck photo.

Brooke Army Medical Center; Institute of Surgical Research; Army Medical Command; Army Medical Dept. Center and School; 5th Recruiting Brigade; 12th Brigade, Western Region (ROTC); Camp Bullis (est. 1917), training area.

Red River Army Depot
Location: 18 miles west of Texarkana (est. 1941).
Address: Red River Army Depot, Texarkana 75507
Main phone number: (903) 334-2141
Personnel: 186 active-duty; 2,640 civilians; 2,278 other.
Major unit: Defense Distribution Center; U.S. Army Tank-Automotive and Armaments Command.

U.S. AIR FORCE

Brooks City-Base
Location: San Antonio (est. 1917, in 2002 the property was conveyed to the Brooks Development Authority for commercial use, but retains military missions.).
Address: Brooks City-Base, San Antonio 78235
Main phone number: (210) 536-1110
Personnel: 807 active-duty; 1,294 civilians.
Major units: 311th Human Systems Wing; 311th Mission Support Group; School of Aerospace Medicine; Air Force Institute for Occupational Health; 59th Medical Squadron; 68th Information Operations Squadron; 710th Intelligence Flight.

Dyess Air Force Base
Location: Abilene (est. 1942 as Tye Army Airfield, closed at end of World War II, re-established in 1956).
Address: Dyess Air Force Base, Texas 79607
Main phone number: (915) 696-0212
Personnel: 4,918 active-duty; 391 civilians.
Major units: 7th Bomb Wing (Air Combat Command); 317th Airlift Group.

Goodfellow Air Force Base
Location: San Angelo (est. 1940).
Address: Goodfellow AFB, San Angelo 76908
Main phone number: (915) 654-3231
Personnel: 1,308 active-duty, approximately 1,200 trainees; 585 civilians.
Major units: 17th Training Wing; 344th Military Intelligence Battalion.

Lackland Air Force Base
Location: San Antonio (est. 1942 when separated from Kelly Field).
Address: Lackland Air Force Base, Texas 78236
Main phone number: (210) 671-1110
Personnel: 11,701 active-duty; 4,508 civilians.
Major units: 37th Training Wing; 433d Airlift Wing; Defense Language Institute; Inter-American Air Force Academy; Kelly Field Annex (was Kelly Air Force Base, est. 1916, closed as base 2001).

Laughlin Air Force Base
Location: Del Rio (est. 1942).
Address: Laughlin Air Force Base, Texas 78843
Main phone number: (830) 298-3511
Personnel: 956 active-duty; 961 civilians.
Major units: 47th Flying Training Wing.

Randolph Air Force Base
Location: San Antonio (est. 1930).
Address: Randolph Air Force Base, Texas 78150
Main phone number: (210) 652-1110
Personnel: 2,910 active-duty; 5,804 civilians.
Major units: 12th Flying Training Wing; Air Education and Training Command; Air Force Personnel Center; Air Force Recruiting Service; Air Force Manpower Agency.

Sheppard Air Force Base
Location: Four miles north of Wichita Falls (est. 1941).

Congressional Medal Honors DeBakey

Renowned Houston heart surgeon Dr. Michael DeBakey was voted the highest civilian honor awarded by Congress in late 2007, the Congressional Gold Medal of Honor.

In an April 2008 ceremony in Washington, just weeks before his death on July 11, Dr. DeBakey was presented with the medal, which dates back to 1776 when the Continental Congress awarded the first medal to Gen. George Washington.

Michael E. DeBakey was born Michel Dabaghi Sept. 7, 1908, in Lake Charles, La., to immigrants from Lebanon. The family name was later Anglicized.

Dr. DeBakey joined Baylor College in Medicine in Houston in 1948 where he performed more than 60,000 surgeries. Besides he work in Houston, he is credited with developing from his World War II experience the concept of bringing mobile hospitals, later known as MASH units, to the battlefield.

Dr. Michael DeBakey.

He received the Presidential Medal of Freedom in 1969, and, in 1987 President Ronald Reagan awarded him the National Medal of Science.

Legislation to award a Congressional Gold Medal of Honor must be co-sponsored by two-thirds of the House and at least 67 senators must also cosponsor the proposal in that chamber.

The gold medal was originally a military honor until the Medal of Honor (commonly called the Congressional Medal of Honor) was instituted during the Civil War for military valor.

Texans previously receiving the Congressional Gold Medal have been Norman Borlaug, international agriculture professor at Texas A&M University, and the golf legend Byron Nelson of Fort Worth in 2006.

Also, Lady Bird Johnson in 1984, Sam Rayburn in 1962, and Howard Hughes, who was raised in Houston, in 1939. ☆

Address: Sheppard Air Force Base, Texas 76311
Main phone number: (940) 676-2511
Personnel: 2,603 active-duty; 1,304 civilians.
Major units: 82nd Training Wing;
  80th Flying Training Wing.

TEXAS MILITARY FORCES

Camp Mabry

Location: 2210 W. 35th St. in Austin. Just west of
  MoPac Blvd.
Address: Box 5218, Austin, Texas 78763
Main phone number: (512) 465-5101
Web site: www.agd.state.tx.us
Personnel: 1,876 guard, 527 civilians, 238 other.

Adjutant General of Texas:
  Lt. General Charles G. Rodriguez.
Major units:
  Joint Force Headquarters, the Standing Joint
  Interagency Task Force, the 36th Infantry Divi-
  sion, the 147th Reconnaissance Wing, 149th
  Fighter Wing, and the 136th Airlift Wing.
  Texas Air National Guard.

Texas Military Forces Museum,
  open Wednesday–Sunday, 10 a.m. - 4 p.m.

Tracing their history to early frontier days, the
Texas Military Forces are organized into the Army and
Air National Guard, the Texas State Guard and the Ad-
jutant General's Department.

When not in active federal service, Camp Mabry, in
northwest Austin, is the main storage maintenance and
administrative headquarters.

Camp Mabry was established in the early 1890s as
a summer encampment of the Texas Volunteer Guard,
a forerunner of the Texas National Guard. The name,
Camp Mabry, honors Woodford Haywood Mabry, adjutant general of Texas from 1891-98.

The Texas State Guard, an all-volunteer backup
force, was originally created by the Texas Legislature
in 1941. It became an active element of the state military forces in 1965 with a mission of reinforcing the
National Guard in state emergencies, and of replacing
National Guard units called into federal service.

The Texas State Guard has a membership of approximately 1,100 personnel.

When the forces were reorganized following World
War II, the Texas Air National Guard was added. Texas
Air National Guard units serve as augmentation units
to major Air Force commands, including the Air Combat Command, and the Air Mobility Command.

Approximately 3,500 men and women made up the
Air Guard in 2009.

The Army National Guard is available for either
national or state emergencies and has been used extensively during hurricanes, tornadoes and floods. There
are more than 117 armories throughout Texas, with
many units serving in recent years in Afghanistan,
Iraq, Kosovo, Bosnia and the Sinai.

The governor of Texas is commander-in-chief of
the Texas National and State Guards. This command
function is exercised through the adjutant general appointed by the governor and approved by both federal
and state legislative authority.

The adjutant general is the active administrative
head of the Texas Military Forces. In 2009, Adjutant
General Rodriguez was responsible for commanding
a total of 23,500 soldiers, airmen and civilians in the
Texas Army and Air National Guard, the State Guard
and the Adjutant General's Department.

When called into active federal service, National
Guard units come within the chain of command of the
Army and Air Force units. ☆

The VA Medical Center in Big Spring, one of ten hospitals that the U.S. Department of Veterans Affairs has in Texas. The others are at Amarillo, Bonham, Dallas, El Paso, Houston, Kerrville, San Antonio, Temple and Waco. In addition, the VA has numerous outpatient clinics in the state. Robert Plocheck photo.

Federal Courts in Texas

Source: The following list of U.S. appeals and district court judges and officials was compiled from court Web sites.

Texas is divided into four federal judicial districts, each of which is comprised of several divisions. Appeal from all Texas federal courts is to the **U.S. Fifth Circuit Court of Appeals** in New Orleans.

U.S. COURT OF APPEALS, FIFTH CIRCUIT

The Fifth Circuit is composed of Louisiana, Mississippi and Texas. Sessions are held in each of the states at least once a year and may be scheduled at any location having adequate facilities. U.S. circuit judges are appointed for life and received a salary of $184,500 in 2009.

Circuit Judges — Chief Judge, Edith H. Jones, Houston. **Judges**: Fortunato P. Benavides and Priscilla R. Owen, Austin; Catharina Haynes, Dallas; Carolyn Dineen King, Jerry E. Smith and Jennifer Walker Elrod, Houston; Rhesa H. Barksdale, Leslie H. Southwick and E. Grady Jolly, Jackson, Miss.; W. Eugene Davis, Lafayette, La.; Jacques L. Wiener Jr., James L. Dennis and Edith Brown Clement, New Orleans; Emilio M. Garza and Edward C. Prado, San Antonio; Carl E. Stewart, Shreveport, La. **Senior Judges**: Harold R. DeMoss Jr., and Thomas M. Reavley, Houston; Will Garwood and Patrick E. Higginbotham, Austin. **Clerk of Court**: Charles R. Fulbruge III, New Orleans.

U.S. DISTRICT COURTS

U.S. district judges are appointed for life and received a salary in 2009 of $174,000.

Northern Texas District
www.txnd.uscourts.gov

District Judges — Chief Judge, Sidney A. Fitzwater, Dallas. **Judges**: Mary Lou Robinson, Amarillo; Jorge A. Solis, Sam A. Lindsay, Barbara M.G. Lynn, David C. Godbey, Ed Kinkeade, Jane Boyle, Reed O'Connor, Dallas; John H. McBryde, Terry R. Means, Fort Worth; Sam R. Cummings, Lubbock. **Senior Judges**: A. Joe Fish, Robert B. Maloney, Jerry Buchmeyer, Dallas. **Clerk of District Court**: Karen Mitchell, Dallas. **U.S. Attorney** (acting): James Jacks, Dallas. **Federal Public Defender**: Richard A. Anderson. **U.S. Marshal**: Randy Ely, Dallas. **Bankruptcy Judges**: Harlan D. Hale, Barbara J. Houser and Stacey G.C. Jernigan, Dallas; D. Michael Lynn and Russell F. Nelms, Fort Worth; Robert Jones, Lubbock. Court is in continuous session in each division of the Northern Texas District.

Following are the different divisions of the Northern District and the counties in each division:

Abilene Division
Callahan, Eastland, Fisher, Haskell, Howard, Jones, Mitchell, Nolan, Shackelford, Stephens, Stonewall, Taylor and Throckmorton. **Magistrate**: Phillip R. Lane, San Angelo. **Deputy-in-charge**: Marsha Elliott.

Amarillo Division
Armstrong, Briscoe, Carson, Castro, Childress, Collingsworth, Dallam, Deaf Smith, Donley, Gray, Hall, Hansford, Hartley, Hemphill, Hutchinson, Lipscomb, Moore, Ochiltree, Oldham, Parmer, Potter, Randall, Roberts, Sherman, Swisher and Wheeler. **Magistrate**: Clinton E. Averitte, Amarillo. **Deputy-in-charge**: Jeanetta Hetrick.

Dallas Division
Dallas, Ellis, Hunt, Johnson, Kaufman, Navarro and Rockwall. **Magistrates**: William F. Sanderson Jr., Jeff Kaplan, Paul Stickney and Irma C. Ramirez, Dallas.

Fort Worth Division
Comanche, Erath, Hood, Jack, Palo Pinto, Parker, Tarrant and Wise. **Magistrate**: Charles Bleil, Fort Worth. **Manager:** Lynn Sherman.

Lubbock Division
Bailey, Borden, Cochran, Crosby, Dawson, Dickens, Floyd, Gaines, Garza, Hale, Hockley, Kent, Lamb, Lubbock, Lynn, Motley, Scurry, Terry and Yoakum. **U.S. District Judge**: Sam R. Cummings, Lubbock. **Magistrate**: Nancy M. Koenig, Lubbock. **Deputy-in-charge**: Margaret Malone.

San Angelo Division
Brown, Coke, Coleman, Concho, Crockett, Glasscock, Irion, Menard, Mills, Reagan, Runnels, Schleicher, Sterling, Sutton and Tom Green. **Deputy-in-charge**: vacant.

Wichita Falls Division
Archer, Baylor, Clay, Cottle, Foard, Hardeman, King, Knox, Montague, Wichita, Wilbarger and Young. **Magistrate**: R. Kerry Roach, Wichita Falls. **Deputy-in-Charge**: Teena McNeely.

Western Texas District
www.txwd.uscourts.gov

District Judges — Chief Judge, Walter S. Smith Jr., Waco. **Judges**: Xavier Rodriguez, Orlando Garcia, Fred Biery and W. Royal Furgeson, San Antonio; Kathleen Cardone, Frank J. Montalvo, Philip R. Martinez and David Briones, El Paso; Sam Sparks and Lee Yeakel, Austin; Alia M. Ludlum, Del Rio; Robert A. Junell, Midland-Odessa. **Senior Judges**: Harry Lee Hudspeth, William Wayne Justice and James R. Nowlin, Austin. **Clerk of District Court**: William G. Putnicki, San Antonio. **U.S. Attorney**: vacant. **Federal Public Defender**: Henry J. Bemorad. **U.S. Marshal**: Lafayette Collins, San Antonio. **Bankruptcy Judges**: Craig A. Gargotta and Frank P. Monroe, Austin; Lief M. Clark and Ronald B. King, San Antonio.

Following are the different divisions of the Western District, and the counties in each division.

Austin Division
Bastrop, Blanco, Burleson, Burnet, Caldwell, Gillespie, Hays, Kimble, Lampasas, Lee, Llano, Mason, McCulloch, San Saba, Travis, Washington and Williamson. **Magistrates**: Andrew W. Austin and Robert Pitman, Austin. **Divisional Office Manager**: David O'Toole. **Bankruptcy Court Deputy-in-charge**: Maria Dozauer.

Del Rio Division

Edwards, Kinney, Maverick, Terrell, Uvalde, Val Verde and Zavala. **Magistrate**: Dennis Green and Victor R. Garcia, Del Rio. **Divisional Office Manager**: Rebecca Moore.

El Paso Division

El Paso County only. **Magistrates**: Norbert J. Garney, Michael S. McDonald and Richard P. Mesa, El Paso. **Divisional Office Manager**: Tom Hilburger. **Bankruptcy Court Deputy-in-charge**: Julie Herrera.

Midland-Odessa Division

Andrews, Crane, Ector, Martin, Midland and Upton. Court for the Midland-Odessa Division is held at Midland, but may, at the discretion of the court, be held in Odessa. **Magistrate**: L. Stuart Platt, Midland. **Divisional Office Manager**: Laura Fowler-Gonzales, Midland. **Bankruptcy Court Deputy-in-charge**: Christy L. Carouth.

Pecos Division

Brewster, Culberson, Hudspeth, Jeff Davis, Loving, Pecos, Presidio, Reeves, Ward and Winkler. **Magistrate**: B. Dwight Goains, Alpine. **Divisional Office Manager**: Karen J. White.

San Antonio Division

Atascosa, Bandera, Bexar, Comal, Dimmit, Frio, Gonzales, Guadalupe, Karnes, Kendall, Kerr, Medina, Real and Wilson. **Magistrates**: Pamela A. Mathy, John W. Primomo and Nancy Stein Nowak, San Antonio. **Divisional Office Manager**: Michael F. Oakes. **Bankruptcy Court Deputy-in-Charge**: Mary Croy, San Antonio.

Waco Division

Bell, Bosque, Coryell, Falls, Freestone, Hamilton, Hill, Leon, Limestone, McLennan, Milam, Robertson and Somervell. **Magistrate**: Jeffrey C. Manske, Waco. **Divisional Office Manager**: Mark G. Borchardt. **Bankruptcy Court Deputy-in-charge**: Bridget Hardage.

Eastern Texas District
www.txed.uscourts.gov

District Judges — Chief Judge, David J. Folsom, Texarkana. **Judges**: Ron Clark, Marcia A. Crone and Thad Heartfield, Beaumont; Michael H. Schneider and Leonard Davis, Tyler; T. John Ward, Marshall; Richard A. Schell, Sherman. **Clerk of District Court**: David J. Maland, Tyler. **U.S. Attorney**: Rebecca A. Gregory. **Federal Public Defender**: G. Patrick Black. **U.S. Marshal** (acting): Gary Brown. **Bankruptcy Judges**: William Parker, Tyler, and Brenda T. Roades, Plano.

Following are the divisions of the Eastern District and the counties in each division:

Beaumont Division
Hardin, Jasper, Jefferson, Liberty, Newton, Orange. **Magistrates**: Earl Hines.

Lufkin Division
Angelina, Houston, Nacogdoches, Polk, Sabine, San Augustine, Shelby, Trinity, Tyler.

Marshall Division
Camp, Cass, Harrison, Hopkins, Marion, Morris, Upshur. **Magistrate**: Charles Everingham IV.

Sherman Division
Collin, Cooke, Delta, Denton, Fannin, Grayson, Hopkins and Lamar. **Magistrate**: Don Bush.

Texarkana Division
Bowie, Franklin, Red River and Titus. **Magistrate**: Caroline M. Craven.

Tyler Division
Anderson, Cherokee, Gregg, Henderson, Panola, Rains, Rusk, Smith, Van Zandt and Wood. **Magistrates**: Judith Guthrie and John Love, Tyler.

Southern Texas District
www.txs.uscourts.gov

District Judges — Chief Judge, Hayden W. Head Jr., Corpus Christi. **Judges**: Nancy F. Atlas, Keith Ellison, Vanessa Gilmore, Melinda Harmon, Kenneth M. Hoyt, Lynn N. Hughes, Sim Lake, Gray H. Miller, John D. Rainey, Lee H. Rosenthal, Houston; Janis Graham Jack, Corpus Christi; Hilda G. Tagle and Andrew S. Hanen, Brownsville; Ricardo H. Hinojosa and Randy Crane, McAllen; George P. Kazen and Micaela Alvarez, Laredo; John D. Rainey, Victoria. **Senior Judges**: David Hittner and Ewing Werlein Jr., Houston. **Clerk of Court**: Michael N. Milby, Houston. **U. S. Attorney** (acting): Tim Johnson, Houston. **Federal Public Defender**: Marjorie A. Meyers. **U.S. Marshal**: vacant. **Bankruptcy Judges**: Chief, Karen K. Brown, Houston; Jeff Bohm, Marvin Isgur and Wesley W. Steen, Houston; Richard S. Schmidt, Corpus Christi, and Letitia Z. Clark, Galveston.

Following are the different divisions of the Southern District and the counties in each division:

Brownsville Division
Cameron and Willacy. **Magistrates**: John Wm. Black, Felix Recio. **Deputy-in-charge**: Rosalina D'Venturi.

Corpus Christi Division
Aransas, Bee, Brooks, Duval, Jim Wells, Kenedy, Kleberg, Live Oak, Nueces and San Patricio. **Magistrates**: B. Janice Ellington and Brian L. Owsley.

Galveston Division
Brazoria, Chambers, Galveston and Matagorda. **Magistrate**: John R. Froeschner.

Houston Division
Austin, Brazos, Colorado, Fayette, Fort Bend, Grimes, Harris, Madison, Montgomery, San Jacinto, Walker, Waller and Wharton. **Magistrates**: Calvin Botley, Frances H. Stacy, Nancy Johnson, Mary Milloy and Stephen W. Smith. **Deputy-in-charge**: Nathan Ochsner.

Laredo Division
Jim Hogg, La Salle, McMullen, Webb and Zapata. **Magistrates**: J. Scott Hacker and Diana Saldaña.

McAllen Division
Hidalgo and Starr. **Magistrates**: Dorina Ramos and Peter Ormsby. **Deputy-in-charge**: Ed Leandro.

Victoria Division
Calhoun, DeWitt, Goliad, Jackson, Lavaca, Refugio and Victoria. **Magistrate**: Nancy K. Johnson. **Deputy-in-charge**: Joyce Richards. ☆

Crime in Texas — 2008

Source: Texas Department of Public Safety, Austin; www.txdps.state.tx.us

The **total number of major crimes** committed in Texas in 2008 decreased 1.2 percent compared to 2007. In addition, the **2008 major crime rate** — the number of crimes per 100,000 population — decreased 2.9 percent from 2007. In 2008, there were 4,494.7 crimes per 100,000 people, compared with 4,631.1 in 2007.

The **violent crime rate** decreased 0.6 percent from 2007 to 2008. The number of murders in 2008 was down 3 percent from 2007, and the number of rapes decreased 5.1 percent from 2007.

The **nonviolent, or property, crime rate** decreased 3.2 percent from 2007 to 2008. The value of property stolen during the commission of index crimes in 2008 was more than $2 billion. The **value of stolen property recovered** by Texas law-enforcement agencies in 2008 was more than $552 million.

The total number of arrests in Texas increased 1.6 percent in 2008 over 2007. The number of juvenile arrests decreased 1.2 percent, while adult arrests increased 2 percent. There were 1.19 million arrests in 2008 compared with 1.17 million arrests in 2007.

The crime rate is tabulated on seven major offenses designated Index Crimes by the Federal Bureau of Investigation's **Uniform Crime Reporting program**. These seven categories include four violent offenses (murder, rape, robbery and aggravated assault) and three non-violent crimes (burglary, larceny-theft and motor-vehicle theft). In Texas, these figures are collected by the Texas Department of Public Safety for the national UCR program. In 2008, 1,031 Texas law enforcement agencies (99.9 percent) participated in the Texas UCR program. Data are estimated for non-reporting agencies.

Arson in 2008

In 2008, reported arson offenses increased 6 percent from 2007. Property damage from arson was reported at more than $128 million in 2008. There were 6,363 arsons in 2008, an increase from 6,003 arsons in 2007.

Family Violence in Texas in 2008

Family violence increased by about 2.1 percent in 2008 from 2007. In 2008, there were 193,505 reported incidents of family violence committed against 208,073 victims by 203,682 offenders. In 2007, there were 189,439 incidents of family violence committed against 201,526 victims by 197,299 offenders. In 45.4 percent of the 2008 incidents, the relationship of victim to offender was marital. Of these victims, 18.9 percent were wives and 14.7 percent were common-law wives.

Of the remaining offenses, 15.7 percent involved parents against children or children against parents; and 38.9 involved other family/household relationships, such as grandparents, grandchildren, siblings, step-siblings, roommates or in-laws. The 77th Legislature amended the Texas Family Code to include violence in a "dating relationship."

There are six general categories of family violence: assault, homicide, kidnapping, robbery, forcible sex offenses and nonforcible sex offenses. Assaults (including aggravated, simple and intimidation) accounted for 96.9 percent of all family violence in 2008. Investigation of reports of domestic violence can be hazardous to police officers. During 2008, 342 Texas law officers were assaulted while investigating such reports.

Hate Crimes in Texas in 2008

There were 246 reported incidents of hate crime in Texas in 2008. This is an increase of 1.2 percent from the 243 incidents in 2007. These crimes involved 276 victims, 233 offenders, resulting in a total of 258 offenses.

These crimes were motivated by race (53%), sexual orientation (22.3%), ethnicity/national origin (14.6%) and religion (10.1%). There were no reports of hate crimes toward the disabled in 2007 or 2008.

Hate crimes, as defined by the Texas Hate Crimes Act, are crimes motivated by prejudice and hatred. The Texas Hate Crimes Act directs all law enforcement agencies in Texas to report bias offenses to the DPS.

Law Enforcement Deaths, Injuries

In 2008, three Texas law enforcement officers were killed in the line of duty because of criminal activity, and nine officers were killed in duty-related accidents.

There were 5,184 officers assaulted during 2008 compared to 4,396 in 2007. This represents an increase of 17.9 percent. ☆

Texas Crime History 1988–2008

Year	Murder	Rape	Robbery	Aggravated Assault	Burglary	Larceny-Theft	Motor Vehicle Theft	Rate per 100,000 Population
1988	2,021	8,122	39,307	60,084	362,099	739,784	134,271	8,019.6
1989	2,029	7,953	37,910	63,978	342,360	741,642	150,974	7,926.8
1990	2,388	8,746	44,316	73,860	314,346	730,926	154,387	7,823.7
1991	2,651	9,265	49,698	84,104	312,719	734,177	163,837	7,818.6
1992	2,240	9,368	44,582	86,067	268,864	689,515	145,039	7,055.1
1993	2,149	9,923	40,464	84,892	233,944	664,738	124,822	6,438.5
1994	2,023	9,101	37,639	81,079	214,698	624,048	110,772	5,873.1
1995	1,694	8,526	33,666	80,377	202,637	632,523	104,939	5,684.5
1996	1,476	8,374	32,796	80,572	204,335	659,397	104,928	5,708.3
1997	1,328	8,007	30,513	77,239	200,966	645,174	101,687	5,478.2
1998	1,343	7,914	28,672	73,648	194,872	606,805	96,614	5,110.7
1999	1,218	7,629	29,424	74,165	190,347	614,478	91,992	5,035.2
2000	1,236	7,821	30,186	73,987	188,205	634,575	92,878	4,952.4
2001	1,331	8,191	35,330	77,221	204,240	669,587	102,838	5,152.3
2002	1,305	8,541	37,599	78,713	212,702	690,028	102,943	5,196.7
2003	1,417	7,986	37,000	75,706	219,733	697,790	98,174	5,144.1
2004	1,360	8,401	35,811	75,983	220,079	696,220	93,844	5,032.0
2005	1,405	8,505	35,781	75,409	219,733	676,022	93,471	4,857.1
2006	1,385	8,407	37,271	74,624	215,754	648,083	95,750	4,599.6
2007	1,415	8,430	38,777	73,570	228,325	662,481	94,026	4,631.1
2008	1,373	8.004	37,757	76,487	230,263	654,133	85,411	4,494.7

Sources: Texas Department of Public Safety, Austin, and the Federal Bureau of Investigation, Washington. The crime rate is based on the estimated 2008 Texas population of 24,326,974.

Crime Profile of Texas Counties for 2008

County	Agencies	Commissioned Personnel †	Murder	Rape	Robbery	Assault	Burglary	Larceny-Theft	Auto Theft	Total Index Crimes (see page 540 for definition)	Crime Rate per 100,000
Anderson	3	77	2	18	22	151	437	830	91	1,551	2,722.1
Andrews	2	28	0	14	2	44	95	217	15	387	2,938.7
Angelina	5	148	1	28	53	242	779	1,795	123	3,021	3,633.6
Aransas	2	44	2	5	5	34	287	538	47	918	3,839.2
Archer	2	10	2	0	1	7	35	52	7	104	1,153.6
Armstrong	1	3	0	0	0	0	4	6	0	10	485.4
Atascosa	5	66	4	9	14	73	260	596	53	1,009	2,261.1
Austin	4	67	1	9	1	32	108	276	51	478	1,770.9
Bailey	2	14	0	6	1	9	39	77	12	144	2,275.2
Bandera	1	28	1	2	0	9	76	132	1	221	1,077.2
Bastrop	4	126	3	35	20	223	467	1,008	121	1,877	2,516.7
Baylor	2	10	1	4	3	16	32	45	0	101	2,653.0
Bee	2	37	0	13	10	68	179	369	35	674	2,058.3
Bell ‡	14	542	16	134	358	820	2,867	6,772	433	11,400	4,027.6
Bexar	28	3,247	138	542	2,970	6,981	22,241	80,087	8,790	121,749	7,512.1
Blanco	3	18	0	1	0	13	30	75	6	125	1,366.6
Borden	1	2	0	0	0	0	2	3	0	5	875.7
Bosque ‡	4	26	1	6	2	19	50	102	5	185	1,025.2
Bowie	7	164	3	29	85	508	970	2,101	215	3,911	4,258.2
Brazoria	20	555	7	73	126	380	1,680	4,796	407	7,469	2,438.8
Brazos	4	370	5	92	157	634	1,849	5,457	325	8,519	4,914.2
Brewster	3	28	1	5	2	15	54	77	7	161	1,734.0
Briscoe	1	2	0	0	0	0	2	11	2	15	1,037.3
Brooks	2	20	1	0	0	40	78	115	14	248	3,286.5
Brown	4	71	2	8	6	101	262	769	31	1,179	3,046.8
Burleson	3	29	2	18	5	33	112	94	22	286	1,722.3
Burnet	7	120	1	17	4	85	244	666	50	1,067	2,271.2
Caldwell	4	67	0	16	18	126	212	446	14	832	2,314.3
Calhoun ‡	4	46	1	5	1	50	156	297	29	539	2,653.3
Callahan	3	15	0	0	1	9	30	74	6	120	883.4
Cameron ‡	16	627	13	133	321	1,199	4,081	14,323	764	20,834	5,287.0
Camp	2	17	0	7	8	16	105	197	17	350	2,759.6
Carson	2	10	0	2	1	15	24	43	4	89	1,403.8
Cass	5	46	1	13	11	60	250	354	47	736	2,517.6
Castro ‡	3	17	1	1	0	10	80	138	11	241	3,397.7
Chambers	2	50	1	9	9	60	248	314	60	701	2,690.3
Cherokee ‡	6	75	1	25	29	155	404	844	101	1,559	3,234.2
Childress	2	11	0	0	0	28	44	75	11	158	2,095.8
Clay	1	11	1	5	1	9	62	114	11	203	1,824.7
Cochran	1	7	0	1	2	4	30	42	5	84	2,783.3
Coke	1	5	0	0	0	5	4	1	0	10	283.5
Coleman	3	18	0	1	0	10	93	121	7	232	2,737.5
Collin	15	1,016	14	158	221	819	3,602	12,934	768	18,516	2,646.0
Collingsworth	1	3	0	3	1	0	3	0	0	7	237.6
Colorado	4	44	0	15	8	61	111	257	18	470	2,270.0
Comal	3	232	6	22	39	239	635	2,385	148	3,474	3,130.2
Comanche	3	21	2	3	0	21	72	136	14	248	1,838.9
Concho	2	8	0	0	0	5	19	27	1	52	1,461.9
Cooke ‡	4	59	2	19	25	57	345	563	56	1,067	2,753.7
Coryell	3	89	0	11	23	124	489	947	73	1,667	2,294.4
Cottle	2	3	1	0	0	3	17	4	0	25	1,584.3
Crane	2	11	1	2	0	5	19	35	2	64	1,661.5
Crockett	1	8	1	4	0	6	15	38	3	67	1,781.4
Crosby	3	9	1	1	0	8	15	17	5	47	755.3
Culberson	1	7	0	0	1	0	2	0	0	3	123.4
Dallam	2	18	0	0	0	15	56	97	10	178	2,107.5
Dallas	36	6,266	225	815	8,071	6,614	33,914	79,278	17,835	146,752	5,557.6
Dawson	2	22	0	3	2	25	99	183	18	330	2,419.5
Deaf Smith	2	34	2	1	9	72	182	326	28	620	3,361.2
Delta	1	10	0	0	1	7	48	22	7	85	1,579.9
Denton ‡	21	870	5	139	231	508	2,113	7,781	742	11,519	2,278.4
DeWitt	3	26	0	7	1	22	86	210	5	331	1,876.3
Dickens	2	3	0	2	0	1	3	5	0	11	442.7
Dimmit	1	21	0	5	5	77	110	160	8	365	3,724.1
Donley	1	6	0	0	0	4	13	38	3	58	1,478.8
Duval	3	28	1	3	3	58	179	195	10	449	3,463.2

Crime Profile of Texas Counties for 2008

County	Agencies	Commissioned Personnel †	Murder	Rape	Robbery	Assault	Burglary	Larceny-Theft	Auto Theft	Total Index Crimes (see page 540 for definition)	Crime Rate per 100,000
Eastland	6	35	1	1	4	20	82	223	11	342	1,864.6
Ector	4	270	10	4	89	682	1,206	3,701	379	6,071	4,597.7
Edwards	1	4	0	0	0	3	27	22	2	54	2,821.3
Ellis	9	234	7	22	71	295	1,138	2,506	320	4,359	3,135.1
El Paso	10	1,541	19	212	517	2,494	2,734	17,225	3,105	26,306	3,546.9
Erath	4	77	0	24	2	53	188	662	44	973	2,705.0
Falls	4	28	0	4	3	23	50	69	14	163	959.8
Fannin	2	34	2	11	7	46	211	375	29	681	2,045.7
Fayette	3	31	2	1	3	9	62	182	12	271	1,197.6
Fisher	1	5	0	8	0	7	15	32	4	66	1,687.1
Floyd	3	12	1	4	1	17	36	55	4	118	1,806.8
Foard	2	4	0	0	0	0	4	8	0	12	858.4
Fort Bend ‡	11	836	11	113	312	1,157	2,576	6,073	721	10,963	2195.2
Franklin	1	10	0	0	2	6	61	43	13	125	1,189.9
Freestone	4	39	0	2	2	27	81	196	24	332	1,755.7
Frio	3	28	4	0	2	32	102	191	8	339	2,102.3
Gaines	3	27	1	3	0	10	33	152	10	209	1,394.4
Galveston	15	572	20	177	378	606	2,775	6,907	716	11,579	3,882.3
Garza	1	7	0	1	0	2	16	36	6	61	1,302.9
Gillespie	2	51	0	4	3	8	45	286	5	351	1,471.5
Glasscock	1	3	1	0	0	0	1	3	0	5	435.2
Goliad	1	13	0	2	2	2	20	27	2	55	766.3
Gonzales	3	36	0	4	15	98	133	218	4	472	2,448.1
Gray	2	36	2	4	8	139	212	676	43	1,084	4,931.1
Grayson	11	212	3	15	47	270	898	2,429	153	3,815	3,187.9
Gregg	5	324	13	69	258	664	1,559	4,925	614	8,102	6,488.2
Grimes	2	42	0	4	13	46	208	451	31	753	2,911.4
Guadalupe	5	190	1	40	49	231	687	2,186	152	3,346	2,898.8
Hale	4	54	1	10	10	80	305	867	36	1,309	3,605.5
Hall	2	5	2	0	0	3	64	39	5	113	3,276.3
Hamilton ‡	2	14	0	0	0	18	58	80	18	174	2,141.0
Hansford	3	9	0	1	0	12	17	40	6	76	1,455.7
Hardeman	2	9	0	3	3	4	52	47	4	113	2,786.0
Hardin	5	74	0	7	11	58	264	601	89	1,030	1,979.1
Harris ‡	39	9,053	388	1,277	13,575	19,335	43,315	111,263	22,565	211,718	5,254.1
Harrison	4	99	4	9	42	188	703	1,189	96	2,231	3,601.8
Hartley	1	5	0	0	0	0	8	11	1	20	713.3
Haskell	2	6	0	0	0	2	21	51	1	75	1,465.1
Hays	4	271	0	24	41	313	798	2,570	133	3,879	2,612.5
Hemphill	1	8	0	2	0	10	13	41	7	73	2,170.0
Henderson ‡	9	139	3	19	25	260	741	1,251	172	2,471	3,104.4
Hidalgo ‡	21	1,164	51	176	667	1,730	7,427	23,352	2,861	36,264	4,968.9
Hill	5	67	0	7	6	27	208	443	40	731	2,046.8
Hockley	5	40	0	20	8	79	180	345	29	661	2,981.1
Hood	3	76	2	0	4	60	218	792	60	1,136	2,261.6
Hopkins	2	54	0	20	12	61	164	268	44	569	1,673.8
Houston	3	40	2	3	5	46	152	308	56	572	2,517.5
Howard	2	50	2	19	36	128	455	1,165	86	1,891	5,881.1
Hudspeth	1	16	0	0	1	2	18	16	0	37	1,125.3
Hunt	9	142	3	21	94	273	1,009	2,059	222	3,681	4,396.3
Hutchinson ‡	3	35	0	9	7	200	178	446	32	872	4,033.9
Irion	1	4	0	0	0	6	8	18	0	32	1,839.1
Jack	2	21	0	2	0	2	38	74	13	129	1,458.8
Jackson	3	27	0	5	3	33	82	153	15	291	2,070.6
Jasper	3	44	1	5	10	63	194	365	38	676	1,963.6
Jeff Davis	1	2	0	3	0	5	6	5	0	19	837.7
Jefferson	7	577	17	127	490	934	3,416	6,841	626	12,451	5,170.6
Jim Hogg	1	20	0	0	0	10	22	50	11	93	1,883.7
Jim Wells	4	69	0	15	16	254	626	1,480	109	2,500	6,178.6
Johnson	7	235	2	29	42	372	897	2,358	276	3,976	2,564.3
Jones	5	25	0	3	4	25	57	111	16	216	1,624.8
Karnes	3	22	2	5	2	27	104	166	16	322	2,143.5
Kaufman	7	175	4	14	76	329	1,166	1,895	271	3,755	3,766.6
Kendall	2	77	1	11	8	17	86	362	23	508	1,619.9
Kenedy	1	11	0	1	1	1	3	4	2	12	3,069.1
Kent	1	1	0	1	0	6	2	9	0	18	2,489.6

Crime Profile of Texas Counties for 2008

County	Agencies	Commissioned Personnel †	Murder	Rape	Robbery	Assault	Burglary	Larceny-Theft	Auto Theft	Total Index Crimes (see page 540 for definition)	Crime Rate per 100,000
Kerr	3	100	5	14	13	85	274	823	66	1,280	2,645.2
Kimble	2	17	0	4	0	14	20	37	0	75	1,682.7
King	1	2	0	0	0	0	1	2	0	3	1,056.3
Kinney	1	6	0	0	0	4	12	16	0	32	966.2
Kleberg	3	79	1	25	16	180	465	1,269	36	1,992	6,630.5
Knox	3	5	0	4	0	8	7	25	3	47	1,365.1
Lamar	4	92	1	11	46	141	538	1,269	65	2,071	4,197.7
Lamb	5	31	1	1	3	44	81	194	16	340	2,462.0
Lampasas	3	37	0	3	1	21	71	196	14	306	1,496.4
La Salle	1	13	0	0	1	3	40	68	0	112	1,858.6
Lavaca	3	27	0	0	3	32	73	172	9	289	1,392.0
Lee	3	24	0	8	2	41	64	232	8	355	2,159.8
Leon	1	22	0	5	3	18	45	50	11	132	795.4
Liberty	4	100	4	31	25	246	686	1,608	261	2,861	3,761.1
Limestone	4	45	1	23	17	54	184	500	23	802	3,569.5
Lipscomb	1	6	0	0	0	3	9	4	0	16	527.4
Live Oak	2	16	0	0	0	8	48	38	6	100	889.8
Llano	3	35	0	3	0	20	93	262	11	389	2,346.3
Loving	1	2	0	0	0	0	0	12	0	12	2,222.2
Lubbock	9	589	8	108	312	1,829	3,614	9,379	679	15,929	6,067.2
Lynn	3	12	0	3	0	3	25	49	2	82	1,386.5
Madison	2	20	1	4	2	35	75	181	19	317	2,359.0
Marion	2	21	2	3	4	25	103	139	9	285	2,659.6
Martin	2	8	1	2	1	3	8	20	5	40	969.2
Mason	1	4	0	0	0	6	9	21	0	36	921.0
Matagorda	4	86	1	14	47	136	405	1,032	33	1,668	4,519.1
Maverick	2	61	1	6	15	249	413	1,234	58	1,976	3,783.8
McCulloch	2	15	0	4	4	13	54	129	8	212	2,709.3
McLennan	17	523	15	153	294	953	2,792	7,427	544	12,178	5,296.4
McMullen	1	3	0	0	0	1	0	0	0	1	113.9
Medina	4	58	2	13	8	77	205	495	27	827	1,878.8
Menard	1	5	0	0	0	3	1	7	0	11	521.8
Midland	3	235	4	71	99	336	1,057	2,880	182	4,629	3,649.4
Milam	4	332	1	0	11	37	155	511	50	765	3,068.1
Mills	1	6	0	0	0	3	11	22	1	37	737.2
Mitchell	2	12	0	4	2	12	19	123	9	169	1,830.8
Montague ‡	4	27	1	1	2	26	140	317	31	518	2,626.5
Montgomery	9	580	12	71	228	720	2,854	6,794	563	11,242	2,618.4
Moore	3	44	0	14	8	50	106	451	33	662	3,297.0
Morris ‡	4	23	1	4	4	34	120	111	26	300	2,295.5
Motley	1	2	0	0	0	2	7	2	1	12	945.6
Nacogdoches	3	127	2	29	27	155	492	1,273	115	2,093	3,330.4
Navarro	3	95	2	26	36	70	589	1,348	92	2,163	4,331.8
Newton	1	11	2	3	2	8	41	112	5	173	1,264.3
Nolan	3	33	0	10	7	133	104	283	19	556	3,840.3
Nueces	8	600	19	210	509	1,666	4,034	14,723	729	21,890	6,794.9
Ochiltree	2	15	0	4	0	7	27	63	8	109	1,127.7
Oldham	1	6	0	0	0	4	11	14	1	30	1,455.6
Orange	7	152	1	34	98	256	857	1,546	261	3,053	3,705.3
Palo Pinto	2	47	2	24	10	71	220	568	50	945	3,196.6
Panola	2	41	1	5	2	40	88	255	61	452	1,981.1
Parker	5	170	2	24	9	93	542	1,334	103	2,107	1,968.4
Parmer	4	16	0	3	0	12	39	80	3	137	1,464.1
Pecos	2	36	1	0	3	23	133	170	15	345	2,172.7
Polk	4	77	1	22	13	63	315	751	78	1,243	2,646.5
Potter	4	429	15	123	326	1,030	2,493	7,316	762	12,065	5,955.5
Presidio	3	12	0	0	2	7	19	33	1	62	815.3
Rains	1	10	3	6	0	13	41	81	7	151	1,314.2
Randall	3	98	0	9	3	35	108	323	43	521	1,568.2
Reagan	1	8	0	0	0	1	6	13	1	21	694.4
Real	1	3	1	0	0	1	1	3	0	9	304.7
Red River	3	28	0	0	1	7	41	97	11	157	1,210.7
Reeves	2	33	2	0	1	17	61	146	15	242	2,206.0
Refugio	2	26	0	0	2	14	24	76	9	125	1,711.9
Roberts	1	5	0	1	0	1	1	17	0	20	2,424.2
Robertson	4	29	3	3	9	57	100	227	34	433	2,741.4

Crime Profile of Texas Counties for 2008

County	Agencies	Commissioned Personnel †	Murder	Rape	Robbery	Assault	Burglary	Larceny-Theft	Auto Theft	Total Index Crimes (see page 540 for definition)	Crime Rate per 100,000
Rockwall	4	135	1	18	16	117	273	1,272	114	1,811	2,575.5
Runnels	3	17	0	0	0	11	36	80	3	130	1,270.6
Rusk	4	81	2	15	23	179	385	907	119	1,630	3,510.3
Sabine	3	12	0	2	1	32	48	58	9	150	1,485.1
San Augustine	2	11	1	0	4	33	50	80	14	182	2,116.0
San Jacinto	1	21	0	1	4	50	226	271	92	644	2,562.5
San Patricio	9	132	0	28	25	127	563	1,576	86	2,405	3,438.0
San Saba	2	8	0	0	0	3	16	20	3	42	707.1
Schleicher	1	5	0	0	0	1	8	9	0	18	643.1
Scurry	3	30	1	11	2	118	107	247	13	499	3,121.9
Shackelford	1	5	0	0	0	0	7	6	2	15	477.1
Shelby	2	31	1	11	7	73	130	444	44	710	2,662.0
Sherman	2	6	0	1	0	2	3	5	0	11	383.0
Smith ‡	11	394	14	80	156	737	1,554	4,848	422	7,811	3,870.2
Somervell	1	20	0	0	0	8	26	70	4	108	1,370.4
Starr	3	79	6	22	17	136	427	578	235	1,421	2,258.5
Stephens	2	17	0	1	3	12	53	91	7	167	1,753.1
Sterling	1	3	0	0	0	2	4	9	0	15	1,219.5
Stonewall	1	2	0	0	0	3	4	4	1	12	872.7
Sutton	2	7	1	5	0	17	5	34	2	64	1,475.3
Swisher	3	14	1	2	1	16	44	103	14	181	2,375.0
Tarrant	38	4,068	84	677	2,826	5,203	17,773	53,840	5,781	86,184	5,010.8
Taylor	6	281	7	92	183	392	1,330	3,259	242	5,505	4,157.2
Terrell	1	6	0	0	0	2	4	9	4	19	2,067.5
Terry	2	23	0	1	7	21	55	78	14	176	1,451.5
Throckmorton	1	2	0	1	0	0	4	1	0	6	365.0
Titus	2	47	2	11	16	128	235	508	51	951	3,217.2
Tom Green	3	215	6	69	66	251	1,121	3,395	243	5,151	4,830.6
Travis	16	2,545	26	324	1,392	2,617	10,163	38,476	2,911	55,909	5,546.1
Trinity	2	16	2	0	2	29	56	96	21	206	1,449.5
Tyler	2	29	1	9	8	38	170	119	23	368	1,808.7
Upshur	5	67	0	14	8	73	311	507	71	984	2,759.8
Upton	1	11	0	0	0	6	2	12	0	20	663.6
Uvalde	3	56	0	11	18	82	275	807	36	1,229	4,609.0
Val Verde	2	107	3	0	9	82	216	731	82	1,123	2,319.2
Van Zandt	6	76	3	4	11	92	381	755	101	1,347	2,563.8
Victoria	2	197	1	54	70	401	1,025	2,775	148	4,474	5,167.4
Walker	2	83	1	19	39	164	414	1,108	101	1,846	2,876.3
Waller	6	69	3	11	36	99	386	505	76	1,116	3,132.3
Ward	2	22	0	3	3	76	121	238	6	447	4,381.5
Washington	3	73	3	17	11	78	221	413	33	776	2,406.7
Webb	6	512	11	82	322	1,021	2,239	10,755	1,767	16,197	6,791.5
Wharton	3	91	0	9	19	143	407	695	60	1,333	3,262.6
Wheeler	2	8	0	0	1	8	11	29	8	57	1,202.3
Wichita	6	266	4	51	211	343	1,725	5,262	557	8,153	6,390.1
Wilbarger	2	26	0	7	3	35	70	272	14	401	2,871.7
Willacy	3	23	1	2	15	257	254	396	11	936	4,549.9
Williamson	12	565	4	75	76	357	1,348	5,327	298	7,485	1,976.7
Wilson	3	47	3	4	1	56	97	351	23	535	1,331.7
Winkler	3	21	0	3	0	8	19	84	3	117	1,805.6
Wise	4	96	0	25	7	135	233	612	30	1,042	1,783.9
Wood ‡	5	46	1	1	7	110	240	396	54	809	1,859.3
Yoakum	2	16	0	1	0	20	18	83	5	127	1,700.4
Young	3	40	1	8	1	37	164	207	22	440	2,492.2
Zapata	1	41	1	1	3	41	75	56	14	191	1,384.9
Zavala	2	22	0	1	3	43	107	167	18	339	2,903.9
STATE TOTAL		52,589	1,373	8,004	37,757	76,487	230,263	654,133	85,411	1,093,428	4,494.7

* County population figures used for calculation of crime rate are the U.S. Census Bureau revised figures for 2008.
† The commissioned officers listed here are those employed by sheriffs' offices and police departments of municipalities; universities, colleges and public-school districts; transit systems; park departments; and medical facilities. The Texas Department of Public Safety also has 3,506 commissioned personnel stationed statewide.
‡ County in which one or more law-enforcement agencies did not report data for all of 2008 to the DPS. The number of commissioned officers listed for this county does not include those employed by nonreporting agencies. The numbers of index crimes for the county includes estimates for nonreporting agencies to enable the DPS to provide comparable data for 2008.

Culture & the Arts

Youngsters at the Bob Bullock Texas State History Museum in Austin. Robert Plocheck photo.

Museums

Performing Arts Organizations

Film and Television

Honored Artists

Religion

Scandinavians in Texas

Early Scandinavian-Texans

Norway	Denmark	Sweden
	1830 Christian Hillebrandt brings his cattle into Texas from Louisiana and establishes claim to land near Beaumont.	
	1835 Charles Zanco arrives from Denmark to farm in Harris County. Enters the Alamo Feb. 23, 1836, where he died on March 6.	
	1835 George L. Hammeken, persuaded by Stephen F. Austin, arrives in October from Mexico City as a business agent.	
	1836 Peter Johnson moves his shipping business to Galveston from Mobile, Ala. In 1850, relocates to Indianola and Lamar.	**1838** Swen Magnus Swenson sets up business in Brazoria, later in Houston. Acquires plantation near Richmond. Later resides in Austin.
	late 1830s John Edward Henrichson settles near Corpus Christi Bay with his three children. Henrichson was of both Danish and Swedish ancestry.	
1841 Johannes Nordboe is first permanent Norwegian settler in Texas a short distance south of Dallas.		
1845 Johan Reinert Reiersen brings first Norwegian colony to Brownsboro.	**late 1840s** Danes settle individually, many in the Lower Rio Grande Valley (Family names; Loez, Miller, Bedstrup).	**1844** Svante Palm arrives at invitation of nephew S.M. Swenson. Settles in Austin where he serves as Swedish-Norwegian vice consul.
	around 1850 John C. Trube, after working on steamers between Galveston and Houston, establishes mercantile business in Galveston.	**1848** 25 Swedes arrive at Swenson plantation in Fort Bend County. Resettle just east of Austin.
1854 Cleng Peerson, Canutesons and a few other Norwegian families, who had joined Johannes Nordboe near Dallas in 1849, move on to establish Norse (Bosque County).	**early 1850s** Christian Dorbrandt serves in Army at Fort Croghan near Burnet. Retires from Army and settles at Marble Falls 1855. Later moves to community of South Gabriel (Burnet County).	
	1853 Lovenskiold family settles in Corpus Christi.	
1855 Johan F.G. Streigler, of both Danish and Norwegian ancestry, settles his family at Rocky Hill (Gillespie County) at the invitation of schoolmate from Denmark, Rasmus Frandsen, who preceded him by a year.		
1872 Several Norwegian families migrate to the Lower Rio Grande Valley from other sections of the United States.	**late 1860s** Danish families settle in what is now Lee County.	**1870s** Swedes from other states relocate to Texas at Fort Worth, Dallas, Waco.
	1880s Danes settle at Hutto (Williamson County) from other parts of Texas.	**1880s** S.M. Swenson's massive SMS Ranches bring Swedes to Northwest Texas area including Stamford.
1884 Norwegians found Normanna in Bee County.	**around 1890** Danes settle at Stonewall (Gillespie County).	
	1894 Danevang founded in Wharton County.	
1908 Anders Mordt recruits Norwegians from Midwestern states to a Panhandle site he named Olso in Hansford County.	**1918** Bentsen family relocates from South Dakota to Lower Rio Grande Valley.	*Photo top left: Austin's historic Gethsemane Lutheran Church founded by Swedish immigrants.*

Scandinavian Settlement, Contributions Diverse

Texans of Swedish descent are the tenth largest ethnic group in the state, according to both the 1990 and 2000 censuses, with the latest U.S. census estimate, the 2007 American Community Survey, putting their number at 155, 949.

The same 2007 survey estimates 137,342 Texans of Norwegian ancestry and 50,689 Danish-Texans.

Although many of the early Scandinavian immigrants came to Texas directly from Europe, this group more than any other ethnic group had successive waves move to Texas from other states in the union.

For example, the family of the late Sen. Lloyd Bentsen, perhaps the most well-known Danish-Texan, came to the Lower Rio Grande Valley from South Dakota in 1918.

The Scandinavian Evangelical Lutheran Church School in Clifton, 1900–1910.
Courtesy of Bosque County Collection; Bosque County Historical Commission; Meridian, Tex.

And, Swen Mangus Swenson, who would eventually establish the massive SMS Ranches in Northwest Texas, left Sweden in 1836 for New York and Baltimore before arriving in Texas in 1838.

Johannes Nordboe, the first permanent Norwegian settler, arrived in Galveston at age 73 after nine years in New York state. He, his wife and three of his sons began farming a short distance south of Dallas in 1841.

Charles Hillebrant, born in Denmark in 1793, drove his cattle herd across the Sabine River from Abbeville, Louisiana, in 1830 to settle on the bayous south of present-day Beaumont, and a few years later brought his family to join him.

Among those who came directly to Texas were Charles Zanco and his father Frederick, who arrived in Galveston from Denmark in the summer of 1835 and began farming in Harris County.

Within months, Charles joined the Lynchburg Volunteers in the Texas Revolution. He entered the Alamo on Feb. 23, 1836, where he died in the battle of March 6.

Swedes

Swen (Sven, Svante, Swante) Magnus Swenson is called the father of Swedish immigration to Texas because many of the first Swedes to follow his arrival in 1838 were either related to him or received financial support from him. He first worked as a clerk in

Danish-Texan Lloyd Bentsen, U.S. senator and secretary of the Treasury. Department of Treasury portrait.

Galveston, working his way up to be able to buy land set aside to fund railroads and schools in Texas.

His uncle Swante Palm arrived in 1844 to open mercantile businesses in La Grange and Austin where S.M. had established his business headquarters. Swante would later serve as Swedish-Norwegian vice consul in Austin, and through the years, acquire one of the largest book collections in the state, which he left to the University of Texas.

The Austin area attracted other Swedes who settled in Hutto, Swedish Hill, East Sweden and other communities in Travis and Williamson counties.

In 1848 S.M. recruited 25 Swedes who went directly to the plantation near Richmond in Fort Bend County that S.M. had acquired through marriage. Some of these immigrants were related to S.M. and many were related to each other.

S.M. Swenson had to flee to Mexico during the Civil War because of the Unionist sympathies he shared with his old friend Sam Houston. Although after the war he would relocate to New York, he continued to help Swedes move to Texas, especially to work on his ranches in Northwest Texas.

The SMS ranches, which would eventually include the Spur, Tongue River, Flat Mountain, and Ericsdahl ranches, were operated by his sons Eric and Albin and managed by relatives, including for many years his nephew A.J. Swenson and A.J.'s sons Willie and Swede.

The town of Stamford was established nearby and many residents of Swedish or Scandinavian descent came there to work.

The New York branch of the family — S.M., Eric and Albin

— would be major investors in the First National City Bank of New York where Eric would serve as chairman of the board. It is the bank we now know as Citibank.

Norwegians

Bosque County is the "home place" for many Texas Norwegians, although it was not the first area of Norwegian communities.

After Johannes Nordboe began farming south of Dallas, Johan Reinert Reiersen (Reierson) in 1845 brought the first group of colonists to an area in eastern Henderson County they called Normandy. The settlement would merge into nearby Brownsboro, as many if not most of the immigrant families decided to leave the bottomlands of the Neches River tributaries for higher ground just 50 miles to the west at the line between Van Zandt and Kaufman counties. Here at Four Mile Prairie and Prairieville the Norwegians started anew in 1848.

By 1850, some of the Norwegians who had settled near Nordboe, began to look westward for land. Cleng Peerson and Ole Canuteson found the vacant land in Bosque County attractive and in 1854 began persuading their neighbors to move there. Norse was founded in 1853-54 and soon some of the families from the Van Zandt and Kaufman counties were moving there, as well.

Both Peerson and Reiersen contributed much to the emigration from Norway by publicizing the opportunities available on the American frontier. Peerson, sometimes called the "father of Norwegian immigration to America" had traveled extensively across North America in the 1820s and returned to Norway to recruit many who settled in the north-central United States. He himself settled there, but in 1849, at 67, moved on to Texas.

Reiersen promoted immigration in his newspaper *Christiansandsposton*, and, in 1844, collected his essays into a book, *Veiviser — Pathfinder for Norwegian Immigrants to the United North American States and Texas*. The book was a great catalyst toward Norwegian emigration.

Danes

Most Danes came to Texas as individuals or a single family, although there were a few settlements. After the Civil War, two Texans, Travis Shaw and John Hester, whose wife was Danish, traveled to Denmark and promoted Central Texas as a good place to farm. By the late 1870s, several Danish families settled in the northern part of Lee County, an area that would come to be called Little Denmark.

Rocky Hill near Fredericksburg in Gillespie County, which was already settled by Germans, attracted some Danish families.

The most extensive Danish settlement began in

Hammeken, of Danish extraction, important figure in Texas history

George Louis Hammeken Jr. had a significant and ubiquitous role in the early history of the Republic of Texas. His father, who had served as Danish consul in New York and Philadelphia, was born in Tunis, Africa, where his father Ludvig (Louis) Hammeken was serving as Danish consul.

George Jr., born in 1811, was in Mexico City in 1833 when he was persuaded by Stephen F. Austin to come to Texas. Arriving in Galveston in October 1835, he was employed briefly as an agent for an English bank before departing for New Orleans; then he returned to Texas in December 1836.

In 1837, he translated Gen. Vicente Filisola's *Evacuation from Texas*. Filisola, Santa Anna's second in command, wrote the account to explain that he was following Santa Anna's orders in retreating from Texas. The book was widely popular in Texas, in part, because it supported the legitimacy of the terms of Mexican surrender and was critical of Santa Anna. Hammeken would

also write "Recollections of Stephen F. Austin" in 1844.

In 1838, Hammeken was among a group of businessmen granted one of the first railroad charters in the new republic, the Brazos-Galveston Railroad Company. Emily Austin Perry, upon the death of her brother Stephen F. Austin, became the sole owner of the Dollar Point tract on Galveston Bay where the railroad was to terminate.

She deeded to her son, William Joel Bryan, and Hammeken part of the town site there, "Austinia," to help finance the project. Bryan and Hammeken would later buy the rest of Austinia and Dollar Point peninsula. Plans were changed to build a canal instead, but the effort was abandoned in 1843 with neither railroad nor canal built.

Hammeken was named secretary to the Texas agents dispatched to Mexico in 1839 and 1841, and served as interpreter and secretary to Gen. Alexander Somervell in the retaliatory expedition of 1842 against Mexico.

In 1848, Hammeken married

Maria Adelaida Matilda Mexía, daughter José Antonio Mexía, the Mexican general executed by Santa Anna. She and her brother Enrique had received in 1833 large tracts of land in Limestone, Freestone and Anderson counties from the Pedro Varela grant. Some accounts put the combined acreage at more than 243,000. Enrique Mexía, who served as a general in the Mexican struggle against the French in the 1860s, moved to the lands in 1871 to manage his properties and those of his sister and brother-in-law. The town of Mexia was named to honor the family in 1870.

From the 1850s, Hammeken continued to develop railroads in Mexico while retaining a connection to the Mexía land grant. An 1877 article in the *Galveston Daily News* refers to "Geo. L. Hammeken of Mexia."

George and Adelaida had one son to live to adulthood, Jorge Hammeken y Mexía, who upon his death left his inherited Texas properties to his uncle Enrique.

George Hammeken died in Mexico City in 1881. — RP

1894 at Danevang on the coastal plain in Wharton County. Most of the initial colonists were Danes from the north-central United States but some others followed directly from Denmark.

Customs

Scandinavians assimilated quickly into the American culture. Danevang, which was founded by a faction of the Danish Lutheran Church of America that was protective of its heritage, was using English rather than Danish in its church services within 50 years of settlement.

But the Scandinavian foods, music and customs are maintained through festivals and clubs in Texas.

Danes now living in the larger cities return to Danevang to commemorate the Constitution Day of Denmark each June 5, as well as at Christmas.

Smorgasbords, a type of Scandinavian meal served buffet-style, can include flaeskesteg (roast pork), aebleskiver (Danish doughnuts) and brune kager (brown cookies).

A big smorgasbord is held each November in Norse in Bosque County. Norway's Constitution Day is also celebrated there each May.

The view from a stained-glass ornamented window in St. Olaf's Kierke reveals the rolling countryside of Bosque County where Norwegian pioneers settled in the 1850s. The structure, also known as the Rock Church, was built in 1886. Mary Ramos photo.

In the last few decades in some of the larger cities of Texas, Scandinavian social clubs have been formed. There is a Danish Club and a Swedish Club of Houston, where annual events include a pancake dinner, and, in a blending with Texas Gulf Coast culture, a Swedish Crawfish Party in April.

The Norwegian Society of Texas has several chapters throughout the state, from Houston to El Paso, and Vasa, a Swedish-American fraternal organization, has chapters in Dallas, Austin and Waco.

Prominent Scandinavian Texans

Lloyd Bentsen (1921–2006), served in Congress, first in the House for three terms, and then in the Senate from 1971-1993, when resigned to become U.S. secretary of the Treasury. In 1988, he was the Democratic nominee for vice president. His grandfather, Peter Bentsen, an immigrant from Denmark, brought the family in 1918 from South Dakota to Texas, where they participated in the economic development of the Lower Rio Grande Valley.

Babe Didrikson Zaharias (1911–1956), daughter of Norwegian immigrants, born Mildred Didrikson in Port Arthur and raised in Beaumont. Olympic medalist and professional golf champion.

Erik Jonsson (1901–1995), son of Swedish immigrants, co-founder of Texas Instruments and Dallas civic leader, who served as mayor of the city from 1964-1971.

George Dahl (1894–1987), son of Norwegian immigrants, architect who designed two dozen buildings at the University of Texas at Austin. He is best known for his work on the 1936 Texas Centennial at Fair Park in Dallas, where his art deco buildings remain.

Andrew Hans Thaison (1849–1898), at the age of 19 emigrated from Denmark and later became mayor of Laredo in the late 1890s.

Hans Peter Neilsen Gammel (1854-1931), left Denmark as a young man. Was an early Texas bookseller and collector of Texana. When the Texas Capitol burned in 1881, he salvaged the scattered documents and published them as the first ten volumes of *Laws of Texas, 1822–1897*, which became an invaluable basic reference item in law libraries across the state.

Carl G. Cromwell (1889–1931), oilman born to Swedish immigrants. Called the Big Swede, he was contracted by the Texon Oil and Land Company to drill the famed Santa Rita No. 1 oil well in 1923 with a constantly changing crew. He became drilling superintendent of Texon's field where he drilled wells to record depths at the time. This businessman and entrepreneur later established the airport in San Angelo.
— RP

Sources

New Handbook of Texas, various, Texas State Historical Association, 1996.

Southwestern Historical Quarterly, various, Texas State Historical Association.

Swedes in Texas in Words and Pictures 1838–1918, Ernest Severin, 1918, Web translation by Christine Andreason, 2007.

The Danish Texans, John L. Davis, The University of Texas Institute of Texan Cultures at San Antonio, 1979.

The Norwegian Texans, The University of Texas Institute of Texan Cultures at San Antonio, 1970.

For more on people and subjects discussed in this article, go to the New Handbook of Texas online and the Southwestern Historical Quarterly online at www.tshaonline.org.

THE HANDBOOK OF TEXAS Online

www.TSHAonline.org

The Handbook of Texas Online is the country's oldest, most comprehensive, and most respected state encyclopedia. The *Handbook* offers over 25,000 articles.

The Digital Gateway is designed to provide the public with a one-stop address for online Texas History materials, including in addition to the *Handbook*, the *Southwestern Historical Quarterly Online*, *Texas Day by Day*, lesson plans, educational content, and event information.

In the future, with your support, the site will incorporate greater interactivity, new media, and content such as back issues of the *Texas Almanac* and TSHA books.

Texas Day by Day

SHQ Online

State Cultural Agencies Assist the Arts

Source: Principally, the Texas Commission on the Arts, along with other state cultural agencies.

Culture in Texas, as in any market, is a mixture of activity generated by both the commercial and the nonprofit sectors.

The commercial sector encompasses Texas-based profit-making businesses including commercial recording artists, nightclubs, record companies, private galleries, assorted boutiques that carry fine art collectibles and private dance and music halls.

Texas also has extensive cultural resources offered by nonprofit organizations that are engaged in charitable, educational and/or humanitarian activities.

The Texas Legislature has authorized five state agencies to administer cultural services and funds for the public good. The agencies are:

Texas Commission on the Arts, Box 13406, Austin (78711); Texas Film Commission, Box 13246, Austin (78711); Texas Historical Commission, Box 12276, Austin (78711); Texas State Library and Archives Commission, Box 12927, Austin (78711); and the State Preservation Board, Box 13286, Austin (78711). Although not a state agency, another organization that provides cultural services to the citizens of Texas is Humanities Texas, 1410 Rio Grande, Austin 78701.

The Texas Commission on the Arts was established in 1965 to develop a receptive climate for the arts through the conservation and advancement of Texas' rich and diverse arts and cultural industries.

The Texas Commission on the Arts' primary goals are:

• provide grants for the arts and cultural industries in Texas.

• provide the financial, human, and technical resources necessary to ensure viable arts and cultural communities

• promote widespread attendance at arts and cultural performances and exhibitions in Texas.

• ensure access to arts in Texas through marketing, fund raising, and cultural tourism.

The arts commission is responsible for several initiatives including:

• Arts Education – programs that serve the curricular and training needs of the state's school districts, private schools, and home schools.

• Technology – a full service network providing a one-stop location for the arts and cultural industry of Texas.

• Marketing and Public Relations – marketing and fund-raising expertise to generate funds for agency operations and increase visibility of the arts in Texas.

• Cultural Tourism – programs that develop and promote tourism destinations featuring the arts.

Additional information on programs and services is available on the Texas Commission on the Arts' Web site at www.arts.state.tx.us or by calling (800) 252-9415 or (512) 463-5535. ☆

Texas Performing Arts Organizations

Below are Internet links, listed by city, to Web sites of Texas performing arts organizations — theatre, dance and music. The information is from the Texas Commission on the Arts.

Abilene
Abilene Christian University Theatre
  www.acu.edu/academics/cas/
  theatre/index.html
Abilene Community Theatre
  abilenecommunitytheatre.com/
Abilene Philharmonic
  abilenephilharmonic.org/
Classical Chorus of Abilene
  classicalchorus.org/
Paramount Theatre
  paramount-abilene.org/

Addison
Theatre Britain
  theatre-britain.com/
Water Tower Theatre
  watertowertheatre.org/

Allen
Allen Philharmonic Symphony
  allenphilharmonic.com/

Alpine
Theatre of the Big Bend
  www.sulross.edu/pages/
  3627.asp

Amarillo
Amarillo Boy Choir
  boychoirs.org/amarillo/
Amarillo Little Theatre
  amarillolittletheatre.org/
Amarillo Opera
  amarilloopera.org/
Amarillo Symphony
  amarillosymphony.org/
Chamber Music Amarillo
  www.cmama.org/
Lone Star Ballet
  lonestarballet.org/

Archer City
Royal Theater
  royaltheater.org/

Arlington
Creative Arts Theatre/School
  creativearts.org/
Pantagleize Theatre Co.
  pantatheatre.org/
Texas Radio Theatre Company
  texasradiotheatre.com/
Theatre Arlington
  theatrearlington.org/
UT-Arlington
  www.uta.edu/theatre/

Athens
Henderson County Performing Arts
  Center
  hcpac.org/index_files/

Page772.html
Trinity Valley Community College
  trinityvalleytheatre.com/

Austin
A. Mozart Fest
  amozartfest.org
Austin Cabaret Theatre
  austincabaret.blogspot.com/
Austin Chamber Music Center
  austinchambermusic.org/
Austin Circle of Theaters
  acotonline.org/Pages/Home.html
Austin Civic Orchestra
  austincivicorchestra.org/
Austin Classical Guitar Society
  austinclassicalguitar.org
Austin Lyric Opera
  austinlyricopera.org
Austin Symphonic Band
  asband.org/
Austin Symphony Orchestra
  austinsymphony.org/
Aztlan Dance Company
  aztlandance.com/
Ballet Austin
  balletaustin.org/
Ballet East Dance Theatre
  balleteast.org/
Blue Lapis Light
  bluelapislight.org/
Capital City Men's Chorus

ccmcaustin.org/
Capital City Mystery Players
  capcitymystery.com/
Chorus Austin
  chorusaustin.org/
Conspirare Choir
  conspirare.org/
Creative Opportunity Orchestra
  creop.org/
Different Stages
  main.org/diffstages/
Forklift Danceworks
  forkliftdanceworks.org/
Gilbert and Sullivan Society
  gilbertsullivan.org/
Gobotrick Theatre Co.
  gobotrick.org/
Hyde Park Theatre
  hydeparktheatre.org/
Kathy Dunn Hamrick Dance Co.
  kdhdance.com/
Mary Moody Northen Theatre
  stedwards.edu/hum/thtr/
    index.html
One World Theatre
  www.oneworldtheatre.org/
Onstage Theatre Company
  onstagetheatreco.org/
Paradox Players
  paradoxplayers.org/
Paramount Theater/State Theater
  austintheatre.org/
Physical Plant Theater
  physicalplant.org/
Puerto Rican Folkloric Dance
  prfdance.org/
Roy Lozano Ballet Folklorico
    of Texas
  rlbft.org/
Rude Mechanicals Theatre
    Collective
  rudemechs.com/
Salvage Vanguard Theater
  salvagevanguard.org/
Second Youth Family Theatre
  secondyouth.com/
Tapestry Dance Company
  www.tapestry.org/
Theatre Action Project
  theatreactionproject.org/
Teatro Humanidad
  teatrohumanidad.com/
Teatro Vivo
  teatrovivo.org/
UT Performing Arts Center
  utpac.org/
Vestige Group
  vestigegroup.org/
Violet Crown Radio Players
  violetcrownradio.com/
Vortex Theatre
  vortexrep.org/
Weird City Theatre Company
  weirdcitytheatre.com/
Zachary Scott Theatre Center
  zachscott.com/
Zilker Theatre Productions
  zilker.org/

Azle
Azle Arts Association Popcorn

The giant Guadalupe mosaic candle by Jesse Treviño, a veladora sculpture at the Guadalupe Theater in San Antonio. Robert Plocheck photo.

Players
  azlearts.org/
Bastrop
Bastrop Opera House
  bastropoperahouse.com/
Bay City
Community Actors of South Texas
  communityactors.com/
Baytown
Baytown Little Theater
  baytown.littletheater.org/
Beaumont
Beaumont Community Players
  beaumontcommunityplayers.
    com/
Lamar University
  dept.lamar.edu/cofac/
    depttheatre/
Symphony of Southeast Texas
  sost.org/
Bedford
Onstage in Bedford
  onstageinbedford.com/
Regal Opera Company
  regalopera.org/
Big Spring
Big Spring Symphony
  bigspringsymphony.com/
Boerne
Boerne Community Theatre
  boernetheatre.org/

Bonham
Red River Theatre Company
  redrivertheatre.com/
Brenham
Unity Theatre Company
  unitybrenham.org/
Bridgeport
Off 380 Players
  off380players.org/
Brownsville
Camille Playhouse
  camilleplayers.cjb.net/
Bryan-College Station
Brazos Valley Chorale
  bvchorale.org/
Brazos Valley Symphony Orchestra
  bvso.org/
Brazos Valley Troupe
  bvtroupe.com/
StageCenter Theater
  stagecenter.net/home/
The Theatre Company
  thetheatrecompany.com/
Bulverde
Spotlight Theatre Arts
  stagebulverde.org/
Cameron
Millam Community Theatre
  milamcommunitytheater.com/
Carrollton
Audacity Theatre Lab

audacitytheatrelab.com/
Texas Chamber Orchestra
wwoww.com/csm/

Carthage
Panola College Theatre
www.panola.edu/fine_arts
/mason/liz/index.htm

Claude
Armstrong County Gem Theatre
armstrongcountymuseum.org/

Cleburne
Carnegie Players
carnegieplayers.com/
Plaza Theatre Company
plaza-theatre.com/

Clute
Brazosport Center Stages
bcfas.org/

Commerce
Texas A&M University-Commerce
www7.tamu-commerce.edu/
mmct/theatre/default.asp?ID=1

Conroe
Crighton Players
crightonplayers.org/

Coppell
Coppell Community Theatre
theatrecoppell.com/
Theatre Coppell
theatrecoppell.com/

Copperas Cove
Cove Live Community Theatre
covelive.com/

Corpus Christi
Corpus Christi Ballet
corpuschristiballet.com/
Corpus Christi Symphony
Orchestra
ccsymphony.org/
Fryderyk Chopin Society of Texas
fryderykchopinsocietyoftexas.
org/
Harbor Playhouse
harborplayhouse.com/

Corsicana
Palace Theater
corsicanapalace.com/
Warehouse Living Arts Center
warehouselivingartscenter.com/

Crockett
Piney Woods Fine Arts Association
pwfaa.org/

Dalhart
La Rita Performing Arts Theatre
larita.org/
Anita Martinez Ballet Folklorico
anmbf.org/

Dallas
Beckles Dancing Company
becklesdancingcompany.org/
Black Academy of Arts and Letters
tbaal.org/
Bootstraps Comedy Theater
bootstrapscomedy.com/
Cara Mia Theatre
caramiatheatre.com/
Contemporary Theatre of Dallas
contemporarytheatreofdallas.
com/
Core Performance Manufactory

coreperformancemanufactory.
com/
Dallas Bach Society
dallasbach.org/
Dallas Black Dance Theatre
dbdt.com/
Dallas Chamber Music Society
dallaschambermusic.org/
Dallas Chamber Orchestra
dallaschamberorchestra.org/
Dallas Children's Theater
dct.org/
Dallas Hub Theater
dallashubtheater.org/
Dallas Opera
dallasopera.org/
Dallas Theater Center
dallastheatercenter.org/
Dallas Wind Symphony
dws.org/
Echo Theatre
echotheatre.org/
Fine Arts Chamber Players
fineartschamberplayers.org/
Greater Dallas Youth Orchestra
gdyo.org/
Kitchen Dog Theater
kitchendogtheater.org/
Maharlika Dancers
geocities.com/
maharlika_dancers
Majestic Theatre
liveatthemajestic.com/
Metropolitan Winds
metropolitanwinds.org/
Music Hall at Fair Park
liveatthemusichall.com/
Orchestra of New Spain
orchestraofnewspain.org/
Pegasus Theatre
pegasustheatre.org/
Pocket Sandwich Theatre
dallas.net/~pst/
Second Thought Theatre
secondthoughttheatre.com/
Shakespeare Dallas
shakespearedallas.org/
Shane Arts Theater
shane-arts.com/
Teatro Dallas
teatrodallas.org/
Teco Theatrical Productions
tecotheater.org/
Texas Ballet Theatre
texasballettheater.com/
Theatre Three
theatre3dallas.com/
Turtle Creek Chorale
turtlecreek.org/
Undermain Theatre
undermain.org/
Uptown Players
uptownplayers.org/
WingSpan Theatre Co.
wingspantheatre.com/
Women's Chorus of Dallas
twcd.org/

Deer Park
Art Park Players
artparkplayers.com/

Center Stage
slightlyoffcenterplayers.com/

Del Rio
Del Rio Council for the Arts
delrioarts.com/
The Upstagers
upstagers.org/

Denton
Campus Theatre
campustheatre.com/
Denton Community Theatre
main.org/diffstages/
Music Theatre of Denton
musictheatreofdenton.com/
Texas Women's University
www.twu.edu/soa/drama/
UNT Dept of Dance & Theatre
www.danceandtheatre.unt.edu/

Dickinson
Bay Area Harbour Playhouse
harbourplayhouse.com/

Duncanville
Duncanville Community Theatre
dctheatre.org/

Edinburg
University Theatre
portal.utpa.edu/utpa_main/
daa_home/coah_home/
theatre_home

El Paso
El Paso Opera
epopera.org/
El Paso Performing Arts Center
elpasocvb.com/cpac_index.sstg
El Paso Playhouse
elpasoplayhouse.com/
El Paso Pro-Musica
eppm.org/
El Paso Symphony Orchestra
epso.org/
Outrageous Fortune Theatre
Company
outfortheatre.org/home/

Ennis
Ennis Public Theatre
ennispublictheatre.com/

Flower Mound
Performing Arts Theatre
fmpat.org/

Fort Worth
Amphibian Stage Productions
amphibianproductions.org/
Ballet Concerto
balletconcerto.com/
Bass Performance Hall
basshall.com/indexa.html
Bruce Wood Dance Company
brucedance.org/
Casa Mañana
casamanana.org/
Circle Theatre
circletheatre.com/
Contemporary Dance/Fort Worth
cdfw.org/
Fort Worth Opera
fwopera.org/
Fort Worth Symphony
fwsymphony.org/
Fort Worth Theatre
fortworththeatre.org/

Hip Pocket Theatre
hippocket.org/
Jubilee Theatre
jubileetheatre.org/
Schola Cantorum
scholatexas.com/
Stage West
stagewest.org/
Texas Ballet Theatre
texasballettheater.org/
Texas Boys Choir
texasboyschoir.org/
Texas Camerata
musichost.com/txcam/
Texas Christian University
www.theatre.tcu.edu/
Theatre Wesleyan
web3.txwes.edu/theatrearts/
theatrewesleyan/home.htm
Van Cliburn Foundation
cliburn.org/

Fredericksburg
Fredericksburg Theater Company
fredericksburgtheater.org/

Frisco
Frisco Community Theatre
friscocommunitytheatre.com/
World of Mouth Productions
womproductions.com/

Gainesville
Butterfield Stage Players Theatre
butterfieldstage.org/

Galveston
East-End Theatre Company
islandetc.org/
Galveston Symphony Orchestra
galvestonsymphony.org/
Grand 1894 Opera House
thegrand.com/
Strand Theatre
strandtheatregalveston.org/

Garland
Garland Civic Theatre
garlandcivictheatre.org/
Garland Symphony Orchestra
garlandsymphony.org/

Georgetown
Palace Theater
georgetownpalace.com/

Goodlett
Pease River Productions
peaseriverproductions.org/

Graham
Graham Regional Theatre
grahamregionaltheatre.com/

Granbury
Granbury Opera House
granburyoperahouse.org/

Grand Prairie
Grand Prairie Arts Council
artsgp.com/

Grapevine
Runway Theatre
runwaytheatre.com/

Harlingen
Harlingen Performing Arts Theatre
harlingenplays.com/
Fryderyk Chopin Society of Texas
fryderykchopinsocietyoftexas.
org/

Houston
A.D. Players
adplayers.org/main.html
Alley Theatre
alleytheatre.org/alley/
Default_EN.asp
Applause Theatre Company
applausetheatre.com/
Bayou City Performing Arts
gmch.org/
Bere'sheet Ballet
beresheetballet.com/
Bobbindoctrin Puppet Theatre
bobbindoctrin.org/
City Dance Company
houstoncitydance.com/
Classical Theatre Company
classicaltheatre.org/
Company OnStage
companyonstage.org/
De Camera
dacamera.com/
Dominic Walsh Dance Theater
dwdt.org/
Ensemble Theatre
ensemblehouston.com/
Express Children's Theatre
expresstheatre.com/
Fly Dance Company
flydance.com/
Gilbert and Sullivan Society
gilbertandsullivan.net/
Houston Ballet
houstonballet.org/
Houston Chamber Choir
houstonchamberchoir.org/
Houston Children's Chorus
houstonchildren.org/
Houston Civic Symphony
civicsymphony.org/
Houston Early Music
houstonearlymusic.org/
Houston Grand Opera
houstongrandopera.com/
Houston Metropolitan Dance
Company
houstonmetdance.com/
Houston Repertoire Ballet
www.hrbdance.org/
Houston Symphony
houstonsymphony.org/
Illuminations Theatre with the Deaf
illuminationstheatre.org/
Kuumba House
kuumbahouse.org/
Main Street Theater
mainstreettheater.com/
Masquerade Theatre
masqueradetheatre.com/
Mercury Baroque Ensemble
mercurybaroque.org/
Mildred's Umbrella Theater
Company
mildredsumbrella.com/
Opera in the Heights
operaintheheights.org/
Playhouse 1960
ph1960.com/
Rice Players
players.rice.edu/home/

Radio Music Theatre
radiomusictheatre.com/
Samskriti Indian Performing Arts
samskritihouston.org/
Sandra Organ Dance Company
organdance.org/
Several Dancers Core
severaldancerscore.org/
Stages Repertory Theatre
stagestheatre.com/
Suchu Dance
suchudance.org/
The Houston Sinfonietta
houstonsinfonietta.org/
Theater LaB Houston
theaterlabhouston.com/
Theatre Southwest
theatresouthwest.org/
Theatre Suburbia
theatresuburbia.com/
Theatre Under the Stars
tuts.org/
Thurderbird Theatre
tbirdth.com/
U of H School of Theatre
theatredance.uh.edu/about.asp
Upstage Theatre
upstagetheatre.org/

Huntsville
Huntsville Community Theatre
huntsvillecommunitytheatre.org/

Hurst
Artisan Center Theater
artisanct.com/

Ingram
Hill Country Arts Foundation
hcaf.com/

Irving
Irving Community Theater
irvingtheatre.org/
Las Colinas Symphony
Orchestra
lascolinassymphony.org/
Lyric Stage
lyricstage.org/
New Philharmonic Orchestra
home.earthlink.net/~youngj1/
npoi.htm

Kerrville
Playouse 2000
caillouxtheater.com/

Kilgore
Texas Shakespeare Festival
texasshakespeare.com

Killeen
Killeen Civic Art Guild
kcag.net/
Vive Les Arts
vlatheatre.com/

Lamesa
Lamesa Community Players
pics.net/~lamesaplayers/

Leander
Way Off Broadway Community
Players
wobcp.org/

Lewisville
Greater Lewisville Community
Theatre
glct.org/

Livingston
Piney Woods Players
pineywoodsplayers.com/
Lockhart
Gaslight Baker Theater
gaslightbakertheatre.org/
Longview
Longview Community Theatre
longviewcommunitytheatre.com/
Longview Symphony
longviewsymphony.org/
Lubbock
Ballet Lubbock
balletlubbock.org/
Lubbock Community Theatre
lubbockcommunitytheatre.org/
Lubbock Symphony Orchestra
lubbocksymphony.org/
Texas Tech University Theatre
www.depts.ttu.edu/
theatreanddance/

Marble Falls
Hill Country Community Theatre
hcct.org/
Marfa
Marfa Theatre
themarfatheatre.org/
Marlin
Palace Theatre
palacetheatremarlin.com/
Marshall
Marshall Regional Arts Council
marshallartscouncil.org/
Marshall Symphony
marshall-chamber.com/pages/
symphony.php
McAllen
South Texas Symphony
valleyorchestra.org/
Mesquite
Mesquite Community Theatre
mctweb.org/
Mesquite Symphony Orchestra
mesquitesymphony.org
Midland
Maverick Players
maverickplayers.org/
Midland Community Threatre
mctmidland.org/
Midland-Odessa Symphony &
Chorale
mosc.org/
Mineola
Lake Country Playhouse
lakecountryplayhouse.org/
Mount Pleasant
Whatley Center for Performing Arts
ntcc.edu/Whatley/index.htm
Nacogdoches
Lamp-Lite Theatre
lamplitetheatre.org/
Nassau Bay
Clear Creek Community Theatre
clearcreekcountrytheatre.org/
Clear Lake Symphony Orchestra
nassaubay.com/clsymphony.htm
Navasota
Navasota Theatre Alliance
nta-stage.org/

New Braunfels
Circle Arts Theatre
circleartstheatre.org/
Mid-Texas Symphony
mtsymphony.org/
New Braunfels Theatre Company
newbraunfelstheatreco.org/
Odessa
Globe of the Great Southwest
globesw.org/
Midland-Odessa Symphony &
Chorale
mosc.org/
Permian Playhouse
permianplayhouse.com/
Orange
Lutcher Theater
lutcher.org/
Palestine
Texas Theater
thetexastheater.com/
Pasadena
Pasadena Little Theatre
pasadenalittletheatre.org/
Stage Door
stagedoorinc.com/
Pampa
Community Center for the Arts
createabeat.org/
Paris
Paris Community Theatre
paristheatreonline.com/
Plano
Chamberlain Ballet Company
chamberlainperformingarts.com/
Collin Theatre Center
collintheatrecenter.org/
The Living Opera
thelivingopera.org/
Plano Civic Chorus
planocivicchorus.org/
Plano Symphony Orchestra
planosymphony.org/
Rover Dramawerks
roverdramawerks.com/
Younger Generation Chorus
youngergeneration.org/
Port Arthur
Little Theatre
palt.org/
Port Lavaca
Main Street Theatre
plmainstreet.org/theatre.
html#start
Post
Garza Theatre
garzatheatre.com/
Richardson
Chamber Music International
chambermusicinternational.org/
Labyrinth Theatre
thelabyrinththeatre.org/
Repertory Company Theatre
rcttheatre.com/
Richardson Symphony
richardsonsymphony.org/
Richardson Theatre Centre
richardsontheatrecentre.com/
Tuzer Ballet
tuzerballet.com/

Rockwall
Rockwall Community Playhouse
rockwallcommunityplayhouse.
org/
Round Rock
Sam Bass Community Theatre
sambasstheatre.org/
Round Top
James Dick Foundation
festivalhill.org/
Rowlett
Amateur Community Theatre
actortx.com/
Corp Theatre
corptheatre.com/
Rusk
Cherokee Civic Theatre
cherokeetheatre.net/
San Angelo
Angelo Civic Theatre
angelocivictheatre.com/
San Angelo Symphony
sanangelosymphony.org/
San Antonio
Alamo City Men's Chorale
imagen-design.com/acmc/
default.asp
AtticRep
atticrep.org/
Ballet San Antonio
balletsanantonio.org/
Cameo Theatre
cameocenter.com/
Company Theatre
thecompanytheatre.org/
Guadalupe Cultural Arts Center
guadalupeculturalarts.org/
Josephine Theatrical Company
josephinetheatre.org/
Magik Children's Theatre
magiktheatre.org/
Overtime Theater
theovertimetheater.net/
Renaissance Guild
therenaissanceguild.org/
San Antonio Symphony
sasymphony.org/
San Antonio Theater Coalition
satheatre.com/
San Pedro Playhouse
sanpedroplayhouse.com/
Shoestring Shakespeare Company
shoestringshakespeare.com/
Texas Bach Choir
texasbachchoir.org/
Texas Photographic Society
texasphoto.org/
Youth Orchestras of San Antonio
yosa.org/
University of the Incarnate Word
www.uiw.edu/theatre/
San Marcos
Texas State University
www.theatreanddance.txstate.
edu/
Seguin
Mid-Texas Symphony
mtsymphony.org/
Seguin Art Center
seguinartcenter.com/

Sherman
Austin College Theatre
www.austincollege.edu/Category.
asp?1770
Sherman Community Players
scptheater.org/
Southlake
Southlake Community Band
southlakeband.com/
Stephenville
Cross Timbers Fine Arts Council
crosstimbersarts.org/
Sugar Land
Fort Bend Symphony Orchestra
fbso.org/
Fort Bend Theater
fortbendtheatre.com/
Temple
Temple Civic Theatre
artstemple.com/
Temple Symphony Orchestra
templesymphony.org/
Terrell
Kaufman County Civic Theatre
kcct.org/
Texarkana
Perot Theatre
trahc.org/perot.shtml
Texas Repertory Company
texrep.org/
Texas City
College of the Mainland Theatre
www.com.edu/campus-life/
theatre.cfm
The Colony

Lakeside Community Theatre
lctthecolony.org/
The Woodlands
Class Act Productions
classicaltheatre.org/
Woodlands Center for the
Performing Arts
woodlandscenter.org/
Tyler
Ballet Tyler
ballettyler.org/
East Texas Symphony Orchestra
etso.org/
Tyler Civic Theatre Center
tylercivictheatre.com/
Uvalde
Grand Opera House
prosites-stebmaster.homestead.
com/OperaHouse.html
Victoria
Theatre Victoria
theatrevictoria.org/
Victoria Ballet Theatre
victoriaballettheatre.com/
Victoria Symphony
victoriasymphony.com/
Waco
Baylor Theatre
baylor.edu/theatre/
McLennan Theatre
mclennan.edu/departments/
a&s/dram/
Waco Civic Theatre
wacocivictheatre.org/
Waco Children's Theatre

wacochildrenstheatre.com/
Waco Performing Arts
wacoperformingarts.org/
Waco Symphony Orchestra
wacosymphony.com/
Waxahachie
Waxahachie Community Theatre
waxahachiecommunitytheatre.
com/
Weatherford
Theatre Off the Square
weatherfordtots.org/
Webster
Bay Area Houston Ballet & Theatre
bahbt.org/
Wharton
Plaza Theatre
whartonplazatheatre.org/
Wichita Falls
Backdoor Theatre
backdoortheatre.org/
Wichita Falls Theatre/Opera House
wichitatheatre.com/
Wills Point
Van Zandt Community Theatre
vanzandtcommunitytheatre.com/
Wimberley
EmilyAnn Theatre
emilyann.org/
Wimberley Players
wimberleyplayers.org/
Texas
Texas Living History Association
texanalivinghistory.org/ ☆

Texas Museums of Art, Science, History

Listed below are links to the Web pages of Texas museums. Where required some have indication of the area of emphasis of the exhibits.

Abilene
Frontier Texas! (History)
frontiertexas.com
Grace Museum (Art, History)
thegracemuseum.org
National Center for Children's
Illustrated Literature
nccil.org
Addison
Cavanaugh Flight Museum
cavanaughflightmuseum.com/
Albany
Old Jail Art Center
theoldjailartcenter.org/
Alpine
Museum of the Big Bend (History)
sulross.edu/~museum/
Amarillo
Amarillo Museum of Art
amarilloart.org/
American Quarter Horse Heritage
Center & Museum
aqha.com/foundation/museum/
Don Harrington Discovery Center
(Science, Children's)
dhdc.org/
Texas Pharmacy Museum

ttuhsc.edu/sop/prospective/
visitors/museum.aspx
Angleton
Brazoria County Historical Museum
bchm.org/
Arlington
Legends of the Game Baseball
Museum
texas.rangers.mlb.com/tex/
ballpark/museum.jsp
Austin
Austin Children's Museum
austinkids.org/
Austin Museum of Art
amoa.org/
Bob Bullock Texas State History
Museum
thestoryoftexas.com/
Capitol Visitors Center (Historical)
tspb.state.tx.us/CVC/home/
home.html
Elisabet Ney Museum (Art)
ci.austin.tx.us/elisabetney/html/
main.html
French Legation Museum (History)
frenchlegationmuseum.org/
Harry Ransom Humanities Research
Center (History, Literature)
hrc.utexas.edu/
Jack S. Blanton Museum of Art
blantonmuseum.org/
Jacob Fontaine Religious Museum

rootsweb.com/~txjfrm/
Jourdan-Bachman Pioneer Farms
pioneerfarms.org/
Lady Bird Johnson Wildflower Center
wildflower.org/
Lyndon B. Johnson Library
lbjlib.utexas.edu/
Mexic-Arte Museum (Art)
mexic-artemuseum.org/
O. Henry Museum (History)
ci.austin.tx.us/parks/ohenry.htm
Texas Memorial Museum (History,
Natural History)
utexas.edu/tmm/
Texas Military Forces Museum
texasmilitaryforcesmuseum.org/
Texas Music Museum
texasmusicmuseum.org
Umlauf Sculpture Garden & Museum
umlaufsculpture.org
Wild Basin Wilderness Preserve
wildbasin.org/
Women and Their Work
womenandtheirwork.org/
Bay City
Matagorda County Museum
matagordacountymuseum.org/
Beaumont
Art Museum of Southeast Texas
amset.org/
Edison Museum (Science)
edisonmuseum.org/

Fire Museum of Texas
firemuseumoftexas.org/
McFaddin-Ward House (History)
mcfaddin-ward.org/
Spindletop/Gladys City Boomtown
Museum (History)
spindletop.org/
Texas Energy Museum (History)
texasenergymuseum.org

Belton
Bell County Museum
bellcountytx.com/Museum/
themuseum_directions.html

Big Spring
Heritage of Big Spring
bigspringmuseum.com/

Bonham
Sam Rayburn Library/Museum
cah.utexas.edu/museums/
rayburn.php

Borger
Hutchinson County Historial Museum
hutchinsoncountymuseum.org/

Brownsville
Brownsville Museum of Fine Art
brownsvillemfa.org
Historic Brownsville Museum
brownsvillemuseum.org

Brownwood
Brown County Museum of History
browncountyhistory.org/
bcmoh.html

Bryan
Brazos Valley Museum of Natural
History
brazosvalleymuseum.org/

Buffalo Gap
Buffalo Gap Historic Village
mcwhiney.org/buffgap/bghome.
html

Burton
Burton Cotton Gin and Museum
cottonginmuseum.org/

Canadian
River Valley Pioneer Museum
rivervalleymuseum.org/

Canyon
Panhandle-Plains Historical Museum
panhandleplains.org

Carthage
Texas Country Music Hall of Fame
& Tex Ritter Museum
carthagetexas.com/HallofFame/
index.html

Clarendon
Saints' Roost Museum (Historical)
saintsroost.org

Clifton
Bosque Museum (History)
bosquemuseum.org/

College Station
George Bush Presidential Library
bushlibrary.tamu.edu/
Stark University Center Galleries
stark.tamu.edu/
Virtual Museum of Nautical
Archaeology
ina.tamu.edu/vm.htm

Conroe
Heritage Museum of Montgomery
County
heritagemuseum.us/

Corpus Christi
Art Museum of South Texas
stia.org/
Corpus Christi Museum of Science
and History
ccmuseum.com/museum/
index.cfm
Texas State Aquarium
texasstateaquarium.org/
Texas State Museum of Asian
Cultures
asianculturesmuseum.org/
USS Lexington Museum
usslexington.com/

Corsicana
Pearce Western Art/Civil War
Museum
pearcecollections.us/

Cotulla
Brush Country Historical Museum
historicdistrict.com/museum/

Dalhart
XIT Museum (Historical)
xitmuseum.com/

Dallas
African American Museum
aamdallas.org/
Museum of the American Railroad
dallasrailwaymuseum.com
Dallas Historical Society (Fair Park)
dallashistory.org/
Dallas Museum of Art
dallasmuseumofart.org/
Dallas Museum of Natural History
natureandscience.org
Frontiers of Flight Museum
flightmuseum.com/
International Museum of Cultures
internationalmuseumofcultures.
org/
Meadows Museum (Art)

smu.edu/meadows/museum/
Dallas Heritage Village
dallasheritagevillage.org/
The Sixth Floor Museum (History)
jfk.org/

Denison
Red River Railroad Museum
redriverrailmuseum.org

Denton
Courthouse-on-the-Square Museum
(Historical)
dentoncounty.com/dept/main.
asp?Dept=72
UNT Art Galleries
gallery.unt.edu/
Denton County Historical Museum
dentoncountyhistoricalmuseum.
com

Dublin
Dr Pepper Bottling CompanyMuseum
dublindrpepper.com/

Edgewood
Edgewood Heritage Park and
Historical Village
vzinet.com/heritage/

Edinburg
Museum of South Texas History
mosthistory.org/

El Campo
El Campo Museum of Natural History
elcampomuseum.com/

El Paso
Centennial Museum/Chihuahuan
Desert Gardens
museum.utep.edu/
El Paso Museum of Art
elpasoartmuseum.org/

Fort Davis
Chihuahuan Desert Research
Institute and Visitor Center
cdri.org/

The Houston Museum of Natural Science. Robert Plocheck photo.

Fort Stockton
Annie Riggs Museum (Historical)
tourtexas.com/fortstockton/
ftstockriggs.html
Fort Worth
Amon Carter Museum (Art)
cartermuseum.org/
Cattle Raisers Museum
cattleraisersmuseum.org/
Fort Worth Museum of Science
and History
fwmuseum.org/
Kimbell Art Museum
kimbellart.org/
Log Cabin Village (Historical)
logcabinvillage.org
Modern Art Museum of Fort Worth
mamfw.org/
National Cowgirl Museum
and Hall of Fame
cowgirl.net/
Sid Richardson Collection
of Western Art
sidrmuseum.org/
Texas Civil War Museum
texascivilwarmuseum.com/
Fredericksburg
Gillespie County Historical Society
pioneermuseum.com/
National Museum of the Pacific War
nimitz-museum.org/
Galveston
Lone Star Flight Museum
lsfm.org/
Offshore Energy Center/Ocean Star
(Science, Industry)
oceanstaroec.com/
Texas Seaport Museum and Tallship
"Elissa"
tsm-elissa.org/
Gilmer
Flight of Phoenix Aviation Museum
flightofthephoenix.org/
Greenville
Audie Murphy/American Cotton
Museum
cottonmuseum.com/
Henderson
The Depot Museum (Historical)
depotmuseum.com/
Houston
Blaffer Gallery, University of Houston
class.uh.edu/blaffer/
Children's Museum of Houston
cmhouston.org/
Contemporary Arts Museum
camh.org/
Houston Center for Comtemporary
Craft
crafthouston.org/default.asp?ID=1
Houston Center for Photography
hcponline.org/
Houston Fire Museum (History)
houstonfiremuseum.com/
Houston Museum of Natural Science
hmns.org/
Lawndale Art Center
lawndaleartcenter.org/
The Menil Collection (Art)
menil.org/
Museum of Fine Arts
mfah.org/
Museum of Health and Medical

Science
mhms.org/
Museum of Printing History
printingmuseum.org/
Rice University Art Gallery
ricegallery.org/
San Jacinto Museum of History
sanjacinto-museum.org/
Space Center Houston
spacecenter.org/
Huntsville
Sam Houston Memorial Museum
shsu.edu/~smm_www/
Texas Prison Museum
txprisonmuseum.org/
Kerrville
Museum of Western Art
museumofwesternart.org/
Kilgore
East Texas Oil Museum
easttexasoilmuseum.com/
Lake Jackson
Lake Jackson Historical Museum
lakejacksonmuseum.org/
Laredo
Republic of the Rio Grande Museum
webbheritage.org/riograndehistory.
htm
Texas A&M International University
Planetarium
tamiu.edu/coas/planetarium/
League City
West Bay Common School
Children's Museum (Historical)
oneroomschoolhouse.org/
Longview
Longview Museum of Fine Arts
lmfa.org/
Lubbock
American Museum of Agriculture
agriculturehistory.org/
Buddy Holly Center (Historical)
www.buddyhollycenter.com/
Museum of Texas Tech University
(Art, Humanities, Science)
www.depts.ttu.edu/museumttu/
National Ranching Heritage Center
www.depts.ttu.edu/ranchhc/
home.htm
Science Spectrum
sciencespectrum.com/
Lufkin
Texas Forestry Museum
treetexas.com/
Marfa
Chinati Foundation (Art)
chinati.org/
Marshall
Harrison County Historical Museum
txgenes.com/TXHarrison/
NewHome.htm
Michelson Museum of Art
michelsonmuseum.org/
McAllen
International Museum of Art&Science
imasonline.org/
McKinney
Heard Natural Science Museum
heardmuseum.org/
Midland
American Airpower Heritage
Museum/Commerative Air Force
airpowermuseum.org/

Museum of the Southwest
(Art, Science, Children's)
museumsw.org/
Petroleum Museum
petroleummuseum.org/
Mobeetie
Old Mobeetie Texas Association
mobeetie.com/
New Braunfels
New Braunfels Sophienburg
Museum (History)
sophienburg.org/
Odessa
Ellen Noel Art Museum
noelartmuseum.org/
Orange
Stark Museum of Art
starkmuseum.org/
Panhandle
Square House Museum
squarehousemuseum.org/
Plano
Heritage Farmstead Museum
heritagefarmstead.org/
Port Arthur
Museum of the Gulf Coast (Historical)
museumofthegulfcoast.org/
Port Lavaca
Calhoun County Museum (Historical)
calhouncountymuseum.org/
Richmond
George Ranch Historical Park
georgeranch.org/
Rockport
Texas Maritime Museum
texasmaritimemuseum.org/
Round Top
Henkel Square (History)
texaspioneerarts.org/
henkel_square.html
Winedale Historical Center
www.cah.utexas.edu/museums/
winedale.php
San Angelo
San Angelo Museum of Fine Arts
and Children's Art Museum
samfa.org/
San Antonio
The Alamo
thealamo.org/
Hertzberg Circus Collection/Museum
www.sat.lib.tx.us/Hertzberg/
hzmain.html
Institute of Texan Cultures
texancultures.utsa.edu/
public/index.htm
Magic Lantern Castle Museum
magiclanterns.org/
Museo Alameda
thealameda.org/
The McNay Art Museum
mcnayart.org/
San Antonio Art League Museum
saalm.org/
San Antonio Museum of Art
samuseum.org/main/
Witte Museum (Science, Historical)
wittemuseum.org/
San Marcos
Southwestern Writers Collection and
Wittliff Gallery of Southwestern
& Mexican Photography
library.txstate.edu/swwc/

The Texas Maritime Museum in Rockport. Robert Plocheck photo.

Sarita
Kenedy Ranch Museum of
South Texas
kenedymuseum.org/
Serbin
Texas Wendish Heritage Museum
wendish.concordia.edu
Sherman
Red River Historical Museum
hosting.texoma.net/rrhms/
Sulphur Springs
Southwest Dairy Center/Museum
southwestdairyfarmers.com/
Teague
The B-RI Railroad Museum
therailroadmuseum.com/
Temple
Railroad and Heritage Museum
rrhm.org/
Texarkana
Museum of Regional History
texarkanamuseums.org/

Thurber
W.K. Gordon Center for Industrial
History of Texas
tarleton.edu/~gordoncenter/
Tyler
Discovery Science Place
discoveryscienceplace.com/
Smith County Historical Museum
smithcountyhistoricalsociety.
org/index.php
Tyler Museum of Art
tylermuseum.org
Victoria
Museum of the Coastal Bend
(Historical)
www.museumofthecoastalbend.
org/
Waco
Dr Pepper Museum (History)
drpeppermuseum.com/
Mayborn Museum Complex
(History, Science)

baylor.edu/mayborn/
Texas Ranger Hall of Fame/ Museum
texasranger.org/
Texas Sports Hall of Fame
tshof.org/
Washington
Star of the Republic Museum
(Historical)
starmuseum.org/
Weatherford
Museum of the Americas
museumoftheamericas.com/
White Settlement
White Settlement Historical Museum
wsmuseum.com/
Wichita Falls
Kell House Museum (History)
wichitaheritage.org/kellhouse.html
Museum of Art
mwsu.edu/wfma/ ☆

Public Libraries in Texas

The following information was furnished by the Library Development Division of the Texas State Library, Austin.

Texas public libraries continue to strive to meet the education and information needs of Texans by providing library services of high quality with oftentimes-limited resources.

Each year, services provided by public libraries increase, with more visits to public libraries and higher attendance in library programs.

The challenges facing the public libraries in Texas are many and varied. The costs for providing electronic and on-line sources, in addition to traditional library services, are growing faster than library budgets.

Urban libraries are trying to serve growing populations, while libraries in rural areas are trying to serve remote populations and provide distance learning where possible.

National rankings of public libraries are published by the National Center for Education Statistics. These rankings may be found at:

http://nces.ed.gov/globallocator.

When comparing Texas statistics to those nationally, Texas continues to rank below most of the other states in most categories, with the exception of Reference Transactions and Public Use Internet Terminals.

Complete statistical information on public libraries is available on the Texas State Library's Web page at: **www.tsl.state.tx.us**.

Many Texas public libraries have established pages on the Internet. You can find a list of Web addresses at:

www.tsl.state.tx.us/texshare/pl/texlibs.html. ☆

Alamo Village, a permanent movie set near Brackettville, was built for John Wayne's The Alamo. *It has also been used for* Lonesome Dove, Barbarosa *and* The Good Old Boys, *among other productions. Robert Plocheck photo.*

Film and Television Work in Texas

Source: Texas Film Commission at governor.state.tx.us/film

For almost a century, Texas has been one of the nation's top film-making states, after California and New York.

More than 1,300 projects have been made in Texas since 1910, including **Wings**, the first film to win an Academy Award for Best Picture, which was made in San Antonio in 1927.

Texas' attractions to filmmakers are its diverse locations, abundant sunshine and moderate winter weather, and a variety of support services. The economic benefits of hosting on-location filming over the past decade are estimated at more than $2.79 billion.

Besides salaries paid to locally hired technicians and actors, as well as fees paid to location owners, the production companies do business with hotels, car rental agencies, lumberyards, restaurants, grocery stores, utilities, office furniture suppliers, gas stations, security services and florists.

All types of projects come to Texas besides feature films, including television specials, commercials, corporate films and game videos.

Many projects made in Texas originate in California studios, but Texas is also the home of many independent filmmakers who make films outside the studio system.

Some films and television shows made in Texas have become icons. **Giant**, John Wayne's **The Alamo**, and the long-running TV series **Dallas** all made their mark on the world's perception of Texas and continue to draw tourists to their film locations.

The Texas Film Commission, a division of the Office of the Governor, markets to Hollywood Texas' locations, support services and workforce.

The commission's free services include location research, employment referrals, red-tape-cutting, and information on laws, weather, travel and other topics affecting filmmakers.

The on-line Texas Production Manual includes more than 1,200 individuals and businesses serving every facet of the film industry. ☆

Regional Commissions

Amarillo Film Office
1000 S. Polk, Amarillo 79101
(806) 374-1497
amarillofilm.org

Austin Film Office
301 Congress Ave. Ste. 200
Austin 78701, (800) 926-2282
austintexas.org

Brownsville Border Film Comm.
P.O. Box 911, City Hall
Brownsville 78520, (956) 548-6176
filmbrownsville.com

Dallas Film Commission
325 N. St. Paul Ste. 700
Dallas 75201, (214) 571-1050
filmdfw.com

El Paso Film Commission
One Civic Center Plaza
El Paso 79901, (800) 351-6024
elpasocvb.com

Houston Film Commission
901 Bagby Ste. 100
Houston 77002, (800) 365-7575
filmhouston.texaswebhost.com

Northeast Texas Film Commission
P.O. Box 247

Jefferson 75657, (903) 214-1144
netexasmovies.com

San Antonio Film Commission
203 S. St. Mary's, 2nd Floor
San Antonio 78205, (800)447-3372
filmsanantonio.com

South Padre Island Film Comm.
7355 Padre Blvd.
South Padre Island 78597
(800) 657-2373, sopadre.com

Texas Panhandle Film Commission
P.O. Box 3293, Amarillo 79116
(806) 679-1116
txpanhandlefilm.com

Recent Movies Made in Texas

Following is a partial list of recent major productions filmed in Texas, in descending order by date. The date is for the year of release of the film, while actual location shots occurred often a year or two earlier.

Location information is from the Texas Film Commission and other sources.

When only a small portion of the movie is known to have been filmed in Texas, "(part)" is listed next to the movie title.

Some of the major artists who worked on the project are listed in the far right column.

Sources: Texas Film Commission, and online.

YEAR	MOVIE	LOCATIONS	ARTISTS
2006	**No Country for Old Men** (part)	Marfa	Daniel Day-Lewis
2006	**There Will Be Blood** (part)	Marfa, Big Bend National Park	Ethan and Joel Coen, Tommy Lee Jones
2005	**The Three Burials of Melquiades Estrada**	Van Horn, Monahans, Santa Elena Canyon, Lajitas, Shafter, Midland/Odessa	Tommy Lee Jones
2004	**The Alamo**	Dripping Springs, Wimberley, Pedernales Falls State Park, Bastrop, Austin	Dennis Quaid, Jason Patric
2004	**Friday Night Lights**	Odessa, Notrees, Austin, Houston	Billy Bob Thornton
2003	**Texas Chainsaw Massacre**	Martindale, Taylor, Austin	
2002	**The Rookie**	Thorndale, Taylor, Arlington, Big Lake	Dennis Quaid
2001	**Pearl Harbor** (part)	Battleship Texas, Houston, and USS Lexington, Corpus Christi	Ben Affleck, Cuba Gooding Jr.
2000	**All the Pretty Horses**	Boerne, Helotes, Pipe Creek, Big Bend	Matt Damon, Sam Shepard
2000	**Miss Congeniality**	Austin, San Antonio	Sandra Bullock, Michael Caine
1999	**Where the Heart Is**	Austin, Baylor University, Lockhart, Taylor, Kyle, Driftwood, Bastrop, Georgetown	Natalie Portman, Ashley Judd
1999	**Boys Don't Cry**	Greenville, Dallas area	Hilary Swank
1999	**Office Space**	Austin, Dallas	Jennifer Aniston, Ron Livingston
1999	**Varsity Blues**	Elgin, Coupland, Taylor, Georgetown	John Van Der Beek, Jon Voight
1998	**Dancer, Texas Pop. 81**	Fort Davis, Alpine	Breckin Meyer, Peter Facinelli
1998	**Home Fries**	Coupland, Taylor, Bastrop, Austin, El Paso	Drew Barrymore, Luke Wilson
1998	**Hope Floats**	Smithville, Austin	Sandra Bullock, Harry Connick Jr.
1998	**The Newton Boys**	Bertram, Martindale, Bartlett, Lockhart, Austin, San Antonio	Matthew McConaughey, Ethan Hawke
1996	**Bottle Rocket**	Hillsboro, Grand Prairie, Dallas	Luke and Owen Wilson, James Caan
1996	**Courage Under Fire**	Bertram, Bastrop, San Marcos, Austin, El Paso	Denzel Washington, Meg Ryan
1996	**Lone Star**	Eagle Pass, Del Rio, Laredo	Matthew McConaughey, Kris Kristofferson
1996	**Michael**	Gruene, Muldoon, Granger, New Corn Hill, Gonzales, La Grange, Georgetown	John Travolta, William Hurt
1995	**Apollo 13**	Houston area	Tom Hanks, Kevin Bacon
1993	**Dazed and Confused**	Austin, Georgetown, Seguin	Richard Linklater (director), Matthew McConaughey
1993	**What's Eating Gilbert Grape**	Manor, Lockhart, Austin	Johnny Depp, Leonardo DiCaprio

Number of Production Projects in Texas by Year

	1999	2000	2001	2002	2003	2004	2005	2006	2007
Studio Feature Films	6	9	5	4	8	8	6	8	3
Independent Feature Films	16	27	29	25	13	22	25	37	33
TV Series	3	4	6	8	6	7	13	11	14
TV Single Episodes/Segments	3	5	7	21	12	14	1	63	38
TV Pilots	-	-	-	1	1	3	2	8	7
TV Movies	4	2	4	1	1	1	2	1	-
TV Miniseries	-	-	-	-	-	-	-	2	-
TV Specials	1	1	1	-	3	4	1	3	2
Other TV projects	-	2	2	1	2	3	1	5	7
TOTAL Film/TV projects	33	50	54	61	46	62	51	138	104

Source: Texas Film Commission (revised 2008).

Television series produced in Texas include **Friday Nights Lights** (locations include Pflugerville, Del Valle and San Marcos) and **Prison Break** (locations include Pottsboro, South Padre Island, Decatur, Mineral Wells and Galveston), and syndicated programs such as **Judge Alex**, in addition to the long-running **Austin City Limits**.

Texas Medal of the Arts Awards

Source: Texas Commission on the Arts

The Texas Medals of the Arts were presented to artists and arts patrons with Texas ties in April 2009.

The awards are administered by the Texas Cultural Trust Council. The council was established to raise money and awareness for the Texas Cultural Trust Fund, which was created by the Legislature in 1993 to support cultural arts in Texas (www.txculturaltrust. org).

The medals, awarded every two years, were first presented in 2001. A concurrent proclamation by the state Senate and House of Representatives honors the recipients, and the governor presents the awards in Austin.

2009

A **Standing Ovation Award** was presented to former First Lady Laura Bush of Midland and Dallas.

Lifetime Achievement Award: posthumously to artist Robert Rauschenberg, born in Port Arthur.

Music: Clint Black of Katy, country music singer/songwriter.

Literary: T.R. Fehrenbach of San Antonio. Mr. Fehrenbach, born in San Benito, is the author of 18 nonfiction books, including *Lone Star: A History of Texas and Texans.*

Visual arts: Keith Carter of Beaumont, photographer.

Theater arts: Betty Buckley of Fort Worth, Tony Award winner and film actress.

Multimedia: Austin City Limits, the 30-year television series.

Film: Robert Rodriguez of Austin. Mr. Rodriguez, born in San Antonio, is a film director and writer.

Architecture: David Lake of Austin and Ted Flato of Corpus Christi, both now working in San Antonio.

Arts education: Pianist James Dick of Round Top, founder of the International Festival-Institute there.

Individual arts patron: Edith O'Donnell of Dallas.

Corporate arts patron: Anheuser-Busch of St. Louis and Houston.

2007

Lifetime Achievement Award: Broadcast newsman Walter Cronkite of Houston.

Music: Ornette Coleman of Fort Worth, jazz saxophonist.

Dance: Alvin Ailey American Dance Theater. The late Alvin Ailey, born in Rogers, was a creator of African American dance works.

Literary: writer Sandra Brown of Waco.

Visual arts: Jesús Moroles of Corpus Christi/Rockport, sculptor.

Theater arts: actress Judith Ivey of El Paso.

Multimedia: Bill Wittliff of Taft and Austin, publisher, writer, photographer, director, producer.

Arts education: Paul Baker of Hereford/Waelder. Headed drama departments at Baylor and Trinity universities.

Individual arts patron: Diana and Bill Hobby of Houston.

Corporate arts patron: Neiman Marcus, Dallas.

Foundation arts patron: Sid W. Richardson Foundation of Fort Worth.

2005

Lifetime Achievement Award: singer Vikki Carr of El Paso.

Television/theater: actress Phylicia Rashad of Houston.

Music: singer/songwriter Lyle Lovett of Klein.

Dance: Ben Stevenson of Houston and Fort Worth.

Literary arts: Naomi Shihab Nye of San Antonio.

Visual arts: Jose Cisneros of El Paso.

Theater: Robert Wilson of Waco.

Arts education: Ginger Head-Gearheart of Fort Worth, advocate of arts education in public schools.

Individual arts patrons: Joe R. and Teresa Lozano Long of Austin, philanthropists.

Foundation arts patron: Nasher Foundation/Dallas.

2003

Lifetime Achievement: John Graves of Glen Rose, author of *Goodbye to A River.*

Media-film/television acting: Fess Parker of Fort Worth.

Music: country singer Charley Pride of Dallas.

Dance: Tommy Tune of Wichita Falls and Houston.

Theater: Enid Holm of Odessa, actress and former executive director of Texas Nonprofit Theatres.

Literary arts: Sandra Cisneros of San Antonio.

Visual arts: sculptor Glenna Goodacre of Dallas.

Folk arts: Tejano singer Lydia Mendoza of San Antonio.

Architecture: State Capitol Preservation Project of Austin, headed by Dealey Herndon.

Arts education: theater teacher Marca Lee Bircher of Dallas.

Individual arts patron: philanthropist Nancy B. Hamon of Dallas.

Corporate arts patron: Exxon/Mobil based in Irving.

Foundation arts patron: Houston Endowment Inc.

2001

Lifetime Achievement: Van Cliburn of Fort Worth.

Film: actor Tommy Lee Jones of San Saba.

Music: singer-songwriter Willie Nelson of Austin.

Dance: Debbie Allen of Houston, choreographer, director, actress and composer.

Theater: *Texas* musical-drama producer Neil Hess of Amarillo.

Literary arts: playwright Horton Foote of Wharton.

Visual arts: muralist John Biggers of Houston.

Folk arts: musician brothers Santiago Jimenez Jr. and Flaco Jimenez of San Antonio.

Architecture: restoration architect Wayne Bell of Austin.

Arts education: theater arts director Gilberto Zepeda Jr. of Pharr.

Individual arts patron: philanthropist Jack Blanton of Houston.

Corporate arts patron: SBC Communications Inc. of San Antonio.

Foundation arts patron: Meadows Foundation of Dallas. ☆

Texas Institute of Letters Awards

Each year since 1939, the **Texas Institute of Letters** (texasinstituteofletters.org/) has honored outstanding literature and journalism that is either by Texans or about Texas subjects.

Awards have been made for fiction, nonfiction, Southwest history, general information, magazine and newspaper journalism, children's books, translation, poetry and book design. The awards of recent years are listed below:

Writer/Designer: Title

2008

Brendan M. Greeley Jr.: *The Two Thousand Yard Stare: Tom Lea's World War II Paintings, Drawings, and Eyewitness Accounts*

Thomas Cobb: *Shavetail*

Ann Weisgarber: *The Personal History of Rachel DuPree*

Rick Bass: "Mary Katherine's First Deer" in *Gray's Sporting Journal*

Todd Benson and Guillermo Contreras: "Texas' Deadliest Export" in the *San Antonio Express-News*

Benjamin Alire Saenz: *The Perfect Season for Dreaming*

Claudia Guadalupe Martinez: *The Smell of Old Lady Perfume*

James Allen Hall: *Now You're the Enemy*

Kerry Neville Bakken: "Indignity" in *Gettysburg Review*

James M. Smallwood: *The Feud that Wasn't: The Taylor Ring, Bill Sutton, John Wesley Hardin, and Violence in Texas*

Barbara Whitehead: *Traces of Forgotten Places*

Reginald Gibbons: translator of *Sophocles, Selected Poems: Odes and Fragments*

Lon Tinkle Award (for career): Carolyn Osborn

2007

Robert Krueger and Kathleen Tobin Krueger: *From Bloodshed to Hope in Burundi: Our Embassy Years During Genocide*

John J. McLaughlin: *Run in the Fam'ly*

Todd Benson: "Breaching America" in the *San Antonio Express-News*

DJ Stout and Julie Savasky: *Reflections of a Man: The Photographs of Stanley Marcus*

Rick Bass: "The Lives of the Browns" in *Southern Review*

Rick Bass: "The Elephant"

Arturo O. Martinez: *Perdito's Way*

Naomi Shihab Nye: *I'll Ask You Three Times, Are You OK?*

Jerry Thompson: *Cortina: Defending the Mexican Name in Texas*

Cate Marvin: *Fragment of the Head of a Queen*

Lon Tinkle Award (for career): David J. Weber

2006

Lawrence Wright: *The Looming Tower: Al-Qaeda and the Road to 9/11*

Cormac McCarthy: *The Road*

Dominic Smith: *The Mercury Visions of Louis Daguerre*

Marian Schwartz: translator of *White on Black* by Ruben Gallego

Tony Freemantle: "The Gulf Coast Revisited" in the *Houston Chronicle*

Mary Ann Jacob: *Timeless Texas*

John Sprong: "The Good Book and the Bad Book" in *Texas Monthly*

Mark Wisniewski: "Prisoners of War"

Tim Tingle: *Crossing Bok Chitto: A Choctaw Tale of Friendship and Freedom*

Heather Hepler: *Scrambled Eggs at Midnight*

Jerry Thompson: *Civil War to the Bloody End: The Life and Times of Major Samuel P. Heintzelman*

Christopher Bakken: *Goat Funeral*

Lon Tinkle Award (for career): William D. Wittliff

Special Citation: Allen Maxwell

2005

Stephen Graham Jones: *Bleed Into Me: A Bood of Stories*

Karen Olsson: *Waterloo*

Nate Blakeslee: *Tulia*

Thad Sitton and James H. Conrad: *Freedom Colonies: Independent Black Texans in the Time of Jim Crow*

John Bricuth: *As Long As It's Big*

DJ Stout and Julie Savasky: *Conjunto*

Edward Hegstrom, Tony Freemantle and Elena Vega: "One Nation: Two Worlds" in the *Houston Chronicle*

Kelly Bennett: *Not Norman: A Goldfish Story*

Pamela Porter: *The Crazy Man*

Rick Bass: "The Lives of Rocks"

Pamela Colloff: "Unholy Act" in *Texas Monthly*

Harvey Yunis: translator *Demosthenes: Speeches 18 and 19*

Lon Tinkle Award (for career): James Hoggard

2004

Steven Mintz: *Huck's Raft*

Laurie Lynn Drummond: *Anything You Say Can and Will Be*

Robert Rauschenberg was honored posthumously with a 2009 Texas Medal of Arts. See obituary, p. 706. File photo.

Held Against You
Bret Anthony Johnston: *Corpus Christi*
William Wenthe: *Not Till We Are Lost*
Andres Resendez: *Changing National Identities at the Frontier: Texas and New Mexico, 1800–1850*
Philip Boehm: translator of *Death in Danzig* by Stefan Chwin
Mike Nichols: *Balaam Gimble's Gumption*
Ben Fountain: "Bouki and the Cocaine"
Zanto Peabody: "The Search for Eddie Peabody" in the *Houston Chronicle*
DJ Stout and Julie Savasky: *Maps of the Imagination*
Lawrence Wright: "The Kingdom of Silence" in the *New Yorker*
Diane Stanley: *Jack and the Beanstalk*
Susan Abraham and Denise Gonzales: *Cecilia's Year*
Lon Tinkle Award (for career): T.R. Fehrenbach

2003

Betty Lou Phillips: *Emily Goes Wild*
Brian Yansky: *My Road Trip to the Pretty Girl Capital of the Word*
DJ Stout and Julie Savasky: *The Texas Cowboy Kitchen*
Steve Barthelme: "Claire"
Dick J. Reavis: articles on homelessness in the *San Antonio Express-News*
Jan Reid: "End of the River" in *Texas Monthly*
John Blair: *The Green Girls*
Jennifer Grotz: *Cusp*
Lynn Hoggard: translator of *Nelida* by Marie D'Agoult
B.H. Fairchild: *Early Occult Memory Systems of the Lower Midwest*
Jack Jackson: *Almonte's Texas*, translated by John Wheat
Don Graham: *Kings of Texas*
Robert Ford: *The Student Conductor*
Joseph Skibell: *The English Disease*
Lon Tinkle Award (for career): Bud Shrake

2002

Kathi Appelt: *Where, Where Is Swamp Bear?*
Carolee Dean: *Comfort*
Juan Rulfo: *Pedro Paramo*
Ben Fountain III: "Near-Extinct Birds of the Central Cordillera"
Mark Lisheron and Bill Bishop: "Cities of Ideas" in the *Austin American-Statesman*
Lawrence Wright: "The Man Behind Bin Laden" in the *New Yorker*
Dan Rifenburgh: *Advent*
Reginald Gibbons: *It's Time*
Kinky Friedman: *Meanwhile Back at the Ranch*
Michael Gagarin: *Antiphon the Athenian: Oratory, Law, and Justice in the Age of the Sophists*
Ray Gonzalez: *The Underground Heart: A Return to a Hidden Landscape*
Lisa Schamess: *Borrowed Light*
Rick Bass: *Hermit's Story*
Lon Tinkle Award: Shelby Hearon

2001

Carmen Bredeson: *Animals that Migrate*
Lori Aurelia Williams: *When Kambia Elaine Flew from Neptune*
Vicki Trego Hill: *Folktales of the Zapatista Revolution*
Tom McNeely: "Tickle Torture"
Mike Tolson, James Kimberly, Steve Brewer, Allan Turner: "A Deadly Distinction" in the *Houston Chronicle*
Larry L. King: "The Book on Willie Morris" in *Texas Monthly*
Ted Genoways: *Bullroarer*
Susan Wood: *Asunder*
Wendy Barker and Saranindranath Tagore: *Final Poems* by Rabindranath Tagore
Marco Perela: *Adventures of a No Name Actor*
Betje Klier: *Pavie in the Borderlands*
Larry McMurtry: *Sacagawea's Nickname: Essays on the American West*
Katherine Tannery: *Carousel of Progress*
Sarah Bird: *The Yokota Officers Club*

Lon Tinkle Award: William H. Goetzmann

2000

Rosa Shand: *The Gravity of Sunlight*
Laura Wilson: *Hutterites of Montana*
Richard V. Francaviglia: *The Cast Iron Forest*
Corey Marks: *Renunciation*
Edward Snow: *The Duino Elegies* by Rainer Maria Rilke
Glen Pourciau: "Deep Wilderness"
Pamela Colloff: "Sins of the Father"
Joe Holley: "The Hill Country: Loving It to Death"
Anne Coyle: *Crookwood*
Molly Ivins and Lou DuBose: *Shrub*
Bradley Hutchinson: *Willard Clark: Printer and Printmaker*
D.J. Stout and Julie Savasky: *John Graves and the Making of Goodbye to a River*
Lon Tinkle Award: Leon Hale

1999

Rick DeMarinis: *New and Selected Stories*
Robert Draper: *Hadrian's Walls*
Ann Rowe Seaman: *Swaggart: The Unauthorized Biography of an American Evangelist*
J.Gilberto Quezada: *Border Boss: Manuel B. Bravo and Zapata County*
Walt McDonald: "Whatever the Wind Delivers"
Jenny Lind Porter: *Verses on Death by Helinand of Froidmont*
Tracy Daugherty: *Comfort Me With Apples*
Steven and Rick Barthelme: "Good Losers"
James Hoggard: "Greetings from Cuba"
Benjamin Alire Saenz: *Grandma Fina and Her Wonderful Umbrellas/La Abuelita Fina y Sus Sombrillas Maravillosas*
Neil Barrett Jr.: *Interstate Dreams*
Margerie Adkins West: *Angels on High: Marton Varo's Limestone Angels on Bass Performance Hall*
Peter Brown: *On the Plains*
Lon Tinkle Award: Walt McDonald

1998

C.W. Smith: *Understanding Women*
Susan Choi: *The Foreign Student*
William C. Davis: *Three Roads to the Alamo: The Lives and Fortunes of David Crockett, James Bowie, and William Barret Travis*
Don Carleton: *A Breed So Rare: The Life of J.R. Parten, Liberal Texas Oil Man, 1896-1992*
B.H. Fairchild: "The Art of the Lathe"
Marian Schwartz: *The Ladies from St. Petersburg: Three Novellas*
James Hoggard: *Poems from Cuba: Alone Against the Sea*
Jane Roberts Wood: "My Mother Had a Maid"
Rick Bass: "Into the Fire"
Patrick Beach: "The Struggle for the Soul of Kreuz Market"
Bryan Woolley: "A Legend Runs Through It"
Pat Mora: *The Big Sky*
Lon Tinkle Award: Robert Flynn

1997

Lisa Sandlin: *A Message to the Nurse of Dreams*
Joseph Skibell: *A Blessing on the Moon*
Tara Holley with Joe Holley: *My Mother's Keeper: A Daughter's Memoir of Growing up in the Shadow of Schizophrenia*
John Miller Morris: *El Llano Estacado*
Bruce Bond: "Radiography"
Debbie Nathan and Willavaldo Delgadillo: *The Moon Will Forever Be a Distant Love*
Clifford Hudder: "Misplacement"
Skip Hollandsworth: "The Curse of Romeo and Juliet"
Michael Leahy: "Oswald: A Brother's Burden"
Jerry Herring: *Charles Schorre*
David Timmons: *The Wild and Vivid Land*
Naomi Shihab Nye: *Habibi*
Lon Tinkle Award: Rolando Hinojosa-Smith ☆

National Arts Medal Honors Corpus Christi native Moroles

The 2008 National Medal of Arts honored Jesús Moroles, the sculptor, among nine recipients.

In the award presentation, Mr. Moroles was cited for "his enduring achievements as a sculptor of stone. His granite monuments grace America's landscape."

He was born in Corpus Christi in 1950 and recieved a Bachelor's of Fine Arts from North Texas State University, now the University of North Texas in Denton.

His monumental works include the Houston Police Officers Memorial, the Floating Mesa Fountain in Albuquerque, the Lapstrake at CBS Plaza in New York, and the Granite Landscape in Wichita, Kan.

He now lives and works in Rockport.

At the White House awards ceremony in November 2008, President Bush also surprised two Texans with Presidential Citizens Medals. Robert Martin received a medal for his work as director of the national Institute of Museum and Library Services from 2001 to 2005. Mr. Martin served on the faculty of Texas Woman's University in Denton. A citizens medal also went to Adair Margo of El Paso who headed the President's Committee on the Arts and Humanities.

The Medal of Arts was established by Congress in 1984 to honor those who make outstanding contributions to the arts.

Each year, the National Endowment for the Arts seeks nominations from across the country. The president selects the recipients.

Previous Texas recipients include Lydia Mendoza, Tejano recording star beginning in the 1920s (see obituary, p. 706); country singer George Strait, dancer Tommy Tune, as well as the *Austin City Limits* concert TV series, and dancer/actress Cyd Charisse (see obituary, p. 704. ☆

The Houston Police Officers Memorial by Jesús Moroles. Robert Plocheck photo.

Van Cliburn Piano Competition

The Van Cliburn International Piano Competition was initiated in 1962 by music teachers and community leaders in Fort Worth. The event is held every four years. It commemorates Van Cliburn's victory in the Tchaikovsky International Piano Competition in Moscow in 1958.

Gold medalists receive cash prizes, tour engagements and free management for two years.

Past gold medalists are as follows:

1962	Ralph Votapek, USA
1966	Radu Lupu, Romania
1969	Christina Ortiz, Brazil
1973	Vladimir Viardo, USSR
1977	Steven De Groote, South Africa
1981	André-Michel Schub, USA
1985	José Feghali, Brazil
1989	Alexei Sultanov, USSR
1993	Simone Pedroni, Italy
1997	Jon Nakamatsu, USA
2001	Olga Kern of Russia, and Stanislav Ioudenitch of Uzbekistan
2005	Alexander Kobrin, Russia
2009	Nobuyuki Tsujiii of Japan, and Haochen Zhang of China

Poets Laureate of Texas

Since 2001, a committee of seven members appointed by the governor, lieutenant governor, and speaker of the House selects the poet laureate, state artists and state musician based on recommendations from the Texas Commission on the Arts.

Earlier, the Legislature made the nominations.

The state historian is appointed by the governor and is recommended by both the Texas State Historical Association and the Texas Historical Commission.

Sources: Texas State Library and Archives; Texas Commission on the Arts; The Dallas Morning News.

1932-34	Judd Mortimer Lewis, Houston
1934-36	Aline T. Michaelis, Austin
1936-39	Grace Noll Crowell, Dallas
1939-41	Lexie Dean Robertson, Rising Star
1941-43	Nancy Richey Ranson, Dallas
1943-45	Dollilee Davis Smith, Cleburne
1945-47	DavidRiley Russell, Dallas
1947-49	Aline B. Carter, San Antonio
1949-51	Carlos Ashley, Llano
1951-53	Arthur M. Sampley, Denton
1953-55	Mildred Lindsey Raiborn, San Angelo Dee Walker, Texas City, alternate
1955-57	Pierre Bernard Hill, Hunt
1957-59	Margaret Royalty Edwards, Waco
1959-61	J.V. Chandler, Kingsville Edna Coe Majors, Colorado City, alternate
1961	Lorena Simon, Port Arthur
1962	Marvin Davis Winsett, Dallas
1963	Gwendolyn Bennett Pappas, Houston Vassar Miller, Houston, alternate
1964-65	Jenny Lind Porter, Austin Edith Rayzor Canant, Texas City, alternate
1966	Bessie Maas Rowe, Port Arthur Grace Marie Scott, Abilene, alternate
1967	William E. Bard, Dallas Bessie Maas Rowe, Port Arthur, alternate
1968	Kathryn Henry Harris, Waco Sybil Leonard Armes, El Paso, alternate
1969-70	Anne B. Marely, Austin Rose Davidson Speer, Brady, alternate
1970-71	Mrs. Robby K. Mitchell, McKinney Faye Carr Adams, Dallas, alternate
1971-72	Terry Fontenot, Port Arthur Faye Carr Adams, Dallas, alternate
1972-73	Mrs. Clark Gresham, Burkburnett Marion McDaniel, Sidney, alternate
1973-74	Violette Newton, Beaumont Stella Woodall, San Antonio, alternate
1974-75	Lila Todd O'Neil, Port Arthur C.W. Miller, San Antonio, alternate

1975-76	Ethel Osborn Hill, Port Arthur Gene Shuford, Denton, alternate
1976-77	Florice Stripling Jeffers, Burkburnett Vera L. Eckert, San Angelo, alternate
1977-78	Ruth Carruth, Vernon Joy Gresham Hagstrom, Burkburnett, alternate
1978-79	Patsy Stodghill, Dallas Dorothy B. Elfstroman, Galveston, alternate
1979-80	Dorothy B. Elfstroman, Galveston Ruth Carruth, Vernon, alternate
1980-81	Weems S. Dykes, McCamey Mildred Crabree Speer, Amarillo, alternate
1981-82	*none designated*
1982-83	William D. Barney, Fort Worth Vassar Miller, Houston, alternate
1983-87	*none designated*
1987-88	Ruth E. Reuther, Wichita Falls
1988-89	Vassar Miller, Houston
1989-93	*none designated*
1993-94	Mildred Baass, Victoria
1994-99	*none designated*
2000	James Hoggard, Wichita Falls
2001	Walter McDonald, Lubbock
2002	*none designated*
2003	Jack Myers, Mesquite
2004	Cleatus Rattan, Cisco
2005	Alan Birkelbach, Plano
2006	Red Steagall, Fort Worth
2007	Steven Fromholz, Kopperl, Sugar Land
2008	Larry Thomas, Houston
2009	Paul Ruffin, Huntsville
2010	Karla K. Morton, Denton, Fort Worth

State Historians of Texas

2007-09	Jesús de la Teja, San Marcos
2009-11	Light Cummins, Sherman

State Musicians of Texas

2003	James Dick, Round Top
2004	Ray Benson, Austin
2005	Johnny Gimble, Tyler
2006	Billy Joe Shaver, Waco
2007	Dale Watson, Pasadena, Austin
2008	Shelley King, Austin
2009	Willie Nelson, Austin, Abbott
2010	Sara Hickman, Austin

State Artists of Texas

1971-72	Joe Ruiz Grandee, Arlington
1972-73	Melvin C. Warren, Clifton
1973-74	Ronald Thomason, Weatherford A.C. Gentry Jr., Tyler, alternate
1974-75	Joe Rader Roberts, Dripping Springs Bette Lou Voorhis, Austin, alternate
1975-76	Jack White, New Braunfels
July 4, 1975 –July 4, 1976	Robert Summers, Glen Rose Bicentennial Artist
1976-77	James Boren, Clifton Kenneth Wyatt, Lubbock, alternate
1977-78	Edward "Buck" Schiwetz, DeWitt County Renne Hughes, Tarrant County, alternate
1978-79	Jack Cowan, Rockport Gary Henry, Palo Pinto County, alternate Joyce Tally, Caldwell County, alternate
1979-80	Dalhart Windberg, Travis County Grant Lathe, Canyon Lake, alternate
1980-81	Harry Ahysen, Huntsville Jim Reno, Simonton, alternate
1981-82	Jerry Newman, Beaumont Raul Guiterrez, San Antonio, alternate
1982-83	Dr. James H. Johnson, Bryan Armando Hinojosa, Laredo, alternate
1983-84	Raul Gutierrez, San Antonio James Eddleman, Lubbock, alternate
1984-85	Covelle Jones, Lubbock Ragan Gennusa, Austin, alternate
1986-87	Chuck DeHaan, Graford
1987-88	Neil Caldwell, Angleton Rey Gaytan, Austin, alternate

1988-89	George Hallmark, Walnut Springs Tony Eubanks, Grapevine, alternate	
	Two-dimensional	**Three-dimensional**
1990-91	Mondel Rogers, Sweetwater	Ron Wells, Cleveland
1991-92	Woodrow Foster, Center	Kent Ullberg, Corpus Christi
	Harold Phenix, Houston, alternate	Mark Clapham, Conroe, alternate
1993-94	Roy Lee Ward, Hunt	James Eddleman, Lubbock
1994-95	Frederick Carter, El Paso	Garland A. Weeks, Wichita Falls
1998-99	Carl Rice Embrey, San Antonio	Edd Hayes, Humble
2000-02	*none designated*	
2003	Ralph White, Austin	Dixie Friend Gay, Houston
2004	Sam Caldwell, Houston	David Hickman, Dallas
2005	Kathy Vargas, San Antonio	Sharon Kopriva, Houston
2006	George Boutwell, Bosque	James Surls, Athens
2007	Lee Herring, Rockwall	David Keens, Arlington
2008	Janet Eager Krueger, Encinal	Damian Priour, Austin
2009	René Alvarado, San Angelo	Eliseo Garcia, Farmers Branch
2010	Marc Burckhardt, Austin	John Bennett, Fredericksburg

The concert hall of the International Festival-Institute at Round Top, founded by James Dick. Robert Plocheck photo.

Holidays, Anniversaries and Festivals, 2010 and 2011

Below are listed the principal federal and state government holidays; Christian, Jewish and Islamic holidays and festivals; and special recognition days for 2010 and 2011. Technically, the United States does not observe national holidays. Each state has jurisdiction over its holidays, which are usually designated by its legislature. This list was compiled partially from the Texas Government Code, the U.S. Office of Personnel Management, and *Astronomical Phenomena 2010* and *Astronomical Phenomena 2011,* which are published jointly by the U.S. Naval Observatory and the United Kingdom Hydrographic Office. See the footnotes for explanations of the symbols.

2010

New Year's Day § †	Fri., Jan. 1
Epiphany	Wed., Jan. 6
Sam Rayburn Day ‡	Wed., Jan. 6
Martin Luther King Jr. Day § †	Mon., Jan. 18
Confederate Heroes Day † *	Tues., Jan. 19
Valentine's Day	Sun., Feb. 14
Presidents' Day § † **	Mon., Feb. 15
Ash Wednesday	Wed., Feb. 17
Texas Independence Day †	Tues., March 2
Sam Houston Day ‡	Tues., March 2
Texas Flag Day ‡	Tues., March 2
Primary Election Day	Tues., March 2
Palm Sunday	Sun., March 28
Passover (Pesach), first day of ¶	Tues., March 30
César Chávez Day †	Wed., March 31
Good Friday †	Fri., April 2
Easter Day	Sun., April 4
Former Prisoners of War Recognition Day ‡	Fri., April 9
San Jacinto Day †	Wed., April 21
Mother's Day	Sun., May 9
Ascension Day	Thurs., May 13
Armed Forces Day	Sat., May 15
Shavuot (Feast of Weeks) ¶	Wed., May 19
Whit Sunday — Pentecost	Sun., May 23
Trinity Sunday	Sun., May 30
Memorial Day § †	Mon., May 31
Flag Day (U.S.)	Mon., June 14
Emancipation Day in Texas (Juneteenth) †	Sat., June 19
Father's Day	Sun., June 20
Independence Day § †	Sun., July 4
Ramadan, first day of §§	Wed., Aug. 11
Lyndon Baines Johnson Day †	Fri., Aug. 27
Labor Day § †	Mon., Sept. 6
Rosh Hashanah (Jewish New Year) ¶	Thurs., Sept. 9
Grandparents Day	Sun., Sept. 12
Yom Kippur (Day of Atonement) ¶	Sat., Sept. 18
Sukkot (Tabernacles), first day of ¶	Thurs., Sept. 23
Columbus Day § ‡	Mon., Oct. 11
Halloween	Sun., Oct. 31
General Election Day †	Tues., Nov. 2
Father of Texas (Stephen F. Austin) Day ‡	Wed., Nov. 3
Veterans Day § †	Thurs., Nov. 11
Thanksgiving Day § † ††	Thurs., Nov. 25
First Sunday in Advent	Sun., Nov. 28
Hanukkah, first day of ¶	Thurs., Dec. 2
Islamic New Year §§	Wed., Dec. 8
Christmas Day § †	Sat., Dec. 25

2011

New Year's Day § †	Sat., Jan. 1
Epiphany	Thurs., Jan. 6
Sam Rayburn Day ‡	Thurs., Jan. 6
Martin Luther King Jr. Day § †	Mon., Jan. 17
Confederate Heroes Day † *	Wed., Jan. 19
Valentine's Day	Mon., Feb. 14
Presidents' Day § † **	Mon., Feb. 21
Texas Independence Day †	Wed., March 2
Sam Houston Day ‡	Wed., March 2
Texas Flag Day ‡	Wed., March 2
Ash Wednesday	Wed., March 9
César Chávez Day †	Thurs., March 31
Former Prisoners of War Recognition Day ‡	Sat., April 9
Palm Sunday	Sun., April 17
Passover (Pesach), first day of ¶	Tues., April 19
San Jacinto Day †	Thurs., April 21
Good Friday †	Fri., April 22
Easter Day	Sun., April 24
Mother's Day	Sun., May 8
Armed Forces Day	Sat., May 21
Memorial Day § †	Mon., May 30
Ascension Day	Thurs., June 2
Shavuot (Feast of Weeks) ¶	Wed., June 8
Whit Sunday — Pentecost	Sun., June 12
Flag Day (U.S.)	Tues., June 14
Trinity Sunday	Sun., June 19
Father's Day	Sun., June 19
Emancipation Day in Texas (Juneteenth) †	Sun., June 19
Independence Day § †	Mon., July 4
Ramadan, first day of §§	Mon., Aug. 1
Lyndon Baines Johnson Day †	Sat., Aug. 27
Labor Day § †	Mon., Sept. 5
Grandparents Day	Sun., Sept. 11
Rosh Hashanah (Jewish New Year) ¶	Thurs., Sept. 29
Yom Kippur (Day of Atonement) ¶	Sat., Oct. 8
Columbus Day § ‡	Mon., Oct. 10
Sukkot (Tabernacles), first day of ¶	Thurs., Oct. 13
Halloween	Mon., Oct. 31
Father of Texas (Stephen F. Austin) Day ‡	Thurs., Nov. 3
Veterans Day § †	Fri., Nov. 11
Thanksgiving Day § † ††	Thurs., Nov. 24
First Sunday in Advent	Sun., Nov. 27
Islamic New Year §§	Sun., Nov. 27
Hanukkah, first day of ¶	Wed., Dec. 21
Christmas Day § †	Sun., Dec. 25

§ Federal legal public holiday. If the holiday falls on a Sunday, the following Monday may be treated as a holiday. If the holiday falls on a Saturday, the preceding Friday may be treated as a holiday.

† State holiday in Texas. For state employees, the Friday after Thanksgiving Day, Dec. 24 and Dec. 26 are also holidays. *Optional holidays* are César Chávez Day, Good Friday, Rosh Hashanah and Yom Kippur. *Partial-staffing holidays* are Confederate Heroes Day, Texas Independence Day, San Jacinto Day, Emancipation Day in Texas and Lyndon Baines Johnson Day. State offices will be open on optional holidays and partial-staffing holidays.

‡ State Recognition Days, as designated by the Texas Legislature.

* Confederate Heroes Day combines the birthdays of Robert E. Lee (Jan. 19) and Jefferson Davis (June 3).

** Presidents' Day combines the birthdays of George Washington (Feb. 22) and Abraham Lincoln (Feb. 12).

¶ §§ Jewish (¶) and Islamic (§§) holidays are tabular, which in this case means they begin at sunset on the previous day.

†† Between 1939 and 1957, Texas observed **Thanksgiving Day** on the last Thursday in November. As a result, in a November having five Thursdays, Texas celebrated national Thanksgiving on the fourth Thursday and Texas Thanksgiving on the fifth Thursday. In 1957, Texas changed the state observance to coincide with the national holiday. ☆

"Coronado's Camp at Blanco Canyon" by William K. Hartmann. Floyd County Museum.

Coronado Expedition at Blanco Canyon in 1541

Artifacts and recent historical research now point to Blanco Canyon in south Floyd County as the probable site of an encampment of the Coronado Expedition in the late spring of 1541.

Spanish explorer Francisco Vásquez de Coronado made his 1540-42 journey through the High Plains of Texas in search of the rumored seven golden cities.

Archaeologist Donald J. Blakeslee, professor in the Department of Anthropology at Wichita State University, Kansas, has spent several years working at the Blanco Canyon site near Floydada. What brought Dr. Blakeslee to the canyon were two pieces of chain mail discovered there by local ranchers in the 1960s, and copper crossbow arrow points found there in 1993 by Jimmy Owens, a local metal-detector buff.

The crossbow artifacts are significant because later Spanish expeditions had guns, making crossbows obsolete. In addition, Spanish coins and Mesoamerican pottery sherds have been found at the Owens site, named for Jimmy Owens, as well as a camp layout indicative of the Spanish military and unlike the camps of Indian tribes. This evidence supports the theory that this is one of the two Texas campsites of Coronado's expedition, an enterprise that included 1,200 Indian allies and 300 Spanish soldiers.

Also on the expedition were Franciscan friars, including Fray Juan de Padilla, who celebrated the Mass of Ascension Day 1541 in the canyon for those assembled there.

Fray Padilla, a native of Andalucia, chose to remain in the Southwest after Coronado abandoned his search, and the Franciscan, who would later be killed there, is called the first Christian martyr in what is now the United States.

Bishop Plácido Rodríquez of the Catholic Diocese of Lubbock celebrated a commemorative Mass in the canyon May 12, 2008. The event marked the anniversary of the Mass celebrated there by Fray Padilla. — RP.

A chain mail gauntlet found near Blanco Canyon. Floyd County Museum.

A cross is planted to commemorate the Ascension Mass of 1541 in Blanco Canyon. Robert Plocheck photo.

Church Affiliation Change: 1990 to 2000

Texas remains one of the nation's more "churched" states, even though there is a declining proportion of Texans affiliated with a church.

Texas ranks 18th among the states in percentage of the population belonging to a denomination. According to *Churches and Church Membership in the United States 2000*, at least 55.5 percent of Texans are adherents to a religion.

The survey, from the Glenmary Research Center in Nashville, is the only U.S. survey to report church membership at the state and county level. It relies on reports from the different denominations for membership numbers.

But in 2000, the African-American churches did not participate in the study. This probably leaves out more than one million church-going Texans.

In 1990, when the survey was previously done, it was estimated that there were 815,000 black Baptists in Texas. A conservative estimate of the membership in black Pentecostal churches in 2000 would be about 300,000. And, an estimate for black Methodists in Texas would be approximately 200,000.

Adjusting for those additions, then the percentage of Texans that are members of a religion would be closer to 61.7 percent. Although that is higher than the 55.5 percent figure compiled from the reporting churches, still, it would be down from 67.1 percent ten years before, indicating a move away from church membership.

This decrease occurred while many indicators have been showing that Americans are more interested in their spiritual lives than at any time in recent decades. Churches reported an increase of 1.5 million members while the total population of Texas increased by 4 million from 1990 to 2000. During the same period, the number of Texans not attached to a religion rose by 2.5 million.

Thus, according to the Texas Almanac analysis

According to *Churches And Church Membership in the United States 2000*, **Texas ranks**:

- **First** in number of Evangelical Protestants, with 5,083,087. California, which ranks second, has less than half as many, with 2,432,285.
- **Second**, behind Pennsylvania, in number of Mainline Protestants at 1,705,394.
- **Third** in number of Catholics, behind California and New York.
- **Third** in number of Buddhist congregations.
- **Fifth** in number of Muslims.
- **Fifth** in number of Hindu congregations.
- **Sixth** in number of Mormons.
- **Tenth** in number of Jews.

from a variety of sources, there are 7.9 million persons in the state who are not claimed by a church and about 13 million who are church members. (The U.S. census counted 20,851,820 persons in Texas in 2000.)

From the 2000 church survey, diversity among religious believers can be seen in the congregations of Muslims, Hindus, Buddhists and other non-Christian faiths. In 1990, these groups were not surveyed, so increases cannot be determined.

The estimate of Jewish Texans, 128,000, is from the congregations in the state. The number increased by 20,000 from 1990.

During the 1990s, the number of Catholics increased by almost 800,000, the greatest numerical gain among the churches. However, the percentage of Texans who are Catholic remained at 21 percent.

The largest faith group, the Baptists, increased by 314,761 members, a rate less than the statewide population increase. Thus in 2000, Baptists made up 21.8

The former Whitt Seminary in Parker County was built in 1880–81 and later used as a church for the Disciples of Christ congregation there until 1937. Robert Plocheck photo.

percent of the population, down from 24.9 percent in 1990.

The trend in the state's two largest denominations, Roman Catholic and Southern Baptist, which together make up over 40 percent of the population, was especially noticeable in the four largest metropolitan areas. More than half of all Texans live in these areas.

In the eight-county Houston metro area, the percentage of Catholics rose from 17.3 percent to 18.2 percent, while the percentage of Southern Baptists went down slightly from 14.9 percent to 14.8.

In the five-county Austin metro area, the percentage of Catholics increased from 13.6 percent to 18.4 percent. The percentage of Southern Baptists decreased from 13.5 percent to 10.2 percent.

In the four-county San Antonio metro area, the percentage of Catholics increased from 36.0 to 38.8, while the percentage of Southern Baptists decreased from 10.4 to 8.8.

The 12-county Dallas-Forth Worth metro area is the only one of the four where the number of Southern Baptists, 855,680, is higher than Catholics, 808,167. But, here also, the percentage of Southern Baptists declined from 19.0 to 16.4, while the percentage of Catholics rose from 9.0 in 1990 to 15.5 in 2000.

As noted, while these shifts in religious make-up were occurring, the number of persons not affiliated with a religious group was increasing.

In Houston in 1990, the percentage of the population not counted as church members was 43.1. In 2000, that had risen to 50.1 percent.

In Austin, the figure increased from 52.4 percent to 55.3 percent.

In San Antonio, the percentage of non-adherents to a religion was 36.2 in 1990. In 2000, it had risen

slightly to 37.0 percent.

In the Dallas-Fort Worth area, it increased from 43.6 percent in 1990, to 47.7 percent in 2000.

These trends reflect what was happening in the nation at large, where the percentage of the population not affiliated with a church rose from 44.9 to 55.1.

The Southern Baptists and Catholics also were the largest religious groups in the nation. And the percentage of Catholics remained about the same, 21.5 in 1990 and 22.0 in 2000, while the percentage of the total population that was Southern Baptist declined from 13.8 to 7.1.

The Glenmary study is a combined effort of the Catholic research center and the Church of the Nazarene, a Protestant denomination with headquarters in Kansas City, Mo..

The study distinguishes between members, which it defines as adult members only, and adherents, which includes adults and children. **All figures for members used by the Texas Almanac refer to children and adults.**

Sources

Churches and Church Membership in the United States 2000, Glenmary Research Center, Nashville, Tenn., 2002.

National Council of Churches of Christ in the USA, New York, *Yearbook of American and Canadian Churches*, annual.

New Handbook of Texas, 1996, various: "Christian Methodist Episcopal Church," by Charles E. Tatum; "African-American Churches," "African Methodist Episcopal Church," and "African Methodist Episcopal Zion Church," by William E. Montgomery; "Religion," by John W. Storey. — *Robert Plocheck*

Numbers of Members by Denomination

Religious Groups in Texas	1990	Change	2000
Baha'i			**10,777**
Baptist	**4,223,157**	**+ 314,761**	**4,537,918**
American Baptist Association			61,272
American Baptist Churches in the USA	12,905	- 5,848	7,057
Baptist General Conference	278	+ 62	340
Baptist Missionary Association of America	125,323	- 2,125	123,198
Conservative Baptist Association of America (1 congregation)			
Free Will Baptist, National Association of, Inc.	4,936	- 2,114	2,822
Interstate & Foreign Landmark Missionary Baptists Association	76	+ 17	93
Landmark Baptist, Indep. Assns. & Unaffil. Churches			964
National Primitive Baptist Convention, USA			4,463
North American Baptist Conference	1,634	- 65	1,569
Primitive Baptists Associations	2,544		
Primitive Baptist Church — Old Line (118 congregations)			NR
Progressive Primitive Baptists			197
Reformed Baptist Churches (10 congregations)			
Regular Baptist Churches, General Association of			684
Seventh Day Baptist General Conference	242		
Southern Baptist Convention	3,259,395	+ 260,064	3,519,459
Southwide Baptist Fellowship (13 congregations)			
Two-Seed-in-the-Spirit Predestinarian Baptists	53	- 24	29
(Black Baptists Estimate)*	(815,771)*	—	(815,771)*

Religious Groups in Texas	1990	Change	2000
Buddhism (88 congregations)			NR
Catholic Church	3,574,728	+ 794,241	4,368,969
(Independent) Christian Churches & Churches of Christ	33,766	+ 9,836	43,602
Churches of Christ	380,948	- 3,684	377,264
(Disciples of Christ) Christian Church	105,495	+ 5,793	111,288
Episcopal	169,227	+ 8,683	177,910
Episcopal Church, The	169,112	+ 8,798	177,910
Reformed Episcopal Church	115		
Hindu (34 congregations)			NR
Holiness	61,487	+ 25,052	86,539
Christian & Missionary Alliance, The	3,082	+ 776	3,858
Church of God (Anderson, Ind.)	5,854	- 1,185	4,669
Free Methodist Church of North America	886	- 12	874
Nazarene, Church of the	45,097	+ 5,431	50,528
Salvation Army	5,676	+ 19,394	25,070
Wesleyan Church, The	892	+648	1,540
Independent Non-Charismatic Churches	132,292	+ 12,957	145,249
Jain (6 congregations)			NR
Jewish, estimate	107,980	+ 20,020	128,000
Lutheran	294,524	+ 6,994	301,518
Church of the Lutheran Brethren of America	71		
Church of the Lutheran Confession	144		
Evangelical Lutheran Church in America	155,276	- 257	155,019
Evangelical Lutheran Synod	146		
Free Lutheran Congregations, The Association of	144	+ 224	368
Lutheran Church–Missouri Synod, The	134,280	+ 5,826	140,106
Wisconsin Evangelical Lutheran Synod	4,463	+ 1,562	6,025
Mennonite/Amish	2,608	+ 2,011	4,619
Amish, Old Order	400	- 376	24
Amish, other			68
Beachy Amish Mennonite Churches	70	+ 57	127
Church of God in Christ (Mennonite)	522	+ 327	849
Conservative Mennonite Conference			191
Evangelical Bible Churches, Fellowship of (was Ev. Menn. Bre.)	20		
Eastern Pennsylvania Mennonite Church	39	+ 26	65
Mennonite Brethren Churches, U.S. Conference of	329	+ 96	425
Mennonite, other			1,655
Mennonite Church USA	1,228	- 13	1,215
Methodist	1,202,991	+ 16,542	1,219,533
African Methodist Episcopal Zion	2,191	—	(2,191)*
(African Methodist Episcopal estimate)*(300 congregations)	(150,000)*	—	(150,000)*
(Christian Methodist Episcopal estimate)*	(45,000)*	—	(45,000)*
Evangelical Methodist Church	1,482		
United Methodist Church, The	1,004,318	+ 18,024	1,022,342
(Mormons) Church of Jesus Christ of Latter-day Saints	111,276	+ 44,175	155,451
Muslim, estimate			114,999
Orthodox	2,082	+ 20,673	22,755
Antiochian Orthodox of North America			4,642
Armenian Apostolic Church/Cilicia			80
Armenian Apostolic Church/Etchmiadzin			1,275
Assyrian Apostolic Church	282		
Coptic Orthodox Church (8 congregations)			NR
Greek Orthodox Archdiocese of America			9,444
Greek Orthodox Archdiocese of Vasiloupulis			135
Malankara Archdiocese/Syrian Orthodox Church in North Amer.			825
Malankara Orthodox Syrian Church, American Diocese of the			2,675
Orthodox Church in America (Romanian Diocese)			413
Orthodox Church in America (Territorial Dioceses)			2,096
Russian Orthodox Church Outside of Russia (4 congregations)			NR

Religious Groups in Texas	1990	Change	2000
Serbian Orthodox Church in the USA			1,110
Serbian Orthodox Ch./New Gracanica Metropolitanate (1 cong)			NR
Syrian Orthodox Church of Antioch	1,800	- 1,740	60
Pentecostal/Charismatic	**682,769**	**+ 80,301**	**763,070**
Assemblies of God	202,082	+ 26,016	228,098
Pentecostal Church of God	12,296	- 704	11,592
Pentecostal Holiness Church, International	5,517	+ 4,748	10,265
Church of God (Cleveland, Tenn.)	27,828	+ 10,431	38,259
Church of God of Prophecy	2,918	- 12	2,906
(Church of God in Christ estimate)*(268 congregations)	(300,000)*	—	(300,000)*
International Church of the Foursquare Gospel	4,278	+ 8,223	12,501
Independent Charismatic Churches	127,850	+ 31,599	159,449
Presbyterian	**217,277**	**- 12,473**	**204,804**
Associate Reformed Presbyterian Church			28
Cumberland Presbyterian Church	10,373	- 1,951	8,422
Evangelical Presbyterian Church	490	+ 959	1,449
Orthodox Presbyterian Church, The			644
Presbyterian Church (USA)	200,969	- 20,654	180,315
Presbyterian Church in America	5,445	+ 8,501	13,946
(Quakers) Friends	**2,548**	**- 1,474**	**1,074**
Seventh-day Adventists	**41,470**	**+ 4,798**	**46,268**
Sikh (13 congregations)			**NR**
Tao (1 congregation)			**NR**
United Church of Christ	**20,950**	**- 4,363**	**16,587**
Zoroastrian (3 congregations)			**NR**
OTHERS (less than 12,000 reported)			
Advent Christian Church	221		
Apostolic Christian Churches of America	13	+ 14	27
Brethren In Christ Church	73		
Calvary Chapel Fellowship Church (19 congregations)			NR
Christ Catholic Church	3		
Christian (Plymouth) Brethren	6,766		
Christian Reformed Church	866	+ 1,070	1,936
Church of Christ, Scientist (93 congregations)			NR
Church of God General Conference, Abrahamic Faith	93	- 38	55
Church of God (Seventh Day) Denver, Col., The	1,743		
Church of the Brethren	302	- 18	284
Community of Christ			2,817
Congregational Christian Churches, National Association of	721		
Congregational Christian Churches (Not part of CCC body)	23		
Conservative Congregational Christian Conference	104	- 79	25
Evangelical Covenant Church, The			1,022
Evangelical Free Church of America, The	5,463	+ 4,257	9,720
Independent Fundamental Churches of America (4 cong.)			NR
International Churches of Christ			4,041
International Council of Community Churches			1,152
Metropolitan Community Churches, Universal Fellowship of			5,570
Missionary Church USA			403
Open Bible Standard Churches, Inc. (2 congregations)			NR
Reformed Church in America	1,592	+ 448	2,040
Unitarian Universalist Association	5,843	+ 1,029	6,872
Vineyard USA			11,637
Statewide Totals	**11,391,401**	**+ 1,483,617**	**12,875,018**
Unclaimed (not counted as adherent to religion)	5,460,358	+ 2,516,444	7,976,802

*Compiled principally from Glenmary Research Center, also other sources. NR, not reported. *Almanac estimates.*

Health & Science

"Old Red", begun in 1890, is the original building at the University of Texas Medical Branch in Galveston. Robert Plocheck photo.

Honored Scientists

Research Funding in Texas

Vital Statistics

Hospitals

Drug Treatment

Mental Health Care

Texans in the National Academy of Sciences

Source: National Academy of Sciences

The National Academy of Sciences is a private organization of scientists and engineers dedicated to the furtherance of science and its use for the general welfare. A total of 79 scientists affiliated with Texas institutions have been named members or associates.

Established by congressional acts of incorporation, which were signed by Abraham Lincoln in 1863, the academy acts as official adviser to the federal government in matters of science or technology.

Selected to the academy in 2009 were: **Thomas J.R. Hughes**, professor of aerospace engineering and engineering mechanics at the University of Texas at Austin, and **David J. Meltzer**, professor of prehistory and executive director of the archaelogical program of the department of anthropology at Southern Methodist University in Dallas.

Selected to the academy in 2008 were: **Richard W. Aldrich**, professor and chairman of neurobiol-

ogy in the school of biological sciences at UT-Austin; **Wilson S. Geisler**, professor of psychology and biomedical engineering at UT-Austin; **David M. Hillis,** professor and director of the center for computational biology and bioinformatics at UT-Austin. Also, **David J. Mangelsdorf**, chairman of pharmacology at the University of Texas Southwestern Medical Center in Dallas.

Election to the academy is one of the highest honors that can be accorded a scientist. As of May 2009, the number of active members was 2,150.

In addition, 404 scientists with citizenship outside the United States are nonvoting foreign associates. In 1970, D.H.R. Barton from Texas A&M University, and, in 1997, Johann Deisenhofer of the UT Southwestern Medical Center, Dallas, were elected as foreign associates.

In 1948, Karl Folkers of UT-Austin became the first Texan elected to the science academy. ☆

Academy Member	Affiliation*	Year Elected
Perry L. Adkisson	A&M	1979
Richard W. Aldrich	UT-Austin	2008
Abram Amsel	UT-Austin	1992
Neal R. Amundson	U of H	1992
Charles J. Arntzen	A&M	1983
David H. Auston	Rice	1991
Paul F. Barbara	UT-Austin	2006
Allen J. Bard	UT-Austin	1982
Brian J.L. Berry	UT-Dallas	1975
Lewis R. Binford	SMU	2001
Norman E. Borlaug	A&M	1968
Michael S. Brown	UTSWMC	1980
Karl W. Butzer	UT-Austin	1996
Luis A. Caffarelli	UT-Austin	1991
C. Thomas Caskey	Baylor Medical	1993
Joseph W. Chamberlain †	Rice	1965
C.W. Chu	U of H	1989
Melanie H. Cobb	UTSWMC	2006
F. Albert Cotton †	A&M	1967
Robert F. Curl	Rice	1997
Gerard H. de Vaucouleurs †	UT-Austin	1986
Bryce DeWitt †	UT-Austin	1990
Stephen J. Elledge	Baylor Medical	2003
Ronald W. Estabrook	UTSWMC	1979
Mary K. Estes	Baylor Medical	2007
Karl Folkers †	UT-Austin	1948
Marye Anne Fox	UT-Austin	1994
David L. Garbers	UTSWMC	1993
Wilson S. Geisler	UT-Austin	2008
Quentin H. Gibson	Rice	1982
Alfred G. Gilman	UTSWMC	1985
Joseph L. Goldstein	UTSWMC	1980
William E. Gordon	Rice	1968
Verne E. Grant †	UT-Austin	1968
Norman Hackerman †	Welch	1971
Dudley Herschbach	A&M	1967
David M. Hillis	UT-Austin	2008
Helen H. Hobbs	UTSWMC	2007
A. James Hudspeth	UTSWMC	1991
Thomas J.R. Hughes	UT-Austin	2009
James L. Kinsey	Rice	1991
Ernst Knobil †	UTHSC-Houston	1986
Jay K. Kochi †	U of H	1982
Alan M. Lambowitz	UT-Austin	2004

Academy Member	Affiliation*	Year Elected
Alan G. MacDiarmid †	UT-Dallas	2002
David J. Mangelsdorf	UT-Austin	2008
John L. Margrave †	Rice	1974
S.M. McCann	UTSWMC	1983
Steven L. McKnight	UTSWMC	1992
David J. Meltzer	SMU	2009
Ferid Murad	UTHSC-Houston	1997
Jack Myers †	UT-Austin	1975
Eric N. Olson	UTSWMC	2000
Bert W. O'Malley	Baylor Medical	1992
Kenneth L. Pike †	SIL	1985
Lester J. Reed	UT-Austin	1973
David W. Russell	UTSWMC	2006
Marlan O. Scully	A&M	2001
Richard E. Smalley †	Rice	1990
Esmond E. Snell †	UT-Austin	1955
Richard C. Starr †	UT-Austin	1976
Thomas Südhof	UTSWMC	2002
Max D. Summers	A&M	1989
Harry L. Swinney	UT-Austin	1992
John T. Tate	UT-Austin	1969
Karen K. Uhlenbeck	UT-Austin	1986
Jonathan W. Uhr	UTSWMC	1984
Roger H. Unger	UTSWMC	1986
Ellen S. Vitetta	UTSWMC	1994
Salih J. Wakil	Baylor Medical	1990
Xiaodong Wang	UTSWMC	2004
Steven Weinberg	UT-Austin	1972
D. Fred Wendorf	SMU	1987
Jean D. Wilson	UTSWMC	1983
James E. Womack	A&M	1999
Masahi Yanagisawa	UTSWMC	2003
Huda Y. Zoghbi	Baylor Medical	2004
		† Deceased

A&M - Texas A&M University
UT-Austin - The University of Texas at Austin
U of H - University of Houston
UT-Dallas - The University of Texas at Dallas
UTSWMC - The University of Texas Southwestern Medical Center at Dallas
Baylor Medical - Baylor College of Medicine, Houston
Rice - Rice University
Welch - Robert A. Welch Foundation
UTHSC - Houston - The University of Texas Health Science Center at Houston
SIL - Summer Institute of Linguistics
SMU - Southern Methodist University

Science Research Funding at Universities

The following chart shows funding for research and development by source at universities in Texas, in order of total R&D funding. The figures are from the National Science Foundation and are for fiscal year 2007.

(Thousands of dollars, $ 000)	All R&D expenditures	Federal gov.	State/local gov.	Industry	Institutional funds	All other sources
United States	$ 49,430,767	$ 30,440,745	$3,145,376	$2,672,333	$ 9,655,290	$ 3,517,023
Texas (statewide)	3,415,419	1,842,323	430,984	203,112	575,926	363,074
1. Texas A&M University	543,888	228,363	121,498	36,465	146,757	10,805
2. U. Texas M.D. Anderson Cancer Ctr.	496,539	190,508	131,884	34,308	78,752	61,087
3. University of Texas-Austin	446,765	289,331	22,120	35,593	76,412	23,309
4. Baylor College of Medicine	438,280	263,146	2,801	18,383	66,790	87,160
5. U. Texas Southwestern Med. Dallas	341,090	191,687	37,687	19,036	11,678	81,002
6. U. Texas Health Sci. Houston	191,724	131,879	13,256	7,861	19,591	19,137
7. U. Texas Medical Branch Galveston	183,492	118,173	7,425	6,659	30,810	20,425
8. U. Texas Health Sci. San Antonio	160,282	95,610	5,846	8,622	36,102	14,102
9. Texas A&M Health Sci. Ctr.	77,957	35,004	1,378	4,551	23,939	13,085
10. University of Houston	73,542	40,116	7,466	3,125	18,146	4,689
11. Rice University	69,772	54,301	967	2,260	7,288	4,956
12. Texas Tech University	57,878	22,874	16,978	4,034	10,744	3,248
13. University of Texas-Dallas	46,477	17,783	15,319	4,140	2,297	6,938
14. University of Texas-El Paso	39,965	21,018	12,274	4,061	2,612	0
15. University of Texas-Arlington	32,734	19,774	1,916	4,625	6,419	0
16. University of Texas-San Antonio	30,542	20,545	7,858	636	1,503	0
17. U. North Texas Health Sci. Ft.Worth	28,187	19,203	1,452	807	4,704	2,021
18. Texas Tech Health Science Center	21,006	8,765	836	1,710	7,720	1,975
19. University of North Texas	14,207	7,192	41	655	5,064	1,255
20. Texas A&M University-Kingsville	13,794	5,067	1,066	199	6,767	695
21. Southern Methodist University	13,381	10,304	126	300	1,918	733
22. Prairie View A&M University	12,019	9,217	1,815	108	879	0
23. Texas A&M U.-Corpus Christi	11,933	6,609	2,908	86	260	2,070
24. Tarleton State University	9,151	4,852	3,475	172	652	0
25. Baylor University	8,951	2,829	846	1,873	2,444	959
26. Texas State University-San Marcos	7,890	2,528	2,913	241	1,397	811
27. Stephen F. Austin State University	6,957	3,285	1,410	150	1,729	383

Colleges and universities not listed received less. Source: National Science Foundation, 2009.

Science and Engineering Profile of Texas

The following chart shows academic degrees in the state and spending on research and development (R&D).

Characteristic	Texas	U.S. total	Texas rank
Employed SEH* doctorate holders, 2006	36,000	620,143	3
S&E* doctorates awarded, 2006	1,930	29,854	3
Engineering	28 %	24 %	-
Life sciences	26 %	26 %	-
Physical sciences	12 %	13 %	-
SEH postdoctorates in doctorate-granting institutions, 2006	3,189	49,201	4
SEH graduate students in doctorate-granting institutions, 2006	37,004	542,073	3
Federal R&D spending, 2005 (in $ millions)	$ 4,989	$ 106,845	5
Total R&D performance, 2005 (in $ millions)	$ 15,867	$ 310,194	4
Industry R&D, 2005 (in $ millions)	$ 12,438	$ 222,427	5
Academic R&D, 2006 (in $ millions)	$ 3,271	$ 47,735	3
Life Sciences	67 %	60 %	-
Engineering	14 %	15 %	-
Physical sciences	6 %	8 %	-
Utility patents issued to state residents, 2006	6,308	89,820	2

*SEH = science, engineering, and health, S&E = science and engineering. Source: National Science Foundation/Division of Science Resources Statistics, 2009, compiled from various sources.

Death, Birth Rates Continue Trends in Texas Vital Statistics

Source: Texas Department of State Health Services.

Heart disease and cancer remained the major causes of death in 2006, the latest year for which statistical breakdowns were available from the Bureau of Vital Statistics, Texas Department of State Health Services.

Of the 156,525 deaths, heart disease claimed 38,487 lives, and cancer claimed 34,776 lives. These two diseases have been the leading causes of death in Texas and the nation since 1950.

Cerebrovascular diseases (strokes), accidents and chronic lower respiratory diseases ranked third, fourth and fifth, respectively. Together, these five leading causes of death represented 63.5 percent of all deaths.

While the number of babies born to Texas mothers continued to increase in 2005 (385,537), the state's birth rate was at an all-time low of 16.9 per 1,000 population. In 1960, that figure was 25.7. *(See chart comparing other state and world birth rates, page 580.)*

Although there was a general decrease from 1990 to 2005 in the number of abortions, there was an increasing trend since, with 77,811 abortions in 2007.

Health Care and Deaths in Texas Counties

County	2008 Physicians	2006 Hospital Beds	Total Deaths 2006	2005 Pregnancy rate*	2007 Abortions
Statewide Total	**46,476**	**61,904**	**156,525**	**91.6**	**77,811***
Anderson	80	120	594	90.9	83
Andrews	13	44	124	89.5	17
Angelina	150	343	783	90.4	151
Aransas	16	0	306	89.5	54
Archer	1	0	73	62.1	8
Armstrong	0	0	25	58.7	3
Atascosa	34	67	307	86.2	111
Austin	8	25	262	76.4	142
Bailey	5	25	64	121.3	10
Bandera	6	0	180	58.7	19
Bastrop	38	48	501	71.7	108
Baylor	5	38	52	89.9	11
Bee	20	63	209	82.0	52
Bell	909	829	1,691	106.9	832
Bexar	4,475	4,550	10,626	96.6	7,372
Blanco	44	0	89	94.4	25
Borden	0	0	5	63.5	1
Bosque	14	40	242	87.3	29
Bowie	245	612	876	69.9	49
Brazoria	250	221	1,832	87.9	557
Brazos	413	415	778	66.3	495
Brewster	12	27	66	69.6	18
Briscoe	0	0	17	121.7	8
Brooks	2	0	85	113.2	18
Brown	71	168	457	73.6	29
Burleson	4	25	162	76.3	26
Burnet	55	25	388	75.5	68
Caldwell	15	59	293	78.1	65
Calhoun	19	25	199	79.2	33
Callahan	3	0	156	65.6	5
Cameron	518	1,084	2,032	114.5	895
Camp	13	25	135	91.1	17
Carson	0	0	70	63.8	1
Cass	14	81	361	62.8	10
Castro	5	25	54	95.4	6
Chambers	5	39	181	69.7	98
Cherokee	75	78	455	93.0	46
Childress	9	35	79	85.1	3
Clay	4	25	101	52.9	11
Cochran	1	18	28	81.2	0
Coke	2	0	63	80.1	8

County	2008 Physicians	2006 Hospital Beds	Total Deaths 2006	2005 Pregnancy rate*	2007 Abortions
Coleman	3	25	158	67.7	5
Collin	1,348	1,355	2,475	80.9	1,914
Collingswrth	2	16	39	99.8	3
Colorado	26	85	229	79.9	36
Comal	150	132	759	77.0	185
Comanche	16	38	193	76.8	20
Concho	2	16	26	67.6	3
Cooke	31	78	382	85.7	62
Coryell	27	138	364	53.3	127
Cottle	0	0	35	122.7	11
Crane	2	25	39	76.3	8
Crockett	1	0	30	102.0	14
Crosby	2	25	78	92.3	13
Culberson	1	14	17	74.9	2
Dallam	5	0	64	99.5	5
Dallas	6,936	6,611	13,873	101.7	11,152
Dawson	7	29	132	102.5	16
Deaf Smith	12	35	149	107.8	20
Delta	2	0	69	70.1	10
Denton	666	939	2,187	73.1	1,654
DeWitt	18	58	264	81.5	15
Dickens	0	0	33	90.9	3
Dimmit	7	35	83	94.0	20
Donley	1	0	51	59.5	10
Duval	1	0	118	97.6	39
Eastland	13	40	237	83.3	18
Ector	241	539	1,120	94.6	323
Edwards	1	0	18	83.6	1
Ellis	96	114	890	78.4	294
El Paso	1,035	1,793	4,356	101.1	2,251
Erath	39	99	323	73.7	76
Falls	4	32	247	59.5	37
Fannin	27	25	467	80.1	36
Fayette	24	48	308	70.0	23
Fisher	3	9	62	57.3	1
Floyd	7	25	74	80.9	0
Foard	0	0	22	54.7	1
Fort Bend	529	486	1,941	79.2	1,250
Franklin	9	30	116	79.9	15
Freestone	11	20	194	86.0	28
Frio	9	40	128	107.3	36
Gaines	5	25	107	99.3	11
Galveston	783	914	2,348	81.2	741

County	2008 Physicians	2006 Hospital Beds	Total Deaths 2006	2005 Pregnancy rate*	2007 Abortions	County	2008 Physicians	2006 Hospital Beds	Total Deaths 2006	2005 Pregnancy rate*	2007 Abortions
Garza	1	0	43	69.7	2	Leon	3	0	191	88.3	18
Gillespie	67	78	270	78.0	31	Liberty	57	123	664	67.5	136
Glasscock	0	0	4	45.3	0	Limestone	21	67	273	88.9	51
Goliad	2	0	78	57.8	9	Lipscomb	0	0	30	84.8	3
Gonzales	11	34	187	106.0	23	Live Oak	2	0	97	70.1	16
Gray	28	91	290	91.7	22	Llano	21	30	29	78.9	16
Grayson	232	504	1,281	76.4	184	Loving	0	0	0	–	0
Gregg	305	558	1,163	84.2	134	Lubbock	831	1,553	2,031	79.3	604
Grimes	14	25	187	89.0	55	Lynn	2	19	55	72.2	8
Guadalupe	76	101	733	73.6	193	Madison	6	25	136	78.5	6
Hale	32	32	301	95.2	39	Marion	5	0	164	50.1	7
Hall	1	0	52	81.4	5	Martin	2	20	51	84.3	6
Hamilton	9	34	132	83.0	13	Mason	0	0	44	66.3	2
Hansford	2	25	45	113.4	3	Matagorda	39	77	326	80.7	46
Hardeman	6	45	40	76.6	7	Maverick	30	101	300	99.2	49
Hardin	16	0	485	72.3	114	McCulloch	6	25	100	81.7	9
Harris	10,272	12,213	20,573	100.4	17,956	McLennan	449	444	2,023	79.8	657
Harrison	45	122	569	65.2	30	McMullen	0	0	9	83.3	1
Hartley	0	21	57	97.1	2	Medina	16	25	331	79.4	78
Haskell	2	25	76	64.6	14	Menard	2	0	39	74.2	2
Hays	153	113	656	64.1	418	Midland	186	301	912	89.4	283
Hemphill	4	19	39	118.3	4	Milam	11	59	335	77.9	33
Henderson	61	117	894	79.0	98	Mills	4	0	75	61.2	1
Hidalgo	791	1,972	3,303	120.8	1,662	Mitchell	3	25	88	74.5	5
Hill	19	112	441	87.7	60	Montague	14	77	233	80.7	22
Hockley	17	22	202	88.1	18	Montgomery	605	885	2,566	80.3	680
Hood	60	59	540	71.4	68	Moore	17	102	144	100.9	17
Hopkins	36	54	310	79.3	56	Morris	2	0	180	81.9	16
Houston	11	48	274	71.4	177	Motley	1	0	23	81.1	3
Howard	45	122	369	95.9	50	Nacgdoches	131	245	561	72.6	134
Hudspeth	0	0	17	71.9	2	Navarro	47	148	524	82.2	83
Hunt	74	178	791	75.2	157	Newton	5	0	166	51.5	27
Hutchinson	17	25	256	73.2	27	Nolan	15	54	179	94.6	24
Irion	0	0	13	29.6	5	Nueces	816	1,495	2,477	90.0	1,253
Jack	4	17	97	69.4	4	Ochiltree	5	42	74	101.9	3
Jackson	5	25	159	83.4	24	Oldham	0	0	14	49.1	2
Jasper	35	77	369	75.1	50	Orange	45	103	831	70.6	136
Jeff Davis	1	0	15	48.4	3	Palo Pinto	27	42	314	89.4	43
Jefferson	554	1,486	2,501	79.3	646	Panola	16	37	278	69.8	9
Jim Hogg	1	0	43	111.2	11	Parker	77	77	799	65.1	201
Jim Wells	36	144	340	96.0	112	Parmer	3	15	79	85.1	8
Johnson	125	48	1,072	74.2	289	Pecos	11	36	111	79.9	19
Jones	8	79	182	77.0	19	Polk	47	48	627	77.4	50
Karnes	4	21	154	97.7	17	Potter	473	982	1,174	101.8	209
Kaufman	78	198	763	82.3	176	Presidio	0	0	44	107.2	6
Kendall	50	0	303	69.7	43	Rains	2	0	113	71.1	15
Kenedy	0	0	2	55.6	2	Randall	96	4	825	66.0	152
Kent	0	0	18	25.0	0	Reagan	1	14	26	84.5	5
Kerr	138	118	661	91.4	77	Real	0	0	44	57.5	3
Kimble	4	15	73	73.5	3	Red River	5	36	201	58.4	16
King	0	0	1	40.5	2	Reeves	7	30	104	79.7	23
Kinney	1	0	32	76.9	4	Refugio	3	20	88	74.8	14
Kleberg	23	100	202	87.7	98	Roberts	0	0	9	91.5	0
Knox	3	14	51	61.3	3	Robertson	4	0	191	93.1	21
Lamar	106	316	563	70.6	60	Rockwall	71	99	381	85.5	143
Lamb	4	41	168	92.2	15	Runnels	4	37	137	85.6	12
Lampasas	11	25	182	69.6	16	Rusk	26	82	507	80.8	33
La Salle	2	0	51	108.8	17	Sabine	3	25	165	63.7	8
Lavaca	18	50	294	80.2	22	S. Augustine	4	18	119	75.8	7
Lee	5	0	162	73.6	27	San Jacinto	3	0	263	70.0	25

County	2008 Physicians	2006 Hospital Beds	Total Deaths 2006	2005 Pregnancy rate*	2007 Abortions
San Patricio	24	58	493	88.2	171
San Saba	1	0	76	72.1	4
Schleicher	2	14	36	78.7	4
Scurry	13	49	145	88.6	23
Shackelford	2	0	32	62.3	6
Shelby	9	46	284	76.5	4
Sherman	0	0	26	98.5	12
Smith	714	1,112	1,675	83.4	377
Somervell	12	16	75	66.0	11
Starr	24	48	276	114.1	101
Stephens	7	33	97	97.3	19
Sterling	0	0	12	50.0	1
Stonewall	4	12	25	56.3	3
Sutton	2	12	30	82.4	10
Swisher	4	20	83	97.8	7
Tarrant	3,205	4,050	10,028	91.8	6,257
Taylor	290	571	1,169	77.9	202
Terrell	1	0	11	145.6	12
Terry	6	26	104	93.0	10
Throckmortn	1	14	19	42.6	3
Titus	51	144	240	101.9	84
Tom Green	233	471	933	78.3	216
Travis	2,688	2,174	4,339	88.0	3,675
Trinity	4	22	220	70.1	17
Tyler	6	25	230	82.0	68
Upshur	10	37	381	75.1	22
Upton	1	20	35	78.6	4
Uvalde	28	50	206	97.1	55
Val Verde	37	86	315	97.1	70
Van Zandt	15	24	575	104.4	61

County	2008 Physicians	2006 Hospital Beds	Total Deaths 2006	2005 Pregnancy rate*	2007 Abortions
Victoria	216	569	742	70.3	169
Walker	77	88	423	81.8	151
Waller	6	0	262	63.5	78
Ward	3	25	115	78.6	17
Washington	39	60	337	83.2	68
Webb	211	551	1,031	118.9	356
Wharton	59	126	302	86.9	56
Wheeler	7	29	83	101.3	4
Wichita	283	512	1,282	79.2	236
Wilbarger	21	47	177	88.5	25
Willacy	8	0	117	98.4	51
Williamson	451	227	1,550	82.5	834
Wilson	15	44	302	69.3	100
Winkler	4	15	83	78.0	16
Wise	53	133	433	68.0	87
Wood	29	68	511	76.8	41
Yoakum	6	22	43	92.6	5
Young	20	60	280	78.4	22
Zapata	5	0	64	112.7	25
Zavala	4	0	94	111.8	21

Sources: Texas Department of Health: Vital Statistics, 2006-2007(by county of residence) and **Center for Health Statistics**, January 2009. **Texas Medical Board**, September 2008.
Physicians - All practicing licensed M.D.s and D.O.s.
Hospital Beds - Staffed beds not including military and veteran's hospitals. (Previous lists reported licensed beds.)
*Pregnancy Rate figured per 1,000 women age 15-44.
*Abortion total statewide includes abortions performed in Texas but county of residence unknown, plus abortions obtained outside the state by Texas residents.

Marriage and Divorce

These charts are for certain years, including 1946 when there was a significant increase in marriages after World War II as well as a significant increase in divorces. Also included are the years 1979-81 when the marriage and divorce rates reached another peak. *Source: Statistical Abstracts of the United States, various, and U.S. Census.*

Texas

Year	Total marriages	Marriage rate*	Total divorces	Divorce rate*
1940	86,500	13.5	27,500	4.3
1946	143,092	**20.5**	57,112	**8.4**
1950	89,155	11.6	37,400	4.9
1955	91,210	10.4	34,921	4.0
1960	91,700	9.6	34,732	3.6
1965	111,500	10.5	41,300	3.9
1970	139,500	12.5	51,500	4.6
1975	153,200	12.5	76,700	6.3
1979	172,800	**12.9**	92,400	**6.9**
1980	181,800	**12.8**	96,800	**6.8**
1981	194,800	**13.2**	101,900	**6.9**
1985	213,800	13.1	101,200	6.2
1990	182,800	10.5	94,000	5.5
1995	188,500	10.1	98,400	5.3
2000	196,400	9.6	85,200	4.2
2005	169,300	7.4	74,000	3.2
2006	175,000	7.5	78,100	3.3

*Rate per 1,000 population.

United States

Year	Total marriages	Marriage rate*	Total divorces	Divorce rate*
1940	1,595,879	12.1	264,000	2.0
1946	2,291,045	**16.4**	610,000	**4.3**
1950	1,667,231	11.1	385,144	2.6
1955	1,531,000	9.3	377,000	2.3
1960	1,523,381	8.5	393,000	2.2
1965	1,800,200	9.3	479,000	2.5
1970	2,159,000	10.6	708,000	3.5
1975	2,152,700	10.1	1,036,000	4.9
1979	2,331,300	**10.6**	1,181,000	**5.4**
1980	2,390,300	**10.6**	1,189,000	**5.2**
1981	2,422,100	**10.6**	1,213,000	**5.3**
1985	2,425,000	10.2	1,187,000	5.0
1990	2,443,000	9.8	1,182,000	4.7
1995	2,336,000	8.9	1,169,000	4.4
2000	2,329,000	8.2	**NA	4.1
2005	2,230,000	7.5	NA	3.6
2006	2,160,000	7.5	NA	3.6

**Not Available. Since 1995, the federal government no longer publishes information on the total number of divorces.

National Health Expenditures

Type of Expenditure	1990	1995	2000	2006
Total ($ billions)	$ 714.0	$ 1,016.5	$1,353.3	$ 2,105.5
Percent of gross domestic product	12.3	13.7	13.8	16.0
Private expenditures	$ 427.3	$ 551.7	$ 757.1	$ 1,135.2
Insurance premiums*	$ 233.7	$ 325.2	$ 455.2	$ 723.4
Out-of-pocket payments	$ 136.1	$ 146.3	$ 192.9	$ 256.5
Public expenditures	$ 286.7	$ 464.8	$ 596.1	$ 970.3
Percent federal of public	67.6	70.4	70.0	72.6

*Covers insurance benefits and amount retained by insurance companies for expenses, additions to reserves and profits.

Source: Statistical Abstract of the United States 2008/2009, from U.S. Centers for Medicare and Medicaid Services.

Comparison of Vital Statistics

The most current data available, with selected states; those bordering Texas and other large states. **Lowest and highest with number in bold.**

State/Country	BIRTH rate*	DEATH rate*	LIFE expectancy
Texas	17.0	6.7	77.5
Alaska	16.4	**5.0**	-
Arkansas	14.6	9.9	-
California	15.4	6.5	-
Florida	13.1	9.4	-
Georgia	15.9	7.2	-
Illinois	14.1	8.0	-
Louisiana	14.8	9.3	-
Michigan	12.6	8.5	-
New Mexico	15.3	7.8	-
New York	13.0	7.7	-
Ohio	13.1	9.3	-
Oklahoma	15.1	9.9	-
Utah	**21.0**	5.4	-
Vermont	**10.4**	8.1	-
West Virginia	11.5	**11.4**	-
United States	14.2	8.1	78.1
Afghanistan	45.5	19.2	43.3
Brazil	18.4	6.4	72.0
Canada	10.3	7.8	81.2
Germany	8.2	10.9	79.3
Italy	8.2	10.7	80.2
Japan	**7.6**	9.5	**82.1**
Mexico	19.7	4.8	76.1
Niger	**51.6**	14.8	52.6
Russia	11.1	16.1	66.0
Swaziland	26.3	**30.8**	**31.9**
United Arab Em.	16.0	**2.11**	76.1
United Kingdom	10.7	10.0	79.0
World	20.0	8.2	66.6

*Rates are number during 1 year per 1,000 persons. Sources: U.S. Statistical Abstract 2009; CIA World Factbook, 2009; Texas Vital Statistics Annual Report 2006. Statistics are from 2005-2009.

Life Expectancy for Texans by Group

	All	Whites	Blacks	Hispanics
Total population	77.5	77.9	72.7	78.5
Males	74.9	75.4	69.8	75.8
Females	80.1	80.3	75.4	81.1

Source: Texas Department of State Health Services, 2005.

Texas Births by Race/Ethnicity and Sex

	2005	2000	1990	1980
All Races	385,537	363,325	316,257	273,433
All Male	197,491	185,591	161,522	139,999
All Female	188,046	177,734	154,735	133,434
White Total	137,156	142,553	150,461	151,725
White Male	70,786	72,972	77,134	78,086
White Female	66,370	69,581	73,327	73,639
Black Total	42,335	41,180	43,342	38,544
Black Male	21,323	21,128	21,951	19,501
Black Female	21,012	20,052	21,391	19,043
Hispanic Total	191,488	166,440	115,576	79,324
Hispanic Male	97,890	84,750	58,846	40,475
Hispanic Female	93,598	81,690	56,730	38,849
Other* Total	14,558	13,152	6,687	3,840
Other Male	7,492	6,741	3,591	1,937
Other Female	7,066	6,411	3,287	1,903

*Other includes births of unknown race/ethnicity.
Source: Texas Department of State Health Services, 2005.

Disposition of Bodies in Texas by Percent of Deaths

Year	Burial	Cremation	Donation of body	Removal from state/other
1989	83.7	7.1	0.7	8.5
1991	83.6	8.5	1.0	7.1
1993	82.8	10.1	0.9	6.2
1995	81.7	11.6	0.8	5.8
1997	79.9	12.9	1.0	6.2
1999	78.0	14.9	0.9	6.2
2001	75.5	17.3	0.8	6.3
2003	73.1	19.7	0.9	6.2

Source: Texas Department of State Health Services, 2005.

M.D. Anderson Cancer Center and St. Luke's Hospital in Houston's Texas Medical Center. Robert Plocheck photo.

Community Hospitals in Texas

Source: The Texas Hospital Association

– Of the 583 reporting hospitals in Texas in 2007, 409 were considered community hospitals.

(A community hospital is defined as either a non-federal, short-term general hospital or a special hospital whose facilities and services are available to the public. A hospital may include a nursing home-type unit and still be classified as short-term, provided that the majority of its patients are admitted to units where the average length-of-stay is less than 30 days.)

– These 409 hospitals employed 293,000 full-time equivalent people (FTEs) with a payroll, including benefits, of more than $17.9 billion.

– These hospitals contained some 58,000 beds.

– The average length-of-stay was 5.2 days in 2007, compared to 6.8 days in 1975. This was less than the U.S. average of 5.5 days.

– The average cost per adjusted admission in Texas was $9,140 or $1,806 per day. This was 2.2 percent less than the U.S. average of $9,341.

– There were 2,468,000 admissions in Texas, which accounted for 12,817,000 inpatient days.

– There were 32,499,999 outpatient visits in 2007, of which 8,444,000 were emergency room visits.

– Of the FTEs working in community hospitals within Texas, there were 81,150 registered nurses and 11,320 licensed vocational nurses. ☆

U.S. Hospital Care: Source of Payments

Source of payment	1990	1995	2000	2006
Hospital care, total ($ billions)	$ 251.6	$ 340.7	$ 417.0	$ 648.2
Out-of-pocket payments	$ 11.3	$ 10.4	$ 13.6	$ 21.4
Private health insurance	$ 97.8	$ 110.6	$ 143.6	$ 234.8
Federal Government	$ 101.7	$ 166.0	$ 192.9	$ 290.2
State/Local Government	$ 30.3	$ 39.2	$ 45.2	$ 72.4
Physician and clinical services, total ($ billions)	$ 157.5	$ 220.5	$ 288.6	$ 447.6
Out-of-pocket payments	$ 30.2	$ 26.0	$ 32.2	$ 46.2
Private health insurance	$ 67.3	$ 106.1	$ 136.8	$ 219.7
Federal Government	$ 38.0	$ 56.2	$ 79.0	$ 126.4
State/Local Government	$ 10.7	$ 14.7	$ 18.4	$ 26.6

Source: Statistical Abstract of the United States 2009, from U.S. Centers for Medicare and Medicaid Services.

Substance Abuse and Mental Health Admissions

Drug Treatment in State-Funded Programs: 2007

Primary Drug	Total Admissions	White	Black	Hispanic	Percent Employed over last 12 months	Average education (years)	Percent homeless
		(percent)					
All Drugs	88,452	46.8	19.3	32.5	33.4	11.4	10.6
Heroin	8,622	35.7	8.6	54.5	16.7	11.2	13.5
Other opiates	4,529	80.6	8.3	9.8	18.8	12.2	8.1
Alcohol	22,073	54.6	12.5	31.4	31.8	11.8	13.5
Barbiturates	99	58.6	10.1	27.3	33.3	11.3	5.1
Other sedatives	1,328	68.9	11.0	18.0	25.2	11.4	6.2
Amphet/Methamph	9,560	84.4	1.6	12.1	29.4	11.7	5.1
Cocaine (powder)	9,799	32.7	18.0	47.8	33.5	11.2	6.0
Crack	11,128	35.1	46.2	17.7	14.3	11.7	21.1
Ecstasy	217	37.8	42.9	15.2	40.1	11.2	6.0
Marijuana	20,048	30.0	27.0	41.6	54.2	10.5	4.9

Source: Texas Department of State Health Services, 2009.

Estimated Use of Drugs in Texas and Bordering States: 2005-2006

State	Any illicit drug	Marijuana	Other than marijuana[1]	Cigarettes	Binge alcohol[2]
	*Current users[3] as **percent of population**. Selected states.*				
U.S. total	8.2	6.0	3.8	25.0	22.8
Texas	6.8	4.4	3.9	25.5	24.1
Arkansas	8.4	5.7	4.5	29.1	20.7
Louisana	8.4	5.6	4.6	27.1	23.5
Oklahoma	8.4	5.3	4.0	31.3	21.1
New Mexico	8.3	6.1	3.8	24.2	20.3

[1]Marijuana users who have also used another drug are included. [2]Binge use is defined as drinking five or more drinks on the same occasion on a least one day in the past 30 days. [3]Used drugs at least once within month. *Source: U.S. Substance Abuse and Mental Health Services Administration,* National Household Survey on Drug Use and Health, 2005-06.

Primary Diagnosis of Clients in Texas and Bordering States: 2007

State	Schizophrenia	Other Psychoses	Bipolar and Mood Disorders	No Diagnosis	All Other
	In Percent of clients.				
U.S. total	15.1	3.8	41.5	10.5	29.0
Texas	21.2	0.5	56.8	18.5	3.0
Arkansas	NA	NA	NA	NA	NA
Louisana	26.6	4.7	60.9	1.2*	6.6
Oklahoma	16.3	2.4	61.9	1.5*	17.9
New Mexico	5.8	0.7	29.0	5.2	59.2

˙Data from Outcome Domain. NA, not available. *Source: U.S. Department of Health and Human Services, Center for Mental Health Services,* Uniform Reporting System, 2007.

Readmission within 180 Days of Treatment: 2007

Age	Civil* Texas	Civil U.S.	States reporting	Forensic* Texas	Forensic U.S.
	In Percent of clients.				
0 to 12	13.6 %	15.8 %	20	-	18.8 %
13 to 17	14.1 %	15.1 %	30	15.5 %	11.2 %
18 to 20	19.5 %	19.3 %	42	13.9 %	11.7 %
21 to 64	22.4 %	20.6 %	47	19.1 %	13.3 %
65 to 74	14.0 %	17.1 %	36	8.0 %	14.5 %
75 and over	8.5 %	11.3 %	24	50.0 %	11.1 %
age not available	-	21.1 %	1	-	-
Total	21.2%	19.9 %	48	18.7%	13.2%

˙Forensic services are mental health services provided to persons directed into treatment by the criminal justice system, others are listed as "Civil". *Source: U.S. Department of Health and Human Services, Center for Mental Health Services,* Uniform Reporting System, 2007.

State Institutions for Mental Health Services

Source: Texas Department of State Health Services.

Mental health services are provided to some 100,000 Texans each year in various institutions. In 2009, the Texas Department of State Health Services (TDSHS) budget included $374.5 million for mental hospitals and $653.5 million for community mental health centers and substance-abuse treatment.

On Sept. 1, 2004, the TDSHS was created, bringing together:

— the Texas Department of Health,
— the Texas Department of Mental Health and Mental Retardation (MHMR),
— Commission on Alcohol and Drug Abuse,
— the Texas Health Care Information Council.

With the consolidation of the four agencies, TDSHS, with more than 11,500 employees, now includes treatment and prevention for mental illness and substance abuse in its public health framework. The Web address is: www.dshs.state.tx.us

Following is a list of state hospitals, the year each was founded and numbers of admissions of patients in fiscal year 2008.

Hospitals for Persons with Mental Illness
Austin State Hospital — Austin; 1857; 3,665 patients.
Big Spring State Hospital — Big Spring; 1937; 1,042 patients.
El Paso Psychiatric Center — El Paso; 1974; 1,025 patients.
Kerrville State Hospital — Kerrville; 1950; 306 patients.
North Texas State Hospital — Wichita Falls (1922) and Vernon (1969); 2,504 patients.
Rio Grande State Center — Harlingen; 1962; 1,183 patients.
Rusk State Hospital — Rusk; 1919; 1,805 patients.
San Antonio State Hospital — San Antonio; 1892; 2,655 patients.
Terrell State Hospital — Terrell; 1885; 2,727 patients.
Waco Center for Youth — Waco; 1979; 176 patients.

Following is a list of community mental health centers, the year each was founded, and the counties each serves.

Community Mental Health Centers

Abilene — Betty Hardwick Center; 1971; Callahan, Jones, Shackleford, Stephens and Taylor.
Amarillo — Texas Panhandle MHMR; 1968; Armstrong, Carson, Collingsworth, Dallam, Deaf Smith, Donley, Gray, Hall, Hansford, Hartley, Hemphill, Hutchinson, Lipscomb, Moore, Ochiltree, Oldham, Potter, Randall, Roberts, Sherman and Wheeler.
Austin — Austin-Travis County Center; 1967; Travis.
Beaumont — Spindletop MHMR Services; 1967; Chambers, Hardin, Jefferson and Orange.
Big Spring — West Texas Centers; 1997; Andrews, Borden, Crane, Dawson, Fisher, Gaines, Garza, Glasscock, Howard, Kent, Loving, Martin, Mitchell, Nolan, Reeves, Runnels, Scurry, Terrell, Terry, Upton, Ward, Winkler and Yoakum.
Brownwood — Center for Life Resources; 1969; Brown, Coleman, Comanche, Eastland, McCulloch, Mills and San Saba.
Bryan-College Station — MHMR Authority of Brazos Valley; 1972; Brazos, Burleson, Grimes, Leon, Madison, Robertson and Washington.
Cleburne — Johnson-Ellis-Navarro County Center; 1985; Ellis, Johnson, Navarro.

Conroe — Tri-County Services; 1983; Liberty, Montgomery and Walker.
Corpus Christi — Nueces County Community Center; 1970; Nueces.
Dallas — Dallas MetroCare; 1967; Dallas.
Denton — Denton County Center; 1987; Denton.
Edinburg — Tropical Texas Center; 1967; Cameron, Hidalgo and Willacy.
El Paso — Community Center; 1968; El Paso.
Fort Worth — MHMR of Tarrant County; 1969; Tarrant.
Galveston — Gulf Coast Center; 1969; Brazoria and Galveston.
Houston — MHMR Authority/Harris County; 1965; Harris.
Jacksonville — Anderson-Cherokee Community Enrichment Services; 1995; Anderson, Cherokee.
Kerrville — Hill Country Community Center; 1997; Bandera, Blanco, Comal, Edwards, Gillespie, Hays, Kendall, Kerr, Kimble, Kinney, Llano, Mason, Medina, Menard, Real, Schleicher, Sutton, Uvalde and Val Verde.
Laredo — Border Region Community Center; 1969; Jim Hogg, Starr, Webb and Zapata.
Longview — Sabine Valley Center; 1970; Gregg, Harrison, Marion, Panola, Rusk and Upshur.
Lubbock — Lubbock Regional Center; 1969; Cochran, Crosby, Hockley, Lubbock and Lynn.
Lufkin — Burke Center; 1975; Angelina, Houston, Jasper, Nacogdoches, Newton, Polk, Sabine, San Augustine, San Jacinto, Shelby, Trinity and Tyler.
Lytle — Camino Real Community Center; 1996; Atascosa, Dimmit, Frio, La Salle, Karnes, Maverick, McMullen, Wilson and Zavala.
McKinney — LifePath Systems; 1986; Collin.
Midland — Permian Basin Community Centers; 1969; Brewster, Culberson, Ector, Hudspeth, Jeff Davis, Midland, Pecos and Presidio.
Plainview — Central Plains Center; 1969; Bailey, Briscoe, Castro, Floyd, Hale, Lamb, Motley, Parmer and Swisher.
Portland — Coastal Plains Community; 1996; Aransas, Bee, Brooks, Duval, Jim Wells, Kenedy, Kleberg, Live Oak and San Patricio.
Rosenberg — Texana Center; 1996; Austin, Colorado, Fort Bend, Matagorda, Waller and Wharton.
Round Rock — Bluebonnet Trails Community Center; 1997; Bastroop, Burnet, Caldwell, Fayette, Gonzales, Guadalupe, Lee and Williamson.
San Angelo — MHMR Services for the Concho Valley; 1969; Coke, Concho, Crockett, Irion, Reagan, Sterling and Tom Green.
San Antonio — The Center for Health Care Services; 1966; Bexar.
Sherman — MHMR Services of Texoma; 1974; Cooke, Fannin and Grayson.
Stephenville — Pecan Valley Region; 1977; Erath, Hood, palo Pinto, Parker and Somervell.
Temple — Central Counties Center; 1967; Bell, Coryell, Hamilton, Lampasas and Milam.
Terrell — Lakes Regional Center; 1996; Camp, Delta, Franklin, Hopkins, Hunt, Kaufman, Lamar, Morris, Rockwall and Titus.
Texarkana — Northeast Texas Center; 1974; Bowie, Cass and Red River.
Tyler — Andrews Center; 1970; Henderson, Rains, Smith, Van Zandt and Wood.
Victoria — Gulf Bend Center; 1970; Calhoun, DeWitt, Jackson, Lavaca, Refugio and Victoria.
Waco — Heart of Texas Region Center; 1969; Bosque, Falls, Freestone, Hill, Limestone and McLennan.
Wichita Falls — Helen Farabee Regional Centers; 1969; Archer, Bayor, Childress, Clay, Cottle, Dickens, Foard, Hardeman, Haskell, Jack, King, Knox, Montague, Stonewall, Throckmorton, Wichita, Wilbarger and Young. ☆

Education

Students walk past the W.A. Baker Chemistry Building on The University of Texas at Arlington campus. Photo courtesy of UT Arlington/University Publications.

Texas Public Schools

UIL Winning Schools for 2007–2008 & 2008–2009

Higher Education in Texas

Universities and Colleges

Texas Public Schools

Source: Texas Education Agency; www.tea.state.tx.us

Enrollment in the Texas public schools **reached a peak of 4,594,942 in 2006–2007**, according to the Texas Education Agency. That is an increase of almost 600,000 students over the last six years; enrollment was 4,059,619 in 2000–2001.

The **seven largest districts** (listed in descending order by average daily attendance) are: Houston, Dallas, Cypress-Fairbanks (Harris Co.), Northside (Bexar County), Austin, Fort Worth and Fort Bend (Fort Bend Co.)

In Texas, there are **1,031 independent and common school districts** and **198 charter districts**. Independent school districts are administered by an elected board of trustees and deal directly with the Texas Education Agency. Common districts are supervised by elected county school superintendents and county trustees. Charter schools are discussed later in this article.

Brief History of Public Education

Public education was one of the primary goals of the early settlers of Texas, who listed the failure to provide education as one of their grievances in the Texas Declaration of Independence from Mexico.

As early as 1838, President Mirabeau B. Lamar's message to the Republic of Texas Congress advocated setting aside public domain for public schools. His interest caused him to be called the "Father of Education in Texas." In 1839 Congress designated three leagues of land to support public schools for each Texas county and 50 leagues for a state university. In 1840 each county was allocated one more league of land.

The Republic, however, did not establish a public school system or a university. After being admitted into the Union, the 1845 Texas State Constitution advocated public education, instructing the Legislature to designate at least 10 percent of the tax revenue for schools. Further delay occurred until Gov. Elisha M. Pease, on Jan. 31, 1854, signed the bill setting up the Texas public school system.

The public school system was made possible by setting aside $2 million out of $10 million Texas received for relinquishing its claim to land north and west of its present boundaries in the Compromise of 1850 (see map on page 44).

During 1854, legislation provided for state apportionment of funds based upon an annual census. Also, railroads receiving grants were required to survey alternate sections to be set aside for public-school financing. The first school census that year showed 65,463 students; state fund apportionment was 62 cents per student.

When adopted in 1876, the present Texas Constitution provided: "All funds, lands and other property heretofore set apart and appropriated for the support of public schools; all the alternate sections of land reserved by the state of grants heretofore made or that may hereafter be made to railroads, or other corporations, of any nature whatsoever; one half of the public domain of the state, and all sums of money that may come to the state from the sale of any portion of the same shall constitute a perpetual public school fund."

More than 52 million acres of the Texas public domain were allotted for school purposes. (See table, Distribution of the Public Lands of Texas on page 480.)

The Constitution also provided for one-fourth of occupation taxes and a poll tax of one dollar for school support and made provisions for local taxation.

No provision was made for direct ad valorem taxation for maintenance of an available school fund, but a maximum 20-cent state ad valorem school tax was ad-

Enrollment and Expenditures per Student

School Year	Enrollment	Spending per student
2007–2008	4,651,516	$10,162
2006–2007	4,576,933	9,629
2005–2006	4,505,572	9,269
2004–2005	4,383,871	8,916
2003–2004	4,311,502	7,708
2002–2003	4,239,911	7,088
2001–2002	4,146,653	6,913
2000–2001	4,059,619	6,638
1999–2000	3,991,783	6,354
1998–1999	3,945,367	5,853
1997–1998	3,900,488	5,597

Graduates and Dropouts

School Year	Graduates	*Dropouts
2006–2007	241,193	55,306
2005–2006	240,485	51,841
2004–2005	239,716	18,290
2003–2004	244,165	16,434
2002–2003	238,109	15,117
2001–2002	225,167	16,622
2000–2001	215,316	17,563
1999–2000	212,925	23,457
1998–1999	203,393	27,592
1997–1998	197,186	27,550
1996–1997	181,794	26,901

*Grades 7–12.

opted in 1883 and raised to 35 cents in connection with provision of free textbooks in the amendment of 1918.

In 1949, the Gilmer-Aikin Laws reorganized the state system of public schools by making sweeping changes in administration and financing. The Texas Education Agency, headed by the governor-appointed Commissioner of Education, administers the public-school system.

The policy-making body for public education is the 15-member State Board of Education, which is elected from separate districts for overlapping four-year terms. Current membership of the board may be found in the State Government section of this Almanac.

Recent Changes in Public Education

Members of the 68th Legislature passed a historic education-reform bill in the summer of 1984. House Bill 72 came in response to growing concern over deteriorating literacy among Texas' schoolchildren over two decades, reflected in students' scores on standardized tests.

Provisions of HB 72 raised teachers' salaries, but tied those raises to teacher performance. It also introduced more stringent teacher certification and initiated competency testing for teachers.

Academic achievement was set as a priority in public education with stricter attendance rules; adoption of a no-pass, no-play rule prohibiting students who were failing courses from participating in sports and other extracurricular activities for a six-week period; and national norm-referenced testing throughout all grades to assure parents of individual schools' performance through a common frame of reference.

No-pass, no-play now requires only a three-week suspension for a failing course grade, during which time the student can continue to practice, but not participate in competition.

The 74th Legislature passed the Public Schools Reform Act of 1995, which increased local control of public schools by limiting the Texas Education Agency to recommending and reporting on educational goals; overseeing charter schools; managing the permanent, foundation and available school funds; administering an accountability system; creating and implementing the student testing program; recommending educator appraisal and counselor evaluation instruments; and developing plans for special, bilingual, compensatory, gifted and talented, vocational and technology education.

Texas students, beginning with the Class of 1987, have been required to pass an exit-level exam, along with their courses, in order to receive a diploma from a Texas public high school. Beginning with the Class of 2005, Texas students must pass the exit-level Texas Assessment of Knowledge and Skills (TAKS) to meet this graduation requirement. TAKS, which is the most rigorous graduation test ever given to Texas students, covers English language arts, mathematics, science and social studies.

To give Texas residents a sense of how schools are performing, the state has issued ratings for its public school districts and campuses since 1993. The new system is based on state test scores and high school completion rates.

A teacher also may remove a disruptive student from class and, subject to review by a campus committee, veto the student's return to class. The district must provide alternative education for students removed from class. A student must be placed in alternative education for assault, selling drugs or alcohol, substance abuse or public lewdness. A student must be expelled and referred to the appropriate court for serious offenses, such as murder or aggravated assault.

Actions of the 81st Legislature Affecting Public Schools

Although a smaller-than-usual number of public education bills were approved by lawmakers during the 81st Legislature, the bills' impact will be widespread.

Texas School Personnel & Salaries

Year/ Personnel Type	Personnel (Full-Time Equivalent)*	Average Total Salaries†
2007–2006 Personnel		
Teachers	321,730	$47,283
Campus Administrators	17,861	67,895
Central Administrators	6,447	84,544
Support Staff*	52,637	55,252
Total Professionals	***398,675***	***49,861***
Educational Aides	62,669	17,850
Auxiliary Staff	172,003	21,579
2006–2007 Personnel		
Teachers	311,466	$45,971
Campus Administrators	17,098	66,037
Central Administrators	6,202	81,827
Support Staff*	50,334	53,653
Total Professionals	***385,100***	***48,444***
Educational Aides	61,345	17,313
Auxiliary Staff	167,469	21,009

*Support staff includes supervisors, counselors, educational diagnosticians, librarians, nurses/physicians, therapists and psychologists.
†Supplements for non-teaching duties and career-ladder supplements are not included in this figure.

Lawmakers provided more flexibility in the state's primary graduation plan by reducing the number of required courses and increasing the number of electives. The changes were effective immediately. In the 26-credit, Recommended High School Graduation Program which most students follow, the number of electives increased from 3.5 to six.

Students are no longer required to take a health class or a technology application class. The number of required physical education credits was also reduced for this degree program.

Beginning with the 2009–2010 entering freshman class, students who follow the 22-credit Minimum

Students of Nancy Moseley Elementary School in Dallas enjoy an outing to Green Meadows Petting Farm in Lynn Creek Park at Joe Pool Lake in Grand Prairie. Irwin Thompson photo.

Graduation Plan will be required to earn one fine arts credit. The 26-credit Distinguished Achievement Program, the state's third graduation plan, was not changed by the new legislation.

HB3, which included the graduation changes, contained a number of other revisions. It eliminated testing requirements tied to third-grade promotion. Previously, third-grade students were required to pass the reading Texas Assessment of Knowledge and Skills (TAKS) in order to be promoted. Fifth and eighth-grade students still must pass the reading and math TAKS to be promoted.

The bill requires a revamping of the state's assessment program for grades 3–8, which will result in the development of a replacement test for TAKS over the next several years.

Sanctions for schools or districts that earn the state's lowest school rating were also revised. Previously, a school that received the state's lowest rating for five years in a row was required to be closed under state law. HB3 makes the closure permissible but not mandatory.

Another major bill approved this session, HB3646, updates the state's school finance system.

SB174 provides consumers with more information about educator preparation programs, which will help prospective teachers select the best possible teacher training program. The bill revised the Accountability System for Educator Preparation Programs (ASEP) to include certification exam results, performance results for beginning teachers, student achievement information and information provided by field supervisors of teachers in training.

Numerous bills provide expanded avenues for the purchase of textbooks or other instructional material to be used in Texas classrooms. Although electronic materials have been available for use in the state's classrooms since the early 1990s, HB 4294 would allow expenditure of state textbook funds for equipment, such as laptops, necessary to utilize electronic instructional material.

Charter Schools

Charter-school legislation in Texas provides for three types of charter schools: the home-rule school district charter, the campus or campus-program charter

and the open-enrollment charter.

As of April 2007, no district has expressed official interest in home-rule charter status, because of its complex developmental procedures. Houston, Dallas, Nacogdoches, San Antonio, Clear Creek, Colorado, Corpus Christi and Spring Branch school districts have created campus charter schools, which are overseen by each school district's board of trustees.

Open-enrollment charter schools are public schools released from some Texas education laws and regulations. These schools are granted by the State Board of Education (SBOE). This charter contract is typically granted for 5 years and can be revoked if the school violates its charter.

Many charter schools have focused tefforts on educating young people who are at risk of dropping out of school or who have dropped out and then returned to school. ☆

PSF Apportionment, 1854–2008

The first apportionment by Texas to public schools was for school year 1854–1855

Years	Amount of P.S.F. Distributed to Schools	Years	Amount of P.S.F. Distributed to Schools
1854–55	$ 40,587	1992–93	739,494,967
1880–81	679,317	1993–94	737,677,545
1900–01	3,002,820	1994–95	737,008,244
1910–11	5,931,287	1995–96	739,996,574
1920–21	18,431,716	1996–97	692,678,412
1930–31	27,342,473	1997–98	690,802,024
1940–41	34,580,475	1998–99	661,892,466
1950–51	93,996,600	1999–00	698,487,305
1960–61	164,188,461	2000–01	794,284,231
1970–71	287,159,758	2001–02	764,554,567
1980–81	3,042,476	2002–03	896,810,915
1985–86	807,680,617	2003–04	825,059,655
1988–89	882,999,623	2004–05	879,981,965
1989–90	917,608,395	2005–06	841,878,709
1990–91	700,276,846	2006–07	843,136,949
1991–92	739,200,044	2007–08	716,534,543

Source: Texas Education Agency.

Permanent School Fund

The Texas public school system was established and the permanent fund set up by the Fifth Legislature, Jan. 31, 1854.

Year	Total Investment Fund*	Total Income Earned by P.S.F.	Year	Total Investment Fund*	Total Income Earned by P.S.F.
1854	$ 2,000,000	. . .	1993	11,822,465,497	739,494,967
1880	3,542,126	. . .	1994	11,330,590,652	737,677,545
1900	9,102,873	$ 783,142	1995	12,273,168,900	737,008,244
1910	16,752,407	1,970,527	1996	12,995,820,070	762,569,466
1920	25,698,282	2,888,555	1997	15,496,646,498	692,678,412
1930	38,718,106	2,769,547	1998	16,296,199,389	690,802,024
1940	68,299,082	3,331,874	1999	19,615,730,341	661,892,466
1950	161,179,979	3,985,974	2000	22,275,586,452	698,487,305
1961	454,391,643	13,766,436	2001	19,021,750,040	794,284,231
1970	842,217,721	34,762,955	2002	17,047,245,212	764,554,567
1980	2,464,579,397	166,475,426	2003	18,037,320,374	896,810,915
1985	5,095,802,979	417,080,383	2004	19,261,799,285	54,922,310
1988	6,493,070,622	572,665,253	2005	21,354,333,727	0
1989	6,873,610,771	614,786,823	2006	22,802,708,177	0
1990	8,930,703,666	674,634,994	2007	25,311,835,346	0
1991	10,227,777,535	700,276,846	2008	23,142,393,002	0
1992	10,944,944,872	739,200,044			

*For years before 1991, includes cash, bonds at par and stocks at book value. For years beginning with 1991, includes cash, bonds and stocks at fair value.

University Interscholastic League Winning Schools for the 2007–2008 to 2008–2009 School Years

Winners in the academic, music and the arts categories are listed first, then winners in sports categories. A dash (—) in the box means there was no competition in that conference in that category for that year. Source: University Interscholastic League. http://www.uil.utexas.edu/

Academics

Year	Conference A	Conference AA	Conference AAA	Conference AAAA	Conference AAAAA
Overall State Meet Academic Champions					
2007–08	Lindsay	Tuscola Jim Ned	Argyle	Friendswood	Fort Bend Clements
2008–09	Lindsay	Holliday	Argyle	Friendswood	Fort Bend Clements
Accounting					
2007–08	Sudan	Tuscola Jim Ned	Snyder	Brownwood	Keller
2008–09	Sudan	Caddo Mills	Dalhart	Hallsville	Edinburg
Accounting Team					
2007–08	Happy	Rosebud-Lott	Hamshire-Fannett	Brownwood	Keller
2008–09	Happy	Rosebud-Lott	Snyder	Magnolia	Fort Bend Dulles
Calculator Applications					
2007–08	Lindsay	Tuscola Jim Ned	Bridge City	Nederland	Pharr-San Juan-Alamo
2008–09	Lindsay	Caddo Mills	Argyle	Cor. Christi Flour Bluff	Klein
Calculator Applications Team					
2007–08	San Isidro	Elkhart	Bridge City	Nederland	Klein
2008–09	Lindsay	Elkhart	Argyle	Longview Pine Tree	Fort Bend Clements
Computer Applications					
2007–08	Earth Springlake	Grandview	Hamshire-Fannett	Sherman	Mission Sharyland
2008–09	Garden City	Shelbyville	Lubbock Cooper	Friendswood	Kingwood
Computer Science					
2007–08	Martin's Mill	Wall	Gonzales	Katy Seven Lakes	Arlington Martin
2008–09	Port Aransas	Refugio	Gonzales	Denton	Klein
Computer Science Team					
2007–08	Garden City	Wall	Gonzales	Katy Seven Lakes	Fort Bend Clements
2008–09	Port Aransas	Wall	Lucas Lovejoy	Friendswood	Fort Bend Clements
Number Sense					
2007–08	Lindsay	Caddo Mills	Argyle	Nederland	Klein
2008–09	Lindsay	Caddo Mills	Wichita Falls Hirschi	Big Spring	Fort Bend Clements
Number Sense Team					
2007–08	Lindsay	Caddo Mills	Argyle	Katy Seven Lakes	Klein
2008–09	Lindsay	Caddo Mills	Wichita Falls Hirschi	Longview Pine Tree	Fort Bend Clements
Mathematics					
2007–08	Lindsay	Caddo Mills	Bridge City	Port Lavaca Calhoun	Klein
2008–09	Lindsay	Caddo Mills	Argyle	Port Lavaca Calhoun	Keller
Mathematics Team					
2007–08	Lindsay	Caddo Mills	Argyle	Katy Seven Lakes	Klein
2008–09	Lindsay	Caddo Mills	Argyle	Port Lavaca Calhoun	Fort Bend Clements
Science					
2007–08	Moulton	Vanderbilt Industrial	Wimberley	Friendswood	Fort Bend Clements
2008–09	Canadian	White Oak	Wimberley	Austin Lake Travis	Arlington Martin
Science Team					
2007–08	Harper	Floydada	Argyle	Dallas Highland Park	Fort Bend Clements
2008–09	Lindsay	Irving North Hills	Whitney	Dallas Highland Park	Fort Bend Dulles
Social Studies					
2007–08	Roby	Colorado City	Emory Rains	Katy Seven Lakes	El Paso Franklin
2008–09	San Isidro	Paris Chisum	China Spring	Whitehouse	Katy Taylor
Social Studies Team					
2007–08	San Isidro	Tuscola Jim Ned	Wimberley	Katy Seven Lakes	Katy Taylor
2008–09	Anton	Paris Chisum	Abilene Wylie	Whitehouse	Katy Taylor
Current Issues & Events					
2007–08	Muenster	Sadler S&S Consolidated	Wimberley	Pflugerville Hendrickson	Houston Clear Lake
2008–09	Latexo	Tuscola Jim Ned	Hidalgo Early College	Houston Kerr	Katy Taylor
Current Issues & Events Team					
2007–08	Apple Springs	Sadler S&S Consolidated	Abilene Wylie	Pflugerville Hendrickson	Houston Clear Lake
2008–09	Apple Springs	Tuscola Jim Ned	Hidalgo Early College	Aledo	Katy Taylor
Literary Criticism					
2007–08	Frost	Weimar	Iowa Park	Lindale	Cedar Park

Year	Conference A	Conference AA	Conference AAA	Conference AAAA	Conference AAAAA
2008–09	Winters	Dimmitt	Liberty	Lindale	Southlake Carroll
Literary Criticism Team					
2007–08	Martin's Mill	Sadler S&S Consol.	Atlanta	Friendswood	Southlake Carroll
2008–09	Martin's Mill	Weimar	Liberty	Aledo	Lewisville
Poetry Interpretation					
2007–08	Wink	Holliday	Van	Wolfforth Frenship	Plano
2008–09	Wellman-Union	Hebbronville	Athens	Ennis	Alief Elsik
Prose Interpretation					
2007–08	Tolar	Holliday	Athens	Cleburne	Harlingen South
2008–09	Simm Bowie	Holliday	Iowa Park	Stephenville	South Grand Prairie
Ready Writing					
2007–08	Fort Worth Acad. of Fine Arts	Hico	Wimberley	Alice	Arlington Martin
2008–09	Mason	Cooper	Bullard	Crosby	San Antonio Churchill
Speech Team					
2007–08	Lindsay	Holliday	Seminole	Friendswood	Plano
2008–09	Lindsay	Holliday	Iowa Park	Lindale	College Station A&M
Informative Speaking					
2007–08	Lindsay	Bishop	Wills Point	Friendswood	Houston Lamar
2008–09	Lindsay	Bishop	Gatesville	Houston Kerr	Plano
Persuasive Speaking					
2007–08	Apple Springs	Rogers	Devine	Lindale	Houston Cypress Ridge
2008–09	Lometa	Holliday	Paris North Lamar	San Marcos	Plano East
Lincoln-Douglas Debate					
2007–08	Farwell	Blanco	Van	Paris North Lamar	Round Rock Westwood
2008–09	Wolfe City	Woden	La Vernia	Lindale	Houston Cypress Falls
Cross Examination Team Debate					
2007–08	Gail Borden	Blanco	Palestine	Bay City	Round Rock Westwood
2008–09	Thorndale	Lago Vista	Bandera	Hallsville	Fort Bend Dulles
Spelling & Vocabulary					
2007–08	Albany	Sadler S&S Consol.	Pearland Dawson	Waxahachie	Fort Bend Clements
2008–09	Albany	Vanderbilt Industrial	Giddings	Texarkana Texas	Garland
Spelling & Vocabulary Team					
2007–08	Groveton	East Bernard	Giddings	Aledo	Klein
2008–09	Martin's Mill	Vanderbilt Industrial	Giddings	Sulphur Springs	Fort Bend Clements
Journalism Team					
2007–08	Nazareth	New Boston	Brownsboro	Lindale	Flower Mound Marcus
2008–09	Thrall	Buffalo	Carthage	Big Spring	Klein Collins
Editorial Writing					
2007–08	Iola	Sanford-Fritch	Lytle	Hallsville	Flower Mound Marcus
2008–09	Utopia	Hebbronville	Carthage	Whitehouse	Klein Collins
Feature Writing					
2007–08	Nazareth	New Boston	Carthage	Big Spring	Corpus Christi King
2008–09	Albany	Univ. City Randolph	Emory Rains	Longview Pine Tree	San Antonio Churchill
Headline Writing					
2007–08	Quanah	Mildred	Canton	San Antonio Jefferson	South Grand Prairie
2008–09	Happy	East Bernard	Giddings	Pleasanton	San Antonio Marshall
News Writing					
2007–08	Clarendon	Redwater	Fabens	Lindale	Flower Mound Marcus
2008–09	D'Hanis	Buffalo	Carthage	Big Spring	Houston Cypress Creek

Publications

Year	Yearbooks (Gold Awards)	Newspapers (Gold Awards)
2007–08	Connally, Duncanville, McKinney, Pleasant Grove, St. Mark's School of Texas, Austin Westlake, White Oak	Albany, Burges, Connally, Liberal Arts & Science Academy, St. Mark's School of Texas, Austin Westlake
2008–09	Abilene, Burges, Duncanville, McKinney, Pleasant Grove, Westlake, White Oak	Albany, Burges, Crandall, Liberal Arts & Science Academy, Pleasant Grove, St. Mark's School of Texas, Westlake

Music and Theater

Year	Conference A	Conference AA	Conference AAA	Conference AAAA	Conference AAAAA
One-Act Play					
2007–08	Fort Worth Acad. of Fine Arts	Rogers	Mexia	Clemens	Mansfield
2008–09	Lindsay	Rogers	Athens	Friendswood	Austin
State Marching Band Contest					
2007–08	Forsan	Queen City	—	Mesquite Poteet	—
2008–09	—	—	Argyle	—	Flower Mound Marcus

Athletics

Year	Conference A	Conference AA	Conference AAA	Conference AAAA	Conference AAAAA
Baseball					
2007–08	Bosqueville	Salado	Snyder	Corpus Christi Calallen	Plano West
2008–09	Miles	Danbury	Carthage	Texarkana Texas	El Paso Socorro
Basketball, Boys					
2007–08	I: Thorndale II: Laneville	Ponder	Kennedale	Dallas South Oak Cliff	North Crowley
2008–09	I: Roscoe II: Elkhart Slocum	Ponder	Dallas Madison	Houston Yates	DeSoto
Basketball, Girls					
2007–08	I: Martin's Mill II: Follett	Tuscola Jim Ned	Canyon	Dallas Lincoln	Houston Cypress-Fairbanks
2008–09	I: Sudan II: Roby	Brock	Robinson	Waco Midway	Mansfield Summit
Cross Country Team, Boys					
2007–08	Sundown	Wallis Brazos	Argyle	Katy Seven Lakes	Conroe The Woodlands
2008–09	Sundown	Wall	Argyle	Boerne Champion	Conroe The Woodlands
Cross Country Individual, Boys					
2007–08	Big Sandy	Paradise	Argyle	Lockhart	Southlake Carroll
2008–09	Big Sandy	Holliday	Argyle	Big Spring	Conroe The Woodlands
Cross Country Team, Girls					
2007–08	Lindsay	Wall	Humble Kingwood Park	Hereford	Southlake Carroll
2008–09	Sundown	Spearman	Decatur	Humble Kingwood Park	Conroe The Woodlands
Cross Country Individual, Girls					
2007–08	Seymour	Hamilton	Prosper	Dallas Highland Park	Clute Brazoswood
2008–09	Shamrock	Universal City Randolph	Prosper	Midlothian	Conroe The Woodlands
Golf Team, Boys					
2007–08	Robert Lee	Salado	Graham	Dallas Highland Park	Plano West
2008–09	Robert Lee	Salado	Gatesville	Richardson Pearce	Austin Westlake
Golf Individual, Boys					
2007–08	Grapeland	Salado	Robinson	Dallas Highland Park	Houston Memorial
2008–09	Robert Lee	Salado	Devine	Dallas Highland Park	Dallas Jesuit
Golf Team, Girls					
2007–08	Martin's Mill	Wall	Andrews	Dallas Highland Park	Southlake Carroll
2008–09	Baird	Wall	Monahans	Montgomery	Southlake Carroll
Golf Individual, Girls					
2007–08	Chilton	San Saba	Andrews	Montgomery	College Station A&M
2008–09	Chilton	Callisburg	Monahans	Arlington Heights	Fort Bend Clements
Softball					
2007–08	Shiner	East Bernard	Huntington	Aledo	Alvin
2008–09	Forsan	Brock	Needville	New Braunfels Canyon	Spring Branch Smithson Valley
Tennis, Team					
2007–08	—	—	—	New Braunfels	Austin Westlake
2008–09	—	—	—	New Braunfels	Dallas Highland Park
Tennis, Boys Singles					
2007–08	Avery	Franklin	Vernon	New Braunfels	Laredo United
2008–09	Mason	Tuscola Jim Ned	Argyle	Texarkana Texas	Klein Collins
Tennis, Boys Doubles					
2007–08	Menard	Lexington	Robinson	Boerne	Plano West
2008–09	Mason	Brock	Vernon	Richardson Pearce	Plano West
Tennis, Girls Singles					
2007–08	Miles	Peaster	Liberty	New Braunfels	Conroe Woodlands College Park
2008–09	Mason	Franklin	Abilene Wylie	Austin Lake Travis	New Braunfels
Tennis, Girls Doubles					
2007–08	Menard	Mason	Abilene Wylie	Dallas Highland Park	Katy Taylor
2008–09	Mason	Big Lake Reagan Co.	Abilene Wylie	Dallas Highland Park	Klein
Tennis, Mixed Doubles					
2007–08	Lenorah Grady	Franklin	Abilene Wylie	New Braunfels	Klein
2008–09	Menard	Franklin	Van	Richardson Pearce	New Braunfels
Track & Field, Boys Team					
2007–08	Rule	Arp	Cuero	Lancaster	Garland Rowlett
2008–09	Canadian	Corrigan-Camden	West Orange-Stark	Lancaster	Garland Rowlett

Year	Conference A	Conference AA	Conference AAA	Conference AAAA	Conference AAAAA
Track & Field, Girls Team					
2007–08	Rochelle	Universal City Randolph	Canyon	Lancaster	Dallas Skyline
2008–09	Rochelle	Wallis Brazos	Waco Connally	Mansfield Timberview	Dallas Skyline
Volleyball					
2007–08	Windthorst	Bushland	Wimberley	Waco Midway	Amarillo
2008–09	Windhorst	Bushland	Lucas Lovejoy	Hereford	Amarillo

Duncanville's Brigetta Barrett wins the Girls 5A high jump in the UIL Track and Field Championships at the Mike A. Myers Stadium in Austin in May 2008. Erich Schlegel photo.

Football					
Year	6-man	A	AA	AAA	AAAA	AAAAA
2007–08	I: Richland Springs II: Matador Motley County	I: Alto II: Munday	I: Farmersville II: Canadian	I: Liberty Hill II: Celina	I: Rosenberg Lamar Consolidated II: Austin Lake Travis	I: Euless Trinity II: Katy
2008–09	I: Strawn II: Borden County	I: Canadian II: Stratford	I: Muleshoe II: Daingerfield	I: Prosper II: Carthage	I: Lake Travis II: Sulphur Springs	I: Allen II: Katy

Soccer				
	Girls		Boys	
Year	AAAA	AAAAA	AAAA	AAAAA
2007–08	McKinney Boyd	Southlake Carroll	El Paso Del Valle	Flower Mound Marcus
2008–09	Richardson Pearce	Coppell	Hidalgo Early College	Plano

Swimming & Diving, Team				
	Girls		Boys	
Year	AAAA	AAAAA	AAAA	AAAAA
2007–08	Dallas Highland Park	Austin Westlake	Frisco	San Antonio Churchill
2008–09	Dallas Highland Park	Conroe The Woodlands	Humble Kingwood Park	Humble Kingwood

Wrestling, Boys	
2007–08	**Team**: Canyon Randall; **Weight Class 103**: Grapevine; **112**: Canyon Randall; **119**: Arlington; **125**: Conroe The Woodlands; **130**: Colleyville Heritage; **135**: Euless Trinity; **140**: Flower Mound Marcus; **145**: Amarillo Tascosa; **152**: Arlington Lamar; **160**: Houston Westside; **171**: Houston Westside; **180**: Katy Cinco Ranch; **189**: Southlake Carroll; **215**: Dallas Molina; **285**: Katy Cinco Ranch
2008–09	**Team**: Canyon Randall; **Weight Class 103**: Allen; **112**: Amarillo Tascosa; **119**: Lubbock Monterey; **125**: Canyon Randall; **130**: Conroe The Woodlands; **135**: Cedar Park Vista Ridge; **140**: Canyon Randall; **145**: Flower Mound Marcus; **152**: Austin Westlake; **160**: Canyon Randall; **171**: Southlake Carroll; **180**: McAllen; **189**: Canyon Randall; **215**: Conroe The Woodlands; **285**: Katy Taylor

Wrestling, Girls	
2007–08	**Team**: Amarillo Caprock; **Weight Class 95**: Houston Cypress Ridge; **102**: Amarillo Caprock; **110**: Frisco Centennial; **119**: El Paso Del Valle; **128**: El Paso Irvin; **138**: Coppell; **148**: Amarillo Tascosa; **165**: Katy; **185**: Arlington Martin; **215**: Arlington
2008–09	**Team**: Amarillo Caprock; **Weight Class 95**: Amarillo Caprock; **102**: Frisco Centennial; **110**: Amarillo Tascosa; **119**: El Paso Del Valle; **128**: El Paso Irvin; **138**: Arlington Lamar; **148**: Amarillo Caprock; **165**: Katy; **185**: Klein Collins; **215**: Cedar Park

TEXAS A&M UNIVERSITY PRESS

Texas A&M University was the state's first publically supported college. Ron Billings photo; Texas Forest Service.

Brief History of Higher Education in Texas

While there were earlier efforts toward higher education, the first permanent institutions established were church-supported schools:

• Rutersville University, established in 1840 by Methodist minister Martin Ruter in Fayette County, predecessor of Southwestern University, Georgetown, established in 1843;

• Baylor University, now at Waco, but established in 1845 at Independence, Washington County, by the Texas Union Baptist Association; and

• Austin College, now at Sherman, but founded in 1849 at Huntsville by the Brazos Presbytery of the Old School Presbyterian Church.

Other historic Texas schools of collegiate rank included:

Larissa College, 1848, at Larissa, Cherokee County; McKenzie College, 1841, Clarksville; Chappell Hill Male and Female Institute, 1850, Chappell Hill; Soule University, 1855, Chappell Hill;

Johnson Institute, 1852, Driftwood, Hays County; Nacogdoches University, 1845, Nacogdoches; Salado College, 1859, Salado, Bell County. Add-Ran College, established at Thorp Spring, Hood County, in 1873, was the predecessor of present Texas Christian University, Fort Worth.

Texas A&M University and
The University of Texas

The Agricultural and Mechanical College of Texas (now Texas A&M University), authorized by the Legislature in 1871, opened its doors in 1876 to become the first publicly supported institution of higher education.

In 1881, Texans established the University of Texas in Austin, with a medical branch in Galveston. The Austin institution opened Sept. 15, 1883, the Galveston school in 1891.

First College for Women

In 1901, the 27th Legislature established the Girls Industrial College, which began classes at its campus in Denton in 1903. A campaign to establish a state industrial college for women was led by the State Grange and Patrons of Husbandry.

A bill was signed into law on April 6, 1901, creating the college. It was charged with a dual mission, which continues to guide the university today, to provide a liberal education and to prepare young women with a specialized education "for the practical industries of the age."

In 1905 the name of the college was changed to the College of Industrial Arts; in 1934, it was changed to Texas State College for Women.

Since 1957 the institution, which is now the largest university principally for women in the United States, has been the Texas Woman's University.

Historic, Primarily Black Colleges

A number of Texas schools were established primarily for blacks, although collegiate racial integration is now complete in the state.

The black-oriented institutions include state-supported Prairie View A&M University (originally established as Alta Vista Agricultural College in 1876), Prairie View; Texas Southern University, Houston; and privately supported Huston-Tillotson College, Austin; Jarvis Christian College, Hawkins; Wiley College, Marshall; Paul Quinn College, originally located in Waco, now in Dallas; and Texas College, Tyler.

Predominantly black colleges that are important in the history of higher education in Texas, but which have ceased operations, include Bishop College, established in Marshall in 1881, then moved to Dallas; Mary Allen College, established in Crockett in 1886; and Butler College, originally named the Texas Baptist Academy, in 1905 in Tyler.

Recent Developments in Texas Higher Education

Source: Texas Higher Education Coordinating Board; **www.thecb.state.tx.us/**

State Appropriations

For the 2010–2011 biennium, beginning Sept. 1, 2009, and ending Aug. 31, 2011, total funding for higher education was $22.7 billion (including American Recovery and Reinvestment Act funds), an increase of $1.56 billion, or 7.4 percent, over the 2008–2009 appropriation of $21.18 billion. Higher education for 2010–2011 was 12.5 percent of the total state budget, compared with about 14 percent of the state budget for 2008–2009.

Enrollment

Enrollment in Texas public and independent, or private, colleges and universities in fall 2008 totaled 1,299,058 students, an increase of 44,075 from fall 2007. Enrollment in the **35 public universities** increased by 11,941 students to 509,136 students. Twenty-four universities reported enrollment increases, while 11 reported decreases. The state's **public community college districts and Lamar State Colleges,** which offer two-year degree programs, reported fall 2008 enrollments totaling 604,163 students, an increase of 28,529 over fall 2007. The public **Texas State Technical College System,** which also offers two-year degree programs, reported fall 2008 enrollments totaling 13,344 students, an increase of 1,734 students over fall 2007. Enrollments for fall 2008 at the state's 37 **independent senior colleges and universities** increased to 116,607 students, up 980 students from fall 2007. The state's two **independent junior colleges** reported 615 students in fall 2008, an increase of 36 students from the previous fall. Public medical, dental, nursing, and allied **health institutions** of higher education reported enrollments totaling 17,684 students in fall 2008, up 949 from fall 2007. Enrollment at **independent health-related insti-** tutions totaled 2,737 students, down 22 students from the previous fall.

Actions of the 81st Legislature

HB 51 was a major piece of legislation intended to raise the excellence of public universities and develop, fund and maintain major research universities in Texas.

SB 175 authorizes The University of Texas at Austin (UT-Austin) to place a cap on the number of students admitted under the Top Ten Percent Law. Beginning with the 2011–2012 academic year, UT-Austin is not required to offer admission to applicants qualifying under the Top Ten Percent Law in excess of the number needed to fill 75 percent of enrollment capacity for first-time resident undergraduate students.

HB 3 establishes two performance standards for high school end-of-course examinations: a standard performance and, for Algebra II and English III, a college readiness performance standard.

SB 956 authorizes the board of the University of North Texas System to establish and operate a school of law in Dallas as a professional school of the system.

SB 98 establishes The University of Texas Health Science Center-South Texas, which includes The University of Texas Medical School-South Texas. The UT System is directed to convert the current Lower Rio Grande Valley Regional Academic Health Center to The University of Texas Health Science Center-South Texas as a component institution of the system.

SB 629 removes statutory barriers to the establishment of three new universities that had been operating as system centers: Texas A&M San Antonio, Texas A&M Central Texas and University of North Texas at Dallas. These institutions have been approved but are not yet operating, pending accreditation.

Universities and Colleges

Sources: Texas Higher Education Coordinating Board and individual institutions. Dates of establishment may differ from Brief History on page 593 because schools use the date when authorization was given rather than date of first classes. **For explanation of type of institution and other symbols, see notes at end of table. www.thecb.state.tx.us**

		Enrollment		
Name of Institution — Location; (*type or ownership, if private sectarian institution); date of founding; president (unless otherwise noted)	Number of Faculty †	Fall Term 2008	Summer Sessions 2008 §	Extension or Continuing Ed.
Abilene Christian University — Abilene; (3–Church of Christ); 1906 (as Childers Classical Institute; as Abilene Christian College, 1914; as university, 1976); Dr. Royce Money	368	4,683	1,428	NA
ALAMO COLLEGES (9) — Dr. Bruce H. Leslie, chancellor. 1978 (as San Antonio Community College District; 1982, as Alamo Community College District; current name, 2009). System consists of following colleges and presidents:	2,752	52,306	25,934	4,950
Northeast Lakeview College — San Antonio; (7); 2007; Dr. Eric Reno		416	NA	NA
Northwest Vista College — San Antonio; (7); 1995; Dr. Jacqueline Claunch	298	12,034	2,817	285
Palo Alto College — San Antonio; (7); 1983; Dr. Ana M. (Cha) Guzmán	337	7,829	4,307	1,516
St. Philip's College — San Antonio; (7); 1898; Dr. Adena Williams Loston	601	10,337	4,928	5,396
San Antonio College — San Antonio; (7); 1925; Dr. Robert E. Zeigler	1,051	21,766	11,461	4,337
Alvin Community College — Alvin; (7); 1949; Dr. A. Rodney Allbright	**92	4,348	2,114	491
Amarillo College — Amarillo; (7); 1929; Dr. Paul Matney, acting president	384	10,150	3,393	25,000
Amberton University — Garland; (3); 1971 (as Amber University; current name, 2001); Dr. Melinda H. Reagan	40	1,562	1,378	NA
Angelina College — Lufkin; (7); 1968; Dr. Larry Phillips	110	4,940	2,613	2,574
Angelo State University — San Angelo (*See* **Texas Tech University**)				
Arlington Baptist College — Arlington; (3–Baptist); 1939 (as Bible Baptist Seminary; name changed to current in 1965); Dr. David Bryant	20	175	80	75
Austin College — Sherman; (3–Presbyterian USA); 1849; Dr. Marjorie Hass	106	1,330	**	**
Austin Community College — Austin; (7); 1972; Dr. Stephen B. Kinslow	1,842	35,798	24,407	16,002
Austin Presbyterian Theological Seminary — Austin; (3–Presbyterian); 1902 (successor of Austin School of Theology, est. 1884); Theodore J. Wardlaw	25	255	52	388

Name of Institution — Location; (*type or ownership, if private sectarian institution); date of founding; president (unless otherwise noted)	Number of Faculty †	Enrollment		
		Fall Term 2008	Summer Sessions 2008 §	Extension or Continuing Ed.
Baptist Missionary Association Theological Seminary — Jacksonville; (3–Baptist Missionary); 1955; Dr. Charley Holmes	15	145	NA	30
Baylor College of Medicine — Houston; (5); 1903 (in Dallas; moved to Houston, 1943; Baptist until 1969); Dr. William T. Butler, interim president	3,696	1,385	NA	~17,901
Baylor University — Waco; (3–Southern Baptist); 1845 (in Independence; merged with Waco University and moved to Waco, 1887); Dr. David E. Garland, interim president	823	14,653	4,789	NA
Bee County College — Beeville (See **Coastal Bend College**)				
Blinn College — Brenham; (7); 1883 (as academy; jr. college, 1927); Dr. Daniel J. Holt	575	14,046	10,783	900
Brazosport College — Lake Jackson; (7); 1967; Dr. Millicent M. Valek	86	3,887	2,434	1,088
Brookhaven College — Farmers Branch (See **Dallas County Community College District**)				
Cedar Valley College — Lancaster (See **Dallas County Community College District**)				
Central Texas College — Killeen; (7); 1965; Dr. James R. Anderson, chancellor	2,316	11,083	17,477	721
Cisco College — Cisco; (7); 1909 (as Cisco Junior College, a private institution; became state school in 1939; name changed to current in 2009); Dr. Colleen Smith	195	3,761	1,435	67
Clarendon College — Clarendon; (7); 1898 (as church school; became state school in 1927); Dr. William R. Auvenshine	**69	1,240	428	376
Coastal Bend College — Beeville; (7); (1966 as Bee County College, name changed in 1999); Dr. Thomas Baynum	99	3,821	2,266	588
College of the Mainland — Texas City; (7); 1967; Dr. J. Lawrence Durrence, interim president	89	3,961	2,949	**
College of St. Thomas More, The — Fort Worth; (3–Roman Catholic); 1981 (as St. Thomas More Institute; as college, 1989); Dr. James A. Patrick, chancellor	9	45	4	NA
Collin College — McKinney; (7); 1985 (as Collin County Community College); Dr. Cary A. Israel	1,102	31,952	14,174	13,452
Concordia University Texas— Austin; (3–Lutheran Church–Missouri Synod); 1926 (as Concordia Lutheran College; current name, 1995); part of Concordia University System. Dr. Thomas Cedel	358	2,170	1,256	314
Cooke County College — Gainesville (See **North Central Texas College**)				
Corpus Christi State University — (See **Texas A&M University–Corpus Christi** under **Texas A&M University System**)				
Cy-Fair College — Houston (See **Lone Star College System**)				
Dallas Baptist University — Dallas; (3–Southern Baptist); 1891 (as Northwest Texas Bible College; name changed to Decatur Baptist College, 1897; moved to Dallas, name changed to Dallas Baptist College, 1965; became university, 1985); Dr. Gary R. Cook	523	5,297	2,461	NA
Dallas Christian College — Dallas; (3–Christian); 1950; Dr. Dustin D. Rubeck	60	268	116	NA
DALLAS COUNTY COMMUNITY COLLEGE DISTRICT (9) — Dr. Wright Lassiter, chancellor. System consists of following colleges and presidents:	3,163	61.964	36,448	22,186
Brookhaven College — Farmers Branch; (7); 1978; Dr. Richard D. McCrary	585	10,531	8,706	3,204
Cedar Valley College — Lancaster; (7); 1977; Dr. Jennifer B. Wimbish	†† 100	4,800	**	2,500
Eastfield College — Mesquite; (7); 1970; Dr. Jean Conway	460	10,279	8,077	2,177
El Centro College — Dallas; (7); 1966; Dr. Paul J. McCarthy	408	7,270	4,079	10,441
Mountain View College — Dallas; (7); 1970; Dr. Felix A. Zamora	382	6,598	3,786	2,631
North Lake College — Irving; (7); 1977; Dr. Herlinda M. Glassock	550	9,769	6,606	3,092
Richland College — Dallas; (7); 1972; Dr. Stephen K. Mittelstet	903	14,128	16,946	8,200
Dallas Theological Seminary — Dallas; (3–Christian); 1924 (as Evangelical Theological College; current name, 1936); Dr. Mark L. Bailey	119	2,036	1,144	493
Del Mar College — Corpus Christi; (7); 1935; Dr. Mark Escamilla	314	11,310	7,256	2,188
Eastfield College — Mesquite (See **Dallas County Community College District**)				
East Texas Baptist University — Marshall; (3–Baptist); 1913 (as College of Marshall; as East Texas Baptist College, 1944; as university, 1984); Dr. Samuel (Dub) Oliver	64	1,210	NA	NA
East Texas State University — Commerce (See **Texas A&M University–Commerce** under **Texas A&M University System**)				
East Texas State University at Texarkana — Texarkana (See **Texas A&M University–Texarkana** under **Texas A&M University System**)				
El Centro College — Dallas (See **Dallas County Community College District**)				
El Paso Community College — El Paso; (7); 1969; *five campuses:* **Mission del Paso, Northwest, Rio Grande, Transmountain** and **Valle Verde**; Dr. Richard M. Rhodes	# 1,337	25,011	15,586	**
Episcopal Theological Seminary of the Southwest — Austin; (3–Episcopal); 1952; Dr. Doug Travis	38	109	55	NA
Frank Phillips College — Borger; (7); 1948; Dr. Herbert J. Swender.	92	1,236	586	1,886
Galveston College — Galveston; (7); 1967; Dr. W. Myles Shelton	70	2,229	1,643	154
Grayson County College — Denison; (7); 1963; Dr. Alan Scheibmeir	¶ 104	4,026	2,128	450
Hardin-Simmons University — Abilene; (3–Southern Baptist); 1891 (as Simmons College; as Simmons University, 1925; current name, 1934); Dr. Lanny Hall	157	2,392	1,123	NA
Hill College — Hillsboro; (7); 1923 (as Hillsboro Junior College; name changed to current, 1962); Dr. Sheryl Smith Kappus	195	3,714	1,512	161
Houston Baptist University — Houston; (3–Baptist); 1960; Dr. Robert B. Sloan Jr.	139	2,564	1,052	NA
HOUSTON COMMUNITY COLLEGE (9) — Dr. Mary S. Spangler, chancellor. Houston; 1971. System consists of following colleges and presidents:	2,878	48,169	40,905	4,649
Central College — Houston; (7); Dr. William W. Harmon				
Coleman College for Health Sciences — Houston; (7); 2004; Dr. William W. Harmon, interim president	**	**	1,058	2,116

Name of Institution — Location; (*type or ownership, if private sectarian institution); date of founding; president (unless otherwise noted)	Number of Faculty †	Enrollment		
		Fall Term 2008	Summer Sessions 2008 §	Extension or Continuing Ed.
Northeast College — Houston; (7); Dr. Margaret Ford Fisher				
Northwest College — Houston; (7); Dr. Zachary R. Hodges				
Southeast College — Houston; (7); Dr. Irene M. Porcarello, interim president				
Southwest College — Houston; (7); Dr. Orfelina (Fena) Garza				
Howard College — Big Spring; (7); 1945; Dr. Cheryl T. Sparks; (*includes* campuses in Big Spring, Lamesa and San Angelo, and the **Southwest Collegiate Institute for the Deaf**, Mark J. Myers, provost)	# 309	3,573	**	**
Howard Payne University — Brownwood; (3–Baptist); 1889; Dr. Lanny Hall	146	1,388	251	172
Huston-Tillotson University — Austin; (3–United Church of Christ and United Methodist); 1952 (as Huston-Tillotson College, the merger of Tillotson College, 1875, and Samuel Huston College, 1876; current name, 2005); Dr. Larry L. Earvin	71	785	146	NA
International Bible College — San Antonio; (3–Christian); 1944; Rev. David W. Cook	15	75	NA	NA
Jacksonville College — Jacksonville; (8–Missionary Baptist); 1899; Dr. Edwin Crank	27	274	171	24
Jarvis Christian College — Hawkins; (3); 1912; Dr. Cornell Thomas	**	538	**	**
Kilgore College — Kilgore; (7); 1935; Dr. William M. Holda	139	4,968		4,968
Kingwood College — Kingwood (*See* **Lone Star College System**)				
Lamar University and all branches (*See* **Texas State University System**)				
Laredo Community College — Laredo; (7); 1946; Dr. Juan L. Maldonado	337	9,030	4,480	3,545
Lee College — Baytown; (7); 1934; Dr. Dennis Topper, interim president	364	5,854	4,615	2,616
LeTourneau University — Longview; (3); 1946 (as LeTourneau Technical Institute; became 4-yr. college, 1961); Dr. Dale A. Lunsford	¶ 76	3,661	472	1,035
Lon Morris College — Jacksonville; (8–Methodist); 1854 (as Danville Academy; changed name in 1873 to Alexander Institution; name changed to present, 1923); Dr. Miles McCall	**	437	NA	NA
LONE STAR COLLEGE SYSTEM (9) — Dr. Richard Carpenter, chancellor. (Formerly North Harris Montgomery Community College District.) System consists of following colleges and presidents:	2,798	51,494	28,876	35,797
Lone Star College–Cy-Fair — Houston; (7); Dr. Audre Levy	661	12,755	9,161	683
Lone Star College–Kingwood — Humble; (7); Dr. Katherine Persson	442	8,000	4,434	5,300
Lone Star College–Montgomery — Conroe; (7); Dr. Penny Westerfeld, interim	700	9,700	**	†† 2,500
Lone Star College–North Harris — Houston; (7); Dr. Stephen C. Head	10,114			
Lone Star College–Tomball — Tomball; (7); Dr. Raymond H. Hawkins	**	7,406	4,637	**
Lubbock Christian University — Lubbock; (3–Church of Christ); 1957; Dr. L. Ken Jones	172	1,868	588	NA
McLennan Community College — Waco; (7); 1965; Dr. Johnette McKown	386	7,884	6,743	900
McMurry University — Abilene; (3–Methodist); 1923; Dr. John H. Russell	104	1,386	612	NA
Midland College — Midland; (7); 1972; Dr. Steve Thomas	290	6,005	4,513	2,404
Midwestern State University — Wichita Falls; (2); 1922; Dr. Jesse W. Rogers	¶ 224	6,093	3,997	1,422
Montgomery College — Conroe (*See* **Lone Star College System**)				
Mountain View College — Dallas (*See* **Dallas County Community College District**)				
Navarro College — Corsicana; (7); 1946; *four campuses:* **Corsicana, Mexia, Midlothian** and **Waxahachie**; Dr. Richard M. Sanchez	738	8,328	4,720	658
North Central Texas College — Gainesville; (7); 1924 (as Gainesville Jr. College; Cooke County College, 1960; present name, 1994); Dr. Eddie Hadlock	372	8,040	4,343	4,434
Northeast Lakeview College — San Antonio (*See* **Alamo Colleges**)				
Northeast Texas Community College — Mount Pleasant; (7); 1984; Dr. Bradley W. Johnson	135	2,474	1,678	2,533
North Harris College — Houston (*See* **Lone Star College System**)				
North Lake College — Irving (*See* **Dallas County Community College District**)				
Northwest Vista College — San Antonio (*See* **Alamo Colleges**)				
Northwood University — Cedar Hill; (3); 1966; Dr. Kevin Fegan		57	1,135	524
Oblate School of Theology — San Antonio; (3–Roman Catholic); 1903 (formerly Scholasticate); the Rev. Ronald Rolheiser	24	166	78	**
Odessa College — Odessa; (7); 1946; Dr. Gregory Williams	191	4,674	2,858	1,934
Our Lady of the Lake University of San Antonio — San Antonio; (3–Roman Catholic); 1895 (as school for girls; as senior college, 1911; as university, 1975); *two campuses:* San Antonio and Houston; Dr. Tessa Martinez Pollock	256	2,642	**	**
Palo Alto College — San Antonio (*See* **Alamo Colleges**)				
Panola College — Carthage; (7); 1947 (as Panola Junior College; name changed, 1988); Dr. Gregory S. Powell	177	1,983	1,142	510
Parker College of Chiropractic — Dallas; (5); 1982; Dr. Dr. Fabrizio Mancini	92	986	981	424
Paris Junior College — Paris; (7); 1924; Dr. Pamela Anglin	¶ 95	4,733	2,582	773
Paul Quinn College — Dallas; (3–African Methodist Episcopal Church); 1872 (in Waco; moved to Dallas, 1990); Dr. Michael J. Sorrell	55	441	**	NA
Prairie View A&M University — Prairie View (*See* **Texas A&M University System**)				
Ranger College — Ranger; (7); 1926; Dr. James McDonald, interim president	23	894	398	NA
Rice University — Houston; (3); chartered, 1891; opened, 1912 (as Rice Institute; as William Marsh Rice University, 1960); Dr. David W. Leebron	741	5,456	NA	5,432
Richland College — Dallas (*See* **Dallas County Community College District**)				
St. Edward's University — Austin; (3–Catholic); 1885; Dr. George E. Martin	522	5,317	**	1,886

Rice University in Houston was chartered in 1891 and opened in 1912. Robert Plocheck photo.

Name of Institution — Location; (*type or ownership, if private sectarian institution); date of founding; president (unless otherwise noted)	Number of Faculty †	Enrollment		
		Fall Term 2008	Summer Sessions 2008 §	Extension or Contin-ing Ed.
St. Mary's University of San Antonio — San Antonio; (3–Roman Catholic); 1852; Dr. Charles L. Cotrell	351	3,889	1,153	**
St. Philip's College — San Antonio (*See* **Alamo Colleges**)				
Sam Houston State University — Huntsville (*See* **Texas State University System**)				
San Antonio College — San Antonio (*See* **Alamo Colleges**)				
SAN JACINTO COLLEGE DISTRICT (9) — **Dr. Brenda Lang Hellyer, chancellor.** System consists of following colleges and presidents:	1,072	24,616	9,985	2,005
Central — Pasadena; (7); Dr. Neil Matkin				
North — Houston; (7); Dr. Allatia Harris				
South — Houston; (7); Dr. Maureen Murphy	¶ 145	9,200	**	**
Schreiner University — Kerrville; (3–Presbyterian); 1923; Dr. Charles Timothy Sum-merlin	94	930	125	NA
South Plains College — Levelland; (7); 1957; Dr. Kevin Sharp	289	9,561	2,500	**
South Texas College — McAllen; (7); NA; Dr. Shirley A. Reed	760	22,066	10,775	1,678
South Texas College of Law — Houston; (3); 1923; Dr. James J. Alfini	124	1,267	589	NA
Southern Methodist University — Dallas; (3–Methodist); 1911; Dr. R. Gerald Turner	¶ 656	10,965	4,458	2,186
Southwest Collegiate Institute for the Deaf — Big Spring (*See* **Howard College**)	20	120	NA	NA
Southwest Texas Junior College — Uvalde; (7); 1946; Dr. Ismael Sosa Jr.	**	5,202	**	**
Southwest Texas State University — San Marcos (*See* **Texas State University–San Marcos** under **Texas State University System**)				
Southwestern Adventist University — Keene; (3–Seventh-Day Adventist); 1893 (as Keene Industrial Academy; as Southwestern Junior College, 1916; as Southwestern Union College, 1963; as Southwestern Adventist College,1980; as university, 1996); Dr. Eric Anderson	75	894	260	289
Southwestern Assemblies of God University — Waxahachie; (3–Assemblies of God); 1927 (in Enid, Okla., as Southwestern Bible School; moved to Fort Worth and merged with South Central Bible Institute, 1941; moved to Waxahachie as Southwestern Bible Institute, 1943; as Southwestern Assemblies of God College,1963; as university, 1996); Dr. Kermit S. Bridges	96	1,702	**	NA
Southwestern Baptist Theological Seminary — Fort Worth; (3–Southern Baptist); 1908; Dr. Kenneth Hemphill	91	3,005	1,179	26
Southwestern Christian College — Terrell; (3–Church of Christ); 1948 (as Southern Bible Institute in Fort Worth; moved to Terrell and changed name, 1950); Dr. Jack Evans Sr.	20	220	NA	NA
Southwestern University — Georgetown; (3–Methodist); 1840 (merger of Rutersville College, 1840; McKenzie College, 1841; Wesleyan College, 1846; and Soule Univer-sity, 1855; first named Texas University; current name, 1875); Dr. Jake B. Schrum	127	1,270	NA	NA
Stephen F. Austin State University — Nacogdoches; (2); 1921; Dr. Baker Pattillo	712	11,990	8,527	NA
Sul Ross State University — Alpine (*See* **Texas State University System**)				
Sul Ross State University–Rio Grande College — Uvalde (*See* **Texas State Univer-sity System**)				
Tarleton State University — Stephenville (*See* **Texas A&M University System**)				
TARRANT COUNTY COLLEGE DISTRICT (9) — **Dr. Erma Johnson Hadley, interim chancellor.** Fort Worth; 1965 (as Tarrant County Junior College; name changed, 1999). System consists of following colleges and presidents:	1,756	39,596	7,980	21,571
Northeast Campus — Hurst; (7); Dr. Larry Darlage	412	10,975	7,130	5,553
Northwest Campus — Fort Worth; (7); Dr. Elva Concha LeBlanc	261	5,259	2,987	8,597

Name of Institution — Location; (*type or ownership, if private sectarian institution); date of founding; president (unless otherwise noted)	Number of Faculty †	Enrollment		
		Fall Term 2008	Summer Sessions 2008 §	Extension or Contin- ing Ed.
South Campus — Fort Worth, (7); Dr. Ernest L. Thomas				
Southeast Campus — Arlington, (7); Dr. Judith J. Carrier				
Trinity River Campus — Fort Worth, (7);				
Temple College — Temple; (7); 1926; Dr. Glenda O. Barron	261	5,128	2,065	1,163
Texarkana College — Texarkana; (7); 1927; Dr. Alan Rasco	215	4,924	1,812	4,000
Texas A&I University — Kingsville (See Texas A&M University–Kingsville under Texas A&M University System)				
TEXAS A&M UNIVERSITY SYSTEM (1) — Dr. Michael D. McKinney, chancellor. System consists of following colleges and presidents:				
Prairie View A&M University — Prairie View; (2); 1876 (as Alta Vista Agricultural Col- lege; as Prairie View State Normal Institute, 1879; as Prairie View Normal and Indus- trial College; as Prairie View A&M College, 1947, as branch of Texas A&M University System; current name, 1973); Dr. George C. Wright	467	8,350	3,389	NA
Tarleton State University — Stephenville; (2); 1899 (as John Tarleton College; as state- run John Tarleton Agricultural College,1917; as Tarleton State College, 1949; current name, 1973); includes campus in Killeen; Dr. F. Dominic Dottavio	585	9,634	5,352	NA
Texas A&M International University — Laredo; (2); 1970 (as Laredo State University; current name, 1993); Dr. Ray M. Keck III	300	5,856	4,324	NA
Texas A&M University — College Station; (2); 1876 (as Agricultural and Mechanical of Texas; current name,1963); includes College of Veterinary Medicine and College of Medicine at College Station; Dr. R. Bowen Loftin, acting president	3,730	48,039	18,622	NA
Texas A&M University–Commerce — Commerce; (2); 1889 (as East Texas Normal College; as East Texas State Teachers College, 1923; as East Texas State College, 1957; university status conferred and named changed to East Texas State University, 1965; transferred to Texas A&M System, 1995); includes ETSU Metroplex Commuter Facility, Mesquite; Dr. Dan R. Jones	330	8,566	4,834	152
Texas A&M University–Corpus Christi — Corpus Christi; (2); 1973 (as upper-level Corpus Christi State University; current name, 1993; 4-year in 1994); Dr. Flavius C. Killebrew	580	8,584	4,728	NA
Texas A&M University at Galveston — Galveston; (2); 1962 (as Texas Maritime Acad- emy; as 4-yr. Moody College of Marine Sciences and Maritime Resources, 1971); Dr. R. Bowen Loftin, CEO	170	1,772	803	NA
Texas A&M University–Kingsville — Kingsville; (2); 1925 (as South Texas Teachers College; as Texas College of Arts and Industries, 1929; as Texas A&I University, 1967; joined University of South Texas System, 1977; joined Texas A&M University System, 1993); Dr. Steven H. Tallant	471	7,134	5,443	1,312
Texas A&M University Health Science Center — (4); Includes Baylor College of Dentistry, College of Medicine, Graduate School of Biomedical Sciences, Institute of Biosciences and Technology, School of Rural Public Health, and HSC Statellite loca- tions; Dr. Nancy W. Dickey	1,077	1,695	NA	NA
Texas A&M University–Texarkana — Texarkana; (2); 1971 (as East Texas State Uni- versity at Texarkana; transferred to Texas A&M System and name changed, 1996); Dr. Carlisle Baxter (Bix) Rathburn III	135	1,666	1,444	NA
West Texas A&M University — Canyon; (2); 1910 (as West Texas State Normal Col- lege; as West Texas State Teachers College, 1923; as West Texas State College, 1949; as West Texas State Univ., 1949; currentt name, 1993); Dr. J. Patrick O'Brien	374	7,535	4,425	191
Texas Baptist Institute-Seminary — Henderson; (3–Calvary Baptist); 1948; Dr. Ray O. Brooks	16	50	NA	20
Texas Christian University — Fort Worth; (3–Disciples of Christ); 1873 (as AddRan Male and Female College at Thorp Spring; moved to Waco, 1895; as AddRan Chris- tian University, 1889; current name,1902; moved to Fort Worth, 1910); Dr. Victor J. Boschini Jr., chancellor	811	8,696	2,604	2,050
Texas Chiropractic College — Pasadena; (5); 1908; Dr. Richard G. Brassard	39	350	352	NA
Texas College — Tyler; (3–C.M.E.); 1894; Dr. Billy C. Hawkins	42	757	109	0
Texas College of Osteopathic Medicine — Fort Worth (See University of North Texas Health Science Center at Fort Worth)				
Texas Lutheran University — Seguin; (3–Evangelical Lutheran); 1891 (as Evangeli- cal Lutheran College in Brenham; as Lutheran College of Seguin, 1912; as Texas Lutheran College,1932; as university, 1996); Rev. Ann M. Svennungsen	142	1,432	217	161
Texas Southern University — Houston; (2); 1926 (as Houston Colored Junior College; as 4-yr. Houston College for Negroes, mid-1930s; as Texas State University for Negroes, 1947; present name, 1951); Dr. John M. Rudley	578	11,224	2,818	50
Texas Southmost College — Brownsville (See The University of Texas at Browns- ville under University of Texas System)				
TEXAS STATE TECHNICAL COLLEGE SYSTEM (6) — Dr. Willaim Segura, chancellor. System consists of following colleges and presidents:	534	13,394	7,551	4,089
Texas State Technical College–Harlingen — Harlingen; 1967; Dr. J. Gilbert Leal	**	4,350	**	**
Texas State Technical College–Marshall — Marshall; 1991 (as extension center; as independent college, 1999); Dr. Randall Wooten	46	687	393	246
Texas State Technical College–Waco — Waco; 1965 (as James Connally Technical Institute; current name, 1969); Dr. Elton E. Stuckly Jr.	280	4,491	2,602	88
Texas State Technical College–West Texas — Abilene, Breckenridge, Brownwood and Sweetwater; 1970; Dr. Mike Reeser	123	1,725	1,208	1,990

Name of Institution — Location; (*type or ownership, if private sectarian institution); date of founding; president (unless otherwise noted)	Number of Faculty †	Enrollment		
		Fall Term 2008	Summer Sessions 2008 §	Extension or Continuing Ed.
TEXAS STATE UNIVERSITY SYSTEM (1) — Dr. Charles R. Matthews, chancellor. System consists of following colleges and presidents:				
Lamar University — Beaumont; (2); 1923 (as South Park Junior College; as Lamar College, 1932; as Lamar State College of Technology, 1951; present name, 1971; transferred from Lamar University System, 1995); Dr. James M. Simmons	561	13,280	6,836	4,263
Lamar State College–Orange — Orange; (10); 1969 (transferred from Lamar University System, 1995; current name, 2000); Dr. J. Michael Shahan	97	2,011	694	97
Lamar State College–Port Arthur — Port Arthur; (10); 1909 (as Port Arthur College; joined Lamar University System, 1975; joined TSU System, 1995; current name, 2000); Dr. W. Sam Monroe	115	1,985	1,772	485
Lamar Institute of Technology — Beaumont; (10); (joined TSU System, 1995); Dr. Paul Szuch	162	2,885	889	650
Sam Houston State University — Huntsville; (2); 1879; Dr. James F. Gaertner	669	16,663	10,722	NA
Sul Ross State University — Alpine; (2); 1917 (as Sul Ross State Normal College; as Sul Ross State Teachers College, 1923; as Sul Ross State College, 1949; current name, 1969); Dr. R. Vic Morgan	148	1,937	1,024	NA
Sul Ross State University – Rio Grande College — Uvalde, Eagle Pass, Del Rio (2); 1973 (current name, 1995); Dr. R. Vic Morgan	30	938	1,020	NA
Texas State University–San Marcos — San Marcos; (2); 1903 (as Southwest Texas Normal School; as Southwest Texas State Normal College, 1918; as Southwest Texas State Teachers College, 1923; as Southwest Texas State College, 1959; as Southwest Texas State University, 1969; current name, 2003); Dr. Denise M. Trauth	1,300	29,105	17,011	1,759
TEXAS TECH UNIVERSITY SYSTEM (1) —Kent Hance, chancellor. System consists of following colleges and presidents:				
Angelo State University — San Angelo; (2); 1928 (was part of Texas State University System; joined Texas Tech system, 2007); Dr. Joseph C. Rallo	336	6,155	3,362	1,340
Texas Tech University — Lubbock; (2); 1923 (as Texas Technological College; current name, 1969); Dr. Guy Bailey	2,488	28,422	16,990	**
Texas Tech University Health Sciences Center — Lubbock; (4); 1972; Dr. John Charles Baldwin	596	2,272	**	NA
Texas Wesleyan University — Fort Worth; (3–United Methodist); 1891 (as college; current name, 1989); Dr. Harold G. Jeffcoat	266	3,202	695	NA
Texas Woman's University — Denton; (2); 1901 (as College of Industrial Arts; as Texas State College for Women, 1934; current name, 1957); Dr. Ann Stuart, chancellor	†† 700	12,500	17,000	NA
Tomball College — Tomball (*See* **Lone Star College System**)				
Trinity University — San Antonio; (3–Presbyterian); 1869 (at Tehuacana; moved to Waxahachie, 1902; to San Antonio, 1942); Dr. John R. Brazil	243	2,703	356	NA
Trinity Valley Community College — Athens; (7); 1946 (as Henderson County Junior College); includes campus at Terrell; Dr. Glendon S. Forgey	124	6,456	2,500	1,400
Tyler Junior College — Tyler; (7); 1926; Dr. Mike Metke	492	9,422	3,951	1,782
University of Central Texas — Killeen (*See* **Tarleton State University** under **Texas A&M University System**)				
University of Dallas — Irving; (3–Catholic); 1956; Dr. Francis M. Lazarus	244	2,977	1,526	200
UNIVERSITY OF HOUSTON SYSTEM (1) — Dr. Renu Khator, chancellor. System consists of following colleges and presidents:				
University of Houston — Houston; (2); 1927; Dr. Renu Khator	3,036	35,100	NA	NA
University of Houston–Clear Lake — Houston; (2); 1974; Dr. William A. Staples	687	7,658	4,350	NA
University of Houston–Downtown — Houston; (2); 1948 (as South Texas College; joined University of Houston System, 1974); Dr. William V. Flores	570	12,283	7,505	2,177
University of Houston–Victoria — Victoria; (2); 1973; Dr. Tim Hudson	176	3,174	2,033	NA
University of the Incarnate Word — San Antonio; (3–Catholic); 1881 (as Incarnate Word College; current name, 1996); Dr. Louis J. Agnese Jr.	¶ 200	6,702	NA	1,012
University of Mary Hardin–Baylor — Belton; (3–Baptist); 1845; Dr. Randy O'Rear	238	2,701	742	NA
UNIVERSITY OF NORTH TEXAS SYSTEM (1) — Lee F. Jackson, chancellor. System consists of following colleges and presidents:				
University of North Texas — Denton; (2); 1890 (as North Texas Normal College; as North Texas State Teachers College, 1923; as North Texas State College, 1949; as university, 1961; current name, 1988); Dr. Gretchen M. Bataille	2,098	33,443	15,823	
University of North Texas Dallas Campus — Dallas; (2); (2000); Dr. John Ellis Price, CEO				
University of North Texas Health Science Center at Fort Worth — Fort Worth; (4);1966 (as private college; part of North Texas State University, 1975; current name, 1993); Dr. Scott B. Ransom		222	1,021	777
University of St. Thomas — Houston; (3); 1947; Dr. Robert R. Ivany	273	3,246	2,106	NA
THE UNIVERSITY OF TEXAS SYSTEM (1) — Dr. Francisco G. Cigarroa, chancellor. System consists of following colleges and presidents:	18,198	201,058	**	5,951
University of Texas at Arlington, The — Arlington; (2); 1895 (as Arlington College; as state-run Grubbs Vocational College, 1917; as North Texas Agricultural and Mechanical College, 1923; as Arlington State College, 1949; current name, 1967); Dr. James D. Spaniolo	1,973	25,084	11,164	7,468
University of Texas at Austin, The — Austin; (2); 1883; Dr. William Powers Jr.	2,137	50,403	**	**

Name of Institution — Location; (*type or ownership, if private sectarian institution); date of founding; president (unless otherwise noted)	Number of Faculty †	Enrollment Fall Term 2008	Enrollment Summer Sessions 2008 §	Enrollment Extension or Contin- ing Ed.
University of Texas at Brownsville, The, and Texas Southmost College — (2); 1973 (as branch of Pan American College; as University of Texas–Pan American at Brownsville, 1989; present name, 1991); Dr. Juliet V. Garcia **Texas Southmost College** — Brownsville; (7); 1926 (as Brownsville Junior College; current name, 1949); Dr. Juliet V. Garcia	¶ 216	19,923	7,653	1,651
University of Texas at Dallas, The — Richardson; (2); 1961 (as Graduate Research of the Southwest; as Southwest Center for Advanced Studies, 1967; joined UT System with current name, 1969; full undergraduate program, 1975); Dr. David Daniel	772	14,944	**	NA
University of Texas at El Paso, The — El Paso; (2); 1913 (as Texas College of Mines and Metallurgy; as Texas Western College of UT, 1949; current name, 1967); Dr. Diana S. Natalicio	1,083	19,842	8,716	2,921
University of Texas–Pan American, The — Edinburg; (2); 1927 (as Edinburg Junior College; as 4-yr. Pan American College, 1952; as Pan American University, 1971; current name, 1991); Dr. Charles Sorber, interim president	819	17,534	15,165	50
University of Texas of the Permian Basin, The — Odessa; (2); 1969 (as 2-yr., upper-level institution; expanded to 4-yr., 1991); Dr. W. David Watts	128	3,615	2,156	140
University of Texas at San Antonio, The — San Antonio; (2); 1969; Dr. Ricardo Romo	1,271	28,413	**	**
University of Texas at Tyler, The — Tyler; (2); 1971 (as Tyler State College; as Texas Eastern University, 1975; joined UT System, 1979); Dr. Rodney H. Mabry	399	6,117	2,034	NA
University of Texas Telecampus, The — 1998; Exec. Vice-Chancellor Dr. David Prior	NA	5,093	2,898	NA
University of Texas Health Science Center at Houston, The — Houston; (4); 1972; *includes* Dental Branch (1905); Graduate School of Biomedical Sciences (1963); Medical School (1970); School of Allied Health Sciences (1973); School of Nursing (1972); School of Public Health (1967); Division of Continuing Education (1958); Dr. Larry R. Kaiser	1,389	3,865	2,306	24,875
University of Texas Health Science Center at San Antonio, The — San Antonio; (4) 1968; *includes* Dental School (1970); Graduate School of Biomedical Sciences (1970); Health Science Center (1972); Medical School (1959 as South Texas Medical School of UT; present name, 1966); School of Allied Health Sciences (1976); School of Nursing (1969); Dr. William L. Henrich, interim president	1,400	2,845	NA	NA
University of Texas Health Science Center at Tyler, The — Tyler; (4); 1949 (as East Texas Tuberculosis Sanatorium; as East Texas Chest Hospital, 1971; joined UT system with current name, 1977); Dr. Kirk A. Calhoun	125	75	NA	NA
University of Texas M.D. Anderson Cancer Center, The — Houston; (4); 1941; Dr. John Mendelsohn	1,050	70	NA	2,252
University of Texas Medical Branch at Galveston, The — Galveston; (4) 1891; *includes* Graduate School of Biomedical Sciences (1952); Medical School (1891); School of Allied Health Sciences (1968); School of Nursing (1890); Dr. David L. Callender	1,885	2,338	NA	NA
University of Texas Southwestern Medical Center at Dallas, The — Dallas; (4); 1943 (as private institution; as Southwestern Medical College of UT, 1948; as UT Southwestern Medical School at Dallas, 1967; joined UT Health Science Center at Dallas, 1972; *includes* Graduate School of Biomedical Sciences (1947); School of Allied Health Sciences (1968); Southwestern Medical School (1943); Dr. Daniel Podolsky	2,223	4,327	NA	NA
Vernon College — Vernon; (7); 1970; includes Wichita Falls campus; Dr. Dusty R. Johnston	139	2,960	2,180	930
Victoria College, The — Victoria; (7); 1925; Dr. Thomas Butler	111	3,991	2,211	3,181
Wayland Baptist University — Plainview; (3–Southern Baptist); 1910; Dr. Paul Armes	329	6,039	4,516	NA
Weatherford College — Weatherford; (7); 1869 (as branch of Southwestern University; as denominational junior college, 1922; as municipal junior college, 1949); Dr. Joseph Birmingham	225	4,801	2,319	1,012
Western Texas College — Snyder; (7); 1969; Dr. Michael Dreith	72	1,698	1,099	876
Wharton County Junior College — Wharton; (7); 1946; Dr. Betty A. McCrohan	293	6,115	4,006	300
Wiley College — Marshall; (3–Methodist); 1873; Dr. Haywood L. Strickland	85	967	182	20

Key to Table Symbols

*Type:
(1) Public University System
(2) Public University
(3) Independent Senior College or University
(4) Public Medical School or Health Science Center
(5) Independent Medical, Dental or Chiropractic School

(6) Public Technical College System
(7) Public Community College
(8) Independent Junior College
(9) Public Community College System
(10) Public Lower-Level Institution

NA — Not applicable
† Unless otherwise noted, faculty count includes professors, associate professors, adjunct professors, instructors and tutors, both full- and part-time, but does not include voluntary instructors.
‡ No reply received to questionnaire. Name of president and number of students enrolled in fall 2008 obtained from the institution's website or the Texas Higher Education Coordinating Board website: www.txhighereddata.org/Interactive/Institutions.cfm.
# Includes faculty and enrollment at all branches or divisions.

§ Figure may combine multiple summer sessions.
¶ Full-time faculty only.
** Information not supplied by institution.
†† Approximate count.
§§ Latest figures available from institution's website were for 2008–2009 school year.
§§§ Enrollment in online courses only.
~ Number of students in extension courses or continuing education for all of fiscal year 2008.

Business

The Mary Kay Inc. world headquarters in Addison/North Dallas. Robert Plocheck photo.

Economy & Employment

Banking & Insurance

Oil & Gas

Minerals

Media

Construction

Commercial Fishing

Utilities

Energy Prices Benefit Texas Economy in 2008

Source: Excepted from the State of Texas Annual Cash Report 2008, Comptroller of Public Accounts.

The Texas economy continued growing during fiscal 2008, despite the weakening national economy. While the nation lost 0.2 percent of its jobs, Texas' nonfarm employment advanced by 2.4 percent, the fifth consecutive year of job growth.

Texas' economy benefited greatly from hiring in the natural resources and mining industry, as well as service jobs that support the energy industry. The New York Mercantile Exchange (NYMEX) energy prices spiked in fiscal 2008, with oil hitting $145.29 per barrel and natural gas reaching $13.53 per 1,000 cubic feet, bringing economic vitality to the state's energy sector. The prices have since dropped, but remain high enough for active oil and gas exploration to continue.

Increasing fuel prices had negative effects on the nation's consumers, but the oil and natural gas industry — five times more concentrated in Texas than in the nation — provided Texas with a large number of high-paying jobs.

As a result, the downside on Texas' consuming sectors was to some extent offset by the positive effects for energy businesses and producers, reducing the effect on the state economy's bottom line as measured by the gross domestic product.

The Consumer Confidence Index, a monthly measure of the level of optimism that consumers have in the economy, dropped precipitously in this region during the fiscal year, but the decline was even steeper elsewhere. The rise in the price of fuels and other commodities, declining stock market and housing prices, and an increasingly deep fallout from the nation's sub-prime mortgage predicament kept consumers uncertain and shaky about the status of the economy and its outlook. Texas' West South Central regional index ended the year 22 percent lower than at the beginning, while the national index dropped 46 percent.

As the nation's mortgage lending and housing crisis deepened, housing construction starts fell precipitously. Fortunately, road and other non-residential construction in Texas remained very active, buffering residential construction job losses.

Utility system construction was the fastest in job growth, prompted by extensive construction of pipelines, petrochemical refineries and other facilities related to the state's oil and natural gas industry. Employment in heavy engineering construction grew rapidly (7.1 percent) as well.

Highway construction was one of the areas where employment jumped by 4.0 percent. And, while the U.S. construction industry saw a second consecutive year of job declines (down 5.7 percent in the recent year), Texas construction employment rose by 23,800 jobs or 3.7 percent.

Even with a substantial 35 percent drop in single-family housing starts in Texas, jobs related to the construction of buildings actually rose by 3.4 percent, owing to a 22 percent increase in the value of non-residential buildings being put in place. Nonresidential buildings include commercial and industrial buildings.

Although Texas fared better than many other states because single-family housing here has not been overvalued, defaults in sub-prime mortgages kept home foreclosures higher than normal (but at half the national rate), increasing both the number of homes on the market and the demand for apartments. Consequently housing permits grew by 0.8 percent during the 2008 fiscal year, keeping construction jobs growing in the multi-family segment of the residential market.

Texas' service-providing industries, which account for more than 83 percent of the state's total nonfarm employment, remain the primary driver of employment growth, accounting for seven-eighths of the net job growth. ☆

Gross Domestic Product in Current Dollars

	Millions of $ dollars			Percent of U.S. total			GDP* 2008	
	2003	2005	2007	2003	2005	2007	European Union	14,960,000
United States	**10,896,356**	**12,346,871**	**13,743,021**	**100.0**	**100.0**	**100.0**	United States	14,580,000
1. California	1,410,539	1,632,822	1,812,968	12.9	13.2	13.2	China	7,800,000
2. Texas	**828,456**	**979,311**	**1,141,965**	**7.6**	**7.9**	**8.3**	Japan	4,487,000
3. New York	847,123	953,641	1,103,024	7.8	7.7	8.0	India	3,319,000
4. Florida	556,748	670,237	734,519	5.1	5.4	5.3	Germany	2,863,000
5. Illinois	509,161	554,099	609,570	4.7	4.5	4.4	United Kingdom	2,281,000
6. Pennsylvania	439,241	482,413	531,110	4.0	3.9	3.9	Russia	2,225,000
7. Ohio	402,607	439,271	466,309	3.7	3.6	3.4	Brazil	2,030,000
8. New Jersey	388,645	425,497	465,484	3.6	3.4	3.4	Italy	1,801,000
9. North Carolina	307,871	349,216	399,446	2.8	2.8	2.9	Mexico	1,578,000
10. Georgia	317,490	359,694	396,504	2.9	2.9	2.9	Spain	1,378,000

Source: Bureau of Economic Analysis, U.S. Department of Commerce.

*Estimated Gross Domestic Product in millions of U.S. dollars from the World Factbook of the CIA.

Texas Gross Domestic Product, 1999–2008, By Industry (in millions)

Industry	1999	2000	2001	2002	2003	2004	2005	2006	2007	2008
Agriculture, Forestry, Fishing/Hunting	$6,752	$6,470	$6,394	$7,457	$8,094	$9,878	$8,707	$7,807	$9,651	$10,596
% change*	11.6	(4.2)	(1.2)	16.6	8.5	21.0	(11.9)	(10.3)	23.6	9.8
Natural Resources and Mining	27,652	45,182	44,072	39,219	57,917	68,248	91,549	104,167	110,336	121,108
% change	19.0	63.4	(2.5)	(11.0)	47.7	19.1	34.1	13.8	5.9	9.8
Construction	32,836	36,882	40,259	41,871	43,475	45,648	50,577	55,324	52,203	52,283
% change	11.1	12.3	9.2	4.0	3.8	3.7	10.8	9.4	(5.6)	0.2
Manufacturing	91,601	92,981	92,273	94,462	93,158	119,028	126,490	142,846	153,180	160,783
% change	(6.5)	1.5	(0.8)	2.4	(1.4)	27.6	6.3	12.9	7.2	5.0
Trade, Transportation, Utilities	146,595	155,785	160,789	164,723	170,757	181,596	191,652	206,664	222,262	235,138
% change	8.2	6.3	3.2	2.4	3.7	5.3	5.5	6.6	7.2	5.8
Information	33,295	35,865	36,992	36,531	36,040	38,545	41,122	43,829	48,069	51,109
% change	8.8	7.7	3.1	(1.2)	(1.3)	7.7	6.7	6.6	9.7	6.3
Financial Activities	107,929	117,200	125,928	128,219	133,439	137,454	145,254	157,743	167,219	177,303
% change	8.7	8.6	7.4	1.8	4.1	4.7	5.7	8.6	6.0	6.0
Professional and Business Services	69,387	73,208	82,195	83,937	88,719	93,307	104,248	114,443	128,415	140,082
% change	10.3	5.5	12.3	2.1	3.9	7.7	11.7	9.8	12.2	9.1
Educational and Health Services	39,357	42,359	46,797	51,380	54,761	59,440	61,674	65,744	70,939	75,821
% change	5.8	7.6	10.5	9.8	6.6	7.8	3.8	6.6	7.9	6.9
Leisure and Hospitality Services	21,764	23,106	23,993	25,492	26,479	27,877	29,551	32,109	34,011	36,167
% change	9.0	6.2	3.8	6.2	3.9	4.6	6.0	8.7	5.9	6.3
Other Private Services	16,576	17,603	18,106	18,679	19,644	19,889	21,143	22,458	23,805	25,150
% change	4.1	6.2	2.9	3.2	5.2	1.4	6.3	6.2	6.0	5.7
Government and Schools	75,249	80,590	84,448	91,512	96,326	100,759	107,343	114,970	121,866	128,635
% change	5.9	7.1	4.8	8.4	5.3	5.0	5.9	5.5	4.4	4.4
TOTAL	$668,993	$727,231	$762,246	$783,482	$828,809	$901,669	$979,330	$1,068,104	$1,141,956	$1,215,175
% change	6.3	8.7	4.8	2.8	5.8	9.1	9.4	9.1	6.9	6.4
TOTAL (in 2000 chained dollars)**	$699,101	$727,229	$745,325	$760,588	$770,975	$806,055	$825,217	$867,791	$903,383	$940,334
% change	4.9	4.0	2.5	2.0	1.4	4.8	2.4	5.2	4.1	4.1

*Percent change from the previous year. ** In 1996, the U.S. Department of Commerce introduced the chained-dollar measure. The new measure is based on the average weights of goods and services in successive pairs of years. It is "chained" because the second year in each pair, with its weights, becomes the first year of the next pair. Source: 2008 Comprehensive Annual Financial Report for the State of Texas.

Per Capita Income by County, 2007

Below are listed data for 2007 for total personal income and per capita income by county. Total income is reported in millions of dollars. The middle column indicates the percent of change in total income from 2006 to 2007.

In the far right column is the county's rank in the state for per capita income. Loving County, a unique case — with a total population in 2007 of 54, leads in per capita income with $99,593. Midland County, also in the Permian Basin, is second with $52,974.

The lowest per capita income is in Starr County, along the Rio Grande, at $13,854.

Source: Bureau of Economic Analysis, U.S. Department of Commerce.

County	Total Income ($ mil)	% change 06/07	Per capita income	Rank
United States	$11,634,322	6.0	$ 38,615	–
Metropolitan	10,213,729	6.0	40,544	–
Nonmetro	1,420,593	6.1	28,773	–
Texas	$ 884,191	7.6	$ 37,083	–
Metropolitan	801,656	7.6	38,398	–
Nonmetro	82,535	8.0	27,828	–
Anderson	$ 1,327	9.2	$ 23,399	220
Andrews	446	13.6	33,971	51
Angelina	2,694	5.9	32,627	62
Aransas	825	7.2	33,602	55
Archer	324	6.7	36,236	30
Armstrong	62	–0.5	29,943	101
Atascosa	1,103	6.8	25,358	195
Austin	943	9.1	35,580	37
Bailey	173	5.5	27,444	156
Bandera	636	6.2	31,632	81
Bastrop	1,876	6.7	26,011	183
Baylor	103	16.8	26,746	167
Bee	682	8.5	20,887	237
Bell	9,559	10.2	34,414	48
Bexar	54,324	6.1	34,163	50
Blanco	334	10.0	37,135	26
Borden	18	43.8	31,604	82
Bosque	486	7.4	27,274	160
Bowie	2,770	6.4	30,291	97
Brazoria	10,120	8.3	34,529	47
Brazos	4,468	6.2	26,147	179
Brewster	269	2.9	29,103	125
Briscoe	43	16.1	28,896	131
Brooks	159	8.0	21,016	236
Brown	1,001	5.2	26,171	178
Burleson	480	6.5	28,960	127
Burnet	1,456	8.1	33,413	59
Caldwell	873	4.8	23,849	218
Calhoun	571	6.4	28,187	140
Callahan	377	9.4	28,046	144
Cameron	7,570	7.5	19,667	244
Camp	371	6.5	29,824	107
Carson	206	19.8	32,550	63
Cass	818	6.8	27,892	147
Castro	278	10.6	38,645	20
Chambers	1,117	8.5	38,856	18
Cherokee	1,319	5.9	27,439	157
Childress	140	7.5	18,603	248
Clay	350	6.1	31,473	70

County	Total Income ($ mil)	% change 06/07	Per capita income	Rank
Cochran	$ 98	8,0	$ 31,913	70
Coke	80	9.0	23,036	226
Coleman	231	10.2	27,152	163
Collin	35,116	10.4	48,044	6
Collingsworth	94	12.4	31,669	78
Colorado	649	8.2	31,660	79
Comal	3,814	9.5	36,414	29
Comanche	388	9.6	28,783	132
Concho	73	18.0	20,405	241
Cooke	1,411	10.0	36,787	27
Coryell	2,282	8.0	31,643	80
Cottle	50	11.6	31,688	76
Crane	113	9.7	29,186	124
Crockett	88	13.3	23,317	223
Crosby	195	9.3	31,146	87
Culberson	54	11.2	21,887	230
Dallam	206	18.9	33,534	56
Dallas	107,556	5.0	45,131	7
Dawson	322	9.2	23,372	221
Deaf Smith	465	8.5	25,287	196
Delta	135	13.2	25,066	202
Denton	24,127	8.7	39,316	16
DeWitt	528	8.0	26,770	165
Dickens	50	6.9	20,042	243
Dimmit	210	9.3	21,490	232
Donley	101	9.1	25,823	186
Duval	302	9.4	24,845	204
Eastland	590	6.5	32,213	68
Ector	4,114	11.5	31,787	73
Edwards	41	10.1	21,054	235
Ellis	4,427	8.7	30,958	94
El Paso	19,406	6.7	26,585	169
Erath	1,008	11.9	28,331	137
Falls	391	5.1	23,091	225
Fannin	832	6.8	25,258	197
Fayette	790	7.1	35,196	39
Fisher	109	22.2	27,655	152
Floyd	198	18.5	29,847	106
Foard	37	19.9	26,318	175
Fort Bend	21,206	10.0	41,779	10
Franklin	317	6.7	28,517	135
Freestone	489	5.4	26,107	180
Frio	333	8.2	20,718	239
Gaines	397	13.1	26,807	164
Galveston	10,914	6.7	38,553	21
Garza	147	14.6	31,362	86
Gillespie	874	7.1	37,366	25

County	Total Income ($ mil)	% change 06/07	Per capita income	Rank	County	Total Income ($ mil)	% change 06/07	Per capita income	Rank
Glasscock	$ 46	26.0	$ 39,825	14	Lee	$ 497	7.6	$ 30,524	96
Goliad	188	6.6	26,489	172	Leon	469	9.1	28,588	134
Gonzales	510	3.7	26,757	166	Liberty	2,296	6.3	30,638	95
Gray	793	14.0	36,035	33	Limestone	595	6.8	26,669	168
Grayson	3,412	6.3	28,901	130	Lipscomb	100	14.6	33,609	54
Gregg	4,525	7.5	38,717	19	Live Oak	292	9.1	25,880	185
Grimes	630	7.9	24,565	212	Llano	581	8.2	31,698	75
Guadalupe	3,605	9.8	32,083	69	Loving	5	13.3	99,593	1
Hale	845	3.9	23,758	219	Lubbock	7,910	5.1	30,212	98
Hall	71	6.5	20,449	240	Lynn	181	43.9	31,043	90
Hamilton	238	5.1	29,532	112	Madison	330	7.4	24,786	206
Hansford	189	10.2	36,735	28	Marion	260	6.9	24,366	216
Hardeman	111	7.2	27,179	162	Martin	124	12.8	27,854	149
Hardin	1,669	6.7	32,380	67	Mason	102	4.4	26,351	174
Harris	194,178	9.1	49,634	5	Matagorda	959	7.3	26,027	182
Harrison	2,050	9.1	32,435	66	Maverick	862	8.1	16,789	252
Hartley	152	2.3	29,444	116	McCulloch	218	9.9	27,837	151
Haskell	152	13.9	29,103	125	McLennan	6,773	5.8	29,730	109
Hays	4,078	9.3	28,729	133	McMullen	24	3.5	27,212	161
Hemphill	169	20.8	50,319	3	Medina	1,162	7.8	26,557	170
Henderson	2,175	5.2	27,627	153	Menard	54	10.0	25,680	187
Hidalgo	12,922	8.3	18,316	249	Midland	6,688	10.6	52,974	2
Hill	923	7.9	26,240	176	Milam	693	8.1	27,970	146
Hockley	664	7.9	29,906	103	Mills	132	4.6	26,388	173
Hood	1,772	7.8	36,142	31	Mitchell	181	12.0	19,460	246
Hopkins	938	8.8	27,843	150	Montague	640	10.2	32,648	61
Houston	563	7.6	24,807	205	Montgomery	17,562	9.7	42,704	9
Howard	911	7.8	28,262	138	Moore	588	8.0	29,542	111
Hudspeth	75	43.6	23,252	224	Morris	378	6.4	28,912	129
Hunt	2,394	5.3	28,944	128	Motley	32	19.1	25,216	200
Hutchinson	752	6.4	34,600	45	Nacogdoches	1,524	6.5	24,491	214
Irion	55	4.5	31,785	74	Navarro	1,238	6.8	25,228	199
Jack	260	12.7	29,509	114	Newton	308	6.1	22,376	229
Jackson	384	7.6	27,370	158	Nolan	401	10.4	27,539	154
Jasper	973	6.3	28,230	139	Nueces	10,875	6.3	33,970	52
Jeff Davis	56	10.3	24,746	208	Ochiltree	359	10.8	37,838	24
Jefferson	8,191	5.0	33,795	53	Oldham	53	9.0	25,628	189
Jim Hogg	135	9.7	27,298	159	Orange	2,565	6.2	31,076	89
Jim Wells	1,214	10.3	29,523	113	Palo Pinto	820	5.2	30,068	99
Johnson	4,383	6.6	29,347	120	Panola	731	10.8	31,882	71
Jones	450	11.7	23,368	222	Parker	3,801	10.5	35,053	42
Karnes	303	8.2	20,175	242	Parmer	242	5.9	25,953	184
Kaufman	2,839	8.9	29,430	117	Pecos	307	8.1	19,306	247
Kendall	1,382	10.2	44,325	8	Polk	1,471	6.5	31,832	72
Kenedy	11	−9.0	28,398	136	Potter	3,531	6.2	29,331	121
Kent	16	−2.3	22,390	228	Presidio	132	8.3	17,601	251
Kerr	1,832	6.6	38,431	23	Rains	277	8.6	24,768	207
Kimble	113	6.2	25,491	192	Randall	3,916	8.3	34,548	46
King	7	−1.5	24,959	203	Reagan	101	24.2	33,478	57
Kinney	76	6.7	22,984	227	Real	72	5.3	24,233	217
Kleberg	861	6.2	28,095	142	Red River	322	6.9	24,629	210
Knox	103	9.0	29,415	118	Reeves	244	10.7	21,804	231
Lamar	1,350	8.1	27,500	155	Refugio	228	10.0	31,015	93
Lamb	351	6.5	25,367	194	Roberts	26	25.1	31,022	92
Lampasas	732	12.4	35,078	41	Robertson	469	8.6	29,753	108
La Salle	116	4.3	19,467	245	Rockwall	2,997	12.0	40,665	11
Lavaca	608	7.0	32,450	65	Runnels	264	9.4	25,636	188

County	Total Income ($ mil)	% change 06/07	Per capita income	Rank	County	Total Income ($ mil)	% change 06/07	Per capita income	Rank
Rusk	1,361	8.1	28,081	143	Trinity	347	6.1	24,520	213
Sabine	296	7.6	29,372	119	Tyler	521	6.2	25,607	190
San Augustine	217	7.3	25,198	201	Upshur	1,067	9.0	28,164	141
San Jacinto	693	7.2	27,996	145	Upton	101	16.9	33,421	58
San Patricio	2,002	8.1	29,272	122	Uvalde	668	7.2	25,238	198
San Saba	146	8.9	24,596	211	Val Verde	1,212	7.2	25,381	193
Schleicher	68	15.0	24,413	215	Van Zandt	1,636	5.6	31,585	83
Scurry	502	13.1	31,436	85	Victoria	3,026	6.6	35,121	40
Shackelford	124	16.4	39,133	17	Walker	1,367	6.4	21,385	234
Shelby	690	6.9	26,190	177	Waller	1,111	7.2	31,025	91
Sherman	144	35.7	50,114	4	Ward	306	13.0	30,025	100
Smith	6,872	6.3	34,713	44	Washington	1,137	7.4	35,618	36
Somervell	245	8.1	31,676	77	Webb	4,959	8.1	21,423	233
Starr	850	7.5	13,854	254	Wharton	1,216	6.3	29,861	105
Stephens	281	9.2	29,589	110	Wheeler	193	13.1	40,572	12
Sterling	32	22.2	25,509	191	Wichita	4,461	5.8	34,889	43
Stonewall	51	14.6	35,968	34	Wilbarger	414	5.6	29,890	104
Sutton	169	21.1	39,469	15	Willacy	424	11.1	20,765	238
Swisher	190	–2.1	24,695	209	Williamson	13,266	12.6	35,659	35
Tarrant	65,870	6.5	38,538	22	Wilson	1,153	9.3	29,455	115
Taylor	4,179	7.7	33,047	60	Winkler	211	12.1	32,488	64
Terrell	24	9.9	26,042	181	Wise	1,719	8.5	29,918	102
Terry	355	11.8	29,197	123	Wood	1,110	8.2	26,537	171
Throckmorton	57	22.2	34,299	49	Yoakum	262	15.4	35,320	38
Titus	815	4.9	27,885	148	Young	637	6.6	36,111	32
Tom Green	3,315	5.6	31,090	88	Zapata	239	10.9	17,637	250
Travis	39,213	4.5	40,430	13	Zavala	184	8.2	15,815	253

Average Work Hours and Earnings

The following table compares the **average weekly earnings**, **hours worked per week** and **average hourly wage** in Texas for selected industries in January 2009 and January 2008. Figures are provided by the Texas Workforce Commission.

Industry	Avg. Weekly Earnings		Avg. Weekly Hours		Avg. Hourly Earnings	
	Jan. 09	Jan. 08	Jan. 09	Jan. 08	Jan. 09	Jan. 08
Mining and Logging	$ 640.37	$ 685.72	40.3	43.4	$ 15.89	$ 15.80
Mining (including Oil & Gas)	687.98	717.84	41.0	43.4	16.78	16.54
Manufacturing	595.33	588.28	41.4	41.9	14.38	14.04
Durable Goods	586.98	578.43	41.6	42.5	14.11	13.61
Fabricated Metal Product Mfg.	540.55	604.49	40.1	47.3	13.48	12.78
Aerospace Products/Parts	1,643.79	NA	44.9	NA	36.61	NA
Non-Durable Goods	615.82	608.18	41.0	40.9	15.02	14.87
Trade, Transportation, Utilities						
Wholesale Trade	616.53	634.37	38.8	39.5	15.89	16.06
Machinery, Equipment, Supplies	551.45	581.99	37.9	41.9	14.55	13.89
Retail Trade						
Auto Dealers/Parts	578.92	593.25	35.3	35.0	16.40	16.95
Building Material/Garden Equip.	418.54	386.48	36.3	34.6	11.53	11.17
Food/Beverage Stores	343.66	303.95	33.3	31.4	10.32	9.68
Gasoline Stations	310.49	308.09	36.4	35.7	8.53	8.63
Clothing/Accessories Stores	215.59	234.23	20.3	22.5	10.62	10.41
Information						
Telecommunications	935.70	434.97	34.1	27.0	27.44	16.11

NA – Not Available

Employment in Texas by Industry

Employment in Texas increased to 10,461,200 in January 2009, up from 10,439,700 in January 2008. The following table shows Texas Workforce Commission estimates of the nonagricultural labor force by industry for January 2008 and 2009. The column at the extreme right shows the percent change during the year in the number employed. *Source: Texas Workforce Commission. Additional information available at the website www.twc.state.ts.us.*

Industry	2009	2008	Chng.	Industry	2009	2008	Chng.
(in thousands, 000)				Transportation/Utilities	428.4	433.4	−1.2
GOODS PRODUCING	1,757.3	1,799.1	−2.3	Utilities	48.8	46.4	5.2
				Transportation	379.6	387.0	−1.9
Mining	231.6	216.8	6.8	Air	63.9	64.9	−1.5
Oil & Gas Extraction	84.6	78.5	7.8	Trucking	113.9	116.7	−2.4
Support Activities	137.7	127.4	8.1	Pipeline	13.1	12.4	5.6
Construction	631.5	653.8	−3.4	Support Activities	73.1	69.5	5.2
Manufacturing	891.3	926.7	−3.8	Couriers/Messengers	35.6	37.5	−5.1
Durable Goods	586.5	609.3	−3.7	Warehousing/Storage	47.4	47.3	0.2
Wood Products	22.9	25.7	−10.9	Information	208.6	219.0	−4.7
Furniture/Fixtures	27.4	29.9	−8.4	Publishing	46.2	48.7	−5.1
Primary Metals	24.8	25.7	−3.5	Telecommunications	96.7	97.7	−1.0
Fabricated Metal Industries	130.2	132.4	−1.7	Internet/Data Search	28.1	29.4	−4.4
Machinery	94.6	94.4	0.2	**Financial Activities**	645.9	641.7	0.7
Computers/Electronics	105.3	110.0	−4.3	Finance/Insurance	463.1	459.2	0.8
Electric/Appliances	20.6	20.0	3.0	Credit Intermediation	241.6	241.8	−0.1
Transportation Equipment	91.8	97.4	−5.7	Securities/Investments	50.0	48.2	3.7
Misc. Manufacturing	28.9	30.7	−5.9	Insurance Carriers	159.1	158.9	0.1
Non-Durable Goods	304.8	317.4	−4.0	Real Estate/Rental	182.8	182.5	0.2
Food	87.5	87.5	0.0	Real Estate	121.0	119.2	1.5
Beverage/Tobacco	11.2	11.4	−1.8	Rental/Leasing	59.1	60.9	−3.0
Paper	18.8	19.5	−3.6	**Professional Services**	1,313.2	1,313.4	0.0
Printing	31.9	33.6	−5.1	Scientific/Tech	582.4	583.9	−0.3
Petroleum/Coal Products	26.3	25.4	3.5	Management/Enterprises	77.5	73.9	4.9
Chemicals	76.5	75.9	0.8	Administration/Support	653.3	655.6	−0.4
Rubber/Plastics	41.5	44.6	−7.0	**Education/Health**	1,313.9	1,258.1	4.4
				Educational Services	147.6	145.2	1.7
SERVICE PROVIDING	8,703.9	8,640.6	0.7	Health Care	1,166.3	1,112.9	4.8
				Ambulatory	549.4	509.8	7.8
Trade/Transport/Utilities	2,100.8	2,129.8	−1.4	Hospitals	281.6	271.4	3.8
Wholesale Trade	510.0	525.0	−2.9	Residential Care	162.5	154.2	5.4
Merchants/Durable Goods	289.5	304.5	−4.9	Social Assistance	172.8	177.5	−2.6
Merchants/Non-Durable	156.9	160.9	−2.5	**Leisure/Hospitality**	983.4	961.6	2.3
Retail Trade	1,162.4	1,171.4	−0.8	Accommodations	99.4	97.6	1.8
Building/Garden Supplies	93.2	89.3	4.4	Food/Drinking Places	780.8	768.1	1.7
General Merchandise	266.4	266.0	0.2	Amusements/Recreation	72.4	70.4	2.8
Food/Beverage Stores	201.9	198.1	1.9	**Other Services**	353.8	355.2	−0.4
Motor Vehicles/Parts	149.6	156.5	−4.4	Repair/Maintenance	107.1	108.0	−0.8
Clothing/Accessories	113.5	118.0	−3.8	Personal/Laundry	94.8	93.5	1.4
Furniture	43.1	45.8	−5.9	Religious/Civic	151.9	153.7	−1.2
Electronics/Appliances	47.1	47.8	−1.5	**Total Government**	1,784.3	1,761.8	1.3
Gasoline Stations	65.7	67.4	−2.5	Federal	194.9	187.1	4.2
Sporting/Books/Music	39.8	39.1	1.8	State	366.8	358.2	2.4
Misc. Store Retailers	56.8	59.8	−5.0	Local	1,222.6	1,216.5	0.5
Nonstore Retailers	21.1	21.1	0.0				

Cost of Living Index for Metro Areas

The comparison standard of all values is for the **United States set at 100**. Data are an annual average for 2007. The overall composite is excluding taxes. The column at the far right refers to miscellaneous goods and services.

Metro area	Overall	Groceries	Housing	Utilities	Transport	Health	Goods/Services
Austin	94.5	89.8	80.8	94.7	99.2	98.1	105.3
Brownsville	85.9	86.4	71.4	104.7	98.4	95.9	87.2
Corpus Christi	88.2	82.0	79.9	98.2	93.3	87.4	92.8
Dallas	91.2	99.0	71.5	98.6	103.4	101.6	97.4
El Paso	93.0	112.1	78.5	95.6	99.2	100.3	94.3
Fort Worth	88.2	95.3	74.0	97.9	97.7	90.1	91.1
Houston	87.7	83.1	73.5	100.6	96.2	101.2	93.0
Lubbock	86.4	91.3	71.1	83.7	102.8	98.7	91.5
San Antonio	94.1	83.7	84.1	83.5	100.1	102.5	106.4

Source: Statistical Abstract of the United States 2009.

Largest Banks Operating in Texas by Asset Size

Source: Texas Department of Banking, Dec. 31, 2008

Abbreviations: NA, not available; N.A. National Association.

	Name	City	Class	Assets	Loans
				(in thousands, 000)	
1	Comerica Bank	Dallas	State	$ 67,597,552	$ 50,505,646
2	JP Morgan Chase Bank	New York NY	National	67,332,000	NA
3	Bank of America	Charlotte NC	National	59,931,000	NA
4	Wells Fargo Bank	San Francisco CA	National	29,865,000	NA
5	Compass Bank	Birmingham AL	State	22,351,000	NA
6	Frost National Bank	San Antonio	National	15,112,135	8,816,927
7	Amergy Bank N.A.	Houston	National	12,354,037	9,079,822
8	Wachovia Bank	Charlotte NC	National	11,276,000	NA
9	International Bank of Commerce	Laredo	State	10,638,109	5,196,089
10	Prosperity Bank	El Campo	State	9,070,227	3,566,853
11	Capital One	New Orleans LA	National	6,016,000	NA
12	Texas Capital Bank N.A.	Dallas	National	5,131,657	4,027,870
13	Sterling Bank	Houston	State	5,081,614	3,792,290
14	Bank of Texas N.A.	Dallas	National	4,280,804	3,257,949
15	First National Bank	Edinburg	National	4,184,844	2,838,578
16	PlainsCapital Bank	Lubbock	State	3,937,307	2,966,699
17	Citibank	Las Vegas NV	National	3,654,000	NA
18	Regions Bank	Birmingham AL	State	2,962,000	NA
19	Woodforest National Bank	Houston	National	2,928,263	1,958,838
20	Amarillo National Bank	Amarillo	National	2,711,761	2,004,293
21	Southside Bank	Tyler	State	2,695,678	1,022,549
22	American State Bank	Lubbock	State	2,200,542	990,827
23	TIB Independent BankersBank	Irving	State	2,089,946	891,575
24	American National Bank of Texas	Terrell	National	2,024,897	1,268,522
25	Broadway National Bank	San Antonio	National	1,876,520	1,052,171
26	City Bank	Lubbock	State	1,863,661	1,684,516
27	Lone Star National Bank	Pharr	National	1,776,124	1,160,879
28	Inter National Bank	McAllen	National	1,746,144	1,135,230
29	Legacy Texas Bank	Plano	State	1,631,599	1,293,438
30	Century Bank N.A.	Texarkana	National	1,616,614	1,247,884
31	Encore Bank N.A.	Houston	National	1,579,951	1,218,404
32	First Victoria National Bank	Victoria	National	1,445,577	1,101,569
33	Inwood National Bank	Dallas	National	1,362,660	967,262
34	Town North Bank N.A.	Dallas	National	1,216,762	644,168
35	Metrobank N.A.	Houston	National	1,157,128	974,164
36	First Financial Bank N.A.	Abilene	National	1,105,537	420,708
37	Extraco Banks N.A.	Temple	National	1,084,558	723,606
38	Texas Bank and Trust Co.	Longview	State	1,062,798	805,202
30	American Bank of Texas	Sherman	State	1,058,077	835,601
40	Austin Bank Texas N.A.	Jacksonville	National	1,046,808	762,505
41	United Central Bank	Garland	State	1,011,386	774,783
42	First State Bank Central Texas	Austin	State	993,054	673,149
43	Happy State Bank	Happy	State	981,332	616,140
44	North Dallas Bank & Trust Co.	Dallas	State	974,294	382,776
45	Patriot Bank	Houston	State	963,902	890,280
46	Western National Bank	Odessa	National	952,649	681,539
47	Northern Trust	Miami FL	National	928,000	NA
48	Falcon International Bank	Laredo	State	914,173	745,610
49	American Bank N.A.	Corpus Christi	National	859,286	610,060
50	International Bank of Commerce	Brownsville	State	847,833	390,832

Deposits/Assets of Commercial Banks by County

Source: Federal Reserve Bank of Dallas as of Dec. 31, 2008.
(thousands of dollars, 000)

COUNTY	Banks	Deposits	Assets	COUNTY	Banks	Deposits	Assets
Anderson	3	$ 273,459	$ 307,797	Dimmit	1	$ 29,909	$ 36,908
Andrews	2	438,660	480,028	Donley	2	46,615	57,694
Angelina	2	807,876	904,478	Duval	2	88,688	97,282
Armstrong	1	80,787	90,869	Eastland	1	127,132	153,029
Atascosa	3	155,446	192,635	Ector	4	1,347,449	1,622,664
Austin	5	728,911	927,936	Edwards	1	50,075	57,084
Bailey	2	167,890	187,936	Ellis	5	670,472	796,159
Bandera	1	32,815	37,409	El Paso	3	957,468	1,135,126
Bastrop	2	284,763	349,369	Erath	4	495,723	573,848
Baylor	2	92,709	104,259	Fannin	2	164,374	202,161
Bee	1	150,173	164,032	Fayette	4	509,996	566,721
Bell	5	1,878,109	2,336,019	Fisher	1	44,496	51,331
Bexar	7	14,125,647	18,055,498	Floyd	1	89,918	102,301
Blanco	3	256,245	287,864	Foard	1	21,434	24,518
Bosque	3	329,928	370,998	Fort Bend	2	511,229	613,770
Bowie	4	1,657,031	2,117,508	Franklin	1	104,074	131,662
Brazoria	7	766,546	912,938	Freestone	1	88,311	112,640
Brazos	2	151,082	178,425	Frio	2	209,738	424,697
Briscoe	1	36,788	43,578	Galveston	6	1,571,852	1,788,349
Brooks	3	108,543	125,653	Gillespie	1	474,120	600,392
Brown	2	414,985	475,687	Gonzales	2	255,033	286,169
Burleson	1	251,246	276,743	Gray	1	13,664	16,115
Burnet	3	743,330	883,386	Grayson	5	1,256,182	1,458,890
Caldwell	2	157,377	181,308	Gregg	6	1,453,066	1,679,227
Calhoun	1	148,711	173,573	Grimes	2	192,101	216,067
Callahan	2	240,268	273,351	Guadalupe	3	253,065	295,551
Cameron	4	779,712	1,132,144	Hale	2	306,828	360,304
Camp	1	253,291	302,261	Hall	2	69,693	85,834
Carson	1	32,289	35,066	Hamilton	1	30,182	33,709
Cass	4	252,389	314,546	Hansford	3	222,740	262,109
Castro	1	704,063	827,646	Hardeman	2	75,674	86,929
Chambers	3	214,620	251,153	Harris	33	22,089,894	31,113,525
Cherokee	2	1,055,118	1,218,528	Harrison	2	127,600	145,050
Childress	1	69,645	75,982	Haskell	1	57,517	65,140
Clay	1	73,024	83,430	Hemphill	2	244,377	266,864
Coke	1	45,965	52,083	Henderson	2	366,828	412,158
Coleman	3	130,085	153,622	Hidalgo	8	6,602,449	8,356,617
Collin	13	3,413,519	4,318,856	Hill	2	137,924	203,986
Collingsworth	1	154,246	170,836	Hockley	2	117,018	132,207
Colorado	4	319,225	385,705	Hood	3	723,587	821,158
Comal	1	198,298	234,015	Hopkins	2	698,350	823,259
Comanche	2	239,314	278,135	Houston	4	295,784	346,469
Concho	2	104,845	121,804	Howard	2	321,956	362,364
Cooke	2	467,939	539,824	Hunt	1	37,647	41,105
Coryell	3	470,189	517,813	Hutchinson	1	36,952	41,289
Cottle	1	58,431	64,548	Irion	1	164,833	181,113
Crockett	2	387,636	463,123	Jack	2	434,963	655,083
Crosby	2	155,137	181,599	Jackson	1	53,895	58,497
Dallam	1	52,543	56,866	Jasper	1	179,006	224,879
Dallas	39	55,198,964	88,769,049	Jeff Davis	1	51,632	58,959
Dawson	1	194,635	220,446	Jefferson	1	633,351	725,043
Deaf Smith	2	212,520	255,777	Jim Hogg	1	87,642	103,061
Delta	2	47,932	55,898	Jim Wells	1	237,810	311,878
Denton	7	1,265,065	1,485,555	Johnson	3	505,170	565,826
DeWitt	2	210,451	245,090	Jones	2	124,926	145,417
Dickens	1	29,825	33,644	Karnes	2	186,688	213,759

Total bank assets in Dallas County were $88.8 billion, up from $16.6 billion in 2006. This was due to the relocation of Comerica Bank in 2007 from Detroit. In Bexar County (San Antonio), assets were $18.1 billion, and, in Harris County (Houston), assets were $31.1 billion.

Besides the major metropolitan areas, banks in two counties had assets over $10 billion, Lubbock and Webb (Laredo).

No independent banks were reported in 41 counties: Aransas, Archer, Borden, Brewster, Cochran, Crane, Culberson, Falls, Gaines, Garza, Glasscock, Goliad, Hardin, Hartley, Hays, Hudspeth, Kendall, Kenedy, King, Kinney, Lipscomb, Loving, Marion, Maverick, McMullen, Moore, Motley, Newton, Oldham, Randall, Reagan, Real, Robertson, San Augustine, Somervell, Terrell, Terry, Upton, Waller, Willacy and Winkler.

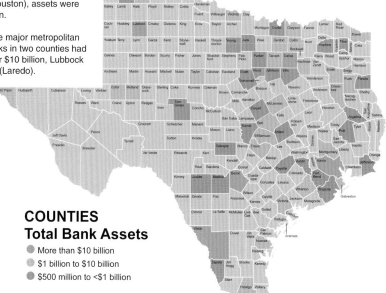

COUNTIES
Total Bank Assets

- More than $10 billion
- $1 billion to $10 billion
- $500 million to <$1 billion

COUNTY	Banks	Deposits	Assets
Kaufman	2	$ 1,699,387	$ 2,078,014
Kent	1	12,872	14,856
Kerr	2	63,313	71,991
Kimble	2	64,257	75,378
Kleberg	1	277,868	353,170
Knox	1	68,581	75,468
Lamar	4	392,012	480,000
Lamb	3	240,230	274,394
Lampasas	1	90,752	106,025
La Salle	1	38,702	43,508
Lavaca	2	243,943	290,176
Lee	1	112,974	138,983
Leon	3	298,726	337,550
Liberty	2	245,035	288,217
Limestone	3	216,291	250,804
Live Oak	2	207,062	239,133
Llano	2	191,345	215,771
Lubbock	12	8,297,719	10,679,467
Lynn	1	56,382	62,813
Madison	1	189,830	244,411
Martin	1	62,040	71,575
Mason	2	90,249	112,099
Matagorda	1	38,169	43,627
McCulloch	2	152,408	172,800
McLennan	12	2,187,075	2,549,857
Medina	7	452,756	529,174
Menard	1	26,905	30,724
Midland	3	1,289,638	1,428,048
Milam	3	461,817	531,644

COUNTY	Banks	Deposits	Assets
Mills	1	$ 154,701	$ 179,040
Mitchell	2	93,835	106,203
Montague	1	454,490	519,561
Montgomery	3	906,600	1,027,369
Morris	3	175,438	213,626
Nacogdoches	1	282,932	335,341
Navarro	5	382,549	450,687
Nolan	3	280,068	317,428
Nueces	4	1,234,753	1,398,496
Ochiltree	1	107,063	120,787
Orange	1	118,574	130,398
Palo Pinto	3	243,997	292,438
Panola	2	449,402	513,236
Parker	3	579,899	647,811
Parmer	2	161,237	184,771
Pecos	3	180,103	213,368
Polk	3	500,615	599,713
Potter	3	3,137,954	3,748,229
Presidio	1	61,206	72,161
Rains	1	81,321	94,375
Red River	1	16,527	25,041
Reeves	1	128,045	142,404
Refugio	2	206,088	263,240
Roberts	1	31,840	34,789
Rockwall	2	89,132	104,111
Runnels	4	229,528	254,665
Rusk	3	962,071	1,081,419
Sabine	1	41,838	49,411
San Jacinto	2	116,376	127,151

COUNTY	Banks	Deposits	Assets
San Patrico	1	$ 71,136	$ 79,049
San Saba	1	49,885	58,018
Schleicher	1	46,053	52,599
Scurry	2	234,974	266,770
Shackelford	1	317,105	349,530
Shelby	3	381,260	427,105
Sherman	1	149,746	181,620
Smith	5	2,369,717	3,872,698
Starr	1	56,931	66,036
Stephens	1	87,142	97,239
Sterling	1	71,339	80,257
Stonewall	1	26,353	37,293
Sutton	1	175,756	196,970
Swisher	2	801,673	1,013,727
Tarrant	19	2,636,814	3,219,631
Taylor	4	967,094	1,242,814
Throckmorton	1	25,288	27,978
Titus	2	624,638	804,096
Tom Green	2	422,937	503,375
Travis	6	1,081,112	1,366,790
Trinity	1	43,886	48,164
Tyler	1	110,992	119,662

COUNTY	Banks	Deposits	Assets
Upshur	3	$ 379,339	$ 436,020
Uvalde	2	471,687	528,037
Val Verde	1	10,295	15,286
Van Zandt	5	280,116	317,310
Victoria	1	1,200,337	1,445,577
Walker	2	402,552	450,114
Ward	1	177,627	228,663
Washington	4	291,458	349,671
Webb	4	7,504,553	12,651,824
Wharton	4	7,969,112	9,771,840
Wheeler	1	79,485	84,213
Wichita	5	1,059,497	1,253,132
Wilbarger	2	213,928	258,312
Williamson	7	873,472	1,000,507
Wilson	1	24,234	30,868
Wise	3	250,051	285,220
Wood	4	329,090	427,118
Yoakum	1	44,055	60,129
Young	5	451,419	534,450
Zapata	2	483,620	557,324
Zavala	1	44,854	52,704

Texas Total Bank Resources and Deposits: 1905–2008

On Dec. 31, 2008, Texas had a total of 594 national and state banks, the lowest number since 1906 when there were 619. In 1986, the number of independent banks in the state peaked at 1,972. In 2007 and 2008, total assets were the highest since 1997, when assets were $235 billion. *Source: Federal Reserve Bank of Dallas*

Date	National Banks			State Banks			Combined Total		
	No. Banks	Assets (add 000)	Deposits (add 000)	No. Banks	Assets (add 000)	Deposits (add 000)	No. Banks	Assets (add 000)	Deposits (add 000)
Sept. 30, 1905	440	$ 189,484	$ 101,285	29	$ 4,341	$ 2,213	469	$ 193,825	$ 103,498
Nov. 10, 1910	516	293,245	145,249	621	88,103	59,766	1,137	381,348	205,015
Dec. 29, 1920	556	780,246	564,135	1,031	391,127	280,429	1,587	1,171,373	844,564
Dec. 31, 1930	560	1,028,420	826,723	655	299,012	231,909	1,215	1,327,432	1,058,632
Dec. 31, 1940	446	1,695,662	1,534,702	393	227,866	179,027	839	1,923,528	1,713,729
Dec. 31, 1950	442	6,467,275	6,076,006	449	1,427,680	1,338,540	891	7,894,955	7,414,546
Dec. 31, 1960	468	10,520,690	9,560,668	532	2,997,609	2,735,726	1,000	13,518,299	12,296,394
Dec. 31, 1970	530	22,087,890	18,384,922	653	8,907,039	7,958,133	1,183	30,994,929	26,343,055
Dec. 31, 1980	641	75,540,334	58,378,669	825	35,186,113	31,055,648	1,466	110,726,447	89,434,317
Dec. 31, 1985	1,058	144,674,908	111,903,178	878	64,349,869	56,392,634	1,936	209,024,777	168,295,812
Dec. 31, 1986	1,077	141,397,037	106,973,189	895	65,989,944	57,739,091	1,972	207,386,981	164,712,280
Dec. 31, 1987	953	135,690,678	103,930,262	812	54,361,514	47,283,855	1,765	190,052,192	151,214,117
Dec. 31, 1988	802	130,310,243	106,740,461	690	40,791,310	36,655,253	1,492	171,101,553	143,395,714
Dec. 31, 1989	687	133,163,016	104,091,836	626	40,893,848	36,652,675	1,313	174,056,864	140,744,511
Dec. 31, 1990	605	125,808,263	103,573,445	578	45,021,304	40,116,662	1,183	170,829,567	143,690,107
Dec. 31, 1991	579	123,022,314	106,153,441	546	46,279,752	41,315,420	1,125	169,302,066	147,468,861
Dec. 31, 1992	562	135,507,244	112,468,203	529	40,088,963	35,767,858	1,091	175,596,207	148,236,061
Dec. 31, 1993	502	139,409,250	111,993,205	510	44,566,815	39,190,373	1,012	183,976,065	151,183,578
Dec. 31, 1994	481	140,374,540	111,881,041	502	47,769,694	41,522,943	983	188,144,234	153,403,984
Dec. 31, 1995	456	152,750,093	112,557,468	479	49,967,946	42,728,454	935	202,718,039	155,285,922
Dec. 31, 1996	432	152,299,695	122,242,990	445	52,868,263	45,970,674	877	205,167,958	168,213,664
Dec. 31, 1997	417	180,252,942	145,588,677	421	54,845,186	46,202,808	838	235,098,128	191,791,485
Dec. 31, 1998	402	128,609,813	106,704,893	395	50,966,996	42,277,367	797	179,576,809	148,982,260
Dec. 31, 1999	380	128,878,607	99,383,776	373	52,266,148	42,579,986	753	181,144,755	141,963,762
Dec. 31, 2000	358	112,793,856	88,591,657	351	53,561,550	43,835,525	709	166,355,406	132,427,182
Dec. 31, 2001	342	85,625,768	72,812,548	344	59,047,520	47,843,799	686	144,673,288	120,656,347
Dec. 31, 2002	332	95,308,420	79,183,418	337	62,093,220	49,715,186	669	157,401,640	128,898,604
Dec. 31, 2003	316	75,003,613	62,567,943	337	61,448,617	49,790,333	653	136,452,230	112,358,276
Dec. 31, 2004	311	82,333,800	67,977,669	328	69,127,411	54,950,601	639	151,461,211	122,928,270
Dec. 31, 2005	302	96,505,262	77,688,463	324	76,697,256	61,257,128	626	173,202,518	138,945,591
Dec. 31, 2006	286	97,936,270	79,389,737	322	83,910,356	66,132,394	608	181,846,626	145,522,131
Dec. 31, 2007	282	107,260,539	83,637,302	330	154,283,181	114,537,280	612	261,543,720	198,174,582
Dec. 31, 2008	267	$108,816,852	$84,802,191	327	$164,658,101	$115,186,285	594	$273,474,953	$199,988,476

Texas State Banks

Consolidated Statement, Foreign and Domestic
Offices, as of Dec. 31, 2008
Source: Federal Reserve Bank of Dallas

Number of Banks	327

(thousands of dollars, 000)

Assets

Cash and balances due from banks:
Non-interest-bearing balances
and currency and coin .... $ 3,760,217
Interest-bearing balances 4,138,344
Held-to-maturity securities 6,887,437
Available-for sale securities 28,806,719
Federal funds sold in domestic offices 1,888,966
Securities purchases under agreements to resell 1,850
Loans and lease financing receivables:
Loans and leases held for sale 373,250
Loans and leases, net of unearned income ..108,366,178
Less: allowance for loan and lease losses 1,436,757
Loans and leases, net 106,929,421
Trading Assets 773,557
Premises and fixed assets 2,733,951
Other real estate owned 328,079
Investments in unconsolidated subsidiaries
and associated companies 36,320
Intangible assets:
Goodwill 1,967,774
Other 203,377
Other assets 5,828,839

   Total Assets .... $ 164,658,101

Liabilities

Deposits:
In domestic offices .... $ 115,186,285
Non-interest-bearing 27,304,626
Interest-bearing 87,881,656
In foreign offices, edge & agreement subsidiaries
and IBFs 3,304,922
Non-interest-bearing 103,166
Interest-bearing balances 3,201,756
Federal funds purchased and securities sold under
agreements to repurchase:
funds in domestic offices 1,850,556
securities sold under agreement to repurchase .2,944,740
Trading liabilities 661,555
Other borrowed money (mortgages/leases) 20,413,495
Subordinated notes and debentures 2,360,582
Other liabilities 1,848,105

   Total Liabilities .... $ 148,570,240
Minority interest in consolidated subsidiaries 22,554

Equity Capital

Perpetual preferred stock .... $ 320,600
Common stock 664,032
Surplus (exclude surplus related to
preferred stock) 7,925,652
Retained earnings 7,346,291
Accumulated other comprehensive income .... -190,567
Other equity capital components .... -701

   Total Equity Capital .... $ 16,065,307

**Total liabilities, minority interest and
equity capital** .... $ 164,658,101

Texas National Banks

Consolidated Statement, Foreign and Domestic
Offices, as of Dec. 31, 2008
Source: Federal Reserve Bank of Dallas

Number of Banks	267

(thousands of dollars, 000)

Assets

Cash and balances due from banks:
Non-interest-bearing balances
and currency and coin .... $ 4,088,427
Interest-bearing balances 2,367,677
Held-to-maturity securities 1,774,617
Available-for sale securities 19,474,286
Federal funds sold in domestic offices 1,774,089
Securities purchases under agreements to resell 10,000
Loans and lease financing receivables:
Loans and leases held for sale 860,565
Loans and leases, net of unearned income 70,652,530
Less: allowance for loan and lease losses 939,798
Loans and leases, net 69,712,732
Trading Assets 280,538
Premises and fixed assets 2,334,331
Other real estate owned 219,886
Investments in unconsolidated subsidiaries
and associated companies 15,366
Intangible assets:
Goodwill 2,615,567
Other 255,661
Other assets 3,033,114

   Total Assets .... $ 108,816,856

Liabilities

Deposits:
In domestic offices .... $ 84,802,191
Non-interest-bearing 20,155,326
Interest-bearing 64,646,867
In foreign offices, edge & agreement subsidiaries
and IBFs 1,823,394
Non-interest-bearing 0
Interest-bearing balances 1,823,394
Federal funds purchased and securities sold under
agreements to repurchase:
funds in domestic offices 1,507,043
securities sold under agreement to repurchase .2,210,576
Trading liabilities 188,580
Other borrowed money (mortgages/leases) 4,784,352
Subordinated notes and debentures 391,000
Other liabilities 758,028

   Total Liabilities .... $ 96,465,164
Minority interest in consolidated subsidiaries 652

Equity Capital

Perpetual preferred stock .... $ 80,760
Common stock 520,863
Surplus (exclude surplus related to
preferred stock) 6,137,004
Retained earnings 5,427,114
Accumulated other comprehensive income 205,528
Other equity capital components .... -20,229

   Total Equity Capital .... $ 12,351,040

**Total liabilities, minority interest and
equity capital** .... $ 108,816,856

Credit Unions: Mid-Year 2008

	#Credit Unions	State Charter	Federal Charter	Members	Percent of Pop.*	Savings (000)	Loans (000)	Assets (000)
Texas	579	213	366	7,126,703	29.8	$47,443,160	$37,083,731	$56,217,184
U.S.	8,260	3,305	4,955	90,163,004	29.5	$694,406,930	$560,406,886	$822,131,836

* Percent of population, each member counted once for every credit union they belong to. Source: Credit Union National Association.

	U.S. Credit Union History				**Texas Credit Union History**			
Year	# Credit Unions	Members	Savings ($ millions)	Loans ($ millions)	# Credit Unions	Members	Savings ($ millions)	Loans ($ millions)
2007	8,538	89,053,757	$ 650,879	$ 522,904	595	6,993,043	$ 44,018	$ 35,984
2006	8,853	87,895,738	613,297	492,635	610	6,880,403	41,228	33,894
2005	9,198	86,987,764	591,388	449,891	625	6,832,172	40,273	32,745
2004	9,542	85,639,535	567,827	407,937	641	7,130,609	40,749	31,709
2003	9,875	84,240,057	538,033	367,065	667	7,000,010	39,148	29,199
2002	10,174	82,557,258	483,527	343,400	683	6,801,810	36,591	26,383
2001	10,514	80,937,530	427,411	318,027	695	6,626,098	32,838	24,128
2000	10,860	78,865,715	380,858	295,251	714	6,454,376	28,400	22,562
1995	12,230	69,305,876	278,813	198,337	819	5,360,020	20,306	14,701
1990	14,549	61,610,057	201,082	141,889	954	4,379,982	13,875	8,946
1980	21,465	43,930,569	61,724	48,703	1,379	3,202,066	4,818	3,691
1970	23,687	22,775,511	15,411	14,068	1,435	1,452,416	1,034	951
1960	20,094	12,025,393	4,976	4,376	1,159	688,517	282	265
1950	10,586	4,617,086	862	679	484	179,956	38	35

Source: Credit Union National Association.

Credit Unions in Texas

Source: Texas Credit Union Department, National Credit Union Administration and Credit Union National Association.

Credit unions are chartered at federal and state levels. The National Credit Union Administration (NCUA) is the regulatory agency for the federal-chartered credit unions in Texas.

The Texas Credit Union Department is the regulatory agency for the state-chartered credit unions. It was established in 1969 as a separate agency by the 61st Legislature. In 2008, it supervised 213 active state-chartered credit unions.

These state-chartered credit unions served 2.7 million Texans and had approximately $19.3 billion in assets in 2008.

The department is supervised by the nine-member Texas Credit Union Commission, which is appointed by the governor to staggered terms of six years, with the terms of one-third of the members expiring Feb. 15 of each odd-numbered year.

The Texas Credit Union League has been the state association for federal and state chartered credit unions since October 1934.

The league's address is 4455 LBJ Freeway Ste. 909, Farmers Branch, 75244-5998.

The address for the Texas Credit Union Department is 914 East Anderson Lane, Austin, 78752-1699. Their Web site is www.tcud.state.tx.us. ☆

Distribution of Consumer Savings

$ billions. Mid-Year 2008

	Savings	Market share
Commercial banks	$ 4,416.3	59.0%
Money Market Mutual Funds	1,285.4	17.2%
Savings Institutions	894.7	12.0%
Credit Unions	694.4	**9.3%**
US Savings Securities	195.0	2.6%
Total	$ 7,485.8	

Credit Outstanding by Lenders

	Outstanding	Market share
Commercial banks	$ 814.6	31.5%
Pool of Securitized Assets	690.3	26.7%
Finance Companies	585.4	22.6%
Credit Unions	254.0	**9.8%**
Student Loans	104.3	4.0%
Savings Institutions	89.2	3.4%
Nonfinancial business	51.4	2.0%
Total	$ 2,589.2	

Source: Credit Union National Association.

Savings and Loan Associations in Texas

This table includes all thrifts that are not also classified as banks under federal law: that is, it includes federal savings and loan associations and federal savings banks. *Source: Texas Department of Savings and Mortgage Lending.*

Year ending	Number of Institutions	Total Assets	Mortgage Loans	Cash/ Securities	Deposits	FHLB/ Borrowed Money	†Net Worth
				in thousands of dollars (000)			
Dec. 31, 2008	22	$ 87,572,855	$ 49,816,471	$ 31,763,898	$ 52,606,655	$27,137,730	$ 6,582,759
Dec. 31, 2007	21	74,346,114	38,795,098	15,444,116	43,442,843	23,264,570	5,628,255
Dec. 31, 2006	20	64,692,927	22,908,898	12,709,276	39,661,286	18,817,750	4,993,335
Dec. 31, 2005	19	55,755,096	42,027,293	9,140,789	30,565,411	11,299,136	4,228,103
Dec. 31, 2004	20	51,000,806	40,740,030	6,648,858	26,526,138	12,786,086	3,647,046
Dec. 31, 2003	21	45,941,356	16,840,610	17,362,664	23,954,623	10,725,209	3,130,442
Dec. 31, 2002	24	43,940,058	31,604,285	4,900,880	23,264,510	11,662,118	3,189,629
Dec. 31, 2001	24	42,716,060	35,823,258	9,542,688	22,182,152	15,531,159	3,608,222
Dec. 31, 2000	25	55,709,391	43,515,610	1,512,444	28,914,234	17,093,369	4,449,097
Dec. 31, 1999	25	45,508,256	40,283,186	2,615,072	26,369,005	14,790,241	3,802,977
Dec. 31, 1998	30	40,021,239	35,419,110	5,236,596	21,693,469	15,224,654	3,101,795
Dec. 31, 1997	32	40,284,148	33,451,365	4,556,626	21,854,620	15,190,014	3,089,458
Dec. 31, 1996	37	54,427,896	27,514,639	5,112,995	28,053,292	20,210,616	4,345,257
Dec. 31, 1995	45	52,292,519	27,509,933	5,971,364	28,635,799	15,837,632	3,827,249
Dec. 31, 1994	50	50,014,102	24,148,760	6,790,416	29,394,433	15,973,056	3,447,110
Dec. 31, 1993	62	42,983,595	14,784,215	10,769,889	25,503,656	13,356,018	2,968,840
Dec. 31, 1992	64	47,565,516	14,137,191	14,527,573	33,299,278	10,490,144	2,917,881
Dec. 31, 1991	80	53,500,091	15,417,895	11,422,071	41,985,117	8,189,800	2,257,329
Dec. 31, 1990 §	131	72,041,456	27,475,664	20,569,770	56,994,387	17,738,041	-4,566,656
Conservatorship	51	14,952,402	6,397,466	2,188,820	16,581,525	4,304,033	-6,637,882
Privately Owned	80	57,089,054	21,078,198	18,380,950	40,412,862	13,434,008	2,071,226
Dec. 31, 1989 §	196	90,606,100	37,793,043	21,218,130	70,823,464	27,158,238	-9,356,209
Conservatorship	81	22,159,752	11,793,445	2,605,080	25,381,494	7,103,657	-10,866,213
Privately Owned	115	68,446,348	25,999,598	18,613,050	45,441,970	20,054,581	1,510,004
Dec. 31, 1988	204	110,499,276	50,920,006	26,181,917	83,950,314	28,381,573	-4,088,355
Dec. 31, 1987	279	99,613,666	56,884,564	12,559,154	85,324,796	19,235,506	-6,677,338
Dec. 31, 1986	281	96,919,775	61,489,463	9,989,918	80,429,758	14,528,311	109,807
Dec. 31, 1985	273	91,798,890	* 60,866,666	10,426,464	72,806,067	13,194,147	3,903,611
Dec. 31, 1980	318	34,954,129	$ 27,717,383	$ 3,066,791	$ 28,439,210	$ 3,187,638	$ 1,711,201

Texas Savings Banks

The savings bank charter was approved by the Legislature in 1993 and the first savings bank was chartered in 1994. Savings banks operate similarly to savings and loans associations in that they are housing-oriented lenders. Under federal law a savings bank is categorized as a commercial bank and not a thrift. Therefore savings-bank information is also reported with state and national bank information. *Source: Texas Department of Savings and Mortgage Lending.*

				in thousands of dollars (000)			
Dec. 31, 2008	28	$ 3,988,377	$ 1,980,651	$ 538,162	$ 3,119,082	$ 411,119	$ 434,893
Dec. 31, 2007	26	9,967,678	6,471,833	1,027,709	6,162,709	2,328,467	1,372,231
Dec. 31, 2006	22	9,393,482	6,444,178	836,821	5,721,314	2,453,757	1,138,780
Dec. 31, 2005	19	8,720,497	5,605,678	985,535	5,308,639	1,967,673	1,352,882
Dec. 31, 2004	22	12,981,650	6,035,081	1,654,978	8,377,409	3,000,318	1,482,078
Dec. 31, 2003	23	17,780,413	8,396,606	3,380,565	11,901,441	3,315,544	2,422,317
Dec. 31, 2002	24	15,445,211	7,028,139	3,147,381	10,009,861	3,422,600	1,910,660
Dec. 31, 2001	25	11,956,074	5,845,605	1,305,731	8,742,372	1,850,076	1,270,273
Dec. 31, 2000	25	11,315,961	9,613,164	514,818	8,644,826	1,455,497	1,059,638
Dec. 31, 1999	28	13,474,299	8,870,291	4,101,480	7,330,776	4,822,372	1,188,852
Dec. 31, 1998	23	12,843,828	7,806,738	193,992	7,299,636	4,477,546	1,067,977
Dec. 31, 1997	17	7,952,703	6,125,467	892,556	5,608,429	1,615,311	745,515
Dec. 31, 1996	15	7,872,238	6,227,811	856,970	5,329,919	1,930,378	611,941
Dec. 31, 1995	13	7,348,647	5,644,591	1,106,557	4,603,026	2,225,793	519,827
Dec. 31, 1994	8	$ 6,347,505	$ 2,825,012	$ 3,139,573	$ 3,227,886	$ 2,628,847	$ 352,363

* Beginning in 1982, net of loans in process.
† Net worth includes permanent stock and paid-in surplus general reserves, surplus and undivided profits.
§ In 1989 and 1990, the Office of Thrift Supervision, U.S. Department of the Treasury, separated data on savings and loans (thrifts) into two categories: those under the supervision of the Office of Thrift Supervision (Conservatorship Thrifts) and those still under private management (Privately Owned).

Insurance in Texas

Source: 2008 Annual Report, Texas Dept. of Insurance.

The Texas Department of Insurance reported that on Aug. 31, 2008, there were 2,716 firms licensed to handle insurance business in Texas and 306,036 insurance agents.

From 1957 to 1993, a three-member State Board of Insurance administered legislation relating to the insurance industry. This board, appointed by the governor, hired a commissioner of insurance. The establishment of the system followed discovery of irregularities in some firms. It succeeded two previous regulatory groups, established in 1913 and changed in 1927.

Under reforms in 1993-94, the board was replaced by the Texas Department of Insurance with a Commissioner of Insurance appointed by the governor for a two-year term in each odd-numbered year and confirmed by the Texas Senate.

On Sept. 1, 2005, legislation passed by the 79th Legislature took effect, transferring functions of the Texas Workers' Compensation Commission to the Texas Department of Insurance and creating within it the Division of Worker's Compensation.

Also established was the office of Commissioner of Workers' Compensation, appointed by the governor, to enforce and implement the Texas Workers' Compensation Act. The division consists of five sections: dispute resolution, field services, legal/compliance, medical advisor, and workplace and medical services.

Companies in Texas

The following table shows the number and kinds of insurance companies licensed in Texas on Aug. 31, 2008.

Type of Insurance	Texas	Out-of-State	Total
Stock Life	110	462	572
Mutual Life	3	32	35
Stipulated Premium Life	30	0	30
Non-Profit Life	0	1	1
Stock Fire	2	4	6
Stock Fire & Casualty	110	666	776
Mutual Fire & Casualty	4	55	59
Stock Casualty	10	158	168
Mexican Casualty	0	13	13
Lloyds	57	0	57
Reciprocal Exchanges	8	15	23
Fraternal Benefit Societies	8	24	32
Title Insurance	5	28	33
Non-Profit Legal Services	3	0	3
Health Maintenance Organizations	51	3	54
Risk Retention Groups	2	0	2
Multiple Employer Welfare Arrang.	4	1	5
Joint Underwriting Associations	3	3	6
Third Party Administrators	269	479	748
Workers' Comp. Self Insurance	8	0	8
Continuing Care Retirement Communities	25	4	29
Total	**712**	**1,948**	**2,660**
Local Mutual Associations	3	0	3
Exempt Associations	8	0	8
Non-Profit Hospital Service	2	0	2
County Mutual Fire	24	0	24
Farm Mutual Fire	17	0	17
Total	**56**	**0**	**56**
Grand Total	**768**	**1,948**	**2,716**

Source: 2006 Annual Report, Texas Department of Insurance.

Premium Income and Losses Paid, 2007

(Texas business only)	Texas Companies	Out-of-State Companies
Legal Reserve Life Insurance Companies		
Life premiums	$ 686,426,886	$ 7,913,288,553
Claims & benefits paid	$2,266,753,825	$ 22,557,991,037
Accident & health premiums	$ 766,621,833	$ 35,542,852,007
Accident & health loss paid	$ 501,188,524	$ 28,082,182,019
Mutual Fire & Casualty Companies		
Premiums	$1,227,389,572	$ 3,394,547,654
Losses	$ 319,246,875	$ 2,033,445,231
Lloyds Insurance		
Premiums	$4,828,000,853	. . . .
Losses	$1,823,005,445	. . . .
Reciprocal Insurance Companies		
Premiums	$ 839,867,732	$ 623,956,449
Losses	$ 469,421,354	$ 241,032,345
Fraternal Benefit Societies		
Life Certificates Issued	9,230	18,635
Amount issued 2007	$ 164,290,916	$ 1,962,869,238
Considerations from members:		
Life	$ 55,420,793	$ 260,965,942
Accident/Health	$ 114,955	$ 34,200,598
Benefits paid to members:		
Life	$ 65,098,833	$ 284,051,426
Accident/Health	$ 17,919	$ 19,315,018
Insurance in force	$3,243,029,000	$284,769,099,000
Title Companies		
Premiums	$ 437,496,096	$ 1,184,150,991
Paid losses	$ 10,170,096	$ 44,793,755
Stock Fire, Stock Casualty, and Stock Fire & Casualty Companies		
Premiums	$2,401,603,752	$13,814,603,065
Losses	$1,038,310,527	$6,064,035,723

Texas Top 5 Auto Insurers

Company	% of market
1. State Farm Mutual	18.58
2. Farmers Texas County Mutual	9.76
3. Progressive County Mutual	7.39
4. Allstate Indemnity	4.80
5. Allstate County Mutual	3.98

Texas Top 5 Homeowners Insurers

1. State Farm Lloyds	29.30
2. Allstate Texas Lloyds	12.30
3. Travelers Lloyds of Texas	5.40
4. Texas Farmers	4.88
5. United Services	4.31

Texas Top 5 Accident/Health Insurers

1. Blue Cross/Blue Shield	25.12
2. United Healthcare	16.09
3. Humana	7.60
4. Aetna Life	6.59
5. Unicare	2.92

Texas Top 5 HMOs

1. Pacificare of Texas	16.47
2. Amerigroup Texas	11.55
3. Aetna Health	9.70
4. Superior Healthplan	6.90
5. Humana	6.46

Texas Top 5 Life Insurers

1. Metropolitan Life	6.28
2. Northwestern Mutual Life	4.75
3. Lincoln National Life	3.20
4. American General Life	3.16
5. New York Life	3.06

Source: 2008 Annual Report, Texas Department of Insurance.

Homeowners Insurance: Average Premiums by State, 2005

The U.S. average is $764. Idaho has the least expensive at $457.

1. Texas.............................**$ 1,372**
2. Louisiana 1,144
3. Florida............................. 1,083
4. Oklahoma 996
5. District of Columbia........... 963
6. Mississippi 939
7. California......................... 895
8. Rhode Island.................... 849
9. Alabama.......................... 847
10. New York........................ 842

In dollars. The Texas Insurance Commissioner promulgates residential policy forms which are similar but not identical to the standard national forms. Source: U.S. Statistical Abstract 2009.

Auto Insurance: Average for Coverage by State, 2005

The U.S. average is $829. North Dakota has the least expensive at $554.

1. New Jersey................................$ 1,184
2. District of Columbia 1,182
3. New York 1,122
4. Massachusetts 1,113
5. Louisiana...................................... 1,076
6. Florida 1,063
7. Rhode Island................................. 1,059
8. Delaware 1,028
9. Connecticut 991
10. Nevada 983
17. Texas 845

In dollars. The figures are actually reported as 'average expenditures', which equals total premiums divided by liability car-years. A car-year is equal to 365 days of insured coverage for a single vehicle. Source: U.S. Statistical Abstract 2009.

Ten-year history, number of insurance companies operating in Texas

	1999	2000	2001	2002	2003	2004	2005	2006	2007	2008
Life/Health										
In-State	233	220	216	213	206	196	190	186	175	170
Out-of-State	649	639	625	607	580	561	552	546	529	520
subtotal	882	859	841	820	786	757	742	732	704	690
Property/Casualty										
In-State	250	250	245	243	244	245	250	248	252	250
Out-of-State	877	888	910	913	916	915	917	926	932	942
subtotal	1,127	1,138	1,155	1,156	1,160	1,160	1,167	1,174	1,184	1,192
Other*										
In-State	359	367	373	368	362	348	352	341	341	348
Out-of-State	390	414	426	436	456	462	479	485	471	486
subtotal	749	481	799	804	818	810	831	826	812	834
Grand Total	**2,758**	**2,778**	**2,795**	**2,780**	**2,764**	**2,727**	**2,740**	**2,732**	**2,700**	**2,716****

*Other includes: Non-profit legal services corporations, third party administrators, continuing care retirement communities and health maintenance organizations.

**Does not include 250 premium finance companies and their 21 branch offices.

Source: 2008 Annual Report, Texas Department of Insurance.

Construction Industry: Comparison of Awards, 1945–2009

The chart below shows the total value of construction contract awards in Texas by year: *Source Texas Contractor, 2009.*

Year	Total Awards	Year	Total Awards	Year	Total Awards
2009	$ 29,892,995,000	1995	$ 4,771,332,413	1981	$ 3,700,112,809
2008	30,790,000,000	1994	4,396,199,988	1980	3,543,117,615
2007	25,785,189,283	1993	5,394,342,718	1979	3,353,243,234
2006	20,566,889,250	1992	4,747,666,912	1978	2,684,743,190
2005	18,923,051,000	1991	3,926,799,801	1977	2,270,788,842
2004	13,014,672,068	1990	3,922,781,630	1976	1,966,553,804
2003	12,897,933,353	1989	4,176,355,929	1975	1,737,036,682
2002	7,297,909,363	1988	3,562,336,666	1970	1,458,708,492
2001	6,067,377,351	1987	4,607,051,270	1965	1,254,638,051
2000	5,232,788,835	1986	4,636,310,266	1960	1,047,943,630
1999	4,941,352,362	1985	4,806,998,065	1955	949,213,349
1998	4,951,275,224	1984	3,424,721,025	1950	1,059,457,667
1997	5,088,017,435	1983	4,074,910,947	1945	245,438,277
1996	4,383,336,574	1982	3,453,784,388		

Approved Texas Construction, 2009

Federal:

Department of Defense	$ 385,000,000
Federal Aviation Administration	98,000,000
General Services Administration	4,200,000
Department of Energy	6,500,000
NASA	4,125,000
Department of Veterans Affairs	16,550,000
Rural Utilities Service	107,000,000
Natural Res. Conserv. Service	5,000,000
U.S. Department of Agriculture	123,000,000
Department of Justice	1,300,000
Department of the Interior	1,270,000
Federal Highway Administration	2,500,000,000
Total Federal	$ 3,251,495,000

State:

Texas Dept. of Transportation	$ 3,500,000,000
State Agencies	350,000,000
State Colleges and Universities	1,435,000,000
Total State	$ 4,285,000,000

Water Projects:

Corps of Engineers	$ 110,000,000
Bureau of Reclamation	500,000
River Authorities	910,000,000
Clean Water StateRevolvingFund	695,000,000
Drinking WaterState Revolving Fund	411,000,000
Total Water Projects	$ 2,126,500,000

Buildings Total ... $ 20,230,000,000

Grand Total ... **$ 29,892,995,000**

Source: Texas Contractor Web site, 2009.

Texas Single-Family Building Permits

Year	No. of Dwelling Units		Avg. Value per Unit ($)	
	Units	% change	Value	% change
1981	66,161	–	$ 55,700	–
1982	78,714	19	53,800	-3
1983	103,252	31	63,400	18
1984	84,565	-18	68,000	7
1985	67,964	-20	71,000	4
1986	59,143	-13	72,200	2
1987	43,975	-26	77,700	8
1988	35,908	-18	83,900	8
1989	36,658	2	90,400	8
1990	38,233	4	95,500	6
1991	46,209	21	92,800	-3
1992	59,543	29	95,400	3
1993	69,964	18	96,400	1
1994	70,452	1	99,500	3
1995	70,421	0	100,300	1
1996	83,132	18	102,100	2
1997	82,228	-1	108,900	7
1998	99,912	22	112,800	4
1999	101,928	2	118,800	5
2000	108,782	7	127,100	7
2001	111,915	3	124,700	-2
2002	122,913	10	126,400	1
2003	137,493	12	128,800	2
2004	151,384	10	137,600	7
2005	166,203	10	144,300	5
2006	163,032	-2	155,100	7
2007	120,366	-26	169,000	9
2008	81,107	-34	$174,100	3

Source: U.S. Bureau of Census and Real Estate Center at Texas A&M University, 2008.

Federal Aid to States for Highway Trust Fund, 2006

The chart below shows dispersement of federal funds for highway construction and maintenance in **millions of dollars** in the middle column. The column at right shows dollars per capita based on estimated population. *Source: U.S. Bureau of Census.*

State	Highway Fund		State	Highway Fund		State	Highway Fund	
	Total	Per capita		Total	Per capita		Total	Per capita
U.S.	$33,126	$110	Pennsylvania	$1,427	$115	New Jersey	$747	$86
Texas	**2,892**	**124**	N. Carolina	908	102	Missouri	747	128
California	2,750	76	Ohio	1,302	114	S. Carolina	733	169
Florida	1,895	105	Michigan	999	99	Tennessee	670	110
New York	1,496	128	Georgia	923	99	Illinois	986	77

Texas Commercial Fishery Landings by Species

Species	2005 Pounds	2005 Value	2006 Pounds	2006 Value	2007 Pounds	2007 Value
Shrimp, Brown	40,441,245	$80,726,617	71,033,067	$105,372,321	42,841,648	$84,258,622
Shrimp, White	27,532,112	57,464,870	31,525,199	58,214,024	27,160,444	56,847,983
Oyster, Eastern	5,007,472	15,882,977	4,922,882	17,262,696	5,187,631	17,759,573
Snapper, Red	1,939,953	5,344,722	2,158,396	6,168,022	1,214,664	3,769,518
Shrimp, Dendrobranchiata	1,231,858	3,675,740	1,034,867	3,096,119	1,051,026	3,127,202
Crab, Blue	3,119,000	2,410,342	1,965,694	1,458,894	3,309,044	2,660,051
Drum, Black	2,077,446	1,917,329	2,211,757	2,012,550	1,684,400	1,656,699
Snapper, Vermilion	278,803	570,543	273,026	642,421	664,095	1,535,104
Croaker, Atlantic	58,174	415,399	67,331	500,365	54,926	417,341
Grouper, Yellowedge	200,105	558,089	144,104	436,720	89,973	288,690
Total, including others	**84,289,291**	**$172,336,642**	**117,131,191**	**$197,290,989**	**84,937,097**	**$174,346,556**

Source: National Ocean Economics Program, 2009.

An oyster boat moves into Fulton Harbor in Aransas County. Robert Plocheck photo.

Commercial Fisheries in Texas

Total coastwide landings in 2007 were more than 84 million pounds, valued at more than $174 million. Shrimp accounted for most of the weight and value of all seafood landed *(see chart above).*

The Coastal Fisheries Division of the Texas Parks and Wildlife Department manages the marine fishery resources of Texas' four million acres of saltwater, including the bays and estuaries and out to nine nautical miles in the Gulf of Mexico.

The division works toward sustaining fisheries populations at levels that are necessary to ensure replenishable stocks of commercially and recreationally important species. It also focuses on habitat conservation and restoration and leads the agency research on all water-related issues, including assuring adequate in-stream flows for rivers and sufficient freshwater inflows for bays and estuaries. ☆

Landings by State 2007

Rank	States	Pounds (000)	Dollars (000)
	Total, U.S.	9,231,833	$ 4,089,012
1	Alaska	5,314,743	1,494,242
2	Massachusetts	303,006	417,795
3	Maine	176,006	319,523
4	Louisiana	951,240	259,564
5	Washington	456,243	214,270
6	**Texas**	**87,374**	**179,502**

Source: National Maritime Fisheries Service, 2009.

Top Fishing Ports for Texas in 2006

Rank	Landing Weight Port	Pounds (000)	Landed Value Port	Dollars (000)
1	Brownsville–Port Isabel	30,500	Brownsville–Port Isabel	$ 52,000
2	Port Arthur	25,000	Port Arthur	42,800
3	Palacios	22,300	Galveston	40,700
4	Galveston	22,000	Palacios	32,600
5	Freeport	5,900	Freeport	9,200

Source: National Ocean Economics Program, 2009.

U.S. Ports in 2006

Rank	Fishery Landed Value Port	Dollars (000,000)
1	New Bedford, MA	$ 281.2
2	Dutch Harbor–Unalaska, AK	165.2
3	Kodiak, AK	101.4
4	Honolulu, HI	54.6
5	Key West, FL	54.4
6	Sitka, AK	53.2
7	**Brownsville–Port Isabel, TX**	**52.0**

Source: National Maritime Fisheries Service, 2009.

Tourism Impact Estimates by County, 2007

This analysis covers most travel in Texas including business, pleasure, shopping, to attend meetings and other destinations. Visitor **spending** is for purchases including lodging taxes and other applicable local and state taxes. **Earnings** are wages and salaries of employees and income of proprietors of businesses that receive travel expenditures. Employment associated with these businesses are listed under **jobs**. **Local tax** receipts are from hotel taxes, local sales taxes, auto rental taxes, etc, as separate from state tax receipts. *Source: Office of the Governor, Economic Development and Tourism.*

County	Spending ($000)	Earnings ($000)	Jobs	Local tax ($000)	County	Spending ($000)	Earnings ($000)	Jobs	Local tax ($000)
Anderson	$ 48,630	$ 11,080	670	$ 730	Crane	$ 1,530	$ 300	20	$ 30
Andrews	9,140	2,110	150	110	Crockett	27,660	2,140	160	110
Angelina	118,700	23,630	1,400	1,460	Crosby	1,510	380	30	10
Aransas	91,600	25,120	1,230	1,740	Culberson	35,580	4,020	180	330
Archer	1,850	320	20	20	Dallam	16,280	5,340	270	360
Armstrong	1,310	80	10	0	Dallas	7,085,500	2,401,800	66,220	185,300
Atascosa	26,250	6,270	310	300	Dawson	13,730	2,050	160	120
Austin	39,070	8,160	460	350	Deaf Smith	15,470	3,010	200	230
Bailey	4,010	1,040	80	70	Delta	1,210	220	10	10
Bandera	27,800	16,770	820	590	Denton	476,480	126,870	4,360	9,340
Bastrop	119,740	42,220	1,600	2,760	DeWitt	40,330	6,080	310	280
Baylor	7,030	790	40	40	Dickens	640	180	10	10
Bee	27,730	6,270	340	380	Dimmit	14,790	1,750	110	140
Bell	367,140	86,120	5,160	6,500	Donley	6,170	1,650	120	120
Bexar	5,250,310	1,433,340	52,370	116,890	Duval	12,260	1,220	70	150
Blanco	10,280	2,450	150	170	Eastland	13,150	2,970	200	240
Borden	100	10	0	0	Ector	232,180	64,000	2,790	4,670
Bosque	14,130	6,230	220	240	Edwards	1,250	280	20	20
Bowie	162,510	22,200	1,420	1,690	Ellis	129,140	28,080	890	1,980
Brazoria	252,630	62,540	3,670	3,700	El Paso	1,259,820	303,470	11,810	19,870
Brazos	343,140	74,450	4,280	5,800	Erath	42,060	9,730	470	610
Brewster	47,900	21,850	1,340	990	Falls	7,680	1,510	80	90
Briscoe	1,330	140	10	0	Fannin	11,870	1,690	100	110
Brooks	13,750	1,810	110	160	Fayette	32,720	5,500	340	350
Brown	43,250	12,280	640	790	Fisher	1,080	160	10	10
Burleson	12,020	2,830	150	120	Floyd	5,320	630	40	20
Burnet	60,680	19,240	860	1,280	Foard	350	80	10	0
Caldwell	27,540	5,580	210	250	Fort Bend	349,120	92,430	3,610	6,520
Calhoun	31,190	8,990	420	590	Franklin	8,330	1,400	100	100
Callahan	3,690	920	60	50	Freestone	53,080	6,020	490	580
Cameron	689,530	151,240	8,230	15,330	Frio	11,570	2,250	140	160
Camp	15,750	1,120	60	40	Gaines	10,740	1,620	110	90
Carson	7,160	490	40	20	Galveston	736,700	194,520	9,500	19,590
Cass	20,790	4,770	220	230	Garza	9,920	2,930	120	90
Castro	3,150	550	40	30	Gillespie	72,900	20,510	1,030	1,880
Chambers	25,870	4,670	200	580	Glasscock	200	30	0	0
Cherokee	34,440	7,100	460	400	Goliad	8,640	1,340	60	70
Childress	10,860	2,300	170	310	Gonzales	19,500	2,010	120	120
Clay	21,220	1,280	90	30	Gray	44,780	12,010	740	770
Cochran	890	180	20	10	Grayson	193,120	29,130	1,550	2,180
Coke	3,360	630	50	20	Gregg	216,140	51,050	2,810	3,190
Coleman	6,880	1,240	80	100	Grimes	16,200	4,000	190	210
Collin	888,930	278,410	10,150	18,840	Guadalupe	100,410	33,110	1,270	1,710
Collingswrth	2,190	300	20	10	Hale	53,860	12,330	950	840
Colorado	52,040	9,410	510	480	Hall	2,470	290	20	20
Comal	254,670	69,640	2,830	5,150	Hamilton	5,170	1,070	60	80
Comanche	12,150	1,900	130	100	Hansford	1,890	290	20	30
Concho	1,430	770	30	20	Hardeman	6,250	920	70	70
Cooke	50,470	10,950	520	730	Hardin	40,290	7,680	470	580
Coryell	38,470	8,880	470	510	Harris	8,835,220	4,071,690	96,220	215,010
Cottle	1,710	130	10	0	Harrison	94,350	14,150	790	590

Moody Gardens, a popular tourist attraction in Galveston.

Lamberto Alvarez photo.

Travelers' Top Attractions, 2007

Most visited sites by Texans (traveling more than 50 miles) and non-residents. *Source: Survey for Office of Governor.*

Rank	Texans	Rank	Non Texans
1.	Alamo	1.	Galveston Island
2.	River Walk	2.	Alamo
3.	Galveston Island	3.	San Marcos Outlets
4.	State Capitol	4.	River Walk
5.(T)	South Padre Island	5.	State Capitol
5.(T)	Six Flags	6.	South Padre Island
7.	NASA Space Center	7.	Cabela's*
8.	Ft. Worth Stockyards	8.	Sea World
9.	Fort Worth Zoo	9.	State Fair
10.	Cabela's*	10.	Six Flags
11.(T)	Sea World	11.	Kemah Boardwalk
11.(T)	Moody Gardens	12.	Ft. Worth Stockyards
13.	Ballpark at Arlington	13.	Fiesta Texas
14.	Kemah Boardwalk	14.	Moody Gardens
15.	San Marcos Outlets	15.	Ballpark at Arlington

* Includes Fort Worth and Buda locations.

Top Counties, 2007

The counties with the most visitor spending in 2007 are listed below, by rank.

Rank	County/Cities	($ Millions)
1.	Harris (Houston)	$ 8,835.2
2.	Dallas	7,085.5
3.	Bexar (San Antonio)	5,250.3
4.	Tarrant (Ft. Worth/Arlington)	3,978.9
5.	Travis (Austin)	3,318.8
6.	El Paso	1,259.8
7.	Hidalgo (McAllen)	1,060.4
8.	Collin (Plano/Frisco)	888.9
9.	Nueces (Corpus Christi)	820.8
10.	Galveston	736.7
11.	Cameron (South Padre Is.)	689.5
12.	Potter (Amarillo)	640.7
13.	Lubbock	571.9
14.	Denton	476.5
15.	Webb (Laredo)	472.0

County	Spending ($000)	Earnings ($000)	Jobs	Local tax ($000)
Hartley	$ 1,010	$ 180	10	$ 10
Haskell	4,260	880	70	80
Hays	187,430	46,430	1,950	2,980
Hemphill	4,210	710	40	120
Henderson	112,830	16,910	500	810
Hidalgo	1,060,400	262,300	13,970	18,740
Hill	61,090	9,510	580	560
Hockley	22,310	5,280	350	220
Hood	59,290	13,980	560	1,020
Hopkins	60,020	8,930	510	440
Houston	37,580	6,980	370	310
Howard	84,340	11,440	690	930
Hudspeth	5,640	330	20	0
Hunt	98,540	20,410	700	1,080
Hutchinson	36,860	7,470	480	510
Irion	11,110	300	20	0
Jack	4,680	710	50	40
Jackson	9,480	1,730	100	110

County	Spending ($000)	Earnings ($000)	Jobs	Local tax ($000)
Jasper	$ 39,250	$ 10,450	670	$ 750
Jeff Davis	7,670	2,720	100	0
Jefferson	461,610	87,940	4,870	7,290
Jim Hogg	5,370	1,210	60	60
Jim Wells	62,520	12,590	690	490
Johnson	128,900	19,890	870	1,400
Jones	8,400	2,070	120	90
Karnes	17,050	2,390	120	100
Kaufman	121,900	15,690	570	970
Kendall	67,110	16,940	920	1,030
Kenedy	830	270	20	0
Kent	780	120	10	0
Kerr	90,330	34,080	1,820	1,790
Kimble	16,960	2,280	180	230
King	40	10	0	0
Kinney	5,340	1,590	100	60
Kleberg	49,050	11,010	530	620
Knox	3,240	420	20	30

County	Spending ($000)	Earnings ($000)	Jobs	Local tax ($000)
La Salle	$6,940	$1,200	70	$80
Lamar	60,770	14,990	740	810
Lamb	11,330	1,140	80	60
Lampasas	13,040	2,240	160	180
Lavaca	14,740	3,140	150	220
Lee	21,750	4,270	200	160
Leon	32,180	4,240	270	360
Liberty	45,650	13,420	450	580
Limestone	17,030	2,170	130	240
Lipscomb	2,400	150	10	0
Live Oak	30,000	3,140	190	290
Llano	85,620	31,950	1,820	1,820
Loving	30	10	0	0
Lubbock	571,880	163,250	6,700	7,780
Lynn	1,090	220	20	10
Madison	10,410	2,160	140	210
Marion	8,290	2,070	170	150
Martin	14,960	540	30	10
Mason	2,560	570	50	30
Matagorda	43,120	13,750	860	960
Maverick	48,460	10,000	570	840
McCulloch	14,700	1,700	140	150
McLennan	435,130	88,420	4,910	6,020
McMullen	750	140	10	0
Medina	40,260	6,580	350	320
Menard	2,900	310	20	20
Midland	277,260	60,360	3,030	3,610
Milam	28,510	5,930	310	310
Mills	3,030	510	30	40
Mitchell	7,980	1,390	60	70
Montague	16,780	3,820	300	230
Montgomery	395,800	156,530	4,860	8,860
Moore	38,170	5,430	390	640
Morris	5,150	830	50	40
Motley	700	80	10	0
Nacgdoches	73,720	18,260	1,200	1,500
Navarro	41,940	9,500	540	650
Newton	4,920	700	30	40
Nolan	22,140	6,560	420	640
Nueces	820,780	213,800	10,410	19,880
Ochiltree	20,050	3,240	220	390
Oldham	9,990	950	70	70
Orange	107,800	20,310	1,090	1,220
Palo Pinto	74,220	12,480	590	600
Panola	14,560	2,700	180	310
Parker	112,820	20,960	840	1,340
Parmer	4,980	580	40	30
Pecos	48,470	6,500	530	1,050
Polk	52,590	13,890	770	550
Potter	640,730	128,010	7,350	12,320
Presidio	8,630	1,590	60	210
Rains	6,560	1,670	70	60
Randall	103,420	16,600	1,080	990
Reagan	2,210	400	30	10
Real	5,740	1,700	80	50
Red River	4,820	1,150	50	40
Reeves	38,370	4,500	340	520
Refugio	22,560	2,040	120	150
Roberts	1,090	30	0	0

County	Spending ($000)	Earnings ($000)	Jobs	Local tax ($000)
Robertson	$20,150	$3,390	230	$420
Rockwall	52,610	11,450	450	860
Runnels	6,640	1,080	80	50
Rusk	37,080	6,110	320	400
Sabine	11,630	2,080	160	30
S.Augustne	7,920	1,820	100	70
SanJacinto	11,830	2,320	170	70
SanPatricio	94,330	18,670	920	1,560
San Saba	3,930	880	60	40
Schleicher	470	120	10	10
Scurry	27,280	7,370	480	360
Shackelford	2,100	1,330	90	40
Shelby	27,730	5,270	390	330
Sherman	5,710	440	40	20
Smith	292,550	62,470	3,160	4,190
Somervell	15,330	3,440	180	370
Starr	26,010	4,910	270	410
Stephens	6,210	1,450	110	100
Sterling	2,330	150	10	10
Stonewall	1,000	240	20	10
Sutton	10,770	2,760	230	320
Swisher	3,550	720	40	30
Tarrant	3,978,860	2,956,040	62,130	71,340
Taylor	361,980	65,630	3,540	6,000
Terrell	1,470	280	20	0
Terry	5,930	1,600	120	110
Throckmrton	3,660	170	10	0
Titus	49,540	8,240	460	600
Tom Green	171,770	47,150	2,890	2,200
Travis	3,318,770	970,680	36,840	84,260
Trinity	11,150	5,490	330	140
Tyler	10,550	2,330	180	130
Upshur	22,080	2,940	180	180
Upton	2,490	580	50	40
Uvalde	59,820	10,230	630	940
Val Verde	57,350	16,330	830	1,210
Van Zandt	47,690	7,880	460	440
Victoria	178,180	34,840	1,740	2,410
Walker	90,020	16,810	1,140	960
Waller	38,890	4,270	160	300
Ward	12,520	3,120	220	250
Washington	85,220	11,540	620	730
Webb	472,020	112,210	5,520	7,180
Wharton	32,120	8,160	530	540
Wheeler	19,260	2,660	180	230
Wichita	194,090	41,990	2,990	3,520
Wilbarger	19,060	3,990	260	310
Willacy	23,780	3,190	160	170
Williamson	408,870	88,600	3,800	7,800
Wilson	23,770	4,220	230	150
Winkler	4,350	700	50	50
Wise	50,340	13,280	760	860
Wood	26,630	8,160	450	260
Yoakum	4,480	880	60	60
Young	24,620	6,800	390	340
Zapata	14,700	2,450	160	130
Zavala	7,700	820	50	60

Telecommunications Trends to High-Speed, Wireless

The chart below shows the move since the beginning of the decade to wireless communications, and the decline in the number of telephone land lines in Texas and nationwide. The chart also shows the growth of high-speed Internet use in the state and in the United States. *Sources: Trends in Telephone Service, Federal Communications Commission, February 2008; and National Exchange Carrier Association 2008 Study Results.*

	2000	2002	2003	2004	2005	2006	2007
Mobile Wireless Telephone Subscribers							
Texas	6,705,423	9,650,715	10,776,234	12,091,134	14,424,353	16,927,880	18,792,225
U.S.	90,643,058	130,751,459	147,623,734	167,313,001	192,053,067	217,418,404	238,229,953
Local Telephone Lines							
Texas	13,657,444	12,949,056	12,717,073	11,590,497	10,945,498	10,308,842	9,692,891
U.S.	188,499,586	180,095,333	173,140,710	165,978,892	157,041,487	146,848,926	135,121,037
High-Speed Lines for Internet							
Texas	252,721	1,015,245	1,571,250	2,203,490	2,943,487	4,357,437	6,855,680
U.S.	4,106,918	15,787,647	22,995,444	31,950,574	42,517,810	65,270,912	100,921,647

High-Speed Lines by Technology as of June 2007

	DSL	Cable Modem	Traditional Wireline	Fiber	Satellite	Fixed Wireless	Mobile Wireless	Power Line	Total
Texas	2,194,456	2,081,963	37,066	169,821	*	72,403	*	0	6,855,680
U.S.	27,836,103	34,408,533	708,722	1,402,652	668,803	586,141	35,305,253	5,420	100,921,647

* Data withheld to maintain firm confidentiality.

Percent of U.S. Households with Internet Connections

Year	Internet			Dail-Up			High-Speed			Other		
	Rural	Urban	Total	Rural	Urban	Total	Rural	Urban	Total	Rural	Urban	Total
2003	54.1	54.8	54.6	40.4	32.3	34.3	13.2	21.8	19.9	0.4	0.5	0.4
2007	58.3	62.6	61.7	19.3	8.5	10.7	38.8	53.8	50.8	0.3	0.3	0.3

Source: Trends in Telephone Service, Federal Communications Commission, February 2008.

Summary Statistics for Natural Gas in Texas

	2002	2003	2004	2005	2006	2007
Total Supply (MMcf, million cubic feet)	7,136,599	7,349,612	7,320,094	7,058,461	6,868,572	7,485,099
Consumption (million cubic feet) delivered to consumers						
Residential	209,951	206,694	191,507	185,124	166,225	199,680
Commercial	226,273	218,565	192,901	159,972	147,366	161,199
Industrial	1,978,184	1,866,138	1,814,173	1,341,461	1,288,887	1,296,251
Vehicle Fuel	1,811	2,2183	2,485	1,811	1,866	1,966
Electric Power	1,550,292	1,453,858	1,394,408	1,466,263	1,463,658	1,473,555
Number of Consumers						
Residential	3,809,370	3,859,647	3,939,101	3,984,481	4,067,508	4,155,204
Commercial	317,446	320,786	322,242	322,999	329,918	326,762
Industrial	9,143	9,015	9,359	9,136	8,664	11,043
Average Price for Natural Gas (dollars per Mcf, thousand cubic feet)						
Residential	$ 7.29	$ 9.22	$ 10.37	$ 12.48	$ 13.11	$ 12.00
Commercial	5.49	7.59	8.36	10.47	10.25	9.77
Industrial	3.40	5.36	5.91	7.62	6.69	6.76
Vehicle Fuel	5.67	8.09	8.58	10.52	10.07	9.76
Electric Power	3.41	5.47	5.90	8.12	6.55	6.77

Source: Federal Energy Information Administration, Natural Gas Annual 2007.

Texas Electric Grids: Demand and Capacity

- The Electric Reliability Council of Texas (**ERCOT**) operates the electric grid for 75 percent of the state.
- The Panhandle, South Plains and a small corner of Northeast Texas are under the Southwest Power Pool (**SPP**).
- El Paso and the far western corner of the Trans Pecos are under the Western Electric Coordinating Council (**WECC**).
- The southeast corner of Texas is under the **SERC** Reliability Corporation.

The councils were first formed in 1968 to ensure adequate bulk power supply.

History *(in megawatts)*							**Projections**		
	2002	**2003**	**2004**	**2005**	**2006**	**2007**	**2008**	**2009**	**2010**
ERCOT demand	55,833	59,282	58,531	59,060	62,669	64,010	65,383	66,830	68,331
capacity	76,849	74,764	73,850	66,724	71,156	71,510	71,405	71,839	72,553
% margin*	27.3	20.7	20.7	11.5	11.9	10.5	8.4	7.0	5.8
SPP demand	38,298	39,428	39,383	41,079	42,266	43,196	44,073	44,911	45,711
capacity	47,233	45,802	48,000	46,376	46,564	47,758	48,097	50,309	51,544
% margin	18.9	13.9	18.0	11.4	9.2	9.6	14.5	14.3	13.8
WECC demand	117,032	120,894	121,205	128,464	134,157	136,804	139,704	142,514	145,237
capacity	142,624	150,277	155,455	160,026	169,950	173,695	175,753	179,070	180,214
% margin	17.9	19.6	22.0	19.7	21.1	21.2	20.5	20.4	19.4
SERC demand	154,459	148,380	153,024	186,049	196,111	200,073	204,432	208,908	212,603
capacity	172,485	177,231	182,861	219,749	231,123	230,489	235,229	242,315	246,919
% margin	10.5	16.3	16.3	15.3	15.1	13.2	13.1	13.8	13.9
U.S. demand	696,376	696,752	692,908	746,470	760,108	774,926	791,828	807,165	821,612
capacity	833,380	856,131	875,870	882,125	906,155	913.738	925,916	942,084	953,221
% margin	16.4	18.6	20.9	15.4	16.1	15.2	14.5	14.3	13.8

Capacity Margin is the amount of unused available capability of an electric power system at peak load as a percentage of capacity resources. Source: Federal Energy Information Administration, 2007.

Transmission lines at the South Texas Nuclear Plant in Matagorda County. Robert Plocheck photo.

Nuclear Power Plants

	Texas	**U.S.**
Units	4**	104

NET GENERATION				
Year	**Total mil. kWh**	**% of total**	**Total mil. kWh**	**% of total**
2006	41,264	10.3	787,219	19.4
2004	40,435	10.4	788,528	19.9
2002	35,618	9.2	780,064	20.2

NET SUMMER CAPACITY				
	Total mil. kW	**% of total**	**Total mil. kW**	**% of total**
2006	4.86	4.8	100.33	10.2
2004	4.86	4.8	99.63	10.3
2002	4.74	5.0	98.66	10.9

**Texas has two nuclear plants; South Texas near Bay City and Comanche Peak near Glen Rose. Each has two units.

Electric Cooperatives

Source: Texas Electric Cooperatives, 2009.

Electric cooperatives are nonprofit, consumer-owned utilities providing electric service primarily in rural areas. Rates are regulated by the Public Utility Commission of Texas.

The nation's first electric cooperative was established in 1935 at Bartlett in Central Texas. It and others were organized when investor-owned utilities neglected or refused to serve farms and rural communities. By 1940 there were 567 cooperatives in 46 states.

Today Texas is home to 65 distribution co-ops and nine generation and transmission co-ops serving nearly 3 million member-customers.

And, there are more than 286,000 miles of lines linking 232 of the 254 counties. ☆

The Horse Hollow wind farm in Nolan and Taylor counties. Robert Plocheck photo.

Wind Energy Continues Expansion in State

Source: State Energy Conservation Office, Austin, 2009, and other sources.

In 2006, Texas surpassed California to lead the nation in wind-generating capacity and in that year accounted for almost a third of new installed wind capacity in the U.S.

By the end of 2007, U.S. installed wind capacity had grown to 16,596 MW, enough to power about 5 million homes based on their average household consumption in 2006. In 2007, Texas had installed wind capacity of 4,296 MW, enough to power about 1 million homes, based on average electric use in 2006.

At least 1,557 additional MW of installed wind capacity projects came on line in West Texas in 2007, with an additional 1,396 MW currently under construction in Texas.

As of 2007, all of Texas' utility-scale wind projects were in the western parts of the state. The McCamey area, south of Odessa and Midland, saw the first wave of wind development in Texas.

West Central Texas continues to experience rapid growth and is home to the largest single onshore wind farm in the world, FPL Energy's 735 MW Horse Hollow site, which has 428 wind turbines covering about 47,000 acres of Nolan and Taylor counties, near Sweetwater and Abilene.

Along the Gulf Coast, plans are under way to build wind farms both on land and offshore. Phase I of the Peñascal Wind Power project and the Gulf Winds wind farm, both in Kenedy County, began partial operations in early 2009. Peñascal will have 84 turbines and Gulf Winds will have 118 when fully operational.

The Electric Reliability Council of Texas (ERCOT), which manages the state's largest power grid, reports that wind energy accounted for 2.1 percent of

Installed Wind Capacity in megawatts (MW)			
YEAR	Texas	California	U.S.
2007	4,296	2,439	16,596
2006	2,739	2,376	11,575
2005	1,995	2,150	9,149
2004	1,293	2,096	6,740
2003	1,293	2,043	6,374
2002	1,096	1,822	4,685
2001	1,096	1,714	4,261
2000	181	1,646	2,566
1999	180	1,646	2,500
Source: U.S. Department of Energy			

electricity generated in its region in 2006, compared with just 1.1 percent in 2004. In the U.S., by contrast, wind power provided just 0.8 percent of electricity at the end of 2006. By 2007, wind energy accounted for 2.9 percent of electricity generated in the Texas ERCOT region.

Since ERCOT is responsible for ensuring the reliability and adequacy of the electric grid, it makes capacity calculations to determine if it will have sufficient generating capacity on the grid. Wind power is variable and ERCOT historical wind generation data reveals that there is often less wind blowing on summer afternoons that coincide with peak electrical demand.

For planning purposes, ERCOT determined that in the future, it can count on just 8.7 percent of its installed wind capacity to alleviate Texas' peak summer demand. It also notes that conventional generation must be available to meet forecast load and reserve requirements. ☆

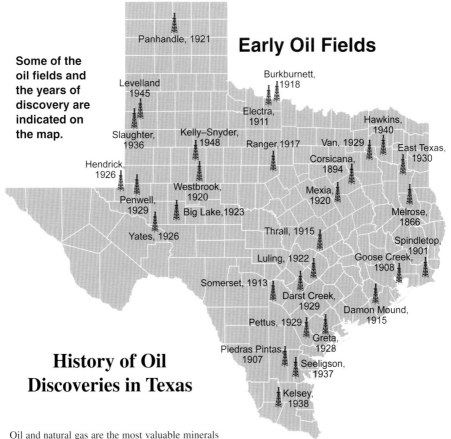

Early Oil Fields

Some of the oil fields and the years of discovery are indicated on the map.

Panhandle, 1921
Burkburnett, 1918
Levelland 1945
Electra, 1911
Hawkins, 1940
Slaughter, 1936
Kelly–Snyder, 1948
Ranger, 1917
Van, 1929
East Texas, 1930
Hendrick, 1926
Corsicana, 1894
Penwell, 1929
Westbrook, 1920
Big Lake, 1923
Mexia, 1920
Melrose, 1866
Yates, 1926
Thrall, 1915
Spindletop, 1901
Luling, 1922
Goose Creek, 1908
Somerset, 1913
Darst Creek, 1929
Damon Mound, 1915
Pettus, 1929
Greta, 1928
Piedras Pintas, 1907
Seeligson, 1937
Kelsey, 1938

History of Oil Discoveries in Texas

Oil and natural gas are the most valuable minerals produced in Texas, contributing 18.2 percent of the oil production in the United States in 2006, and nearly 30 percent of the gas production in the nation in 2005, the latest figures available.

Oil and gas have been produced from most areas of Texas and from rocks of all geologic eras except the Precambrian. All of the major sedimentary basins of Texas have produced some oil or gas.

The Permian Basin of West Texas has yielded large quantities of oil since the Big Lake discovery in 1923, although there was a smaller discovery in the Westbrook field in Mitchell County three years earlier.

The 1923 discovery, Santa Rita No. 1 in Reagan County, was on University of Texas land, and it and Texas A&M University both have benefitted from the royalties.

Although large quantities of petroleum have been produced from rocks of Permian age, production in the area also occurs from older Paleozoic rocks. Production from rocks of Paleozoic age occurs primarily from North Central Texas westward to New Mexico and southwestward to the Rio Grande, but there is also significant Paleozoic production in North Texas.

Mesozoic rocks are the primary hydrocarbon reservoirs of the East Texas Basin and the area south and east of the Balcones Fault Zone. Cenozoic sandstones are the main reservoirs along the Gulf Coast and offshore state waters.

Earliest Oil

Indians found oil seeping from the soils of Texas long before the first Europeans arrived. They told explorers that the fluid had medicinal values. The first record of Europeans using crude oil, however, was the caulking of boats in 1543 by survivors of the DeSoto expedition near Sabine Pass.

Melrose, in Nacogdoches County, was the site in 1866 of the first drilled well to produce oil in Texas. The driller was Lyne T. Barret.

Barret used an auger, fastened to a pipe and rotated by a cogwheel driven by a steam engine — a basic principle of rotary drilling that has been used since, although with much improvement.

In 1867 Amory (Emory) Starr and Peyton F. Edwards brought in a well at Oil Springs, in the same area.

Other wells followed and Nacogdoches County was the site of Texas' first commercial oil field, pipeline and effort to refine crude. Several thousand barrels of oil were produced there during these years.

First major refinery, 1899

Other oil was found in crudely dug wells in Bexar County in 1889 and in Hardin County in 1893. The three small wells in Hardin County led to the creation of two small refineries in 1896 and 1898.

Spindletop field in Jefferson County in 1902. Texas Energy Museum, Beaumont, photo.

But it was not until June 9, 1894, that Texas had a major discovery. This occurred in the drilling of a water well for the city of Corsicana. Oil caused that well to be abandoned, but a company formed in 1895 drilled several producing oil wells.

The first well-equipped refinery in Texas was built there in 1898, and this plant, which shipped its first production in 1899, usually is called the state's first refinery, despite the earlier efforts. Discovery of the Powell Field, also near Corsicana, followed in 1900.

Spindletop, 1901

Jan. 10, 1901, is the most famous date in Texas petroleum history. This is the date that the great gusher erupted in the oil well being drilled at Spindletop, near Beaumont, by a mining engineer, Capt. A. F. Lucas.

Thousands of barrels of oil flowed before the well could be capped. This was the first salt dome oil discovery. Spindletop created a sensation throughout the world, and encouraged exploration and drilling in Texas that has continued since.

Texas oil production increased from 836,039 barrels in 1900 to 4,393,658 in 1901; and in 1902 Spindletop alone produced 17,421,000 barrels, or 94 percent of the state's production. Prices dropped to 3 cents a barrel, an all-time low.

Offshore, 1908

The first offshore drilling was in shallow northern Galveston Bay, where the Goose Creek Field was discovered in 1908. Several dry holes followed and the field was abandoned. But a gusher in 1916 created the real boom there. A water-well drilling outfit on the W. T. Waggoner Ranch in Wichita County hit oil, bringing in the Electra Field in 1911.

Salt dome oil fields followed at Damon Mound in 1915, Barbers Hill in 1916, and Blue Ridge in 1919.

In 1917 came the discovery of the Ranger Field in Eastland County. The Burkburnett Field in Wichita County was discovered in 1919.

About this time, oil discoveries brought a short era of swindling, with oil stock promotion and selling on a nationwide scale. It ended after a series of trials in federal courts.

The Mexia Field in Limestone County was discovered in 1920, and the second Powell Field in Navarro County in 1924.

Another great area really developed in 1921 in the Panhandle, a field with sensational oil and gas discoveries in Hutchinson and contiguous counties and the booming of Borger.

The Luling Field was opened in 1922, and 1925 saw the comeback of Spindletop with a production larger than that of the original field.

In 1925 Howard County was opened for production. Hendricks in Winkler County opened in 1926 and Raccoon Bend, Austin County, opened in 1927. Sugar Land was the most important Texas oil development in 1928.

The Darst Creek Field was opened in 1929. In the same year, new records of productive sand thickness were set for the industry at Van, Van Zandt County. Pettus was another contribution of 1929 in Bee County.

East Texas Field

The East Texas field, biggest of them all, was discovered near Turnertown and Joinerville, Rusk County, by veteran wildcatter C. M. (Dad) Joiner, in October 1930. The success of this well — drilled on land condemned many times by geologists of the major companies — was followed by the biggest leasing campaign in history.

The field soon was extended to Kilgore, Longview and northward. The East Texas field brought overproduction and a rapid sinking of the price. Private attempts were made to prorate production, but without much success.

On Aug. 17, 1931, Gov. Ross S. Sterling ordered the National Guard into the field, which he placed under martial law. This drastic action was taken after the Texas Railroad Commission had been enjoined from enforcing production restrictions. After the complete shutdown, the Texas Legislature enacted legal proration, the system of regulation still utilized.

West Texas

The most significant subsequent oil discoveries in Texas were those in West Texas. In 1936, oil was discovered west of Lubbock in the Duggan Field in Cochran County.

Originally it was thought to be one of two fields, it and the adjacent Slaughter Field, but in 1940 the Railroad Commission ruled that the two produced from one reservoir, called Slaughter. The prolific Levelland Field, in Cochran and Hockley counties, was discovered in 1945. A discovery well in Scurry County on Nov. 21, 1948, was the first of several major developments in that region. Many of the leading Texas counties in minerals value are in that section.

Austin Chalk

The Giddings Field on the Austin Chalk in Lee, Fayette and Burleson counties had significant drilling in the 1970s that continued into the 1980s. ☆

Chronological Listing of Major Oil Discoveries

The following list gives the name of the field, county and discovery date. Sources include Texas Mid-Continent Oil and Gas Association from records of the U.S. Bureau of Mines; the Oil and Gas Journal; previous Texas Almanacs, the New Handbook of Texas, and the Energy Information Administration of the U.S. Department of Energy.

FIELD	COUNTY	Year	FIELD	COUNTY	Year
Corsicana	Navarro	1894	Salt Flat	Caldwell	1928
Powell	Navarro	1900	Sugarland	Fort Bend	1928
Spindletop	Jefferson	1901	Darst Creek	Guadalupe	1929
Sour Lake	Hardin	1902	Penwell	Ector	1929
Batson-Old	Hardin	1903	Pettus	Bee	1929
Humble	Harris	1905	Van	Van Zandt	1929
Mission	Bexar	1907	Cowden North	Ector	1930
Piedras Pintas	Duval	1907	East Texas	Cherokee-Gregg-Rusk-Smith-Upshur	1930
Goose Creek	Harris	1908			
Panhandle Osborne	Wheeler	1910	Fuhrman-Mascho	Andrews	1930
Archer County	Archer	1911	Sand Hills	Crane	1930
Electra	Wichita	1911	Conroe	Montgomery	1931
Burk	Wichita	1912	Manvel	Brazoria	1931
Iowa Park	Wichita	1913	Tomball	Harris	1933
Orange	Orange	1913	Dickinson	Galveston	1934
Somerset	Bexar	1913	Hastings East	Brazoria	1934
Damon Mound	Brazoria	1915	Means	Andrews	1934
Thrall	Williamson	1915	Old Ocean	Brazoria	1934
Wilbarger County	Wilbarger	1915	Tom O'Connor	Refugio	1934
Barbers Hill	Chambers	1916	Anahuac	Chambers	1935
Stephens County Regular	Stephens	1916	Goldsmith	Ector	1935
			Keystone	Winkler	1935
Ranger	Eastland	1917	Plymouth	San Patricio	1935
Young County	Young	1917	Withers	Wharton	1936
Burkburnett Townsite	Wichita	1918	Pearsall	Frio	1936
Desdemona	Eastland	1918	Seminole	Gaines	1936
Hull	Liberty	1918	Slaughter	Cochran-Hockley	1936
West Columbia	Brazoria	1918	Talco	Titus-Franklin	1936
Blue Ridge	Fort Bend	1919	Wasson	Gaines	1936
KMA (Kemp-Munger-Allen)	Wichita	1919	Webster	Harris	1936
			Jordan	Crane-Ector	1937
Mexia	Limestone-Freestone	1920	Seeligson	Jim Wells-Kleberg	1937
Refugio	Refugio	1920	Dune	Crane	1938
Westbrook	Mitchell	1920	Kelsey	Brooks-Jim Hogg-Starr	1938
Panhandle	Carson-Collingsworth-Gray-Hutchinson-Moore-Potter-Wheeler	1921	Walnut Bend	Cooke	1938
			West Ranch	Jackson	1938
			Diamond M	Scurry	1940
Currie	Navarro	1921	Hawkins	Wood	1940
Mirando City	Webb	1921	Fullerton	Andrews	1941
Pierce Junction	Harris	1921	Oyster Bayou	Chambers	1941
Thompsons	Fort Bend	1921	Tijerina-Canales-Blucher	Jim Wells-Kleberg	1941
Aviators	Webb	1922			
High Island	Galveston-Chambers	1922	Quitman	Wood	1942
Luling-Branyon	Caldwell-Guadalupe	1923	Welch	Dawson	1942
Big Lake	Reagan	1923	Russell	Gaines	1943
Cooke County	Cooke	1924	Anton-Irish	Hale-Lamb-Lubbock	1944
Richland	Navarro	1924	Mabee	Andrews-Martin	1944
Wortham	Freestone	1924	Midland Farms	Andrews	1944
Boling	Wharton	1925	TXL Devonian	Ector	1944
Howard-Glasscock	Howard	1925	Block 31	Crane	1945
Lytton Springs	Caldwell	1925	Borregos	Kleberg	1945
McCamey	Upton	1925	Dollarhide	Andrews	1945
Hendrick	Winkler	1926	Levelland	Cochran-Hockley	1945
Iatan East	Howard	1926	Andector	Ector	1946
McElroy	Crane	1926	Kelly-Snyder	Scurry	1948
Yates	Pecos	1926	Cogdell Area	Scurry	1949
Raccoon Bend	Austin	1927	Pegasus	Upton-Midland	1949
Waddell	Crane	1927	Spraberry Trend	Glasscock-Midland	1949
Agua Dulce-Stratton	Nueces	1928	Prentice	Yoakum	1950
Greta	Refugio	1928	Salt Creek	Kent	1950
Kermit	Winkler	1928	Dora Roberts	Midland	1954

Top Oil Producing Counties since Discovery

There are 34 counties that have produced more than 500 million barrels of oil since discovery. The counties are ranked below. The column at right lists the number of producing oil wells in the county in February 2009.

Rank	County	Barrels	Oil Wells	Rank	County	Barrels	Oil Wells
1.	Gregg	3,296,738,687	3,262	19.	Howard	833,920,513	3,432
2.	Ector	3,162,302,882	5,854	20.	Montgomery	778,946,236	148
3.	Andrews	2,878,421,083	7,123	21.	Ward	778,506,194	3,107
4.	Gaines	2,280,700,372	3,474	22.	Fort Bend	698,774,158	290
5.	Yoakum	2,159,145,183	3,542	23.	Jackson	685,451,542	262
6.	Scurry	2,093,199,012	2,601	24.	Gray	677,040,379	2,794
7.	Rusk	1,839,978,556	1,876	25.	Midland	660,759,505	4,799
8.	Pecos	1,800,674,586	3,046	26.	Duval	591,490,998	703
9.	Crane	1,780,451,476	4,135	27.	Kent	586,800,402	565
10.	Hockley	1,707,774,562	4,243	28.	Nueces	567,042,580	197
11.	Harris	1,381,741,090	338	29.	Van Zandt	553,868,680	537
12.	Refugio	1,335,849,189	716	30.	Jefferson	547,949,678	170
13.	Brazoria	1,280,656,566	347	31.	Liberty	543,535,175	652
14.	Wood	1,215,758,738	577	32.	Hutchinson	533,783,323	3,118
15.	Winkler	1,088,894,404	1,788	33.	Reagan	524,916,946	3,969
16.	Chambers	912,513,077	170	34.	Cochran	518,124,825	1,964
17.	Upton	876,660,507	2,973		Source: Texas Railroad Commission.		
18.	Wichita	835,867,684	5,736				

Oil Production since Discovery

- More than 1 billion barrels
- 500 million to 1 billion
- 250 million to 500 million

Texas Oil Production History

The table shows the year of oil or gas discovery in each county, oil production in 2007 and 2008 and total oil production from date of discovery to Jan. 1, 2009. **The 16 counties omitted have not produced oil.**

The table has been compiled by the Texas Almanac from information provided in past years by the Texas Mid-Continent Oil & Gas Assoc., which used data from the U.S. Bureau of Mines and the Texas state comptroller. Since 1970, production figures have been compiled from records of the Railroad Commission of Texas. The figures in the final column are cumulative of all previously published figures. The change in sources, due to different techniques, may create some discrepancies in year-to-year comparisons among counties.

County	Year of Discovery	Production in Barrels*		Total Production to Jan. 1, 2009	County	Year of Discovery	Production in Barrels*		Total Production to Jan. 1, 2009
		2007	2008				2007	2008	
Anderson	1928	762,135	686,177	302,790,904	Crockett	1925	5,651,859	5,186,358	382,769,418
Andrews	1929	24,185,685	22,113,471	2,878,421,083	Crosby	1955	517,025	505,555	26,579,652
Angelina	1936	15,025	18,836	922,232	Culberson	1953	103,574	89,541	25,181,629
Aransas	1936	577,199	415,312	86,752,078	Dallas	1986	0	0	231
Archer	1911	1,045,828	989,991	498,259,755	Dawson	1934	4,437,665	3,854,398	396,991,802
Atascosa	1917	635,658	539,260	152,629,270	Delta	1984	0	0	65,089
Austin	1915	318,226	307,315	116,148,291	Denton	1937	527,508	460,645	8,180,034
Bandera	1995	1,226	1,419	28,056	DeWitt	1930	629,894	521,182	69,215,469
Bastrop	1913	196,192	454,969	17,407,047	Dickens	1953	1,340,613	1,166,336	22,585,708
Baylor	1924	105,332	97,940	58,412,627	Dimmit	1943	1,110,469	808,408	109,686,567
Bee	1929	539,760	470,094	109,961,653	Donley	1967	361	418	1,040
Bell	1980	0	0	446	Duval	1905	1,581,803	1,408,350	591,490,998
Bexar	1889	119,502	105,708	36,307,189	Eastland	1917	403,954	312,285	157,880,111
Borden	1949	3,675,854	3,310,756	420,834,833	Ector	1926	18,014,345	17,309,614	3,162,302,882
Bosque	2006	73	20	128	Edwards	1946	3,048	3,578	541,140
Bowie	1944	58,250	45,389	6,695,881	Ellis	1953	12	105	840,141
Brazoria	1902	2,505,089	2,402,836	1,280,656,566	Erath	1917	18,314	29,816	2,152,326
Brazos	1942	1,576,444	1,421,850	143,862,406	Falls	1937	1,541	2,971	856,806
Brewster	1969	0	0	56	Fannin	1980	0	0	13,281
Briscoe	1982	0	0	3,554	Fayette	1943	1,500,130	1,198,030	157,066,085
Brooks	1935	1,300,727	950,311	174,760,104	Fisher	1928	593,769	721,346	250,838,875
Brown	1917	111,294	96,654	53,691,485	Floyd	1952	1,182	1,318	161,461
Burleson	1938	1,883,385	1,894,940	200,305,339	Foard	1929	89,381	95,868	24,460,905
Caldwell	1922	888,840	839,889	284,965,062	Fort Bend	1919	2,126,074	1,818,131	698,774,158
Calhoun	1935	471,609	493,818	105,864,221	Franklin	1936	362,435	358,076	178,414,790
Callahan	1923	223,760	206,931	86,728,390	Freestone	1916	261,857	227,954	45,948,502
Cameron	1944	668	624	469,582	Frio	1934	525,338	545,139	148,017,467
Camp	1940	253,565	221,712	29,936,048	Gaines	1935	26,942,743	23,305,460	2,280,700,372
Carson	1921	285,315	259,653	181,028,897	Galveston	1922	1,524,558	1,403,858	458,658,287
Cass	1936	297,054	237,523	115,311,488	Garza	1926	3,641,734	3,303,006	349,670,353
Chambers	1916	1,160,161	862,720	912,513,007	Glasscock	1925	3,755,663	3,271,027	280,296,886
Cherokee	1926	279,740	227,283	71,829,670	Goliad	1930	747,490	536,983	85,722,059
Childress	1961	23,214	0	1,666,975	Gonzales	1902	228,418	212,247	44,505,620
Clay	1917	626,766	561,242	206,682,104	Gray	1925	1,178,573	1,029,275	677,040,379
Cochran	1936	3,875,846	3,460,813	518,124,825	Grayson	1930	1,164,437	1,057,786	260,508,926
Coke	1942	474,260	504,665	225,151,572	Gregg	1931	2,729,987	2,478,611	3,296,738,687
Coleman	1902	248,183	249,868	95,750,052	Grimes	1952	138,866	128,357	18,812,239
Collin	1963	0	0	53,000	Guadalupe	1922	1,209,456	1,051,739	208,764,736
Collingswrth	1936	2,250	2,139	1,246,354	Hale	1946	2,799,659	2,583,943	186,828,055
Colorado	1932	446,194	382,409	42,873,523	Hamilton	1938	587	576	154,617
Comanche	1918	9,679	8,147	5,994,295	Hansford	1937	154,863	195,835	39,724,057
Concho	1940	438,735	370,634	27,623,937	Hardeman	1944	1,247,753	1,088,843	87,692,145
Cooke	1924	1,983,107	1,964,108	395,728,965	Hardin	1893	2,298,675	2,354,886	446,459,483
Coryell	1964	0	0	1,100	Harris	1905	1,891,882	1,610,674	1,381,741,090
Cottle	1955	153,820	171,535	5,089,505	Harrison	1928	1,340,899	1,315,234	93,846,180
Crane	1926	9,425,930	8,722,797	1,780,451,476					

*Total includes condensate production.

County	Year of Discovery	Production in Barrels* 2007	2008	Total Production to Jan. 1, 2009
Hartley	1937	207,034	194,327	8,137,744
Haskell	1929	313,200	275,853	117,845,564
Hays	1956	0	0	296
Hemphill	1955	1,510,525	1,460,045	42,603,845
Henderson	1934	443,571	348,309	179,160,344
Hidalgo	1934	3,372,645	2,795,774	121,802,723
Hill	1929	114	581	76,090
Hockley	1937	18,945,325	16,796,250	1,707,774,562
Hood	1958	221,938	406,892	896,887
Hopkins	1936	258,390	200,629	90,574,108
Houston	1934	745,419	651,272	59,438,605
Howard	1925	5,470,673	4,887,113	833,920,513
Hudspeth	2008	0	59	59
Hunt	1942	0	0	2,024,660
Hutchinson	1923	840,184	786,761	533,783,323
Irion	1928	2,033,665	2,208,404	108,072,771
Jack	1923	755,191	769,648	206,693,261
Jackson	1934	1,007,409	1,108,061	685,451,542
Jasper	1928	554,816	394,868	36,668,915
Jeff Davis	1980	0	0	20,866
Jefferson	1901	4,036,911	3,663,329	547,949,678
Jim Hogg	1921	278,367	221,044	113,330,938
Jim Wells	1931	151,721	156,583	463,257,600
Johnson	1962	23,121	37,055	290,667
Jones	1926	770,751	694,420	223,545,352
Karnes	1930	367,997	348,035	109,679,348
Kaufman	1948	60,955	55,648	24,839,040
Kenedy	1947	321,332	247,747	40,191,863
Kent	1946	4,377,254	3,669,856	586,800,402
Kerr	1982	0	0	78,946
Kimble	1939	400	317	99,116
King	1943	2,054,336	1,772,603	184,540,228
Kinney	1960	0	0	402
Kleberg	1919	600,211	352,465	338,172,317
Knox	1946	221,951	202,501	62,593,203
Lamb	1945	575,540	628,564	40,304,321
Lampasas	1985	0	0	111
La Salle	1940	321,812	260,240	28,762,343
Lavaca	1941	711,495	716,154	33,376,692
Lee	1939	1,184,805	1,044,667	139,231,097
Leon	1936	972,600	765,442	66,329,623
Liberty	1904	3,572,962	2,687,188	543,535,175
Limestone	1920	212,479	166,414	120,118,010
Lipscomb	1956	1,609,218	1,808,591	65,155,771
Live Oak	1930	810,498	673,847	86,661,948
Llano	1978	0	0	647
Loving	1921	1,382,881	1,441,041	115,382,529
Lubbock	1941	1,458,595	1,292,260	74,343,601
Lynn	1950	263,484	243,793	19,994,058
Madison	1946	534,988	426,669	35,029,975
Marion	1910	185,894	179,910	56,333,390
Martin	1945	6,386,234	8,091,394	333,661,443
Matagorda	1901	1,205,468	1,224,891	284,847,197
Maverick	1929	1,681,487	1,754,187	57,752,900
McCulloch	1938	67,747	52,236	2,100,031
McLennan	1902	1,230	1,365	341,798

County	Year of Discovery	Production in Barrels* 2007	2008	Total Production to Jan. 1, 2009
McMullen	1922	1,384,192	1,393,965	109,155,713
Medina	1901	85,696	76,896	11,081,878
Menard	1946	114,850	134,511	7,793,511
Midland	1945	11,028,772	10,120,793	660,759,505
Milam	1921	412,131	369,934	22,393,390
Mills	1982	0	0	28,122
Mitchell	1920	3,341,818	3,264,353	237,440,481
Montague	1919	1,631,829	1,626,135	296,653,156
Montgomery	1931	964,095	1,085,908	778,946,236
Moore	1926	319,718	306,155	31,033,832
Morris	2004	1,747	1,651	9,782
Motley	1957	31,115	24,546	11,118,790
Nacgdoches	1866	348,164	506,391	5,455,385
Navarro	1894	881,315	356,548	219,670,847
Newton	1937	1,165,030	708,191	66,394,780
Nolan	1939	1,165,030	1,189,310	202,754,338
Nueces	1930	1,179,688	1,121,914	567,042,580
Ochiltree	1951	1,329,510	1,281,138	164,641,462
Oldham	1957	150,902	170,987	14,253,625
Orange	1913	1,074,788	844,572	161,338,833
Palo Pinto	1902	224,464	319,257	24,669,055
Panola	1917	2,584,705	2,300,548	101,798,224
Parker	1942	366,657	323,091	3,841,060
Parmer	1963	0	0	144,000
Pecos	1926	12,108,813	11,449,449	1,800,674,586
Polk	1930	1,670,023	1,548,784	129,934,743
Potter	1925	189,289	193,110	10,516,503
Presidio	1980	0	0	4,377
Rains	1955	0	0	148,897
Reagan	1923	5,668,643	5,451,291	524,916,946
Real	2003	1,723	1,093	26,072
Red River	1951	136,907	122,311	8,341,906
Reeves	1939	884,997	808,161	81,288,507
Refugio	1920	3,805,634	3,319,524	1,335,849,189
Roberts	1945	1,090,063	1,047,909	51,002,194
Robertson	1944	914,177	1,279,449	30,314,166
Runnels	1927	670,759	601,374	149,505,350
Rusk	1930	3,074,997	2,829,601	1,839,978,556
Sabine	1981	5,985	4,705	4,927,038
S.Augustine	1947	14,335	40,863	2,537,501
San Jacinto	1940	299,813	353,209	27,056,282
SanPatricio	1930	1,016,142	943,150	489,702,826
San Saba	1982	0	0	32,362
Schleicher	1934	475,779	416,708	89,587,660
Scurry	1923	14,736,137	13,545,618	2,093,199,012
Shackelford	1910	689,561	644,498	184,917,837
Shelby	1917	337,480	278,038	4,085,407
Sherman	1938	91,758	78,503	9,653,689
Smith	1931	1,543,692	1,312,558	270,590,739
Somervell	1978	6,530	8,253	14,955
Starr	1929	2,281,983	2,133,925	303,646,547
Stephens	1916	2,307,290	2,156,532	348,394,536
Sterling	1947	1,206,641	954,903	92,552,315
Stonewall	1938	893,641	866,649	266,055,123

*Total includes condensate production.

County	Year of Discovery	Production in Barrels*		Total Production to Jan. 1, 2009
		2007	2008	
Sutton	1948	91,394	89,343	8,109,965
Swisher	1981	0	0	6
Tarrant	1969	36,063	47,802	108,668
Taylor	1929	479,755	415,917	146,280,114
Terrell	1952	217,859	174,872	9,804,536
Terry	1940	4,018,035	3,879,461	454,448,008
Throckmrton	1925	703,125	607,810	223,823,500
Titus	1936	435,999	440,338	213,096,887
Tom Green	1940	625,476	549,208	94,412,845
Travis	1934	1,881	1,813	758,875
Trinity	1946	65,250	69,688	1,171,632
Tyler	1937	3,457,985	2,922,234	54,617,600
Upshur	1931	638,764	578,726	289,830,449
Upton	1925	12,630,170	13,361,158	876,660,507
Uvalde	1950	0	0	1,814
Val Verde	1935	2,379	1,370	147,091
Van Zandt	1929	767,173	657,963	553,868,680
Victoria	1931	749,775	746,011	256,086,329
Walker	1934	4,631	3,027	541,557
Waller	1934	892,378	667,316	31,561,342

County	Year of Discovery	Production in Barrels*		Total Production to Jan. 1, 2009
		2007	2008	
Ward	1928	5,608,654	5,965,307	778,,506,194
Washington	1915	503,599	407,989	33,262,559
Webb	1921	1,089,607	963,667	165,279,540
Wharton	1925	1,632,050	1,670,378	349,935,768
Wheeler	1910	1,827,798	2,091,356	107,925,620
Wichita	1910	2,053,530	1,934,556	835,867,684
Wilbarger	1915	730,843	643,043	266,350,561
Willacy	1936	886,097	699,153	117,187,001
Williamson	1915	8,186	7,065	9,576,044
Wilson	1941	273,936	259,709	49,940,119
Winkler	1926	3,869,293	3,401,149	1,088,894,404
Wise	1942	1,146,921	1,130,591	105,004,402
Wood	1940	3,959,644	3,321,179	1,215,758,738
Yoakum	1936	23,722,461	21,534,310	2,159,145,183
Young	1917	1,250,501	1,242,949	314,516,517
Zapata	1919	339,682	275,602	48,784,797
Zavala	1937	1,062,312	643,518	49,659,379

Source: Railroad Commission, 2007-08 production reports.

*Total includes condensate production.

Rig Counts and Wells Drilled by Year

Year	Rotary rigs active*		Permits	Texas wells completed		Wells drilled**
	Texas	U.S.	Texas	Oil	Gas	Texas
1982	994	3,117	41,224	16,296	6,273	27,648
1983	796	2,232	45,550	15,941	5,027	26,882
1984	850	2,428	37,507	18,716	5,489	30,898
1985	680	1,980	30,878	16,543	4,605	27,124
1986	313	964	15,894	10,373	3,304	18,707
1987	293	1,090	15,297	7,327	2,542	13,121
1988	280	936	† 13,493	6,441	2,665	12,261
1989	264	871	12,756	4,914	2,760	10,054
1990	348	1,009	14,033	5,593	2,894	11,231
1991	315	860	12,494	6,025	2,755	11,295
1992	251	721	12,089	5,031	2,537	9,498
1993	264	754	11,612	4,646	3,295	9,969
1994	274	775	11,030	3,962	3,553	9,299
1995	251	723	11,244	4,334	3,778	9,785
1996	283	779	12,669	4,061	4,060	9,747
1997	358	945	13,933	4,482	4,594	10,778
1998	303	827	9,385	4,509	4,907	11,057
1999	226	622	8,430	2,049	3,566	6,658
2000	343	918	12,021	3,111	4,580	8,854
2001	462	1,156	12,227	3,082	5,787	10,005
2002	338	830	9,716	3,268	5,474	9,877
2003	449	1,032	12,664	3,111	6,336	10,420
2004	506	1,192	14,700	3,446	7,118	11,587
2005	614	1,381	16,914	3,454	7,197	11,154
2006	746	1,649	18,952	4,761	8,534	12,764
2007	834	1,769	19,994	5,084	8,643	13,778
2008	898	1,880	24,073	6,208	10,361	16,641

Source for rig count: Baker Hughes Inc. This is an annual average from monthly reports.
†Totals shown for 1988 and after are number of drilling permits issued; data for previous years were total drilling applications received.
Wells drilled are oil and gas well **completions and dry holes drilled/plugged.

Oil and Gas Production by County, 2008

In 2008 in Texas, the total natural gas production from gas wells was 5,868,822,481 thousand cubic feet (MCF) and total crude oil production was 315,895,813 barrels (BBL). Total condensate was 43,273,184 barrels. Total casinghead production was 677,943,212 MCF. **Counties not listed in the chart below had no production in 2008.** *Source: Texas Railroad Commission.*

County	Oil (BBL)	Casing-head (MCF)	GW Gas (MCF)	Conden-sate (BBL)	County	Oil (BBL)	Casing-head (MCF)	GW Gas (MCF)	Conden-sate (BBL)
Anderson	619,085	4,510,217	6,616,060	67,092	Eastland	244,464	675,502	4,156,159	67,821
Andrews	22,102,151	24,746,824	1,403,147	11,320	Ector	17,304,762	28,522,868	8,512,595	4,852
Angelina	1,987	3,934	9,609,000	16,849	Edwards	2,463	60	15,292,130	1,115
Aransas	73,589	558,291	10,398,105	341,723	Ellis	104	17,797	4,666,912	1
Archer	989,869	425,958	20,808	122	Erath	4,594	104,961	5,884,932	25,222
Atascosa	509,567	185,140	5,419,392	29,693	Falls	2,971	0	0	0
Austin	232,943	54,523	7,180,676	74,372	Fayette	1,001,433	7,089,587	8,996,899	196,597
Bandera	1,419	0	0	0	Fisher	719,522	1,151,216	206,672	1,824
Bastrop	437,370	168,526	137,091	17,599	Floyd	1,318	0	0	0
Baylor	97,940	11	0	0	Foard	95,505	22	383,295	363
Bee	301,207	331,329	33,133,301	168,887	Fort Bend	1,504,226	2,003,870	19,803,912	313,905
Bexar	105,708	33	0	0	Franklin	311,298	314,301	2,893,950	46,778
Borden	3,310,756	2,616,324	0	0	Freestone	58,354	107,106	252,346,905	169,600
Bosque	0	0	219,967	20	Frio	542,930	616,486	1,033,353	2,200
Bowie	41,367	16,758	106,387	4,022	Gaines	23,292,067	19,141,645	13,594,270	13,393
Brazoria	1,784,624	1,722,207	25,613,345	613,212	Galveston	490,042	702,191	12,127,156	913,816
Brazos	1,328,142	4,620,813	5,109,198	93,708	Garza	3,303,006	685,448	0	0
Brooks	205,944	552,398	43,904,610	744,367	Glasscock	3,248,742	10,345,797	1,304,101	22,285
Brown	95,755	342,723	962,626	899	Goliad	228,470	373,860	47,017,248	308,513
Burleson	1,854,843	8,470,537	2,436,938	40,061	Gonzales	203,428	95,017	852,117	8,819
Caldwell	839,889	369,660	10,265	0	Gray	1,024,678	2,707,163	8,826,005	4,597
Calhoun	204,817	448,798	9,901,827	289,001	Grayson	1,045,300	3,678,326	1,491,974	12,486
Callahan	198,678	287,296	732,887	8,253	Gregg	2,220,288	2,597,272	48,484,238	258,323
Cameron	527	2,070	94,034	97	Grimes	93,107	548,421	18,283,726	35,250
Camp	221,688	2,278	597,453	24	Guadalupe	1,051,489	60,268	9,678	250
Carson	256,183	1,699,341	13,668,156	3,470	Hale	2,583,943	1,362,714	0	0
Cass	223,175	432,816	1,361,812	14,348	Hamilton	57	0	139,553	519
Chambers	692,769	1,231,708	7,711,517	169,951	Hansford	178,544	709,837	19,204,885	17,291
Cherokee	160,350	186,571	22,316,805	66,933	Hardeman	1,088,353	210,448	27,701	490
Childress	40,650	0	0	0	Hardin	1,406,780	2,322,583	14,877,826	948,106
Clay	552,650	365,390	250,654	8,592	Harris	1,280,655	901,321	19,341,985	330,019
Cochran	3,479,557	2,059,217	221,198	1,256	Harrison	340,552	2,377,389	122,437,949	974,682
Coke	502,486	2,962,162	579,268	2,179	Hartley	194,327	0	1,983,809	0
Coleman	246,554	606,503	878,406	3,314	Haskell	275,853	28,508	0	0
Collingswth	2,139	17,189	1,183,421	0	Hemphill	213,151	2,773,756	117,639,865	1,246,894
Colorado	173,678	397,007	20,460,414	208,731	Henderson	284,997	8,331,622	19,731,154	63,312
Comanche	6,708	42,219	508,625	1,439	Hidalgo	61,293	550,900	221,935,744	2,734,481
Concho	368,623	429,803	812,997	2,011	Hill	364	0	14,320,858	217
Cooke	1,956,264	3,638,695	255,022	7,844	Hockley	16,794,390	8,307,313	84,969	1,860
Cottle	60,037	39,331	6,221,664	111,498	Hood	557	40,484	51,028,493	406,335
Crane	8,619,654	48,536,103	11,116,965	103,143	Hopkins	199,009	135,930	364,304	1,620
Crockett	4,849,467	5,730,120	91,611,834	336,891	Houston	622,553	224,650	9,297,317	28,719
Crosby	505,555	44,769	0	0	Howard	4,876,200	5,403,719	497,568	10,913
Culberson	87,197	181,084	1,264,817	2,344	Hudspeth	0	0	2,676	59
Dallas	0	0	2,388,563	0	Hutchinson	769,650	4,688,107	8,973,451	17,111
Dawson	3,854,398	2,206,640	0	0	Irion	2,163,236	9,307,820	4,106,864	45,168
Denton	65,845	915,166	184,937,420	394,800	Jack	636,854	2,055,284	15,953,077	132,794
DeWitt	74,844	37,728	41,615,444	446,338	Jackson	658,639	891,107	15,515,835	449,422
Dickens	1,166,336	106,421	0	0	Jasper	112,370	389,985	9,602,811	282,498
Dimmit	778,687	1,560,416	2,608,119	29,721	Jefferson	807,396	1,312,696	55,182,862	2,855,933
Donley	0	0	14,002	418	Jim hogg	40,290	42,697	16,278,385	180,754
Duval	901,947	410,233	61,764,501	506,403	Jim wells	116,996	350,977	5,881,784	39,587

County	Oil (BBL)	Casing-head (MCF)	GW Gas (MCF)	Condensate (BBL)
Johnson	0	0	387,382,869	37,055
Jones	693,244	335,623	21,186	1,176
Karnes	220,169	505,482	7,178,250	127,866
Kaufman	55,648	5,361	0	0
Kenedy	55,513	124,489	42,996,737	192,234
Kent	3,669,856	6,665,714	0	0
Kimble	317	0	83,771	0
King	1,766,120	95,388	717,260	6,483
Kinney	0	0	0	0
Kleberg	27,530	65,055	29,612,638	324,935
Knox	202,501	42	0	0
La Salle	130,795	780,420	12,346,439	129,445
Lamb	628,564	174,111	0	0
Lavaca	151,742	242,744	59,225,064	564,412
Lee	1,003,359	7,973,209	2,056,012	41,308
Leon	571,434	1,485,935	66,803,067	194,008
Liberty	1,470,330	1,490,395	39,129,392	1,216,858
Limestone	82,370	1,661	89,010,177	84,044
Lipscomb	1,230,346	8,654,173	54,160,525	578,245
Live Oak	439,217	529,708	21,428,929	234,630
Loving	1,247,455	2,825,694	88,285,161	193,586
Lubbock	1,292,260	81,559	0	0
Lynn	243,793	95,295	0	0
Madison	403,580	355,325	5,349,809	23,089
Marion	132,504	486,683	3,167,742	47,406
Martin	8,091,233	12,059,889	24,010	161
Matagorda	306,763	652,262	40,311,608	918,128
Maverick	1,742,656	174,272	2,505,636	11,531
McCulloch	52,236	1,000	6,985	0
McLennan	1,365	0	0	0
McMullen	1,262,668	3,170,578	19,016,322	131,297
Medina	76,896	241	121,468	0
Menard	134,511	21,711	22,913	0
Midland	9,908,757	30,444,559	11,681,543	212,036
Milam	369,648	329,757	12,270	286
Mills	0	0	7,547	0
Mitchell	3,264,353	337,322	0	0
Montague	1,620,225	4,634,264	282,207	5,910
Montgomery	1,012,826	1,422,932	5,958,210	73,082
Moore	305,137	2,347,464	32,368,619	1,018
Morris	1,651	0	0	0
Motley	24,546	0	0	0
Nacgdoches	6,630	246,873	106,999,992	499,761
Navarro	328,504	65,485	687,583	28,044
Newton	668,921	1,871,134	1,649,138	39,270
Nolan	1,187,548	1,869,504	403,980	1,762
Nueces	394,659	1,179,724	34,069,256	727,255
Ochiltree	1,179,429	4,485,553	20,833,554	101,709
Oldham	170,987	0	123,274	0
Orange	431,478	818,299	7,559,769	413,094
Palo Pinto	163,170	1,111,593	14,620,120	156,087
Panola	306,498	3,067,012	261,729,338	1,994,050
Parker	12,475	607,257	90,303,218	310,616
Pecos	11,257,927	92,635,536	153,746,637	191,522
Polk	460,284	323,224	23,627,269	1,088,500
Potter	192,764	267,489	13,760,467	346
Rains	0	0	4,290,071	0
Reagan	5,409,648	24,235,939	1,663,842	41,643
Real	1,093	14,080	54,277	0

County	Oil (BBL)	Casing-head (MCF)	GW Gas (MCF)	Condensate (BBL)
Red River	122,311	7,700	0	0
Reeves	778,976	2,006,939	21,254,845	29,185
Refugio	3,084,196	18,539,700	14,552,492	235,328
Roberts	473,664	5,432,769	43,380,137	574,245
Robertson	1,255,450	709,753	215,228,038	23,999
Runnels	600,429	2,024,768	238,584	945
Rusk	1,957,386	2,142,583	138,231,818	872,215
Sabine	4,705	28,865	0	0
S. Augustine	31,260	216,584	11,522,451	9,603
San Jacinto	24,263	88,901	12,823,850	328,946
San Patricio	365,101	878,460	16,428,646	578,049
Schleicher	342,066	1,277,030	10,085,759	74,642
Scurry	13,545,618	28,677,738	0	0
Shackelford	626,177	777,505	2,426,437	18,321
Shelby	123,383	1,724,958	50,587,336	154,655
Sherman	73,276	115,724	20,827,863	5,227
Smith	1,096,776	1,293,735	37,653,028	215,782
Somervell	0	0	3,945,469	8,253
Starr	360,227	759,264	113,811,687	1,773,698
Stephens	2,090,759	3,075,351	10,875,254	65,773
Sterling	908,138	7,484,424	4,764,293	46,765
Stonewall	866,649	381,815	0	0
Sutton	12,173	71,901	74,359,292	77,170
Tarrant	0	0	352,270,389	47,802
Taylor	415,917	150,557	19,149	0
Terrell	14,718	515,294	57,470,741	160,154
Terry	3,879,461	1,052,072	0	0
Throckmrton	606,749	1,112,005	219,161	1,061
Titus	440,338	1,888	0	0
Tom Green	529,387	1,386,317	1,343,052	19,821
Travis	1,813	0	0	0
Trinity	65,343	46,753	316,644	4,345
Tyler	226,552	304,496	27,858,267	2,695,682
Upshur	126,129	72,786	40,601,543	452,597
Upton	12,613,178	34,338,167	32,617,207	747,980
Uvalde	0	0	803	0
Val Verde	1,034	3,251	13,287,244	336
Van Zandt	650,001	722,261	3,383,178	7,962
Victoria	657,837	681,176	15,423,737	88,174
Walker	1,612	2,273	765,159	1,415
Waller	564,284	73,459	8,400,604	103,032
Ward	5,884,281	15,764,559	26,348,416	81,026
Washington	313,958	2,217,345	14,097,832	94,031
Webb	109,899	174,079	187,537,863	853,768
Wharton	1,002,104	810,917	39,893,365	668,274
Wheeler	414,311	1,002,917	125,990,701	1,677,245
Wichita	1,934,556	265,384	0	0
Wilbarger	643,043	24,262	6,332	0
Willacy	354,595	375,036	21,179,246	344,558
Williamson	7,065	0	0	0
Wilson	259,358	23,732	23,970	351
Winkler	3,339,168	13,403,148	22,196,473	62,011
Wise	413,434	5,784,266	180,559,745	717,157
Wood	3,288,356	13,362,016	6,435,799	32,823
Yoakum	21,534,222	24,262,549	880,363	88
Young	1,231,538	1,547,923	1,281,072	11,411
Zapata	31,981	20,644	269,446,109	243,621
Zavala	643,487	823,883	636,194	31

Top Gas Producing Counties, 1993–2008

In all, 48 counties have produced more than 500 billion cubic feet of natural gas from 1993–2008. The top 36 counties are listed in the chart below. The fourth column at the right lists the number of producing gas wells in the county in February 2009. (**MCF** is thousand cubic feet.)

Rank	County	Gas (MCF)	Gas Wells	Rank	County	Gas (MCF)	Gas Wells
1.	Zapata	4,886,731,644	3,072	20.	Brooks	1,008,248,136	448
2.	Webb	4,570,697,792	4,700	21.	Johnson	957,539,867	1,895
3.	Panola	4,101,448,232	5,070	22.	Limestone	915,632,284	1,054
4.	Hidalgo	4,094,670,250	1,488	23.	Wharton	915,304,271	514
5.	Pecos	2,995,995,169	1,196	24.	Gregg	915,233,710	1,005
6.	Freestone	2,574,476,582	2,725	25.	Upshur	878,609,650	775
7.	Starr	2,297,522,961	1,258	26.	Wheeler	873,333,052	1,590
8.	Crockett	1,907,387,177	5,627	27.	Moore	868,820,349	1,287
9.	Wise	1,798,159,652	3,860	28.	Harris	815,964,217	158
10.	Hemphill	1,468,162,015	2,380	29.	Nueces	769,888,193	757
11.	Rusk	1,353,087,810	2,508	30.	Ward	734,369,184	279
12.	Lavaca	1,192,006,275	589	31.	Washington	732,808,995	172
13.	Denton	1,188,726,411	2,461	32.	Nacogdoches	696,304,485	1,336
14.	Harrison	1,141,796,452	2,392	33.	Kenedy	694,374,177	198
15.	Sutton	1,141,552,917	5,980	34.	Lipscomb	666,124,126	1,277
16.	Robertson	1,069,597,164	722	35.	Goliad	664,819,510	575
17.	Terrell	1,062,158,817	658	36.	Brazoria	646,315,288	191
18.	Tarrant	1,060,976,427	1,708			*Source: Texas Railroad Commission.*	
19.	Duval	1,059,035,533	645				

Natural Gas Produced since 1993

- 2 trillion cubic feet or more
- 1 trillion to 2 trillion cubic feet
- 750 billion to 1 trillion cubic feet
- 500 billion to 750 billion cubic feet

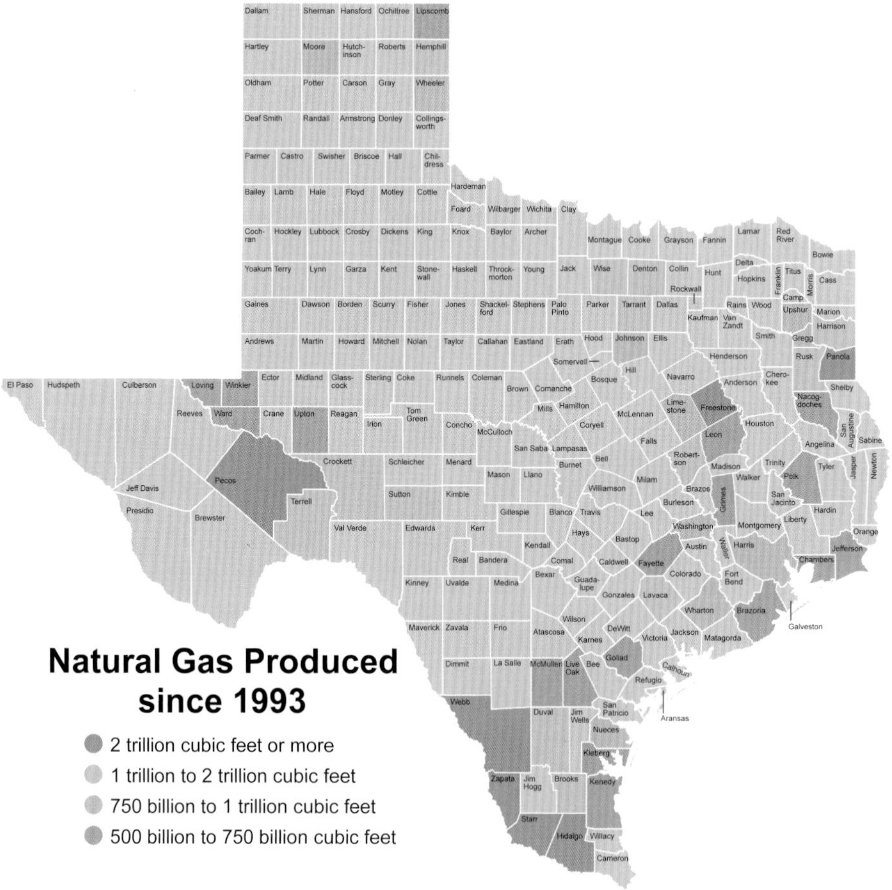

Petroleum Production and Income in Texas

Year	Crude Oil				Natural Gas		
	Production (thousand barrels)	Value (add 000)	Average Price per barrel (nominal)	*Average price per barrel (2000 $)	Production (million cubic feet)	Value (add 000)	Average Price (cents per **MCF)
1915	24,943	$ 13,027	$ 0 .52	NA	13,324	$ 2,594	19.5
1925	144,648	262,270	1.81	NA	134,872	7,040	5.2
1935	392,666	367,820	0.94	NA	642,366	13,233	2.1
1945	754,710	914,410	1.21	NA	1,711,401	44,839	2.6
1955	1,053,297	2,989,330	2.84	NA	4,730,798	378,464	8.0
1965	1,000,749	2,962,119	2.96	NA	6,636,555	858,396	12.9
1970	1,249,697	4,104,005	3.28	NA	8,357,716	1,203,511	14.4
1971	1,222,926	4,261,775	3.48	NA	8,550,705	1,376,664	16.1
1972	1,301,685	4,536,077	3.48	NA	8,657,840	1,419,886	16.4
1973	1,294,671	5,157,623	3.98	NA	8,513,850	1,735,221	20.4
1974	1,262,126	8,773,003	6.95	NA	8,170,798	2,541,118	31.1
1975	1,221,929	9,336,570	7.64	NA	7,485,764	3,885,112	51.9
1976	1,189,523	10,217,702	8.59	NA	7,191,859	5,163,755	71.8
1977	1,137,880	9,986,002	8.78	$ 20.07	7,051,027	6,367,077	90.3
1978	1,074,050	9,980,333	9.29	20.30	6,548,184	6,515,443	99.5
1979	1,018,094	12,715,994	12.49	25.53	7,174,623	8,509,103	118.6
1980	977,436	21,259,233	21.75	40.41	7,115,889	10,673,834	150.0
1981	945,132	32,692,116	34.59	59.30	7,050,207	12,598,712	178.7
1982	923,868	29,074,126	31.47	50.65	6,497,678	13,567,151	208.8
1983	876,205	22,947,814	26.19	45.01	5,643,183	14,672,275	260.0
1984	874,079	25,138,520	28.76	42.67	5,864,224	13,487,715	230.0
1985	860,300	23,159,286	26.92	38.44	5,805,098	12,665,114	218.0
1986	813,620	11,976,488	14.72	20.67	5,663,491	8,778,410	155.0
1987	754,213	13,221,345	17.53	23.98	5,516,224	7,612,389	138.0
1988	727,928	10,729,660	14.74	19.43	5,702,643	7,983,700	140.0
1989	679,575	12,123,624	17.84	22.67	5,595,190	8,113,026	145.0
1990	672,081	15,047,902	22.39	27.42	5,520,915	8,281,372	150.0
1991	672,810	12,836,080	19.05	22.55	5,509,990	7,713,986	140.0
1992	642,059	11,820,306	18.41	21.21	5,436,408	8,643,888	159.0
1993	572,600	9,288,800	16.22	18.32	4,062,500	7,365,800	181.0
1994	533,900	7,977,500	14.94	16.60	3,842,500	6,220,300	162.0
1995	503,200	8,177,700	16.25	17.78	3,690,000	5,305,200	143.0
1996	478,100	9,560,800	20.00	21.64	3,458,100	6,945,000	200.0
1997	464,900	8,516,800	18.32	19.56	3,672,300	8,134,200	221.5
1998	440,600	5,472,400	12.42	12.73	3,557,900	6,362,900	178.8
1999	337,100	5,855,800	17.37	17.67	3,321,600	6,789,700	204.4
2000	348,900	10,037,300	28.60	28.60	3,552,000	12,837,600	361.4
2001	325,500	7,770,500	23.87	22.86	3,732,700	13,708,700	367.3
2002	335,600	8,150,400	24.29	22.81	3,476,800	9,840,800	283.0
2003	333,300	9,708,600	29.13	27.38	3,272,800	14,797,800	452.1
2004	327,910	12,762,650	38.79	35.44	3,336,200	17,077,700	511.9
2005	327,600	12,744,600	52.61	46.54	3,206,600	16,399,400	511.4
2006	314,600	19,353,500	61.31	52.55	4,029,300	23,500,800	583.2
2007	311,830	21,341,100	68.30	57.00	4,059,320	22,968,420	565.8
2008	315,896	$ 30,409,170	$ 96.86	$ 79.12	5,868,822	$ 34,415,890	586.4

*In chained (2000) dollars, as calculated by the federal Energy Information Administration. (NA, not available.) **MCF (thousand cubic feet).
Sources: Previously from the Texas Railroad Commission, Texas Mid-Continent Oil & Gas Association and, beginning in 1979, data are from Department of Energy. Data since 1993 are from the state comptroller. DOE figures do not include gas that is vented or flared or used for pressure maintenance and repressuring, but do include non-hydrocarbon gases.

Offshore Production History – Oil and Gas

The cumulative offshore natural gas production as of Nov. 1, 2008, was **4,019,674,418** thousand cubic feet (Mcf). The cumulative offshore oil production was **39,027,178** barrels.

Production in Recent Years

YEAR	Crude Oil BBL	Casing-head Mcf	Gas Well Gas Mcf	Conden-sate BBL
1993	1,685,177	1,370,634	86,264,924	275,945
1994	1,367,850	1,068,230	87,315,422	303,451
1995	1,108,868	807,468	64,295,758	223,103
1996	908,743	724,651	68,159,547	212,048
1997	765,283	698,488	76,974,574	328,025
1998	586,999	611,882	60,080,329	233,044
1999	448,207	431,690	48,816,099	132,827
2000	548,046	335,415	44,086,237	220,309
2001	530,261	408,163	53,526,532	475,387
2002	1,144,389	2,404,329	54,988,278	405,577
2003	760,824	1,370,696	52,572,194	436,442
2004	442,462	325,345	46,539,253	396,096
2005	450,378	389,301	28,589,312	452,049
2006	310,625	262,049	26,870,964	295,034
2007	232,602	124,942	30,051,725	410,375

2008 Production by Area

Offshore Area	Crude Oil BBL	Casing-head Mcf	Gas Well Gas Mcf	Conden-sate BBL
Brazos-LB	0	0	2,404,673	1,684
Brazos-SB	0	0	445,461	223
Galveston-LB	0	0	7,237,105	80,291
Galveston-SB	0	0	25,006	1
High Island-LB	64,058	53,619	19,154,828	139,750
High Island-SB	35,544	27,333	49,412	0
Matagrda Island-LB	86,313	0	6,466,035	52,611
Matagrda Island-SB	0	0	660,798	10,511
Mustang Island-LB	39	0	2,258,337	10,151
Mustang Island-SB	24,982	40,034	2,885,696	84,945
N. Padre Island-LB	0	0	441,728	13,427
S. Padre Island-LB	0	0	0	0
Sabine Pass	0	0	0	0
Total	**210,897**	**120,986**	**42,029,079**	**393,594**

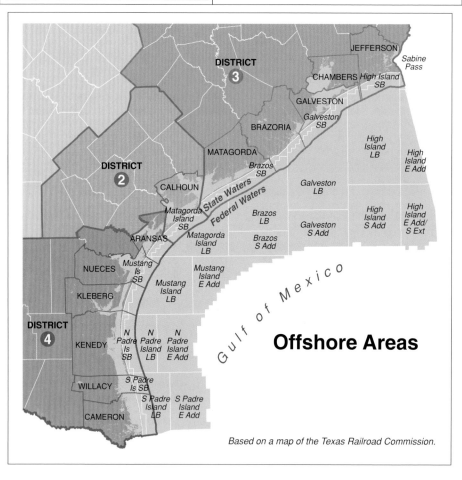

Offshore Areas

Based on a map of the Texas Railroad Commission.

Receipts by Texas from Tidelands

The Republic of Texas had proclaimed its Gulf boundaries as three marine leagues, recognized by international law as traditional national boundaries. These boundaries were never seriously questioned when Texas joined the Union in 1845. But, in 1930 a congressional resolution authorized the U.S. Attorney General to file suit to establish offshore lands as properties of the federal government. Congress returned the disputed lands to Texas in 1953, and the U.S. Supreme Court confirmed Texas' ownership in 1960. In 1978, the federal government also granted states a "fair and equitable" share of the revenues from offshore leases within three miles of the states' outermost boundary. States did not receive any such revenue until 1986.

The following table shows receipts from tidelands in the Gulf of Mexico by the Texas General Land Office to Aug. 31, 2007. It does not include revenue from bays and other submerged area owned by Texas. Source: General Land Office.

From	To	Total	Bonus	Rental	Royalty	Lease
6-09-1922	9-28-1945	$ 924,363.81	$ 814,055.70	$ 61,973.75	$ 48,334.36	...
9-29-1945	6-23-1947	296,400.30	272,700.00	7,680.00	16,020.30	...
6-24-1947	6-05-1950	7,695,552.22	7,231,755.48	377,355.00	86,441.74	...
6-06-1950	5-22-1953	55,095.04	—	9,176.00	45,919.04	...
5-23-1953	6-30-1958	54,264,553.11	49,788,639.03	3,852,726.98	623,187.10	...
7-01-1958	8-31-1959	771,064.75	—	143,857.00	627,207.75	...
9-01-1959	8-31-1960	983,335.32	257,900.00	98,226.00	627,209.32	...
9-01-1960	8-31-1961	3,890,800.15	3,228,639.51	68,578.00	593,582.64	...
9-01-1961	8-31-1962	1,121,925.09	297,129.88	127,105.00	697,690.21	...
9-01-1962	8-31-1963	3,575,888.64	2,617,057.14	177,174.91	781,656.59	...
9-01-1963	8-31-1964	3,656,236.75	2,435,244.36	525,315.00	695,677.39	...
9-01-1964	8-31-1965	54,654,576.96	53,114,943.63	755,050.12	784,583.21	...
9-01-1965	8-31-1966	22,148,825.44	18,223,357.84	3,163,475.00	761,992.60	...
9-01-1966	8-31-1967	8,469,680.86	3,641,414.96	3,711,092.65	1,117,173.25	...
9-01-1967	8-31-1968	6,305,851.00	1,251,852.50	2,683,732.50	2,370,266.00	...
9-01-1968	8-31-1969	6,372,268.28	1,838,118.33	1,491,592.50	3,042,557.45	...
9-01-1969	8-31-1970	10,311,030.48	5,994,666.32	618,362.50	3,698,001.66	...
9-01-1970	8-31-1971	9,969,629.17	4,326,120.11	726,294.15	4,917,214.91	...
9-01-1971	8-31-1972	7,558,327.21	1,360,212.64	963,367.60	5,234,746.97	...
9-01-1972	8-31-1973	9,267,975.68	3,701,737.30	920,121.60	4,646,116.78	...
9-01-1973	8-31-1974	41,717,670.04	32,981,619.28	1,065,516.60	7,670,534.16	...
9-01-1974	8-31-1975	27,321,536.62	5,319,762.85	2,935,295.60	19,066,478.17	...
9-01-1975	8-31-1976	38,747,074.09	6,197,853.00	3,222,535.84	29,326,685.25	...
9-01-1976	8-31-1977	84,196,228.27	41,343,114.81	2,404,988.80	40,448,124.66	...
9-01-1977	8-31-1978	118,266,812.05	49,807,750.45	4,775,509.92	63,683,551.68	...
9-01-1978	8-31-1979	100,410,268.68	34,578,340.94	7,318,748.40	58,513,179.34	...
9-01-1979	8-31-1980	200,263,803.03	34,733,270.02	10,293,153.80	155,237,379.21	...
9-01-1980	8-31-1981	219,126,876.54	37,467,196.97	13,100,484.25	168,559,195.32	...
9-01-1981	8-31-1982	250,824,581.69	27,529,516.33	14,214,478.97	209,080,586.39	...
9-01-1982	8-31-1983	165,197,734.83	10,180,696.40	12,007,476.70	143,009,561.73	...
9-01-1983	8-31-1984	152,755,934.29	32,864,122.19	8,573,996.87	111,317,815.23	...
9-01-1984	8-31-1985	140,568,090.79	32,650,127.75	6,837,603.70	101,073,959.34	...
9-01-1985	8-31-1986	516,503,771.05	6,365,426.23	4,241,892.75	78,289,592.27	$427,606,859.83
9-01-1986	8-31-1987	60,066,571.05	4,186,561.63	1,933,752.50	44,691,907.22	9,254,349.70
9-01-1987	8-31-1988	56,875,069.22	14,195,274.28	1,817,058.90	28,068,202.53	12,794,533.51
9-01-1988	8-31-1989	61,793,380.04	12,995,892.74	1,290,984.37	35,160,568.40	12,345,934.53
9-01-1989	8-31-1990	68,701,751.51	7,708,449.54	1,289,849.87	40,331,537.06	19,371,915.04
9-01-1990	8-31-1991	90,885,856.99	3,791,832.77	1,345,711.07	70,023,601.01	15,724,712.14
9-01-1991	8-31-1992	51,154,511.34	4,450,850.00	1,123,585.54	26,776,191.35	18,803,884.45
9-01-1992	8-31-1993	60,287,712.60	3,394,230.00	904,359.58	34,853,679.68	21,135,443.34
9-01-1993	8-31-1994	57,825,043.59	3,570,657.60	694,029.30	32,244,987.95	21,315,368.74
9-01-1994	8-31-1995	62,143,227.78	8,824,722.93	674,479.79	34,691,023.35	17,951,001.71
9-01-1995	8-31-1996	68,166,645.51	13,919,246.80	1,102,591.39	32,681,315.73	20,463,491.59
9-01-1996	8-31-1997	90,614,935.93	22,007,378.46	1,319,614.78	41,605,792.50	25,682,150.19
9-01-1997	8-31-1998	104,016,006.75	36,946,312.49	2,070,802.90	38,760,320.91	26,238,570.45
9-01-1998	8-31-1999	53,565,810.30	5,402,171.00	2,471,128.47	23,346,515.93	22,345,994.90
9-01-1999	8-31-2000	55,465,763.99	3,487,564.80	2,171,636.35	24,314,241.99	25,492,320.85
9-01-2000	8-31-2001	68,226,347.58	9,963,608.68	1,830,378.11	23,244,034.74	33,188,326.05
9-01-2001	8-31-2002	30,910,283.91	9,286,015.20	1,545,583.01	13,369,771.56	6,708,914.14
9-01-2002	8-31-2003	50,881,515.90	15,152,092.40	1,071,377.60	19,648,641.39	15,009,404.51
9-01-2003	8-31-2004	54,379,791.20	14,448,555.70	1,094,201.41	25,199,635.21	13,637,398.88
9-01-2004	8-31-2005	53,594,809.87	9,148,220.20	1,624,666.50	32,406,328.78	10,415,594.39
9-01-2005	8-31-2006	60,829,271.63	22,565,845.14	1,605,090.30	23,287,994.53	13,370,341.66
9-01-2006	8-31-2007	52,513,621.85	15,879,784.44	2,022,859.80	18,785,626.55	15,825,351.06
Totals		$3,581,085,290.80	$753,739,608.75	$142,479,680.00	$1,880,184,140.39	$804,681,861.66
Inside three-mile line		$ 507,912,858.02	$174,484,671.15	$37,812,696.73	$ 295,615,490.14	0
Between three-mile and three marine-league line		$2,265,665,205.54	$576,602,853.21	$104,493,702.08	$1,584,568,650.25	0
Outside three marine-league line		$ 807,507,227.24	$ 2,652,084.39	$ 173,281.19	0	$804,681,861.66

Nonfuel Mineral Production and Value,
2004, 2005 and 2006

Source: U.S. Geological Survey and the Texas Bureau of Economic Geology.

*Production is measured by mine shipments, sales or marketable production, including consumption by producers. Production and value data is given in **thousand metric tons** and **thousand dollars**, unless otherwise specified.*

MINERAL	2004		2005		2006	
	Production	Value	Production	Value	Production	Value
Cement:						
Masonry	319	$ 38,000*	395	$ 48,500*	382	$ 50,700*
Portland	11,200	800,000*	11,600	951,000*	11,300	1,070,000*
Clays:						
Ball	W	W	W	7,730	W	W
Bentonite	W	W	W	W	71	2,300
Common	2,160	8,890	2,340	8,680	2,360	12,600
Gemstones, natural	NA	201	NA	201	NA	202
Gypsum, crude	2,450	18,800	1,540	11,800	1,430	11,800
Lime	1,630	115,000	1,610	112,000	1,650	130,000
Salt	9,780	118,000	9,600	118,000	9,570	132,000
Sand and gravel:						
Construction	81,700	436,000	80,700	472,000	99,500	603,000
Industrial	2,790	109,000	2,840	114,000	1,530	65,600
Stone:						
Crushed	122,000	621,000	137,000	820,000	136,000	824,000
Dimension	64	15,200	44	12,200	31	12,600
Talc, crude	258	W	W	W	W	W
‡Combined value	§	46,300	§	41,500	§	68,200
††Total Texas Values	§	**$2,330,000**	§	**$2,720,000**	§	**2,980,000**

** Estimated. † Preliminary. **NA**: not available. **W**: data withheld to avoid disclosing proprietary data; value included with "Combined value." § Not applicable. ‡ Includes values of brucite, clays (fuller's earth, kaolin), helium, zeolites and values indicated by symbol W. †† Data do not add to total shown because of independent rounding.*

Nonpetroleum Minerals

The nonpetroleum, or nonfuel, minerals that occur in Texas constitute a long list. Some are currently mined; some may have a potential for future development; some are minor occurrences only. Although overshadowed by the petroleum, natural gas and natural gas liquids that are produced in the state, many of the non-petroleum minerals are, nonetheless, important to the economy. In 2006, they were valued at an estimated $2.9 billion, representing a 17 percent increase from 2005 and ranking Texas fifth in overall U.S. production.

The **Bureau of Economic Geology**, which functions as the state geological survey of Texas, revised the following information about nonpetroleum minerals for this edition of the *Texas Almanac*. Publications of the Bureau, on file in many libraries, contain more detailed information. Among the items available is the Bureau map, "Mineral Resources of Texas," showing locations of resource access of many nonpetroleum minerals.

A catalog of Bureau publications is also available free on request from the Bureau Publications Sales, University Station, Box X, Austin, TX 78713-7508; 512-471-1534. On the Web: **www.beg.utexas.edu/**.

Texas' nonpetroleum minerals are as follows:

ALUMINUM — No aluminum ores are mined in Texas, but three Texas plants process aluminum materials in one or more ways. Plants in San Patricio and Calhoun counties produce **aluminum oxide (alumina)** from imported raw ore **(bauxite)**, and a plant in Milam County reduces the oxide to aluminum.

ASBESTOS — Small occurrences of amphibole-type asbestos have been found in the state. In West Texas, **richterite**, a white, long-fibered amphibole, is associated with some of the **talc deposits** northwest of **Allamoore** in Hudspeth County. Another type, **tremolite**, has been found in the **Llano Uplift** of Central Texas where it is associated with **serpentinite** in eastern Gillespie and western Blanco County. No asbestos is mined in Texas.

ASPHALT (Native) — Asphalt-bearing Cretaceous limestones crop out in Burnet, Kinney, Pecos, Reeves, Uvalde and other counties. The most significant deposit is in southwestern Uvalde County where asphalt occurs naturally in the pore spaces of the Anacacho Limestone. The material is quarried and used extensively as **road-paving material**. Asphalt-bearing sandstones occur in Anderson, Angelina, Cooke, Jasper, Maverick, Montague, Nacogdoches, Uvalde, Zavala and other counties.

BARITE — Deposits of a heavy, nonmetallic mineral, barite (barium sulphate), have been found in many localities, including Baylor, Brown, Brewster, Culberson, Gillespie, Howard, Hudspeth, Jeff Davis, Kinney, Llano, Live Oak, Taylor, Val Verde and Webb counties. During the 1960s, there was small, intermittent production in the **Seven Heart Gap** area of the **Apache Mountains** in Culberson County, where barite was mined from open pits. Most of the deposits are known to be relatively small, but the Webb County deposit has not been evaluated. Grinding plants, which prepare barite mined outside of Texas for use chiefly as a **weighting agent** in well-drilling muds and as a **filler**, are located in Brownsville, Corpus Christi, El Paso, Galena Park, Galveston, and Houston.

BASALT (TRAP ROCK) — Masses of basalt — a hard, dark-colored, fine-grained igneous rock — crop out in Kinney, Travis, Uvalde and several other counties along the **Balcones Fault Zone**, and also in the Trans-Pecos area of West Texas. Basalt is quarried near Knippa in Uvalde County for use as **road-building material, railroad ballast and other aggregate**.

BENTONITE (see **CLAYS**).

BERYLLIUM — Occurrences of beryllium minerals at several Trans-Pecos localities have been recognized for several years.

BRINE (see also **SALT, SODIUM SULPHATE**) — Many wells in Texas produce brine by solution mining of subsurface salt deposits, mostly in West Texas counties such as Andrews, Crane, Ector, Loving, Midland, Pecos, Reeves, Ward and others. These wells in the Permian Basin dissolve salt from the Salado Formation, an enormous salt deposit that extends in the subsurface from north of the Big Bend northward to Kansas, has an east-west width of 150 to 200 miles, and may have several hundred feet of net salt thickness. The majority of the brine is used in the petroleum industry, but it also is used in water softening, the chemical industry and other uses. Three Gulf Coast counties, Fort Bend, Duval and Jefferson, have brine stations that produce from salt domes.

BUILDING STONE (DIMENSION STONE) — **Granite** and **limestone** currently are quarried for use as dimension stone. The granite quarries are located in Burnet, Gillespie, Llano and Mason counties; the limestone quarries are in Shackelford and Williamson counties. Past production of limestone for use as dimension stone has been reported in Burnet, Gillespie, Jones, Tarrant, Travis and several other counties. There has also been production of **sandstone** in various counties for use as dimension stone.

CEMENT MATERIALS — Cement is currently manufactured in Bexar, Comal, Dallas, Ector, Ellis, Hays, McLennan, Nolan and Potter counties. Many of these plants utilize Cretaceous limestones and shales or clays as raw materials for the cement. On the Texas High Plains, a cement plant near Amarillo uses impure **caliche** as the chief raw material. Iron oxide, also a constituent of cement, is available from the iron ore deposits of East Texas and from smelter slag. **Gypsum**, added to the cement as a retarder, is found chiefly in North Central Texas, Central Texas and the Trans-Pecos area.

CHROMIUM — Chromite-bearing rock has been found in several small deposits around the margin of the Coal Creek **serpentinite** mass in northeastern Gillespie County and northwestern Blanco County. Exploration has not revealed significant deposits.

CLAYS — Texas has an abundance and variety of ceramic and non-ceramic clays and is one of the country's leading producers of clay products.

Almost any kind of clay, ranging from common clay used to make ordinary brick and tile to clays suitable for manufacture of specialty whitewares, can be used for ceramic purposes. **Fire clay** suitable for use as **refractories** occurs chiefly in East and North Central Texas; **ball clay**, a high-quality plastic ceramic clay, is found locally in East Texas.

Ceramic clay suitable for quality structural clay products such as **structural building brick, paving brick and drain tile** is especially abundant in East and North Central Texas. Common clay suitable for use in the manufacture of cement and ordinary brick is found in most counties of the state. Many of the Texas clays will expand or bloat upon rapid firing and are suitable for the manufacture of lightweight aggregate, which is used mainly in concrete blocks and highway surfacing.

Nonceramic clays are utilized without firing. They are used primarily as **bleaching and absorbent clays, fillers, coaters, additives, bonding clays, drilling muds, catalysts** and potentially as sources of alumina. Most of the nonceramic clays in Texas are **bentonites** and **fuller's earth**. These occur extensively in the Coastal Plain and locally in the High Plains and Big Bend areas. **Kaolin clays** in parts of East Texas are potential sources of such nonceramic products as **paper coaters and fillers,** **rubber fillers and drilling agents**. Relatively high in alumina, these clays also are a potential source of metallic aluminum.

COAL (see also LIGNITE) — **Bituminous coal**, which occurs in North Central, South and West Texas, was a significant energy source in Texas prior to the large-scale development of oil and gas. During the period from 1895 to 1943, Texas mines produced more than 25 million tons of coal. The mines were inactive for many years, but the renewed interest in coal as a major energy source prompted a revaluation of Texas' coal deposits. In the late 1970s, bituminous coal production resumed in the state on a limited scale when mines were opened in Coleman, Erath and Webb counties.

Much of the state's bituminous coal occurs in North Central Texas. Deposits are found there in Pennsylvanian rocks within a large area that includes Coleman, Eastland, Erath, Jack, McCulloch, Montague, Palo Pinto, Parker, Throckmorton, Wise, Young and other counties. Before the general availability of oil and gas, underground coal mines near **Thurber, Bridgeport, Newcastle, Strawn** and other points annually produced significant tonnages. Preliminary evaluations indicate substantial amounts of coal may remain in the North Central Texas area. The coal seams there are generally no more than 30 inches thick and are commonly covered by well-consolidated overburden. Ash and sulphur content are high. Beginning in 1979, two bituminous coal mine operations in North Central Texas — one in southern Coleman County and one in northwestern Erath County — produced coal to be used as fuel by the cement industry. Neither mine is currently operating.

In South Texas, bituminous coal occurs in the Eagle Pass district of Maverick County, and bituminous **cannel coal** is present in the **Santo Tomas district** of Webb County. The Eagle Pass area was a leading coal-producing district in Texas during the late 1800s and early 1900s. The bituminous coal in that area, which occurs in the Upper Cretaceous Olmos Formation, has a high ash content and a moderate moisture and sulfur content. According to reports, Maverick County coal beds range from four to seven feet thick.

The **cannel coals** of western Webb County occur near the Rio Grande in middle Eocene strata. They were mined for more than 50 years and used primarily as a boiler fuel. Mining ceased from 1939 until 1978, when a surface mine was opened 30 miles northwest of Laredo to produce cannel coal for use as fuel in the cement industry and for export. An additional mine has since been opened in that county. Tests show that the coals of the Webb County Santo Tomas district have a high hydrogen content and yield significant amounts of gas and oil when distilled. They also have a high sulfur content. A potential use might be as a source of various petrochemical products.

Coal deposits in the Trans-Pecos country of West Texas include those in the Cretaceous rocks of the Terlingua area of Brewster County, the Eagle Spring area of Hudspeth County and the **San Carlos** area of Presidio County. The coal deposits in these areas are believed to have relatively little potential for development as a fuel. They have been sold in the past as a soil amendment (see **LEONARDITE**).

See map of coal mining locations and mine production in Texas on page 640.

COPPER — Copper minerals have been found in the **Trans-Pecos** area of West Texas, in the **Llano Uplift** area of Central Texas and in redbed deposits of North Texas. No copper has been mined in Texas during recent years, and the total copper produced in the state has been relatively small. Past attempts to mine the North Texas and Llano Uplift copper deposits resulted in small shipments, but practically all the copper production in the state has been from the **Van Horn-Allamoore** district of Culberson and Hudspeth Counties in the Trans-Pecos area.

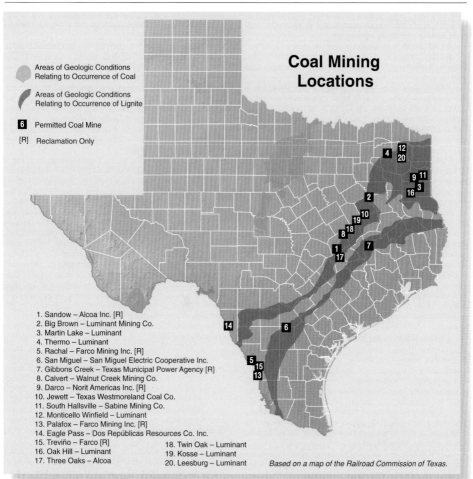

Coal Mining Locations

Areas of Geologic Conditions Relating to Occurrence of Coal

Areas of Geologic Conditions Relating to Occurrence of Lignite

6 Permitted Coal Mine

[R] Reclamation Only

1. Sandow – Alcoa Inc. [R]
2. Big Brown – Luminant Mining Co.
3. Martin Lake – Luminant
4. Thermo – Luminant
5. Rachal – Farco Mining Inc. [R]
6. San Miguel – San Miguel Electric Cooperative Inc.
7. Gibbons Creek – Texas Municipal Power Agency [R]
8. Calvert – Walnut Creek Mining Co.
9. Darco – Norit Americas Inc. [R]
10. Jewett – Texas Westmoreland Coal Co.
11. South Hallsville – Sabine Mining Co.
12. Monticello Winfield – Luminant
13. Palafox – Farco Mining Inc. [R]
14. Eagle Pass – Dos Repúblicas Resources Co. Inc.
15. Treviño – Farco [R]
16. Oak Hill – Luminant
17. Three Oaks – Alcoa
18. Twin Oak – Luminant
19. Kosse – Luminant
20. Leesburg – Luminant

Based on a map of the Railroad Commission of Texas.

Mine Production (in tons)

Mine	2007	Cumulative
Sandow	0	150,966,982
Big Brown	3,515,809	160,688,997
Martin Lake	7,677,112	265,916,057
Thermo	2,090,370	35,414,085
Rachal	0	963,827
San Miguel	2,899,523	80,248,344
Gibbons Creek	0	42,978,785
Calvert	1,902,877	32,643,244
Darco	0	6,798,881
Jewett	6,800,668	167,693,510
South Hallsville	4,153,485	80,376,323
Monticello-Winfield	3,502,720	268,096,803
Palafox	0	95,355,519
Eagle Pass	0	0
Treviño	0	890,453
Oak Hill	3,761,434	101,154,229
Three Oaks	4,284,599	13,672,715
Twin Oak	0	236
Kosse	196,806	196,806
Leesburg	0	0
Little Bull Creek (Coleman Co.)	No longer permitted	428,932
Powell Bend (Bastrop Co.)	No longer permitted	1,569,875
Thurber (Erath Co.)	No longer permitted	465,984
Statewide total	40,785,403	1,416,520,587
Lignite for Electricity	40,785,403	1,315,257,300

Source: Railroad Commission of Texas, 2008.

Coal Production by State, 2008
(million short tons)

Total	United States	1,171.5
1.	Wyoming	467.6
2.	West Virginia	158.0
3.	Kentucky	119.9
4.	Pennsylvania	65.3
5.	Montana	44.8
6.	**Texas**	**39.0**
7.	Indiana	36.2

Source: U.S. Department of Energy.

Texas Coal Consumption
(million tons)

Year	Total	Percent from out of state
2001	96.89	52.9%
2002	99.32	55.0%
2003	104.54	53.9%
2004	105.92	56.7%
2005	105.33	56.7%
2006	103.76	56.1%
2007	104.78	60.1%

Source: U.S. Energy Information Administration.

Chief output was from the **Hazel copper-silver mine** of Culberson County that yielded over 1 million pounds of copper during 1891–1947. Copper ores and concentrates from outside of Texas are processed at **smelters** in El Paso and Amarillo.

CRUSHED STONE — Texas is among the leading states in the production of crushed stone. Most production consists of **limestone**; other kinds of crushed stone produced in the state include **basalt (trap rock), dolomite, granite, marble, rhyolite, sandstone and serpentinite**. Large tonnages of crushed stone are used as **aggregate** in concrete, as **road material** and in the manufacture of cement and lime. Some is used as **riprap, terrazzo, roofing chips, filter material, fillers** and for other purposes.

Fredericksburg granite is often used creatively, as well as in construction. Dallas Morning News photo.

DIATOMITE (DIATOMACEOUS EARTH) — Diatomite is a very lightweight siliceous material consisting of the remains of microscopic aquatic plants (diatoms). It is used chiefly as a **filter and filler**; other uses are for **thermal insulation**, as an **abrasive**, as an **insecticide carrier** and as a **lightweight aggregate**, and for other purposes. The diatomite was deposited in shallow fresh-water lakes that were present in the High Plains during portions of the Pliocene and Pleistocene epochs. Deposits have been found in Armstrong, Crosby, Dickens, Ector, Hartley and Lamb counties. No diatomite is mined in Texas.

DOLOMITE ROCK — Dolomite rock, which consists largely of the mineral dolomite (calcium-magnesium carbonate), commonly is associated with limestone in Texas. Areas in which dolomite rock occurs include Central Texas, the Callahan Divide and parts of the Edwards Plateau, High Plains and West Texas. Some of the principal deposits of dolomite rock are found in Bell, Brown, Burnet, Comanche, Edwards, El Paso, Gillespie, Lampasas, Mills, Nolan, Taylor and Williamson counties. Dolomite rock can be used as crushed stone (although much of Texas dolomite is soft and not a good aggregate material), in the manufacture of lime and as a source of **magnesium**.

FELDSPAR — Large crystals and crystal fragments of feldspar minerals occur in the Precambrian pegmatite rocks that crop out in the **Llano Uplift** area of Central Texas — including Blanco, Burnet, Gillespie, Llano and Mason counties — and in the **Van Horn area** of Culberson and Hudspeth Counties in West Texas. Feldspar has been mined in Llano County for use as **roofing granules** and as a **ceramic material**. Feldspar is currently mined in Burnet County for use as an aggregate.

FLUORSPAR — The mineral fluorite (calcium fluoride), which is known commercially as fluorspar, occurs in both Central and West Texas. In Central Texas, the deposits that have been found in Burnet, Gillespie and Mason counties are not considered adequate to sustain mining operations. In West Texas, deposits have been found in Brewster, El Paso, Hudspeth, Jeff Davis and Presidio counties. Fluorspar has been mined in the **Christmas Mountains** of Brewster County and processed in Marathon. Former West Texas mining activity in the **Eagle Mountains** district of Hudspeth County resulted in the production of approximately 15,000 short tons of fluorspar during the peak years of 1942-1950. No production has been reported in Hudspeth County since that period. Imported fluorspar is processed in Brownsville, Eagle Pass, El Paso and Houston. Fluorspar is used in the **steel,** chemical, aluminum, magnesium, ceramics and glass **industries** and for various other purposes.

FULLER'S EARTH (see **CLAY**).

GOLD — No major deposits of gold are known in Texas. Small amounts have been found in the **Llano Uplift** region of Central Texas and in West Texas; minor occurrences have been reported on the **Edwards Plateau** and the **Gulf Coastal Plain** of Texas. Nearly all of the gold produced in the state came as a by-product of silver and lead mining at **Presidio mine**, near **Shafter**, in Presidio County. Additional small quantities were produced as a by-product of copper mining in Culberson County and from residual soils developed from gold-bearing quartz stringers in metamorphic rocks in Llano County. No gold mining has been reported in Texas since 1952. Total **gold production** in the state, 1889-1952, amounted to more than 8,419 troy ounces according to U.S. Bureau of Mines figures. Most of the production — at least 73 percent and probably more — came from the Presidio mine.

GRANITE — Granites in shades of red and gray and related intrusive igneous rocks occur in the **Llano Uplift** of Central Texas and in the **Trans-Pecos** country of West Texas. Deposits are found in Blanco, Brewster, Burnet, El Paso, Gillespie, Hudspeth, Llano, McCulloch, Mason, Presidio and other counties. Quarries in Burnet, Gillespie, Llano and Mason counties produce Precambrian granite for a variety of uses as **dimension stone and crushed stone**.

GRAPHITE — Graphite, a soft, dark-gray mineral, is a form of very high-grade carbon. It occurs in Precambrian schist rocks of the **Llano Uplift** of Central Texas, notably in Burnet and Llano counties. Crystalline-flake graphite ore formerly was mined from open pits in the **Clear Creek area** of western Burnet County and processed at a plant near the mine. The mill now occasionally grinds imported material. Uses of natural crystalline graphite are **refractories, steel production, pencil leads, lubricants, foundry facings and crucibles** and for other purposes.

GRINDING PEBBLES (ABRASIVE STONES) — Flint pebbles, suitable for use in **tube-mill grinding**, are found in the **Gulf Coastal Plain** where they occur in gravel deposits along rivers and in upland areas. Grinding pebbles are produced from **Frio River terrace** deposits near the McMullen-Live Oak county line, but the area is now part of the Choke Canyon Reservoir area.

GYPSUM — Gypsum is widely distributed in Texas. Chief deposits are bedded gypsum in the area east of the **High Plains**, in the **Trans-Pecos** country and in **Central Texas**. It also occurs in **salt-dome caprocks** of the Gulf

Coast. The massive, granular variety, which is known as rock gypsum, is the kind most commonly used by industry. Other varieties include **alabaster, satin spar and selenite**.

Gypsum is one of the important industrial minerals in Texas. Bedded gypsum is produced from surface mines in Culberson, Fisher, Gillespie, Hardeman, Hudspeth, Kimble, Nolan and Stonewall counties. Gypsum was formerly mined at **Gyp Hill salt dome** in Brooks County and at **Hockley salt dome** in Harris County. Most of the gypsum is calcined and used in the manufacture of **gypsum wallboard, plaster, joint compounds** and other construction products. Crude gypsum is used chiefly as a **retarder in portland cement** and as a **soil conditioner**.

HELIUM — Helium is a very light, nonflammable, chemically inert gas. The **U.S. Interior Department has ended its helium operation** near Masterson in the Panhandle. The storage facility at **Cliffside gas field** near Amarillo and the 425-mile pipeline system will remain in operation until the government sells its remaining unrefined, crude helium. Helium is used in **cryogenics, welding, pressurizing and purging, leak detection, synthetic breathing mixtures** and for other purposes.

IRON — Iron oxide (**limonite, goethite and hematite**) and **iron carbonate (siderite)** deposits occur widely in East Texas, notably in Cass, Cherokee, Marion and Morris counties, and also in Anderson, Camp, Harrison, Henderson, Nacogdoches, Smith, Upshur and other counties. **Magnetite (magnetic, black iron oxide)** occurs in Central Texas, including a deposit at **Iron Mountain** in Llano County. Hematite occurs in the **Trans-Pecos** area and in the **Llano Uplift** of Central Texas. The extensive deposits of **glauconite** (a complex silicate containing iron) that occur in East Texas and the hematitic and goethitic Cambrian sandstone that crops out in the northwestern Llano Uplift region are potential sources of low-grade iron ore.

Limonite and other East Texas iron ores are mined from open pits in Cherokee and Henderson counties for use in the preparation of **portland cement**, as a **weighting agent in well-drilling fluids**, as an **animal feed supplement** and for other purposes. East Texas iron ores also were mined in the past for use in the iron-steel industry.

KAOLIN (see **CLAY**).

LEAD AND ZINC — The lead mineral **galena (lead sulfide)** commonly is associated with zinc and silver. It formerly was produced as a by-product of West Texas silver mining, chiefly from the **Presidio mine at Shafter** in Presidio County, although lesser amounts were obtained at several other mines and prospects. Deposits of galena also are known to occur in Blanco, Brewster, Burnet, Gillespie and Hudspeth counties.

Zinc, primarily from the mineral **sphalerite (zinc sulphide)**, was produced chiefly from the **Bonanza** and **Alice Ray** mines in the **Quitman Mountains** of Hudspeth County. In addition, small production was reported from several other areas, including the **Chinati** and **Montezuma mines** of Presidio County and the **Buck Prospect** in the **Apache Mountains** of Culberson County. Zinc mineralization also occurs in association with the lead deposits in Cambrian rocks of Central Texas.

LEONARDITE — Deposits of weathered (oxidized) low-Btu value bituminous coals, generally referred to as "leonardite," occur in Brewster County. The name leonardite is used for a mixture of chemical compounds that is high in humic acids. In the past, material from these deposits was sold as **soil conditioner**. Other uses of leonardite include **modification of viscosity of drill fluids and as sorbants in water-treatment**.

LIGHTWEIGHT AGGREGATE (see CLAY, DIATOMITE, PERLITE, VERMICULITE).

LIGNITE — Almost all current coal production in Texas is located in the Tertiary-aged lignite belts that extend across the Texas Gulf Coastal Plain from the Rio Grande in South Texas to the Arkansas and Louisiana borders in East Texas. The Railroad Commission of Texas (RRC) reported that in 2005 Texas produced 47.2 million short tons of lignite in 13 mines. Cumulative production in 2005 was 1.33 billion short tons of lignite and coal. According to U.S. Energy Information Administration (EIA) 2005 preliminary numbers, Texas continued to rank as the fifth-largest coal-producing state.

The near-surface lignite resources, occurring at depths of less than 200 feet in seams of three feet or thicker, are estimated at 23 billion short tons. **Recoverable reserves of strippable lignite** — those that can be economically mined under current conditions of price and technology — are estimated by the EIA to be 722 million short tons.

Additional lignite resources of the Texas Gulf Coastal Plain occur as deep-basin deposits. Deep-basin resources, those that occur at depths of 200 to 2,000 feet in seams of five feet or thicker, are comparable in magnitude to near-surface resources. The deep-basin lignites are a potential energy resource that conceivably could be utilized by in situ (in place) recovery methods such as underground gasification.

As with bituminous coal, lignite production was significant prior to the general availability of oil and gas. Remnants of old underground mines are common throughout the area of lignite occurrence. Large reserves of strippable lignite have again attracted the attention of energy suppliers, and Texas is now the nation's **5th leading producer of coal**, 99 percent of it lignite. Eleven large strip mines are now producing lignite that is burned for **mine-mouth electric-power generation**, and additional mines are planned. One of the currently operating mines is located in Bastrop, Milam and Lee counties, where part of the electric power is used for **alumina reduction**. Other mines are in Atascosa, Franklin, Freestone, Harrison, Hopkins, Leon, Limestone, McMullen, Panola, Robertson, Rusk and Titus counties. New permit applications have been submitted to the Railroad Commission of Texas for Freestone, Lee, Leon and Robertson counties.

LIME MATERIAL — Limestones, which are abundant in some areas of Texas, are heated to produce lime (calcium oxide) at a number of plants in the state. High-magnesium limestone and dolomite are used to prepare lime at a plant in Burnet County. Other lime plants are located in Bexar, Bosque, Comal, Hill, Johnson and Travis counties. Lime production captive to the kiln's operator occurs in several Texas counties. Lime is used in **soil stabilization, water purification, paper and pulp manufacture, metallurgy, sugar refining, agriculture, construction, removal of sulfur from stack gases** and for many other purposes.

LIMESTONE (see also **BUILDING STONE**) — Texas is one of the nation's leading producers of limestone, which is quarried in more than 60 counties. Limestone occurs in nearly all areas of the state with the exception of most of the Gulf Coastal Plain and High Plains. Although some of the limestone is quarried for use as **dimension stone**, most of the output is crushed for uses such as **bulk building materials (crushed stone, road base, concrete aggregate), chemical raw materials, fillers or extenders, lime and portland cement raw materials, agricultural limestone and removal of sulfur from stack gases.**

MAGNESITE — Small deposits of magnesite (natural magnesium carbonate) have been found in Precambrian rocks in Llano and Mason counties of Central Texas. At one time there was small-scale mining of magnesite in the area; some of the material was used as **agricultural stone** and as **terrazzo chips**. Magnesite also can be calcined to form magnesia, which is used in metallurgical furnace refractories and other products.

MAGNESIUM — On the Texas Gulf Coast in Brazoria County, magnesium chloride is **extracted from sea water** at a plant in Freeport and used to produce **magnesium**

compounds and magnesium metal. During World War II, high-magnesium Ellenburger dolomite rock from Burnet County was used as magnesium ore at a plant near Austin.

MANGANESE — Deposits of manganese minerals, such as **braunite, hollandite and pyrolusite**, have been found in several areas, including Jeff Davis, Llano, Mason, Presidio and Val Verde counties. Known deposits are not large. Small shipments have been made from Jeff Davis, Mason and Val Verde counties, but no manganese mining has been reported in Texas since 1954.

MARBLE — Metamorphic and sedimentary marbles suitable for **monument and building stone** are found in the **Llano Uplift** and nearby areas of Central Texas and the **Trans-Pecos** area of West Texas. Gray, white, black, greenish black, light green, brown and cream-colored marbles occur in Central Texas in Burnet, Gillespie, Llano and Mason counties. West Texas metamorphic marbles include the bluish-white and the black marbles found southwest of Alpine in Brewster County and the white marble from **Marble Canyon** north of Van Horn in Culberson County. Marble can be used as **dimension stone, terrazzo and roofing aggregate** and for other purposes.

MERCURY (QUICKSILVER) — Mercury minerals, chiefly **cinnabar**, occur in the **Terlingua district** and nearby districts of southern Brewster and southeastern Presidio counties. Mining began there about 1894, and from 1905 to 1935, Texas was one of the nation's leading producers of quicksilver. Following World War II, a sharp drop in demand and price, along with depletion of developed ore reserves, caused abandonment of all the Texas mercury mines.

With a rise in the price, sporadic mining took place between 1951-1960. In 1965, when the price of mercury moved to a record high, renewed interest in the Texas mercury districts resulted in the reopening of several mines and the discovery of new ore reserves. By April 1972, however, the price had declined and the mines have reported no production since 1973.

MICA — Large crystals of flexible, transparent mica minerals in igneous pegmatite rocks and mica flakes in metamorphic schist rocks are found in the **Llano area** of Central Texas and the **Van Horn area** of West Texas. Most Central Texas deposits do not meet specifications for sheet mica, and although several attempts have been made to produce West Texas sheet mica in Culberson and Hudspeth counties, sustained production has not been achieved. A mica quarry operated for a short time in the early 1980s in the Van Horn Mountains of Culberson and Hudspeth counties to mine mica schist for use as an **additive in rotary drilling fluids**.

MOLYBDENUM — Small occurrences of molybdenite have been found in Burnet and Llano counties, and **wulfenite**, another molybdenum mineral, has been noted in rocks in the **Quitman Mountains** of Hudspeth County. Molybdenum minerals also occur at **Cave Peak** north of Van Horn in Culberson County, in the **Altuda Mountain area** of northwestern Brewster County and in association with uranium ores of the Gulf Coastal Plain.

PEAT — This spongy organic substance forms in bogs from plant remains. It has been found in the **Gulf Coastal Plain** in several localities including Gonzales, Guadalupe, Lee, Milam, Polk and San Jacinto counties. There has been intermittent, small-scale production of some of the peat for use as a **soil conditioner**.

PERLITE — Perlite, a glassy igneous rock, expands to a lightweight, porous mass when heated. It can be used as **lightweight aggregate, filter aid, horticultural aggregate** and for other purposes. Perlite occurs in Presidio County, where it has been mined in the **Pinto Canyon area** north of **the Chinati Mountains**. No perlite is currently mined in Texas, but perlite mined outside of Texas is expanded at plants in Bexar, Dallas, El Paso, Guadalupe, Harris and Nolan counties.

PHOSPHATE — Rock phosphate is present in Paleo-

zoic rocks in several areas of Brewster and Presidio counties in West Texas and in Central Texas, but the known deposits are not large. In Northeast Texas, sedimentary rock phosphate occurs in thin conglomeratic lenses in Upper Cretaceous and Tertiary rock units; possibly some of these low-grade phosphorites could be processed on a small scale for local use as a **fertilizer**. Imported phosphate rock is processed at a plant in Brownsville.

POTASH — The potassium mineral **polyhalite** is widely distributed in the subsurface Permian Basin of West Texas and has been found in many wells in that area. During 1927-1931, the federal government drilled a series of potash-test wells in Crane, Crockett, Ector, Glasscock, Loving, Reagan, Upton and Winkler counties. In addition to polyhalite, which was found in all of the counties, these wells revealed the presence of the potassium minerals **carnallite and sylvite** in Loving County and carnallite in Winkler County. The known Texas potash deposits are not as rich as those in the New Mexico portion of the Permian Basin and have not been developed.

PUMICITE (VOLCANIC ASH) — Deposits of volcanic ash occur in Brazos, Fayette, Gonzales, Karnes, Polk, Starr and other counties of the Texas Coastal Plain. Deposits also have been found in the Trans-Pecos area, High Plains and in several counties east of the High Plains. Volcanic ash is used to prepare **pozzolan cement, cleansing and scouring compounds and soaps and sweeping compounds**; as a **carrier for insecticides**, and for other purposes. It has been mined in Dickens, Lynn, Scurry, Starr and other counties.

QUICKSILVER (see **MERCURY**).

RARE-EARTH ELEMENTS AND METALS — The term, "rare-earth elements," is commonly applied to elements of the **lanthanide** group (atomic numbers 57 through 71) plus **yttrium**. Yttrium, atomic number 39 and not a member of the lanthanide group, is included as a rare-earth element because it has similar properties to members of that group and usually occurs in nature with them. The metals **thorium and scandium** are sometimes termed "rare metals" because their occurence is often associated with the rare-earth elements.

The majority of rare-earth elements are consumed as **catalysts** in petroleum cracking and other chemical industries. Rare earths are widely used in the **glass industry for tableware, specialty glasses, optics and fiber optics**. Cerium oxide has growing use as a **polishing compound** for glass, gem stones, cathode-ray tube faceplates, and other polishing. Rare earths are alloyed with various metals to produce materials used in the **aeronautic, space and electronics** industries. Addition of rare-earth elements may improve resistance to metal fatigue at high temperatures, reduce potential for corrosion, and selectively increase conductivity and magnetism of the metal.

Various members of this group, including **thorium**, have anomalous concentrations in the **rhyolitic and related igneous rocks** of the **Quitman Mountains** and the **Sierra Blanca area** of Trans-Pecos.

SALT (SODIUM CHLORIDE) (see also **BRINES**) — Salt resources of Texas are virtually inexhaustible. Enormous deposits occur in the subsurface **Permian Basin** of West Texas and in the **salt domes of the Gulf Coastal Plain**. Salt also is found in the alkali **playa lakes** of the High Plains, the **alkali flats or salt lakes in the Salt Basin** of Culberson and Hudspeth counties and along some of the bays and lagoons of the South Texas **Gulf Coast**.

Texas is one of the leading salt-producing states. **Rock salt** is obtained from underground mines in **salt domes at Grand Saline** in Van Zandt County. Approximately one-third of the salt produced in the state is from rock salt; most of the salt is produced by solution mining as brines from wells drilled into the underground salt deposits.

SAND, INDUSTRIAL — Sands used for special purposes, due to **high silica content** or to unique physical properties, command higher prices than common sand. Industrial sands in Texas occur mainly in the **Central Gulf Coastal Plain** and in **North Central Texas**. They include **abrasive, blast, chemical, engine, filtration, foundry, glass, hydraulic-fracturing (propant), molding and pottery sands**. Recent production of industrial sands has been from Atascosa, Colorado, Hardin, Harris, Liberty, Limestone, McCulloch, Newton, Smith, Somervell and Upshur counties.

SAND AND GRAVEL (CONSTRUCTION) — Sand and gravel are among the most extensively utilized resources in Texas. Principal occurrence is along the major streams and in stream terraces. Sand and gravel are important **bulk construction materials, used as railroad ballast, base materials** and for other purposes.

SANDSTONE — Sandstones of a variety of colors and textures are widely distributed in a number of geologic formations in Texas. Some of the sandstones have been quarried for use as **dimension stone** in El Paso, Parker, Terrell, Ward and other counties. **Crushed sandstone** is produced in Freestone, Gaines, Jasper, McMullen, Motley and other counties for use as **road-building material, terrazzo stone and aggregate**.

SERPENTINITE — Several masses of serpentinite, which formed from the alteration of basic igneous rocks, are associated with other Precambrian metamorphic rocks of the **Llano Uplift**. The largest deposit is the **Coal Creek serpentine mass** in northern Blanco and Gillespie counties from which **terrazzo chips** have been produced. Other deposits are present in Gillespie and Llano counties. (The features that are associated with surface and subsurface Cretaceous rocks in several counties in or near the **Balcones Fault Zone** and that are commonly known as "**serpentine plugs**" are not serpentine at all, but are altered igneous volcanic necks and pipes and mounds of altered volcanic ash — **palagonite** — that accumulated around the former **submarine volcanic pipes**.)

SHELL — Oyster shells and other shells in shallow coastal waters and in deposits along the **Texas Gulf Coast** have been produced in the past chiefly by dredging. They were used to a limited extent as raw material in the **manufacture of cement, as concrete aggregate and road base**, and for other purposes. No shell has been produced in Texas since 1981.

SILVER — During the period 1885-1952, the production of silver in Texas, as reported by the U.S. Bureau of Mines, totaled about **33 million troy ounces**. For about 70 years, silver was the most consistently produced metal in Texas, although always in moderate quantities. All of the production came from the **Trans-Pecos country** of West Texas, where the silver was mined in Brewster County (**Altuda Mountain**), Culberson and Hudspeth counties (**Van Horn Mountains and Van Horn-Allamoore district**), Hudspeth County (**Quitman Mountains and Eagle Mountains**) and Presidio County (**Chinati Mountains area, Loma Plata mine and Shafter district**).

Chief producer was the **Presidio mine in the Shafter district**, which began operations in the late 1800s, and, through September 1942, produced more than 30 million ounces of silver — more than 92 percent of Texas' total silver production. Water in the lower mine levels, lean ores and low price of silver resulted in the closing of the mine in 1942. Another important silver producer was the **Hazel copper-silver mine** in the **Van Horn-Allamoore district** in Culberson County, which accounted for more than 2 million ounces.

An increase in the price of silver in the late 1970s stimulated prospecting for new reserves, and exploration began near the old **Presidio mine**, near the old **Plata Verde mine** in the Van Horn Mountains district, at the Bonanza mine in the **Quitman Mountains** district and at the old **Hazel mine**. A decline in the price of silver in the early 1980s, however, resulted in reduction of exploration and mine development in the region. There is no current exploration in these areas.

SOAPSTONE (see **TALC AND SOAPSTONE**).

SODIUM SULFATE (**SALT CAKE**) — Sodium sulfate minerals occur in salt beds and brines of the alkali **playa lakes** of the High Plains in West Texas. In some lakes, the sodium sulfate minerals are present in deposits a few feet beneath the lakebeds. Sodium sulfate also is found in underground brines in the Permian Basin. Current production is from brines and dry salt beds at alkali lakes in Gaines and Terry counties. Past production was reported in Lynn and Ward counties. Sodium sulfate is used chiefly by the **detergent and paper and pulp industries**. Other uses are in the **preparation of glass and other products**.

STONE (see **BUILDING STONE** and **CRUSHED STONE**).

STRONTIUM — Deposits of the mineral **celestite (strontium sulfate)** have been found in a number of places, including localities in Brown, Coke, Comanche, Fisher, Lampasas, Mills, Nolan, Real, Taylor, Travis and Williamson counties. Most of the occurrences are very minor, and no strontium is currently produced in the state.

SULFUR — Texas is **one of the world's principal sulfur-producing areas**. The sulfur is mined from deposits of native sulfur, and it is extracted from sour (sulfur-bearing) natural gas and petroleum. **Recovered sulfur** is a growing industry and accounted for approximately 60 percent of all 1987 sulfur production in the United States, but only approximately 40 percent of Texas production. Native sulfur is found in large deposits in the caprock of some of the **salt domes** along the Texas Gulf Coast and in some of the surface and subsurface Permian strata of West Texas, notably in Culberson and Pecos counties.

Native sulfur obtained from the underground deposits is known as **Frasch sulfur**, so-called because of Herman Frasch, the chemist who devised the method of drilling wells into the deposits, melting the sulfur with superheated water and forcing the molten sulfur to the surface. Most of the production now goes to the users in molten form.

Frasch sulfur is produced from only one Gulf Coast salt dome in Wharton County and from West Texas underground Permian strata in Culberson County. Operations at several Gulf Coast domes have been closed in recent years. In the 1940s, acidic sulfur earth was produced in the **Rustler Springs district** in Culberson County for use as a **fertilizer and soil conditioner**. Sulfur is recovered from sour natural gas and petroleum at plants in numerous Texas counties.

Sulfur is used in the preparation of **fertilizers and organic and inorganic chemicals, in petroleum refining** and for many other purposes.

TALC AND SOAPSTONE — Deposits of talc are found in the Precambrian metamorphic rocks of the **Allamoore area** of eastern Hudspeth and western Culberson counties. Soapstone, containing talc, occurs in the Precambrian metamorphic rocks of the **Llano Uplift** area, notably in Blanco, Gillespie and Llano counties. Current production is from surface mines in the **Allamoore area**. Talc is used in **ceramic, roofing, paint, paper, plastic, synthetic rubber** and other products.

TIN — Tin minerals have been found in El Paso and Mason counties. Small quantities were produced during the early 1900s in the Franklin Mountains north of El Paso. **Cassiterite (tin dioxide)** occurrences in Mason County are believed to be very minor. The **only tin smelter in the United States**, built at **Texas City** by the federal government during World War II and later sold to a private company, processes tin concentrates from ores mined outside of Texas, tin residues and secondary tin-bearing materials.

TITANIUM — The titanium mineral **rutile** has been found in small amounts at the **Mueller prospect** in Jeff Davis County. Another titanium mineral, **ilmenite**, occurs in sandstones in Burleson, Fayette, Lee, Starr and several other counties. Deposits that would be considered commercial under present conditions have not been found.

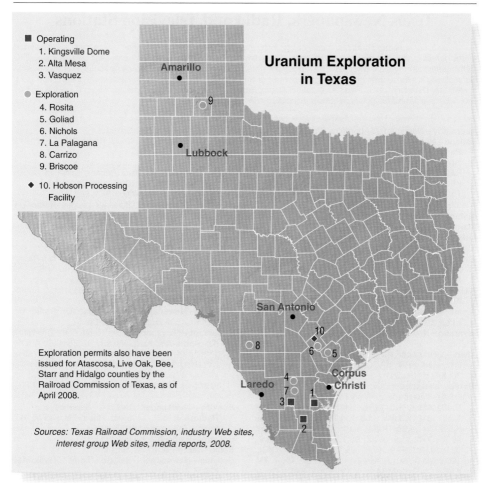

Uranium Exploration
in Texas

■ Operating
1. Kingsville Dome
2. Alta Mesa
3. Vasquez

● Exploration
4. Rosita
5. Goliad
6. Nichols
7. La Palagana
8. Carrizo
9. Briscoe

◆ 10. Hobson Processing
Facility

Exploration permits also have been
issued for Atascosa, Live Oak, Bee,
Starr and Hidalgo counties by the
Railroad Commission of Texas, as of
April 2008.

*Sources: Texas Railroad Commission, industry Web sites,
interest group Web sites, media reports, 2008.*

TRAP ROCK (see **BASALT**).

TUNGSTEN — The tungsten mineral **scheelite** has been found in small deposits in Gillespie and Llano counties and in the **Quitman Mountains** in Hudspeth County. Small deposits of other tungsten minerals have been prospected in the **Cave Peak area** north of Van Horn in Culberson County.

URANIUM — Uranium deposits were discovered in the **Texas Coastal Plain** in 1954 when abnormal radioactivity was detected in the Karnes County area. A number of uranium deposits have since been discovered within a belt of strata extending more than 250 miles from the middle Coastal Plain southwestward to the Rio Grande.

Various uranium minerals also have been found in other areas of Texas, including the **Trans-Pecos**, the **Llano Uplift** and the **High Plains**. With the exception of small shipments from the High Plains during the 1950s, all the uranium production in Texas has been from the Coastal Plain. Uranium has been obtained from surface mines extending from northern Live Oak County, southeastern Atascosa County, across northern Karnes County and into southern Gonzales County. Uranium is produced by in-situ leaching, brought to the surface through wells, and stripped from the solution at recovery operations.

In 1999, uranium mining shut down because of decreased value and demand. Production resumed in Texas in late 2004, when inventories were depleted and market prices rose to economic levels that allowed resumption of production. A total of 1.325 million pounds of eU3O8 was produced in South Texas in 2006. Uranium Resources (URI) in Dallas reported a total of 259 thousand pounds of eU3O8 production. URI has operations at Kingsville Dome in Kleberg County and Vasquez Mine in Duval County. Mesteña Uranium LLC reported 1.066 million pounds of eU3O8 production from its Alta Mesa project in Brooks County. Cumulative production from 2004 through 2006 was 1.7 million pounds.

VERMICULITE — Vermiculite, a mica-like mineral that expands when heated, occurs in Burnet, Gillespie, Llano, Mason and other counties in the **Llano region**. It has been produced at a surface mine in Llano County. Vermiculite, mined outside of Texas, is exfoliated (expanded) at plants in Dallas, Houston and San Antonio. Exfoliated vermiculite is used for **lightweight concrete aggregate, horticulture, insulation** and other purposes.

VOLCANIC ASH (see **PUMICITE**).

ZEOLITES — The zeolite minerals **clinoptilolite** and **analcime** occur in Tertiary lavas and tuffs in Brewster, Jeff Davis and Presidio counties, in West Texas. Clinoptilolite also is found associated with Tertiary tuffs in the southern Texas Coastal Plain, including deposits in Karnes, McMullen and Webb counties, and currently is produced in McMullen County. Zeolites, sometimes called "**molecular sieves**," can be used in **ion-exchange processes to reduce pollution**, as a catalyst in **oil cracking**, in obtaining **high-purity oxygen and nitrogen** from air, in **water purification** and for many other purposes.

ZINC (see **LEAD AND ZINC**). ☆

Texas Newspapers, Radio and Television Stations

In the list of print and broadcast media below, frequency of publication of subscription newspapers is indicated after the names by the following codes: (D), daily; (S), semiweekly; (TW), triweekly; (BW), biweekly; (SM), semimonthly; (M), monthly; all others are weeklies. The radio and TV stations are those with valid operating licenses as of July 2008. Not included are those with only construction permits or with applications pending. Sources: Newspapers: 2009 Texas Newspaper Directory, Texas Press Association, Austin; Broadcast Media: Federal Communications Commission Web site: http://svartifoss2.fcc.gov/prod/cdbs/pubacc/prod/cdbs_pa.htm.

Abernathy—Newspaper: Abernathy Star.

Abilene—Newspaper: Abilene Reporter-News (D). **Radio-AM:** KSLI, 1280 kHz; KWKC, 1340; KYYW, 1470; KZQQ, 1560. **Radio-FM:** KGNZ, 88.1 MHz; KACU, 89.7; KAGT, 90.5; KAQD, 91.3; KULL, 92.5; KFGL, 100.7; KEAN, 105.1; KKHR, 106.3; KEYJ, 107.9. **TV:** KRBC-Ch. 9; KXVA-Ch. 15; KTAB-Ch. 32.

Alamo—Radio-FM: KJAV, 104.9 MHz.

Alamo Heights—Radio-AM: KDRY, 1100 kHz.

Albany—Newspaper: Albany News.

Aledo—Newspaper: The Community News.

Alice—Newspaper: Alice Echo-News Journal (D). **Radio-AM:** KOPY, 1070 kHz. **Radio-FM:** KOPY, 92.1 MHz; KNDA, 102.9.

Allen—Newspaper: The Allen American. **Radio-FM:** KESN, 103.3 MHz.

Alpine—Newspaper: Alpine Avalanche. **Radio-AM:** KVLF, 1240 kHz. **Radio-FM:** KALP, 92.7 MHz.

Alvarado—Newspapers: Alvarado Post; Alvarado Star.

Alvin—Newspaper: Alvin Sun. **Radio-AM:** KTEK, 1110 kHz. **Radio-FM:** KACC, 89.7 MHz. **TV:** KFTH-Ch. 36; KFTH-Ch. 67.

Alvord—Newspaper: Alvord Gazette.

Amarillo—Newspaper: Amarillo Globe-News (D). **Radio-AM:** KGNC, 710 kHz; KIXZ, 940; KTNZ, 1010; KZIP, 1310; KDJW, 1360; KPUR, 1440. **Radio-FM:** KJRT, 88.3 MHz; KXLV, 89.1; KACV, 89.9; KAVW, 90.7; KXRI, 91.9; KQIZ, 93.1; KMXJ, 94.1; KMML, 96.9; KGNC, 97.9; KPRF, 98.7; KBZD, 99.7; KXGL, 100.9; KATP, 101.9; KRGN, 103.1; KJJP, 105.7. **TV:** KACV-Ch. 2; KAMR-Ch. 4; KVII-Ch. 7; KACV-Ch. 8; KFDA-Ch. 9; KFDA-Ch. 10; KCIT-Ch. 14.

Anahuac—Newspaper: The Progress.

Andrews—Newspaper: Andrews County News (S). **Radio-AM:** KACT, 1360 kHz. **Radio-FM:** KACT, 105.5 MHz.

Anna—Newspaper: The Anna-Melissa Tribune.

Anson—Newspaper: Western Observer. **Radio-FM:** KTLT, 98.1 MHz.

Aransas Pass—Newspapers: Aransas Pass Progress.

Archer City—Newspaper: Archer County News.

Arlington—Radio-FM: KLTY, 94.9 MHz. **TV:** KPXD-Ch. 42; KPXD-Ch. 68.

Aspermont—Newspaper: Stonewall County Courier.

Athens—Newspaper: Athens Daily Review (D). **Radio-AM:** KLVQ, 1410 kHz. **Radio-FM:** KATG, 88.1 MHz.

Atlanta—Newspaper: Atlanta Citizens Journal (S). **Radio-AM:** KPYN, 900 kHz. **Radio-FM:** KNRB, 100.1 MHz.

Austin—Newspapers: Austin American-Statesman (D); Austin Business Journal; Austin Chronicle; Daily Texan (D); Texas Observer (BW); Texas Weekly; West Austin News; Westlake Picayune. **Radio-AM:** KLBJ, 590 kHz; KVET, 1300; KFON, 1490. **Radio-FM:** KAZI, 88.7 MHz; KMFA, 89.5; KUT, 90.5; KVRX, 91.7; KLBJ, 93.7; KKMJ, 95.5; KVET, 98.1; KASE, 100.7; KPEZ, 102.3. **TV:** KTBC-Ch. 7; KLRU-Ch. 18; KXAN-CH. 21; KLRU-Ch. 22; KVUE-Ch. 24; KVUE-CH. 33; KXAN-Ch. 36; KEYE-Ch. 42; KEYE-Ch. 43;

KNVA-Ch. 54; KTBC-Ch. 56.

Azle—Newspaper: Azle News. **Radio-FM:** KTCY,101.7 MHz.

Baird—Newspapers: Baird Banner; Callahan County Star. **Radio-FM:** KORQ, 95.1 MHz.

Balch Springs—Radio-AM: KSKY, 660 kHz.

Ballinger—Newspaper: Ballinger Ledger. **Radio-AM:** KRUN, 1400 kHz. **Radio-FM:** KKCN, 103.1 MHz.

Bandera—Newspapers: The Bandera Bulletin; Bandera County Courier. **Radio-FM:** KEEP, 103.1 MHz.

Bartlett —Newspaper: Tribune-Progress.

Bastrop—Newspaper: Bastrop Advertiser (S) **Radio-FM:** KHIB, 88.5 MHz; KGSR, 107.1.

Bay City—Newspaper: The Bay City Tribune (S). **Radio-FM:** KZBJ, 89.5 MHz; KXGJ, 101.7; KMKS, 102.5.

Baytown—Newspaper: Baytown Sun (D). **Radio-AM:** KWWJ, 1360 kHz. **TV:** KAZH-Ch. 57.

Beaumont—Newspaper: The Beaumont Enterprise (D). **Radio-AM:** KLVI, 560 kHz; KZZB, 990; KRCM, 1380; KIKR, 1450. **Radio-FM:** KTXB, 89.7 MHz; KVLU, 91.3; KQXY, 94.1; KYKR, 95.1; KFNC, 97.5; KTCX, 102.5; KQQK, 107.9. **TV:** KFDM-Ch. 6; KBMT-Ch. 12; KFDM-Ch. 21; KITU-Ch. 33; KITU-Ch. 34.

Beeville—Newspaper: Beeville Bee-Picayune (S). **Radio-AM:** KIBL, 1490 kHz. **Radio-FM:** KVFM, 91.3 MHz; KTKO, 105.7; KRXB, 107.1.

Bellaire—Radio-AM: KILE, 1560 kHz.

Bells—Radio-FM: KMKT, 93.1 MHz.

Bellville—Newspaper: Bellville Times. **Radio-AM:** KNUZ, 1090 kHz.

Belton—Newspaper: The Belton Journal. **Radio-AM:** KTON, 940 kHz. **Radio-FM:** KOOC, 106.3 MHz. **TV:** KNCT-Ch. 46.

Benavides—Radio-FM: KXTM, 107.7 MHz.

Benbrook—Radio-FM: KDXX, 107.1 MHz.

Big Lake—Newspaper: Big Lake Wildcat. **Radio-FM:** KPDB, 98.3 MHz; KWTR, 104.1

Big Sandy—Newspaper: Big Sandy–Hawkins Journal. **Radio-FM:** KTAA, 90.7 MHz.

Big Spring—Newspaper: Big Spring Herald (D). **Radio-AM:** KBYG, 1400 kHz; KBST, 1490. **Radio-FM:** KPBD, 89.3 MHz; KBCX, 91.5; KBTS, 94.3; KBST, 95.7. **TV:** KWAB-Ch. 4.

Bishop—Newspaper: Kingsville Record and Bishop News. **Radio-FM:** KMZZ, 106.9 MHz.

Blanco—Newspaper: Blanco County News. **TV:** KNIC-Ch. 17.

Bloomington—Radio-FM: KHVT, 91.5 MHz; KLUB, 106.9.

Blossom—Newspaper: Blossom Times.

Boerne—Newspapers: Boerne Star (S); Hill Country Weekly. **Radio-AM:** KBRN, 1500 kHz.

Bogata—Newspaper: Bogata News.

Bonham—Newspaper: Bonham Journal, Fannin County Special. **Radio-AM:** KFYN, 1420 kHz.

Borger—Newspaper: Borger News-Herald (D). **Radio-AM:** KQTY, 1490 kHz. **Radio-FM:** KASV, 88.7 MHz; KQFX, 104.3; KQTY, 106.7. **TV:** KEYU-Ch. 31.

Bowie—Newspaper: Bowie News (S). **Radio-AM:** KNTX, 1410 kHz.

Above and at left are historic photos from WBAP-TV in Fort Worth, the first television station in the southwest and the first to broadcast local news in Texas. In 1948, publisher and businessman Amon G. Carter founded WBAP (the call letters stood for "We Bring A Program"), and its first broadcast was on Sept. 27, 1948: the visit of President Harry S. Truman to Fort Worth. Original broadcasts were from the Fort Worth Star-Telegram building in downtown Fort Worth, but in June 1949, the staff moved into the first TV facility in the southwest, which is still used today. In 1974, LIN Television bought WBAP and changed the call letters to KXAS, and in 1998, NBC purchased controlling interest. The facility is home to NBC 5, Telemundo 39, Telemundo Production Center, NBC Arthouse, NBC Network News and NBC Universal Television Distribution. Among the station's other milestones: first to carry a local golf tournament and live college and high school football, first to produce a live weather program, and first to show helicopter aerial shots. Photos courtesy of KXAS-TV.

Brackettville—Newspaper: The Brackett News.

Brady—Newspaper: Brady Standard-Herald (S). **Radio-AM:** KNEL, 1490 kHz. **Radio-FM:** KNEL, 95.3 MHz.

Breckenridge—Newspaper: Breckenridge American (S). **Radio-AM:** KROO, 1430 kHz. **Radio-FM:** KLXK, 93.5 MHz.

Bremond—Newspaper: Bremond Press.

Brenham—Newspaper: Brenham Banner-Press (D). **Radio-AM:** KWHI, 1280 kHz. **Radio-FM:** KULF, 94.1 MHz; KTTX, 106.1.

Bridgeport—Newspaper: Bridgeport Index. **Radio-FM:** KBOC, 98.3 MHz.

Brookshire—Newspaper: The Times Tribune. **Radio-AM:** KCHN, 1050 kHz.

Brownfield—Newspaper: Brownfield News (S). **Radio-AM:** KKUB, 1300 kHz. **Radio-FM:** KPBB, 88.5 MHz; KLZK, 104.3.

Brownsboro—Newspaper: Brownsboro and Chandler Statesman.

Brownsville—Newspaper: The Brownsville Herald (D). **Radio-AM:** KVNS, 1700 kHz. **Radio-FM:** KBNR, 88.3 MHz; KKPS, 99.5; KTEX, 100.3. **TV:** KVEO-Ch. 23; KVEO-Ch. 24.

Brownwood—Newspaper: Brownwood Bulletin (D). **Radio-AM:** KXYL, 1240 kHz; KBWD, 1380. **Radio-FM:** KPBE, 89.3 MHz; KBUB, 90.3; KHPU, 91.7; KXYL, 96.9; KPSM, 99.3; KOXE, 101.3.

Bryan—Newspaper: Bryan-College Station Eagle (D). **Radio-AM:** KTAM, 1240 kHz; KAGC, 1510. **Radio-FM:** KORA, 98.3 MHz; KNFX, 99.5; KKYS, 104.7. **TV:** KBTX-Ch. 3; KYLE-Ch. 28.

Buda—Newspaper: Free Press. **Radio-FM:** KROX, 101.5 MHz.

Buffalo—Newspapers: Buffalo Express; Buffalo Press.

Bullard—Newspaper: Bullard Banner News.

Buna—Newspaper: The Buna Beacon.

Burkburnett—Newspaper: Burkburnett Informer Star. **Radio-FM:** KYYI, 104.7 MHz.

Burleson—Newspaper: Burleson Star (S). **Radio-AM:** KHFX, 1460 kHz.

Burnet—Newspapers: Burnet Bulletin; Citizens Gazette. **Radio-AM:** KRHC, 1340 kHz. **Radio-FM:** KBEY, 92.5 MHz; KHLE, 106.9.

Bushland—Radio-FM: KTXP, 91.5 MHz.

Caldwell—Newspaper: Burleson County Tribune. **Radio-FM:** KLTR, 107.3 MHz.
Callisburg—Radio-FM: KPFC, 91.9 MHz.
Calvert—Newspaper: Calvert Tribune.
Cameron—Newspaper: The Cameron Herald. **Radio-AM:** KMIL, 1330 kHz. **Radio-FM:** KNVR, 94.3 MHz; KXCS, 103. 9. **Campbell—Radio-FM:** KRVA, 107.1 MHz.
Camp Wood—Radio-FM: KAYG, 99.1 MHz.
Canadian—Newspaper: Canadian Record.
Canton—Newspapers: Canton Herald; Van Zandt News. **Radio-AM:** KRDH, 1510 kHz.
Canyon—Newspaper: The Canyon News (S). **Radio-AM:** KZRK, 1550 kHz. **Radio-FM:** KWTS, 91.1 MHz; KPUR, 107.1; KZRK, 107.9.
Canyon Lake—Newspaper: Times Guardian.
Carrizo Springs—Newspaper: Carrizo Springs Javelin. **Radio-AM:** KBEN, 1450 kHz. **Radio-FM:** KCZO, 92.1 MHz.
Carrollton—Radio-AM: KJON, 850 kHz.
Carthage—Newspaper: Panola Watchman (S). **Radio-AM:** KGAS, 1590 kHz. **Radio-FM:** KTUX, 98.9 MHz; KGAS, 104.3.
Castroville—Newspaper: Castroville News Bulletin.
Cedar Hill—Newspapers: Cedar Hill Today.
Cedar Park—Newspaper: Hill Country News Weekender. **Radio-FM:** KDHT, 93.3 MHz.
Celina—Newspaper: Celina Record.
Center—Newspaper: The Light & Champion (TW). **Radio-AM:** KDET, 930 kHz. **Radio-FM:** KQBB, 100.5 MHz.
Centerville—Newspaper: Centerville News. **Radio-FM:** KUZN, 105.9 MHz.
Chico—Newspaper: Chico Texan.
Childress—Newspaper: The Childress Index (TW). **Radio-AM:** KCTX, 1510 kHz. **Radio-FM:** KCTX, 96.1 MHz.
Cisco—Newspaper: Cisco Press (S).
Clarendon—Newspaper: Clarendon Enterprise. **Radio-FM:** KEFH, 99.3 MHz.
Clarksville—Newspaper: Clarksville Times. **Radio-AM:** KCAR, 1350 kHz. **Radio-FM:** KGAP, 98.5 MHz.
Claude—Newspaper: The Claude News. **Radio-FM:** KARX, 95.7 MHz.
Clear Lake—Newspaper: The Citizen.
Cleburne—Newspaper: Cleburne Times-Review (D). **Radio-AM:** KCLE, 1140 kHz.
Cleveland—Newspaper: Cleveland Advocate. **Radio-FM:** KTHT, 97.1 MHz.
Clifton—Newspaper: Clifton Record. **Radio-FM:** KWOW, 104.1 MHz.
Clute—Newspaper: The Facts (D).
Clyde—Newspaper: Clyde Journal.
Coahoma—Radio-FM: KWDC, 105.5 MHz.
Cockrell Hill—Radio-AM: KRVA, 1600 kHz.
Coleman—Newspaper: Chronicle & Democrat-Voice (S). **Radio-AM:** KSTA, 1000 kHz. **Radio-FM:** KQBZ, 102.3 MHz.
College Station—Newspaper: The Battalion (D). **Radio-AM:** KZNE, 1150 kHz, WTAW, 1620. **Radio-FM:** KEOS, 89.1 MHz; KLGS, 89.9; KAMU, 90.9; KNDE, 95.1. **TV:** KAMU-Ch. 12; KAMU-Ch. 15.
Colorado City—Newspaper: Colorado City Record. **Radio-AM:** KVMC, 1320 kHz. **Radio-FM:** KAUM, 107.1 MHz.
Columbus—Newspapers: The Banner Press Newspaper; Colorado County Citizen. **Radio-FM:** KULM, 98.3 MHz.
Comanche—Newspaper: Comanche Chief. **Radio-AM:** KCOM, 1550 kHz. **Radio-FM:** KYOX, 94.3 MHz.

Comfort—Newspaper: The Comfort News. **Radio-FM:** KCOR, 95.1 MHz.
Commerce—Newspaper: Commerce Journal. **Radio-FM:** KETR, 88.9 MHz; KYJC, 91.3.
Conroe—Newspaper: The Courier (D). **Radio-AM:** KJOJ, 880 kHz; KYOK, 1140. **Radio-FM:** KAFR, 88.3 MHz; KHPT, 106.9. **TV:** KPXB-Ch. 5; KTBU-Ch. 42; KPXB-Ch. 49; KTBU-CH. 55.
Cooper—Newspaper: Cooper Review.
Coppell—Newspaper: Citizens' Advocate.
Copperas Cove—Newspaper: Copperas Cove Leader-Press (S). **Radio-FM:** KSSM, 103.1 MHz.
Corpus Christi—Newspapers: Corpus Christi Caller-Times (D); Coastal Bend Legal & Business News (D); South Texas Catholic (BW). **Radio-FM:** KCTA, 1030 kHz; KCCT, 1150; KSIX, 1230; KKTX, 1360; KUNO, 1400; KEYS, 1440. **Radio-FM:** KKLM, 88.7 MHz; KEDT, 90.3; KBNJ, 91.7; KMXR, 93.9; KBSO, 94.7; KZFM, 95.5; KLTG, 96.5; KRYS, 99.1. **TV:** KIII-Ch. 3; KRIS-Ch. 6; KZTV-Ch. 10; KEDT-Ch. 16; KORO-Ch. 28.
Corrigan—Newspaper: Corrigan Times.
Corsicana—Newspaper: Corsicana Daily Sun (D). **Radio-AM:** KAND, 1340 kHz.
Crane—Newspaper: Crane News. **Radio-AM:** KXOI, 810 kHz. **Radio-FM:** KMMZ, 101.3 MHz.
Crawford—Newspaper: Lone Star Iconoclast (M).
Creedmoor—Radio-AM: KZNX, 1530 kHz.
Crockett—Newspaper: Houston Co. Courier (S). **Radio-AM:** KIVY, 1290 kHz. **Radio-FM:** KCKT, 88.5 MHz; KIVY, 92.7; KBHT, 93.5.
Cross Plains—Newspaper: Cross Plains Review.
Crowell—Newspaper: Foard Co. News.
Crowley—Newspaper: Crowley Star.
Crystal Beach—Radio-FM: KSTB, 101.5 MHz; KPTI, 105.3.
Crystal City—Newspaper: Zavala County Sentinel. **Radio-FM:** KHER, 94.3 MHz.
Cuero—Newspaper: Cuero Record. **Radio-FM:** KTLZ, 89.9 MHz; KLTO, 97.7.
Cypress—Radio-AM: KYND, 1520 kHz.

Daingerfield—Newspaper: The Bee. **Radio-AM:** KNGR, 1560 kHz.
Dalhart—Newspaper: Dalhart Texan (TW). **Radio-AM:** KXIT, 1240 kHz. **Radio-FM:** KXIT, 96.3 MHz.
Dallas—Newspapers: The Dallas Morning News (D); Al Día; Dallas Business Journal; Daily Campus; Daily Commercial Record (D); Dallas Examiner; Oak Cliff Tribune; Park Cities News; Park Cities People; Texas Jewish Post; Texas Lawyer; The White Rocker. **Radio-AM:** KLIF, 570 kHz; KGGR, 1040; KRLD, 1080; KFXR, 1190; KTCK, 1310; KNIT, 1480. **Radio-FM:** KNON, 89.3 HMz; KERA, 90.1; KCBI, 90.9; KVTT, 91.7; KZPS, 92.5; KBFB, 97.9; KLUV, 98.7; KJKK, 100.3; WRR, 101.1; KDMX, 102.9; KKDA, 104.5; KLLI, 105.3. **TV:** KDFW-Ch. 4; WFAA-Ch. 8; WFAA-Ch. 9; KERA-Ch. 13; KERA-Ch. 14; KDFI-Ch. 27; KDAF-Ch. 32; KDAF-Ch. 33; KDFW-Ch. 35; KXTX-Ch. 39; KXTX-Ch. 40; KDTX-Ch. 58.
Decatur—Newspaper: Wise County Messenger (S). **Radio-FM:** KDKR, 91.3 MHz; KRNB, 105.7. **TV:** KMPX-Ch. 29; KMPX-Ch. 30.
Deer Park—Newspaper: Deer Park Progress.
De Kalb—Newspaper: De Kalb News (S).
De Leon—Newspapers: De Leon Free Press.
Dell City—Newspaper: Hudspeth County Herald.
Del Mar Hills—Radio-AM: KVOZ, 890 kHz.
Del Rio—Newspaper: Del Rio News-Herald (D). **Radio-AM:** KTJK, 1230 kHz; KWMC, 1490. **Radio-FM:** KDLK, 94.1 MHz; KTDR, 96.3. **TV:** KTRG-Ch. 10.
Del Valle—Radio-AM: KIXL, 970 kHz.
Denison—Newspapers: Herald Democrat (D); The

Pottsboro/Denison Press. **Radio-AM:** KYNG, 950 kHz.

Denton—Newspaper: Denton Record-Chronicle (D). **Radio-FM:** KNTU, 88.1 MHz; KFZO, 99.1; KHKS, 106.1. **TV:** KDTN-Ch. 2; KDTN-Ch. 43.

Denver City—Newspaper: Denver City Press.

Deport—Newspaper: Deport Times.

DeSoto—Newspapers: Focus Daily News (D); DeSoto Today.

Detroit—Newspaper: Detroit Weekly.

Devine—Newspaper: Devine News. **Radio-FM:** KRPT, 92.5 MHz.

Diboll—Newspaper: Diboll Free Press. **Radio-AM:** KSML, 1260 kHz. **Radio-FM:** KAFX, 95.5 MHz.

Dilley—Radio-FM: KVWG, 95.3 MHz; KLMO, 98.9.

Dimmitt—Newspaper: Castro County News. **Radio-AM:** KDHN, 1470 kHz. **Radio-FM:** KNNK, 100.5 MHz.

Doss—Radio-FM: KGLF, 88.1 MHz.

Dripping Springs—Newspapers: Dripping Springs Century News; The News-Dispatch. **Radio-FM:** KXXS, 104.9 MHz.

Dublin—Newspaper: Dublin Citizen.

Dumas—Newspaper: Moore County News-Press (S). **Radio-AM:** KDDD, 800 kHz. **Radio-FM:** KDDD, 95.3 MHz.

Duncanville—Newspaper: Duncanville Today.

Eagle Lake—Newspaper: Eagle Lake Headlight.

Eagle Pass—Newspapers: The News Gram; Eagle Pass News-Guide. **Radio-AM:** KEPS, 1270 kHz. **Radio-FM:** KEPI, 88.7 MHz; KEPX, 89.5; KINL, 92.7. **TV:** KVAW-Ch. 16.

East Bernard—Newspaper: East Bernard Express.

Eastland—Newspaper: Eastland Telegram (S). **Radio-AM:** KEAS, 1590 kHz. **Radio-FM:** KATX, 97.7 MHz.

Eden—Newspaper: The Eden Echo.

Edgewood—Newspaper: Edgewood Enterprise.

Edinburg—Radio-AM: KURV, 710 kHz. **Radio-FM:** KOIR, 88.5 MHz; KBFM, 104.1; KVLY, 107.9.

Edna—Newspaper: Jackson Co. Herald-Tribune. **Radio-AM:** KTMR, 1130 kHz. **Radio-FM:** KEZB, 96.1 MHz.

El Campo—Newspaper: El Campo Leader-News (S). **Radio-AM:** KULP, 1390 kHz. **Radio-FM:** KIOX, 96.9 MHz.

Eldorado—Newspaper: Eldorado Success.

Electra—Newspaper: Electra Star-News. **Radio-FM:** KOLI, 94.9 MHz.

Elgin—Newspaper: Elgin Courier. **Radio-FM:** KKLB, 92.5 MHz.

El Paso—Newspaper: El Paso Times (D). **Radio-AM:** KROD, 600 kHz; KTSM, 690; KAMA, 750; KBNA, 920; KXPL, 1060; KSVE, 1150; KVIV, 1340; KHEY, 1380; KELP, 1590; KHRO, 1650. **Radio-FM:** KTEP, 88.5 MHz; KKLY; 89.5; KVER, 91.1; KOFX, 92.3; KSII, 93.1; KINT, 93.9; KYSE, 94.7; KLAQ, 95.5; KHEY, 96.3; KBNA, 97.5; KTSM, 99.9; KPRR, 102.1. **TV:** KDBC-Ch. 4; KVIA-Ch. 7; KTSM-Ch. 9; KCOS-Ch. 13; KFOX-Ch. 14; KFOX-CH. 15; KTSM-Ch. 16; KVIA-Ch. 17; KDBC-Ch. 18; KINT-Ch. 26; KCOS-Ch. 30; KSCE-Ch. 38; KTFN-Ch. 65.

Emory—Newspaper: Rains Co. Leader.

Ennis—Newspaper: Ennis Daily News (D).

Everman—Newspaper: South Tarrant Star.

Fabens—Radio-FM: KPAS, 103.1 MHz.

Fairfield—Newspapers: Freestone County Times; The Fairfield Recorder. **Radio-FM:** KNES, 99.1 MHz.

Falfurrias—Newspaper: Falfurrias Facts. **Radio-AM:** KLDS, 1260 kHz. **Radio-FM:** KDFM, 103.3 MHz; KPSO, 106.3.

Fannett—Radio-FM: KZFT, 90.5 MHz.

Farmersville—Newspaper: Farmersville Times. **Radio-AM:** KFCD, 990 kHz. **Radio-FM:** KXEZ, 92.1 MHz.

Farwell—Newspaper: State Line Tribune. **Radio-AM:** KMUL, 830 kHz; KIJN, 1060. **Radio-FM:** KIJN, 92.3 MHz; KICA, 98.3. **TV:** KPTF-Ch. 18.

Ferris—Newspaper: The Ellis County Press. **Radio-AM:** KDFT, 540 kHz.

Flatonia—Newspaper: The Flatonia Argus.

Floresville—Newspapers: Floresville Chronicle-Journal; Wilson County News. **Radio-FM:** KWCB, 89.7 MHz; KTFM, 94.1.

Flower Mound—Radio-FM: KTYS, 96.7 MHz.

Floydada—Newspaper: Floyd Co. Hesperian-Beacon. **Radio-AM:** KFLP, 900 kHz. **Radio-FM:** KFLP, 106.1 MHz.

Follett—Newspaper: The Golden Spread.

Forney—Newspaper: Forney Messenger.

Fort Davis—Newspaper: Jeff Davis Co. Mt. Dispatch.

Fort Stockton—Newspaper: Fort Stockton Pioneer. **Radio-AM:** KFST, 860 kHz. **Radio-FM:** KFST, 94.3 MHz.

Fort Worth—Newspapers: Fort Worth Business Press; Commercial Recorder (D); Fort Worth Star-Telegram (D); Fort Worth Weekly; NW Tarrant Co. Times-Record. **Radio-AM:** WBAP, 820 kHz; KFJZ, 870; KHVN, 970; KFLC, 1270; KKGM, 1630. **Radio-FM:** KTCU, 88.7 MHz; KLNO, 94.1; KSCS, 96.3; KEGL, 97.1; KPLX, 99.5; KDGE, 102.1; KMVK, 107.5. **TV:** KXAS-Ch. 5; KTVT-Ch. 11; KTXA-Ch. 18; KTVT-Ch. 19; KTXA-Ch. 21; KXAS-Ch. 41; KFWD-Ch. 51; KFWD-Ch. 52.

Franklin—Newspapers: Franklin Advocate; Franklin News Weekly. **Radio-FM:** KZTR, 101.9 MHz.

Frankston—Newspaper: The Frankston Citizen. **Radio-AM:** KKBM, 890 kHz. **Radio-FM:** KOYE, 96.7 MHz.

Fredericksburg—Newspaper: Standard/Radio Post. **Radio-AM:** KNAF, 910 kHz. **Radio-FM:** KNAF, 105.7 MHz. **TV:** KCWX-Ch. 2.

Freeport—Radio-AM: KBRZ, 1460 kHz. **Radio-FM:** KJOJ, 103.3 MHz.

Freer—Newspaper: Freer Press. **Radio-FM:** KPBN, 90.7 MHz; KBRA, 95.9.

Friendswood—Newspapers: Friendswood Journal; Friendswood Reporter News.

Friona—Newspaper: Friona Star. **Radio-FM:** KGRW, 94.7 MHz.

Frisco—Newspaper: The Frisco Enterprise. **Radio-AM:** KATH, 910 kHz.

Fritch—Newspaper: The Eagle Press.

Gail—Newspaper: Borden Star.

Gainesville—Newspaper: Gainesville Daily Register (D). **Radio-AM:** KGAF, 1580 kHz. **Radio-FM:** KSOC, 94.5 MHz.

Galveston—Newspaper: Galveston Co. Daily News (D). **Radio-AM:** KHCB, 1400 kHz; KGBC, 1540. **Radio-FM:** KOVE, 106.5 MHz. **TV:** KLTJ-Ch. 22; KTMD-Ch. 47; KTMD-Ch. 48.

Ganado—Radio-FM: KZAM, 104.7 MHz.

Gardendale—Radio-FM: KFZX, 102.1 MHz.

Garland—Radio-AM: KAAM, 770 kHz. **TV:** KUVN-Ch. 23; KUVN-Ch. 24.

Garrison—Newspaper: Garrison In The News.

Gatesville—Newspaper: Gatesville Messenger and Star Forum (S). **Radio-FM:** KYAR, 98.3 MHz.

Georgetown—Newspapers: Sunday Sun; Williamson Co. Sun. **Radio-FM:** KHFI, 96.7 MHz; KINV, 107.7.

Giddings—Newspaper: Giddings Times & News. **Radio-FM:** KANJ, 91.1 MHz.

Gilmer—Newspaper: Gilmer Mirror (S). **Radio-FM:** KFRO, 95.3 MHz.

Gladewater—Newspaper: Gladewater Mirror. **Radio-AM:** KEES, 1430 kHz.

Glen Rose—Newspaper: Glen Rose Reporter. **Radio-FM:** KTFW, 92.1 MHz.

Goldthwaite—Newspaper: Goldthwaite Eagle.

Goliad—Newspaper: The Texan Express. **Radio-FM:** KHMC, 95.9 MHz.

Gonzales—Newspaper: Gonzales Inquirer (S). **Radio-AM:** KCTI, 1450 kHz. **Radio-FM:** KMLR, 106.3 MHz.

Gorman—Newspaper: Gorman Progress.

Graford—Newspaper: Lake Country Sun.

Graham—Newspaper: The Graham Leader (S). **Radio-AM:** KSWA, 1330 kHz. **Radio-FM:** KWKQ, 94.7 MHz.

Granbury—Newspaper: Hood Co. News (S). **Radio-AM:** KPIR, 1420 kHz.

Grand Prairie—Radio-AM: KKDA, 730 kHz.

Grand Saline—Newspaper: Grand Saline Sun.

Grandview—Newspaper: Grandview Tribune.

Grapeland—Newspaper: Grapeland Messenger.

Greenville—Newspaper: Herald-Banner (D). **Radio-AM:** KGVL, 1400 kHz. **Radio-FM:** KTXG, 90.5 MHz; KIKT, 93.5. **TV:** KTAQ-Ch. 46; KTAQ-Ch. 47.

Gregory—Radio-FM: KPUS, 104.5 MHz.

Groesbeck—Newspaper: Groesbeck Journal.

Groom—Newspaper: Groom/McLean News.

Groves—Radio-FM: KCOL, 92.5 MHz.

Groveton—Newspaper: Groveton News.

Gun Barrel City—Newspaper: Cedar Creek Pilot.

Hale Center—Newspaper: Hale Center American.

Hallettsville—Newspaper: Hallettsville Tribune-Herald. **Radio-AM:** KHLT, 1520 kHz. **Radio-FM:** KTXM, 99.9 MHz.

Haltom City—Radio-FM: KDBN, 93.3 MHz.

Hamilton—Newspaper: Hamilton Herald-News. **Radio-AM:** KCLW, 900 kHz.

Hamlin—Newspaper: Hamlin Herald. **Radio-FM:** KCDD, 103.7 MHz.

Harker Heights—Radio-FM: KUSJ, 105.5 MHz.

Harlingen—Newspaper: Valley Morning Star (D). **Radio-AM:** KGBT, 1530 kHz. **Radio-FM:** KMBH, 88.9 MHz; KFRQ, 94.5; KBTQ, 96.1. **TV:** KGBT-Ch. 4; KGBT-Ch. 31; KMBH-Ch. 38; KLUJ-Ch. 44; KMBH-Ch. 60.

Hart—Newspaper: Hart Beat.

Haskell—Newspaper: Haskell Free Press. **Radio-FM:** KVRP, 97.1 MHz.

Hawkins—Newspaper: Big Sandy-Hawkins Journal.

Hearne—Newspaper: Hearne Democrat. **Radio-FM:** KVJM, 103.1 MHz.

Hebbronville—Newspapers: Hebbronville View; Jim Hogg Co. Enterprise. **Radio-FM:** KAZF, 91.9 MHz; KEKO, 101.7.

Helotes—Radio-FM: KONO, 101.1 MHz.

Hemphill—Newspaper: The Sabine Co. Reporter. **Radio-AM:** KPBL, 1240 kHz. **Radio-FM:** KTHP, 103.9 Mhz.

Hempstead—Newspaper: Waller Co. News-Citizen. **Radio-FM:** KEZB, 105.3 MHz.

Henderson—Newspaper: Henderson Daily News (D). **Radio-AM:** KWRD, 1470 kHz.

Henrietta—Newspaper: Clay County Leader.

Hereford—Newspaper: Hereford Brand (D). **Radio-AM:** KPAN, 860 kHz. **Radio-FM:** KJNZ, 103.5 MHz; KPAN, 106.3.

Hewitt—Newspaper: Hometown News.

Hico—Newspaper: Hico News Review.

Highland Park—Radio-AM: KVCE, 1160 kHz. **Radio-FM:** KVIL, 103.7 MHz.

Highlands—Newspaper: Highlands Star/Crosby Courier.

Highland Village—Radio-FM: KWRD, 100.7 Mhz.

Hillsboro—Newspaper: Hillsboro Reporter (S). **Radio-AM:** KHBR, 1560 kHz. **Radio-FM:** KBRQ, 102.5 MHz.

Holliday—Newspaper: Archer County Advocate.

Hondo—Newspaper: Hondo Anvil Herald. **Radio-AM:** KCWM, 1460 kHz. **Radio-FM:** KMFR, 105.9 MHz.

Honey Grove—Newspaper: Weekly Gazette.

Hooks—Radio-FM: KPWW, 95.9 MHz.

Hornsby—Radio-FM: KOOP, 91.7 MHz.

Houston—Newspapers: Houston Business Journal; Houston Chronicle (D); Daily Court Review (D); Houston Forward Times; Houston Informer & Texas Freeman; Jewish Herald-Voice; Texas Catholic Herald (SM). **Radio-AM:** KILT, 610 kHz; KTRH, 740; KBME, 790; KEYH, 850; KPRC, 950; KLAT, 1010; KNTH, 1070; KQUE, 1230; KXYZ, 1320; KCOH, 1430; KMIC, 1590. **Radio-FM:** KUHF, 88.7 MHz; KPFT, 90.1; KTSU, 90.9; KTRU, 91.7; KKRW, 93.7; KTBZ, 94.5; KHJZ, 95.7; KHMX, 96.5; KBXX, 97.9; KODA, 99.1; KILT, 100.3; KLOL, 101.1; KMJQ, 102.1; KLTN, 102.9; KRBE, 104.1; KHCB, 105.7. **TV:** KPRC-Ch. 2; KUHT-Ch. 8; KUHT-Ch. 9; KHOU-Ch. 11; KTRK-Ch. 13; KETH-CH. 14; KTXH-Ch. 19; KTXH-Ch. 20; KETH-Ch. 24; KRIV-Ch. 26; KRIV-Ch. 27; KHOU-Ch 31; KTRK-Ch. 32; KPRC-Ch. 35; KHCW-Ch. 38; KHCW-Ch. 39; KZJL-Ch. 61.

Howe—Newspaper: Texoma Enterprise. **Radio-FM:** KHYI, 95.3 MHz.

Hubbard—Newspaper: Hubbard City News.

Hudson—Radio-FM: KLSN, 96.3 MHz.

Humble—Radio-AM: KGOL, 1180 kHz. **Radio-FM:** KSBJ, 89.3 MHz.

Huntington—Radio-FM: KSML, 101.9 MHz.

Huntsville—Newspaper: Huntsville Item (D). **Radio-AM:** KHCH, 1410 kHz; KHVL, 1490. **Radio-FM:** KSHU, 90.5 MHz; KSAM, 101.7.

Hurst—Radio-AM: KMNY, 1360 kHz.

Hutto—Radio-FM: KYLR, 92.1 MHz.

Idalou—Newspaper: Idalou Beacon. **Radio-FM:** KRBL, 105.7 MHz.

Ingleside—Newspaper: Ingleside Index. **Radio-FM:** KJKE, 107.3 MHz.

Ingram—Newspaper: West Kerr Current. **Radio-FM:** KTXI, 90.1 MHz.

Iowa Park—Newspaper: Iowa Park Leader.

Irving—TV: KSTR-Ch. 48; KSTR-Ch. 49.

Jacksboro—Newspapers: Jacksboro Gazette-News; Jack County Herald. **Radio-FM:** KJKB, 95.5 MHz.

Jacksonville—Newspaper: Jacksonville Daily Progress (D). **Radio-AM:** KEBE, 1400 kHz. **Radio-FM:** KBJS, 90.3 MHz; KLJT, 102.3; KOOI, 106.5. **TV:** KETK-Ch. 56.

Jasper—Newspaper: The Jasper Newsboy. **Radio-AM:** KCOX, 1350 kHz. **Radio-FM:** KTXJ, 102.7 MHz; KJAS, 107.3.

Jefferson—Newspaper: Jefferson Jimplecute. **Radio-FM:** KHCJ, 91.9 MHz; KJTX, 104.5.

Jewett—Newspaper: Jewett Messenger.

Johnson City—Newspaper: Johnson City Record-Courier. **Radio-FM:** KFAN, 107.9 MHz.

Joshua—Newspaper: Joshua Star.

Jourdanton—Radio-FM: KLEY, 95.7 MHz.

Junction—Newspaper: Junction Eagle. **Radio-AM:** KMBL, 1450 kHz. **Radio-FM:** KOOK, 93.5 MHz.

Karnes City—Newspaper: The Countywide. **Radio-AM:** KAML, 990 kHz. **Radio-FM:** KTXX, 103.1 MHz.

Katy—Newspaper: Katy Times (S). **TV:** KNWS-Ch. 51.

Kaufman—Newspaper: Kaufman Herald.

Keene—Newspaper: Keene Star. **Radio-FM:** KJCR; 88.3 MHz.

Kenedy—Radio-AM: KAML, 990 kHz. **Radio-FM:** KTNR, 92.1 MHz.

Kerens—Newspaper: Kerens Tribune. **Radio-FM:** KRVF, 106.9 MHz.

Kermit—Newspaper: Winkler Co. News. **Radio-AM:** KERB, 600 kHz. **Radio-FM:** KERB, 106.3 MHz.

Kerrville—Newspapers: Kerrville Daily Times (D); Hill Country Community Journal. **Radio-AM:** KERV, 1230 kHz. **Radio-FM:** KKER, 88.7 MHz; KHKV, 91.1; KRNH, 92.3; KRVL, 94.3. **TV:** KMYS-Ch. 35.

Kilgore—Newspaper: Kilgore News Herald (D). **Radio-AM:** KBGE, 1240 kHz. **Radio-FM:** KTPB, 88.7 MHz; KKTX, 96.1.

Killeen—Newspaper: Killeen Daily Herald (D). **Radio-AM:** KRMY, 1050 kHz. **Radio-FM:** KNCT, 91.3 MHz; KIIZ, 92.3. **TV:** KAKW-Ch. 13; KAKW-Ch. 62.

Kingsville—Newspaper: Kingsville Record & Bishop News (S). **Radio-AM:** KINE, 1330 kHz. **Radio-FM:** KTAI, 91.1 MHz; KKBA, 92.7; KFTX, 97.5.

Kirbyville—Newspaper: Kirbyville Banner.

Knox City—Newspaper: Knox Co. News.

Kress—Newspaper: Kress Chronicle.

Krum—Radio-FM: KNOR, 93.7 MHz.

La Feria—Newspaper: La Feria News.

La Grange—Newspaper: The Fayette County Record (S). **Radio-AM:** KVLG, 1570 kHz. **Radio-FM:** KBUK, 104.9 MHz.

Lake Dallas—Newspaper: The Lake Cities Sun. **TV:** KLDT-Ch. 54.

Lake Jackson—Radio-FM: KYBJ, 91.1 MHz; KHTC, 107.5.

Lakeway—Newspaper: Lake Travis View.

Lamesa—Newspaper: Lamesa Press Reporter (S). **Radio-AM:** KPET, 690 kHz. **Radio-FM:** KBKN, 91.3 MHz; KTXC, 104.7.

Lampasas—Newspaper: Lampasas Dispatch Record (S). **Radio-AM:** KCYL, 1450 kHz.

Lancaster—Newspaper: Lancaster Today.

La Porte—Newspaper: Bayshore Sun (S). **Radio-FM:** KIOL, 103.7 MHz.

Laredo—Newspaper: Laredo Morning Times (D). **Radio-AM:** KLAR, 1300 kHz; KLNT, 1490. **Radio-FM:** KHOY, 88.1 MHz; KBNL, 89.9; KJBZ, 92.7; KQUR, 94.9; KRRG, 98.1; KNEX, 106.1. **TV:** KGNS-Ch. 8; KVTV-Ch. 13; KLDO-Ch. 27.

La Vernia—Newspaper: La Vernia News.

Leakey—Newspaper: The Leakey Star (BW). **Radio-FM:** KBLT, 104.3 MHz.

Leander—Radio-FM: KHHL, 98.9 MHz.

Leonard—Newspaper: Leonard Graphic.

Levelland—Newspaper: Levelland and Hockley Co. News-Press (S). **Radio-AM:** KLVT, 1230 kHz. **Radio-FM:** KLVT, 105.3 MHz.

Lewisville—Radio-FM: KESS, 107.9 MHz.

Lexington—Newspaper: Lexington Leader.

Liberty—Newspaper: Liberty Vindicator (S). **Radio-FM:** KSHN, 99.9 MHz.

Liberty Hill—Newspaper: The Liberty Hill Independent.

Lindale—Newspapers: Lindale News & Times.

Linden—Newspaper: Cass County News.

Little Elm—Newspaper: The Little Elm Journal.

Littlefield—Newspaper: Lamb Co. Leader-News (S). **Radio-AM:** KZZN, 1490 kHz.

Livingston—Newspaper: Polk Co. Enterprise (S). **Radio-AM:** KETX, 1440 kHz. **Radio-FM:** KETX, 92.3 MHz.

Llano—Newspaper: Llano News. **Radio-FM:** KAJZ, 96.3 MHz; KITY, 102.9. **TV:** KXAM-Ch. 14.

Lockhart—Newspaper: Lockhart Post-Register;

Lockhart Times-Sentinel. **Radio-AM:** KFIT, 1060 kHz.

Lometa—Radio-FM: KACQ, 101.9 MHz.

Longview—Newspaper: Longview News-Journal (D). **Radio-AM:** KFRO, 1370 kHz. **Radio-FM:** KYKX, 105.7 MHz. **TV:** KFXK-Ch. 51; KCEB-Ch. 54.

Lorenzo—Radio-FM: KKCL, 98.1 MHz.

Lubbock—Newspaper: Lubbock Avalanche-Journal (D). **Radio-AM:** KRFE, 580 kHz; KFYO, 790; KJTV, 950; KKAM, 1340; KJDL, 1420; KBZO, 1460; KDAV, 1590. **Radio-FM:** KTXT, 88.1 MHz; KOHM, 89.1; KAMY, 90.1; KKLU, 90.9; KXTQ, 93.7; KFMX, 94.5; KLLL, 96.3; KQBR, 99.5; KONE, 101.1; KZII, 102.5; KEJS, 106.5. **TV:** KTXT-Ch. 5; KCBD-Ch. 9; KCBD-Ch. 11; KLBK-Ch. 13; KPTB-Ch. 16; KPTB-Ch. 25; KAMC-Ch. 28; KJTV- Ch. 34; KTXT-Ch. 39.

Lufkin—Newspaper: Lufkin Daily News (D). **Radio-AM:** KRBA, 1340 kHz. **Radio-FM:** KLDN, 88.9 MHz; KSWP, 90.9; KAVX, 91.9. KYBI, 100.1; KYKS, 105.1. **TV:** KTRE-Ch. 9; KTRE-CH. 11.

Luling—Newspaper: Luling Newsboy and Signal. **Radio-FM:** KAMX, 94.7 MHz.

Lytle—Newspapers: Leader News; Medina Valley Times. **Radio-FM:** KZLV, 91.3 MHz.

Mabank—Newspaper: The Monitor (S).

Madisonville—Newspaper: Madisonville Meteor. **Radio-AM:** KMVL, 1220 kHz. **Radio-FM:** KHML, 91.5 MHz; KAGG, 96.1; KMVL, 100.5.

Malakoff—Newspaper: Malakoff News. **Radio-FM:** KCKL, 95.9 MHz.

Manor—Radio-AM: KELG, 1440 kHz.

Mansfield—Newspaper: Mansfield News-Mirror.

Marble Falls—Newspapers: The Highlander (S); The River Cities Daily Tribune (D). **Radio-FM:** KBMD, 88.5 MHz.

Marfa—Newspaper: The Big Bend Sentinel.

Marion—Radio-AM: KBIB, 1000 kHz.

Markham—Radio-FM: KZRC, 92.5 MHz.

Marlin—Newspaper: The Marlin Democrat. **Radio-FM:** KLRK, 92.9 MHz.

Marshall—Newspapers: Marshall News Messenger (D); Lone Star Eagle. **Radio-AM:** KCUL, 1410 kHz; KMHT, 1450. **Radio-FM:** KBWC, 91.1 MHz; KCUL, 92.3; KMHT, 103.9.

Mart—Newspaper: Mart Messenger. **Radio-FM:** KSUR, 88.9 MHz.

Mason—Newspaper: Mason County News. **Radio-FM:** KOTY, 95.7 MHz; KHLB, 102.5.

Matador—Newspaper: Motley County Tribune.

Mathis—Newspaper: Mathis News.

McAllen—Newspaper: The Monitor (D). **Radio-AM:** KRIO, 910 kHz. **Radio-FM:** KHID, 88.1 MHz; KVMV, 96.9; KGBT, 98.5. **TV:** KNVO-Ch. 48.

McCamey—Radio-FM: KPBM, 95.3 MHz.

McCook—Radio-FM: KCAS, 91.5 MHz.

McGregor—Newspaper: McGregor Mirror and Crawford Sun.

McKinney—Newspaper: McKinney Courier-Gazette (D); Collin County Commercial Record. **Radio-FM:** KNTU, 88.1 MHz.

Melissa—Newspaper: The Anna/Melissa Tribune.

Memphis—Newspaper: Hall County Herald. **Radio-FM:** KLSR, 105.3 MHz.

Menard—Newspaper: Menard News and Messenger.

Mercedes—Newspaper: Mercedes Enterprise. **Radio-FM:** KHKZ, 106.3 MHz.

Meridian—Newspaper: Bosque Co. News.

Merkel—Newspaper: Merkel Mail. **Radio-AM:** KMXO, 1500 kHz. **Radio-FM:** KHXS, 102.7 MHz.

Mertzon—Radio-FM: KMEO, 91.9 MHz.

Mesquite—Radio-FM: KEOM, 88.5 MHz.

Mexia—Newspaper: Mexia Daily News (D). **Radio-AM:**

KRQX, 1590 kHz. **Radio-FM:** KWGW, 104.9 MHz.

Miami—Newspaper: Miami Chief.

Midland—Newspaper: Midland Reporter-Telegram (D). **Radio-AM:** KCRS, 550 kHz; KWEL, 1070; KJBC, 1150; KMND, 1510. **Radio-FM:** KPBJ, 90.1 MHz; KAQQ, 90.9; KNFM, 92.3; KZBT, 93.3; KQRX, 95.1; KCRS, 103.3; KCHX, 106.7. **TV:** KMID-Ch. 2; KUPB-Ch. 18.

Midlothian—Newspaper: Midlothian Mirror.

Miles—Newspaper: Miles Messenger.

Mineola—Newspaper: Mineola Monitor. **Radio-FM:** KMOO, 99.9 MHz.

Mineral Wells—Newspaper: Mineral Wells Index (D). **Radio-AM:** KJSA, 1120 kHz. **Radio-FM:** KFWR, 95.9 MHz.

Mirando City—Radio-FM: KBDR, 100.5 MHz.

Mission—Newspaper: Progress-Times. **Radio-AM:** KIRT, 1580 kHz. **Radio-FM:** KQXX, 105.5 MHz.

Missouri City—Radio-FM: KPTY, 104.9 MHz.

Monahans—Newspaper: The Monahans News (S). **Radio-AM:** KLBO, 1330 kHz. **Radio-FM:** KBAT, 99.9 MHz.

Moody—Newspaper: The Courier.

Morton—Newspaper: Morton Tribune.

Moulton—Newspaper: Moulton Eagle.

Mount Pleasant—Newspaper: Daily Tribune (D). **Radio-AM:** KIMP, 960 kHz.

Mount Vernon—Newspaper: Mount Vernon Optic-Herald.

Muenster—Newspaper: Muenster Enterprise. **Radio-FM:** KZZA, 106.7 MHz.

Muleshoe—Newspaper: Muleshoe Journal. **Radio-FM:** KMUL, 103.1 MHz.

Munday—Newspaper: The Munday Courier.

Murphy—Newspaper: Murphy Monitor.

Nacogdoches—Newspaper: Nacogdoches Daily Sentinel (D). **Radio-AM:** KSFA, 860 kHz. **Radio-FM:** KSAU, 90.1 MHz; KJCS, 103.3; KTBQ, 107.7. **TV:** KYTX-Ch. 19.

Naples—Newspaper: The Monitor.

Navasota—Newspaper: The Navasota Examiner. **Radio-AM:** KWBC, 1550 kHz. **Radio-FM:** KHTZ, 92.5 MHz.

Nederland—Radio-AM: KBED, 1510 kHz.

Needville—Newspaper: The Gulf Coast Tribune.

New Boston—Newspaper: Bowie County Citizen Tribune (S). **Radio-AM:** KNBO, 1530 kHz. **Radio-FM:** KEWL, 95.1 MHz; KZRB, 103.5.

New Braunfels—Newspaper: Herald-Zeitung (D). **Radio-AM:** KGNB, 1420 kHz. **Radio-FM:** KNBT, 92.1 MHz.

Newton—Newspaper: Newton Co. News.

New Ulm—Newspaper: New Ulm Enterprise. **Radio-FM:** KNRG, 92.3 MHz.

Nixon—Newspaper: Cow Country Courier.

Nocona—Newspaper: Nocona News.

Nolanville—Radio-FM: KLFX, 107.3 MHz.

Normangee—Newspaper: Normangee Star.

Odem—Newspaper: Odem-Edroy Times. **Radio-FM:** KLHB, 98.3 MHz.

Odessa—Newspaper: Odessa American (D). **Radio-AM:** KFLB, 920 kHz; KOZA, 1230; KRIL, 1410. **Radio-FM:** KBMM, 89.5 MHz; KFLB, 90.5 MHz; KOCV, 91.3; KMRK, 96.1; KMCM, 96.9; KODM, 97.9; KHHX, 99.1; KQLM, 107.9. **TV:** KOSA-Ch. 7; KWES-Ch. 9; KPEJ-Ch. 24; KWWT-Ch. 30; KPBT-Ch. 36; KMLM-Ch. 42.

O'Donnell—Newspaper: O'Donnell Index-Press.

Olney—Newspaper: The Olney Enterprise.

Olton—Newspaper: Olton Enterprise.

Orange—Newspaper: Orange Leader (D). **Radio-AM:**

KOGT, 1600 kHz. **Radio-FM:** KKMY, 104.5 MHz; KIOC, 106.1.

Ore City—Radio-FM: KAZE, 106.9 MHz.

Overton—Newspaper: Overton Press. **Radio-FM:** KPXI, 100.7 MHz.

Ozona—Newspaper: Ozona Stockman. **Radio-FM:** KYXX, 94.3 MHz.

Paducah—Newspaper: Paducah Post.

Paint Rock—Newspaper: Concho Herald.

Palacios—Newspaper: Palacios Beacon. **Radio-FM:** KROY, 99.7 MHz.

Palestine—Newspaper: Palestine Herald Press (D). **Radio-AM:** KNET, 1450 kHz. **Radio-FM:** KYFP, 89.1 MHz; KYYK, 98.3.

Pampa—Newspaper: Pampa News (D). **Radio-AM:** KGRO, 1230 kHz. **Radio-FM:** KAVO, 90.9 MHz; KOMX, 100.3.

Panhandle—Newspaper: Panhandle Herald; White Deer News.

Paris—Newspaper: Paris News (D). **Radio-AM:** KZHN, 1250 kHz; KPLT, 1490. **Radio-FM:** KHCP, 89.3 MHz; KOYN, 93.9; KBUS, 101.9; KPLT, 107.7.

Pasadena—Newspaper: Pasadena Citizen (D). **Radio-AM:** KIKK, 650 kHz; KLVL, 1480. **Radio-FM:** KFTG, 88.1 MHz; KKBQ, 92.9.

Pearland—Newspapers: Pearland Journal; Pearland Reporter News.

Pearsall—Newspaper: Frio-Nueces Current. **Radio-AM:** KVWG, 1280 kHz. **Radio-FM:** KRIO, 104.1 MHz.

Pecan Grove—Radio-AM: KREH, 900 kHz.

Pecos—Newspaper: Pecos Enterprise (S). **Radio-AM:** KIUN, 1400 kHz. **Radio-FM:** KGEE, 97.3 MHz; KPTX, 98.3.

Perryton—Newspaper: Perryton Herald (S). **Radio-AM:** KEYE, 1400 kHz. **Radio-FM:** KEYE, 96.1 MHz.

Petersburg—Newspaper: The Paper.

Pflugerville—Newspaper: Pflugerville Pflag. **Radio-AM:** KOKE, 1600 kHz.

Pharr—Newspaper: Advance News Journal. **Radio-AM:** KVJY, 840 kHz.

Pilot Point—Newspaper: Pilot Point Post-Signal. **Radio-FM:** KZMP, 104.9 MHz.

Pittsburg—Newspaper: Pittsburg Gazette. **Radio-FM:** KGWP, 91.1 MHz; KSCN, 96.9; KDVE, 103.1.

Plains—Newspaper: Cowboy Country News. **Radio-FM:** KPHS, 90.3 MHz.

Plainview—Newspaper: Plainview Daily Herald (D). **Radio-AM:** KVOP, 1090 kHz; KREW, 1400. **Radio-FM:** KPMB, 88.5 MHz; KBAH, 90.5; KWLD, 91.5; KSTQ, 97.3; KRIA, 103.9; KKYN, 106.9.

Plano—Newspaper: Plano Star Courier (D). **Radio-AM:** KMKI, 620 kHz.

Pleasanton—Newspaper: Pleasanton Express. **Radio-AM:** KFNI, 1380 kHz.

Point Comfort—Radio-FM: KJAZ, 94.1 MHz.

Port Aransas—Newspaper: Port Aransas South Jetty.

Port Arthur—Newspaper: Port Arthur News (D). **Radio-AM:** KDEI, 1250 kHz; KOLE, 1340. **Radio-FM:** KQBU, 93.3 MHz; KTJM, 98.5. **TV:** KBTV-Ch. 4.

Port Isabel—Newspaper: Port Isabel/South Padre Press (S). **Radio-FM:** KNVO, 101.1 MHz.

Portland—Newspaper: Portland News. **Radio-FM:** KSGR, 91.1 MHz; KMJR, 105.5.

Port Lavaca—Newspaper: Port Lavaca Wave (S). **Radio-FM:** KITE, 93.3 MHz.

Port Neches—Radio-AM: KUHD, 1150 kHz.

Post—Newspaper: Post Dispatch. **Radio-FM:** KPOS, 107.3 MHz.

Pottsboro—Newspaper: Pottsboro/Denison Press.

Prairie View—Radio-FM: KPVU, 91.3 MHz.
Premont—Radio-FM: KMFM, 100.7 MHz.
Presidio—Newspaper: The International Presidio Paper.
Princeton—Newspaper: Princeton Herald.

Quanah—Newspaper: Quanah Tribune-Chief (S). **Radio-AM:** KREL, 1150 kHz. **Radio-FM:** KWFB, 100.9 MHz.
Quinlan—Newspaper: The Quinlan-Tawakoni News.
Quitaque—Newspaper: Valley Tribune.
Quitman—Newspaper: Wood Co. Democrat.

Ralls—Newspaper: Crosby County News. **Radio-AM:** KCLR, 1530 kHz.
Ranger—Newspaper: Ranger Times. **Radio-FM:** KCUB, 98.5 MHz.
Rankin—Newspaper: Rankin News.
Raymondville—Newspaper: Chronicle/Willacy Co. News. **Radio-AM:** KSOX, 1240 kHz. **Radio-FM:** KBUC, 102.1 MHz; KBIC, 105.7.
Red Oak—Newspaper: Ellis Co. Chronicle.
Refugio—Newspaper: Refugio Co. Press. **Radio-FM:** KTKY, 106.1 MHz.
Richardson—Radio-AM: KKLF, 1700 kHz.
Richmond—Newspaper: Radio-AM. (see Rosenberg)
Riesel—Newspaper: Riesel Rustler.
Rio Grande City—Newspaper: Rio Grande Herald. **Radio-FM:** KQBO, 107.5 MHz. **TV:** KTLM-Ch. 40.
Rising Star—Newspaper: Rising Star.
Robert Lee—Newspaper: Observer/Enterprise.
Robinson—Radio-FM: KHCK, 107.9 MHz.
Robstown—Newspaper: Nueces Co. Record-Star. **Radio-AM:** KROB, 1510 kHz. **Radio-FM:** KLUX, 89.5 MHz; KSAB, 99.9; KMIQ, 104.9.
Rochester—Newspaper: Twin Cities News.
Rockdale—Newspaper: Rockdale Reporter. **Radio-FM:** KRXT, 98.5 MHz.
Rockport—Newspapers: Rockport Pilot (S); The Coastal Bend Herald. **Radio-FM:** KKPN, 102.3 MHz.
Rocksprings—Newspaper: Texas Mohair Weekly.
Rockwall—Newspaper: Rockwall County News.
Rollingwood—Radio-AM: KJCE, 1370 kHz.
Roma—Newspaper: South Texas Reporter. **Radio-FM:** KBMI, 97.7 MHz.
Rosebud—Newspaper: Rosebud News.
Rosenberg—Newspaper: Rosenberg Herald-Coaster (D). **Radio-AM:** KRTX, 980 kHz. **TV:** KXLN-Ch. 45; KXLN-Ch. 46.
Rotan—Newspaper: Rotan Advance-Star-Record.
Round Rock—Newspaper: Round Rock Leader (TW). **Radio-FM:** KNLE, 88.1 MHz; KFMK, 105.9.
Rowena—Newspaper: Rowena Press.
Rowlett—Newspaper: The Rowlett Lakeshore Times.
Rudolph—Radio-FM: KTER, 90.7 MHz.
Rusk—Newspaper: Cherokeean Herald. **Radio-AM:** KTLU, 1580 kHz. **Radio-FM:** KWRW, 97.7 MHz.

Sachse—Newspaper: Sachse News.
Saint Jo—Newspaper: Saint Jo Tribune.
San Angelo—Newspaper: San Angelo Standard-Times (D). **Radio-AM:** KGKL, 960 kHz; KKSA, 1260; KCRN, 1340. **Radio-FM:** KLRW, 88.5 MHz; KNAR, 89.3; KUTX, 90.1; KDCD, 92.9; KCRN, 93.9; KIXY, 94.7; KGKL, 97.5; KELI, 98.7; KCLL, 100.1; KWFR, 101.9; KMDX, 106.1; KSJT, 107.5. **TV:** KSAN-Ch. 3; KIDY-Ch. 6; KLST-Ch. 8.
San Antonio—Newspapers: San Antonio Business Journal; Commercial Recorder (D); Express-News (D); North San Antonio Times; Today's Catholic. **Radio-AM:** KTSA, 550 kHz; KSLR, 630; KKYX, 680; KTKR, 760; KONO, 860; KRDY, 1160; WOAI, 1200;

KZDC, 1250; KAHL, 1310; KCOR, 1350; KCHL, 1480; KEDA, 1540. **Radio-FM:** KPAC, 88.3 MHz; KSTX, 89.1; KSYM, 90.1; KYFS, 90.9; KRTU, 91.7; KROM, 92.9; KXXM, 96.1; KAJA, 97.3; KISS, 99.5; KCYY, 100.3; KQXT, 101.9; KJXK, 102.7; KZEP, 104.5; KXTN, 107.5. **TV:** WOAI-Ch. 4; KENS-Ch. 5; KLRN-Ch. 8; KLRN-Ch. 9; KSAT-Ch. 12; KHCE-Ch. 16; KHCE-Ch. 23; KABB-Ch. 29; KVDA-Ch. 38; KWEX-Ch. 39; KWEX-Ch. 41; KSAT-Ch. 48; WOAI-Ch. 58; KVDA-Ch. 60.
San Augustine—Newspaper: San Augustine Tribune. **Radio-FM:** KQSI, 92.5 MHz.
San Benito—Newspaper: San Benito News (S).
San Diego—Newspaper: Duval County Picture (S). **Radio-FM:** KUKA, 105.9 MHz.
Sanger—Newspaper: Sanger Courier. **Radio-FM:** KVRK, 89.7 MHz; KTDK, 104.1.
San Juan—Radio-AM: KUBR, 1210 kHz.
San Marcos—Newspaper: San Marcos Daily Record (D). **Radio-AM:** KUOL, 1470 kHz. **Radio-FM:** KTSW, 89.9 MHz; KBPA, 103.5.
San Saba—Newspaper: San Saba News & Star. **Radio-AM:** KBAL, 1410 kHz. **Radio-FM:** KBAL, 106.1 MHz.
Santa Fe—Radio-FM: KJIC, 90.5 MHz.
Schertz—Radio-FM: KBBT, 98.5 MHz.
Schulenburg—Newspaper: Schulenburg Sticker.
Seabrook—Radio-FM: KROI, 92.1 MHz.
Seadrift—Radio-FM: KMAT, 105.1 MHz.
Seagoville—Newspaper: Suburbia News.
Seagraves—Newspaper: Tri County Tribune.
Sealy—Newspaper: The Sealy News (S).
Seguin—Newspaper: Seguin Gazette-Enterprise (D). **Radio-AM:** KWED, 1580 kHz. **Radio-FM:** KSMG, 105.3 MHz.
Seminole—Newspaper: Seminole Sentinel (S). **Radio-AM:** KIKZ, 1250 kHz. **Radio-FM:** KSEM, 106.3 MHz.
Seymour—Newspaper: Baylor Co. Banner. **Radio-AM:** KSEY, 1230 kHz. **Radio-FM:** KSEY, 94.3 MHz.
Shamrock—Newspaper: County Star-News.
Shepherd—Newspaper: San Jacinto News-Times.
Sherman—Newspaper: Herald Democrat (D). **Radio-AM:** KJIM, 1500 kHz. **TV:** KXII-Ch. 12; KXII-Ch. 20.
Shiner—Newspaper: The Shiner Gazette.
Silsbee—Newspaper: Silsbee Bee. **Radio-AM:** KSET, 1300 kHz. **Radio-FM:** KAYD, 101.7 MHz.
Silverton—Newspaper: Briscoe Co. News.
Sinton—Newspaper: San Patricio Co. News. **Radio-AM:** KDAE, 1590 kHz. **Radio-FM:** KNCN, 101.3 MHz; KOUL, 103.7.
Slaton—Newspaper: Slaton Slatonite. **Radio-FM:** KJAK, 92.7 MHz.
Smithville—Newspaper: Smithville Times.
Snyder—Newspaper: Snyder Daily News (D). **Radio-AM:** KSNY, 1450 kHz. **Radio-FM:** KLYD, 98.9 MHz; KSNY, 101.5. **TV:** KPCB-Ch. 10; KPCB-Ch. 17.
Somerset—Radio-AM: KYTY, 810 kHz.
Sonora—Newspaper: Devil's River News. **Radio-FM:** KHOS, 92.1 MHz.
South Padre Island—Radio-FM: KESO, 92.7 MHz; KZSP, 95.3.
Spearman—Newspaper: Hansford Co. Reporter-Statesman. **Radio-FM:** KTOT, 89.5 MHz; KXDJ, 98.3.
Springtown—Newspaper: Springtown Epigraph. **Radio-FM:** KSQX, 89.1 MHz.
Spur—Newspaper: Texas Spur.
Stamford—Newspaper: Stamford American. **Radio-AM:** KVRP, 1400 kHz. **Radio-FM:** KJTZ, 106.9 MHz.
Stanton—Newspaper: Martin Co. Messenger. **Radio-FM:** KFRI, 88.1 MHz.

Stephenville—Newspaper: Stephenville Empire-Tribune (D). **Radio-AM:** KSTV, 1510 kHz. **Radio-FM:** KQXS, 89.1 MHz; KEQX, 89.7.

Sterling City—Radio-FM: KNRX, 96.5 MHz.

Stratford—Newspaper: Stratford Star.

Sudan—Newspaper: Sudan Beacon-News.

Sugar Land—Newspaper: The Sugar Land Scoop.

Sulphur Springs—Newspaper: News-Telegram (D). **Radio-AM:** KSST, 1230 kHz. **Radio-FM:** KSCH, 95.9 MHz.

Sweetwater—Newspaper: Sweetwater Reporter (D). **Radio-AM:** KXOX, 1240 kHz. **TV:** KTXS-Ch. 12.

Taft—Newspaper: Taft Tribune.

Tahoka—Newspaper: Lynn Co. News. **Radio-FM:** KMMX, 100.3 MHz; KAMZ, 103.5.

Talco—Newspaper: Talco Times.

Tatum—Newspaper: Trammel Trace Tribune. **Radio-FM:** KXAL, 100.3 MHz.

Taylor—Newspaper: Taylor Daily Press (D). **Radio-AM:** KWNX, 1260 kHz. **Radio-FM:** KXBT, 104.3 MHz.

Teague—Newspaper: Teague Chronicle.

Temple—Newspaper: Temple Daily Telegram (D). **Radio-AM:** KTEM, 1400 kHz. **Radio-FM:** KVLT, 88.5 MHz; KBDE, 89.9; KLTD, 101.7. **TV:** KCEN-Ch. 6; KCEN-Ch. 9.

Terrell—Newspaper: Terrell Tribune (D). **Radio-AM:** KPYK, 1570 kHz.

Terrell Hills—Radio-AM: KLUP, 930 kHz. **Radio-FM:** KPWT, 106.7 MHz.

Texarkana—Newspaper: Texarkana Gazette (D). **Radio-AM:** KCMC, 740 kHz; KTFS, 940; KKTK, 1400. **Radio-FM:** KTXK, 91.5 MHz; KTAL, 98.1; KKYR, 102.5. **TV:** KTAL-Ch. 6.

Texas City—Radio-AM: KYST, 920 kHz.

Thorndale—Newspaper: Thorndale Champion. **Radio-FM:** KLGO, 99.3 MHz.

Three Rivers—Newspaper: The Progress. **Radio-FM:** KEMA, 94.5 MHz.

Throckmorton—Newspaper: Throckmorton Tribune.

Timpson—Newspaper: Timpson & Tenaha News.

Tomball—Radio-AM: KSEV, 700 kHz.

Trenton—Newspaper: Trenton Tribune.

Trinity—Newspaper: Trinity Standard.

Tulia—Newspaper: Tulia Herald. **Radio-AM:** KTUE, 1260 kHz. **Radio-FM:** KBTE, 104.9 MHz.

Tuscola—Newspaper: Jim Ned Journal (BW).

Tye—Radio-FM: KBCY, 99.7 MHz.

Tyler—Newspapers: Tyler Morning Telegraph (D); Catholic East Texas (SM). **Radio-AM:** KTBB, 600 kHz; KZEY, 690; KGLD, 1330; KYZS, 1490. **Radio-FM:** KVNE, 89.5 MHz; KGLY, 91.3; KDOK, 92.1; KTYL, 93.1; KNUE, 101.5; KKUS, 104.1. **TV:** KLTV-Ch. 7; KLTV-Ch. 10.

Universal City—Radio-AM: KSAH, 720 kHz.

University Park—Radio-AM: KTNO, 1440 kHz; KZMP, 1540.

Uvalde—Newspaper: Uvalde Leader-News (S). **Radio-AM:** KVOU, 1400 kHz. **Radio-FM:** KBNU, 93.9 MHz; KUVA, 102.3; KVOU, 104.9. **TV:** KPXL-Ch. 26.

Valley Mills—Newspaper: Valley Mills Progress.

Van—Newspaper: Van Banner.

Van Alstyne—Newspaper: Van Alstyne Leader.

Van Horn—Newspaper: Van Horn Advocate.

Vega—Newspaper: Vega Enterprise.

Vernon—Newspaper: Vernon Daily Record (D). **Radio-AM:** KVWC, 1490 kHz. **Radio-FM:** KVWC, 103.1 MHz.

Victoria—Newspaper: Victoria Advocate (D). **Radio-AM:** KVNN, 1340 kHz; KNAL, 1410. **Radio-FM:** KAYK, 88.5 MHz; KXBJ, 89.3; KVRT, 90.7; KQVT, 92.3; KVIC, 95.1; KTXN, 98.7; KEPG, 100.9; KIXS, 107.9. **TV:** KVCT-Ch. 19; KAVU-Ch. 25.

Vidor—Newspaper: Vidor Vidorian.

Waco—Newspapers: The Waco Citizen; Waco Tribune-Herald (D). **Radio-AM:** KBBW, 1010 kHz; KWTX, 1230; KRZI, 1660. **Radio-FM:** KVLW, 88.1 MHz; KBCT, 94.5; KBGO, 95.7; KWTX, 97.5; WACO, 99.9; KWBU, 103.3. **TV:** KWTX-Ch. 10; KWBU-Ch 20; KXXV-Ch. 25; KXXV-Ch. 26; KWBU-Ch. 34; KWKT-Ch. 44; KWTX-Ch. 53.

Wake Village—Radio-FM: KHTA, 92.5 MHz.

Wallis—Newspaper: Wallis News-Review.

Waxahachie—Newspaper: Waxahachie Daily Light (D). **Radio-AM:** KBEC, 1390 kHz.

Weatherford—Newspaper: Weatherford Democrat (D). **Radio-AM:** KZEE, 1220 kHz. **Radio-FM:** KMQX, 88.5 MHz; KYQX, 89.5.

Weimar—Newspaper: Weimar Mercury.

Wells—Radio-FM: KVLL, 94.7 MHz.

Wellington—Newspaper: Wellington Leader.

Weslaco—Radio-AM: KRGE, 1290 kHz. **TV:** KRGV-Ch. 5; KRGV-Ch. 13.

West—Newspaper: West News.

West Lake Hills—Radio-AM: KTXZ, 1560 kHz.

West Odessa—Radio-FM: KLVW, 88.7 MHz.

Wharton—Newspaper: Wharton Journal-Spectator (S). **Radio-AM:** KANI, 1500 kHz.

Wheeler—Newspaper: The Wheeler Times. **Radio-FM:** KPDR, 90.5 MHz.

Whitehouse—Newspaper: Tri County Leader. **Radio-FM:** KISX, 107.3 MHz.

White Oak—Newspaper: White Oak Independent. **Radio-FM:** KAJK, 99.3 MHz.

Whitesboro—Newspaper: Whitesboro News-Record. **Radio-FM:** KMAD, 102.5 MHz.

Whitewright—Newspaper: Whitewright Sun.

Whitney—Newspaper: Lake Whitney Views (M).

Wichita Falls—Newspaper: Times-Record-News (D). **Radio-AM:** KWFS, 1290. **Radio-FM:** KMCU, 88.7 MHz; KMOC, 89.5; KZKL, 90.5; KNIN, 92.9; KLUR, 99.9; KWFS, 102.3; KQXC, 103.9; KBZS, 106.3. **TV:** KFDX-Ch. 3; KAUZ-Ch. 6; KJTL-Ch. 18.

Willis—Radio-FM: KVST, 99.7 MHz.

Wills Point—Newspaper: Wills Point Chronicle.

Wimberley—Newspaper: Wimberley View (S).

Winfield—Radio-FM: KALK, 97.7 MHz.

Winnie—Newspaper: The Hometown Press. **Radio-FM:** KKHT, 100.7 MHz.

Winnsboro—Newspaper: Winnsboro News. **Radio-FM:** KWNS, 104.7 MHz.

Winona—Radio-FM: KBLZ, 102.7 MHz.

Winters—Newspaper: Winters Enterprise. **Radio-FM:** KNCE, 96.1 MHz.

Wolfe City—Newspaper: Wolfe City Mirror.

Wolfforth—Radio-FM: KAIQ, 95.5 MHz. **TV:** KLCW-Ch. 22.

Woodville—Newspaper: Tyler Co. Booster. **Radio-AM:** KWUD, 1490 kHz.

Wylie—Newspaper: The Wylie News. **Radio-AM:** KHSE, 700 kHz.

Yoakum—Newspaper: Yoakum Herald-Times. **Radio-FM:** KYKM, 92.5 MHz.

Yorktown—Newspaper: Yorktown News-View.

Zapata—Newspaper: Zapata Co. News. **Radio-FM:** KBAW, 93.5 MHz.. ☆

Transportation

American Airlines jets at DFW International Airport. Vernon Bryant photo.

Freight Gateways

Highways

Railroads

Aviation

Ports

Foreign Trade Zones

Consulates

Freight Railroads in Texas

In Texas in 2007 there were 45 railroad companies operating, carrying 385 million tons of freight. A complete list of railroads is in the Counties section on page 211. *Source: Association of American Railroads.*

Railroads in State	Miles Operated
Class I (three – *see chart at right*)	12,176
Regional (one – Texas Pacifico)	393
Local (20)	762
Switching & Terminal (21)	1,070
Total	**14,401**
Total excluding trackage rights*	**10,804**

Railroads in State	Miles Operated
Class I	
Union Pacific Railroad Co.	6,344
BNSF Railway Co.	4,940
Kansas City Southern Railway Co.	892

*Trackage rights — track provided by another railroad. Numbers in parentheses represent the number of railroad companies in each category.

Freight Traffic in Texas by Kind – 2007					
Carloads originated		Percent	**Carloads terminated**		Percent
Intermodal	497,960	23%	Intermodal	842,480	27%
Chemicals	441,391	21%	Coal	558,920	18%
Gravel, crushed stone	227,737	11%	Gravel, crushed stone	365,613	12%
Autos, parts	158,360	7%	Chemicals	265,197	8%
Petroleum, coal	124,151	6%	Grain, crops	245,895	8%
All Other	701,404	32%	All Other	885,420	27%
Total	**2,151,003**	**100%**	**Total**	**3,163,525**	**100%**

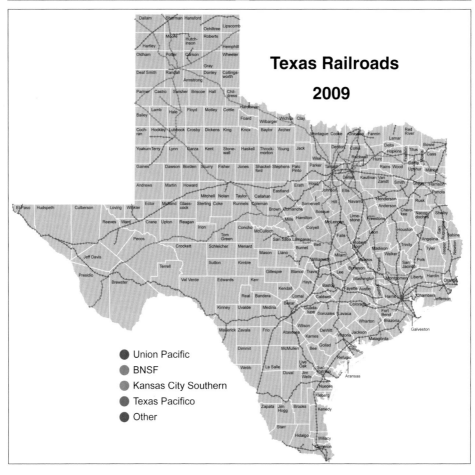

Texas Railroads 2009

- ● Union Pacific
- ● BNSF
- ● Kansas City Southern
- ● Texas Pacifico
- ● Other

A picnic area along FM 170 in Presidio County northwest of Big Bend National Park. The Texas Department of Transportation maintains more than 660 such roadside stops. Robert Plocheck photo.

Highway Miles, Construction, Maintenance, Vehicles: 2008

Texans drove more than 21 million motor vehicles in 2008 over 300,000 miles of roadways, including city- and county-maintained roads. That driving is calculated to have included more than 488.8 million miles driven daily on the 192,000 miles of state-maintained highways alone.

The Texas Department of Transportation (TxDOT) is responsible for state highway construction and maintenance, motor vehicles titles and registration, commercial trucking, automobile dealer licensing and the state's 12 official Texas Travel Information Centers and 100 safety rest areas.

The following mileage, maintenance and construction figures (listed by county) refer only to roads that are maintained by the state: Interstates, U.S. highways, state highways, farm-to-market roads and some loops around urban areas. Not included are city- or county-maintained streets and roads. A lane mile is one lane for one mile; i.e., one mile of four-lane highway equals four lane miles. Source: Texas Department of Transportation, 2009.

County	Vehicles Registered	Lane Miles of Highway	Vehicle Miles Driven Daily	State Construction Expenditures	State/ Contracted Maintenance Expenditures	State Net Receipts	County Net Receipts	Total Vehicle Registration Fees
Anderson	50,002	968	1,319,277	$ 15,418,767	$ 25,596,053	$ 2,019,519	$ 1,053,483	$ 3,078,917
Andrews	16,530	542	492,845	86,034	1,560,940	684,473	456,303	1,142,118
Angelina	83,696	929	2,207,019	20,092,178	45,363,544	3,893,775	1,719,000	5,623,123
Aransas	24,335	205	460,666	324,933	2,342,615	831,012	549,955	1,386,759
Archer	11,485	546	385,563	2,330,870	11,843,034	238,468	482,412	722,710
Armstrong	2,846	378	344,365	5,905,061	7,716,638	4,096	158,387	162,572
Atascosa	39,076	1011	1,498,598	1,898,481	15,202,525	1,341,177	873,189	2,219,829
Austin	37,076	614	1,359,736	5,132,999	10,200,210	1,465,298	840,870	2,311,647
Bailey	6,849	490	222,203	16,582	2,037,907	71,976	396,307	468,571
Bandera	25,087	415	381,130	2,070,874	21,476,329	728,922	632,841	1,366,605
Bastrop	70,894	811	2,043,072	7,551,011	28,644,225	2,784,607	1,460,421	4,258,118
Baylor	4,452	437	181,848	11,038,900	26,392,364	21,803	239,815	261,951
Bee	21,505	649	636,414	13,898,005	29,261,661	631,180	663,406	1,297,683
Bell	256,862	1510	6,268,077	70,540,768	108,600,702	11,145,998	5,308,127	16,521,253
Bexar	1,302,830	3274	27,604,293	211,204,222	401,641,017	63,877,456	25,736,719	89,836,754
Blanco	14,316	462	602,770	599,584	5,047,903	440,148	429,325	872,114

County	Vehicles Registered	Lane Miles of Highway	Vehicle Miles Driven Daily	State Construction Expenditures	State/ Contracted Maintenance Expenditures	State Net Receipts	County Net Receipts	Total Vehicle Registration Fees
Borden	1,092	344	60,914	10,592	1,522,710	1,126	41,751	43,076
Bosque	21,858	695	569,069	380,699	5,098,687	553,967	611,587	1,168,426
Bowie	90,220	1196	2,729,385	27,778,705	43,934,153	3,778,958	1,807,237	5,600,282
Brazoria	279,616	1294	4,679,734	33,986,543	43,658,438	12,840,592	4,831,189	17,725,903
Brazos	131,721	892	3,386,180	43,952,645	66,328,829	6,225,542	2,747,508	9,012,580
Brewster	10,003	591	250,341	759,264	8,457,197	210,617	358,848	574,539
Briscoe	2,330	326	59,205	667,736	6,692,068	3,901	142,502	146,546
Brooks	6,963	317	604,147	6,627,629	9,121,937	101,806	263,779	366,187
Brown	41,387	764	819,096	1,566,079	13,840,570	1,572,342	965,180	2,541,169
Burleson	21,914	522	738,226	4,469,943	12,475,499	637,079	672,995	1,312,311
Burnet	50,007	804	1,436,044	3,160,708	19,187,371	1,937,205	1,143,204	3,090,482
Caldwell	33,757	591	967,085	3,512,529	13,036,507	1,214,014	773,378	1,991,413
Calhoun	21,306	402	440,144	914,210	8,711,919	745,179	672,452	1,421,144
Callahan	16,763	745	859,052	2,856,057	11,310,027	428,781	646,290	1,076,786
Cameron	256,328	1676	6,128,120	75,359,509	104,489,262	11,773,535	5,453,654	17,249,266
Camp	17,335	265	292,888	2,142,538	13,453,491	885,588	529,404	1,416,725
Carson	7,763	776	839,375	1,478,094	22,016,153	71,392	373,042	445,281
Cass	35,145	985	988,095	15,234,874	26,270,464	1,106,593	819,088	1,928,603
Castro	8,255	534	269,915	730,765	2,520,151	151,794	478,004	630,840
Chambers	38,468	744	2,431,195	42,052,866	59,083,812	1,655,362	857,873	2,519,900
Cherokee	45,183	1121	1,378,830	1,555,511	9,699,232	1,669,009	984,684	2,658,614
Childress	6,610	477	359,340	1,907,131	10,857,541	36,348	326,862	363,723
Clay	13,841	791	836,429	642,937	5,875,162	315,730	584,367	901,695
Cochran	3,457	468	96,595	14,652	1,682,880	6,194	196,619	202,978
Coke	4,499	368	189,811	12,953	1,459,568	13,646	218,267	232,019
Coleman	11,579	754	382,556	407,090	3,179,085	142,104	486,075	629,380
Collin	608,341	1517	7,561,147	60,285,332	81,914,335	27,904,409	13,019,445	41,123,060
Collingsworth	3,493	445	101,593	69,174	1,977,585	5,564	202,490	208,490
Colorado	27,082	761	1,600,455	2,404,269	11,232,214	1,013,541	714,362	1,733,459
Comal	116,445	679	3,419,434	8,957,737	25,330,754	5,586,052	2,529,946	8,144,839
Comanche	16,745	737	503,072	3,975,288	13,753,067	410,856	599,209	1,011,138
Concho	3,541	463	238,456	22,075,004	24,188,686	5,326	182,049	187,674
Cooke	46,445	847	1,558,989	3,131,778	12,471,999	2,133,839	1,028,792	3,171,367
Coryell	53,048	684	971,551	7,408,411	26,080,250	1,831,795	1,081,999	2,923,112
Cottle	1,899	390	85,562	527,060	4,792,689	3,131	99,225	102,439
Crane	4,745	318	219,289	639,172	2,722,040	120,042	247,461	367,717
Crockett	5,353	785	510,399	868,947	7,074,655	45,305	275,962	322,130
Crosby	6,464	569	179,826	47,106	2,326,891	26,318	333,382	360,036
Culberson	2,315	748	683,479	245,631	4,777,267	3,417	133,350	136,867
Dallam	6,982	644	312,151	11,807,151	14,715,126	110,095	430,019	540,822
Dallas	1,925,213	3353	38,227,782	587,121,823	673,553,762	100,666,196	36,184,438	137,229,976
Dawson	12,283	715	397,104	866,950	3,485,802	250,265	602,515	855,753
Deaf Smith	19,553	668	377,886	555,208	3,309,982	922,170	669,012	1,593,604
Delta	6,680	603	185,085	10,545,339	12,981,449	77,279	302,415	380,279
Denton	501,039	343	9,167,517	78,244,327	114,423,626	23,400,391	9,326,293	32,856,544
Dewitt	22,233	1558	506,584	2,722,684	10,180,875	625,318	637,397	1,264,217
Dickens	3,160	469	107,122	543,239	6,102,048	3,598	127,396	131,075
Dimmit	8,451	506	333,507	671,780	6,059,713	171,855	377,800	550,633
Donley	3,680	457	528,223	367,486	5,070,575	7,178	218,551	225,997
Duval	12,256	629	444,808	1,700,465	15,785,838	340,028	465,507	806,340
Eastland	24,439	1023	1,153,715	1,753,205	10,990,379	1,684,122	739,433	2,425,332
Ector	138,241	951	1,958,459	14,251,244	26,978,610	7,662,413	3,193,319	10,870,741
Edwards	3,109	499	111,912	681,314	5,368,644	4,392	148,178	152,911
Ellis	155,029	1536	4,705,901	27,394,383	77,736,741	7,329,149	2,357,206	9,707,477
Elpaso	566,539	1621	10,276,798	95,745,342	129,475,712	27,170,791	9,827,665	37,062,346
Erath	37,038	821	1,086,894	3,868,762	14,517,608	1,374,355	901,290	2,281,642
Falls	16,455	733	748,537	20,028,588	26,927,117	363,156	570,566	935,068
Fannin	36,492	965	797,836	967,034	9,899,338	1,263,647	962,942	2,230,774

County	Vehicles Registered	Lane Miles of Highway	Vehicle Miles Driven Daily	State Construction Expenditures	State/ Contracted Maintenance Expenditures	State Net Receipts	County Net Receipts	Total Vehicle Registration Fees
Fayette	31,755	1032	1,506,505	1,264,339	14,154,743	996,741	773,613	1,775,548
Fisher	4,896	555	151,867	88,861	2,542,233	7,302	241,660	249,273
Floyd	7,256	703	187,610	697,376	11,425,398	54,843	384,705	440,421
Foard	1,643	298	62,165	431,967	6,251,007	2,369	80,413	82,782
Fort Bend	429,422	1182	6,381,407	120,265,536	135,429,002	20,882,345	7,823,899	28,813,657
Franklin	11,893	336	459,507	1,128,567	4,489,958	221,867	405,248	628,687
Freestone	24,366	809	1,700,430	1,214,576	14,315,871	720,324	720,700	1,443,132
Frio	12,233	759	981,579	1,904,747	17,955,143	249,106	481,284	731,402
Gaines	17,654	668	513,345	384,812	6,403,364	610,280	433,278	1,044,664
Galveston	259,329	1059	4,880,887	94,313,056	109,429,821	11,444,683	4,347,918	15,855,947
Garza	5,175	459	446,820	29,438	2,497,886	58,306	243,812	302,808
Gillespie	30,843	689	753,808	1,927,269	12,877,829	988,458	768,594	1,763,197
Glasscock	2,421	294	181,532	217,491	1,273,260	10,902	155,719	166,981
Goliad	8,354	505	363,131	11,915,775	18,080,250	80,093	329,732	410,364
Gonzales	21,569	880	1,121,766	902,132	16,491,050	668,786	654,521	1,324,876
Gray	25,851	773	715,241	417,450	6,318,298	923,202	770,943	1,697,356
Grayson	124,685	1210	3,192,827	8,110,467	31,694,017	5,468,568	2,274,093	7,774,440
Gregg	128,732	798	2,874,010	3,880,950	19,471,300	6,803,964	2,909,651	9,732,998
Grimes	29,508	615	969,533	1,037,944	9,871,901	967,198	726,102	1,696,848
Guadalupe	114,254	932	2,873,060	4,986,608	25,894,247	5,110,569	2,018,459	7,156,054
Hale	31,035	1057	819,784	920,022	11,456,880	1,200,225	784,268	1,987,394
Hall	3,485	457	228,027	476,106	2,842,059	5,223	190,294	195,738
Hamilton	11,352	580	386,223	718,837	7,485,880	153,954	489,524	644,200
Hansford	6,872	525	139,831	76,721	2,666,837	73,381	381,185	455,280
Hardeman	4,605	465	351,005	744,771	9,127,125	7,849	257,674	266,076
Hardin	57,469	575	1,457,663	1,163,048	12,695,090	2,350,270	1,295,128	3,653,490
Harris	3,076,623	4882	59,872,287	522,162,848	698,574,727	159,239,064	64,671,525	224,554,969
Harrison	68,466	1184	2,624,975	7,213,873	25,097,208	2,933,546	1,407,285	4,349,188
Hartley	5,791	540	287,658	87,180	1,480,258	115,736	339,490	455,983
Haskell	6,939	670	230,786	1,520,985	4,299,288	42,368	374,338	418,123
Hays	126,149	686	3,725,158	6,610,404	22,855,959	5,618,634	2,511,011	8,159,684
Hemphill	5,825	386	222,776	471,236	4,929,010	53,994	296,252	350,823
Henderson	85,472	1014	1,852,733	27,616,498	45,963,827	3,466,042	1,444,264	4,920,693
Hidalgo	458,300	2227	10,219,261	72,509,550	127,330,319	23,506,070	11,448,634	34,999,547
Hill	40,780	1075	2,240,197	31,560,146	45,144,649	1,515,453	881,098	2,400,733
Hockley	24,797	752	640,932	1,055,098	10,913,400	1,069,511	683,250	1,755,525
Hood	60,430	389	1,027,711	5,939,161	16,287,350	2,632,152	1,361,893	4,007,017
Hopkins	38,757	964	1,491,664	7,266,150	30,305,073	1,504,695	891,780	2,400,478
Houston	23,572	844	654,256	1,511,385	15,717,006	681,908	650,716	1,336,911
Howard	29,136	859	953,221	1,637,798	15,984,355	1,026,871	777,601	1,808,454
Hudspeth	3,566	826	1,223,637	291,873	4,878,294	6,096	180,190	186,588
Hunt	88,258	1308	2,661,259	17,625,236	33,832,806	3,604,358	1,762,765	5,378,451
Hutchinson	27,271	474	391,005	414,632	6,645,455	1,068,448	640,117	1,712,179
Irion	3,501	247	116,563	46,752	1,126,683	56,095	196,301	252,593
Jack	11,872	576	369,427	856,466	6,597,236	414,787	468,721	884,395
Jackson	16,495	636	872,774	710,672	5,849,680	396,897	561,028	959,753
Jasper	39,863	771	1,245,401	11,398,603	28,002,437	1,478,258	894,536	2,377,653
Jeff Davis	3,198	469	193,263	379,058	2,827,102	60,482	166,437	227,880
Jefferson	210,891	1123	5,359,382	7,221,504	45,940,724	10,034,950	4,103,570	14,179,689
Jim Hogg	5,076	288	218,584	0	1,571,386	100,259	280,154	381,097
Jim Wells	39,753	715	1,267,938	1,872,191	19,728,130	1,890,157	1,040,122	2,934,002
Johnson	157,150	950	3,428,463	10,829,003	57,828,945	7,617,296	2,659,196	10,299,742
Jones	17,823	1011	511,972	983,900	9,769,329	556,025	671,660	1,229,454
Karnes	12,802	696	393,855	923,722	5,183,525	183,185	510,690	695,132
Kaufman	97,912	1201	3,793,697	17,297,509	44,481,107	4,018,552	1,910,814	5,943,762
Kendall	46,134	453	960,771	1,323,198	9,215,162	1,785,345	1,523,960	3,325,994
Kenedy	835	188	440,715	0	935,698	1,033	33,148	34,259
Kent	1,206	325	55,949	55,031	2,017,611	2,101	62,741	65,018

County	Vehicles Registered	Lane Miles of Highway	Vehicle Miles Driven Daily	State Construction Expenditures	State/ Contracted Maintenance Expenditures	State Net Receipts	County Net Receipts	Total Vehicle Registration Fees
Kerr	54,239	703	1,145,602	12,800,824	23,280,656	2,140,040	1,166,233	3,321,125
Kimble	6,455	686	514,590	1,458,580	11,958,968	57,893	291,212	349,754
King	623	199	72,471	5,229,056	5,719,271	612	37,512	38,124
Kinney	3,505	407	183,342	1,058,959	4,791,721	39,261	153,716	193,319
Kleberg	26,403	373	830,973	738,584	5,636,499	1,070,270	800,980	1,876,433
Knox	4,805	466	132,838	1,420,488	3,581,157	37,159	286,500	323,994
Lamar	52,581	991	1,228,994	2,704,199	19,317,305	2,200,254	1,155,096	3,361,330
Lamb	14,391	805	454,786	1,277,745	13,264,148	356,597	569,811	927,757
Lampasas	23,303	490	579,554	7,219,423	12,217,910	681,497	755,911	1,442,075
La Salle	5,801	649	718,119	363,773	6,820,461	282,147	339,205	622,317
Lavaca	25,844	641	567,642	11,355,635	25,679,901	813,333	670,640	1,485,952
Lee	21,607	529	731,601	692,802	7,595,606	735,873	616,909	1,355,334
Leon	22,707	833	1,521,701	1,541,487	9,413,638	721,423	587,609	1,310,587
Liberty	76,252	817	2,092,655	10,446,276	46,308,785	3,535,120	1,453,717	4,997,261
Limestone	24,950	769	781,545	4,049,552	20,167,494	763,939	683,187	1,449,290
Lipscomb	3,944	412	129,878	61,084	2,212,954	6,226	245,874	252,498
Live Oak	12,812	1001	1,271,947	19,338,200	37,118,102	276,135	546,436	824,426
Llano	24,932	498	491,637	406,905	6,204,703	711,014	670,180	1,386,776
Loving	248	67	18,807	0	126,196	228	17,709	17,938
Lubbock	220,728	1705	3,745,458	85,792,159	116,598,123	11,175,510	4,594,587	15,839,389
Lynn	6,467	710	352,588	5,752	2,992,647	24,852	324,966	350,969
Madison	12,899	571	965,867	301,854	6,588,081	333,733	589,251	924,609
Marion	11,456	323	353,928	10,836,826	14,588,331	185,207	477,701	664,061
Martin	5,962	574	410,025	842,609	3,942,888	31,287	367,253	399,236
Mason	5,818	423	175,207	31,561	1,908,082	47,018	254,593	302,218
Matagorda	37,396	691	744,092	2,238,774	25,642,178	1,375,898	863,322	2,244,593
Maverick	35,348	476	711,322	8,809,416	22,467,801	1,565,412	804,224	2,374,603
McCulloch	10,212	608	308,569	2,074,574	5,347,777	131,960	466,100	599,706
McLennan	201,880	1670	5,868,411	32,088,027	61,476,496	9,807,939	3,620,933	13,462,198
McMullen	2,637	317	137,000	371,958	5,924,354	53,340	189,969	243,515
Medina	44,900	766	1,225,304	3,013,327	16,704,210	1,616,419	1,082,565	2,704,989
Menard	3,090	346	138,922	320,969	2,667,047	6,988	143,789	151,251
Midland	149,377	1036	2,284,800	6,872,499	24,881,499	8,875,966	2,939,124	11,844,836
Milam	29,308	691	902,620	4,247,503	14,371,809	888,063	715,123	1,606,597
Mills	7,018	451	263,393	423,422	2,780,930	34,268	366,434	401,340
Mitchell	8,000	662	565,850	377,693	3,866,498	72,314	364,983	438,080
Montague	26,037	850	762,323	2,113,908	8,958,014	897,024	723,480	1,623,203

The ferry at Port Aransas. TxDOT operates ferries there and Galveston-Port Bolivar. Robert Plocheck photo.

County	Vehicles Registered	Lane Miles of Highway	Vehicle Miles Driven Daily	State Construction Expenditures	State/ Contracted Maintenance Expenditures	State Net Receipts	County Net Receipts	Total Vehicle Registration Fees
Montgomery	385,240	1219	8,347,427	208,541,616	228,228,196	18,368,318	6,312,306	24,776,991
Moore	21,279	467	468,439	721,991	5,842,726	892,691	610,635	1,505,410
Morris	14,862	356	468,600	896,814	3,528,318	372,969	449,533	823,751
Motley	1,721	331	63,721	906,884	8,626,762	2,651	83,991	86,769
Nacogdoches	55,976	958	1,915,627	3,551,381	25,843,240	2,189,269	1,234,291	3,431,763
Navarro	48,077	1192	1,983,565	18,831,106	42,196,629	1,896,389	1,059,508	2,961,069
Newton	15,133	551	446,603	616,844	7,668,158	256,062	520,264	777,642
Nolan	15,668	694	843,169	1,804,685	19,317,353	423,724	576,828	1,002,025
Nueces	267,474	1495	5,936,483	28,714,084	55,723,585	13,076,038	5,091,513	18,206,106
Ochiltree	13,418	430	265,813	76,380	1,541,388	478,294	570,881	1,051,842
Oldham	2,808	472	588,292	1,797,961	16,689,909	19,169	166,269	185,864
Orange	84,774	619	2,652,566	36,565,772	57,256,545	3,466,468	1,435,534	4,912,939
Palo Pinto	34,603	829	967,107	6,958,947	36,125,645	1,361,286	762,812	2,129,291
Panola	31,039	771	1,170,662	3,195,361	12,359,073	1,388,714	520,105	1,911,654
Parker	123,594	880	3,126,784	8,187,110	28,796,842	5,669,690	2,578,573	8,276,025
Parmer	10,413	614	384,013	3,594,317	6,752,391	186,741	507,933	695,136
Pecos	15,643	1683	940,339	1,684,555	17,604,274	450,137	581,365	1,033,588
Polk	58,778	857	1,815,374	1,665,746	16,878,119	2,878,370	1,284,190	4,170,002
Potter	101,304	901	2,716,423	6,035,579	27,358,938	5,137,457	2,041,772	7,198,956
Presidio	7,469	545	182,369	904,563	9,819,415	122,561	310,168	433,416
Rains	13,461	268	317,309	155,135	3,632,288	300,590	445,674	748,306
Randall	117,443	902	1,320,585	2,558,184	16,452,508	5,421,175	2,545,024	8,000,999
Reagan	4,134	320	127,773	52,470	1,168,872	61,439	252,207	313,862
Real	4,260	296	115,477	1,346,840	9,324,339	42,372	200,203	243,035
Red River	15,385	750	452,837	3,691,504	11,591,772	244,683	523,792	769,901
Reeves	10,006	1180	749,600	835,920	9,020,472	124,123	434,466	559,942
Refugio	8,314	465	824,829	1,384,857	8,049,410	134,818	351,815	487,598
Roberts	1,422	241	106,754	24,388	757,473	2,228	70,096	72,639
Robertson	18,338	627	970,323	9,764,920	22,787,895	429,372	623,689	1,055,331
Rockwall	71,734	339	1,674,060	17,898,445	29,682,427	3,277,340	1,238,860	4,535,528
Runnels	13,371	730	370,840	998,104	9,327,089	361,160	534,529	896,523
Rusk	52,359	1182	1,554,027	1,022,591	16,758,150	2,007,910	1,050,873	3,065,521
Sabine	13,226	487	311,206	1,435,346	15,442,962	247,369	460,151	709,076
SanAugustine	9,584	529	299,091	734,322	7,066,657	135,111	424,179	559,963
San Jacinto	26,042	516	797,233	2,777,542	21,671,778	843,364	665,383	1,511,376
San Patricio	63,179	947	2,002,917	28,803,742	43,739,173	2,689,540	1,389,768	4,089,446
San Saba	7,672	436	165,223	77,860	2,227,585	58,622	389,285	448,524
Schleicher	4,198	361	151,833	306,969	3,205,141	36,232	211,016	247,675
Scurry	20,975	680	657,558	980,459	9,799,997	972,229	672,668	1,647,046
Shackelford	4,746	353	176,221	589,580	6,101,741	56,421	247,596	304,577
Shelby	27,779	861	856,174	4,636,482	19,269,560	917,769	783,512	1,704,342
Sherman	3,101	429	223,481	144,427	2,581,092	4,888	183,639	188,818
Smith	202,082	1599	5,317,254	28,916,903	65,360,160	9,201,165	4,165,548	13,401,927
Somervell	10,066	198	298,973	2,789,906	4,956,685	237,843	332,832	572,530
Starr	42,884	494	1,140,646	4,709,392	11,518,730	1,635,327	962,355	2,600,228
Stephens	11,992	560	248,655	238,694	2,655,769	284,162	470,059	755,258
Sterling	2,092	283	179,118	721,370	2,024,040	3,495	86,020	89,749
Stonewall	2,276	329	94,348	357,212	3,439,766	2,834	128,104	130,980
Sutton	7,100	592	581,232	3,004	1,926,133	169,697	341,669	512,777
Swisher	6,863	807	415,688	15,322	2,707,622	48,229	356,682	405,678
Tarrant	1,482,367	3213	30,079,863	111,352,935	231,818,350	75,757,282	27,622,010	103,791,238
Taylor	124,375	1215	2,306,911	19,225,438	38,273,131	5,865,660	2,573,117	8,459,517
Terrell	1,353	374	97,430	0	730,313	1,673	61,622	63,555
Terry	12,346	630	417,116	736,761	13,859,598	247,143	546,958	795,411
Throckmorton	2,279	341	74,437	1,135,288	5,920,779	3,147	113,357	116,576
Titus	30,376	541	1,042,088	2,970,496	13,479,606	1,146,963	887,523	2,039,566
Tom Green	105,420	1022	1,549,315	7,016,730	32,304,516	4,697,921	2,264,823	6,979,961
Travis	947,473	1955	16,933,316	316,714,988	401,656,003	37,776,631	15,737,427	53,794,220

County	Vehicles Registered	Lane Miles of Highway	Vehicle Miles Driven Daily	State Construction Expenditures	State/ Contracted Maintenance Expenditures	State Net Receipts	County Net Receipts	Total Vehicle Registration Fees
Trinity	15,754	436	340,078	693,544	5,516,079	365,380	506,495	872,661
Tyler	21,807	521	614,766	2,560,173	14,903,558	562,275	601,185	1,165,438
Upshur	42,537	787	1,055,180	3,586,673	25,645,630	1,464,499	886,890	2,355,243
Upton	4,150	391	176,102	109,129	1,846,625	51,849	182,944	235,096
Uvalde	25,046	740	741,610	1,752,382	16,893,594	1,062,703	650,506	1,716,133
Val Verde	41,735	713	488,188	4,604,029	12,061,213	1,647,757	981,908	2,638,418
Van Zandt	62,233	1166	2,199,581	1,901,256	31,012,671	2,419,579	1,136,084	3,561,535
Victoria	86,137	890	2,013,194	7,583,417	20,166,792	4,111,173	1,862,125	5,988,084
Walker	48,341	799	2,342,963	6,228,304	16,770,600	1,762,279	1,097,114	2,866,902
Waller	42,665	584	1,848,701	3,405,546	8,613,284	1,628,055	1,316,808	2,953,556
Ward	12,637	666	612,450	399,956	4,211,887	472,185	331,754	805,231
Washington	40,039	658	1,237,829	1,180,914	14,187,513	1,697,811	959,209	2,663,288
Webb	155,504	1127	3,088,204	59,445,040	94,421,971	8,811,476	3,029,187	11,861,497
Wharton	45,998	885	1,648,643	1,222,096	12,993,124	2,199,687	1,006,947	3,212,014
Wheeler	7,638	672	619,239	1,294,039	13,155,181	66,758	385,287	452,906
Wichita	115,097	1123	2,154,333	15,120,184	34,862,907	5,050,854	2,237,530	7,308,183
Wilbarger	13,904	736	642,709	2,266,984	19,519,496	274,044	584,810	862,325
Willacy	14,211	479	467,396	5,023,653	11,804,327	307,662	550,596	859,520
Williamson	324,180	1657	7,012,908	78,139,046	105,642,562	15,286,011	6,991,045	22,376,930
Wilson	43,547	745	830,780	1,067,092	12,737,611	1,561,717	920,604	2,487,277
Winkler	8,000	294	187,911	31,653	858,989	197,891	327,004	525,790
Wise	77,924	856	2,358,429	9,809,910	21,609,987	4,092,763	1,540,967	5,643,422
Wood	50,898	899	986,302	4,344,097	15,606,836	1,941,040	1,085,612	3,032,773
Yoakum	10,079	431	242,348	57,619	2,199,976	215,469	502,463	718,773
Young	24,553	706	371,842	1,084,472	9,802,944	899,930	691,078	1,594,838
Zapata	12,277	248	426,558	6,087,660	10,977,558	432,471	346,082	779,952
Zavala	8,228	542	304,081	1,195,412	6,771,815	154,781	356,101	511,751
Total	21,171,729	192,542	488,790,361	$4,004,870,195	$7,395,914,005	$971,890,724	$449,875,888	$1,425,954,490

Texas Toll Roads, Bridges

Facility	Operating Authority	2006 Tolls Collected
		(thousands of dollars, 000)
Cameron County International Toll Bridge	Cameron County	$ 17,867
Central Texas Toll Facilities	Central Texas Regional Mobility Authority	NA*
Del Rio International Bridge	City of Del Rio	4,610
Eagle Pass International Bridge	City of Eagle Pass	7,784
Fort Bend Toll Road	Fort Bend Toll Road Authority	11,643
Harris County Toll Facilities	Harris County Toll Road Authority	354,460
Laredo International Bridge	City of Laredo	39,047
McAllen International Toll Bridge	City of McAllen	11,256
North Texas Toll Facilities	North Texas Tollway Authority	191,434
Pharr International Toll Bridge	City of Pharr	7,658
Roma International Toll Bridge	Starr County	2,673
San Luis Pass–Vacek Bridge	Galveston County	675
Zaragosa Bridge	City of El Paso	14,262
	Total	**$ 663,369**

*Not Available: Central Texas roads began operation in late 2006.
Source: Highway Statistics 2007, Federal Highway Administration.

Driver Licenses

The following list shows the number of licensed drivers by year for Texas and for all the states.

Year	Texas licensed drivers	Total U.S. licensed drivers
2008	16,511,156	NA
2007	16,330,825	205,741,845
2006	16,096,985	202,810,438
2005	15,831,852	200,548,972
2004	15,562,484	198,888,912
2003	15,091,776	196,165,666
2002	14,639,132	194,295,633
2001	14,303,799	191,275,719
2000	14,024,305	190,625,023
1995	12,369,243	176,628,482
1990	11,136,694	167,015,250
1985	10,809,078	156,868,277
1980	9,287,286	145,295,036
1975	7,509,497	129,790,666
1970	6,380,057	111,542,787
1965	5,413,887	98,502,152
1960	4,352,168	87,252,563
1955	3,874,834	74,685,949
1950	2,687,349	59,322,278

Sources: Texas Department of Public Safety and the Federal Highway Administration.

Motor Vehicles Crashes, Losses in Texas

Year	Number killed	Number injured	Crashes by Kind				Vehicle Miles Traveled		Economic loss (000,000)
			Fatal	Injury	Non-injury	Total	Number (000,000)	Deaths per 100 mill miles	
1960	2,254	127,980	1,842	71,100	239,300	312,242	46,353	4.9	$ 350
1965	3,028	186,062	2,460	103,368	365,160	470,988	* 52,163	5.8	498
1966	3,406	208,310	2,784	115,728	406,460	524,972	55,261	6.2	557
1967	3,367	† 205,308	2,778	114,060	768,430	885,268	58,124	5.8	793
1968	3,481	216,972	2,902	120,540	816,830	940,272	62,794	5.5	837
1969	3,551	223,000	2,913	124,000	850,000	976,913	67,742	5.2	955
1970	3,560	223,000	2,965	124,000	886,000	1,012,965	* 68,031	5.2	1,042
1971	3,594	224,000	2,993	124,000	890,000	1,016,993	70,709	5.1	1,045
1972	3,688	† 128,158	3,099	83,607	346,292	432,998	76,690	4.8	1,035
1973	3,692	132,635	3,074	87,631	373,521	464,226	80,615	4.6	1,035
1974	3,046	123,611	2,626	83,341	348,227	434,194	78,290	3.9	1,095
1975	3,429	138,962	2,945	92,510	373,141	468,596	84,575	4.1	1,440
1976	3,230	145,282	2,780	96,348	380,075	479,203	91,279	3.5	1,485
1977	3,698	161,635	3,230	106,923	393,848	504,001	96,998	3.8	1,960
1978	‡ 3,980	178,228	‡ 3,468	117,998	§ 304,830	426,296	102,624	3.9	2,430
1979	4,229	184,550	3,685	122,793	322,336	448,814	101,909	4.1	2,580
1980	4,424	185,964	3,863	123,577	305,500	432,940	103,255	4.3	3,010
1981	4,701	206,196	4,137	136,396	317,484	458,017	111,036	4.2	3,430
1982	4,271	204,666	3,752	135,859	312,159	451,770	* 124,910	3.4	3,375
1983	‡ 3,823	208,157	‡ 3,328	137,695	302,876	443,899	129,309	3.0	3,440
1984	3,913	220,720	3,466	145,543	293,285	442,294	137,280	2.9	¶ 3,795
1985	3,682	231,009	3,270	151,657	300,531	452,188	143,500	2.6	3,755
1986	3,568	234,120	3,121	154,514	298,079	452,593	150,474	2.4	3,782
1987	3,261	226,895	2,881	146,913	246,175	395,969	151,221	2.2	3,913
1988	3,395	238,845	3,004	152,004	237,703	392,711	152,819	2.2	4,515
1989	3,361	243,030	2,926	153,356	233,967	390,249	159,679	2.1	4,873
1990	3,243	262,576	2,882	162,424	216,140	381,446	163,103	2.0	4,994
1991	3,079	263,430	2,690	161,470	207,288	371,448	162,780	1.9	5,604
1992	3,057	282,025	2,690	170,513	209,152	382,355	162,769	1.9	6,725
1993	3,037	298,891	2,690	178,194	209,533	390,417	167,988	1.8	¶ 11,784
1994	3,142	326,837	2,710	192,014	219,890	414,614	172,976	1.8	12,505
1995	3,172	334,259	2,790	196,093	152,190	351,073	183,103	1.7	13,005
1996	3,738	350,397	3,247	204,635	§ 90,261	298,143	187,064	2.0	¶ 7,766
1997	3,508	347,881	3,079	205,595	97,315	305,989	194,665	1.8	7,662
1998	3,576	338,661	3,160	202,223	102,732	308,115	201,989	1.8	8,780
1999	3,519	339,448	3,106	203,220	105,375	311,701	213,847	1.6	8,729
2000	3,775	341,097	3,247	205,569	110,174	318,990	210,340	1.8	9,163
2001	3,739	340,554	3,319	207,043	113,596	323,958	216,276	1.73	9,348
2002	3,826	315,061	3,544	196,211	113,089	** 324,651	215,873	1.77	¶ 21,100
2003	3,823	308,543	3,372	190,926	§ 245,607	†† 460,025	218,209	1.75	20,700
2004	3,725	288,715	3,286	180,556	245,000	447,691	229,345	1.62	19,400
2005	3,559	293,583	3,157	184,093	257,532	464,541	234,232	1.52	19,200
2006	3,523	272,779	3,120	173,861	243,970	439,027	236,852	1.49	20,400
2007	3,463	267,305	3,098	173,052	264,098	459,689	241,746	1.43	$ 20,600

(Note: The highest death rate was in 1966.)
*Method of calculating vehicle miles traveled revised. Last changed in 1982 by TxDOT.
†In August 1967, amended estimating formula received from National Safety Council (NCS). Starting 1972, actual reported injuries are listed rather than estimates.
‡Change in counting fatalities. In 1978, counted when injury results in death within 90 days of accident. In 1983, counted when injury results in death within 30 days.

§Change in counting Non-injury accidents. For 1996–2002, only crashes having at least **one vehicle towed** were tabulated.
¶Economic loss formula changed. Last changed in 2002, when figures are calculated using NCS Average Calculable Cost on a per death basis figure for the year identified. Figures are rounded to the nearest hundred million. For 1996–2001, only property damage in crashes having at least one vehicle towed was tabulated.
**Beginning with 2002 data, the "Total"

crash figure includes "Unknown Severity Crashes" which are not included on this chart. Prior to 2002 these crashes were counted in the Non-injury or Injury category.
††Beginning with 2003 crashes, only those resulting in injury or death or damage to property to the apparent extent of $1,000 are tabulated.

Source: Texas Department of Transportation (TxDOT) since 2001. Earlier statistics are from the Texas Department of Public Safety (DPS).

U.S. Freight Gateways, 2005

[In billions of dollars (134.9 represents $134,900,000,000)]. Top gateways ranked by value of shipments, with Texas gateways highlighted. *Source: U.S. Bureau of Transportation Statistics, National Transportation Statistics, annual.*

Rank	Port	Mode	Total trade	Exports	Imports	Exports as a percent of total
1	JFK International Airport, NY	Air	$ 134.9	$ 59.3	$ 75.6	43.9
2	Port of Los Angeles, CA	Water	134.3	18.4	116.0	13.7
3	Port of Detroit, MI	Water	130.5	68.8	61.7	52.7
4	Port of New York, NY and NJ	Water	130.4	26.2	104.2	20.1
5	Port of Long Beach, CA	Water	124.6	21.2	103.4	17.0
6	Port of Laredo, TX	Land	93.7	40.9	52.8	43.7
7	Port of Houston, TX	Water	86.1	33.8	52.3	39.2
8	Chicago, IL	Air	73.4	29.1	44.3	39.7
9	Los Angeles International Airport, CA	Air	72.9	36.5	36.4	50.1
10	Port of Buffalo–Niagra Falls, NY	Land	70.5	32.5	38.0	46.2
11	Port of Huron, MI	Land	68.2	23.6	44.6	34.6
12	San Francisco International Airport, CA	Air	57.2	25.2	32.0	44.0
13	Port of Charleston, SC	Water	52.4	15.9	36.5	30.4
14	Port of El Paso, TX	Land	43.0	18.9	24.1	43.9
15	Port of Norfolk Harbor, VA	Water	43.0	15.0	24.5	37.9
16	Port of Baltimore, MD	Water	35.6	8.6	27.0	24.0
17	Dallas-Fort Worth, TX	Air	35.1	15.4	19.7	44.0
18	Port of Seattle, WA	Water	35.0	7.7	27.3	22.0
19	Anchorage, AK	Air	34.7	8.7	26.0	25.1
20	Port of Tacoma, WA	Water	33.8	5.0	28.7	14.9
21	Port of Savannah, GA	Water	33.4	11.3	22.1	33.7
22	Port of Oakland, CA	Water	32.6	8.9	23.7	27.3
23	Atlanta, GA	Air	29.9	11.6	18.3	38.7
24	New Orleans, LA	Air	29.7	11.8	17.9	39.3
25	Miami International Airport, FL	Air	27.4	17.8	9.7	64.8
33	Port of Hidalgo, TX	Land	18.3	7.6	10.7	41.6
34	Port of Beaumont, TX	Water	17.0	1.2	15.8	7.1
38	Port of Corpus Christi, TX	Water	15.5	2.2	13.3	14.2

Border Crossings at U.S. Ports of Entry, 2006-2007

Below are statistics for selected states as to incoming border traffic at ports of entry into the United States. *Data are from the U.S. Bureau of Transportation Statistics.* (**Total in thousands**. Percent of U.S. total listed with states.)

Entering at border (000)	U.S. total	Texas	%	California	%	Arizona	%	New York	%	Michigan	%
2006											
Persons (total)	295,979	112,022	**37.8**	82,291	27.8	32,291	10.8	22,643	7.7	16,838	5.7
Pedestrians	46,785	19,154	**40.9**	15,518	33.2	11,328	24.2	349	0.7	8	–
Vehicles (total)	130,135	47,880	**36.8**	35,566	27.3	9,134	7.0	11,042	8.5	11,213	8.6
Personal vehicles	118,334	44,570	**37.7**	34,286	29.0	8,747	7.4	9,135	7.7	8,497	7.2
Loaded containers	10,513	2,390	**22.7**	693	6.6	313	3.0	1,934	18.4	2,764	26.3
2007											
Persons (total)	280,089	107,147	**38.3**	75,777	27.1	31,711	11.3	22,031	7.9	15,940	5.7
Pedestrians	49,980	20,915	**41.8**	16,553	33.1	11,806	23.6	279	0.6	12	–
Vehicles (total)	123,395	45,277	**36.7**	32,185	26.1	8,595	7.0	10,940	8.9	10,718	8.7
Personal vehicles	111,551	41,853	**37.5**	30,897	27.7	8,208	7.4	9,094	8.2	8,075	7.2
Loaded containers	10,176	2,380	**23.4**	704	6.9	311	3.1	1,750	17.2	2,699	26.5

Foreign Consulates in Texas

In the list below, these abbreviations appear after the name of the city: (CG) Consulate General; (C) Consulate; (VC) Vice Consulate. The letter "H" before the designation indicates honorary status. Compiled from "Foreign Consular Offices in the United States," U.S. Dept. of State, Summer 2007, and recent Internet sources.

Albania: Houston (HC); 10 Waterway Ct., Ste. 401, The Woodlands, 77380. (281) 548-4740.

Angola: Houston (CG); 3040 Post Oak Blvd., Ste. 780, 77056. (713) 212-3840.

Argentina: Houston (CG); 3050 Post Oak Blvd., Ste. 1625, 77056. (713) 871-8935.

Australia: Houston (HC); 4623 Feagan St., 77007. (713) 782-6009.

Austria: Houston (HCG); 1717 Bissonet St., Ste 306, 77005. (713) 526-0127.

Bangladesh: Houston (HCG); 35 N. Wynden Dr., 77056. (713) 621-8462.

Barbados: Houston (HC); 3027 Sleepy Hollow Dr., Sugar Land 77479. (832) 725-5566.

Belgium: Houston (HC); 2009 Lubbock St., 77007. (713) 426-3933.
Fort Worth (HC); 6201 South Fwy., 76134. (817) 551-8389.
San Antonio (HC); 106 S. St. Mary's, Ste. 200, 78205. (210) 271-8820.

Belize: Houston (HCG); 7101 Breen, 77086. (713) 999-4484.
Dallas (HC); 1315 19th St., Ste. 2A, Plano, 75074. (972) 579-0070.

Bolivia: Houston (HCG); 800 Wilcrest, Ste. 100, 77042 (713) 977-2344.
Dallas (HC); 1881 Sylvan Ave., Ste. 110, 75208. (214) 571-6131.

Botswana: Houston (HC); 10000 Memorial Dr., Ste. 400, 77024. (713) 680-1155.

Brazil: Houston (CG); 1233 West Loop South, Ste. 1150, 77027. (713) 961-3063.

Cameroon: Houston (HC); 1319 Gamma, Crosby 77532. (713) 499-3502.

Canada: Dallas (CG); 750 N. Saint Paul, Ste. 1700, 75201. (214) 922-9806.
Houston (C); 5847 San Felipe St., Ste. 1700, 77057. (713) 821-1442.
San Antonio (HCG); 106 S. St. Mary's, Ste. 800, 78205. (210) 299-3525.

Chile: Houston (CG):1360 Post Oak Blvd., Ste. 1130, 77056; (713) 963-9066.
Dallas (HC); 3500 Oak Lawn, Apt. 200, 75219. (214) 528-2731.

China: Houston (CG); 3417 Montrose, Ste. 700, 77006. (713) 524-0780.

Colombia: Houston (CG); 5851 San Felipe, Ste. 300, 77057; (713) 527-8919.

Costa Rica: Houston (CG); 3000 Wilcrest, Ste. 112, 77042. (713) 266-0484.
Austin (C); 1730 E. Oltorf, 78741. (512) 445-0023.
Dallas (HC); 7777 Forest Lane, Ste. B-445, 75230. (972) 566-7020.

Cyprus: Houston (HCG); 320 S. 66th St., 77011. (713) 928-2264.

Czech Republic: Houston (HC); 11748 Heritage Pkwy., West, 76691. (713) 629-6963.

Denmark: Dallas (HC); 2100 McKinney Ave., Ste. 700, 75201. (214) 661-8399.
Houston (HC); 4545 Post Oak Place, Ste. 347, 77027. (713) 622-9018.

Ecuador: Houston (CG); 4200 Westheimer, Ste. 218, 77027. (713) 622-1787.
Dallas (HCG); 7510 Acorn Lane, Frisco, 75034. (972) 712-9107.

Egypt: Houston (CG); 1990 Post Oak Blvd., Ste. 2180, 77056. (713) 961-4915.

El Salvador: Dallas (CG); 1555 W. Mockingbird Lane, Ste. 216, 75235.
Houston (CG); 1702 Hillendahl Blvd. 77055. (713) 270-6239.

Ethiopia: Houston (HC); 9301 Southwest Freeway, Ste. 250, 77074. (713) 271-7567.

Fiji: Dallas (HC); 3400 Carlisle, Ste. 310, 75204. (214) 954-9993.

Finland: Dallas (HC); 1601 Elm, Ste. 3000, 75201. (214) 999-4472.
Houston (HC); 14 Greenway Plaza, Ste. 22R, 77046. (713) 552-1722.

France: Houston (CG); 777 Post Oak Blvd. Ste. 600, 77056. (713) 572-2799.
Austin (HC); 515 Congress Ave, 78701. (512) 480-5605.
Dallas (HC); 12720 Hillcrest, Ste. 730, 75230. (972) 789-9305.
San Antonio (HC); X Route 1, 78209. 78209. (210) 659-3101.

Georgia: Houston (HC); 3040 Post Oak Blvd., Ste. 700, 77056. (281) 633-3500.

Germany: Houston (CG); 1330 Post Oak Blvd., Ste. 1850, 77056. (713) 627-7770.
Corpus Christi (HC); 615 N. Upper Broadway, Ste. 630,78477. (361) 884-7766.
Dallas (HC); 325 N. St. Paul, Ste. 2300, 75201. (214) 748-8500.
San Antonio (HC); 310 S. St. Mary's, 78205. (210) 226-1788.

Ghana: Houston (HC); 3434 Locke Lane, 77027. (713) 960-8806.

Greece: Houston (CG); 520 Post Oak Blvd., Ste. 450, 77027. (713) 840-7522.

Guatemala: Houston (CG); 3013 Fountain View, Ste 210, 77057. (713) 953-9531.
San Antonio (HC); 4840 Whirlwind, 78217.

Guyana: Houston (HC); 1810 Woodland Park Dr., 77077. (713) 497-4466.

Haiti: Houston (HC); 3535 Sage Rd., 77027.

Honduras: Houston (CG); 5433 Westheimer Rd., Ste. 325, 77056. (713) 667-4693.

Hungary: Houston (HCG); 2221 Potomac B, 77057. (713) 977-8604.

Iceland: Dallas (HC); 17910 Windflower, Apt. 2201, 75252. (214) 540-9135.
Houston (HC); 2348 W. Settler's Way, The Woodlands, 77380. (713) 367-2777.

India: Houston (CG); 1990 Post Oak Blvd., Ste 600, 77056. (713) 626-2148.

Indonesia: Houston (CG); 10900 Richmond Ave., 77042.

Ireland: Houston (HC); 2630 Sutton Ct., 77027. (713) 961-5363.

Israel: Houston (CG); 24 Greenway Plz., Ste. 1500, 77046. (713) 627-3780.

Ivory Coast: Houston (HCG); 412 Hawthorne, 77006. (713) 529-4928.

Italy: Houston (CG); 1300 Post Oak Blvd., Ste. 660, 77056. (713) 850-7520.
Dallas (HVC); 6255 W. Northwest Hwy., Apt. 304, 75225. (214) 368-4113.

Jamaica: Houston (HC); 7737 Southwest Fwy., Suite 580, 77074. (713) 541-3333.
Dallas (HC); 3068 Forest Lane, 75234. (972) 396-7969.

Japan: Houston (CG); 909 Fannin, Ste. 3000,

77010. (713) 652-2977.
Dallas (HCG); 5819 Edinburgh St., 75252.
(972) 713-8683.
Korea: Houston (CG); 1990 Post Oak Blvd., Ste. 1250,
77056. (713) 961-0186.
Dallas (HC); 13111 N. Central Expy., 75243. (214)
454-1112.
Kyrgyzstan: Houston (HCG); 15600 Barkers Landing Rd.,
Apt. 1, 77079. (281) 920-1841.
Latvia: Houston (HC); 5847 San Felipe, Ste. 3400,
77057. (713) 785-0807.
Lebanon: Houston (HC); 2400 Augusta Dr., Ste. 308,
77057. (713) 526-1141.
Lesotho: Austin (HC); 7400 Valburn Dr., 78731.
Lithuania: Houston (HC); 4030 Case, 77005
(713) 665-4218.
Luxembourg: Fort Worth (HC); 48 Valley Ridge Rd.,
76107. (817) 738-8600.
Malaysia: Houston (HC); 700 Louisiana, Floor 46,
77002. (713) 222-1470.
Malta: Houston (HCG); 2602 Commonwealth, 77006.
(713) 654-7900.
Dallas (HC); PO Box 830688, SM-24, Richardson,
75083. (972) 883-4785.
Austin (HC); 3925 W. Braker Lane, Ste. 300, 78759.
(512) 305-0612.
Mexico: Austin (CG); 800 Brazos, Ste. 330, 78701.
(512) 478,2803.
Brownsville (C); 301 Mexico Blvd., Ste. F3, 78520.
(956) 542-4431.
Corpus Christi (C); 800 N. Shoreline, Ste. 410,
78401.
Dallas (CG); 8855 N. Stemmons Fwy, 75247.
(214) 522-9740.
Del Rio (C); 2398 Spur 239, 78840.
(830) 774-5031.
Eagle Pass (C); 2252 E. Garrison, 78852.
(830) 773-9255.
El Paso (CG); 910 E. San Antonio Ave., 79901.
(915) 533-3644.
Houston (CG); 4507 San Jacinto St., 77004.
(713) 271-6800.
Laredo (CG); 1612 Farragut St., 78040.
(956) 723-6369.
McAllen (C); 600 S. Broadway, 78501.
(956) 686-0243.
Midland (C); 511 W. Ohio St., Ste. 121, 79701.
Presidio (C); 6717 Kelley Addition 1 Hwy, 79845.
(915) 229-2788.
San Antonio (CG); 127 Navarro St., 78205. (210)
227-9145.
San Antonio (Office of Mexican Attorney General);
613 NW Loop 410 Ste. 610, 78216.
(210) 344-1131.
Monaco: Dallas (HC); 8350 N. Central Expressway,
Ste. 1900, 75206. (214) 234-4124.
Mongolia: Houston (HCAgent); 1221 Lamar, Ste. 1201,
77010. (713) 759-1922.
Nambia: Houston (HC); 1330 Post Oak Blvd., Ste. 2200,
77056. (713) 965-5119.
Netherlands: Houston (CG); 2200 Post Oak Blvd.,
Ste. 610, 77056. (713) 622-8000.
New Zealand: Houston (HC); 246 Warrenton Dr.,
77024. (713) 973-8680.
Nicaragua: Houston (CG); 8989 Westheimer, Ste. 103,
77063. (713) 789-2762.
Norway: Houston (CG); 2777 Allen Parkway, Ste. 1185,
77019. (713) 521-2900.
Dallas (HC); 5500 Caruth Haven Lane, 75225.
(214) 750-4222.
Pakistan: Houston (C); 11850 Jones Rd. 77070.
(2810 890-8525.
Panama: Houston (CG); 24 Greenway Plaza, Ste. 1307,

77046. (713) 622-4451.
Papua New Guinea: Houston (HCG); 4900 Woodway Dr.
Ste. 1200, 77056. (713) 966-2500.
Peru: Houston (CG); 5177 Richmond Ave., Ste.
695, 77056. (713) 355-9571.
Dallas (CG); 1500 Marilla, Rm D, 75201.
Poland: Houston (HC); 35 Harbor View, Sugar Land,
77479. (281) 565-1507.
Portugal: Houston (HC); 4544 Post Oak Place, Ste. 350,
77027. (713) 759-1188.
Qatar: Houston (CG); 1990 Post Oak Blvd, Ste. 810,
77056. (713) 355-8221.
Romania: Dallas (HC); 220 Ross Ave., Ste. 2200,
75201. (214) 740-8608.
Houston (HCG); 4265 San Felipe, Ste. 220, 77027.
(713) 629-1551.
Russia: Houston (CG); 1333 West Loop South, Ste. 1300,
77027. (713) 337-3300.
Saint Kitts/Nevis: Dallas (HC); 6336 Greenville Ave.,
75206.
Saudi Arabia: Houston (CG); 5718 Westheimer, Ste.
1500, 77057. (713) 785-5577.
Senegal: Houston (CG); 9701 Richmond, Ste. 212, 77042.
Singapore: Houston (HCG); 600 Travis, Ste. 370, 77002.
(713) 512-4488.
Slovenia: Houston (HC); 2925 Briar Park, Floor 7,
77042. (713) 430-7350.
South Africa: Dallas (HC); 400 S. Zang, Ste. 806, 75208.
Spain: Houston (CG); 1800 Bering Dr., Ste. 660,
77057. (713) 783-6200.
Corpus Christi (HC); 7517 Yorkshire Blvd., 78413
(361) 994-7517.
Dallas (HC); 5499 Glen Lakes Dr., Ste. 209, 75231.
(214) 373-1200.
El Paso (HC); 420 Golden Springs Dr., 79912.
(915) 534-0677.
San Antonio (HC); 8350 Delphian, 78148.
Sweden: Houston (HC); 2909 Hillcroft, Ste. 515, 77057.
(713) 953-1417.
Dallas: (HC); 6600 LBJ Fwy, Ste. 183, 75240.
(972) 991-8013.
Switzerland: Houston (CG); 11922 Taylorcrest, 77024.
(713) 467-9889.
Dallas (HC); 2651 N. Harwood, Ste. 455, 75201.
(214) 965-1025.
Syria: Houston (HCG); 5433 Westheimer Rd., Ste. 1020,
77056. (713) 622-8860.
Thailand: Houston (HCG); 600 Travis St., Ste. 2800,
77002. (713) 229-8733.
Dallas (HCG); 1717 Main St., Ste. 4100,
75201.
El Paso (HCG); 4401 N. Mesa, Ste. 204, 79902.
(915) 533-5757.
Trinidad/Tobago: Houston (HC); 2400 Augusta, Ste. 250,
77057. (713) 840-1100.
Tunisia: Dallas (HC); 4227 N. Capistrano Dr., 75287.
(972) 267-4191.
Houston (HC); 12527 Mossycup, 77024.
(713) 935-9427.
Turkey: Houston (CG); 1990 Post Oak Blvd., Ste.1300,
77056. (713) 622-5849.
Ukraine: Houston (HC); 2934 Fairway Dr., Sugar Land,
77478. (281) 242-2842.
United Kingdom: Houston (CG); 1000 Louisiana St.,
Ste. 1900, 77002. (713) 659-6270.
Dallas (C); 2911 Turtle Creek, Ste. 940, 75219.
(214) 637-3600.
San Antonio (HC); 254 Spencer Lane, 78201.
(210) 735-9393.
Uruguay: Houston (HCG); 1220 S. Ripple Creek Dr.,
77057. (713) 974-7855.
Venezuela : Houston (CG); 2925 Briar Park Dr., Ste. 900,
77027. (713) 961-5141. ☆

Foreign Trade Zones in Texas

Source: U.S. Department of Commerce.

Foreign-trade-zone status endows a domestic site with certain customs privileges, causing it to be considered outside customs territory and therefore available for activities that might otherwise be carried on overseas.

Operated as public utilities for qualified corporations, the zones are established under grants of authority from the Foreign-Trade Zones board, which is chaired by the U.S. Secretary of Commerce. Zone facilities are available for operations involving storage, repacking, inspection, exhibition, assembly, manufacturing and other processing.

A foreign-trade zone is especially suitable for export processing or manufacturing operations when foreign components or materials with a high U.S. duty are needed to make the end product competitive in markets abroad.

Source: U.S. Department of Commerce

There were 33 Foreign-Trade Zones in Texas as of November 2008.

Amarillo, FTZ 252
City of Amarillo
801 S. Fillmore, Ste. 2205, Amarillo 79101

Athens, FTZ 269
Athens Economic Development Corp.
100 W. Tyler St., Athens 75751

Austin, FTZ 183
FTZ of Central Texas Inc.
301 W. Bagdad Ave., Round Rock 78664

Beaumont, FTZ 115
Port Arthur, FTZ 116
Orange, FTZ 117
FTZ of Southeast Texas Inc.
P.O. Drawer 2297, Beaumont 77704

Bowie County, FTZ 258
Red River Redevelopment Authority
107 Chapel Lane, New Boston 75570

Brownsville, FTZ 62
Brownsville Navigation District
1000 Foust Road, Brownsville 78521

Calhoun/Victoria Counties FTZ 155
Calhoun-Victoria FTZ Inc.
P.O. Drawer 397, Point Comfort 77978

Conroe, FTZ 265
City of Conroe
PO Box 3066, Conroe 77305

Corpus Christi, FTZ 122
Port of Corpus Christi Authority
1305 N. Shoreline Blvd.
Corpus Christi 78403

Dallas/Ft.Worth, FTZ 39
D/FW International Airport Board
Drawer 619428, D/FW Airport 75261

Dallas/Fort Worth, FTZ 168
FTZ Operating Company of Texas
P.O. Box 742916, Dallas 75374

Eagle Pass, FTZ 96
Maverick County Development Corp.
P.O. Box 3693, Eagle Pass 78853

Edinburg, FTZ 251
City of Edinburg
602 W. University Dr., Ste. B
Edinburg 78539

Ellis County, FTZ 113
Midlothian Trade Zone Corp.
1500 N. Service Road, Hwy. 67
Midlothian 76065

El Paso, FTZ 68
City of El Paso
501 George Perry, Ste. I,
El Paso 79906

El Paso, FTZ 150
Westport Economic Dev. Corp.
1865 Northwestern Dr.. El Paso 79912

Fort Worth, FTZ 196
Alliance Corridor Inc.
13600 Heritage Pkwy., Ste. 200
Fort Worth 76177

Freeport, FTZ 149
Brazos River Harbor Navigation Dist.
Box 615, Freeport 77542

Galveston, FTZ 36
Port of Galveston
P.O. Box 328, Galveston 77553

Gregg County, FTZ 234
Gregg County
269 Terminal Circle, Longview 75603

Harris County, FTZ 84
Port of Houston Authority
111 East Loop North, Houston 77029

Laredo, FTZ 94
Laredo International Airport
5210 Bob Bullock Loop, Laredo 78041

Liberty County, FTZ 171
Liberty Co. Economic Dev. Corp.
P.O. Box 857, Liberty 77575

Lubbock, FTZ 260
City of Lubbock
5401 N. Martin Luther King Blvd.
Lubbock 79403

McAllen, FTZ 12
McAllen Economic Dev. Corp.
6401 South 33rd St., McAllen 78501

Midland, FTZ 165
City of Midland
P.O. Box 60305, Midland 79711

San Antonio, FTZ 80
City of San Antonio
P.O. Box 839966, San Antonio 78283

Starr County, FTZ 95
Starr County Industrial Foundation
P.O. Box 502, Rio Grande City 78582

Texas City, FTZ 199
Texas City Harbor FTZ Corp.
P.O. Box 2608, Texas City 77592

Waco, FTZ 246
City of Waco
P.O. Box 1220, Waco 76703

Weslaco, FTZ 156
City of Weslaco
255 S. Kansas Ave., Weslaco 78596

Ships docked along the Houston Ship Channel. Robert Plocheck photo.

Annual Tonnage Handled by Major/Minor Texas Ports

Table below gives consolidated tonnage (x1,000) handled by Texas ports. All figures are in short tons (2,000 lbs.). Note that " - " indicates no commerce was reported, "0" means tonnage reported was less than 500 tons. *Source: U.S. Corps of Engineers.*

Port	2007	2006	2005	2000	1995	1990	1985
Beaumont	81,384	79,486	78,887	76,894	20,937	26,729	26,842
Brownsville	4,506	5,310	5,105	3,268	2,656	1,372	1,443
Corpus Christi	81,072	77,556	77,637	81,164	70,218	60,165	41,057
Freeport	29,598	32,147	33,602	28,966	19,662	14,526	12,918
Galveston	9,791	9,357	8,008	10,402	10,465	9,620	7,792
Houston	216,064	222,147	211,666	186,567	135,231	126,178	90,669
Matagorda Channel (Port Lavaca)	10,862	10,808	11,607	10,552	9,237	6,097	4,366
Port Arthur	29,262	28,403	26,385	20,524	49,800	30,681	15,755
Sabine Pass	904	902	641	910	231	631	547
Texas City	56,787	48,875	57,839	58,109	50,403	48,052	33,441
Victoria Channel	3,155	3,556	3,224	5,104	4,624	3,740	3,414
Anahuac	-	-	-	-	-	0	53
Aransas Pass	272	90	128	6	181	169	10
Arroyo Colorado	615	349	791	837	994	765	692
Port Isabel	7	1	-	5	130	269	280
Cedar Bayou	1,030	1,054	1,172	1,002	473	219	219
Chocolate Bayou	3,640	3,647	3,537	3,488	3,480	3,463	4,077
Clear Creek	-	-	-	-	-	0	0
Colorado River	434	494	501	445	576	476	480
Dickinson	907	903	688	904	657	556	195
Double Bayou	-	36	257	0	-	0	21
Greens Bayou	6,505	6,075	3,768	0	0	0	0
Harbor Island (Port Aransas)	7	2	10	151	209	na	na
Liberty Channel	-	-	-	-	-	0	0
Orange	682	718	627	681	693	710	648
Palacios	-	-	-	-	-	0	10
Port Mansfield	-	-	-	-	20	102	204
Rockport	-	-	-	-	-	644	0
San Bernard River	625	597	773	633	653	534	519
Other Ports	0	0	0	0	0	0	307
TOTAL*	490,123	488,357	487,100	452,991	371,021	335,312	245,959

Excludes duplication.

Foreign/Domestic Commerce: Breakdown for 2007

Data below represent inbound and outbound tonnage for major ports. Note that "-" means no tonnage was reported. *Does not include Canadian. *Source: U.S. Corps of Engineers*
(All figures in short tons x1000)

| Port | Foreign* | | Domestic | | | | |
| | | | Coastwise | | Internal | | Local |
	Imports	Exports	Receipts	Shipments	Receipts	Shipments	
Beaumont	49,872	6,561	829	2,432	7,459	12,298	1,322
Brownsville	2,439	497	1,570	120	776	562	-
Corpus Christi	47,795	9,950	1,318	6,338	4,334	8,679	2,032
Freeport	20,901	2,739	990	292	3,027	2,115	9
Galveston	1,339	4,071	103	1,421	1,842	845	161
Houston	93,040	50,294	4,182	4,717	29,227	17,948	14,648
Matagorda Chl. (Port Lavaca)	7,027	1,575	142	215	372	1,302	-
Port Arthur	11,788	5,606	903	2,313	2,557	4,182	192
Sabine Pass	0	1	7	27	223	648	-
Texas City	35,777	4,173	348	1,299	6,422	7,526	712
Victoria	-	-	-	-	884	2,271	-

Gulf Intracoastal Waterway by Commodity (Texas portion)

(All figures in short tons x1000) *Source: U.S. Army Corps of Engineers*

Commodity	2007	2006	2005	2000	1995
Coal	197	463	335	121	162
Petroleum products	48,452	44,632	39,538	34,816	40,496
Chemicals	20,434	20,035	20,668	21,382	26,818
Raw materials	4,518	5,038	4,898	5,822	6,544
Manufactured goods	2,403	2,327	2,449	2,301	2,056
Food, farm products	413	475	473	960	1,216
Total	77,361	74,161	69,517	66,440	78,386

U.S. ports ranked by tonnage, 2007
(x1,000)

1. S. Louisiana......... 229,040
2. Houston.............. 216,064
3. New York 157,202
4. Long Beach 85,940
5. Beaumont............. 81,384
6. Corpus Christi...... 81,072
7. Huntington, WV 76,489
8. New Orleans.......... 76,046
9. Los Angeles.......... 65,502
10. Mobile................. 64,494

States ranked by tonnage, 2007
(x1,000)

1. Louisiana 498,256
2. Texas................. 490,123
3. California 232,386
4. New Jersey.......... 134,279
5. Florida................. 124,419
6. Washington.......... 123,992
7. Illinois.................. 120,970
8. Ohio 112,493
9. Pennsylvania 102,084
10. Kentucky............. 100,374

Aviation: Declining Economy Slows Growth

Air transportation is a vital and vigorous part of the Texas economy, and Texans are major users of air transportation. The state's airport system ranks as one of the busiest and largest in the nation.

The economic impact of general aviation in Texas includes total employment of 61,943 jobs, a total payroll of $2,514,708,000, and total economic output of $8,738,586,000.

The state's 48,849 active pilots represent 7.99 percent of the nation's pilots. The number of active general aviation aircraft in the state total 20,235, some 8.74 percent of the nation's total. Collectively they flew nearly 2.5 million hours.

In 2007, more than 90 percent of the state's population lived within 50 miles of an airport with scheduled air passenger service. Dallas/Fort Worth International, Dallas Love Field, Houston George Bush Intercontinental, and Houston's William P. Hobby together accounted for 81 percent of the passengers, or 57,214,280 enplanements.

Air service continues to be an area of concern for some communities as the airlines have worked to remove excess capacity from the system in an effort to return to profitability.

This has been exacerbated by the economic downturn that began in late 2007 and continued through 2008.

None of the 25 cities served by the airlines have seen their air service completely eliminated but some have experienced a decrease in the level of service. Some airlines have reduced the number of flights at airports and stopped serving others but no airport has been left without service altogether.

Adding to the airline's difficulties were the high fuel prices and the return to the more fuel-efficient but older turbo-prop aircraft, in lieu of the regional jets that were once believed to be the future of small community air service.

Despite solid growth from 2005 to 2006, the declining economy began to show in passenger traffic as the growth in enplanements in 2007 slowed.

Airports

Twenty-seven airports continue to provide commercial service to Texas communities including the Texarkana Regional Airport, which is physically located in Arkansas. Scheduled passenger traffic (air carrier and commuters) increased from 2005 to 2007 continuing the trend that began in 2002. Enplanements in Texas increased by more than 5 million, or 8 percent, over the two-year period.

Twenty-three airports saw their enplanements increase, with eleven of them experiencing double-digit growth ranging from 11 percent to 31 percent. Five airports saw increases above 20 percent including Killeen/Fort Hood, Brownsville, McAllen, Abilene, and Laredo *(see chart, page 671.).*

Public Administration

Source: Texas Transportation Institute.

The state of Texas has long been committed to providing air transportation to the public. In 1945, the Texas Aeronautics Commission (TAC) was created and directed by the Legislature to foster the development of aeronautics within the state and to encourage the establishment of airports and air navigational facilities.

The commission's first annual report of Dec. 31, 1946, stated that Texas had 592 designated airports and 7,756 civilian aircraft.

In 1989, the TAC became the Texas Department of Aviation (TDA). And on Sept. 1, 1991, when the Texas Department of Transportation (TxDOT) was created, the TDA became the Aviation Division within the department.

The primary responsibilities of the Aviation Division include providing engineering and technical services for constructing and maintaining aeronautical facilities in the state. It is also responsible for long-range planning on the statewide system of airports and applying for and disbursing federal funds.

One of TxDOT's goals is to develop a statewide system of airports that will provide adequate air access to the population and economic centers of the state.

In the Texas Airport System Plan, TxDOT has identified 300 airports that are needed to meet the forecast aviation demand and to maximize access by aircraft to the state's population, business, and agricultural and mineral resource centers.

Of these 300 airports, 27 are commercial service airports, 25 are reliever airports, and 248 are general aviation airports.

Commercial service airports provide scheduled passenger service. Reliever airports are a special class of general aviation airports designated by the Federal Aviation Administration (FAA).

They provide alternative landing facilities in the metropolitan areas separate from the commercial service airports, and, together with the business service airports, provide access for business and executive turbine-powered aircraft.

The community service and basic service airports provide access for single- and multi-engine, piston-powered aircraft to smaller communities throughout the state. Some community service airports are also capable of accommodating light jets.

TxDOT is charged by the Legislature with planning and implementing improvement projects at the general aviation airports. In carrying out these responsibilities, TxDOT channels Airport Improvement Program (AIP) funds provided by the FAA.

Since 1993, TxDOT has participated in the FAA's state block grant demonstration program. Under this program, TxDOT assumes most of the FAA's responsibility for the administration of the AIP funds.

The Aviation Facilities Development Program (AFDP) oversees planning and research, assists with engineering and technical services, and provides financial assistance through state grants to public bodies operating airports.

The 80th Legislature appropriated funds to TxDOT who subsequently allocated a portion of those funds to the Aviation Division. TxDOT allocated approximately $16 million annually for the 2008-2009 biennium to the Aviation Division to help implement and administer the AFDP.

Security lines at DFW International Airport. Michael Ainsworth photo.

Four airports experienced a decline in passenger traffic; Southeast Texas Regional Airport in Beaumont, Wichita Falls Municipal Airport, Tyler Pounds Regional Airport, and Victoria Regional Airport.

Wichita Falls and Tyler saw their enplanements decrease 2 and 6 percent, respectively. The decreases in Victoria and Beaumont were more significant at 21 and 36 percent, respectively.

Aircraft Production

General aviation continues to be an important part of both the aviation industry and the national economy as the demand for general aviation aircraft is closely related to economic growth.

The current industry data continue to reflect a strong industry, but one that is beginning to show signs of decline related to the global economic recession. Aircraft shipments were mixed in 2008 with total piston deliveries down significantly to 2,119 from 2,755 in 2006. Turbine shipments increased significantly in 2008 rising to 1,850 from 1,298 in 2006. Overall, total shipments were down from 4,053 in 2006 to 3,969 in 2008. This is down from an all-time high of 4,272 in 2007.

Billings for general aviation aircraft worldwide were a slightly different story in 2008. Total billings increased from $17.9 billion in 2006 to $23.9 billion in 2008. Billings for both piston and turbine aircraft continued their upward trend that began in 2002 for the piston market and 2003 for the turbine market.

Airplane shipments for those manufactured in the U.S. showed a decline in 2008 dropping to 3,079 from 3,147 in 2006 and 3,279 in 2007. Billings, however, increased from $10.4 billion in 2006 to $13.3 billion in 2008.

In both worldwide and U.S. manufacturing, turbine aircraft continued to show growth in shipments in 2008 with double-digit increases over 2007, while piston shipments experienced double-digit decreases over the same period. Overall, shipments decreased 7.1 percent and 6.1 percent for aircraft manufactured worldwide and in the U.S., respectively.

Billings, however, increased 13.4 percent and 11.8 percent respectively, reflecting the increases in shipments of the more expensive turbine aircraft, particularly business jets. Billings of U.S manufactured aircraft sent out of the country also surged 27.8 percent from 2007 to 2008 while shipments increased 1.7 percent. U.S. exports accounted for 37.7 percent of the total U.S. manufactured shipments and 43.9 percent of the billings.

Business aviation has long been a leader in the industry and that is not expected to change. The earlier focus on very light jets and the potential of air taxi services has given way to improving the operating efficiencies of a range of business jets to better meet the needs of their customers no matter their utilization.

Technical Changes

New technology and innovation continue to drive general aviation both in terms of aircraft and how they operate in the airspace as well as on and around the airport environment.

This includes new flight information and navigations systems in the cockpit to new satellite and ground-based augmentations systems that enhance the current global positioning system allowing for improved approaches to airports.

These enhancements have provided for a safer and more efficient air transportation system.

Sources: Federal Aviation Administration, General Aviation and Part 135 Activity Survey - CY2007; General Aviation Manufacturer's Association 2008 General Aviation Statistical Databook and Annual Industry Review and Market Outlook; FAA Terminal Area Forecasts 2008; Texas Department of Transportation, Aviation Division; FAA Aerospace Forecasts 2008-2025; Wilbur Smith Associates, 2007.

Passenger Enplanement by Airport

Airport	1997	1999	2001	2003	2005	Percent change*	2007
Abilene	52,864	48,624	57,645	46,166	75,414	20%	90,507
Amarillo	450,432	435,758	440,018	384,829	442,327	3%	455,539
Austin	2,948,701	3,235,560	3,595,173	3,157,961	3,601,135	14%	4,111,614
Beaumont	112,456	100,684	78,215	43,931	55,484	−36%	35,352
Brownsville	81,439	71,530	74,411	60,087	73,361	24%	91,262
Brownwood**	—	1,475	2,232	2,008	603	NA	—
College Station	93,331	92,691	85,875	67,459	83,866	7%	89,830
Corpus Christi	471,914	451,999	425,847	358,843	413,364	1%	418,674
D/FW	28,152,220	28,077,898	26,929,286	24,601,481	27,960,344	2%	28,400,719
Dallas/Love	3,413,519	3,415,785	3,552,419	2,783,787	2,976,972	31%	3,912,738
Del Rio	—	889	0	0	7,638	128%	17,386
El Paso	1,634,578	1,664,123	1,618,128	1,418,974	1,617,793	4%	1,676,693
Harlingen	461,619	465,516	461,067	392,733	429,541	3%	440,332
Houston/Bush	13,212,686	15,026,633	16,693,056	15,934,088	18,636,208	11%	20,680,973
Houston/Hobby	3,949,236	4,222,144	4,265,890	3,691,967	3,947,543	7%	4,219,850
Houston/Ellington	50,503	46,520	31,775	45,748	3,021	NA	—
Killeen†	84,963	86,649	98,574	92,106	—	—	—
Fort Hood/Gray†	—	—	15,176	3,159	153,930	26%	193,722
Laredo	67,664	88,969	82,215	73,210	94,042	18%	110,751
Longview	26,779	28,888	31,436	29,022	23,250	12%	26,076
Lubbock	592,101	565,173	552,726	504,916	545,340	6%	575,774
McAllen	313,506	307,325	306,259	263,431	341,824	20%	411,610
Midland	527,760	486,709	452,889	399,334	439,507	11%	489,845
San Angelo	41,404	40,400	49,140	42,688	63,785	9%	69,738
San Antonio	3,343,818	3,384,107	3,434,894	3,121,545	3,518,786	11%	3,903,642
Texarkana	36,367	40,506	34,799	25,634	33,573	5%	35,280
Tyler	69,639	73,845	65,336	53,854	81,723	−6%	77,117
Victoria	21,656	20,585	16,835	10,775	11,115	−21%	8,829
Waco	58,742	61,668	62,228	49,915	70,851	6%	75,456
Wichita Falls	53,942	54,453	51,286	39,608	47,126	−2%	46,297
Total	**60,329,687**	**62,597,136**	**63,564,830**	**57,699,259**	**65,479,466**	**8%**	**70,665,606**

*Percent change 2005 to 2007. **Not a commercial airport. †Killeen-Fort Hood Regional/Robert Gray AAF replaced Killeen Municipal as the commercial service airport in the area. Calendar year data. Source: FAA Terminal Area Forecast 2008.*

Texas Air History

Passengers enplaned in Texas by scheduled carriers. (Texarkana not included.) Fiscal year data. *FAA.*

1950	1,169,051
1955	2,434,814
1960	3,113,582
1965	5,757,689
1970	10,256,691
1975	13,182,957
1980	26,280,646
1985	40,718,209
1990	49,317,029
1995	57,166,515
1996	58,180,769
1997	60,154,165
1998	61,712,342
1999	62,558,165
2000	65,090,784
2001	63,531,077
2002	57,638,423
2003	57,675,118
2004	62,835,571
2005	65,717,954
2006	69,254,682
2007	70,634,137

Leading U.S. Routes, 2007

Rank	Route	Daily Passengers*
1.	New York to-from Chicago	4,839
2.	New York to-from Fort Lauderdale	4,777
3.	New York to-From Orlando	4,423
4.	New York to-from Los Angeles	3,776
5.	New York to-from Atlanta	3,518
14.	**Dallas/Fort Worth** to-from **Houston**	2,147
17.	**Dallas/Fort Worth** to-from New York	2,001

Average/Each Way. Includes all commercial airports in a metro area. Source: Air Transport Association.

Leading U.S. Airlines, 2007

Rank	Airline	Passengers	Planes
1.	**Southwest**	101,910,000	520
2.	**American**	98,165,000	655
3.	Delta	72,924,000	446
4.	United	68,362,000	460
5.	US Airways	57,829,000	356
6	Northwest	53,678,000	356
7.	**Continental**	48,974,000	365
8.	AirTran	23,741,000	137
9.	SkyWest	22,047,000	272
10.	JetBlue	21,304,000	134

Source: Air Transport Association. Note: Texas-based airlines in bold type. SkyWest data is from July 2008. Scheduled service only.

Agriculture

Belted Galloways on the Fruth organic farm near Cash in Hunt County. Jan. 1, 2009, inventory of cattle and calves in Texas totaled 13.6 million head, valued at $10.47 billion. Cheryl Diaz Meyer photo.

Principal Crops

Vegetable Crops

Fruits & Nuts

Livestock and Their Products

Agriculture in Texas

Information was provided by Texas AgriLife Extension specialists, Texas Agricultural Statistics Service, U.S. Department of Agriculture and U.S. Department of Commerce. Carl G. Anderson, Professor and Extension Specialist–Emeritus, Texas A&M University, coordinated the information. All references are to Texas unless otherwise specified.

Importance of Agriculture to the Texas Economy

Agribusiness, the combined phases of food and fiber production, processing, transporting and marketing, is a leading Texas industry. Most of this article is devoted to the phase of production on farms and ranches.

Agriculture is one of the most important industries in Texas. Many businesses, financial institutions and individuals are involved in providing supplies, credit and services to farmers and ranchers, and in processing and marketing agricultural commodities.

Texas agriculture is a strong industry. **Receipts from farm and ranch marketings in 2008 were estimated at $19.7 billion,** compared with $19.1 billion in 2007.

The potential for further growth is favorable. With the increasing demand for food and fiber throughout the world, and because of the importance of agricultural exports to the U.S. trade balance, agriculture in Texas is destined to play an even greater role in the future.

Major efforts of research and educational programs by the Texas A&M University System are directed toward developing the state's agricultural industry to its fullest potential. The goal is to capitalize on natural advantages that agriculture has in Texas because of the relatively warm climate, productive soils and availability of excellent export and transportation facilities.

Texas Farms

The number and nature of farms have changed over time. The number of farms in Texas has decreased from 420,000 in 1940 to 247,500 in 2008, with an average size of 527 acres. Average value per farm of all farm assets, including land and buildings, has increased from $20,100 in 1950 to $816,646 in 2008. The number of small farms is increasing — but part-time farmers operate them.

Mechanization of farming continues as new and larger machines replace manpower. Although machinery price tags are high relative to times past, machines are technologically advanced and efficient. Tractors,

mechanical harvesters and numerous cropping machines have virtually eliminated menial tasks that for many years were traditional to farming.

Revolutionary agricultural chemicals have appeared along with improved plants and animals, and methods of handling them. Many of the natural hazards of farming and ranching have been reduced by better use of weather information, machinery and other improvements; but rising costs, labor availability and high-energy costs have added to concerns of farmers and ranchers. Changes in Texas agriculture in the last 50 years include:

1. More detailed record keeping that assists in management and marketing decisions;

2. More restrictions on choice or inputs/practices;

3. Precision agriculture will take on new dimensions through the use of satellites, computers, Global Positioning Systems (GPS) and other high-tech tools to help producers manage inputs, such as seed, fertilizers, pesticides and water.

Farms have become fewer, larger, specialized and much more expensive to own and operate, but far more productive. The number of small farms operated by part-time farmers is increasing. Land ownership is becoming more of a lifestyle used mostly for recreational purposes. The number of non-farm landowners are increasing.

Irrigation has become an important factor in crop production.

Crops and livestock have made major changes in production areas, as in the concentration of cotton on the High Plains and livestock increases in central and eastern Texas.

Pest and disease control methods have greatly improved. Herbicides are relied upon for weed control.

Ranchers and farmers are better educated and informed, and more science- and business-oriented. Today, agriculture operates in a global, high-tech, consumer-driven environment.

Feedlot finishing, commercial broiler production,

Mechanization of farming continues as new and larger machines replace manpower. Here, a combine cuts grain sorghum and loads in onto a grain cart near Arroyo City in Cameron County. Joe Hermosa photo/AP.

artificial insemination, improved pastures and brush control, reduced feed requirements, and other changes have greatly increased livestock and poultry efficiency. Biotechnology and genetic engineering promise new breakthroughs in reaching even higher levels of productivity. Horticultural plant and nursery businesses have expanded. Improved wildlife management has increased deer, turkey and other wildlife populations. The use of land for recreation and ecotourism is growing.

Cooperation among farmers in marketing, promotion and other fields has increased.

Agricultural producers have become increasingly dependent on off-the-farm services to supply production inputs, such as feeds, chemicals and credit.

Agribusiness

Texas farmers and ranchers have developed considerable dependence upon agribusiness. With many producers specializing in the production of certain crops and livestock, they look beyond the farm and ranch for supplies and services. On the input side, they rely on suppliers of production needs and services and, on the output side, they need assemblers, processors and distributors. **The impact of production agriculture and related businesses on the Texas economy is about $36.4 billion annually.**

Since 1940, the proportion of Texans whose livelihood is linked to agriculture has changed greatly. In 1940, about 23 percent were producers on farms and ranches, and about 17 percent were suppliers or were engaged in assembly, processing and distribution of agricultural products. The agribusiness alignment in 2008 was less than 2 percent on farms and ranches, with about 15 percent of the labor force providing production or marketing supplies and services, and retailing food and fiber products.

Cash Receipts

Farm and ranch cash receipts in 2007 totaled $19.075 billion. With estimates of $1.348 billion for government payments, $2.636 billion of non-cash income, and

$1.356 billion of other farm-related income included, realized gross farm income totaled $24.415 billion. With farm production expenses of $18.018 billion, **net farm income totaled $7.181 billion.** The value of inventory adjustment was plus-$902.2 million.

Percent of Income from Products

Livestock and livestock products accounted for 59.69 percent of the $19.075 billion cash receipts from farm marketings in 2007, with the remaining 40.31 percent from crops. Receipts from livestock have trended up

Cash Receipts for Commodities, 2003–2007

Commodity *	2003	2004	2005	2006	2007	% of 2007
(All values in thousands of dollars)						
All Commodities:	15,350,018	16,779,771	16,883,919	16,315,289	19,074,827	100.00%
Livestock & products	10,313,219	11,205,449	10,760,110	10,356,008	11,386,493	59.69%
Crops, fruits & others	5,036,799	5,574,322	6,123,809	5,959,281	7,688,334	40.31%
Livestock & Products						
Cattle & calves	7,872,092	8,092,721	7,558,585	7,430,169	7,630,837	40.00%
Milk, wholesale	729,430	975,718	981,801	947,492	1,448,738	7.60%
Broilers	1,031,590	1,424,520	1,436,644	1,198,800	1,404,552	7.36%
Eggs, chicken	310,007	306,322	238,798	254,055	373,403	1.96%
Hogs	66,646	88,556	104,010	107,424	93,807	0.49%
Sheep and lambs	50,428	57,893	60,133	42,267	38,859	0.20%
Wool	5,040	5,712	5,328	4,459	5,324	0.03%
Mohair	2,856	3,402	3,750	4,400	3,600	0.02%
Other livestock †	245,130	250,605	371,061	366,942	387,373	2.03%
Crops:						
Cotton lint	1,114,357	1,158,710	1,703,584	1,720,436	1,774,676	9.30%
Corn	407,784	597,651	364,344	534,638	850,969	4.46%
Wheat	246,390	329,907	277,257	189,016	615,778	3.23%
Hay	294,198	306,751	254,627	326,220	582,037	3.05%
Sorghum grain	294,197	336,592	203,464	189,563	450,041	2.36%
Cottonseed	179,728	243,018	256,411	216,326	343,341	1.80%
Onions	158,712	112,543	149,327	89,424	186,520	0.98%
Peanuts	157,950	154,310	175,500	96,258	166,935	0.88%
Rice	69,503	128,074	98,881	105,082	109,049	0.57%
Potatoes	66,746	53,417	71,968	91,774	74,824	0.39%
Sugarcane for sugar	51,381	45,400	54,241	48,130	41,902	0.22%
Cabbage	53,869	60,208	41,499	42,454	37,325	0.20%
Watermelons	67,760	60,500	74,214	62,195	34,588	0.18%
Soybeans	32,591	44,132	45,973	27,189	19,325	0.10%
Cucumbers	24,231	25,809	11,068	15,866	15,290	0.08%
Cantaloupes	63,444	26,760	34,206	20,236	14,040	0.07%
Peppers, chili	13,703	12,788	10,199	5,250	12,192	0.06%
Honeydew melons	19,437	8,822	2,187	5,642	7,462	0.04%
Dry beans	8,510	6,641	4,018	5,102	6,573	0.03%
Tomatoes, fresh	7,605	7,540	8,625	5,709	6,020	0.03%
Sunflower	7,182	9,197	17,522	17,205	5,896	0.03%
Oats	5,255	4,850	3,839	2,564	5,860	0.03%
Sweet potatoes	8,182	7,253	3,530	2,694	3,311	0.02%
Corn, sweet	5,377	2,736	2,642	2,367	3,203	0.02%
Other crop ‡	251,985	269,014	441,954	486,608	636,822	3.34%
Fruits & Nuts:						
Pecans	63,840	66,760	95,850	75,310	77,600	0.41%
Grapefruit	17,396	34,755	87,356	60,041	50,875	0.27%
Oranges	5,224	7,227	10,961	15,770	17,569	0.09%
Peaches	4,891	15,097	14,047	1,230	13,455	0.07%
Grapes	5,220	7,812	10,625	3,855	4,751	0.02%
Other fruits and nuts	4,931	5,753	8,671	8,180	18,645	0.10%
Other Farm Income:						
Greenhouse/nursery	1,325,220	1,424,295	1,585,219	1,486,947	1,501,460	7.87%

* Commodities are listed in order of importance for 2007 by crop items and by livestock items.
† For 2003–2007, includes milkfat, turkey eggs, equine, goats, goat milk, catfish, honey, farm chickens and other poultry, and livestock.
‡ For 2003–2007, includes miscellaneous vegetables and other field crops.
Source: 2007 Texas Agricultural Statistics, USDA/Texas Agricultural Statistics Service, October 2008; various issues of Texas Agriculture Facts, Texas Agricultural Cash Receipts and Price Statistics, USDA/TASS.

largely because of increased feeding operations and reduced crop acreage associated with farm programs and low prices. However, these relationships change because of variations in commodity prices and volume of marketings.

Meat animals (cattle, hogs and sheep) accounted for 40.7 percent of total cash receipts received by Texas farmers and ranchers in 2007. Most of these receipts were from cattle and calf sales. Dairy products made up 7.6 percent of receipts; poultry and eggs, 9.8 percent; and miscellaneous livestock, 1.6 percent.

Cotton and cottonseed accounted for 11.1 percent of total receipts; feed crops, 9.9 percent; food grains, 3.8 percent; vegetables, 2.8 percent; greenhouse/nursery products, 7.9 percent; oil crops, 1.0 percent; fruits and nuts, 0.96 percent; and other crops, 2.9 percent.

Texas Rank Among States

Measured by cash receipts for farm and ranch marketings, Texas ranked second in 2007, with California ranking first and Iowa third.

Texas normally leads all other states in numbers of farms and ranches and farm and ranch land, cattle

slaughtered, cattle on feed, calf births, sheep and lambs, goats, cash receipts from livestock marketings, cattle and calves, beef cows, wool production, mohair production, and exports of fats, oils, and greases. The state also usually leads in production of cotton.

Texas Agricultural Exports

The value of Texas' share of agricultural exports in fiscal year 2007 was $5.2 billion. Cotton accounted for $1,824 million of the exports; feed grains and products, $492.4 million; wheat and products, $529.1 million; fats, oil and greases, $111.5 million; rice, $65.6 million; cottonseed and products, $53.7 million; hides and skins, $322.2 million; live animals and meat, excluding poultry, $509 million; fruits, $74.8 million; peanuts and products, $49.2 million; soybeans and products, $12.9 million; vegetables and products, $47.9 million; poultry and products, $194.1 million; dairy products, $12.4 million; and miscellaneous and other products, $862.8 million.

In 2006, Texas' exports of $3.625 billion of farm and ranch products compares with $3.622 billion in 2005 and $3.876 billion in 2004.

Hunting

The management of wildlife as an economic enterprise through leasing for hunting makes a significant contribution to the economy of many counties. Leasing the right of ingress on a farm or ranch for the purpose of hunting is the service marketed. After the leasing, the consumer — the hunter — goes onto the land to seek the harvest of the wildlife commodity. Hunting lease income to farmers and ranchers in 2008 was estimated at $504 million.

The demand for hunting opportunities is growing while the land capable of producing huntable wildlife is decreasing. As a result, farmers and ranchers are placing more emphasis on wildlife management practices to help meet requests for hunting leases.

Irrigation

Agricultural irrigation in Texas peaked in 1974 at 8.6 million acres. Over the next 20 years, irrigation declined

*Realized Gross Income and Net Income from Farming, Texas, 1980–2007

Year	**Realized Gross Farm Income	Farm Production Expenses	Net Change In Farm Inventories	***Total Net Farm Income	***Total Net Income Per Farm
	— Millions of Dollars —				Dollars
1980	9,611.4	9,081.1	−542.5	456.9	2,331.0
1981	11,545.7	9,643.1	699.9	1,902.6	9,756.8
1982	11,404.5	10,008.2	−127.8	1,396.3	7,197.6
1983	11,318.1	9,778.9	−590.7	1,539.2	7,933.8
1984	11,692.6	10,257.3	186.1	1,435.3	7,398.3
1985	11,375.3	9,842.8	−9.0	1,532.5	7,981.9
1986	10,450.1	9,272.8	−349.0	1,177.3	6,196.6
1987	12,296.6	10,038.7	563.2	2,257.9	12,010.1
1988	12,842.8	10,331.7	−128.4	2,510.6	13,076.2
1989	12,843.1	10,328.4	−798.6	2,514.7	12,962.1
1990	14,421.5	11,012.9	343.9	3,408.6	17,391.0
1991	14,376.4	11,270.3	150.0	3,106.1	15,767.0
1992	14,482.5	10,617.6	464.1	3,864.9	19,519.8
1993	15,817.0	11,294.6	197.0	4,522.5	20,745.4
1994	15,394.5	11,134.7	107.7	4,259.9	19,363.0
1995	15,678.9	12,537.3	243.7	3,141.6	14,151.3
1996	15,025.0	12,006.6	−290.1	3,018.4	13,475.1
1997	16,430.7	12,718.5	709.2	3,712.3	16,498.9
1998	15,506.0	12,047.4	−817.1	3,458.6	15,269.7
1999	17,469.5	12,441.9	196.0	5,027.6	22,099.3
2000	16,810.1	12,717.6	−50.2	4,092.5	17,926.1
2001	18,089.1	13,116.3	113.4	4,972.8	21,753.4
2002	16,567.7	11,378.9	436.6	5,188.8	22,658.6
2003	19,903.6	13,723.9	−169.9	6,179.7	26,985.4
2004	21,901.6	14,433.7	539.0	7,467.9	32,610.9
2005	22,375.5	15,453.1	328.5	6,922.4	30,097.4
2006	20,890.0	16,030.2	−748.4	4,859.8	21,129.5
2007	24,414.7	18,018.2	902.2	7,181.0	29,014.2

* Details for items may not add to totals because of rounding.
** Cash receipts from farm marketings, government payments, value of home consumption and gross rental value of farm dwellings.
*** Farm income of farm operators.
† A positive value of inventory change represents current-year production not sold by Dec. 31. A negative value is an offset to production from prior years included in current-year sales.
§ Starting in 1977, farms with production of $1,000 or more used to figure income.
Source: "Economic Indicators of the Farm Sector, State Financial Summary, 1985," 1987," 1989," 1993," USDA/ERS; "Farm Business Economics Report," August 1996, "Texas Agricultural Statistics Service, October 2008;" ERS Briefing Room.

Export Shares of Commodities

Commodity*	2004	2005	2006	2007	2007 % of U.S. Total
	Millions of Dollars				
Rice	73.6	75.3	71.3	65.6	4.67
Cotton & Linters	1,486.2	1,341.2	1,247.0	1,824.0	42.37
Fats, oils & greases	89.5	76.7	80.0	111.5	14.88
Hides & skins	279.4	279.6	314.9	322.2	14.92
Meats other than poultry	333.7	280.6	419.2	509.0	7.5
Feed grains	307.8	252.6	259.2	492.4	4.16
Poultry products	140.1	161.7	154.3	194.1	5.14
Fruits	44.9	60.5	64.8	74.8	1.49
Vegetables	44.3	50.1	54.5	47.9	1.11
Wheat & flour	315.3	259.1	156.3	529.1	6.26
Soybeans	24.9	17.2	9.6	12.9	0.12
Cottonseed	34.7	38.1	27.3	53.7	43.42
Peanuts	39.9	43.5	33.4	49.2	19.75
Tree nuts	23.6	26.2	34.3	37.0	1.22
Dairy products	3.9	5.1	5.7	12.4	0.49
† All other	634.0	654.0	692.7	862.8	5.33
Total	**3,875.8**	**3,621.5**	**3,624.5**	**5,198.6**	**6.34**

Totals may not add due to rounding.
* Commodity and related preparations.
† Sunflower-seed and oil, feeds and fodders, seeds, sugar and tropical products, minor oilseeds, essential oils, beverages other than juice, nursery and greenhouse, wine, and vegetable products.
Source: FATUS, Foreign Agricultural Trade of the United States, various issues, web site: www.ers.usda.gov for 2007 data. USDA/ERS.

The annual Texas cotton harvest, which amounts to about 25 percent of total production in the United States, has averaged 5.43 million bales since 1996. David Nance photo; USDA Agricultural Research Service.

due to many factors including poor farm economics, falling water tables and conversion to more efficient technologies. Total irrigated area fluctuates from year to year with current estimates at about 6 million acres. This puts Texas third in the nation, behind California and Nebraska, in agricultural irrigation.

Although some irrigation is practiced in nearly every county of the state, about 50 percent of the total irrigated acreage is on the High Plains. Other concentrated areas of irrigation are the Gulf Coast rice-producing area, the Lower Rio Grande Valley, the Winter Garden area of South Texas, the Trans-Pecos area of West Texas, and the peanut-producing area in North-Central Texas that is centered around Erath, Eastland and Comanche counties.

Sprinkler irrigation is used on about 65 percent of the total irrigated acreage, with surface irrigation methods, primarily furrow and surge methods, being used on the remaining irrigated area. Texas farmers lead the nation in the adoption of efficient irrigation technologies, particularly LEPA (low energy precision application) and LESA (low elevation spray application) center pivot systems, both of which were developed by Texas AgriLife Research and the Texas AgriLife Extension Service.

The use of drip irrigation is increasing, with current acreage estimated to be about 400,000 acres. Drip irrigation is routinely used on vegetables and tree crops, such as citrus, pecans and peaches. Some drip irrigation of cotton, forages and turfgrass is being practiced in West Texas. Farmers continue to experiment with drip irrigation, but the high costs and management requirements are limiting more widespread use.

Agricultural irrigation uses about 60 percent of all fresh water in the state, and landscape irrigation accounts for about 40 percent of total municipal water use. Texas is one of only a handful of states that require a state irrigator's license for the design and installation of landscape and residential irrigation systems. New regulations went into effect January 2009 that requires all cities of 20,000 persons or larger to have irrigation inspectors, and for irrigation dealers to meet new design and installation requirements. However, no license or certification is required for the design or installation of agricultural irrigation systems.

To meet future water demand for our rapidly growing cities and industries, several regions of the state are looking at water transfers from agriculture. In recent years, major water transfer projects have been proposed, including transferring water from the Texas High Plains to the Metroplex and from the Colorado River to San Antonio. However, significant environmental and legal obstacles exist, and the viability of such projects is not known.

Water utilities in San Antonio also have water transfer programs with irrigators in the Edwards Aquifer region. The effects of such transfers on farm and rural economies are uncertain.

In about 20 percent of the irrigated area, water is delivered to farms by irrigation and water districts through canals and pipelines. Many of these delivery networks are aging, in poor condition and have high seepage losses. In 2000, Congress passed Public Law 106-576 that, along with subsequent legislation, authorized federal cost-sharing for rehabilitation of districts along the Rio Grande in Texas. To date, Congress has appropriated about $10 million for such projects.

About 80 percent of the state's irrigated acreage is supplied with water pumped from wells. Surface water sources supply the remaining area. Declining groundwater levels in several of the major aquifers is a serious problem for agriculture, particularly in the Ogallala Aquifer in the Texas High Plains and the southern portion of the Carizo-Wilcox formation. As the water levels decline, well yields decrease and pumping costs increase.

Irrigation is an important factor in the productivity of Texas agriculture. The value of crop production from irrigated acreage is 50–60 percent of the total value of all crop production, although only about 30 percent of the state's total harvested cropland acreage is irrigated.

Principal Crops

In most recent years, the value of crop production in Texas is less than 40 percent of the total value of the state's agricultural output. Cash receipts from farm sales of crops are reduced somewhat because some grain and roughage is fed to livestock on farms where produced. Drought and low prices have reduced receipts in recent years.

Receipts from all Texas crops totaled $7.688 billion in 2007; $5.959 billion in 2006; and $6.124 billion in 2005.

Cotton, corn, grain sorghum and wheat account for a large part of the total crop receipts. In 2007, cotton contributed about 23.1 percent of the crop total; corn, 11.7 percent; grain sorghum, 5.9 percent; and wheat, 8.0 percent. Hay, cottonseed, vegetables, peanuts, rice and soybeans are other important cash crops.

Corn

Interest in corn production throughout the state has increased since the 1970s as yields improved with new varieties. Once the principal grain crop, corn acreage declined as plantings of grain sorghum increased. Only 500,000 acres were harvested annually until the mid-1970s when development of new hybrids occurred.

Harvested acreage was 2.03 million in 2008; 1.97 million in 2007; and 1.45 million in 2006. Yields for those same years were 125, 148 and 121 bushels per acre, respectively.

Most of the acreage and yield increase has occurred in Central and South Texas. In 2008, corn ranked first in value among the state's crops. It was valued at $1.2 billion in 2008; $1.3 billion in 2007; and $561.44 million in 2006. The grain is largely used for livestock feed, but other important uses are in food products.

The leading counties in production for 2007 were Hartley, Dallam, Castro, Sherman and Moore.

Cotton

Cotton has been a major crop in Texas for more than a century. Since 1880, Texas has led all states in cotton production in most years, and today the annual Texas cotton harvest amounts to about 25 percent of total production in the United States. The annual cotton crop has averaged 5.43 million bales since 1996.

Value of Upland cotton produced in Texas in 2008 was $1.142 billion. Cottonseed value in 2008 was $363.6 million, making the value of the Texas crop around $1.505 billion.

Upland cotton was harvested from 3.4 million acres in 2008, and American-Pima cotton from 15,000 acres, for a total of 3.415 million acres. Severe drought reduced harvested acreage from the 5 million acres planted. Yield for Upland cotton in 2008 was 649 pounds per harvested acre, with American-Pima yielding 768 pounds per acre. Cotton acreage harvested in 2007 totaled 4.7 million, with a yield of 843 pounds per acre for Upland cotton and 920 pounds per acre for American-Pima. Total cotton production was 4.624 million bales in 2008 and 8.296 million in 2007. Counties leading in production of Upland cotton in 2007 included Gaines, Lubbock, Hockley, Lynn, Dawson, Hale and Terry.

Cotton is the raw material for processing operations at gins, oil mills, compresses and a small number of textile mills in Texas. Less than 10 percent of the raw cotton produced is processed within the state.

Cotton in Texas is machine harvested. Field storage of harvested seed cotton is gaining in popularity as gins decline in number. Much of the Texas cotton crop is exported. China, Japan, South Korea and Mexico are major buyers. With the continuing development of fiber spinning technology and the improved quality of Texas cotton, more utilization of cotton by mills within the

Value of Cotton and Cottonseed 1900–2008

Crop Year	Upland Cotton Production (Bales)	Upland Cotton Value	Cottonseed Production (Tons)	Cottonseed Value
	(All Figures in Thousands)			
1900	3,438	$157,306	1,531	$20,898
1910	3,047	210,260	1,356	31,050
1920	4,345	376,080	1,934	41,350
1930	4,037	194,080	1,798	40,820
1940	3,234	162,140	1,318	31,852
1950	2,946	574,689	1,232	111,989
1960	4,346	612,224	1,821	75,207
1970	3,191	314,913	1,242	68,310
*1980	3,320	1,091,616	1,361	161,959
1981	5,645	1,259,964	2,438	207,230
1982	2,700	664,848	1,122	90,882
1983	2,380	677,443	1,002	162,324
1984	3,680	927,360	1,563	157,863
1985	3,910	968,429	1,635	102,156
1986	2,535	560,945	1,053	82,118
1987	4,635	1,325,981	1,915	157,971
1988	5,215	1,291,651	2,131	238,672
1989	2,870	812,784	1,189	141,491
1990	4,965	1,506,182	1,943	225,388
1991	4,710	1,211,789	1,903	134,162
1992	3,265	769,495	1,346	145,368
1993	5,095	1,308,396	2,147	255,493
1994	4,915	1,642,003	2,111	215,322
1995	4,460	1,597,037	1,828	201,080
1996	4,345	1,368,154	1,784	230,136
1997	5,140	1,482,787	1,983	226,062
1998	3,600	969,408	1,558	204,098
1999	5,050	993,840	1,987	160,947
2000	3,940	868,061	1,589	162,078
2001	4,260	580,723	1,724	159,470
2002	5,040	967,680	1,855	191,065
2003	4,330	1,199,237	1,616	202,000
2004	7,740	1,493,510	2,895	301,080
2005	8,440	1,879,757	2,869	289,739
2006	5,800	1,288,992	2,066	243,776
2007	8,250	2,391,840	2,861	443,409
2008	4,600	1,141,536	1,595	363,660

* Beginning in 1971, basis for cotton prices was changed from 500 pound gross weight to 480 pound net weight bale; to compute comparable prices for previous years multiply price times 1.04167.
Sources: "A Texas Agricultural Facts," Crop Value Annual Summary, February 2008 and "A Texas Ag Statistics," Texas Agricultural Statistics Service, Austin, Texas, annual summary, March 2009. Also, Texas Cottonseed Crushers historical records; U.S. Commerce Dept.; and USDA.

state may develop. Spinning techniques can efficiently produce high-quality yarn from relatively strong, short or longer staple Upland cotton with fine mature fiber.

The first high-volume instrument cotton classing office in the nation was opened at Lamesa in 1980.

Forest Products

For information on Texas forest products, turn to the section titled "Texas Forest Resources," page 105.

Grain Sorghum

Grain sorghum in 2008 ranked sixth in dollar value. Much of the grain is exported, as well as being used in livestock and poultry feed throughout the state.

Total production of grain sorghum in 2008 was 88.82 million hundredweight (cwt), with a 2,912 pound per acre yield. With an average price of $7.30 per cwt., the total value reached $648.4 million. In 2007, 2.45 million acres of grain sorghum were harvested, yielding an average of 3,640 pounds per acre for a total production of 89.18 million cwt. It was valued at $6.60 per cwt., for a total value of $588.6 million. In 2006, 1.3 million acres were harvested, with an average of 2,688 pounds per acre, or 34.94 million cwt. The season's price was $5.24 per cwt. for a total value of $183.12 million.

Although grown to some extent in all counties where crops are important, the largest concentrations are in the High Plains, Rolling Plains, Blackland Prairie, Coastal Bend and Lower Rio Grande Valley areas. Counties leading in production in 2007 were Nueces, Hidalgo, Willacy, Cameron, San Patricio and Hale.

Hay, Silage and Other Forage Crops

A large proportion of Texas' agricultural land is devoted to forage crop production. This acreage produces forage needs and provides essentially the total feed requirements for most of the state's large domestic livestock population, as well as game animals.

About 87.2 million acres of pasture and rangeland, which are primarily in the western half of Texas, provide grazing for beef cattle, sheep, goats, horses and game animals. An additional 7.8 million acres are devoted to cropland used only for pasture or grazing. The average annual acreage of forage land used for hay, silage and other forms of machine-harvested forage is around 5 million acres.

Hay accounts for a large amount of this production, with some corn and sorghum silage also produced. The most important hay crops are annual and perennial grasses and alfalfa. Production in 2008 totaled 9.21 million tons of hay from 4.43 million harvested acres at a yield of 2.08 tons per acre. Value of hay was $1.015 million, or $122 per ton. In 2007, 14.74 million tons of hay was produced from 5.34 million harvested acres at a yield of 2.76 tons per acre. The value in 2007 was $1.94 billion, or $135 per ton. In 2006, the production of hay was 8.67 million tons from 5.15 million harvested acres with a value of $1.09 billion, or $131 per ton, at a yield of 1.68 tons per acre.

Alfalfa hay production in 2008 totaled 611,000 tons, with 130,000 acres harvested and a yield of 4.7 tons per acre. At a value of $183 per ton, total value was $111.81 million. In 2007, 770,000 tons of alfalfa hay was harvested from 140,000 acres at a yield of 5 tons per acre. Value was $115.5 million, or $165 per ton. Alfalfa hay was harvested from 150,000 acres in 2006, producing an average of 4.50 tons per acre for total production of 675,000 tons, valued at $107.3 million.

An additional sizable acreage of annual forage crops is grazed, as well as much of the small grain acreage. Alfalfa, sweet corn, vetch, arrowleaf clover, grasses and other forage plants also provide income as seed crops.

Nursery Crops

The trend to increase production of nursery crops continues to rise as transportation costs on long-distance hauling increases. This has resulted in a marked increase in the production of container-grown plants in Texas. This increase is noted especially in the production of bedding plants, foliage plants, sod and woody landscape plants.

Plant rental services have become a multi-million dollar business. This relatively new service provides the plants and maintains them in office buildings, shopping malls, public buildings, and even in some homes for a fee. The response has been good as evidenced by the growth of companies providing these services.

Interest in plants for interior landscapes appeals to all age groups; both retail nurseries and florist shops report that people of all ages are buying plants — from the elderly in retirement homes to high school and college students in dormitory rooms and apartments.

Texas AgriLife Extension specialists estimated cash receipts from nursery crops in Texas to be around $1.8 billion in 2008. Ranking counties in specialty crops are Harris, Dallas, Montgomery, Bexar, Fort Bend and Cherokee.

Oats

Oats are grown extensively in Texas for winter pasture, hay, silage and greenchop feeding, and some acreage is harvested for grain.

Of the 600,000 acres planted to oats in 2008, 100,000 acres were harvested. The average yield was 50 bushels per acre. Production totaled 5 million bushels with a value of $19.25 million. In 2007, 710,000 acres were planted and 100,000 acres were harvested. The average yield was 40 bushels per acre for a total production of 4 million bushels. Average price per bushel was $3.47, and total production value was $13.88 million.

Texas farmers planted 760,000 acres of oats in 2006. They harvested 100,000 acres that averaged 37 bushels per acre for a total production of 3.7 million bushels at an average price of $2.43 per bushel and an estimated value of $8.99 million. Most of the acreage was used for grazing.

Almost all oat grain produced in Texas is utilized as

Texas Crop Production 2008

Crop	Harvested Acres (000)	Yield Per Acre	Unit	Total Production (000)	Value (000)
Beans, dry edible	21.8	1,300	lb.,cwt.	283	9,905
Corn, grain	2,030	125	bu.	253,750	1,218,000
Corn, silage	180	21.0	ton	3,780	—
Cotton, American-Pima	15	768	lb./bale	24	—
Cotton, upland	3,400	649	lb., bale	4,600	1,141,536
Cottonseed	—	—	ton	1,595	363,660
Grapefruit *	—	—	box	6,100	31,606
Hay, Alfalfa	130	4.7	ton	611	111,813
Hay, Other	4,300	2.0	ton	8,600	903,000
Hay, all	4,430	2.08	ton	9,211	1,014,813
Oats	100	50	bu.	5,000	19,250
Oranges †	—	—	box	1,734	913
Peaches (utilized)	—	—	ton	7.9	13,230
Peanuts	253	3,400	lb.	860,200	185,803
Pecans	—	—	lb.	30,000	41,700
Potatoes (all)	14.5	304	cwt.	4,410	81,228
Rice	172	6,900	lb., cwt.	11,868	194,635
Sorghum, grain	3,050	52	lb., cwt.	158,600	648,357
Sorghum, silage	130	15	ton	1,950	—
Soybeans	205	24	bu.	4,920	45,510
Sugar cane	41.5	39.8	ton	1,652	††
Sunflowers	87	1,062	lb.	92,400	18,282
Sweet potatoes	1.5	140	cwt.	210	4,305
Vegetables (commercial):					
Fresh market ‡	52.3	—	cwt.	12,700	244,894
Processing §	22.1	—	cwt.	2,894	31,736
Wheat, winter	3,300	30	bu.	99,000	737,550
Total of Listed Crops	**21,935.7**	**—**	**—**	**—**	**7,060,726**

* Grapefruit, Texas 80-lb./box, reflects 2007–2008 crop year. † Oranges, Texas 85-lb./box, reflects 2007–2008 crop year. †† Sugarcane value will be published February 2010. ‡ Total Texas fresh market vegetables include: Bell peppers, cabbage, cantaloupes, carrots, cauliflower, celery, cucumbers, honeydew melons, onions, spinach, sweet corn, tomatoes and watermelons. § Total Texas processing vegetables include carrots, cucumbers, snap beans, spinach and tomatoes.
Source: "A Texas Ag Facts Annual Summary," TASS/USDA, 3/3/2009.

feed for livestock within the state. A small acreage is grown exclusively for planting seed. Leading oat grain–producing counties in 2007 were Falls, McLennan, Hamilton, Coryell, Uvalde and Medina.

Peanuts

Peanuts are grown on more than 250,000 acres in Texas. More than three-fourths of the crop annually produced is on irrigated acreage. Texas ranked second nationally in production of peanuts in 2008. Among Texas crops, peanuts rank ninth in value.

Until 1973, essentially all of the Texas acreage was planted to the Spanish type, which was favored because of its earlier maturity and better drought tolerance than other types. The Spanish variety is also preferred for some uses because of its distinctive flavor. The Florunner variety, a runner market type, is now planted on a sizable proportion of the acreage where soil moisture is favorable. The variety matures later but produces better yields than Spanish varieties under good growing conditions. Florunner peanuts have acceptable quality to compete with the Spanish variety in most products.

In 2008, peanut production totaled 860.2 million pounds from 253,000 harvested acres, yielding 3,400 pounds per acre. At 21.6 cents per pound, value was estimated at $185.8 million. In 2007, peanut production was 691.9 million pounds from 190,000 acres planted and 187,000 harvested. Average yield of 3,700 pounds per acre and average price of 23.5 cents per pound combined for a 2007 value of $162.6 million. Production in 2006 amounted to 514.7 million pounds of peanuts from 155,000 acres planted and 145,000 acres harvested, or an average of 3,550 pounds per harvested acre valued at 18.7 cents per pound for a value of $96.26 million.

Leading counties in peanut production in 2007 included Gaines, Yoakum, Terry, Collingsworth, Frio, Haskell and Cochran.

Rice

Rice, which is grown in about 20 counties on the Coastal Prairie of Texas, ranked third in value among Texas crops for a number of years. Recently, however, cotton, grain sorghum, wheat, corn, peanuts and hay have outranked rice.

Farms are highly mechanized, producing rice through irrigation and using airplanes for much of the planting, fertilizing, and application of insecticides and herbicides.

Texas farmers grow long- and medium-grain rice

Rice has ranked third in value among Texas crops for many years. Here, it is harvested in Fort Bend County, one of about 20 counties in the Coastal Plains where rice is grown. David Nance photo; USDA Agricultural Research Service.

only. The Texas rice industry, which has grown from 110 acres in 1850 to a high of 642,000 acres in 1954, has been marked by significant yield increases and improved varieties. Record production was in 1981, with 27.23 million hundredweights harvested. Highest yield was 7,170 pounds per acre in 2006.

Several different types of rice milling procedures are used. The simplest and oldest method produces a product known as regular milled white rice, the most prevalent on the market.

During this process, rice grains are subjected to additional cleaning to remove chaff, dust and foreign seed, and then husks are removed from the grains. This results in a product that is the whole unpolished grain of rice with only the outer hull and a small amount of bran removed. This product is called brown rice and is sometimes sold without further treatment other than grading. It has a delightful nutlike flavor and a slightly chewy texture.

When additional layers of the bran are removed, the

rice becomes white in color and begins to appear as it is normally recognized at retail level. The removal of the bran layer from the grain is performed in a number of steps using two or three types of machines. After the bran is removed, the product is ready for classification as to size. Rice is more valuable if the grains are not broken. In many cases, additional vitamins are added to the grains to produce "enriched rice."

Another process may be used in rice milling to produce a product called parboiled rice. In this process, the rice is subjected to a combination of steam and pressure prior milling. This process gelatinizes the starch in the grain, the treatment aiding in the retention of much of the natural vitamin and mineral content. After cooking, parboiled rice tends to be fluffy, more separate and plump.

Still another type of rice is precooked rice, which is milled rice that, after milling, has been cooked. Then the moisture is removed through a dehydration process. Precooked rice requires a minimum of preparation time because it needs merely to have the moisture restored.

The United States produces only a small part of the world's total rice, but it is one of the leading exporters. American rice is popular abroad and is exported to more than 100 foreign countries.

Rice production in 2008 totaled 11.87 million cwt. from 172,000 harvested acres, with a yield of 6,900 pounds per acre. The crop value totaled $194.63 million. Rice production was 9.5 million cwt. in 2007 on 145,000 harvested acres, yielding 6,550 pounds per acre. Total value in 2007 was $117.8 million. Rice production was 10.76 million cwt. in 2006 on 150,000 harvested acres. Production in 2006 was valued at $107.6 million, with a yield of 7,170 pounds per acre. Counties leading in rice production in 2007 included Wharton, Colorado, Matagorda, Jefferson, Jackson and Brazoria.

Soybeans

Production of soybeans is largely in the areas of the Upper Coast, irrigated High Plains and Red River Valley of northeast Texas. Soybeans are adapted to the same general soil climate conditions as corn, cotton or grain sorghum — provided moisture, disease and insects are not limiting factors. The major counties in soybean production in 2007 were Lamar, Fannin, Ellis, Wharton, Bowie, Dallas and Victoria.

In low-rainfall areas, yields have been too low or inconsistent for profitable production under dryland conditions. Soybeans' need for moisture in late summer minimizes economic crop possibilities in the Blacklands and Rolling Plains. In the Blacklands, cotton root rot seriously hinders soybean production. Limited moisture at critical growth stages may occasionally prevent economical yields, even in high-rainfall areas of northeast Texas and the Coastal Prairie.

Because of day length sensitivity, soybeans should be planted in Texas during the long days of May and June to obtain sufficient vegetative growth for optimum yields. Varieties planted during this period usually cease vegetative development and initiate reproductive processes during the hot, usually dry months of July and August. When moisture is insufficient during the blooming and fruiting period, yields are drastically reduced. In most areas of the state, July and August rainfall is insufficient to permit economical dryland production. The risk of dryland soybean production in the Coastal Prairie and northeast Texas is considerably less when compared to other dryland areas because moisture is available more often during the critical fruiting period.

The 2008 soybean crop totaled 4.92 million bushels and was valued at $45.51 million, or $9.25 per bushel. Of the 230,000 acres planted, 205,000 were harvested with an average yield of 24 bushels per acre. In 2007, the Texas soybean crop averaged 37.5 bushels per acre

from 92,000 acres harvested. Total production of 3.45 million bushels was valued at $35.88 million, or $10.4 per bushel. In 2006, the soybean crop averaged 24 bushels per acre from 155,000 acres harvested. Total production of 3.72 million bushels was valued at $20.09 million, or $5.40 per bushel.

Sugarcane

Sugarcane is grown from seed cane planted in late summer or fall. It is harvested 12 months later and milled to produce raw sugar and molasses. Raw sugar requires additional refining before it is in final form and can be offered to consumers.

The sugarcane grinding mill operated at Santa Rosa, Cameron County, is considered one of the most modern mills in the United States. Texas sugarcane-producing counties are Hidalgo, Cameron and Willacy.

At a yield of 39.8 tons per acre, sugarcane production in 2008 totaled 1.65 million tons from 41,500 harvested acres. In 2007, 43,700 acres were harvested for total production of 1.46 million tons valued at $34.16 million, or $23.40 per ton. The yield was 33.4 tons per acre. In 2006, 40,700 acres were harvested, from which 1.68 million tons of sugarcane were milled. The yield averaged 41.2 tons per acre. The price averaged $28.70 per ton for a total value of $48.13 million.

Sunflowers

Sunflowers constitute one of the most important annual oilseed crops in the world. The cultivated types, which are thought to be descendants of the common wild sunflower native to Texas, have been successfully grown in several countries including Russia, Argentina, Romania, Bulgaria, Uruguay, Western Canada and portions of the northern United States. Extensive trial plantings conducted in the Cotton Belt states since 1968 showed sunflowers have considerable potential as an oilseed crop in much of this area, including Texas. This crop exhibits good cold and drought tolerance, is adapted to a wide range of soil and climate conditions, and tolerates higher levels of hail, wind and sand abrasion than other crops.

In 2008, sunflower production totaled 92.4 million pounds and was harvested from 87,000 acres at a yield of 1,062 pounds per acre. With an average price of $19.80 per cwt., the crop was valued at $18.28 million. In 2007, 38,500 of the 42,000 acres planted to sunflowers were harvested with an average yield of 1,308 pounds per acre. Total production of 50.34 million pounds was valued at $9.84 million, or $19.50 per cwt.

In 2006, of 52,000 acres planted to sunflowers, 24,000 acres were harvested, yielding 890 pounds per acre for a total yield of 21.35 million pounds, valued at $3.27 million, or $15.30 per cwt. The leading counties in production in 2007 were Lamb, Bailey, Hale, Hartley, Cochran and Dallam.

Reasons for growing sunflowers include the need for an additional cash crop with low water and plant nutrient requirements, the development of sunflower hybrids, and interest by food processors in Texas sunflower oil, which has high oleic acid content. Commercial users have found many advantages in this high oleic oil, including excellent cooking stability, particularly for use as a deep-frying medium for potato chips, corn chips and similar products.

Sunflower meal is a high-quality protein source free of nutritional toxins that can be included in rations for swine, poultry and ruminants. The hulls constitute a source of roughage, which can also be included in livestock rations.

Wheat

Wheat for grain is one of the state's most valuable cash crops. In 2008, wheat was exceeded in value by corn, cotton and hay. Wheat pastures also provide considerable winter forage for cattle that is reflected in value of livestock produced.

Texas wheat production totaled 99 million bushels in 2008, as yield averaged 30 bushels per acre. Planted acreage totaled 5.8 million acres and 3.3 million acres were harvested. With an average price of $7.45 per bushel, the 2008 wheat value totaled $737.55 million. In 2007, Texas wheat growers planted 6.2 million acres and harvested 3.8 million acres. The yield was 37 bushels per acre, with total production of 140.6 million bushels at $6.40 per bushel valued at $899.84 million.

Texas wheat growers planted 5.55 million acres in 2006 and harvested grain from 1.4 million acres. The yield was 24 bushels per acre for a total production of 33.6 million bushels valued at $150.19 million.

Leading wheat-producing counties in 2007 were Hansford, Ochiltree, Deaf Smith, Parmer, Sherman and Dallam. The leading counties, based on acreage planted in 2007, were Deaf Smith, Hansford, Parmer, Ochiltree, Castro and Swisher.

Wheat was first grown commercially in Texas near Sherman about 1833. The acreage expanded greatly in North-Central Texas after 1850 because of rapid settlement of the state and introduction of the well-adapted Mediterranean strain of wheat. A major family flour industry was developed in the area around Fort Worth, Dallas and Sherman between 1875 and 1900. Now, around half of the state's acreage is planted on the High Plains and about a third of this is irrigated. Most of the Texas wheat acreage is of the hard red winter class. Because of the development of varieties with improved disease resistance and the use of wheat for winter pasture, there has been a sizable expansion of acreage in Central and South Texas.

John Jifon, a plant physiologist at the Texas A&M Experiment Station, measures photosynthetic activity of plants sprayed with potassium. Peggy Greb photo; USDA Agricultural Research Service.

Most all wheat harvested for grain is used in some phase of the milling industry. The better-quality hard red winter wheat is used in the production of commercial bakery flour. Lower grades and varieties of soft red winter wheat are used in family flours. By-products of milled wheat are used for feed.

Vegetable Crops

Some market vegetables are produced in almost all Texas counties, but most of the commercial crop comes from about 200 counties. Hidalgo County is the leading Texas county in vegetable acres harvested, followed by Parmer and Uvalde counties. Other leading producing counties are: Hale, Frio, Yoakum, Zavala, Hudspeth and Gaines.

Texas is one of the seven leading states in the production of fresh market vegetables. Nationally, in 2008, Texas ranked seventh in production, exceeded by California, Florida, Arizona, Georgia, New York and Washington. Texas also ranked seventh in value of fresh-market vegetables. Texas had 2.8 percent of the production and 2.4 percent of the value of fresh-market vegetables produced. Onions were the top cash crop, with watermelons second. Other vegetables leading in value of production for 2008 were cabbage, carrots, squash, cantaloupes honeydew melons.

In 2008, total vegetable production of 15.59 million cwt. was valued at $276.63 million from 74,400 acres harvested. In 2007, Texas growers harvested total commercial vegetable crops valued at $356.54 million from 76,550 acres with a production of 13.74 million cwt. In 2006, Texas growers harvested 18.68 million cwt. of commercial vegetable crops from 85,100 acres, valued at $287.29 million.

Cabbage

In 2008, 7,100 acres were harvested and yielded total production of 2.27 million cwt. that was valued at $46.12 million. Yield was 320 cwt. per acre. In 2007, 6,000 acres of cabbage were harvested yielding total production of 1.62 million cwt., or 270 cwt. per acre, valued at $41.47 million. In 2006, the 7,600 acres of cabbage harvested in Texas brought a value of $42.45 million. At a yield of 380 cwt. per acre, total production was 2.89 million cwt.

Cantaloupe & Honeydew Melons

Cantaloupe production in 2008 totaled 198,000 cwt. from 1,800 harvested acres and was valued at $6.73 million at a yield of 110 cwt. per acre. In 2007, cantaloupes were harvested from 3,600 acres for total production of 432,000 cwt., valued at $14.04 million, yielding 120 cwt. per acre. Of the 4,300 harvested acres in 2006, 559,000 cwt. cantaloupes were produced at a yield of 130 cwt. per acre and were valued at $20.24 million.

Honeydew production totaled 189,000 cwt. and was valued at $5.54 million at a yield of 270 cwt. per acre in 2008. In 2007, 182,000 cwt. of honeydew melons were harvested from 650 acres for total value of $7.46 million, yielding 280 cwt. per acre. In 2006, honeydew melons valued at $5.64 million were harvested on 700 acres, producing a yield of 260 cwt. per acre for a total production of 182,000 cwt.

Carrots

Carrot production in 2008 totaled 312,000 cwt. from 1,300 harvested acres at a yield of 240 cwt. per acre. Production was valued at $7.8 million. In 2007, carrots were harvested from 1,500 acres with a value of $8.4 million. At a yield of 200 cwt. per acre, 2007 production was 300,000 cwt. In 2006, carrot production was valued at $12.33 million from 2,000 acres harvested. Production was 620,000 cwt. at a yield of 310 cwt. per acre.

The winter carrot production from South Texas accounts for about three-fourths of total production during the winter season.

Cucumbers

In 2008, 1,000 acres of cucumbers were harvested. Production totaled 104,000 cwt. and was valued at $2.39 million. The 2008 yield was 104 cwt. per acre. In 2007, 1,100 acres of cucumbers were harvested with a value of $2.78 million. Production was 121,000 cwt. with a yield of 110 cwt. per acre. In 2006, 1,300 acres were harvested with a value of $3.37 million. Production was 143,000 cwt. with a yield of 110 cwt. per acre.

Onions

Onion production in 2008 totaled 2.68 million cwt. from 9,600 harvested acres and was valued at $82.16 million, at a yield of 279 cwt. per acre. In 2007, 3.52 million cwt. of onions were harvested from 11,400 acres and valued at $186.52 million, at a yield of 309 cwt. per acre. A total of 4.32 million cwt. of onions were produced from 16,100 harvested acres and valued at $89.42 million in 2006, yielding 268 cwt. per acre.

Potatoes

In 2008, all potatoes were harvested from 14,500 acres with production of 4.41 million cwt. valued at $81.23 million and a yield of 304 cwt. per acre. In 2007, potatoes were harvested from 18,800 acres with production of 5.94 million cwt. valued at $69.11 million, yielding 316 cwt. per acre. This compares with 19,900 acres harvested and valued at $93.58 million in 2006, with production of 7.12 million cwt. and a yield of 358 cwt. per acre.

Spinach

Spinach production is primarily concentrated in the Winter Garden area of South Texas. The 2008 production value of spinach was estimated at $3.43 million. Production of 132,000 cwt. was harvested from 1,100 acres with a yield of 120 cwt. per acre. In 2007, 800 acres were harvested with a value of $2.4 million. At a yield of 125 cwt. per acre, production was 100,000 cwt. The 2,200 acres harvested in 2006 produced 176,000 cwt. at a yield of 80 cwt. per acre and valued at $4.68 million.

Sweet Corn

In 2008, 161,000 cwt. of sweet corn was harvested from 2,400 acres. Value of production was estimated at $3.54 million, with a yield of 67 cwt. per acre. In 2007, 185,000 cwt. of sweet corn was produced from 2,400 harvested acres at a yield of 77 cwt. per acre and valued

Texas Vegetable Production 2008

Crop	Harvested Acres (000)	Yield Per Acre, Cwt.	Production (000) Cwt.	Value (000)
Cabbage	7,100	320	2,272	46,122
Cantaloupes	1,800	110	198	6,732
Carrots	1,300	240	312	7,800
Chile Peppers ‡	5,300	33	174	13,883
Cucumbers	1,000	104	104	2,392
Honeydew Melons	700	270	189	5,538
Onions, Spring	8,900	270	2,403	72,811
Onions, Summer	700	400	280	9,352
Spinach	1,100	120	132	3,432
Squash	1,500	200	300	12,690
Sweet Corn	2,400	67	161	3,542
Tomatoes	1,000	130	130	8,008
Watermelons	19,500	310	6,045	52,592
*Total Fresh Market**	52,300	—	12,700	244,894
Processed †	22,100	—	2,894	31,736
Total Vegetables	**74,400**	—	**15,594**	**276,630**

* Includes some quantities processed.
† Carrots, cucumbers, snap beans and spinach.
‡ Chile peppers are defined as all peppers, excluding bell peppers. Estimates include both fresh and dry product combined.
Source: "Texas Ag Facts", Texas Agricultural Statistics Service/USDA. February 2009.

at $3.85 million. In 2006, sweet corn was harvested from 1,800 acres and valued at $2.37 million. Production was 97,000 cwt. at a yield of 54 cwt. per acre.

Sweet Potatoes

In 2008, 210,000 cwt. of sweet potatoes were harvested from 1,500 acres for a value of $4.3 million at a yield of 140 cwt. per acre. Sweet potatoes in 2007 produced 162,000 cwt. from 1,800 harvested acres, with a value of $3.2 million. Yield was 90 cwt. per acre. This compared with 137,000 cwt. produced in 2006 at a yield of 65 cwt. from 2,100 harvested acres and valued at $3.11 million.

Tomatoes

Commercial tomatoes are marketed throughout the year from Texas partly as a result of recent increases in greenhouse production during the winter.

In 2008, 1,000 harvested acres of tomatoes at a yield of 130 cwt. per acre produced 130,000 cwt. of tomatoes with a value of $8 million. In 2007, 1,100 acres of tomatoes were harvested, producing 143,000 cwt. at a yield of 130 cwt. per acre for a value of $6.02 million. The tomato crop in 2006 was valued at $5.7 million from 1,100 harvested acres. Tomato production was 110,000 cwt. at a yield of 100 cwt. per acre.

Watermelons

Watermelon production in 2008 was 6.04 million cwt. from 19,500 acres, with a value of $52.59 million, yielding 310 cwt. per acre. In 2007, at a yield of 190 cwt. per acre, 4.37 million cwt. of watermelons were harvested from 23,000 acres and valued at $35.83 million. Watermelon production in 2006 was 7.23 million cwt. from 22,600 acres, with a value of $62.2 million, at a yield of 320 cwt. per acre.

Vegetables for Processing

In 2008, 2.89 million cwt. of cucumbers, carrots, snap beans and spinach for processing were harvested from 22,100 acres and valued at $31.73 million. In 2007, 19,100 acres were harvested and valued at $20.86 million, with a production of 2.29 million cwt. In 2006, 20,400 acres were harvested and valued at $20.41 million, producing 1.91 million cwt.

Citrus farmer Jimmy Steidinger samples a Rio Red grapefruit in one of his orchards near Donna in Hidalgo County. In 2007–2008, grapefruit production was estimated at 6.1 million boxes. Erich Schlegel photo.

Fruits and Nuts

Texas is noted for producing a wide variety of fruits. The pecan is the only commercial nut crop in the state. The pecan is native to most of the state's river valleys and is the Texas state tree. Citrus is produced in the three southernmost counties in the Lower Rio Grande Valley. Peaches represent the next most important Texas fruit crop, yet there is a considerable amount of interest in growing apples.

Citrus

Texas ranks with Florida, California and Arizona as leading states in the production of citrus. Most of the Texas production is in Cameron, Hidalgo and Willacy counties of the Lower Rio Grande Valley. In 2007–2008, grapefruit production was estimated at 6.1 million boxes. At $5.18 per box, value of production was $31.6 million. Grapefruit production in 2006–2007, was 7.1 million boxes at $6.82 per box for a total value of $48.4 million. Production in 2005–2006 was 5.2 million boxes at $12.17 per box with a value of $63.29 million.

Production of oranges in 2007–2008 was 1.73 million boxes. At 53 cents per box, total value was $913,000. In 2006–2007, production was 1.98 million boxes at $12.21 per box for a total value of $24.18 million. Production was 1.6 million boxes in 2005–2006 at $6.62 per box

for a value of $10.6 million.

Peaches

Primary production areas are East Texas, the Hill Country and the West Cross Timbers. Production varies substantially due to adverse weather conditions. Low-chilling varieties for early marketings are being grown in Atascosa, Frio, Webb, Karnes and Duval counties.

The Texas peach crop's utilized production totaled 6,300 tons in 2008 for a value of $13.23 million or $2,100 per ton. In 2007, utilized production was 5,700 tons. Value of production was $11.11 million or $1,950 per ton. In 2006, utilized production was 750 tons that was valued at $1.23 million or $1,640 per ton.

The demand for high-quality Texas peaches greatly exceeds the supply. Texas ranked 10th nationally in peach production in 2008. Leading Texas counties in production are Gillespie, Parker, Montague, Comanche, Limestone and Eastland.

Pecans

The pecan, the state tree, is one of the most widely distributed trees in Texas. It is native to over 150 counties and is grown commercially in some 30 additional counties. The pecan is also widely used as a dual-purpose yard tree. The commercial plantings of pecans have accelerated in Central and West Texas, with

A youngster picks peaches at the Barsana Dham peach orchard in Austin. Texas ranked 10th nationally in peach production in 2008. Taylor Jones photo.

many of the new orchards being irrigated. Many new pecan plantings are being established under trickle-irrigation systems.

In 2008, utilized pecan production totaled 30 million pounds and was valued at $41.7 million, or $1.39 per pound. In 2007, 70 million pounds were produced. Total value was estimated at $77.6 million, and price averaged $1.11 per pound. The 2006 crop totaled 47 million pounds, valued at $75.31 million or $1.56 per pound.

Nationally, Texas ranked third behind Georgia and New Mexico in pecan production in 2008. Leading Texas counties in pecan production are Hood, El Paso, Pecos, San Saba, Mills, Comanche, Wharton and Gonzales.

Livestock and Their Products

Livestock and their products accounted for about 59.7 percent of the agricultural cash receipts in Texas in 2007. The state ranks first nationally in all cattle, beef cattle, cattle on feed, sheep and lambs, wool, goats and mohair.

Meat animals account for around 68.2 percent of cash receipts from marketings of livestock and their products. Sales of livestock and products in 2007 totaled $11.39 billion, up from $10.36 billion in 2006.

Cattle and calves dominate livestock production in Texas, contributing more than 67 percent of cash receipts from livestock and products each year. The Jan. 1, 2009, inventory of all cattle and calves in Texas totaled 13.6 million head, valued at $10.47 billion, compared to 13.6 million as of Jan. 1, 2008, valued at $11.7 billion.

On Jan. 1, 2009, the sheep and lamb inventory stood at 870,000 head, valued at $87.87 million, compared with 960,000 head as of Jan. 1, 2008, valued at $97.92 million. Sheep and lambs numbered 3.21 million on Jan. 1, 1973, down from a high of 10.83 million in 1943. Sheep and lamb production fell from 148.29 million pounds in 1973 to 28.4 million pounds on Jan. 1, 2009. Wool production decreased from 26.35 million pounds valued at $23.19 million in 1973 to 4.2 million pounds valued at $4.87 million in 2008. Production was 4.5 million pounds in 2007, valued at $5.45 million. The price of wool per pound was 88 cents in 1973, $1.21 cents in 2007, and $1.16 cents in 2008.

Lamb prices averaged $99.30 per cwt. as of Jan. 1, 2009, $98.10 per cwt. in 2008, and $92.40 per cwt. in 2007. The average price of sheep was $30.40 per cwt. as of Jan. 1, 2009, $35.30 in 2008, and $37.10 in 2007.

Mohair production in Texas has dropped from a 1965 high of 31.58 million pounds to 820,000 pounds in 2008. Production was valued at $3.12 million or $3.80 per pound. In 2007, production was 960,000 pounds, valued at $3.84 million, or $4 per pound. Mohair production in 2006 was 1.1 million pounds, valued at $4.4 million, or $4 per pound.

Beef Cattle

Raising beef cattle is the most extensive agricultural operation in Texas. In 2007, 40 percent of total cash receipts from farm and ranch marketings — $7.63 million of $19.07 million — came from cattle and calves, compared with $7.43 million of $16.32 million in 2005 (45.5 percent), and $7.56 million of $16.88 million in 2005 (44.8 percent). The next leading commodity is cotton.

Texas Cattle Marketed by Size of Feedlots, 1965–2007

Year	Feedlot Capacity (head)						Total
	Under 1,000	1,000– 1,999	2000– 3,999	4,000– 7,999	8,000– 15,999	16,000 & Over	
	Cattle Marketed — 1,000 head —						
1965	104	108	205	324	107	246	1,094
1970	98	53	112	281	727	1,867	3,138
1975	50	22	51	134	485	2,325	3,067
1976	60	33	62	170	583	3,039	3,947
1977	146	22	38	206	604	3,211	4,277
1978	80	20	50	242	697	3,826	4,915
1979	54	19	46	227	556	3,543	4,445
1980	51	18	47	226	533	3,285	4,160
1981	50	20	50	220	510	3,110	3,960
1982	55	20	60	210	540	3,190	4,075
1983	100	20	80	130	490	3,580	4,400
1984	60	20	180	150	540	4,140	5,090
1985	70	10	20	170	620	4,140	5,030
1986	90	10	40	180	550	4,390	5,260
1987	90	20	35	170	625	4,375	5,255
1988	30	15	35	185	650	4,120	5,035
1989	40	15	40	165	675	3,810	4,745
1990	35	24	56	180	605	3,940	4,840
1991	35	25	45	225	500	4,250	5,080
1992	50	10	25	140	505	4,065	4,795
1993	30	20	70	160	640	4,370	5,290
1994	14	13	55	173	725	4,680	5,660
1995	12	24	43	166	630	4,665	5,540
1996	NA	17	43	180	460	4,800	5,500
1997	NA	17	48	250	485	5,000	5,800
1998	NA	10	20	140	420	5,470	6,060
1999	NA	10	20	140	385	5,510	6,065
2000	NA	8	17	125	470	5,570	6,190
2001	NA	8	22	90	450	5,460	6,030
2002	NA	10	15	85	390	5,480	5,980
2003	NA	10	15	75	420	5,450	5,970
2004	NA	20	20	485	485	5,180	5,685
2005	NA	20	20	475	475	5,260	5,755
2006	NA	25	25	470	470	5,280	5,755
2007	NA	20	20	400	400	5,265	5,685

Number of feedlots with 1,000 head or more capacity is number of lots operating any time during the year. Number under 1,000 head capacity and total number of all feedlots is number at end of year.
* Beginning in 2004 report, cattle marketed as 1,000–3,999 and 4,000– 15,999 in feedlot capacity.
Source: "Texas Agricultural Facts, 1997," Texas Agricultural Statistics Service, September 1998. Numbers for 1986, '87, '88, '89, '90, '91, '92. 1993 Texas Livestock Statistics, Bulletin 252, August 1994; Cattle on Feed annual summary, USDA/NASS, February 2009.

Nearly all of the 254 counties in Texas derive more revenue from cattle than from any other agricultural commodity, and those that don't usually rank cattle second in importance.

Texas contains 14.4 percent of all the U.S. cattle, 16.3 percent of the beef breeding cows, and 13.3 percent of the calf crop, as of the Jan. 1, 2009, inventory.

The number of all cattle in Texas on Jan. 1, 2009, totaled 13.6 million, compared with 13.6 million on Jan. 1, 2008; and 14 million in 2007.

Calves born on Texas farms and ranches by Jan. 1, 2009, totaled 4.8 million, compared with 4.8 million in 2008; and 4.9 million in 2007.

Sale of cattle and calves at approximately 147 livestock auctions inspected by the Texas Animal Health Commission totaled 4.15 million head in 2008; 4.05 million head in 2007; and 5.22 million in 2006. The number of cattle and calves shipped into Texas totaled 1.75 million head in 2008; 1.89 million head in 2007; and 2.06 million head in 2006.

Livestock Industries

A large portion of Texas livestock is sold through local auction markets. In 2007, the Texas Animal Health

Agricultural engineer Nolan Clark programs automatic runoff samplers at an experimental feedlot near Bushland in Potter County, which was built to study environmental effects of feedlots. Peggy Greb photo; USDA Agricultural Research Service.

Commission reported 147 livestock auctions. In 2008, auctions sold 4.15 million head of cattle and calves; 32,000 hogs; and 1.03 million sheep and goats. This compared with 2007 figures of 4.05 million cattle and calves; 35,000 hogs; and 1.15 million sheep and goats. Figures for 2006 were 5.22 million cattle and calves; 43,000 hogs; 1.37 million sheep and goats.

During 2008, the commission reported 715,060 cattle and calves shipped from Texas to other states and 1.75 million shipped in; compared with 852,313 shipped out and 1.89 million shipped in during 2007; and 1.06 million shipped out and 2.07 million shipped in during 2006. (Figures exclude cattle shipped direct to slaughter where no health certificates are required.)

During 2008, Texas shipped out 25,093 sheep and lambs and shipped in 12,107; compared with 91,570 shipped out and 42,842 shipped in during 2007; and 129,388 shipped out and 46,835 shipped in during 2006.

Feedlot Production

Feedlot production of livestock, mainly cattle, is a major industry in Texas. Annual fed cattle marketings totaled 5.73 million for feedlot capacity (head) of 1,000 and over in 2008. Texas lots marketed a total of 5.69 million head of grain-fed cattle in 2007, compared with 5.78 million in 2006 and 5.76 million in 2005. In recent years, more cattle have been fed in Texas than any other state in the United States.

During 2008, there were 128 feedlots in Texas with capacity of 1,000 animals or more. This compared with 128 in 2007, 130 in 2006, and 130 in 2005.

Federally inspected slaughter plants in Texas numbered 47 in 2008. This compared with 45 in 2007 and 43 in 2006. In 2008, the number of cattle slaughtered in Texas totaled 6.72 million cattle, 369,500 hogs, 5,200 sheep and lambs, and 18,700 calves. This compared with 6.09 million cattle, 356,500 hogs, 3,000 sheep and lambs, and 11,400 calves in 2007; and 6.46

million cattle, 334,000 hogs, 41,300 sheep and lambs, and 8,300 calves in 2006.

Feeding of cattle in commercial feedlots is a major economic development that has stimulated the establishment and expansion of beef slaughtering plants. Most of this development is in the Northern High Plains area of northwest Texas. This area alone accounts for around 91 percent of the cattle fed in the state as of Jan. 1, 2009.

Total feedlot marketings represented about 26 percent of total U.S. fed cattle marketings in Jan. 1, 2009. Large amounts of capital are required for feedlot operations. This has forced many lots to become custom feeding facilities.

Feedlots are concentrated on the High Plains largely because of extensive supplies of corn, sorghum and other feed. Beef breeding herds have increased most in East Texas, where grazing is abundant.

Dairying

The state's dairy industry is spread out across the northern half of Texas, with the trend toward larger operations. As of the Jan. 1, 2007, inventory, leading counties in milk production are Erath, Deaf Smith, Parmer, Hopkins, Castro, Comanche and Lubbock. Combined, these seven counties produce 58 percent of the milk in Texas, with Erath producing 16 percent of the total.

All the milk sold by Texas dairy farmers is marketed under the terms of Federal Marketing Orders. Most Texas dairymen are members of one of four marketing cooperatives. Associate Milk Producers, Inc., is the largest, representing the majority of the state's producers.

Texas dairy farmers received an average price for milk of $18.80 per hundred pounds in 2008, $19.70 in 2007, and $13.30 in 2006. A total of 8.389 billion pounds of milk was sold to plants and dealers in 2008, bringing in cash receipts from milk to dairy farmers of $1.569 billion. This compared with 7.379 billion pounds sold

Anne Jones raises dairy goats in Denton County and sells her goat cheese to local stores. Spanish and other types of goats numbered about 1 million in January 2009. The rest of the Texas goat herd are Angora goats, which are used for mohair production. More than half of the world's mohair is produced in Texas. Rex C. Curry photo.

in 2007 that brought in $1.45 billion in cash receipts. In 2006, Texas dairymen sold 7.124 billion pounds of milk, which brought in cash receipts of $947.5 million.

The annual average number of milk cows in Texas was 430,000 head as of Jan. 1, 2009, inventory. This compared with 418,000 head as of Jan. 1, 2008, and 389,000 as of Jan. 1, 2007. Average milk production per cow in the state has increased steadily over the past several decades. The average milk production per cow was 20,134 pounds in 2008, 18,982 pounds in 2007, and 21,328 pounds in 2006. Total milk production in Texas was 8.416 billion pounds in 2008, 7.384 billion pounds in 2007, and 7.145 billion pounds in 2006.

There were 1,200 operations reporting milk cows in Texas in 2007, 1,300 in 2006, and 1,500 in 2005.

Dairy Manufacturing

The major dairy products manufactured in Texas include condensed, evaporated and dry milk; creamery butter; and cheese. However, this data are not available because of the small number of manufacturing plants producing these products.

Frozen Desserts

Production of frozen desserts in Texas totaled 90.07 million gallons in 2007, 96.87 million gallons in 2006, and 82.61 million gallons in 2005. Production for regular ice cream in Texas in 2007 amounted to 61.5 million gallons, compared to 64.57 million gallons in 2006, and 54.8 million gallons in 2005. Regular ice cream mix produced in Texas in 2007 amounted to 33.08 million gallons; 35.26 million gallons in 2006; and 30.85 million gallons in 2005.

Sherbet mix in Texas totaled 916,000 gallons in 2007, 709,000 gallons in 2006, and 470,000 gallons in 2005. Sherbet production in 2007 totaled 1.29 million gallons, compared with 939,000 gallons in 2006, and 719,000 gallons in 2005.

Goats and Mohair

Goats in Texas numbered 1.12 million on Jan. 1, 2009. This compares with 1.185 million on Jan. 1, 2008, and 1.3 million on Jan. 1, 2007. They had a value of $129.92 million or $116 per head in 2009; $120.87 million or $102 per head in 2008; and $150.8 million or $116 per head as of Jan. 1, 2007.

The goat herd consists of Angora goats for mohair production. Angora goats totaled 120,000 as of Jan. 1, 2009; 134,000 as of Jan. 1, 2008; and 180,000 as of Jan. 1, 2007. Spanish goats and others numbered 1 million as of Jan. 1, 2009; 1.05 million as of 2008; and 1.12 million as of Jan. 1, 2007.

Mohair production during 2008 totaled 820,000 pounds. This compares with 960,000 in 2007, and 1.1 million pounds in 2006. Average price per pound in 2008 was $3.80 from 130,000 goats clipped for a total value of $3.116 million. In 2007, producers received $4 per pound from 150,000 goats clipped for a total value of $3.84 million. In 2006, producers received $4 per pound from 170,000 goats clipped for a total value of $4.4 million. This is a sharp drop from 16.2 million pounds with a value of $42.6 million in 1987.

More than half of the world's mohair and 67 percent of the U.S. clip are produced in Texas. The leading Texas counties in Angora goats as of Jan. 1, 2008, are: Edwards, Sutton, Val Verde, Kinney, Uvalde and Terrell.

Horses

Nationally, Texas ranks as one of the leading states in horse numbers and is the headquarters for many national horse organizations. The largest single-breed registry in America, the American Quarter Horse Association, has its headquarters in Amarillo.

The headquarters of the National Cutting Horse Association and the American Paint Horse Association are both located in Fort Worth. In addition to these

Goats and Mohair
1900–2009

Year	Goats		Mohair	
	Number	Farm Value	Production (lbs)	Value
1900	627,000	$924,000	961,000	$268,000
1910	1,135,000	2,514,000	1,998,000	468,000
1920	1,753,000	9,967,000	6,786,000	1,816,000
1930	2,965,000	14,528,000	14,800,000	4,995,000
1940	3,300,000	10,560,000	18,250,000	9,308,000
1950	2,295,000	13,082,000	12,643,000	9,735,000
1960	3,339,000	29,383,000	23,750,000	21,375,000
1970	2,572,000	19,033,000	17,985,000	7,032,000
1980	1,400,000	64,400,000	8,800,000	30,800,000
1981	1,380,000	53,130,000	10,100,000	35,350,000
1982	1,410,000	57,810,000	10,000,000	25,500,000
1983	1,420,000	53,250,000	10,600,000	42,930,000
1984	1,450,000	82,215,000	10,600,000	48,160,000
1985	1,590,000	76,797,000	13,300,000	45,885,000
1986	1,770,000	70,977,000	16,000,000	40,160,000
1987	1,780,000	82,592,000	16,200,000	42,606,000
1988	1,800,000	108,180,000	15,400,000	29,876,000
1989	1,850,000	100,270,000	15,400,000	24,794,000
1990	1,900,000	93,100,000	14,500,000	13,775,000
1991	1,830,000	73,200,000	14,800,000	19,388,000
1992	2,000,000	84,000,000	14,200,000	12,354,000
1993	1,960,000	84,280,000	13,490,000	11,197,000
1994	1,960,000	74,480,000	11,680,000	30,602,000
1995	1,850,000	81,400,000	11,319,000	20,940,000
1996	1,900,000	89,300,000	7,490,000	14,606,000
1997	1,650,000	70,950,000	6,384,000	14,556,000
1998	1,400,000	71,400,000	4,650,000	12,044,000
1999	1,350,000	71,550,000	2,550,000	9,384,000
2000	1,300,000	74,100,000	2,346,000	10,088,000
2001	1,400,000	105,000,000	1,716,000	3,775,000
2002	1,250,000	106,250,000	1,944,000	3,110,400
2003	1,200,000	110,400,000	1,680,000	2,856,000
2004	1,200,000	115,200,000	1,620,000	3,402,000
2005	1,270,000	138,430,000	1,250,000	3,750,000
2006	1,310,000	140,170,000	1,100,000	4,400,000
2007	1,300,000	150,800,000	960,000	3,840,000
2008	1,185,000	120,870,000	820,000	3,116,000
2009	1,120,000	129,920,000	NA	NA

NA = not available.
Source: "1985 Texas Livestock, Dairy and Poultry Statistics,"
USDA Bulletin 235, June 1986. "Texas Agricultural Facts,"
Crop and Livestock Reporting Service, various years; "1993
Texas Livestock Statistics," Texas Agricultural Statistics
Service, Bulletin 252, August 1994; "Texas Agricultural
Statistics, 2007," October 2008; "Texas Ag Facts," February
and March 2009.

national associations, Texas also has active state associations that include Palominos, Arabians, Thoroughbreds, Appaloosa and Ponies.

Horses are still used to support the state's giant beef cattle and sheep industries. However, the largest horse numbers within the state are near urban and suburban areas, where they are mostly used for recreation. State participation activities consist of horse shows, trail rides, play days, rodeos, polo and horse racing. Residential subdivisions have been developed within the state to provide facilities for urban and suburban horse owners.

Poultry and Eggs

Poultry and eggs contributed about 9.1 percent to the average yearly cash receipts of Texas farmers in 2007. On Jan. 1, 2008, Texas ranked sixth among the states in broilers produced, fifth in eggs produced and seventh in hens produced.

In 2007, cash receipts to Texas producers from the production of poultry and eggs totaled $1.865 billion. This compares with $1.528 billion in 2006 and $1.731 billion in 2005.

Value of production from eggs was $460.3 million in 2008; $373.5 million in 2007; and $254.05 million in 2006. Eggs produced in 2008 totaled 4.93 billion, compared with 5 billion in 2007 and 5.05 billion in 2006. The average price received per dozen in 2008 was $1.12, compared with 89.7 cents in 2007, and 60.3 cents in 2006.

Broiler production in 2008 totaled 640.8 million birds, compared with 616.3 million in 2007, and 628.3 million in 2006. Value of production from broilers totaled $1.557 billion in 2008, $1.405 billion in 2007, and $1.199 billion in 2006. Price per pound averaged 45 cents in 2008, 43 cents in 2007, and 36 cents in 2006.

Sheep and Wool

Sheep and lambs in Texas numbered 870,000 head on Jan. 1, 2009, compared to 960,000 as of Jan. 1, 2008, and 1.05 million as of Jan. 1, 2007. All sheep were valued at $87.87 million or $101 per head on Jan. 1, 2009, compared with $97.92 million or $102 per head as of Jan. 1, 2008, and $111.3 million or $106 per head as of Jan. 1, 2007.

Breeding ewes one year old and over numbered 666,000 as of Jan. 1, 2009; 730,000 as of Jan. 1, 2008; and 810,000 as of Jan. 1, 2007. Replacement lambs less than one year old totaled 100,000 head as of Jan. 1, 2009; 100,000 as of Jan. 1, 2008; and 105,000 as of Jan. 1, 2007. Sheep and lamb operations in Texas were

There were 4.93 billion eggs produced in Texas in 2008, which were valued at $460.3 million. Texas ranks fifth in the United States in eggs production. Cheryl Diaz Meyer photo.

Research assistant Anna Johnson of Texas Tech University secures a video camera on top of a farrowing hut to moni-tor the behavior of a sow and her piglets at the university's Sustainable Pork Farm near Lubbock. The farm allows the animals to roam freely, and they are not treated with antibiotics. Scott Bauer photo; USDA Agricultural Research Service.

estimated to be 8,700 as of Jan. 1, 2009; 7,300 as of Jan. 1, 2008; and 7,200 as of Jan. 1, 2007.

Texas wool production in 2008 was 4.2 million pounds from 600,000 sheep. Value totaled $4.87 million or $1.16 per pound. This compared with 4.5 million pounds of wool from 620,000 sheep valued at $5.45 million or $1.21 per pound in 2007; and 4.9 million pounds from 700,000 sheep valued at $4.46 million or 91 cents per pound in 2006.

Most sheep and lambs in Texas are concentrated in the Edwards Plateau area of West-Central Texas and nearby counties. As of Jan. 1, 2008, the 10 leading counties are: Crockett, Val Verde, Tom Green, Pecos, Gillespie, Schleicher, Concho, Sutton, Mills and Edwards. Sheep production largely has a dual purpose, for both wool and lamb production.

San Angelo long has been the largest sheep and wool market in the United States and the center for wool and mohair warehouses, scouring plants and slaughterhouses.

Swine

Texas had 1.12 million head of swine on hand, Dec. 1, 2008 — only 1.7 percent of the U.S. swine herd. Swine producers in the state produce about 1.69 million head marketed annually.

Although the number of farms producing hogs has steadily decreased over the years, the size of production units has increased substantially.

In 2008, 1.69 million head of hogs were marketed in Texas, producing 315.52 million pounds of pork valued at $40.50 per 100 pounds, or $127.9 million. In 2007, 1.48 million head of hogs were marketed, producing 273.21 million pounds of pork valued at $107.82 million, or $39.70 per 100 pounds.

Figures for 2006 were 1.45 million head marketed, and 257.64 million pounds of pork produced with a value of $104.9 million, or $40.80 per 100 pounds. ☆

Hog Production 1960–2008

Year	Production (1,000 Pounds)	Avg. Market Wt. (Pounds)	Avg. Price Per Cwt. (Dollars)	Gross Income (1,000 Dollars)
1960	288,844	228	$14.70	$44,634
1970	385,502	241	22.50	75,288
1980	315,827	259	35.90	111,700
1981	264,693	256	41.70	121,054
1982	205,656	256	49.60	112,726
1983	209,621	256	45.20	95,343
1984	189,620	262	45.50	95,657
1985	168,950	266	43.40	72,512
1986	176,660	269	47.30	82,885
1987	216,834	NA	50.60	103,983
1988	236,658	NA	41.30	100,029
1989	224,229	NA	39.90	93,178
1990	196,225	NA	48.20	92,222
1991	207,023	NA	45.10	97,398
1992	217,554	NA	36.40	79,436
1993	221,130	NA	39.90	90,561
1994	224,397	NA	35.10	78,394
1995	221,323	NA	35.50	81,509
1996	203,761	NA	45.90	93,526
1997	224,131	NA	47.40	106,238
1998	270,977	NA	30.70	83,190
1999	274,572	NA	27.50	71,604
2000	328,732	NA	36.60	115,105
2001	260,875	NA	39.10	105,217
2002	223,441	NA	28.70	67,255
2003	197,876	NA	33.60	67,998
2004	202,199	NA	44.90	90,349
2005	223,375	NA	45.40	105,989
2006	259,989	NA	40.80	109,318
2007	273,213	NA	39.70	95,581
2008	315,521	NA	NA	132,435

NA = not available.
Source: "1985 Texas Livestock, Dairy and Poultry Statistics," USDA, Bulletin 235, June 1986, pp. 32, 46; 1991 "Texas Livestock Statistics"; USDA, "Meat Animals—Prod., Dips., & Income," April 2008 and May 2009; "1993 Texas Livestock Statistics," Bulletin 252, Texas Agricultural Statistics Service, August 1994; "Texas Agricultural Facts, 2007," October, 2008; "Texas Ag Facts", various years (Dec. 1 previous year).

Texas Sheep and Wool Production
1850–2007

Year	Sheep *Number	Sheep Value	Wool Production (lbs)	Wool Value	Year	Sheep *Number	Sheep Value	Wool Production (lbs)	Wool Value
1850	100,530	N A	131,917	N A	1989	1,870,000	133,445,000	18,000,000	27,180,000
1860	753,363	N A	1,493,363	N A	1990	2,090,000	133,760,000	17,400,000	19,662,000
1870	1,223,000	$2,079,000	N A	N A	1991	2,000,000	108,000,000	16,700,000	13,861,000
1880	6,024,000	12,048,000	N A	N A	1992	2,140,000	111,280,000	17,600,000	16,896,000
1890	4,752,000	7,128,000	N A	N A	1993	2,040,000	118,320,000	17,000,000	11,050,000
1900	2,416,000	4,590,000	9,630,000	N A	1994	1,895,000	106,120,000	14,840,000	15,582,000
1910	1,909,000	5,536,000	8,943,000	$1,699,170	1995	1,700,000	100,300,000	13,468,000	15,488,000
1920	3,360,000	33,600,000	22,813,000	5,019,000	1996	1,650,000	108,900,000	9,900,000	8,316,000
1930	6,304,000	44,758,000	48,262,000	10,135,000	1997	1,400,000	100,800,000	10,950,000	11,607,000
1940	10,069,000	49,413,000	79,900,000	23,171,000	1998	1,530,000	122,400,000	9,230,000	5,815,000
1950	6,756,000	103,877,000	51,480,000	32,947,000	1999	1,350,000	95,850,000	7,956,000	3,898,000
1960	5,938,000	85,801,000	51,980,000	21,832,000	2000	1,200,000	94,800,000	7,506,000	3,678,000
1970	3,708,000	73,602,000	30,784,000	11,082,000	2001	1,150,000	92,000,000	6,003,000	3,122,000
1980	2,400,000	138,000,000	18,300,000	17,751,000	2002	1,130,000	88,140,000	5,950,000	4,046,000
1981	2,360,000	116,820,000	20,500,000	24,600,000	2003	1,040,000	82,160,000	5,600,000	5,040,000
1982	2,400,000	100,800,000	19,300,000	16,212,000	2004	1,100,000	105,600,000	5,600,000	5,712,000
1983	2,225,000	86,775,000	18,600,000	15,438,000	2005	1,070,000	112,350,000	5,550,000	5,328,000
1984	1,970,000	76,830,000	17,500,000	16,100,000	2006	1,090,000	124,260,000	4,900,000	4,459,000
1985	1,930,000	110,975,000	16,200,000	13,284,000	2007	1,050,000	111,300,000	4,500,000	5,445,000
1986	1,850,000	107,300,000	16,400,000	13,284,000	2008	960,000	97,920,000	4,200,000	4,872,000
1987	2,050,000	133,250,000	16,400,000	19,844,000	2009	870,000	87,870,000	NA	NA
1988	2,040,000	155,040,000	18,200,000	35,854,000					

NA = not available.
Source: "1985 Texas Livestock, Dairy and Poultry Statistics," USDA Bulletin 235, June 1986. "Texas Agricultural Facts" Annual Summary, Crop and Livestock Reporting Service, various years, "1993 Texas Livestock Statistics," Texas Agricultural Statistics Service, Bulletin 252, August 1994; "Texas Agricultural Statistics, 2007", October 2008, "Texas Ag Facts," February and March 2009.

The running of the sheep takes place each September in San Angelo in Tom Green County. San Angelo long has been the largest sheep and wool market in the United States and the center for wool and mohair warehouses, scouring plants and slaughterhouses. Photo courtesy of the San Angelo Convention & Visitor's Bureau.

Appendix

The Guadalupe Mountains from Dell City. Robert Plocheck photo.

Pronunciation Guide

State Obituaries

Index of Entries

Texas Pronunciation Guide

Texas' rich cultural diversity is reflected nowhere better than in the names of places. Standard pronunciation is used in many cases, but purely colloquial pronunciation often is used, too.

In the late 1940s, George Mitchel Stokes, a graduate student at Baylor University, developed a list of pronunciations of 2,300 place names across the state. Stokes earned his doctorate and served as director of the speech division in the communications studies department at Baylor University. He retired in 1983.

In the following list based on Stokes longer list, pronunciation is by respelling and diacritical marking. Respelling is employed as follows: "ah" as in the exclamation, ah, or the "o" in tot; "ee" as in meet; "oo" as in moot; "yoo" as in use; "ow" as in cow; "oi" as in oil; "uh" as in mud.

Note that ah, uh and the apostrophe(') are used for varying degrees of neutral vowel sounds, the apostrophe being used where the vowel is barely sounded. Diacritical markings are used as follows: bāle, băd, lĕt, rīse, rĭll, ōak, broōd, foŏt.

The stressed syllable is capitalized. Secondary stress is indicated by an underline as in Atascosa — <u>ăt</u> uhs KŌ suh.

A

Abbott — Ă buht
Abernathy — Ă ber nă thĭ
Abilene — ĂB uh leen
Acala — uh KĀ luh
Ackerly — ĂK er lĭ
Acme — ĂK mĭ
Acton — ĂK t'n
Acuff — Ā kuhf
Adamsville — Ă d'mz vĭl
Addicks — Ă dĭks
Addielou — ă dĭ LŌŌ
Addison — A di s'n
Adkins — ĂT kĭnz
Adrian — Ā drĭ uhn
Afton — ĀF t'n
Agua Dulce — ah wuh DŌŌL sĭ
Agua Nueva — ah wuh nyoō Ā vuh
Aiken — Ā kĭn
Alamo — ĂL uh mō
Alamo Heights — ăl uh mō HĬTS
Alanreed — ĂL uhn <u>reed</u>
Alba — ĂL buh
Albany — AWL buh nĭ
Albert — ĂL bert
Aledo — uh LEE dō
Alexander — ĕl ĭg ZĂN der
Alfred — ĂL frĕd
Algoa — ăl GŌ uh
Alice — Ă lĭs
Alief — Ă leef
Allen — Ă lĭn
Allenfarm — ălĭn FAHRM
Alleyton — Ă lĭ t'n
Allison — ĂL uh s'n
Alma — AHL muh
Alpine — ĂL pĭn
Altair — awl TĂR
Alta Loma — ăl tuh LŌ muh
Alto — ĂL tō
Altoga — ăl TŌ guh
Alvarado — ăl vuh RĂ dō
Alvin — ĂL vĭn
Alvord — ĂL vord
Amarillo — <u>ăm</u> uh RĬL ō
Amherst — AM <u>herst</u>
Ammannsville — ĂM 'nz vĭl
Anahuac — ĂN uh wăk

Anderson — ĂN der s'n
Andice — ĂN dĭs
Andrews — ĂN drooz
Angelina — <u>ăn</u> juh LEE nuh
Angleton — ĂNG g'l t'n
Anna — ĂN uh
Annona — ă NŌ nuh
Anson — ĂN s'n
Antelope — ĂNT uh lōp
Anton — ĂNT n
Appleby — Ă p'l bĭ
Apple Springs — <u>ă</u> p'l SPRĬNGZ
Aquilla — uh KWĬL uh
Aransas — uh RĂN zuhs
Aransas Pass — uh <u>răn</u> zuhs PĂS
Arbala — ahr BĀ luh
Arcadia — ahr KĂ dĭ uh
Archer — AHR cher
Archer City — ahr cher SĬT ĭ
Arcola — ahr KŌ luh
Argo — AHR gō
Argyle — ahr GĬL
Arlington — AHR lĭng t'n
Arneckeville — AHR nĭ kĭ vĭl
Arnett — AHR nĭt
Arp — ahrp
Artesia Wells — ahr <u>tee</u> zh' WĔLZ
Arthur City — ahr ther SĬT ĭ
Asherton — ĂSH er t'n
Aspermont — ĂS per mahnt
Atascosa — <u>ăt</u> uhs KŌ suh
Athens — Ă thĕnz
Atlanta — ăt LĂN tuh
Atlas — ĂT l's
Attoyac — AT uh yăk
Aubrey — AW brĭ
Augusta — aw GUHS tuh
Austin — AWS t'n
Austonio — aws TŌ nĭ ō
Austwell — AWS wĕl
Avalon — ĀV uhl n
Avery — Ā vuh rĭ
Avinger — Ă vĭn jer
Avoca — uh VŌ kuh
Axtell — ĂKS t'l
Azle — Ā z'l

B

Bagwell — BĂG w'l

Bailey — BĀ lĭ
Baileyboro — BĀ lĭ <u>ber</u> ruh
Baileyville — BĀ lĭ vĭl
Baird — bărd
Bakersfield — BĀ kers <u>feeld</u>
Balch Springs — bawlch or bawlk SPRĬNGZ
Ballinger — BĂL ĭn jer
Balmorhea — băl muh RĂ
Bandera — băn DĔR uh
Bangs — băngz
Banquete — băn KĔ tĭ
Barclay — BAHRK lĭ
Bardwell — BAHRD w'l
Barker — BAHR ker
Barksdale — BAHRKS dāl
Barnhart — BAHRN hahrt
Barnum — BAHR n'm
Barry — BĂ rĭ
Barstow — BAHRS tō
Bartlett — BAHRT lĭt
Bassett — BĂ sĭt
Bastrop — BĂS trahp
Batesville — BĀTS v'l
Batson — BĂT s'n
Baxter — BĂKS ter
Bay City — ba SĬT ĭ
Baylor — BĀ ler
Bayside — BĀ sīd
Baytown — BĀ town
Beasley — BEEZ lĭ
Beaukiss — bō KĬS
Beaumont — BŌ mahnt
Bebe — bee bee
Beckville — BĔK v'l
Becton — BĔK t'n
Bedias — BEE dĭs
Bee — bee
Beehouse — BEE hows
Beeville — BEE vĭl
Belcherville — BĔL cher vĭl
Bell — bĕl
Bellaire — bĕl ĂR
Bellevue — BĔL vyoō
Bellmead — bĕl MEED
Bells — bĕlz
Bellville — BĔL vĭl
Belmont — BĔL mahnt
Belton — BĔL t'n

Ben Arnold — bĕn AHR n'ld
Benavides — <u>bĕn</u> uh VEE d's
Ben Bolt — bĕn BŌLT
Benbrook — BĬN brŏŏk
Benchley — BĔNCH lĭ
Bend — bĕnd
Ben Franklin — bĕn FRĂNGk lĭn
Ben Hur — bĕn HER
Benjamin — BĔN juh m'n
Bennett — BĔN ĭt
Bentonville — BĔNT n vĭl
Ben Wheeler — bĭn HWEE ler
Berclair — ber KLĂR
Bertram — BERT r'm
Bessmay — bĕs MĂ
Best — bĕst
Bettie — BĔT ĭ
Bexar — BA är or băr
Beyersville — BĬRZ vĭl
Biardstown — BĂRDZ t'n
Bigfoot — BĬG fŏŏt
Big Lake — bĭg LĂK
Big Sandy — bĭg SĂN dĭ
Big Spring — bĭg SPRĬNG
Big Wells — bĭg WĔLZ
Birdville — BERD vĭl
Birome — bī RŌM
Birthright — BERTH rĭt
Bishop — BĬ sh'p
Bivins — BĬ vĭnz
Black — blăk
Blackfoot — BLĂK fŏŏt
Blackwell — BLĂK w'l
Blair — blăr
Blanchard — BLĂN cherd
Blanco — BLĂNG kō
Blanket — BLĂNG kĭt
Bleakwood — BLEEK wŏŏd
Bledsoe — BLĔD sō
Blessing — BLĔ sĭng
Blewett — BLŌŌ ĭt
Blooming Grove — <u>blŏŏ</u> mĭng
   GRŌV
Bloomington — BLŌŌM ĭng t'n
Blossom — BLAH s'm
Blue Grove — blŏŏ GRŌV
Blue Ridge — blŏŏ RĬJ
Bluff Dale — BLUHF dāl
Bluffton — BLUHF t'n
Blum — bluhm
Boerne — BER nĭ
Bogata — buh GŌ duh
Boling — BŌL ĭng
Bolivar — BAH lĭ ver
Bomarton — BŌ mer t'n
Bonham — BAH n'm
Bonita — bō NEE tuh
Bonney — BAH nĭ
Bonus — BŌ n's
Bon Wier — bahn WEER
Booker — BŌŌ ker
Boonsville — BŌŌNZ vĭl
Booth — bŏŏth
Borden — BAWRD n
Borger — BŌR ger
Bosque — BAHS kĭ

Boston — BAWS t'n
Bovina — bō VEE nuh
Bowie — BŌŌ Ĭ
Boxelder — bahks ĔL der
Boyce — bawĭs
Boyd — boĭd
Brachfield — BRĂCH feeld
Bracken — BRĂ kĭn
Brackettville — BRĂ kĭt vĭl
Bradford — BRĂD ferd
Bradshaw — BRĂD shaw
Brady — BRĂ dĭ
Brandon — BRĂN d'n
Brashear — bruh SHĬR
Brazoria — bruh ZŌ rĭ uh
Brazos — BRĂZ uhs
Breckenridge — BRĔK uhn rĭj
Bremond — <u>bree</u> MAHND
Brenham — BRĔ n'm
Brewster — BRŌŌ ster
Brice — brĭs
Bridgeport — BRĬJ pōrt
Briggs — brĭgz
Briscoe — BRĬS kō
Britton — BRĬT n
Broaddus — BRAW d's
Brock — brahk
Bronson — BRAHN s'n
Bronte — brahnt
Brookeland — BRŌŌK l'nd
Brookesmith — BRŌŌK smith
Brooks — brŏŏks
Brookshire — BRŌŌK sher
Brookston — BRŌŌKS t'n
Brown — brown
Browndel — brown DĔL
Brownfield — BROWN feeld
Brownsboro — BROWNZ <u>buh</u> ruh
Brownsville — BROWNZ vĭl
Brownwood — BROWN wŏŏd
Bruceville — BRŌŌS v'l
Brundage — BRUHN dĭj
Bruni — BRŌŌ nĭ
Brushy Creek — bruh shĭ KREEK
Bryan — BRĪ uhn
Bryans Mill — brī 'nz MĬL
Bryarly — BRĪ er lĭ
Bryson — BRĪ s'n
Buchanan Dam — buhk <u>hăn</u> uhn
   DĂM
Buckholts — BUHK hōlts
Buckhorn — BUHK hawrn
Buda — BYŌŌ duh
Buena Vista — <u>bwā</u> nuh VEES tuh
Buffalo — BUHF uh lō
Buffalo Gap — <u>buhf</u> uh lō GĂP
Buffalo Springs — <u>buhf</u> uh lō
   SPRĬNGZ
Bula — BYŌŌ luh
Bullard — BŎŎL erd
Bulverde — bŏŏl VER dĭ
Buna — BYŌŌ nuh
Burkburnett — <u>berk</u> ber NET
Burkett — BER kĭt
Burkeville — BERK vĭl
Burleson — BER luh s'n

Burlington — BER lĭng t'n
Burnet — BER nĕt
Burton — BERT n
Bushland — BŎŎSH l'nd
Bustamante — <u>buhs</u> tuh MAHN tĭ
Butler — BUHT ler
Byers — BĪ erz
Bynum — BĪ n'm
Byrd — berd

C

Cactus — KĂK t's
Caddo Mills — <u>kă</u> dō MĬLZ
Calallen — kăl ĂL ĭn
Calaveras — kăl uh VĔR's
Caldwell — KAHL wĕl
Calhoun — kăl HŌŌN
Call — kawl
Calliham — KĂL uh hăm
Callisburg — KĂ lĭs berg
Call Junction — kawl JUHNGK sh'n
Calvert — KĂL vert
Camden — KĂM dĭn
Cameron — KĂM uh r'n
Camilla — kuh MEEL yuh
Camp — kămp
Campbell — KĂM uhl
Campbellton — KĂM uhl t'n
Camp Wood — kămp WŎŎD
Canadian — <u>kuh</u> NĂ dĭ uhn
Candelaria — kăn duh LĔ rĭ uh
Canton — KĂNT n
Canyon — KĂN y'n
Caplen — KĂP lĭn
Caps — kăps
Caradan — KĂR uh dăn
Carbon — KAHR b'n
Carey — KĂ rĭ
Carlisle — KAHR lĭl
Carlsbad — KAHR uhlz băd
Carlton — KAHR uhl t'n
Carmine — kahr MEEN
Carmona — <u>kahr</u> MŌ nuh
Caro — KAH rō
Carrizo Springs — kuh <u>ree</u> zuh
   SPRĬNGZ
Carrollton — KĂR 'l t'n
Carson — KAHR s'n
Carthage — KAHR thĭj
Cash — kăsh
Cason — KĂ s'n
Cass — kăs
Castell — kăs TĔL
Castro — KĂS trō
Castroville — KĂS tro vĭl
Catarina — kăt uh REE nuh
Cat Spring — kăt SPRĬNG
Caviness — KĂ vĭ nĕs
Cayuga — kă YŌŌ guh
Cedar Bayou — <u>see</u> der BĪ ō
Cedar Creek — <u>see</u> der KREEK
Cedar Hill — <u>see</u> der HĬL
Cedar Lake — <u>see</u> der LĂK
Cedar Lane — <u>see</u> der LĂN
Cedar Park — <u>see</u> der PAHRK
Cedar Valley — <u>see</u> der VA lĭ

Diacritical markings are used as follows: bāle, băd, lĕt, rise, rĭll, ōak, brŏŏd, fŏŏt. The stressed syllable is capitalized. Secondary stress is indicated by an underline as in Atascosa — <u>ăt</u> uhs KŌ suh. TEXAS ALMANAC ©.

Painted buffaloes in Midland. Robert Plocheck photo.

coons

Cee Vee — <u>see</u> VEE
Celeste — suh LĔST
Celina — suh LĪ nuh
Center — SENT er
Center City — sĕn ter SĬT ĭ
Center Point — sĕn ter POINT
Centerville — sĕn ter vĭl
Centralia — sĕn TRĀL yuh
Chalk — chawlk
Chalk Mountain — chawlk MOWNT n
Chambers — CHĂM berz
Chandler — CHĂND ler
Channelview — <u>chăn</u> uhl VYŌŌ
Channing — CHĂN ĭng
Chapman Ranch — chăp m'n RĂNCH
Chappell Hill — chă p'l HĬL
Charco — CHAHR kō
Charleston — CHAHR uhls t'n
Charlie — CHAHR lĭ
Charlotte — SHAHR l't
Chatfield — CHĂT feeld
Cheapside — CHEEP sīd
Cheek — cheek
Cherokee — CHĔR uh <u>kee</u>
Chester — CHĔS ter
Chico — CHEE kō
Chicota — chĭ KŌ tuh
Childress — CHĬL drĕs
Chillicothe — <u>chĭl</u> ĭ KAH thĭ
Chilton — CHĬL t'n
China — CHĪ nuh
China Spring — chī nuh SPRĬNG
Chireno — sh' REE nō
Chisholm — CHĬZ uhm
Chita — CHEE tuh
Chocolate Bayou — <u>chah</u> kuh lĭt BĪ ō
Choice — chois
Chriesman — KRĬS m'n
Christine — krĭs TEEN
Christoval — krĭs TŌ v'l
Cibolo — SEE bō lō
Circle Back — SER k'l băk
Circleville — SER k'l vĭl
Cisco — SĬS kō

Cistern — SĬS tern
Clairemont — KLĂR mahnt
Clairette — klăr ĭ ĔT
Clarendon — KLĂR ĭn d'n
Clareville — KLĂR vĭl
Clarksville — KLAHRKS vĭl
Clarkwood — KLAHRK wŏŏd
Claude — klawd
Clawson — KLAW s'n
Clay — klā
Clayton — KLĀT n
Clear Lake — KLĬR lăk
Clear Spring — klĭr SPRĬNG
Cleburne — KLEE bern
Clemville — KLĔM vĭl
Cleveland — KLEEV l'nd
Clifton — KLĬF t'n
Cline — klīn
Clint — klĭnt
Clodine — klaw DEEN
Clute — klŏŏt
Clyde — klīd
Coahoma — kuh HŌ muh
Cockrell Hill — kahk ruhl HĬL
Coke — kōk
Coldspring — KŌLD sprĭng
Coleman — KŌL m'n
Colfax — KAHL făks
Collegeport — kah lĭj PŌRT
College Station — <u>kah</u> lĭj STĀ sh'n
Collin — KAH lĭn
Collingsworth — KAH lĭnz werth
Collinsville — KAH lĭnz vĭl
Colmesneil — KŌL m's neel
Colorado — <u>kahl</u> uh RAH dō
Colorado City — kah luh <u>ră</u> duh SĬT ĭ
Columbus — kuh LUHM b's
Comal — KŌ măl
Comanche — kuh MĂN chĭ
Combes — kōmz
Comfort — KUHM fert
Commerce — KAH mers
Como — KŌ mō
Comstock — KAHM stahk
Concan — KAHN kăn
Concepcion — kuhn sep sĭ ŌN

Concho — KAHN chō
Concord — KAHN kawrd
Concrete — kahn KREET
Cone — kōn
Conlen — KAHN lĭn
Conroe — KAHN rō
Converse — KAHN vers
Conway — KAHN wā
Cooke — kŏŏk
Cookville — KŌŌK vĭl
Coolidge — KŌŌ lĭj
Cooper — KŌŌ per
Copeville — KŌP v'l
Coppell — kuhp PĔL or kuh PĔL
Copperas Cove — kahp ruhs KŌV
Corbett — KAWR bĭt
Cordele — kawr DĔL
Corinth — KAH rĭnth
Corley — KAWR lĭ
Corpus Christi — <u>kawr</u> p's KRĬS tĭ
Corrigan — KAWR uh g'n
Corsicana — <u>kawr</u> sĭ KĂN uh
Coryell — kō rĭ ĔL
Cost — kawst
Cottle — KAH t'l
Cotton Center — <u>kaht</u> n SĔNT er
Cotton Gin — KAHT n jĭn
Cottonwood — KAHT n wŏŏd
Cotulla — kuh TŌŌ luh
Coupland — KŌP l'n
Courtney — KŌRT nĭ
Covington — KUHV ĭng t'n
Coy City — koi SĬT ĭ
Craft — krăft
Crafton — KRĂF t'n
Crandall — KRĂN d'l
Crane — krān
Cranfills Gap — krăn f'lz GĂP
Crawford — KRAW ferd
Creedmore — KREED mōr
Cresson — KRĔ s'n
Crisp — krĭsp
Crockett — KRAH kĭt
Crosby — KRAWZ bĭ
Crosbyton — KRAWZ bĭ t'n
Cross — kraws
Cross Cut — KRAWS kuht

Diacritical markings are used as follows: bāle, băd, lĕt, rīse, rĭll, ōak, brōōd, fŏŏt. The stressed syllable is capitalized. Secondary stress is indicated by an underline as in Atascosa — <u>ăt</u> uhs KŌ suh. TEXAS ALMANAC ©.

Cross Plains — kraws PLĂNZ
Cross Roads — KRAWS rōdz
Crow — krō
Crowell — KRŌ uhl
Crowley — KROW li
Crystal City — krĭs t'l SĬT ĭ
Crystal Falls — krĭs t'l FAWLZ
Cuero — KWĔR o
Culberson — KUHL ber s'n
Cumby — KUHM bĭ
Cuney — KYŌŌ nĭ
Cunningham — KUHN ĭng hăm
Currie — KER rĭ
Cushing — KŌŌ shĭng
Cuthand — KUHT hănd
Cyclone — SĪ klōn
Cypress — SĪ prĕs

D

Dabney — DĂB nĭ
Dacosta — duh KAHS tuh
Dacus — DĂ k's
Daingerfield — DĂN jer feeld
Daisetta — dā ZĔT uh
Dalby Springs — dĂl bĭ SPRĬNGZ
Dale — dāl
Dalhart — DĂL hahrt
Dallam — DĂL uhm
Dallas — DĂ luhs
Damon — DĂ m'n
Danbury — DĂN bĕrĭ
Danciger — DĂN sĭ ger
Danevang — DĂN uh văng
Darrouzett — dăr uh ZĔT
Davilla — duh VĬL uh
Dawn — dawn
Dawson — DAW s'n
Dayton — DĀT n
Deadwood — DĔD wŏŏd
Deaf Smith — dĕf SMĬTH
Deanville — DEEN vĭl
DeBerry — duh BĔ rĭ
Decatur — dee KĀT er
Deer Park — dĭr PAHRK
De Kalb — dĭ KĂB
De Leon — da lee AHN
Del Rio — dĕl REE ō
Delta — DĔL tuh
Del Valle — dĕl VĂ lĭ
Delwin — DĔl wĭn
Denhawken — DĬN haw kĭn
Denison — DĔN uh s'n
Denning — DĔN ĭng
Dennis — DĔ nĭs
Denton — DĔNT n
Denver City — dĕn ver SĬT ĭ
Deport — dĭ PŌRT
Derby — DER bĭ
Desdemona — dĕz dĭ MŌ nuh
DeSoto — dĭ SŌ tuh
Detroit — dee TROIT
Devers — DĔ vers
Devine — duh VĬN
Dew — dyōō
Deweyville — DYŌŌ ĭ vĭl
DeWitt — dĭ WĬT

Dewville — DYŌŌ vĭl
Dexter — DĔKS ter
D'Hanis — duh HĂ nĭs
Dialville — DĬ uhl vil
Diboll — DĬ bawl
Dickens — DĬK Ĭnz
Dickinson — DĬK ĭn s'n
Dike — dĭk
Dilley — DĬL i
Dilworth — DĬL werth
Dimebox — dĩm BAHKS
Dimmit — DĬM ĭt
Dinero — dĭ NĔ rō
Direct — duh RĔKT
Dixon — DĬK s'n
Dobbin — DAH bĬn
Dobrowolski — dah bruh WAHL skĭ
Dodd City — dahd SĬT ĭ
Dodge — DAH j
Dodson — DAHD s'n
Donie — DŌ nĭ
Donley — DAHN lĭ
Donna — dah nuh
Doole — DOO lĭ
Dorchester — dawr CHĔS ter
Doss — daws
Doucette — DŌŌ sĕt
Dougherty — DAHR tĭ
Douglass — DUHG l's
Douglassville — DUHG lĭs vĭl
Downing — DOWN ĭng
Downsville — DOWNZ vĭl
Dozier — DŌ zher
Draw — draw
Driftwood — DRĬFT wŏŏd
Dripping Springs — drĭp ĭng SPRĬNGZ
Driscoll — DRĬS k'l
Dryden — DRĬD n
Dublin — DUHB lĭn
Duffau — DUHF ō
Dumas — DŌŌ m's
Dumont — DYŌŌ mahnt
Dundee — DUHN dĭ
Dunlap — DUHN lăp
Dunlay — DUHN lĭ
Dunn — duhn
Durango — duh RĂNG gō
Duval — DŌŌ vawl

E

Eagle — EE g'l
Eagle Lake — ee g'l LĀK
Eagle Pass — ee g'l PĂS
Earth — erth
East Bernard — eest ber NAHRD
Easterly — EES ter lĭ
Eastland — EEST l'nd
Easton — EES t'n
Ector — ĔK ter
Edcouch — ĕd KOWCH
Eddy — E di
Eden — EED n
Edge — ĕj
Edgewood — ĔJ wŏŏd
Edinburg — ĔD n berg

Edmonson — ĔD m'n s'n
Edna — ED nuh
Edom — EE d'm
Edroy — ĔD roi
Edwards — ĔD werdz
Egan — EE g'n
Egypt — EE juhpt
Elbert — ĔL bert
El Campo — ĕl KĂM pō
Eldorado — ĕl duh RĂ duh
Electra — ĭ LĔK truh
Elgin — ĔL gĭn
Eliasville — ee LĪ uhs vĭl
El Indio — ĕl ĬN dĭ ō
Elkhart — ĔLK hahrt
Ellinger — ĔL ĭn jer
Elliott — ĔL ĭ 't
Ellis — ĔL uhs
Elmendorf — ĔLM 'n dawrf
Elm Mott — ĕl MAHT
Elmo — ĔL mō
Eloise — ĔL o eez
El Paso — ĕl PĂS ō
Elsa — ĔL suh
Elysian Fields — uh lee zh'n FEELDZ
Emhouse — ĔM hows
Emory — ĔM uh rĭ
Encinal — ĕn suh NAHL
Encino — ĕn SEE nō
Energy — ĔN er jĭ
Engle — ĔN g'l
English — ĬNG glĭsh
Enloe — ĔN lō
Ennis — ĔN ĭs
Enochs — EE nuhks
Eola — ee Ō luh
Era — EE ruh
Erath — EE răth
Esperanza — ĕs per RĂN zuh
Estelline — ĔS tuh leen
Etoile — ĭ TOIL
Etter — ĔT er
Eula — YŌŌ luh
Euless — YŌŌ lĭs
Eureka — yōō REE kuh
Eustace — YŌŌS t's
Evadale — ĔE vuh dāl
Evant — EE vănt
Evergreen — Ĕ ver green
Everman — Ĕ ver m'n

F

Fabens — FĂ b'nz
Fairbanks — FĂR bangks
Fairfield — FĂR feeld
Fairlie — FĂR lee
Fair Play — făr PLĂ
Fairview — FĂR vyōō
Fairy — FĂ rĭ
Falfurrias — făl FYŌŌ rĭ uhs
Falls — fawlz
Falls City — fawlz SĬT ĭ
Fannett — fă NĔT
Fannin — FĂN ĭn
Fargo — FAHR gō

Farmers Branch — fahr merz BRĂNCH
Farmersville — FAHRM erz vĭl
Farnsworth — FAHRNZ werth
Farrar — FĂR uh
Farrsville — FAHRZ vĭl
Farwell — FAHR w'l
Fashing — FĂ shĭng
Fate — fāt
Fayette — fā ĔT
Fayetteville — FĀ uht vĭl
Fentress — FĔN trĭs
Ferris — FĔR ĭs
Field Creek — feeld KREEK
Fieldton — FEEL t'n
Fife — fīf
Fischer — FĬ sher
Fisher — FĬSH er
Fisk — fĭsk
Flagg — flăg
Flat — flăt
Flatonia — flă TŌN yuh
Flint — flĭnt
Flomot — FLŌ maht
Florence — FLAH ruhns
Floresville — FLŌRZ vil
Florey — FLŌ ri
Floyd — floid
Floydada — floi DĂ duh
Fluvanna — flo͞o VĂN uh
Flynn — flĭn
Foard — fōrd
Foard City — fōrd SĬT ĭ
Fodice — FŌ dĭs
Follett — fah LĔT
Fordtran — fōrd TRĂN
Forest — FAW rĕst
Forestburg — FAW rĕst berg
Forney — FAWR nĭ
Forreston — FAW rĕs t'n
Forsan — FŌR săn
Fort Bend — fōrt BĔND
Fort Chadbourne — fōrt CHĂD bern
Fort Davis — fōrt DĂ vĭs
Fort Griffin — fōrt GRĬF ĭn
Fort Hancock — fōrt HĂN kahk
Fort McKavett — fōrt muh KĂ vĕt
Fort Stockton — fōrt STAHK t'n
Fort Worth — fōrt WERTH
Fowlerton — FOW ler t'n
Francitas — frăn SEE t's
Franklin — FRĂNGK lĭn
Frankston — FRĂNGS t'n
Fred — frĕd
Fredericksburg — FRĔD er rĭks berg
Fredonia — free DŌN yuh
Freeport — FREE pōrt
Freer — FREE er
Freestone — FREE stōn
Frelsburg — FRĔLZ berg
Fresno — FRĔZ nō
Friday — FRĬ dī
Friendswood — FRĔNZ wo͞od
Frio — FREE ō
Friona — free Ō nuh

Pagoda-style architecture of the Kronkosky Tower in Boerne. Robert Plocheck photo.

Frisco — FRĬS kō
Fritch — frĭch
Frost — frawst
Fruitland — FRO͞OT lănd
Fruitvale — FRO͞OT văl
Frydek — FRĪ dĕk
Fulbright — FO͞OL brĭt
Fulshear — FUHL sher
Fulton — FO͞OL t'n

G

Gail — gāl
Gaines — gānz
Gainesville — GĀNZ vuhl
Galena Park — guh lee nuh PAHRK
Gallatin — GĂL uh t'n
Galveston — GĂL vĕs t'n
Ganado — guh NĂ dō
Garceno — gahr SĂ nō
Garciasville — gahr SEE uhs vĭl
Garden City — GAHRD n sĭt ĭ
Gardendale — GAHRD n dāl
Garden Valley — gahrd n VĂ lĭ
Garland — GAHR l'nd
Garner — GAHR ner
Garrett — GĂR ĭt
Garrison — GĂ rĭ s'n
Garwood — GAHR wo͞od
Gary — GĔ rĭ
Garza — GAHR zuh
Gatesville — GĀTS vil
Gause — gawz
Gay Hill — gā HĬL
Geneva — juh NEE vuh
Georgetown — JAWRJ town
George West — jawrj WĔST
Geronimo — juh RAH nĭ mō
Giddings — GĬD ĭngz
Gillespie — guh LĔS pĭ
Gillett — juh LĔT
Gilliland — GĬL ĭ l'nd
Gilmer — GĬL mer
Ginger — JĬN jer
Girard — juh RAHRD
Girvin — GER vĭn
Gladewater — GLĀD wah ter
Glasscock — GLĂS kahk
Glazier — GLĂ zher

Glen Cove — glĕn KŌV
Glendale — GLĔN dāl
Glenfawn — glĕn FAWN
Glen Flora — glĕn FLŌ ruh
Glenn — glĕn
Glen Rose — GLĔN rōz
Glidden — GLĬD n
Gober — GŌ ber
Godley — GAHD lĭ
Golden — GŌL d'n
Goldfinch — GŌLD fĭnch
Goldsboro — GŌLZ buh ruh
Goldsmith — GŌL smith
Goldthwaite — GŌLTH wāt
Goliad — GŌ lĭ ăd
Golinda — gō LĬN duh
Gonzales — guhn ZAH l's
Goodland — GO͞OD l'n
Goodlett — GO͞OD lĕt
Goodnight — GO͞OD nĭt
Goodrich — GO͞OD rĭch
Gordon — GAWRD n
Gordonville — GAWRD n vĭl
Goree — GŌ ree
Gorman — GAWR m'n
Gouldbusk — GO͞OLD buhsk
Graford — GRĂ ferd
Graham — GRĂ 'm
Granbury — GRĂN bĕ rĭ
Grandfalls — gränd FAWLZ
Grand Saline — grăn suh LEEN
Grandview — GRĂN vyo͞o
Granger — GRĂN jer
Grapeland — GRĂP l'nd
Grapevine — GRĂP vīn
Grassland — GRĂS l'nd
Grassyville — GRĂ sĭ vĭl
Gray — grā
Grayburg — GRĂ berg
Grayson — GRA s'n
Green — green
Greenville — GREEN v'l
Greenwood — GREEN wo͞od
Gregg — grĕg
Gregory — GRĔG uh rĭ
Grimes — grīmz
Groesbeck — GRŌZ bĕk
Groom — gro͞om

Groveton — GRŌV t'n
Grow — grō
Gruene — green
Grulla — GRŌŌL yuh
Gruver — GRŌŌ ver
Guadalupe — gwah duh LŌŌ pĭ
  or gwah duh LŌŌ pä
Guerra — GWĔ ruh
Gunter — GUHN ter
Gustine — GUHS teen
Guthrie — GUHTH rĭ
Guy — gī

H

Hackberry — HĂK bĕ rĭ
Hagansport — HĂ gĭnz pōrt
Hainesville — HĀNZ v'l
Hale — hāl
Hale Center — hāl SĔNT er
Hall — hawl
Hallettsville — HĂL ĕts vĭl
Hallsville — HAWLZ vĭl
Hamilton — HĂM uhl t'n
Hamlin — HĂM lĭn
Hammond — HĂM 'nd
Hamon — HĂ m'n
Hamshire — HĂM sher
Handley — HĂND lĭ
Hankamer — HĂN kăm er
Hansford — HĂNZ ferd
Happy — HĂ pĭ
Hardeman — HAHR duh m'n
Hardin — HAHRD n
Hare — hăr
Hargill — HAHR gĭl
Harleton — HAHR uhl t'n
Harlingen — HAHR lĭn juhn
Harper — HAHR per
Harris — HĂ rĭs
Harrison — HĂ rĭ s'n
Harrold — HĂR 'ld
Hart — hahrt
Hartburg — HAHRT berg
Hartley — HAHRT lĭ
Harwood — HAHR wŏŏd
Haskell — HĂS k'l
Haslam — HĂZ l'm
Haslet — HĂS lĕt
Hasse — HĂ sĭ
Hatchell — HĂ ch'l
Hawkins — HAW kĭnz
Hawley — HAW lĭ
Hays — hāz
Hearne — hern
Heath — heeth
Hebbronville — HĔB r'n vĭl
Hebron — HEE br'n
Hedley — HĔD lĭ
Heidenheimer — HĬD n hīmer
Helena — HĔL uh nuh
Helotes — hĕl Ō tĭs
Hemphill — HĔMP hĭl
Hempstead — HĔM stĕd
Henderson — HĔN der s'n
Henly — HĔN lĭ
Henrietta — hĕn rĭ Ĕ tuh
Hereford — HER ferd

The snackateria in Balmorhea. Robert Plocheck photo.

Hermleigh — HER muh lee
Hewitt — HYŌŌ ĭt
Hicks — hĭks
Hico — HĬ kō
Hidalgo — hĭ DĂL gō
Higgins — HĬ gĭnz
High — hī
Highbank — HĬ băngk
High Island — hī Ī l'nd
Highlands — HĬ l'ndz
Hightower — HĬ tow er
Hill — hĭl
Hillister — HĬL ĭs ter
Hillsboro — HĬLZ buh ruh
Hindes — hĭndz
Hiram — HĬ r'm
Hitchcock — HĬCH kahk
Hitchland — HĬCH l'nd
Hobson — HAHB s'n
Hochheim — HŌ hīm
Hockley — HAHK lĭ
Holland — HAHL 'nd
Holliday — HAH luh dā
Hondo — HAHN dō
Honey Grove — HUHN ĭ grōv
Honey Island — huhn ĭ Ī l'nd
Honey Springs — huhn ĭ SPRĬNGZ
Hood — hŏŏd
Hooks — hŏŏks
Hopkins — HAHP kĭnz
Houston — HYŌŌS t'n or YŌŌS t'n
Howard — HOW erd
Howe — how
Howland — HOW l'nd
Hubbard — HUH berd
Huckabay — HUHK uh bĭ
Hudspeth — HUHD sp'th
Huffman — HUHF m'n
Hufsmith — HUHF smĭth
Hughes Springs — hyŏŏz SPRĬNGZ
Hull — huhl
Humble — UHM b'l

Hungerford — HUHNG ger ferd
Hunt — huhnt
Hunter — HUHNT er
Huntington — HUHNT ĭng t'n
Huntsville — HUHNTS v'l
Hurlwood — HERL wŏŏd
Hutchins — HUH chĭnz
Hutchinson — HUH chĭn s'n
Hutto — HUH tō
Hye — hī
Hylton — HĬL t'n

I

Iago — ī Ā gō
Idalou — Ī duh lōō
Imperial — ĭm PĬR ĭ uhl
Inadale — Ī nuh dāl
Independence — ĭn duh PĔN d'ns
Indian Creek — ĭn dĭ uhn KREEK
Indian Gap — ĭn dĭ uhn GĂP
Industry — ĬN duhs trĭ
Inez — ī NĔZ
Ingleside — ĬNG g'l sīd
Ingram — ĬNG gr'm
Iola — ī Ō luh
Iowa Park — ī uh wuh PAHRK
Ira — Ī ruh
Iraan — ī ruh ĂN
Iredell — Ī ruh dĕl
Ireland — Ī rĭ l'nd
Irene — ī REEN
Irion — ĪR i uhn
Ironton — ĪRN t'n
Irving — ER vĭng
Italy — ĬT uh lĭ
Itasca — ī TĂS kuh
Ivan — Ī v'n
Ivanhoe — Ī v'n hō

J

Jack — jăk
Jacksboro — JĂKS buh ruh

Jackson — JĂK s'n
Jacksonville — JĂK s'n vĭl
Jamestown — JĀMZ town
Jardin — JAHRD n
Jarrell — JĂR uhl
Jasper — JĂS per
Jayton — JĀT n
Jean — jeen
Jeddo — JĔ dō
Jeff Davis — jĕf DA vĭs
Jefferson — JĔF er s'n
Jericho — JĔ rĭ kō
Jermyn — JER m'n
Jewett — JOO ĭt
Jiba — HEE buh
Jim Hogg — jĭm HAWG
Jim Wells — jĭm WĔLZ
Joaquin — waw KEEN
Johnson — JAHN s'n
Johnson City — jahn s'n SĬT ĭ
Johntown — JAHN town
Johnsville — JAHNZ vĭl
Joinerville — JOI ner vĭl
Jolly — JAH lĭ
Jollyville — JAH lĭ vĭl
Jonah — JŌ nuh
Jones — jōnz
Jonesboro — JŌNZ buh ruh
Jonesville — JŌNZ vĭl
Josephine — JŌ suh feen
Joshua — JAH sh' wa
Jourdanton — JERD n t'n
Joy — joi
Joyce — jawĭs
Juliff — JOO lĭf
Junction — JUHNGK sh'n
Juno — JOO nō
Justiceburg — JUHS tĭs berg
Justin — JUHS tĭn

K

Kalgary — KĂL gĕ rĭ
Kamay — KĀ ĭm ā
Kanawha — KAHN uh wah
Karnack — KAHR năk
Karnes — kahrnz
Karnes City — kahrnz SĬT ĭ
Katemcy — kuh TĔM sĭ
Katy — KĀ tĭ
Kaufman — KAWF m'n
Keechi — KEE chĭ
Keene — keen
Kellerville — KĔL er vĭl
Kemah — KEE muh
Kemp — kĕmp or kĭmp
Kemp City — kĕmp SĬT ĭ
Kempner — KĔMP ner
Kendalia — kĔn DĀL yuh
Kenedy — KĔN uh dĭ
Kennard — kuh NAHRD
Kennedale — KĔN uh dāl
Kent — kĕnt
Kerens — KER 'nz
Kermit — KER mĭt
Kerr — ker
Kerrville — KER vĭl
Kildare — KĬL där

Kilgore — KĬL gōr
Killeen — kuh LEEN
Kimble — KĬM b'l
King — kĭng
Kingsbury — KĬNGZ bĕ rĭ
Kingsland — KĬNGZ l'nd
Kingsmill — kĭngz MĬL
Kingston — KĬNGZ t'n
Kingsville — KĬNGZ vĭl
Kinney — KĬN ĭ
Kirby — KER bĭ
Kirbyville — KER bĭ vĭl
Kirkland — KERK l'nd
Kirvin — KER vĭn
Kleberg — KLĀ berg
Klondike — KLAHN dīk
Knickerbocker — NĬK uh bah ker
Knippa — kuh NĬP uh
Knott — naht
Knox — nahks
Knox City — nahks SĬT ĭ
Kosciusko — kuh SHOOS kō
Kosse — KAH sĭ
Kountze — kōōntz
Kress — kres
Krum — kruhm
Kurten — KER t'n
Kyle — kīl

L

La Blanca — lah BLAHN kuh
La Coste — luh KAWST
Ladonia — luh DŌN yuh
LaFayette — lah fĭ ĔT
Laferia — luh FĔ rĭ uh
Lagarto — luh GAHR tō
La Gloria — lah GLŌ rĭ uh
La Grange — luh GRĂNJ
Laguna — luh GOO nuh
Laird Hill — lärd HĬL
La Joya — luh HŌ yuh
Lake Creek — lāk KREEK
Lake Dallas — lāk DĂL uhs
Lake Jackson — lāk JĂK s'n
Laketon — LĀK t'n
Lake Victor — lāk VĬK ter
Lakeview — LĀK vyōō
Lamar — luh MAHR
La Marque — luh MAHRK
Lamasco — luh MĂS kō
Lamb — lăm
Lamesa — luh MEE suh
Lamkin — LĂM kĭn
Lampasas — lăm PĂ s's
Lancaster — LĂNG k's ter
Land City — lăn SĬT ĭ
Laneville — LĀN vĭl
Langtry — LĂNG trĭ
Lanier — luh NĬR
La Paloma — lah puh LŌ muh
La Porte — luh PŌRT
La Pryor — luh PRĬ er
Laredo — luh RĀ dō
Lariat — LĂ ri uht
Larue — luh RŌŌ
LaSalle — luh SĂL

Lasara — luh SĔ ruh
Lassater — LĂ sĭ ter
Latch — lĂch
Latexo — luh TĔKS ō
Lavaca — luh VĂ kuh
La Vernia — luh VER nĭ uh
La Villa — lah VĬL uh
Lavon — luh VAHN
La Ward — luh WAWRD
Lawn — lawn
Lawrence — LAH r'ns
Lazbuddie — LĂZ buh dĭ
League City — leeg SĬT ĭ
Leakey — LĀ kĭ
Leander — lee ĂN der
Leary — LĬ er ĭ
Ledbetter — LĔD bĕt er
Lee — lee
Leesburg — LEEZ berg
Leesville — LEEZ vĭl
Lefors — lĭ FŌRZ
Leggett — LĔ gĭt
Leigh — lee
Lela — LEE luh
Lelia Lake — leel yuh LĀK
Leming — LĔ mĭng
Lenorah — lĕ NŌ ruh
Leo — LEE ō
Leon — lee AHN
Leona — lee Ō nuh
Leonard — LĔN erd
Leon Springs — lee ahn SPRĬNGZ
Leroy — LEE roi
Levelland — LĔ v'l lănd
Levita — luh VĬ tuh
Lewisville — LOO ĭs vĭl
Lexington — LĔKS ĭng t'n
Liberty — LĬB er tĭ
Liberty Hill — lĬ ber tĭ HĬL
Lillian — LĬL yuhn
Limestone — LĬM stōn
Lincoln — LĬNG k'n
Lindale — LĬN dāl
Linden — LĬN d'n
Lindenau — lĭn duh NOW
Lindsay — LĬN zĭ
Lingleville — LĬNG g'l vĭl
Linn — lĭn
Lipan — lĭ PĂN
Lipscomb — LĬPS k'm
Lissie — LĬ sĭ
Little Elm — lĭt l ĔLM
Littlefield — LĬT uhl feeld
Little River — lĭt uhl RĬV er
Live Oak — LĬV ōk
Liverpool — LĬ ver pōōl
Livingston — LĬV ĭngz t'n
Llano — LĂ nō
Locker — LAH ker
Lockett — LAH kĭt
Lockhart — LAHK hahrt
Lockney — LAHK nĭ
Lodi — LŌ dĭ
Lohn — lahn
Lolita — lō LEE tuh
Loma Alto — lō muh ĂL tō
Lometa — lō MEE tuh

London — LUHN d'n
Lone Grove — lōn GRŌV
Lone Oak — LŌN ōk
Long Branch — lawng BRĂNCH
Long Mott — lawng MAHT
Longview — LAWNG vyōō
Longworth — LAWNG werth
Loop — lōōp
Lopeno — lō PEE nō
Loraine — lō RĂN
Lorena — lō REE nuh
Los Angeles — laws AN juh l's
Los Ebanos — lōs ĔB uh nōs
Los Fresnos — lōs FRĔZ nōs
Los Indios — lōs ĬN dī ōs
Losoya — luh SAW yuh
Lott — laht
Louise — LŌŌ eez
Lovelady — LUHV lā dī
Loving — LUH vǐng
Lubbock — LUH buhk   or   LUH b'k
Lueders — LŌŌ derz
Luella — lōō ĔL uh
Lufkin — LUHF kǐn
Luling — LŌŌ lǐng
Lund — luhnd
Lutie — LŌŌ tǐ
Lyford — LĪ ferd
Lynn — lǐn
Lyons — LĪ 'nz
Lytton Springs — lǐt n SPRĬNGZ

M

Mabank — MĂ băngk
Macune — muh KŌŌN
Madison — MĂ dǐ s'n
Madisonville — MĂ duh s'n vǐl
Magnolia — măg NŌL yuh
Magnolia Springs — măg nol yuh SPRINGZ
Malakoff — MĂL uh kawf
Malone — muh LŌN
Malta — MAWL tuh
Manchaca — MĂN shăk
Manchester — MĂN chěs ter
Manheim — MĂN hīm
Mankins — MĂN kǐnz
Manor — MĂ ner
Mansfield — MĂNZ feeld
Manvel — MĂN v'l
Maple — MĂ puhl
Marathon — MĂR uh th'n
Marble Falls — mahr b'l FAWLZ
Marfa — MAHR fuh
Margaret — MAHR guh rǐt
Marietta — mě rǐ Ĕ tuh
Marion — MĔ rǐ uhn
Markham — MAHR k'm
Marlin — MAHR lǐn
Marquez — mahr KĂ
Marshall — MAHR sh'l
Mart — mahrt
Martin — MAHRT n
Martindale — MAHRT n dāl
Martinsville — MAHRT nz vǐl
Maryneal — mā rǐ NEEL
Marysville — MĂ rǐz vǐl

Mason — MĂ s'n
Matador — MĂT uh dōr
Matagorda — măt uh GAWR duh
Mathis — MĂ thǐs
Maud — mawd
Mauriceville — maw REES vǐl
Maverick — MĂV rǐk
Maxey — MĂKS ǐ
Maxwell — MĂKS w'l
May — mā
Maydell — MĂ děl
Maypearl — mā PERL
Maysfield — MĂZ feeld
McAdoo — MĂK uh dōō
McAllen — măk ĂL ǐn
McCamey — muh KĂ mǐ
McCaulley — muh KAW lǐ
McCoy — muh KOI
McCulloch — muh KUH luhk
McFaddin — măk FĂD n
McGregor — muh GRĔ ger
McKinney — muh KĬN ǐ
McLean — muh KLĂN
McLennan — muhk LĔN uhn
McLeod — măk LOWD
McMahan — măk MĂN
McMullen — măk MUHL ǐn
McNary — măk NĂ rǐ
McNeil — măk NEEL
McQueeney — muh KWEE nǐ
Meadow — MĔ dō
Medicine Mound — měd uhs n MOWND
Medill — mě DĬL
Medina — muh DEE nuh
Megargel — muh GAHR g'l
Melissa — muh LĬS uh
Melrose — MĔL rōz
Melvin — MĔL vǐn
Memphis — MĔM fǐs
Menard — muh NAHRD
Mendoza — měn DŌ zuh
Mentone — měn TŌN
Mercedes — mer SĂ deez
Mercury — MER kyuh ri
Mereta — muh RĔT uh
Meridian — muh RĬ dǐ uhn
Merit — MĔR ǐt
Merkel — MER k'l
Mertens — mer TĔNZ
Mertzon — MERTS n
Mesquite — muhs KEET
Mexia — muh HĂ uh
Meyersville — MĪRZ vǐl
Miami — mī ĂM uh or mī ĂM ǐ
Mico — MEE kō
Middleton — MĬD uhl t'n
Midfields — MĬD feeldz
Midland — MĬD l'nd
Midlothian — mǐd LŌ thǐ n
Midway — MĬD wā
Milam — MĬ l'm
Milano — mī LĂ nō
Mildred — MĬL drěd
Miles — mīlz
Milford — MĬL ferd
Miller Grove — mǐl er GRŌV

Millersview — MĬL erz vyōō
Millett — MĬL ǐt
Millheim — MĬL hīm
Millican — MĬL uh kuhn
Mills — mǐlz
Millsap — MĬL săp
Minden — MĬN d'n
Mineola — mǐn ǐ Ō luh
Mineral — MĬN er uhl
Mineral Wells — mǐn er uhl WĔLZ
Minerva — mǐ NER vuh
Mingus — MĬNG guhs
Minter — MĬNT er
Mirando City — mǐ răn duh SĬT ǐ
Mission — MĬSH uhn
Mission Valley — mǐsh uhn VĂ lǐ
Missouri City — muh zōōr uh SĬT ǐ
Mitchell — MĬ ch'l
Mobeetie — mō BEE tǐ
Moline — mō LEEN
Monahans — MAH nuh hănz
Monaville — MŌ nuh vǐl
Monkstown — MUHNGKS town
Monroe — MAHN rō
Monroe City — mahn rō SĬT ǐ
Montague — mahn TĂG
Montalba — mahnt ĂL buh
Mont Belvieu — mahnt BĔL vyōō
Montell — mahn TĔL
Montgomery — mahnt GUHM er ǐ
Monthalia — mahn THĂL yuh
Moody — MŌŌ dǐ
Moore — mōr
Morales — muh RAH lěs
Moran — mō RĂN
Morgan — MAWR g'n
Morgan Mill — mawr g'n MĬL
Morse — mawrs
Morton — MAWRT n
Moscow — MAHS kow
Mosheim — MŌ shǐm
Moss Bluff — maws BLUHF
Motley — MAHT lǐ
Moulton — MŌL t'n
Mound — mownd
Mountain Home — mownt n HŌM
Mount Calm — mownt KAHM
Mount Enterprise — mownt ĔN ter prīz
Mount Pleasant — mownt PLĔ z'nt
Mount Selman — mownt SĔL m'n
Mount Sylvan — mownt SĬL v'n
Mount Vernon — mownt VER n'n
Muenster — MYŌŌNS ter
Muldoon — muhl DŌŌN
Muleshoe — MYŌŌL shōō
Mullin — MUHL ǐn
Mumford — MUHM ferd
Munday — MUHN dǐ
Murchison — MER kuh s'n
Murphy — MER fǐ
Mykawa — mī KAH wuh
Myra — MĪ ruh
Myrtle Springs — mert l SPRĬNGZ

N

Nacogdoches — năk uh DŌ chǐs

Diacritical markings are used as follows: bāle, băd, lĕt, rīse, rĭll, ōak, brōōd, fŏŏt. The stressed syllable is capitalized. Secondary stress is indicated by an underline as in Atascosa — ăt uhs KŌ suh. TEXAS ALMANAC ©.

Bicyclists experience winter in the Lower Rio Grande Valley at Mission. Robert Plocheck photo.

Nada — NĀ duh
Naples — NĀ p'lz
Nash — năsh
Natalia — nuh TĂL yuh
Navarro — nuh VĂ rō
Navasota — năv uh SŌ tuh
Nazareth — NĂZ uh r'th
Neches — NĀ chĭs
Nederland — NEE der l'nd
Needville — NEED vĭl
Nelsonville — NĔL s'n vĭl
Neuville — NYŌŌ v'l
Nevada — nuh VĂ duh
Newark — NŌŌ erk
New Baden — nyōō BĀD n
New Berlin — nyōō BER lin
New Boston — nyōō BAWS t'n
New Braunfels — nyōō BRAHN f'ls
   or BROWN fĕlz
Newby — NYŌŌ bĭ
New Caney — nyōō KĀ nĭ
Newcastle — NYŌŌ kăs uhl
New Gulf — nyōō GUHLF
New Home — NYŌŌ hōm
New Hope — nyōō HŌP
Newlin — NYŌŌ lĭn
New London — nyōō LUHN d'n
Newman — NYŌŌ m'n
Newport — NYŌŌ pōrt
New Salem — nyōō SĀ l'm
Newsome — NYŌŌ s'm
New Summerfield — nyōō
   SUHM er feeld
Newton — NYŌŌT n
New Ulm — nyōō UHLM
New Waverly — nyōō WĀ ver lĭ
New Willard — nyōō WĬL erd
Nimrod — NĬM rahd
Nineveh — NĬN uh vuh
Nixon — NĬKS uhn
Nocona — nō KŌ nuh
Nolan — NŌ l'n
Nolanville — NŌ l'n vĭl
Nome — nōm
Noonday — NŌŌN dā
Nopal — NŌ păl
Nordheim — NAWRD hīm
Normandy — NAWR m'n dĭ
Normangee — NAWR m'n jee
Normanna — nawr MĂN uh
Northrup — NAWR thr'p
North Zulch — nawrth ZŌŌLCH

Norton — NAWRT n
Novice — NAH vĭs
Nueces — nyōō Ā sĭs
Nugent — NYŌŌ j'nt
Nursery — NER suh rĭ

O

Oakalla — ō KĂL uh
Oak Grove — ōk GRŌV
Oak Hill — ōk HĬL
Oakhurst — ŌK herst
Oakland — ŌK l'nd
Oakville — ŌK vĭl
Oakwood — ŌK wōōd
O'Brien — ō BRĪ uhn
Ochiltree — AH k'l tree
Odell — Ō dĕl or ō DĔL
Odem — Ō d'm
Odessa — ō DĔS uh
O'Donnell — ō DAH n'l
Oenaville — ō EEN uh v'l
Oglesby — Ō g'lz bĭ
Oilton — OIL t'n
Oklaunion — ōk luh YŌŌN y'n
Olden — ŌL d'n
Oldenburg — ŌL dĭn berg
Oldham — ŌL d'm
Old Glory — ōld GLŌ rĭ
Olivia — ō LĬV ĭ uh
Olmito — awl MEE tuh
Olmos Park — ahl m's PAHRK
Olney — AHL nĭ
Olton — ŌL t'n
Omaha — Ō muh haw
Omen — Ō mĭn
Onalaska — uhn uh LĂS kuh
Oplin — AHP lĭn
Orange — AHR ĭnj
Orangefield — AHR ĭnj feeld
Orange Grove — AHR ĭnj GRŌV
Orchard — AWR cherd
Ore City — ōr SĬT ĭ
Osceola — ō sĭ Ō luh
Otey — Ō tĭ
Otis Chalk — ō tĭs CHAWLK
Ottine — ah TEEN
Otto — AH tō
Ovalo — ō VĂL uh
Overton — Ō ver t'n
Owens — Ō ĭnz
Ozona — ō ZŌ nuh

P

Paducah — puh DYŌŌ kuh
Paige — pāj
Paint Rock — pănt RAHK
Palacios — puh LĂ sh's
Palestine — PAL uhs teen
Palito Blanco — p' lee to
   BLAHNG kō
Palmer — PAH mer
Palo Pinto — pă lō PĬN tō
Paluxy — puh LUHK sĭ
Pampa — PĂM puh
Pandora — păn DŌR uh
Panhandle — PĂN hăn d'l
Panna Maria — păn uh
   muh REE uh
Papalote — pah puh LŌ tĭ
Paradise — PĂR uh dīs
Paris — PĂ rĭs
Parker — PAHR ker
Parmer — PAH mer
Parnell — pahr NĔL
Parsley Hill — pahrs lĭ HĬL
Pasadena — păs uh DEE nuh
Patricia — puh TRĬ shuh
Patroon — puh TRŌŌN
Pattison — PĂT uh s'n
Pattonville — PĂT n vĭl
Pawnee — paw NEE
Paxton — PĂKS t'n
Peacock — PEE kahk
Pearl — perl
Pearland — PĂR lănd
Pearsall — PEER sawl
Peaster — PEES ter
Pecan Gap — pĭ kahn GĂP
Pecos — PĀ k's
Penelope — puh NĔL uh pĭ
Penitas — puh NEE t's
Pennington — PĔN ĭng t'n
Penwell — PĬN wĕl
Peoria — pee Ō rĭ uh
Percilla — per SĬL uh
Perrin — PĔR ĭn
Perry — PĔ rĭ
Perryton — PĔ rĭ t'n
Peters — PEET erz
Petersburg — PEET erz berg
Petrolia — puh TRŌL yuh
Petteway — PĔT uh wā
Pettit — PĔT ĭt

Diacritical markings are used as follows: bāle, băd, lĕt, rīse, rĭll, ōak, brōōd, fōōt. The stressed syllable is capitalized. Secondary stress is indicated by an underline as in Atascosa — ăt uhs KŌ suh. TEXAS ALMANAC ©.

Pettus — PĔT uhs
Petty — PĔT ĭ
Pflugerville — FLŌŌ ger vĭl
Pharr — fahr
Phelps — fĕlps
Phillips — FĬL uhps
Pickton — PĬK t'n
Pidcoke — PĬD kŏk
Piedmont — PEED mahnt
Pierce — PĬ ers
Pilot Point — pī l't POINT
Pine Forest — pīn FAW rĕst
Pine Hill — pīn HĬL
Pinehurst — PĬN herst
Pineland — PĬN land
Pine Mills — pīn MĬLZ
Pine Springs — pīn SPRĬNGZ
Pioneer — pī uh NĬR
Pipecreek — pīp KREEK
Pittsburg — PĬTS berg
Placedo — PLĂS ĭ dō
Placid — PLĂ sĭd
Plains — plānz
Plainview — PLĂN vyōō
Plano — PLĂ nō
Plantersville — PLĂN terz vĭl
Plaska — PLĂS kuh
Plateau — plă TŌ
Pleasant Grove—plĕ z'nt GRŌV
Pleasanton — PLĔZ uhn t'n
Pledger — PLĔ jer
Plum — pluhm
Point — point
Pointblank — pint BLĂNGK
Polk — pōlk
Pollock — PAHL uhk
Ponder — PAHN der
Ponta — pahn TĂ
Pontotoc — PAHNT uh tahk
Poolville — PŌŌL vĭl
Port Aransas — pōrt uh RĂN zuhs
Port Arthur — pōrt AHR ther
Port Bolivar — pōrt BAH lĭ ver
Porter Springs — pōr ter SPRĬNGZ
Port Isabel — pōrt ĬZ uh bĕl
Portland — PŌRT l'nd
Port Lavaca — pōrt luh VĂ kuh
Port Neches — pōrt NĂ chĭs
Port O'Connor — pōrt ō KAH ner
Posey — PŌ zĭ
Post — pōst
Postoak — PŌST ōk
Poteet — pō TEET
Poth — pōth
Potosi — puh TŌ sĭ
Potter — PAHT er
Pottsboro — PAHTS buh ruh
Pottsville — PAHTS vĭl
Powderly — POW der lĭ
Powell — POW w'l
Poynor — POI ner
Prairie Dell — prĕr ĭ DĔL
Prairie Hill — prĕr ĭ HĬL
Prairie Lea — prĕr ĭ LEE
Prairie View — prĕr ĭ VYŌŌ
Prairieville — PRĔR ĭ vĭl

Premont — PREE mahnt
Presidio — pruh SĬ dĭ ō
Priddy — PRĬ dĭ
Primera — pree MĚ ruh
Princeton — PRĬNS t'n
Pritchett — PRĬ chĭt
Proctor — PRAHK ter
Progreso — prō GRĔ sō
Prosper — PRAHS per
Purdon — PERD n
Purley — PER lĭ
Purmela — per MEE luh
Putnam — PUHT n'm
Pyote — PĬ ōt

Q

Quail — kwāl
Quanah — KWAH nuh
Queen City — kween SĬT ĭ
Quemado — kuh MAH dō
Quihi — KWEE hee
Quinlan — KWĬN l'n
Quintana — kwĭn TAH nuh
Quitaque — KĬT uh kwa
Quitman — KWĬT m'n

R

Rainbow — RĂN bō
Rains — rānz
Ralls — rahlz
Randall — RĂN d'l
Randolph — RĂN dahlf
Ranger — RĂN jer
Rangerville — RĂN jer vĭl
Rankin — RĂNG kĭn
Ratcliff — RĂT klĭf
Ravenna — rĭ VĚN uh
Rayburn — RĂ bern
Raymondville — RĂ m'nd vĭl
Raywood — RĂ wŏŏd
Reagan — RĂ g'n
Real — REE awl
Realitos — ree uh LEE t's
Redford — RĔD ferd
Red Oak — RĔD ōk
Red River — rĕd RĬ ver
Red Rock — rĕd RAHK
Red Springs — rĕd SPRĬNGZ
Red Water — RĔD wah ter
Reeves — reevz
Refugio — rĕ FYŌŌ rĭ ō
Reilly Springs — rĭ lĭ SPRĬNGZ
Reklaw — RĔK law
Reno — REE nō
Rhineland — RĬN l'nd
Rhome — rōm
Rhonesboro — RŌNZ buh ruh
Ricardo — rĭ KAHR dō
Rice — rīs
Richards — RĬCH erdz
Richardson — RĬCH erd s'n
Richland — RĬCH l'nd
Richland Springs — rĭch l'nd SPRĬNGZ
Richmond — RĬCH m'nd
Ridge — rĭj

Ridgeway — RĬJ wā
Riesel — REE s'l
Ringgold — RĬNG gōld
Rio Frio — ree ō FREE ō
Rio Grande City — ree ō grahn dĭ
    or ree ō grän SĬT ĭ
Rio Hondo — ree ō HAHN dō
Riomedina — ree ō muh DEE nuh
Rios — REE ōs
Rio Vista — ree ō VĬS tuh
Rising Star — rĭ zĭng STAHR
River Oaks — rĭ ver ŌKS
Riverside — RĬ ver sĭd
Riviera — ruh VĬR uh
Roane — rōn
Roanoke — RŌN ōk or
    RŌ uh nōk
Roans Prairie — rōnz PRĔR ĭ
Roaring Springs — rōr ĭng SPRĬNGZ
Robert Lee — rah bert LEE
Roberts — RAH berts
Robertson — RAH bert s'n
Robinson — RAH bĭn s'n
Robstown — RAHBZ town
Roby — RŌ bĭ
Rochelle — rō SHĔL
Rochester — RAH chĕs ter
Rockdale — RAHK dāl
Rock Island — rahk Ī l'nd
Rockland — RAHK l'nd
Rockport — rahk PŌRT
Rocksprings — rahk SPRĬNGZ
Rockwall — rahk WAWL
Rockwood — RAHK wŏŏd
Roganville — RŌ g'n vĭl
Rogers — RAH jerz
Roma — RŌ muh
Romayor — rō MĂ er
Roosevelt — RŌŌ suh v'lt
Ropesville — RŌPS vĭl
Rosanky — rō ZĂNG kĭ
Roscoe — RAHS kō
Rosebud — RŌZ b'd
Rose Hill — rōz HĬL
Rosenberg — RŌZ n berg
Rosenthal — RŌZ uhn thawl
Rosewood — RŌZ wŏŏd
Rosharon — rō SHĔ r'n
Rosita — rō SEE tuh
Ross — raws
Rosser — RAW ser
Rosston — RAWS t'n
Rossville — RAWS vĭl
Roswell — RAHZ w'l
Rotan — rō TĂN
Round Rock — ROWND rahk
Round Top — ROWN tahp
Rowena — rō EE nuh
Rowlett — ROW lĭt
Roxton — RAHKS t'n
Royalty — ROI uhl tĭ
Royse City — roi SĬT ĭ
Royston — ROIS t'n
Rugby — RUHG bĭ
Ruidosa — ree uh DŌ suh

Rule — ro͞ol
Runge — RUHNG ĭ
Runnels — RUHN 'lz
Rural Shade — ro͞or uhl SHĀD
Rusk — ruhsk
Rutersville — RO͞O ter vĭl
Rye — rī

S

Sabinal — SĂB uh năl
Sabine — suh BEEN
Sabine Pass — suh <u>been</u> PĂS
Sabinetown — suh <u>been</u> TOWN
Sachse — SĂK sĭ
Sacul — SĂ k'l
Sadler — SĂD ler
Sagerton — SĂ ger t'n
Saginaw — SĂ guh naw
Saint Jo — sănt JŌ
Saint Paul — sănt PAWL
Salado — suh LĀ dŏ
Salesville — SĂLZ vĭl
Salineno — suh LEEN yŏ
Salmon — SĂL m'n
Salt Gap — sawlt GĂP
Saltillo — săl TĬL ō
Samfordyce — săm FOR dis
Sample — SĂM p'l
Samnorwood — săm NAWR wo͞od
San Angelo — <u>săn</u> ĂN juh lō
San Antonio — <u>săn</u> ăn TŌ nĭ ō
San Augustine — <u>săn</u> AW g's teen
San Benito — săn buh NEE tuh
Sanderson — SĂN der s'n
Sandia — săn DEE uh
San Diego — <u>săn</u> dĭ Ā gō
Sandy Point — săn dĭ POINT
San Elizario — săn ĕl ĭ ZAH rĭ ō
San Felipe — <u>săn</u> fuh LEEP
Sanford — SĂN ferd
San Gabriel — săn GĀ brĭ uhl
Sanger — SĂNG er
San Jacinto — <u>săn</u> juh SĬN tuh
   or juh SĬN tō
San Juan — săn WAHN
San Marcos — <u>săn</u> MAHR k's
San Patricio — <u>săn</u> puh TRĬSH ĭ ō
San Perlita — <u>săn</u> per LEE tuh
San Saba — <u>săn</u> SĂ buh
Santa Anna — <u>săn</u> tuh ĂN uh
Santa Elena — săn tuh LEE nuh
Santa Maria — <u>săn</u> tuh
   muh REE uh
Santa Rosa — <u>săn</u> tuh RŌ suh
Santo — SĂN tō
San Ygnacio — <u>săn</u> ĭg NAH sĭ ō
Saragosa — <u>sĕ</u> ruh GŌ suh
Saratoga — <u>sĕ</u> ruh TŌ guh
Sargent — SAHR juhnt
Sarita — suh REE tuh
Saspamco — suh SPĂM kŏ
Satin — SĂT n
Savoy — suh VOI
Schattel — SHĂT uhl
Schertz — sherts
Schleicher — SHLĪ ker

Carnival at Oysterfest, Fulton. Robert Plocheck photo.

Schroeder — SHRĀ der
Schulenburg — SHO͞O lĭn berg
Schwertner — SWERT ner
Scotland — SKAHT l'nd
Scottsville — SKAHTS vĭl
Scranton — SKRĂNT n
Scurry — SKUH rĭ
Scyene — sĭ EEN
Seabrook — SEE bro͞ok
Seadrift — SEE drĭft
Seagoville — SEE gō vĭl
Seagraves — SEE grăvz
Seale — seel
Sealy — SEE lĭ
Sebastopol — suh BĂS tuh po͞ol
Sebastian — suh BĂS tĭ 'n
Security — sĭ KYO͞OR ĭ tĭ
Segno — SĔG nō
Segovia — sĭ GŌ vĭ uh
Seguin — sĭ GEEN
Selfs — sĕlfs
Selma — SĔL muh
Seminole — SĔM uh nōl
Seymour — SEE mōr
Shackelford — SHĂK uhl ferd
Shady Grove — shā dĭ GRŌV
Shafter — SHĂF ter
Shallowater — SHĂL uh wah ter
Shamrock — SHĂM rahk
Shannon — SHĂN uhn
Sharp — shahrp
Sheffield — SHĔ feeld
Shelby — SHĔL bĭ
Shelbyville — SHĔL bĭ vĭl
Sheldon — SHĔL d'n
Shepherd — SHĔ perd
Sheridan — SHĔ rĭ dn
Sherman — SHER m'n
Sherwood — SHER wood
Shiner — SHĪ ner
Shiro — SHĪ rō
Shive — shĭv
Sidney — SĬD nĭ

Sierra Blanca — sĭer ruh
   BLĂNG kuh
Siloam — suh LŌM
Silsbee — SĬLZ bĭ
Silver Lake — sĭl ver LĀK
Silverton — SĬL ver t'n
Silver Valley — <u>sĭl</u> ver VĂ lĭ
Simms — sĭmz
Simonton — SĪ m'n t'n
Singleton — SĬNG g'l t'n
Sinton — SĬNT n
Sipe Springs — SEEP sprĭngz
Sisterdale — SĬS ter dāl
Sivells Bend — <u>sĭ</u> v'lz BĔND
Skellytown — SKĔ lĭ town
Skidmore — SKĬD mōr
Slaton — SLĀT n
Slayden — SLĀD n
Slidell — slī DĔL
Slocum — SLŌ k'm
Smiley — SMĪ lĭ
Smith — smĭth
Smithfield — SMĬTH feeld
Smithland — SMĬTH l'nd
Smithson Valley — smĭth s'n VĂ lĭ
Smithville — SMĬTH vĭl
Smyer — SMĪ er
Snook — sno͞ok
Snyder — SNĪ der
Somerset — SUH mer sĕt
Somervell — SUH mer vĕl
Somerville — SUH mer vĭl
Sonora — suh NŌ ruh
Sour Lake — sowr LĀK
South Bend — sowth BĔND
South Bosque — sowth BAHS kĭ
South Houston — sowth HYO͞OS t'n
Southland — SOWTH l'nd
Southmayd — sowth MĀD
South Plains — sowth PLĂNZ
Spade — spād
Spanish Fort — spă nĭsh FŌRT
Sparenberg — SPĂR ĭn berg

Speaks — speeks
Spearman — SPĬR m'n
Spicewood — SPĬS wōōd
Splendora — splĕn DŌ ruh
Spofford — SPAH ferd
Spring — sprĭng
Springdale — SPRĬNG dāl
Springlake — sprĭng LĀK
Springtown — SPRĬNG town
Spur — sper
Spurger — SPER ger
Stacy — STĀ sĭ
Stafford — STĂ ferd
Stamford — STĂM ferd
Stanton — STĂNT n
Staples — STĀ p'lz
Starr — stahr
Stephens — STEE vĕnz
Stephenville — STEEV n vĭl
Sterley — STER lĭ
Sterling — STER lĭng
Sterling City — ster lĭng SĬT ĭ
Stiles — stīlz
Stinnett — stĭ NĔT
Stockdale — STAHK dāl
Stoneburg — STŌN berg
Stoneham — STŌN uhm
Stone Point — stōn POINT
Stonewall — STŌN wawl
Stout — stowt
Stowell — STO w'l
Stranger — STRĂN jer
Stratford — STRĂT ferd
Strawn — strawn
Streeter — STREET er
Streetman — STREET m'n
Study Butte — styōō dĭ BYŌŌT
Sublime — s'b LĬM
Sudan — SŌŌ dăn
Sugar Land — SHŌŌ ger lănd
Sullivan City — suh luh v'n SĬT ĭ
Sulphur Bluff — suhl fer BLUHF
Sulphur Springs — suhl fer
  SPRĬNGZ
Summerfield — SUHM er feeld
Sumner — SUHM ner
Sundown — SUHN down
Suniland — SUH nĭ lănd
Sunny Side — SUH nĭ sīd
Sunray — SUHN rā
Sunset — SUHN sĕt
Sutherland Springs — suh ther l'nd
  SPRĬNGZ
Sutton — SUHT n
Swan — swahn
Sweeny — SWEE nĭ
Sweet Home — sweet HŌM
Sweetwater — SWEET wah ter
Swenson — SWĔN s'n
Swift — swĭft
Swisher — SWĬ sher
Sylvester — sil VES ter

T

Taft — tăft
Tahoka — tuh HŌ kuh
Talco — TĂL kō

Talpa — TĂL puh
Tanglewood — TĂNG g'l wōōd
Tankersley — TĂNG kers lĭ
Tarrant — TAR uhnt
Tarzan — TAHR z'n
Tascosa — tăs KŌ suh
Tatum — TĂ t'm
Tavener — TĂV uh ner
Taylor — TĂ ler
Teague — teeg
Tehuacana — tuh WAW kuh nuh
Telephone — TĔL uh fōn
Telferner — TĔLF ner
Tell — tĕl
Temple — TĔM p'l
Tenaha — TĔN uh haw
Tennyson — TĔN uh s'n
Terlingua — TER lĭng guh
Terrell — TĔR uhl
Terrell Hills — ter uhl HILZ
Terry — TĔR ĭ
Texarkana — tĕks ahr KĂN uh
Texas City — tĕks ĕz SĬT ĭ
Texhoma — tĕks Ō muh
Texline — TĔKS līn
Texon — tĕks AHN
Thalia — THĂL yuh
The Grove — th' GRŌV
Thicket — THĬ kĭt
Thomaston — TAHM uhs t'n
Thompsons — TAHMP s'nz
Thorndale — THAWRN dāl
Thornton — THAWRN t'n
Thorp Spring — thawrp SPRĬNG
Thrall — thrawl
Three Rivers — three RĬ verz
Throckmorton — THRAHK mawrt n
Thurber — THER ber
Tilden — TĬL d'n
Timpson — TĬM s'n
Tioga — tĭ Ō guh
Titus — TĪT uhs
Tivoli — tĭ VŌ luh
Tokio — TŌ kĭ ō
Tolar — TŌ ler
Tolbert — TAHL bert
Tolosa — tuh LŌ suh
Tomball — TAHM bawl
Tom Bean — tahm BEEN
Tom Green — tahm GREEN
Tool — tōōl
Topsey — TAHP sĭ
Tornillo — tawr NEE yō
Tow — tow
Toyah — TOI yuh
Toyahvale — TOI yuh vāl
Trawick — TRĂ wĭk
Travis — TRĂ vĭs
Trent — trĕnt
Trenton — TRĔNT n
Trickham — TRĬK uhm
Trinidad — TRĬN uh dăd
Trinity — TRĬN ĭ tĭ
Troup — trōōp
Troy — TRAW ĭ
Truby — TRŌŌ bĭ
Trumbull — TRUHM b'l

Truscott — TRUHS k't
Tucker — TUHK er
Tuleta — tōō LEE tuh
Tulia — TŌŌL yuh
Tulsita — tuhl SEE tuh
Tundra — TUHN druh
Tunis — TŌŌ nĭs
Turkey — TER kĭ
Turlington — TER lĭng t'n
Turnersville — TER nerz vĭl
Turnertown — TER ner town
Turney — TER nĭ
Tuscola — tuhs KŌ luh
Tuxedo — TUHKS ĭ dō
Twin Sisters — twĭn SĬS terz
Twitty — TWĬ tĭ
Tye — tī
Tyler — TĬ ler
Tynan — TĬ nuhn

U

Uhland — YŌŌ l'nd
Umbarger — UHM bahr ger
Union — YŌŌN y'n
Upshur — UHP sher
Upton — UHP t'n
Urbana — er BĂ nuh
Utley — YŌŌT lĭ
Utopia — yōō TŌ pĭ uh
Uvalde — yōō VĂL dĭ

V

Valdasta — văl DĂS tuh
Valentine — VĂL uhn tīn
Valera — vuh LĬ ruh
Valley Mills — vă lĭ MĬLZ
Valley Spring — vă lĭ SPRĬNG
Valley View — vă lĭ VYŌŌ
Van — văn
Van Alstyne — văn AWLZ teen
Vancourt — VĂN kört
Vanderbilt — VĂN der bĭlt
Vanderpool — VĂN der pōōl
Van Horn — văn hawrn
Van Vleck — văn VLĔK
Van Zandt — văn ZĂNT
Vashti — VĂSH tĭ
Vaughan — vawn
Vega — VĂ guh
Velasco — vuh LĂS kō
Venus — VEE n's
Vera — VĬ ruh
Verhalen — ver HĂ lĭn
Veribest — VĔR ĭ bĕst
Vernon — VER n'n
Vickery — VĬK er ĭ
Victoria — vĭk TŌ rĭ uh
Vidor — VĬ der
Vienna — vee ĔN uh
View — vyōō
Village Mills — vĭl ĭj MĬLZ
Vincent — VĬN s'nt
Vinegarone — vĭn er guh RŌN
Vineyard — VĬN yerd
Violet — VĬ ō lĕt
Voca — VŌ kuh

Diacritical markings are used as follows: bāle, băd, lĕt, rīse, rĭll, ōak, brōōd, fōōt. The stressed syllable is capitalized. Secondary stress is indicated by an underline as in Atascosa — ăt uhs KŌ suh. TEXAS ALMANAC ©.

Von Ormy — vahn AHR mĭ
Voss — vaws
Votaw — VŌ taw

W

Waco — WĀ kō
Wadsworth — WAHDZ werth
Waelder — WĔL der
Waka — WAH kuh
Walberg — WAWL berg
Waldeck — WAWL dĕk
Walker — WAWL ker
Wall — wawl
Waller — WAW ler
Wallis — WAH lĭs
Wallisville — WAH lĭs vĭl
Walnut Springs — wawl n't
  SPRĬNGZ
Walton — WAWL t'n
Warda — WAWR duh
Ward — wawrd
Waring — WĂR ĭng
Warren — WAW rĭn
Warrenton — WAW rĭn t'n
Washburn — WAHSH bern
Washington — WAHSH ĭng t'n
Waskom — WAHS k'm
Wastella — wahs TĔL uh
Watauga — wuh TAW guh
Water Valley — <u>wah</u> ter VĂ lĭ
Waxahachie — <u>wawks</u> uh HĂ chĭ
Wayland — WĀ l'nd
Weatherford — WĔ ther ferd
Weaver — WEE ver
Webb — wĕb
Webberville — WĔ ber vĭl
Webster — WĔBS ter
Weches — WEE chĭz
Weesatche — WEE săch
Weimar — WĪ mer
Weinert — WĪ nert
Weir — weer
Welch — wĕlch
Welcome — WĔL k'm
Weldon — WĔL d'n
Wellborn — WĔL bern
Wellington — WĔL ĭng t'n
Wellman — WĔL m'n
Wells — wĕlz
Weser — WEE zer
Weslaco — WĔS luh kō
West — wĕst
Westbrook — WĔST brŏŏk
Westfield — WĔST feeld
Westhoff — WĔS tawf
Westminster — wĕst MĬN ster
Weston — WĔS t'n
Westover — WĔS tō ver
Westphalia — <u>wĕst</u> FĀL yuh
West Point — wĕst POINT
Wetmore — WĔT mōr
Wharton — HWAWRT n
Wheeler — HWEE ler
Wheelock — HWEE lahk
White Deer — HWĪT Deer
Whiteface — HWĪT fās

"Watch for alligators" at Seadrift. Robert Plocheck photo.

Whiteflat — hwĭt FLĂT
Whitehouse — HWĪT hows
Whitesboro — HWĪTS <u>buh</u> ruh
Whitewright — HWĪT rĭt
Whitharral — HWĪT hăr uhl
Whitney — HWĪT nĭ
Whitsett — HWĪT sĭt
Whitson — HWĪT s'n
Whitt — hwĭt
Whon — hwahn
Wichita — WĬCH ĭ taw
Wichita Falls — <u>wĭch</u> ĭ taw FAWLZ
Wickett — WĬ kĭt
Wiergate — WEER gāt
Wilbarger — WĬL bahr ger
Wildorado — wĭl duh RĂ dō
Willacy — WĬL uh sĭ
Williamson — WĬL yuhm s'n
Willis — WĬ lĭs
Wills Point — wĭlz POINT
Wilmer — WĬL mer
Wilson — WĬL s'n
Wimberley — WĬM ber lĭ
Winchester — WĬN ches ter
Windom — WĬN d'm
Windthorst — WĬN thr'st
Winfield — WĬN feeld
Wingate — WĬN gāt
Wink — wĭngk
Winkler — WĬNGK ler
Winnie — WĬ nĭ
Winnsboro — WĬNZ buh ruh
Winona — wĭ NŌ nuh
Winterhaven — WĬN ter <u>hă</u> v'n
Winters — WĬN terz
Wise — wīz

Wizard Wells — wĭ zerd WĔLZ
Woden — WŌD n
Wolfe City — wŏŏlf SĬT ĭ
Wolfforth — WŌOL forth
Wood — wŏŏd
Woodbine — WŌŎD bīn
Woodlake — wŏŏd LĀK
Woodland — WŌŎD l'nd
Woodlawn — wŏŏd LAWN
Woodrow — WŌŎD rō
Woodsboro — WŌŎDZ buh ruh
Woodson — WŌŎD s'n
Woodville — WŌŎD v'l
Wortham — WERTH uhm
Wright City — rĭt SĬT ĭ
Wrightsboro — RĬTS buh ruh
Wylie — WĪ lĭ

Y

Yancey — YĂN sĭ
Yantis — YĂN tĭs
Yoakum — YŌ k'm
Yorktown — YAWRK town
Young — yuhng
Youngsport — YUHNGZ pōrt
Ysleta — īs LĔT uh

Z

Zapata — zuh PAH tuh
Zavalla — zuh VĂL uh
Zephyr — ZĔF er
Zuehl — ZEE uhl

Diacritical markings are used as follows: bāle, băd, lĕt, rīse, rĭll, ōak, brŏŏd, fŏŏt. The stressed syllable is capitalized. Secondary stress is indicated by an underline as in Atascosa — <u>ăt</u> uhs KŌ suh. TEXAS ALMANAC ©.

Obituaries: July 2007–July 2009

Ammerman, Dan, 76; television news anchor at Houston's KTRK in 1960s and 1970s, actor with roles including doctor who dug the bullet out of J.R. on *Dallas*, in the film *Local Hero* and in several TV movies; in Houston, May 11, 2009.

Andrews, William "Rooster," 84; diminutive UT Longhorn booster, team manager, player in 1940s, became giant in sporting goods retailing; in Austin, Jan. 21, 2008.

Armstrong, Anne, 80; Texas Republican stalwart, born Anne Legendre in New Orleans, married into South Texas ranch family, adviser to four presidents, served as U.S. ambassador to Great Britain, was Kenedy County commissioner at time of her death; in Houston, July 30, 2008.

Ballard, Clint Jr., 77; songwriter born in El Paso, attended University of North Texas, graduated from UTEP, best known for 1965 hit "Game of Love" and Linda Ronstadt's hit "You're No Good;" in Denton, Dec. 23, 2008.

Barrios, Viola B., 76; matriarch of San Antonio restaurant family, started in 1979 Los Barrios, one of the city's best-known Mexican restaurants; in San Antonio, April 24, 2008.

Baugh, Sammy, 94; record-setting quarterback "Slingin' Sammy" led TCU and Washington Redskins to national championships in 1930s–40s, born near Temple, completed high school in Sweetwater; in Rotan, Dec. 17, 2008.

Blanchard, Doc, 84; Heisman Trophy winner and three-time All-American at Army in 1944–46 where he was "Mr. Inside" to Glenn Davis' "Mr. Outside;" in Bulverde where he had lived the last 20 years, April 19, 2009.

Brinker, Norman, 78; Dallas restaurateur who launched Steak & Ale in 1966, built Brinker International empire of more than 1,000

restaurants including Chili's and On the Border; while on vacation in Colorado Springs, June 9, 2009.

Cade, J. Robert, 80; San Antonio native and graduate of UT-Austin and UT Southwestern Medical School who with other researchers developed Gatorade in 1965, became spokesman in TV commercial; in Florida, Nov. 27, 2007.

Campbell, George H. Jr., 89; Fort Worth native, songwriter/arranger for big band music at New York's Copacabana Club in 1940s, but best known as writer of 1957 country classic "Four Walls"; in Fort Worth, April 9, 2008.

Cantu, Margarita Contreras, 93; organized Mexican-American families in 1956 in Kenedy and Atascosa counties to oppose segregation in schools, later took up the same struggle in Kendall County; in Boerne, Dec. 22, 2007.

Chagra, Jamiel A. "Jimmy," 63; drug kingpin accused of conspiracy to kill U.S. District Judge John Wood Jr. in 1979 in San Antonio, paroled in 2003 after serving prison term on lesser charges; in Mesa, Ariz., July 25, 2008.

Charisse, Cyd, 86; born Tula Finklea in Amarillo in 1922, left for the West Coast as a teenager to pursue dancing career, became star in Hollywood musicals including, *Singin' in the Rain* and *Brigadoon*; in Los Angeles, June 17, 2008.

Cronkite, Walter, 92; famed CBS anchorman grew up in Houston from age 10, attended San Jacinto High School and UT-Austin where he worked on the campus newspaper *The Daily Texan* in the 1930s, worked for *The Houston Post* and *Houston Press*; in New York, July 17, 2009.

Crow, Trammell, 94; legendary Dallas real estate magnate, developed city's Apparel Mart, World Trade Mart and others, also Atlanta's Peachtree Center,

Brussels' Trade Mart, co-founded National Tree Trust; in Tyler, Jan. 14, 2009.

Cummins, Jim, 62; Emmy-winning correspondent for NBC, opened the network's Southwest bureau in Dallas in 1989 and provided coverage of assault on the Branch Davidian compound near Waco in 1993; in Plano, Oct. 27, 2007.

DeBakey, Michael E., 99; born Michel Dabaghi to Lebanese immigrants, internationally acclaimed as the father of modern cardiovascular surgery and instrumental in laying the foundation for the Texas Medical Center, beginning in 1949 *(see story, p. 536)*; in Houston, July 11, 2008.

Dial, Gilbert "Buddy," 71; Rice University All-American in late 1950s, All-Pro with Pittsburgh Steelers 1959–63, ended career with Dallas Cowboys; in Houston, Feb. 29, 2008.

Doolin, Mary Kathryn Coleman "Kitty," 89; helped husband build Frito corn-chip empire beginning in 1941 with expansion from Texas to California and nationwide; in Dallas, June 22, 2009.

Doss, Noble, 88; UT Longhorn football legend best known for "Impossible Catch" that upset Texas Aggies in 1940, played for NFL Philadephia Eagles and New York Yankees of All-American Conference; in Austin, Feb. 15, 2009.

Edwards, George, 60; began teaching music at Prairie View A&M University in 1978, five years later started the "Marching Storm," the marching band and dance troupe he directed until his death; May, 20, 2009.

Fath, Creekmore, 93; Austin lawyer was leader among liberal Democrats working under Sam Rayburn and Lyndon B. Johnson and with Ralph Yarborough, Bob Eckhardt and Frances "Sissy" Farenthold; in Austin, June 25, 2009.

Fawcett, Farrah, 62; born and raised in Corpus Christi, discovered as UT-Austin "most beautiful coed," was one of *Charlie's Angels*, with later dramatic roles, known for celebrated 1970s pinup poster; in Santa Monica, Calif., June 25, 2009.

Foote, Horton, 93; Oscar- and Pulitzer Prize-winning playwright and screenwriter of works including *Tender Mercies, Trip to Bountiful,* born in Wharton where he maintained a home; in Hartford, Conn., while working on adapting a play,

Former Ambassador Anne Armstrong, left, NBC's Jim Cummins, center, and dancer and actress Cyd Charisse, right.

Sports broadcaster Charlie Jones, left, actor Pat Hingle, center, and playwright Horton Foote, right.

March 4, 2009.

Foreman, Wilson, 81; Eastland native represented Austin in the Legislature for 16 years beginning in 1957, raised in Edinburg, student body president at UT-Austin; in Liberty Hill, March 14, 2008.

Freund, Carl, 82; Penelope native, UT-Austin graduate, was journalist for 60 years including 20 years with *The Dallas Morning News*, covered JFK assassination, pallbearer for Lee Harvey Oswald, interviewed Jack Ruby; in Plano, Feb. 24, 2008.

Gabler, Norma, 84; wielded national influence through four decades over textbook selections as founder, with her husband, of the Longview-based Educational Research Analysts, a conservative Christian organization; in Phoenix, Ariz., July 22, 2007.

Garner, Porter S. Jr., 83; owner of Nuevo Laredo's legendary Cadillac Bar purchased by his father-in-law in 1926, a destination through the decades for Texans; in Kerrville, July 30, 2007.

Gaylor, Alan Blum, 81; turned his 1950s tuxedo shop into a statewide empire with more than 100 Al's Formal Wear locations renting attire to generations of Texans; in Houston, April 15, 2008.

Giuffre, Jimmy, 86; Dallas native was clarinetist and composer who infused jazz with blues and classical notes, graduated from University of North Texas; in Pittsfield, Mass., April 24, 2008.

Guerrero, Lena, 50; Mission native was legislator from 1984–91, first woman and first Hispanic appointed to Texas Railroad Commission in 1991, later resigned after it was revealed she lied about having graduated from UT-Austin; of cancer in Austin, April 23, 2008.

Hale, Monte, 89; San Angelo native became singing cowboy in Hollywood Westerns in the 1940s, played Bale Clinch in *Giant*; in Los Angeles, March 29, 2009.

Haney, Paul, 80; the voice of Mission Control at Houston Space Center during the Gemini and Apollo flights in the 1960s; in Alamogordo, N.M., May 28, 2009.

Haskins, Don, 78; Hall of Fame basketball coach who drew attention to racial exclusionary policies in college sports when he started five black players on Texas Western's team that defeated all-white University of Kentucky in 1966; in El Paso, Sept. 7, 2008.

Hazlewood, Lee, 78; singer/songwriter wrote Nancy Sinatra hit "These Boots Are Made for Walkin'" and "Houston" for Dean Martin, spent teen years in Port Neches, studied at SMU; in Nevada, Aug. 4, 2007.

Henckel, Donald L. 79; an engineer for eight years of the legendary Brackenridge Eagle miniature train that has been a tourist attraction in San Antonio for more than 50 years; in San Antonio, May 23, 2008.

Hill, David L. "Tex," 92; Flying Tigers fighter pilot who was youngest brigadier general in the history of the Texas Air National Guard; in Terrell Hills, Oct. 11, 2007.

Hillaker, Harry J., 89; led the design team for the F-16 aircraft at General Dynamics where he worked for 44 years; in Fort Worth, Feb. 8, 2009.

Hingle, Pat, 84; character actor who attended Weslaco High School, graduated UT-Austin 1949, had recurring role in *Batman* as Commissioner Gordon; in Carolina Beach, N.C., Jan. 3, 2009.

Hlavaty, Deane, 89; one of the famed carhops in scanty shorts and towering hats at Prince's Hamburgers in the 1930s, later worked for decades as a travel agent; in Houston, July 17, 2009.

Hoffman, Philip G., 93; president of the University of Houston for 16 years beginning in 1961 during era of expansion and state affiliation; in Houston, Oct. 29, 2008.

Hunt, Tom, 85; former chairman of Hunt Petroleum and adviser to his uncle, famed wildcatter H.L. Hunt; in Dallas, Nov. 11, 2008.

Jameson, Betty, 89; child prodigy in golf, won first tournament at 13, grew up in Dallas and San Antonio, attended UT-Austin 1939–40, founding member of women's professional tour in 1950; in Boynton Beach, Fla., Feb. 7, 2009.

Johnson, Robert H. "Bob," 84; Colorado City native, Associated Press editor and executive for 42 years mostly in Dallas, wrote first bulletin on the assassination of President John F. Kennedy; in Albuquerque, N. M., Aug. 25, 2007.

Johnson, Ken, 74; former *Dallas Times Herald* executive editor in the 1970s and '80s during a spirited fight against rival *The Dallas Morning News*; in Dallas, Nov. 8, 2008.

Jones, Charlie, 77; TV sports anchor at Dallas' WFAA five years, announcer for AFL Dallas Texans beginning in 1960, called AFC games for NBC 1965–97; in La Jolla, Calif., June 12, 2008.

Jones, Grace, 87; born Grace Rosanky in Waelder, fashion maven whose boutique in Salado sold merchandise to customers across the globe, entered Baylor University at age 15, ferried aircraft during World War II; in Gonzales, Feb. 16, 2008.

Keyes, Evelyn, 91; Port Arthur native played Scarlet O'Hara's younger sister in *Gone With the Wind*, was married to Artie Shaw; in California, July 4, 2008.

Kocurek, Willie, 98; Austin civic icon, bow-tie-wearing pitchman in

Writer Bud Shrake, left, broadcaster Ray Miller, center, and Tejano singer Lydia Mendoza, right.

his appliance store commercials, served on school board 1946–54 including four years as president; in Austin, Jan. 1, 2009.

Koy Kistler, Margaret, 63; part of legendary Koy sports family, hired out of UT-Austin in 1967 at the *Abilene Reporter-News,* becoming one of first female sportswriters in Texas; in Bellville, Feb. 22, 2008.

Lea, Sarah C. Dighton, 96; widow of celebrated artist Tom Lea who served as a subject for his paintings, first woman to become a bank director in El Paso in 1974, headed many local civic and service groups including YWCA; in El Paso, May 2, 2008.

Leeds Swanson, Lana, 63; was known as Lana Phillips in 1966 when she was hit in the UT Tower shooting, became music teacher and founded Austin Children's Repertoire Company; in Austin, Feb. 15, 2009.

Locke, Randall, "Poodie," 60; Willie Nelson's stage manager for 34 years and owner of Poodie's Hilltop Bar in Spicewood where Willie's crew hung out between tours; at Briarcliff, May 6, 2009.

Locklin, Hank, 91; Grand Ole Opry member who hosted TV shows in Houston and Dallas in 1970s, had hits "Send Me the Pillow You Dream On" and "Please Help Me I'm Falling;" in Alabama, March 8, 2009.

Long, Huey, 105; jazz great born in Sealy, played guitar with Dizzy Gillespie and Charlie Parker and as part of the famed Ink Spots vocal group; in Houston, June 10, 2009.

Longoria, Beatrice, 88; widow of war hero Pvt. Felix Longoria whose reburial in 1949 became a national incident when a South Texas funeral home refused use of its chapel because the Longoria's were Mexican-American; in Colo-

rado, March 27, 2008.

Magness, B. Don, 75; Miss Texas pageant showman, named manager of Will Rogers Auditorium in 1965, spent 33 years with city of Fort Worth as promoter of events, coached contestants to Miss America; in Fort Worth, July 17, 2008.

Mancuso, Frank, 89; served 30 years (1963–93) on the Houston city council; catcher for St. Louis Browns 1944 American League champs and for Houston Buffs; in Houston, Aug. 4, 2007.

Martinez, Reuben D., 77; headed El Fenix restaurant chain founded by his father in Dallas in 1918, philanthropist who assisted generations of students at Dallas Jesuit school; in Dallas, May 9, 2008.

Mascolo, Guy, 65; co-founder of the international hair salon Toni & Guy started with his brother Toni in London in 1963, came to Dallas in 1983; in Dallas, May, 9, 2009.

Mattox, Jim, 65; crusading populist former Texas attorney general, part of "Dirty Thirty" reforming faction in Legislature, three-term congressman, lost Democratic primary race for governor against Ann Richards in 1990; in Dripping Springs, Nov. 20, 2008.

Mendoza, Lydia, 91; first star of Mexican-American Tejano music with first hit "Mal Hombre" in the 1930s, received National Medal of Arts in 1999; in San Antonio, Dec. 20, 2007.

Mersky, Roy, 82; led the University of Texas law library as director beginning in 1965, making it one of the best in the nation, veteran of Battle of the Bulge; in Austin, May, 8, 2008.

Miles, Buddy, 60; drummer on Jimi Hendrix's *Electric Ladyland* album, sang on the California Raisins commercials in 1980s, wrote and

performed song "Them Changes"; in Austin, Feb. 26, 2008.

Miller, Ray, 89; broadcast newsman in Houston beginning in 1951, created *The Eyes of Texas* TV program in 1969 and wrote accompanying travel guides; in Houston, Sept. 27, 2008.

Moreland, Ralph, 82; Stamford native founded in 1962 Austin's Holiday House chain, home of the "flame-kissed burger," reaching 26 restaurants before closing in 2004; in Austin, March 29, 2009.

Mueller, Robert L. "Bobby," 69; owner and pitmaster of iconic barbecue joint in Taylor started by his father Louie in 1949; in Taylor, Sept. 6, 2008.

Neuhaus, Richard John, 72; liberal Lutheran pastor in civil rights struggle who became Catholic priest/theologian beacon for conservatives, as teenager ran store in Cisco, graduated from Concordia College in Austin in 1950s; in New York, Jan. 8, 2009.

Oliphant, Benjamin, 83; Methodist bishop of Houston area 1984–92, supported civil rights struggle in 1950s and '60s as pastor in Louisiana, encouraged women in ministry; in Houston, July 7, 2007.

Patman, Bill, 81; state senator for 20 years and U.S. congressman for two terms 1981–85 representing the Coastal Bend, son of longtime U.S. Rep. Wright Patman; in Houston, Dec. 9, 2008.

Plummer, Matthew W. Sr., 87; born in San Antonio to a former slave, practiced law in Houston for nearly 50 years, fought to integrate the Harris County Courthouse cafeteria when a cross was burned in his yard, was flight instructor to the famous Tuskegee Airmen in World War II; in Houston, Oct. 22, 2007.

Rauschenberg, Robert, 82; Port Arthur native, attended UT-Austin, renowned and prolific artist who crossed boundaries to also sculpt, choreograph, perform (*see photo, p. 563);* in Florida, May 12, 2008.

Robertson, J.M. "Tex," 98; UT-Austin's first swim coach beginning in 1936, Sweetwater native founded Camp Longhorn in 1939 where thousands of youngsters learned to swim; in Burnet, Aug. 27, 2007.

Rogers, Lorene, 94; Prosper native, biochemist who was first woman to head a major research university when she became president of the University of Texas in 1975; in Dallas, Jan. 11, 2009.

Rostow, Elspeth, 90; dean of LBJ School of Public Affairs at UT-Austin 1977–83, began teaching at UT in 1969, appointed to national advisory panels by President Reagan; in Austin, Dec. 9, 2007.

Ruby, Lloyd, 81; Indianapolis 500, Daytona and Sebring racing veteran 1960–77; in Wichita Falls, March 23, 2009.

Sanders, H. Barefoot, 83; federal judge who oversaw desegregation of Dallas schools, served in U.S. Justice Department in Johnson administration, former legislator lost race for U.S. Senate in 1972; in Dallas, Sept. 21, 2008.

Seals, Dan, 61; McCamey native was pop/country singer "England Dan" who with John Ford Coley had 1976 hit "I'd Really Rather See You Tonight," older brother Jimmy was in Seals & Crofts; in Nashville, Tenn., March 25, 2009.

Shepherd, Mark Jr., 86; engineer and Dallas native who as CEO of Texas Instruments led it to power as a maker of semiconductors and consumer electronics; in Quitman, Feb. 4, 2009.

Shrake, Edwin "Bud," 77; sportswriter for *Sports Illustrated* and novelist, *Blessed McGill* and other

works, collaborated on best-selling sports title of all time, *Harvey Penick's Little Red Book,* buried in the Texas State Cemetery next to his longtime companion, former Gov. Ann Richards: in Austin, May 8, 2009.

Stone, Ron, 72; television newsman over four decades at Houston's KHOU and KPRC, began hosting *The Eyes of Texas* TV program in 1970s; in Houston, May 13, 2008.

Storm, Gale, 87; 1950s TV star of *My Little Margie* and *Oh! Susanna,* born Josephine Cottle in Bloomington, raised in Houston where she performed in the drama club at San Jacinto High School; in California, June 27, 2009.

Thompson, Hank, 82; Waco native, country music Hall of Famer who with his Brazos Valley Boys blended honky-tonk and Western swing in hits including "The Wild Side of Life" and "Six Pack to Go;" in Keller, Nov. 6, 2007.

Tschoepe, Thomas A., 93; Pilot Point farm boy who spent 24 years living simply as Catholic bishop, first in San Angelo 1966–69, then in Dallas retiring in 1990, criticized for transferring to new positions priests accused of sexual molestation; in Dallas, Jan. 24, 2009.

Upshaw, Gene, 63; Hall of Fame football star, Robstown native and lineman at Texas A&I University and for Oakland Raiders, led NFL Players Association since 1983, guiding the union toward winning free-agency rights for players; at his home at Lake Tahoe, Calif., Aug. 20, 2008.

Walker, Charlie, 81; Grand Ole Opry member and well-known disc jockey at KMAC in San Antonio starting in 1951, born in Copeville, had singing hit "Pick Me Up on Your Way Down;" in Hendersonville, Tenn., Sept. 12, 2008.

Welch, Louie, 89; five-term mayor of Houston 1963–73 after four terms on the city council beginning in 1949, led city's chamber of commerce after leaving political office; in Houston, Jan. 27, 2008.

Wells, Henrietta Bell, 96; only female member of the 1930 Wiley College team that took part in the first interracial collegiate debate, Houston native later taught in public schools and served as dean of women at Dillard University; in Baytown, Feb. 27, 2008.

West, Buddy, 71; eight-term legislator from Odessa, supported UT-Permian Basin and Presidential Museum there; in Odessa, June 25, 2008.

Wheeler, John A., 96; nuclear physicist taught at UT-Austin 1976–86, involved in Manhattan Project, coined term "black hole" in 1967; in New Jersey, April 13, 2008.

Williams, Lawton, 85; composer of 1957 country hit "Fraulein," performer and emcee in early 1960s of "Big D Jamboree," which was broadcast from Dallas; in Fort Worth, July 26, 2007.

Williams, Milton Redd "Chief," 72; Texas high school basketball legend led Dallardsville-Big Sandy to state championship in 1952, member of Alabama-Coushatta tribe; in Woodville, Oct. 31, 2007.

Williamson, Ric, 55; chairman of the Texas Transportation Commission who championed toll roads, Abilene native was former legislator 1985–98; of a heart attack in Weatherford, Dec. 30, 2007.

Zindler, Marvin, 85; flamboyant Houston TV personality, newsman and longtime consumer advocate, his crusade against the Chicken Ranch in La Grange became basis for the movie and Broadway play *Best Little Whorehouse in Texas;* in Houston, July 29, 2007. ☆

Singer Hank Thompson, left, NFL Players chief Gene Upshaw, center, and TV personality Marvin Zindler, right.

Advertiser Index

General Index

For cities and towns not listed in the Index, see list in the Population section, pages 398–426, and the Mayors list, pages 500–510.

— A —

Abbott, 291, 398, 500
Abbott, Greg, 464
Abernathy, 279, 320, 398, 500
Abilene, 304, 370, 398, 500
   metro area map, 397
Abilene, Lake, 94
Abilene Christian University, 594
Abilene State Park, 162, 166
Abortions, 577–579
Abshier (Candy) Wildlife Management
   Area, 122, 123
Academy (Little River-), 220, 398, 505
Accidents, 663
Accountancy, State Board of Public,
   486
Ackerly, 253, 322, 398, 500
Acton State Historic Sites, 162, 166
Acupuncture Examiners, State Board
   of, 486
Addicks Reservoir, 94
Addison, 252, 253, 398, 500
Adjutant General, 486
Administrative Hearings, State Office
   of, 486
Administrative Judicial Districts,
   475–477, 486
Admiral Nimitz Museum State Historic
   Site. *See* National Museum
   of the Pacific War
Admiral Nimitz State Historic Site,
   167, 173
Adrian, 340, 398, 500
Adult Offender Supervision, Interstate
   Commission, 492
Ad Valorem Tax Rate, Board to
   Calculate, 486
Aerial cable-car tramway, 169
Aeronautics Commission, 669
Affordable Housing Corporation, 492
African Americans. *See* Blacks
Age of majority, 57
Aggravated assault, 540–544
Aging and Disability Services,
   Department of, 467
Aging and Disability Services Board,
   486
Agricultural Finance Authority, 486
Agriculture, 673–689. *See also*
   Ranching; and specific
   crops
   agribusiness, 673–675

cash receipts for commodities,
   674–675
cash receipts of farms and
   ranches, 673, 674
comparative ranking with other
   states, 15, 675
cotton production, 64, 65
by county, 210–393
crop production statistics
   (2008), 678
exports of agricultural
   products, 675
fruits and nuts, 674, 675, 678,
   683–684
gross domestic product
   (1999–2008), 603
growing season by county,
   143–150
history of, 36, 44, 45, 47–53,
   54
hunting lease income and, 675
income from, 675
irrigation, 83–85, 88, 675–676
livestock and their products,
   674–675, 684–689
number and nature of farms,
   673–674
principal crops, 14, 674,
   677–684
rice production, 88
in soil subdivisions, 78–82
statistics, 14
vegetables, 674, 675, 678,
   681–682

Agriculture, Department of, 467
Agriculture Commissioner, 465
Agua Dulce, 339, 398, 500
Agustín de Iturbide, Emperor, 35
Ailey, Alvin, 562
Air Force, U.S., 536
Airlines, 669, 671. *See also* Airports
Airports, 669–671
Alabama/Coushatta Indians, 346
Alabama Creek Wildlife Management
   Area, 122, 123
Alamo (city), 290, 398, 500
The Alamo (film), 560
Alamo (mission), 33, 620
Alamo, battle of, 37–38
Alamo Area Council of Governments,
   511
Alamo Colleges, 594

Alamo Heights, 221, 398, 500
Alan Henry, Lake, 94
Alba, 348, 391, 398, 500
Albania, consular office, 665
Albany, 360, 398, 500
Alcoa Lake, 94
Alcohol
   binge alcohol, 582
   liquor-by-the-drink, 57, 517
   local-option clause for, 50, 54
   prohibition movement and,
      50–52, 54
   and repeal of prohibition, 54
   rum distillery, 175
   treatment programs, 582
   wet-or-dry status of counties,
      517
Alcohol and Drug Abuse, Commission
   on, 486, 583
Alcoholic Beverage Commission, 486
Aldrich, Richard W., 575
Aledo, 343, 398, 500
Alger, Bruce, 56–57
Alibates Flint Quarries National
   Monument, 176
Alice, 302, 398, 500
Allen, 242, 398, 500
Allen, Debbie, 562
Alligators, 119, 163, 164
Allred, James V., 54
Alluvial fans, 74
Alma, 261, 398, 500
Alpine, 227, 398, 500
Alternative Dispute Resolution
   Centers, 471
Altitude of counties, 210–393
Alto, 237, 398, 500
Alton, 290, 398, 501
Aluminum, 638
Alvarado, 303, 398, 501
Alvin, 225, 398, 501
Alvin Ailey American Dance Theater,
   562
Alvin Community College, 594
Alvord, 390, 398, 501
Alzheimer's Disease & Related
   Disorders, Council on, 486
Amarillo, 346, 348, 398, 501
   metro area map, 397
Amarillo College, 594
Amberton University, 594
American Indians. *See* Indians

For CITIES and TOWNS not listed in the Index, see complete list on pages 398–426.

For CITIES and TOWNS not listed in the Index, see complete list on pages 398–426.

For CITIES and TOWNS not listed in the Index, see complete list on pages 398–426.

Coons, Benjamin Franklin, 262

For CITIES and TOWNS not listed in the Index, see complete list on pages 398–426.

For CITIES and TOWNS not listed in the Index, see complete list on pages 398–426.

For CITIES and TOWNS not listed in the Index, see complete list on pages 398–426.

For CITIES and TOWNS not listed in the Index, see complete list on pages 398–426.

For CITIES and TOWNS not listed in the Index, see complete list on pages 398–426.

For CITIES and TOWNS not listed in the Index, see complete list on pages 398–426.

For CITIES and TOWNS not listed in the Index, see complete list on pages 398–426.

For CITIES and TOWNS not listed in the Index, see complete list on pages 398–426.

Justin, 255, 411, 504
Juvenile Justice Advisory Board, 493
Juvenile Probation Commission, 493

— K —

Karnes City, 304, 411, 504
Karnes County, map, profile, 304
Katy, 267, 284, 285, 382, 411, 504
Kaufman (city), 305, 411, 504
Kaufman County, 396
    map, profile, 305
Keechi Creek Wildlife Management
    Area, 122, 123
Keene, 303, 411, 504
Keller (town), 368, 369, 411, 504
Kelly base site, 221
Kemah, 271, 411, 504, 620
Kemp, 305, 411, 504
Kemp, Lake, 98
Kempner, 313, 411, 504
Kendall County, 396
    map, profile, 306
Kendleton, 267, 411, 504
Kenedy (city), 304, 411, 504
Kenedy, Mifflin, 43
Kenedy County, map, profile, 307
Kenefick, 316, 411, 504
Kennard, 294, 411, 504
Kennedale, 368, 369, 411, 504
Kennedy, John F., 25–26, 28, 56
Kennedy, Robert, 25
Kent County, 396
    map, profile, 307
Kerens, 337, 411, 504
Kermit, 389, 411, 504
Kerr County, 217
    map, profile, 308
Kerrville, 308, 411, 504
Kerr Wildlife Management Area, 122,
    123
Keyes, Evelyn, 705
Kickapoo, Lake, 98
Kickapoo Cavern State Park, 166,
    170
Kickapoo Indians, 325
Kilby, Jack St. Clair, 56
Kilgore, 277, 355, 411, 504
Kilgore College, 596
Killeen, 220, 411, 504
    Killeen-Temple-Fort Hood MSA
        (metro area), 397
Kimble County, map, profile, 309
King, Richard, 43
King County, 396
    map, profile, 309
Kingsland, 319, 411, 504
Kingsville, 310, 311, 411, 504
Kingwood College, 596
Kinney County, map, profile, 310
Kiowa, Lake, 98
Kirby, 221, 411, 504
Kirby, Lake, 98
Kirby (John Henry) State Forest, 110,
    111, 175
Kirbyville, 299, 411, 504
Kirk, Ron, 429
Kirvin, 268, 411, 504
Kleberg, Richard, 25
Kleberg County, map, profile, 311
Knollwood, 276, 411, 504
Know-Nothing Party, 44–45
Knox, Frank, 55
Knox City, 311, 411, 505
Knox County, 396
    map, profile, 311

Kocurek, Willie, 705–706
Korea, consular offices, 666
Kosse, 317, 411, 505
Kountze, 283, 411, 505
Koy Kistler, Margaret, 706
Kreische Brewery State Historic Site,
    167, 172–173
Kress, 367, 411, 505
Krugerville, 255, 411, 505
Krum, 255, 411, 505
Ku Klux Klan (KKK), 52
Kurten, 226, 411, 505
Kurth, Lake, 98
Kyle, 288, 411, 505
Kyrgyzstan, consular office, 666

— L —

La Bahía, 38, 169, 274
La Blanca, 290, 411, 505
Labor. See Employment
Lackland Air Force Base, 221, 536
La Coste, 328, 411, 505
Lacy-Lakeview, 327, 411, 505
Ladonia, 264, 411, 505
Lady Bird Lake, 29, 65, 87, 98
La Feria, 233, 411, 505
Lafitte, Jean, 135
Lago Vista, 375, 411, 505
La Grange, 265, 411, 505
La Grulla, 364, 411, 505
Laguna Atascosa National Wildlife
    Refuge, 120–121
Laguna Vista, 233, 411, 505
La Joya, 290, 411, 505
La Junta, 343, 411, 505
Lake, David, 562
Lake Arrowhead State Park, 167, 170
Lake Bob Sandlin State Park, 167,
    170
Lake Bridgeport, 390, 411, 505
Lake Brownwood State Park, 167,
    170–171
Lake Casa Blanca International State
    Park, 167, 171
Lake City, 357, 412, 505
Lake Colorado City State Park, 167,
    171
Lake Corpus Christi State Park, 167,
    171
Lake Creek Lake, 98
Lake Dallas (town), 255, 412, 505
Lake Davy Crockett Recreation Area,
    179
Lake Fork Reservoir, 98
Lake Jackson (town), 225, 412, 505
Lake Livingston State Park, 167, 171
Lake Meredith National Recreation
    Area, 177
Lake Mineral Wells State Park, 167,
    171
Lake O' the Pines, 89, 98, 179
Lakeport, 277, 412, 505
Lakes and reservoirs. See also
    specific lakes and
    reservoirs, such as
    Meredith, Lake
    Corps of Engineers lakes, 179
    list of, 94–100
    natural lakes, 94
    recreational facilities of Corps
        of Engineers lakes,
        179
    statistics on, 94
Lakeside (Tarrant County), 368, 369,
    412, 505

Lakeside (San Patricio County), 357,
    412, 505
Lakeside City, 214, 412, 505
Lake Somerville State Park, 167, 171
Lake Tanglewood, 348, 412, 505
Lake Tawakoni State Park, 167, 171
Lake Texana State Park, 167, 171
Lakeview (Hall County), 280, 412, 505
Lakeview (McLennan), 327, 412, 505
Lakeway, 375, 412, 505
Lake Whitney State Park, 167, 171
Lakewood Village, 255, 412, 505
Lake Worth, 368, 369, 412, 505
Lamar, Mirabeau B., 17, 40, 41, 456,
    585
Lamar County, map, profile, 312
Lamar Institute of Technology, 599
La Marque, 271, 412, 505
Lamar State College, 599
Lamar University, 599
Lamb County, map, profile, 313
Lamesa, 253, 412, 505
Lampasas (town), 313, 412, 505
Lampasas County, map, profile, 313
Lancaster, 252, 253, 412, 505
Land area of Texas, 14, 60
Land Board, School, 493
Land Board, Veterans', 493
Land Commissioner, 464
Landmark Inn State Historic Site,
    167, 171
Land Office. See General Land Office
Lands, Board for Lease of University,
    493
Land Surveying, Board of
    Professional, 493
Land use, 78–82, 101, 480–481
Lanham, Fritz G., 54
La Porte, 284, 285, 412, 505
Larceny-theft, 540–544
Laredo, 384, 412, 505
    metro area map, 397
Laredo Community College, 596
La Salle, René Robert Cavelier, Sieur
    de, 32, 298
La Salle County, map, profile, 314
Las Palomas Wildlife Management
    Area, 122, 123
Latexo, 294, 412, 505
Latitude and longitude of Texas, 60
Latvia, consular office, 666
Laughlin Air Force Base, 379, 536
Lava, 74
Lavaca Bay, 298
Lavaca County, map, profile, 314
Lavaca-Navidad River Authority, 493
Lavaca River, 86, 87
La Vernia, 389, 412, 505
La Villa, 290, 412, 505
Lavon, 242, 412, 505
Lavon Lake, 88, 98, 179
La Ward, 299, 412, 505
Law enforcement. See also Crime
    by county, 541–544
    deaths and injuries of law
        enforcement officers,
        540
    sheriffs and sheriffs' offices,
        541–544
Law Enforcement Officer Standards
    & Education, Commission
    on, 493
Law Examiners, Board of, 493
Law Library Board, 493
Lawn (town), 370, 412, 505

For CITIES and TOWNS not listed in the Index, see complete list on pages 398–426.

For CITIES and TOWNS not listed in the Index, see complete list on pages 398–426.

For CITIES and TOWNS not listed in the Index, see complete list on pages 398–426.

For CITIES and TOWNS not listed in the Index, see complete list on pages 398–426.

For CITIES and TOWNS not listed in the Index, see complete list on pages 398–426.

For CITIES and TOWNS not listed in the Index, see complete list on pages 398–426.

For CITIES and TOWNS not listed in the Index, see complete list on pages 398–426.

For CITIES and TOWNS not listed in the Index, see complete list on pages 398–426.

For CITIES and TOWNS not listed in the Index, see complete list on pages 398–426.

For CITIES and TOWNS not listed in the Index, see complete list on pages 398–426.

For CITIES and TOWNS not listed in the Index, see complete list on pages 398–426.

Texas Lakes

Bodies of water with a normal capacity of 5,000 acre-feet or larger. Italicized reservoirs usually dry.

● PANHANDLE PLAINS
1. Palo Duro Reservoir
2. Lake Rita Blanca
3. Lake Meredith
4. Bivins Lake
5. Buffalo Lake
6. Mackenzie Reservoir
7. Greenbelt Lake
8. Baylor Creek Lake
9. White River Lake
10. Lake Alan Henry
11. Lake J.B. Thomas
12. Sulphur Springs Draw Reservoir
13. Natural Dam Lake
14. Red Draw Reservoir
15. Lake Colorado City
16. Champion Creek Reservoir
17. Mitchell County Reservoir
18. Lake Sweetwater
19. E.V. Spence Reservoir
20. Oak Creek Reservoir
21. O.C. Fisher Lake
22. Twin Buttes Reservoir
23. Lake Nasworthy
24. Lake Ballinger/ Moonen
25. O.H. Ivie Reservoir
26. Hords Creek Lake
27. Lake Winters
28. Lake Abilene
29. Lake Coleman
30. Lake Brownwood
31. Lake Clyde
32. Lake Kirby
33. Lake Fort Phantom Hill
34. Lake Stamford
35. Lake Davis
36. Truscott Brine Lake
37. Santa Rosa Lake
38. Lake Electra
39. Lake Kemp
40. Lake Diversion
41. Lake Kickapoo
42. North Fork Buffalo Creek Reservoir
43. Lake Wichita
44. Lake Arrowhead
45. Millers Creek Reservoir
46. Lake Cooper/Olney
47. Lake Graham
48. Lost Creek Reservoir
49. Possum Kingdom Lake
50. Hubbard Creek Reservoir
51. Lake Daniel
52. Lake Cisco

53. Lake Palo Pinto
54. Lake Leon
55. Proctor Lake

● BIG BEND
56. Red Bluff Reservoir
57. Balmorhea Lake
58. Imperial Reservoir
59. Amistad International Reservoir

● HILL COUNTRY
60. Brady Creek Reservoir
61. Lake Buchanan
62. Inks Lake
63. Lake Lyndon B. Johnson
64. Lake Marble Falls
65. Lake Travis
66. Lake Austin
67. Town Lake
68. Lake Walter E. Long
69. Lake Georgetown
70. Granger Lake
71. Canyon Lake
72. Medina Lake

● PRAIRIES AND LAKES
73. Lake Nocona
74. Hubert H. Moss Lake
75. Lake Texoma
76. Randell Lake
77. Valley Lake
78. Lake Bonham
79. Coffee Mill Lake
80. Pat Mayse Lake
81. Lake Crook
82. River Crest Lake
83. Big Creek Reservoir
84. Cooper Lake
85. Lake Sulphur Springs
86. Lake Cypress Springs
87. Greenville City Lakes
88. Lake Tawakoni
89. Terrell City Lake
90. Lake Lavon
91. Lake Ray Hubbard
92. Lake Kiowa
93. Lake Ray Roberts
94. Lewisville Lake
95. Grapevine Lake
96. North Lake
97. White Rock Lake
98. Mountain Creek Lake
99. Joe Pool Reservoir
100. Lake Arlington
101. Lake Worth
102. Eagle Mountain Lake
103. Lake Weatherford

104. Lake Amon G. Carter
105. Lake Bridgeport
106. Lake Mineral Wells
107. Benbrook Lake
108. Lake Granbury
109. Squaw Creek Reservoir
110. Lake Pat Cleburne
111. Lake Waxahachie
112. Bardwell Lake
113. Cedar Creek Reservoir
114. Forest Grove Reservoir
115. Lake Athens
116. Trinidad Lake
117. Lake Halbert
118. Richland-Chambers Reservoir
119. Fairfield Lake
120. Navarro Mills Lake
121. Aquilla Lake
122. Lake Whitney
123. Lake Waco
124. Tradinghouse Creek Reservoir

125. Lake Creek Lake
126. Belton Lake
127. Stillhouse Hollow Lake
128. Alcoa Lake
129. Lake Limestone
130. Twin Oaks Reservoir
131. Camp Creek Lake
132. Bryan Lake
133. Gibbons Creek Reservoir
134. Somerville Lake
135. Lake Bastrop
136. Fayette County Reservoir
137. Lake Dunlap
138. Lake Gonzales
139. Eagle Lake

● PINEYWOODS
140. Wright Patman Lake
141. Monticello Reservoir
142. Lake Winnsboro
143. Lake Bob Sandlin
144. Welsh Reservoir
145. Ellison Creek Reservoir
146. Lake O' the Pines
147. Johnson Creek Reservoir
148. Caddo Lake
149. Lake Fork Reservoir
150. Lake Quitman
151. Lake Holbrook
152. Lake Hawkins
153. Gilmer Reservoir
154. Lake Gladewater
155. Eastman Lakes
156. Brandy Branch Reservoir
157. Lake Cherokee
158. Martin Creek Lake

Dallam | Sh
Hartley 2 | M
Oldham | Po
Deaf Smith | Ra
5
Parmer | Castro
Bailey | Lamb
Cochran | Hockley
Yoakum | Terry | L
Gaines | Da
Andrews | Ma
Ector | Midla
El Paso | Hudspeth | Culberson | 56 Loving | Winkler
Reeves | Ward | Crane | Upto
58
57 Pecos
Jeff Davis | Terrell
Presidio | Brewster